A Bibliography of Finance

A Bibliography of Finance

Richard Brealey

Helen Edwards

The MIT Press
Cambridge, Massachusetts
London, England

An ASCII version of the bibliography in this book is available. For more information please contact

Professor Richard A. Brealey
Midland Bank Professor of Corporate Finance
London Business School
Sussex Place
Regent's Park
London NW1 4SA
United Kingdom

©1991 Massachusetts Institute of Technology

This book was printed and bound in the United States of America.

Library of Congress Cataloging-in-Publication Data

Brealey, Richard A.
  A bibliography of finance / Richard Brealey, Helen Edwards.
    p.   cm.
  Includes index.
  ISBN 0-262-02319-9
  1. Finance—Bibliography. I. Edwards, Helen. II. Title.
Z7164.F5B76 1991
[HG173]
016.332—dc20   90-13523
                                                                CIP

Contents

Introduction

This bibliography is about finance. That may sound straightforward but the boundaries of the subject are ill-defined and we were continuously obliged to make arbitrary rulings lest we encroach on such adjoining kingdoms as accounting, law and monetary economics. As a result we have provided less comprehensive coverage of topics such as these that lie on the borders of our subject. While we could never make up our minds where the subject stopped, at least we felt confident that articles which are written by financial economists and published in finance journals are probably about finance and these therefore form the core of this book.

Since usefulness seems more important than neatness, we have also included a small number of works that are not directly about finance but that are frequently referenced by finance authors. For example, we have included Keynes's General Theory (together with the chapter numbers of Keynes's criticisms of the stock market). We have also included a number of papers about information asymmetry and signalling equilibria as well as some of the more frequently referenced works on statistics and econometrics.

Our second main criterion for inclusion was that the work should be concerned with issues of lasting importance and this in turn means that it should be analytical rather than just descriptive. We sought to avoid obtruding our own opinions about a publication's quality. Thus in the case of the major finance journals, such as the Journal of Finance and Journal of Financial Economics, we have included essentially all articles. But particularly where we were concerned with the professional journals we could not avoid making many, somewhat arbitrary, judgements as to the possible interest in the article. In such cases a recent publication date was more likely to ensure inclusion.

We have not limited our selection to the publications of any one country nor was our interest restricted to the capital markets of any one country. However, with minor exceptions all works are in the English language or, if this was not the original language of publication, they are available in translated form.

Our final criterion was that the work should be published. This means that we have excluded inter alia working papers and doctoral papers. Again there are a handful of occasions where we broke our own rules and included an unpublished but seminal paper such as Treynor's unpublished paper on the capital asset pricing model.

Some brief statistics may be of interest. The bibliography contains 12,037 entries. Approximately 120 periodicals are represented.

Of these periodicals the following are most commonly represented:

No. of articles
Journal of Finance   1539
Journal of Financial Economics   413
Journal of Financial and Quantitative
Economics   931

Our earliest included work is Bernoulli's famous paper of 1730 and our latest entries are works published at the end of 1989. As the following table indicates, the bulk of the publications are very recent.

Number of entries

Before 1950	92
1950-1959	253
1960-1969	1325
1970-1979	3613
1980-1989	6754

It would be disingenuous to pretend that we have avoided errors both of omission and commission. Our worries about omissions center largely on books where we had no cost-effective way of ensuring that all seminal books were included or that we had identified the latest edition. The principal sins of commission undoubtedly involve the misallocation of publications to subject headings. Subjects merge imperceptibly into one another and we recommend that the user consults more than one subject heading. We can only hope that the user finds that such sins are outweighed by the bibliography's virtues.

We received help from a number of quarters. In particular we are grateful to Diana Hughes who undertook a substantial proportion of the compilation. We made extensive use of the facilities of the London Business School Library and are especially grateful to Stephen Hume, Systems Librarian, who helped with a number of computing problems and Gill Dwyer, Technical Services Librarian, who advised on online searching. The Institute for Quantitative Research in Finance (The Q Group) generously provided assistance in the form of a grant and for this also we are grateful.

Lay-out of Bibliography

Works are listed under two principal files. One of these consists of an alphabetical listing by author. Cross-references are included for second and third authors. Here again we should include a word of warning. The author, J.H. Smith, may be listed under both 'J. Smith' and 'J.H. Smith'. Conversely, different authors with the same initial may be listed as one author.

The other file consists of a subject index. Entries have been divided into 373 subject areas and within each of these areas articles are listed by year of publication and within each year alphabetically by author. The average number of articles per subject classification is 34 and in no case does the number exceed 260.

There are 40 main subject areas and these in turn are subdivided up to 3 more times. Thus the figure 9 indicates that a work is concerned with market efficiency, 9.6 indicates that it is concerned with empirical regularities, 9.63 that it is concerned with seasonal regularities in security prices and 9.631 that it is concerned with month-of-the-year effects.

A list of the subject headings is provided on page 1. Since articles stubbornly refused to fit into our a priori classes, our choice of headings was entirely pragmatic. To prevent undue length, articles have rarely been filed under more than one subject heading. Conversely, like some modern-day Procrustes we attempted to force each article into some subject classification.

To facilitate identification of the appropriate subject heading, we have provided an index on pages iv to xxxiv that links keywords with the appropriate subject heading. For example, anyone looking up 'bankruptcy' in the index will be directed to '31.7 Bankruptcy', '27.23 Bankruptcy and capital structure', '8.13 Bank failure, capital adequacy and deposit insurance' and '30.32 Credit analysis'.

Index of Keywords

Under each of the following keywords we show in bold face the primary subject heading(s) under which articles are likely to be listed. In non-bold face we show some of the secondary headings under which further references may be found.

For economy we show in each case only one node on the tree of subject headings. For example, we show that the primary reference for preferred stock is '**18.48 Preferred stock**'. However, the reader may also wish to consult the broader classification '18.4 Types of debt and preferred' as well as the finer classifications '18.481 Floating rate preferred' and '18.482 Auction rate preferred'. These are not separately itemised in the following index.

Index of keywords

Index of keywords

Index of keywords

Index of keywords

Index of keywords

Index of keywords

Index of keywords

Index of keywords

Index of keywords

Index of keywords

Journal Abbreviations

AE	Applied Economics
AER	American Economic Review
AJM	Australian Journal of Management
AJP	American Journal of Psychology
AR	The Accounting Review
B	Barron's
BellJ	Bell Journal of Economics and Management Science
BEQB	Bank of England Quarterly Bulletin
BNLQR	Banca Nazionale di Lavoro Quarterly Review
CFQ	Chase Financial Quarterly
CJWB	Canadian Journal of World Business
CMR	California Management Review
Ec	Economica
EE	Engineering Economist
EER	European Economic Review
EJ	Economic Journal
EJOR	European Journal of Operation Research
Em	Econometrica
ERA	Empirical Research in Accounting: Selected Studies
F	Fortune
FAJ	Financial Analysts Journal
FD	Finance and Development
FE	Financial Executive
FIN MGMT	Financial Management
FR	Financial Review
F R Bk Atlanta Ec Rev	
	Federal Reserve Bank of Atlanta Economic Review
F R Bk Bus Rev Philadelphia	
	Federal Reserve Bank Business Review of Philadelphia
F R Bk Chicago, Bus Cond	
	Business Conditions, Federal Reserve Bank of Chicago
F R Bk Cleveland Mo Bus Rev	
	Federal Reserve Bank of Cleveland Monthly Business Review
F R Bk Dallas Ec Rev	
	Federal Reserve Bank of Dallas Economic Review
F R Bk Kansas City Mo Rev	
	Federal Reserve Bank of Kansas City Monthly Review
F R Bk Minneapolis Q Rev	
	Federal Reserve Bank of Minneapolis Quarterly Review
F R Bk New York Mo Rev	
	Federal Reserve Bank of New York Monthly Review
F R Bk New York Q Rev	
	Federal Reserve Bank of New York Quarterly Review
F R Bk Richmond Ec Rev	
	Federal Reserve Bank of Richmond Economic Review
F R Bk San Francisco Ec Rev	
	Federal Reserve Bank of San Francisco Economic Review

Journal abbreviations

F R Bk St Louis Rev
        Federal Reserve Bank of St Louis Review
F R Bul   Federal Reserve Bulletin
FRIS   Food Research Institute Studies
FS   Fiscal Studies

HBR   Harvard Business Review
HFR   Housing Finance Review
HLR   Harvard Law Review

II   Institutional Investor
IMF   Staff Papers, International Monetary Fund
IMR   Industrial Management Review
IntER   International Economic Review

JACF   Journal of Applied Corporate Finance
JAE   Journal of Accounting and Economics
JAR   Journal of Accounting Research
JASA   American Statistical Association, Journal
JB   Journal of Business
JBankF   Journal of Banking and Finance
JBF   Journal of Business Finance
JBFA   Journal of Business Finance and Accounting
JBR   Journal of Bank Research
JBusR   Journal of Business Research
JCBL   Journal of Commercial Bank Lending
JCM   Journal of Cash Management
JEL   Journal of Economic Literature
JEP   Journal of Economic Perspectives
JET   Journal of Economic Theory
JF   Journal of Finance
JFarmE   Journal of Farm Economics
JFE   Journal of Financial Economics
JFM   Journal of Futures Markets
JFQA   Journal of Financial and Quantitative Analysis
JFR   Journal of Financial Research
JFSR   Journal of Financial Services Research
JIBS   Journal of International Business Studies
JIE   Journal of Industrial Economics
JIMF   Journal of International Money and Finance
JIntE   Journal of International Economics
JLE   Journal of Law and Economics
JMCB   Journal of Money, Credit and Banking
JME   Journal of Monetary Economics
JPE   Journal of Political Economy
JPM   Journal of Portfolio Management
JRSS   Royal Statistical Society, Journal

Kyk   Kyklos

LBR   Lloyds Bank Review
LCP   Law and Contemporary Problems

Met	Metroeconomica
MF	Managerial Finance
MCFJ	Midland Corporate Finance Journal
MIR	Management International Review
MS	Manchester School of Economic and Social Studies
MSci	Management Science
NBR	National Banking Review
NTJ	National Tax Journal
NWBQR	National Westminster Bank Quarterly Review
OEP	Oxford Economic Papers
OR	Operations Research
PUF	Public Utilities Fortnightly
QJE	Quarterly Journal of Economics
QREB	Quarterly Review of Economics and Business
RandJ	Rand Journal of Economics
RBER	Review of Business and Economic Research
REStat	Review of Economics and Statistics
REStud	Review of Economic Studies
RFS	Review of Financial Studies
SEJ	Southern Economic Journal
SJE	Swedish Journal of Economics
SMJ	Strategic Management Journal
SMR	Sloan Management Review
VLR	Virginia Law Review
WEJ	Western Economic Journal
Wheat	Wheat Studies of the Food Research Institute
YEE	Yale Economic Essays

Table of Contents

Table of contents

Table of contents

1 Finance - general

(1)
Brown S J, Kritzman M, Kubota M
Quantitative methods for financial analysis
Tokyo Keizai Shinposa, 1989.

(2)
Sarwal A K comp.
KPMG international handbook of financial instruments and transactions
Butterworth, 1989.

(3)
Byland T
Understanding finance with the Financial Times
Harrap, 1988.

(4)
Copeland T E, Weston J F
Financial theory and corporate policy. 3rd ed
Addison-Wes, 1988.

(5)
Duffie D
Security markets: Stochastic models
Academic Pr, 1988.

(6)
Huang C F, Litzenberger R H
Foundations for financial economics
N Holland, 1988.

(7)
Martin J D, Cox S H, MacMinn R D
The theory of finance: Evidence and applications
Dryden Pr, 1988.

(8)
Renshaw E F
The rationality model revisited
JFM 1988 APR VOL 8:2 p 157-166.

(9)
Cooley P L, Heck J L
A survey of the introductory business finance course: The professor's viewpoint
Journal of Financial Education 1987 FALL.

(10)
Emery G W
An optimal financial response to variable demand
JFQA 1987 JUN VOL 22 p 209.

(11)
Gibbons M R
The interrelations of finance and economics
AER 1987 MAY VOL 77:2 p 35-41.

(12)
Helfert E A
Techniques of financial analysis. 6th ed
Irwin, 1987.

(13)
Ingersoll J E
Theory of financial decision making
Rowman and Littlefield, 1987.

(14)
MacMinn R D
Forward markets, stock markets, and the theory of the firm
JF 1987 DEC VOL 42:5 p 1167-1186.

(15)
Ross S A
The interrelations of finance and economics
AER 1987 MAY VOL 77:2 p 29-34.

(16)
McCutcheon J J, Scott W F
An introduction to the mathematics of finance
Heinemann, 1986.

(17)
Summers H L
On economics and finance
JF 1985 JUL VOL 40:3 p 633-635.

(18)
Allen D E
Finance: a theoretical introduction
Oxford: Martin Robertson, 1983.

(19)
Hempel G H
Teaching and research in finance: Perceptions, conflicts and the future
FIN MGMT 1983 WINTER VOL 12 p 5-10.

(20)
Merton R C
Financial economics
(in Brown E C and Solow R M eds., Paul Samuelson and modern economic theory. McGraw, 1983.)

(21)
Weston J F
Developments in finance theory
FIN MGMT 1981 SUPP VOL 10 p 5-22.

(22)
Coghlan R
The theory of money and finance
Macmillan, 1980.

(23)
Findlay M C III, Williams E E
A positivist evaluation of the new finance
FIN MGMT 1980 SUMMER VOL 9 p 7.

(24)
Hakansson N H
The fantastic world of finance: Progress and the
free lunch
JFQA 1979 NOV VOL 14 p 717.

(25)
Cissell R et al.
Mathematics of finance. 5th ed
HM, 1978.

(26)
Friedland S, Lawson W M
Principles of financial management: corporate
finance, investments and macrofinance
Cambridge, Mass.: Winthrop Publishers, 1978.

(27)
Krainer R E
Wealth redistribution risk and the modern theory
of finance
JMCB 1977 AUG VOL 9:3 p 460-468.

(28)
Haley C W
A theoretical foundation for the basic finance
course
JFQA 1975 NOV VOL 10 p 691.

(29)
Merton R C
Theory of finance from the perspective of
continuous time
JFQA 1975 NOV VOL 10 p 659.

(30)
Wert J E
Content orientation in the introductory finance
course
JFQA 1975 NOV VOL 10 p 695.

(31)
Weston J F
A management orientation in the first finance
course
JFQA 1975 NOV VOL 10 p 699.

(32)
Findlay M C III
Beyond shareholder wealth maximization
FIN MGMT 1974 WINTER VOL 4 p 25.

(33)
Friend I
Mythodology in finance
JF 1973 VOL 28 p 257.

(34)
Haley C W, Schall L D
The theory of financial decisions
McGraw, 1973.

(35)
Mossin J
Theory of financial markets
P-H, 1973.

(36)
Weber J A
A note on keeping abreast of developments in the
field of finance
JF 1973 VOL 28 p 161.

(37)
Fama E F, Miller M H
The theory of finance
HR & W, 1972.

(38)
Hummel P M, Seebeck C L
Mathematics of finance. 3rd ed
McGraw, 1971.

(39)
Dewey D
Modern capital theory
Columbia U Pr, 1965.

(40)
Bogen J I ed.
Financial handbook. 4th ed
Ronald, 1964.

(41)
Hicks J R
Value and capital: an inquiry into some fundamental principles of economic theory. 2nd ed
Oxford U Pr, 1946.

1.01 Finance - readings and conference proceedings.

(42)
Bhattacharya S, Constantinides G eds.
Frontiers of financial theory
Littlefield, 1987.

(43)
Copeland T E ed.
Modern finance and industrial economics: papers in honor of J. Fred Weston
Blackwell, 1987.

(44)
Fischer S, Dornbusch R, Bossons J eds.
Macroeconomics and finance: Essays in Honor of Franco Modigliani
MIT Pr, 1987.

(45)
Fair D E ed.
Shifting frontiers in financial markets
Martinus Nijhoff, 1986.

(46)
Firth M, Keane S M eds.
Issues in finance
Philip Allan, 1986.

(47)
Sharpe W F, Cootner C M eds.
Financial economics: essays in honor of Paul Cootner
P-H, 1982.

(48)
Dean J W, Schwindt R eds.
Finance I: financial theory, financial institutions and money markets
Durham, NC: Eno River Press, 1981.

(49)
Dean J W, Schwindt R eds.
Finance II: corporate finance and investments
Durham, NC: Eno River Press, 1981.

(50)
Levy H ed.
Research in finance: a research annual: volume 3
JAI Pr, 1981.

(51)
Levy H ed.
Research in finance: a research annual: volume 2
JAI Pr, 1980.

(52)
Bicksler J L ed.
Handbook of financial economics
N Holland, 1979.

(53)
Levy H ed.
Research in finance: a research annual: volume 1
JAI Pr, 1979..

Bicksler J L ed.
Capital market equilibrium and efficiency: implications for accounting, financial and portfolio decision making
Lexington Bks, 1977.

(54)
Friend I, Bicksler J L ed.
Risk and return in finance
Ballinger, 1977.

(55)
Levy H, Sarnat M eds.
Financial decision making under uncertainty
Academic Pr, 1977.

(56)
Szego G P, Shell K eds.
Mathematical methods in investment and finance
N Holland, 1972.

(57)
Wolf H A, Richardson L eds.
Readings in finance
Appleton, 1966.

1.02   Finance - cases

(58)
Barnes P ed.
Case studies in finance
Philip Allan, 1989.

(59)
Butters J K, Fruhan W E Jr, Mullins D W et al.
Case problems in finance. 9th ed
Irwin, 1987.

1.03   Finance - bibliographies and glossaries

(60)
Edwards H ed.
London Business School bibliography of financial markets: 1987-88
London Bus Library, 1989.

(61)
Heck J L
Finance literature index
McGraw, 1988.

(62)
Edwards H ed.
London Business School bibliography of financial markets: 1985-86
London Bus Library, 1987.

(63)
Reuters
Reuters glossary of international economic and financial terms
Heinemann, 1982.

(64)
Perry F E
A selected vocabulary of financial terms
Waterlow, 1981.

(65)
Standard & Poors Corporation
A glossary of financial investment terms
S & P, nd.

1.04   Finance - research and publications

(66)
Heck J L, Cooley P L
Most frequent contributors to the finance literature
FIN MGMT 1988 AUTUMN VOL 17 p 100.

(67)
Cudd M, Morris J
Bias in journal ratings
FR 1988 FEB VOL 23:1.

(68)
Niemi A W Jr
Institutional contributions to the leading finance journals, 1975 through 1986: a note
JF 1987 DEC VOL 42:5 p 1389-1398.

(69)
Heck J L, Cooley P L, Hubbard C M
Contributing authors and institutions to the Journal of Finance : 1946-1985.
JF 1986 DEC VOL 41:5 p 1129-1140.

(70)
Kaufman G G
Rankings of finance departments by faculty representation on editorial boards of professional journals : a note
JF 1984 SEP VOL 39:4 p 1189-1197.

(71)
Beranek W
Research directions in finance
QREB 1981 SPRING VOL 21:1 p 6-24

(72)
Cooley P L, Heck J L
Significant contributions to finance literature
FIN MGMT 1981 SUPP VOL 10 p 23-33.

(73)
Petry G H
A history and analysis of scholarly papers presented at the seven Academic Finance Associations from 1939 through 1980
FIN MGMT 1981 SUPP VOL 10 p 93-104.

(74)
Farrelly G
A behavioral science approach to financial research
FIN MGMT 1980 AUTUMN VOL 9 p 15.

(75)
Moore L J, Taylor B W
A study of the institutional publications in business-related academic journals
QREB 1980 SPRING VOL 20 p 87.

(76)
Ederington L H
Aspects of the production of significant financial research
JF 1979 JUN VOL 34:3 p 777-786.

(77)
Carleton W T
An agenda for more effective research in corporate finance
FIN MGMT 1978 WINTER VOL 7 p 7

(78)
Fuller R J, Petry G H
The geographic distribution of papers at the seven academic finance associations in the United States
JFQA 1978 NOV VOL 13 p 785.

(79)
Klemkosky R C, Tuttle D L
A ranking of doctoral programs by financial research contributions of graduates
JFQA 1977 SEP VOL 12 p 491.

(80)
Klemkosky R C, Tuttle D L
The institutional source and concentration of financial research
JF 1977 VOL 32 p 901.

(81)
Schweser C
The doctoral origins of contributors to the Journal of Finance from 1964 through 1975
JF 1977 VOL 32 p 908.

(82)
Hamelman P W, Mazze E M
Citation patterns in finance journals
JF 1974 VOL 29 p 1295.

(83)
National Bureau of Economic Research
Research in the capital markets
JF 1964 MAY VOL 19 Suppl p 1-43.

1.1 Investment management - general

(84)
Adams A
Investment
Graham & Trotman, 1989.

(85)
Alexander G J, Sharpe W F
Fundamentals of investments
P-H, 1989.

(86)
Amling F
Investments: an introduction to analysis and management. 6th ed
P-H, 1989.

(87)
Bodie Z, Kane A, Marcus A J
Investments
Irwin, 1989.

(88)
Brimson J A
Activity-based investment management
AMA, 1989.

(89)
Arnott R D
The future for quantitative investment products
JPM 1988 WINTER VOL 14:2 p 52-56.

(90)
Francis J C
Management of investments. 2nd ed
McGraw, 1988.

(91)
Gitman L J, Joehnk M D
Fundamentals of investing. 3rd ed
Har-Row, 1988.

(92)
Jacob N L, Pettit R R
Investments. 2nd ed
Irwin, 1988.

(93)
Jones C P
Investments: analysis and management. 2nd ed
Wiley, 1988.

(94)
Levine S N ed.
The financial analyst's handbook. 2nd ed
Dow Jones-Irwin, 1988.

(95)
Mayo H
Investments: An introduction. 2nd ed
Dryden Pr, 1988.

(96)
Perold A F
The implementation shortfall: paper versus reality
JPM 1988 SPRING VOL 14:3 p 4-9.

(97)
Valentine J L
Applying expert systems to investment
FAJ 1988 NOV-DEC VOL 44 p 48-53.

(98)
Wagner W ed.
A complete guide to securities transactions:
Controlling costs and enhancing performance
Wiley, 1988.

(99)
Bank of England
Management of UK equity portfolios
BEQB 1987 VOL 27 p 253-260.

(100)
Beidleman C R ed.
Handbook of international investing
Gower, 1987.

(101)
Berkowitz S A, Logue D E
The portfolio turnover explosion explored
JPM 1987 SPRING VOL 13:3 p 38-45.

(102)
Cohen J B, Zinbarg E D, Zeikel A
Investment analysis and portfolio management.
5th ed
Irwin, 1987.

(103)
Elton E J, Gruber M J
Modern portfolio theory and investment analysis.
3rd ed
Wiley, 1987.

(104)
Fischer D E, Jordan R J
Security analysis and portfolio management. 4th
ed
P-H, 1987.

(105)
Fuller R J, Farrell J L
Modern investments and security analysis
McGraw, 1987..

(106)**Huang S S C, Randall M R**
Investment analysis and management. 2nd ed
Allyn, 1987.

(107)
Ibbotson R G, Brinson G P
Investment markets: Gaining the performance
advantage
McGraw, 1987.

(108)
Pound J, Shiller R J
Are institutional investors speculators
JPM 1987 SPRING VOL 13:3 p 46-52.

(109)
Radcliffe R C
Investment: concepts, analysis and strategy. 2nd ed
Scott, Foresman, 1987.

(110)
Samuelson P A
Paradise lost & refound: the Harvard ABC barometers
JPM 1987 SPRING VOL 13:3 p 4-9.

(111)
Sobel R
The new game on Wall Street
Wiley, 1987.

(112)
Veale S R ed.
Stocks, bonds, options, futures: investments and their markets
P-H, for the New York Institute of Finance, 1987.

(113)
Winfield R G, Curry S J
Success in investment. 3rd ed
John Murray, 1987.

(114)
Francis J C
Investments: analysis and management. 4th ed
McGraw, 1986.

(115)
Hirt G A, Block S B
Fundamentals of investment management. 2nd ed
Irwin, 1986.

(116)
Meyers T A
The Dow Jones-Irwin guide to on-line investing: sources, services and strategies
Dow Jones-Irwin, 1986.

(117)
Bank of England
Investment management in the United Kingdom
BEQB 1985 VOL 25 p 212-216.

(118)
Hardy C C ed.
Dun & Bradstreet 's guide to your investments: 1985
Har-Row, 1985.

(119)
Lorie J H, Dodd P, Kimpton M H
The Stock Market: theories and evidence. 2nd ed
Irwin, 1985.

(120)
Malkiel B G
A random walk down Wall Street. 4th ed
Norton, 1985.

(121)
Pfleiderer P
Finance anthropology
JPM 1985 FALL VOL 12:1 p 52.

(122)
Reilly F K
Investment analysis and portfolio management. 2nd ed
Dryden Pr, 1985.

(123)
Sharpe W F
Investments. 3rd ed
P-H, 1985.

(124)
Fogler H R, Bayston D M eds.
Improving the investment decision process: Quantitative assistance for the practitioner - and for the firm
Institute of Chartered Financial Analysts, 1984.

(125)
George F H
The science of investment
Abacus Pr, 1984.

(126)
Stevenson R A, Jennings E H
Fundamentals of investments. 3rd ed
West Pub, 1984.

(127)
Vertin J ed.
International equity investing
Dow Jones-Irwin, 1984

(128)
Brealey R A
An introduction to risk and return from common stocks. 2nd ed
MIT Pr, 1983.

(129)
Farrell J L
Guide to portfolio management
McGraw, 1983.

(130)
Johnson T E
Investment principles. 2nd ed
P-H, 1983.

(131)
Rutterford J
Introduction to stock exchange investment
Macmillan, 1983.

(132)
Christy G A, Clendenin J C
Introduction to investments. 8th ed
McGraw, 1982.

(133)
Ittensohn J
Back to the drawing board!
JPM 1982 FALL VOL 9:1 p 28.

(134)
Rudd A, Clasing H K
Modern portfolio theory: the principles of
investment management
Dow Jones-Irwin, 1982.

(135)
Bernstein J
The investor's quotient: the psychology of
successful investing in commodities and stocks
Wiley, 1980.

(136)
Craig M
Successful investment
Allen, 1979.

(137)
Francis J, Archer S
Portfolio analysis
P-H, 1979.

(138)
Lewellen W G, Lease R C, Schlarbaum G G
The personal investments of professional
managers
FIN MGMT 1979 WINTER VOL 8 p 28.

(139)
Tinic S M, West R R
Investing in securities: an efficient markets
approach
Addison-Wes, 1979.

(140)
Coates C R
Investment strategy
McGraw, 1978.

(141)
Davis D W, Boatsman J R, Baskin E F
On generalizing stock market research to a
broader class of markets
AR 1978 JAN VOL 53:1 p 1-10.

(142)
Dougall H E, Corrigan F J
Investments. 10th ed
P-H, 1978.

(143)
Hoffland D L
A model bank investment policy
FAJ 1978 MAY-JUN p 64-76.

(144)
Black F
The investment policy spectrum: Individuals,
endowment funds and pension funds
FAJ 1976 JAN-FEB VOL 32 p 23-31.

(145)
Fama E F
Foundations of finance: portfolio decisions and
securities prices
Basic, 1976.

(146)
Hayes D A, Bauman W S
Investments: analysis and management. 3rd ed
Macmillan, 1976.

(147)
Bernhard A
Investing in common stocks
Arnold Bernhard & Co., Inc., New York, 1975.

(148)
Briston R J
The Stock Exchange and investment analysis. 3rd
ed
Allen, 1975.

(149)
Ellis C D
The loser's game
FAJ 1975 JUL-AUG VOL 31 p 19-26.

(150)
Valentine J L
Investment analysis and capital market theory
Research Foundation of the Institute of Chartered
Financial Analysts, 1975.

(151)
Christy G A
Teaching of investments: A "Utilitarian" view
JFQA 1974 NOV VOL 9 p 781.

(152)
Eiteman D K, Smith K V
A portfolio analysis of the teaching of
investments
JFQA 1974 NOV VOL 9 p 771.

(153)
West R R
The teaching of investment - is "witchcraft" still
appropriate?
JFQA 1974 NOV VOL 9 p 789.

(154)
Graham B
The intelligent investor: a book of practical
counsel. 4th ed
Har-Row, 1973.

(155)
Lorie J H, Hamilton M T
New focus for investment counselling to pension
and endowment portfolios
FAJ 1973 JUL-AUG VOL 29 p 46-51.

(156)
Bolten S
Security analysis and portfolio management
HR & W, 1972.

(157)
Carol A
An investment paradox
JFQA 1972 JAN VOL 7 p 1421.

(158)
Elton E J, Gruber M J eds.
Security evaluation and portfolio analysis
P-H, 1972..

(159)**Levy H, Sarnat M**
Investment and portfolio analysis
Wiley, 1972.

(160)
Wagner W H, Quay S R
New concepts in portfolio management
JBR 1972 SUMMER VOL 3:2.

(161)
Brealey R A
Security prices in a competitive market: more
about risk and return from common stocks
MIT Pr, 1971.

(162)
Ellis C D
Institutional investing
Dow Jones-Irwin, 1971.

(163)
Latane H A, Tuttle D L
Security analysis and portfolio management
Ronald, 1971.

(164)
Renwick F B
Introduction to investments and finance: theory
and analysis
Macmillan, 1971.

(165)
Smith K V
Portfolio management: theoretical and empirical
studies of portfolio decision-making
HR & W, 1971.

(166)
Weaver D
Investment analysis
Longman, 1971.

(167)
Williamson J P
Investments: new analytic techniques
Longman, 1971.

(168)
Lishan J M, Crary D T eds.
The investment process
Intext, 1970.

(169)
Smith K V, Goudzwaard M B
Survey of investment management: teaching versus
practice
JF 1970 MAY VOL 25 p 329-348.

(170)
Van Horne J C
The function and analysis of capital market rates
P-H, 1970.

(171)
Badger R E et al.
Investment principles and practices. 6th ed
P-H, 1969.

(172)
Clendenin J C
Introduction to investments. 5th ed
McGraw, 1969.

(173)
Bookbinder A I A
Investment decision-making
Programmed Pr, 1968.

(174)
Badger R E, Coffman P B
The complete guide to investment analysis
McGraw, 1967.

(175)
Sauvain H C
Investment management. 3rd ed
P-H, 1967.

(176)
Vaughn D E
Survey of investments
HR & W, 1967.

(177)
Bowyer J W
Investment analysis and management. 3rd ed
Irwin, 1966.

(178)
Freund W C
Investment fundamentals
New York: American Bankers Association, 1966.

(179)
Lerner E M, Carleton W T
A theory of financial analysis
HarBraceJ, 1966.

(180)
Vaughn D E
Investment principles, practices and techniques
HR & W, 1965.

(181)
Leffler G L
The stock market. 3rd ed / rev by Farwell L C
Ronald, 1963.

(182)
Wyckoff P
The psychology of stock market timing
P-H, 1963.

(183)
Graham B, Dodd D L, Cottle S
Security analysis: principles and technique. 4th ed
McGraw, 1962.

(184)
Dowrie G W et al.
Investments. 3rd ed
Wiley, 1961.

(185)
Plum L V, Humphrey J H, Bowyer J W
Investment analysis and management. 2nd ed
Irwin, 1961.

(186)
Rose H B
The economic background to investment
Cambridge U Pr, 1960.

(187)
Osborn R
The mathematics of investment
Har-Row, 1957.

(188)
Cottle S, Whitman W T
Investment timing
McGraw, 1953.

(189)
Smith E L
Common stocks as long term investments
Macmillan, 1924.

1.11   Investment management - readings and conference proceedings

(190)
Fabozzi F J ed.
Selected topics in investment management
Ballinger, 1988.

(191)
Fabozzi F J ed.
The institutional investor focus on investment management
Ballinger, 1988.

(192)
Vertin J R ed.
Managing the investment organization
Institute of Chartered Financial Analysts, 1988.

(193)
Brown S J, Kritzman M P
Quantitative methods for financial analysis
Research Foundation of the Institute of Chartered Financial Analysts, 1987.

(194)
Troughton G H ed.
Asset/liability management
Institute of Chartered Financial Analysts, 1986.

(195)
Vertin J R ed.
Applying economic analysis to portfolio management: Improving the investment decision process
Institute of Chartered Financial Analysts, 1985.

(196)
Institute of Chartered Financial Analysts
CFA readings in financial analysis
Institute of Chartered Financial Analysts, 1984.

(197)
Vertin J R ed.
Managing the investment professional
Institute of Chartered Financial Analysts, 1984.

(198)
Fabozzi F J
Readings in investment management
Irwin, 1983.

(199)
Maginn J L, Tuttle D L eds
Managing investment portfolios: A dynamic process
Warren Gorham & Lamont, 1983

(200)
Vertin J R ed.
Management skills for investment managers
Institute of Chartered Financial Analysts, 1983.

(201)
Lorie J H, Brealey R A eds.
Modern developments in investment management: a book of readings. 2nd ed
Dryden Pr, 1978.

(202)
Bicksler J L, Samuelson P A eds.
Investment portfolio decision-making
Lexington Bks, 1974.

(203)
Bicksler J L ed.
Methodology in finance: investments
Lexington Bks, 1972.

(204)
Fredrikson E B ed.
Frontiers of investment analysis. Rev ed
Intext, 1971.

(205)
Taylor B F ed.
Investment analysis and portfolio management: readings from British Publications
Elek, 1970.

(206)
Ball R E ed.
Readings in investments
Allyn, 1965.

(207)
Wu H-K, Zakon A J eds.
Elements of investments: selected readings
HR & W, 1965.

(208)
Lerner E M
Readings in financial analysis and investment management
Irwin, 1963.

1.12 Investment management - cases

(209)
Vandell R F
Cases in portfolio management
Irwin, 1988.

(210)
Twark A J et al.
Security analysis and portfolio management: a casebook
Holden-Day, 1973.

(211)
Bates G E
Investment management: a casebook
McGraw, 1959..

(212)**Calkins F J**
Cases and problems in investments
P-H, 1957.

1.13 Investment management bibliographies and glossaries

(213)
Rosenberg J M
The investor's dictionary
Wiley, 1986.

(214)
Pratt S P
Bibliography on risks and rates of return for common stocks
FAJ 1968 MAY-JUN VOL 24 p 151-166.

(215)
Society of Investment Analysts
A bibliography for investment and economic analysis
Society of Investment Analysts, London, 1965.

(216)
Wyckoff P
Dictionary of stock market terms
P-H, 1964.

(217)
European Federation of Financial Analysts Societies
A concise bibliography for investment analysis in Europe
Paris: The Federation, 1963.

1.2 Corporate finance - general

(218)
Block S B, Hirt G A
Foundations of financial management. 5th ed
Irwin, 1989.

(219)
Bruce R et al.
Handbook of Australian corporate finance. 3rd ed
Butterworth, 1989.

(220)
Gitman L J
Basic managerial finance. 2nd ed
Har-Row, 1989.

(221)
Hampton J J
Financial decision making: concepts, problems, and cases. 4th ed
P-H, 1989.

(222)
Harrington D R, Wilson B D
Corporate financial analysis. 3rd ed
Dow Jones-Irwin, 1989.

(223)
Higgins R C
Analysis for financial management. 2nd ed
Irwin, 1989.

(224)
Schlosser M
Corporate finance: A model-building approach
P-H, 1989.

(225)
Van Horne J C
Fundamentals of financial management. 7th ed
P-H, 1989.

(226)
Van Horne J C
Financial management and policy. 8th ed
P-H, 1989.

(227)
Allen D
Strategic financial management: managing for long-term financial success
Financial Times Business Information, 1988.

(228)
Ballon R J, Tomita I
The financial behavior of Japanese corporations
New York: Kodansha International, 1988.

(229)
Brealey R A, Myers S C
Principles of corporate finance. 3rd ed
McGraw, 1988.

(230)
Brigham E F, Gapenski L C
Financial management: theory and practice. 5th ed
Dryden Pr, 1988.

(231)
Cary W L, Eisenberg M A
Cases and materials on corporations
Foundation Press, 1988.

(232)
Clarke R G, Wilson B D, Daines R D et al.
Strategic financial management
Irwin, 1988.

(233)
Cooley P L
Business financial management
Dryden Pr, 1988.

(234)
Deschamps B, Mehta D
Chief financial officer: Strategy formulation and implementation
Wiley, 1988.

(235)
Dobbins R, Witt S F
Practical financial management
Blackwell, 1988.

(236)
Heertje A ed.
Innovation, technology and finance
Blackwell, 1988.

(237)
Kolb B A, DeMong R F
Principles of financial management. 2nd ed
Irwin, 1988.

(238)
Kolb R W
Principles of finance
Scott, Foresman, 1988.

(239)
Maness T S
Introduction to corporate finance
McGraw, 1988.

(240)
Mayer C
New issues in corporate finance: comments
EER 1988 VOL 32:5.

(241)
Neveu R P
Fundamentals of managerial finance. 3rd ed
SW Pub, 1988.

(242)
Reichert A K, Moore J S, Byler E
Financial analysis among large U S corporations: Recent trends and the impact of the personal computer
JBFA 1988 WINTER VOL 15:4 p 469-486.

(243)
Ross S A, Westerfield R W
Corporate finance
Irwin, 1988.

(244)
Rutterford J et al., eds.
Handbook of UK corporate finance
Butterworth, 1988.

(245)
Schall L D, Haley C W
Introduction to financial management. 5th ed
McGraw, 1988.

(246)
Vale P A ed.
Financial management handbook. 3rd ed
Gower, 1988.

(247)
Brigham E F, Gapenski L C
Intermediate financial management. 2nd ed
Dryden Pr, 1987.

(248)
Brooks L D
FINGAME: the financial management decision
game. 3rd ed
Irwin, 1987.

(249)
Cooper I A, Franks J R
Treasury performance measurement
MCFJ 1987 WINTER VOL 4 p 29-43.

(250)
Cornell B, Shapiro A C
Corporate stakeholders and corporate finance
FIN MGMT 1987 SPRING VOL 16 p 5-14.

(251)
Gup B E
Principles of financial management. 2nd ed
Wiley, 1987.

(252)
Kolb R W
Financial management
Scott, Foresman, 1987.

(253)
Pringle J J, Harris R S
Essentials of managerial finance. 2nd ed
Scott, Foresman, 1987.

(254)
Rao R K S
Financial management: Concepts and applications
Macmillan, 1987.

(255)
Stewart J C
Corporate finance and fiscal policy in Ireland
Gower, 1987.

(256)
Weston J F, Brigham E F
Essentials of managerial finance. 8th ed
Dryden Pr, 1987.

(257)
Altman E I, McKinney M J eds.
Handbook of corporate finance
Wiley, 1986.

(258)
Brigham E F
Fundamentals of financial management. 4th ed
Dryden Pr, 1986.

(259)
Chew D H
Six roundtable discussions of corporate finance
with Joel Stern
Quorum Bks, 1986.

(260)
Higson C J
Business finance
Butterworth, 1986.

(261)
Law W A
A corporation is more than its stock
HBR 1986 MAY-JUN VOL 64:3 p 80-83.

(262)
Levy H, Sarnat M
Capital investment and financial decisions. 3rd ed
P-H, 1986.

(263)
Mayo H B
Finance: an introduction. 2nd ed
Dryden Pr, 1986.

(264)
McLaney E J
Business finance: theory and practice
Pitman, 1986..

(265)
Samuels J M, Wilkes F M
Management of company finance. 4th ed
Van N-Rein, 1986.

(266)
Trueman B
The relationship between the level of capital expenditures and firm value
JFQA 1986 JUN VOL 21:2 p 115-129

(267)
Watson A, Altringham R
Treasury management: international banking operations
Institute of Bankers, 1986.

(268)
Weston J F, Copeland T E
Managerial finance. 8th ed
CBS International, 1986.

(269)
Dotan A, Ravid S A
On the interaction of real and financial decisions of the firm under uncertainty
JF 1985 JUN VOL 40:2 p 501-517

(270)
Franks J R et al.
Corporate finance: concepts and applications
Kent Publishing, 1985.

(271)
Gitman L J, Maxwell C E
Financial activities of major U S firms: Survey and analysis of Fortune's 1000
FIN MGMT 1985 WINTER VOL 14 p 57-65.

(272)
Taylor T W
The financing of industry and commerce
Heinemann, 1985.

(273)
Bar-Yosef S, Landskroner Y
The impact of the government sector on financial equilibrium and corporate financial decisions
JBFA 1984 VOL 11:1 p 13.

(274)
Davis E W, Pointon J
Finance and the firm
Oxford U Pr, 1984.

(275)
Hodson D ed.
Corporate finance and treasury management
Gee, 1984.

(276)
Lumby S P
Investment appraisal. 2nd ed
Van N-Rein, 1984.

(277)
Moyer R C, McGuigan J R, Kretlow W J
Contemporary financial management. 2nd ed
West Pub, 1984.

(278)
Archer S H et al.
Financial management. 2nd ed
Wiley, 1983.

(279)
Broyles J et al., eds.
Financial management handbook. 2nd ed
Gower, 1983.

(280)
Clarkson G P E, Elliott B J
Managing money and finance. 3rd ed / by Alan Johnson
Gower, 1983.

(281)
Davey P J
New patterns in organizing for financial management
New York: Conference Board, 1983.

(282)
Joy O M
Introduction to financial management. 3rd ed
Irwin, 1983.

(283)
Moore J S, Reichert A K
An analysis of the financial management techniques currently employed by large US corporations
JBFA 1983 WINTER VOL 10:4 p 623-645

(284)
Johnson R W, Melicher R W
Financial management. 5th ed
Allyn, 1982.

(285)
McInnes J M, Carlton W J
Theory, models and implementation in financial
management
MSci 1982 SEP VOL 28:9 p 957-978

(286)
Hargreaves R L, Smith R H
Managing your company's finances
Heinemann, 1981.

(287)
Norgaard R L
The evolution of business finance textbooks
FIN MGMT 1981 SUPP VOL 10 p 34-45.

(288)
Vause R, Woodward N
Finance for managers. 2nd ed
Macmillan, 1981.

(289)
Freear J
The management of business finance
Pitman, 1980.

(290)
Solomon E, Pringle J J
An introduction to financial management. 2nd ed
Scott, Foresman, 1980.

(291)
Franks J R, Broyles J E
Modern managerial finance
Wiley, 1979.

(292)
Gitman L J
Principles of managerial finance. 2nd ed
Har-Row, 1979.

(293)
Heyel C ed.
The VNR concise guide to financial management
Van N-Rein, 1979.

(294)
Midgley K, Burns R G
Business finance and the capital market. 3rd ed
Macmillan, 1979.

(295)
Murphy J E Jr, Osborne M F M
Games of chance and the probability of corporate
profit or loss
FIN MGMT 1979 SUMMER VOL 8 p 82.

(296)
Prodhan B
The Board and financial management
Business Bks, 1979.

(297)
Gibbs J
A practical approach to financial management
Financial Training Publications, 1978.

(298)
Kroncke C O et al.
Managerial finance: essentials. 2nd ed
West Pub, 1978.

(299)
Walker E W, Petty J W
Financial management of the small firm
P-H, 1978.

(300)
Boudreaux K J, Long H W
The basic theory of corporate finance
P-H, 1977.

(301)
Desmond G M, Kelley R E
Business valuation handbook
Llano, Ca.: Valuation Press, 1977.

(302)
Franks J R, Scholefield H H
Corporate financial management. 2nd ed
Gower, 1977.

(303)
Higgins R C
How much growth can a firm afford?
FIN MGMT 1977 AUTUMN VOL 6 p 7.

(304)
Pritchard R E
Operational financial management
P-H, 1977.

(305)
Schwartzman S D, Ball R E
Elements of financial analysis
Van N-Rein, 1977.

(306)
Aydon C
How to finance your company
Business Bks, 1976.

(307)
Bolten S E
Managerial finance: principles and practice
HM, 1976.

(308)
Findlay M C III
Corporate finance and normalised price
JBFA 1976 SUMMER VOL 3:2 P 115-130.

(309)
Gerstner L V Jr, Anderson H M
The chief financial officer as activist
HBR 1976 SEP-OCT VOL 54:5 p 100-106.

(310)
Mao J C T
Corporate financial decisions
Palo Alto, Calif.: Pavan Publishers, 1976.

(311)
Petty J W, Bowlin O D
The financial manager and quantitative decision
models
FIN MGMT 1976 WINTER VOL 5 p 32.

(312)
Kreps C H, Wacht R F
Financial administration
Dryden Pr, 1975.

(313)
Bradley J F
Administrative financial management. 3rd ed
Dryden Pr, 1974.

(314)
Pogue G A, Lall K
Corporate finance: An overview
SMR 1974 SPRING p 19-38.

(315)
West R R, Tinic S M
Corporate finance and the changing stock market
FIN MGMT 1974 AUTUMN VOL 3 p 14.

(316)
Francis D P
The foundations of financial management
Pitman, 1973.

(317)
Hopkins R W
"Predictions"   and   "hindsights"   relevant   to
corporate financial performance
JBF 1973 SPRING VOL 5:1 p 31-37..

(318)**Jean W H**
Finance
Dryden Pr, 1973.

(319)
Lusztig P A, Schwab B
Managerial finance in a Canadian setting
HR & W, 1973.

(320)
O'Herlihy C St. J
Towards a practical theory of finance for the firm
(with some of its implications)
JBF 1973 SUMMER VOL 5:2 p 49-55.

(321)
Shuckett D H, Mock E J
Decision strategies in financial management
New York: AMACOM, 1973.

(322)
Archer S H, D'Ambrosio C A
Business finance: theory and management. 2nd ed
Macmillan, 1972.

(323)
Brandt L K
Analysis for financial management
P-H, 1972.

(324)
Committe T C
Managerial finance for the seventies
McGraw, 1972.

(325)
Elliott J W
Control, size, growth and financial performance in the firm
JFQA 1972 JAN VOL 7 p 1309-1320.

(326)
Elliott J W
Forecasting and analysis of corporate financial performance with an econometric model of the firm
JFQA 1972 MAR VOL 7 p 1499-1526.

(327)
Dobrovolsky S P
The economics of corporation finance
McGraw, 1971.

(328)
Hunt P et al.
Basic business finance: text and cases. 4th ed
Irwin, 1971.

(329)
Lerner E M
Managerial finance: a systems approach
HarBraceJ, 1971.

(330)
Prather C L, Wert J E
Financing business firms. 4th ed
Irwin, 1971.

(331)
Bierman H Jr
Financial policy decisions
Collier Macmillan, 1970.

(332)
Curran W S
Principles of financial management
McGraw, 1970.

(333)
Grunewald A E, Nemmers E E
Basic managerial finance
HR & W, 1970.

(334)
Jackson A S, Townsend E C
Financial management
Harrap, 1970.

(335)
Newbould G D
Business finance
Harrap, 1970.

(336)
Robinson R I, Johnson R W
Self correcting problems in finance. 2nd ed
Allyn, 1970.

(337)
Stapleton R C
The theory of corporate finance
Harrap, 1970.

(338)
Vancil R F ed.
Financial executive's handbook
Dow Jones-Irwin, 1970.

(339)
Wright M G
Financial management
McGraw, 1970.

(340)
Bierman H Jr, Fouraker L E, Jaedicke R K
Quantitative analysis for business decisions. 3rd ed
Irwin, 1969.

(341)
Donaldson E F, Pfahl J K
Corporate finance: policy and management. 3rd ed
Ronald, 1969.

(342)
Flink S J, Grunewald D
Managerial finance
Wiley, 1969.

(343)
Kent R P
Corporate financial management. 3rd ed
Irwin, 1969.

(344)
Mao J C T
Quantitative analysis of financial decisions
Macmillan, 1969.

(345)
Paish F W
Business finance. 4th ed
Pitman, 1968.

(346)
Van Arsdell P M
Corporation finance
Ronald, 1968.

(347)
Chambers R J
Financial management
Law Book, 1967.

(348)
Cooke G W, Bomeli E C
Business and financial management
HM, 1967.

(349)
Lindsay R, Sametz A W
Financial management--an analytical approach.
Rev ed
Irwin, 1967.

(350)
Cohen J B, Robbins S M
The financial manager - basic aspects of financial
administration
Har-Row, 1966.

(351)
Friedland S
The economics of corporate finance
P-H, 1966.

(352)
Hastings P G
The management of business finance
Van N-Rein, 1966.

(353)
Husband W H, Dockeray J C
Modern corporation finance. 6th ed
Irwin, 1966.

(354)
Lerner E M, Carleton W T
A theory of financial analysis
HarBraceJ, 1966.

(355)
Page C S, Canaway E E
Finance for management
Heinemann, 1966.

(356)
Potter C C
Finance and business administration in Canada
P-H, 1966.

(357)
Weston J F
The scope and methodology of finance
P-H, 1966.

(358)
Brandt L K
Business finance, a management approach
P-H, 1965.

(359)
Childs J F
Long-term financing
P-H, 1965.

(360)
Osborn R C
Business finance: the management approach
Appleton, 1965.

(361)
Porterfield J T S
Investment decisions and capital costs
P-H, 1965.

(362)
Robichek A A, Myers S C
Optimal financing decisions
P-H, 1965.

(363)
Walker E W
Essentials of financial management
P-H, 1965.

(364)
Burtchett F F et al.
Corporation finance. Rev ed
Johnsen, 1964.

(365)
Dauten C A, Welshans M T
Principles of finance: functions, problems, institutions, 3rd ed.
SW Pub, 1964.

(366)
Gordon M J
The investment, financing and valuation of the corporation
Irwin, 1964.

(367)
Meiselman D, Shapiro E
The measurement of corporate sources and uses of funds
Natl Bur Econ Res, 1964.

(368)
Mock E J
Short problems in business finance and financial management
Intext, 1964.

(369)
Taylor M
General financing knowledge: the principles and practice of finance
Textbooks, 1964.

(370)
Walker E W, Baughn W H
Financial planning and policy
Har-Row, 1964..

(371)
White K K
Financing company expansion
AMA, 1964.

(372)
Beranek W
Analysis for financial decision
Irwin, 1963.

(373)
Corrigan F J, Ward H A eds.
Financial management: policies and practices
HM, 1963.

(374)
Solomon E
The theory of financial management
Columbia U Pr, 1963.

(375)
Curtis E T
Company organization of the finance function
AMA, 1962.

(376)
Guthmann H G, Dougall H E
Corporate financial policy. 4th ed
P-H, 1962.

(377)
Kimball M
Corporate finance
Littlefield, 1962.

(378)
O'Donnell J L, Goldberg M S eds.
Elements of financial administration
Merrill, 1962.

(379)
Schwartz E
Corporation finance
St Martin, 1962.

(380)
Wessel R H
Principles of financial analysis: a study of financial management: text with cases
Macmillan, 1961.

(381)
Prentice-Hall Editorial Staff
Encyclopedic dictionary of business finance
P-H, 1960.

(382)
Bradley J F
Fundamentals of corporation finance. Rev ed
HR & W, 1959.

(383)
Gerstenberg C W
Financial organisation and management of business. 4th ed
P-H, 1959.

(384)
Osborn R C
Corporation finance
Har-Row, 1959.

(385)
Tew B, Henderson R F eds.
Studies in company finance
Cambridge U Pr, 1959.

(386)
Dauten C A
Business finance: the fundamentals of financial
management. 2nd ed
P-H, 1956.

(387)
Dewing A S
The financial policy of corporations, 2 vols. 5th
ed
Ronald, 1953.

(388)
Howard B B, Upton M
Introduction to business finance
McGraw, 1953.

(389)
Dean J
Managerial economics
P-H, 1951.

(390)
Lutz F A, Lutz V C
The theory of investment of the firm
Princeton U Pr, 1951.

1.21 Corporate finance - readings and conference proceedings

(391)
Jensen M C, Smith C W eds.
Modern theory of corporate finance. 2nd ed
McGraw, 1989.

(392)
Johnson R E ed.
Issues and readings in managerial finance. 3rd ed
Dryden Pr, 1987.

(393)
Edwards J, Franks J R, Mayer C et al., eds.
Recent developments in corporate finance
Cambridge U Pr, 1986.

(394)
Ivison S et al., eds.
British readings in financial management
Har-Row, 1986.

(395)
Stern J M, Chew D H eds.
The revolution in corporate finance
Blackwell, 1986.

(396)
Altman E I, Subrahmanyam M eds.
Recent advances in corporate finance
Irwin, 1985.

(397)
Lee C F ed.
Financial analysis and planning: theory and
application: a book of readings
Addison-Wes, 1983.

(398)
Scott D F Jr et al., eds.
Readings in financial management
Academic Pr, 1982.

(399)
Derkinderen F G J, Crum R L eds.
Risk, capital costs and project financing decisions
Martinus Nijhoff, 1981.

(400)
Van Dam C ed.
Trends in financial decision-making: planning and
capital investment decisions
Martinus Nijhoff, 1978.

(401)
Myers S C ed.
Modern developments in financial management
Praeger, 1976.

(402)
Brigham E F, Ricks M B eds.
Readings in the essentials of management finance
HR & W, 1971.

(403)
Serraino W J et al., eds.
Frontiers of financial management: selected readings
SW Pub, 1971.

(404)
Carsberg B V, Edey H C eds.
Modern financial management: selected readings
Penguin, 1969.

(405)
Hunt P, Andrews V L
Financial management: cases and readings
Irwin, 1968.

(406)
Archer S H, D'Ambrosio C A eds.
The theory of business finance: a book of readings
Macmillan, 1967.

(407)
Ball R E, Melnyk Z L eds.
Theory of managerial finance: selected readings
Allyn, 1967.

(408)
Chen H C ed.
Frontiers of managerial finance
Gulf Pub, 1967.

(409)
Mock E J ed.
Financial decision-making
Intext, 1967.

(410)
Robichek A A ed.
Financial research and management decisions
Wiley, 1967.

(411)
Weston J F, Woods D H eds.
Basic financial management: selected readings
Wadsworth Pub, 1967.

(412)
Weston J F, Woods D H eds.
Theory of business finance: advanced readings
Wadsworth Pub, 1967.

(413)
Van Horne J C ed.
Foundations for financial management: a book of readings
Irwin, 1966.

(414)
Mock E J ed.
Readings in financial management
Intext, 1964.

(415)
Solomon E ed.
The management of corporate capital
Free Pr, 1964.

(416)
Weston J F ed.
Readings in finance from Fortune
HR & W, 1958.

1.22 Corporate finance - cases

(417)
Archer S, Kerr H S
Readings and cases in corporate finance
McGraw, 1988.

(418)
Crum R L, Brigham E F
Cases in managerial finance. 6th ed
Dryden Pr, 1987.

(419)
Dimson E, Marsh P
Cases in corporate finance
Wiley, 1987.

(420)
Harrington D R
Case studies in financial decision making
Dryden Pr, 1985.

(421)
Hamilton R W
Corporation finance: Cases and materials
West Pub, 1984.

(422)
Gitman L J, Moses E A
Financial management: cases
West Pub, 1978.

(423)
Scott D F Jr et al.
Cases in finance
P-H, 1977..

(424)**Cohan A B, Wyman H E**
Cases in financial management
P-H, 1972.

(425)
Midgley K, Burns R G
Case studies in business finance and financial
analysis
Macmillan, 1971.

(426)
Bush R C et al.
Case problems in financial management
Appleton, 1968.

(427)
Mock E J et al.
Basic financial management: text, problems and
cases
Intext, 1968.

(428)
Walker E W et al.
Case problems in financial management
Appleton, 1968.

(429)
Norgaard R L, Vaughn D E
Cases in financial decision making
P-H, 1967.

(430)
Howard B B, Jones S L eds.
Managerial problems in finance; cases in decision
making
McGraw, 1964.

(431)
Nemmers E E
Cases in finance
Allyn, 1964.

(432)
Norgaard R L, Longstreet J R
Cases in financial management. 2nd ed
Wadsworth Pub, 1964.

(433)
Vandell R F, Coleman A B
Case problems in finance. 4th ed
Irwin, 1962.

(434)
Longstreet J R
Cases in financial management
Wadsworth Pub, 1961.

(435)
Masson R L, Hunt P, Anthony R N
Cases in financial management
Irwin, 1960.

1.23 Corporate finance - bibliographies and glossaries

(436)
IFR Publishing
The IFR financial glossary
IFR Publishing, 1988.

1.3 International finance - general

(437)
Aliber R Z ed.
The handbook of international financial
management
Dow Jones-Irwin, 1989.

(438)
Chuppe T M, Haworth H R, Watkins M G
Global finance: causes, consequences and
prospects of the future
Global Finance Journal 1989 VOL 1:1.

(439)
Eiteman D K, Stonehill A I
Multinational business finance. 5th ed
Addison-Wes, 1989.

(440)
Stoakes C, Freeman A eds.
Managing global portfolios
Euromoney Publications, 1989.

(441)
Business International
Automating global financial management
Wiley, 1988.

(442)
Kane D R
Principles of international finance
Croom Helm, 1988.

(443)
Shapiro A C
International corporate finance. 2nd ed
Ballinger, 1988.

(444)
Solnik B H
International investments
Addison-Wes, 1988.

(445)
Watson M et al.
International capital markets: developments and prospects
Washington, DC: International Monetary Fund, 1988.

(446)
Abdullah F A
Financial management for the multinational firm
P-H, 1987.

(447)
Bryant R C
International financial intermediation
Brookings, 1987.

(448)
Myers S C
Finance theory and financial strategy
MCFJ 1987 SPRING VOL 5 p 6-13.

(449)
Officer D T, Hoffmeister J R
ADRs: A substitute for the real thing
JPM 1987 WINTER VOL 13:2 p 61-65.

(450)
Ross D et al.
International treasury management
Woodhead-Faulkner, 1987.

(451)
Stonehill A I, Eiteman D K
Finance: an international perspective
Irwin, 1987.

(452)
Adler M, Simon D
Exchange rate surprises in international portfolios
JPM 1986 WINTER VOL 12 p 44-53.

(453)
Ayling D E
The internationalisation of stockmarkets: the trend towards greater foreign borrowing and investment
Gower, 1986.

(454)
Buckley A
Multinational finance
Philip Allan, 1986.

(455)
Capie F, Wood G E eds.
Financial crises and the world banking system
Macmillan, 1986.

(456)
Gaab W, Granziol M J, Horner M
On some international parity conditions: an empirical investment
EER 1986 VOL 30:3.

(457)
Grabbe O
International financial markets
Elsevier, 1986.

(458)
Holland J
International financial management
Blackwell, 1986.

(459)
Tapley M ed.
International portfolio management
Euromoney Publications, 1986.

(460)
Zenoff D B ed.
Corporate finance in multinational companies
Euromoney Publications, 1986.

(461)
Mattione R P
OPEC's investments and the international financial system
Brookings, 1985.

(462)
Melvin M
International money and finance
Har-Row, 1985.

(463)
Oxelheim L
International financial market fluctuations: corporate forecasting and reporting problems
Wiley, 1985.

(464)
Rugman A M, Eden L eds.
Multinationals and transfer pricing
Croom Helm, 1985.

(465)
Tsoukalis L ed.
Political economy of international money: in search of a new order
Sage, 1985.

(466)
Moffitt M
The world's money: international banking from Bretton Woods to the brink of insolvency
Michael Joseph, 1984.

(467)
Putnam B H
Perspectives on country risk
MCFJ 1984 FALL VOL 2 p 59-63.

(468)
Rodriguez R M, Carter E E
International financial management. 3rd ed
P-H, 1984.

(469)
Shapiro A C
The evaluation and control of foreign affiliates
MCFJ 1984 SPRING VOL 2 p 13-25.

(470)
Aliber R Z
The international money game. 4th ed
Macmillan, 1983.

(471)
George A M, Giddy I H eds.
International finance handbook: volumes 1 and 2
Wiley, 1983.

(472)
Hawkins R G et al., eds.
Internationalization of financial markets and national economic policy
JAI Pr, 1983.

(473)
Herring R J ed.
Managing international risk: essays commissioned in honor of the Centenary of the Wharton School, University of Pennsylvania
Cambridge U Pr, 1983.

(474)
Lessard D R, Shapiro A C
Guidelines for global financing choices
MCFJ 1983 WINTER VOL 1 p 68-79.

(475)
Levi M D
International finance: financial management and the international economy
McGraw, 1983.

(476)
Rosenthal L
An empirical test of the efficiency of the ADR market
JBankF 1983 VOL 7 p 17..

(477)**Stewart B**
A proposal for measuring international performance
MCFJ 1983 SUMMER VOL 1 p 56-71.

(478)
OECD
Controls on international capital movements: the experience with controls on international financial credits, loans and deposits
OECD, 1982.

(479)
Shapiro A C
Multinational financial management
Allyn, 1982.

(480)
Dean J W, Schwindt R eds.
International banking and finance
Durham, NC: Eno River Pr, 1981.

(481)
Wood D, Byrne J
International business finance
Macmillan, 1981.

(482)
Mendelsohn M S
Money on the move: the modern international
capital market
McGraw, 1980.

(483)
OECD
Experience with controls on international
portfolio operations in shares and bonds
OECD, 1980.

(484)
Kettell B
The finance of international business
Graham & Trotman, 1979.

(485)
Roll R, Solnik B
On some international parity conditions
Journal of Macroeconomics 1979 SUMMER.

(486)
Rugman A M
International diversification and the multinational
enterprise
Lexington Bks, 1979.

(487)
Black F
The ins and outs of foreign investment
FAJ 1978 MAY-JUN p 25-33.

(488)
Baker M R
Teaching international finance - an economist's
perspective
JFQA 1977 NOV VOL 12 p 607.

(489)
Choi F D S
Teaching international finance - an accountant's
perspective
JFQA 1977 NOV VOL 12 p 609.

(490)
Esslen R
The complete book of international investing:
how to buy foreign securities and who's who on
the international investment scene
McGraw, 1977.

(491)
Folks W R Jr
Integrating international finance into a unified
business program
JFQA 1977 NOV VOL 12 p 599.

(492)
Giddy I H
A note on the macroeconomic assumptions of
international financial management
JFQA 1977 NOV VOL 12 p 601.

(493)
Weston J F
Guide to international financial management
McGraw, 1977.

(494)
Coombs C A
The arena of international finance
Wiley, 1976.

(495)
Obersteiner E
Should the foreign affiliate remit dividends or
reinvest?
FIN MGMT 1973 SPRING VOL 2 p 88.

(496)
Solnik B H
European capital markets: towards a general
theory of international investment
Lexington Bks, 1973.

(497)
Petty J W, Walker E W
Optimal transfer pricing for the multinational
firm
FIN MGMT 1972 WINTER VOL 1 p 74.

(498)
Weston J F, Sorge B W
International managerial finance
Irwin, 1972.

(499)
Zenoff D B, Zwick J
International financial management
P-H, 1969.

1.31 International finance - readings and conference proceedings

(500)
Poniachek H A ed.
International corporate finance: markets, transactions, and financial management
Unwin Hyman, 1989.

(501)
Stern J M, Chew D H eds.
New developments in international finance
Blackwell, 1988.

(502)
Lessard D R ed.
International financial management: theory and application
Wiley, 1985.

(503)
Agmon T et al., eds.
Future of the International Monetary System
Lexington Bks, 1984.

(504)
Vertin J R ed.
International equity investing
Institute of Chartered Financial Analysts, 1984.

(505)
Sarnat M, Szego G P eds.
International finance and trade, Vols I and II
Ballinger, 1979.

(506)
Elton E J, Gruber M J eds.
International capital markets
N Holland, 1975.

(507)
Dunning J H ed.
International investment: selected readings
Penguin, 1972.

1.32 International finance - cases

(508)
Dufey G, Giddy I H
50 cases in international finance
Addison-Wes, 1987.

(509)
Feiger G, Jacquillat B
International finance: text and cases
Allyn, 1982.

(510)
Carlson R S et al.
International finance: cases and simulation
Addison-Wes, 1980.

1.33 International finance bibliographies and glossaries

(511)
Walmsley J
Macmillan dictionary of international finance.
2nd ed
Macmillan, 1985.

(512)
Aggarwal R
The literature of international business finance: a bibliography of selected business and academic sources
Praeger, 1984.

1.4 Personal finance - general

(513)
Aliber R Z
Your money and your life
Dow Jones-Irwin, 1989.

(514)
Boone L E, Kurtz D L
Personal financial management
Irwin, 1989.

(515)
Edwards J
Personal finance: the A-Z of investment and money management
Grafton, 1989.

(516)
Widicus W W, Stitzel T E
Personal investing. 5th ed
Irwin, 1989.

(517)
Bayston D M ed.
Serving the individual investor
Institute of Chartered Financial Analysts, 1988.

(518)
Kapoor J R, Dlabay L R, Hughes R J
Personal finance
Irwin, 1988.

(519)
Lang L R
Strategy for personal finance. 4th ed
McGraw, 1988.

(520)
Mathur I
Personal finance. 2nd ed
SW Pub, 1988

(521)
Droms W G ed.
Asset allocation for the individual investor
Institute of Chartered Financial Analysts, 1987.

(522)
Gitman L J
Personal financial planning. 4th ed
Dryden Pr, 1987.

(523)
Amling F, Droms W G
Personal financial management. 2nd ed
Irwin, 1986.

(524)
Matatko J, Stafford D
Key developments in personal finance
Blackwell, 1985.

(525)
Rosefsky R S
Personal finance and money management
Wiley, 1978.

(526)
Loomis C J
Fortune's guide to personal investing
McGraw, 1963.

2 Decisions under uncertainty

(527)
Jewitt I
Choosing between risky prospects: the characterization of comparaive statics results, and location independent risk
MSci 1989 VOL 35 p 60.

(528)
Machina M J
Dynamic consistency and non-expected utility models of choice under uncertainty
JEL 1989 DEC VOL 27:4 1622-1668.

(529)
Eichenbaum M S, Hansen L P, Singleton K J
Time series analysis of representative agent models of consumption and leisure choice under uncertainty
QJE 1988 VOL 103 p 51..

(530)**Feivel G ed.**
Essays in honor of Kenneth Arrow
Macmillan, 1987.

(531)
Friedman B M, Roley V V
Aspects of investor behavior under risk
(in Feiwel G ed., Essays in honor of Kenneth Arrow. Macmillan, 1987.)

(532)
Robison L J, Barry P J
The competitive firm's response to risk
Macmillan, 1987.

(533)
Sandler T, Sterbenz F P, Posnett J
Free riding and uncertainty
EER 1987 VOL 31:8.

(534)
Greenberg E, Marshall W J, Yawitz J B
Firm behavior under conditions of uncertainty and the theory of finance
QREB 1983 SUMMER VOL 23:2 p 6-22

(535)
Kahneman D, Slovic P, Tversky A eds.
Judgement under uncertainty: Heuristics and biases
Cambridge U Pr, 1982.

(536)
Merton R C
On the microeconomic theory of investment under uncertainty
(in Arrow K J and Intrilagator M D eds., Handbook of mathematical economics. N Holland, 1982.)

(537)
Tversky A, Kahneman D
The framing of decisions and the psychology of choice
Science 1981 p 453-458.

(538)
Lee W Y, Senchak A J Jr
On the social optimality of the value maximization criterion
JFQA 1980 JUN VOL 15 p 379.

(539)
Lippman S A, McCall J J, Winston W L
Constant absolute risk aversion bankruptcy and wealth-dependent decisions.
JB 1980 JUL VOL 53:3 p 285-296.

(540)
Sanders G S
An integration of shifts toward risk and caution in gambling situations
Journal of Experimental Social Psychology 1978 JUL VOL 14 p 409-416.

(541)
Heal G
Guarantees and risk-sharing
REStud 1977 VOL 44 p 549.

(542)
Levy H, Sarnat M eds.
Financial decision making under uncertainty
Academic Pr, 1977.

2.1 Utility theory

(543)
Chew S H, Epstein L G
A unifying approach to axiomatic non-expected utility theories
JET 1989 DEC VOL 49:2 p 207-240.

(544)
Cox J C, Epstein S
Preference reversals without the independence axiom
AER 1989 VOL 79:3 p 408-426.

(545)
Currim I S, Sarin R K
Prospect versus utility
MSci 1989 VOL 35 p 22.

(546)
Johnson E J, Schkade D A
Bias in utility assessments: further evidence and explanations
MSci 1989 VOL 35 p 406.

(547)
Knetsch J L
The endowment effect and evidence of nonreversible indifference curves
AER 1989 VOL 79:5 p 1277-1284.

(548)
Omberg E
The expected utility of the doubling strategy
JF 1989 JUN VOL 44:2 p 515-524.

(549)
Bell D E
The value of pre-decision side bets for utility mazimizers
MSci 1988 VOL 34 p 797.

(550)
Bell D E
One-switch utility functions and a measure of risk
MSci 1988 VOL 34 p 1416.

(551)
Bordley R F
An additive group utility for a fund manager
MSci 1988 VOL 34 p 836.

(552)
Busche K, Hall C D
An exception to the risk preference anomaly
JB 1988 VOL 61 p 337.

(553)
Fishburn P C, LaValle I H
Transitivity is equivalent to independence for states-additive SSB utilities
JET 1988 FEB VOL 44:1 p 202-208.

(554)
Harvey C M
Utility functions for infinite-period planning
MSci 1988 VOL 34 p 645.

(555)
Rubinstein A
Similarity and decision-making under risk (is there a utility theory resolution to the Allais paradox?)
JET 1988 OCT VOL 46:1 p 145-153.

(556)
Allen B
Smooth preferences and the approximate expected utility hypothesis
JET 1987 APR VOL 41:2 p 340-355.

(557)
Green J
"Making book against oneself", the independence axiom and nonlinear utility theory
QJE 1987 VOL 102 p 785.

(558)
Hong C S, Karni E, Safra Z
Risk aversion in the theory of expected utility with rank dependent probabilities
JET 1987 AUG VOL 42:2 p 370-381.

(559)
LeRoy S F, Singell L D Jr
Knight on risk and uncertainty
JPE 1987 VOL 95 p 394-406.

(560)
Loomes G, Sugden R
Some implications of a more general form of regret theory
JET 1987 APR VOL 41:2 p 270-287.

(561)
Machina M J
Choice under uncertainty: problems solved and unsolved
JEP 1987 VOL 1:1 p 121-154.

(562)
Swofford J L, Whitney G A
Nonparametric tests of utility maximization and weak separability for consumption, leisure and money
REStat 1987 VOL 69 p 458.

(563)
Green R C, Srivastava S
Expected utility maximization and demand behavior
JET 1986 APR VOL 38:2 p 313-323.

(564)
Jackson M O
Integration of demand and continuous utility functions
JET 1986 APR VOL 38:2 p 298-312.

(565)
Polemarchakis H M, Selden L, Zipkin P et al.
Approximate aggregation under uncertainty
JET 1986 APR VOL 38:2 p 189-210.

(566)
Arkes H R, Bulmer C
The psychology of sunk cost
Organizational Behavior and Human Decision Processes 1985 FEB VOL 35 p 124-140.

(567)
Brookshire D S, Thayer M A, Tschirhart J
A test of the expected utility model: Evidence from earth-quake risks
JPE 1985 VOL 93 p 369.

(568)
Green R C, Srivastava S
Risk aversion and arbitrage
JF 1985 MAR VOL 40:1 p 257-268

(569)
Horvath P A, Scott R C
An expected utility explanation of plunging and dumping behavior
FR 1985 MAY VOL 20:2.

(570)
Martin L J
Uncertain? how do you spell relief?
JPM 1985 SPRING VOL 11:3 p 5-8.

(571)
Stadt H van de, Kapteyn A, Geer S van de
The relativity of utility: evidence from panel data
REStat 1985 VOL 67 p 179.

(572)
Aivazian V A
Mean-variance utility functions and the demand for risky assets : an empirical analysis using flexible functional forms
JFQA 1983 DEC VOL 18:4 p 411-424

(573)
Ang J S, Chua J H, Woodward R S
A note on investment decision rules based on utility functions
JBFA 1983 WINTER VOL 10:4 p 657-661

(574)
Katz E
Relative risk aversion in comparative statics
AER 1983 VOL 73 P 452-454.

(575)
Morin R A, Suarez A F
Risk aversion revisited
JF 1983 SEP VOL 38:4 p 1201-1216

(576)
Yilmaz M R
The use of risk and return models for multiattribute decisions with decomposable utilities
JFQA 1983 SEP VOL 18:3 p 279-285

(577)
Basu K
Determinateness of the utility function: Revisiting a controversy of the thirties
REStud 1982 VOL 49 p 307.

(578)
Bell D
Regret in decision making under uncertainty
OR 1982 SEP-OCT VOL 30 p 961-981.

(579)
Bodily S E, White C C
Optimal consumption and portfolio strategies in a discrete-time model with summary-dependent preferences
JFQA 1982 MAR VOL 17:1 p 1-15

(580)
Siegel F W, Hoban J P Jr
Relative risk aversion revisited
REStat 1982 VOL 64 p 481.

(581)
Sinn H-W
Kinked utility and the demand for human wealth
and liability insurance
EER 1982 VOL 17:2.

(582)
Bernhard R H
Avoiding irrationality in the use of two-parameter
risk-benefit   models   for   investment   under
uncertainty
FIN MGMT 1981 SPRING VOL 10 p 77..

(583)**Crum R L, Laughhunn D J, Payne J W**
Risk-seeking behavior and its implications for
financial models
FIN MGMT 1981 WINTER VOL 10 p 20-27.

(584)
Dybvig P H, Polemarchakis H
Recovering cardinal utility
REStud 1981 JAN VOL 48:1 NO 151 p 159-166.

(585)
Friedman D
Why there are no risk preferrers
JPE 1981 VOL 89 p 600.

(586)
Kihlstrom R E, Mirman L J
Constant, increasing and decreasing risk aversion
with many commodities
REStud 1981 APR VOL 48:2 NO 152 p 271-280.

(587)
Thaler R H, Shefrin H M
An economic theory of self-control
JPE 1981 VOL 89 p 392.

(588)
Amihud Y
General risk aversion and attitude towards risk
JF 1980 JUN VOL 25:3 p 685-691.

(589)
Bailey M J, Olson M, Wonnacott P
The marginal utility of income does not increase:
Borrowing, lending and Friedman-Savage gambles
AER 1980 VOL 70 p 372-389.

(590)
Barrager S M
Assessment of simple joint time/risk preference
functions
MSci 1980 JUN VOL 26:6 p 620-632.

(591)
Jones-Lee M W
Maximum acceptable physical risk and a new
measure of financial risk-aversion
EJ 1980 SEP VOL 90:359 p 550-568.

(592)
Keeney R L
Utility functions for equity and public risk
MSci 1980 APR VOL 26:4 p 345-353.

(593)
Norgaard R, Killeen T
Expected utility and the truncated normal
distribution
MSci 1980 SEP VOL 26:9 p 901-909.

(594)
Payne J W, Laughhaun D J, Crum R
Translation of gambles and aspiration level effects
in risky choice behavior
MSci 1980 OCT VOL 26:10 p 1039-1060.

(595)
Selden L
A new approach to the joint consumption
portfolio problem
JMCB 1980 AUG VOL 12:3 p 429-447.

(596)
Eden B
An expected utility function for the insurance
buying gambler
REStud 1979 VOL 46 p 741.

(597)
Graves P E
Relative risk aversion: Increasing or decreasing
JFQA 1979 JUN VOL 14 p 205.

(598)
Kraus A, Sick G A
Communication of aggregate preferences through
market prices
JFQA 1979 NOV VOL 14 p 695.

(599)
Levy H, Markowitz H M
Approximating expected utility by a function of
mean and variance
AER 1979 VOL 69 p 308-317.

(600)
Shapiro P, Braithwait S D
Empirical tests for the existence of group utility
functions
REStud 1979 VOL 46 p 653.

(601)
Suits D B
The elasticity of demand for gambling
QJE 1979 VOL 93 p 155.

(602)
Eliashberg J, Winkler R L
The role of attitude toward risk in strictly
competitive decison making situations
MSci 1978 DEC VOL 24:16 p 1231.

(603)
Fishburn P C
On Handa's "New Theory of Cardinal Utility" and
the maximization of expected return
JPE 1978 VOL 86 p 321.

(604)
Grauer R R
The inference of tastes and beliefs from bond and
stock market data
JFQA 1978 JUN VOL 13 p 273.

(605)
Rossman M, Selden L
Time preferences, conditional risk preferences,
and two-period cardinal utility
JET 1978 OCT VOL 19:1 p 64-83.

(606)
Russell W R, Seo T K
Ordering uncertain prospects: The multivariate
utility functions case
REStud 1978 VOL 45 p 605.

(607)
Amihud Y
A note on risk aversion and indifference curves
JFQA 1977 SEP VOL 12 p 509.

(608)
Baker H K, Hargrove M B, Haslem J A
An empirical analysis of the risk-return
preferences of individual investors
JFQA 1977 SEP VOL 12 p 377.

(609)
Engelbrecht R
A note on multivariate risk and separable utility
functions
MSci 1977 AUG VOL 23:12 p 1143.

(610)
Handa J
Risk, probabilities and a new theory of cardinal
utility
JPE 1977 VOL 85 p 97.

(611)
Howitt P W
Intertemporal utility maximization and the timing
of transactions
AER 1977 VOL 67 p 156-165.

(612)
Keeney R L
A group preference axiomatization with cardinal
utility
MSci 1977 AUG VOL 23:12 p 140.

(613)
Prakash P
On the consistency of a gambler with time
preference
JET 1977 JUN VOL 15:1 p 92-98.

(614)
Sakai Y
Revealed favorability, indirect utility, and direct
utility
JET 1977 FEB VOL 14:1 p 113-129.

(615)
Samuelson P A
St. Petersburg paradoxes: defanged, dissected, and
historically described
JEL 1977 VOL 15 p 24-55.

(616)
Schofield N
Transitivity of preferences on a smooth manifold
of alternatives
JET 1977 FEB VOL 14:1 p 149-171.

(617)
Shapley L S
The St. Petersburg paradox: a con game?
JET 1977 APR VOL 14:2 p 439-442.

(618)
Suzumura K
Houthakker's axiom in the theory of rational
choice
JET 1977 APR VOL 14:2 p 284-290.

(619)
Weisbrod B A
Comparing utility functions in efficiency terms or,
what kind of utility functions do we want?
AER 1977 VOL 67 p 991-995.

(620)
Fishburn P C
Unbounded utility functions in expected utility
theory
QJE 1976 VOL 90 p 163.

(621)
Loistl O
The erroneous approximation of expected utility
by means of a Taylor's series expansion: Analytic
and computational results
AER 1976 VOL 66 p 904-910.

(622)
Schwartz T
Choice functions, "rationality" conditions, and
variations on the weak axiom of revealed
preference
JET 1976 DEC VOL 13:3 p 414-427.

(623)
Bowman R G
The role of utility in the state-preference
framework
JFQA 1975 JUN VOL 10 p 341.

(624)
Glustoff E
On continuous utility
QJE 1975 VOL 89 p 512.

(625)
Kallio M, Ohlson J A
A note on the representation of bounded utility
functions defined on (a,oo)
JFQA 1975 JUN VOL 10 p 377.

(626)
Miller S M
Measures of risk aversion: Some clarifying
comments
JFQA 1975 JUN VOL 10 p 299.

(627)
Nachman D C
Risk aversion, impatience, and optimal timing
decisions
JET 1975 OCT VOL 11:2 p 196-246.

(628)
Paroush J
Risk premium with many commodities
JET 1975 OCT VOL 11:2 p 283-286.

(629)
Chipman J S
Homothetic preferences and aggregation
JET 1974 MAY VOL 8:1 p 26-38.

(630)
Diamond P A, Stiglitz J E
Increases in risk and in risk aversion
JET 1974 JUL VOL 8:3 p 337-360.

(631)
Hammond J S III
Simplifying the choice between uncertain
prospects where preference is nonlinear
MSci 1974 JUL VOL 20:11 p 1047.

(632)
Kihlstrom R E, Mirman L J
Risk aversion with many commodities
JET 1974 JUL VOL 8:3 p 361-388.

(633)
Borch K
Uncertainty and indifference curves
REStud 1973 VOL 40 p 141.

(634)
Hoskins C G
Distinctions between risk and uncertainty
JBF 1973 SPRING VOL 5:1 p 10-12.

(635)
Fama E F
Ordinal and measurable utility
(in Jensen M C ed., Studies in the theory of
capital markets. Praeger, 1972.).

(636)**Foldes L**
Expected utility and continuity
REStud 1972 VOL 39 p 407.

(637)
Glustoff E, Nigro N
Liquidity preference and risk aversion with an
exponential utility function
REStud 1972 VOL 39 p 113

(638)
Kamien M I, Schwartz N L
A direct approach to choice under uncertainty
MSci 1972 VOL 18 p B470-B477.

(639)
Keeney R L
Utility functions for multiattributed consequences
MSci 1972 JUL VOL 18:11 p 276.

(640)
Sato K
Additive utility functions with double-log
consumer demand functions
JPE 1972 VOL 80 p 102.

(641)
Tarascio V J, Murphy J L
Uncertainty, learning, and dynamic utility theory
QREB 1972 VOL 12:3 p 19.

(642)
Arrow K J
Essays in the theory of risk-bearing
N Holland, 1971.

(643)
Luce R W, Krantz D H
Conditional expected utility
Em 1971 MAR VOL 39 p 253-272.

(644)
Pollak R A
Habit formation and dynamic demand functions
JPE 1970 VOL 78 p 745-763.

(645)
Shackle G L S
Decision order and time in human affairs. 2nd ed
Cambridge U Pr, 1970.

(646)
Zeckhauser R, Keeler E
Another type of risk aversion
Em 1970 SEP VOL 38 p 661-665.

(647)
Fishburn P C
A general theory of subjective probabilities and
expected utilities
Annals of Mathematical Statistics 1969 VOL 40
p 1419-1429.

(648)
Stiglitz J E
Behavior towards risk with many commodities
Em 1969 OCT VOL 37 p 660-667.

(649)
Borch K
Indifference curves and uncertainty
SJE 1968 MAR VOL 70 p 19-24.

(650)
Enzer H
A utility measure based on time preference
EJ 1968 DEC VOL 78 p 888-897.

(651)
Feldstein M
On the measurement of risk aversion
SJE 1968 JUL VOL 35 p 58-59.

(652)
Latane H A, Tuttle D L
Framework for forming probability beliefs
FAJ 1968 JUL-AUG VOL 24 p 51-61.

(653)
MacCrimmon K R
Descriptive and normative implications of the decision-theory postulates
(in Borch K and Mossin J eds., Risk and uncertainty. Macmillan Int, 1968.)

(654)
Moore B J
An introduction to the theory of finance--assetholder behavior under uncertainty
Free Pr, 1968.

(655)
Raiffa H
Decision analysis: introductory lectures on choices under uncertainty
Addison-Wes, 1968.

(656)
Borch K
The theory of risk
JRSS 1967 VOL 29 p B432-B452.

(657)
Fishburn P C
Methods of estimating additive utilities
MSci 1967 MAR VOL 13 p 435-453.

(658)
Lloyd C, Rohr R J, Walker M
A calculus proof of the existence of a continuous utility function
Met 1967 VOL 19 p 103-112.

(659)
Rosett R N
Estimating the utility of wealth from call option transactions
(in Hester D D and Tobin J eds., Risk aversion and portfolio choice. Wiley, 1967.)

(660)
Royama S, Hamada K
Substitution and complementarity in the choice of risky assets
(in Hester D D and Tobin J eds., Risk aversion and portfolio choice. Wiley, 1967.)

(661)
Bierwag G O, Groves M A
Indifference curves in asset analysis
EJ 1966 JUN VOL 76 p 337-343.

(662)
Borch K
A utility function derived from a survival game
MSci 1966 APR VOL 12 p B287-B295.

(663)
Latane H A, Tuttle D L
Decision theory and financial management
JF 1966 MAY VOL 21 p 228-244.

(664)
Swalm R O
Utility theory--insights into risk taking
HBR 1966 NOV-DEC VOL 44 p 123-136.

(665)
Thompson H E, Beranek W
The efficient use of an imperfect forecast
MSci 1966 NOV VOL 13 p 233-243.

(666)
Arrow K J
Aspects of the theory of risk bearing
Jahnssonin, 1965.

(667)
Brewer K R W, Fellner W
The slanting of subjective probabilities--agreement on some essentials
QJE 1965 NOV VOL 79 p 657-663.

(668)
Naslund B
Mathematical programming under risk
SJE 1965 SEP VOL 67 p 240-255.

(669)
Ozga S A
Expectations in economic theory
Weidenfeld & N, 1965.

(670)
Roberts H V
Probabilistic prediction
JASA 1965 MAR VOL 60 p 50-62.

(671)
Rosett R N
Gambling and rationality
JPE 1965 DEC VOL 73 p 595-607.

(672)
Yaari M E
Convexity in the theory of choice under risk
QJE 1965 MAY VOL 79 p 278-290.

(673)
Cootner P H
Rationality and risk in financial decision making
(in Fisk G ed., The frontiers of management
psychology. Har-Row, 1964.)

(674)
Kogan N, Wallach M A
Risk taking: a study in cognition and personality
HR & W, 1964.

(675)
Naslund B, Whinston A
Model of decision-making under risk
Met 1964 MAY-AUG VOL 16 p 81-94.

(676)
Pratt J W
Risk aversion in the small and in the large
Em 1964 JAN-APR VOL 32 p 122-136.

(677)
Pratt J W, Raiffa H, Schlaifer R
The foundations of decision under uncertainty
JASA 1964 JUN VOL 59 p 353-375.

(678)
Borch K
A note on utility and attitudes to risk
MSci 1963 JUL VOL 9 p 697-700.

(679)
DeGroot M H
Some   comments   on   the   experimental
measurement of utility
Behavioral Science 1963 APR VOL 8 p 146-149.

(680)
Tisdell C
Notes upon some of the present theories of
choice under uncertainty
Met 1963 AUG-DEC VOL 15 p 125-135.

(681)
Pollak R A
Additive   Von-Neumann-Morgenstern   utility
functions
Em 1962 OCT VOL 30 p 729-743.

(682)
Quirk J P, Saposnik R
Admissibility and measurable utility functions
REStud 1962 FEB VOL 29 p 140-146.

(683)
Eisenberg E
Aggregation of utility functions
MSci 1961 JUL VOL 7 p 337-350.

(684)
Ellsberg D
Risk, ambiguity, and the Savage axioms
QJE 1961 NOV VOL 75 p 643-669.

(685)
Suppes P
Behavioristic foundations of utility
Em 1961 APR VOL 29 p 186-202.

(686)
Chipman J S
The foundations of utility
Em 1960 APR VOL 28 p 193-224.

(687)
Egerton R A D
Investment decisions under uncertainty
Liverpool U Pr, 1960.

(688)
Grayson C J
Decision under uncertainty: drilling decisions by
oil and gas operators
Harvard Busn, 1960..

(689)**Koopmans T C**
Stationary ordinal utility and impatience
Em 1960 APR VOL 28 p 287-309.

(690)
Haring J E, Smith G C
Utility theory, decision theory, and profit
maximization
AER 1959 SEP VOL 49 p 566-583.

(691)
Majumdar T
The measurement of utility
St Martin, 1958.

(692)
Carter C F, Meredith G P, Shackle G L S eds.
Uncertainty and business decisions: the logic, philosophy and psychology of business decision-making under uncertainty: a symposium. 2nd ed
Liverpool U Pr, 1957.

(693)
Egerton R A D
The holding of assets: gambler preference or "safety first"?
OEP 1956 FEB VOL 8 p 51-59.

(694)
Egerton R A D
Investment, uncertainty and expectations
REStud 1955 SUMMER VOL 22 p 143-150.

(695)
Bernoulli D
Exposition of a new theory on the measurement of risk.   Papers of the Imperial Academy of Science in Petersburg 1730 VOL 2 p 175-192.
Translated into English by Sommer L in Em 1954 JAN p 23-36.

(696)
Edwards W
The theory of decision making
Psychological Bulletin 1954 JUL p 380-417.

(697)
Edwards W
Variance preferences in gambling
AJP 1954 VOL 67 p 441-452.

(698)
Ellsberg D
Classic and current notions of "measurable utility"
EJ 1954 SEP VOL 64.

(699)
Alchian A A
The meaning of utility measurement
AER 1953 MAR VOL 43 p 26-50.

(700)
Edwards W
Probability preferences in gambling
AJP 1953 JUL VOL 66 p 349-364.

(701)
Herstein I N, Milnor J
An axiomatic approach to measurable utility
Em 1953 APR VOL 21 p 291-297.

(702)
Strotz R H
Cardinal utility
AER 1953 MAY VOL 43 p 390-391.

(703)
Von Neumann J, Morgenstern O
Theory of games and economic behavior. 3rd ed
Princeton U Pr, 1953.

(704)
Friedman M, Savage L J
The expected utility hypothesis and the measurability of utility
JPE 1952 DEC VOL 60 p 463-475.

(705)
Markowitz H M
The utility of wealth
JPE 1952 APR VOL 60 p 151-158.

(706)
Samuelson P A
Probability, utility and the independence axiom
Em 1952 OCT VOL 20.

(707)
Arrow K J
Alternative approaches to the theory of choice in risk-taking situations
Em 1951 OCT VOL 19 p 404-437.

(708)
Mosteller F, Nogee P
An experimental measurement of utility
JPE 1951 OCT VOL 59 p 371-404.

(709)
Marschak J
Rational behavior, uncertain prospects and measurable utility
Em 1950 APR VOL 18 p 111-141.

(710)
Stigler G J
The development of utility theory
JPE 1950 AUG VOL 58 p 307-327.

(711)
Shackle G L S
Expectations in economics
Cambridge U Pr, 1949.

(712)
Armstrong W E
Uncertainty and the utility function
EJ 1948 MAR VOL 58 p 1-10.

(713)
Friedman M, Savage L J
The utility analysis of choices involving risk
JPE 1948 AUG VOL 56 p 279-304.

(714)
Vickrey W S
Measuring marginal utility by reactions to risk
Em 1945 OCT VOL 13 p 319-333.

(715)
Tintner G
A contribution to the non-static theory of choice
QJE 1942 FEB VOL 55 p 274-306.

(716)
Tintner G
The theory of choice under subjective risk and
uncertainty
Em 1941 JUL-OCT VOL 9 p 298-304.

(717)
Finetti B de
La prevision: ses lois logiques, ses sources
subjectives. Annales de l'Institut Henri Poincare
1937 VOL 7 p 1-68.
Translated into English in Kyburg H E Jr and
Smokler H E, Studies in subjective probability.
Wiley, 1964.

(718)
Ramsey F P
Truth and probability
(in The foundations of mathematics and other
logical essays. Paul Trench, 1931.)

2.2 Stochastic dominance

(719)
Jean W H, Helms B P
The identification of stochastic dominance
efficient sets by moment combination orderings
JBankF 1988 VOL 12 p 243-253.

(720)
Jean W H, Helms B P
Moment orderings and stochastic dominance tests
JBFA 1988 WINTER VOL 15:4 p 573-584.

(721)
Stein W E, Pfaffenberger R C, French D W
Sampling error in first order stochastic dominance
JFR 1987 VOL 10:3 p 259-268.

(722)
Jarrow R A
The relationship between arbitrage and first order
stochastic dominance
JF 1986 SEP VOL 41:4 p 915-921.

(723)
Bawa V S
On determination of stochastic dominance
optimal sets
JF 1985 JUN VOL 40:2 p 417-431.

(724)
Henin C G, Rentz W F
Subjective stochastic dominance put writing and
stock purchases with extensions to option pricing
and portfolio composition
MSci 1985 AUG VOL 31:8 p 919-927.

(725)
Scarsini M
Stochastic deminance and regret
Giornale degli Economisti e Annali di Economia
1985 VOL 44:3-4.

(726)
Jean W H
The harmonic mean and other necessary
conditions for stochastic dominance
JF 1984 JUN VOL 39:2 p 527-534.

(727)
Stein W E, Pfaffenberger R C, Kumar P C
On the estimation risk in first-order stochastic dominance : a note
JFQA 1983 DEC VOL 18:4 p 471-476.

(728)
Wilkes F M
Dominance criteria for the ranking of projects with an imperfect capital market
JBFA 1983 SPRING VOL 10:1 p 105-126

(729)
Ashton D J
Stochastic dominance and mean variance rules in the selection of risky investment
JBFA 1982 WINTER VOL 9:4 p 471-481.

(730)
Bawa V S
Stochastic dominance: a research bibliography
MSci 1982 JUN VOL 28:6 p 698-712.

(731)
Hughes J S
Agency theory and stochastic dominance
JFQA 1982 SEP VOL 17:3 p 341-361.

(732)
Kroll Y, Levy H
Stochastic dominance: a note
JF 1982 JUN VOL 37:3 p 871-875.

(733)
Levy H
Stochastic dominance rules for truncated normal distributions: a note
JF 1982 DEC VOL 37:5 p 1299-1303.

(734)
Levy H, Levy A
Stochastic dominance and the investment horizon with riskless assets
REStud 1982 VOL 49 p 427-438.

(735)
Tehranian H, Helms B P
An empirical comparison of stochastic dominance among lognormal prospects
JFQA 1982 JUN VOL 17:2 p 217-226.

(736)
Yitzhaki S
Stochastic dominance, mean variance and Gini's mean difference
AER 1982 VOL 72 p 178-185.

(737)
Gandhi D K, Saunders A
The superiority of stochastic dominance over mean variance efficiency criteria: Some clarification
JBFA 1981 SPRING VOL 8:1 p 51.

(738)
Jean W H
The geometric mean and stochastic dominance
JF 1980 MAR VOL 35:1 p 151-158.

(739)
Kira D, Ziemba W T
The demand for a risky asset
MSci 1980 NOV VOL 26:11 p 1158-1165.

(740)
Saunders A, Ward C, Woodward R
Stochastic dominance and the performance of U K unit trusts
JFQA 1980 JUN VOL 15 p 323.

(741)
Tehranian H
Empirical studies in porfolio performance using higher degrees of stochastic dominance
JF 1980 MAR VOL 35:1 p 159-171..

(742)**Bey R P**
Estimating the optimal stochastic dominance efficient set with a mean semi-variance algorithm
JFQA 1979 DEC VOL 14 p 1059.

(743)
Kroll Y, Levy H
Stochastic dominance with a riskless asset: An imperfect market
JFQA 1979 JUN VOL 14 p 179.

(744)
Bawa V S
Safety-first, stochastic dominance and optimal portfolio choice
JFQA 1978 JUN VOL 13 p 255.

(745)
Fishburn P C
Stochastic dominance without transitive preferences
MSci 1978 DEC VOL 24:16 p 1268.

(746)
Huang C C, Kira D, Vertinsky I
Stochastic dominance rules for multi-attribute utility functions
REStud 1978 VOL 45 p 611.

(747)
Huang C C, Vertinsky I, Ziemba W T
On multiperiod stochastic dominance
JFQA 1978 MAR VOL 13 p 1.

(748)
Robison L J, Barry P J
Risk efficiency using stochastic dominance and expected gain-confidence limits
JF 1978 VOL 33 p 1244.

(749)
Altman M, Vickson R G
On the relative effectiveness of stochastic dominance rules: Extension to decreasingly risk-averse utility functions
JFQA 1977 MAR VOL 12 p 73.

(750)
Meyer J
Further applications of stochastic dominance to mutual fund performance
JFQA 1977 JUN VOL 12 p 235.

(751)
Brooks L D
Stochastic dominance tests for selecting acceptable debt issuance strategies
MSci 1976 AUG VOL 22:12 p 477.

(752)
Kroll Y, Levy H
Stochastic dominance with riskless assets
JFQA 1976 DEC VOL 11 p 743.

(753)
Rentz W F, Westin R B
A note on first-degree stochastic dominance and portfolio composition
MSci 1976 AUG VOL 22:12 p 501.

(754)
Tesfatsion L
Stochastic dominance and the maximization of expected utility
REStud 1976 VOL 43 p 301.

(755)
Ali M M
Stochastic dominance and portfolio analysis
JFE 1975 VOL 2 p 205.

(756)
Jean W H
Comparison of moment and stochastic dominance ranking methods
JFQA 1975 MAR VOL 10 p 151.

(757)
Vickson R G
Stochastic dominance for decreasing absolute risk aversion
JFQA 1975 DEC VOL 10 p 799.

(758)
Vickson R G
Stochastic dominance tests for decreasing absolute risk aversion. I. Discrete random variables
MSci 1975 AUG VOL 21:12 p 1438.

(759)
Fishburn P C
Convex stochastic dominance with continuous distribution functions
JET 1974 FEB VOL 7:2 p 143-158.

(760)
Joy O M, Porter R B
Stochastic dominance and mutual fund performance
JFQA 1974 JAN VOL 9 p 25.

(761)
Porter R B
Semivariance and stochastic dominance: A comparison
AER 1974 VOL 64 p 200-204.

(762)
Levy H
Stochastic dominance, efficiency criteria and efficient portfolios: The multi-period case
AER 1973 VOL 63 p 986-994.

(763)
Porter R B
An empirical comparison of stochastic dominance
and mean-variance portfolio choice criteria
JFQA 1973 SEP VOL 8:4 p 587.

(764)
Porter R B, Wart J R, Ferguson D L
Efficient algorithms for conducting stochastic
dominance tests on large numbers of portfolios
JFQA 1973 JAN VOL 8:1 p 71-82.

(765)
Porter R B, Gaumnitz J E
Stochastic dominance vs. mean-variance portfolio
analysis: an empirical evaluation
AER 1972 JUN VOL 62 p 438-446.

(766)
Hadar J, Russell W R
Rules for ordering uncertain prospects
AER 1969 MAR VOL 59 p 25-34.

(767)
Hanoch G, Levy H
The efficiency analysis of choices involving risk
REStud 1969 JUL VOL 36 p 335-346.

2.3 General equilibrium under uncertainty

(768)
Aliprantis C D, Brown D J, Burkinshaw O
Existence and optimality of competitive equilibria
Springer-Verlag, 1989.

(769)
Dumas B
Two-person dynamic equilibrium in the capital
market
RFS 1989 VOL 2:2 p 157-188.

(770)
Geanakoplos J, Mas-Colell A
Real indeterminacy with financial assets
JET 1989 FEB VOL 47:1 p 22-38.

(771)
Binmore K G, Herrero M J
Security equilibrium
REStud 1988 VOL 55 p 33.

(772)
Boyle G W, Young L
Asset prices, commodity prices and money: A
general equilibrium, rational expectations model
AER 1988 MAR VOL 78:1 p 24-45.

(773)
Chae S
Existence of competitive equilibrium with
incomplete markets
JET 1988 FEB VOL 44:1 p 179-188.

(774)
Grandmont J-M ed.
Temporary equilibrium: selected readings
Academic Pr, 1988.

(775)
Madan D B
Risk measurement in semimartingale models with
multiple consumption goods
JET 1988 APR VOL 44:2 p 398-412.

(776)
Repullo R
A new characterization of the efficiency of
equilibrium with incomplete markets
JET 1988 APR VOL 44:2 p 217-230.

(777)
Svensson L E O
Trade in risky assets
AER 1988 JUN VOL 78:3 p 375-394.

(778)
Asch P, Quandt R E
Efficiency and profitability in exotic bets
Ec 1987 AUG VOL 54:215 p 289-298.

(779)
Becker R A, Foias C
A characterization of Ramsey equilibrium
JET 1987 FEB VOL 41:1 p 173-184.

(780)
Dammon R M, Green R C
Tax arbitrage and the existence of equilibrium
prices for financial assets
JF 1987 DEC VOL 42:5 p 1143-1166.

(781)
Duffie D
Stochastic equilibria with incomplete financial
markets
JET 1987 APR VOL 41:2 p 405-416.

(782)
Epstein L G
A simple dynamic general equilibrium model
JET 1987 FEB VOL 41:1 p 68-95.

(783)
Green R C, Jarrow R A
Spanning and completeness in markets with
contingent claims
JET 1987 FEB VOL 41:1 p 202-210.

(784)
Heath D C, Jarrow R A
Arbitrage, continuous trading, and margin
requirements
JF 1987 DEC VOL 42:5 p 1129-1142.

(785)
Huffman G W
A dynamic equilibrium model of asset prices and
transaction volume
JPE 1987 FEB VOL 95:1 p 138-159.

(786)
Jewitt I
Risk aversion and the choice between risky
projects: The preservation of comparative statics
results
REStud 1987 VOL 54 p 73.

(787)
Kolstad C D, Mathiesen L
Necessary and sufficient conditions for uniqueness
of a Cournot equilibrium
REStud 1987 VOL 54 p 681.

(788)
Merton R C
A simple model of capital market equilibrium
with incomplete information
JF 1987 JUL VOL 42:3 p 483-510

(789)
Page F H Jr
On equilibrium in Hart's securities exchange
model
JET 1987 APR VOL 41:2 p 392-404.

(790)
Wright R D
Market structure and competitive equilibrium in
dynamic economic models
JET 1987 FEB VOL 41:1 p 189-201.

(791)
Appelbaum E, Katz E
Measures of risk aversion and comparative statics
of industry equilibrium
AER 1986 VOL 76 p 524-529.

(792)
Campbell J Y
Bond and stock returns in a simple exchange
model
QJE 1986 VOL 101 p 785.

(793)
Deneckere R, Pelikan S
Competitive chaos
JET 1986 OCT VOL 40:1 p 13-25.

(794)
Detemple J B
Asset pricing in a production economy with
incomplete information
JF 1986 JUN VOL 41:2 p 383-391..

(795)**Gal-Or E**
Information transmission-Cournot and Bertrand
equilibria
REStud 1986 VOL 53 p 85.

(796)
Grossman S J, Perry M
Perfect sequential equilibrium
JET 1986 JUN VOL 39:1 p 97-119.

(797)
Amershi A H
A complete analysis of full Pareto efficiency in financial markets for arbitary preferences
JF 1985 SEP VOL 40:4 p 1235-1243

(798)
Bergstrom T C, Varian H R
When are Nash equilibria independent of the distribution of agents' characteristics?
REStud 1985 VOL 52 p 715.

(799)
Sprenkle C M
On the precautionary demand for assets
JBankF 1985 VOL 9 p 499.

(800)
Ushio Y
Approximate efficiency of Cournot equilibria in large markets
REStud 1985 VOL 52 p 547.

(801)
Werner J
Equilibrium in economies with incomplete financial markets
JET 1985 JUN VOL 36:1 p 110-119.

(802)
Allen B
Expectations equilibria with dispersed information: Existence with approximate rationality in a model with a continuum of agents and finitely many states of the world
REStud 1983 VOL 50 p 267.

(803)
Marcus A J
Risk sharing and the theory of the firm
BellJ 1982 AUTUMN VOL 13:2 p 369-378.

(804)
Newbery D M G, Stiglitz J E
The choice of techniques and the optimality of market equilibrium with rational expectations
JPE 1982 VOL 90 p 223.

(805)
Newbery D M G, Stiglitz J E
Risk aversion, supply response and the optimality of random prices: A diagrammatic analysis
QJE 1982 VOL 97 p 1.

(806)
Stiglitz J E
The inefficiency of the stock market equilibrium.
REStud 1982 APR VOL 49 p 241-261.

(807)
Zusman P
The equilibrium configuration of pure risk sharing contracts in markets with diverse transactors
EER 1982 VOL 19:2-3.

(808)
DeAngelo H
Competition and unanimity
AER 1981 VOL 71 p 18-27.

(809)
Laumas G S
Discount rate and wealth
JPE 1981 VOL 89 p 196.

(810)
Stiglitz J E
Pareto optimality and competition
JF 1981 MAY VOL 36:2 p 235-251

(811)
Beja A, Goldman M B
On the dynamic behavior of prices in disequilibrium
JF 1980 MAY VOL 35:2 p 235-248

(812)
Epstein L G, Turnbull S M
Capital asset prices and the temporal resolution of uncertainty
JF 1980 JUN VOL 25:3 p 627-643

(813)
Lin W T, Jen F C
Consumption investment market price of risk and the risk-free rate
JFQA 1980 DEC VOL 15:5 p 1025-1040

(814)
Milne F
Short selling default risk and the existence of equilibrium in a securities model
IntER 1980 JUN VOL 21:2 p 255-267.

(815)
Baron D P
On the relationship between complete and incomplete financial market models
IntER 1979 FEB VOL 20:1 p 105-117.

(816)
Benninga A
General equilibrium with financial markets: existence uniqueness and implications for corporate finance
JF 1979 MAY VOL 34:2 p 325-339.

(817)
Cootner P H, Pyle D H
Capital asset pricing in a general equilibrium framework
JFQA 1978 NOV VOL 13 p 613.

(818)
Dubey P, Shubik M
A theory of money and financial institutions
JET 1978 FEB VOL 17:1 p 1-20.

(819)
Helpman E, Razin A
Participation equilibrium and the efficiency of stock market allocations
IntER 1978 FEB VOL 19:1 p 129-140.

(820)
Leland H E
Information, managerial choice and stockholder unanimity.
REStud 1978 OCT VOL 45 p 527-534.

(821)
Rubinstein M
Competition and approximation
BellJ 1978 SPRING VOL 9:1 p 280-286.

(822)
Burmeister E, Long N V
Some unresolved questions in capital theory
QJE 1977 VOL 91 p 289.

(823)
Cootner P H
The theorems of modern finance in a general equilibrium setting: Paradoxes resolved
JFQA 1977 NOV VOL 12 p 553.

(824)
Danforth J P
Wealth and the value of generalized lotteries
JET 1977 JUN VOL 15:1 p 54-71.

(825)
Grossman S J
A characterization of the optimality of equilibrium in incomplete markets
JET 1977 JUN VOL 15:1 p 1-15.

(826)
Ohlson J A
Equilibrium in stable markets
JPE 1977 VOL 85 p 859.

(827)
Shubik M
On competitive equilibrium, contingent commodities and information
JF 1977 VOL 32 p 189.

(828)
Svensson L E O
The stock market, the objective function of the firm, and intertemporal Pareto efficiency: the certainty case
BellJ 1977 SPRING VOL 8:1 p 207-216.

(829)
Benveniste L M
A complete characterization of efficiency for a general capital accumulation model
JET 1976 APR VOL 12:2 p 325-337..

(830)**Birch E M, Siebert C D**
Uncertainty, permanent demand, and investment behavior
AER 1976 MAR VOL 66:1 p 15-27.

(831)
Green J, Polemarchakis H
A brief note on the efficiency of equilibria with costly transactions
REStud 1976 VOL 43 p 537.

(832)
Levy H
Multi period consumption decision under conditions of uncertainty
MSci 1976 JUL VOL 22:11 p 1258-1267.

(833)
Svensson L E O
Sequences of temporary equilibria, stationary point expectations, and Pareto efficiency
JET 1976 OCT VOL 13:2 p 169-183.

(834)
Boadway R W
Cost-benefit rules in general equilibrium
REStud 1975 VOL 42 p 361.

(835)
Friend I, Blume M E
The demand for risky assets
AER 1975 DEC VOL 65:5 p 900-922.

(836)
Shafer W, Sonnenschein H
Some theorems on the existence of competitive equilibrium
JET 1975 AUG VOL 11:1 p 83-93.

(837)
Varian H L
On persistent disequilibrium
JET 1975 APR VOL 10:2 p 218-228.

(838)
Hart O D
On the existence of equilibrium in a securities model
JET 1974 NOV VOL 9:3 p 293-311.

(839)
Kurz M
Equilibrium with transaction cost and money in a single market exchange economy
JET 1974 APR VOL 7:4 p 418-452.

(840)
Leland H E
Production theory and the stock market
BellJ 1974 SPRING VOL 5:1 p 125-144.

(841)
Levy H, Paroush J
Toward multivariate efficiency criteria
JET 1974 FEB VOL 7:2 p 129-142.

(842)
Rubinstein M
An aggregation theorem for securities markets
JFE 1974 VOL 1 p 225.

(843)
Shoven J B
A proof of the existence of a general equilibrium with ad valorem commodity taxes
JET 1974 MAY VOL 8:1 p 1-25.

(844)
Douglas A J
Stochastic returns and the theory of the firm
AER 1973 VOL 63 P+P p 129-133.

(845)
Bierman H Jr
The resolution of investment uncertainty through time
MSci 1972 AUG VOL 18:12 p B654.

(846)
Diamond P A, Yaari M E
Implications of the theory of rationing for consumer choice under uncertainty
AER 1972 JUN VOL 62 p 333-343.

(847)
Fama E F
Perfect competition and optimal production decisions under uncertainty
BellJ 1972 FALL VOL 3:2 p 509-530.

(848)
Jensen M C, Long J B Jr
Corporate investment under uncertainty and pareto optimality in the capital markets
BellJ 1972 SPRING VOL 3:1 p 151-174.

(849)
Katzner D W
A simple approach to existence and uniqueness of competitive equilibria
AER 1972 VOL 62 p 432-437.

(850)
Long J B Jr
Consumption-investment decisions and equilibrium in the securities market
(in Jensen M C ed., Studies in the theory of capital markets. Praeger, 1972.)

(851)
Long J B Jr, Jensen M C
Corporate investment under uncertainty and Pareto optimality in the capital markets
BellJ 1972 APR VOL 3.

(852)
Masson R T
The creation of risk aversion by imperfect capital markets
AER 1972 MAR VOL 62 p 77-86.

(853)
Stiglitz J E
On the optimality of stock market allocation
QJE 1972 FEB VOL 86 p 25-60.

(854)
Baron D P
Price uncertainty, utility and industry equilibrium in pure competition
IntER 1970 OCT VOL 11 p 463-480.

(855)
Dreze J H
Market allocation under uncertainty
EER 1970-71 WINTER VOL 2 p 133-165.

(856)
Hirshleifer J
Investment, interest, and capital
P-H, 1970.

(857)
Radner R
Problems in the theory of markets under uncertainty
AER 1970 MAY VOL 60 p 454-464.

(858)
Borch K
Equilibrium, optimum and prejudice in capital markets
JFQA 1969 MAR VOL 4 p 1-14.

(859)
Litzenberger R H
Equilibrium in the equity market under uncertainty
JF 1969 SEP VOL 24 p 663-671.

(860)
Machol R E, Lerner E M
Risk, ruin and investment analysis
JFQA 1969 DEC VOL 4 p 473-492.

(861)
Schmeidler D
Competitive equilibria in markets with a continuum of traders and incomplete preferences
Em 1969 OCT VOL 37 p 578-585.

(862)
Stignum B P
Competitive equilibria under uncertainty
QJE 1969 NOV VOL 83 p 533-561.

(863)
Borch K
The economics of uncertainty
Princeton U Pr, 1968.

(864)
Borch K
General equilibrium in the economics of uncertainty
(in Borch K and Mossin J eds., Risk and uncertainty. Macmillan Int, 1968.)

(865)
Freimer M, Gordon M J
Investment behavior with utility a concave function of wealth
(in Borch K and Mossin J eds., Risk and uncertainty. Macmillan Int, 1968.)

(866)
Myers S C
Effects of uncertainty on the valuation of securities and the financial decisions of the firm
JF 1968 MAR VOL 23 p 205-206.

(867)
Myers S C
A time-state preference model for security valuation
JFQA 1968 MAR VOL 3 p 1-34.

(868)
Radner R
Competitive equilibrium under uncertainty
Em 1968 JAN VOL 36 p 31-58.

(869)
Chen A H
Valuation under uncertainty
JFQA 1967 SEP VOL 2 p 313-326.

(870)
Diamond P A
The role of a stock market in a general
equilibrium model with technological uncertainty
AER 1967 SEP VOL 57 p 759-776.

(871)
Puu T
Some reflections on the theories of choice
between alternative investment opportunities
Weltswirtschaftliches Archiv 1967 VOL 99 p
107-123.

(872)
Aumann R J
Existence of competitive equilibria in markets
with a continuum of traders
Em 1966 JAN VOL 34 p 1-17.

(873)
Hirshleifer J
Investment   decision   under   uncertainty:
applications of the state--preference approach
QJE 1966 MAY VOL 80 p 252-277.

(874)
Hirshleifer J
Investment   decision   under   uncertainty:
choice--theoretic approaches
QJE 1965 NOV VOL 79 p 509-536.

(875)
Arrow K J
The role of securities in the optimal allocation of
risk-bearing
REStud 1964 APR VOL 31 p 91-96.

(876)
Becker S W, Brownson F O
What price ambiguity? or the role of ambiguity in
decision making
JPE 1964 FEB VOL 72 p 62-73.

(877)
Arrow K J
Uncertainty and the welfare economics of medical
care
AER 1963 DEC VOL 53 p 941-973.

(878)
Debreu G
New concepts and techniques for equilibrium
analysis
IntER 1962 VOL 3 p 257-273.

(879)
Smith V L
Time preference and risk in investment theory
AER 1961 MAY VOL 51 p 124-127.

(880)
Debreu G
Theory of value: an axiomatic analysis of
economic equilibrium
Wiley, 1959.

(881)
McKenzie L W
On the existence of general equilibrium for a
competitive market
Em 1959 JAN VOL 27 p 54-71.

(882)
McGlothlin W H
Stability of choices among uncertain alternatives
AJP 1956 DEC VOL 69 p 604-615..

(883)**Nash J**
The bargaining problem
Em 1950 VOL 18 p 155-162.

2.31   Rational expectations

(884)
Chow G C
Rational versus adaptive expectations in present
value models
REStat 1989 VOL 71 p 376.

(885)
West K D
Estimation of linear rational expectations models,
in the presence of deterministic terms
JME 1989 VOL 24 p 437.

(886)
Chari V V, Jagannathan R
Banking, panics, information and rational
expectations equilibrium
JF 1988 JUL VOL 43:3 p 749-760.

(887)
Neilsen M T
The Pareto domination of irrational expectations
over rational expectations
JET 1988 DEC VOL 46:2 p 322-334.

(888)
Bhattacharya G
Notes on optimality of rational expectations
equilibrium with incomplete markets
JET 1987 AUG VOL 42:2 p 191-208.

(889)
Coutinho P C
Non-optimality of rational expectations
equilibrium: The complete markets case
REStud 1986 VOL 53.

(890)
Lovell M C
Tests of the rational expectations hypothesis
AER 1986 VOL 76 p 110-124.

(891)
Allen B
The existence of fully rational expectations
approximate equilibria with noisy price
observations
JET 1985 DEC VOL 37:2 p 213-253.

(892)
Banks J S
Price-conveyed information versus observed
insider behavior: A note on rational expectations
convergence
JPE 1985 VOL 93 p 807.

(893)
Evans G
Expectational stability and the multiple equilibria
problem in linear rational expectations models
QJE 1985 VOL 100 p 1217.

(894)
Haltiwanger J, Waldman M
Rational expectations and the limits of rationality:
an analysis of heterogeneity
AER 1985 VOL 75 p 326-340.

(895)
Scarth W M
A note on non-uniqueness in rational
expectations models
JME 1985 VOL 15 p 247.

(896)
Jennings R H, Barry C B
On information dissemination and equilibrium
asset prices : a note
JFQA 1984 DEC VOL 19:4 p 395-402

(897)
Cesarano F
The rational expectations hypothesis in retrospect
AER 1983 VOL 73 p 198-203.

(898)
Figlewski S, Wachtel P
Rational expectations, informational efficiency,
and tests using survey data: a reply
REStat 1983 VOL 65 p 529.

(899)
Walsh C E
Asset prices, asset stocks and rational expectations
JME 1983 VOL 11 p 337.

(900)
Frydman R
Toward an understanding of market processes:
Individual expectations, learning and convergence
to rational expectations equilibrium
AER 1982 VOL 72 p 652-668.

(901)
Hansen L P, Singleton K J
Generalized instrumental variables estimation of
nonlinear expectations models
Em 1982 SEP VOL 50 p 1269-1286.

(902)
LeRoy S F
Expectations models of asset prices : a survey of theory
JF 1982 MAR VOL 37:1 p 185-217

(903)
Tirole J
On the possibility of speculation under rational expectations
Em 1982 SEP VOL 50 p 1162-1181.

(904)
Chow G C
Estimation and control of rational expectation models
AER 1981 VOL 71 P+P p 211-216.

(905)
Elton E J, Gruber M J, Gultekin M
Expectations and share prices
MSci 1981 SEP VOL 27:9 p 975-987

(906)
Kraus A, Sick G A
Distinguishing beliefs and preferences in equilibrium prices
JF 1980 MAY VOL 35:2 p 335-346

(907)
Anderson P A
Rational expectations forecasts from nonrational models
JME 1979 VOL 5 p 67.

(908)
DeCanio S J
Rational expectations and learning from experience
QJE 1979 VOL 93 p 47.

(909)
Feiger G M
Divergent rational expectations equilibrium in a dynamic model of a futures market
JET 1978 APR VOL 17:2 p 164-178.

(910)
Mussa M
On the inherent stability of rationally adaptive expectations
JME 1978 VOL 4 p 307.

(911)
Cukierman A
A test of expectational processes using information from the capital markets: the Israeli case
IntER 1977 OCT VOL 18:3 p 737-753.

(912)
Jordan J S
Expectations equilibrium and informational efficiency for stochastic environments
JET 1977 DEC VOL 16:2 p 354-372.

(913)
Jordan J S
Temporary competitive equilibrium and the existence of self-fulfilling expectations
JET 1976 JUN VOL 12:3 p 455-471.

(914)
Cyert R M, DeGroot M H
Rational expectations and Bayesian analysis
JPR 1974 VOL 82 p 521.

(915)
Black S W
The use of rational expectations in models of speculation
REStat 1972 MAY VOL 54 p 161-165.

(916)
Muth J F
Rational expectations and the theory of price movements
Em 1961 JUL VOL 29 p 315-335.

2.32   Speculation and stability

(917)
Kosmicke R, Opsal S D
The effect of volatility on investment returns
JPM 1988 WINTER VOL 14:2 p 14-19.

(918)
Woodward R S
Some new evidence on the profitability of one-way versus round-trip arbitrage
JMCB 1988 NOV VOL 20:4 p 645-652.

(919)
Milne F, Shefrin H M
Information and securities: a note on Pareto dominance and the second best
JET 1987 DEC VOL 43:2 p 314-328.

(920)
Stein J C
Informational externalities and welfare-reducing speculation
JPE 1987 VOL 95 p 1123.

(921)
Danthine J-P
Information, futures prices, and stabilizing speculation
JET 1978 FEB VOL 17:1 p 79-98.

(922)
Hart O D
The profitability of speculation
QJE 1977 VOL 91 p 579.

(923)
Miller R M, Plott C R, Smith V L
Intertemporal competitive equilibrium: An empirical study of speculation
QJE 1977 VOL 91 p 599.

(924)
Johnson H G
Destabilizing speculation: a general equilibrium approach
JPE 1976 FEB VOL 84:1 p 101-108.

(925)
Francis J C
Speculative markets: valuable institutions or dens of iniquity?
F R Bk Bus Rev Philadelphia 1972 JUL.

(926)
Gray W R
Price effects of a lack of speculation
FRIS 1967 VOL 7 Suppl p 177-194.

(927)
Obst N P
A connection between speculation and stability in the foreign exchange market
SEJ 1967 JUL VOL 34 p 146-149.

(928)
Farrell M J
Profitable speculation
Ec 1966 MAY VOL 46 p 183-193.

(929)
Glahe F R
Professional and non-professional speculation, profitability, and stability
SEJ 1966 JUL VOL 33 p 43-44.

(930)
Cowing C B
Populists, plungers and progressives: social history of stock and commodity speculation
Princeton U Pr, 1965.

(931)
Aliber R Z
Speculation and price stability again
JPE 1964 DEC VOL 72 p 607-609.

(932)
Fishman G S
Price behavior under alternative forms of price expectations
QJE 1964 MAY VOL 78 p 281-298.

(933)
Kemp M C
Speculation, profitability and price stability
REStat 1963 MAY VOL 45 p 185-189.

(934)
Friedman M
In defense of destabilizing speculation
(in Prouts R W ed., Essays in economics and econometrics. U of NC Pr, 1960.)

(935)
Telser L G
A theory of speculation relating profitability and stability
REStat 1959 AUG VOL 41 p 295-301..

(936)**Baumol W J**
Speculation, profitability and stability
REStat 1957 AUG VOL 39 p 263-271.

(937)
Meade J
Degrees of competitive speculation
REStud 1949-1950 VOL 17.

(938)
Kaldor N
Speculation and economic stability
REStud 1939 OCT VOL 7 p 13-16.

2.33   Bubbles and fads

(939)
Casella A
Testing for rational bubbles with exogenous or endogenous fundamentals: the German hyperinflation once more
JME 1989 VOL 24 p 109.

(940)
Evans G W
The fragility of sunspots and bubbles
JME 1989 VOL 23 p 297.

(941)
Garber P M
Tulipmania
JPE 1989 VOL 97 p 535.

(942)
Garber P M
Who put the mania in tulipmania?
JPM 1989 FALL VOL 16:1 p 53-60.

(943)
Diba B T, Grossman H I
Rational inflationary bubbles
JME 1988 VOL 21 p 35.

(944)
Diba B T, Grossman H I
Explosive rational bubbles in stock prices?
AER 1988 VOL 78:3 p 520-530.

(945)
Hardouvelis G A
Evidence on stock market speculative bubbles: Japan, the United States, and Great Britain
F R Bk New York Q Rev 1988 SUMMER VOL 13:2.

(946)
Savit R
When random is not random: an introduction to chaos in market prices
JFM 1988 JUN VOL 8:3 p 271-290.

(947)
West K D
Bubbles, fads, and stock price volatility tests: a partial evaluation
JF 1988 JUL VOL 43:3 p 639-655.

(948)
Diba B T, Grossman H I
On the inception of rational bubbles
QJE 1987 VOL 102 p 697-700.

(949)
West K D
A specification test for speculative bubbles
QJE 1987 AUG VOL 102 p 553-580.

(950)
Woo W T
Some evidence of speculative bubbles in the foreign exchange markets
JMCB 1987 NOV VOL 19:4 p 499-514.

(951)
Evans G W
A test for speculative bubbles and the sterling-dollar exchange rate 1981-84
AER 1986 VOL 76 p 621-636.

(952)
Flood R P, Hodrick R J
Asset price volatility bubbles and process switching.
JF 1986 SEP VOL 41:4 p 831-842.

(953)
Meese R A
Testing for bubbles in exchange markets: A case of sparkling rates?
JPE 1986 VOL 94 p 345.

(954)
Obstfeld M, Rogoff K
Ruling out divergent speculative bubbles
JME 1986 VOL 17 p 349-362.

(955)
Tirole J
Asset bubbles and overlapping generations
Em 1986 SEP VOL 53 p 1071-1100.

(956)
Le Bon G
The mind of crowds
JPM 1980 SUMMER VOL 6:4 p 69.

2.34 Continuous trading, martingales and arbitrage

(957)
Ross S A
Information and volatility: the no-arbitrage martingale approach to timing and resolution irrelevancy
JF 1989 MAR VOL 44:1 p 1-18.

(958)
Milne F
The induced preference approach to arbitrage and diversification arguments in finance
EER 1987 VOL 31:1-2.

(959)
Ross S A
Arbitrage and martingales with taxation
JPE 1987 APR VOL 95:2 p 371-393

(960)
Varian H R
The arbitrage principle in financial economics
JEP 1987 VOL 1:2 p 55-72.

(961)
Deshmukh S D, Pliska S R
A Martingale characterization of the price of a nonrenewable resource with decisions involving uncertainty
JET 1985 APR VOL 35:2 p 322-342.

(962)
Harrison J M, Pittbladdo R, Schaefer S M
Continuous price processes in frictionless markets have infinite variation
JB 1984 JUL VOL 57:3 p 353-365.

(963)
Harrison J M, Pliska S R
A stochastic calculus model of continuous trading: Complete markets
Stochastic Processes and their Applications 1983 VOL 15 p 313-316.

(964)
Harrison J M, Pliska S R
Martingales and stochastic integrals in the theory of continuous trading
Stochastic Processes and their Applications 1981 VOL 11 p 215-260.

(965)
Kreps D M
Arbitrage and equilibrium in economies with infinitely many commodities
Journal of Mathematical Economics 1981 MAR VOL 8 p 15-35.

(966)
Malliaris A G
Martingale methods in financial decision-making
SIAM Review 1981 VOL 23 p 434-443.

3 Economics of information

(967)**Philips L**
The economics of imperfect information
Cambridge U Pr, 1989.

(968)
Thakor A V
Strategic issues in financial contracting: an overview
FIN MGMT 1989 SUMMER VOL 18 p 39-58.

(969)
Feltham G, Amershi A, Ziemba W eds.
Economic analysis of information and contracts: Essays in honor of John E. Butterworth
Kluwer Academic, 1988.

(970)
Gal-Or E
The advantages of imprecise information
RandJ 1988 SUMMER VOL 19:2 p 266-275.

(971)
Bhattacharya S
Financial markets and incomplete information: A review of some recent developments
(in Bhattacharya S and Constantinides G eds., Frontiers of financial theory. Littlefield, 1987.)

(972)
Gal-Or E
First mover disadvantages with private information
REStud 1987 VOL 54 p 279.

(973)
Hoffer G E, Pruitt S W, Reilly R J
Automotive recalls and informational efficiency
FR 1987 NOV VOL 22:4.

(974)
Larcker D F, Lys T
An empirical analysis of the incentives to engage in costly information acquisition: the case of risk arbitrage
JFE 1987 VOL 18 p 111-126.

(975)
Antonovitz F, Roe T
A theoretical and empirical approach to the value of information in risky markets
REStat 1986 VOL 68 p 105.

(976)
Arrow K J
Informational structure of the firm
AER 1985 VOL 75 P+P p 303-307.

(977)
Farmer R E A
Implicit contracts with asymmetric information and bankruptcy: The effect of interest rates on layoffs
REStud 1985 VOL 52 p 427.

(978)
Freixas X, Guesnerie R, Tirole J
Planning under incomplete information and the ratchet effect
REStud 1985 VOL 52 p 173.

(979)
Stiglitz J E
Information and economic analysis: A perspective
EJ 1985 VOL 95 SUPPL p 21-42.

(980)
Baron D P, Besanko D
Regulation, asymmetric information and auditing
RandJ 1984 WINTER VOL 15:4 p 447-470.

(981)
Greenwald B, Stiglitz J E, Weiss A
Informational imperfections in the capital market and macroeconomic fluctuations
AER 1984 VOL 74 P+P p 194-199.

(982)
Schmalensee R
Imperfect information and the quitability of competitive prices
QJE 1984 VOL 99 p 441.

(983)
Clarke R N
Collusion and the incentives for information sharing
BellJ 1983 AUTUMN VOL 14:2 p 383-414.

(984)
Grossman S J, Hart O D
Implicit contracts under asymmetric information
QJE 1983 VOL 98 p 123.

(985)
Holmstrom B, Myerson R
Efficient and durable decision rules with incomplete information
Em 1983 NOV VOL 51 p 1799-1819.

(986)
Tandon P
Rivalry and the excessive allocation of resources to research
BellJ 1983 SPRING VOL 14:1 p 152-165.

(987)
Trueman B
Motivating management to reveal inside information
JF 1983 SEP VOL 38:4 p 1253-1269.

(988)
Jovanovic B
Truthful disclosure of information
BellJ 1982 SPRING VOL 13:1 p 36-44..

(989)**McCall J J ed.**
The economics of information and uncertainty
U of Chicago Pr, 1982.

(990)
Sappington D
Optimal regulation of research and development under imperfect information
BellJ 1982 AUTUMN VOL 13:2 p 354-368.

(991)
Shapiro C
Consumer information, product quality and seller reputation
BellJ 1982 SPRING VOL 13:1 P 20-35.

(992)
Grossman S J
The information role of warranties and private disclosure about product quality
JLE 1981 VOL 24:3 p 461.

(993)
Ordover J, Weiss A
Information and the law: Evaluating legal restrictions on competitive contracts
AER 1981 VOL 71 P+P p 399-404.

(994)
Conrad J M
Quasi-option value and the expected value of information
QJE 1980 VOL 94 p 813.

(995)
Barzel Y
Some fallacies in the interpretation of information costs
JLE 1977 VOL 20 p 291.

(996)
Beja A, Hakansson N H
Dynamic market processes and the rewards of up-to-date information
JF 1977 MAY VOL 32:2 p 291-303.

(997)
Grossman S J, Kihlstrom R E, Mirman L J
A Bayesian approach to the production of information and learning by doing
REStud 1977 VOL 44.

(998)
Leland H E
Quality choice and competition
AER 1977 VOL 67 p 127-135.

(999)
Merkhofer M W
The value of information given decision flexibility
MSci 1977 AUG VOL 23:12 p 716.

(1000)
Akerlof G
The economics of caste and of the rat race and other woeful tales
QJE 1976 VOL 90 p 599.

(1001)
Salop S
Information and monopolistic competition
AER 1976 VOL 66 P+P p 240-245.

(1002)
Winsen J K
Investor behavior and information
JFQA 1976 MAR VOL 11 p 13.

(1003)
Hirshleifer J
Speculation and equilibrium information, risk and markets
QJE 1975 VOL 89 p 519.

(1004)
Jaffe J F, Merville L J
The value of risk-reducing information
JFQA 1974 NOV VOL 9 p 697.

(1005)
Hirshleifer J
Where are we in the theory of information
AER 1973 VOL 63 P+P p 31-39.

(1006)
Hurwicz L
On informationally decentralized systems
(in McGuire C B and Radner R eds., Decision and organization. N Holland, 1972.)

(1007)
Fama E F, Laffer A B
Information and capital markets
JB 1971 JUL VOL 44 p 289-298.

(1008)
Spence M, Zeckhauser R
Insurance, information, and individual action
AER 1971 VOL 16 p 119-132.

(1009)
Stigler G J
The economics of information
JPE 1961 JUN VOL 69 p 213-225.

(1010)
Kelly J
A new interpretation of information rate
Bell Systems Technical Journal 1956 JUL VOL 35 p 917-926.

(1011)
Hayek F
The use of knowledge in society
AER 1945 SEP.

3.1   Social   and   private   value   of information

(1012)
Admati A R, Pfleiderer P
A monopolistic market for information
JET 1986 AUG VOL 39:2 p 400-438.

(1013)
Antonovitz F, Roe T
A theoretical and empirical approach to the value of information in risky markets
REStat 1986 FEB VOL 68:1 p 105-114

(1014)
Trueman B
Optimality of the disclosure of private information in a production-exchange economy
JF 1983 JUN VOL 38:3 p 913-924

(1015)
Hakansson N H, Kunkel J G, Ohlson J A
Sufficient and necessary conditions for information to have social value in pure exchange
JF 1982 DEC VOL 37:5 p 1169-1181.

(1016)
Ng D S
Pareto-optimality of authentic information
JF 1977 VOL 32 p 1717.

(1017)
Ng D S
Information accuracy and social welfare under homogeneous beliefs
JFE 1975 VOL 2 p 53.

(1018)
Gould J P
Risk, stochastic preference, and the value of information
JET 1974 MAY VOL 8:1 p 64-84.

3.2   Aggregation of information

(1019)
Admati A R, Pfleiderer P
Viable allocations of information in financial markets
JET 1987 OCT VOL 43:1 p 76-115.

(1020)
Polemarchakis H M, Selden L, Zipkin P et al.
Approximate aggregation under uncertainty
JET 1986 APR VOL 38:2 p 189-210.

(1021)
Ashton D J
Disagreements on conditions for unanimity
JBFA 1985 WINTER VOL 12:4 p 507-513

(1022)
Krouse C G
Competition and unanimity revisited, again
AER 1985 VOL 75 p 1109-1114.

(1023)
Makowski L, Pepall L
Easy proof of unanimity and optimality without spanning : A pedagogical note
JF 1985 SEP VOL 40:4 p 1245-1250.

(1024)
Ohlson J A
Ex post stockholder unanimity: A complete and simplified treatment
JBankF 1985 VOL 9 p 387.

(1025)
Friedman D, Harrison G W, Salmon J W
The informational efficiency of experimental asset markets
JPE 1984 VOL 92 p 349.

(1026)
Makowski L
Competition and unanimity revisited
AER 1983 VOL 73 p 329-339.

(1027)
Aivazian V A, Callen J L
The "unanimity" literature and the security market line criterion: The additive risk case
JBFA 1981 SUMMER VOL 8:2 p 177-184

(1028)
Diamond D W, Verrecchia R E
Information aggregation in a noisy rational expectations economy
JFE 1981 VOL 9 p 221.

(1029)
Satterthwaite M A
On the scope of the stockholder unanimity theorems
IntER 1981 FEB VOL 22:1 p 119-133.

(1030)
Grossman S J, Stiglitz J E
Stockholder unanimity in making production and financial decisions
QJE 1980 VOL 94 p 543.

(1031)
Grossman S J, Stiglitz J E
On the impossibility of informationally efficient markets
AER 1980 VOL 70 p 393-408.

(1032)
Verrecchia R E
Consensus beliefs, information acquisition and market information efficiency
AER 1980 VOL 70 p 874-884.

(1033)
Garbade K D, Pomrenze J L, Silber W L
On the information content of prices
AER 1979 VOL 69 p 50-59.

(1034)
Verrecchia R E
A proof of the existence of "consensus beliefs"
JF 1979 SEP VOL 34:4 p 957-963.

(1035)
Brennan M J, Kraus A
Necessary conditions for aggregation in securities markets
JFQA 1978 SEP VOL 13 p 407.

(1036)
Grossman S J
Further results on the informational efficiency of competitive stock markets
JET 1978 JUN VOL 18:1 p 81-101.

(1037)
Leland H E
Information, managerial choice and stockholder unanimity.
REStud 1978 OCT VOL 45 p 527-534.

(1038)
Green J
The non-existence of informational equilibria
REStud 1977 VOL 44 p 451.

(1039)
Grossman S J, Stiglitz J E
Information and competitive price systems
AER 1976 VOL 66 P+P p 246-253.

(1040)
Wilson R
On the theory of aggregation
JET 1975 FEB VOL 10:1 p 89-99.

(1041)
Lintner J
The aggregation of investor's diverse judgments and preferences in purely competitive security markets
JFQA 1969 DEC VOL 4 p 347-400.

3.3   Incomplete markets with heterogeneous information

(1042)
Trueman B
A theory of noise trading in securities markets
JF 1988 MAR VOL 43:1 p 83-96.

(1043)
Black F
Noise
JF 1986 JUL VOL 41:3 p 529-543

(1044)
Detemple J B
A general equilibrium model of asset pricing with partial or heterogeneous information
Finance 1986 DEC VOL 7 p 183-201.

(1045)
John K
Market resolution and valuation in incomplete markets
JFQA 1984 MAR VOL 19:1 p 29-44

(1046)
Mayshar J
On divergence of opinion and imperfections in capital markets
AER 1983 VOL 73 p 114-128.

(1047)
Figlewski S
Information diversity and market behavior
JF 1982 MAR VOL 37:1 p 87-102.

(1048)
Jarrow R A
Heterogeneous expectations restrictions on short sales and equilibrium asset prices
JF 1980 DEC VOL 35:5 p 1105-1113.

(1049)
Bart J T
The nature of the conflict between transactors' expectations of capital gain
JF 1978 VOL 33 p 1095.

(1050)
Figlewski S
Market "efficiency" in a market with heterogeneous information
JPE 1978 VOL 86 p 581.

(1051)
Harrison J M, Kreps D M
Speculative investor behavior in a stock market with heterogeneous expectations
QJE 1978 VOL 92 p 323.

(1052)
Rabinovitch R, Owen J
Nonhomogeneous expectations and information in the capital asset market
JF 1978 VOL 33 p 575.

(1053)
Miller E M
Risk, uncertainty and divergence of opinion
JF 1977 VOL 32 p 1551.

3.4   Prices with asymmetric information

(1054)
Hellwig M
Asymmetric information, financial markets and financial institutions: where are we currently going?
EER 1989 VOL 33 p 277.

(1055)
Admati A R, Pfleiderer P
Selling and trading on information in financial markets
AER 1988 MAY VOL 78:2 p 96-103.

(1056)
Allen F
A theory of price rigidities when quality is unobservable
REStud 1988 VOL 55 p 139.

(1057)
Arnott R, Stiglitz J E
Randomization with asymmetric information
RandJ 1988 AUTUMN VOL 19:3 p 344-362.

(1058)
Ho T S Y, Michaely R
Information quality and market efficiency
JFQA 1988 MAR VOL 23:1 p 53-70.

(1059)
Chatterjee K, Samuelson L
Bargaining with two-sided incomplete information: An infinite horizon model with alternating offers
REStud 1987 VOL 54 p 175.

(1060)
Nalebuff B, Scharfstein D
Testing in models of asymmetric information
REStud 1987 VOL 54 p 265.

(1061)
Harris M, Townsend R
Resource allocation under asymmetric information
Em 1985 NOV VOL 49 p 33-64.

(1062)
Kim J-C
The market for "lemons" reconsidered: A model of the used car market with asymmetric information
AER 1985 VOL 75 p 836-843.

(1063)
Varian H R
Divergence of opinion in complete markets : a note
JF 1985 MAR VOL 40:1 p 309-317

(1064)
Allen F
Reputation and product quality
RandJ 1984 AUTUMN VOL 15:3 p 311-327.

(1065)
Riordan M H
Uncertainty, asymmetric information and bilateral contracts
REStud 1984 VOL 51 p 83.

(1066)
Rosenthal R W, Weiss A
Mixed-strategy equilibrium in a market with asymmetric information
REStud 1984 VOL 51 p 333.

(1067)
Bond E W
A direct test of the "lemons" model: The market for used pickup trucks
AER 1982 VOL 72 p 836-840.

(1068)
Chan Y S, Leland H
Prices and qualities in markets with costly information
REStud 1982 VOL 49 p 499.

(1069)
Jovanovic B
Favorable selection with asymmetric information
QJE 1982 VOL 97 P 535.

(1070)
Kambhu J
Optimal product quality under asymmetric information and moral hazard
BellJ 1982 AUTUMN VOL 13:2 p 483-492.

(1071)
Plott C R, Sunder S
Efficiency of experimental security markets with
insider information: An   application   of
rational-expectations models
JPE 1982 VOL 90 p 663.

(1072)
Baron D P
Price   regulation,   quality   and   asymmetric
information
AER 1981 VOL 71 p 212-220.

(1073)
Riley J G
Informational equilibrium
Em 1979 VOL 47 p 331-359.

(1074)
Smallwood D E, Conlisk J
Product quality in markets where consumers are
imperfectly informed
QJE 1979 VOL 93 p 1.

(1075)
Hughart D
Informational asymmetry, bidding strategies and
the marketing of offshore petroleum leases
JPE 1975 VOL 83 p 969.

(1076)
Albin P S
Information exchange in security markets and the
assumption of "homogeneous beliefs"
JF 1974 VOL 29 p 1217.

(1077)
Akerlof G
The market for lemons: Qualitative uncertainty
and the market mechanism
QJE 1970 AUG VOL 84 p 488-500.

3.5 Signalling and self-selection

(1078)
Poitevin M
Financial signalling and the "deep-pocket"
argument
RandJ 1989 SPRING VOL 20:1 p 26-40.

(1079)
Acharya S
A generalized econometric model and tests of a
signalling hypothesis with two discrete signals
JF 1988 JUN VOL 43:2 p 413-430.

(1080)
Gertner R, Gibbons R, Scharfstein D
Simultaneous signalling to the capital and product
markets
RandJ 1988 SUMMER VOL 19:2 p 173-190.

(1081)
Milde H, Riley J G
Signaling in credit markets
QJE 1988 FEB VOL 103:1 p 101-130.

(1082)
Wernerfelt B
Umbrella branding as a signal of new product
quality: an example of signalling by posting a
bond
RandJ 1988 AUTUMN VOL 19:3 p 458-466.

(1083)
Cho I-K, Kreps D M
Signaling games and stable equilibria
QJE 1987 VOL 102 p 179.

(1084)
Franke G
Costless signalling in financial markets
JF 1987 SEP VOL 42:4 p 809-822.

(1085)
Diamond D W
Optimal release of information by firms
JF 1985 SEP VOL 40:4 p 1071-1094

(1086)
John K, Nachman D C
Risky debt investment incentives and reputation
in a sequential equilibrium
JF 1985 JUL VOL 40:3 p 863-880

(1087)
Brennan M J, Kraus A
Notes on costless signalling
(in Bamberg S and Spremann eds., Risk and
capital. Springer, 1984.)

(1088)
Brennan M J, Kraus A
Notes on costless financial signaling
(in Spremann K ed., Lecture notes in economics
and mathematical systems, Vol 127. Springer,
1984.)

(1089)
Waldman M
Job assignments, signalling and efficiency
RandJ 1984 SUMMER VOL 15:2 p 255-270.

(1090)
Bhattacharya S, Ritter J R
Innovation and communication: Signalling with
partial disclosure
REStud 1983 VOL 50 p 331-346.

(1091)
Chamley C
Entrepreneurial abilities and liabilities in a model
of self-selection
BellJ 1983 SPRING VOL 14:1 p 70-80.

(1092)
Thakor A V
An exploration of competitive signalling equilibria
with "third party" information production: the
case of debt insurance
JF 1982 JUN VOL 37:3 p 717-739.

(1093)
Guasch J L, Weiss A
Self-selection in the labor market
AER 1981 VOL 71 p 275-284.

(1094)
Leland H E
Quacks, lemons and licensing: A theory of
minimum quality standards
JPE 1979 VOL 87 p 1328..

(1095)**Riley J G**
Noncooperative equilibrium and market signalling
AER 1979 VOL 69 p 303.

(1096)
Ross S A
Disclosure regulation in financial markets: Some
implications of modern signalling theory
(in Edwards F ed., Issues in financial regulation.
McGraw, 1979.)

(1097)
Willis R J, Rosen S
Education and self-selection
JPE 1979 VOL 87 Suppl p 7.

(1098)
Riley J G
Information, screening and human capital
AER 1976 VOL 66 P+P p 254-260.

(1099)
Rothschild M, Stiglitz J E
Equilibrium in competitive insurance markets: An
essay in the economics of imperfect information
QJE 1976 NOV VOL 80 p 629-649.

(1100)
Salop J, Salop S
Self-selection and turnover in the labor market
QJE 1976 VOL 90 p 619-627.

(1101)
Spence M
Competition in salaries and signaling prerequisites
for jobs
QJE 1976 VOL 90 p 51.

(1102)
Riley J G
Competitive signalling
JET 1975 APR VOL 10:2 p 174-186.

(1103)
Spence M
Competitive and optimal responses to signals: an
analysis of efficiency and distribution
JET 1974 MAR VOL 7:3 p 296-332.

(1104)
Spence M
Job-market signalling
QJE 1973 AUG VOL 87 p 355-379.

3.6 Search costs

(1105)
Benabou R
Search, price setting and inflation
REStud 1988 VOL 55 p 353.

(1106)
Vishwanath T
Parallel search and information gathering
AER 1988 MAY VOL 78:2 p 110-116.

(1107)
De Meza D, Webb D C
Labour turnover, job-specific skills and efficiency
in a search model
QJE 1987 VOL 102 p 281.

(1108)
Zeira J
Investment as a process of search
JPE 1987 VOL 95 p 204-210.

(1109)
Hey J D, McKenna C J
Consumer search with uncertain product quality
JPE 1985 VOL 89 p 54.

(1110)
Cothren R
Job search and implicit contracts
JPE 1983 VOL 91 p 494.

(1111)
Wilde L L
Information costs, duration of search and
turnover: Theory and application
JPE 1981 VOL 89 p 1122.

(1112)
MacMinn R D
Search and market equilibrium
JPE 1980 VOL 88 p 308.

(1113)
Karni E, Schwartz A
Search theory: the case of search with uncertain
recall
JET 1977 OCT VOL 16:1 p 38-52.

(1114)
Landsberger M, Peled D
Duration of offers, price structure, and the gain
from search
JET 1977 OCT VOL 16:1 p 17-37.

(1115)
Ioannides Y M
Market allocation through search: equilibrium
adjustment and price dispersion
JET 1975 OCT VOL 11:2 p 247-262.

(1116)
Kohn M G, Shavell S
The theory of search
JET 1974 OCT VOL 9:2 p 93-123.

(1117)
Telser L G
Searching for the lowest price
AER 1973 VOL 63 P+P p 40-49.

4 The principal-agent relationship

(1118)
Brioschi F, Buzzacchi L, Colombo M G
Risk capital financing and the separation of ownership and control in business groups
JBankF 1989 SEP VOL 13:4-5 p 747-772.

(1119)
Crutchley C E, Hansen R S
A test of the agency theory of managerial ownership, corporate leverage, and corporate dividends
FIN MGMT 1989 WINTER VOL 18 p 36-46.

(1120)
Karpoff J M, Rice E M
Organizatiional form, share transferability, and firm performance: evidence from the ANCSA corporations
JFE 1989 SEP VOL 24:1 p 69-106.

(1121)
Kirby R G
Whose company is it, anyway?
JPM 1989 FALL VOL 16:1 p 13-18.

(1122)
Lewis T R, Sappington D E M
Countervailing incentives in agency problems
JET 1989 DEC VOL 49:2 p 294-313.

(1123)
Moyer R C, Chatfield R E, Sisneros P M
Security analyst monitoring activity: agency costs and information demands
JFQA 1989 DEC VOL 24:4 p 503-512.

(1124)
Demsetz H
The theory of the firm revisited
Journal of Law, Economics and Organization 1988 SPRING VOL 4.

(1125)
Hagerty K M, Siegel D R
On the observational equivalence of managerial contracts under conditions of moral hazard and self-selection
QJE 1988 VOL 103 p 425.

(1126)
Hart O, Moore J H H
Incomplete contracts and renegotiation
EM 1988 JUL VOL 56 p 755-785.

(1127)
Hart O D
Incomplete contracts and the theory of the firm
Journal of Law, Economics and Organization 1988 SPRING VOL 4.

(1128)
Kumar P
Shareholder-manager conflict and the information content of dividends
RFS 1988 SUMMER VOL 1:2 p 111-136.

(1129)
Ma C-T
Unique implementation of incentive contracts with many agents
REStud 1988 VOL 55 p 555.

(1130)
Ma C-T, Moore J, Turnbull S
Stopping agents from "cheating"
JET 1988 DEC VOL 46:2 p 355-372.

(1131)
Malcomson J M, Spinnewyn F
The multiperiod principal-agent problem
REStud 1988 VOL 54 p 391.

(1132)
Moore J H H
Contracting between two parties with private information
REStud 1988 JAN VOL 55 p 49-69.

(1133)
Williamson O E
The logic of economic organization
Journal of Law, Economics and Organization 1988 SPRING VOL 4.

(1134)
Wood A S
Manager vs. client: what's the difference
JPM 1988 SUMMER VOL 14:4 p 63-65.

(1135)
Bamberg G, Spremann K eds.
Agency theory, information, and incentives
Springer-Verlag, 1987.

(1136)
Hart O D, Holmstrom B
The theory of contracts
(in Bewley T ed., Advances in economic theory.
Cambridge U Pr, 1987.)

(1137)
Laffont J-J, Tirole J
Auctioning incentive contracts
JPE 1987 VOL 95 p 921.

(1138)
Ross S A
Equilibrium and agency - inadmissible agents in
the public agency problem
AER 1987 VOL 77 P+P p 308-312.

(1139)
Shaban R A
Testing   between   competing   models   of
sharecropping
JPE 1987 VOL 95 p 893.

(1140)
Williams S R
Efficient performance in two agent bargaining
JET 1987 FEB VOL 41:1 p 154-172.

(1141)
Williamson O E
Transaction cost economics: the comparative
contracting perspective
Journal of Economic Behavior and Organization
1987 VOL 8:4 p 617-626.

(1142)
Jensen M C
Agency costs of free cash flow, corporate finance
and takeovers
AER 1986 VOL 76 P+P p 323-329.

(1143)
Malcomson J M
Rank order contracts for a principal with many
agents
REStud 1986 VOL 53 p 807.

(1144)
McAfee R P, McMillan J
Bidding for contracts:a principal-agent analysis
RandJ 1986 AUTUMN VOL 17:3 p 326-338.

(1145)
Arrow K J
The economics of agency
(in Pratt J and Zeckhauser R eds., Principals and
agents: The structure of business. Harvard Busn,
1985.)

(1146)
Barnea A, Haugen R A, Senbet L W
Agency problems and financial contracting
P-H, 1985.

(1147)
Benston G J
The self-serving management hypothesis: Some
evidence
JAE 1985 APR VOL p 67-84..

(1148)DeJong D V, Forsythe R, Lundholm R J
Ripoffs, lemons and reputation formation in
agency relationships: a laboratory market study
JF 1985 JUL VOL 40:3 p 809-823.

(1149)
Fama E F, Jensen M C
Organizational forms and investment decisions.
JFE 1985 VOL 14:1 p 101-119.

(1150)
Jensen M C, Smith C W
Stockholder, manager and creditor interests:
Applications of agency theory
(in Altman E and Subrahmanyam M eds., Recent
advances in corporate finance. Irwin, 1985.)

(1151)
Joskow P
Vertical integration and long-term contracts
Journal of Law, Economics and Organization
1985 SPRING VOL 1.

(1152)
Manne H G
Controlling the giant corporation: myths and
realities
MCFJ 1985 SPRING VOL 3 p 6-12.

(1153)
Manne H G
The   American   Law   Institute's   corporate
governance proposals: reform or revenge?
MCFJ 1985 SPRING VOL 3 p 13-21.

(1154)
Pratt J, Zeckhauser R eds.
Principals and agents: The structure of business
Harvard Bus Pr, 1985.

(1155)
Riordan M, Williamson O
Asset specificity and economic organization
International Journal of Industrial Organization
1985 VOL 3 p 365-378.

(1156)
Singh N
Monitoring and hierarchies: The marginal value of
information in a principal-agent model
JPE 1985 VOL 85 p 599.

(1157)
Williamson O E
The economic institutions of capitalism
Free Pr, 1985.

(1158)
Beer M, Spector B, Lawrence P R et al.
Managing human assets
Free Pr, 1984.

(1159)
Mookherjee D
Optimal incentive schemes with many agents
REStud 1984 VOL 51 p 433.

(1160)
Amihud Y, Kamin J Y, Ronen J
"Managerialism", "ownership" and risk
JBankF 1983 VOL 7 p 189.

(1161)
Cheung S N S
The contractual nature of the firm
JLE 1983 VOL 26:1 p 1-22.

(1162)
Demsetz H
The structure of ownership and the theory of the
firm
JLE 1983 VOL 26:2 p 375-390.

(1163)
Fama E F, Jensen M C
Separation of ownership and control
JLE 1983 JUN VOL 26 p 301-325.

(1164)
Fama E F, Jensen M C
Agency problems and residual claims
JLE 1983 VOL 26:2 p 327-350.

(1165)
Jemison D B, Oakley R A
Corporate governance in mutual insurance
companies
JBusR 1983 VOL 11 p 501-522.

(1166)
Klein B
Contracting costs and residual claims: the
separation of ownership and control
JLE 1983 VOL 26:2 p 367-374.

(1167)
Means G C
Corporate power in the marketplace
JLE 1983 VOL 26:2 p 467-486.

(1168)
Meckling W H, Jensen M C
Reflections on the corporation as a social
invention
MCFJ 1983 FALL VOL 1 p 6-15.

(1169)
Stiglitz J E, Weiss A
Incentive effects of termination: Applications to
the credit and labor markets
AER 1983 VOL 73 p 912-927.

(1170)
Williamson O E
Organizational form, residual claimants, and
corporate control
JLE 1983 VOL 26:2 p 351-366.

(1171)
Forsythe R, Suchanek G L
The impossibility of efficient decision rules for
firms in competitive stock market economies
JFQA 1982 NOV VOL 17:4 p 555-577.

(1172)
Hand J H, Lloyd W P, Rogow R B
Agency relationships in the close corporation
FIN MGMT 1982 SPRING VOL 11 p 25-30.

(1173)
Harris M, Kriebel C H, Raviv A
Asymmetric information, incentives and intrafirm resource allocation
MSci 1982 JUN VOL 28:6 p 604-620

(1174)
Hughes J S
Agency theory and stochastic dominance
JFQA 1982 SEP VOL 17:3 p 341-361.

(1175)
Myerson R
Optimal coordination mechanisms in generalized principal-agent problems
Journal of Mathematical Economics 1982 VOL 10 p 67-81.

(1176)
Ramakrishnan R T S, Thakor A V
Moral hazard, agency costs, and asset prices in a competitive equilibrium
JFQA 1982 NOV VOL 17:4 p 503-532.

(1177)
Milgrom P R
Good news and bad news: representation theorems and applications
BellJ 1981 AUTUMN VOL 12:2 p 380-391.

(1178)
Williamson O
The modern corporation: origins, evolution, attributes
JEL 1981 DEC VOL 19 p 1537-1568.

(1179)
Fama E F
Agency problems and the theory of the firm
JPE 1980 VOL 88 p 288.

(1180)
Klein B
Transaction cost determinants of "unfair" contractual arrangements
AER 1980 MAY VOL 70 p 356-362.

(1181)
Weitzman M L
Efficient incentive contracts
QJE 1980 VOL 94 p 719.

(1182)
Fellingham J C, Newman D P
Monitoring decisions in an agency setting
JBFA 1979 SUMMER VOL 6:2 p 203-221

(1183)
Haugen R A, Senbet L W
New perspectives on informational asymmetry and agency relationships
JFQA 1979 NOV VOL 14 p 671.

(1184)
Draper D W, Hoag J W
Financial intermediation and the theory of agency
JFQA 1978 NOV VOL 13 p 595.

(1185)
Harris M, Raviv A
Some results on incentive contracts with applications to education and employment, health insurance and law enforcement
AER 1978 VOL 68 p 20-30.

(1186)
Barrett M E, Fraser L B II
Conflicting roles in budgeting for operations
HBR 1977 JUL-AUG VOL 55:4 p 137-146.

(1187)
Jensen M C, Meckling W H
Theory of the firm: Managerial behavior, agency costs and ownership structure
JFE 1976 VOL 3 p 305.

(1188)
Heckerman D G
Motivating managers to make investment decisions
JFE 1975 VOL 2 p 273.

(1189)
Radner R, Rothschild M
On the allocation of effort
JET 1975 JUN VOL 10:3 p 358-376.

(1190)
Stiglitz J E
Incentives, risk and information: notes towards a theory of hierarchy
BellJ 1975 AUTUMN VOL 6:2 p 582-585.

(1191)
Williamson O E
Markets and hierarchies: analysis and antitrust implications
Free Pr, 1975.

(1192)
Stiglitz J E
Incentives and risk sharing in sharecropping
REStud 1974 VOL 41 p 219.

(1193)
Ross S A
The economic theory of agency: The principal's problem
AER 1973 VOL 63 P+P p 134-139.

(1194)
Williamson O E
Markets and hierarchies: Some elementary considerations
AER 1973 VOL 63 P+P p 316-325.

(1195)
Alchian A A, Demsetz H
Production, information costs, and economic organization
AER 1972 DEC p 777-795.

(1196)
Marschak J, Radner R
Economic theory of teams
Yale U Pr, 1972.

(1197)
Williamson O E
The vertical integration of production: market failure considerations
AER 1971 MAY VOL 61 p 112-123.

(1198)
Berle A A, Means G C
The modern corporation and private property. Rev ed
HarBraceJ, 1969.

(1199)
Marris R
The economic theory of managerial capitalism
Free Pr, 1964.

(1200)
Williamson O
The economics of discretionary behavior: managerial objectives in a theory of the firm
P-H, 1964..

Donaldson G
Financial goals: management vs stockholders
HBR 1963 MAY-JUN VOL 41 p 116-129.

(1201)
Coase R H
The nature of the firm
(in Stigler J and Boulding K E eds., Readings in price theory. Irwin, 1952. Also Economica N.S. 1973 VOL 4 p 386-405.)

4.1 Moral hazard and adverse selection

(1202)
Boyer M, Dionne G
An empirical analysis of moral hazard and experience rating
REStat 1989 VOL 71 p 128.

(1203)
Demougin D M
A renegotiation-proof mechanism for a principal-agent model with moral hazard and adverse selection
RandJ 1989 SUMMER VOL 20:2 p 256-267.

(1204)
Guesnerie R, Picard P, Rey P
Adverse selection and moral hazard with risk neutral agents
EER 1989 VOL 33 p 807.

(1205)
Lutz N A
Warranties as signals under consumer moral hazard
RandJ 1989 SUMMER VOL 20:2 p 239-255.

(1206)
Aron D J
Ability, moral hazard, firm size and diversification
RandJ 1988 SPRING VOL 19:1 p 72-87.

(1207)
Crocker K J, Masten S E
Mitigating contractual hazards: unilateral options and contract length
RandJ 1988 AUTUMN VOL 19:3 p 327-343.

(1208)
Emons W
Warranties, moral hazard, and the Lemons problem
JET 1988 OCT VOL 46:1 p 16-33.

(1209)
Mann D P, Wissink J P
Money-back contracts with double moral hazard
RandJ 1988 SUMMER VOL 19:2 p 285-292.

(1210)
Chan Y S, Thakor A V
Collateral and competitive equilibria with moral hazard and private information
JF 1987 JUN VOL 42:2 p 345-363.

(1211)
Eichenbaum M S, Peled D
Capital accumulation and annuities in an adverse selection economy
JPE 1987 APR VOL 95:2 p 334-354.

(1212)
Rasmusen E
Moral hazard in risk-averse teams
RandJ 1987 AUTUMN VOL 18:3 p 428-435.

(1213)
Spear S E, Srivastava S
On repeated moral hazard with discounting
REStud 1987 VOL 54 p 599.

(1214)
Wilson C A
Equilibrium and adverse selection
AER 1987 VOL 77 P+P p 313-317.

(1215)
Farrell J
Moral hazard as an entry barrier
RandJ 1986 AUTUMN VOL 17:3 p 440-449.

(1216)
Greenwald B C
Adverse selection in the labour market
REStud 1986 VOL 53 p 325.

(1217)
Shapiro C
Investment, moral hazard and occupational licensing
REStud 1986 VOL 53 p 843.

(1218)
Dionne G, Lasserre P
Adverse selection, repeated insurance contracts and announcement strategy
REStud 1985 VOL 52 p 719.

(1219)
Ramakrishnan R T S, Thakor A V
The valuation of assets under moral hazard
JF 1984 MAR VOL 39:1 p 229-238.

(1220)
Lambert R A
Long-term contracts and moral hazard
BellJ 1983 AUTUMN VOL 14:2 p 441-452.

(1221)
Holmstrom B
Moral hazard in teams
BellJ 1982 AUTUMN VOL 13:2 p 324-340.

(1222)
Guasch J L, Weiss A
Adverse selection by markets and the advantage of being late
QJE 1980 VOL 94 p 453.

(1223)
Shavell S
On moral hazard and insurance
QJE 1979 VOL 93 p 541.

(1224)
Marshall J M
Moral hazard
AER 1976 DEC VOL 66:5 p 880-890.

(1225)
Helpman E, Laffont J-J
On moral hazard in general equilibrium theory
JET 1975 FEB VOL 10:1 p 8-23.

(1226)
Laffont J-J
Optimism and experts against adverse selection in
a competitive economy
JET 1975 JUN VOL 10:3 p 284-308.

4.2 Value of control

(1227)
Morck R, Shliefer A, Vishny R W
Alternative mechanisms for corporate control
AER 1989 VOL 79:4 p 842-852.

(1228)
Holderness C G, Sheehan D P
The role of majority shareholders in publicly held
corporations: an exploratory analysis
JFE 1988 VOL 20 p 317-346.

(1229)
Jarrell G A, Poulsen A B
Dual-class   recapitalizations   as   antitakeover
mechanisms: the recent evidence
JFE 1988 VOL 20 p 129-152.

(1230)
Jensen M C, Warner J B
The distribution of power among corporate
managers, shareholders, and directors
JFE 1988 VOL 20 p 3-24.

(1231)
Klein A, Rosenfeld J
Targeted share repurchases and top management
changes
JFE 1988 VOL 20 p 493-506.

(1232)
Leech D
Relationship between shareholding concentration
and shareholder voting power in British
companies: a study of the application of power
indices for simple games
MSci 1988 VOL 34 p 509.

(1233)
Morck R, Schleifer A, Vishny R W
Management ownership and market valuation: an
empirical analysis
JFE 1988 VOL 20 p 293-316.

(1234)
Ruback R S
Coercive dual-class exchange offers
JFE 1988 VOL 20 p 153-174..

(1235)**Stulz R M**
Managerial control of voting rights: financing
policies and the market for corporate control
JFE 1988 VOL 20 p 25-54.

(1236)
Warner J B, Watts R L, Wruck K H
Stock prices and top management changes
JFE 1988 VOL 20 p 461-492.

(1237)
Weisbach M S
Outside directors and CEO turnover
JFE 1988 VOL 20 p 431-460.

(1238)
Furtado E P H, Rozeff M S
The wealth effects of company initiated
management changes
JFE 1987 VOL 18 p 147-160.

(1239)
Shleifer A, Vishny R W
Large shareholders and corporate control
JPE 1986 VOL 94 p 461.

(1240)
Lease R C, McConnell J J, Mikkelson W H
The market value of control in publicly-traded
corporations.
JFE 1983 APR VOL 11 p 439-471

(1241)
Levy H
Economic evaluation of voting power of common
stock
JF 1983 MAR VOL 38:1 p 79-93.

(1242)
Midgley K ed.
Management   accountability   and   corporate
governance: selected readings
Macmillan, 1982.

(1243)
Stiglitz J E
Ownership, control and efficient markets: Some paradoxes in the theory of capital markets
(in Boyer K and Shepherd W eds., Economic regulation: Essays in honour of James R. Nelson. Michigan State U Pr, 1982.)

(1244)
Treynor J L
The financial objective in the widely held corporation
FAJ 1981 MAR-APR VOL 37 p 68-72.

(1245)
Dodd P, Leftwich R
The market for corporate charters: "unhealthy competition" versus federal regulation
JB 1980 JUL VOL 53:3 p 259-283.

(1246)
Meeker L G, Joy O M
Price premiums for controlling shares of closely held bank stock
JB 1980 JUL VOL 53:3 p 297-314.

(1247)
Benninga S, Muller E
Majority choice and the objective function of the firm under uncertainty
BellJ 1979 AUTUMN VOL 10:2 p 670-682.

(1248)
Smith E D, Salamon G L
Corporate control and managerial misrepresentation of firm performance
BellJ 1979 SPRING VOL 10:1 p 319-328.

(1249)
Jensen M C, Meckling W H
Can the corporation survive?
FAJ 1978 JAN-FEB p 31-37.

(1250)
Fishburn P C
Majority voting on risky investments
JET 1974 MAY VOL 8:1 p 85ff.

(1251)
Palmer J
The profit-performance effects of the separation of ownership from control in large U S industrial corporation
BellJ 1973 SPRING VOL 4:1 p 293-303.

(1252)
Palmer J P
The separation of ownership from control in large US industrial corporations
QREB 1972 VOL 12:3 p 55.

4.21 Voting rights and proxy contests

(1253)
DeAngelo H, DeAngelo L
Proxy contests and the governance of publicly held corporations
JFE 1989 VOL 23 p 29.

(1254)
Murphy J A
Analyzing sub-classes of General Motors common stock
FIN MGMT 1989 SPRING VOL 18 p 64.

(1255)
Brickley J A, Lease R C, Smith C W Jr
Ownership structure and voting on antitakeover amendments
JFE 1988 VOL 20 p 267-292.

(1256)
Grossman S J, Hart O D
One share-one vote and the market for corporate control
JFE 1988 VOL 20 p 175-202.

(1257)
Harris M, Raviv A
Corporate governance: voting rights and majority rules
JFE 1988 VOL 20 p 203-236.

(1258)
Horner M R
The value of the corporate voting right: evidence from Switzerland
JBankF 1988 VOL 12 p 69-83.

(1259)
Pound J
Proxy contests and the efficiency of shareholder oversight
JFE 1988 VOL 20 p 237-266.

(1260)
Partch M M
The creation of a class of limited voting common stock and shareholder wealth
JFE 1987 JUN VOL 18:2 p 313-339.

(1261)
Bickley J A
Interpreting common stock returns around proxy statement disclosure and annual shareholder meetings.
JFQA 1986 SEP VOL 21:3 p 343-349

(1262)
Jog V M, Riding A L
Price effects of dual-class shares
FAJ 1986 JAN-FEB VOL 42:1 p 58-67.

(1263)
Lease R C, McConnell J J, Mikkelson W H
The evidence of limited voting stock: motives and consequences
MCFJ 1986 SUMMER VOL 4 p 66-71.

(1264)
DeAngelo H, DeAngelo L
Managerial ownership of voting rights: A study of public corporations with dual classes of common stock
JFE 1985 VOL 14:1 p 33-69.

(1265)
Mikkelson W H, Partch M M
An examination of evidence on voting rights and the market for corporate control
AJM 1985 DEC VOL 10 p 67-82.

(1266)
Bhagat S, Brickley J A
Cumulative voting: the value of minority shareholding voting rights
JLE 1984 VOL 27:2 p 339-367.

(1267)
Dodd P, Warner J B
On corporate governance: a study of proxy contests.
JFE 1983 APR VOL 11 p 401-438

(1268)
Easterbrook F H, Fischel D R
Voting in corporate law
JLE 1983 VOL 26:2 p 395-428.

(1269)
Meeker L G, Joy O M, Cogger K O
Valuation of controlling shares in closely held banks
JBankF 1983 VOL 7 p 175.

(1270)
Duvall R M, Austin D V
Predicting the results of proxy contests
JF 1965 SEP VOL 20 p 464-471.

(1271)
Von Mehren R B, McCarroll J C
The proxy rules: a case study in administrative process
LCP 1964 JUN VOL 29 p 728-748.

4.3   Executive   compensation   and incentives

(1272)
Lambert R A, Lanen W N, Larcker D F
Executive stock option plans and corporate dividend policy
JFQA 1989 DEC VOL 24:4 p 409-426.

(1273)
Ricart i Costa J E
On managerial contracting with asymmetric information
EER 1989 VOL 33 p 1805.

(1274)
Baker G P, Jensen M C, Murphy K J
Compensation and incentives: practice vs. theory
JF 1988 JUL VOL 43:3 p 593-616.

(1275)
Demski J S, Sappington D E M, Spiller P T
Incentive schemes with multiple agents and
bankruptcy constraints
JET 1988 FEB VOL 44:1 p 156-167.

(1276)
Laffont J-J, Tirole J
Repeated auctions of incentive contracts,
investment, and bidding parity with an application
to takeovers
RandJ 1988 WINTER VOL 19:4 p 516-537.

(1277)
Riordan M H, Sappington D E M
Optimal contracts with public ex post information
JET 1988 JUN VOL 45:1 p 189-199.

(1278)
Stern J M, Stewart G B, Chew D H eds.
Corporate restructuring and executive
compensation
Ballinger, 1988.

(1279)
Agrawal A, Mandelker G N
Managerial incentives and corporate investment
and financing decisions
JF 1987 SEP VOL 42:4 p 823-837.

(1280)
Campbell T S, Kracaw W A
Optimal managerial incentive contracts and the
value of corporate insurance.
JFQA 1987 SEP VOL 22:3 p 315-328.

(1281)
Larcker D F
Short-term compensation contracts and executive
expenditure decisions : the case of commercial
banks
JFQA 1987 MAR VOL 22:1 p 33-50.

(1282)
Meyer M A, Mookherjee D
Incentives, compensation and social welfare
REStud 1987 VOL 54 p 209.

(1283)
Skivas S D
The strategic choice of managerial incentives
RandJ 1987 AUTUMN VOL 18:3 p 452-460.

(1284)
Strong J S, Meyer J R
Asset writedowns : Managerial incentives and
security returns
JF 1987 JUL VOL 42:3 p 643-661.

(1285)
Holmstrom B, Costa J R I
Managerial incentives and capital management
QJE 1986 VOL 101 p 835.

(1286)
Santerre R E, Neun S P
Stock dispersion and executive compensation
REStat 1986 VOL 68 p 685.

(1287)
Brickley J A, Bhagat S, Lease R C
The impact of long-range managerial
compensation plans on shareholder wealth
JAE 1985 APR VOL 7 p 85-107..

(1288)**Brindisi L J**
Creating shareholder value: a new mission for
executive compensation
MCFJ 1985 WINTER VOL 2 p 56-66.

(1289)
Bulmash S B, Mehrez A
Sharing rule contracts between management and
investors and their effect on the management's
attitude towards risk
JBFA 1985 AUTUMN VOL 12:3 p 399-413

(1290)
Campbell T S, Kracaw W A
The market for managerial labor services and
capital market equilibrium
JFQA 1985 SEP VOL 20:3 p 277-297.

(1291)
Lambert R A, Larker D F
Executive compensation, corporate
decision-making and shareholder wealth: a review
of the evidence
MCFJ 1985 WINTER VOL 2 p 6-22.

(1292)
Murphy K J
Corporate performance and managerial
remuneration: An empirical analysis
JAE 1985 APR VOL 7 p 11-42.

(1293)
Narayanan M P
Managerial incentives for short-term results
JF 1985 DEC VOL 40:5 p 1469-1484.

(1294)
Stewart B
Performance measurement and incentive compensation
MCFJ 1985 WINTER VOL 2 p 76-81.

(1295)
Ubelhart M C
Business strategy, performance measurement and compensation
MCFJ 1985 WINTER VOL 2 p 67-75.

(1296)
Donaldson G
Managing corporate wealth
Harvard U Pr, 1984.

(1297)
O'Keeffe M, Viscusi W K, Zeckhauser R J
Economic contests: comparative reward schemes
Journal of Labor Economics 1984 JAN VOL 2 p 27-56.

(1298)
Eaton J, Rosen H S
Agency delay compensation and the structure of executive remuneration
JF 1983 DEC VOL 38:5 p 1489-1505.

(1299)
Hart O D
The market mechanism as an incentive scheme
BellJ 1983 AUTUMN VOL 14:2 p 366-282.

(1300)
Beck P J, Zorn T S
Managerial incentives in a stock market economy
JF 1982 DEC VOL 37:5 p 1151-1167.

(1301)
Cooley P L, Edwards C E
Ownership effects on managerial salaries in small business
FIN MGMT 1982 WINTER VOL 11 p 5-9.

(1302)
Diamond D W, Verrecchia R E
Optimal managerial contracts and equilibrium security prices
JF 1982 MAY VOL 37:2 p 275-287.

(1303)
Hite G, Long M
Taxes and executive stock options
JAE 1982 JUL VOL 4 p 3-14.

(1304)
Smith C W Jr, Watts R L
Incentive and tax effects of U.S. executive compensation plans
AJM 1982 VOL 7 p 139-157.

(1305)
Euske K J, Jackson D W Jr, Reif W E
Performance and satisfaction of bank managers
JBR 1980 SPRING VOL 11:1.

(1306)
Jennergren L P
On the design of incentives in business firms - a survey of some research
MSci 1980 FEB VOL 26:2 p 180-201.

(1307)
Medoff J L, Abraham D G
Experience, performance and earnings
QJE 1980 DEC VOL 95 p 703-736.

(1308)
Sarin R K, Winkler R L
Performance-based incentive plans
MSci 1980 NOV VOL 26:11 p 1131-1144.

(1309)
Veit E T, Avey M L, Corley J L
The role of stock options in the bank trust departments: fifth Federal Reserve District banks
JBR 1980 WINTER VOL 10:4.

(1310)
Holt C A Jr
Uncertainty and the bidding for incentive contracts
AER 1979 VOL 69 p 697-705.

(1311)
McAlister M K, Overstreet G A
Comparative job satisfaction levels among bank managers
JBR 1979 WINTER VOL 9:4.

(1312)
Murrell P
The performance of multiperiod managerial incentive schemes
AER 1979 VOL 69 p 934-940.

(1313)
Rappaport A
Executive incentives vs corporate growth
HBR 1978 JUL-AUG VOL 56:4 p 81-88.

(1314)
Edwards F R
Managerial objectives in regulated industries: expense-preference behavior in banking
JPE 1977 FEB VOL 85:1 p 147-162.

(1315)
Itami H
Analysis of implied risk-taking behavior under a goal-based incentive scheme
MSci 1977 AUG VOL 23:12 p 183.

(1316)
Bonin J P
On the design of managerial incentive structures in a decentralized planning enviroment
AER 1976 VOL 66 p 682-687.

(1317)
De Alessi L
Managerial tenure under private and government ownership in the electric power industry
JPE 1974 VOL 82 p 645.

(1318)
Baron D P
Incentive contracts and competitive bidding
AER 1972 VOL 62 p 384-394.

(1319)
Slocum J W Jr, Strawer R H
The impact of job level, geographical location and organisational size on the managerial satisfaction of bankers
JBR 1970 AUTUMN VOL 1:3 p 41-49.

5 Social responsibility

(1320)
Maldonado-Bear R
Free markets: Finance, ethics and public policy
P-H, 1989.

(1321)
Bruyn S T
The field of social investment
Cambridge U Pr, 1987.

(1322)
Ennis R M, Parkhill R L
South African divestment: Social responsibility or
fiduciary folly
FAJ 1986 JUL-AUG VOL 42 p 30-38.

(1323)
Grossman B R, Sharpe W F
Financial implications of South African
divestment
FAJ 1986 JUL-AUG VOL 42 p 15-29.

(1324)
Block H R, Lareau T J
Should we invest in "socially irresponsible" firms?
JPM 1985 WINTER VOL 11:4 p 27-32.

(1325)
Mahapatra S
Investor reaction to a corporate social accounting
JBFA 1984 SPRING VOL 11:1 p 29-40

(1326)
Mills D L, Gardner M J
Financial profiles and the disclosure of
expenditures for socially responsible purposes
JBusR 1984 VOL 12 p 407-424.

(1327)
Wagner W H, Emkin A, Dixon R L
South African divestment: The investment issues
FAJ 1984 NOV-DEC VOL 40 p 14-22.

(1328)
Curzan M P, Pelesh M L
Revitalizing corporate democracy: control of
investment managers' voting on social
responsibility proxy issues
HLR 1980 VOL 93:4 p 670-700.

(1329)
Schotland R A
Divergent investing for pension funds
FAJ 1980 SEP-OCT VOL 36 p 29-40.

(1330)
Buzby S L, Falk H
Demand for social responsibility information by
university investors
AR 1979 JAN VOL 54:1 p 23-37.

(1331)
Purcell T V
Management and the ethical investors
HBR 1979 SEP-OCT VOL 57:7 p 24-44.

(1332)
Ingram R W
An investigation of the information content of
(certain) social responsibility disclosures
JAR 1978 AUTUMN VOL 16:2 p 270-285.

(1333)
Spicer B H
Investors, corporate social performance and
information disclosure: an empirical study
AR 1978 JAN VOL 53:1 p 94-111.

(1334)
Spicer B H
Market risk, accounting data and companies'
pollution control records
JBFA 1978 SPRING VOL 5:1 p 67-84.

(1335)
Simon J G et al.
The ethical investor: universities and corporate
responsibility
Yale U Pr, 1972.

6 Capital markets and securities markets

(1336)
Jappelli T, Pagano M
Consumption and capital market imperfections: an international comparison
AER 1989 VOL 79:5 p 1088-1105.

(1337)
Moylan J J, Ukman L A, Lake P S
Exchange memberships: an overview of the issues pertaining to the property rights of a bankrupt member and his creditors
JFM 1989 VOL 9:5 p 461-468.

(1338)
Walter I
Competitive positioning in international financial services
Journal of International Financial Management & Accounting 1989 SPRING VOL 1:1 p 15-40.

(1339)
Valentine S
International dictionary of the securities industry. 2nd ed
Macmillan, 1988.

(1340)
Wilcox J A
Current readings on money, banking, and financial markets
Scott, Foresman, 1988..

(1341)**Altman E I, McKinney M J eds.**
Handbook of financial markets and institutions. 6th ed
Wiley, 1987.

(1342)
Snowden K A
American stock market development and performance, 1871-1929
Explorations in Economic History 1987 VOL 24:4.

(1343)
Cooper S K, Fraser D R
The financial marketplace. 2nd ed
Addison-Wes, 1986.

(1344)
Gilpin A
Dictionary of economics and financial markets. 5th ed
Butterworth, 1986.

(1345)
Kaufman H
Interest rates, the markets, and the new financial world
Tauris, 1986.

(1346)
Frankel J A
Portfolio crowding out empirically estimated
QJE 1985 VOL 100 Suppl p 1041-1065.

(1347)
Grinblatt M S, Ross S A
Market power in a securities market with endogenous information
QJE 1985 VOL 100 p 1143.

(1348)
Henning C N et al.
Financial markets and the economy. 4th ed
P-H, 1984.

(1349)
Khoury S J
Speculative markets
Woodbridge, Ill.: McMillan Pubs, 1984.

(1350)
Milne F, Shefrin H M
Clarifying some misconceptions about stock market economies
QJE 1984 VOL 99 p 615.

(1351)
Tobin J
On the efficiency of the financial system
LBR 1984 JUL 153 p 1-15

(1352)
Harberger A C
Vignettes on the world capital market
AER 1980 VOL 70 P+P p 336-337.

(1353)
Robinson R I, Wrightsman D
Financial markets: The accumulation and allocation of wealth
McGraw, 1980.

(1354)
Lauer J R, Singleton J C
The implications of recursiveness in capital markets - theory and empirical tests
JFQA 1979 MAR VOL 14 p 59.

(1355)
Hendershott P H, Kidwell D S
The impact of relative security supplies
JMCB 1978 AUG VOL 10:3 p 337-347.

(1356)
Kindleberger C P
Manias, panics and crashes: a history of financial crises
Macmillan, 1978.

(1357)
Altman E I, Sametz A W eds.
Financial crises: institutions and markets in a fragile environment
Wiley, 1977.

(1358)
Hirshleifer J
The theory of speculation under alternative regimes of markets
JF 1977 VOL 32 p 975.

(1359)
Mossin J
The economic efficiency of financial markets
Lexington Bks, 1977.

(1360)
Schwert G W
Stock exchange seats as capital assets
JFE 1977 VOL 4 p 51.

(1361)
Dieffenbach B C
A theory of securities markets under uncertainty
REStud 1976 VOL 43 p 317.

(1362)
Hamilton J L
Competition, scale economies and transaction cost in the stock market
JFQA 1976 DEC VOL 11 p 779.

(1363)
Scott R H
Teaching the financial markets course
JFQA 1976 NOV VOL 11.

(1364)
Moore B J
Equities, capital gains and the role of finance in accumulation
AER 1975 VOL 65 p 872-886.

(1365)
Ishikawa T
Imperfection in the capital market and the institutional arrangement of inheritance
REStud 1974 VOL 41 p 383.

(1366)
Shane M
Capital markets and the dynamics of growth
AER 1974 VOL 64 p 162-169.

(1367)
Friend I
The economic consequences of the stock market
AER 1972 VOL 62 P+P p 212-219.

(1368)
Rasche R
Impact of the stock market on private demand
AER 1972 VOL 62 P+P p 220-228.

(1369)
Dunning J H, Morgan E V eds.
An economic study of the City of London.
Economists Advisory Group (EAG)
Allen, 1971.

(1370)
Dougall H E
Capital markets and institutions. 2nd ed
P-H, 1970.

(1371)
Brooks J
Once in Golconda: a true drama of Wall Street
1920-1938
Har-Row, 1969.

(1372)
Rosen L R
Go where the money is: a guide to understanding
and entering the securities business
Dow Jones-Irwin, 1969.

(1373)
Sobel R
Panic on Wall Street: a history of America's
financial disasters
Macmillan, 1968.

(1374)
Vickers D
The theory of the firm; production, capital and
finance
McGraw, 1968.

(1375)
Grant A T K
A study of the capital market in Britain from
1919-1936. 2nd ed
Cass, 1967.

(1376)
Hester D D, Tobin J eds.
Financial markets and economic activity
Wiley, 1967.

(1377)
Wilson J S G
Some aspects of the development of capital
markets
BNLQR 1966 DEC VOL 19 p 263-310.

(1378)
Baumol W J
The stock market and economic efficiency
Fordham, 1965.

(1379)
Solow R M
Capital theory and the rate of return
Chicago: Rand McNally, 1965.

(1380)
Hirshleifer J
Efficient allocation of capital in an uncertain
world
AER 1964 MAY VOL 54 p 77-85.

(1381)
Leeuw F de
Financial markets in business cycles: a simulation
study
AER 1964 DEC VOL 54 p 309-323.

(1382)
Sametz A W
Trends in the volume and composition of equity
finance
JF 1964 SEP VOL 19 p 450-469.

(1383)
Deane P
Long-term trends in capital formation and
financing
EJ 1962 DEC VOL 72 p 926-930.

(1384)
Kuznets S
Capital in the American economy: its formation
and financing
(Dist by Princeton U Pr) Natl Bur Econ Res,
1961.

(1385)
**Committee on the Working of the Monetary
System**
Report command 827 (The Radcliffe report)
HMSO, 1959.

(1386)
Brooks J
The 7 fat years: chronicles of Wall Street
Magee, 1958.

(1387)
Galbraith J K
The great crash
HM, 1955.

(1388)
Machlup F
The stock market, credit and capital formation.
Translated from a revised version of the German
edition by V C Smith
Macmillan, 1940.

6.1 Innovation in capital markets

(1389)
Blair D H, Golbe D L, Gerard J M
Unbundling the voting rights and profit claims of
common shares
JPE 1989 VOL 97 p 420.

(1390)
Finnerty J D, Borun V M
An analysis of unbundled stock units
Global Finance Journal 1989 VOL 1:1.

(1391)
Levich R
Recent international financial innovations:
implications for financial management
Journal of International Financial Management &
Accounting 1989 SPRING VOL 1:1 p 1-14.

(1392)
Ross S A
Presidential address: Institutional markets,
financial marketing, and financial innovation
JF 1989 JUL VOL 44:3 p 541-556.

(1393)
Allen F, Gale D
Optimal security design
RFS 1988 FALL VOL 1:3 p 229-264..

(1394) **Kabir M, Mangla I**
Effects of financial innovations on the money
demand function: a Canadian evidence
AE 1988 SEP VOL 20:9 p 1263-1274.

(1395)
Kane E J
Interaction of financial and regulatory innovation
AER 1988 MAY VOL 78:2 p 328-334.

(1396)
Petruzzi C, Del Valle M, Judlowe S
Patent and copyright protection for innovations in
finance
FIN MGMT 1988 WINTER VOL 17 p 66-71.

(1397)
Anderson R W, Harris C J
A model of innovation with application to new
financial products
OEP 1986 NOV VOL 38 Suppl p 203-218.

(1398)
Bank for International Settlements
Recent innovations in international banking
Basle: Bank for International Settlements, 1986.

(1399)
Cooper I A
Innovations: New market instruments
Oxford Review of Economic Policy 1986 VOL 2
p 1-17.

(1400)
Milbourne R, Moore H A
Some statistical evidence on the effects of
financial innovation
REStat 1986 VOL 68 p 521.

(1401)
Miller M H
Financial innovation : the last twenty years and
the next
JFQA 1986 DEC VOL 21:4 p 459-471.

(1402)
Germany J D, Morton J E
Financial innovation and deregulation in foreign
industrial countries
F R Bul 1985 VOL 71:10.

(1403)
Van Horne J C
Of financial innovations and excesses.
JF 1985 JUL VOL 40:3 p 621-631.

(1404)
Wenninger J
Financial innovation - a complex problem even in
a simple framework
F R Bk New York Q Rev 1984 SUMMER VOL
9:2.

(1405)
Freedman C
Financial innovation in Canada: Causes and consequences
AER 1983 VOL 73 P+P p 101-106.

(1406)
Niehans J
Financial innovation, multinational banking and monetary policy
JBankF 1983 VOL 7 p 537.

(1407)
Silber W L
The process of financial innovation
AER 1983 VOL 73 P+P p 89-95.

(1408)
Arak M
Innovations in the financial markets
F R Bk New York Q Rev 1981-82 WINTER VOL 6:4.

(1409)
Hakansson N H
Changes in the financial market : welfare and price effects and basic theorems of value conservation
JF 1982 SEP VOL 37:4 p 977-1005

(1410)
Christelow D B
Financial innovation and monetary indicators in Japan
F R Bk New York Q Rev 1981 SPRING VOL 6:1.

(1411)
Landy L
Financial innovation in Canada
F R Bk New York Q Rev 1980 AUTUMN VOL 5:3.

(1412)
Burns J M
On the effects of financial innovations
QREB 1971 VOL 11:2 p 83.

6.2 Structure of capital markets

(1413)
Allen M et al.
International capital markets: developments and prospects
IMF, 1989.

(1414)
Allingham M
Theory of markets
Macmillan, 1989.

(1415)
Arthur Andersen & Co
European capital markets: a strategic forecast
Economist Publications, 1989.

(1416)
Bank of England
London as an international financial centre
BEQB 1989 NOV VOL 29:4 p 516-528.

(1417)
Buckland R, Davis E W
The Unlisted Securities Market
Oxford U Pr, 1989.

(1418)
Coggan P
The money machine: how the city works. 2nd ed
Penguin, 1989.

(1419)
de Caires B ed.
The GT guide to world equity markets: 1989
Euromoney Publications, 1989.

(1420)
Economist
European financial centres: no 1: France
Economist Publications, 1989.

(1421)
Economist
European financial centres: no 2: Italy
Economist Publications, 1989.

(1422)
Economist Conference Unit
Restructuring Europe's financial services: 1992 and beyond
Stanstead Abbotts, Herts: Rooster Books, 1989.

(1423)
Elton E J, Gruber M J
Japanese security markets
Ballinger, 1989.

(1424)
Eurofi
1992: planning for financial services and the insurance sector
Butterworth, 1989.

(1425)
Gammill J F Jr, Perold A F
The changing character of stock market liquidity
JPM 1989 SPRING VOL 15:3 p 13-18.

(1426)
Geisst C R
A guide to the financial markets. 2nd ed
Macmillan, 1989.

(1427)
Goldberg L G, Keenan M, Schrier L
Relative revenue distribution in the securities industry
QREB 1989 AUTUMN VOL 29:3 p 86-94.

(1428)
Group of Thirty
Clearance and settlement systems in the world's securities markets
Group of Thirty, 1989.

(1429)
Honeygold D
International financial markets
Woodhead-Faulkner, 1989.

(1430)
Kaufman G G
The US financial system: money, markets, and institutions. 4th ed
P-H, 1989.

(1431)
Kaushik S K ed.
International capital markets: new directions
New York Institute of Finance, 1989.

(1432)
Kessides C et al, eds.
Financial reform in socialist economies
Washington, DC: World Bank, 1989.

(1433)
Noyelle T
New York's financial markets: the challenges of globalization
Westview Press, 1989.

(1434)
Rose P S
Money and capital markets: the financial system in an increasingly global economy. 3rd ed
Irwin, 1989.

(1435)
Sharp R M
The lore and legends of Wall Street
Dow Jones-Irwin, 1989.

(1436)
Takagi S
The Japanese equity market: past and present
JBankF 1989 SEP VOL 13:4-5 p 537-570.

(1437)
Abdul-Hadi A S F
Stock markets of the Arab world: trends, problems and prospects for integration
Routledge, 1988.

(1438)
Campbell T S
Money and capital markets
Scott, Foresman, 1988.

(1439)
Cargill T F, Royama S
The transition of finance in Japan and the United States
Stanford, Calif: Hoover Institution Press, 1988.

(1440)
Clarke W M
How the City of London works: an introduction
to its financial markets. 2nd ed
Waterlow, 1988.

(1441)
Edwards A ed.
Brazil: a guide to the structure, development and
regulation of financial services
Economist Publications, 1988.

(1442)
England C, Huertas T eds.
The financial services revolution: policy directions
for the future
Kluwer Academic, 1988.

(1443)
Fabozzi F J, Ma C K
The over-the-counter market and New York Stock
Exchange trading halts
FR 1988 NOV VOL 23:4 p 427-438.

(1444)
Fortune
The battle over US market reform
F 1988 FEB 1 VOL 117:3 p 28-31.

(1445)
Gilbody J
The UK monetary and financial system: an
introduction
Routledge, 1988.

(1446)
Harris L et al., eds.
New perspectives on the financial system
Croom Helm, 1988..

(1447)**Hutchinson P, Meric I, Meric G**
The financial characteristics of small firms which
achieve quotation on the U K unlisted securities
market
JBFA 1988 SPRING VOL 15:1 p 9-20.

(1448)
Jonquieres G de
1992: countdown to reality
Financial Times, 1988.

(1449)
Kincaid G R
Policy implications of structural changes in
financial markets
FD 1988 VOL 25:1.

(1450)
Knoll M S
Uncertainty, efficiency, and the brokerage industry
JLE 1988 VOL 31:1 p 249.

(1451)
Mayer M
Markets: who plays, who risks, who gains, who
loses
S & S, 1988.

(1452)
McCullough V
The Economist pocket guide to the new City
Blackwell and The Economist Publications, 1988.

(1453)
Radecki L J, Reinhart V
The globalization of financial markets and the
effectiveness of monetary policy instruments
F R Bk New York Q Rev 1988 AUTUMN VOL
13:3.

(1454)
Reid M I
All-change in the City: the revolution in Britain's
financial sector
Macmillan, 1988.

(1455)
Schwartz R A
Equity markets: Structure, trading, and
performance
Har-Row, 1988.

(1456)
Schwartz R A
A proposal to stabilize stock prices
JPM 1988 FALL VOL 15:1 p 4-11.

(1457)
Spicer & Oppenheim International
The Spicer & Oppenheim guide to securities
markets around the world
Wiley, 1988.

(1458)
Takagi S
The changing Japanese financial system
FD 1988 VOL 25:1.

(1459)
Villanueva D
Issues in financial sector reform
FD 1988 VOL 25:1.

(1460)
Viner A
Inside Japanese financial markets
Dow Jones-Irwin, 1988.

(1461)
Viner A
The financial Samurai: the emerging power of Japanese money
Kogan Page, 1988.

(1462)
Watson M et al.
International capital markets: developments and prospects
IMF, 1988.

(1463)
Whitehead D D
Moving toward 1992: a common financial market for Europe?
F R Bk Atlanta Ec Rev 1988 VOL 73:6.

(1464)
Bench N
Questions and answers about today's securities market
P-H, 1987.

(1465)
Corrigan E G
A perspective on the globalization of financial markets and institutions
F R Bk New York Q Rev 1987 SPRING VOL 12:1.

(1466)
Corrigan E G
A framework for reform of the financial system
F R Bk New York Q Rev 1987 SUMMER VOL 12:2.

(1467)
Edwards A ed.
Hong Kong: a guide to the structure, development and regulation of financial services
Economist Publications, 1987.

(1468)
Edwards A ed.
Singapore: a guide to the structure, development and regulation of financial services
Economist Publications, 1987.

(1469)
Hall M
The City revolution: causes and consequences
Macmillan, 1987.

(1470)
Hamilton J L
Off-board trading of NYSE-listed stocks: the effects of deregulation and the national market system
JF 1987 DEC VOL 42:5 p 1331-1346.

(1471)
Hilton A
City within a state: a portrait of Britain's financial world
Tauris, 1987.

(1472)
Michie R C
The London and New York stock exchanges: 1850-1914
Allen, 1987.

(1473)
OECD
International trade in services: securities
OECD, 1987.

(1474)
Parry R T
Major trends in the U.S. financial system: implications and issues
F R Bk San Francisco Ec Rev 1987 SPRING.

(1475)
Putnam B H, Zimmer S C
The Blackwell guide to Wall Street
Blackwell, 1987.

(1476)
Robins B
Tokyo: a world financial centre
Euromoney Publications, 1987.

(1477)
Rowley E E
The financial system today
Manchester U Pr, 1987.

(1478)
Seznec J-F
The financial markets of the Arabian Gulf
Croom Helm, 1987.

(1479)
Skully M T
Financial institutions and markets in the South
Pacific: a study of New Caledonia, Solomon
Islands, Tonga, Vanuatu and Western Samoa
Macmillan, 1987.

(1480)
Stonham P
Global stock market reforms
Gower, 1987.

(1481)
Suzuki S
The Japanese financial system
Clarendon, 1987.

(1482)
Teweles R J, Bradley E S
The stock market. 5th ed
Wiley, 1987.

(1483)
Chapman C
How the new Stock Exchange works
Hutchinson, 1986.

(1484)
Christensen B V
Switzerland's role as an international financial
center
IMF, 1986.

(1485)
Corrigan E G
Coping with globally integrated financial markets
F R Bk New York Q Rev 1986-87 WINTER
VOL 11:4.

(1486)
Dougall H E, Gaumnitz J E
Capital markets and institutions. 5th ed
P-H, 1986.

(1487)
Economists Advisory Group
Tokyo 2000: the world's third international
financial centre?
Economist Publications, 1986.

(1488)
Feldman R A
Japanese financial markets: deficits, dilemmas, and
deregulation
MIT Pr, 1986.

(1489)
Goldenberg S
Trading: inside the world's leading stock
exchanges
Sidgwick & Jackson, 1986.

(1490)
Hamilton A
The financial revolution: the big bang worldwide
Viking, 1986.

(1491)
Hamilton J D
Stockbroking tomorrow
Macmillan, 1986.

(1492)
Kay W
The Big Bang: an investor's guide to the changing
City
Weidenfeld & N, 1986.

(1493)
Kay W ed.
Stock Exchange: a marketplace for tomorrow
Sterling Publications, 1986.

(1494)
Kerr I M
Big Bang
Euromoney Publications, 1986.

(1495)
Marsh F
Japan's next export success: the financial services
industry
Economist Publications, 1986.

(1496)
Scott R H et al., eds.
Hong Kong's financial institutions and markets
Oxford U Pr, 1986.

(1497)
Thomas W A
The big bang
Philip Allan, 1986.

(1498)
Thomas W A
The stock exchanges of Ireland
Cairns, 1986.

(1499)
Widlake B
In the City
Faber & Faber, 1986..

(1500)**Bank of England**
The unlisted securities market
BEQB 1985 VOL 25 p 537-543.

(1501)
Goobey A R
The City revolution: 'gentlemen vs. players'
Bow Group, 1985.

(1502)
Gould J P, Verrecchia R E
The information content of specialist pricing
JPE 1985 VOL 93 p 66.

(1503)
Hewlett N, Toporowski J
All change in the City: a report on recent
changes and future prospects in London's
financial markets
Economist Publications, 1985.

(1504)
Higgins R C
Introduction to Japanese finance : markets,
institutions, and firms.
JFQA 1985 JUN VOL 20:2 p 169-191

(1505)
Horne J
Japan's financial markets: conflict and consensus
in policymaking
Allen, 1985.

(1506)
Maru J, Takahashi T
Recent developments of interdealer brokerage in
the Japanese secondary bond markets
JFQA 1985 JUN VOL 20:2 p 193-210.

(1507)
McRae H, Cairncross F
Capital city: London as a financial centre. Rev ed
Methuen, 1985.

(1508)
Peasnell K V, Ward C W R
British financial markets and institutions
P-H, 1985.

(1509)
Pessin A H
Fundamentals of the securities industry. Rev ed
New York Institute of Finance, 1985.

(1510)
Research Services Limited
Customer reactions to the City revolution
Wembley: Research Services Ltd, 1985.

(1511)
Skully M T ed.
Financial institutions and markets in the
Southwest Pacific: a study of Australia, Fiji, New
Zealand and Papua New Guinea
Macmillan, 1985.

(1512)
Stoll H R
Alternative views of market making
(in Amihud Y, Ho T, and Schwartz R eds.,
Market making and the changing structure of the
securities industry. Lexington Bks, 1985.)

(1513)
Valin Pollen Limited
The City revolution: report on a survey of City
professionals
Valin Pollen, 1985.

(1514)
Whitcomb D
An international comparison of stock exchange
trading structures
(in Amihud Y, Ho T, and Scwartz R eds., Market
making and the changing structure of the
securities industry. Lexington Bks, 1985.)

(1515)
Wilmot T
Inside the over-the-counter market
Woodhead-Faulkner, 1985.

(1516)
Wood J H, Wood N L
Financial markets
HarBraceJ, 1985.

(1517)
Abdeen A M, Shook D N
The Saudi financial system: in the context of
Western and Islamic finance
Wiley, 1984.

(1518)
Calvin D L
The national market system: a successful
adventure in industry self-improvement
VLR 1984 VOL 70:4 p 785-811.

(1519)
Fortune
The stock market of the future now
F 1984 OCT 29 VOL 110:9 p 89-92.

(1520)
Fortune
The revolution in London's financial markets
F 1984 MAY 14 VOL 109:10 p 76-79.

(1521)
Germidis D, Michalet C-A
International banks and financial markets in
developing countries
OECD, 1984.

(1522)
Kemp L J
The Wardley guide to world money and securities
markets
Euromoney Publications, 1984.

(1523)
**Ontario.   Ministry of Treasury and Economics.
Library**
Financial services industry: emerging issues and
trends, 1973-1984
Monticello, Ill: Vance Bibliographies, 1984.

(1524)
Skully M T ed.
Financial institutions and markets in Southeast
Asia: a study of Brunei, Indonesia, Malaysia,
Philippines, Singapore and Thailand
Macmillan, 1984.

(1525)
Van Horne J C
Financial market rates and flows
P-H, 1984.

(1526)
Coakley J, Harris L
The City of capital: London's role as a financial
centre
Blackwell, 1983.

(1527)
Eiteman D K
International capital markets
(in Roussekis N ed., International banking:
Principles and practices. Praeger, 1983.)

(1528)
Kane E J
Policy implications of structural changes in
financial markets
AER 1983 VOL 73 P+P p 96-100.

(1529)
Makowski L
Competitive stock markets
REStud 1983 VOL 50 p 305.

(1530)
Monti M et al.
The Italian credit and financial system: report by the Commission appointed by the Minister of the Treasury
Rome: Banco Nazionale del Lavoro, 1983.

(1531)
Wachtel P ed
Crises in the economic and financial structure
Lexington Bks, 1983.

(1532)
Burns J M
Electronic trading in futures markets
FAJ 1982 JAN-FEB p 33-42.

(1533)
Garbade K
Securities markets
McGraw, 1982.

(1534)
Kemp L J
A guide to world money and capital markets
McGraw, 1982.

(1535)
Seligman J
The transformation of Wall Street
HM, 1982.

(1536)
Stonham P
Major stock markets of Europe
Gower, 1982.

(1537)
Reed H C
The preeminence of international financial centers
Praeger, 1981

(1538)
Verheirstraeten A ed.
Competition and regulation in financial markets
Macmillan, 1981.

(1539)
Cheng H-S
Financial deepening in Pacific Basin countries
F R Bk San Francisco Ec Rev 1980 SUMMER.

(1540)
Massaro V G
Corporate finance and the changing US financial structure
New York: Conference Board, 1980.

(1541)
Davies B
Business finance and the City of London. 2nd ed
Heinemann Educational, 1979.

(1542)
Hamilton J L
Marketplace fragmentation competition and the efficiency of the stock exchange
JF 1979 MAR VOL 34:1 p 171-187.

(1543)
Mendelson M M, Peake J W
The ABCs of trading on a national market system
FAJ 1979 SEP-OCT VOL 35:5 p 31-42.

(1544)
Mendelson M M, Peake J W
Which way to a national market system?
FAJ 1979 SEP-OCT p 31-43.

(1545)
Morgan E V et al.
City lights: essays on financial institutions and markets in the City of London
Inst Econ Aff, 1979.

(1546)
Garbade K D
Electronic quotation systems and the market for government securities
F R Bk New York Q Rev 1978 SUMMER VOL 3:2.

(1547)
Geyer C T
The abrogation of rule 390
FAJ 1978 JAN-FEB p 22-30.

(1548)
Hamilton J L
Marketplace organization and marketability: NASDAQ, the Stock Exchange and the nation market system
JF 1978 VOL 33 p 487.

(1549)
Kryzanowski L
Misinformation and regulatory actions in the Canadian capital markets: some empirical evidence
BellJ 1978 AUTUMN VOL 9:2 p 355-368.

(1550)
Melton W C
Corporate equities and the national market system
F R Bk New York Q Rev 1978-79 WINTER VOL 3:4.

(1551)
Peake J W
The National Market System
FAJ 1978 JUL-AUG p 25-34.

(1552)
Smith P F
Money and financial intermediation: the theory and structure of financial systems
P-H, 1978..

(1553)**West R R, Tinic S M**
Critique of Schaefer and Warner
FAJ 1978 MAY-JUN p 46.

(1554)
McCurdy C J
The dealer market for United States government securities
F R Bk New York Q Rev 1977-78 WINTER VOL 2:4.

(1555)
Morgan E V, Harrington R
Capital markets in the EEC: the sources and uses of medium and long-term finan
Wilton House Publications, 1977.

(1556)
Schaefer J M, Warner A J
Concentration in the securities industry
FAJ 1977 NOV-DEC p 29-35.

(1557)
Sobel R
Inside Wall Street: continuity and change in the financial district
Norton, 1977.

(1558)
Ellis C D
Negotiated commissions and the structure of the institutional brokerage industry
FAJ 1976 SEP-OCT VOL 32 p 20-24.

(1559)
Runyon H
Equity shares and the financial markets
F R Bk San Francisco Ec Rev 1976 SUMMER.

(1560)
Barnea A
Performance evaluation of New York stock exchange specialists
JFQA 1974 SEP VOL 9 p 511.

(1561)
Farrar D E
Toward a central market system: Wall Street's slow retreat into the future
JFQA 1974 NOV VOL 9 p 815.

(1562)
Hirst R R, Wallace R H eds
The Australian capital market
Melbourne: Cheshire Publishing, 1974.

(1563)
Santomero A
The economic effects of NASDAQ: Some preliminary results
JFQA 1974 JAN VOL 9 p 13.

(1564)
Mendleson M
The Martin report and its aftermath
BellJ 1973 SPRING VOL 4:1 p 250-269.

(1565)
Radman P et al.
The European money puzzle
Michael Joseph, 1973.

(1566)
Revell J R S
The British financial system
Macmillan, 1973.

(1567)
Farrar D
The coming reform on Wall Street
HBR 1972 SEP-OCT VOL 50:4 p 108-117.

(1568)
Freund W C
Issues confronting the stock market in a period of
rising institutionalization
JFQA 1972 MAR VOL 7 Suppl p 1687-1690.

(1569)
Revell J R S
Financial structure and government regulation in
the United Kingdom 1952-1980
Inter-bank Research Organisation, 1972.

(1570)
Sullivan J L Jr
Current trends in the reduction of stock
certificates
JBR 1972 SUMMER VOL 3:2.

(1571)
Tinic S M
The economics of liquidity services
QJE 1972 FEB VOL 86 p 79-93.

(1572)
Weedin D E
Competition: key to market structure
JFQA 1972 MAR VOL 7 Suppl p 1699-1701.

(1573)
Wu H-K
Odd-lot trading in the stock market and its
market impact
JFQA 1972 JAN VOL 7 p 1321-1342.

(1574)
Martin W McC Jr
The securities markets
A report with recommendations submitted to the
Board of Governors of the New York Stock
Exchange, Aug 5, 1971.

(1575)
West R R, Tinic S M
The economics of the stock market
Praeger, 1971.

(1576)
Baker J C
The German stock market: its operations,
problems and prospects
Praeger, 1970.

(1577)
Morgan E V, Thomas W A
The Stock Exchange, its history and functions.
2nd ed
Elek, 1970.

(1578)
Zarb F G, Kerekes G T
The stock market handbook: reference manual for
the securities industry
Dow Jones-Irwin, 1970.

(1579)
Bank of Japan. Economic Research Department
The Japanese financial system, March 1969
Bank of Japan, 1969.

(1580)
Goldsmith R W
Financial structure and development
Yale U Pr, 1969.

(1581)
Ishaq T
The capital market in Pakistan
PEJ 1969 JAN VOL 2 p 102-111.

(1582)
Rose P J
Australian securities markets
U of Melbourne. Institute of Applied Economic
Research, 1969.

(1583)
Eiteman W J, Eiteman S C
Nine leading stock exchanges
U of Mich Bus, 1968.

(1584)
Noritake Y
The Japanese capital market
Bankers' Magazine 1968 MAY VOL 205 p
287-291.

(1585)
OECD Committee for Invisible Transactions
Functioning of capitals markets
OECD, 1968.

(1586)
Smith A (pseud)
The money game
Random, 1968.

(1587)
Sobel R
The great bull market: Wall Street in the 1920's
Norton, 1968.

(1588)
Willett E F
Fundamentals of securities markets
Appleton, 1968.

(1589)
Loll L M, Buckley J
Over-the-counter securities markets. 2nd ed
P-H, 1967.

(1590)
Schwartz R J
You and your stockbroker
Collier Macmillan, 1967.

(1591)
Weiner J M
Developing a European capital market
LBR 1967 JUL VOL 85 p 16-28.

(1592)
Commission of the European Communities
The development of a European capital market:
report of a group of experts appointed by the
EEC Commission
Brussels: ECC, 1966.

(1593)
Eiteman D K
Stock exchanges in Latin America
U of Mich Pr, 1966.

(1594)
Mayer M
Wall Street: men and money. Rev ed
Macmillan, 1966.

(1595)
Robbins S M
The securities market: operations and issues
Collier Macmillan, 1966.

(1596)
Sarnat M
The development of the securities market in
Israel
Kyk 1966.

(1597)
Altman O L
The integration of European capital markets
JF 1965 MAY VOL 20 p 209-221.

(1598)
Sobel R
The big board, a history of the New York Stock
Market
Free Pr, 1965.

(1599)
Williams D
The development of capital markets in Europe
IMF 1965 MAR VOL 12 p 37-62.

(1600)
Cooke G W
The stock market
Simmons-B, 1964.

(1601)
Eiteman W J, Eiteman D K
Leading world stock exchanges: trading practices
and organisation
U of Mich Pr, 1964.

(1602)
Federal Reserve Bank of Chicago
Capital markets--United States and Europe
F R Bk Chicago Bus Cond 1964 SEP p 9-16.

(1603)
Macrae N
The London capital market
Staples, 1964.

(1604)
Spray D E ed.
The principal stock exchanges of the world--their
operation, structure and development
Int Econ, 1964.

(1605)
Treasury Department et al.
A description and analysis of certain European
capital markets, prepared for the Joint Economic
Committee by the Treasury Dept and various
European Consulates
US Govt, 1964.

(1606)
Wise T A
Wall Street's main event: S.E.C. vs. the specialist
F 1964 MAY VOL 76 p 149-152.

(1607)
Schultz B E
The securities market, and how it works. Rev ed
Har-Row, 1963.

(1608)
Securities and Exchange Commission
Report of the special study of the securities
markets
US Govt, 1963.

(1609)
Cormier F
Wall Street's shady side
Pub Affairs, 1962.

(1610)
Doodha K D
Stock exchanges in a developing economy
Bombay U Pr, 1962.

(1611)
Farrell M J
On the structure of the capital market
EJ 1962 DEC VOL 72 p 830-844.

(1612)
James R, James E
Disputed role of the stock exchange specialists
HBR 1962 MAY-JUN VOL 40 p 133-146.

(1613)
Ludtke J B
The American financial system: markets and
institutions. 2nd ed
Allyn, 1961.

(1614)
Manes P
The structure of the Italian stock market
BNLQR 1960 JUN VOL 53 p 171-208.

(1615)
Meltzer A H, Von del Linde G
A study of the dealer market for federal
government securities
US Govt, 1960.

(1616)
Robbins S M, Terleckyj N E
Money metropolis; a locational study of financial
activities in the New York region
Harvard U Pr, 1960.

(1617)
Schwed F
Where are the customers' yachts? or a good hard
look at Wall Street
Magee, 1960.

(1618)
Walter J E, Williamson J P
Organized securities exchanges in Canada
JF 1960 SEP VOL 15 p 307-324.

(1619)
Friend I, Hoffman G W, Winn W J
The over-the-counter securities markets
McGraw, 1958.

(1620)
OECD Committee for Invisible Transactions
The supply of capital funds for industrial
development in Europe: resources, structure and
method
OECD, 1957.

(1621)
Walter J E
The role of regional security exchanges
U of Cal Pr, 1957.

(1622)
Balogh T
Studies in financial organisation
Cambridge U Pr, 1950.

(1623)
Neill H B
The inside story of the Stock Exchange
Forbes B C, 1950.

(1624)
Hirst F W
The Stock Exchange; a short study of investment and speculation, 4th ed
Oxford U Pr, 1948.

(1625)
Securities and Exchange Commission
Stock trading on the New York Stock Exchange
US Govt, SEP 3 1946.

(1626)
Hardy C O
Odd-lot trading on the New York Stock Exchange
Brookings, 1939.

(1627)
Simpson K, Ballinger W
The feasibility and advisability of the complete separation of the functions of dealer and broker
Washington, DC: Securities and Exchange Commission, 1936.

(1628)
Twentieth Century Fund
The security markets
Twentieth Fund, 1935.

6.21 Ownership of capital assets and flow of funds

(1629)
Hamada K, Iwata K
On the international capital ownership pattern at the turn of the twenty-first century
EER 1989 VOL 33 p 1055.

(1630)
McDonald J
The Mochiai effect: Japanese corporate cross-holdings
JPM 1989 FALL VOL 16:1 p 90-95.

(1631)
Wruck K H
Equity ownership concentration and firm value: evidence from private equity financings
JFE 1989 VOL 23 p 3.

(1632)
Krehbiel T L, Yunker J A
Investment analysis by the individual investor
QREB 1988 VOL 28:4 p 90.

(1633)
Noland M
Japanese household portfolio allocation behavior
REStat 1988 VOL 70 p 135.

(1634)
Pitelis C
Corporate capital: control, ownership, saving and crisis
Cambridge U Pr, 1987.

(1635)
Kester W C
Capital and ownership structure: A comparison of United States and Japanese manufacturing corporations
FIN MGMT 1986 SPRING VOL 15 p 5-16.

(1636)
Demsetz H, Lehn K
The structure of corporate ownership: Causes and consquences
JPE 1985 VOL 93 p 1155.

(1637)
Matthews K, Minford P
Private sector expenditure and financial asset accumulation in the UK
JMCB 1980 NOV VOL 12:4 p 644-653.

(1638)
Waters W R
Savings and wealth patterns of employee households approaching retirement
(in Cooper K H and Mills C C eds., Canada at the pension crossroads. Fin Exec, 1979.)

(1639)
Blume M E, Friend I
The changing role of the individual investor: A Twentieth Century Fund Report
Wiley, 1978.

(1640)
Dolde W
Capital markets and the short run behavior of life cycle savers
JF 1978 VOL 33 p 413..

(1641)**Garvy G**
Money, financial flows and credit in the Soviet Union
Ballinger, 1977.

(1642)
Hendershott P H
Understanding capital markets: volume I: A flow-of-funds financial model: estimation and application to financial policies and reform
Heath, 1977.

(1643)
Klemkosky R C
The impact and efficiency of institutional net trading imbalances
JF 1977 VOL 32 p 79.

(1644)
Sametz A W, Wachtel P eds.
Understanding capital markets. Volume II: The financial environment and the flow of funds in the next decade
Heath, 1977.

(1645)
Lease R C, Lewellen W G, Schlarbaum G G
Market segmentation: Evidence on the individual investor
FAJ 1976 SEP-OCT VOL 32 p 53-60.

(1646)
Revell J R S
Savings flows in Europe: personal saving and borrowing
Financial Times, 1976.

(1647)
Bain A D et al.
Company financing in the United Kingdom: a flow of funds model
Martin Robertson, 1975.

(1648)
Blume M E, Friend I
The allocation of wealth to risky assets: The asset structure of individual portfolios and some implications for utility functions
JF 1975 MAY VOL 30:2 p 585-604.

(1649)
Boe W J, Soldofsky R M
Institutional holdings of common stock: 1969, 1972, and new developments
QREB 1975 VOL 15:2 p 47.

(1650)
Cohn R A, Lewellen W G, Lease R C
Individual investor risk aversion and investment portfolio composition
JF 1975 MAY VOL 30:2 p 605-620.

(1651)
Dobbins R, Greenwood M J
Institutional shareholders and equity market stability
JBFA 1975 SUMMER VOL 2:2 p 257-268.

(1652)
Hendershott P H, Lemmon R C
The financial behavior of households: Some empirical estimates
JF 1975 VOL 30 p 733.

(1653)
De Alessi L
Private property and dispersion of ownership in large corporations
JF 1973 VOL 28 p 839.

(1654)
Vernon R A et al.
Who owns the blue chips? A study of shareholding in a leading company
Gower, 1973.

(1655)
Findlay M C III, Williams E E
Capital allocation and the nature of ownership equities
FIN MGMT 1972 SUMMER VOL 1 p 68.

(1656)
Robertson M
A note on the flow of capital in outstanding common and preferred shares between Canada and the United States
JFQA 1972 JAN VOL 7 p 1425.

(1657)
Hendershott P H
A flow of funds model
JMCB 1971 p 815-832.

(1658)
Moyle J
The pattern of ordinary share ownership 1957-1970
Cambridge U Pr, 1971.

(1659)
Soldofsky R M
Institutional holdings of common stock, 1900-2000: history, projection and interpretation
U of Mich, 1971.

(1660)
Hamburger M J
Household demand for financial assets
Em 1968 JUN VOL 36 p 97-118.

(1661)
Lepper S J
Effects of alternative tax structures on individuals' holdings of financial assets
(in Hester D D and Tobin J eds., Risk aversion and portfolio choice. Wiley, 1967.)

(1662)
Larner R J
Ownership and control in the 200 largest nonfinancial corporations, 1929 and 1963
AER 1966 SEP VOL 56 p 777-787.

(1663)
Stone R, Revell J R S, Moyle J
The ownership of quoted ordinary shares--a survey for 1963
Chapman, 1966.

(1664)
Goldsmith R W
The flow of capital funds in the postwar economy
(Dist by Columbia U Pr) Natl Bur Econ Res, 1965.

(1665)
Levy M E
Cycles in government securities: determinants of changes in ownership
Natl Ind Conf Bd, 1965.

(1666)
Morgan J, Barlow R, Brazer H
A survey of investment management and working behavior among high-income individuals
AER 1965 MAY VOL 55 p 252-264.

(1667)
Entine A D
Government securities holdings of selected financial intermediaries, 1954-1962
JF 1964 DEC VOL 19 p 644-651.

(1668)
Cox E B
Trends in the distribution of stock ownership
U of Pa Pr, 1963.

(1669)
Levy M E
Cycles in government securities: federal debt and its ownership
Natl Ind Conf Bd, 1962.

(1670)
Wilson S J
Public participation in the stock market: an analysis of long-term market trends
Fraser, 1962.

(1671)
Jacobs D P
The marketable security portfolios of non-financial corporations, investment practices and trends
JF 1960 SEP VOL 15 p 341-352.

(1672)
Kreinin M E
Factors associated with stock ownership
REStat 1959 FEB VOL 41 p 12-23.

(1673)
Frazer W J
Large manufacturing corporations as suppliers of funds to the United States government securities market
JF 1958 DEC VOL 13 p 499-509.

(1674)
Freund W C
An appraisal of the sources and uses of funds: approach to the analysis of financial markets
JF 1958 MAY VOL 13 p 275-294.

(1675)
Atkinson T R
The pattern of financial assets ownership: Wisconsin individuals
(Dist by Princeton U Pr) Natl Bur Econ Res, 1956.

(1676)
Kimmel L H
Share ownership in the United States; a study prepared at the request of the New York Stock Exchange
Brookings, 1952.

6.22   Market regulation

(1677)
Franks J, Mayer C
Risk, regulation and investor protection: the case of investment management
Clarendon, 1989.

(1678)
Karafiath I, Glascock J
Intra-industry effects of a regulatory shift: capital market evidence from Penn Square
FR 1989 FEB VOL 24:1 p 123-134.

(1679)
Ma C K, Rao R P, Sears R S
Volatility, price resolution, and the effectiveness of price limits
JFSR 1989 VOL 3:2-3 p 165-200.

(1680)
Rider B A K et al.
Guide to the Financial Services Act 1986. 2nd ed
CCH Editions, 1989.

(1681)
Roll R
Price volatility, international market links, and their implications for regulatory policies
JFSR 1989 VOL 3:2-3 p 211-246.

(1682)
Stiglitz J E
Using tax policy to curb speculative short-term trading
JFSR 1989 VOL 3:2-3 p 101-116.

(1683)
Summers L H, Summers V P
When financial markets work too well: a cautious case for a securities transactions tax
JFSR 1989 VOL 3:2-3 p 261-286.

(1684)
Blejer M I, Sagari S B
Sequencing the liberalization of financial markets
FD 1988 VOL 25:1.

(1685)
Ferguson R
What to do, or not do, about the markets
JPM 1988 SUMMER VOL 14:4 p 14-19.

(1686)
Glassman C A et al.
Regulating the new financial services industry
Washington, DC: Center for National Policy Press, 1988.

(1687)
Malkiel B G
The Brady Commission Report: a critique
JPM 1988 SUMMER VOL 14:4 p 9-13.

(1688)
Miller J
Stock Exchange Press dictionary of financial regulation 1988/89
London & International Publishers, 1988.

(1689)
Pettway R H, Tapley T C, Yamada T
The impacts of financial deregulation upon trading efficiency and the levels of risk and return of Japanese banks
FR 1988 AUG VOL 23:3 p 243-268.

(1690)
Seldon A ed.
Financial regulation - or over-regulation?
Inst Econ Aff, 1988.

(1691)
Bank of England
Change in the Stock Exchange and regulation of the City
BEQB 1987 VOL 27 p 54-65.

(1692)
Evans K R
Canada for sale: the Investment Canada Act
Journal of World Trade Law 1987 JUN VOL 21:3 p 85-97.

(1693)
Finley D E, Shaw D
The implication of deregulation of the Canadian securities markets
Business Quarterly 1987 FALL VOL 52:2 p 45-51..

(1694)**Goodhart C A E, Currie D, Llewellyn D T**
The operation and regulation of financial markets
Macmillan, 1987.

(1695)
Hall M
Financial deregulation: a comparative study of Australia and the United Kingdom
Macmillan, 1987.

(1696)
Kohona P T
Investment Protection Agreements: an Australian perspective
Journal of World Trade Law 1987 APR VOL 21:2 p 79-103.

(1697)
Kontkanen E
Trends in Finnish financial market legislation
Bank of Finland Monthly Bulletin 1987 FEB VOL 61:2 p 26-31.

(1698)
Laajanen P
Evolving financial markets and legislation
Kansallis-Osake-Pankki Economic Review 1987 1 p 13-20.

(1699)
Larke R comp.
Financial Services Act 1986; with index
Woodhead-Faulkner, 1987.

(1700)
Lomax D F
London markets after the Financial Services Act
Butterworth, 1987.

(1701)
Morgan G E, Smith S D
The role of capital adequacy regulation in the hedging decisions of financial intermediaries
JFR 1987 SPRING VOL 10:1 p 33-46.

(1702)
Skousen K F
An introduction to the SEC. 4th ed
SW Pub, 1987.

(1703)
Cho Y J
Inefficiencies from financial liberalization in the absence of well functioning equity markets
JMCB 1986 MAY VOL 18:2 p 191-199.

(1704)
Clarke M
Regulating the City: competition, scandal and reform
OUP, 1986.

(1705)
Dale R ed.
Financial deregulation: the proceedings of a conference held by the David Hume Institute in May 1986
Woodhead-Faulkner, 1986.

(1706)
Dale R ed.
Financial deregulation
Cambridge U Pr, 1986.

(1707)
Goode R M ed.
Conflicts of interest in the changing financial world
Institute of Bankers, 1986.

(1708)
Grossman S J, Miller M H
Economic costs and benefits of the proposed one-minute time bracketing regulation
JFM 1986 SPRING VOL 6 p 141-166.

(1709)
Llewellyn D T
The regulation and supervision of financial institutions
Institute of Bankers, 1986.

(1710)
Troughton H
Japanese finance: the impact of deregulation
Euromoney Publications, 1986.

(1711)
Bank of England
Change in the Stock Exchange and regulation of the City
BEQB 1985 VOL 25 p 544-550.

(1712)
Benston G J
Toward a cost-benefit anlysis of the SEC: have the British a better way?
MCFJ 1985 SUMMER VOL 3 p 65-85.

(1713)
Hall M J B
Financial deregulation in Australia
NWBQR 1985 AUG p 18-29.

(1714)
Langevoort D C
Information technology and the structure of securities regulation
HLR 1985 VOL 98:4 p 747-804.

(1715)
Walter I ed.
Deregulating Wall Street: Commercial bank penetration of the corporate securities market
Wiley, 1985.

(1716)
Coffee J C Jr
Market failure and the economic case for a mandatory disclosure system
VLR 1984 VOL 70:4 p 717-753.

(1717)
Easterbrook F H, Fischel D R
Mandatory disclosure and the protection of investors
VLR 1984 VOL 70:4 p 669-715.

(1718)
Fischel D R, Grossman S J
Customer protection in futures and securities markets
JFM 1984 VOL 4.

(1719)
Jarrell G A
Change at the Exchange: the causes and effects of deregulation
JLE 1984 VOL 27:2 p 273-312.

(1720)
Kitch E W
A federal vision of the securities laws
VLR 1984 VOL 70:4 p 857-873.

(1721)
Werner W
The SEC as a market regulator
VLR 1984 VOL 70:4 p 755-784.

(1722)
Cheng H-S
Financial reform in Australia and New Zealand
F R Bk San Francisco Ec Rev 1983 WINTER.

(1723)
Horvitz P M
Reorganization of the financial regulatory agencies
JBR 1983 WINTER VOL 13:4.

(1724)
Kaufman G G, Mote L, Rosenblum H
Implications of deregulation for product lines and geographical markets of financial institutions
JBR 1983 SPRING VOL 14:1.

(1725)
Pigott C
Financial reform in Japan
F R Bk San Francisco Ec Rev 1983 WINTER.

(1726)
Torell J R III
U S financial deregulation: Upheaval and promise
JBankF 1983 VOL 7 p 561.

(1727)
Gower L C B
Review of investor protection: a discussion document
HMSO, 1982.

(1728)
Phillips S M, Zecher J R
The SEC and the public interest
MIT Pr, 1981.

(1729)
Alboini V P
The new Ontario Securities Act
FAJ 1980 NOV-DEC VOL 36 p 64-70.

(1730)
Conway B
Investor power: a guide to shareholder rights
Flame Books, 1980.

(1731)
Horvitz P M, Harper C P
Regulation of the money order industry
FIN MGMT 1980 WINTER VOL 9 p 13.

(1732)
Twentieth Century Fund
Abuse on Wall Street: conflicts of interest in the securities market
Quorum Bks, 1980.

(1733)
Edwards F R ed.
Issues in financial regulation
McGraw, 1979.

(1734)
Lowenfels L D
The case against the proposed federal securities code
VLR 1979 VOL 65:4 p 615-661.

(1735)
Wymeersch E
Control of securities markets in the European Economic Community
EEC, 1978.

(1736)
Harvard Law Review
Securities regulation
HLR 1977 VOL 91:1 p 274-284.

(1737)
Schwert G W
Public regulation of national securities exchanges: a test of the capture hypothesis
BellJ 1977 SPRING VOL 8:1 p 128-150.

(1738)
Benston G J
Required disclosure and the stock market: An evaluation of the Securities Exchange Act of 1934
AER 1973 VOL 63 p 132-155.

(1739)
West R R
Conflicts of interest: substance or subterfuge?
FAJ 1971 NOV-DEC VOL 27 p 31-39.

(1740)
Clare R L Jr ed.
The law, disclosure and the securities markets
Pr Law Inst, 1970.

(1741)
Parrish M E
Securities regulation and the new deal
Yale U Pr, 1970.

(1742)
Manne H G ed.
Economic policy and the regulation of corporate
securities
Washington, DC: American Enterprise Institute
for Public Policy Research, 1969.

(1743)
Naylor G
Guide to shareholders' rights
Allen, 1969.

(1744)
Sowards H L
Comments, cases and materials on securities
regulation
Dennis, 1966.

(1745)
Mundheim R H ed.
Conference on securities regulation
Commerce, 1965.

(1746)
Robinson R I, Bartell R Jr
Uneasy partnership SEC/NYSE
HBR 1965 JAN-FEB VOL 43 p 76-88..

(1747)**Tyler P ed.**
Securities, exchanges and the S.E.C.
Wilson, 1965.

(1748)
Cary W L
A review of the work of the Securities and
Exchange Commission
The Record of the Association of the Bar of the
City of New York 1964 NOV.

(1749)
De Bedts R F
The new deal's SEC: the formative years
Columbia U Pr, 1964.

(1750)
Friend I, Herman E S
The S.E.C. through a glass darkly
JB 1964 OCT VOL 37 p 382-405.

(1751)
Heller H
Integration of the dissemination of information
under the Securities Act of 1933 and the
Securities Act of 1934.
LCP 1964 JUN VOL 29 p 749-776.

(1752)
Jennings R W
Self-regulation in the securities industry: the role
of the Securities and Exchange Commission
LCP 1964 JUN VOL 29 p 663-690.

(1753)
Knaus R L
A reappraisal of the role of disclosure
Michigan Law Review 1964 FEB p 607-648.

(1754)
Robbins S M, Werner W
Professor Stigler revisited
JB 1964 OCT VOL 37 p 406-413.

(1755)
Stigler G J
Public regulation of the securities market
JB 1964 APR VOL 37 p 117-142.

(1756)
Loss L
Securities regulation, vols 1-3
Little, 1961.

(1757)
Securities and Exchange Commission
A 25 year summary of the activities of the
Securities and Exchange Commission, 1934-1959
US Govt, 1961.

(1758)
Williamson J P
Securities regulation in Canada
U of Toronto Pr, 1960.

(1759)
Choka A D
An introduction to securities regulation
Twentieth Press, 1958.

(1760)
Pecora F
Wall Street under oath
S & S, 1939.

6.3   Listings, delistings and suspensions

(1761)
Bhandari A, Grammatikos T, Makhija A K
Risk and return on newly listed stocks: the
post-listing experience
JFR 1989 SUMMER VOL 12:2 p 93-102.

(1762)
Biddle G, Saudagaran S
The effects of financial disclosure levels on firms'
choices among alternative foreign stock exchange
listings
Journal of International Financial Management &
Accounting 1989 SPRING VOL 1:1 p 55-87.

(1763)
Jahera J S Jnr., Lloyd W P
Exchange listing and size: effects on excess
returns
JBFA 1989 WINTER VOL 16:5 p 675.

(1764)
Prakash A J, Parhizgari A M, Perritt G W
The effects of listing on the parameters of
characteristic line models
JBFA 1989 SUMMER VOL 16:3 p 335.

(1765)
Alexander G J, Eun C S, Janakiramanan S
International listings and stock returns: some
empirical evidence
JFQA 1988 JUN VOL 23:2 p 135-152.

(1766)
Howe J S, Kelm K
The stock price impacts of overseas listings
FIN MGMT 1987 AUTUMN VOL 16 p 51-56.

(1767)
McConnell J J, Sanger G C
The puzzle in post-listing common stock returns
JF 1987 MAR VOL 42:1 p 119-140.

(1768)
Boardman C M, Dark F H, Lease R C
On the listing of corporate debt : a note.
JFQA 1986 MAR VOL 21:1 p 107-114.

(1769)
Grammatikos T, Papaioannou G J
The information value of listing on the New York
Stock Exchange
FR 1986 NOV VOL 21:4.

(1770)
Howe J S, Schlarbaum G G
SEC trading suspensions : empirical evidence
JFQA 1986 SEP VOL 21:3 p 323-333.

(1771)
Sanger G C, McConnell J J
Stock exchange listings, firm value, and security
market efficiency : the impact of NASDAQ
JFQA 1986 MAR VOL 21:1 p 1-25.

(1772)
Fraser D R, Groth J C
Listing and the liquidity of bank stocks
JBR 1985 AUTUMN VOL 16:3 p 136-144.

(1773)
McConnell J J, Sanger G C
A trading strategy for new listings on the NYSE
FAJ 1984 JAN-FEB VOL 40 p 34-38.

(1774)
Dhaliwal D S
Exchange-listing effects on a firm's cost of equity
capital
JBusR 1983 VOL 11 p 139-152.

(1775)
Fabozzi F J
Does listing on the AMEX increase the value of
equity?
FIN MGMT 1981 SPRING VOL 10 p 43-50.

(1776)
Kryzanowski L
The efficiency of trading suspension: a regulatory action designed to prevent the exploitation of monopoly information
JF 1979 DEC VOL 34:5 p 1187-1200.

(1777)
Hopewell M H, Schwartz A L
Temporary trading suspensions in individual NYSE securities
JF 1978 VOL 33 p 1355.

(1778)
Lease R C, Ying L K W, Lewellen W G
Stock exchange listings and securities returns
JFQA 1977 SEP VOL 12 p 415.

(1779)
Hopewell M H, Schwartz A H
Stock price movement associated with temporary trading suspensions: Bear market versus bull market
JFQA 1976 NOV VOL 11.

(1780)
Goulet W M
Price changes, managerial action and insider trading at the time of listing
FIN MGMT 1974 SPRING VOL 3 p 30.

(1781)
Blume M E, Husic F
Price, beta and exchange listing
JF 1973 VOL 28 p 283.

(1782)
Reilly F K, Slaughter W C
The effect of dual markets on common stock market making
JFQA 1973 MAR VOL 8:2 p 167-182.

(1783)
Furst R W
Does listing increase the market price of common stocks?
JB 1970 APR VOL 43 p 174-180.

(1784)
Van Horne J C
New listings and their price behavior
JF 1970 SEP VOL 25 p 783-784.

(1785)
O'Donnell J L
Case evidence on the value of a New York Stock Exchange listing
Business Topics (Michigan St U) 1969 SUMMER VOL 17.

(1786)
Merjos A
Going on the big board
B 1967 MAY 1 p 9-10.

(1787)
Newbould G D
The benefits and costs of a stock exchange quotation
Bankers' Magazine 1967 JUN VOL 203 p 359-365.

(1788)
Forbes
That post-listing tired feeling
Forbes 1964 NOV 1.

(1789)
Merjos A
Like money in the bank: big board listing, the record suggests, is a valuable asset
B 1963 JUL 8 p 94ff.

(1790)
Merjos A
Going on the big board: stocks act better before listing than right afterward
B 1962 JAN 29 p 54ff.

6.4 Trading volume and liquidity

(1791)
Bolster P J, Lindsey L B, Mitrusi A
Tax-induced trading: the effect of the 1986 Tax Reform Act on stock market activity
JF 1989 JUN VOL 44:2 p 327-344.

(1792)
Giovannini A
Uncertainty and liquidity
JME 1989 VOL 23 p 239.

(1793)
Lakonishok J, Smidt S
Past price changes and current trading volume
JPM 1989 SUMMER VOL 15:4 p 18-25.

(1794)
Pagano M
Trading volume and asset liquidity
QJE 1989 MAY VOL 104:2 p 255-274.

(1795)
Pagano M
Endogenous market thinness and stock price volatility
REStud 1989 VOL 56 p 269.

(1796)
Admati A R, Pfleiderer P
A theory of intraday patterns: volume and price variability
RFS 1988 SPRING VOL 1:1 p 3-40.

(1797)
Amihud Y, Mendelson H
Liquidity and asset prices: Financial management implications
FIN MGMT 1988 SPRING VOL 17 p 5-15.

(1798)
Anthony J H
The interrelation of stock and options market trading-volume data
JF 1988 SEP VOL 43:4 p 949-964.

(1799)
Ferris S P, Haugen R A, Makhija A K
Predicting contemporary volume with historic volume at differential price levels: evidence supporting the disposition effect
JF 1988 JUL VOL 43:3 p 677-697..

(1800)**Jain P C, Joh G-H**
The dependence between hourly prices and trading volumes
JFQA 1988 SEP VOL 23 p 269.

(1801)
Smirlock M, Starks L
An empirical analysis of the stock price-volume relationship
JBankF 1988 VOL 12:1 p 31-42.

(1802)
Bernstein P L
Liquidity, stock markets and market makers
FIN MGMT 1987 SUMMER VOL 16 p 54-62.

(1803)
Comiskey E E, Walkling R A, Weeks M A
Dispersion of expectations and trading volume
JBFA 1987 SUMMER VOL 14:2 p 229-239.

(1804)
Huffman G W
A dynamic equilibrium model of asset prices and transaction volume
JPE 1987 FEB VOL 95:1 p 138-159.

(1805)
Karpoff J M
The relations between price changes and trading volume: A survey
JFQA 1987 MAR VOL 22 p 109-126.

(1806)
Karpoff J M
A theory of trading volume
JF 1986 DEC VOL 41:5 p 1069-1087.

(1807)
Lakonishok J, Smidt S
Volume for winners and losers : taxation and other motives for stock trading
JF 1986 SEP VOL 41:4 p 951-974.

(1808)
Richardson G, Sefcik S E, Thompson R
A test of dividend irrelevance using volume reactions to a change in dividend policy
JFE 1986 DEC VOL 17:2 p 313-333

(1809)
Slemrod J
Stock transaction volume and the 1978 capital gains tax reduction
Public Finance Quarterly 1986 VOL 14 p 3-16.

(1810)
Banks D W
Information uncertainty and trading volume
FR 1985 FEB VOL 20:1.

(1811)
Lakonishok J, Smidt S
Volume and turn-of-the-year behavior
JFE 1984 SEP VOL 13:3 p 435-455.

(1812)
James C, Edmister R O
The relation between common stock returns,
trading activity and market value
JF 1983 VOL 38:4 p 1075-1086

(1813)
Carpenter M D, Upton D E
Trading volume and beta stability
JPM 1981 WINTER VOL 7:2 p 60-64.

(1814)
Morse D
Asymmetrical information in securities markets
and trading volume
JFQA 1980 DEC VOL 15 p 1129-1148.

(1815)
Copeland T E
Liquidity changes following stock splits
JF 1979 MAR VOL 34:1 p 115-141.

(1816)
Goldman M B, Sosin H B
Information dissemination, market efficiency and
the frequency of transactions
JFE 1979 MAR VOL 7:1 p 29-61.

(1817)
Hanna M
Security price changes and transaction volumes:
Additional evidence
AER 1978 VOL 68 p 692-695.

(1818)
Epps T W
Security price changes and transaction volumes:
Some additional evidence
JFQA 1977 MAR VOL 12 p 141.

(1819)
Fouse W L
Risk and liquidity revisited
FAJ 1977 JAN-FEB p 40-45.

(1820)
Epps T
The demand for brokers' services: the relation
between security trading volume and transaction
cost
BellJ 1976 SPRING VOL 7:1 p 163-194.

(1821)
Epps T W
Security price changes and transaction volumes:
Theory and evidence
AER 1975 VOL 65 p 586-597.

(1822)
Silber W L
Thinness in capital markets: The case of the Tel
Aviv stock exchange
JFQA 1975 MAR VOL 10 p 129.

(1823)
Barnea A, Brenner M
The effect of world events on stock market
volume
FAJ 1974 JUL-AUG VOL 30 p 64-66.

(1824)
Kraus A, Stoll H R
Parallel trading by institutional investors
JFQA 1972 DEC VOL 7 p 2107.

(1825)
Ying C C
Stock market prices and volume of sales
Em 1966 JUL VOL 34 p 676-685.

(1826)
Paukert F
The value of stock exchange transactions in
non-government securities, 1911-1959
Ec 1961 AUG VOL 28 p 303-309.

6.41 Price impact of block trading

(1827)
Ball R, Finn F J
The effect of block transactions on share prices:
Australian evidence
JBankF 1989 JUL VOL 13:3 p 397-420.

(1828)
Burdett K, O'Hara M
Building blocks: an introduction to block trading
JBankF 1987 VOL 11 p 193-212.

(1829)
Holthausen R W, Leftwich R W, Mayers D
The effect of large block transactions on security
prices: A cross-sectional analysis
JFE 1987 VOL 19 p 237-267.

(1830)
Reilly F K, Wright D J
Block trading and aggregate stock price volatility
FAJ 1984 MAR-APR VOL 40 p 54-60.

(1831)
Dann L Y, Mayers D, Raab R J Jr
Trading rules, large blocks and the speed of price
adjustment
JFE 1977 VOL 4 p 3.

(1832)
Close N
Price reaction to large transactions in the
Canadian equity markets
FAJ 1975 NOV-DEC VOL 31 p 50-57.

(1833)
Shitovitz B
On some problems arising in markets with some
large traders and a continuum of small traders
JET 1974 AUG VOL 8:4 p 458-470.

(1834)
Radcliffe R C
Liquidity costs and block trading
FAJ 1973 JUL-AUG VOL 29 p 73-80.

(1835)
Kraus A, Stoll H
Price impacts of block trading on the New York
Stock Exchange
JF 1972 JUN VOL 27 p 569-588.

(1836)
Scholes M
The market for securities: substitution versus
price pressure and the effects of information on
share prices
JB 1972 APR VOL 45 p 179-211.

6.5 Commissions and dealing spreads

(1837)
Fortin R D, Grube R C, Joy M O
Seasonality in NASDAQ dealer spreads
JFQA 1989 SEP VOL 24:3 p 395.

(1838)
Haller A, Stoll H R
Market structure and transaction costs: implied
spreads in the German stock market
JBankF 1989 SEP VOL 13:4-5 p 697-708.

(1839)
Stoll H R
Inferring the components of the bid-ask spread:
theory and empirical tests
JF 1989 MAR VOL 44:1 p 115-134.

(1840)
Berkowitz S A, Logue D E, Noser E A Jr
The total cost of transactions on the NYSE
JF 1988 MAR VOL 43:1 p 97-112.

(1841)
Choi J Y, Salandro D, Shastri K
On the estimation of bid-ask spreads: theory and
evidence
JFQA 1988 JUN VOL 23:2 p 219-230.

(1842)
Hasbrouck J, Schwartz R A
Liquidity and execution costs in equity markets
JPM 1988 SPRING VOL 14:3 p 10-17

(1843)
Salandro D, Choi J Y, Shastri K
On the estimation of bid-ask spreads: Theory and
evidence
JFQA 1988 JUN VOL 23 p 219.

(1844)
Sherrerd K F ed.
Trading strategies and execution costs
Institute of Chartered Financial Analysts, 1988.

(1845)
Saunders A, Smirlock M
Intra and interindustry effects on bank securities
market activities: The case of discount brokerage
JFQA 1987 DEC VOL 22 p 467.

(1846)
Amihud Y, Mendelson H
Asset pricing and the bid-ask spread
JFE 1986 VOL 17 p 223.

(1847)
Blum G A, Krakaw W A, Lewellen W G
Determinants of the execution costs of common
stock trades by individual investors
JFR 1986 WINTER VOL 9 p 291-302.

(1848)
Dubofsky D A, Groth J C
An examination of asked-bid spreads for two
over-the-counter market segments
FR 1986 MAY VOL 21:2.

(1849)
Edmister R O, Walkling R A
Trends in institutional commission costs following
deregulation : evidence from the USA
JBFA 1985 WINTER VOL 12:4 p 553-559

(1850)
Huffman G W
Adjustment costs and capital asset pricing
JF 1985 JUL VOL 40:3 p 691-709.

(1851)
Blum G A, Lewellen W G
Negotiated brokerage commissions and the
individual investor.
JFQA 1983 SEP VOL 18:3 p 331-343

(1852)
Loeb T F
Trading cost: The critical link between investment
information and results
FAJ 1983 MAY-JUN VOL 39 p 39-45..

(1853) **Walkling R A, Edmister R O**
Are there commission cost side-effects from
portfolio management decisions?
FAJ 1983 JUL-AUG VOL 39 p 52-59.

(1854)
Edmister R O, Subramanian N
Determinants of brokerage comission rates for
institutional investors : a note
JF 1982 SEP VOL 37:4 p 1087-1093.

(1855)
Cohen K J, Maier S F, Schwartz R A
Transaction costs, order placement strategy and
existence of the bid-ask spread
JPE 1981 VOL 89 p 287.

(1856)
Condon K A
Measuring equity transaction costs
FAJ 1981 SEP-OCT VOL 37:5 p 57-60.

(1857)
Beebower G L, Priest W W Jr
The tricks of the trade
JPM 1980 WINTER VOL 6:2 p 36-42.

(1858)
Melnik A, Ofer A R
Competitive commission rates, execution quality,
and customer's market power
JMCB 1980 MAY VOL 12:2 p 221-227.

(1859)
Schreiner J C, Smith K V
The impact of Mayday on diversification costs
JPM 1980 SUMMER VOL 6:4 p 28-36.

(1860)
Tinic S M, West R R
The securities industry under negotiated
brokerage commissions: changes in the structure
and performance of New York Stock Exchange
member firms
BellJ 1980 SPRING VOL 11:1 p 29-41.

(1861)
Bildersee J S
Bid ask price spreads in the agency bond market
JMCB 1979 MAY VOL 11:2 p 209-213.

(1862)
Cohen K J, Maier S F, Schwartz R A
Market makers and the market spread: A review
of recent literature
JFQA 1979 NOV VOL 14 p 813.

(1863)
Theobald M
A note on variable transactions costs, the capital
asset pricing model and the corporate dividend
decision
JBFA 1979 SPRING VOL 6:1 p 9-16.

(1864)
Edmister R O
Commission cost structure: Shifts and scale economies
JF 1978 VOL 33 p 477.

(1865)
Grant D, Whaley R
Transactions costs on government bonds: a respecification
JB 1978 JAN VOL 51:1 p 57-64.

(1866)
Ofer A R, Melnick A
Price deregulation in the brokerage industry: an empirical analysis
BellJ 1978 AUTUMN VOL 9:2 p 633-641.

(1867)
Branch B, Freed W
Bid-asked spreads on the AMEX and the big board
JF 1977 VOL 32 p 159.

(1868)
Lechner A B, Londoner D J
Brokerage profits under the pressure of negotiated commissions
FAJ 1976 JAN-FEB VOL 32 p 12-17.

(1869)
Barnea A, Logue D E
The effect of risk on the market maker's spread
FAJ 1975 NOV-DEC VOL 31 p 45-49.

(1870)
Boudreaux K J
Competitive rates, market efficiency, and the economics of security analysis
FAJ 1975 MAR-APR VOL 31 p 18-25.

(1871)
Cuneo L J, Wagner W H
Reducing the cost of stock trading
FAJ 1975 NOV-DEC VOL 31 p 35-44.

(1872)
Smiley R
The effect of the Williams amendment and other factors on transactions costs
Industrial Organization Review 1975 VOL 3 p 138-145.

(1873)
Benston G J, Hagerman R L
Determinants of bid-asked spreads in the over-the-counter market
JFE 1974 VOL 1 p 353.

(1874)
Friend I, Blume M
Competitive commissions on the New York Stock Exchange
JF 1973 VOL 28 p 795.

(1875)
Freund W, Schaeffer J
Negotiated rates and the securities markets
American Statistical Association Proceedings 1972 p 151-158.

(1876)
Tinic S M, West R R
Competition and the pricing of dealer service in the over-the-counter market
JFQA 1972 JUN VOL 7 p 1707-1728.

(1877)
Demsetz H
The cost of transacting
QJE 1968 FEB VOL 82 p 33-53.

(1878)
Jennings R W
The New York Stock Exchange and the commission rate struggle
Business Lawyer 1965 NOV.

6.6 Margin requirements

(1879)
Kupiec P H
Initial margin requirements and stock returns volatility: another look
JFSR 1989 VOL 3:2-3 p 287.

(1880)
Salinger M A
Stock market margin requirements and volatility: implications for regulation of stock index futures
JFSR 1989 VOL 3:2-3 p 121-138.

(1881)
Schwert G W
Margin requirements and stock volatility
JFSR 1989 VOL 3:2-3 p 153-164.

(1882)
Estrella A
Consistent margin requirements: are they feasible?
F R Bk New York Q Rev 1988 SUMMER VOL 13:2.

(1883)
Ferris S, Chance D
Margin requirements and stock market volatility
Economic Letters 1988 VOL 28.

(1884)
Grube R C, Joy O M
Some evidence on the efficacy of security credit regulation in the OTC equity market
JFR 1988 VOL 11:2 p 137-142.

(1885)
Hardouvelis G A
Margin requirements and stock market volatility
F R Bk New York Q Rev 1988 SUMMER VOL 13:2.

(1886)
Sofianos G
Margin requirements on equity instruments
F R Bk New York Q Rev 1988 SUMMER VOL 13:2.

(1887)
Grube R C, Joy O M, Howe J S
Some empirical evidence on stock returns and security credit regulation in the OTC equity market
JBankF 1987 VOL 11 p 17-31..

(1888)**Goldberg M A**
The relevance of margin regulations
JMCB 1985 NOV VOL 17:4 p 521-527.

(1889)
Federal Reserve System
A review and evaluation of federal margin regulation
Washington, DC: Board of Governors, DEC 1984.

(1890)
Luckett D G
On the effectiveness of the Federal Reserve's margin requirement
JF 1982 JUN VOL 37:3 p 783-795.

(1891)
Phillips S M, Tosini P A
A comparison of margin requirements for options and futures
FAJ 1982 NOV-DEC VOL 38 p 54-59.

(1892)
Rudd A, Schroeder M
The calculation of minimum margin
MSci 1982 DEC VOL 28:12 p 1368-1379.

(1893)
Yagil J
Margin trading : a risk-return analysis
JBFA 1982 WINTER VOL 9:4 p 483-487

(1894)
Asay M R
Implied margin requirements on options and stocks
JPM 1981 SPRING VOL 7:3 p 55-62.

(1895)
Jenkins J W
Taxes, margining and bond selection
FAJ 1980 MAY-JUN p 41-48.

(1896)
Grube R C, Joy O M, Panton D B
Market responses to Federal Reserve changes in the initial margin requirement.
JF 1979 JUN VOL 34:3 p 659-674.

(1897)
Eckardt W L Jr, Rogoff D L
100% margins revisited
JF 1976 VOL 31 p 995.

(1898)
Ulrey A P
The structure of margin credit
F R Bul 1975 VOL 61:4.

(1899)
Largay J A
100% margins: Combating speculation in individual security issues
JF 1973 VOL 28 p 973.

(1900)
Largay J A, West R R
Margin changes and stock price behavior
JPE 1973 MAR-APR VOL 81:2 p 328-339.

(1901)
Cohen J
Federal reserve margin requirements and the stock market
JFQA 1966 SEP VOL 1 p 30-54.

(1902)
Moore T G
Stock market margin requirements
JPE 1966 APR VOL 74 p 158-167.

(1903)
Spiegelglas S
Changes in margin requirements and stock market prices
FAJ 1960 NOV-DEC VOL 16 p 35-37.

6.7 Short selling

(1904)
Karpoff J M
Costly short sales and the correlation of returns with volume
JFR 1988 FALL VOL 11:3 p 173-188.

(1905)
Bowlin L, Rozeff M S
Do specialists' short sales predict returns?
JPM 1987 SPRING VOL 13:3 p 59-63.

(1906)
Diamond D W, Verrecchia R E
Constraints on short-selling and asset price adjustment to private information
JFE 1987 JUN VOL 18:2 p 277-311.

(1907)
Reilly F K, Whitford D T
A test of the specialists' short sale ratio
JPM 1982 WINTER VOL 8:2 p 12-18.

(1908)
Figlewski S
The information effects of restrictions on short sales : some empirical evidence
JFQA 1981 NOV VOL 16:4 p 463-476.

(1909)
Milne F
Borrowing, short-sales, consumer default and the creation of new assets
JFQA 1979 JUN VOL 14 p 255.

(1910)
Dyl E A
Short selling and the capital gains tax
FAJ 1978 MAR-APR p 61-64.

(1911)
Hurtado-Sanchez L
Short interest: Its influence as a stabilizer of stock returns
JFQA 1978 DEC VOL 13 p 965.

(1912)
Renshaw E F
Short selling and financial arbitrage
FAJ 1977 JAN-FEB p 58-65.

(1913)
Hanna M
A stock price predictive model based on changes in ratios of short interest to trading volume
JFQA 1976 DEC VOL 11 p 857.

(1914)
Kerrrigan T J
The short interest ratio and its component parts
FAJ 1974 NOV-DEC VOL 30 p 45-49.

(1915)
McDonald J G, Baron D C
Risk and return on short positions in common stocks
JF 1973 VOL 28 p 97.

(1916)
Kisor M Jr, Niederhoffer V
Odd-lot short sales ratio: it signals a market rise
B 1969 SEP 1 p 8.

(1917)
Mayor T H
Short trading activities and the price of equities:
some simulation and regression results
JFQA 1968 SEP VOL 3 p 283-298.

(1918)
Smith R D
Short interest and stock market prices
FAJ 1968 NOV-DEC VOL 24 p 151-154.

(1919)
Seneca J J
Short interest: bearish or bullish?
JF 1967 MAR VOL 22 p 67-70.

(1920)
Weaver M
The technique of short selling
Inv Pr, 1963.

(1921)
Macaulay F R, Durand D
Short selling on the New York Stock Exchange
Twentieth Fund, 1951.

(1922)
Field M J
Security prices and stock exchange holidays in
relation to short selling
JB 1934 OCT VOL 7 p 328.

6.8 Stock market crashes

(1923)
Ferguson R
On crashes
FAJ 1989 MAR-APR VOL 45 p 42-52.

(1924)
Furbush D
Program trading and price movement: evidence
from the October 1987 market crash
FIN MGMT 1989 AUTUMN VOL 18 p 68-83.

(1925)
Harris L
The October 1987 S&P stock-futures basis
JF 1989 MAR VOL 44:1 p 77-100.

(1926)
**Kamphuis R W, Kormendi R C, Watson J W H
eds.**
Black Monday and the future of financial markets
Dow Jones-Irwin, 1989.

(1927)
Kim G, Markowitz H M
Investment rules, margin, and market volatility
JPM 1989 FALL VOL 16:1 p 45-52.

(1928)
Mitchell M L, Netter J M
Triggering the 1987 stock market crash:
antitakeover provisions in the proposed House
Ways and Means bill
JFE 1989 SEP VOL 24:1 p 37-68.

(1929)
Netter J M, Mitchell M L
Stock-repurchase announcements and insider
transactions after the October 1987 stock market
crash
FIN MGMT 1989 AUTUMN VOL 18 p 84-96.

(1930)
Sommariva A, Tullio G
The German depression and the stock market
crash of the thirties: the role of macropolicies and
of the international business cycle
JBankF 1989 SEP VOL 13:4-5 p 515-536.

(1931)
Aderhold R, Cumming C, Harwood A
International linkages among equities markets and
the October 1987 market break
F R Bk New York Q Rev 1988 SUMMER VOL
13:2.

(1932)
Aiyagari S R
Economic fluctuations without shocks to
fundamentals; or, Does the stock market dance to
its own music?
F R Bk Minneapolis Q Rev 1988 VOL 12:1 p
8-24.

(1933)
Bank of England
The equity market crash
BEQB 1988 VOL 28 p 51-58.

(1934)
Barro R, Fama E, Fischel D et al.
Black Monday and the future of financial markets
Irwin, 1988.

(1935)
Bennett P, Kelleher J
The international transmission of stock price disruption in October 1987
F R Bk New York Q Rev 1988 SUMMER VOL 13:2.

(1936)
Bond S R, Devereux M
Financial volatility, the stock market crash and corporate investment
FS 1988 VOL 9:2.

(1937)
Bose M
The crash: the fundamental flaws which caused the 1987-8 world stock market slump and what they mean for future financial stability
Bloomsbury Publishing, 1988.

(1938)
Edward F R
Studies of the 1987 stock market crash: review and appraisal
Journal of Financial Services Research 1988 VOL 1.

(1939)
Gammill J F Jr, Marsh T A
Trading activity and price behavior in the stock and stock index futures markets in October 1987
JEP 1988 VOL 2:3 p 25-44.

(1940)
Greenwald B, Stein J
The task force report: the reasoning behind the recommendations
JEP 1988 VOL 2:3 p 3-24..

(1941)**Leland H E, Rubinstein M**
Comments on the market crash: six months after
JEP 1988 VOL 2:3 p 45-50.

(1942)
Miller M H et al
Final Report of the Committee of Inquiry appointed by the Chicago Mercantile Exchange to examine the events surrounding October 19, 1987
CME, 1988.

(1943)
Roll R
The international crash of October 1987
FAJ 1988 SEP-OCT VOL 44 p 19-35.

(1944)
Rubinstein M
Portfolio insurance and the market crash
FAJ 1988 JAN-FEB VOL 44 p 38-47.

(1945)
Santoni G J
The October crash: some evidence on the cascade theory
F R Bk St Louis Rev 1988 MAY-JUN VOL 70:3.

(1946)
Securities and Exchange Commission
The October 1987 Market Break (A report by the Division of Market Regulation)
SEC FEB 1988.

(1947)
The Presidential Task Force on Market Mechanisms
The "Brady" Report
The Presidential Task Force on Market Mechanisms, 1988.

(1948)
Tosini P A
Stock index futures and stock market activity in October 1987
FAJ 1988 JAN-FEB VOL 44 p 28-37.

(1949)
United States General Accounting Office
Financial markets: Preliminary observations on the October 1987 Crash
GAO JAN 1988.

(1950)
U.S. Commodity Futures Trading Commission
Final report on stock index futures and cash
market activity during October 1987
CFTC 1988.

(1951)
International Stock Exchange of Great Britain
Report on the October 1987 Crash
Quality of Markets Report 1987/88 WINTER p
1-83.

(1952)
Axon G V
The stock market crash of 1929
New York: Mason/Charter, 1974.

(1953)
Galbraith J K
The great crash
HM, 1955.

7 Market microstructure

(1954)
Babcock B
The Dow Jones-Irwin guide to trading systems
Dow Jones-Irwin, 1989.

(1955)
DeLong J B, Shleifer A, Summers L H
The size and incidence of the losses from noise trading
JF 1989 JUL VOL 44:3 p 681-696.

(1956)
Gresik T A, Satterthwaite M A
The rate at which a simple market converges to efficiency as the number of traders increases: an asymptotic result for optimal trading mechanisms
JET 1989 JUN VOL 48:1 p 304-332.

(1957)
Rubinstein M
Market basket alternatives
FAJ 1989 SEP-OCT VOL 45 p 20-29.

(1958)
Grossman S J
An analysis of the implications for stock and futures price volatility of program trading and dynamic hedging strategies
JB 1988 VOL 61 p 295.

(1959)
Grossman S J, Miller M H
Liquidity and market structure
JF 1988 JUL VOL 43:3 p 617-633.

(1960)
Hasbrouck J
Trades, quotes, inventories and information
JFE 1988 VOL 22 p 229.

(1961)
Hill J M, Jones F J
Equity trading, program trading, portfolio insurance, computer trading and all that
FAJ 1988 JUL-AUG VOL 44 p 29-38.

(1962)
Wolinsky A
Dynamic markets with competitive bidding
REStud 1988 VOL 54 p 71.

(1963)
Amihud Y, Mendelson H
Trading mechanisms and stock returns : an empirical investigation.
JF 1987 JUL VOL 42:3 p 533-553.

(1964)
Hagerty K M, Rogerson W P
Robust trading mechanisms
JET 1987 JUN VOL 42:1 p 94-107.

(1965)
Hamilton J L
Market information and price dispersion: Unlisted stocks and NASDAQ
Journal of Economics and Business 1987 FEB VOL 39 p 67-80.

(1966)
Hasbrouck J, Ho T S Y
Order arrival quote behavior and the return-generating process
JF 1987 SEP VOL 42:4 p 1035-1048.

(1967)
Katzenbach N de B
An overview of program trading and its impact on current market practices
New York Stock Exchange, 1987.

(1968)
Santoni G J
Has programmed trading made stock prices more volatile?
F R Bk St Louis Rev 1987 VOL 69:5.

(1969)
Williams A W
The formation of price forecasts in experimental markets
JMCB 1987 FEB VOL 19:1 p 1-18.

(1970)
Cohen K J et al.
The microstructure of securities markets
P-H, 1986.

(1971)
Amihud Y, Ho T, Schwartz R eds.
Market making and the changing structure of the securities industry
Heath, 1985.

(1972)
Copeland T E, Stoll H R
Trading markets
(in Logue D E ed., Handbook of modern finance.
Warren, Gorham and Lamont, 1984.)

(1973)
Cohen K J
Implications of microstructure theory for
empirical research on stock price behavior
JF 1980 MAY VOL 35:2 p 249-257.

(1974)
Van Landingham M H
The day trader: Some additional evidence
JFQA 1980 JUN VOL 15 p 341.

(1975)
Copeland T E
A probability model of asset trading
JFQA 1977 NOV VOL 12 p 563.

(1976)
Copeland T E
A model of asset trading under the assumption of
sequential information arrival
JF 1976 VOL 31 p 1149.

(1977)
Branch B
The optimal price to trade
JFQA 1975 SEP VOL 10 p 497.

(1978)
Bear R M, Curley A J
Day trading and equity market arbitrage
QREB 1974 VOL 14:3 p 61.

(1979)
Rothschild M
A two-armed bandit theory of market pricing
JET 1974 OCT VOL 9:2 p 185-202.

(1980)
Black F
Toward a fully automated stock exchange [Parts
1-2]
FAJ 1971 JUL-AUG VOL 27 p 29-35; FAJ 1971
NOV-DEC VOL 27 p 24ff.

7.1 Dealer markets

(1981)
Glosten L R
Insider trading, liquidity, and the role of the
monopolist specialist
JB 1989 VOL 62:2 p 211-236.

(1982)
Kyle A S
Informed speculation with imperfect competition
REStud 1989 VOL 56 p 317.

(1983)
Admati A R, Pfleiderer P
Selling and trading on information in financial
markets
AER 1988 MAY VOL 78:2 p 96-103.

(1984)
Choi J Y, Salandro D, Shastri K
On the estimation of bid-ask spreads: theory and
evidence
JFQA 1988 JUN VOL 23:2 p 219-230.

(1985)
Glosten L R, Harris L E
Estimating the components of the bid/ask spread
JFE 1988 VOL 21 p 123-142.

(1986)
Easley D, O'Hara M
Price, trade size, and information in securities
markets
JFE 1987 VOL 19 p 69-90.

(1987)
Glosten L R
Components of the bid-ask spread and the
statistical properties of transaction prices
JF 1987 DEC VOL 42:5 p 1293-1308.

(1988)
Treynor J L
The economics of the dealer function
FAJ 1987 NOV-DEC VOL 43 p 27-34.

(1989)
Controy R M, Winkler R L
Market structure: The specialist as dealer and broker
JBankF 1986 VOL 10 p 21.

(1990)
O'Hara M, Oldfield G S
The microeconomics of market making
JFQA 1986 DEC VOL 21:4 p 361-376.

(1991)
Venkatesh P C, Chiang R
Information asymmetry and the dealer's bid-ask spread : a case study of earnings and dividend announcements
JF 1986 DEC VOL 41:5 p 1089-1102.

(1992)
Glosten L R, Milgrom P R
Bid, ask and transaction prices in a specialist market with heterogeneously informed traders.
JFE 1985 VOL 14:1 p 71-100.

(1993)
Hakansson N H, Beja A, Kale J
On the feasibility of automated market making by programmed specialist
JF 1985 MAR VOL 40:1 p 1-20..

(1994)**Ho T S Y, Schwartz R A, Whitcomb D K**
The trading decision and market clearing under transaction price uncertainty
JF 1985 MAR VOL 40:1 p 21-42.

(1995)
Stoll H R
The stock exchange specialist system: an economic analysis
NYU, 1985.

(1996)
Copeland T E, Galai D
Information effects of the bid-ask spread
JF 1983 DEC VOL 38:5 p 1457-1469.

(1997)
Ho T S Y, Stoll H R
The dynamics of dealer markets under competition
JF 1983 VOL 38:4 p 1053-1074.

(1998)
Mildenstein E, Schleef H
The optimal pricing policy of a monopolistic market-maker in the equity market
JF 1983 MAR VOL 38:1 p 218-231.

(1999)
Amihud Y, Mendelson H
Asset price behavior in a dealership market
FAJ 1982 MAY-JUN p 50-59.

(2000)
Archibald B, Baesel J B, Brewer D E
Optimal bid-ask price strategies
Omega 1982 VOL 10:3 p 309-319.

(2001)
Garbade K D, Silber W L
Best execution in securities markets : an application of signaling and agency theory.
JF 1982 MAY VOL 37:2 p 505-517.

(2002)
Conroy R M, Winkler R L
Informational differences between limit and market orders for a market maker
JFQA 1981 DEC VOL 16:5 p 703-724.

(2003)
Ho T S Y, Stoll H R
Optimal dealer pricing under transactions and return uncertainty
JFE 1981 VOL 9 p 47.

(2004)
Treynor J L
What does it take to win the trading game?
FAJ 1981 JAN-FEB VOL 37 p 55-60.

(2005)
Amihud Y, Mendelson H
Dealership market: Market-making with inventory
JFE 1980 VOL 8 p 31-53.

(2006)
Ho T S Y, Stoll H R
On dealer markets under competition
JF 1980 MAY VOL 35:2 p 259-268.

(2007)
Bradfield J
A formal dynamic model of market making
JFQA 1979 JUN VOL 14 p 275.

(2008)
Garbade K D, Silber W L
Structural organisations of secondary markets: clearing frequency dealer activity and liquidity risk.
JF 1979 JUN VOL 34:3 p 577-593.

(2009)
Goldman M B, Beja A
Market prices vs. equilibrium prices: returns' variance serial correlation and the role of the specialist
JF 1979 JUN VOL 34:3 p 595-607.

(2010)
Benston G J, Hagerman R L
Risk, volume and spread
FAJ 1978 JAN-FEB p 46-49.

(2011)
Garbade K D
The effect of interdealer brokerage on the transactional characteristics of dealer markets
JB 1978 JUL VOL 51:3 p 477-498.

(2012)
Guesnerie R, Laffont J-J
Taxing price makers
JET 1978 DEC VOL 19:2 p 423-455.

(2013)
Stoll H R
The supply of dealer services in securities markets
JF 1978 SEP VOL 33:4 p 1133-1151.

(2014)
Stoll H R
The pricing of security dealer services: an empirical study of NASDAQ stocks
JF 1978 SEP VOL 33:4 p 1153-1172.

(2015)
Altman E I
A financial early warning system for over-the-counter broker-dealers
JF 1976 VOL 31 p 1201.

(2016)
Garman M B
Market microstructure
JFE 1976 VOL 3 p 257.

(2017)
Stoll H R
Dealer inventory behavior: An empirical investigation of NASDAQ stocks
JFQA 1976 SEP VOL 11 p 359.

(2018)
Logue D E
Market-making and the assessment of market efficiency
JF 1975 VOL 30 p 115.

(2019)
Reilly F K, Drzycimski E F
The stock exchange specialist and the market impact of major world events
FAJ 1975 JUL-AUG VOL 31 p 27-32.

(2020)
Van Belle J J
The behavior of professional risk bearers: test of a theory
JMCB 1975 MAY VOL 7:2 p 253-257.

(2021)
Tinic S M, West R R
Marketability of common stocks in Canada and the USA: A comparison of agent versus dealer dominated markets
JF 1974 VOL 29 p 729.

(2022)
Bagehot W (pseud for Treynor J L)
The only game in town
FAJ 1971 MAR-APR VOL 27 p 12.

7.2   Auctions

(2023)
Ashenfelter O
How auctions work for wine and art
JEP 1989 SUMMER VOL 3:3 p 23-36.

(2024)
Boyes W J, Happel S K
Auctions as an allocation mechanism in academia:
the case of faculty offices
JEP 1989 SUMMER VOL 3:3 p 37-40.

(2025)
Dyer D, Kagel J H, Levin D
Resolving uncertainty about the number of
bidders in independent private-value auctions: an
experimental analysis
RandJ 1989 SUMMER VOL 20:2 p 268-279.

(2026)
Engelbrecht-Wiggans R
The effect of regret on optimal bidding in
auctions
MSci 1989 VOL 35 p 685.

(2027)
Harrison G W
Theory and misbehavior of first-price auctions
AER 1989 VOL 79:4 p 749-762.

(2028)
Milgrom P
Auctions and bidding: a primer
JEP 1989 SUMMER VOL 3:3 p 3-22.

(2029)
Riley J G
Expected revenues from open and sealed bid
auctions
JEP 1989 SUMMER VOL 3:3 p 41-50.

(2030)
Satterthwaite M A, Williams S R
The rate of converge to efficiency in the buyer's
double bid auction as the market becomes large
REStud 1989 VOL 56 p 477.

(2031)
Bikhchandani S
Reputation in repeated second-price auctions
JET 1988 OCT VOL 46:1 p 97-119.

(2032)
Engelbrecht-Wiggans R
On a possible benefit to bid takers from using
multi-stage auctions
MSci 1988 VOL 34 p 1109.

(2033)
Hansen R G
Auctions with endogenous quantity
RandJ 1988 SPRING VOL 19:1 p 44-58.

(2034)
Hendricks K, Porter R H
An empirical study of an auction with asymmetric
information
AER 1988 VOL 78:5 p 865-883.

(2035)
Riley J G
Ex post information in auctions
REStud 1988 VOL 54 p 409.

(2036)
Thaler R H
Anomalies: The winner's curse
JEP 1988 VOL 2:1 p 191-202.

(2037)
Thiel S E
Some evidence on the winner's curse
AER 1988 VOL 78:5 p 884-895.

(2038)
Engelbrecht-Wiggins R
On optimal reservation prices in auctions
MSci 1987 JUN VOL 33:6 p 763-770.

(2039)
Graham D A, Marshall R C
Collusive bidder behavior at single-object second
price and English auctions
JPE 1987 VOL 95 p 1217.

(2040)
Hausch D B
An asymmetric common-value auction
RandJ 1987 WINTER VOL 18:4 p 611.

(2041)
Laffont J-J, Tirole J
Auctioning incentive contracts
JPE 1987 VOL 95 p 921.

(2042)
McAfee R P, McMillan J
Auctions and bidding
JEL 1987 JUN VOL 25:2 p 699-738.

(2043)
McAffe R P, McMillan J
Auctions with a stochastic number of bidders
JET 1987 OCT VOL 43:1 p 1-19.

(2044)
Demange G, Gale D, Sotomajor M
Multi-item auctions
JPE 1986 VOL 94 p 863.

(2045)
Hausch D B
Multi-object auctions : sequential vs. simultaneous
sales
MSci 1986 DEC VOL 32:12 p 1599-1612.

(2046)
Kagel J H, Levin D
The winner's curse and public information in
common value auctions
AER 1986 VOL 76 p 894-920..

(2047)**Nauss R M**
True interest cost in municipal bond bidding : an
integer programming approach
MSci 1986 JUL VOL 32:7 p 870-877.

(2048)
Feinstein J S, Block M K, Nold F D
Asymmetric information and collusive behavior in
auction markets
AER 1985 VOL 75 p 441-460.

(2049)
Hansen R G
Empirical testing of auction theory
AER 1985 VOL 75 P+P p 156-159.

(2050)
Harstad R M, Levin D
A dominant strategy argument for a class of
common value auctions
REStud 1985 VOL 52 p 525.

(2051)
Maskin E S, Riley J G
Auction theory with private values
AER 1985 VOL 75 P+P p 150-155.

(2052)
Robinson M S
Collusion and the choice of auction
RandJ 1985 SPRING VOL 16:1.

(2053)
Cox J C, Smith V L, Walker J M
Theory and behavior of multiple unit
discriminative auctions.
JF 1984 SEP VOL 39:4 p 983-1010

(2054)
Friedman D
On the efficiency of experimental double auction
markets
AER 1984 VOL 74 p 60-72.

(2055)
Ketcham J, Smith V L, Williams A W
A comparison of posted-offer and double-auction
pricing institutions
REStud 1984 VOL 51 p 595.

(2056)
Moulin H
The conditional auction mechanism for sharing a
surplus
REStud 1984 VOL 51 p 157.

(2057)
Silber W L
Marketmaker behavior in an auction market : an
analysis of scalpers in future markets
JF 1984 SEP VOL 39:4 p 937-953.

(2058)
Holt C A Jr, Sherman R
Waiting-line auctions
JPE 1982 VOL 90 P 280.

(2059)
Hoffman E, Plott C R
The effect of intertemporal speculation on the
outcomes in seller posted offer auction markets
QJE 1981 VOL 96 p 223.

(2060)
Brubaker E R
On the auction mechanism and its incentive
compatibility
JPE 1980 VOL 88 p 617.

(2061)
Engelbrecht-Wiggans R
Auctions and bidding models: A survey
MSci 1980 FEB VOL 26:2 p 119-142.

(2062)
Holt C A Jr
Competitive bidding for contracts under alternative auction procedures
JPE 1980 VOL 88 p 433.

(2063)
Holt C A Jr
Uncertainty and the bidding for incentive contracts
AER 1979 VOL 69 p 697-705.

(2064)
Smidt S
Continuous versus intermittent trading on auction markets
JFQA 1979 NOV VOL 14 p 837.

(2065)
Wilson R
Auctions of shares
QJE 1979 VOL 93 p 675.

(2066)
Barr J L, Shaftel T L
Solution properties of deterministic auctions
JFQA 1976 JUN VOL 11 p 287.

(2067)
Yamey B S
Why £2,310,000 for a Velazquez? An auction bidding rule
JPE 1972 VOL 80 p 1323.

(2068)
Riley J G, Samuelson W F
Optimal auctions
AER 1971 VOL 71 p 381-392.

(2069)
Butler E B
Auction prices: estimated and realized
EJ 1961 MAR VOL 71 p 114-120.

7.3 Sealed bids

(2070)
Forsythe R, Isaac R M, Palfrey T R
Theories and tests of "blind bidding" in sealed-bid auctions
RandJ 1989 SUMMER VOL 20:2 p 214-238.

(2071)
Leininger W, Linhart P B, Radner R
Equilibria of the sealed-bid mechanism for bargaining with incomplete information
JET 1989 JUN VOL 48:1 p 63-106.

(2072)
Matthews S A, Postlewaite A
Pre-play communication in two-person sealed-bid double auctions
JET 1989 JUN VOL 48:1 p 238-263.

(2073)
Radner R, Schotter A
The sealed bid mechanism: an experimental study
JET 1989 JUN VOL 48:1 p 179-220.

(2074)
Satterthwaite M LA, Williams S R
Bilateral trade with the sealed bid k-double auction: existence and efficiency
JET 1989 JUN VOL 48:1 p 107-133.

(2075)
Blumenthal M A
Auctions with constrained information: blind bidding for motion pictures
REStat 1988 VOL 70 p 191.

(2076)
Brown K C, Brown D J
Using order statistics to estimate real estate bid distributions
MSci 1986 MAR VOL 32:3 p 289-297.

(2077)
Engelbrecht-Wiggins R, Dougherty E L, Lohrenz J
A model for the distribution of the number of bids on federal offshore oil leases
MSci 1986 SEP VOL 32:9 p 1087-1094.

(2078)
Gilley O W, Karels G V, Leone R P
Uncertainty experience and the "Winner's Curse"
in OCS lease bidding
MSci 1986 JUN VOL 32:6 p 673-682.

(2079)
McAfee R P, McMillan J
Bidding for contracts:a principal-agent analysis
RandJ 1986 AUTUMN VOL 17:3 p 326-338.

(2080)
Samuelson W
Bidding for contracts
MSci 1986 DEC VOL 32:12 p 1538-1550.

(2081)
Cox J C, Smith V L, Walker J M
Experimental development of sealed-bid auction
theory: Calibrating controls for risk aversion
AER 1985 VOL 75 P+P p 160-165.

(2082)
Mead W J, Moseidjord A, Sorensen P E
Competitive   bidding   under   asymmetrical
information: behavior and performance in Gulf of
Mexico drainage lease sales, 1959-1969
REStat 1984 VOL 66 p 505.

(2083)
Smith V L, Williams A W, Bratton W K
Competitive market institutions: Double auctions
vs. sealed bid-offer auctions
AER 1982 VOL 72 p 58-77.

(2084)
Naykki P
On optimal bidding strategies
MSci 1977 AUG VOL 23:12 p 198.

(2085)
Brown K C
A note on optimal fixed-price bidding with
uncertain production cost
BellJ 1975 AUTUMN VOL 6:2 P 695-697.

(2086)
Hughart D
Informational asymmetry, bidding strategies and
the marketing of offshore petroleum leases
JPE 1975 VOL 83 p 969.

(2087)
Attansi E
Some interpretations of sequential bid pricing
strategies
MSci 1974 JUL VOL 20:11 p 1424.

(2088)
Chen C R, Chan A
Interest rate sensitivity, asymmetry, and the stock returns of financial institutions
FR 1989 AUG VOL 24:3 p 457-474.

(2089)
Economist Conference Unit
Restructuring Europe's financial services: 1992 and beyond
Stanstead Abbotts, Herts: Rooster Books, 1989.

(2090)
Farin T A
Asset and liability management for savings institutions
Dow Jones-Irwin, 1989.

(2091)
Haubrich J G
Financial intermediation: delegated monitoring and long-term relationships
JBankF 1989 MAR VOL 13:1 p 9-20.

(2092)
Hull J
Assessing credit risk in a financial institution's off-balance sheet commitments
JFQA 1989 DEC VOL 24:4 p 489-502.

(2093)
Karim R A A, Ali A E-T
Determinants of the financial strategy of Islamic banks
JBFA 1989 SPRING VOL 16:2 p 193.

(2094)
Ritter L S, Silber W L
Principles of money, banking, and financial markets. 6th ed
Basic, 1989.

(2095)
Santomero A M
The changing structure of financial institutions: a review essay
JME 1989 VOL 24 p 321.

(2096)
Zenoff D B ed.
Marketing financial services
Ballinger, 1989.

(2097)
Balachandran M
A guide to statistical sources in money, banking, and finance
Oryx Press, 1988.

(2098)
Chorafas D N, Steinmann H
Implementing networks in banking and financial services
Macmillan, 1988.

(2099)
England C, Huertas T eds.
The financial services revolution: policy directions for the future
Kluwer Academic, 1988..

(2100)**Gardner M J, Mills D L**
Managing financial institution: An asset/liability approach
Dryden Pr, 1988.

(2101)
Geisst C R
A guide to financial institutions
Macmillan, 1988.

(2102)
Horvath P A
Disintermediation revisited
FR 1988 AUG VOL 23:3 p 301-312.

(2103)
Melicher R W, Welshans M T
Finance: Introduction to markets, institutions and management. 7th ed
SW Pub, 1988.

(2104)
Rose P S, Fraser D R
Financial institutions: understanding and managing financial services. 3rd ed
Irwin, 1988.

(2105)
Rothwell M, Jowett P
Rivalry in retail financial services
Macmillan, 1988.

(2106)
Besanko D, Thakor A V
Competitive equilibrium in the credit market under asymmetric information
JET 1987 JUN VOL 42:1 p 167-182.

(2107)
Bryant R C
International financial intermediation
Brookings, 1987.

(2108)
Dalgaard B R
Money, financial institutions and economic activity
Scott, Foresman, 1987.

(2109)
Fraser D R, Rose P S
Financial institutions and markets in a changing world. 3rd ed
Irwin, 1987.

(2110)
Goacher D J, Curwen P J
British non-bank financial intermediaries
Allen, 1987.

(2111)
Gupta K L
Aggregate savings, financial intermediation and interest rates
REStat 1987 VOL 69 p 303.

(2112)
Herring R J, Vankudre P
Growth opportunities and risk-taking by financial intermediaries
JF 1987 JUL VOL 42:3 p 583-599.

(2113)
Kidwell D S, Peterson R L
Financial institutions, markets, and money. 3rd ed
Dryden Pr, 1987.

(2114)
Morgan G E, Smith S D
Maturity intermediation and intertemporal lending policies of financial intermediaries
JF 1987 SEP VOL 42:4 p 1023-1034.

(2115)
Prager J
Fundamentals of money, banking, and financial institutions. 2nd ed
Har-Row, 1987.

(2116)
Walter I
Global competition in financial services
Ballinger, 1987.

(2117)
Williamson S
Transactions costs, inflation, and the variety of intermediation services.
JMCB 1987 NOV VOL 19:4 p 484-498.

(2118)
Boyd J H, Prescott E C
Financial intermediary-coalitions
JET 1986 APR VOL 38:2 p 211-232.

(2119)
Carter R L et al., eds.
Personal financial markets: an examination of the evolving markets for personal savings and financing in the United Kingdom and the United States
Philip Allan, 1986.

(2120)
Edmister R O
Financial institutions: markets and management. 2nd ed
McGraw, 1986.

(2121)
Maycock J
Financial conglomerates: the new phenomenon
Gower, 1986.

(2122)
Whiteside R M et al., eds.
Major financial institutions of continental Europe: 1986
Graham & Trotman, 1986.

(2123)
Williamson S D
Increasing returns to scale in financial intermediation and the non-neutrality of government policy
REStud 1986 VOL 53 p 863.

(2124)
Gilberto M
Interest rate sensitivity in the common stocks of financial intermediaries: a methodical note
JFQA 1985 MAR VOL 20:1 p 123-126.

(2125)
Hancock D
The financial firm: Production with monetary and nonmonetary goods
JPE 1985 VOL 93 p 859.

(2126)
Rosenberg J M
Dictionary of banking and financial services. 2nd ed
Wiley, 1985.

(2127)
Stiglitz J E
Credit markets and the control of capital
JMCB 1985 MAY VOL 17:2 p 133-152.

(2128)
Teas R K, Deliva W L
Conjoint measurement of consumers' preferences for multiattribute financial services
JBR 1985 SUMMER VOL 16:2 p 99.

(2129)
Ziegel J, Waverman L, Conklin D W eds.
Canadian financial institutions: Changing the regulatory environment
Ontario Economic Council, 1985.

(2130)
Diamond D W
Financial intermediation and delegated monitoring
REStud 1984 VOL 51 p 393.

(2131)
Kane E J
Technological and regulatory forces in the developing fusion of financial-services competition
JF 1984 JUL VOL 39:3 p 759-773.

(2132)
Ramakrishnan R T S, Thakor A V
Information reliability and a theory of financial intermediation
REStud 1984 VOL 51 p 415.

(2133)
Santoni G J
Interest rate risk and the stock prices of financial institutions
F R Bk St Louis Rev 1984 VOL 66:7.

(2134)
Corner D, Mayes D G eds.
Modern portfolio theory and financial institutions
Macmillan, 1983..

(2135)**Elliott J V**
What is the role of government in a major restructuring of financial institutions in the 1980's
JBR 1983 SPRING VOL 14:1.

(2136)
Fama E F
Financial intermediation and price level control
JME 1983 VOL 12 p 7.

(2137)
Kaufman G G, Mote L, Rosenblum H
Implications of deregulation for product lines and geographical markets of financial institutions
JBR 1983 SPRING VOL 14:1.

(2138)
Marlow M L
Entry and performance in financial markets
JBR 1983 AUTUMN VOL 14:3.

(2139)
Munn G G ed.
Encyclopedia of banking and finance. 8th ed, rev by F L Garcia
Bankers, 1983.

(2140)
Steindl F G, Weinrobe M D
Natural hazards and deposit behavior at financial institutions: A note
JBankF 1983 VOL 7 p 111.

(2141)
Farrar D E, Girton L
Institutional investors and concentration of financial power: Berle and Means revisited
JF 1981 MAY VOL 36:2 p 369-381.

(2142)
MacBean A I, Snowden P N
International institutions in trade and finance
Allen, 1981.

(2143)
O'Hara M
Property rights and the financial firm
JLE 1981 VOL 24:3 p 317.

(2144)
Berndt E R, McCurdy T H, Rose D E
On testing theories of financial intermediary portfolio selection
REStud 1980 VOL 47 p 861.

(2145)
Campbell T S, Kracaw W A
Information production, market signalling and the theory of financial intermediation.
JF 1980 SEP VOL 35:4 p 863-882.

(2146)
Meyer R A Jr
The regulated financial firm
QREB 1980 WINTER VOL 20:4 p 44-57

(2147)
Nathan H C
Nonbank organizations and the Mcfadden Act
JBR 1980 SUMMER VOL 11:2.

(2148)
Sarin R K, Winkler R L
Performance-based incentive plans
MSci 1980 NOV VOL 26:11 p 1131-1144.

(2149)
Clark R C
The regulation of financial holding companies
HLR 1979 VOL 92:4 p 787-863.

(2150)
Gilbert R A, Lovati J M
Disintermediation: an old disorder with a new remedy
F R Bk St Louis Rev 1979 VOL 61:1.

(2151)
Murphy N B, Mandell L
Reforming the structure and regulation of financial institutions: the evidence from the State of Maine
JBR 1979 WINTER VOL 9:4.

(2152)
Draper D W, Hoag J W
Financial intermediation and the theory of agency
JFQA 1978 NOV VOL 13 p 595.

(2153)
Morton T G, Duker J M
Black financial institutions: An appraisal
FIN MGMT 1978 SUMMER VOL 7 p 28.

(2154)
Townsend R M
Intermediation with costly bilateral exchange
REStud 1978 OCT VOL 45:141 p 417-425.

(2155)
Hempel G H, Yawitz J B
Financial management of financial institutions
P-H, 1977.

(2156)
Kane E J
Good intentions and unintended evil: the case against selective credit allocation
JMCB 1977 FEB VOL 9:1 p 55-69.

(2157)
Lovati J M
The growing similarity among financial institutions
F R Bk St Louis Rev 1977 VOL 59:10.

(2158)
Runyon H
Real world risk and financial institutions
F R Bk San Francisco Ec Rev 1977 WINTER.

(2159)
Tuccillo J
Taxation by regulation: the case of financial intermediaries
BellJ 1977 AUTUMN VOL 8:2 p 577-587.

(2160)
Hopelain D G, Jones D W
Managing change in the modern investment institution
FAJ 1976 SEP-OCT VOL 32 p 27-34.

(2161)
Kaufman G G
Teaching of the basic money and financial institutions course
JFQA 1976 NOV VOL 11.

(2162)
Courakis A S
Testing theories of discount house portfolio selection
REStud 1975 VOL 42 p 643.

(2163)
Cramer R H, Hawk S L
The consideration of coupon levels, taxes, reinvestment rates and maturity in the investment management of financial institutions
JFQA 1975 MAR VOL 10 p 67.

(2164)
Goldsmith R W ed.
Institutional investors and corporate stock: a background study
Natl Bur Econ Res, 1975.

(2165)
Gibson W E
Reform of financial institutions
JFQA 1974 NOV VOL 9 p 803.

(2166)
Hart O D, Jaffee D M
On the application of portfolio theory to depository financial intermediaries
REStud 1974 VOL 41 p 129.

(2167)
Phillips A
Regulatory reform for the deposit financial institutions: Retrospect and prospects
JFQA 1974 NOV VOL 9 p 795.

(2168)
Rosenberg M
Institutional investors: Holdings, prices and liquidity
FAJ 1974 MAR-APR VOL 30 p 53-59.

(2169)
Stillson R T
An analysis of information and transaction services in financial institutions
JMCB 1974 NOV VOL 6:4 p 517-536.

(2170)
Klein M A
The economics of security divisibility and financial intermediation
JF 1973 VOL 28 p 923.

(2171)
Benston G J
Economies of scale of financial institutions
JMCB 1972 MAY VOL 4 p 312-341.

(2172)
Freund W C
Issues confronting the stock market in a period of rising institutionalization
JFQA 1972 MAR VOL 7 Suppl p 1687-1690.

(2173)
Friend I
Effect of institutionalization of savings on the long-term for the securities industry
JFQA 1972 MAR VOL 7 Suppl p 1691-1695.

(2174)
Jacobs D P et al.
Financial institutions. 5th ed
Irwin, 1972.

(2175)
Jones L D
Some contributions of the institutional investor study
JF 1972 MAY VOL 27 p 305-318.

(2176)
Pyle D H
Descriptive theories of financial institutions under
uncertainty
JFQA 1972 DEC VOL 7 p 2010.

(2177)
Hunt Commission Report
The report of the President's Commission on
Financial Structure and Regulation (The Hunt
Commission report)
Washington, DC: Supt. of Documents, DEC 1971.

(2178)
Krooss H E, Blyn M R
A history of financial intermediaries
Random, 1971.

(2179)
Pyle D H
On the theory of financial intermediation
JF 1971 JUN VOL 26 p 737-747.

(2180)
Securities and Exchange Commission
Institutional investor study report of the
Securities and Exchange Commission
US Govt, 1971.

(2181)
Sheppard D K
The growth and role of U.K. financial institutions
1880-1962
Methuen, 1971.

(2182)
Smith P F
Economics of financial institutions and markets
Irwin, 1971.

(2183)
West R R
Institutional trading and the changing stock
market
FAJ 1971 MAY-JUN VOL 27 p 17ff.

(2184)
Bank of England
The financial institutions. [Parts 1-3]
BEQB 1970 DEC VOL 10 p 419-431; BEQB
1971 MAR VOL 11 p 48-71; BEQB 1971 JUN
VOL 11 p 199-210.

(2185)
Hakansson N H
An induced theory of the firm under risk: the
pure mutual fund
JFQA 1970 JUN VOL 5 p 155-178.

(2186)
Silber W L
Portfolio behavior of financial institutions
HR & W, 1970.

(2187)
Gupta L C
The changing structure of industrial finance in
India: the impact of institutional finance
Oxford U Pr, 1969..

(2188)**Goldsmith R W**
Financial institutions
Random, 1968.

(2189)
West D A
The investor in a changing economy
P-H, 1968.

(2190)
Michaelsen J B, Goshay R C
Portfolio selection in financial intermediaries: a
new approach
JFQA 1967 JUN VOL 2 p 116-199.

(2191)
Robichek A A, Coleman A B
Management of financial institutions: notes and
cases
HR & W, 1967.

(2192)
Baum D J, Stiles N B
The silent partners--institutional investors and
corporate control
Syracuse U Pr, 1965.

(2193)
Ketchum M D, Kendall L T eds.
Readings in financial institutions
HM, 1965.

(2194)
Krainer R E
Financial institutions and the struggle for primary securities
SEJ 1964 APR VOL 30 p 362-376.

(2195)
Seligman D, Wise T A
New forces in the stock market
F 1964 FEB VOL 69 p 92ff.

(2196)
Commission on Money & Credit
Private financial institutions: a series of research studies prepared for the Commission
P-H, 1963.

(2197)
Hanson W C
Capital sources and major investing institutions
Simmons-B, 1963.

(2198)
Clayton G
British financial intermediaries in theory and practice
EJ 1962 DEC VOL 72 p 869-886.

(2199)
Cooke G W et al.
Financial institutions: their role in the American economy
Simmons-B, 1962.

(2200)
Gies T G
Portfolio regulations of selected financial intermediaries: some proposals for change
JF 1962 MAY VOL 17 p 302-310.

(2201)
Mayer T
Is the portfolio control of financial institutions justified?
JF 1962 MAY VOL 17 p 311-317.

(2202)
Robinson R I, Boehmler E W, Gane F H et al., eds.
Financial institutions. 3rd ed
Irwin, 1960.

(2203)
Goldsmith R W
Financial intermediaries in the American economy since 1900
Princeton U Pr, 1958.

(2204)
Neenan W B
Review of institutional activity in the equity market, 1951-54
JF 1957 DEC VOL 12 p 468-488.

(2205)
Prochnow H V ed.
American financial institutions
P-H, 1951.

8.1   Commercial banking

(2206)
Bryant J
Money, banking and intertemporal substitution
JBankF 1989 MAY VOL 13:2 p 171-180.

(2207)
Chorafas D N
Bank profitability: from cost control to pricing financial products and services
Butterworth, 1989.

(2208)
Cotterrell A
Case studies in banking
Pitman, 1989.

(2209)
Friedman D H
Money and banking. 2nd ed.
ABA, 1989.

(2210)
Gup B E, Fraser D R, Kolari J W
Commercial bank management
Wiley, 1989.

(2211)
Hendrie A ed.
Banking in Comecon: structures and sources of finance
Financial Times Business Information, 1989.

(2212)
Johnson F P, Johnson R D
Bank management. 2nd ed.
ABA, 1989.

(2213)
Korsvik W J, Juris H eds.
The new frontier in bank strategy
Dow Jones-Irwin, 1989.

(2214)
Kwast M L
The impact of underwriting and dealing on bank
returns and risks
JBankF 1989 MAR VOL 13:1 p 101-126.

(2215)
Madura J, McDaniel W R
Market reaction to increased loan loss reserves at
money-center banks
JFSR 1989 VOL 3:4 p 359.

(2216)
Pavlopoulos P G, Kouzelis A K
Cost behaviour in the banking industry: evidence
from a Greek commercial bank
AE 1989 VOL 21:3 p 285-294.

(2217)
Steiner T D, Teixeira D B
Technology in banking
Dow Jones-Irwin, 1989.

(2218)
Udell G F
Loan quality, commercial loan review and loan
officer contracting
JBankF 1989 JUL VOL 13:3 p 367-382.

(2219)
Benston G J
The problems and future of commercial banks
MCFJ 1988 WINTER VOL 5 p 6-13.

(2220)
Burstein M L
Studies in banking theory, financial history and
vertical control
Macmillan, 1988.

(2221)
Collins M
Money and banking in the UK: a history
Croom Helm, 1988.

(2222)
Darrat A F
The Islamic interest-free banking system: some
empirical evidence
AE 1988 MAR VOL 20:3 p 417-425.

(2223)
Economopoulos A J
Illinois free banking experience
JMCB 1988 MAY VOL 20.2 p 249.

(2224)
Freeman S
Banking as the provision of liquidity
JB 1988 VOL 61 p 45.

(2225)
Goodhart C
The evolution of central banks
MIT, 1988.

(2226)
Hendrie A ed.
Banking in the EEC, 1988: structures and sources
of finance
Financial Times Business Information, 1988.

(2227)
Koch T W
Bank management
Dryden Pr, 1988.

(2228)
Meinster D R, Elyasiani E
The performance of foreign owned, minority
owned and holding company owned banks in the
US
JBankF 1988 VOL 12:2 p 293-314.

(2229)
Pozdena R J
Banks affiliated with bank holding companies: a
new look at their performance
F R Bk San Francisco Ec Rev 1988 FALL NO 4.

(2230)
Van Fenstermaker J, Malone R P
An analysis of commercial bank stock returns: 1802-97.
AE 1988 JUN VOL 20:6 p 813-842.

(2231)
Wallace N
Another attempt to explain an illiquid banking system: the Diamond and Dybvig model with sequential service taken seriously
F R Bk Minneapolis Q Rev 1988 VOL 12:4.

(2232)
Wilcox J A
Current readings on money, banking, and financial markets
Scott, Foresman, 1988.

(2233)
Arshadi N, Lawrence E C
An empirical investigation of new bank performance
JBankF 1987 VOL 11 p 33-48.

(2234)
Cothren R
Asymmetric information and optimal bank reserves
JMCB 1987 FEB VOL 19:1 p 68-77.

(2235)
Gooptu S, Lombra R
Aggregation across heterogeneous depository institutions
FR 1987 NOV VOL 22:4.

(2236)
Hirtle B
The growth of the financial guarantee market
F R Bk New York Q Rev 1987 SPRING VOL 12:1.

(2237)
James C
Some evidence on the uniqueness of bank loans
JFE 1987 VOL 19 p 217-235.

(2238)
Kareken J H
The emergence and regulation of contingent commitment banking
JBankF 1987 VOL 11 p 359-377.

(2239)
King D
Banking and money
Edward Arnold, 1987.

(2240)
Larcker D F
Short-term compensation contracts and executive expenditure decisions : the case of commercial banks
JFQA 1987 MAR VOL 22:1 p 33-50..

(2241)**Lewis M K, Davis K T**
Domestic and international banking
Philip Allan, 1987.

(2242)
Penn G A et al.
The law relating to domestic banking
Sweet, 1987.

(2243)
Perry F E
Law and practice relating to banking. 5th ed, rev by J E Kelly
Methuen, 1987.

(2244)
Rhoades S A
The effect of nonbank thrift institutions on commercial bank profit performance in local markets
QREB 1987 SPRING VOL 27:1 p 16-28.

(2245)
Tarhan V
Unanticipated interest rates, bank stock returns and the nominal contracting hypothesis
JBankF 1987 VOL 11 p 99-115.

(2246)
Williamson S D
Recent developments in modeling financial intermediation
F R Bk Minneapolis Q Rev 1987 VOL 11:3.

(2247)
Anderlini L
Competitive banking in a simple model
(in Edwards J et al. eds., Recent developments in corporate finance. Cambridge U Pr, 1986.)

(2248)
Ballarin E
Commercial banks amid the financial revolution: developing a competitive strategy
Ballinger, 1986.

(2249)
Boehlje M, Fisher G
A competitive management game for non-metropolitan commercial banks
JBR 1986 SPRING VOL 17:1.

(2250)
Carraro K C, Thornton D L
The cost of checkable deposits in the United States
F R Bk St Louis Rev 1986 VOL 68:4.

(2251)
Chan Y S, Greenbaum S I, Thakor A V
Information reusability, competition and bank asset quality
JBankF 1986 VOL 10 p 243.

(2252)
Davis R G, Korobow L
The pricing of consumer deposit products - the non-rate dimensions
F R Bk New York Q Rev 1986-87 WINTER VOL 11:4.

(2253)
Davis R G, Korobow L, Wenninger J
Bankers on pricing consumer deposits
F R Bk New York Q Rev 1986-87 WINTER VOL 11:4.

(2254)
Goldfield S M, Chandler L V
The economics of money and banking. 9th ed
Har-Row, 1986.

(2255)
Hancock D
Testing price taking in loan and deposit markets by financial firms
FR 1986 MAY VOL 21:2.

(2256)
Hancock D
A model of the financial firm with imperfect asset and deposit elasticities
JBankF 1986 VOL 10 p 37.

(2257)
Lawrence C, Shay R P
Technology and financial intermediation in multiproduct banking firms
(in Lawrence C and Shay R eds., Technology, innovation, regulation and the monetary economy. Ballinger, 1986.)

(2258)
Mishkin F S
The economics of money, banking, and financial markets
Little, 1986.

(2259)
Moran M
The politics of banking: the strange case of competition and credit control. 2nd ed
Macmillan, 1986.

(2260)
Perry F E
The elements of banking. 5th ed, rev by G Klein
Methuen, 1986.

(2261)
Prisman E Z, Slovin M B, Sushka M E
A general model of the banking firm under conditions of monopoly, uncertainty and recourse
JME 1986 VOL 17 p 293.

(2262)
Santoni G J
The effects of inflation on commercial banks
F R Bk St Louis Rev 1986 VOL 68:3.

(2263)
Vittas D
Banks' relations with industry : an international survey
NWBQR 1986 FEB p 2-14.

(2264)
Aspinwall R C, Eisenbeis R A eds.
Handbook for banking strategy
Wiley, 1985.

(2265)
Dermine J
Inflation taxes and banks' market values
JBFA 1985 SPRING VOL 12:1 p 65-73

(2266)
Fama E F
What's different about banks?
JME 1985 VOL 15 p 29-39.

(2267)
Fraser D R, Groth J C
Listing and the liquidity of bank stocks
JBR 1985 AUTUMN VOL 16:3 p 136-144.

(2268)
Gallant P
Electronic treasury management: a guide for corporate and bank treasurers
Woodhead-Faulkner, 1985.

(2269)
Gorton G
Banking theory and free banking history: a review essay
JME 1985 VOL 16 p 267.

(2270)
Hamblin C
Banking law
Sweet, 1985.

(2271)
Hanson D G
Dictionary of banking and finance: a commentary on banking, financial services and corporate and personal finance
Pitman, 1985.

(2272)
Horvitz P M
The combination of banking and insurance: implications for regulation
Growth and Change 1985 VOL 16:4.

(2273)
Kahn J A
Another look at free banking in the United States
AER 1985 VOL 75 p 881-885.

(2274)
Karafiath I
Will a risk-averse competitive bank prefer contemporaneous reserve accounting?
FR 1985 FEB VOL 20:1.

(2275)
Landskroner Y, Ruthenberg D
Optimal bank behavior under uncertain inflation
JF 1985 SEP VOL 40:4 p 1159-1171.

(2276)
Langohr H W, Santomero A M
Commercial bank refinancing and economic stability: An analysis of European features
JBankF 1985 VOL 9 p 535.

(2277)
McShane R W, Sharpe I G
A time series/cross section analysis of the determinants of Australian trading bank loan/deposit interest margins: 1962-1981
JBankF 1985 VOL 9 p 115.

(2278)
Miller R L, Pulsinelli R W
Modern money and banking
McGraw, 1985.

(2279)
Myers F E, Van Walleghem J
Management transferability in rural banks
JBR 1985 WINTER VOL 15:4.

(2280)
Reeday T G
The law relating to banking. 5th ed
Butterworth, 1985.

(2281)
Revell J R S
Costs and margins in banking: statistical
supplement 1978-1982
OECD, 1985.

(2282)
Rockoff H
New evidence on free banking in the United
States
AER 1985 VOL 75 p 886-889.

(2283)
Rose P S, Kolari J W, Riener K W
A national survey study of bank services and
prices arrayed by size and structure
JBR 1985 SUMMER VOL 16:2 p 72-85.

(2284)
Shaw E R, Howcroft J B
Banking law
Blackwell, 1985.

(2285)
Sherman H D, Gold F
Bank branch operating efficiency: Evaluation with
data envelopment analysis
JBankF 1985 VOL 9 p 297.

(2286)
Wall L D
Why are some banks more profitable than others
JBR 1985 WINTER VOL 15:4.

(2287)
Cooper J
The management and regulation of banks
Macmillan, 1984.

(2288)
Dunkelberg W C, Scott J A
Rural versus urban bank performance: an analysis
of market competition for small business loans
JBR 1984 AUTUMN VOL 15:3.

(2289)
Dunkelberg W C, Scott J A
Small business and the value of bank customer
relationships
JBR 1984 WINTER VOL 14:4.

(2290)
Eisenbeis R A, Harris R S, Lakonishok J
Benefits of bank diversification: the evidence from
shareholder returns
JF 1984 JUL VOL 39:3 p 881-894.

(2291)
Gardner M J
Minority owned banks: a managerial and
performance analysis
JBR 1984 SPRING VOL 15:1.

(2292)
Giroux G A, Rose P S
An update of bank planning systems: results of a
nationwide survey of large U S banks
JBR 1984 AUTUMN VOL 15:3.

(2293)
Graddy D B, Homaifar G, Karna A S
Double leverage as a source of systematic risk in
bank holding company stocks
JBR 1984 SUMMER VOL 15:2..

(2294)**Gurel E, Pyle D**
Bank income taxes and interest rate risk
management : a note
JF 1984 SEP VOL 39:4 p 1199-1206.

(2295)
Hannan T H
Competition between commercial banks and thrift
institutions: an empirical examination
JBR 1984 SPRING VOL 15:1.

(2296)
Hannan T H, McDowell J M
The determinants of technology adoption: the
case of the banking firm
RandJ 1984 AUTUMN VOL 15:3 p 328-335.

(2297)
Hu Y-S
Industrial banking and special credit institutions:
a comparative study
Policy Studies Institute, 1984.

(2298)
Reese R M, Stanton W W
Further segmenting a minority bank's customer
set
JBR 1984 WINTER VOL 14:4.

(2299)
Rhoades S A, White A P
Output in relation to labor input in the banking
and savings and loan industries: 1927-1979
JBankF 1984 VOL 8 p 119.

(2300)
Shaffer S
Cross subsidization in checking accounts
JMCB 1984 FEB VOL 16:1 p 100-109.

(2301)
Smith B D
Private information, deposit interest rates and the
"stability" of the banking system
JME 1984 VOL 14 p 293.

(2302)
Barth J R
The effect of government regulations on personal
loan markets : a tobit estimation of a
microeconomic model
JF 1983 SEP VOL 38:4 p 1233-1251

(2303)
Brown D M
Bank holding company performance studies and
the public interest: normative uses for positive
analysis?
F R Bk St Louis Rev 1983 MAR VOL 65:3.

(2304)
Dalton D R, Krackhardt D M, Porter L W
The impact of teller turnover in banking: first
appearances are deceiving
JBR 1983 AUTUMN VOL 14:3.

(2305)
Friedman R M, Roberts W W
The carry-forward provision and management of
bank reserves
JF 1983 JUN VOL 38:3 p 845-855.

(2306)
Gendreau B C
The implicit return on bankers' balances
JMCB 1983 NOV VOL 15:4 p 411-424.

(2307)
Giroux G A, Grossman S, Shearon W
How does inflation affect a BHC's rate of return?
JBR 1983 SUMMER VOL 14:2.

(2308)
Hicks S S
Aggregate bank portfolio statistics: do they tell us
anything?
JBR 1983 AUTUMN VOL 14:3.

(2309)
Keen H Jr
The impact of a dividend cut announcement on
bank share prices
JBR 1983 WINTER VOL 13:4.

(2310)
Martell T F
The accuracy of deposit forecasts generated by the
bank chartering process
JBR 1983 WINTER VOL 13:4.

(2311)
Meeker L G, Joy O M, Cogger K O
Valuation of controlling shares in closely held
banks
JBankF 1983 VOL 7 p 175.

(2312)
O'Hara M
A dynamic theory of the banking firm
JF 1983 MAR VOL 38:1 p 127-140.

(2313)
Orgler Y E, Taggart R A Jr
Implications of corporate capital structure theory
for banking institutions
JMCB 1983 MAY VOL 15:2 p 212-221.

(2314)
Perry F E
A dictionary of banking. 2nd ed
Macdonald and Evans, 1983.

(2315)
Rolnick A J, Weber W E
New evidence on the free banking era
AER 1983 VOL 73 p 1080-1091.

(2316)
Rose J T, Talley S H
Financial transactions within bank holding
companies
F R Bul 1983 VOL 69:5.

(2317)
Sealey C W Jr
Valuation capital structure and shareholder unanimity for depository financial intermediaries
JF 1983 JUN VOL 38:3 p 857-871.

(2318)
Walsh C E
Taxation of interest income deregulation and the banking industry
JF 1983 DEC VOL 38:5 p 1529-1542.

(2319)
Zoltners A A
A manpower sizing and resource allocation model for commercial lending
JBR 1983 SUMMER VOL 14:2.

(2320)
Davis S G, Reutzel E T
Multi-stage scheduling for the banks by mathematical programming
Omega 1982 VOL 10:6 p 663-671.

(2321)
Fortune
How banks lure the rich
F 1982 NOV 1 VOL 106:9 p 60-64.

(2322)
Goodman L S
Bank foreign exchange operations: a portfolio approach
JMCB 1982 FEB VOL 14:1 p 84-91.

(2323)
Holden J M
Banker and customer. 3rd ed
Pitman, 1982.

(2324)
Karna A S, Graddy D B
Bank holding company leverage and the return on stockholders' equity
JBR 1982 SPRING VOL 13:1.

(2325)
Mabert V A, Stocco R
Managing and monitoring a forecasting system: the Chemical Bank experience
JBR 1982 AUTUMN VOL 13:3.

(2326)
Megrah M, Ryder F R ed.
Paget's law of banking. 9th ed
Butterworth, 1982.

(2327)
Nielsen J F
Trading small bank stocks: an Oregon case study
JBR 1982 SPRING VOL 13:1.

(2328)
Reid M I
The secondary banking crisis, 1973-75: its causes and course
Macmillan, 1982.

(2329)
Rose J T
Bank holding company affiliation and market share performance
JME 1982 VOL 9 p 109.

(2330)
Beedles W L, Buschmann N K
Describing bank equity returns: the year by year record
JMCB 1981 MAY VOL 13:2 p 241-247.

(2331)
Cohen K J, Maier S F, Vander Weide J H
Recent developments in management science in banking
MSci 1981 OCT VOL 27:10 p 1097-1119.

(2332)
Doyle P, Fenwick I, Savage G P
A model for evaluating branch location and performance
JBR 1981 SUMMER VOL 12:2.

(2333)
Kwast M L
New minority-owned commercial banks: a statistical analysis
JBR 1981 SPRING VOL 12:1.

(2334)
Opper B N
Profitability of insured commercial banks
F R Bul 1981 VOL 67:9.

(2335)
Ratti R A
Bank attitude toward risk, implicit rates of interest and the behavior of an index of risk aversion for commercial banks
QJE 1981 VOL 95 p 309.

(2336)
Rose J T, Rutz R D
Organizational form and risk in bank affiliated mortgage companies
JMCB 1981 AUG VOL 13:3 p 375-380.

(2337)
Selby E B
The role of director deposits in new bank growth
JBR 1981 SPRING VOL 12:1.

(2338)
Spellman L J
Commercial banks and the profits of savings and loan markets
JBR 1981 SPRING VOL 12:1.

(2339)
Baltensperger E
Alternative approaches to the theory of the banking firm
JME 1980 VOL 6 p 1.

(2340)
Euske K J, Jackson D W Jr, Reif W E
Performance and satisfaction of bank managers
JBR 1980 SPRING VOL 11:1.

(2341)
Fama E F
Banking in the theory of finance
JME 1980 VOL 6 p 39.

(2342)
Fortune
Dark days ahead for banks
F 1980 JUN 30 VOL 101:13 p 86-90.

(2343)
Fortune
How the savings banks can save themselves
F 1980 JAN 28 VOL 101:2 p 76-81.

(2344)
Giroux G A
A survey of forecasting techniques used by commercial banks
JBR 1980 SPRING VOL 11:1.

(2345)
Graddy D B, Kyle R
Affiliated bank performance and the simultaneity of financial decisionmaking
JF 1980 SEP VOL 35:4 p 951-957.

(2346)
Heard E L, Wheat J E
Management engineering in large US banks
JBR 1980 WINTER VOL 10:4..

(2347)**Horvitz P M**
A reconsideration of the role of bank examination
JMCB 1980 NOV VOL 12:4 p 654-659.

(2348)
Jahankhani A, Lynge M J Jr
Commercial bank financial policies and their impact on market-determined measures of risk
JBR 1980 AUTUMN VOL 11:3.

(2349)
Mayne L S
Bank holding company characteristics and the upstreaming of bank funds
JMCB 1980 MAY VOL 12:2 p 209-214.

(2350)
Mayne L S
Bank dividend policy and holding company affiliation
JFQA 1980 JUN VOL 15 p 469.

(2351)
Meeker L G, Joy O M
Price premiums for controlling shares of closely held bank stock
JB 1980 JUL VOL 53:3 p 297-314.

(2352)
Miller R J
Examination man-hour cost for independent joint and divided examination programs
JBR 1980 SPRING VOL 11:1.

(2353)
Mukhergee T K, Austin L M
An empirical investigation of small bank stock
valuation and dividend policy
FIN MGMT 1980 SPRING VOL 9 p 27.

(2354)
Revell J R S
Costs and margins in banking: an international
survey
OECD, 1980.

(2355)
Roley V V
The role of commercial banks' portfolio behavior
in the determination of Treasury security yields
JMCB 1980 MAY VOL 12:2 p 353-369.

(2356)
Sealey C W Jr
Deposit rate-setting risk aversion and the theory
of depository financial intermediaries
JF 1980 DEC VOL 35:5 p 1139-1154.

(2357)
Spindt P A, Tarhan V
Liquidity structure adjustment behavior of large
money center banks
JMCB 1980 MAY VOL 12:2 p 198-208.

(2358)
Veit E T, Avey M L, Corley J L
The role of stock options in the bank trust
departments: fifth Federal Reserve District banks
JBR 1980 WINTER VOL 10:4.

(2359)
Chiang D T
Liquidity planning in a small bank
Omega 1979 VOL 7:4 p 287-295.

(2360)
Fry E R
New measures of commercial bank credit and
bank nondeposit funds
F R Bul 1979 VOL 65:9.

(2361)
Karna A S
Bank holding company profitability: nonbanking
subsidiaries and financial leverage
JBR 1979 SPRING VOL 10:1.

(2362)
McAlister M K, Overstreet G A
Comparative job satisfaction levels among bank
managers
JBR 1979 WINTER VOL 9:4.

(2363)
Myers F E, Hoenig T
Relative operating performance of withdrawing
10th Federal Reserve District member banks
JBR 1979 AUTUMN VOL 10:3.

(2364)
Watne D A
Cross-selling the bank customer
JBR 1979 AUTUMN VOL 10:3.

(2365)
Benbow R F
A new approach for analysis and control of the
yield from commercial customers
JBR 1978 SUMMER VOL 9:2.

(2366)
Cramer R H, Miller R B
Multivariate time series analysis of bank financial
behavior
JFQA 1978 DEC VOL 13 p 1003.

(2367)
Fraser D R, Richards R M
The persistence of bank profitability: evidence and
explanation
QREB 1978 VOL 18:4 p 98.

(2368)
Kopecky K J
Nonmember banks and empirical measures of the
variability of reserves and money: A theoretical
appraisal
JF 1978 VOL 33 p 311.

(2369)
Martell T F, Fitts R L
Determinants of bank trust department usage
JBR 1978 SPRING VOL 9:1.

(2370)
Ricketts D, Stover R
An examination of commercial bank financial
ratios
JBR 1978 SUMMER VOL 9:2.

(2371)
Smith T R, Martin D
The determinants of manpower costs in the examination of banks in the Second Federal Reserve District
JBR 1978 AUTUMN VOL 9:3.

(2372)
Stover R D, Alexander G J
Bank managed equity common trust funds. A performance analysis
JBR 1978 WINTER VOL 8:4.

(2373)
Tinsley D B
Personnel administration in bank holding companies
JBR 1978 SPRING VOL 9:1.

(2374)
Angermueller H H, Taylor M A
Commercial vs investment bankers
HBR 1977 SEPT-OCT VOL 55:5 p 132-144.

(2375)
Beighley H P
The risk perceptions of bank holding company debtholders
JBR 1977 SUMMER VOL 8:2.

(2376)
Boyd K, Mabert V A
A two stage forecasting approach at Chemical Bank of New York for check processing
JBR 1977 SUMMER VOL 8:2.

(2377)
Brown S W, Smith R L II, Zurowski G
The appropriateness and applicability of image research to banking
JBR 1977 SUMMER VOL 8:2.

(2378)
Edwards F R
Managerial objectives in regulated industries: expense-preference behavior in banking
JPE 1977 FEB VOL 85:1 p 147-162.

(2379)
Fortson J C, Dince R R
An application of goal programming to management of a country bank
JBR 1977 WINTER VOL 7:4.

(2380)
Mandell L, Lundsten L L
Diversion of credit life insurance commissions by bankers
JBR 1977 SUMMER VOL 8:2.

(2381)
McCall A S, Peterson M O
The impact of De Novo Commercial Bank entry
JF 1977 VOL 32 p 1587.

(2382)
Savage D T
Money and banking
Wiley, 1977.

(2383)
Sealey C W Jr, Lindley J T
Inputs, outputs and a theory of production and cost at depository financial institutions
JF 1977 VOL 32 p 1251.

(2384)
Spong K, Hoenig T
An examination of individual bank growth
JBR 1977 WINTER VOL 7:4.

(2385)
Anderson R N, Haslem J A, Leonard J B
An empirical analysis of the impact of branching on demand deposit variability
JFQA 1976 SEP VOL 11 p 455.

(2386)
Berman P I
Differentials in discount facility administration: some empirical evidence
JBR 1976 SUMMER VOL 7:2.

(2387)
Boyd J, Breen W
Classroom simulation as a pedagogical device in teaching money and banking
JFQA 1976 NOV VOL 11.

(2388)
DePamphilis D M
Establishing confidence levels for economic indicators used in forecasting bank related variables
JBR 1976 AUTUMN VOL 7:3.

(2389)
Greenbaum S I, Ali M M, Merris R C
Monetary policy and banking profits
JF 1976 VOL 31 p 89.

(2390)
Kane E J
The teaching of money and banking
JFQA 1976 NOV VOL 11.

(2391)
Mayne L S
Management policies of bank holding companies and bank performance
JBR 1976 SPRING VOL 7:1.

(2392)
Milutinovich J S, Stremmel S C
Reduction of terminal response time in an expanding real time banking system
JBR 1976 WINTER VOL 6:4.

(2393)
Moondra S L
An L P model for workforce scheduling for banks
JBR 1976 WINTER VOL 6:4.

(2394)
Pool A A
Attitudes toward consumer banking packages: an empirical analysis
JBR 1976 SPRING VOL 7:1.

(2395)
Reed E W et al.
Commercial banking
P-H, 1976.

(2396)
Simkin M G, Sprague R H Jr
Staffing for bank telephone inquiry systems: a decision analysis
JBR 1976 SUMMER VOL 7:2.

(2397)
Taylor B W III, Moore L J
A simulation approach to planning bank projects
JBR 1976 AUTUMN VOL 7:3.

(2398)
Adar Z, Agmon T et al.
Output mix and jointness in production in the banking firm
JMCB 1975 MAY VOL 7:2 p 235-243.

(2399)
Cupta M C, Walker D A
Dividend disbursal practices in commercial banking
JFQA 1975 SEP VOL 10 p 515..

(2400)**Edelstein R H**
Improving the selection of credit risks: An analysis of a commercial bank minority lending program
JF 1975 VOL 30 p 37.

(2401)
Grandmont J, Laroque G
On money and banking
REStud 1975 VOL 42 p 207.

(2402)
Havrilesky T, Schweitzer R L
Non-price competition among banking firms
JBR 1975 SUMMER VOL 6:2.

(2403)
Jessup P F, Stolz R W
Customer alternatives among rural banks
JBR 1975 SUMMER VOL 6:2.

(2404)
Lovati J M
The changing competition between commercial banks and thrift institutions for deposits
F R Bk St Louis Rev 1975 VOL 57:7.

(2405)
Meinster D R, Mohindru R K
Determinants of the demand for correspondent balances by small and medium sized banks
JBR 1975 SPRING VOL 6:1.

(2406)
Mingo J J
Capital management and profitability of prospective holding company banks
JFQA 1975 JUN VOL 10 p 191.

(2407)
Royer M H
Simulation at Banque de Bruxelles
JBR 1975 WINTER VOL 5:4.

(2408)
Stone B K
Allocating credit lines, planned borrowing and tangible services over a company's banking system
FIN MGMT 1975 SUMMER VOL 4 p 65.

(2409)
Whiting D P
Elements of banking
Macdonald and Evans, 1975.

(2410)
Benson D
Banking's present and future competitors: thrift institutions
JBR 1974 AUTUMN VOL 5:2.

(2411)
Boorman J T
The prospects for minority-owned commercial banks: a comparative performance analysis
JBR 1974 WINTER VOL 4:4 p 263-279.

(2412)
Chalmers E
The money world: a guide to money and banking in the age of inflation
Macmillan, 1974.

(2413)
Fraser D R, Phillips W Jr, Rose P S
A canonical analysis of bank performance
JFQA 1974 MAR VOL 9 p 287.

(2414)
Hinderliter R H
Market access, uncertainty and reserve-position adjustments of large commercial banks in the 1960's
JF 1974 VOL 29 p 41.

(2415)
Hosek W R, Zahn F
Credit and the demand for time deposits
QREB 1974 VOL 14:3 p 109.

(2416)
Hoskins C R
Impact of change on bank personnel and the management process
JBR 1974 AUTUMN VOL 5:2.

(2417)
Lawrence R J
Operating policies of bank holding companies--part II: Nonbanking subsidiaries
F R Bul 1974 VOL 60:3.

(2418)
Long R H
Impact of technological change on bank products and customers
JBR 1974 AUTUMN VOL 5:2.

(2419)
Longbrake W A
Bank holding companies
FIN MGMT 1974 WINTER VOL 3 p 10.

(2420)
Mayer M
The bankers
New York: Weybright and Talley, 1974.

(2421)
Moore W R
Impact of technological change on internal bank operations
JBR 1974 AUTUMN VOL 5:2.

(2422)
Peterson M O, McLaughlin H S
Conflict of interest and the financing of commercial bank stock ownership
JBR 1974 SPRING VOL 5:1 p 7-12.

(2423)
Pringle J
The imperfect-markets model of commercial bank financial management
JFQA 1974 JAN VOL 9 p 69-87.

(2424)
Ryder F R, Jenkins D B eds.
Thomson's dictionary of banking. 12th ed
Pitman, 1974.

(2425)
Towey R E
Money creation and the theory of the banking
firm
JF 1974 VOL 29 p 57.

(2426)
White D L
The present value approach to selecting bank
customers
JBR 1974 SUMMER VOL 5:2 p 96-101.

(2427)
White G C Jr
Bank cooperation and competition: where to draw
the line
JBR 1974 AUTUMN VOL 5:2.

(2428)
Boyd J H
Bank strategies in the retail demand deposit
markets
JBR 1973 SUMMER VOL 4:2.

(2429)
Coyne T J
Commercial bank profitability by function
FIN MGMT 1973 SPRING VOL 2 p 64.

(2430)
Darnell J C
Banking structure: what does the future hold?
F R Bk Bus Rev Philadelphia 1973 AUG.

(2431)
Falkenberg J F
The sources of bank profitability
JBR 1973 SUMMER VOL 4:2.

(2432)
Hagerman R L
The efficiency of the market for bank stocks: an
empirical test
JMCB 1973 AUG VOL 5:3 p 846-855.

(2433)
Harris D G
Some evidence on differential lending practices at
commercial banks
JF 1973 VOL 28 p 1303.

(2434)
Johnson H E
Strategic planning for banks
JBR 1973 SUMMER VOL 4:2.

(2435)
Levy S J
Consumer views of bank services
JBR 1973 SUMMER VOL 4:2.

(2436)
Longbrake W A
Computers and the cost of producing banking
services: planning and control considerations
JBR 1973 AUTUMN VOL 4:3 p 194-202.

(2437)
McCall A S, Walker D A
The effects of control status on commercial bank
profitability
JFQA 1973 SEP VOL 8:4 p 637-646.

(2438)
Nicholson E A, Litschert R L
Long range planning in banking: ten cases in the
U S and Britain
JBR 1973 SPRING VOL 4:1.

(2439)
Pringle J J
A theory of the banking firm
JMCB 1973 NOV VOL 5:4 p 990-996.

(2440)
Walters A A ed.
Money and banking: selected readings
Penguin, 1973.

(2441)
Wentz J, Mazza G
The acquisitive bank holding companies: a bigger
role in mortgage banking
F R Bk Bus Rev Philadelphia 1973 OCT.

(2442)
Baltensperger E
Costs of banking activities, interactions between risk and operating cost
JMCB 1972 AUG VOL 4:3 p 595-611.

(2443)
Benston G J
Overdraft banking: its implications for monetary policy, the commercial banking industry & individual banks
JBR 1972 SPRING VOL 3:1 p 7-25.

(2444)
Cacy J A, Bedford M E
Commercial bank profitability: 1961-71
F R Bk Kansas City Mo Rev 1972 SEP-OCT.

(2445)
Eilon S, Fowkes T R ed.
Applications of management science in banking and finance
Gower, 1972.

(2446)
Eisenbeis R A
Nonlocal banking markets for business loans
JBR 1972 WINTER VOL 2:4 p 41-47.

(2447)
Hagerman R L
The value of regulation F: an empirical test
JBR 1972 AUTUMN VOL 3:3 p 178-185.

(2448)
Herbst A F
Truth in lending, regulation Z: comments on closed-end contract interest rate disclosure requirements
JBR 1972 SUMMER VOL 3:2.

(2449)
Smith K V, Goudzwaard M B
Profitability of bank trust management
JBR 1972 AUTUMN VOL 3:3 p 166-177.

(2450)
Strawser R H
A comparative study of the perceived adequacy of financial reporting practices of commercial banks
JBR 1972 WINTER VOL 2:4 p 48-58.

(2451)
Watson H J, Vroman H W
A heuristic model for processing overdrafts
JBR 1972 AUTUMN VOL 3:3 p 186-188.

(2452)
Bower R S, Downes D H
The time-sharing decision in banking
JBR 1971 AUTUMN VOL 2:3..

(2453)**Gies T G, Apilado V P eds.**
Banking markets and financial institutions
Irwin, 1971.

(2454)
Gilbert G G, Murphy N B
Competition between thrift institutions and commercial banks: an examination of the evidence
JBR 1971 SUMMER VOL 2:2.

(2455)
Haslem J A, Longbrake W A
A discriminant analysis of commercial bank profitability
QREB 1971 VOL 11:3 p 39.

(2456)
Holden J M
Jones and Holden's studies in practical banking.
6th ed
Pitman, 1971.

(2457)
Boughton J M
Econometric models, a decision making tool for bank management
JBR 1970 SUMMER VOL 1:2 p 9-19.

(2458)
Crane D B
Marketing strategy and bank service interaction
JBR 1970 SUMMER VOL 1:2 p 49-56.

(2459)
Reed E W, Woodland D L
Cases in commercial banking
Appleton, 1970.

(2460)
Slocum J W Jr, Strawer R H
The impact of job level, geographical location and
organisational size on the managerial satisfaction
of bankers
JBR 1970 AUTUMN VOL 1:3 p 41-49.

(2461)
Strawser R H
Trends in the financial reporting practices of
commercial banks
JBR 1970 SUMMER VOL 1:2 p 20-29.

(2462)
Masten J T, Haynes W W
Programmed text in money and banking
P-H, 1969.

(2463)
Prather C L
Money and banking. 9th ed
Irwin, 1969.

(2464)
Wolf C R
A model for selecting commercial bank
government security portfolios
REStat 1969 FEB VOL 51 p 40-52.

(2465)
Binhammer H H
Money, banking and the Canadian financial
system
Methuen, 1968.

(2466)
Fiske H S
The banks learn to live with report cards
II 1968 MAY VOL 2.

(2467)
**International Bank for Reconstruction and
Development@aInternational** Development
Association
Multilateral regional financing institutions
The Bank and The Association, 1968.

(2468)
Meznerics I
Banking business in socialist economy with special
regard to East-West trade
Leyden: A W Sijthoff, 1968.

(2469)
Pesek B P, Saving T R
The foundations of money and banking
Macmillan, 1968.

(2470)
Redlich F
The moulding of American banking: men and
ideas
Johnson Reprint, 1968.

(2471)
Smith H M
The essentials of money and banking
Random, 1968.

(2472)
Whittlesey C R, Wilson J S G eds
Essays in money and banking in honour of R S
Sayers
Oxford U Pr, 1968.

(2473)
Whittlesey C R et al.
Money and banking: analysis and policy. 2nd ed
Collier Macmillan, 1968.

(2474)
Wolf H A, Doenges R C eds.
Readings in money and banking
Appleton, 1968.

(2475)
Orsinger R
Banks of the world. Trans. by D S Ault
Macmillan, 1967.

(2476)
Sayers R S
Modern banking. 7th ed
Oxford U Pr, 1967.

(2477)
Scott R H
A conditional theory of banking enterprise
(in Pontecorvo G et al., eds., Issues in banking
and monetary analysis. HR & W, 1967.)

(2478)
Baughn W H, Walker C E eds.
The banker's handbook
Dow Jones-Irwin, 1966.

(2479)
Cohen K J,   Hammer F S eds.
Analytical methods in banking
Irwin, 1966.

(2480)
Frazer W J,   Yohe W P
Introduction to the analytics and institutions of money and banking
Van N-Rein, 1966.

(2481)
Galbraith J A
The economics of banking operations: a Canadian study
McGill-Queens U Pr, 1963.

(2482)
Reed E W
Commercial bank management
Har-Row, 1963.

(2483)
Crosse H D
Management policies for commercial banks
P-H, 1962.

(2484)
Durand D
Bank stock prices and the bank capital problem
Natl Bur Econ Res, 1957.

8.11   Bank market structure

(2485)
Amel D F,   Jacowski M J
Trends in banking structure since the mid-1970s
F R Bul 1989 MAR VOL 75:3.

(2486)
Berger A N,   Hannan T H
The price-concentration relationship in banking
REStat 1989 VOL 71 p 291.

(2487)
Amel D F,   Rhoades S A
Strategic groups in banking
REStat 1988 VOL 70 p 685.

(2488)
Bryan L L
Breaking up the bank: rethinking an industry under siege
Dow Jones-Irwin, 1988.

(2489)
Evanoff D D
Branch banking and service accessibility
JMCB 1988 MAY VOL 20:2 p 191-202

(2490)
Institutional Investor
The remaking of American banks
II 1988 MAR p 98-104.

(2491)
Miller S M
Counterfactual experiments of deregulation on banking structure
QREB 1988 VOL 28:4 p 38.

(2492)
Osborne D K
Competition and geographical integration in commercial bank lending
JBankF 1988 VOL 12:1 p 85-104.

(2493)
Tsutsui W M
Banking policy in Japan: American efforts at reform during the occupation
Routledge, 1988.

(2494)
Ayati M B,   Papazian N
Navigating through a banking complex
Journal of Systems Management 1987 DEC VOL 38:12 p 9-19.

(2495)
Boot A,   Thakor A V,   Udell G F
Competition, risk neutrality and loan commitments
JBankF 1987 VOL 11 p 449-471.

(2496)
Curtis C,   Baker J C
The evolution of the Super Edge: regulation and operations of Edge Act banks
Journal of World Trade Law 1987 DEC VOL 21:6 p 25-36.

(2497)
Jain A K, Gupta S
Some evidence on 'herding' behavior of U.S. banks
JMCB 1987 FEB VOL 19:1 p 78-89.

(2498)
Savage D T
Interstate banking developments
F R Bul 1987 VOL 73:2.

(2499)
Boyd J H, Graham S L
Risk, regulation, and bank holding company expansion into nonbanking
F R Bk Minneapolis Q Rev 1986 VOL 10:2.

(2500)
Grady J, Weale M
British banking, 1960-85
Macmillan, 1986.

(2501)
Howcroft J B, Lavis J
Retail banking: the new revolution in structure and strategy
Blackwell, 1986.

(2502)
Pozdena R J
Structure and performance: some evidence from California banking
F R Bk San Francisco Ec Rev 1986 WINTER.

(2503)
Wilson J S G
Banking policy and structure: a comparative analysis
Croom Helm, 1986.

(2504)
Duncan F H
Intermarket bank expansions: implications for interstate banking
JBR 1985 SPRING VOL 16:1 p 16-21.

(2505)
Keeley M C
The regulation of bank entry
F R Bk San Francisco Ec Rev 1985 SUMMER..

(2506)**Keeley M C, Zimmerman G C**
Determining geographic markets for deposit

competition in banking
F R Bk San Francisco Ec Rev 1985 SUMMER.

(2507)
Korobow L, Budzeika G
Financial limits on interstate bank expansion
F R Bk New York Q Rev 1985 SUMMER VOL 10:2.

(2508)
Walter I
Barriers to trade in banking and financial services
Trade Policy Research Centre, 1985.

(2509)
Billingsley R S, Lamy R E
Market reaction to the formation of one-bank holding companies and the 1970 Bank Holding Company Act amendment
JBankF 1984 VOL 8 p 21.

(2510)
Booth J R, Smith R L II
The impact of the Community Reinvestment Act on branching activity of financial institutions
JBR 1984 SUMMER VOL 15:2.

(2511)
Curry T J, Rose J T
Bank holding company presence and banking market performance
JBR 1984 WINTER VOL 14:4.

(2512)
Francke H-H, Hudson M
Banking and finance in West Germany
Croom Helm, 1984.

(2513)
Ladenson M L, Bombara K J
Entry in commercial banking 1962-78
JMCB 1984 MAY VOL 16:2 p 165-174.

(2514)
Schuster L
Profitability and market share of banks
JBR 1984 SPRING VOL 15:1.

(2515)
Curry T J, Rose J T
Multibank holding companies: recent evidence on
competition and performance in banking markets
JBR 1983 AUTUMN VOL 14:3.

(2516)
Flannery M J
Correspondent services and cost economies in
commercial banking
JBankF 1983 VOL 7 p 83.

(2517)
Rose J T
Branch banking and the state/national charter
decision
JBR 1983 SUMMER VOL 14:2.

(2518)
Rose J T, Savage D T
Bank holding company de novo entry bank
performance and holding company size
QREB 1983 WINTER VOL 23:4 p 54-62

(2519)
Swary I
Bank acquisition of non-bank firms: An empirical
analysis of administrative decisions
JBankF 1983 VOL 7 p 213.

(2520)
Curry T J, Rose J T
Multibank holding companies: recent evidence on
competition and performance in banking markets
F R Bul 1982 VOL 68:1.

(2521)
Faith N
Safety in numbers: the mysterious world of Swiss
banking
Hamilton, 1982.

(2522)
Frieder L A, Apilado V P
Bank holding company research: classification,
synthesis and new directions
JBR 1982 SUMMER VOL 13:2.

(2523)
King B F
Future holding company lead banks: Federal
Reserve standards and records
JBR 1982 SUMMER VOL 13:2.

(2524)
Savage D T
Developments in banking structure, 1970-81
F R Bul 1982 VOL 68:2.

(2525)
Savage D T
Branch banking laws. Deposits, market share and
profitability of new banks
JBR 1982 WINTER VOL 12:4.

(2526)
Aharony J, Swary I
Effects of the 1970 Banks Holding Company Act:
evidence from capital markets
JF 1981 SEP VOL 36:4 p 841-853.

(2527)
Cole R T
Financial performance of small banks, 1977-80
F R Bul 1981 VOL 67:6.

(2528)
Houpt J V
Performance   and   characteristics   of   Edge
corporations
F R Bul 1981 VOL 67:1.

(2529)
Kane E J
Accelerating inflation technological innovation
and the decreasing effectiveness of banking
regulation
JF 1981 MAY VOL 36:2 p 355-367.

(2530)
Prindl A R
Japanese finance: a guide to banking in Japan
Wiley, 1981.

(2531)
Boczar G E
The external growth of multibank holding
companies
JBR 1980 AUTUMN VOL 11:3.

(2532)
McCall A S
The impact of bank structure on bank service to local communities
JBR 1980 SUMMER VOL 11:2.

(2533)
McCall A S, Savage D T
Branching policy: the options
JBR 1980 SUMMER VOL 11:2.

(2534)
Rhoades S A
The competitive effects of interstate banking
F R Bul 1980 VOL 66:1.

(2535)
Savage D T, Solomon E H
Branch banking: the competitive issues
JBR 1980 SUMMER VOL 11:2.

(2536)
Stover R D
The single-subsidiary bank holding company
JBR 1980 SPRING VOL 11:1.

(2537)
Suzuki Y
Money and banking in contemporary Japan: the theoretical setting and its application
Yale U Pr, 1980.

(2538)
Fraser D R, Seaver W L
Branch banking and the availability of banking services in metropolitan areas
JFQA 1979 MAR VOL 14 p 153.

(2539)
Graddy D B, Kyle R
The simultaneity of bank decision-making market structure and bank performance
JF 1979 MAR VOL 34:1 p 1-18.

(2540)
Guenther H
Banking in the United States
Banker Research Unit, 1979.

(2541)
Guttentag J M, Thomas K H
Branch banking and bank structure: some evidence from Alabama
JBR 1979 SPRING VOL 10:1.

(2542)
Olson L M, Lord J D
Market area characteristics and branch bank performance
JBR 1979 SUMMER VOL 10:2.

(2543)
Rhoades S A, Rutz R D
Impact of bank holding companies on competition and performance in banking markets
F R Bul 1979 VOL 65:8.

(2544)
Savage D T, Humphrey D B
Branching laws and banking offices
JMCB 1979 MAY VOL 11:2 p 227-230.

(2545)
Shin T S, Lynge M J Jr
Rural banking markets in Illinois: an empirical test
JBR 1979 SUMMER VOL 10:2.

(2546)
Benson W J
London clearing banks' evidence to the Wilson Committee
NWBQR 1978 MAY p 2-7.

(2547)
Black H A
The dichotomization of bank markets over time: the case of Washington D C
JBR 1978 WINTER VOL 8:4.

(2548)
Burke J
Bank holding company behavior and structural change
JBR 1978 SPRING VOL 9:1.

(2549)
Lackman C L, Minami W N
Market profiles by lending institutions
JBR 1978 AUTUMN VOL 9:3.

(2550)
Mastropasqua S
The banking system in the countries of the EEC:
institutional and structural aspects
Alphen aan den Rijn, Netherlands: Sijthoff &
Noordhoff International, 1978.

(2551)
Ali M M, Greenbaum S M
A spatial model of the banking industry
JF 1977 VOL 32 p 1283.

(2552)
Boczar G E
Market characteristics and multibank holding
company acquisitions
JF 1977 VOL 32 p 131.

(2553)
Ederington L H, Skogstad S L
Measurement of banking competition and
geographic markets
JMCB 1977 AUG VOL 9:3 p 469-482.

(2554)
Heggestad A A
Market structure, risk and profitability in
commercial banking
JF 1977 VOL 32 p 1207.

(2555)
Heggestad A A, Mingo J J
The competitive condition of U S banking
markets and the impact of structural reform
JF 1977 VOL 32 p 649.

(2556)
Mayne L S
A comparative study of bank holding company
affiliates and independent banks, 1969-1972
JF 1977 VOL 32 p 147.

(2557)
Phillips A
CMC, Heller, Hunt, FIA, FRA, and FINE:
the neglected aspect of financial reform
JMCB 1977 NOV VOL 9:4 p 636-641.

(2558)
Robertson D H, Bellenger D N
Identifying bank market segments
JBR 1977 WINTER VOL 7:4..

(2559)**Eisemann P C**
Diversification & the congeneric banking holding
company
JBR 1976 SPRING VOL 7:1.

(2560)
Rhoades S A
Characteristics of banking markets entered by
foothold acquisition
JME 1976 VOL 2 p 399.

(2561)
Boczar G E
The evidence on competition between commercial
banks and finance companies
JBR 1975 SUMMER VOL 6:2.

(2562)
Eisenbeis R A
The allocative effects of branch banking
restrictions on business loan markets
JBR 1975 SPRING VOL 6:1.

(2563)
Holland R C
Bank holding companies and financial stability
JFQA 1975 NOV VOL 10 p 577.

(2564)
Throop A W
Capital investment and entry in commercial
banking
JMCB 1975 MAY VOL 7:2 p 193-211.

(2565)
Weber W E
Monetary assets, net wealth, and banking
structure
JMCB 1975 AUG VOL 7:3 p 331-342.

(2566)
Gilbert G G, Longbrake W A
The effects of branching by financial institutions
on competition, productive efficiency and stability:
an examination of the evidence (Part 2)
JBR 1974 WINTER VOL 4:4 p 298-307.

(2567)
Jacobs D P, Beighley H P
Changing structure of banking and its future impact on banks
JBR 1974 AUTUMN VOL 5:2.

(2568)
Marcus W R
Financing tomorrow's bank growth
JBR 1974 AUTUMN VOL 5:2.

(2569)
Nadler P S
The territorial hunger of our major banks
HBR 1974 MAR-APR VOL 52:2 p 87-98.

(2570)
Scott W L, Shatto G
Social efficiency in banking: a stochastic model of bank growth
QREB 1974 VOL 14:3 p 85.

(2571)
Benston G J
The optimal banking structure: theory and evidence
JBR 1973 WINTER VOL 3:4 p 220-237.

(2572)
Gilbert G G, Longbrake W A
The effects of branching by financial institutions on competition, productive efficiency and stability: an examination of the evidence (Part 1)
JBR 1973 AUTUMN VOL 4:3 p 154-167.

(2573)
Mason J B, Mayer M L
Consumer perceptions of affiliated banking
JBR 1972 AUTUMN VOL 3:3 p 189-191.

(2574)
Chandross R H
The impact of new bank entry on unit banks in one bank towns
JBR 1971 AUTUMN VOL 2:3.

(2575)
Kramer R L
Forecasting branch bank growth patterns
JBR 1971 WINTER VOL 1:4 p 17-24.

(2576)
Eisenbeis R A
A study of geographic banking markets for business loans
JBR 1970 SPRING VOL 1:1.

(2577)
Griffiths B
Competition in banking
Inst Econ Aff, 1970.

(2578)
Nevin E, Davis E W
The London clearing banks
Elek, 1970.

(2579)
Fischer G C
American banking structure
Columbia U Pr, 1968.

(2580)
Whale P B
Joint stock banking in Germany: a study of the German creditbanks before and after the War
Cass, 1968.

(2581)
Dacey W M
The British banking mechanism. 4th ed
Hutchinson, 1967.

(2582)
Guttentag J M, Herman E S
Banking structure and performance
NYU, 1967.

(2583)
Crick W F ed.
Commonwealth banking systems
Oxford U Pr, 1965.

(2584)
Beckhart B H ed.
Banking systems: a definitive comparison and authoritative account of the banking systems of sixteen countries
Columbia U Pr, 1964.

(2585)
American Bankers Association
The commercial banking industry: a monograph prepared for the Commission on Money and Credit
P-H, 1962.

(2586)
Sayers R S ed.
Banking in Western Europe
Oxford U Pr, 1962.

8.111   Economies of scale, market concentration, and bank mergers

(2587)
Bertin W J, Ghazanfari F, Torabzadeh K M
Failed bank acquisitions and successful bidders' returns
FIN MGMT 1989 SUMMER VOL 18 p 93.

(2588)
Bourke P
Concentration and other determinants of bank profitability in Europe, North America and Australia
JBankF 1989 MAR VOL 13:1 p 65-80.

(2589)
Cheng D C, Gup B E, Wall L D
Financial determinants of bank takeovers
JMCB 1989 VOL 21 p 524-536.

(2590)
Dubofsky D A, Fraser D R
The differential impact of two significant court decisions concerning banking consolidation
JBankF 1989 JUL VOL 13:3 p 339-354.

(2591)
Hannan T H, Wolken J D
Returns to bidders and targets in the acquisition process: evidence from the banking industry
JFSR 1989 VOL 3:1 p 5-16.

(2592)
Lawrence C
Banking costs, generalized functional forms, and estimation of economies of scale and scope
JMCB 1989 VOL 21 p 368-379.

(2593)
Rose P S
Diversification of the banking firm
FR 1989 MAY VOL 24:2 p 251-280.

(2594)
Boyd J H, Graham S L
The profitability and risk effects of allowing bank holding companies to merge with other financial firms: a simulation study
F R Bk Minneapolis Q Rev 1988 VOL 12:2.

(2595)
Cebenoyan A S
Multiproduct cost functions and scale economies in banking
FR 1988 NOV VOL 23:4 p 499-512.

(2596)
Goldberg L G, Hanweck G A
What we can expect from interstate banking
JBankF 1988 VOL 12 p 51-67.

(2597)
Gup B E, Walter J R
Profitable large banks: the key to their success
MCFJ 1988 WINTER VOL 5 p 24-29.

(2598)
Sushka M E, Bendeck Y
Bank acquisitions and stockholders' wealth
JBankF 1988 DEC VOL 12:4 p 551-562.

(2599)
Hannan T H, Rhoades S A
Acquisition targets and motives: The case of the banking industry
REStat 1987 VOL 69 p 67.

(2600)
James C, Wier P
Returns to acquirers and competition in the acquisition market : the case of banking
JPE 1987 APR VOL 95:2 p 355-370.

(2601)
Neely W P
Banking aquisitions: Acquirer and target shareholder returns
FIN MGMT 1987 WINTER VOL 16 p 66.

(2602)
Trifts J W, Scanlon K P
Interstate bank mergers: the early evidence
JFR 1987 VOL 10:4 p 305-312.

(2603)
Kilbride B J, McDonald B, Miller R E
A reexamination of economies of scale in banking
using a generalized functional form
JMCB 1986 NOV VOL 18:4 p 519-526.

(2604)
Beatty R P, Reim J F, Schapperie R F
The effect of barriers to entry on bank
shareholder wealth: implications for interstate
banking
JBR 1985 SPRING VOL 16:1 p 8-15.

(2605)
Nelson R W
Branching, scale economies and banking costs
JBankF 1985 VOL 9 p 177.

(2606)
Pettway R H, Trifts J W
Do banks overbid when acquiring failed banks?
FIN MGMT 1985 SUMMER VOL 14 p 5-15.

(2607)
Smirlock M
Evidence on the (non) relationship between
concentration and profitability in banking
JMCB 1985 FEB VOL 17:1 p 69-83.

(2608)
Welch P J, Naes J L Jr
The merger guidelines, concentration and excess
capacity in local commercial banking markets
JBR 1985 AUTUMN VOL 16:3 p 158-160.

(2609)
Gilligan T W, Smirlock M L, Marshall W
Scale and scope economies in the multi-product
banking firm
JME 1984 MAY VOL 13 p 393-405.

(2610)
Gilligan T W, Smirlock M L
An empirical study of joint production and scale
economies in commercial banking
JBankF 1984 VOL 8 p 67.

(2611)
James C
An analysis of the effect of state acquisition laws
on managerial efficiency: the case of the bank
holding company acquisitions
JLE 1984 VOL 27:1 p 211-226..

(2612)**Labue M**
Categorical bank acquisitions
JBR 1984 WINTER VOL 14:4.

(2613)
Murphy N B, Rogers R C
The line of commerce in retail financial
institutions mergers: some evidence from
consumer data in New England
JBR 1984 SPRING VOL 15:1.

(2614)
Rose J T, Savage D T
De novo entry and performance of bank holding
companies versus independent banks
JBR 1984 SUMMER VOL 15:2.

(2615)
Stutzer M J
Probable future competition in banking antitrust
determination: research findings
F R Bk Minneapolis Q Rev 1984 VOL 8:3.

(2616)
Gilbert R A
Economies of scale in correspondent banking
JMCB 1983 NOV VOL 15:4 p 483-488.

(2617)
Hannan T H
Bank profitability and the threat of entry
JBR 1983 SUMMER VOL 14:2.

(2618)
Harvard Law Review
The line of commerce for commercial bank
mergers: a product oriented redefinition
HLR 1983 VOL 96:4 p 907-926.

(2619)
Benston G J, Hanweck G A, Humphrey D B
Scale economies in banking: a restructuring and
reassessment
JMCB 1982 NOV VOL 14:4 p 435-456.

(2620)
Harvard Law Review
Commercial bank mergers: the case for procedural
and substantive deregulation
HLR 1982 VOL 95:8 p 1914-1934.

(2621)
Rhoades S A
Bank expansion and merger activity by state
1960-1975
JBR 1982 WINTER VOL 12:4.

(2622)
Rose J T, Savage D T
Bank holding company de novo entry and banking
market deconcentration
JBR 1982 SUMMER VOL 13:2.

(2623)
Stover R D
A re-examination of bank holding company
acquisitions
JBR 1982 SUMMER VOL 13:2.

(2624)
Curry T J
The pre-acquisition characteristics of banks
acquired by multibank holding companies
JBR 1981 SUMMER VOL 12:2.

(2625)
Fortune
Small banks stand up to the Goliaths
F 1981 JAN 26 VOL 103:2 p 28ff.

(2626)
Koch T W
Commercial bank size. Relative profitability and
the demand for tax-exempt securities
JBR 1981 AUTUMN VOL 12:3.

(2627)
Trebing M E
The new bank-thrift competition: will it affect
bank acquisition and merger analysis?
F R Bk St Louis Rev 1981 VOL 63:2.

(2628)
Fellows J A, Beard T R
Some welfare implications of legal restrictions on
commercial bank entry
JBR 1980 AUTUMN VOL 11:3.

(2629)
McCall A S
Economies of scale. Operating efficiencies and the
organizational structure
JBR 1980 SUMMER VOL 11:2.

(2630)
Schweitzer P, Green J
Determinants and consequences of market entry:
a case study of two Wisconsin banking markets
JBR 1979 WINTER VOL 9:4.

(2631)
Hobson H A, Masten J T, Severiens J T
Holding company acquisitions and bank
performance: a comparative study
JBR 1978 SUMMER VOL 9:2.

(2632)
Mullineaux D J
Economies of scale and organizational efficiency
in banking: A profit-function approach
JF 1978 VOL 33 p 259.

(2633)
Rhoades S A, Schweitzer P
Foothold acquisitions and bank market structure
F R Bul 1978 VOL 64:7.

(2634)
Rose J T
The attractiveness of banking markets for de novo
entry
JBR 1977 WINTER VOL 7:4.

(2635)
Heggestad A A, Mingo J J
Prices, nonprices, and concentration in
commercial banking
JMCB 1976 FEB VOL 8:1 p 107-118.

(2636)
Heggestad A A, Rhoades S A
Concentration and firm stability in commercial
banking
REStat 1976 NOV VOL 58:4 p 446-452.

(2637)
Rose P S
The pattern of bank holding company acquisitions
JBR 1976 AUTUMN VOL 7:3.

(2638)
Carey R G
Evaluation under the Bank Merger Act of 1960 of
the competitive factors involved in bank mergers:
the regulatory agencies compared
JME 1975 VOL 1 p 275.

(2639)
Eisenbeis R A
Differences in federal regulatory agencies' bank
merger policies
JMCB 1975 FEB VOL 7:1 p 93-104.

(2640)
Gilbert G G
An analysis of federal regulatory decisions on
market extension bank mergers
JMCB 1975 FEB VOL 7:1 p 81-92.

(2641)
Longbrake W A, Haslem J A
Productive efficiency in commercial banking: the
effects of size and legal form of organization on
the cost of producing demand deposit services
JMCB 1975 AUG VOL 7:3 p 317-330.

(2642)
Rhoades S A
Clarification of the potential competition doctrine
in bank merger analysis
JBR 1975 SPRING VOL 6:1.

(2643)
Edwards L N, Edwards F R
Measuring the effectiveness of regulation: the case
of bank entry regulation
JLE 1974 VOL 17 p 445.

(2644)
Gilbert G G
Predicting de novo expansion in bank merger
cases
JF 1974 VOL 29 p 151.

(2645)
Jessup P F
Analyzing acquisitions by bank holding companies
JBR 1974 SPRING VOL 5:1 p 55-62.

(2646)
Piper T R, Weiss S J
The profitability of multibank holding company
acquisitions
JF 1974 VOL 29 p 163.

(2647)
Roades S A, Yeats A J
Growth, consolidation and mergers in banking
JF 1974 VOL 29 p 1397.

(2648)
Yeats A J
A framework for evaluating potential competition
as a factor in bank mergers and acquisitions
JMCB 1974 AUG VOL 6:3 p 395-403.

(2649)
Daniel D L, Longbrake W A, Murphy N B
The effect of technology on bank economies of
scale for demand deposits
JF 1973 VOL 28 p 131.

(2650)
Darnell J C
Bank mergers: prices paid to marriage partners
F R Bk Bus Rev Philadelphia 1973 JUL.

(2651)
Johnson R D, Meinster D R
The analysis of bank holding company
acquisitions: some methodological issues
JBR 1973 SPRING VOL 4:1.

(2652)
Moyer R C, Sussna E
Registered bank holding company acquisitions: A
cross-selection analysis
JFQA 1973 SEP VOL 8:4 p 647-664.

(2653)
Snider T E
The effect of merger on the lending behavior of
rural unit banks in Virginia
JBR 1973 SPRING VOL 4:1.

(2654)
Yeats A J
An analysis of the effect of mergers on banking
market structure
JMCB 1973 MAY VOL 5:2 p 623-636.

(2655)
Baltensperger E
Economies of scale, firm size and concentration
in banking
JMCB 1972 AUG VOL 4:3 p 467-488.

(2656)
Kaufman G G
Deposit variability and bank size
JFQA 1972 DEC VOL 7 p 2087.

(2657)
Cohen K J,   Reid S R
The benefits and costs of bank mergers
JFQA 1966 DEC VOL 1 p 15-57.

8.112   Bank regulation/ deregulation

(2658)
Bundt T P,   Schweitzer R
Deregulation, deposit markets, and banks' costs of
funds
FR 1989 AUG VOL 24:3 p 417-430.

(2659)
Hall M J B
Handbook of banking regulation and supervision
Woodhead-Faulkner, 1989.

(2660)
Millon-Cornett M H
Stock   market   reactions   to   the   depository
institutions deregulation and monetary control act
of 1980
JBankF 1989 MAR VOL 13:1 p 81-100.

(2661)
Aharony J, Saunders A, Swary I
The effects of DIDMCA on bank stockholders'
returns and risk
JBankF 1988 VOL 12:3 1988 p 317-332.

(2662)
Avery R B, Belton T M, Goldberg M A
Market discipline in regulating bank risk: new
evidence from the capital markets
JMCB 1988 NOV VOL 20:4 p 597-610.

(2663)
Greenspan A
Innovation and regulation of banks in the 1990s
F R Bul 1988 DEC VOL 74:12.

(2664)
VanHoose D D
Deregulation and oligopolistic rivalry in bank
deposit markets
JBankF 1988 VOL 12:3 p 379-388..

(2665)**Cosimano T F**
The federal funds market under bank deregulation
JMCB 1987 AUG VOL 19:3 p 326-339.

(2666)
Kareken J H
The   emergence   and   regulation   of   contingent
commitment banking
JBankF 1987 VOL 11 p 359-377.

(2667)
Lucas D,   McDonald R L
Bank portfolio choice with private information
about loan quality: theory and implications for
regulation
JBankF 1987 VOL 11 p 473-497.

(2668)
Martin J D,   Keown A J
One-bank   holding   company   formation   and   the
1970 Bank Holding Company Act Amendment: an
empirical examination allowing for industry group
effects
JBankF 1987 VOL 11 p 213-221.

(2669)
Mullineux A W
UK banking after deregulation
Croom Helm, 1987.

(2670)
Schaefer S M
The design of bank regulations and supervision,
some lessons from the theory of finance
(in Portes R and Swoboda A, Threats to
international financial stability. Cambridge U Pr,
1987.)

(2671)
Cooper K, Fraser D R
Banking deregulation and the new competition in financial services
Ballinger, 1986.

(2672)
Jehle G A
Regulation and the public interest in banking
JBankF 1986 VOL 10 p 549.

(2673)
Keeley M C, Furlong F T
Bank regulation and the public interest
F R Bk San Francisco Ec Rev 1986 SPRING.

(2674)
Miron J A
Financial panics, the seasonality of the nominal interest rate, and the founding of the Fed
AER 1986 VOL 76 p 125-140.

(2675)
Poulsen A B
Japanese bank regulation and the activities of U.S. offices of Japanese banks
JMCB 1986 AUG VOL 18:3 p 366-373.

(2676)
Seidman W L
The American experience: Bank supervision in the United States
(in Dale R ed., Financial deregulation. Cambridge U Pr, 1986.)

(2677)
Corrigan E G
Bank supervision in a changing financial environment
F R Bk New York Q Rev 1985-86 WINTER VOL 10:4.

(2678)
Fraser D R, Richards R M, Fosberg R H
A note on deposit rate deregulation, super nows and bank security returns
JBankF 1985 VOL 9 p 585.

(2679)
Harvard Law Review
The demise of the bank/nonbank distinction: an argument for deregulating the activities of bank holding companies
HLR 1985 VOL 98:3 p 650-668.

(2680)
Kolari J, DiClemente J
A case study of geographic deregulation: the new Illinois Bank Holding Company Act
JBR 1985 AUTUMN VOL 16:3 p 150-157.

(2681)
Lam C H, Chen A H
Joint effects of interest rate deregulation and capital requirements on optimal bank portfolio adjustments
JF 1985 JUN VOL 40:2 p 563-575.

(2682)
Pozdena R J, Hotti K L
Developments in British banking: lessons for regulation and supervision
F R Bk San Francisco Ec Rev 1985 FALL.

(2683)
Rolnick A J, Weber W E
Banking instability and regulation in the U.S. free banking era
F R Bk Minneapolis Q Rev 1985 VOL 9:3.

(2684)
Dale R
The regulation of international banking
Woodhead-Faulkner, 1984.

(2685)
Huertas T
An economic brief against Glass-Steagall
JBR 1984 AUTUMN VOL 15:3.

(2686)
Kaufman G G, Mote L R, Rosenblum H
Consequences of deregulation for commercial banking
JF 1984 JUL VOL 39:3 p 789-805.

(2687)
Mahajan A, Rose P S
Banking in North America : regulation and innovation
CJWB 1984 WINTER VOL 19:4 p 69-82.

(2688)
Marcus A J
Deregulation and bank financial policy
JBankF 1984 VOL 8 p 557.

(2689)
McCarthy F W Jr
The evolution of the bank regulatory structure: a reappraisal
F R Bk Richmond Ec Rev 1984 VOL 70:3.

(2690)
Solomon A M
Banking deregulation - where do we go from here?
F R Bk New York Q Rev 1984 AUTUMN VOL 9:3.

(2691)
Benston G J
Federal regulation of banking: analysis and policy recommendations
JBR 1983 WINTER VOL 13:4.

(2692)
Cohen K J
Reform of banking regulation: an overview
JBR 1983 SPRING VOL 14:1.

(2693)
Hester D D
Deregulation and locational rents in banking
JBR 1983 SPRING VOL 14:1.

(2694)
Rigelman B
National banks and the brokerage business: the Comptroller's new reading of the Glass-Steagall Act
VLR 1983 VOL 69:7 p 1303-1349.

(2695)
Struck P L, Mandell L
The effect of bank deregulation on small business : a note
JF 1983 JUN VOL 38:3 p 1025-1031.

(2696)
Walker D A
U S banking regulations and foreign banks' entry into the United States
JBankF 1983 VOL 7 p 569.

(2697)
Crafton S M
An empirical test of the effect of usury laws
JLE 1980 VOL 23:1 p 135.

(2698)
Goldberg L G, White L J eds.
The deregulation of the banking and securities industries
Lexington Bks, 1979.

(2699)
Miller R J
A note on the cost analysis of a commercial bank regulatory agency as a multiproduct firm: implications for regulatory reorganization
JBR 1979 WINTER VOL 9:4..

(2700)**Juncker G R**
A new supervisory system for rating banks
F R Bk New York Q Rev 1978 SUMMER VOL 3:2.

(2701)
OECD
Regulations affecting international banking operations of banks and non-banks in France, Germany, the Netherlands, Switzerland, the UK
OECD, 1978.

(2702)
Mingo J J, Wolkowitz B
The effects of regulation on bank balance sheet decisions
JF 1977 VOL 32 p 1605.

(2703)
Brown M V
The prospects for banking reform
FAJ 1976 MAR-APR p 14-25.

(2704)
Bank of England
The supervision of the UK banking system
BEQB 1975 VOL 15 p 188.

(2705)
Chase S B Jr, Mingo J J
Diversification of commercial bank and non-bank activities: The regulation of bank holding companies
JF 1975 MAY VOL 30:2 p 281-292.

(2706)
Goldberg L G
The effect of state banking regulations on bank credit card use
JMCB 1975 FEB VOL 7:1 p 105-112.

(2707)
Mingo J J
Regulatory influence on bank capital investment
JF 1975 VOL 30 p 1111.

(2708)
Senate Committee on Banking, Housing and Urban Affairs
Compendium of major issues in bank regulation
US Govt, 1975.

(2709)
Storrs T I
Freedom for banks
JF 1975 MAY VOL 30:2 p 293.

(2710)
Melvin D J
Future direction of bank regulation and legislation
JBR 1974 AUTUMN VOL 5:2.

(2711)
Kalish L III, Gilbert R A
The influence of bank regulation on the operating efficiency of commercial banks
JF 1973 VOL 28 p 1287.

(2712)
Meltzer A H
Aggregative consequences of removing restrictions
JBR 1972 SUMMER VOL 3:2.

8.113 Federal Reserve membership and reserve requirements

(2713)
Kolari J, Mahajan A, Saunders E M
The effect of changes in reserve requirements on bank stock prices
JBankF 1988 VOL 12:2 p 183-198.

(2714)
Kopecky K J
A mean-variance framework for analyzing reserve requirements and monetary control
JBankF 1988 VOL 12 p 151-160.

(2715)
Kanatas G
Commercial paper, bank reserve requirements, and the informational role of loan commitments
JBankF 1987 VOL 11 p 425-448.

(2716)
Humphrey D B
Resource use in federal reserve check and ACH operations after pricing
JBR 1985 SPRING VOL 16:1 p 45.

(2717)
Vogt M G, Hanna R S
Variation of the federal funds rate and bank reserve management
JBR 1984 AUTUMN VOL 15:3.

(2718)
Greenbaum S I
Legal reserve requirements: a case study in bank regulation
JBR 1983 SPRING VOL 14:1.

(2719)
Mitchell D W
The effects of interest-bearing required reserves on bank portfolio riskiness
JFQA 1982 JUN VOL 17:2 p 209-216.

(2720)
Benston G J
Federal reserve membership: consequences, cost benefits and alternatives
JBR 1980 SPRING VOL 11:1.

(2721)
Gambs C M
State reserve requirements and bank cash assets
JMCB 1980 AUG VOL 12:3 p 462-470.

(2722)
D'Antonia L J, Melicher R W
Changes in Federal Reserve membership: a risk-return profitability analysis
JF 1979 SEP VOL 34:4 p 987-997.

(2723)
Rose J T
Federal reserve system attrition since 1960
JBR 1979 SPRING VOL 10:1.

(2724)
Goldberg L G, Rose J T
Do state reserve requirements matter?
JBR 1977 SPRING VOL 8:1.

(2725)
Rose P S
Banker attitudes toward the federal reserve system: survey results
JBR 1977 SUMMER VOL 8:2.

(2726)
Coats W L Jr
What do reserve carry-overs mean for bank management and for free reserves?
JBR 1976 SUMMER VOL 7:2.

(2727)
Goldberg L G
The effect on nonmember banks of the imposition of member bank reserve requirements-with and without federal reserve services
JF 1976 VOL 31 p 1457.

(2728)
Mayne L S
Deposit reserve requirements: time for change
JBR 1976 WINTER VOL 6:4.

(2729)
Poole W
A proposal for reforming bank reserve requirements in the United States
JMCB 1976 MAY VOL 8:2 p 137-147.

(2730)
Prestopino C J
Do higher reserve requirements discourage federal reserve membership?
JF 1976 VOL 31 p 1471.

(2731)
Thurston T B
Regional interaction and the reserve adjustment lag within the commercial banking sector
JF 1976 VOL 31 p 1443.

(2732)
Fraser D R, Rose P S, Schugart G L
Federal reserve membership and bank performance: The evidence from Texas
JF 1975 MAY VOL 30:2 p 641-658.

(2733)
Gilbert G G, Peterson M O
The impact of changes in federal reserve membership on commercial bank performance
JF 1975 VOL 30 p 713.

(2734)
Fulmer J
The effect of Federal Reserve System membership on the earnings of commercial banks in South Carolina
JBR 1974 WINTER VOL 4:4 p 314-315.

(2735)
Gilbert G G, Peterson M O
Uniform reserve requirements on demand deposits: some policy issues
JBR 1974 SPRING VOL 5:1 p 38-44.

(2736)
Burns A F
The structure of reserve requirements
F R Bul 1973 VOL 59:5.

(2737)
Mayne L S
The deposit reserve requirement recommendations of the Commission on Financial Structure & Regulation: analysis and critique
JBR 1973 SPRING VOL 4:1.

(2738)
Mayne L S
The effect of Federal Reserve System membership
on the profitability of Illinois banks, 1961-1963
Penn St U, 1967.

(2739)
Federal Reserve System
The Federal Reserve System: purposes and
functions. 5th ed
Washington, DC: Board of Governors, 1963.

8.12 Bank asset and liability structure

(2740)
Rosen R J, Lloyd-Davies P, Humphrey D B
New banking powers: a portfolio analysis of bank
investment in real estate
JBankF 1989 JUL VOL 13:3 p 355-366.

(2741)
Brodt A I
Optimal bank asset and liability management with
financial futures
JFM 1988 AUG VOL 8:4 p 457-482.

(2742)
Kaufman G G
Securities activities of commercial banks: recent
changes in the economic and legal environments
MCFJ 1988 WINTER VOL 5 p 14-23.

(2743)
Morgan G E, Shome D K, Smith S D
Optimal futures positions for large banking firms
JF 1988 MAR VOL 43:1 p 175-196.

(2744)
Pennachi G G
Loan sales and the cost of bank capital
JF 1988 JUN VOL 43:2 p 375-396.

(2745)
Wilson J S G ed.
Managing bank assets and liabilities
Euromoney Publications, 1988.

(2746)
Bedoni M
Strategies simulation in an aggregate bank model
EJOR 1987 JUN VOL 30:1 p 24-29.

(2747)
Greenbaum S I, Thakor A V
Bank funding modes: securitization versus
deposits
JBankF 1987 VOL 11 p 379-401.

(2748)
James C
Off-balance sheet banking
F R Bk San Francisco Ec Rev 1987 FALL.

(2749)
Kolari J, Zardkoohi A
Bank costs, structure, and performance
Heath, 1987.

(2750)
Korhonen A
A dynamic bank portfolio planning model with
multiple scenarios multiple goals and changing
priorities
EJOR 1987 JAN VOL 30:1 p 13-23.

(2751)
Lucas D, McDonald R L
Bank portfolio choice with private information
about loan quality: theory and implications for
regulation
JBankF 1987 VOL 11 p 473-497.

(2752)
McCormick J M
The role of securitization in transforming banks
into more efficient financial intermediaries
MCFJ 1987 FALL VOL 5 p 50-61..

(2753)**Meeker L G, Gray L**
A note on non-performing loans as an indicator
of asset quality
JBankF 1987 VOL 11 p 161-168.

(2754)
Smith S D, Gregory D W, Weiss K A
A note on quantity versus price risk and the
theory of financial intermediation
JF 1987 DEC VOL 42:5 p 1377-1384.

(2755)
Sprenkle C M
Liability and asset uncertainty for banks
JBankF 1987 VOL 11 p 147-159.

(2756)
Fortune
Banks seek life beyond lending
F 1986 MAR 3 VOL 113:5 p 54-57.

(2757)
Keeley M C, Zimmerman G C
Deposit rate deregulation and the demand for
transactions media
F R Bk San Francisco Ec Rev 1986 SUMMER.

(2758)
Stanhouse B
Commercial bank portfolio behaviour and
endogenous uncertainty
JF 1986 DEC VOL 41:5 p 1103-1114.

(2759)
Szego G P
Bank asset management and financial insurance
JBankF 1986 VOL 10 p 295.

(2760)
Koppenhaver G D
A note on managing deposit flows with cash and
futures market decisions
JBankF 1985 VOL 9 p 323.

(2761)
Scott J A, Hempel G H, Peavy J W III
The effect of stock-for-debt swaps on bank
holding companies
JBankF 1985 VOL 9 p 233.

(2762)
Borio C E V
A test of the mean-variance model of bank
behaviour on Italian data
Greek Economic Review 1984 VOL 6:1.

(2763)
Flannery M J, James C M
Market evidence on the effective maturity of bank
assets and liabilities
JMCB 1984 NOV VOL 16:4 p 435-445.

(2764)
Jacobs R L
The rate maturity of prime and other indexed
assets or liabilities
JBR 1984 SUMMER VOL 15:2.

(2765)
Jahera J S Jr, Sinkey J F Jr
A note on the intracyclical balance-sheet behavior
of large commercial banks: 1972-1978
JBankF 1984 VOL 8 p 109.

(2766)
Bruni F
Interest and exchange rate volatility: implications
for bank management
Giornale degli Economisti e Annali di Economia
1983 VOL 42:7-8.

(2767)
Deshmukh S D, Greenbaum S I, Kanatas G
Lending policies of financial intermediaries facing
credit and funding risk
JF 1983 JUN VOL 38:3 p 873-886.

(2768)
Simonson D G, Stowe J D, Watson C J
A canonical correlation analysis of commercial
bank asset/liability structures
JFQA 1983 MAR VOL 18:1 p 125-140.

(2769)
Bashir B A
Portfolio management of Islamic banks: "Certainty
model"
JBankF 1983 VOL 7 p 339.

(2770)
Cargill T F, Meyer R A
Dynamic portfolio behavior of commercial banks
: an integrated analysis
QREB 1982 SPRING VOL 22:1 p 67-80

(2771)
Howard D H
The British banking system's demand for cash
reserves
JME 1982 VOL 9 p 21

(2772)
Judd J P, Scadding J L
Liability management, bank loans and deposit
"market" disequilibrium
F R Bk San Francisco Ec Rev 1981 SUMMER.

(2773)
Priewasser E
Implementation of OR/MS models in German
banks
JBR 1981 SUMMER VOL 12:2.

(2774)
Buser S A
Efficient risk/return management in commercial
banking
JBR 1980 WINTER VOL 10:4.

(2775)
LaForge R L, Wood Jr. D R
Use of operations research in the planning
activities of large U S banks
JBR 1980 AUTUMN VOL 11:3.

(2776)
Rush M
Comment and further evidence on "implicit
interest" on demand deposits
JME 1980 VOL 6 p 437.

(2777)
Schweser C, Cole J, D'Antonio L
Hedging opportunities in bank risk management
programs
JCBL 1980 JAN VOL 62 p 29-41.

(2778)
Cohen K J, Lam C H
A linear programming planning model for bank
holding companies
JBR 1979 AUTUMN VOL 10:3.

(2779)
Eatman J L, Sealey C W Jr
A multiobjective linear programming model for
commercial bank balance sheet management
JBR 1979 WINTER VOL 9:4.

(2780)
Fielitz B D, Loeffler T A
A linear programming model for commercial bank
liquidity management
FIN MGMT 1979 AUTUMN VOL 8 p 41.

(2781)
Kane E J, Buser S A
Portfolio diversification at commercial banks
JF 1979 MAR VOL 34:1 p 19-34.

(2782)
Melnik A
Demand deposit variability in banks: a time series
analysis
JBR 1979 SUMMER VOL 10:2.

(2783)
Santomero A M
The role of transaction costs and rates of return
on the demand deposit decision
JME 1979 VOL 5 p 343.

(2784)
Startz R
Implicit interest on demand deposits
JME 1979 VOL 5 p 515.

(2785)
Francis J C
Portfolio analysis of asset and liability
management in small-medium and large-sized
banks
JME 1978 VOL 4 p 459.

(2786)
Fraser D R, Rose P S
Commercial bank adjustments to monetary policy:
the speed of response
JBR 1978 WINTER VOL 8:4.

(2787)
Heggestad A A, Mingo J J
On the usefulness of functional cost analysis data
JBR 1978 WINTER VOL 8:4.

(2788)
Roering K J, Smith P E
A distributed lag forecasting model for bank loans
and the money supply
JBR 1978 SUMMER VOL 9:2.

(2789)
Barth J R, Kraft A et al.
A utility maximization approach to individual bank asset selection
JMCB 1977 MAY VOL 9:2 p 316-327.

(2790)
Eatman J L, Sealey C W Jr
A spectral analysis of aggregate commercial bank liability management and its relationship to short-run earning asset behavior
JFQA 1977 DEC VOL 12 p 767.

(2791)
Harrison W B
Observed characteristics of fifth district member banks' deposit distributions
JBR 1977 AUTUMN VOL 8:3.

(2792)
McKinney G
Use of models in the management of bank funds
JBR 1977 SUMMER VOL 8:2.

(2793)
Sutherland R J
Income velocity and commercial bank portfolios
JF 1977 VOL 32 p 1752.

(2794)
Watson R D
The marginal cost of funds concept in banking
JBR 1977 AUTUMN VOL 8:3.

(2795)
Baltensperger E, Milde H
Predictability of reserve demand, information costs and portfolio behavior of commercial banks
JF 1976 VOL 31 p 835.

(2796)
Echols M E, Elliott J W
Forecasting vs. allocation efficiency in bank asset planning
JBR 1976 WINTER VOL 6:4.

(2797)
Fabozzi F J, Trovato S
The use of quantitative techniques in commercial banks
JBR 1976 SUMMER VOL 7:2.

(2798)
Hendershott P H, Orlando F S
The interest rate behavior of flow of funds and bank reserves financial models
JMCB 1976 NOV VOL 8:4 p 497-512.

(2799)
McCallum J S
The Canadian chartered banks & the government of Canada bond market: ex post efficient portfolios & actual holdings
JBR 1976 SPRING 76 VOL 7:1.

(2800)
Serfaty A
The kinked supply function for savings banks deposits
JBR 1976 SPRING VOL 7:1.

(2801)
Watson R D, Oldfield G S, Santomero A M
A symposium on the capital structure of banks
FIN MGMT 1976 WINTER VOL 5 P 53.

(2802)
Aghili P, Cramer R H, Thompson H E
Asset-liability management-applying two-stage programming models
JBR 1975 WINTER VOL 5:4.

(2803)
Balzano R V
A model to forecast a bank's daily net clearing house liability
JBR 1975 AUTUMN VOL 6:3.

(2804)
Barth J R, Bennett J T
Deposit variability and commercial bank cash holdings
REStat 1975 MAY VOL 57:2 p 238-241.

(2805)
Black F
Bank funds management in an efficient market
JFE 1975 VOL 2 p 323..

(2806)**Clinch J H M Jr**
Liquidity imbalances: profits & penalties
JBR 1975 AUTUMN VOL 6:3.

(2807)
Moag J S, Jacobs D P
The effects of direct payroll deposits on the use of bank services
JBR 1975 WINTER VOL 5:4.

(2808)
Wood J H
Commercial bank loan and investment behaviour
Wiley, 1975.

(2809)
Feige E L
Alternative temporal cross-section specifications of the demand for demand deposits
JF 1974 VOL 29 p 923.

(2810)
Fry C L
An explanation of short-run fluctuations in the ratio of currency to demand deposits
JMCB 1974 AUG VOL 6:3 p 403-412.

(2811)
Greenbaum S I, Ali M M
Need interest rates on bank loans and deposits move sympathetically?
JF 1974 VOL 29 p 963.

(2812)
Lane M
Short-term money management for bank portfolios
JBR 1974 SUMMER VOL 5:2 p 102-119.

(2813)
Pattison J C
Bank deposit variability: some further evidence
JBR 1974 WINTER VOL 4:4 p 308-310.

(2814)
Bradley S P, Crane D B
Management of commercial bank goverment security portfolios: an optimization approach under uncertainty
JBR 1973 SPRING VOL 4:1.

(2815)
Coats W L Jr
Regulation D and the vault cash game
JF 1973 VOL 28 p 601.

(2816)
Cramer R H, Miller R B
Development of a deposit forecasting procedure for use in bank financial management
JBR 1973 SUMMER VOL 4:2.

(2817)
Fraser D R, Rose P S
Short-run bank portfolio behavior: An examination of selected liquid assets
JF 1973 VOL 28 p 531.

(2818)
Lifson K A, Blackmarr B R
Simulation and optimization models for asset deployment and funds sources balancing profit, liquidity and growth
JBR 1973 AUTUMN VOL 4:3 p 239-255.

(2819)
Longbrake W A
Murphy's method for determining the weights assigned to demand deposit items: a clarification and extension
JBR 1973 SUMMER VOL 4:2.

(2820)
Pye G
Sequential policies for bank money management
MSci 1973 NOV VOL 20:3 p 385-395.

(2821)
Robinson R S
BANKMOD: an interactive simulation aid for bank financial planning
JBR 1973 AUTUMN VOL 4:3 p 212-224.

(2822)
Silverberg S C
Deposit costs and bank portfolio policy
JF 1973 VOL 28 p 881.

(2823)
Verbrugge J A
The effects of pledging regulations on bank asset composition
JBR 1973 AUTUMN VOL 4:3 p 168-176.

(2824)
Booth G G
Programming bank portfolios under uncertainty:
an extension
JBR 1972 WINTER VOL 2:4 p 28-40.

(2825)
Brown G F
Optimal management of bank reserves
JFQA 1972 DEC VOL 7 p 2031.

(2826)
Cohen K J
Dynamic balance sheet management: a
management science approach
JBR 1972 WINTER VOL 2:4 p 9-19.

(2827)
Derwa L
Computer models: aids to management at Societe
Generale de Banque
JBR 1972 SUMMER VOL 3:2.

(2828)
Walker D A
A recursive programming approach to bank asset
management
JFQA 1972 DEC VOL 7 p 2055.

(2829)
Aigner D J, Bryan W R
A model of short-run bank behavior
QJE 1971 FEB VOL 85 p 97-118.

(2830)
Budzeika G
A model of business loan behavior of large New
York City banks
JBR 1971 WINTER VOL 1:4 p 58-72.

(2831)
Cohen K J, Rutenberg D P
Toward a comprehensive framework for bank
financial planning
JBR 1971 WINTER VOL 1:4 p 41-57.

(2832)
Crane D B
A stochastic programming model for commercial
bank bond portfolio management
JFQA 1971 JUN VOL 6 p 955-976.

(2833)
Jacobs D P, Lerner E M, Moag J S
Guidelines for designing bank planning models
and information systems
JBR 1971 SPRING VOL 2:1.

(2834)
Lastavica J
Asset management and other financial simulation
models
JBR 1971 SPRING VOL 2:1.

(2835)
Magen S D
The cost of funds to commercial banks: an
econometric analysis
New York: Dunellen, 1971.

(2836)
Murphy N B
A statistical approach to determining the weights
to be assigned activity items in the demand
deposit function
JBR 1971 AUTUMN VOL 2:3.

(2837)
Renwick F B et al.
Portfolio management for commercial banks
Presidents, 1971.

(2838)
Cohen K J, Thore S
Programming bank portfolios under uncertainty
JBR 1970 SPRING VOL 1 p 42-61.

(2839)
Fried J S
Bank portfolio selection
JFQA 1970 JUN VOL 5 p 203-228.

(2840)
Gray K B Jr
Managing the balance sheet: a mathematical
approach to decision making
JBR 1970 SPRING VOL 1:1 p 35-42.

(2841)
Melnik A
Short run determinants of commercial bank
investment portfolios: an empirical analysis
JF 1970 JUN VOL 25 p 639-649.

(2842)
Reich K E, Gray K B Jr, Hochenwarter W P
Balance sheet management: a simulation approach
JBR 1970 AUTUMN VOL 1:3.

(2843)
Bryan W R, Carleton W T
Short-run adjustments of an individual bank
Em 1967 APR VOL 35 p 321-347.

(2844)
Cohen K J, Hammer F S
Linear programming and optimal bank asset
management decisions
JF 1967 MAY VOL 22 p 147-165.

(2845)
Pierce J L
An empirical model of commercial bank portfolio
management
(in Hester D D and Tobin J eds., Studies of
portfolio behavior. Wiley, 1967.)

(2846)
Ruffin R J
Free reserves, vault cash and the portfolio
behavior of banks
JPE 1967 DEC VOL 75 p 889-892.

(2847)
Woodworth G W
The management of cyclical liquidity of
commercial banks
Bankers, 1967.

(2848)
Haydon R B, Wicks J M
A model of commercial bank earnings assets
selection
JFQA 1966 JUN VOL 1 p 99-113.

(2849)
Hester D D, Zoellner J F
The relation between bank portfolios and
earnings: an econometric analysis
REStat 1966 NOV VOL 48 p 372-386.

(2850)
Morrison G R
Liquidity preferences of commercial banks
U of Chicago Pr, 1966.

(2851)
Beazer W F
Optimizing of bank portfolios and response to
monetary policy
Northwestern U, 1965.

(2852)
Kane E J, Malkiel B G
Bank portfolio allocation, deposit variability and
the availability doctrine
QJE 1965 FEB VOL 79 p 113-134.

(2853)
Meigs J A
The changing role of banks in the market for
equities
JF 1965 MAY VOL 20 p 368-378.

(2854)
Russell W R
Commercial bank portfolio adjustments
AER 1964 MAY VOL 56 p 547-550.

(2855)
Hodgman D R
Commercial bank loan and investment policy
U of Ill Pr, 1963.

(2856)
Luckett D G
Compensatory cyclical bank asset adjustments
JF 1962 MAR VOL 17 p 53-62.

(2857)
Robinson R I
The management of bank funds. 2nd ed
McGraw, 1962.

(2858)
Bogen J I
The changing composition of bank assets
Graduate School of Business Administration,
NYU, 1961..

(2859)**Chambers D J, Charnes A**
Intertemporal analysis and optimization of bank
portfolios
MSci 1961 JUL VOL 7 p 393-410.

(2860)
Porter R C
A model of bank portfolio selection
YEE 1961 FALL VOL 1 p 323-359.

(2861)
Lyon R A
Investment portfolio management in the commercial bank
Rutgers U Pr, 1960.

(2862)
Federal Reserve Bank of Kansas City
Commercial bank investments in recession and expansion
F R Bk Kansas City Mo Rev 1959 MAR.

(2863)
Parks R H
Portfolio operations of commercial banks and the level of Treasury security prices
JF 1959 MAR VOL 14 p 52-66.

(2864)
Parks R H
Income and tax aspects of commercial bank portfolio operations in Treasury securities
NTJ 1958 MAR VOL 11 p 21-34.

(2865)
Scott I O Jr
The changing significance of Treasury bill obligations in commercial bank portfolios
JF 1957 MAY VOL 12 p 213-222.

(2866)
McEvoy R H
Variation in bank asset portfolios
JF 1956 DEC VOL 11 p 463-473.

(2867)
Coleman G W
Lending and investment practices of commercial banks
LCP 1952 WINTER VOL 17 p 108-127.

(2868)
Hunt P
Portfolio policies of commercial banks in the United States, 1920-1939
Harvard Busn, 1940.

8.121 Interest rates and bank profitability

(2869)
Mitchell K
Interest rate risk at commercial banks: an empirical investigation
FR 1989 AUG VOL 24:3 p 431-456.

(2870)
Thistle P D, McLeod R W, Conrad B L
Interest rates and bank portfolio adjustments
JBankF 1989 MAR VOL 13:1 p 151-162.

(2871)
Allen L
The determinants of bank interest margins: a note
JFQA 1988 JUN VOL 23:2 p 231-235.

(2872)
Goldfarb D R
Hedging interest rate risk in banking
JFM 1987 FEB VOL 7:1 p 35-48.

(2873)
Meyer zu Selhausen H
Exploring and controlling a bank's interest risk : Sensitivity analysis of an asset and liability co-ordination model
EJOR 1987 MAR VOL 28:3 p 261-278.

(2874)
Dermine J
The measurement of interest-rate risk by financial intermediaries
JBR 1985 SUMMER VOL 16:2 p 86-90.

(2875)
Graddy D B, Karna A S
Net interest margin sensitivity among banks of different sizes
JBR 1984 WINTER VOL 14:4.

(2876)
Deshmukh S D, Greenbaum S I, Kanatas G
Interest rate uncertainty and the financial intermediary's choice of exposure
JF 1983 MAR VOL 38:1 p 141-147

(2877)
Flannery M J
Interest rates and bank profitability: additional evidence
JMCB 1983 AUG VOL 15:3 p 355-362.

(2878)
Olson R L, Simonson D G
Gap management and market rate sensitivity in banks
JBR 1982 SPRING VOL 13:1.

(2879)
Simonson D G, Hempel G H
Improving gap management for controlling interest rate risk
JBR 1982 SUMMER VOL 13:2.

(2880)
Flannery M J
Market interest rates and commercial bank profitability : an empirical investigation
JF 1981 DEC VOL 36:5 p 1085-1101.

(2881)
Lynge M J Jr, Zumalt J K
An empirical study of the interest rate sensitivity of commercial bank returns: A multi-index approach
JFQA 1980 SEP VOL 15 p 731.

(2882)
Jacobson R, Maisel S J
Interest rate changes and commercial bank revenues and costs
JFQA 1978 NOV VOL 13 p 687.

8.13 Bank failure, capital adequacy and deposit insurance

(2883)
Arshadi N
Capital structure, agency problems, and deposit insurance in banking firms
FR 1989 FEB VOL 24:1 p 31-52.

(2884)
Engineer M
Bank runs and the suspension of deposit convertibility
JME 1989 VOL 24 p 443.

(2885)
Flannery M J
Capital regulation and insured banks' choice of individual loan default risks
JME 1989 VOL 24 p 235.

(2886)
Gilbert R A, Kochin L A
Local economic effects of bank failures
JFSR 1989 VOL 3:4 p 333-346.

(2887)
Giliberto S M, Varaiya N P
The winner's curse and bidder competition in acquisitions: evidence from failed bank auctions
JF 1989 MAR VOL 44:1 p 59-76.

(2888)
Karels G V, Prakash A J, Roussakis E
The relationship between bank capital adequacy and market measures of risk
JBFA 1989 WINTER VOL 16:5 p 663.

(2889)
Ronn E I, Verma A K
Risk-based capital adequacy standards for a sample of 43 major banks
JBankF 1989 MAR VOL 13:1 p 21-30.

(2890)
Furlong F T
Changes in bank risk-taking
F R Bk San Francisco Ec Rev 1988 SPRING.

(2891)
Hannan T H, Hanweck G A
Bank insolvency risk and the market for large certificates of deposit
JMCB 1988 MAY VOL 20:2 p 203-211.

(2892)
Jacklin C J, Bhattacharya S
Distinguishing panics and information-based bank runs: Welfare and policy implications
JPE 1988 JUN VOL 96:3 p 568-592.

(2893)
Kane E J, Unal H
Change   in   market   assessment   of
deposit-institution riskiness
Journal of Financial Services Research 1988 VOL
1.

(2894)
Keeley M C
Bank capital regulation in the 1980s: effective or
ineffective?
F R Bk San Francisco Ec Rev 1988 WINTER.

(2895)
Kim D, Santomero A M
Risk in banking and capital regulation
JF 1988 DEC VOL 43:5 p 1219-1234.

(2896)
Lawrence E C, Arshadi N
The distributional impact of foreign deposits on
federal deposit insurance premia
JBankF 1988 VOL 12 p 105-115.

(2897)
Paroush J
The domino effect and the supervision of the
banking system
JF 1988 DEC VOL 43:5 p 1207-1218.

(2898)
Peavy J W III, Hempel G H
The   Penn   Square   Bank   failure: effect   on
commercial bank security returns: a note
JBankF 1988 VOL 12 p 141-150.

(2899)
Tallman E
Some unanswered questions about bank panics
F R Bk Atlanta Ec Rev 1988 VOL 73:6.

(2900)
Belongia M T, Gilbert R A
Agricultural banks: causes of failures and the
condition of survivors
F R Bk St Louis Rev 1987 VOL 69:5.

(2901)
Benston G J
Why continue to regulate banks?: an historical
assessment of federal banking regulation
MCFJ 1987 FALL VOL 5 p 67-82.

(2902)
Benveniste L M, Berger A N
Securitization with recourse: an instrument that
offers uninsured bank depositors sequential claims
JBankF 1987 VOL 11 p 403-424.

(2903)
Furlong F T, Keeley M C
Bank capital regulation and asset risk
F R Bk San Francisco Ec Rev 1987 SPRING.

(2904)
Greenbaum S I, Thakor A V
Bank   funding   modes: securitization   versus
deposits
JBankF 1987 VOL 11 p 379-401.

(2905)
Haberman G
Capital   requirements   of   commercial   and
investment banks: contrasts in regulation
F R Bk New York Q Rev 1987 AUTUMN VOL
12:3.

(2906)
Hall M J B
The Deposit Protection Scheme : the case for
reform
NWBQR 1987 AUG p 45-54.

(2907)
James C, Wier P
An analysis of failed bank auctions
JME 1987 VOL 20 p 141.

(2908)
Lomax D F
Risk asset ratios - a new departure in supervisory
policy
NWBQR 1987 AUG p 14-25.

(2909)
Morgan G E, Smith S D
The role of capital adequacy regulation in the
hedging decisions of financial intermediaries
JFR 1987 SPRING VOL 10:1 p 33-46.

(2910)
Pecchioli R M
Prudential supervision in banking
OECD, 1987.

(2911)
Pennacchi G G
A reexamination of the over (or under) pricing of
deposit insurance
JMCB 1987 AUG VOL 19:3 p 340-360..

(2912)Pennacchi G G
Alternative forms of deposit insurance: pricing
and bank incentive issues
JBankF 1987 VOL 11 p 291-312.

(2913)
Postlewaite A, Vives X
Bank runs as an equilibrium phenomenon
JPE 1987 JUN VOL 95:3 p 485-491.

(2914)
Ronn E I, Verma A K
A multi-attribute comparative evaluation of
relative risk for a sample of banks
JBankF 1987 VOL 11 p 499-523.

(2915)
Short E D
Bank problems and financial safety nets
F R Bk Dallas Ec Rev 1987 MAR.

(2916)
Thomson J B
The use of market information in pricing deposit
insurance
JMCB 1987 NOV VOL 19:4 p 528-537.

(2917)
Wall L D, Peterson D R
The effect of capital adequacy guidelines on large
bank holding companies
JBankF 1987 VOL 11 p 581-600.

(2918)
Bennett B
Off balance sheet risk in banking: the case of
standby letters of credit
F R Bk San Francisco Ec Rev 1986 WINTER.

(2919)
Benston G J et al.
Perspectives on safe and sound banking - past,
present and future
MIT Pr, 1986.

(2920)
Brickley J A, James C M
Access to deposit insurance, insolvency rules and
the stock returns of financial institutions.
JFE 1986 JUL VOL 16:3 p 345-371.

(2921)
Crouhy M, Galai D
An economic assessment of capital requirements
in the banking industry
JBankF 1986 VOL 10 p 231.

(2922)
Dermine J
Deposit rates, credit rates and bank capital: The
Klein-Monti model revisited
JBankF 1986 VOL 10 p 99.

(2923)
Fortune
Banks are safer than you think
F 1986 AUG 18 VOL 114:4 p 41-43.

(2924)
Gardener E P M ed.
UK banking supervision: evolution, practice and
issues
Allen, 1986.

(2925)
Gilbert R A, Wood G E
Coping with bank failures: some lessons from the
United States and the United Kingdom
F R Bk St Louis Rev 1986 VOL 68:10.

(2926)
Goodman L S, Santomero A M
Variable-rate deposit insurance: A re-examination
JBankF 1986 VOL 10 p 203.

(2927)
Kanatas G
Deposit insurance and the discount window :
pricing under asymmetric information
JF 1986 JUN VOL 41:2 p 437-450.

(2928)
Kane E J
Risk-related premiums
(in Benston G et al., Perspectives on safe and
sound banking, past, present and future. MIT Pr,
1986.)

(2929)
Kane E J
Appearance and reality in deposit insurance: The case for reform
JBankF 1986 VOL 10 p 175.

(2930)
Lackman C L
The impact of capital adequacy constraints on bank portfolios
JBFA 1986 WINTER VOL 13:4 p 587-596

(2931)
Lane W R, Looney S W, Wansley J W
An application of the Cox proportional hazards model to bank failure
JBankF 1986 VOL 10 p 511.

(2932)
Lefebvre O
Risk sharing in the bank deposit contract
JBFA 1986 WINTER VOL 13:4 p 547-559

(2933)
Mitchell D W
Some regulatory determinants of bank risk behavior
JMCB 1986 AUG VOL 18:3 p 374-382.

(2934)
Ronn E I, Verma A K
Pricing risk-adjusted deposit insurance : an optionbased model
JF 1986 SEP VOL 41:4 p 871-895.

(2935)
Chan Y S, Mak K-T
Depositors' welfare : deposit insurance and deregulation
JF 1985 JUL VOL 40:3 p 959-975.

(2936)
Cumming C
Federal deposit insurance and deposits at foreign branches of U.S. banks
F R Bk New York Q Rev 1985 AUTUMN VOL 10:3.

(2937)
Fortune
More capital won't cure what ails banks
F 1985 JAN 7 VOL 111:1 p 62-65.

(2938)
Gilbert R A
Recent changes in handling bank failures and their effects on the banking industry
F R Bk St Louis Rev 1985 VOL 67:6.

(2939)
Gilbert R A, Stone C C, Trebing M E
The new bank capital adequacy standards
F R Bk St Louis Rev 1985 VOL 67:5.

(2940)
Kane E
The gathering crisis in federal deposit insurance
MIT Pr, 1985.

(2941)
Short E D
FDIC settlement practices and the size of failed banks
F R Bk Dallas Ec Rev 1985 MAR.

(2942)
Van Leeuwen R H
The prediction of business failure at Rabobank
JBR 1985 SUMMER VOL 16:2 p 91-98.

(2943)
Waldo D G
Bank runs, the deposit-currency ratio and the interest rate
JME 1985 VOL 15 p 269.

(2944)
West R C
A factor-analytic approach to bank condition
JBankF 1985 VOL 9 p 253.

(2945)
Bennett B A
Bank regulation and deposit insurance: controlling the FDIC's losses
F R Bk San Francisco Ec Rev 1984 SPRING.

(2946)
Campbell T S, Glenn D
Deposit insurance in a deregulated environment
JF 1984 JUL VOL 39:3 p 775-787.

(2947)
Fortune
Putting more pain into bank failures
F 1984 FEB 20 VOL 109:4 p 89-96.

(2948)
Furlong F T
A view on deposit insurance coverage
F R Bk San Francisco Ec Rev 1984 SPRING.

(2949)
Marcus A J, Shaked I
The valuation of FDIC deposit insurance using
option pricing estimates
JMCB 1984 NOV VOL 16:4 p 446-460.

(2950)
Marcus A J, Shaked I
The relationship between accounting measures
and prospective probabilities of insolvency: an
application to the banking industry
FR 1984 MAR VOL 19:1.

(2951)
Morgan G E
On the adequacy of bank capital regulation
JFQA 1984 JUN VOL 19:2 p 141-162.

(2952)
Pyle D H
Deregulation and deposit insurance reform
F R Bk San Francisco Ec Rev 1984 SPRING.

(2953)
Rolnick A J, Weber W E
The causes of free bank failures; a detailed
examination
JME 1984 VOL 14 p 267.

(2954)
Wu H-K, Helms B P
Confidential bank examination data and the
efficiency of bank share prices
FAJ 1984 NOV-DEC VOL 40 p 31-33.

(2955)
Beebe J H
Bank capital risk in the post-1979 monetary and
deregulatory environment
F R Bk San Francisco Ec Rev 1983 SUMMER.

(2956)
Diamond D W, Dybvig P H
Bank runs, deposit insurance and liquidity
JPE 1983 VOL 91 p 401.

(2957)
Dietrich J K, James C
Regulation and the determination of bank capital
changes : a note
JF 1983 DEC VOL 38:5 p 1651-1658.

(2958)
Flannery M J
Can state bank examination data replace FDIC
examination visits?
JBR 1983 WINTER VOL 13:4.

(2959)
Guttentag J M, Herring R J
The   insolvency   of   financial   institutions:
Assessment and regulatory disposition
(in Wachtel P ed., Crises in the economic and
financial structure. Lexington Bks, 1983.)

(2960)
Kareken J H
Deposit insurance reform or deregulation is the
cart, not the horse
F R Bk Minneapolis Q Rev 1983 SPRING VOL
7:3.

(2961)
Kareken J H
The first step in bank deregulation: What about
the FDIC?
AER 1983 VOL 73 P+P p 198-204.

(2962)
Marcus A J
The bank capital decision : a time series-cross
section analysis
JF 1983 SEP VOL 38:4 p 1217-1232.

(2963)
Santomero A M
Current views of the bank capital issue
Association of Reserve City Bankers, Washington,
1983.

(2964)
Short E D, O'Driscoll G P Jr
Deregulation and deposit insurance
F R Bk Dallas Ec Rev 1983 SEP..

(2965)Sinkey J F Jr
Performance of First Pennsylvania Bank prior to
its bail out
JBR 1983 SUMMER VOL 14:2.

(2966)
Stover R D, Miller J M
Additional evidence on the capital market effect
of bank failures
FIN MGMT 1983 SPRING VOL 12 p 36-41.

(2967)
Talley S H
Bank capital trends and financing
F R Bul 1983 VOL 69:2.

(2968)
Fortune
The swinger who broke Penn Square Bank
F 1982 AUG 23 VOL 106:4 p 122-126.

(2969)
Gardener E P M
Capital adequacy and banking supervision
towards a practical system
JBR 1982 SUMMER VOL 13:2.

(2970)
Gheva D, Sokoler M
An alternative approach to the problem of
classification-the case of bank failures in Israel
JBR 1982 WINTER VOL 12:4.

(2971)
Buser S A, Chen A H, Kane E J
Federal deposit insurance regulatory policy and
optimal bank capital
JF 1981 MAR VOL 36:1 p 51-60.

(2972)
Dale R
Prudential regulation of multinational banking:
The problem outlined
NWBQR 1981 FEB p 14-24.

(2973)
Maisel S J ed.
Risk and capital adequacy in commercial banks
U of Chicago Pr, 1981.

(2974)
Bryant J
A model of bank reserves, bank runs and deposit
insurance
JBankF 1980 VOL 4 p 335-44.

(2975)
Fortune
The bet that almost broke a bank
F 1980 JUN 2 VOL 101:11 p 48-50.

(2976)
Ho T S Y, Saunders A
A catastrophe model of bank failure
JF 1980 DEC VOL 35:5 p 1189-1207.

(2977)
Koehn M, Santomero A M
Regulation of bank capital and portfolio risk
JF 1980 DEC VOL 35:5 p 1235-1244.

(2978)
McCall A S, Lane J T
Multi-office banking and the safety and soundness
of commercial banks
JBR 1980 SUMMER VOL 11:2.

(2979)
Pettway R H
Potential insolvency, market efficiency and bank
regulation of large commercial banks
JFQA 1980 MAR VOL 15 p 219.

(2980)
Pettway R H, Sinkey J F
Establishing on-site bank examination priorities:
an early-warning system using accounting and
market information
JF 1980 MAR VOL 35:1 p 137-150.

(2981)
Shick R A, Sherman L F
Bank stock prices as an early warning system for
changes in condition
JBR 1980 AUTUMN VOL 11:3.

(2982)
Talmor E
A normative approach to bank capital adequacy
JFQA 1980 NOV VOL 15 p 785.

(2983)
Haslem J A, Sachlis J M
Commercial bank capital debt, business risk, and
stock price
QREB 1979 VOL 19:4 p 53.

(2984)
Meinster D R, Johnson R D
Bank holding company diversification and the risk
of capital impairment
BellJ 1979 AUTUMN VOL 10:2 p 683-694.

(2985)
Murphy N B
Disclosure of the problem bank lists: a test of the
impact
JBR 1979 SUMMER VOL 10:2.

(2986)
Pany K, Sherman L F
Information analysis of several large failed banks
JBR 1979 AUTUMN VOL 10:3.

(2987)
Blair R D, Heggestad A A
Bank portfolio regulation and the probability of
bank failure
JMCB 1978 FEB VOL 10:1 p 88-93.

(2988)
Fraser D R, McCormack J P
Large bank failure and investor risk perceptions:
Evidence from the debt market
JFQA 1978 SEP VOL 13 p 527.

(2989)
Gardener E P M
Capital adequacy and bank prudential regulation
JBR 1978 AUTUMN VOL 9:3.

(2990)
Graham D R, Humphrey D B
Bank examination data as predictors of bank net
loan losses
JMCB 1978 NOV VOL 10:4 p 491-504.

(2991)
Sharpe W F
Bank capital adequacy, deposit insurance and
security values
JFQA 1978 NOV VOL 13 p 701.

(2992)
Sinkey J F Jr
Identifying "problem" banks: how do the banking
authorities measure a bank's risk exposure?
JMCB 1978 MAY VOL 10:2 p 184-193.

(2993)
Taggart R A, Greenbaum S I
Bank capital and public regulation
JMCB 1978 MAY VOL 10:2 p 158-169.

(2994)
Beebe J H
A perspective on liability management and bank
risk
F R Bk San Francisco Ec Rev 1977 WINTER.

(2995)
Johnson J M, Weber P G
The impact of the problem bank disclosure on
bank share prices
JBR 1977 AUTUMN VOL 8:3.

(2996)
Santomero A M, Watson R D
Determining an optimal capital standard for the
banking industry
JF 1977 VOL 32 p 1267.

(2997)
Sinkey J F Jr
Identifying large problem/failed banks: The case of
Franklin National Bank of New York
JFQA 1977 DEC VOL 12 p 779.

(2998)
Humphrey D B
100% deposit insurance: what would it cost?
JBR 1976 AUTUMN VOL 7:3.

(2999)
Pettway R H
The effects of large bank failures upon investors'
risk cognizance in the commercial banking
industry
JFQA 1976 SEP VOL 11 p 465.

(3000)
Pettway R H
Market tests of capital adequacy of large
commercial banks
JF 1976 VOL 31 p 865.

(3001)
Sinkey J F Jr
The collapse of Franklin National Bank of New
York
JBR 1976 SUMMER VOL 7:2.

(3002)
Beighley H P, Boyd J H, Jacobs D P
Bank equities and investor risk perceptions: some
entailments for capital adequacy regulation
JBR 1975 AUTUMN VOL 6:3.

(3003)
Carey G V
Reassessing the role of bank capital
JBR 1975 AUTUMN VOL 6:3.

(3004)
Friedman B M, Formuzis P
Bank capital:the deposit-protection incentive
JBR 1975 AUTUMN VOL 6:3.

(3005)
Gilbert R A
Bank failures and public policy
F R Bk St Louis Rev 1975 VOL 57:11.

(3006)
Horvitz P M
Failures of large banks: Implications for banking
supervision and deposit insurance
JFQA 1975 NOV VOL 10 p 589.

(3007)
Mayer T
Preventing the failure of large banks
(in Compendium of major issues in bank
regulation, Senate Committee on Banking,
Housing and Urban Affairs. Government Printing
Office, 1975.)

(3008)
Mayer T
Should large banks be allowed to fail
JFQA 1975 DEC VOL 10 p 603.

(3009)
Orgler Y E
Capital adequacy and recoveries from failed banks
JF 1975 VOL 30 p 1366.

(3010)
Revell J R S
Solvency and regulation of banks: theoretical and
practical implications
U of Wales Pr, 1975.

(3011)
Silverberg S C
Bank holding companies and capital adequacy
JBR 1975 AUTUMN VOL 6:3.

(3012)
Sinkey J F Jr
Adverse publicity and bank deposit flows: the
cases of Franklin National Bank of New York
and United States National Bank of San Diego
JBR 1975 SUMMER VOL 6:2.

(3013)
Sinkey J F Jr
The failure of United States National Bank of
San Diego
JBR 1975 SPRING VOL 6:1.

(3014)
Sinkey J F Jr
A multivariate statistical analysis of the
characteristics of problem banks
JF 1975 VOL 30 p 21.

(3015)
Sinkey J F Jr, Walker D A
Problem banks: identification and characteristics
JBR 1975 WINTER VOL 5:4.

(3016)
Watson J T
A regulatory view of capital adequacy
JBR 1975 AUTUMN VOL 6:3.

(3017)
Benston G J, Marlin J T
Bank examiners' evaluation of credit: an analysis
of the usefulness of substandard loan data
JMCB 1974 FEB VOL 6:1 p 23-44..

(3018)**Pringle J J**
The capital decision in commercial banks

JF 1974 VOL 29 p 779.

(3019)
Kurtz R D, Sinkey J F Jr
Bank disclosure policy and procedures, adverse
publicity and bank deposit flows
JBR 1973 AUTUMN VOL 4:3 p 177-184.

(3020)
Dince R R, Fortson J C
The use of discriminant analysis to predict the
capital adequacy of commercial banks
JBR 1972 SPRING VOL 3:1 p 54-62.

(3021)
Gibson W E
Deposit insurance in the United States:
Evaluation and reform
JFQA 1972 MAR VOL 7 p 1575.

(3022)
Cohen K J
Improving the capital adequacy formula
JBR 1970 SPRING VOL 1:1.

(3023)
Meyer P A, Pifer H W
Prediction of bank failures
JF 1970 SEP VOL 25 p 853-868.

(3024)
Durand D
Bank stock prices and the bank capital problem
Natl Bur Econ Res, 1966.

(3025)
Hahn P J
The capital adequacy of commercial banks
Am Pr, 1966.

(3026)
Federal Reserve Bank of Kansas City
Bank reactions to security losses
F R Bk Kansas City Mo Rev 1960 JUN.

8.14   Interest rate ceilings

(3027)
Unal H
Impact of deposit-rate ceiling changes on bank
stock returns
JMCB 1989 VOL 21 p 206-220.

(3028)
Rolnick A J
The benefits of bank deposit rate ceilings: new
evidence on bank rates and risk in the 1920s
F R Bk Minneapolis Q Rev 1987 VOL 11:3.

(3029)
Taylor T W, Evans J W
Islamic banking and the prohibition of usury in
Western economic thought
NWBQR 1987 NOV p 15-27.

(3030)
Gilbert R A
Requiem for Regulation Q: what it did and why
it passed away
F R Bk St Louis Rev 1986 VOL 68:2.

(3031)
Smirlock M
An analysis of bank risk and deposit rate ceilings:
evidence from the capital markets
JME 1984 VOL 13 p 195.

(3032)
Peterson R L
Usury laws and consumer credit : a note
JF 1983 SEP VOL 38:4 p 1299-1304.

(3033)
Startz R
Competition and interest rate ceilings in
commercial banking
QJE 1983 MAY VOL 98:2 p 255-265.

(3034)
Villegas D J
An analysis of the impact of interest rate ceilings
JF 1982 SEP VOL 37:4 p 941-954.

(3035)
Gilbert R A
Will the removal of regulation Q raise mortgage interest rates?
F R Bk St Louis Rev 1981 VOL 63:10.

(3036)
Lawrence E C, Elliehausen G E
The impact of Federal interest rate regulations on the small saver: further evidence
JF 1981 JUN VOL 36:3 p 677-684.

(3037)
Nathan H C
Economic analysis of usury laws
JBR 1980 WINTER VOL 10:4.

(3038)
Spellman L J
Deposit ceilings and the efficiency of financial intermediation
JF 1980 MAR VOL 35:1 p 129-136.

(3039)
Lovati J M, Gilbert R A
Do floating ceilings solve the usury rate problem?
F R Bk St Louis Rev 1979 VOL 61:4.

(3040)
Clotfelter C, Lieberman C
On the distributional impact of federal interest rate restrictions
JF 1978 VOL 33 p 199.

(3041)
Taggart R A
Effects of deposit rate ceilings
JMCB 1978 MAY VOL 10:2 p 139-157.

(3042)
Jadlow J M
Adam Smith on usury laws
JF 1977 VOL 32 p 1195.

(3043)
Murphy N B
Removing deposit interest ceilings: an analysis of deposit flows, portfolio response and income effects in Boston co-operative banks
JBR 1977 WINTER VOL 7:4.

(3044)
Sushka M E, Slovin M B
The macroeconomic impact of changes in the ceilings on deposit rates
JF 1977 VOL 32 p 117.

(3045)
Long M S
Effect of lending rate ceilings and money costs on extensions of consumer credit
JBR 1976 AUTUMN VOL 7:3.

(3046)
Longbrake W A
Commercial bank capacity to pay interest on demand deposits [Part 1]
JBR 1976 SPRING VOL 7:1.

(3047)
Longbrake W A
Commercial bank capacity to pay interest on demand deposits: earnings and cost analysis [Part II]
JBR 1976 SUMMER VOL 7:2.

(3048)
Greer D F
Rate ceilings and loan turndowns
JF 1975 VOL 30 p 1376.

(3049)
Avio K L
On the effects of statutory interest rate ceilings
JF 1974 VOL 29 p 1383.

(3050)
Pyle D H
The losses on savings deposits from interest rate regulation
BellJ 1974 AUTUMN VOL 5:2 p 614-622.

(3051)
Towey R E
The prohibition of interest on demand deposits
JBR 1971 WINTER VOL 1:4 p 8-16.

8.141   Interest-bearing deposits and compensating balances

(3052)
Clark J A, Speaker P J
Compensating balance requirements and the firm's demand for transactions balances
JBankF 1986 VOL 10 p 411.

(3053)
Keeley M C, Zimmerman G C
Competition for money market deposit accounts
F R Bk San Francisco Mo Rev 1985 SPRING.

(3054)
McCulloch J H
Interest-risk sensitive deposit insurance premia: Stable ACH estimates
JBankF 1985 VOL 9 p 137.

(3055)
Merris R C
Explicit interest and demand deposit service charges
JMCB 1985 NOV VOL 17:4 p 528-533.

(3056)
Sealey C W Jr, Heinkel R
Asymmetric information and a theory of compensating balances
JBankF 1985 VOL 9 p 193.

(3057)
Rogowski R J
Pricing the money market deposit and super-now accounts in 1983
JBR 1984 SUMMER VOL 15:2.

(3058)
Basch D L
Regulatory transition and depositor inertia: the response of Massachusetts commercial banks to NOW accounts
JBR 1983 WINTER VOL 13:4.

(3059)
Booth J R
NOW accounts: the competitive battle in the western States
JBR 1983 WINTER VOL 13:4.

(3060)
Lam C H, Boudreaux K J
Compensating balances, deficiency fees and lines of credit
JBankF 1983 VOL 7 p 307.

(3061)
Tatom J A
Money market deposit accounts, super-NOWs and monetary policy
F R Bk St Louis Rev 1983 MAR VOL 65:3.

(3062)
Basch D L
Circumventive innovation: The case of NOW accounts in Massachusetts
JBR 1982 AUTUMN VOL 13:3.

(3063)
Edmister R O
Margin analysis for consumer deposit interest rate policy
JBR 1982 AUTUMN VOL 13:3.

(3064)
Morgan G E, Becker S M
Enviromental factors in pricing NOW accounts in 1981
JBR 1982 AUTUMN VOL 13:3.

(3065)
James C
Self-selection and the pricing of bank services : an analysis of the market for loan commitments and the role of compensating balance requirements
JFQA 1981 DEC VOL 16:5 p 725.

(3066)
Simonson D G, Marks P C
Breakeven balances on NOW accounts: perils in pricing
JBR 1980 AUTUMN VOL 11:3.

(3067)
Campbell T S, Brendsel L
The impact of compensating balance requirements on the cash balances of manufacturing corporations: An empirical study
JF 1977 VOL 32 p 31.

(3068)
Gilbert R A
Effects of interest on demand deposits: implications of compensating balances
F R Bk St Louis Rev 1977 VOL 59:11.

(3069)
Kolodny R, Seeley P, Polakoff M E
The effect of compensating balance requirements on the profitability of borrowers and lenders
JFQA 1977 DEC VOL 12 p 801.

(3070)
Spellman L J
Nonrate competition for savings deposits
JBR 1977 AUTUMN VOL 8:3.

(3071)
Klein B
Competitive interest payments on bank deposits and the long-run demand for money
AER 1974 VOL 64 p 931-949.

(3072)
Longbrake W A, Cohan S B
The NOW account experiment
JBR 1974 SUMMER VOL 5:2 p 71-85.

(3073)
Batra H
Dynamic interdependence in demand for savings deposits
JF 1973 VOL 28 p 507.

(3074)
Nadler P S
Compensating balances and the prime at twilight
HBR 1972 JAN-FEB VOL 50:1 p 112ff.

(3075)
O'Brien J M
Interest ban on demand deposits: victim of the profit motive?
F R Bk Bus Rev Philadelphia 1972 AUG.

8.15 Money transmission

(3076)
Bank for International Settlements
Payment systems in eleven developed countries
Basle: Bank for International Settlements, 1989.

(3077)
Banca d'Italia
White Paper on the payment system in Italy
Rome: Banca d'Italia, 1988.

(3078)
Mitchell J
Electronic banking and the consumer: the European dimension
Policy Studies Institute, 1988.

(3079)
De Mattia R
The forces at work in the evaluation of payment systems in the 1980's
JBR 1985 WINTER VOL 15:4.

(3080)
Frazer P
Plastic and electronic money: new payment systems and their implications
Woodhead-Faulkner, 1985.

(3081)
Harvard Law Review
Consumer protection and payment systems: regulatory policy for the technological era
HLR 1985 VOL 98:8 p 1870-1889.

(3082)
Nauss R M, Markland R E
Optimization of bank transit check clearing operations
MSci 1985 SEP VOL 31:9 p 1072-1083.

(3083)
Reichert A, Strauss W, Morris R C
An economic analysis of short-run fluctuations in federal reserve wire transfer volume
JBR 1985 WINTER VOL 15:4.

(3084)
Revell J R S
Payment systems over the next decade
JBR 1985 WINTER VOL 15:4.

(3085)
Drury T, Ferrier C W
Credit cards
Butterworth, 1984.

(3086)
Davis S G, Kochenberger G A, Reutzel E T
Expressend: a check clearing decision support
system for endpoint selection
JBR 1983 AUTUMN VOL 14:3.

(3087)
Hopton D
Payment systems: a case for consensus
Basle: Bank for International Settlements, 1983.

(3088)
Davis S G, Ceto N Jr, Rabb J M
A comprehensive check processing simulation
model
JBR 1982 AUTUMN VOL 13:3.

(3089)
Stone B K, Hill N C
Alternative cash transfer mechanisms and
methods: Evaluation frameworks
JBR 1982 SPRING VOL 13 p 7-16.

(3090)
Engler R
Automation of payments in the Federal Republic
of Germany: status and future prospects
JBR 1981 WINTER VOL 11:4.

(3091)
Hogg G H J
Payment systems developments in New Zealand
JBR 1981 WINTER VOL 11:4.

(3092)
Humphrey D B
Scale economies at automated clearinghouses
JBR 1981 SUMMER VOL 12:2.

(3093)
Journal of Bank Research
Payment systems in Norway
JBR 1981 WINTER VOL 11:4.

(3094)
Kearney K J
The new payment technology
JBR 1981 WINTER VOL 11:4.

(3095)
Marbacher J
Characteristics and problems of modern payment
systems
JBR 1981 WINTER VOL 11:4.

(3096)
Starke W
Payment methods of the future
JBR 1981 WINTER VOL 11:4.

(3097)
White G C Jr
Developments in United States payment systems
JBR 1981 WINTER VOL 11:4.

(3098)
Williamson J M
Pricing money transfer services
JBR 1981 WINTER VOL 11:4.

(3099)
Fortune
Explosion in the bank-card cafeteria
F 1980 SEP 8 VOL 102:5 p 76-82.

(3100)
Humphrey D B
Are there economies of scale in check processing
at the Federal Reserve?
JBR 1980 SPRING VOL 11:1.

(3101)
Mayne L S
Funds transfer between bank holding companies
and their affiliates
JBR 1980 SPRING VOL 11:1.

(3102)
Etzel M J, Jones W H
A method for developing promotional themes based on attitudes and usage pattern of bank credit card holders
JBR 1978 WINTER VOL 8:4.

(3103)
Lewin W B
The check collection system: present and future status
JBR 1978 SUMMER VOL 9:2.

(3104)
Trolle-schultz E
International money transfer developments
JBR 1978 SUMMER VOL 9:2.

(3105)
Cornuejols G, Fisher M L, Nemhauser G L
Location of bank accounts to optimize float: an analytic study of exact and approximate algorithms
MSci 1977 VOL 23 p 789-810..

(3106)**Haas G, Zoltners A A**
A computerized bank check collection vehicle routing system
JBR 1977 AUTUMN VOL 8:3.

(3107)
Peterson R L
Factors affecting the growth of bank credit card and check credit
JF 1977 MAY VOL 32:2 p 553-564.

(3108)
Boyd J H
Household demand for checking account money
JME 1976 VOL 2 p 81.

(3109)
Fitzpatrick D B
An analysis of bank credit card profits
JBR 1976 AUTUMN VOL 7:3.

(3110)
Gambs C M
The cost of the U S payment system
JBR 1976 WINTER VOL 6:4.

(3111)
Powers R W
A survey of bank check volume
JBR 1976 WINTER VOL 6:4.

(3112)
Awh R Y, Waters D
A discriminant analysis of economic, demographic and attitudinal characteristics of bank charge-card holders: A case study
JF 1974 VOL 29 p 973.

(3113)
Mathews H L, Slocum J W Jr
Correlatives of commercial bank credit card use
JBR 1972 WINTER VOL 2:4 p 20-27.

(3114)
Fenner L M
The status of payment services today
JBR 1971 SPRING VOL 2:1.

(3115)
Van Fenstermaker J, Perry D
An examination of a charge card system operating in a smaller community through correspondent banks
JBR 1971 SPRING VOL 2:1.

(3116)
Black F
Banking and interest rates in a world without money. The effects of uncontrolled banking
JBR 1970 AUTUMN VOL 1:3.

(3117)
Fenner L M
Payment services in transition
JBR 1970 SUMMER VOL 1:2.

(3118)
Federal Reserve System
Bank credit-card and check-credit plans
Washington, DC: Board of Governors, 1968.

8.151   Electronic funds transfer and automatic teller machines

(3119)
Bright R
Smart cards: principles, practice, applications
Chichester: Ellis Horwood, 1988.

(3120)
Chorafas D N
Electronic funds transfer
Butterworth, 1988.

(3121)
Summers B J
Electronic payments in retrospect
F R Bk Richmond Ec Rev 1988 VOL 74:2.

(3122)
Kirkman P
Electronic funds transfer systems: the revolution in cashless banking and payment methods
Blackwell, 1987.

(3123)
Kouzelis A
On the determinants of ATM performance
EJOR 1987 JUN VOL 30:1 p 89-94.

(3124)
Solomon E
Electronic funds, transfers and payments: The public policy issues
Kluwer Academic, 1987.

(3125)
Reichert A, Northcutt D, Spector W
The impact of economic conditions and electronic payments technology on federal reserve check volume
JBR 1984 WINTER VOL 14:4.

(3126)
Fortune
Here comes the smart card
F 1983 AUG 8 VOL 108:3 p 74-81.

(3127)
Murphy N B
Determinants of ATM activity: the impact of card base, location, time in place and system
JBR 1983 AUTUMN VOL 14:3.

(3128)
Revell J R S
Banking and electronic fund transfers
OECD, 1983.

(3129)
Schroeder F J
Developments in consumer electronic funds transfer
F R Bul 1983 VOL 69:6.

(3130)
Weber C H
Overcoming the obstacles to implementation of point-of-sale electronic fund transfer systems: EFTA and the new uniform payments code
VLR 1983 VOL 69:7 p 1351-1379.

(3131)
Soleil M
A new payment technique: the memory card
JBR 1981 WINTER VOL 11:4.

(3132)
Colton K W, Kraemer K L eds.
Computers and banking: electronic funds transfer systems and public policy
Plenum, 1980.

(3133)
Smith D S
Electronic funds transfers: new protections for consumers, new duties for financial institutions
F R Bul 1980 VOL 66:4.

(3134)
Guenther H, White J
EFT system privacy safeguards: a preliminary inquiry into the privacy-leisure time trade-off
JBR 1979 AUTUMN VOL 10:3.

(3135)
Bernard J E, Gilbert G G, Rogers R P
Final report of the national commission on
electronic fund transfers: implications for federal
regulation of depository institutions
JBR 1978 WINTER VOL 8:4.

(3136)
Fortune
The unexpected fallout from electronic banking
F 1978 APR 8 VOL 97 p 82-87.

(3137)
Hunt A L
Corporate cash management; including electronic
funds transfer
New York: AMACOM, 1978.

(3138)
Mears P, McCarty D E, Osborn R
An empirical investigation of banking customers'
perception of bank machines
JBR 1978 SUMMER VOL 9:2.

(3139)
Morris R D
An empirical analysis of costs and revenue
requirements for a point-of-sale EFTS
JBR 1978 AUTUMN VOL 9:3.

(3140)
White G C Jr
Evaluation of the final report of the national
commission on electronic fund transfers
JBR 1978 WINTER VOL 8:4.

(3141)
Wolkowitz B
The case for the federal reserve actively
participating in electronic funds transfer
JBR 1978 SPRING VOL 9:1.

(3142)
Baxter W F, Cootner P H, Scott K E
Retail banking in the electronic age: The law and
economics of electronic funds transfer
Allanheld, Osmun & Co., 1977.

(3143)
Benton J B
Electronic funds transfer: pitfalls and payoffs
HBR 1977 JUL-AUG VOL 55:4 p 16-32, 164.

(3144)
Mandell L
Diffusion of EFTS among national banks
JMCB 1977 MAY VOL 9:2 p 341-348.

(3145)
Rhoades S A
Sharing arrangements in an electronic funds
transfer system
JBR 1977 SPRING VOL 8:1.

(3146)
Walker D A
An analysis of cash dispenser and automated
teller activity levels
JBR 1977 WINTER VOL 7:4.

(3147)
Walker D A
Contrasts among banks with retail electronic
banking machines and all insured banks: 1974
versus 1976
JBR 1977 AUTUMN VOL 8:3.

(3148)
Dingle J F
The public policy implications of EFTS
JBR 1976 SPRING VOL 7:1.

(3149)
Niblack W C
Development of electronic funds transfer systems
F R Bk St Louis Rev 1976 VOL 58:9.

(3150)
Morris R D
The Fed's RCPC performance: what does it imply
for electronic funds transfer?
JBR 1974 SUMMER VOL 5:2 p 86-91.

(3151)
Pool A A
Application of discriminant analysis in
formulation of promotional strategy for cash
dispensing machines
JBR 1974 SPRING VOL 5:1 p 13-19.

(3152)
Szatrowski Z T
A conceptual overview of the electronic fund
transfer system
JBR 1974 AUTUMN VOL 5:2.

(3153)
Richardson D W
The emerging era of electronic money: some
implications for monetary policy
JBR 1973 WINTER VOL 3:4 p 261-264.

(3154)
Hosemann M J
Measuring the impact of electronic funds transfer
system on float
JBR 1972 AUTUMN VOL 3:3 p 136-154.

(3155)
Anderson A H et al.
An electronic cash and credit system
AMA, 1966.

8.16   International banking

(3156)
Aggarwal R, Durnford J
Market assessment of international banking
activity: a study of US bank holding companies
QREB 1989 VOL 29:1 p 58.

(3157)
Ahmed S
Islamic banking and finance: a review essay
JME 1989 VOL 24 p 157.

(3158)
Bird G
Commercial bank lending and third-world debt
Macmillan, 1989..

(3159)**Blackman W**
Swiss banking in an international context
Macmillan, 1989.

(3160)
Broker G
Competition in banking
OECD, 1989.

(3161)
Hultman C W, McGee L R
Factors affecting the foreign banking presence in
the US
JBankF 1989 JUL VOL 13:3 p 383-396.

(3162)
Mathieson D J et al.
Managing financial risks in indebted developing
countries
Washington, DC: International Monetary Fund,
1989.

(3163)
Moffett M, Stonehill A
International banking facilities revisited
Journal of International Financial Management &
Accounting 1989 SPRING VOL 1:1 p 88.

(3164)
Ozler S
On the relation between reschedulings and bank
value
AER 1989 VOL 79:5 p 1117-1131.

(3165)
Power E ed.
Who owns what in world banking: 1989
Financial Times Business Information, 1989.

(3166)
Arthur Young International Banking Group
Managing international bank taxation
Euromoney Publications, 1988.

(3167)
Channon D F
Global banking strategy
Wiley, 1988.

(3168)
Donaldson T H
Lending in international commercial banking.
2nd ed
Macmillan, 1988.

(3169)
Krayenbuehl T E
Country risk: assessment and monitoring. 2nd ed
Woodhead-Faulkner, 1988.

(3170)
Lessard D R, Tschoegl A E
Panama's International Banking Center: the direct
employment effects
JBankF 1988 VOL 12 p 43-50.

(3171)
Mikdashi Z ed.
International banking: innovations and new policies
Macmillan, 1988.

(3172)
Weisbrod S R
Regulation of international banking: a review essay
JME 1988 VOL 22:2 p 347.

(3173)
Bank of England
Japanese banks in London
BEQB 1987 VOL 27 p 518-524.

(3174)
Khoury S J, Gosh A eds.
Recent developments in international banking and finance
Heath, 1987.

(3175)
Mullineux A
International banking and financial systems: a comparison
Graham & Trotman, 1987.

(3176)
Penn G A et al.
The law and practice of international banking
Sweet, 1987.

(3177)
Tschoegl A E
International retail banking as a strategy : an assessment
JIBS 1987 SUMMER VOL 18:2 p 67-88.

(3178)
Bank of England
International banking in London, 1975-85
BEQB 1986 VOL 26 p 367-378.

(3179)
Cornell B, Shapiro A C
The reaction of bank stock prices to the international debt crisis
JBankF 1986 VOL 10 p 55.

(3180)
Eaton J, Gersovitz M, Stiglitz J E
The pure theory of country risk
EER 1986 VOL 30:3.

(3181)
Guttentag J M, Herring R J
Disclosure policy and international banking
JBankF 1986 VOL 10 p 75.

(3182)
Savona P, Sutija G eds.
Strategic planning in international banking
Macmillan, 1986.

(3183)
Shapiro A C
International banking and country risk analysis
MCFJ 1986 FALL VOL 4 p 56-64.

(3184)
White B, Vittas D
Barriers in international banking
LBR 1986 JUL 161 p 19-31

(3185)
Aharony J, Saunders A, Swary I
The effects of the International Banking Act on domestic bank profitability and risk
JMCB 1985 NOV VOL 17:4 p 493-506.

(3186)
Snowden P N
Emerging risk in international banking: origins of financial vulnerability in the 1980s
Allen, 1985.

(3187)
Zenoff D B et al.
International banking management and strategies
Euromoney Publications, 1985.

(3188)
Bennett P
Applying portfolio theory to global bank lending
JBankF 1984 VOL 8 p 153.

(3189)
Brodt A I
International bank asset and liability management
JBR 1984 SUMMER VOL 15:2.

(3190)
Coulbeck N S
The multinational banking industry
Croom Helm, 1984.

(3191)
Dufey G, Giddy I H
Eurocurrency deposit risk
JBankF 1984 VOL 8 p 567.

(3192)
Born K E
International banking in the 19th and 20th centuries
Berg, 1983.

(3193)
Conybeare J A C
International bank lending: political risk and portfolio diversification
JBusR 1983 VOL 12 p 363-376.

(3194)
Crane D B, Hayes S L III
The evolution of international banking competition and its implication for regulation
JBR 1983 SPRING VOL 14:1.

(3195)
Davis S I
The management of international banks. 2nd ed
Macmillan, 1983.

(3196)
Heimann J G
The effects of political, economic and institutional development on international banks
JBankF 1983 VOL 7 p 615.

(3197)
Houpt J A
Foreign ownership of U S banks: trends and effects
JBR 1983 SUMMER VOL 14:2.

(3198)
Johnson G G
Aspects of the safety net for international banking
FD 1983 VOL 20:3.

(3199)
McKenzie G, Thomas S
Liquidity, credit creation and international banking: An econometric investigation
JBankF 1983 VOL 7 P 467.

(3200)
Niehans J
Financial innovation, multinational banking and monetary policy
JBankF 1983 VOL 7 p 537.

(3201)
Pecchioli R M
The internationalisation of banking: the policy issues
OECD, 1983.

(3202)
Roussekis N ed.
International banking: Principles and practices
Praeger, 1983

(3203)
Teeters N
The role of banks in the international financial system
JBankF 1983 VOL 7 p 453.

(3204)
Walter I, Gray H P
Protectionism and international banking: Sectoral efficiency, competitive structure and national policy
JBankF 1983 VOL 7 p 597.

(3205)
Zecher J R
The effects of the current turbulent times on American multinational banking: An overview
JBankF 1983 VOL 7 p 625.

(3206)
Ball C A, Tschoegl A E
The decision to establish a foreign bank branch or subsidiary : an application of binary classification procedures.
JFQA 1982 SEP VOL 17:3 p 411-424.

(3207)
Goldberg E S
Comparative cost analysis of foreign owned U S
banks
JBR 1982 AUTUMN VOL 13:3.

(3208)
Johns R A
The British Isle offshore finance centres
NWBQR 1982 NOV p 53-65.

(3209)
Key S J
International banking facilities
F R Bul 1982 VOL 68:10.

(3210)
Shapiro A C
Risk in international banking.
JFQA 1982 DEC VOL 17:5 p 727-739.

(3211)
White B B
Foreign banking in the United States: a
regulatory and supervisory perspective
F R Bk New York Q Rev 1982 SUMMER VOL
7:2..

(3212)**Abrams R K**
The role of regional banks in international
banking
CJWB 1981 SUMMER VOL 16:2 p 62-72.

(3213)
Bank of England
Eurobanks and the inter-bank market
BEQB 1981 VOL 21 p 351-364.

(3214)
Edwards F R
The new "international banking facility" : a study
in regulatory frustration
CJWB 1981 WINTER VOL 16:4 p 6-18.

(3215)
Goldberg L G, Saunders A
The growth of organizational forms of foreign
banks in the US
JMCB 1981 AUG VOL 13:3 p 365-374.

(3216)
Rabino S
The growth strategies of New York based foreign
banks
CJWB 1981 WINTER VOL 16:4 p 29-35.

(3217)
**United   Nations.   Centre   on   Transnational
Corporations**
Transnational banks: operations, strategies and
their effects in developing countries
UNCTC, 1981.

(3218)
Goldberg L G, Saunders A
The causes of US bank expansion overseas: the
case of Great Britain
JMCB 1980 NOV VOL 12:4 p 630-643.

(3219)
Ogilvie N R
Foreign banks in the U S and geographic
restrictions on banking
JBR 1980 SUMMER VOL 11:2.

(3220)
Mayer H
Credit and liquidity creation in the international
banking sector
Basle: Bank for International Settlements, 1979.

(3221)
Moskowitz W E
Global   asset   and   liability   management   at
commercial banks
F R Bk New York Q Rev 1979 SPRING VOL
4:1.

(3222)
Virginia Law Review
The regulation of foreign banking in the United
States after the International Banking Act of 1978
VLR 1979 VOL 65:5 p 993-1030.

(3223)
Fortune
Foreign banks are cracking the facade of US
banking
F 1978 AUG 4 VOL 98 p 94-99.

(3224)
Chandler L V, Jaffee D M
Regulating the regulators: a review of the FINE
regulatory reforms
JMCB 1977 NOV VOL 9:4 p 619-635.

(3225)
Freedman C
The FINE proposals on foreign banks in the
United States and American banks abroad
JMCB 1977 NOV VOL 9:4 p 642-651.

(3226)
Kelly J
Bankers and borders: the case of American banks
in Britain
Ballinger, 1977.

(3227)
Aliber R Z
Towards a theory of international banking
F R Bk San Francisco Ec Rev 1976 SPRING.

(3228)
Cheng H-S
U.S. West Coast as an international financial
center
F R Bk San Francisco Ec Rev 1976 SPRING.

(3229)
Johnston R
Proposals for federal control of foreign banks
F R Bk San Francisco Ec Rev 1976 SPRING.

(3230)
Steuber U
International banking: the foreign activities of the
banks of principal industrial countries
Leyden: A W Sijthoff, 1976.

(3231)
Brimmer A F, Dahl F R
Internationalization of commercial banking growth
of American international banking: Implications
for public policy
JF 1975 MAY VOL 30:2 p 341-364.

(3232)
Steib S B
The demand for Euro-Dollar borrowings by U S
banks
JF 1973 VOL 28 p 875.

(3233)
Robinson S W
Multinational banking: a study of certain legal
and financial aspects of the postwar operations of
the US branch banks in Western Europe
Leyden: A W Sijthoff, 1972.

8.2 Credit unions

(3234)
Berthoud R, Hinton T
Credit unions in the United Kingdom
Policy Studies Institute, 1989.

(3235)
Bundt T, Keating B
Depository institution competition in the
deregulation environment: the case of a large
credit union
AE 1988 OCT VOL 20:10 p 1333-1342.

(3236)
Smith D J
Credit union rate and earnings retention decisions
under uncertainty and taxation
JMCB 1988 FEB VOL 20:1 p 119.

(3237)
Clair R T
Deposit insurance, moral hazard, and credit
unions
F R Bk Dallas Ec Rev 1984 JUL.

(3238)
Murray J D, White R W
Economies of scale and economies of scope in
multiproduct financial institution : a study of
British Columbia credit unions
JF 1983 JUN VOL 38:3 p 887-902.

(3239)
Fry C L, Harper C P, Stansell S R
An analysis of credit union costs: a new approach
to analyzing costs of financial institutions
JBR 1982 WINTER VOL 12:4.

(3240)
Black H, Dugger R H
Credit union structure growth and regulatory
problems
JF 1981 MAY VOL 36:2 p 529-538.

(3241)
Navratil F J
An aggregate model of the credit union industry
JF 1981 MAY VOL 36:2 p 539-549.

(3242)
Smith D J, Cargill T F, Meyer R A
An economic theory of a credit union
JF 1981 MAY VOL 36:2 p 519-528.

(3243)
Wolken J D, Navratil F J
The economic impact of the federal credit union
usury ceiling
JF 1981 DEC VOL 36:5 p 1157-1168.

(3244)
Wolken J D, Navratil F J
Economies of scale in credit unions: further
evidence
JF 1980 JUN VOL 25:3 p 769-777.

(3245)
Koot R S
On economies of scale in credit unions
JF 1978 VOL 33 p 1087-1094.

(3246)
Koot R S
The demand for credit union shares
JFQA 1976 MAR VOL 11 p 133.

(3247)
Holmes D N Jr
Excess demand, undercapitalization and the true
interest rate for credit union loans in unorganized
money markets
JF 1974 VOL 29 p 1063.

(3248)
Taylor R A
The demand for credit union shares: A
cross-sectional analysis
JFQA 1972 JUN VOL 7 p 1749.

8.3   Savings and loan associations

(3249)
Building Societies Association
The building societies and 1992
Building Society Association, 1989.

(3250)
Drake L
The building society industry in transition
Macmillan, 1989.

(3251)
Drake L M
Building societies in the 1980s
Macmillan, 1989.

(3252)
Hendershott P H, Shilling J D
Reforming conforming loan limits: the impact on
thrift earnings and taxpayer outlays
JFSR 1989 VOL 3:4 p 311-332.

(3253)
Norkett P
Building societies and their subsidiaries
Routledge, 1989.

(3254)
Akella S R, Greenbaum S I
Savings and loan ownership structure and
expense-preference
JBankF 1988 VOL 12:3 p 419-438.

(3255)
Brumbaugh R D
Thrifts under siege: Restoring order to American
banking
Ballinger, 1988.

(3256)
Jordan B D, Verbrugge J A, Burns R M
Returns to initial shareholders in savings
institution conversions: evidence and regulatory
implications
JFR 1988 VOL 11:2 p 125-136.

(3257)
Boleat M
Building societies : the new supervisory framework
NWBQR 1987 AUG p 26-34.

(3258)
Fortune
How to steal an S&L legally
F 1987 OCT 12 VOL 116:8 p 41-46.

(3259)
Masulis R W
Changes in ownership structure: conversions of mutual savings and loans to stock charter
JFE 1987 VOL 18 p 29-59.

(3260)
Mester L J
Multiproduct cost study of savings and loans
JF 1987 JUN VOL 42:2 p 423-445.

(3261)
Mester L J
Multiple market contact between savings and loans.
JMCB 1987 NOV VOL 19:4 p 538-549.

(3262)
Neely W P, Rochester D P
Operating performance and merger benefits: the savings and loan experience
FR 1987 FEB VOL 22:1.

(3263)
Boleat M
The building society industry. 2nd ed
Allen, 1986.

(3264)
Welker D L
Thrift competition: does it matter?
F R Bk Richmond Ec Rev 1986 VOL 72:1..

(3265)**Barnes P**
UK building societies - a study of the gains from merger
JBFA 1985 SPRING VOL 12:1 p 75-91

(3266)
Bulmash S B
Loan default risk return on equity and size effects and ownership control - empirical evidence on savings and loans associations in the USA
JBFA 1985 SUMMER VOL 12:2 p 313-326

(3267)
Furlong F T
Savings and loan asset composition and the mortgage market
F R Bk San Francisco Ec Rev 1985 SUMMER.

(3268)
Mahoney P I, White A P
The thrift industry in transition
F R Bul 1985 VOL 71:3.

(3269)
Barnes P
Building societies: the myth of mutuality
Pluto Pr, 1984.

(3270)
Hadaway B L, Hadaway S C
Implications of savings and loan conversions in a deregulated world
JBR 1984 SPRING VOL 15:1.

(3271)
Hannan T H
Competition between commercial banks and thrift institutions: an empirical examination
JBR 1984 SPRING VOL 15:1.

(3272)
King A T
Thrift institution deposits: the influence of MMCs and MMMFs
JMCB 1984 AUG VOL 16:3 p 328-334.

(3273)
Rhoades S A, White A P
Output in relation to labor input in the banking and savings and loan industries: 1927-1979
JBankF 1984 VOL 8 p 119.

(3274)
Barnes P
The consequences of growth maximisation and expense preference policies of managers: evidence from UK building societies. A study of the causes of profit insufficiency during a period of increased competition using discriminant analysis
JBFA 1983 WINTER VOL 10:4 p 521-530.

(3275)
Barnes P, Dodds C
The structure and performance of the UK building society industry 1970-78
JBFA 1983 SPRING VOL 10:1 p 37-56

(3276)
Bradford W D
The deposit demand of minority savings and loan associations
JBR 1982 SPRING VOL 13:1.

(3277)
Carron A S
The plight of the thrift institution
Brookings, 1982.

(3278)
Dann L Y, James C M
An analysis of the impact of deposit rate ceilings on the market values of thrift institutions
JF 1982 DEC VOL 37:5 p 1259-1275.

(3279)
Fortune
The baleful bailout bandwagon (the Savings and Loan industry)
F 1982 JUN 14 VOL 105:12 p 140-147.

(3280)
Gough T J
The economics of building societies
Macmillan, 1982.

(3281)
Moran M J
Thrift institutions in recent years
F R Bul 1982 VOL 68:12.

(3282)
Smith G, Brainard W
A disequilibrium model of savings and loan associations
JF 1982 DEC VOL 37:5 p 1277-1293.

(3283)
McNulty J E
Economies of scale in the savings and loan industry: new evidence and implications for profitability
Federal Home Loan Bank Board Journal 1981 FEB VOL 14 p 2-8.

(3284)
Spellman L J
Commercial banks and the profits of savings and loan markets
JBR 1981 SPRING VOL 12:1.

(3285)
Trebing M E
The new bank-thrift competition: will it affect bank acquisition and merger analysis?
F R Bk St Louis Rev 1981 VOL 63:2.

(3286)
Verbrugge J A, Jahera J S Jr
Expense preference behavior in the savings and loan industry
JMCB 1981 NOV VOL 13:4 p 465-476.

(3287)
Boleat M
Competition between banks and building societies
NWBQR 1980 NOV p 43-57.

(3288)
Murray J D, White R W
Economies of scale and deposit taking financial institutions in Canada
JMCB 1980 FEB VOL 12:1 p 58-70.

(3289)
Gough T J, Taylor T W
The building society price cartel
Inst Econ Aff, 1979.

(3290)
Hartzog B G Jr
The impact of NOW accounts on savings and
loan behavior and performance
QREB 1979 VOL 19:3 p 97.

(3291)
Kalish L, McKenzie J A
Portfolio drag and savings and loan lending policy
QREB 1979 VOL 19:2 p 71.

(3292)
Llewellyn D T
Do building societies take deposits away from
banks?
LBR 1979 JAN 131 p 21-34

(3293)
Bradford W D
The performance of merging savings and loan
associations
JB 1978 JAN VOL 51:1 p 115-125.

(3294)
Bradford W D
Minority savings and loan associations: Hypothesis
and tests
JFQA 1978 SEP VOL 13 p 533.

(3295)
Lapp J S
The determination of savings and loan association
deposit rates in the absence of rate ceilings: A
cross-section approach
JF 1978 VOL 33 p 215.

(3296)
Spellman L J
Entry and profitability in a rate-free savings and
loan market
QREB 1978 VOL 18:2 p 87.

(3297)
Altman E I
Predicting performance in the savings and loan
association industry
JME 1977 VOL 3 p 443.

(3298)
Spellman L J, Osborne A E Jr, Bradford W D
The comparative operating efficiency of black
savings and loans associations
JF 1977 MAY VOL 32:2 p 565-574.

(3299)
Cassidy H J
Estimates of the aggregate impact of expected
windfalls for a portion of the S & L industry
JMCB 1976 NOV VOL 8:4 p 477-485..

(3300)Fortune P
The effect of FHLB bond operations on savings
inflows at savings and loan associations: Comment
JF 1976 VOL 31 p 963.

(3301)
Gonyer G H, Weiss S J
The competitive effects of demand deposit powers
for thrift institutions in Connecticut
JBR 1976 SUMMER VOL 7:2.

(3302)
Lapp J S
Market structure and advertising in the savings
and loan industry
REStat 1976 MAY VOL 58:2 p 202-208.

(3303)
Shick R A, Verbrugge J A
Market structure and savings and loan
profitability
QREB 1976 VOL 16:2 p 79.

(3304)
Stigum M L
Some further implications of profit maximization
by a savings and loan association
JF 1976 VOL 31 p 1405.

(3305)
Verbrugge J A, Shick R A, Thygerson K J
An analysis of savings and loan profit
performance
JF 1976 VOL 31 p 1427.

(3306)
Fortune P
The effectiveness of recent policies to maintain
thrift deposit flows
JMCB 1975 AUG VOL 7:3 p 297-315.

(3307)
Lovati J M
The changing competition between commercial
banks and thrift institutions for deposits
F R Bk St Louis Rev 1975 VOL 57:7.

(3308)
Benson D
Banking's present and future competitors: thrift
institutions
JBR 1974 AUTUMN VOL 5:2.

(3309)
Jaffee D M
What to do about savings and loan associations?
JMCB 1974 NOV VOL 6:4 p 537-550.

(3310)
Boyd J H
Some recent developments in the savings and
loan deposit market
JMCB 1973 AUG VOL 5:3 p 730-750.

(3311)
Building Societies Institute
Building society management. 5th ed
Franey, 1973.

(3312)
Gramlich E M, Jaffee D M eds.
Savings deposits, mortgages and housing: studies
for the Federal Reserve-MIT-Penn economic
model
Heath, 1972.

(3313)
Kaufman G G
The thrift institution problem reconsidered
JBR 1972 SPRING VOL 3:1 p 26-33.

(3314)
Gilbert G G, Murphy N B
Competition between thrift institutions and
commercial banks: an examination of the evidence
JBR 1971 SUMMER VOL 2:2.

(3315)
Teck A
Mutual savings banks and savings and loan
associations: aspects of growth
Columbia U Pr, 1968.

(3316)
Cleary E J
The Building Society movement
Elek, 1965.

8.4 Finance companies and personal loan markets

(3317)
McShane R W, Sharpe I G
Australian finance company profitability: Tests of
the hedging and SCP models
AJM 1987 JUN VOL 12 p 69-90.

(3318)
Barth J R, Cordes J J, Yezer A M J
Benefits and costs of legal restrictions on personal
loan markets
JLE 1986 VOL 29:2 p 357-380.

(3319)
Goldfaden L C, Hurst G P
Regulatory responses to changes in the consumer
financial services industry
F R Bul 1985 VOL 71:2.

(3320)
Calderon-Rossell J R
Optimal financial structure of finance companies
in a regulated environment of a developing
country
JBankF 1984 VOL 8 p 443.

(3321)
Harris M
Finance companies as business lenders
F R Bk New York Q Rev 1979 SUMMER VOL
4:2.

(3322)
Boczar G E
Competition between banks and finance
companies: A cross section study of personal loan
debtors
JF 1978 VOL 33 p 245.

(3323)
Benston G
Risk on consumer finance company personal loans
JF 1977 MAY VOL 32:2 p 593-608.

(3324)
Benston G J
Graduated interest rate ceilings and operating costs by size of small consumer cash loans
JF 1977 VOL 32 p 1169.

(3325)
Benston G J
Rate ceiling implications of the cost structure of consumer finance companies
JF 1977 VOL 32 p 1169.

(3326)
Durkin T A
Consumer costs and the regulatory basis of loan sharking
JBR 1977 SUMMER VOL 8:2.

(3327)
Smith J F
The Equal Credit Opportunity Act of 1974: a cost/benefit analysis
JF 1977 MAY VOL 32:2 p 609-621.

(3328)
Boczar G E
The evidence on competition between commercial banks and finance companies
JBR 1975 SUMMER VOL 6:2.

(3329)
Apilado V P, Warner D C, Dauten J J
Evaluation techniques in consumer finance - experimental results and policy implications for financial institutions
JFQA 1974 MAR VOL 9 p 275.

(3330)
Greer D F
Rate ceilings, market structure and the supply of finance company personal loans
JF 1974 VOL 29 p 1363.

(3331)
Hammer F S
Banking present and future competitors: finance and insurance companies
JBR 1974 AUTUMN VOL 5:2.

(3332)
Parker G C, Shay R P
Some factors affecting awareness of annual percentage rates in consumer installment credit transactions
JF 1974 VOL 29 p 217.

(3333)
Russell T
The effects of improvements in the consumer loan market
JET 1974 NOV VOL 9:3 p 327-339.

(3334)
Sartoris W L
The effect of regulation, population characteristics and competition on the market for personal cash loans
JFQA 1972 SEP VOL 7 p 1931.

(3335)
Chapman J M, Shay R P eds.
The consumer finance industry: its costs and regulation
Columbia U Pr, 1967.

(3336)
Smith P F
Consumer credit costs 1949-59: a study by the National Bureau of Economic Research
Princeton U Pr, 1964.

(3337)
Harris R et al.
Hire purchase in a free society. 3rd ed
Hutchinson, 1961.

(3338)
Young R A
Personal finance companies and their credit practices
Natl Bur Econ Res, 1940.

8.41   Captive finance companies

(3339)
Brennan M J, Maksimovic V, Zechner J
Vendor financing
JF 1988 DEC VOL 43:5 p 1127-1142.

(3340)
Comiskey E E, McEwen R A, Mulford C W
A test of pro forma consolidation of finance
subsidiaries
FIN MGMT 1987 AUTUMN VOL 16 p 45-50.

(3341)
Fooladi I, Roberts G, Viscione J
Captive finance subsidiaries: overview and
synthesis
FR 1986 MAY VOL 21:2.

(3342)
Livnat J, Sondhi A C
Finance subsidiaries : their formation and
consolidation
JBFA 1986 SPRING VOL 13:1 p 137-147

(3343)
Roberts G S, Viscione J A
Captive finance subsidiaries and M form
hypothesis
BellJ 1981 SPRING VOL 12:1 p 285-295.

(3344)
Roberts G S, Viscione J A
Captive finance subsidiaries: The manager's view
FIN MGMT 1981 SPRING VOL 10 p 36-42.

(3345)
Lewellen W G
Finance subsidiaries and corporate borrowing
capacity
FIN MGMT 1972 SPRING VOL 1 p 21.

8.5   Insurance

(3346)
Smith M L
Investment returns and yields to holders of
insurance
JB 1989 VOL 62:1 p 81-98.

(3347)
Walker K L
Guaranteed investment contracts
Dow Jones-Irwin, 1989.

(3348)
Cummins J D
Risk-based premiums for insurance guaranty funds
JF 1988 SEP VOL 43:4 p 823-840.

(3349)
Doherty N A, Kang H B
Interest rates and insurance price cycles
JBankF 1988 VOL 12.2 p 199-214.

(3350)
Hellwig M F
A note on the specification of inter-firm
communication in insurance markets with adverse
selection
JET 1988 OCT VOL 46:1 p 154-163.

(3351)
Malueg D
Repeated insurance contracts with differential
learning
REStud 1988 VOL 54 p 177.

(3352)
Cozzolino J M, Jacque L L
Foreign exchange risk in international insurance
and reinsurance
MF 1987 VOL 13:1 p 18-22..

(3353)**Pullinger H, Hare A P G**
Corporate financial planning in insurance - a case
study
Journal of the Operational Research Society 1987
OCT VOL 38:10 p 957-964.

(3354)
Abraham K S
Distributing risk: insurance, legal theory, and
public policy
Yale U Pr, 1986.

(3355)
Hammond J D
Essays in the theory of risk and insurance
Scott, Foresman, 1986.

(3356)
Schlesinger H, Venezian E
Insurance markets with loss-prevention activity:
Profits, market structure, and consumer welfare
RandJ 1986 SUMMER VOL 17:2 p 227-238.

(3357)
Briys E P, Louberge H
On the theory of rational insurance purchasing :
a note
JF 1985 JUN VOL 40:2 p 577-581.

(3358)
Dionne G, Lasserre P
Adverse selection, repeated insurance contracts
and announcement strategy
REStud 1985 VOL 52 p 719.

(3359)
Hogarth R M, Kunreuther H
Ambiguity and insurance decisions
AER 1985 VOL 75 P+P p 386-390.

(3360)
Palfrey T R, Spratt C S
Repeated insurance contracts and learning
RandJ 1985 AUTUMN VOL 16:3 p 356-367.

(3361)
Beard R E, Pentikainen T, Pesonen E
Risk theory. 3rd ed
Chapman, 1984.

(3362)
Borch K
Premiums in a competitive insurance market
JBankF 1984 VOL 8 p 431.

(3363)
Bickelhaupt D L
General insurance. 11th ed
Irwin, 1983.

(3364)
Davids L E
Dictionary of insurance. 6th ed
Rowman & Allanheld, 1983.

(3365)
Doherty N A, Schlesinger H
Optimal insurance in incomplete markets
JPE 1983 VOL 91 p 1045.

(3366)
Jemison D B, Oakley R A
Corporate governance in mutual insurance
companies
JBusR 1983 VOL 11 p 501-522.

(3367)
Mayers D, Smith C W
The interdependence of individual portfolio
decisions and demand for insurance
JPE 1983 APR VOL 91:2 p 304-311

(3368)
OECD
International trade in services: insurance:
identification and analysis of obstacles
OECD, 1983.

(3369)
Turnbull S M
Additional aspects of rational insurance
purchasing
JB 1983 APR VOL 56:2 p 217-229.

(3370)
Borch K
Additive insurance premiums: a note
JF 1982 DEC VOL 37:5 p 1295-1298.

(3371)
Crouch E A C, Wilson R
Risk/benefit analysis
Ballinger, 1982.

(3372)
Goldstein A B, Markowitz B C
SOFASIM: a dynamic insurance model with
investment structure policy benefits and taxes
JF 1982 MAY VOL 37:2 p 595-604.

(3373)
Weber N ed.
Insurance deregulation: issues and perspectives:
essays on the regulation-deregulation controversy
and its significance for insurance companies,
agents and consumers
New York: Conference Board, 1982.

(3374)
Bannister J E, Bawcutt P A
Practical risk management
Witherby & Co, 1981.

(3375)
Dickson G C A, Steele J T
Elements of insurance
Macdonald and Evans, 1981.

(3376)
Doherty N A, Tinic S M
Reinsurance under conditions of capital market
equilibrium: a note
JF 1981 SEP VOL 36:4 p 949-953.

(3377)
Mayers D, Smith C W
Contractual provisions, organizational structure
and conflict control in insurance markets
JB 1981 JUL VOL 54:3 p 407-434.

(3378)
Cockerell H
Witherby's dictionary of insurance
Witherby & Co, 1980.

(3379)
Ulph D, Hemming R
Uncertain lifetime, imperfect insurance markets
and the valuation of pension wealth
REStud 1980 VOL 47 p 587.

(3380)
Raviv A
The design of an optimal insurance policy
AER 1979 VOL 69 p 84-96.

(3381)
Shavell S
On moral hazard and insurance
QJE 1979 VOL 93 p 541.

(3382)
Young J S
New York's insurance industry: perspective and
prospects
F R Bk New York Q Rev 1979 SPRING VOL
4:1.

(3383)
Jaynes G D
Equilibria in monopolistically competitive
insurance markets
JET 1978 DEC VOL 19:2 p 394-422.

(3384)
Vaughan E J, Elliott C M
Fundamentals of risk and insurance. 2nd ed
Wiley, 1978.

(3385)
Doherty N A
Stochastic choice in insurance and risk sharing
JF 1977 VOL 32 p 921.

(3386)
Eden B
The role of insurance and gambling in allocating
risk over time
JET 1977 DEC VOL 16:2 p 228-246.

(3387)
Mandell L, Lundsten L L
Diversion of credit life insurance commissions by
bankers
JBR 1977 SUMMER VOL 8:2..

(3388)**Wilson C**
A model of insurance markets with incomplete
information
JET 1977 DEC VOL 16:2 p 167-207.

(3389)
Razin A
Rational insurance purchasing
JF 1976 VOL 31 p 133.

(3390)
Gentry J A
Capital market line theory, insurance company
portfolio performance, and empirical anomalies
QREB 1975 VOL 15:1 p 7.

(3391)
Huefner R J
Alternative approaches to casualty loss
recognition
FIN MGMT 1975 SPRING VOL 4 p 50.

(3392)
Quirin G D, Waters W R
Market efficiency and the cost of capital: The
strange case of fire and casualty insurance
companies
JF 1975 MAY VOL 30:2 p 427-445.

(3393)
Borch K
The mathematical theory of insurance: an annotated selection of papers on insurance published 1960-1972
Lexington Bks, 1974.

(3394)
Hammer F S
Banking present and future competitors: finance and insurance companies
JBR 1974 AUTUMN VOL 5:2.

(3395)
Marshall J M
Insurance as a market in contingent claims: structure and performance
BellJ 1974 AUTUMN VOL 5:2 p 670-682.

(3396)
Pfeffer I, Klock D R
Perspectives on insurance
P-H, 1974.

(3397)
Bain A D, Harris A G, Makower M S
The management of liquid assets in general insurance companies
JBF 1973 SPRING VOL 5:1 p 52-65.

(3398)
Goshay R C, Sandor R L
An inquiry into the feasibility of a reinsurance futures market
JBF 1973 SUMMER VOL 5:2 p 56.

(3399)
Lippman S A
Optimal reinsurance
JFQA 1972 DEC VOL 7 p 2151.

(3400)
Miller R B
Insurance contracts as two-person games
MSci 1972 JUL VOL 18:11 p 444.

(3401)
Parkin J M, Wu S Y
Choice involving unwanted risky events and optimal insurance
AER 1972 VOL 62 p 982-987.

(3402)
Clayton G
British insurance
Elek, 1971.

(3403)
Dunning J H
Insurance in the economy
Inst Econ Aff, 1971.

(3404)
Greene M R
Risk aversion, insurance and the future
Indiana U Bus, 1971.

(3405)
Haugen R A, Kroncke C O
Rate regulation and the cost of capital in the insurance industry
JFQA 1971 DEC VOL 6 p 1283-1305.

(3406)
Haugen R A, Kroncke C O
A portfolio approach to optimizing the structure of assets and claims of a stock insurance company
Journal of Risk and Insurance 1970 MAR VOL 37 p 41-48.

(3407)
Krouse C G
Portfolio balancing corporate assets and liabilities with special application to insurance management
JFQA 1970 MAR VOL 5 p 77-104.

(3408)
Athearn J L
Risk and insurance. 2nd ed
Appleton, 1969.

(3409)
Mowbray A H et al.
Insurance: its theory and practice in the United States. 6th ed
McGraw, 1969.

(3410)
Kulp C A, Hall J W
Casualty insurance. 4th ed
Ronald, 1968.

(3411)
Borch K
The economic theory of insurance
The Astin Bulletin 1967 JUL p 252-264.

(3412)
Mehr R I, Cammack E
Principles of insurance. 4th ed
Irwin, 1966.

(3413)
Regel R, Miller J S
Insurance principles and practices. 5th ed
P-H, 1966.

(3414)
Clayton G, Osborn W T
Insurance company investment, principles and
policy
Allen, 1965.

(3415)
Wherry R H, Newman M
Insurance and risk
HR & W, 1964.

(3416)
Federal Reserve Bank of Cleveland
Investment patterns of fire and casualty insurance
companies
F R Bk Cleveland Mo Bus Rev 1963 MAY.

(3417)
Carter R L
Economics and insurance: an introduction to the
economic aspects of insurance
Stockport, Cheshire: PH Press, nd.

8.51   Corporate insurance and captive insurance companies

(3418)
Bawcutt P A
Captive insurance companies: establishment,
operation and management. 2nd ed
Woodhead-Faulkner, 1987.

(3419)
Campbell T S, Kracaw W A
Optimal managerial incentive contracts and the
value of corporate insurance.
JFQA 1987 SEP VOL 22:3 p 315-328.

(3420)
Cross M L, Davidson W N III, Thornton J H
The impact of a captive insurance company's
formation on a firm's value after the Carnation
case
JBusR 1987 AUG VOL 15:4 p 329-338.

(3421)
Fortune
Danger signals for Bermuda's happy captives
F 1984 JAN 23 VOL 109:2 p 153-160.

(3422)
Mayers D, Smith C W
On the corporate demand for insurance
JB 1982 APR VOL 55:2 p 281-296.

(3423)
Mayers D, Smith C W
The corporate insurance decision
CFQ 1982 SPRING VOL 1 p 47-65.

8.52   Life insurance

(3424)
Lewis F D
Dependents and the demand for life insurance
AER 1989 VOL 79:3 p 452-467.

(3425)
Mehr R I, Gustavson S G
Life insurance: theory and practice. 4th ed
Irwin, 1987.

(3426)
Curry T, Warshawsky M
Life insurance companies in a changing
environment
F R Bul 1986 VOL 72:7.

(3427)
Dorfman M S, Adelman S W
Life insurance and financial planning
Irwin, 1986.

(3428)
Mayers D, Smith C W
Ownership   structure   and   control.   The
mutualization of stock life insurance companies
JFE 1986 MAY VOL 16:1 p 73-98.

(3429)
Babbel D F
The price elasticity of demand for whole life
insurance
JF 1985 MAR VOL 40:1 p 225-239.

(3430)
Babbel D F, Staking K B
A capital budgeting analysis of life insurance costs
in the United States: 1950-1979.
JF 1983 MAR VOL 38:1 p 149-170

(3431)
Kellner S, Mathewson G F
Entry size distribution scale and scope economies
in the life insurance industry.
JB 1983 JAN VOL 56:1 p 25-44

(3432)
Schleef H J
The joint determination of marginal rate of
return and interest adjusted cost for whole life
insurance
MSci 1983 MAY VOL 29:5 p 610-621.

(3433)
Winter R A
On the rate structure of the American life
insurance market
JF 1981 MAR VOL 36:1 p 81-96.

(3434)
Campbell R A
The demand for life insurance: an application of
the economics of uncertainty
JF 1980 DEC VOL 35:5 p 1155-1172.

(3435)
Franklin P J, Woodhead C
The UK assurance industry: a study in applied
economics
Croom Helm, 1980.

(3436)
Brennan M J, Schwartz E S
Alternative investment strategies for the insurers
of equity linked life insurance policies with an
asset value guarantee
JB 1979 JAN VOL 52:1 p 63-93.

(3437)
Brennan M J, Schwartz E S
Pricing and investment strategies for guaranteed
equity-linked life insurance
Irwin, 1979.

(3438)
Cummins J D
Investment activities of life insurance companies
Irwin, 1977.

(3439)
Brennan M J, Schwartz E S
The pricing of equity-linked life insurance policies
with an asset value guarantee
JFE 1976 VOL 3 p 195.

(3440)
Richard S F
Optimal consumption, portfolio and life insurance
rules for an uncertain lived individual in a
continuous time model
JFE 1975 VOL 2 p 187..

(3441)**Pesando J E**
The interest sensitivity of the flow of funds
through life insurance companies: An econometric
analysis
JF 1974 VOL 29 p 1105.

(3442)
Fortune P
A theory of optimal life insurance: Development
and tests
JF 1973 VOL 28 p 587.

(3443)
Greider J E, Beadles W T
Principles of life insurance
Irwin, 1972.

(3444)
Jones L D
Investment policies of life insurance companies
Harvard Busn, 1968.

(3445)
McGill D M
Life insurance. Rev ed
Irwin, 1967.

(3446)
Black K et al.
Cases in life insurance
Irwin, 1965.

(3447)
Hart O H
Life insurance companies and the equity capital
markets
JF 1965 MAY VOL 20 p 358-367.

(3448)
Yaari M E
Uncertain lifetime, life insurance and the theory
of the consumer
REStud 1965 VOL 32 p 137-150.

(3449)
Brimmer A F
Life insurance companies in the capital markets
Mich St U Busn, 1962.

(3450)
Rejda G E
The role of dollar averaging in the common stock
investment operations of life insurance companies
Journal of Insurance 1962 DEC.

(3451)
Walter J E
The investment process, as characterized by
leading life insurance companies
Harvard Busn, 1962.

(3452)
Wehrle L S
Life insurance investment: the experiences of four
companies
YEE 1961 SPRING VOL 1 p 70-136.

(3453)
Wright J F
Gross flows of funds through life insurance
companies
JF 1960 MAY VOL 15 p 140-156.

(3454)
Federal Reserve Bank of New York
Life insurance companies in the postwar capital
markets
F R Bk New York Mo Rev 1958 SEP.

(3455)
Wehrle L S
A theory of life insurance portfolio selection
Cowles Foundation Discussion Paper, No 60,
DEC 1958.

(3456)
McCahan D ed.
Investment of life insurance funds
Irwin, 1953.

(3457)
Federal Reserve Bank of New York
Life insurance companies and the securities
markets [Parts 1-2]
F R Bk New York Mo Rev 1952 MAR; 1952
APR.

8.53   Property liability insurance

(3458)
Doherty N A, D'Arcy S P
The financial theory of pricing property-liability
contracts
Irwin, 1988.

(3459)
Mayers D, Smith C W Jr
Ownership   structure   across   lines   of
property-casualty insurance
JLE 1988 VOL 31:2 p 351-378.

(3460)
Doherty N A, Garven J R
Price regulation in property-liability insurance : a
contingent-claims approach
JF 1986 DEC VOL 41:5 p 1031-1050.

(3461)
Cummins J D
Strategic   planning   and   modeling   in
property-liability insurance
Kluwer-Nijhoff, 1984.

(3462)
Kraus A, Ross S A
The determination of fair profits for the property-liability insurance firm.
JF 1982 SEP VOL 37:4 p 1015-1028

(3463)
Cummins J D, Nye D J
Portfolio optimization models for property-liability insurance companies: an analysis and some extensions.
MSci 1981 APR VOL 27:4 p 414-431.

(3464)
Munch P, Smallwood D E
Solvency regulation in the property liability insurance industry: empirical evidence
BellJ 1980 SPRING VOL 11:1 p 261-279.

(3465)
Fairley W B
Investment income and profit margins in property liability insurance: theory and empirical results
BellJ 1979 SPRING VOL 10:1 p 192-210.

(3466)
Hill R D
Profit regulation in property liability insurance
BellJ 1979 SPRING VOL 10:1 p 172-191.

(3467)
Shick R A, Trieschmann J S
Some future evidence on the performance of property-liability insurance companies' stock portfolios
JFQA 1978 MAR VOL 13 p 157.

(3468)
Foster G
Valuation parameters of property-liability companies
JF 1977 VOL 32 p 823.

(3469)
Kahane Y
Rate making and regulation in property liability insurance
QREB 1977 VOL 17:2 p 97.

(3470)
Schlarbaum G G
The investment performance of the common stock portfolios of property-liability insurance companies
JFQA 1974 JAN VOL 9 p 89.

(3471)
Monroe R J, Trieschmann J
Portfolio performance of property-liability insurance companies
JFQA 1972 MAR VOL 7 p 1595.

(3472)
Institute of Chartered Financial Analysts
Property and liability insurance investment management
Irwin, 1971.

8.6   Investment and merchant banking

(3473)
Ang J S
On merchant banking
JFSR 1989 VOL 3:1 p 33-52.

(3474)
Bloch E
Inside investment banking
Dow Jones-Irwin, 1988.

(3475)
Eccles R G, Crane D B
Doing deals: investment banks at work
Harvard Busn Pr, 1988.

(3476)
Hunter W C, Walker M B
Assessing the fairness of investment bankers' fees
F R Bk Atlanta Ec Rev 1988 VOL 73:2.

(3477)
Auerbach J, Hayes S L
Investment banking and diligence: what price deregulation?
Harvard Bus Pr, 1986.

(3478)
Hakim J
The international investment banking revolution: strategies for global securities trading
Economist Publications, 1986.

(3479)
Rogowski R J, Sorensen E H
The new competitive environment of investment banking
MCFJ 1986 SPRING VOL 4 p 64-71.

(3480)
Chapman S D
The rise of merchant banking
Allen, 1984.

(3481)
Ferris P
Gentlemen of fortune: the world's merchant and investment bankers
Weidenfeld & N, 1984.

(3482)
Clay C J J, Wheble B S eds.
Modern merchant banking: a guide to the workings of the accepting houses of the City of London and their services to industry and commerce. 2nd ed
Woodhead-Faulkner, 1983.

(3483)
Hayes S L, Spence A M, Marks D van P
Competition in the investment banking industry
Harvard U Pr, 1983.

(3484)
Ehrbar A F
Upheaval in investment banking
F 1982 AUG 23 VOL 106 p 90-95.

(3485)
Hayes S L
The transformation of investment banking
HBR 1979 JAN-FEB VOL 57:1 p 153-170.

(3486)
Angermueller H H, Taylor M A
Commercial vs investment bankers
HBR 1977 SEPT-OCT VOL 55:5 p 132-144.

(3487)
Kellett R
The merchant banking arena with case studies
Macmillan, 1976.

(3488)
Wolfson N
Conflicts of interest: Investment banking
Twentieth Fund, 1976.

(3489)
Logue D E, Lindvall J R
The behavior of investment bankers: An econometric investigation
JF 1974 VOL 29 p 203.

(3490)
Young G K
Merchant banking: practice and prospects. 2nd ed
Weidenfeld & N, 1971.

(3491)
Carosso V P
Investment banking in America: a history
Harvard U Pr, 1970.

(3492)
Wechsberg J
The merchant bankers
Weidenfeld & N, 1967.

(3493)
Waterman M H
Investment banking functions, their evolution and adaptation to business finance
U of Mich Busn Res, 1958.

8.7   Investment companies

(3494)
Elton E J, Gruber M J, Rentzler J C
Professionally managed publicly traded commodity funds
JB 1987 APR VOL 60:2 p 175-199.

(3495)
Seligman B
Choosing an investment company
Ballinger, 1987.

(3496)
Jenkins J W
Incentive compensation and REIT financial leverage and asset risk
FIN MGMT 1980 SPRING VOL 9 p 81.

(3497)
Ferretti A P ed.
Investment company portfolio management
Irwin, 1970.

(3498)
Burton H, Corner D C
Investment and unit trusts in Britain and America
Elek, 1968.

(3499)
Securities and Exchange Commission
Public policy implications of investment company growth
US Govt, 1966.

8.71 Closed-end funds

(3500)
Weiss K
The post-offering price performance of closed-end funds
FIN MGMT 1989 AUTUMN VOL 18 p 57-67.

(3501)
Brauer G A
Closed-end fund shares' abnormal returns and the information content of discounts and premiums
JF 1988 MAR VOL 43:1 p 113-128.

(3502)
Brickley J A, Schallheim J S
Lifting the lid on closed-end investment companies : a case of abnormal returns
JFQA 1985 MAR VOL 20:1 p 107-117.

(3503)
Brauer G A
"Open-ending" closed-end funds
JFE 1984 VOL 13 p 491.

(3504)
Woodward R S
The performance of U K investment trusts as internationally diversified portfolios over the period 1968-1977
JBankF 1983 VOL 7 p 417.

(3505)
Richards R M, Fraser D R, Groth J C
The attractions of closed-end bond funds
JPM 1982 WINTER VOL 8:2 p 56-61.

(3506)
Woodward R S, Matatko J
Factors affecting the behaviour of UK closed end fund discounts 1968-1977
JBFA 1982 WINTER VOL 9:4 p 501-509.

(3507)
Herzfeld J
The investor's guide to closed end funds
McGraw, 1980.

(3508)
Richards R M, Fraser D R, Groth J C
Winning strategies for closed-end funds
JPM 1980 FALL VOL 7:1 p 50-55.

(3509)
Guy J R F
The performance of the British investment trust industry
JF 1978 VOL 33 p 443.

(3510)
Thompson R
The information content of discounts and premiums on closed-end fund shares
JFE 1978 VOL 6 p 151-186.

(3511)
Malkiel B G
The valuation of closed-end investment-company shares
JF 1977 VOL 32 p 847.

(3512)
Boudreaux K J
Discounts and premiums on closed-end mutual funds: A study in valuation
JF 1973 VOL 28 p 515.

(3513)
Zweig M E
An investor expectations stock price productive model using closed-end fund premiums
JF 1973 VOL 28 p 67.

8.72   Mutual funds

(3514)
Stopp C ed.
Unit trust industry review and directory: 1989
Professional and Business Information with the Unit Trust Association, 1989.

(3515)
Touche Ross Management Consultants
Unit trust management companies: cost and overhead review 1989
Touche Ross, 1989.

(3516)
Draper P R
Unit trusts homogeneous beliefs and the separation property : a note
JBFA 1984 WINTER VOL 11:4 p 485-492

(3517)
Patel R C, Olsen R A
Financial determinants of systematic risk in real estate investment trusts
JBusR 1984 VOL 12 p 481-482.

(3518)
Alexander G J, Benson P G, Eger E E
Timing decisions and the behavior of mutual fund systematic risk
JFQA 1982 NOV VOL 17:4 p 579-602.

(3519)
Ang J S, Chua J H
Mutual funds: different strokes for different folks?
JPM 1982 WINTER VOL 8:2 p 43-50.

(3520)
Appleyard A R, Strong N, Walker M
Mutual fund performance in the context of models of equilibrium capital asset pricing
JBFA 1982 AUTUMN VOL 9:3 p 289-295

(3521)
Martin J D, Keown A J Jr, Farrell J L Jr
Do fund objectives affect diversification policies?
JPM 1982 WINTER VOL 8:2 p 19-28.

(3522)
Shawky H A
An update on mutual funds: better grades
JPM 1982 WINTER VOL 8:2 p 29-34.

(3523)
Veit E T, Cheney J M
Are mutual funds market timers?
JPM 1982 WINTER VOL 8:2 p 35-42.

(3524)
Woerheide W
Investor response to suggested criteria for the selection of mutual funds
JFQA 1982 MAR VOL 17:1 p 129-137.

(3525)
Calvet A L, Lefoll J
Performance and systematic risk stability of Canadian mutual funds under inflation
JBFA 1981 SUMMER VOL 8:2 p 279-289.

(3526)
Lakonishok J
Performance of mutual funds versus their expenses
JBR 1981 SUMMER VOL 12:2.

(3527)
Fabozzi F J, Francis J C, Lee C F
Generalized functional form for mutual fund returns
JFQA 1980 DEC VOL 15 p 1107-1120.

(3528)
Gatto M A, Geske R, Litzenberger R
Mutual fund insurance
JFE 1980 VOL 8 p 283-317..

(3529)**Gressis N, Miller T W**
Nonstationarity and evaluation of mutual fund performance
JFQA 1980 SEP VOL 15 p 639.

(3530)
Saunders A, Ward C, Woodward R
Stochastic dominance and the performance of U
K unit trusts
JFQA 1980 JUN VOL 15 p 323.

(3531)
Kon S J, Jen F C
The investment performance of mutual funds: an
empirical investigation of timing selectivity and
market efficiency
JB 1979 APR VOL 52:2 p 263-289.

(3532)
Peasnell K V, Skerratt L C L, Taylor P A
An arbitrage rationale for tests of mutual fund
performance
JBFA 1979 AUTUMN VOL 6:3 p 373-400.

(3533)
Dhingra H L
Portfolio volatility adjustment by Canadian mutual
funds
JBFA 1978 WINTER VOL 5:4 p 305-333.

(3534)
Kim T
An assessment of the performance of mutual fund
management: 1969-1975
JFQA 1978 SEP VOL 13 p 385.

(3535)
Firth M
The investment performance of unit trusts in the
period 1965-75
JMCB 1977 NOV VOL 9:4 p 597-604.

(3536)
Meyer J
Further applications of stochastic dominance to
mutual fund performance
JFQA 1977 JUN VOL 12 p 235.

(3537)
Ward C W R, Saunders A
U K unit trust performance 1964-74.
JBFA 1976 WINTER VOL 3:4 p 83-100.

(3538)
Boudreaux K J
The pricing of mutual fund shares
FAJ 1974 JAN-FEB VOL 30 p 26-32.

(3539)
Day M J, Harris P I
Unit trusts
Oyez Publishing, 1974.

(3540)
Joy O M, Porter R B
Stochastic   dominance   and   mutual   fund
performance
JFQA 1974 JAN VOL 9 p 25.

(3541)
Simonson D G
The speculative behavior of mutual funds
JF 1972 MAY VOL 27 p 381-391.

(3542)
Friend I, Blume M E, Crockett J
Mutual funds and other institutional investors
McGraw, 1971.

(3543)
Raw C et al.
Do you sincerely want to be rich?: Bernard
Cornfeld and IOS, an international swindle
Deutsch, 1971.

(3544)
Allerdice F B, Farrer D E
Factors that affect mutual fund growth
JFQA 1967 DEC VOL 2 p 365-382.

(3545)
Horowitz I
Popularity versus performance: the mutual funds
QREB 1966 SPRING VOL 6 p 45-57.

(3546)
Merriman C O
Mutual funds and unit trusts; a global view
Pitman, 1965.

(3547)
Jaretzki A Jr
Duties and responsibilities of directors of mutual
funds
LCP 1964 JUN VOL 29 p 777-794.

(3548)
Stutchbury O P
The management of unit trusts
Skinner, 1964.

(3549)
Brown E E, Vickers D
Mutual funds portfolio activity, performance and
market impact
JF 1963 MAY VOL 18 p 377-391.

(3550)
Herman E S
Mutual fund management fee rates
JF 1963 MAY VOL 18 p 360-376.

(3551)
Smith R L
The grim truth about mutual funds
Putnam, 1963.

(3552)
Securities and Exchange Commission
Study of mutual funds prepared for the Securities
and Exchange Commission by the Wharton
School of Finance and Commerce. House Report
No 2274
US Govt, 1962.

8.721   Hedge funds

(3553)
Fortune
Hedge-fund miseries
F 1971 MAY VOL 83.

(3554)
Loomis C J
Hard times come to the hedge funds
F 1970 JAN VOL 81 p 100.

8.722   Dual purpose funds

(3555)
Kumar P, Philippatos G C, Ezzell J R
Goal programming and the selection of portfolios
by dual-purpose funds
JF 1978 VOL 33 p 303.

(3556)
Litzenberger R H, Sosin H B
The structure and management of dual purpose
funds
JFE 1977 VOL 4 p 203.

(3557)
Litzenberger R H, Sosin H B
The theory of recapitalizations and the evidence
of dual purpose funds
JF 1977 VOL 32 p 1433.

(3558)
Ingersoll J E
A theoretical and empirical investigation of the
dual   purpose   funds: An   application   of
contingent-claims analysis
JFE 1976 VOL 3 p 83.

(3559)
Gentry J A, Pike J R
Dual funds revisited
FAJ 1968 MAR-APR VOL 24 p 149-157.

(3560)
Johnston G S, Curley M L, McIndoe R A
Dual-purpose funds undervalued?
FAJ 1968 NOV-DEC VOL 24 p 157-164.

(3561)
Shelton J P, Brigham E F, Hofflander A E Jr
Dual funds
FAJ 1967 MAY-JUN VOL 23 p 131-139.

8.723   Money market funds

(3562)
Lown C S
Money market deposit accounts versus money
market mutual funds
F R Bk Dallas Ec Rev 1987 NOV.

(3563)
Lyon A B
Money market funds and shareholder dilution
JF 1984 SEP VOL 39:4 p 1011-1020.

(3564)
Hubbard C M
Money market funds money supply and monetary control : a note
JF 1983 SEP VOL 38:4 p 1305-1310.

(3565)
Rosen K T, Katz L
Money market mutual funds : an experiment in ad hoc deregulation : a note
JF 1983 JUN VOL 38:3 p 1011-1017.

(3566)
Langrehr F W
Money market mutual fund investors' saving account holdings and demographic profile
JBR 1982 AUTUMN VOL 13:3.

(3567)
Ferri M G, Oberhelman H D
How well do money market funds perform?
JPM 1981 SPRING VOL 7:3 p 18-26.

(3568)
Ferri M G, Oberhelman H D
A study of the management of money market mutual funds, 1975-1980
FIN MGMT 1981 AUTUMN VOL 10 p 24-29.

8.8   Employee benefit plans

(3569)
Ippolito R A
The economics of pension insurance
Irwin, 1989.

(3570)
Makin J H, Couch K A
Saving, pension contributions, and the real interest rate
REStat 1989 VOL 71 p 401.

(3571)
McGill D M
Fundamentals of private pensions. 6th ed
Irwin, 1989.

(3572)
Mitchell M L, Mulherin J H
The stock price response to pension terminations and the relation of terminations with corporate takeovers
FIN MGMT 1989 AUTUMN VOL 18 p 41-56.

(3573)
Revsine L
Understanding Financial Accounting Standard 87
FAJ 1989 JAN-FEB VOL 45 p 61-68.

(3574)
Allen E T Jr, Melone J J, Rosenbloom J S et al.
Pension planning: pensions, profit-sharing, and other deferred compensation plans. 6th ed
Irwin, 1988.

(3575)
Ambachtsheer K P et al.
The pension dollar report
B 1988 JUN 20 p 2-17.

(3576)
Beam B T Jr, McFadden J J
Employee benefits. 2nd ed
Irwin, 1988.

(3577)
Bodie Z, Shoven J B, Wise D A eds.
Pensions in the U.S. economy
U of Chicago Pr, 1988.

(3578)
Estrella A, Hirtle B
Estimating the funding gap of the Pension Benefit Guaranty Corporation
F R Bk New York Q Rev 1988 AUTUMN VOL 13:3.

(3579)
Haw I-M, Ruland W, Hamdallah A
Investor evaluation of overfunded pension plan terminations
JFR 1988 VOL 11:1 p 81-88.

(3580)
Ippolito R A
A study of the regulatory effect of the Employee Retirement Income Security Act
JLE 1988 VOL 31:1 p 85-126.

(3581)
McFadden J J
Retirement plans for employees
Irwin, 1988..

(3582) **Warshawshy M J**
Pension plans: funding, assets, and regulatory environment
F R Bul 1988 NOV VOL 74:11.

(3583)
Wentzell D
The brave new world of Canadian pension fund fiduciaries
Canadian Investment Review 1988 FALL VOL 1 p 25-28.

(3584)
Alderson M J, Chen K C
The stockholder consequences of terminating the pension fund
MCFJ 1987 WINTER VOL 4 p 55-61.

(3585)
Benjamin B et al.
Pensions: the problems of today and tomorrow
Allen, 1987.

(3586)
Bodie Z, Shoven J B, Wise D A eds.
Issues in pensions economics
U of Chicago Pr, 1987.

(3587)
Allen S G, Clark R L, Sumner D A
Post-retirement adjustments of pension benefits
Journal of Human Resources 1986 WINTER VOL 21 p 118-137.

(3588)
Gabrielli G, Fano D
The challenge of private pension funds: present trends and future prospects in industrialised countries
Economist Publications, 1986.

(3589)
Hubbard R G
Pension wealth and individual saving: some new evidence
JMCB 1986 MAY VOL 18:2 p 167-178.

(3590)
McMillan H M
Nonassignable pensions and the price of risk
JMCB 1986 FEB VOL 18:1 p 60-75.

(3591)
Michas N A
The performance measurement and evaluation of a corporate retirement plan: a case study
FR 1986 NOV VOL 21:4.

(3592)
Rashid M, Gandhi D K
Tax and savings implications of the Canadian registered retirement savings plans
FR 1986 NOV VOL 21:4.

(3593)
Bicksler J L, Chen A H
The integration of insurance and taxes in corporate pension strategy
JF 1985 JUL VOL 40:3 p 943-957.

(3594)
Bodie Z, Light J O, Morck R and Taggart R A
Corporate pension policy: An empirical investigation
FAJ 1985 SEP-OCT VOL 41 p 10-16.

(3595)
Hubbard R G
Personal taxation, pension wealth, and portfolio composition
REStat 1985 VOL 67 p 53.

(3596)
Marcus A J
Spinoff/terminations and the value of pension insurance
JF 1985 JUL VOL 40:3 p 911-926.

(3597)
Pesando J E
The usefulness of the wind-up measure of pension liabilities : a labor market perspective
JF 1985 JUL VOL 40:3 p 927-942.

(3598)
Bodie Z, Shoven J B eds.
Financial aspects of the United States pension system
U of Chicago Pr, 1984.

(3599)
Fortune
The battle for Japan's pension stash has begun
F 1984 AUG 6 VOL 110:3 p 48-50.

(3600)
Kotlikoff L J, Smith D E
Pensions in the American economy
U of Chicago Pr, 1984.

(3601)
Mennis E A, Clark C D
Understanding corporate pension plans
Research Foundation of the Institute of Chartered
Financial Analysts, 1983.

(3602)
Bulow J I
What are corporate pension liabilities?
QJE 1982 VOL 97 p 435-452.

(3603)
Munnell A H
The economics of private pensions
Brookings, 1982.

(3604)
Pesando J E
Investment risk bankruptcy risk and pension
reform in Canada
JF 1982 JUN VOL 37:3 p 741-749.

(3605)
Quinn J F
Pension wealth of government and private sector
workers
AER 1982 VOL 72 P+P p 283-287.

(3606)
Feldstein M
Private pensions and inflation
AER 1981 VOL 71 P+P p 424-428.

(3607)
Bodie V
An innovation for stable real retirement income
JPM 1980 FALL VOL 7:1 p 5-13.

(3608)
Ulph D, Hemming R
Uncertain lifetime, imperfect insurance markets
and the valuation of pension wealth
REStud 1980 VOL 47 p 587.

(3609)
Barnow B S, Ehrenberg R G
The costs of defined benefit pension plans and
firm adjustments
QJE 1979 VOL 93 p 523.

(3610)
Cooper K H, Mills C C eds.
Canada at the pension crossroads
Fin Exec, 1979.

(3611)
Schiller B R, Weiss R D
The impact of private pensions on firm
attachment
REStat 1979 AUG VOL 61:3 p 369-380.

(3612)
Brown M V
Prudence under ERISA: what regulators say
FAJ 1977 JAN-FEB p 33-39.

(3613)
Gray W S
The major shortfall of ERISA
FAJ 1977 JAN-FEB p 18-20.

(3614)
Hall J P III
Celi-another government time bomb
FAJ 1977 SEP-OCT p 30-34.

(3615)
Harvard Law Review
Public employee pensions in times of fiscal
distress
HLR 1977 VOL 90:5 p 992-1017.

(3616)
Hemming R C L
The effect of state and private pensions on
retirement behaviour and personal capital
accumulation
REStud 1977 VOL 44 p 169.

(3617)
Klesch A G
Interpreting the prudent man of ERISA
FAJ 1977 JAN-FEB p 26-32.

(3618)
Korschot B C
Prudence before and after ERISA
FAJ 1977 JUL-AUG p 18-21.

(3619)
Oldfield G S
Financial aspects of the private pension system
JMCB 1977 FEB VOL 9:1 p 48-54.

(3620)
Pozen R C
The prudent man rule and ERISA
FAJ 1977 MAR-APR p30-35.

(3621)
Treynor J
The principles of corporate pension finance
JF 1977 MAY VOL 32:2 p 627-638.

(3622)
Drucker P F
The unseen revolution: how pension fund
socialism came to America
Heinemann, 1976.

(3623)
Munnell A H
Private pensions and saving: New evidence
JPE 1976 VOL 84 p 1013.

(3624)
Paul R D
Can private pension plans deliver?
HBR 1974 SEP-OCT VOL 52:5 p 22-28, 32-34.

(3625)
Murray R F
Pension funds: newest among major financial
institutions
JBR 1973 WINTER VOL 3:4 p 247-260.

(3626)
Bagehot W (pseud for Treynor J L)
Risk and reward in corporate pension funds
FAJ 1972 JAN-FEB VOL 28 p 80-84.

(3627)
Schoeplein R N
The effect of pension plans on other retirement
saving
JF 1970 JUN VOL 25 p 633-638.

(3628)
Gibb W T
Critical evaluation of pension plans
JF 1968 MAY VOL 23 p 337-343.

(3629)
Murray R F
Pension funds in the American economy
JF 1968 MAY VOL 23 p 331-336.

(3630)
Murray R F
Economic aspects of pensions: a summary report
Natl Bur Econ Res, 1968.

(3631)
Antliff J C, Freund W C
Some basic research into historical results under
pension plans with benefits based on common
stock performance
JF 1967 MAY VOL 22 p 169-191.

(3632)
Holland D M
Private pension funds: projected growth
Natl Bur Econ Res, 1966.

(3633)
Polakoff M E
Public pension funds
FAJ 1966 MAY-JUN VOL 22 p 75-81.

(3634)
Sarnat M
Saving and investment through retirement funds
in Israel
Jerusalem: Maurice Falk Institute for Economic
Research in Israel, 1966..

(3635)**Cagan P**
Effect of pension plans on aggregate saving:
evidence from a sample survey
(Dist by Columbia U Pr) Natl Bur Econ Res,
1965.

(3636)
Mundheim R H, Henderson G D
Applicability of the federal securities laws to
pension and profit sharing plans
LCP 1964 JUN VOL 29 p 795-841.

(3637)
Anderson W M
Group accumulation through equities for pensions
JF 1962 MAY VOL 17 p 194-202.

(3638)
McGill D M
Fulfilling pension expectations
Irwin, 1962.

(3639)
Andrews V L
The supply of loanable funds from non-insured
corporate state- and city-administered employee
pension funds
JF 1961 MAY VOL 16 p 328-350.

(3640)
Miller E
Trends in private pension funds
JF 1961 MAY VOL 16 p 313-327.

(3641)
Harbrecht P P
Pension funds and economic power
Twentieth Fund, 1959.

8.81 Pension funding

(3642)
Barrett W B
Term structure modeling for pension liability
discounting
FAJ 1988 NOV-DEC VOL 44 p 63-67.

(3643)
Ennis R M
Is a statewide pension fund a person or a cookie
jar? The answer has implications for investment
policy
FAJ 1988 NOV-DEC VOL 44 p 21-27.

(3644)
Ezra D D
Economic values: a pension pentateuch
FAJ 1988 MAR-APR VOL 44 p 58-67.

(3645)
Hutchison B
Paying for pensions: Can Canada cope?
Canadian Investment Review 1988 FALL VOL 1
p 9-16.

(3646)
Ezra D D, Ambachtsheer K P
Pension funds: Rich or poor?
FAJ 1985 MAR-APR VOL 41 p 43-57.

(3647)
Estrella A
Corporate use of pension overfunding
F R Bk New York Q Rev 1984 SPRING VOL
9:1.

(3648)
Feldstein M, Morck R
Pension   funding   decisions,   interest   rate
assumptions and share prices
(in Bodie Z and Shoven J eds., Financial aspects
of the United States pension system.   U of
Chicago Pr, 1983.)

(3649)
Feldstein M, Morck R
Pension funds and the value of equities
FAJ 1983 SEP-OCT VOL 39 p 29-40.

(3650)
Martin L J, Henderson G V
On bond ratings and pension obligations : a note.
JFQA 1983 DEC VOL 18:4 p 463-470

(3651)
Colvin G
How sick companies are endangering the pension
system
F 1982 OCT 4 VOL 106:7 p 72-78.

(3652)
Ippolito R A
The economic burden of corporate pension
liabilities
FAJ 1986 JAN-FEB p 22-34.

(3653)
Langetieg T C, Findlay M C, Motta L F J da
Multiperiod pension plans and ERISA
JFQA 1982 NOV VOL 17:4 p 603-635.

(3654)
Tepper I
The future of private funding
FAJ 1982 JAN-FEB p 25-32.

(3655)
Ehrbar A F
How to slash your company's tax bill
F 1981 FEB 23 p 122-124.

(3656)
Feldstein M, Seligman S
Pension funding share prices and national savings
JF 1981 SEP VOL 36:4 p 801-824.

(3657)
Ezra D D
How actuaries determine the unfunded pension
liability
FAJ 1980 JUL-AUG VOL 36 p 43-50.

(3658)
Tepper I, Paul R D
How much funding for your company's pension
plan?
HBR 1978 NOV-DEC VOL 56:6 p 6-8.

(3659)
Treynor J L, Regan P, Priest W
Pension claims and corporate assets
FAJ 1978 MAY-JUN p 84.

(3660)
Regan P J
The pension burden under ERISA
FAJ 1976 MAR-APR p 26-32.

(3661)
Sharpe W F
Corporate pension funding policy
JFE 1976 VOL 3 p 183.

(3662)
Treynor J L, Priest W, Regan P
The financial reality of pension funding under
ERISA
Dow Jones-Irwin, 1976.

(3663)
Trowbridge C L
ABC's of pension funding
HBR 1966 MAR-APR VOL 44 p 115-126.

8.811 Simulation models of pension funding

(3664)
Leibowitz M L, Henriksson R D
Portfolio optimisation within a surplus framework
FAJ 1988 MAR-APR VOL 44 p 43-51.

(3665)
Kingsland L
Projecting the financial condition of a pension
using plan simulation analysis
JF 1982 MAY VOL 37:2 p 577-584.

(3666)
Winklevoss H E
PLASM: pension liability and asset simulation
model
JF 1982 MAY VOL 37:2 p 585-594.

(3667)
Tepper I
Risk vs return in pension fund investment
HBR 1977 MAR-APR VOL 55:2 p 100-107.

(3668)
Tepper I, Affleck A R P
Pension plan liabilities and corporate financial
strategies
JF 1974 VOL 29 p 1549.

8.82 Pension fund investment policy

(3669)
Haugen R A
Pension management in the context of corporate
risk management
JPM 1989 FALL VOL 16:1 p 72-78.

(3670)
Arnott R D, Bernstein P L
The right way to manage your pension fund
HBR 1988 JAN-FEB VOL 66:1 p 95-102.

(3671)
Ambachtsheer K P
Pension fund asset allocation: In defense of a
60/40 equity/debt asset mix
FAJ 1987 SEP-OCT VOL 43 p 14-24.

(3672)
Hagigi M, Kluger B
Assessing risk and return of pension funds'
portfolios by the Telser safety-first approach
JBFA 1987 VOL 14:2 p 241.

(3673)
Leibowitz M L
Pension   asset   allocation   through   surplus
management
FAJ 1987 MAR-APR VOL 43 p 29-40.

(3674)
Shepherd A G ed.
Pension fund investment
Woodhead-Faulkner, 1987.

(3675)
Ambachtsheer K P
Pension funds and the bottom line: Managing the
corporate pension fund as a financial business
Dow Jones-Irwin, 1986.

(3676)
Leibowitz M L
Total portfolio duration: A new perspective on
asset allocation
FAJ 1986 SEP-OCT VOL 42 p 18-31.

(3677)
Leibowitz M L
The dedicated bond portfolio in pension funds -
Part 1: motivations and basics
FAJ 1986 JAN-FEB p 69.

(3678)
Malley S L, Jayson S
Why do financial executives manage pension funds
the way they do
FAJ 1986 MAR-APR VOL 42 p 56-62.

(3679)
Copeland T
An   economic   approach   to   pension   fund
management
MCFJ 1984 SPRING VOL 2 p 26-39.

(3680)
Curatola A P, Fields K T, Samson W D
The benefits of the salary reduction plan
FAJ 1984 MAY-JUN VOL 40 p 53-59.

(3681)
Doyle R J
IRAs and the capital-gains tax effect
FAJ 1984 MAY-JUN VOL 40 p 60-66.

(3682)
Good W R
Accountability for pension fund performance
FAJ 1984 JAN-FEB VOL 40 p 39-42.

(3683)
Bird R, Chin H, McCrae M
The performance of Australian superannuation
funds
AJM 1983 JUN VOL 8 p 49-70.

(3684)
Black F, Dewhurst M P
A new investment strategy for pension funds
JPM 1981 SUMMER VOL 7:4 p 26-34.

(3685)
Mennis E A, Valentine J L, Mennis D L
New perspectives on pension fund management
JPM 1981 SPRING VOL 7:3 p 46-50.

(3686)
Tepper I
Taxation and corporate pension policy
JF 1981 MAR VOL 36:1 p 1-13.

(3687)
Black F
The tax consequences of long-run pension policy
FAJ 1980 JUL-AUG VOL 36 p 21-29..

(3688)**Crowell R A, Mainer R E**
Pension fund management: external or internal?
HBR 1980 NOV-DEC VOL 58:6 p 180-182.

(3689)
Ellis C D
Pension funds need management management
FAJ 1979 MAY-JUN VOL 35 p 25-30.

(3690)
Kent G H
Team management of pension money
HBR 1979 MAY-JUN VOL 57:3 p 162-167.

(3691)
Dietz P O, Fogler H R
Pension portfolio objective- Connecting the loop
FIN MGMT 1978 SUMMER VOL 7 p 56.

(3692)
Aldrich P C, Upton K
Real estate investment for pension funds
HBR 1977 MAY-JUN VOL 55:3 p 14-16.

(3693)
Beebower G L, Bergstrom G L
Pension performance 1966-1975
FAJ 1977 MAY-JUN p 31-42.

(3694)
Cottle S
The future of pension management
FAJ 1977 MAY-JUN p 23-26.

(3695)
Langbein J H, Posner R A
Market funds and trust-investment law
American Bar Foundation Journal 1976 (Part I);
1977 (Part II).

(3696)
McWilliams J D
A closer look at incentive fees for bank managed
pension funds
JBR 1973 WINTER VOL 3:4 p 238-246.

(3697)
Williams G P Jr
An incentive plan for bank managed pension
funds
JBR 1971 SPRING VOL 2:1.

(3698)
Gardner E B ed.
Pension fund investment management: CFA
research seminar, September 13-14 1968, Virginia
Irwin, 1969.

(3699)
Nursaw W G
Principles of pension fund investment
Hutchinson, 1965.

(3700)
Howell P L
A re-examination of pension fund investment
policies
JF 1958 MAY VOL 13 p 261-274.

8.83 Employee stock ownership plans (ESOPs) and Keogh plans

(3701)
Cheeks J E
The Dow Jones-Irwin guide to Keoghs
Dow Jones-Irwin, 1989.

(3702)
Bruner R F
Leveraged ESOPs and corporate restructuring
JACF 1988 SPRING VOL 1 p 54-66.

(3703)
Chen A H, Kensinger J W
Beyond the tax benefits of ESOPs
JACF 1988 SPRING VOL 1 p 67-75.

(3704)
Rosen C, Klein K, Young K
Employee ownership in America: the equity
solution
Lexington Bks, 1986.

(3705)
Chen A H, Kensinger J W
Innovations in corporate financing: Tax-deductible
equity
FIN MGMT 1985 WINTER VOL 14 p 44-51.

(3706)
Owens R W, Willinger G L
Investment potential of an individual retirement account
JBR 1985 AUTUMN VOL 16:3 p 161.

(3707)
Mano R M, Burr T
IRAs versus nonsheltered alternatives for retirement savings goals
FAJ 1984 MAY-JUN VOL 40 p 67-75.

(3708)
Dean K, Miller J J
Paysops - are they in your company's future?
FE 1983 JAN VOL 51:1 p 12-18.

(3709)
Rosen C
ESOPs: New growth for your firm
FE 1983 JUL p 10-20.

(3710)
Bogan E C, Bogan T R
Individual Retirement Accounts and preretirement savings goals
FAJ 1982 NOV-DEC VOL 38 p 45-48.

(3711)
Roth T P
Employee stock ownership trusts, myopia, and intertemporal profit maximization
QREB 1978 VOL 18:2 p 73.

(3712)
Lund H A, Casey W J, Chamberlain P K
A financial analysis of the ESOT
FAJ 1976 JAN-FEB VOL 32 p 55-61.

(3713)
Monahan J P, Monahan K B
Company contributions to disretionary profit-sharing plans: A quantitative approach
JF 1974 VOL 29 p 981.

(3714)
Jehring J J
The investment and administration of profit sharing trust funds: a research study of 208 profit sharing trust funds
Profit Sharing, 1957.

8.9 Trust funds

(3715)
Institute of Chartered Financial Analysts
Personal trust investment management. Proceedings, C.F.A. Research Seminar, May 4-6, 1967, Charlottesville, Va.
Irwin, 1968.

(3716)
Kennedy W, Searle P F
The management of a trust department
Bankers, 1967.

(3717)
Goldsmith R W, Shapiro E
An estimate of bank-administered personal trust funds
JF 1959 MAR VOL 14 p 11-17.

8.91 Foundations and endowment funds

(3718)
Garland J P
A market-yield spending rule for endowments and trusts
FAJ 1989 JUL-AUG VOL 45 p 50-60.

(3719)
Kittell C E ed.
The challenges of investing for endowment funds
Institute of Chartered Financial Analysts, 1987.

(3720)
Lipton D A
Significant private foundations and the need for public selection of their trustees
VLR 1978 VOL 64:6 p 779-832.

(3721)
Kim T
Investment performance of college endowment funds
QREB 1976 VOL 16:3 p 73.

(3722)
Litvack J M, Malkiel B G, Quandt R E
A plan for the definition of endowment income
AER 1974 VOL 64 P+P p 433-437.

(3723)
Nichols D A
The investment income formula of the American
Economic Association
AER 1974 VOL 64 P+P p 420-426.

(3724)
Tobin J
What is permanent endowment income?
AER 1974 VOL 64 P+P p 427.

(3725)
Whitaker B
The foundations: an anatomy of philanthropy and
society
Eyre Methuen, 1974.

(3726)
Neuhoff K, Pavel U eds.
Trusts and foundations in Europe: a comparative
study
Bedford Square Pr, 1971.

(3727)
Meckling W H, Jensen M C
University endowments and spending policies
U of Rochester, Jan 1970.

(3728)
Advisory Committee on Endowment Management
Managing educational endowments: report to the
Ford Foundation
Ford, 1969.

(3729)
Cary W L, Bright C B
The law and the lore of endowment funds
Ford, 1969.

(3730)
Malkiel B G
The definition of endowment income
Report of a special faculty-administrative
committee, Princeton U, unp, 1969.

(3731)
Nelson R L
The investment policies of foundations
Russell Sage, 1967.

(3732)
Welles C
University endowments: revolution comes to the
ivory tower
II 1967 SEP VOL 1.

9 Efficiency of securities markets

(3733)
Kamarotou H, O'Hanlon J
Informational efficiency in the UK, US, Canadian and Japanese equity markets: a note
JBFA 1989 SPRING VOL 16:2 p 183.

(3734)
LeRoy S F
Efficient capital markets and martingales
JEL 1989 DEC VOL 27:4 1583-1621.

(3735)
Samuelson P A
The judgment of economic science on rational portfolio management: indexing, timing, and long-horizon effects
JPM 1989 FALL VOL 16:1 p 4-12.

(3736)
Stein J C
Efficient capital markets, inefficient firms: a model of myopic corporate behavior
QJE 1989 NOV VOL 104:4 p 655-670.

(3737)
Aiyagari S R
Economic fluctuations without shocks to fundamentals; or, Does the stock market dance to its own music?
F R Bk Minneapolis Q Rev 1988 VOL 12:1 p 8-24.

(3738)
Brown K C, Harlow W V, Tinic S M
Risk aversion, uncertain information and market efficiency
JFE 1988 VOL 22 p 355.

(3739)
Brown R M
A comparison of market efficiency among stock exchanges
JBFA 1988 AUTUMN VOL 15:3 p373-384.

(3740)
Business Week
The efficient market was a good idea - and then came the crash
Business Week 1988 FEB 22 p 140-142..

(3741)**Campbell J Y, Shiller R J**
The dividend-price ratio and expectations of future dividends and discount factors
RFS 1988 FALL VOL 1:3 p 195-228.

(3742)
Ho T S Y, Michaely R
Information quality and market efficiency
JFQA 1988 MAR VOL 23:1 p 53-70.

(3743)
Jurin B
Raising the equity in an efficient market
MCFJ 1988 WINTER VOL 5 p 53-60.

(3744)
Michaely R, Ho T S Y
Information quality and market efficiency
JFQA 1988 MAR VOL 23 p 53.

(3745)
Taylor S, Kingsman B, Guimaraes R eds.
A reappraisal of the efficiency of financial markets
Springer-Verlag, 1988.

(3746)
Amihud Y, Mendelson H
Are trading profits feasible
JPM 1987 FALL VOL 14:1 p 77-78.

(3747)
Joy O M
Hunting the stock market snark
SMR 1987 SPRING VOL 28:3 p 17-24.

(3748)
Merton R C
On the current state of the stock market rationality hypothesis
(in Fischer S and Dornbusch R eds., Macroeconomics and finance: Essays in honor of Franco Modigliani. MIT Pr, 1987.)

(3749)
Miller E M
Bounded efficient markets: a new wrinkle to the EMH
JPM 1987 SUMMER VOL 13:4 p 4-13.

(3750)
Mookerjee R
Monetary policy and the informational efficiency of the stock market: the evidence from many countries
AE 1987 NOV VOL 19:11 p 1521-1532.

(3751)
Treynor J L
Market efficiency and the bean jar experiment
FAJ 1987 MAY-JUN VOL 43 p 50-53.

(3752)
Keane S M
The efficient market hypothesis on trial
FAJ 1986 MAR-APR VOL 42 p 58-63.

(3753)
Summers L H
Does the Stock Market rationally reflect
fundamental values?
JF 1986 JUL VOL 41:3 p 591-602.

(3754)
Summers L H
Do we really know that financial markets are
efficient?
(in Edwards J et al. eds., Recent developments in
corporate finance. Cambridge U Pr, 1986.)

(3755)
Haugen R A, Ortiz E, Arjona E
Market efficiency: Mexico versus the U.S.
JPM 1985 FALL VOL 12:1 p 28.

(3756)
Smirlock M, Yawitz J B
Asset returns, discount rate changes and market
efficiency
JF 1985 SEP VOL 40:4 p 1141-1158

(3757)
Boldt B L, Arbit H L
Efficient markets and the professional investor
FAJ 1984 JUL-AUG VOL 40 p 22-35.

(3758)
Dawson S M
The trend toward efficiency for less developed
stock exchanges : Hong Kong
JBFA 1984 SUMMER VOL 11:2 p 151-161

(3759)
Gilson R J, Kraakman R H
The mechanisms of market efficiency
VLR 1984 VOL 70:4 p 549-644.

(3760)
Hawawini G A
European equity markets: price behavior and
efficiency
NYU, 1984.

(3761)
Hawawini G A, Michel P A eds.
European equity markets: risk, return, and
efficiency
Garland, 1984.

(3762)
Levmore S
Efficient markets and puzzling intermediaries
VLR 1984 VOL 70:4 p 645-667.

(3763)
Renshaw E F
Stock market panics: A test of the efficient
market hypothesis
FAJ 1984 MAY-JUN VOL 40 p 48-52.

(3764)
Shiller R J
Stock prices and social dynamics
Brookings Papers on Economic Activity 1984 NO
2 p 457-498.

(3765)
Stewart G B, Glassman D M
How to communicate with an efficient market
MCFJ 1984 SPRING VOL 2 p 73-79.

(3766)
Brown R L, Shevlin T J
Stock market efficiency and price predictions
implicit in option trading
AJM 1983 DEC VOL 8 p 71-94.

(3767)
Ferguson R
An efficient stock market? ridiculous!
JPM 1983 SUMMER VOL 9:4 p 31-38.

(3768)
Fortune
Can you beat the stock market?
F 1983 DEC 26 VOL 108:13 p 82-96.

(3769)
Keane S M
Stock market efficiency: theory, evidence and implications
Philip Allan, 1983.

(3770)
Nichols W D
Semantics and capital market efficiency: testing the market's reaction to the naming of stock distributions as splits
JBusR 1983 VOL 11 p 11-20.

(3771)
Sorensen R A
An "essential reservation" about the EMH
JPM 1983 SUMMER VOL 9:4 p 29-30.

(3772)
Oppenheimer H R, Schlarbaum G G
Investing with Ben Graham: an ex ante test of the efficient markets hypothesis.
JFQA 1981 SEP VOL 16:3 p 341-360.

(3773)
Kripke H
Inside information, market information and efficient markets
FAJ 1980 MAR-APR VOL 36 p 20-24.

(3774)
Goldman M B, Sosin H B
Information dissemination, market efficiency and the frequency of transactions
JFE 1979 MAR VOL 7:1 p 29-61.

(3775)
Groth J C
Security-relative information market efficiency: Some empirical evidence
JFQA 1979 SEP VOL 14 p 573.

(3776)
Mayer-Sommer A P
Understanding and acceptance of the efficient markets hypothesis and its accounting implications
AR 1979 JAN VOL 54:1 p 88-106.

(3777)
Miller E M
A simple counter example to the random walk theory
FAJ 1979 JUL-AUG VOL 35 p 55-56.

(3778)
Richards P H
UK & European share price behaviour: the evidence
Kogan Page, 1979.

(3779)
Jensen M C
Some anomalous evidence regarding market efficiency
JFE 1978 VOL 6 p 95.

(3780)
John K
Market efficiency in an Arrow-Debreu economy: A closer look
AER 1978 VOL 68 p 419-422.

(3781)
Laffer A B, Ranson R D
Some practical applications of the efficient-market concept
FIN MGMT 1978 SUMMER VOL 7 p 63.

(3782)
Mayshar J
Investors' time horizon and the inefficiency of capital markets
QJE 1978 VOL 92 p 187.

(3783)
Jaffe J F, Winkler R L
Optimal speculation against an efficient market
JF 1976 VOL 31 p 49.

(3784)
Kessel R A, Clark T A
A study of expectational errors in the money and capital markets, 1921-1970
JLE 1976 VOL 19 p 1.

(3785)
Treynor J L
Long-term investing
FAJ 1976 MAY-JUN VOL 32 p 56-59.

(3786)
Dyckman T R et al.
Efficient capital markets and accounting: a
critical analysis
P-H, 1975.

(3787)
West R R
On the difference between internal and external
market efficiency
FAJ 1975 NOV-DEC VOL 31 p 30-34.

(3788)
Hagerman R L
The efficiency of the market for bank stocks: an
empirical test
JMCB 1973 AUG VOL 5:3 p 846-855.

(3789)
Smidt S
Which road to an efficient stock market?
FAJ 1971 SEP-OCT VOL 27 p 18ff.

(3790)
Vasicek O A, McQuown J A
The efficient market model
FAJ 1971 SEP-OCT VOL 28 p 71-84.

(3791)
Fama E F
Efficient capital markets: a review of theory and
empirical work
JF 1970 MAY VOL 25 p 383-417.

(3792)
Semah J, Serres C, Tessier B
L'ordinateur speculateur
Dunod, 1970.

(3793)
Keynes J M
The general theory of employment, interest and
money (See especially Chapter 12 for Keynes's
comments on the stock market)
Macmillan, 1936.

9.1   Conditions for efficiency

(3794)
Diamond D W, Verrecchia R E
Constraints on short-selling and asset price
adjustment to private information
JFE 1987 JUN VOL 18:2 p 277-311.

(3795)
Latham M
Informational efficiency and information subsets
JF 1986 MAR VOL 41:1 p 39-52.

(3796)
Easley D, Jarrow R A
Consensus beliefs equilibrium and market
efficiency
JF 1983 JUN VOL 38:3 p 903-911.

(3797)
Stiglitz J E
The inefficiency of the stock market equilibrium.
REStud 1982 APR VOL 49 p 241-261.

(3798)
Beaver W H
Market efficiency
AR 1981 JAN VOL 56:1 p 23-37.

(3799)
Bilson J F O
The speculative efficiency hypothesis.
JB 1981 JUL VOL 54:3 p 435-451.

(3800)
Fama E F
Reply (to LeRoy)
JF 1976 MAR VOL 31 p 143-145.

(3801)
LeRoy S F
Efficient capital markets: comment
JF 1976 MAR VOL 31 p 139-141.

(3802)
Rubinstein M
Securities market efficiency in an Arrow-Debreu
economy
AER 1975 DEC VOL 65:5 p 812-824.

9.2   Variance bounds

(3803)
Brown K C, Harlow W V
Market overreaction: magnitude and intensity
JPM 1988 WINTER VOL 14:2 p 6-13.

(3804)
Frankel J A, Stock J J
Regression vs. volatility tests of the efficiency of
foreign exchange markets
JIMF 1987 MAR VOL 6:1 p 31-48.

(3805)
Kleidon A W
Variance bounds tests and stock price valuation
models
JPE 1986 VOL 94 p 953.

(3806)
Marsh T A, Merton R C
Dividend variability and variance bounds tests for
the rationality of stock market prices
AER 1986 VOL 76 p 483-498.

(3807)
Poterba J M, Summers L H
The persistence of volatility and stock market
fluctuations
AER 1986 VOL 76 p 1142-1151.

(3808)
Bondt W F M de, Thaler R H
Does the stock market overreact?
JF 1985 JUL VOL 40:3 p 793-808.

(3809)
Mankiw N G, Romer D, Shapiro M D
An unbiased reexamination of stock market
efficiency
JF 1985 JUL VOL 40:3 p 677-689

(3810)
LeRoy S F
Efficiency and the variability of asset prices
AER 1984 VOL 74 P+P p 183-187.

(3811)
Flavin M A
Excess volatility in the financial markets: A
reassessment of the empirical evidence
JPE 1983 VOL 91 p 929.

(3812)
Michener R W
Variance bounds in a simple model of asset
pricing
JPE 1982 VOL 90 p 166.

(3813)
Grossman S J, Shiller R J
The determinants of the variability of stock
market prices
AER 1981 VOL 71 P+P p 222-227.

(3814)
Shiller R J
The use of volatility measures in assessing market
efficiency
JF 1981 MAY VOL 36:2 p 291-304.

(3815)
Shiller R J
Do stock prices move too much to be justified by
subsequent changes in dividends?
AER 1981 VOL 71 p 421-436.

(3816)
Singleton K J
Expectations models of the term structure and
implied variance bounds
JPE 1980 VOL 88 p 1159.

9.3   Weak-form efficiency

(3817)
Conrad J, Kaul G
Mean reversion in short-horizon expected returns
RFS 1989 VOL 2:2 p 225-240.

(3818)
Davidson W N, Dutia I, Dutia D
A note on the behavior of security returns: a test
of stock market overreaction and efficiency
JFR 1989 FALL VOL 12:3 p 245-252.

(3819)
De Bondt W F M, Thaler R H
Anomalies: a mean-reverting walk down Wall
Street
JEP 1989 WINTER VOL 3:1 p 189-202.

(3820)
Jacobs B I, Levy K N
The complexity of the stock market
JPM 1989 FALL VOL 16:1 p 19-27.

(3821)
Lukac L P, Brorsen B W
The usefulness of historical data in selecting
parameters for technical trading systems
JFM 1989 VOL 9:1 p 55-66.

(3822)
Pruitt S W, White R E
Exchange-traded options and CRISMA trading
JPM 1989 SUMMER VOL 15:4 p 55-57.

(3823)
Berglund T, Liljeblom E
Market serial correlation in a small security
market: a note
JF 1988 DEC VOL 43:5 p 1265-1274.

(3824)
Billingsley R S, Chance D M
Put-call ratios and market timing effectiveness
JPM 1988 FALL VOL 15:1 p 25-28.

(3825)
Chan K C
On the contrarian investment strategy
JB 1988 VOL 61 p 147.

(3826)
Conrad J, Kaul G
Time-variation in expected returns
JB 1988 VOL 61 p 409.

(3827)
Fama E F, French K R
Permanent and temporary components of stock
prices
JPE 1988 APR VOL 96:2 p 246-273.

(3828)
Frankfurter G M, Lamoureux C G
Stock selection and timing - a new look at market
efficiency
JBFA 1988 AUTUMN VOL 15:3 p 385-400.

(3829)
Lo A W, MacKinlay A C
Stock market prices do not follow random walks:
evidence from a simple specification test
RFS 1988 SPRING VOL 1:1 p 41-66.

(3830)
Poterba J M, Summers L H
Mean reversion in stock prices: Evidence and
implications
JFE 1988 VOL 22 p 27.

(3831)
Pruitt S W, White R E
Who says technical analysis can't beat the market
JPM 1988 SPRING VOL 14:3 p 55-58.

(3832)
Sweeney R J
Some new filter rule tests: Methods and results
JFQA 1988 SEP VOL 23 p 285.

(3833)
Atchison M D, Butler K C, Simonds R R
Nonsynchronous security trading and market index
auto correlation
JF 1987 MAR VOL 42:1 p 111-112.

(3834)
Alderson M J, Chen K C
Excess asset reversions and shareholder wealth
JF 1986 MAR VOL 41:1 p 225-241

(3835)
Ashley R, Patterson D M
A nonparametric, distribution-free test for serial
independence in stock returns
JFQA 1986 JUN VOL 21:2 p 221-227.

(3836)
Barnes P
Thin trading and stock market efficiency : the
case of the Kuala Lumpur Stock Exchange
JBFA 1986 WINTER VOL 13:4 p 609-617

(3837)
Dubofsky D A, Groth J C
Relative information accessibility for OTC stocks
and security returns
FR 1986 FEB VOL 21:1.

(3838)
Laurence M M
Weak-form efficiency in the Kuala Lumpur and
Singapore stock markets
JBankF 1986 VOL 10 p 431.

(3839)
Taylor S
Modelling financial time series
Wiley, 1986.

(3840)
Shefrin H M, Statman M
The disposition to sell winners too early and ride
losers too long : theory and evidence
JF 1985 JUL VOL 40:3 p 777-792.

(3841)
Treynor J L, Ferguson R
In defense of technical analysis
JF 1985 JUL VOL 40:3 p 757-775

(3842)
Berglund T, Wahlroos B, Ornmark A
The weak form efficiency of the Finnish and the
Scandinavian stock exchanges: A comparative note
on thin trading
Scandinavian Journal of Economics 1983 VOL
85:4 p 30-41.

(3843)
Taylor S J
Tests of the random walk hypotheses against a
price-trend hypothesis
JFQA 1982 MAR VOL 17:1 p 37-61.

(3844)
Cohen K J, Maier S F, Schwartz R A et al.
On the existence of serial correlation in an
efficient securities market
(in Elton E J and Gruber M J eds., Portfolio
theory, 25 years after: Essays in honor of Harry
Markowitz. N Holland, 1979.)

(3845)
Praetz P D
Testing for a flat spectrum on efficient market
price data
JF 1979 JUN VOL 34:3 p 645-658.

(3846)
Praetz P D
A general test of a filter effect
JFQA 1979 JUN VOL 14 p 385..

(3847)**Arditti F D, McCollough W A**
Real versus randomly generated stock prices
FAJ 1978 NOV-DEC p 70.

(3848)
Meade N
The random walk and a thin market
JBFA 1978 AUTUMN VOL 5:3 p 321-328.

(3849)
Roux F J P, Gilbertson B P
The behaviour of share prices on the
Johannesburg Stock Exchange
JBFA 1978 SUMMER VOL 5:2 p 223-232.

(3850)
Greene M T, Fielitz B D
Long-term dependence in common stock returns
JFE 1977 VOL 4 p 339.

(3851)
Kennedy R E, Sharma J L
A comparative analysis of stock price behavior on
the Bombay, London and New York stock
exchanges
JFQA 1977 SEP VOL 12 p 391.

(3852)
Ohlson J A
Risk aversion and the Martingale property of
stock prices: comments
IntER 1977 FEB VOL 18:1 p 229-234.

(3853)
Oldfield G S, Rogalski R J, Jarrow R A
An autoregressive jump process for common stock
returns
JFE 1977 VOL 5 p 389.

(3854)
Schwartz R A
The time-variance relationship: evidence on autocorrelation in common stock returns
JF 1977 VOL 32 p 41.

(3855)
Branch B
The predictive power of stock market indicators
JFQA 1976 JUN VOL 11 p 269.

(3856)
Praetz P D
Rates of return on filter tests
JF 1976 VOL 31 p 71.

(3857)
Fielitz B D
On the stationarity of transition probability matrices of common stocks
JFQA 1975 JUN VOL 10 p 327.

(3858)
Girmes D H, Benjamin A E
Random walk hypothesis for 543 stocks and shares registered on the London Stock Exchange
JBFA 1975 SPRING VOL 2:1 p 135-146.

(3859)
Emery J T
The information content of daily market indicators
JFQA 1973 MAR VOL 8:2 p 183-190.

(3860)
Hagerman R L, Richmond R D
Random walks, martingales and the OTC
JF 1973 VOL 28 p 897.

(3861)
Philippatos G C, Nawrocki D N
The information inaccuracy of stock market forecasts: Some new evidence of dependence on the New York stock exchange
JFQA 1973 JUN VOL 8:3 p 445-458.

(3862)
Ryan T M
Security prices as Markov processes
JFQA 1973 JAN VOL 8:1 p 17-36.

(3863)
Solnik B H
Note on the validity of the random walk for European stock prices
JF 1973 VOL 28 p 1151.

(3864)
Black F
Implications of the random walk hypothesis for portfolio management
FAJ 1971 MAR-APR VOL 27 p 16-22.

(3865)
Cheng P L, Deets M K
Portfolio returns and the random walk theory
JF 1971 MAR VOL 26 p 11-30.

(3866)
Kemp A G, Reid G C
The random walk hypothesis and the recent behaviour of equity prices in Britain
Ec 1971 VOL 38 p 28-51.

(3867)
Levy R A
The predictive significance of five-point chart patterns
JB 1971 JUL VOL 44 p 316-323.

(3868)
Mandelbrot B
When can price be arbitraged efficiently? A limit to the validity of the random walk and Martingale models
REStat 1971 AUG VOL 53 p 225-236.

(3869)
Young W E
Random walk of stock prices: a test of the variance-time function
Em 1971 SEP VOL 39 p 797-812.

(3870)
Brealey R A
The distribution and independence of successive rates of return in the U.K. equity market
JBF 1970 SUMMER VOL 2 p 29-40.

(3871)
Dryden M M
Filter tests of UK share prices
AE 1970 JAN VOL 1 p 261-276.

(3872)
Dryden M M
A statistical study of U.K. share prices
Scottish Journal of Political Economy 1970 NOV
VOL 17 p 369-389.

(3873)
Granger C W J, Morgenstern O
Predictability of stock market prices
Heath, 1970.

(3874)
Jensen M C, Bennington G A
Random walks and technical theories: some
additional evidence
JF 1970 MAY VOL 25 p 469-482.

(3875)
Dryden M M
Share price movements: a Markovian approach
JF 1969 MAR VOL 24 p 49-60.

(3876)
Dryden M M
A source of bias in filter tests of share prices
JB 1969 JUL VOL 42 p 321-325.

(3877)
Praetz P D
Australian share prices and the random walk
hypothesis
Australian Journal of Statistics 1969 VOL 11 p
123-129.

(3878)
Dryden M M
Short term forecasting of share prices: an
information theory approach
Scottish Journal of Political Economy 1968 NOV
VOL 15 p 227-249.

(3879)
Evans J L
The random walk hypothesis, portfolio analysis
and the buy-and-hold criterion
JFQA 1968 SEP VOL 3 p 327-342.

(3880)
Granger C W J
Some aspects of the random walk model of stock
market prices
IntER 1968 JUN VOL 9 p 253-257.

(3881)
James F E Jr
Monthly averages--an effective investment tool?
JFQA 1968 SEP VOL 3 p 315-326.

(3882)
Mandelbrot B
Some aspects of the random walk model of stock
market prices: comment
IntER 1968 JUN VOL 9 p 258-259.

(3883)
Owen J
Analysis of variance tests for local trends in the
Standard and Poor's Index
JF 1968 JAN VOL 23 p 509-514.

(3884)
Seelenfreund A, Parker G G C, Van Horne J C
Stock price behavior and trading
JFQA 1968 SEP VOL 3 p 263-282.

(3885)
Smidt S
A new look at the random walk hypothesis
JFQA 1968 SEP VOL 3 p 235-262.

(3886)
Van Horne J C, Parker G G C
Technical trading rules: a comment
FAJ 1968 JUL-AUG VOL 24 p 128-132.

(3887)
Zakon A J, Pennypacker J C
An analysis of the advance-decline line as a stock
market indicator
JFQA 1968 SEP VOL 3 p 299-314.

(3888)
Cullity J P
An alternative measure of the diffusion of stock
prices
QREB 1967 AUTUMN VOL 7 p 47-55.

(3889)
Levy R A
The principle of portfolio upgrading
IMR 1967 FALL VOL 7 p 82-96.

(3890)
Levy R A
Random walks: reality or myth
FAJ 1967 NOV-DEC VOL 23 p 69-77.

(3891)
Levy R A
Relative strength as a criterion for investment selection
JF 1967 DEC VOL 22 p 595-610.

(3892)
Osborne M F M
Some quantitative tests for stock price generating models and trading folklore
JASA 1967 JUN VOL 62 p 321-340.

(3893)
Van Horne J C, Parker G G C
The random walk theory: an empirical test
FAJ 1967 NOV-DEC VOL 23 p 87-92.

(3894)
Fama E F, Blume M E
Filter rules and stock market trading
JB 1966 JAN VOL 39 p 226-241.

(3895)
Mandelbrot B
Forecasts of future prices, unbiased markets, and Martingale models
JB 1966 JAN VOL 39 Suppl p 242-255.

(3896)
Niederhoffer V, Osborne M F M
Market making and reversal on the stock exchange
JASA 1966 DEC VOL 61 p 897-916.

(3897)
Fama E F
Random walks in stock market prices
FAJ 1965 SEP-OCT VOL 21 p 55-59.

(3898)
Fama E F
Tomorrow on the New York Stock Exchange
JB 1965 JUL VOL 38 p 285-299.

(3899)
Fama E F
The behavior of stock market prices
JB 1965 JAN VOL 38 p 34-105..

(3900)**Osborne M F M**
The dynamics of stock trading
Em 1965 JAN VOL 33 p 88-113.

(3901)
Samuelson P A
Proof that properly anticipated prices fluctuate randomly
IMR 1965 SPRING VOL 6 p 41-49.

(3902)
Theil H, Leenders C T
Tomorrow on the Amsterdam Exchange
JB 1965 JUL VOL 38 p 277-284.

(3903)
Alexander S S
Price movements in speculative markets: trends or random walks, number 2
IMR 1964 SPRING VOL 5 p 25-46.

(3904)
Borch K
Price movements in the stock market
Skandinavisk Aktuarietidskrift 1964 VOL 47 p 41-50.

(3905)
Cootner P H ed.
The random character of stock market prices
MIT Pr, 1964.

(3906)
Godfrey M D, Granger C W J, Morgenstern O
The random walk hypothesis of stock market behaviour
Kyk 1964 VOL 17 p 1-30.

(3907)
Moore A B
Some characteristics of changes in common stock prices
(in Cootner P H ed., The random character of stock market prices. MIT Pr, 1964.)

(3908)
Steiger W
A test of nonrandomness in stock price changes
(in Cootner P H ed., The random character of
stock market prices. MIT Pr, 1964.)

(3909)
Granger C W J, Morgenstern O
Spectral analysis of New York stock market prices
Kyk 1963 VOL 16 p 1-27.

(3910)
Weintraub R E
On speculative prices and random walks: a denial
JF 1963 MAR VOL 18 p 59-66.

(3911)
Cootner P H
Stock prices: random walks vs finite Markov
chains
IMR 1962 SPRING VOL 3 p 24-45.

(3912)
Osborne M F M
Periodic structure in the Brownian motion of
stock prices
OR 1962 MAY-JUN VOL 10 p 345-379.

(3913)
Seligman D
Playing the market with charts
F 1962 FEB VOL 67.

(3914)
Alexander S S
Price movements in speculative markets: trends or
random walks
IMR 1961 MAY VOL 2 p 7-26.

(3915)
Cowles A
A revision of previous conclusions regarding stock
price behavior
Em 1960 OCT VOL 28 p 909-915.

(3916)
Working H
Note on the correlation of first differences of
averages in a random chain
Em 1960 OCT VOL 28 p 916-918.

(3917)
Osborne M F M
Brownian motion in the stock market
OR 1959 MAR-APR VOL 7 p 145-173.

(3918)
Roberts H V
Stock market 'patterns' and financial analysis:
methodological suggestions
JF 1959 MAR VOL 14 p 1-10.

(3919)
St Laurent A G
Comments on 'Brownian motion in the stock
market'
OR 1959 VOL 7 p 806-807.

(3920)
Working H
A theory of anticipatory prices
AER 1958 VOL 48 p 188-199.

(3921)
Samuelson P A
Intertemporal price equilibrium: a prologue to the
theory of speculation
Weltswirtschaftliches Archiv 1957 VOL 79 p
181-221.

(3922)
Working H
New ideas and methods for price research
JFarmE 1956 VOL 38 p 1427-1436.

(3923)
Kendall M G
The analysis of economic time series, part 1
JRSS 1953 VOL 96 p 11-25.

(3924)
Working H
The investigation of economic expectations
AER 1949 MAY VOL 39 p 150-166.

(3925)
Cowles A, Jones H E
Some a posteriori probabilities in stock market
action
Em 1937 JUL p 280-294.

(3926)
Taussig F W
Is market price determinate?
QJE 1921 MAY VOL 35 p 394-411.

(3927)
Bachelier L
Theorie de la speculation. Docteur des Sciences
Mathematiques diss, University of Paris, 1900.
Originally published in Annales de l'Ecole
Normale Superieure, Sec. 3, 1900, p 21-86.
English translation by Boness A J, Theory of
speculation
(in Cootner P H ed., The random character of
stock market prices. MIT Pr, 1964.)

9.4   Event studies and semi-strong-form efficiency

(3928)
Gross M
A semi-strong test of the efficiency of the
aluminum and copper markets at the LME
JFM 1988 FEB VOL 8:1 p 67-78.

(3929)
Jain P C
Response of hourly stock prices and trading
volume to economic news
JB 1988 VOL 61 p 219.

(3930)
Barrett W B et al.
The adjustment of stock prices to completely
unanticipated events
FR 1987 NOV VOL 22:4.

(3931)
Copeland T E, Friedman D
The effect of sequential information arrival on
asset prices : an experimental study
JF 1987 JUL VOL 42:3 p 763-797.

(3932)
Etebari A, Horrigan J O, Landwehr J L
To be or not to be - reaction of stock returns to
sudden deaths of corporate chief executive officers
JBFA 1987 SUMMER VOL 14:2 p 255-278.

(3933)
Kim M K, Wu C
Macro-economic factors and stock returns
JFR 1987 SUMMER VOL 10:2 p 87-98.

(3934)
Peterson D R
Security price reactions to initial reviews of
common stock by the Value Line investment
survey
JFQA 1987 DEC VOL 22 p 483..

(3935)**French K R, Roll R**
Stock return variances. The arrival of information
and the reaction of traders
JFE 1986 SEP VOL 17:1 p 5-26.

(3936)
Chandy P R, Davidson W N, Garrison S
Bad news = good news! who can tell?
JPM 1985 FALL VOL 12:1 p 24-27.

(3937)
Goodhart C A E, Smith R G
The impact of news on financial markets in the
United Kingdom
JMCB 1985 NOV VOL 17:4 p 507-511.

(3938)
Patell J M, Wolfson M A
The intraday speed of adjustment of stock prices
to earnings and dividend announcements
JFE 1984 VOL 13 p 223-252.

(3939)
Sharpe I G
New information and Australian equity returns: A
multivariate analysis
AJM 1983 JUN VOL 8 p 21-34.

(3940)
Morse D
Wall Street Journal announcements and the
securities markets
FAJ 1982 MAR-APR VOL 38:2 p 69-76

(3941)
Nichols W D, Brown S L
Assimilating earnings and split information: Is the
capital market becoming more efficient?
JFE 1981 VOL 9 p 309.

(3942)
Hillmer S C, Yu P L
The market speed of adjustment to new information.
JFE 1979 DEC VOL 7:4 p 321-345

(3943)
Abdel-Khalik A R, McKeown C
Understanding accounting changes in an efficient market: evidence of differential reaction
AR 1978 OCT VOL 53:4 p 851-868.

(3944)
Ball R J
Anomalies in relationships between securities' yields and yield-surrogates
JFE 1978 JUN-SEP VOL 6:2-3 p 103-126.

(3945)
Charest G
Split information, stock returns and market efficiency
JFE 1978 JUN-SEP VOL 6:2-3 p 265-296.

(3946)
Collins D W
SEC product-line reporting and market efficiency
JFE 1975 VOL 2 p 125.

(3947)
Jaffe J F
On the use of public information in financial markets
JF 1975 VOL 30 p 831.

(3948)
Emery J T
Efficient capital markets and the information content of accounting numbers
JFQA 1974 MAR VOL 9 p 139.

(3949)
Waud R N
Public interpretation of discount rate changes: evidence on the "announcement" effect
Em 1970 MAR VOL 38 p 231-250.

(3950)
Coen P J, Gomme E D, Kendall M G
Lagged relationships in economic forecasting
JRSS 1969 VOL 31 p A133-A163.

(3951)
Fama E F, Fisher L, Jensen M C
The adjustment of stock prices to new information
IntER 1969 FEB VOL 10 p 1-21.

(3952)
Ball R J, Brown P
An empirical evaluation of accounting income numbers
JAR 1968 AUTUMN VOL 6 p 159-178.

(3953)
Spiegelglas S
Changes in margin requirements and stock market prices
FAJ 1960 NOV-DEC VOL 16 p 35-37.

9.41 Event-study methodology

(3954)
Brick I E, Statman M, Weaver D G
Event studies and model misspecification
JBFA 1989 SUMMER VOL 16:3 p 399.

(3955)
Corrado C J
A nonparametric test for abnormal security-price performance in event studies
JFE 1989 VOL 23 p 385.

(3956)
Thompson J E
An alternative control model for event studies
JBFA 1989 AUTUMN VOL 16:4 p 507.

(3957)
Ball C A, Torous W N
Investigating security-price performance in the presence of event-date uncertainty
JFE 1988 VOL 22 p 123.

(3958)
Heinkel R, Kraus A
Measuring event impacts in thinly traded stocks
JFQA 1988 MAR VOL 23:1 p 71-88.

(3959)
Karafiath I
Using dummy variables in the event methodology
FR 1988 AUG VOL 23:3 p 351-358.

(3960)
Thompson J E
More methods that make little difference in event studies
JBFA 1988 SPRING VOL 15:1 p 77-86.

(3961)
Klein A, Rosenfeld J
The influence of market conditions on event-study residuals.
JFQA 1987 SEP VOL 22:3 p 345-351.

(3962)
McDonald B
Event studies and systems methods: Some additional evidence
JFQA 1987 DEC VOL 22 p 495.

(3963)
Dimson E, Marsh P
Event study methodologies and the size effect. The case of UK press recommendations
JFE 1986 SEP VOL 17:1 p 113-142.

(3964)
Malatesta P H
Measuring abnormal performance : the event parameter approach using joint generalized least squares
JFQA 1986 MAR VOL 21:1 p 27-38.

(3965)
Brown K C, Lockwood L J, Lummer S L
An examination of event dependency and structural change in security pricing models
JFQA 1985 SEP VOL 20:3 p 315-334

(3966)
Brown S J, Warner J B
Using daily stock returns: The case of event studies.
JFE 1985 VOL 14:1 p 3-31.

(3967)
Brown S J, Weinstein M I
Derived factors in event studies
JFE 1985 VOL 14 p 491.

(3968)
Thompson R
Conditioning the return-generating process on firm-specific events : a discussion of event study methods
JFQA 1985 JUN VOL 20:2 p 151-168.

(3969)
Wood R A, McInish T H, Ord J K
An investigation of transactions data for NYSE Stocks
JF 1985 JUL VOL 40:3 p 723-741

(3970)
Bowman R G
Understanding and conducting event studies
JBFA 1983 VOL 10:4 p 561.

(3971)
Brown S J, Warner J B
Measuring security price performance.
JFE 1980 SEP VOL 8:3 p 205-258

(3972)
Gordon L A, Larcker D F, Pinches G E
Testing for market efficiency: A comparison of the cumulative average residual methodology and intervention analysis
JFQA 1980 JUN VOL 15 p 267.

(3973)
Brenner M
The sensitivity of the efficient market hypothesis to alternative specifications of the market model
JF 1979 SEP VOL 34:4 p 915-929.

(3974)
Morgan I G
Market proxies and the conditional prediction of returns
JFE 1978 VOL 6 p 385.

(3975)
Brenner M
The effect of model misspecification on tests of the efficient market hypothesis
JF 1977 VOL 32 p 57.

9.5   Strong-form efficiency

(3976)
Sinclair N A, Fatseas V A, Trotman K T
Security price reaction to qualitative forecast information
AJM 1986 DEC VOL 11 p 231-240.

(3977)
Stickel S E
The effect of Value Line investment survey rank changes on common stock prices
JFE 1985 VOL 14 p 121.

(3978)
Brown P, Walter T
Share market efficiency and the experts: Some Australian findings
AJM 1982 JUN VOL 7 p 19-32.

(3979)
Copeland T E, Mayers D
The Value Line enigma (1965-1978): A case study of performance evaluation issues
JFE 1982 NOV VOL 10:3 p 289-321.

(3980)
Holloway C
A note on testing an aggressive investment strategy using Value Line ranks
JF 1981 JUN VOL 36:3 p 711-719

(3981)
Hausman W H
A note on "The Value Line contest: a test of the predictability of stock price changes"
JB 1969 JUL VOL 42 p 317-320.

(3982)
Money Which
Share tipsters
Money Which 1968 SEP.

(3983)
Stoffels J D
Stock recommendations by investment advisory services: immediate effects on market pricing
FAJ 1966 MAR-APR VOL 22 p 77-86.

9.51   Insider trading

(3984)
Lee M H, Bishara H
Recent Canadian experience on the profitability of insider trades
FR 1989 MAY VOL 24:2 p 235-250.

(3985)
Manove M
The harm from insider trading and informed speculation
QJE 1989 NOV VOL 104:4 p 823-846.

(3986)
Mitchell P L
Insider dealing and directors' duties. 2nd ed
Butterworth, 1989.

(3987)
Suter J A C
The regulation of insider dealing in Britain
Butterworth, 1989..

(3988)**Gupta A, Misra L**
Illegal insider trading: is it rampant before corporate takeovers?
FR 1988 NOV VOL 23:4 p 453-464.

(3989)
Oppenheimer H R, Dielman T E
Firm dividend policy and insider activity: Some empirical results
JBFA 1988 WINTER VOL 15:4 p 525-542.

(3990)
Rozeff M S, Zaman M A
Market efficiency and insider trading: new evidence
JB 1988 VOL 61 p 25.

(3991)
Seyhun H N
The information content of aggregate insider trading
JB 1988 VOL 61 p 1.

(3992)
Seyhun H N
The January effect and aggregate insider trading
JF 1988 MAR VOL 43:1 p 129-142.

(3993)
Benesh G A, Pari R A
Performance of stocks recommended on the basis
of insider trading activity
FR 1987 FEB VOL 22:1.

(3994)
Cleeton D L, Reeder P A
Stock and option markets : are insider trading
regulations effective?
QREB 1987 SPRING VOL 27:1 p 63-76.

(3995)
Haddock D D, Macey J R
Regulation on demand: a private interest model,
with an application to insider trading regulation
JLE 1987 VOL 30:2 p 311-352.

(3996)
Herzel L, Katz L
Insider trading: who loses?
LBR 1987 JUL 165 p 15-26.

(3997)
Demsetz H
Corporate control, insider trading and rates of
return
AER 1986 VOL 76 P+P p 313-316.

(3998)
Seyhun N H
Insiders' profits, costs of trading and market
efficiency
JFE 1986 VOL 16 p 189-212.

(3999)
Banks J S
Price-conveyed information versus observed
insider behavior: A note on rational expectations
convergence
JPE 1985 VOL 93 p 807.

(4000)
Penham S H
A comparison of the information content of
insider trading and management earnings forecasts
JFQA 1985 MAR VOL 20:1 p 1-17.

(4001)
Virginia Law Review
A critique of the Insider Trading Sanctions Act of
1984
VLR 1985 VOL 71:3 p 455-498.

(4002)
Elliott J, Morse D, Richardson G
The association between insider trading and
information announcements
RandJ 1984 WINTER VOL 15:4 p 521-536.

(4003)
Harvard Law Review
The Supreme Court, 1982 term: Insider trading
HLR 1983 VOL 97:1 p 286-294.

(4004)
Fortune
The unwinnable war on insider trading
F 1981 JUL 13 VOL 104:1 p 72-82.

(4005)
Keown A J, Pinkerton J M
Merger announcements and insider trading
activity: an empirical investigation
JF 1981 SEP VOL 36:4 p 855-869.

(4006)
Kerr H S
The battle of insider trading vs. market efficiency
JPM 1980 SUMMER VOL 6:4 p 47-50.

(4007)
Trivoli G W
How to profit from insider trading information
JPM 1980 SUMMER VOL 6:4 p 51-57.

(4008)
Baesel J B, Stein G R
The value of information: Inferences from the
profitability of insider trading
JFQA 1979 SEP VOL 14 p 553.

(4009)
Hazen T L
A look beyond the pruning of Rule 10b-5:
implied remedies and Section 17(a) of the
Securities Acts of 1933
VLR 1978 VOL 64:5 p 641-689.

(4010)
Finnerty J E
Insiders' activity and inside information: A multivariate analysis
JFQA 1976 JUN VOL 11 p 205.

(4011)
Finnerty J E
Insiders and market efficiency
JF 1976 VOL 31 p 141.

(4012)
Firth M
The information content of large investment holdings
JF 1975 VOL 30 p 1265.

(4013)
Goulet W M
Price changes, managerial action and insider trading at the time of listing
FIN MGMT 1974 SPRING VOL 3 p 30.

(4014)
Edwards K B
Insider trading
Accountancy 1970 JAN VOL 81 p 46-49.

(4015)
Lorie J H, Niederhoffer V
Predictive and statistical properties of insider trading
JLE 1968 APR VOL 11 p 35-53.

(4016)
Pratt S P, DeVere C W
Relationship between insider trading and rates of return for NYSE common stocks, 1960-1966
Paper for the Seminar on the Analysis of Security Prices, U of Chicago, May 1968.

(4017)
Manne H G
Insider trading and the stock market
Free Pr, 1966.

(4018)
Smith F P
Management trading, stock-market prices and profits
Yale U Pr, 1941.

9.6 Empirical regularities

(4019)
Dowen R J
The relation of firm size, security analyst bias, and neglect
AE 1989 VOL 21:1 p 19-24.

(4020)
Levis M
Stock market anomalies: a re-assessment based on the UK evidence
JBankF 1989 SEP VOL 13:4-5 p 675-696.

(4021)
Zarowin P
Short-run overreaction: size and seasonality effects
JPM 1989 SPRING VOL 15:3 p 26-29.

(4022)
Beedles W L, Dodd P, Officer R R
Regularities in Australian share returns
AJM 1988 JUN VOL 13 p 1-30.

(4023)
Corhay A, Hawawini G, Michel P
The pricing of equity on the London Stock Exchange: Seasonality and size premium
(in Dimson E ed., Stock market anomalies. Cambridge U Pr, 1988.)

(4024)
Dimson E ed.
Stock market anomalies
Cambridge U Pr, 1988.

(4025)
Jacobs B I, Levy K N
Disentangling equity return regularities: new insights and investment opportunities
FAJ 1988 MAY-JUN VOL 44 p 18-44.

(4026)
Nalebuff B
Puzzles: Penny stocks, discount brokers, better bidding, and more
JEP 1988 VOL 2:1 p 179-186.

(4027)
Tseng K C
Low price, price-earnings ratio, market value, and abnormal stock returns
FR 1988 AUG VOL 23:3 p 333-344.

(4028)
Carvell S A, Strebel P J
Is there a neglected firm effect?
JBFA 1987 SUMMER VOL 14:2 p 279-290.

(4029)
Edelman R B, Baker H K
The dynamics of neglect and return
JPM 1987 FALL VOL 14:1 p 52-55.

(4030)
Amihud Y, Mendelson H
Liquidity and stock returns
FAJ 1986 MAY-JUN VOL 42 p 43-48.

(4031)
Dowen R J, Bauman W S
A fundamental multifactor asset pricing model
FAJ 1986 JUL-AUG VOL 42 p 45-51.

(4032)
Keim D B
The CAPM and equity return anomalies
FAJ 1986 MAY-JUN VOL 42 p 19-34.

(4033)
Keim D B, Stambaugh R F
Predicting returns in the stock and bond markets.
JFE 1986 DEC VOL 17:2 p 357-390

(4034)
Smirlock M, Starks L
Day-of-the-week and intraday effects in stock returns
JFE 1986 SEP VOL 17:1 p 197-210.

(4035)
Arbel A
Generic stocks: the key to market anomalies
JPM 1985 SUMMER VOL 11:4 p 4-13.

(4036)
Kato K, Schallheim J S
Seasonal and size anomalies in the Japanese stock market.
JFQA 1985 JUN VOL 20:2 p 243-260.

(4037)
Rosenberg B, Reid K, Lanstein R
Persuasive evidence of market inefficiency
JPM 1985 SPRING VOL 11:3 p 9-17.

(4038)
Brown S J, Barry C B
Anomalies in security returns and the specification of the market model
JF 1984 JUL VOL 39:3 p 807-817.

(4039)
Hobbs G R, Riley W B
Profiting from a presidential election
FAJ 1984 MAR-APR VOL 40:2 p 46-52.

(4040)
Arbel A, Carvell S, Strebel P
Giraffes, institutions and neglected firms
FAJ 1983 MAY-JUN VOL 39 p 57-63..

(4041)**Keim D B**
Size-related anomalies and stock return seasonality: Further empirical evidence
JFE 1983 VOL 12 p 13-32.

(4042)
Reinganum M R
The anomalous stock market behavior of small firms in January : empirical tests for tax-loss selling effects
JFE 1983 JUN VOL 12:1 p 89-104.

(4043)
Arbel A, Strebel P
The neglected and small firm effects
FR 1982 NOV VOL 17 p 201-218.

(4044)
Allvine F C, O'Neill D E
Stock market returns and the presidential election cycle: implications for market efficiency
FAJ 1980 SEP-OCT VOL 36:5 p 49-56.

9.61   Size effect

(4045)
Dwyer H J, Lynn R
Small capitalization companies: what does financial analysis tell us about them?
FR 1989 AUG VOL 24:3 p 397-416.

(4046)
Handa P, Kothari S P, Wasley C
The relation between the return interval and betas: implications for the size effect
JFE 1989 VOL 23 p 79.

(4047)
Jacobs B I, Levy K N
Forecasting the size effect
FAJ 1989 MAY-JUN VOL 45 p 38-54.

(4048)
Chan K C, Chen N-F
An unconditional asset-pricing test and the role of firm size as an instrumental variable for risk
JF 1988 JUN VOL 43:2 p 309-326.

(4049)
Chen N-F
Equilibrium asset pricing models and the firm size effect
(in Dimson E ed., Stock market anomalies. Cambridge U Pr, 1988.)

(4050)
Friend I, Lang L H P
The size effect of stock returns: is it simply a risk effect not adequately reflected by the usual measures?
JBankF 1988 VOL 12 p 13-30.

(4051)
Levis M
Size related anomalies and trading activity of UK institutional investors
(in Dimson E ed., Stock market anomalies. Cambridge U Pr, 1988.)

(4052)
Booth J R, Smith R L II
An examination of the small-firm effect on the basis of skewness preference
JFR 1987 VOL 10:1 p 77-86.

(4053)
Keim D B
The daily returns-size connection
JPM 1987 WINTER VOL 13:2 p 41-47.

(4054)
Zivney T L, Thompson D J
Relative stock prices and the firm size effect
JFR 1987 SUMMER VOL 10:2 p 99-110.

(4055)
Brauer G A
Using Jump-diffusion return models to measure differential information by firm size
JFQA 1986 DEC VOL 21:4 p 447-458

(4056)
Dimson E, Marsh P
Event study methodologies and the size effect. The case of UK press recommendations
JFE 1986 SEP VOL 17:1 p 113-142.

(4057)
Korkie B
Market line deviations and market anomalies with reference to small and large firms
JFQA 1986 JUN VOL 21:2 p 161-180.

(4058)
Rogalski R J, Tinic S M
The January size effect: Anomaly or risk mismeasurement?
FAJ 1986 MAR-APR VOL 42 p 63-70.

(4059)
Boolt J R, Smith R L
The application of errors-in-variables methodology to capital market research : evidence on the small-firm effect
JFQA 1985 DEC VOL 20:4 p 501-515.

(4060)
Chan K C, Chen N, Hsieh D A
An exploratory investigation of the firm size effect
JFE 1985 VOL 14 p 451.

(4061)
Barry C B, Brown S J
Differential information and the small firm effect
JFE 1984 VOL 13 p 283-294.

(4062)
Lakonishok J, Shapiro A C
Stock returns beta variance and size : An empirical analysis
FAJ 1984 JUL-AUG VOL 40:4 p 36-41.

(4063)
Rozeff M S, Cook T J
Size and earnings/price ratio anomalies: one effect or two?
JFQA 1984 DEC VOL 19:4 p 449-466.

(4064)
Blume M E, Stambaugh R F
Biases in computed returns: An application to the size effect
JFE 1983 VOL 12 p 387-404.

(4065)
Brown P, Kleidon A W, Marsh T A
New evidence on the nature of size-related anomalies in stock prices
JFE 1983 VOL 12 p 33-56.

(4066)
Edmister R O, James C
Is illiquidity a bar to buying small cap stocks?
JPM 1983 SUMMER VOL 9:4 p 14-19.

(4067)
Lustig I L, Leinbach P A
The small firm effect
FAJ 1983 MAY-JUN VOL 39 p 46-49.

(4068)
Reinganum M R, Smith J
Investor preference for large firms: New evidence on economies of size
JIE 1983 DEC VOL 32 p 213-227.

(4069)
Roll R
On computing mean returns and the small firm premium
JFE 1983 NOV VOL 12:3 p 371-386.

(4070)
Schwert G W
Size and stock returns and other empirical regularities
JFE 1983 VOL 12 p 3.

(4071)
Stoll H R, Whaley R E
Transaction costs and the small firm effect
JFE 1983 VOL 12 p 57-79.

(4072)
Reinganum M R
A direct test of Roll's conjecture on the firm size effect
JF 1982 MAR VOL 37:1 p 27-35.

(4073)
Banz R W
The relationship between return and market value of common stocks
JFE 1981 VOL 9 p 3.

(4074)
Greenblatt J M, Pzena R, Newberg B L
How the small investor can beat the market
JPM 1981 SUMMER VOL 7:4 p 48-52.

(4075)
Reinganum M R
Misspecification of capital asset pricing: Empirical anomalies based on earnings' yields and market values
JFE 1981 VOL 9 p 19.

(4076)
Reinganum M R
Abnormal returns in small firm portfolios
FAJ 1981 MAR-APR VOL 37 p 52-57.

(4077)
Roll R
A possible explanation of the small firm effect
JF 1981 SEP VOL 36:4 p 879-888.

(4078)
Alberts W W, Archer S H
Some evidence on the effect of company size on the cost of equity capital
JFQA 1973 MAR VOL 8:2 p 229-242.

9.62 P/E and price-level effects

(4079)
Bleiberg S
How little we know
JPM 1989 SUMMER VOL 15:4 p 26-31.

(4080)
Jaffe J, Keim D B, Westerfield R
Earnings yields, market values, and stock returns
JF 1989 MAR VOL 44:1 p 135-148.

(4081)
Johnson R S, Fiore L C, Zuber R
The investment performance of common stocks in
relation to their price-earnings ratios: an update
of the Basu study
FR 1989 AUG VOL 24:3 p 499-506.

(4082)
Elgers P, Callahan C, Strock E
The effect of earnings yields upon the association
between unexpected earnings and security returns
: a re-examination
AR 1987 OCT VOL 62:4 p 763-773.

(4083)
Jahnke G, Klaffke S, Oppenheimer H R
Price earnings ratios and security performance
JPM 1987 FALL VOL 14:1 p 39-47.

(4084)
Keown A J, Pinkerton J M, Chen S N
Portfolio selection based upon P/E ratios:
diversification,   risk   decomposition   and
implications
JBFA 1987 SUMMER VOL 14:2 p 187-198

(4085)
Goodman D A, Peavy III J W
The risk universal nature of the P/E effect
JPM 1985 SUMMER VOL 11:4 p 14-17.

(4086)
Basu S
The relationship between earnings' yield, market
value and return for NYSE common stocks:
Further evidence
JFE 1983 VOL 12 p 129-156.

(4087)
Edmister R O, Greene J B
Performance of super-low-price stocks
JPM 1980 FALL VOL 7:1 p 36-41.

(4088)
Basu S
The effect of earnings yield on assessments of the
association between annual accounting income
numbers and security prices
AR 1978 JUL VOL 53:3 p 599-625.

(4089)
Basu S
Investment performance of common stocks in
relation to their price-earnings ratios: A test of
the efficient market hypothesis
JF 1977 VOL 32 p 663.

(4090)
Basu S
The information content of price-earnings ratios
FIN MGMT 1975 SUMMER VOL 4 p 53.

(4091)
Levy R A
A note on the safety of low P/E stocks
FAJ 1973 JAN-FEB VOL 29 p 57-63.

(4092)
Pinches G E, Simon G M
An analysis of portfolio accumulation strategies
employing low-priced common stocks
JFQA 1972 JUN VOL 7 p 1773-1796.

(4093)
Joy O M, Jones C P
Predictive value of p/e ratios
FAJ 1970 SEP-OCT VOL 26 p 61-68..

(4094)**Latane H A, Tuttle D L, Jones C P**
E/p ratios v changes in earnings
FAJ 1969 JAN-FEB VOL 25 p 117-120.

(4095)
Breen W J
Low price-earnings ratios and industry relatives
FAJ 1968 JUL-AUG VOL 24 p 125-127.

(4096)
Fluegel F K
The rate of return on high and low p/e ratio stocks
FAJ 1968 NOV-DEC VOL 24 p 130-133.

(4097)
Nicholson S F
Price ratios in relation to investment results
FAJ 1968 JAN-FEB VOL 24 p 105-109.

(4098)
McWilliams J D
Prices, earnings and p/e ratios
FAJ 1966 MAY-JUN VOL 22 p 137-142.

(4099)
Nicholson S F
Price-earnings ratios
FAJ 1960 JUL-AUG VOL 16 p 43-45.

9.63   Seasonal regularities

(4100)
Jacobs B I,   Levy K N
Calendar anomalies: abnormal returns at calendar turning points
FAJ 1988 NOV-DEC VOL 44 p 28-39.

(4101)
Linn S C,   Lockwood L J
Short-term stock price patterns: NYSE, AMEX, OTC
JPM 1988 WINTER VOL 14:2 p 30-34.

(4102)
Pettengill G N,   Jordan B D
A comprehensive examination of volume effects and seasonality in daily security returns
JFR 1988 VOL 11:1 p 57-70.

(4103)
Bondt W F M de,   Thaler R H
Further evidence on investor overreaction and stock market seasonality
JF 1987 JUL VOL 42:3 p 557-581.

(4104)
Thaler R H
Anomalies: Weekend, holiday, turn of the month, and intraday effects
JEP 1987 VOL 1:2 p 169-178.

(4105)
Harris L
A transaction data study of weekly and intradaily patterns in stock returns
JFE 1986 MAY VOL 16:1 p 99-117.

(4106)
Park S Y,   Reinganum M R
The puzzling price behavior of Treasury bills that mature at the turn of calendar months
JFE 1986 JUN VOL 16:2 p 267-283.

(4107)
Pettengill G N
Persistent seasonal return patterns
FR 1985 NOV VOL 20:4.

(4108)
Hadaway S C Jr,   Rochester D P
Further evidence of seasonal adjustment of times series data
JFQA 1978 MAR VOL 13 p 133.

9.631   Month-of-the-year effects

(4109)
Chang E C,   Pinegar J M
Seasonal fluctuations in industrial production and stock market seasonals
JFQA 1989 MAR VOL 24:1 p 59-74.

(4110)
Jaffe J,   Westerfield R
Is there a monthly effect in stock market returns?: evidence from foreign countries
JBankF 1989 MAY VOL 13:2 p 237-244.

(4111)
Ritter J R,   Chopra N
Portfolio rebalancing and the turn-of-the-year effect
JF 1989 MAR VOL 44:1 p 149-166.

(4112)
Thomson J B
Errors in recorded security prices and the turn-of-the-year effect
JFQA 1989 DEC VOL 24:4 p 513-526.

(4113)
Chang E C, Pinegar J M
Does the market reward risk in non-January months?
JPM 1988 FALL VOL 15:1 p 55-57.

(4114)
Chari V V, Jagannathan R, Ofer A R
Seasonalities in security returns: the case of earnings announcements
JFE 1988 VOL 21 p 101-122.

(4115)
Clark R, Ziemba W
Playing the turn of the year effect with index futures
OR 1988 JAN-FEB VOL 36.

(4116)
Condoyanni L, McLeay S, O'Hanlon J
Seasonality in the Greek equity market
(in Taylor S, Kingsman B and Guimares R eds., A reappraisal of the efficiency of financial markets. Springer, 1988.)

(4117)
Ritter J R
The buying and selling behavior of individual investors at the turn of the year
JF 1988 JUL VOL 43:3 p 701-716.

(4118)
Seyhun H N
The January effect and aggregate insider trading
JF 1988 MAR VOL 43:1 p 129-142.

(4119)
Tinic S M, Barone-Adesi G
Stock return seasonality and the tests of asset pricing models: Canadian evidence
(in Dimson E ed., Stock market anomalies. Cambridge U Pr, 1988.)

(4120)
Ariel R A
A monthly effect in stock returns
JFE 1987 VOL 18 p 161-174.

(4121)
Barone-Adesi G, Tinic S M, West R R
Seasonality in Canadian stock prices: A test of the "tax-loss-selling" hypothesis
JFQA 1987 MAR VOL 22 p 51.

(4122)
Corhay A, Hawawini G, Michel P
Seasonality in the risk-return relationship: some international evidence
JF 1987 MAR VOL 42:1 p 49-68.

(4123)
Haugen R A, Lakonishok J
The incredible January effect
Dow Jones-Irwin, 1987.

(4124)
Penman S H
The distribution of earnings news over time and seasonalities in aggregate stock returns
JFE 1987 JUN VOL 18:2 p 199-228.

(4125)
Thaler R H
Anomalies: The January effect
JEP 1987 VOL 1:1 p 197.

(4126)
Tinic S M, Barone-Adesi G, West R R
Seasonality in Canadian stock prices : a test of the "Tax-Loss-Selling" hypothesis
JFQA 1987 MAR VOL 22:1 p 51-63.

(4127)
Chan K C
Can tax-loss selling explain the January seasonal in stock returns?
JF 1986 DEC VOL 41:5 p 1115-1128.

(4128)
Chang E C, Pinegar J M
Return seasonality and tax-loss selling in the market for long-term government and corporate bonds.
JFE 1986 DEC VOL 17:2 p 391-415

(4129)
Keim D B
Dividend yields and the January effect
Journal of Financial Management 1986 p 61-65.

(4130)
Pettengill G N
A non-tax cause for the January effect? Evidence
from early data
Quarterly Journal of Business and Economics
1986 SUMMER VOL 25 p 15-33.

(4131)
Santesmases M
An investigation of the Spanish stock market
seasonalities
JBFA 1986 SUMMER VOL 13:2 p 267-276

(4132)
Slemrod J
The effect of capital gains taxation on year-end
stock market behavior
NTJ 1986 VOL 39 p 69-77.

(4133)
Bergh W M van den, Wessels R E
Stock   market   seasonality   and   taxes   :   an
examination of the tax-loss selling hypothesis
JBFA 1985 WINTER VOL 12:4 p 515-530

(4134)
Jaffe J F, Westerfield R
Patterns in Japanese common stock returns : day
of the week and turn of the year effects.
JFQA 1985 JUN VOL 20:2 p 261-272

(4135)
Keim D B
Dividend yields and stock returns: Implications of
abnormal January returns
JFE 1985 VOL 14 p 473

(4136)
Schultz P
Personal income taxes and the January effect :
small firm stock returns before the war revenue
act of 1917 : a note
JF 1985 MAR VOL 40:1 p 333-343.

(4137)
Berges A, McConnell J J, Schlarbaum G G
The turn-of-the-year in Canada
JF 1984 MAR VOL 39:1 p 185-192.

(4138)
Lakonishok J, Smidt S
Volume and turn-of-the-year behavior
JFE 1984 SEP VOL 13:3 p 435-455.

(4139)
Price V, Theobald M
Seasonality estimation in thin markets
JF 1984 JUN VOL 39:2 p 377-392.

(4140)
Tinic S M, West R R
Risk and return: January vs. the rest of the year
JFE 1984 VOL 13 p 561-574.

(4141)
Brown P, Keim D B, Kleidon A W et al.
Stock return seasonalities and the tax-loss selling
hypothesis : analysis of the arguments and
Australian evidence.
JFE 1983 JUN VOL 12:1 p 105-127.

(4142)
Givoly D, Ovaida A
Year-end tax induced sales and stock market
seasonality
JF 1983 MAR VOL 38:1 p 171-185.

(4143)
Gultekin M N, Gultekin N B
Stock market seasonality: International evidence
JFE 1983 VOL 12 p 469-481.

(4144)
Schneeweis T, Woolridge J R
Capital market seasonality: The case of bond
returns
JFQA 1979 DEC VOL 14 p 939.

(4145)
Dyl E A
Capital gains taxation and year-end stock market
behavior
JF 1977 VOL 32 p 165.

(4146)
Rozeff M S, Kinney W R Jr
Capital market seasonality: The case of stock returns
JFE 1976 VOL 3 p 379..

(4147)**Officer R R**
Seasonality in Australian capital markets: Market efficiency and empirical issues
JFE 1975 VOL 2 p 29.

(4148)
Bonin J M, Moses E A
Seasonal variations in prices of individual Dow Jones industrial stocks
JFQA 1974 DEC VOL 9 p 963.

(4149)
Jones C P, Litzenberger R H
Earnings seasonality and stock prices
FAJ 1969 NOV-DEC VOL 25 p 57-59.

(4150)
Shiskin J
Systematic aspects of stock price fluctuations
Paper for the Seminar on the Analysis of Security Prices, U of Chicago, May 1967.

(4151)
Fortune
Buying stocks by the calendar
F 1965 JUN VOL 71.

(4152)
Zinbarg E D, Harrington J J Jr
The stock market's seasonal pattern
FAJ 1964 JAN-FEB VOL 20 p 53-56.

(4153)
Leffler G L
Seasonal patterns
B 1953 MAR 30 p 27.

9.632   Day-of-the-week effects

(4154)
Admati A R, Pfleiderer P
Divide and conquer: a theory of intraday and day-of-the-week mean effects
RFS 1989 VOL 2:2 p 189-224.

(4155)
Choy A Y F, O'Hanlon J
Day of the week effects in the UK equity market: a cross sectional analysis
JBFA 1989 SPRING VOL 16:1 p 89.

(4156)
Connolly R A
An examination of the robustness of the weekend effect
JFQA 1989 JUN VOL 24:2 p 133-170.

(4157)
Jaffe J F, Westerfield R, Ma C
A twist on the Monday effect in stock prices: evidence from the US and foreign stock markets
JBankF 1989 SEP VOL 13:4-5 p 641-650.

(4158)
Pettengill G N
Holiday closings and security returns
JFR 1989 SPRING VOL 12:1 p 57-68.

(4159)
Wingender J, Groff J E
On stochastic dominance analysis of day-of-the-week return patterns
JFR 1989 SPRING VOL 12:1 p 51-56.

(4160)
Ball R J, Bowers J
Daily seasonals in equity and fixed-interest returns: Australian evidence and tests of plausible hypotheses
(in Dimson E ed., Stock market anomalies. Cambridge U Pr, 1988.)

(4161)
Board J L G, Sutcliffe C M S
The weekend effect in U K stock market returns
JBFA 1988 SUMMER VOL 15:2 p 199-214.

(4162)
Chang E C, Kim C-W
Day of the week effects and commodity price changes
JFM 1988 APR VOL 8:2 p 229-242.

(4163)
Condoyanni L, O'Hanlon J, Ward C W R
Weekend effects in stock market returns:
international evidence
(in Dimson E ed., Stock market anomalies.
Cambridge U Pr, 1988.)

(4164)
Flannery M J, Protopapadakis A A
From T-bills to common stocks: investigating the
generality of intra-week return seasonality
JF 1988 JUN VOL 43:2 p 431-450.

(4165)
Kim S-W
Capitalizing on the week-end effect
JPM 1988 SPRING VOL 14:3 p 59-63.

(4166)
Miller E M
Why a weekend effect
JPM 1988 SUMMER VOL 14:4 p 43-49.

(4167)
Pettengill G N, Jordan B D
A comprehensive examination of volume effects
and seasonality in daily security returns
JFR 1988 VOL 11:1 p 57-70.

(4168)
Phillips-Patrick F J, Schneeweis T
The "weekend effect" for stock indexes and stock
index futures: dividend and interest rate effects
JFM 1988 FEB VOL 8:1 p 115-122.

(4169)
Saunders A, Urich T
Weekly variation in the Federal funds market:
The weekend game and other effects
(in Dimson E ed., Stock market anomalies.
Cambridge U Pr, 1988.)

(4170)
Condoyanni L, O'Hanlon J, Ward C W R
Day of the week effects on stock returns :
international evidence
JBFA 1987 SUMMER VOL 14:2 p 159-174.

(4171)
Kolb R W, Rodriguez R J
Friday the thirteenth: part VIV: a note
JF 1987 DEC VOL 42:5 p 1385-1388.

(4172)
Dyl E A, Maberly E D
The weekly pattern in stock index futures: a
further note
JF 1986 DEC VOL 41:5 p 1149-1155.

(4173)
Cornell B
The weekly pattern in stock returns : cash versus
futures : a note
JF 1985 JUN VOL 40:2 p 583-588.

(4174)
Jaffe J, Westerfield R
The week-end effect in common stock returns :
the international evidence
JF 1985 JUN VOL 40:2 p 433-454.

(4175)
Jaffe J F, Westerfield R
Patterns in Japanese common stock returns : day
of the week and turn of the year effects.
JFQA 1985 JUN VOL 20:2 p 261-272

(4176)
French D W
The weekend effect on the distribution of stock
prices: Implications for option pricing
JFE 1984 VOL 13 p 547-559.

(4177)
Keim D B, Stambaugh R F
A further investigation of the weekend effect in
stock returns
JF 1984 JUL VOL 39:3 p 819-839.

(4178)
Rogalski R J
New findings regarding day-of-the-week returns
over trading and non-trading periods
JF 1984 DEC VOL 39:5 p 1603-1614.

(4179)
Lakonishok J, Levi M
Weekend effects on stock returns: a note
JF 1982 JUN VOL 37:3 p 883-889.

(4180)
Gibbons M R, Hess P
Day of the week effects and asset returns
JB 1981 OCT VOL 54:4 p 579-596.

(4181)
French K R
Stock returns and the weekend effect
JFE 1980 VOL 8 p 55-69.

(4182)
Cross F
The behavior of stock prices on Fridays and
Mondays
FAJ 1973 NOV-DEC VOL 29 p 67-79.

9.633   Time-of-day effects

(4183)
Harris L
A day-end transaction price anomaly
JFQA 1989 MAR VOL 24:1 p 29-46.

(4184)
Miller E M
Explaining intra-day and overnight price behavior
JPM 1989 SUMMER VOL 15:4 p 10-17.

(4185)
Oldfield G S, Rogalski R J
A theory of common stock returns over trading
and non-trading periods
JF 1980 JUN VOL 25:3 p 729-751.

10 Rates of return on securities

(4186)
Hamao Y
Japanese stocks, bonds, bills, and inflation, 1973-1987
JPM 1989 WINTER VOL 15:2 p 20-26.

(4187)
Ibbotson Associates
Stocks, bonds, bills, and inflation: 1989 yearbook
Ibbotson Associates, 1989.

(4188)
Wydler D
Swiss stocks, bonds, and inflation, 1926-1987
JPM 1989 WINTER VOL 15:2 p 27-32.

(4189)
Barclays de Zoete Wedd
BZW equity-gilt study: investment in the London stock market since 1918
Barclays de Zoete Wedd, 1988.

(4190)
Bey R P, Collins J M
The relationship between before- and after-tax yields on financial assets
FR 1988 AUG VOL 23:3 p 313-332.

(4191)
Hatch J E, White R W
Canadian stocks, bonds, bills and inflation: 1950-1987
Research Foundation of the Institute of Chartered Financial Analysts, 1988.

(4192)
Leibowitz M L, Krasker W S
The persistence of risk: stocks versus bonds over the long term
FAJ 1988 NOV-DEC VOL 44 p 40-47.

(4193)
Damordaran A
The impact of information structure on stock returns
JPM 1987 SPRING VOL 13:3 p 53-58.

(4194)
Jones C P, Wilson J W
Stocks, bonds, paper, and inflation: 1870-1985
JPM 1987 FALL VOL 14:1 p 20-24.

(4195)
Kawaller I G
A note: debunking the myth of the risk free return
JFM 1987 JUN VOL 7:3 p 327-332.

(4196)
Statman M, Ushman N
Another look at bonds versus stocks
JPM 1987 WINTER VOL 13:2 p 33-38.

(4197)
Wilson J W, Jones C P
A comparison of annual common stock returns : 1871-1925 with 1926-85
JB 1987 APR VOL 60:2 p 239-258.

(4198)
Ball R J, Bowers J
Shares, bonds, treasury notes, property trusts and inflation: Historical returns and risks, 1974-1985
AJM 1986 DEC VOL 11 p 117-137.

(4199)
Grauer R R, Hakansson N H
A half century of returns on levered and unlevered portfolios of stocks bonds and bills with and without small stocks
JB 1986 APR VOL 59:2 p 287-318..

(4200)**Hatch J E, White R W**
A Canadian perspective on Canadian and United States capital market returns: 1950-1983
FAJ 1986 MAY-JUN VOL 42 p 60-68.

(4201)
Ang J S, Peterson D R
Return risk and yield : evidence from ex ante data
JF 1985 JUN VOL 40:2 p 537-548

(4202)
Carleton W T, Lakonishok J
Risk and return on equity: The use and misuse of historical estimates
FAJ 1985 JAN-FEB VOL 41 p 38-47.

(4203)
Grauer R R, Hakansson N H
Returns on levered, actively managed long-run portfolios of stocks, bonds and bills, 1934-1983
FAJ 1985 SEP-OCT VOL 41 p 24-46.

(4204)
Hatch J E, White R W
Canadian stocks, bonds, bills and inflation:
1950-1983
Charlottesville, Va.: Financial Analysts Research
Foundation, 1985.

(4205)
Ibbotson R G, Siegel L B, Love K S
World wealth: market values and returns
JPM 1985 FALL VOL 12:1 p 4-23.

(4206)
Cheng P L
Unbiased estimators of long-run expected returns
revisited
JFQA 1984 DEC VOL 19:4 p 375-393

(4207)
Friend I, Hasbrouck J
Savings and after-tax rates of return
REStat 1983 VOL 65 p 537.

(4208)
Hasbrouck J
An estimate of long-run rates of return : a note
JFQA 1983 DEC VOL 18:4 p 455-461

(4209)
Copeland B L
Inflation, interest rates and equity risk premia
FAJ 1982 MAY-JUN p 32-44.

(4210)
Grauer R R, Hakansson N H
Higher return, lower risk: historical returns on
long-run actively managed portfolios of stocks,
bonds and bills 1936-1978
FAJ 1982 MAR-APR p 39-54.

(4211)
Hawawini G A, Vora A
Yield approximations : a historical perspective
JF 1982 MAR VOL 37:1 p 145-156.

(4212)
Perry P R
The time-variance relationship of security returns:
implications for the return-generating stochastic
process
JF 1982 JUN VOL 37:3 p 857-870.

(4213)
Peterson D R, Peterson P P
The effect of changing expectations upon stock
returns
JFQA 1982 DEC VOL 17:5 p 799-813.

(4214)
Ball R J, Brown P
Risk and return from equity investments in the
Australian mining industry: January 1958 -
February 1979
AJM 1980 VOL 5 p 45-66.

(4215)
Lakonishok J
Stock market return expectations: some general
properties
JF 1980 SEP VOL 35:4 p 921-931

(4216)
Schlarbaum G G, Lewellen W G, Lease R C
Realized returns on common stock investments:
the experience of individual investors.
JB 1978 APR VOL 51:2 p 299-325.

(4217)
Fisher L, Lorie J H
A half century of returns on stocks and bonds:
rates of return on investments in common stocks
and on U.S. Treasury securities, 1926-1976
U of Chicago Bus, 1977.

(4218)
Froewiss K C
Risk premiums in international securities markets:
the Canadian-U.S. experience
F R Bk San Francisco Ec Rev 1977 SUMMER.

(4219)
Huang C J
An unbiased estimator of the N-Period relative
JFQA 1977 SEP VOL 12 p 505.

(4220)
Johnson G L, Reilly F K, Smith R E
A year-by-year analysis of "real" rates of return on
common stocks
QREB 1974 VOL 14:1 p 79.

(4221)
Norgaard R L
An examination of the yields of corporate bonds
and stocks
JF 1974 VOL 29 p 1275.

(4222)
Pinches G E, Simon G M
An analysis of portfolio accumulation strategies
employing low-priced common stocks
JFQA 1972 JUN VOL 7 p 1773-1796.

(4223)
Robichek A A, Cohn R A, Pringle J J
Returns on alternative investment media and
implications for portfolio construction
JB 1972 JUL VOL 45 p 427-443.

(4224)
Cheng P L, Deets M K
Statistical biases and security rates of return
JFQA 1971 JUN VOL 6 p 977-994.

(4225)
Fisher L, Lorie J H
Some studies of variability of returns on
investments in common stocks
JB 1970 APR VOL 43 p 99-134.

(4226)
Fisher L, Lorie J H
Rates of return on investments in common stock.
The year by year record, 1926-65
JB 1968 JUL VOL 41 p 291-316.

(4227)
Ben-Shanar H, Sarnat M
Reinvestment and the rate of return on common
stocks
JF 1966 DEC VOL 21 p 737-742.

(4228)
Edwards C E, Hilton J G
High-low averages as an estimator of annual
average stock prices
JF 1966 MAR VOL 21 p 112-115.

(4229)
Fisher L
An algorithm for finding exact rates of return
JB 1966 JAN VOL 39 Suppl p 111-118.

(4230)
Marris R, Singh A
A measure of a firm's average share price
JRSS 1966 VOL 129 Series A p 74-97.

(4231)
Merrett A J, Sykes A
Return on equities and fixed interest securities
1919-1966
District Bank Review 1966 JUN VOL 158 p
29-45.

(4232)
Fisher L
Outcomes for "random" investments in common
stocks listed on the New York Stock Exchange
JB 1965 APR VOL 38 p 149-161.

(4233)
Fisher L, Lorie J H
Rates of return on investments in common stocks
JB 1964 JAN VOL 37 p 1-17.

(4234)
Merrett A J, Sykes A
Return on equities and fixed interest securities
1919-1963
District Bank Review 1963 DEC.

(4235)
Eiteman W J, Eiteman D S
Common stock values and yields 1950-61
U of Mich Busn Res, 1962.

(4236)
Ortner R
An estimate of the time horizon and expected
yield for a selected group of common shares,
1935-1955
IntER 1961 MAY VOL 2 p 179-198.

10.1 Price indexes

(4237)
Pruitt S W, Wei K C J
Institutional ownership and changes in the S&P
500
JF 1989 JUN VOL 44:2 p 509-514.

(4238)
Toy W W, Zurack M A
Tracking the Euro-Pac index
JPM 1989 WINTER VOL 15:2 p 55-58.

(4239)
Bierman H Jr
The Dow Jones industrials: do you get what you see?
JPM 1988 FALL VOL 15:1 p 58.

(4240)
Stock Exchange
The FT-SE 100 Share Index
Stock Exchange, 1988.

(4241)
Ball R J, Bowers J
A corrected Statex-Actuaries daily accumulated index
AJM 1987 JUN VOL 12 p 1-8.

(4242)
Financial Times et al., comps.
FT-Actuaries world indices: an introduction
Goldman Sachs, 1987.

(4243)
Lamoureux C G, Wansley J W
Market effects of changes in the Standard & Poor's 500 index
FR 1987 FEB VOL 22:1 p 53-69.

(4244)
Butler H L, DeMong R F
The changing Dow Jones Industrial Average
FAJ 1986 JUL-AUG VOL 42 p 59-62.

(4245)
Harris L, Gurel E
Price and volume effects associated with changes in the S&P 500 list : new evidence for the existence of price pressures
JF 1986 SEP VOL 41:4 p 815-829

(4246)
Pierce P S ed.
The Dow Jones averages 1885-1985: centennial edition
Dow Jones-Irwin, 1986.

(4247)
Brennan M J, Schwartz E S
On the geometric mean index: a note
JFQA 1985 MAR VOL 20:1 p 119-122.

(4248)
Witt S F, Dobbins R
A note on the effect of institutional trading activities on the real value of the Financial Times All-Share Index
JBFA 1983 AUTUMN VOL 10:3 p 351-358

(4249)
Ohlson J A, Rosenberg B
Systematic risk of the CRSP equal-weighted common stock index : a history estimated by stochastic-parameter regression
JB 1982 JAN VOL 55:1 p 121-145.

(4250)
Sikorsky N
The origin and construction of the Capital International indices
CJWB 1982 SUMMER VOL 17:2 p 24-41.

(4251)
Butler H L, Allen J D
The Dow Jones Industrial Average reexamined
FAJ 1979 NOV-DEC VOL 35 p 23-32.

(4252)
Rudd A T
The revised Dow Jones Industrial Average: New wine in old bottles?
FAJ 1979 NOV-DEC VOL 35 p 57-63..

(4253)**Burgess R C, O'Dell B T**
An empirical examination of index efficiency: Implications for index funds
JFQA 1978 MAR VOL 13 p 93.

(4254)
Hodges S D, Schaefer S M
On the interpretation of the geometric mean
JFQA 1974 JUN VOL 9 p 497-504.

(4255)
Shashua L, Goldschmidt Y
An index for evaluating financial performance
JF 1974 VOL 29 p 797.

(4256)
Schwartz R A, Altman E I
Volatility behavior of industrial stock price indices
JF 1973 VOL 28 p 957.

(4257)
Latane H A, Tuttle D L, Young W E
Market indexes and their implications for portfolio management
FAJ 1971 SEP-OCT VOL 27 p 75-85.

(4258)
Marks P, Stuart A
An arithmetic version of the FT Index
Journal of the Institute of Actuaries 1971 DEC VOL 97 p 297-324.

(4259)
Carter E E, Cohen K J
Stock averages, stock splits, and bias
FAJ 1967 MAY-JUN VOL 23 p 77-81.

(4260)
Schellbach L L
When did the DJIA top 1200?
FAJ 1967 MAY-JUN VOL 23 p 71-73.

(4261)
Carter E E, Cohen K J
Bias in the DJIA caused by stock splits
FAJ 1966 NOV-DEC VOL 22 p 90-94.

(4262)
Cohen K J, Fitch B
The average investment performance index
MSci 1966 FEB VOL 12 p B195-B215.

(4263)
Cootner P H
Stock market indexes--fallacies and illusions
Commercial and Financial Chronicle 1966 SEP 29.

(4264)
Fisher L
Some new stock-market indexes
JB 1966 JAN VOL 39 Suppl p 191-225.

(4265)
Comer H D
Is the "Dow" already above 1200?
FAJ 1964 MAY-JUN VOL 20 p 69-70.

(4266)
Drakatos C
London share prices indices
Bankers' Magazine 1962 JUN VOL 193 p 465-473.

(4267)
Kendall M G, Stuart A
Measuring share price changes
Times 1960 APR 20.

(4268)
Rich C D
The rationale of the use of the geometric average as an investment index
Journal of the Institute of Actuaries 1948 VOL 74 p 338-339.

(4269)
Cowles A et al.
Common stock indexes. 2nd ed
Bloomington, In.: Principia Press, 1939.

(4270)
Mitchell W C
A critique of index numbers of the prices of stocks
JPE 1916 JUL VOL 24 p 685.

10.2   Stock price databases

(4271)
Choi F D S
International data sources for empirical research in financial management
FIN MGMT 1988 SUMMER VOL 17 p 80.

(4272)
Nunn K P Jr, Hill J, Schneeweis T
Corporate bond price data sources and return/risk measurement
JFQA 1986 JUN VOL 21:2 p 197-208.

(4273)
Roehl T
Data sources for research in Japanese finance
JFQA 1985 JUN VOL 20:2 p 273-276.

(4274)
Bennin R
Error rates in CRSP and Compustat; a second look
JF 1980 DEC VOL 35:5 p 1267-1271.

(4275)
Rosenberg B, Houglet M
Error rates in CRSP and Compustat data bases and their implications
JF 1974 VOL 29 p 1303.

10.3 Frequency distribution of returns

(4276)
Aggarwal R, Rao R P, Hiraki T
Skewness and kurtosis in Japanese equity returns: empirical evidence
JFR 1989 FALL VOL 12:3 p 253-260.

(4277)
Hall J A, Brorsen B W, Irwin S H
The distribution of futures prices: a test of the stable Paretian and mixture of normals hypotheses
JFQA 1989 MAR VOL 24:1 p 105-116.

(4278)
Lau H-S, Wingender J R, Lau A H-L
On estimating skewness in stock returns
MSci 1989 VOL 35 p 1139.

(4279)
Lau H-S, Wingender J R
The analytics of the intervaling effect on skewness and kurtosis of stock returns
FR 1989 MAY VOL 24:2 p 215-234.

(4280)
Badrinath S G, Chatterjee S
On measuring skewness and elongation in common stock return distributions
JB 1988 VOL 61 p 451.

(4281)
Homaifar G, Graddy D B
Equity yields in models considering higher moments of the return distribution
AE 1988 MAR VOL 20:3 p 325-334.

(4282)
Akgiray V, Booth G G
Compound distribution models of stock returns: an empirical comparison
JFR 1987 FALL VOL 10:3 p 269-280.

(4283)
Bookstaber R M, McDonald J B
A general distribution for describing security price returns
JB 1987 JUL VOL 60:3 p 401-424.

(4284)
Frankfurter G M, Lamoureux C G
The relevance of the distributional form of common stock returns to the construction of optimal portfolios
JFQA 1987 DEC VOL 22:4 p 505-511.

(4285)
Harris L
Transaction data tests of the mixture of distributions hypothesis
JFQA 1987 JUN VOL 22:2 p 127-141.

(4286)
Beedles W L
Asymmetry in Australian equity returns
AJM 1986 JUN VOL 11 p 1-12.

(4287)
Grauer R R
Normality, solvency and portfolio choice.
JFQA 1986 SEP VOL 21:3 p 265-278.

(4288)
Harris L
Cross-security tests of the mixture of distributions hypothesis
JFQA 1986 MAR VOL 21:1 p 39-46.

(4289)
Singleton J C, Wingender J
Skewness persistence in common stock returns
JFQA 1986 SEP VOL 21:3 p 335-341.

(4290)
Gottlieb G, Kalay A
Implications of the discreteness of observed stock prices
JF 1985 MAR VOL 40:1 p 135-153.

(4291)
Hsu D A
The behavior of stock returns: is it stationary or evolutionary?
JFQA 1984 MAR VOL 19:1 p 11-28.

(4292)
Owen J, Rabinovitch R
On the class of elliptical distributions and their applications to the theory of portfolio choice
JF 1983 JUN VOL 38:3 p 745-752.

(4293)
Perry P R
More evidence on the nature of the distribution of security returns.
JFQA 1983 JUN VOL 18:2 p 211-221.

(4294)
Stokie M D
Parameter stationarity in the distribution of stock market returns
AJM 1983 JUN VOL 8 p 83-92.

(4295)
Stokie M D
The distribution of stock market returns: Tests of normality
AJM 1982 DEC VOL 7 p 159-178.

(4296)
Simkowitz M A, Beedles W L
Asymmetric stable distributed security returns
JASA 1980 JUN VOL 75 p 306-312.

(4297)
Bawa V S, Elton E J, Gruber M J
Simple rules for optimal portfolio selection in stable paretian markets
JF 1979 SEP VOL 34:4 p 1041-1047.

(4298)
Beedles W L
On the assymetry of market returns
JFQA 1979 SEP VOL 14 p 653.

(4299)
Upton D E, Shannon D S
The stable paretian distribution subordinated stochastic processes and asymptotic lognormality: an empirical investigation
JF 1979 SEP VOL 34.

(4300)
Beedles W L, Simkowitz M A
A note on skewness and data errors
JF 1978 VOL 33 p 288.

(4301)
Cohen K J, Maier S F, Schwartz R A
The returns generation process, returns variance and the effect of thinness in securities markets
JF 1978 VOL 33 p 149.

(4302)
Dowell C D, Grube R C
Common stock return distributions during homoegeneous activity periods
JFQA 1978 MAR VOL 13 p 79.

(4303)
Hagerman R L
More evidence on the distribution of security returns
JF 1978 VOL 33 p 1213.

(4304)
Hayya J C, Saniga E M
Simple goodness-of-fit tests for symmetric stable distributions
JFQA 1977 JUN VOL 12 p 276.

(4305)
Hilliard J E, Leitch R A
Analysis of the warrant hedge in a stable paretian market
JFQA 1977 MAR VOL 12 p 85..

(4306)**Westerfield R**
The distribution of common stock price changes: An application of transaction time and subordinated stochastic models
JFQA 1977 DEC VOL 12 p 743.

(4307)
Fielitz B D
Further results on asymmetric stable distributions
of stock price changes
JFQA 1976 MAR VOL 11 p 39.

(4308)
Ohlson J A, Rosenberg B
The stationary distribution of returns and
portfolio separation in capital markets: A
fundamental contradiction
JFQA 1976 SEP VOL 11 p 393.

(4309)
Samuelson P A
Limited liability, short selling, bounded utility and
infinite-variance stable distributions
JFQA 1976 SEP VOL 11 p 485.

(4310)
Corbeau A B, Meyer C F
The application of spectral analysis to
demonstrate the stochastic distortion in the Delta
midrange of price series
JFQA 1975 JUN VOL 10 p 221.

(4311)
Barnea A, Downes D H
A reexamination of the empirical distribution of
stock price changes
JASA 1973 JUN VOL 68 p 348-356.

(4312)
Clark P K
A subordinated stochastic process model with
finite variance for speculative prices
Em 1973 JAN VOL 41 p 135-155.

(4313)
Praetz P D
The distribution of price changes
JB 1972 JAN VOL 45 p 49-55.

(4314)
Fielitz B D
Stationarity of random data: some implications for
the distribution of stock prices changes
JFQA 1971 JUN VOL 6 p 1025-1034.

(4315)
Rosenberg B
Statistical analysis of price series obscured by
averaging measures
JFQA 1971 SEP VOL 6 p 1083-1094.

(4316)
Teichmoeller J
A note on the distribution of stock price changes
JASA 1971 JUN VOL 66 p 282-284.

(4317)
Brealey R A
The distribution and independence of successive
rates of return in the U.K. equity market
JBF 1970 SUMMER VOL 2 p 29-40.

(4318)
Press S J
A compound events model for security prices
JB 1968 JUL VOL 40 p 317-335.

(4319)
Renwick F B
Theory of investment behavior and empirical
analysis of stock market price relatives
Msci 1968 SEP VOL 15 p 57-71.

(4320)
Mandelbrot B
The variation of some other speculative prices
JB 1967 OCT VOL 40 p 393-413.

(4321)
Mandelbrot B, Taylor H M
On the distribution of stock price differences
OR 1967 NOV-DEC p 1057-1062.

(4322)
Brada J C, Ernst H, Van Tassel J
The distribution of stock price differences:
Gaussian after all?
OR 1966 APR VOL 14 p 334-340.

(4323)
Fama E F
The behavior of stock market prices
JB 1965 JAN VOL 38 p 34-105.

(4324)
Fama E F
Portfolio analysis in a stable Paretian market
MSci 1965 JAN VOL 11 p 404-419.

(4325)
Renwick F B
Economic growth and distributions of change in
stock market prices
IMR 1965 SPRING VOL 9 p 39-68.

(4326)
Fama E F
Mandelbrot and the stable Paretian hypothesis
JB 1963 OCT VOL 36 p 420-429.

(4327)
Mandelbrot B
The variation of certain speculative prices
JB 1963 OCT VOL 36 p 394-419.

(4328)
Niederhoffer V
Clustering of stock prices
OR 1959 VOL 13 p 258-265.

10.4 Factor structure of returns

(4329)
Barsky R B
Why don't the prices of stocks and bonds move
together?
AER 1989 VOL 79:5 p 1132-1145.

(4330)
Bodurtha J N Jr, Cho D C, Senbet L W
Economic forces in the stock market: an
international perspective
Global Finance Journal 1989 VOL 1:1.

(4331)
Elton E J, Gruber M J
A multi-index risk model of the Japanese stock
market
Japan and the World Economy 1989 JAN.

(4332)
Grinold R, Rudd A, Stefek D
Global factors: fact or fiction?
JPM 1989 FALL VOL 16:1 p 79-89.

(4333)
Conway D A, Reinganum M R
Capital market factor structure: identification
through cross validation
Journal of Business and Economic Statistics 1988
JAN VOL 6.

(4334)
Eun C S, Resnick B G
Estimating the dependence structure of share
prices: a comparative study of the United States
and Japan
FR 1988 NOV VOL 23:4 p 387-402.

(4335)
Karathanassis G, Philippas N
Estimation of bank stock price parameters and
the variance components model
AE 1988 APR VOL 20:4 p 497-508.

(4336)
Roll R
R2
JF 1988 JUL VOL 43:3 p 541-566.

(4337)
Campbell J Y
Stock returns and the term structure
JFE 1987 JUN VOL 18:2 p 373-399.

(4338)
Cho D C, Taylor W M
The seasonal stability of the factor structure of
stock returns
JF 1987 DEC VOL 42:5 p 1195-1213.

(4339)
Kim M K, Wu C
Macro-economic factors and stock returns
JFR 1987 SUMMER VOL 10:2 p 87-98.

(4340)
Shanken J
Nonsynchronous data and the covariance-factor
structure of returns
JF 1987 JUN VOL 42:2 p 221-231

(4341)
Yang H C, Wansley J W Lane W R
Stock market recognition of multinationality of a
firm and international events
JBFA 1985 SUMMER VOL 12:2 p 263-274

(4342)
Sinclair N A
Aspects of the factor structure implicit in the Australian equity industrial equity market: Feb 1958 to Aug 1977
AJM 1984 JUN VOL 9 p 23-36.

(4343)
Kryzanowski L, To M C
General factor models and the structure of security returns.
JFQA 1983 MAR VOL 18:1 p 31-52.

(4344)
Rosenberg B, Rudd A
Factor related and specific returns of common stocks : serial correlation and market efficiency
JF 1982 MAY VOL 37:2 p 543-554

(4345)
Sharpe W F
Factors in NYSE security return, 1931-1979
JPM 1982 SUMMER VOL 8:4 p 5-19.

(4346)
Folger H R, John K, Tipton J
Three factors interest rate differentials and stock groups
JF 1981 MAY VOL 36:2 p 323-335.

(4347)
Oldfield G S, Rogalski R J
Treasury bills and common stock returns
JF 1981 MAY VOL 36:2 p 337-350.

(4348)
Arnott R D
Cluster analysis and stock price movement
FAJ 1980 NOV-DEC VOL 36 p 56-63.

(4349)
Ho P C, Paulson A S
Portfolio selection via factor analysis
JPM 1980 SPRING VOL 6:3 p 27-30.

(4350)
Livingston M
Industry movements of common stocks
JF 1977 VOL 32 p 861.

(4351)
Lloyd W P, Shick R A
A test of Stone's two-index model of return
JFQA 1977 SEP VOL 12 p 363.

(4352)
Abe J W
Industry effects and multivariate stock price behavior
JFQA 1976 NOV VOL 11.

(4353)
Farrell J L
The multi-index model and practical portfolio analysis
Research Foundation of the Institute of Chartered Financial Analysts, 1976.

(4354)
Lee C F
A note on the interdependent structure of security returns
JFQA 1976 MAR VOL 11 p 73.

(4355)
Draper P R
Industry influences on share price variability
JBFA 1975 SUMMER VOL 2:2 p 169-186.

(4356)
Farrell J L
Homogeneous stock groupings
FAJ 1975 MAY-JUN VOL 31 p 50-62.

(4357)
Fertuck L
A test of industry indices based on SIC codes
JFQA 1975 DEC VOL 10 p 837.

(4358)
Stone B K
Systematic interest-rate risk in a two-index model of returns
JFQA 1974 NOV VOL 9 p 709..

(4359)**Meyers S L**
A re-examination of market and industry factors in stock price behavior
JF 1973 VOL 28 p 695.

(4360)
Reilly F K
The misdirected emphasis in security valuation
FAJ 1973 JAN-FEB VOL 29 p 54-56.

(4361)
Simkowitz M A, Logue D E
The interdependent structure of security returns
JFQA 1973 MAR VOL 8:2 p 259-272.

(4362)
Tysseland M S
Further tests of the validity of the industry
approach to investment analysis
JFQA 1971 MAR VOL 6 p 835-848.

(4363)
Williams W N, Goodman M L
A statistical grouping of corporations by their
financial characteristics
JFQA 1971 SEP VOL 6 p 1095-1104.

(4364)
Feeney G J, Hester D D
Stock market indices: a principal components
analysis
(in Hester D D and Tobin J eds., Risk aversion
and portfolio choice. Wiley, 1967.)

(4365)
King B F
Market and industry factors in stock price
behavior
JB 1966 JAN VOL 39 p 139-190.

(4366)
Durand D
Bank stocks and the analysis of covariance
Em 1955 JAN VOL 23 p 30-45.

10.41 Market model

(4367)
Huang R D, Jo H
Tests of market models: Heteroskedasticity or
misspecification?
JBankF 1988 VOL 12:3 p 439-456.

(4368)
Hays P A, Upton D E
A shifting regimes approach to the stationarity of
the market model parameters of individual
securities
JFQA 1986 SEP VOL 21:3 p 307-321.

(4369)
Lee C-W J
Market model stationarity and timing of structural
change
FR 1985 NOV VOL 20:4.

(4370)
Beedles W L
Electric utility returns and the market model
JBusR 1984 VOL 12 p 463-480.

(4371)
Brown S J, Barry C B
Anomalies   in   security   returns   and   the
specification of the market model
JF 1984 JUL VOL 39:3 p 807-817.

(4372)
Copley R E, Cooley P L, Roenfeldt R L
Autocorrelation in market model residuals
JBFA 1984 AUTUMN VOL 11:3 p 409-417

(4373)
Tomczyk S, Chatterjee S
Estimating the market model robustly
JBFA 1984 WINTER VOL 11:4 p 563-573

(4374)
Bey R P
Market model stationarity of individual public
utilities
JFQA 1983 MAR VOL 18:1 p 67-85.

(4375)
Stapleton R C, Subrahmanyam M G
The market model and capital asset pricing theory
: a note
JF 1983 DEC VOL 38:5 p 1637-1642.

(4376)
Giacotto C, Ali M M
Optimum distribution-free tests and further
evidence of heteroscedasticity in the market
model
JF 1982 DEC VOL 37:5 p 1247-1257.

(4377)
Rosenberg B
The capital asset pricing model and the market model
JPM 1981 WINTER VOL 7:2 p 5-16.

(4378)
Alexander G J
Applying the market model to long-term corporate bonds
JFQA 1980 DEC VOL 15 p 1063-1080.

(4379)
Bey R P, Pinches G E
Additional evidence of heteroscedasticity in the market model
JFQA 1980 JUN VOL 15 p 299.

(4380)
Emmanuel D M
The market model in New Zealand
JBFA 1980 WINTER VOL 7:4 p 591-602.

(4381)
Rudd A, Rosenberg B
The market model in investment management
JF 1980 MAY VOL 35:2 p 597-609.

(4382)
Schallheim J, DeMagistris R
New estimates of the market parameters
FIN MGMT 1980 AUTUMN VOL 9 p 60.

(4383)
Theobald M
An analysis of market model and beta factors using UK equity share data
JBFA 1980 SPRING VOL 7:1 p 46-64

(4384)
Fabozzi F J, Francis J C
The effects of changing macroeconomic conditions on the parameters of single index market model
JFQA 1979 JUN VOL 14 p 351.

(4385)
Morgan I G
Market proxies and the conditional prediction of returns
JFE 1978 VOL 6 p 385.

(4386)
Belkaoui A
Canadian evidence of heteroscedasticity in the market model
JF 1977 VOL 32 p 1320.

(4387)
Fabozzi F J, Francis J C
Stability tests for alphas and betas over bull and bear market conditions
JF 1977 VOL 32 p 1093.

(4388)
Schwartz R A, Whitcomb D K
Evidence on the presence and causes of serial correlation in market model residuals
JFQA 1977 JUN VOL 12 p 291.

(4389)
Brenner M
On the stability of the distribution of the market component in stock price changes
JFQA 1974 DEC VOL 9 p 945.

(4390)
Pogue G A, Solnik B H
The market model applied to European common stocks: Some empirical results
JFQA 1974 DEC VOL 9 p 917.

(4391)
Solnik B H
An international market model of security price behavior
JFQA 1974 SEP VOL 9 p 537.

(4392)
Fama E F
A note on the market model and the two-parameter model
JF 1973 VOL 28 p 1181.

11 Risk

(4393)
Ambachtsheer K P
The persistence of investment risk
JPM 1989 FALL VOL 16:1 p 69-71.

(4394)
Kraus A, Smith M
Market created risk
JF 1989 JUL VOL 44:3 p 557-570.

(4395)
LeBaron D, Farrelly G, Gula S
Facilitating a dialogue on risk: a questionnaire approach
FAJ 1989 MAY-JUN VOL 45 p 19-24.

(4396)
Dhaliwal D S
The effect of the firm's business risk on the choice of accounting methods
JBFA 1988 SUMMER VOL 15:2 p 289.

(4397)
Federal Reserve Bank of Kansas City
Financial market volatility: A symposium
Federal Reserve Bank of Kansas City, 1988.

(4398)
Fuller R J, Wong G W
Traditional versus theoretical risk measures
FAJ 1988 MAR-APR VOL 44 p 52-57.

(4399)
Joerding W
Excess stock price volatility as a misspecified Euler equation
JFQA 1988 SEP VOL 23 p 253.

(4400)
Stone C C ed.
Financial risk: Theory, evidence and implications
Kluwer Academic, 1988.

(4401)
Wagner W H
The many dimensions of risk
JPM 1988 WINTER VOL 14:2 p 35-39.

(4402)
Smith V K, Desvousges W H
An empirical analysis of the economic value of risk changes
JPE 1987 VOL 95 p 89.

(4403)
Ang J S, Schwarz T
Risk aversion and information structure : an experimental study of price variability in the securities markets
JF 1985 JUL VOL 40:3 p 825-846.

(4404)
Izan H Y
Testing for changes in relative risk
AJM 1985 JUN VOL 10 p 39-48.

(4405)
Leonard H B, Zeckhauser R J
Financial risk and the burdens of contracts
AER 1985 VOL 75 P+P p 375-380.

(4406)
Farrelly G E, Reichenstein W R
Risk perceptions of institutional investors
JPM 1984 SUMMER VOL 10:4 p 5-12.

(4407)
Speakes J K
Risk measurement and risk management
JPM 1984 WINTER VOL 10:2 p 66-71.

(4408)
Estep T, Hanson N, Johnson C
Sources of value and risk in common stocks
JPM 1983 SUMMER VOL 9:4 p 5-13.

(4409)
Muller F L, Fielitz B D, Green M T
S&P quality group rankings: risk and return
JPM 1983 SUMMER VOL 9:4 p 39-42.

(4410)
Nawrocki D
A comparison of risk measures when used in a simple portfolio selection heuristic
JBFA 1983 SUMMER VOL 10:2 p 183-194

(4411)
Weinstein M I
Bond systematic risk and the option pricing model
JF 1983 DEC VOL 38:5 p 1415-1429..

(4412)**Arrow K J**
Risk perception in psychology and economics
Economic Inquiry 1982 p 1-9.

(4413)
Williams A O, Pfeifer P E
Estimating security price risk using duration and price elasticity
JF 1982 MAY VOL 37:2 p 399-411.

(4414)
Bart J, Masse I J
Divergence of opinion and risk.
JFQA 1981 MAR VOL 16:1 p 23-34

(4415)
Chen S-N
Residual variance heteroscedasticity portfolio diversification and trading rules
QREB 1981 AUTUMN VOL 21:3 p 87-97.

(4416)
Chen S-N, Keown A J
Pure residual and market risk : a note
JF 1981 DEC VOL 36:5 p 1203-1209.

(4417)
Moore P G
Some financial implications of risk in the UK
Omega 1981 VOL 9:2 p 113-125.

(4418)
Trczinka C
On revising ex-ante estimates of portfolio risk
EE 1981 SUMMER VOL 26:4 p 316-322.

(4419)
Ben-Horim M, Levy H
Total risk, diversifiable risk and non-diversifiable risk: A pedagogic note
JFQA 1980 JUN VOL 15 p 289.

(4420)
Modani N K, Cooley P L, Roenfeldt R L
Covariation of risk measures under inflation
JBFA 1980 AUTUMN VOL 7:3 p 393-400.

(4421)
Blandon P R, Ward C W R
Investors' perception of risk: A re-assessment
JBFA 1979 WINTER VOL 6:4 p 443-454.

(4422)
Castanias R
Macroinformation and variability of stock market prices
JF 1979 MAY VOL 34:2 p 439-450.

(4423)
Francis J C
Statistical analysis of risk surrogates for NYSE stocks
JFQA 1979 DEC VOL 14 p 981.

(4424)
Gehr A K
Risk and return
JF 1979 SEP VOL 34:4 p 1027-1030

(4425)
Martin J D, Scott D F Jr, Vandell R F
Equivalent risk classes: A multidimensional examination
JFQA 1979 MAR VOL 14 p 101.

(4426)
Moore P G
Handling financial risks
Omega 1979 VOL 7:3 p 183-190.

(4427)
Dhingra H L
Portfolio volatility adjustment by Canadian mutual funds
JBFA 1978 WINTER VOL 5:4 p 305-333.

(4428)
Klemkosky R C, Maness T S
The predictability of real portfolio risk levels
JF 1978 VOL 33 p 631.

(4429)
Falk H, Heintz J A
The predictability of relative risk over time
JBFA 1977 SPRING VOL 4:1 p 5-28.

(4430)
Fouse W L
Risk and liquidity revisited
FAJ 1977 JAN-FEB p 40-45.

(4431)
Keown A J, Martin J D
Interest rate sensitivity and portfolio risk
JFQA 1977 JUN VOL 12 p 181.

(4432)
Pappas J L
A note on the inclusion of earnings risk in
measures of return
JF 1977 VOL 32 p 1363.

(4433)
Barefield R M, Comiskey E E
The association of forecast error with other risk
measures
JBFA 1975 AUTUMN VOL 2:3 p 315-326.

(4434)
Ben-Zion U, Shalit S S
Size, leverage and dividend record as determinants
of equity risk
JF 1975 VOL 30 p 1015.

(4435)
Fewings D R
The impact of growth on the risk of common
stocks
JF 1975 MAY VOL 30:2 p 525-531.

(4436)
Hughes J S, Logue D E, Sweeney R J
Corporate international diversification and market
assigned measures of risk and diversification
JFQA 1975 NOV VOL 10 p 627.

(4437)
McDonald J G
Investment objectives: Diversification, risk and
exposure to surprise
FAJ 1975 MAR-APR VOL 31 p 42-50.

(4438)
Meyer J
Increasing risk
JET 1975 AUG VOL 11:1 p 119-132.

(4439)
Perrakis S
Certainty equivalents and timing uncertainty
JFQA 1975 MAR VOL 10 p 109.

(4440)
Schwendiman C J, Pinches G E
An analysis of alternative measures of investment
risk
JF 1975 VOL 30 p 193.

(4441)
Dickenson J P ed.
Risk and uncertainty in accounting and finance: a
book of readings
Saxon House, 1974.

(4442)
Rosenberg B
Extra-market components of covariance in security
returns
JFQA 1974 MAR VOL 9 p 263.

(4443)
McEnally R W
Some portfolio-relevant risk characteristics of
long-term marketable securities
JFQA 1973 SEP VOL 8:4 p 565-586.

(4444)
Rosenberg B, McKibben W
The prediction of systematic and specific risk in
common stocks
JFQA 1973 MAR VOL 8:2 p 317-334.

(4445)
Stone B K
A general class of three-parameter risk measurers
JF 1973 VOL 28 p 675.

(4446)
Beja A
On systematic and unsystematic components of
financial risk
JF 1972 MAR VOL 27 p 37-46.

(4447)
Bierman H Jr, Hausman W H
The resolution of investment uncertainty through
time
MSci 1972 AUG VOL 18 p B654-B662.

(4448)
Rao N K
Equivalent-risk class hypothesis: An empirical
study
JFQA 1972 JUN VOL 7 p 1763-1772.

(4449)
Haugen R A
Expected growth, required return, and the variability of stock prices
JFQA 1970 SEP VOL 5 p 297-308.

(4450)
Jacob N L
The measurement of market similarity for securities under uncertainty
JB 1970 JUL VOL 43 p 328-340.

(4451)
Joyce J M, Vogel R C
The uncertainty in risk: is variance unambiguous?
JF 1970 MAR VOL 25 p 127-134.

(4452)
Bierman H Jr
Using investment portfolios to change risk
JFQA 1968 JUN VOL 3 p 151-156.

(4453)
Breen W J
Homogenous risk measures and the construction of composite assets
JFQA 1968 DEC VOL 3 p 405-414.

(4454)
Rosett R N
Measuring the perception of risk
(in Borch K and Mossin J eds., Risk and uncertainty. Macmillan Int, 1968.)

(4455)
Fellner W
Probability and profit
Irwin, 1965.

(4456)
Boehm G A W
The science of being almost certain
F 1964 FEB VOL 76 p 104ff.

(4457)
Fellner W
Distortion of subjective probabilities as a reaction to uncertainty
QJE 1961 NOV VOL 75 p 670-689.

(4458)
Coombs C H, Pruitt D G
Components of risk in decision-making: probability and variance preferences
Journal of Experimental Psychology 1960 VOL 60 p 265-277.

(4459)
Redlich F
Towards a better theory of risk
Explorations in Entrepreneurial History 1957 OCT p 33-39.

(4460)
Freund R J
The introduction of risk into a programming model
Em 1956 JUL VOL 24 p 253-263.

(4461)
Shackle G L S
Uncertainty in economics and other reflections
Cambridge U Pr, 1955.

(4462)
Clendenin J C
Quality versus price as factors influencing common stock prices
JF 1951 DEC VOL 6 p 398-405.

(4463)
Hart A G
Risk, uncertainty and the unprofitability of compounding probabilities
(in Studies in mathematical economics and econometrics. U of Chicago Pr, 1942.)

(4464)
Steindl J
On risk
OEP 1941 JUN p 43-53..

(4465)**Hart A G**
Anticipations, uncertainty, and dynamic planning
U of Chicago Pr, 1940.

(4466)
Kalecki M
The principle of increasing risk
Ec 1937 NOV VOL 4 p 440-447.

(4467)
Knight F H
Risk, uncertainty and profit
Kelley, 1921.

(4468)
Haynes J
Risk as an economic factor
QJE 1895 JUL VOL 9 p 409-449.

11.1   Total risk/variance

(4469)
Akgiray V
Conditional heteroscedasticity in time series of stock returns: evidence and forecasts
JB 1989 VOL 62:1 p 55-80.

(4470)
Baillie R T, DeGennaro R P
The impact of delivery terms on stock return volatility
JFSR 1989 VOL 3:1 p 53-74.

(4471)
Merville L J, Pieptea D R
Stock-price volatility, mean-reverting diffusion, and noise
JFE 1989 SEP VOL 24:1 p 193.

(4472)
Ball C A
Estimation bias induced by discrete security prices
JF 1988 SEP VOL 43:4 p 841-866.

(4473)
Van Zijl T
Risk decomposition: Variance or standard deviation - a reexamination and extension
JFQA 1987 JUN VOL 22 p 237.

(4474)
Ronn E I
On the rationality of common stock return volatility
FR 1986 NOV VOL 21:4.

(4475)
Greer W R Jr, Largay J A III
Interim inventory estimation error and the volatility of stock prices
JBFA 1980 AUTUMN VOL 7:3 p 401-414

11.11   Risk of market

(4476)
Bookstaber R M, Pomerantz S
An information-based model of market volatility
FAJ 1989 NOV-DEC VOL 45 p 37-46.

(4477)
Jones C P, Wilson J W
Is stock price volatility increasing?
FAJ 1989 NOV-DEC VOL 45 p 20-26.

(4478)
Grossman S J
Program trading and market volatility: a report on interday relationships
FAJ 1988 JUL-AUG VOL 44 p 18-28.

(4479)
Brown K C, Brown G D
Does the market portfolio's composition matter
JPM 1987 WINTER VOL 13:2 p 26-32.

(4480)
Davis C D, White A P
Stock market volatility
F R Bul 1987 VOL 73:9.

(4481)
McClay M
Is the equity market becoming more volatile?
JPM 1981 SPRING VOL 7:3 p 51-55.

(4482)
Lee S L, Ward C W R
The association of stock market volatility and parallel trading by UK institutional investors
JBFA 1980 AUTUMN VOL 7:3 p 415-425

11.12 Risk of individual securities

(4483)
Baskin J
Dividend policy and the volatility of common stocks
JPM 1989 SPRING VOL 15:3 p 19-25.

(4484)
Callaway R E
Evidence of the nonstationarity of the variance rate of return of New York Stock Exchange listed common stock
FR 1989 MAY VOL 24:2 p 199-214.

(4485)
Scott L O
Stock price changes with random volatility and jumps: some empirical evidence
QREB 1989 VOL 29:1 p 21.

(4486)
Cho D C, Frees E W
Estimating the volatility of discrete stock prices
JF 1988 JUN VOL 43:2 p 451-466.

(4487)
Reichenstein W
On standard deviation and risk
JPM 1987 WINTER VOL 13:2 p 39-40.

(4488)
French K R, Roll R
Stock return variances. The arrival of information and the reaction of traders
JFE 1986 SEP VOL 17:1 p 5-26.

(4489)
Marsh T A, Rosenfeld E R
Non-trading market making and estimates of stock price volatility
JFE 1986 VOL 15 p 359.

(4490)
Beckers S
Variances of security price returns based on high low and closing prices
JB 1983 JAN VOL 56:1 p 97-112.

(4491)
Christie A A
The stochastic behavior of common stock variances: Value, leverage and interest rate effects
JFE 1982 DEC VOL 10:4 p 407-432.

(4492)
Parkinson M
The extreme value method for estimating the variance of the rate of return.
JB 1980 JAN VOL 53:1 p 61-65.

(4493)
Black F
Study of stock price volatility changes
Proceedings of the 1976 Meetings of the American Statistical Association, Business and Economic Statistics Section, Aug 1976.

(4494)
Mokkelbost P B
Unsystematic risk over time
JFQA 1971 MAR VOL 6 p 785-796.

(4495)
Heins A J, Allison S L
Some factors affecting stock price variability
JB 1966 JAN VOL 39 p 19-23.

(4496)
Dyckman T R, Stekler H O
Firm size and variability
JIE 1965 JUN VOL 13 p 214-218.

(4497)
Fritzemeier L H
Relative price fluctuations of industrial stocks in different price groups
JB 1936 APR VOL 9 p 133-154.

11.2 Systematic risk

(4498)
Callahan C M, Mohr R M
The determinants of systematic risk: a synthesis
FR 1989 MAY VOL 24:2 p 157-182.

(4499)
D'Souza R E, Brooks L D, Oberhelman H D
A general stationary stochastic regression model
for estimating and predicting beta
FR 1989 MAY VOL 24:2 p 299-318.

(4500)
Kolb R W, Rodriguez R J
The regression tendencies of betas: a reappraisal
FR 1989 MAY VOL 24:2 p 319.

(4501)
Aharony J, Swary I
A note on corporate bankruptcy and the market
model risk measures
JBFA 1988 SUMMER VOL 15:2 p 275-282.

(4502)
Crum R L, Bi K
An observation on estimating the systematic risk
of an industry segment
FIN MGMT 1988 SPRING VOL 17 p 60.

(4503)
Foster T W, Hansen D R, Vickrey D W
Additional evidence on the abatement of errors in
predicting beta through increases in portfolio size
and on the regression tendency
JBFA 1988 SUMMER VOL 15:2 p 185-198.

(4504)
Miller E M
On the systematic risk of expansion investment
QREB 1988 VOL 28:3 p 67.

(4505)
Reilly F K, Wright D J
A comparison of published betas
JPM 1988 SPRING VOL 14:3 p 64-69.

(4506)
Wei K C J, Lee C F
The generalized Stein/Rubinstein covariance
formula and its application to estimating real
systematic risk
MSci 1988 VOL 34 p 1266.

(4507)
Graham D, Jennings R
Systematic risk, dividend yield and the hedging
performance of stock index futures
JFM 1987 FEB VOL 7:1 p 1-14.

(4508)
Johnson L J, Brick J R, Price K
The interest rate sensitivity of equity prices with
respect to systematic risk and leverage
JBusR 1987 FEB VOL 15:1 p 85-92.

(4509)
Jose M L, Stevens J L
Product market structure, capital intensity, and
systematic risk: empirical results from the theory
of the firm
JFR 1987 VOL 10:2 p 161-176.

(4510)
Rahman A, Kryzanowski L, Sim A B
Systematic risk in purely random market model:
some empirical evidence for individual public
utilities
JFR 1987 VOL 10:2 p 143-152.

(4511)
Ushman N L
A comparison of cross-sectional and time-series
beta adjustment techniques
JBFA 1987 AUTUMN VOL 14:3 p 355-375.

(4512)
Yagil J
Divisional beta estimation under the old and new
tax laws
FIN MGMT 1987 WINTER VOL 16 p 16-21.

(4513)
Knight R F, Affleck-Graves J F
The impact of disclosure requirements on the
systematic risk of South African companies
JBFA 1986 SPRING VOL 13:1 p 87-94

(4514)
Kryzanowski L, Jalilvand A
Statistical tests of the accuracy of alternative
forecasts: some results for U.S. utility betas
FR 1986 MAY VOL 21:2.

(4515)
McInish T H, Wood R A
Adjusting for beta bias: an assessment of alternate
techniques: a note
JF 1986 MAR VOL 41:1 p 277-286.

(4516)
Miles J A
Growth options and the real determinants of
systematic risk
JBFA 1986 SPRING VOL 13:1 p 95-105

(4517)
Myer R L, Antia M J
A note on the calculation of probabilistic betas
FR 1986 FEB VOL 21:1..

(4518)**Simonds R R, LaMotte L R, McWhorter
A**
Testing for nonstationarity of market risk : an
exact test and power considerations
JFQA 1986 JUN VOL 21:2 p 209-220.

(4519)
Uselton G C, Kolari J W, Fraser D R
Long-term trends in the riskiness of electric
utility shares
JBFA 1986 AUTUMN VOL 13:3 p 453-459

(4520)
Chen S-N, Keown A J
Group effects and beta nonstationarity
JBFA 1985 WINTER VOL 12:4 p 595-608

(4521)
DeJong D V, Collins D W
Explanations for the instability of equity beta :
risk-free rate changes and leverage effects
JFQA 1985 MAR VOL 20:1 p 73-94.

(4522)
Fisher L, Kamin J H
Forecasting systematic risk : estimates of "raw"
beta that take account of the tendency of beta to
change and the heteroskedasticity of residual
returns.
JFQA 1985 JUN VOL 20:2 p 127-149.

(4523)
Goldenberg D H
Beta instability and stochastic market weights
MSci 1985 APR VOL 31:4 p 415-421.

(4524)
Grauer R R
Beta in linear risk tolerance economies
MSci 1985 NOV VOL 31:11 p 1390-1402.

(4525)
Hawawini G A, Michel P A, Corhay A
New evidence on beta stationarity and forecast for
Belgian common stocks
JBankF 1985 VOL 9 p 553.

(4526)
Lee C F, Wu C
The impacts of kurtosis on risk stationarity: some
empirical evidence
FR 1985 NOV VOL 20:4.

(4527)
McDonald B
Estimating market model betas : a comparison of
random coefficient methods and their ability to
correctly identify random variation
MSci 1985 NOV VOL 31:11 p 1403-1408.

(4528)
Mohr R M
The operating beta of a US multi-activity firm :
an empirical investigation
JBFA 1985 WINTER VOL 12:4 p 575-593

(4529)
Castagna A D, Greenwood L H, Matolcsy Z P
An evaluation of alternative methods for
estimating systematic risk
AJM 1984 DEC VOL 9 p 1-14.

(4530)
Dotan A, Ofer A
Variable versus stationary beta in the market
model: A comparative analysis
JBankF 1984 VOL 8 p 525.

(4531)
Graddy D B, Homaifar G, Karna A S
Double leverage as a source of systematic risk in
bank holding company stocks
JBR 1984 SUMMER VOL 15:2.

(4532)
Kryzanowski L, To M C
The telescopic effect of past return realizations on
ex-post beta estimates
FR 1984 MAR VOL 19:1.

(4533)
Lee C F
Random coefficient and errors-in-variables models
for beta estimates: methods and applications
JBusR 1984 VOL 12 p 505-516.

(4534)
Boquist J A, Moore W T
Estimating the systematic risk of an industry
segment: A mathematical programming approach
FIN MGMT 1983 WINTER VOL 12 p 11-18.

(4535)
Harrington D R
Whose beta is best?
FAJ 1983 JUL-AUG VOL 39 p 67-73.

(4536)
Madura J
Empirical measurement of exchange rate betas
JPM 1983 SUMMER VOL 9:4 p 43-46.

(4537)
McDonald B
Beta nonstationarity and the use of the Chen and
Lee estimator : a note
JF 1983 JUN VOL 38:3 p 1005-1009.

(4538)
Schneller M I
Are better betas worth the trouble?
FAJ 1983 JUL-AUG VOL 39 p 74-77.

(4539)
Alexander G W, Benson P G
More on beta as a random coefficient
JFQA 1982 MAR VOL 17:1 p 27-36.

(4540)
Chance M D
Evidence on a simplified model of systematic risk
FIN MGMT 1982 AUTUMN VOL 11 p 53-63.

(4541)
Chen C R
Time-series analysis of beta stationarity and its
determinants: A case of public utilities
FIN MGMT 1982 AUTUMN VOL 11 p 64-70.

(4542)
Chen S-N
An examination of risk-return relationship in bull
and bear markets using time-varying betas
JFQA 1982 JUN VOL 17:2 p 265-286.

(4543)
Harpaz G, Thomadakis S B
Systematic risk and the firm's experimental
strategy
JFQA 1982 SEP VOL 17:3 p 363-389.

(4544)
MacQueen J
Beta is dead! Long live beta!
CFQ 1982 SUMMER VOL 1 p 63-74.

(4545)
Maier S F, Peterson D W, Vander Weide J H
An empirical Bayes estimate of market risk
MSci 1982 JUL VOL 28:7 p 728-737.

(4546)
Mehta C R, Beranek W
Tracking asset volatility by means of a Bayesian
switching regression.
JFQA 1982 JUN VOL 17:2 p 241-263.

(4547)
Ohlson J A, Rosenberg B
Systematic risk of the CRSP equal-weighted
common stock index : a history estimated by
stochastic-parameter regression
JB 1982 JAN VOL 55:1 p 121-145.

(4548)
Price K, Price B, Nantell T J
Variance and lower partial moment measures of
systematic risk: some analytical and empirical
results
JF 1982 JUN VOL 37:3 p 843-855.

(4549)
Rosenberg B, Rudd A
The corporate uses of beta
CFQ 1982 SUMMER VOL 1 p 75-96.

(4550)
Theobald M
On estimating betas that change
JPM 1982 FALL VOL 9:1 p 62.

(4551)
Bildersee J S, Roberts G S
Beta instability when interest rate levels change
JFQA 1981 SEP VOL 16:3 p 375-380.

(4552)
Camp R C, Eubank A A Jr
The beta quotient: a new measure of portfolio risk
JPM 1981 SUMMER VOL 7:4 p 53-58..

(4553) **Chen S-N, Keowne A J**
Risk decomposition and portfolio diversification when beta is nonstationary: a note
JF 1981 SEP VOL 36:4 p 941-947.

(4554)
Cooley P L
A review of the use of beta in regulatory proceedings
FIN MGMT 1981 WINTER VOL 10 p 75-81.

(4555)
Fuller R J, Kerr H S
Estimating the divisional cost of capital : an analysis of the pure-play technique
JF 1981 DEC VOL 36:5 p 997-1009.

(4556)
Garbade K, Rentzler J
Testing the hypothesis of beta stationarity
IntER 1981 OCT VOL 22:3 p 577-587.

(4557)
Statman M
Betas compared: Merrill Lynch vs. Value Line
JPM 1981 WINTER VOL 7:2 p 41-44.

(4558)
Theobald M
Beta stationarity and estimation period : some analytical results
JFQA 1981 DEC VOL 16:5 p 747-757.

(4559)
Tole T M
How to maximize stationarity of beta
JPM 1981 WINTER VOL 7:2 p 45-49.

(4560)
Umstead D A
Volatility, growth, and investment policy
JPM 1981 WINTER VOL 7:2 p 55-59.

(4561)
Vandell R F
Is beta a useful measure of security risk?
JPM 1981 WINTER VOL 7:2 p 23-31.

(4562)
Alexander G J, Chervany N L
On the estimation and stability of beta
JFQA 1980 MAR VOL 15 p 123.

(4563)
Chen S-N
Time aggregation, autocorrelation and systematic risk estimates - additive versus multiplicative assumptions
JFQA 1980 MAR VOL 15 p 151.

(4564)
Clarke R G
The effect of fuel adjustment clauses on the systematic risk and market values of electric utilities
JF 1980 MAY VOL 35:2 p 347-358.

(4565)
Garman M B, Klass M J
On the estimation of security price volatilities from historical data
JB 1980 JAN VOL 53:1 p 67-78.

(4566)
Greene M T, Fielitz B D
Long-term dependence and least squares regression in investment analysis
MSci 1980 OCT VOL 26:10 p 1031-1038.

(4567)
Lavely J, Wakefield G, Barrett B
Toward enhancing beta estimates
JPM 1980 SUMMER VOL 6:4 p 43-46.

(4568)
Levy H
The CAPM and beta in an imperfect market
JPM 1980 WINTER VOL 6:2 p 5-11.

(4569)
Scott E, Brown S
Biased estimators and unstable betas
JF 1980 MAR VOL 35:1 p 49-55.

(4570)
Subrahmanyam M G, Thomakakis S B
Systematic risk and the theory of the firm
QJE 1980 VOL 94 p 437.

(4571)
Sunder S
Stationarity of market risk: random coefficients
tests for individual stocks
JF 1980 SEP VOL 35:4 p 883-896.

(4572)
Theobald M
An analysis of market model and beta factors
using UK equity share data
JBFA 1980 SPRING VOL 7:1 p 46-64

(4573)
Wallace A
Is beta dead?
II 1980 JUL p 23-30.

(4574)
Bar-Yosef S, Brown L D
Share price levels and beta
FIN MGMT 1979 SPRING VOL 8 p 60.

(4575)
Bergstrom G L, Umstead D A
Dynamic estimation of portfolio betas
JFQA 1979 SEP VOL 14 p 595.

(4576)
Eubank A A, Zunwalt J K
An analysis of the forecast error impact of
alternative beta adjustment techniques and risk
classes
JF 1979 JUN VOL 34:3 p 761-776.

(4577)
Fabozzi F J, Francis J C
Industry effects and the determinants of beta
QREB 1979 VOL 19:3 p 61.

(4578)
Gahlon J H, Stover R D
Diversification, financial leverage and
conglomerate systematic risk
JFQA 1979 DEC VOL 14 p 999.

(4579)
Haugen R A
Do common stock quality ratings predict risk?
FAJ 1979 MAR-APR VOL 35 p 68-71.

(4580)
Kim M K, Zumwalt J K
An analysis of risk in Bull and Bear markets
JFQA 1979 DEC VOL 14 p 1015.

(4581)
Cornell B, Dietrich J K
Mean-absolute-deviation versus least-squares
regression estimation of beta coefficients
JFQA 1978 MAR VOL 13 p 123.

(4582)
Eddy A R
Interest rate risk and systematic risk: An
interpretation
JF 1978 VOL 33 p 626.

(4583)
Elton E J, Gruber M J
Are betas best?
JF 1978 VOL 33 p 1375.

(4584)
Fabozzi F J, Francis J C
Beta as a random coefficient
JFQA 1978 MAR VOL 13 p 101.

(4585)
Gilster J E Jr, Linke C M
More on the estimation of beta for public
utilities: Biases resulting from structural shifts in
true beta
FIN MGMT 1978 AUTUMN VOL 7 p 60.

(4586)
Griepentrog G L, Roenfeldt R L, Pflaum C C
Further evidence on the stationarity of beta
coefficients
JFQA 1978 MAR VOL 13 p 117.

(4587)
Spicer B H
Market risk, accounting data and companies'
pollution control records
JBFA 1978 SPRING VOL 5:1 p 67-84.

(4588)
Brenner M, Smidt S
A simple model of non-stationarity of systematic
risk
JF 1977 VOL 32 p 1081.

(4589)
Gooding A E, O'Malley T P
Market phase and the stationarity of beta
JFQA 1977 DEC VOL 12 p 833.

(4590)
Lee C F
On the relationship between the systematic risk
and the investment horizon
JFQA 1976 DEC VOL 11 p 803.

(4591)
Blume M E
Beta and their regression tendencies
JF 1975 VOL 30 p 785.

(4592)
Hasty J M Jr, Fielitz B D
Systematic risk for heterogeneous time horizons
JF 1975 MAY VOL 30:2 p 659-673.

(4593)
Klemkosky R C, Martin J D
The adjustment of beta forecasts
JF 1975 VOL 30 p 1123.

(4594)
Reints W W, Vandenberg P A
The impact of changes in trading location on a
security's systematic risk
JFQA 1975 DEC VOL 10 p 881.

(4595)
Schaefer S M, Brealey R A, Hodges S D
Alternative models of systematic risk
(in Elton E J and Gruber M J eds., International
capital markets. N Holland, 1975.)

(4596)
Schneller M I
Regression analysis for multiplicative phenomena
and its implication for the measurement of
investment risk
MSci 1975 DEC VOL 22:4 p 422-426.

(4597)
Altman E I, Jacquillat B, Levasseur M
Comparative analysis of risk measures: France and
the United States
JF 1974 VOL 29 p 1495.

(4598)
Baesel J B
On the assessment of risk: Some further
considerations
JF 1974 VOL 29 p 1491.

(4599)
Fouse W L, Jahnke W W, Rosenberg B
Is beta phlogiston?
FAJ 1974 JAN-FEB VOL 30 p 70-81.

(4600)
Joehnk M D, Nielsen J F
The effects of conglomerate merger activity on
systematic risk
JFQA 1974 MAR VOL 9 p 215.

(4601)
Levitz G D
Market risk and the management of institutional
equity portfolios
FAJ 1974 JAN-FEB VOL 30 p 53-60.

(4602)
Levy R A
Beta coefficients as predictors of return
FAJ 1974 JAN-FEB VOL 30 p 61-69.

(4603)
Melicher R W
Financial factors which influence beta variations
within an homogenous industry environment
JFQA 1974 MAR VOL 9 p 231.

(4604)
Aber J W
Beta coefficients and models of security return
Heath, 1973.

(4605)
Cheng P L, Deets M K
Systematic risk and the horizon problem
JFQA 1973 MAR VOL 8:2 p 299-316..

(4606)**Crowell R A**
Risk measurement: Five applications
FAJ 1973 JUL-AUG VOL 29 p 81-95.

(4607)
Vasicek O A
A note on using cross-sectional information in
Bayesian estimation of security betas
JF 1973 VOL 28 p 1233.

(4608)
Babcock G C
A note on justifying beta as a measure of risk
JF 1972 JUN VOL 27 p 699-702.

(4609)
Campanella F B
The measurement of portfolio risk exposure: use
of beta coefficient
Lexington Bks, 1972.

(4610)
Hamada R S
The effect of the firm's capital structure on the
systematic risk of common stocks
JF 1972 MAY VOL 27 p 435-452.

(4611)
Blume M E
On the assessment of risk
JF 1971 MAR VOL 26 p 1-10.

(4612)
Jacob N L
The measurement of systematic risk for securities
and portfolios: some empirical results
JFQA 1971 MAR VOL 6 p 815-834.

(4613)
Kantor M
Market sensitivities
FAJ 1971 JAN-FEB VOL 27 p 64-68.

(4614)
Levy R A
On the short-term stationarity of beta coefficients
FAJ 1971 NOV-DEC VOL 27 p 55-62.

(4615)
Pinches G E, Kinney W R
The measurement of the volatility of common
stock prices
JF 1971 MAR VOL 26 p 119-126.

(4616)
Sharpe W F
Mean-absolute-deviation characteristic lines for
securities and portfolios
MSci 1971 OCT VOL 18 p B1-B13.

(4617)
Welles C
The beta revolution: learning to live with risk
II 1971 SEP VOL 5 p 21ff.

(4618)
Altman E I, Schwartz R A
Common stock price volatility measures and
patterns
JFQA 1970 JAN VOL 4 p 603-626.

(4619)
Treynor J L, Priest W W Jr, Fisher L et al.
Using portfolio composition to estimate risk
FAJ 1968 SEP-OCT VOL 24 p 93-100.

11.21 Thin trading, index autocorrelation and risk measurement

(4620)
Berglund T, Liljeblom E, Loflund A
Estimating betas on daily data for a small stock
market
JBankF 1989 MAR VOL 13:1 p 41-64.

(4621)
Fowler D J, Rorke C H, Jog V M
A bias-correcting procedure for beta estimation in
the presence of thin trading
JFR 1989 SPRING VOL 12:1 p 23-32.

(4622)
Handa P, Kothari S P, Wasley C
The relation between the return interval and
betas: implications for the size effect
JFE 1989 VOL 23 p 79.

(4623)
Larson J C, Morse J N
Intervalling effects in Hong Kong stocks
JFR 1987 VOL 10:4 p 353-362.

(4624)
Jog V M, Riding A L
Some Canadian findings regarding infrequent trading and instability in the single factor market model
JBFA 1986 SPRING VOL 13:1 p 125-135

(4625)
Fung W K H, Schwartz R A, Whitcomb D K
Adjusting for the intervalling effect bias in beta: A test using Paris Bourse data
JBankF 1985 VOL 9 p 443.

(4626)
Perry P R
Portfolio serial correlation and nonsynchronous trading
JFQA 1985 DEC VOL 20:4 p 517-523.

(4627)
Roden P F
Beta sensitivity to specification of the market index
RBER 1985 VOL 20 p 101-110.

(4628)
Cohen K J
Intervalling-effect bias in beta
MSci 1983 JAN VOL 29:1 p 135-148.

(4629)
Cohen K J, Hawawini G S, Maier S F
Friction in the trading process and the estimation of systematic risk
JFE 1983 VOL 12 p 263-278.

(4630)
Dimson E, Marsh P
The stability of UK risk measures and the problem of thin trading
JF 1983 JUN VOL 38:3 p 753-783.

(4631)
Fowler D J, Rorke C H
Risk measurement when shares are subject to infrequent trading.
JFE 1983 AUG VOL 12:2 p 279-283.

(4632)
Hawawini G A
Why beta shifts as the return interval changes
FAJ 1983 MAY-JUN VOL 39 p 73-77.

(4633)
Theobald M
The analytic relationship between intervaling and nontrading effects in continuous time
JFQA 1983 JUN VOL 18:2 p 199-209.

(4634)
Papaioannou G J
Thinness and short-run price dependence in the Athens Stock Exchange
Greek Economic Review 1982 VOL 4:2.

(4635)
Carpenter M D, Upton D E
Trading volume and beta stability
JPM 1981 WINTER VOL 7:2 p 60-64.

(4636)
Fowler D J, Rorke C H, Jog V M
A note on beta stability and thin trading on the Toronto stock exchange
JBFA 1981 SUMMER VOL 8:2 p 267-278

(4637)
Saniga E M, McInish T H, Gouldey B K
The effect of differencing interval length on beta
JFR 1981 VOL 4 p 121-135.

(4638)
Hawanini G A
An analytical examination of the intervaling effect on skewness and other moments
JFQA 1980 DEC VOL 15 p 1121.

(4639)
Hawawini G A
Intertemporal cross-dependence in securities daily returns and the short-run intervaling effect on systematic risk
JFQA 1980 MAR VOL 15 p 139.

(4640)
Hawawini G A, Vora A
Evidence of intertemporal systematic risks in the daily price movements of NYSE and AMEX common stocks
JFQA 1980 JUN VOL 15 p 331.

(4641)
Dimson E
Risk measurement when shares are subject to infrequent trading
JFE 1979 JUN VOL 7:2 p 197-226.

(4642)
Smith K V
The effect of intervaling on estimating parameters of the capital asset pricing model
JFQA 1978 JUN VOL 13 p 313.

(4643)
Scholes M, Williams J
Estimating betas from nonsynchronous data
JFE 1977 VOL 5 p 309.

11.22 Accounting measures of systematic risk

(4644)
Chung K H
The impact of the demand volatility and leverages on the systematic risk of common stocks
JBFA 1989 SUMMER VOL 16:3 p 343.

(4645)
Dugan M T, Shriver K A
The effects of estimation period, industry, and proxy on the calculation of the degree of operating leverage
FR 1989 FEB VOL 24:1 p 109-122.

(4646)
Blann J, Balachandran B V
An empirical test of the statistical association of market risk and financial accounting allocation
JBFA 1988 SPRING VOL 15:1 p 101-114.

(4647)
Nunthirapakorn T, Millar J A
Changing prices accounting earnings and systematic risk
JBFA 1987 SPRING VOL 14:1 p 1-25

(4648)
Comiskey E E, Mulford C W, Porter T L
Forecast error earnings variability and systematic risk : additional evidence
JBFA 1986 SUMMER VOL 13:2 p 257-265

(4649)
Dyl E A, Hoffmeister J R
A note on dividend policy and beta
JBFA 1986 SPRING VOL 13:1 p 107-115

(4650)
Lee C F et al.
On accounting-based, market-based and composite-based beta predictions: methods and implications
FR 1986 FEB VOL 21:1.

(4651)
Dubofsky D A
The effects of maturing debt on equity risk
QREB 1985 AUTUMN VOL 25:3 p 36-47

(4652)
Mandelker G N, Rhee S G
The impact of the degrees of operating and financial leverage on systematic risk of common stock.
JFQA 1984 MAR VOL 19:1 p 45-57.

(4653)
McDaniel W R
Operating leverage and operating risk
JBFA 1984 SPRING VOL 11:1 p 113-125

(4654)
Conine T E Jr
On the theoretical relationship between systematic risk and price elasticity of demand
JBFA 1983 SUMMER VOL 10:2 p 173-182

(4655)
Conine T E Jr
On the theoretical relationship between business risk and systematic risk
JBFA 1982 SUMMER VOL 9:2 p 199-205.

(4656)
Gahlon J M, Gentry J A
On the relationship between systematic risk and the degrees of operating and financial leverage
FIN MGMT 1982 SUMMER VOL 11 p 15-23.

(4657)
Douglas Smith L, Markland R E
Measurement of business risk for inter-industry comparisons
FIN MGMT 1981 SUMMER VOL 10 p 49-63.

(4658)
Ruland W
The behavior of changes in accounting risk measurers
JBFA 1981 AUTUMN VOL 8:3 p 373..

(4659)**Hill N C, Stone B K**
Accounting betas, systematic operating risk and financial leverage: A risk-composition approach to the determinants of systematic risk
JFQA 1980 SEP VOL 15 p 595.

(4660)
Barefield R M, Comiskey E E
The differential association of forecast error and earnings variability with systematic risk
JBFA 1979 SPRING VOL 6:1 p 1-8

(4661)
Bowman R G
The theoretical relationship between systematic risk and financial (accounting) variables.
JF 1979 JUN VOL 34:3 p 617-630.

(4662)
Eskew R K
The forecasting ability of accounting risk measures: some additional evidence
AR 1979 JAN VOL 54:1 p 107-118.

(4663)
Garsombke H P
The relationship between corporate disclosure and firm risk
JBFA 1979 SPRING VOL 6:1 p 53-70.

(4664)
Brenner M, Smidt S
Asset characterisics and systematic risk
FIN MGMT 1978 WINTER VOL 7 p 33.

(4665)
Griffin P A
The association between relative risk and risk estimates derived from quarterly earnings and dividends
AR 1976 JUL VOL 51:3 p 499-515.

(4666)
Rosenberg B, Guy J
Prediction of beta from investment fundamentals - I
FAJ 1976 MAY-JUN VOL 32 p 60-72.

(4667)
Rosenberg B, Guy J
Prediction of beta from investment fundamentals - II
FAJ 1976 JUL-AUG VOL 32 p 62-71.

(4668)
Beaver W H, Manegold J
The association between market-determined and accounting-determined measures of systematic risk: Some further evidence
JFQA 1975 JUN VOL 10 p 231.

(4669)
Bildersee J S
The association between a market determined measure of risk and alternative measures of risk
AR 1975 JUN VOL 50:1 p 81-98.

(4670)
Gonedes N J
A note on accounting-based and market-based estimates of systematic risk
JFQA 1975 JUN VOL 10 p 355.

(4671)
Gonedes N J
Evidence on the information content of accounting numbers: Accounting based and market-based estimates of systematic risk.
JFQA 1974 JUN VOL 9 p 407.

(4672)
Lev B
On the association between operating leverage and risk
JFQA 1974 SEP VOL 9 p 627.

(4673)
Pettit R R, Westerfield R
A model of capital asset risk
JFQA 1972 MAR VOL 7 p 1649-1668.

(4674)
Beaver W H, Kettler P, Scholes M
The association between market determined and
accounting determined risk measures
AR 1970 OCT VOL 45 p 654-682.

11.23   Consumption betas

(4675)
Mankiw N G, Shapiro M D
Risk and return: Consumption beta versus market
beta
REStat 1986 AUG VOL 68:3 p 452-459.

(4676)
Hazuka T B
Consumption   betas   and   backwardation   in
commodity markets
JF 1984 JUL VOL 39:3 p 647-657.

(4677)
Breeden D T
Consumption risk in futures markets
JF 1980 MAY VOL 35:2 p 503-520.

11.24   Factor sensitivities

(4678)
Berry M A, Burmeister E, McElroy M B
Sorting out risks using known APT factors
FAJ 1988 MAR-APR VOL 44 p 29-42.

11.3   Diversification

(4679)
Statman M
How many stocks make a diversified portfolio?
JFQA 1987 SEP VOL 22:3 p 353-363.

(4680)
Bird R, Tippett M
Naive diversification and portfolio risk - a note
MSci 1986 FEB VOL 32:2 p 244-253.

(4681)
Board J L G, Sutcliffe C M S
Optimal portfolio diversification and the effects of
differing intra sample measures of return
JBFA 1985 WINTER VOL 12:4 p 561-574

(4682)
McEnally R W
Time diversification: the surest route to lower
risk?
JPM 1985 SUMMER VOL 11:4 p 24-26.

(4683)
MacMinn R D
A general diversification theorem : a note
JF 1984 JUN VOL 39:2 p 541-550.

(4684)
Tole T M
You can't diversify without diversifying
JPM 1982 WINTER VOL 8:2 p 5-11.

(4685)
Conine T E Jr, Tamarkin M
On diversification given asymmetry in returns
JF 1981 DEC VOL 36:5 p 1143-1155.

(4686)
Bierman H Jr
How much diversification is desirable?
JPM 1980 FALL VOL 7:1 p 42-44.

(4687)
Lloyd W P, Hanley R L Jr
Time diversification: surest route to lower risk
JPM 1980 SPRING VOL 6:3 p 5-9.

(4688)
Russell W R, Seo T K
Diversification   theorems   for   subsets   of   risk
averters
REStud 1979 JUL VOL 46 p 555-559.·

(4689)
Beedles W L, Simkowitz M A
Diversification in a three-moment world
JFQA 1978 DEC VOL 13 p 927.

(4690)
Hadar J, Russell W R, Seo T K
Gains from diversification
REStud 1977 VOL 44 p 363.

(4691)
Evans J L
An examination of the principle of diversification
JBFA 1975 SUMMER VOL 2:2 p 243-256.

(4692)
Fisher L
Using modern portfolio theory to maintain an
efficiently diversified portfolio
FAJ 1975 MAY-JUN VOL 31 p 73-85.

(4693)
Klemkosky R C, Martin J D
The effect of market risk on portfolio
diversification
JF 1975 VOL 30 p 147.

(4694)
Upson R B, Jessup P F, Matsumoto K
Portfolio diversification strategies
FAJ 1975 MAY-JUN VOL 31 p 86-92.

(4695)
Hadar J, Russell W R
Diversification of interdependent prospects
JET 1974 MAR VOL 7:3 p 231-240.

(4696)
Johnson K H
A note on diversification and the reduction of
dispersion
JFE 1974 VOL 1 p 365.

(4697)
Pye G
A note on diversification
JFQA 1974 JAN VOL 9 p 131.

(4698)
Sarnat M
The gains from risk diversification on the London
Stock Exchange
JBF 1972 AUTUMN VOL 4 p 54-64.

(4699)
Sharpe W F
Risk, market sensitivity and diversification
FAJ 1972 JAN-FEB VOL 28 p 74-79.

(4700)
Jennings E H
An empirical analysis of some aspects of common
stock diversification
JFQA 1971 MAR VOL 6 p 797-814.

(4701)
Wagner W H, Lau S C
The effect of diversification on risk
FAJ 1971 NOV-DEC VOL 27 p 48-53.

(4702)
Mao J C T
Essentials of portfolio diversification strategy
JF 1970 DEC VOL 25 p 1109-1122.

(4703)
Whitmore G A
Diversification and the reduction of dispersion: a
note
JFQA 1970 JUN VOL 5 p 263-264.

(4704)
Evans J L, Archer S H
Diversification and the reduction of dispersion: an
empirical analysis
JF 1968 DEC VOL 23 p 761-767.

(4705)
Samuelson P A
General proof that diversification pays
JFQA 1967 MAR VOL 2 p 1-13.

(4706)
West R R
"Homemade" diversification vs. corporate
diversification
JFQA 1967 DEC VOL 2 p 417-420.

(4707)
Ansoff H I
A model for diversification
MSci 1958 VOL 4 p 392ff.

(4708)
Leavens D H
Diversification of planning
Trusts and Estates 1945 VOL 80 p 469-473.

11.31   International diversification

(4709)
Eun C S, Shim S
International transmission of stock market movements
JFQA 1989 JUN VOL 24:2 p 241-256.

(4710)
Jorion P
Asset allocation with hedged and unhedged foreign stocks and bonds
JPM 1989 SUMMER VOL 15:4 p 49-54.

(4711)
Meric I, Meric G
Potential gains from international portfolio diversification and intertemporal stability and seasonality in international stock market relationships
JBankF 1989 SEP VOL 13:4-5 p 627-640.

(4712)
Defusco R A, Philippatos G C, Choi D
Risk, return and international investment by US corporations
AE 1988 SEP VOL 20:9 p 1199-1210.

(4713)
Dwyer G P Jr, Hafer R W
Are national stock markets linked?
F R Bk St Louis Rev 1988 NOV-DEC VOL 70:6.

(4714)
Eun C S, Resnick B G
Exchange rate uncertainty, forward contracts, and international portfolio selection
JF 1988 MAR VOL 43:1 p 197-216.

(4715)
Kaplanis E C
Stability and forecasting of the comovement measures of international stock market returns
JIMF 1988 MAR VOL 7:1 p 63-76.

(4716)
Levy H, Lerman Z
The benefits of international diversification in bonds
FAJ 1988 SEP-OCT VOL 44 p 56-64.

(4717)
Doukas J, Melhem M
Canadian banks: risk reduction by international diversification
AE 1987 DEC VOL 19:12 p 1561-1570.

(4718)
Errunza V R, Losq E
How risky are emerging markets?
JPM 1987 FALL VOL 14:1 p 62-67.

(4719)
Eun C S, Resnick B G
International diversification under estimation risk: Actual vs. potential gains
(in Khoury S and Gosh A eds., Recent developments in international banking and finance, Vol 1. Lexington Bks, 1987.)

(4720)
Grauer R R, Hakkansson N H
Gains from international diversification: 1968-85 returns on portfolios of stocks and bonds
JF 1987 JUL VOL 42:3 p 721-738.

(4721)
Lee A F
International asset and currency allocation
JPM 1987 FALL VOL 14:1 p 68-73.

(4722)
Jorion P
Why buy international bonds?
Investment Management Review Summer 1986.

(4723)
Errunza V R, Losq E
The behavior of stock prices on LDC markets
JBankF 1985 VOL 9 p 561.

(4724)
Eun C S, Resnick B G
Currency factor in international portfolio diversification
CJWB 1985 SUMMER VOL 20 p 45-53.

(4725)
Jorion P
International portfolio diversification with estimation risk
JB 1985 JUL VOL 58:3 p 259-278.

(4726)
Madura J
International portfolio construction
JBusR 1985 FEB VOL 13:1 p 87-96.

(4727)
Errunza V R, Senbet L W
International corporate diversification market valuation and size-adjusted evidence
JF 1984 JUL VOL 39:3 p 727-745.

(4728)
Eun C S, Resnick B G
Estimating the correlation structure of international share prices
JF 1984 DEC VOL 39:5 p 1311-1324.

(4729)
Fatemi A M
Shareholder benefits from corporate international diversification
JF 1984 DEC VOL 39:5 p 1325-1344.

(4730)
Adler M
Global fixed-income portfolio management
FAJ 1983 SEP-OCT VOL 39 p 41-50.

(4731)
Erhlich E E
Foreign pension fund investments in the United States
F R Bk New York Q Rev 1983 SPRING VOL 8:1.

(4732)
Errunza V R
Emerging markets: A new opportunity for improving global portfolio performance
FAJ 1983 SEP-OCT VOL 39 p 51-58.

(4733)
Philippatos G C, Christofi A, Christofi P
The inter-temporal stability of international stock market relationships: Another view
FIN MGMT 1983 WINTER VOL 12 p 63.

(4734)
Agtmael A W van, Errunza V R
Foreign portfolio investment in emerging securities markets
CJWB 1982 SUMMER VOL 17:2 p 58-63.

(4735)
Errunza V R, Rosenberg B
Investment in developed and less developed countries
JFQA 1982 DEC VOL 17:5 p 741-762.

(4736)
Logue D E
An experiment in international diversification
JPM 1982 FALL VOL 9:1 p 22-27.

(4737)
Tapley M, Simmonds M
International diversification in the nineteenth century
CJWB 1982 SUMMER VOL 17:2 p 64-70.

(4738)
Brewer H L
Investor benefits from corporate international diversification
JFQA 1981 MAR VOL 16:1 p 113-126.

(4739)
Ehrlich E E
International diversification by United States pension funds
F R Bk New York Q Rev 1981 AUTUMN VOL 6:3.

(4740)
Maldonado R, Saunders A
International portfolio diversification and the inter-temporal stability of international stock market relationships, 1957-1978
FIN MGMT 1981 AUTUMN VOL 10 p 54-64.

(4741)
Hana J
Why Americans should have diversified
Euromoney 1980 MAR.

(4742)
Senchack A J Jr, Beedles W L
Is indirect international diversification desirable?
JPM 1980 WINTER VOL 6:2 p 49-57.

(4743)
Watson J
The stationarity of inter-country correlation coefficients: a note
JBFA 1980 SUMMER VOL 7:2 p 297-303

(4744)
Hilliard J E
The relationship between equity indices on world exchanges
JF 1979 MAR VOL 34:1 p 103-114.

(4745)
Guy J R F
An examination of the effects of international diversification from the British viewpoint on both hypothetical and real portfolios
JF 1978 VOL 33 p 1425.

(4746)
Watson J
A study of possible gains from international investment
JBFA 1978 SUMMER VOL 5:2 p 195-205.

(4747) Agmon T, Lessard D
Investor recognition of corporate international diversification
JF 1977 VOL 32 p 1049.

(4748)
Saunders A, Woodward R S
Gains from international portfolio diversification: U K evidence 1971-75
JBFA 1977 AUTUMN VOL 4:3 p 299-310.

(4749)
Joy O M, Panton D B, Lessig V P
Comovement of international equity markets: A taxonomic approach
JFQA 1976 SEP VOL 11 p 415.

(4750)
Lessard D R
World, country, and industry relationships in equity returns
FAJ 1976 JAN-FEB VOL 32 p 32-38.

(4751)
Levy H, Sarnat M
Devaluation risk and the portfolio analysis of international investment
(in Elton E J and Gruber M J eds., International capital markets. N Holland, 1975.)

(4752)
Koning J
Netherlands company pension funds international portfolio diversification: an empirical analysis 1967 I-1972 II
EER 1974 VOL 5:3.

(4753)
Madridakis S G, Wheelwright S C
An analysis of the interrelationships among the major world stock exchanges
JBFA 1974 SUMMER VOL 1:2 p 195-216.

(4754)
Solnik B H
Why not diversify internationally rather than domestically?
FAJ 1974 JUL-AUG VOL 30 p 48-54.

(4755)
Lessard D R
International portfolio diversification: A multivariate analysis for a group of Latin American countries
JF 1973 VOL 28 p 619.

(4756)
Ripley D M
Systematic elements in the linkage of national stock market indices
REStat 1973 AUG VOL 55:3 p 356-361.

(4757)
Agmon T
The relations among equity markets: a study of share price co-movements in the United States, United Kingdom, Germany and Japan
JF 1972 SEP VOL 27 p 839-856.

(4758)
Grubel H G, Fadner K
The interdependence of international equity markets
JF 1971 MAR VOL 26 p 89-94.

(4759)
Levy H, Sarnat M
International diversification of investment portfolios
AER 1970 SEP VOL 60 p 668-675.

(4760)
Grubel H G
Internationally diversified portfolios: welfare gains
and capital flows
AER 1968 DEC VOL 58 p 1299-1314.

12 Portfolio selection

(4761)
Khaksari S, Kamath R, Grieves R
A new approach to determining optimum portfolio mix
JPM 1989 SPRING VOL 15:3 p 43-49.

(4762)
Krehbiel T L, McCarthy P
An analysis of the determinants of portfolio selection
QREB 1989 AUTUMN VOL 29:3 p 43-56.

(4763)
Li Y, Ziemba W T
Characterizations of optimal portfolios by univariate and multivariate risk aversion
MSci 1989 VOL 35 p 259.

(4764)
Nawrocki D, Staples K
A customized LPM risk measure for portfolio analysis
AE 1989 VOL 21:2 p 205-218.

(4765)
Cheung C S, Kwan C C Y
A note on simple criteria for optimal portfolio selection
JF 1988 MAR VOL 43:1 p 241-246.

(4766)
Dybvig P H
Distributional analysis of portfolio choice
JB 1988 VOL 61 p 369.

(4767)
Chen S-N
Simple optimal asset allocation under uncertainty
JPM 1987 SUMMER VOL 13:4 p 69-76.

(4768)
Frankfurter G M, Lamoureux C G
The relevance of the distributional form of common stock returns to the construction of optimal portfolios
JFQA 1987 DEC VOL 22:4 p 505-511.

(4769)
Geanakoplos J, Polemarchakis H
Existence, regularity, and constrained suboptimality of competitive portfolio allocations when the asset market is incomplete
(in Heller W ed., Uncertainty, information and communication: Essays in honor of Kenneth J. Arrow, Vol 3. Cambridge U Pr, 1987.)

(4770)
Kritzman M
How to build a normal portfolio in three easy steps
JPM 1987 SUMMER VOL 13:4 p 21-23.

(4771)
Gennotte G
Optimal portfolio choice under incomplete information
JF 1986 JUL VOL 41:3 p 733-749.

(4772)
Grauer R R
Normality, solvency and portfolio choice.
JFQA 1986 SEP VOL 21:3 p 265-278.

(4773)
Grauer R R, Hakansson N H
A half century of returns on levered and unlevered portfolios of stocks bonds and bills with and without small stocks
JB 1986 APR VOL 59:2 p 287-318.

(4774)
Friedman B M
Portfolio choice and the debt-to-income relationship
AER 1985 VOL 75 P+P p 338-343.

(4775)
Bey R P, Howe K M
Gini's mean difference and portfolio selection : an empirical evaluation.
JFQA 1984 SEP VOL 19:3 p 329-338.

(4776)
Hamermesh R G, White R E
Manage beyond portfolio analysis
HBR 1984 JAN-FEB VOL 62:1 p 103-109

(4777)
Howe J S, Beedles W L
Defensive investing using fundamental data
JPM 1984 WINTER VOL 10:2 p 14-17.

(4778)
Kroll Y, Levy H, Markowitz H M
Mean-variance versus direct utility maximization
JF 1984 MAR VOL 39:1 p 47-61.

(4779)
Shalit H, Yitzhaki S
Mean-Gini Portfolio theory and the pricing of
risky assets
JF 1984 DEC VOL 39:5 p 1449-1468.

(4780)
Gavish B, Kalay A
On the asset substitution problem
JFQA 1983 MAR VOL 18:1 p 21-30

(4781)
Jennings R H, Barry C B
Information dissemination and portfolio choice
JFQA 1983 MAR VOL 18:1 p 1-19

(4782)
Kallberg J G, Ziemba W T
Comparison of alternative utility functions in
portfolio selection problems
MSci 1983 NOV VOL 29:11 p 1257-1276.

(4783)
Owen J, Rabinovitch R
On the class of elliptical distributions and their
applications to the theory of portfolio choice
JF 1983 JUN VOL 38:3 p 745-752.

(4784)
Poncet P
Optimum consumption and portfolio rules with
money as an asset
JBankF 1983 VOL 7 p 231.

(4785)
Ayers H F, Barry J Y
Prologue to a unified portfolio theory
JF 1982 MAY VOL 37:2 p 625-635.

(4786)
Frankfurter G M, Phillips H E
MPT plus security analysis for better performance
JPM 1982 SUMMER VOL 8:4 p 29-36.

(4787)
Grauer R R, Hakansson N H
Higher return, lower risk: historical returns on
long-run actively managed portfolios of stocks,
bonds and bills 1936-1978
FAJ 1982 MAR-APR p 39-54.

(4788)
Kane A
Skewness preference and portfolio choice
JFQA 1982 MAR VOL 17:1 p 15-25.

(4789)
Krasker W S
Minimax behavior in portfolio selection
JF 1982 MAY VOL 37:2 p 609-614.

(4790)
Ekern S
Time dominance efficiency analysis
JF 1981 DEC VOL 36:5 p 1023-1034.

(4791)
Gitman L J et al.
Portstrat: a portfolio strategy simulation
Wiley, 1981.

(4792)
Shrieves R E, Wachowichz J M
A utility theoretic basis for "generalized"
mean-coefficient of variation (MCV) analysis.
JFQA 1981 DEC VOL 16:5 p 671-683

(4793)
Hill J M
Reducing forecast error in portfolio management:
Sample clustering and alternative risk
specifications
FIN MGMT 1980 WINTER VOL 9 p 42.

(4794)
Lee S M, Chesser D L
Goal programming for portfolio selection
JPM 1980 SPRING VOL 6:3 p 22-26.

(4795)
Saaty T, Rogers P C, Pell R
Portfolio selection through hierarchies
JPM 1980 SPRING VOL 6:3 p 16-21.

(4796)
Scott R C, Horvath A
On the direction of preference for moments of higher order than the variance
JF 1980 SEP VOL 35:4 p 915-919.

(4797)
Goldman M B
Anti-diversification or optimal programmes for infrequently revised portfolios
JF 1979 MAY VOL 34:2 p 505-516.

(4798)
Hill N C, Stone B K
Portfolio management and the shrinking knapsack algorithm.
JFQA 1979 DEC VOL 14 p 1071.

(4799)
Mitra T
On the value maximizing property of infinite horizon efficient programs
IntER 1979 OCT VOL 20:3 p 635-642..

(4800)**Nantell T J, Price B**
An analytical comparison of variance and semivariance capital market theories
JFQA 1979 JUN VOL 14 p 221.

(4801)
Rorke C H
On the portfolio effects of nonmarketable assets: Government transfers and human capital payments
JFQA 1979 JUN VOL 14 p 167.

(4802)
Katz E, Vanags A
Money, saving and portfolio choice under uncertainty
AER 1978 VOL 68 p 386-388.

(4803)
Miller E M
Portfolio selection in a fluctuating economy
FAJ 1978 MAY-JUNE p 77-83.

(4804)
Chen A H
Portfolio selection with stochastic cash demand
JFQA 1977 JUN VOL 12 p 197.

(4805)
Morgan I G
Grouping procedures for portfolio formations
JF 1977 VOL 32 p 1759.

(4806)
Bawa V S
Admissible portfolios for all individuals
JF 1976 VOL 31 p 1169.

(4807)
Fishburn P C
Mean-risk analysis with risk associated with below-target returns
AER 1977 VOL 67 p 116-126.

(4808)
Fishburn P C, Porter R B
Optimal portfolios with one safe and one risky asset: effects of changes in rate of return and risk
MSci 1976 JUN VOL 22:10 p 1064-1073.

(4809)
Harris M
Optimal planning under transaction costs: the demand for money and other assets
JET 1976 APR VOL 12:2 p 298-314.

(4810)
James J A
Portfolio selection with an imperfectly competitive asset market
JFQA 1976 DEC VOL 11 p 831.

(4811)
Magill M J P, Constantinides G M
Portfolio selection with transactions costs
JET 1976 OCT VOL 13:2 p 245-263.

(4812)
Ohlson J A, Ziemba W T
Portfolio selection in a lognormal market when the investor has a power utility function
JFQA 1976 MAR VOL 11 p 57.

(4813)
Stuck B W
Explicit solutions to some single-period investment problems for risky logstable stocks
JFE 1976 VOL 3 p277.

(4814)
Arditti F D, Levy H
Portfolio efficiency analysis in three moments: The multiperiod case
JF 1975 VOL 30 p 797.

(4815)
Biger N
Recognizing the impact of inflation: The assessment of inflation and portfolio selection
JF 1975 MAY VOL 30:2 p 451-468.

(4816)
Foley D K, Hellwig M F
Asset management with trading uncertainty
REStud 1975 VOL 42 p 327.

(4817)
Francis J C
Skewness and investors' decisions
JFQA 1975 MAR VOL 10 p 163.

(4818)
Hart O D
Some negative results on the existence of comparative static results in portfolio theory
REStud 1975 VOL 42 p 615.

(4819)
Levhari D, Paroush J, Peleg B
Efficiency analysis for multivariate distributions
REStud 1975 VOL 42 p 87.

(4820)
Long N V
Risk aversion and wealth effects on portfolios with many assets: An extension
REStud 1975 VOL 42 p 473.

(4821)
Ohlson J A
The complete ordering of information alternatives for a class of portfolio selection models
JAR 1975 AUTUMN VOL 13:2 p 267-282.

(4822)
Ohlson J A
Portfolio selection in a log-stable market
JFQA 1975 JUN VOL 10 p 285.

(4823)
Stone B K, Reback R
Constructing a model for managing portfolio revisions
JBR 1975 SPRING VOL 6:1.

(4824)
Elton E J, Gruber M J
Portfolio theory when investment relatives are lognormally distributed
JF 1974 VOL 29 p 1265.

(4825)
Jean W H
More on multidimensional portfolio analysis
JFQA 1974 JUN VOL 9 p 475.

(4826)
Bicksler J L, Barnea A, Babad J
Portfolio choice, the horizon problem and the investment opportunity set
AER 1973 VOL 63 P+P p 140-144.

(4827)
Ziskind R, Boldin R
A computer simulation model for investment portfolio management
FIN MGMT 1973 AUTUMN VOL 2 p 23.

(4828)
Cass D, Stiglitz J E
Risk aversion and wealth effects on portfolios with many assets
REStud 1972 VOL 39 p 331.

(4829)
Gordon M J, Paradis G E, Rorke C H
Experimental evidence on alternative portfolio decision rules
AER 1972 MAY VOL 62 p 107-118.

(4830)
Jean W H
The extension of portfolio analysis to three or more parameters
JFQA 1971 JAN VOL 6 p 505-516.

(4831)
Pye G
Minimax portfolio policies
FAJ 1972 MAR-APR VOL 28 p 56-60.

(4832)
Samuelson P A
The fundamental approximation theorem of portfolio analysis in terms of means, variances and higher moments
REStud 1970 OCT VOL 37 p 537-542.

(4833)
Breen W J
Specific versus general models of portfolio selection
OEP 1968 NOV VOL 20 p 361-368.

(4834)
Bierwag G O, Grove M A
Portfolio selection and taxation
OEP 1967 JUL VOL 19 p 215-221.

(4835)
Hester D D, Tobin J eds.
Risk aversion and portfolio choice
Wiley, 1967.

(4836)
Roskamp K W
Factors influencing portfolio selection: a simple model
Kyk 1967 VOL 20 p 502-510.

(4837)
Mao J C T, Sarndal C E
A decision theory approach to portfolio selection
MSci 1966 APR VOL 12 p B323-B333.

(4838)
Smith K V
Selection and revision decision rules for portfolio management
Purdue U, 1966.

(4839)
Clarkson G P E
Portfolio selection: a simulation of trust investment
P-H, 1962.

(4840)
Clarkson G P E, Meltzer A H
Portfolio selection: a heuristic approach
JF 1960 DEC VOL 15 p 465-480.

(4841)
Latane H A
Individual risk preference in portfolio selection
JF 1960 MAR VOL 15 p 45-52.

12.1   Portfolio separation and mutual-fund theorems

(4842)
Mak K
Approximate separability and aggregation
JET 1988 JUN VOL 45:1 p 200-206.

(4843)
Huang C F, Litzenberger R
On the necessary condition for linear sharing and separation : a note.
JFQA 1985 SEP VOL 20:3 p 381-384.

(4844)
Sealey C W Jr
Portfolio separation for stockholder owned depository financial intermediaries
JBankF 1985 VOL 9 p 477.

(4845)
White J R
Unit trusts, homogenous beliefs and the separation property
JBFA 1981 SPRING VOL 8:1 p 61-78.

(4846)
Litzenberger R H, Ramaswamy K
On distributional restrictions for two fund separation
TIMS Studies in the Management Sciences 1979 VOL 11 p 99-107.

(4847)
Ross S A
Mutual fund separation in financial theory--the separating distributions
JET 1978 APR VOL 17:2 p 254-286.

(4848)
Brennan M J, Kraus A
The geometry of separation and myopia
JFQA 1976 JUN VOL 11 p 171.

(4849)
Magill M J P
The preferability of investment through a mutual fund
JET 1976 OCT VOL 13:2 p 264-271.

(4850)
Ohlson J A, Rosenberg B
The stationary distribution of returns and portfolio separation in capital markets: A fundamental contradiction
JFQA 1976 SEP VOL 11 p 393.

(4851)
Fishburn P C
Separation theorems and expected utilities
JET 1975 AUG VOL 11:1 p 16-34.

(4852)
Hakansson N H
Risk disposition and the separation property in portfolio selection
JFQA 1969 DEC VOL 4 p 401-416..

(4853)**Tobin J**
Liquidity preference as behavior toward risk
REStud 1958 FEB VOL 25 p 65-86.

12.2   Mean-variance selection

(4854)
Frankfurter G M, Lamoureux C G
Estimation and selection bias in mean-variance portfolio selection
JFR 1989 SUMMER VOL 12:2 p 173-182.

(4855)
Grinold R C
The fundamental law of active management
JPM 1989 SPRING VOL 15:3 p 30-37.

(4856)
Jobson J D, Korkie B
A performance interpretation of multivariate tests of asset set intersection, spanning, and mean-variance efficiency
JFQA 1989 JUN VOL 24:2 p 185-204.

(4857)
Leibowitz M L, Henriksson R D
Portfolio optimization with shortfall constraints: a confidence-limit approach to managing downside risk
FAJ 1989 MAR-APR VOL 45 p 34-41.

(4858)
Michaud R O
The Markowitz optimization enigma: is "optimized" optimal?
FAJ 1989 JAN-FEB VOL 45 p 31-42.

(4859)
Richardson H R
A minimum variance result in continuous trading portfolio optimization
MSci 1989 VOL 35 p 1045.

(4860)
Speidell L S, Miller D H, Ullman J R
Portfolio optimization: a primer
FAJ 1989 JAN-FEB VOL 45 p 22-30.

(4861)
Burgess R C, Bey R P
Optimal portfolios: Markowitz full covariance versus simple selection rules
JFR 1988 VOL 11:2 p 153-164.

(4862)
Dowen R J
Beta, non-systematic risk and portfolio selection
AE 1988 FEB VOL 20:2 p 221-228.

(4863)
Frost P A, Savarino J E
For better performance: constrain portfolio weights
JPM 1988 FALL VOL 15:1 p 29-34.

(4864)
Levy H, Lerman Z
Testing the predictive power of ex-post efficient portfolios
JFR 1988 FALL VOL 11:3 p 241-254.

(4865)
Lewis A L
A simple algorithm for the portfolio selection problem
JF 1988 MAR VOL 43:1 p 71-82.

(4866)
Aldrich P C
Active versus passive: a new look
JPM 1987 FALL VOL 14:1 p 9-11.

(4867)
Elton E J, Gruber M J
Portfolio analysis with partial information : the case of grouped data
MSci 1987 OCT VOL 33:10 p 1238-1246.

(4868)
Elton E J, Gruber M J
Modern portfolio theory and investment analysis. 3rd ed
Wiley, 1987.

(4869)
Huberman G, Kandel S
Mean-variance spanning
JF 1987 SEP VOL 42:4 p 873-888.

(4870)
Kandel S, Stambaugh R F
On correlations and inferences about mean-variance efficiency
JFE 1987 VOL 18 p 61-90.

(4871)
Kryzanowski L, To M C
The E-V stationarity of security returns: some empirical evidence
JBankF 1987 VOL 11 p 117-135.

(4872)
Lehmann B N
Orthogonal frontiers and alternative mean-variance efficiency tests
JF 1987 JUL VOL 42:3 p 601-619.

(4873)
Markowitz H M
Mean-variance analysis in portfolio choice and capital markets
Blackwell, 1987.

(4874)
Nielsen L T
Portfolio selection in the mean-variance model: a note
JF 1987 DEC VOL 42:5 p 1371-1376.

(4875)
Shanken J
A Bayesian approach to testing portfolio efficiency
JFE 1987 VOL 19 p 195-215.

(4876)
Tew B V, Reid D W
More evidence on expected value-variance analysis versus direct utility maximization
JFR 1987 FALL VOL 10:3 p 249-257.

(4877)
Zilcha I
Characterizing the efficient set when preferences are state-dependent
JET 1987 APR VOL 41:2 p 417-423.

(4878)
Alexander G J, Francis J C
Portfolio analysis. 3rd ed
P-H, 1986.

(4879)
Frost P A, Savarino J E
An empirical Bayes approach to efficient portfolio
JFQA 1986 SEP VOL 21:3 p 293-305.

(4880)
Green R C
Positively weighted portfolios on the minimum-variance frontier
JF 1986 DEC VOL 41:5 p 1051-1068.

(4881)
Jorion P
Bayes-Stein estimation for portfolio analysis
JFQA 1986 SEP VOL 21:3 p 279-292.

(4882)
Alexander G J, Resnick B G
More on estimation risk and simple rules for
optimal portfolio selection
JF 1985 MAR VOL 40:1 p 125-133.

(4883)
Chen S-N, Moore W T
Uncertain inflation and optimal portfolio
selection: a simplified approach
FR 1985 NOV VOL 20:4.

(4884)
Cheung C S, Kwan C C Y, Yip P C Y
A note on optimal portfolio selection under
stable paretian distributions
Decision Sciences 1985 FALL VOL 16 p 435-441.

(4885)
Frankfurter G M, Booth G G
Further evidence of the role of nonsystematic risk
in efficient portfolios
QREB 1985 SPRING VOL 25:2 p 38-48

(4886)
Pari R A, Chen S
Estimation risk and optimal portfolios
JPM 1985 FALL VOL 12:1 p 40-43.

(4887)
Bennett P
Applying portfolio theory to global bank lending
JBankF 1984 VOL 8 p 153.

(4888)
Dybvig P H
Short sales restrictions and kinks on the mean
variance frontier.
JF 1984 MAR VOL 39:1 p 239-244.

(4889)
Kandel S
The likelihood ratio test statistic of mean-variance
efficiency without a riskless asset
JFE 1984 DEC VOL 13:4 p 575-592.

(4890)
Kwan C C Y
Portfolio analysis using single index multi-index
and constant correlation models : a unified
treatment
JF 1984 DEC VOL 39:5 p 1469-1483.

(4891)
McEntire P L
Portfolio theory for independent assets
MSci 1984 AUG VOL 30:8 p 952-963.

(4892)
McInish T H, Srivastav R K
Ex-ante expectations and portfolio selection
FR 1984 MAR VOL 19:1.

(4893)
Perold A F
Large-scale portfolio optimization
MSci 1984 OCT VOL 30:10 p 1143-1160.

(4894)
Bernstein P L
Markowitz marked to market
FAJ 1983 JAN-FEB VOL 39 p 18-23.

(4895)
Blog B
The optimal selection of small portfolios
MSci 1983 JUL VOL 29:7 p 792-798.

(4896)
Chen S, Brown S J
Estimation risk and simple rules for optimal
portfolio selection
JF 1983 VOL 38:4 p 1087-1093.

(4897)
Dalal A J
On the use of a covariance function in a portfolio
model
JFQA 1983 JUN VOL 18:2 p 223-227.

(4898)
Jobson J D, Korkie B
Statistical inference in two-parameter portfolio
theory with regression software
JFQA 1983 JUN VOL 18:2 p 189-197.

(4899)
Levary R R, Avery M L
A practical LP model for equity portfolios
Omega 1983 VOL 11:1 p 41-48.

(4900)
Ashton D J
Stochastic dominance and mean variance rules in the selection of risky investment
JBFA 1982 WINTER VOL 9:4 p 471-481.

(4901)
Dybvig P H, Ingersoll J E
Mean-variance theory in complete markets
JB 1982 APR VOL 55:2 p 233-251.

(4902)
Jobson J D, Korkie B
Potential performance and tests of portfolio efficiency
JFE 1982 VOL 10 p 433-466.

(4903)
Patel N R, Subrahmanyam M G
A simple algorithm for optimal portfolio selection with fixed transaction costs
MSci 1982 MAR VOL 28:3 p 303-314.

(4904)
Rudd A, Clasing H K
Modern portfolio theory: the principles of investment management
Dow Jones-Irwin, 1982.

(4905)
Yitzhaki S
Stochastic dominance, mean variance and Gini's mean difference
AER 1982 VOL 72 p 178-185..

(4906) **Epps T W**
Necessary and sufficient conditions for the mean-variance portfolio model with constant risk aversion
JFQA 1981 JUN VOL 16:2 p 169-176.

(4907)
Faaland B H, Jacob N L
The linear fractional portfolio selection problem
MSci 1981 DEC VOL 27:12 p 1383-1389.

(4908)
Findlay M C III, McBride R D, Yormark J S
Mean-variance analysis for indivisible assets
Omega 1981 VOL 9:1 p 77-88.

(4909)
Gandhi D K, Saunders A
The superiority of stochastic dominance over mean variance efficiency criteria: Some clarification
JBFA 1981 SPRING VOL 8:1 p 51.

(4910)
Gouldey B K, Gray G J
Implementing mean-variance theory in the selection of U S government bond portfolios
JBR 1981 AUTUMN VOL 12:3.

(4911)
Hessel C A
Extensions to portfolio theory to reflect vast wealth differences among investors
JFQA 1981 MAR VOL 16:1 p 53-70.

(4912)
Hill J M
Is optimal portfolio management worth the candle?
JPM 1981 SUMMER VOL 7:4 p 59-69.

(4913)
Jobson J D, Korkie B
Putting Markowitz theory to work
JPM 1981 SUMMER VOL 7:4 p 70.

(4914)
Markowitz H M, Perold A F
Portfolio analysis with factors and scenarios
JF 1981 SEP VOL 36:4 p 871-877.

(4915)
Pulley L B
A general mean-variance approximation to expected utility for short holding periods
JFQA 1981 SEP VOL 16:3 p 361-373.

(4916)
Sercu P
A note on real and nominal efficients sets
JF 1981 JUN VOL 36:3 p 721-737.

(4917)
Berndt E R, McCurdy T H, Rose D E
On testing theories of financial intermediary portfolio selection
REStud 1980 VOL 47 p 861.

(4918)
Blume M E
The relative efficiency of various portfolios: some further evidence
JF 1980 MAY VOL 35:2 p 269-283.

(4919)
Dhingra H L
Effects of estimation risk on efficient portfolios: a Monte Carlo simulation study
JBFA 1980 SUMMER VOL 7:2 p 277-295

(4920)
Frankfurter G M, Phillips H E
Portfolio selection: An analytic approach for selecting securities from a large universe
JFQA 1980 JUN VOL 15 p 357.

(4921)
Kroll Y, Levy H
Sampling errors and portfolio efficient analysis
JFQA 1980 SEP VOL 15 p 655.

(4922)
Levy H, Kroll Y
Mean-variance efficient portfolios
MSci 1980 NOV VOL 26:11 p 1108-1116.

(4923)
Levy H, Kroll Y
Sample vs. population: Mean-variance efficient portfolios
MSci 1980 NOV VOL 26:11 p 1108-1116.

(4924)
Roll R
Orthogonal portfolios
JFQA 1980 DEC VOL 15 p 1005-1023.

(4925)
Schreiner J
Portfolio   revision: A   turnover-constrained approach
FIN MGMT 1980 SPRING VOL 9 p 67.

(4926)
Bawa V S, Brown S, Klein A
Estimation risk and optimal portfolio choice
N Holland, 1979.

(4927)
Bawa V S, Elton E J, Gruber M J
Simple rules for optimal portfolio selection in stable paretian markets
JF 1979 SEP VOL 34:4 p 1041-1047.

(4928)
Bey R P
Estimating the optimal stochastic dominance efficient set with a mean semi-variance algorithm
JFQA 1979 DEC VOL 14 p 1059.

(4929)
Courtney J F Jr
Differentiating capital appreciation and income in portfolio selection/revision
JBR 1979 SUMMER VOL 10:2.

(4930)
Elton E J, Gruber M J eds.
Portfolio theory, 25 years after: Essays in honor of Harry Markowitz
N Holland, 1979.

(4931)
Frankfurter G M, Frecka T J
Efficient portfolios and superfluous diversification
JFQA 1979 DEC VOL 14 p 925.

(4932)
Frankfurter G M, Phillips H E
Portfolio selection: a procedure for revising ex-ante estimates of portfolio risk
EE 1979 SUMMER VOL 24:4 p 217-234.

(4933)
Gressis N, Saniga E, Hayya J
The effects of sample size and correlation on the accuracy of the EV efficient criterion
JFQA 1979 SEP VOL 14 p 615.

(4934)
Levy H, Markowitz H M
Approximating expected utility by a function of mean and variance
AER 1979 VOL 69 p 308-317.

(4935)
Manaster S
Real and nominal efficient sets
JF 1979 MAR VOL 34:1 p 93-102.

(4936)
Roll R
Testing a portfolio for ex ante mean variance efficiency
(in Elton E J and Gruber M J eds., Portfolio theory, 25 years after: Essays in honor of Harry Markowitz. N Holland, 1979.)

(4937)
Rosenberg B
How active should your portfolio be?
FAJ 1979 JAN-FEB p 49-62.

(4938)
Alexander G J
A reevaluation of alternative portfolio selection models applied to common stocks
JFQA 1978 MAR VOL 13 p 71.

(4939)
Baum S, Carlson R C, Jucker J V
Some problems in applying the continuous portfolio selection model to the discrete capital budgeting problem
JFQA 1978 JUN VOL 13 p 333.

(4940)
Brito N O
Portfolio selection in an economy with marketability and short sales restrictions
JF 1978 VOL 33 p 589.

(4941)
Elton E J, Gruber M J
Taxes and portfolio composition
JFE 1978 VOL 6 p 399.

(4942)
Elton E J, Gruber M J, Padberg M W
Simple criteria for optimal portfolio selection: Tracing out the efficient frontier
JF 1978 VOL 33 p 296.

(4943)
Hawawini G A
A mean-standard deviation exposition of the theory of the firm under uncertainty: A pedagogical note
AER 1978 VOL 68 p 194-202.

(4944)
Perrakis S, Zerbinis J
Identifying the SSD portion of the EV frontier: A note
JFQA 1978 MAR VOL 13 p 167.

(4945)
Solnik B H
Inflation and optimal portfolio choices
JFQA 1978 DEC VOL 13 p 903.

(4946)
Alexander G J
An algorithm for deriving the capital market line
MSci 1977 JUL VOL 23:11 p 1183-1186.

(4947)
Alexander G J
Mixed security testing of alternative portfolio selection models
JFQA 1977 DEC VOL 12 p 817.

(4948)
Baron D P
On the utility theoretic foundations of mean-variance analysis
JF 1977 VOL 32 p 1683.

(4949)
Bawa V S
Mathematical programming of admissible portfolios
MSci 1977 VOL 23 p 779-785.

(4950)
Buser S A
Mean-variance portfolio selection with either a singular or nonsingular variance-covariance matrix
JFQA 1977 SEP VOL 12 p 347.

(4951)
Buser S A
A simplified expression for the efficient frontier in mean-variance portfolio analysis
MSci 1977 AUG VOL 23:12 p 901.

(4952)
Elton E J, Gruber M J, Padberg M W
Simple rules for optimal portfolio selection: The multi group case
JFQA 1977 SEP VOL 12 P 329.

(4953)
Frankfurter G M, Phillips H E, Seagle J P
A proposed normative procedure for portfolio selection under conditions of uncertainty
FIN MGMT 1977 WINTER VOL 6 p 43.

(4954)
Klein R W, Bawa V S
The effect of limited information and estimation risk on optimal portfolio diversification
JFE 1977 VOL 5 p 89.

(4955)
Long J B Jr
Efficient portfolio choice with differential taxation of dividends and capital gains
JFE 1977 VOL 5 p 25.

(4956)
Ohlson J A
Quadratic approximations of the portfolio selection problem when the means and variances of returns are infinite
MSci 1977 VOL 23 p 576-584.

(4957)
Rudd A
A note on qualitative results for investment proportions
JFE 1977 VOL 5 p 259.

(4958)
Stapleton R C, Subrahmanyam M G
Market imperfections, capital market equlibrium, and corporation finance
JF 1977 MAY VOL 32:2 p 307-320..

(4959) **Williams J T**
A note on indifference curves in the mean-variance model
JFQA 1977 MAR VOL 12 p 121.

(4960)
Alexander G J
The derivation of efficient sets
JFQA 1976 DEC VOL 11 p 817.

(4961)
Barry C B, Winkler R L
Nonstationarity and portfolio choice
JFQA 1976 JUN VOL 11 p 217.

(4962)
Biger N
Portfolio selection and purchasing power risk - recent Canadian experience
JFQA 1976 JUN VOL 11 p 251.

(4963)
Bowden R J
A dual concept and associated algorithm in mean variance portfolio analysis
MSci 1976 DEC VOL 23:4 p 423-432.

(4964)
Davies L, Ronning G
A note on the uniqueness of portfolio choice
JFQA 1976 SEP VOL 11 p 481.

(4965)
Elton E J, Gruber M J, Padberg M W
Simple criteria for optimal portfolio selection
JF 1976 VOL 31 p 1341.

(4966)
Frankfurter G M
The effect of "market indexes" on the ex-post performance of the Sharpe portfolio selection model
JF 1976 VOL 31 p 949.

(4967)
Frankfurter G M, Phillips H E, Seagle J P
Performance of the Sharpe portfolio selection model: A comparison
JFQA 1976 JUN VOL 11 p 195.

(4968)
Goldsmith D
Transactions costs and the theory of portfolio selection
JF 1976 VOL 31 p 1127.

(4969)
Hill R R
An algorithm for counting the number of possible portfolios given linear restrictions on the weights
JFQA 1976 SEP VOL 11 p 479.

(4970)
Klein R W, Bawa V S
The effect of estimation risk on optimal portfolio choice
JFE 1976 VOL 3 p 215.

(4971)
Markowitz H M
Markowitz revisited
FAJ 1976 SEP-OCT VOL 32 p 47-52.

(4972)
Barry C B
A Bayesian model for porfolio selection and revision
JF 1975 VOL 30 p 179.

(4973)
Bey R P, Porter R B, Lewis D C
The development of a mean-semivariance approach to capital budgeting
JFQA 1975 NOV VOL 10 p 639.

(4974)
Brealey R A, Hodges S D
Playing with portfolios
JF 1975 VOL 30 p 125.

(4975)
Brennan M J
The optimal number of securities in a risky asset portfolio when there are fixed costs of transacting: Theory and some empirical results
JFQA 1975 SEP VOL 10 p 483.

(4976)
Burgess R C, Johnson K H
The effects of sample sizes on the accuracy of EV and SSD efficiency criteria
JFQA 1975 DEC VOL 10 p 813.

(4977)
Courakis A S
Testing theories of discount house portfolio selection
REStud 1975 VOL 42 p 643.

(4978)
de Faro C, Jucker J V
A simple algorithm for Stone's version of the portfolio selection problem
JFQA 1975 DEC VOL 10 p 859.

(4979)
Ferguson R
Active portfolio management: How to beat the index funds
FAJ 1975 MAY-JUN VOL 31 p 63-72.

(4980)
Kamin J H
Optimal portfolio revision with a proportional transaction cost
MSci 1975 JUL VOL 21:11 p 1263.

(4981)
Philippatos G C, Gressis N
Conditions of equivalence among E-V, SSD, and E-H portfolio selection criteria: The case for uniform normal and lognormal distribution
MSci 1975 AUG VOL 21:12 p 617.

(4982)
Phillips H E, Seagle J P
Data: A mixed blessing in portfolio selection?
FIN MGMT 1975 AUTUMN VOL 4 p 50.

(4983)
Schneller M I
Mean-variance portfolio composition when investors' revision horizon is very long
JF 1975 VOL 30 p 1293.

(4984)
Sibley D
A note on the concavity of the mean-variance problem
REStud 1975 VOL 42 p 479.

(4985)
Ang J S
A note on the E, SL portfolio selection model
JFQA 1974 DEC VOL 10 p 849.

(4986)
Baron D P
Information, investment behavior and efficient portfolios
JFQA 1974 SEP VOL 9 p 555.

(4987)
Faaland B H
An integer programming algorithm for portfolio selection
MSci 1974 VOL 20 p 1376-1384.

(4988)
Hart O D, Jaffee D M
On the application of portfolio theory to depository financial intermediaries
REStud 1974 VOL 41 p 129.

(4989)
Jacob N L
A limited-diversification portfolio selection model
for the small investor
JF 1974 VOL 29 p 847.

(4990)
Porter R B
Semivariance and stochastic dominance: A
comparison
AER 1974 VOL 64 p 200-204.

(4991)
Porter R B, Bey R P
An evaluation of the empirical significance of
optimal seeking algorithms in portfolio selection
JF 1974 VOL 29 p 1479.

(4992)
Reback R
The single index model for portfolio selection
with unstable parameters
JBR 1974 SPRING VOL 5:1 p 35-37.

(4993)
Samuelson P A, Merton R C
Generalized mean-variance tradeoffs for best
perturbation corrections to approximate portfolio
decisions
JF 1974 VOL 29 p 27.

(4994)
Sarnat M
A note on the implications of quadratic utility for
portfolio theory
JFQA 1974 SEP VOL 9 p 687.

(4995)
Sarnat M
Capital market imperfections and the composition
of optimal portfolios
JF 1974 VOL 29 p 1241.

(4996)
Ziemba W T, Parkan C, Brooks-Hill R
Calculation of investment portfolios with risk free
borrowing and lending
MSci 1974 OCT VOL 21:2 p 209-222.

(4997)
Chipman J S
The ordering of portfolios in terms of mean and
variance
REStud 1973 VOL 40 p 167.

(4998)
Elton E J, Gruber M J
Estimating the dependence structure of share
prices-implications for portfolio selection
JF 1973 VOL 28 p 1203.

(4999)
Hodges S D, Brealey R A
Portfolio selection in a dynamic and uncertain
world
FAJ 1973 MAR-APR VOL 29 p 50-65.

(5000)
Lee S M, Lerro A J
Optimizing the portfolio selection for mutual
funds
JF 1973 VOL 28 p 1087.

(5001)
Levy H
Stochastic dominance, efficiency criteria and
efficient portfolios: The multi-period case
AER 1973 VOL 63 p 986-994.

(5002)
Porter R B
An empirical comparison of stochastic dominance
and mean-variance portfolio choice criteria
JFQA 1973 SEP VOL 8:4 p 587.

(5003)
Remaley W
Suboptimization in mean-variance efficient set
analysis
JF 1973 VOL 28 p 397.

(5004)
Treynor J L, Black F
Using security analysis to improve portfolio
selection
JB 1973 JAN VOL 46 p 66-86.

(5005)
Chen A H, Jen F C, Zionts S
Portfolio models with stochastic cash demands
MSci 1972 NOV VOL 19:3 p 319-332.

(5006)
Hakansson N H
Mean-variance analysis in a finite world
JFQA 1972 SEP VOL 7 p 1873.

(5007)
Hogan W W, Warren J M
Computation of the efficient boundary in the E-S
portfolio selection model
JFQA 1972 SEP VOL 7 p 1881.

(5008)
Jacob N L, Smith K V
The value of perfect market forecasts in portfolio
selection
JF 1972 MAY VOL 27 p 355-370.

(5009)
Merton R C
An analytic derivation of the efficient portfolio
frontier
JFQA 1972 SEP VOL 7 p 1851.

(5010)
Porter R B, Gaumnitz J E
Stochastic dominance vs. mean-variance portfolio
analysis: an empirical evaluation
AER 1972 JUN VOL 62 p 438-446.

(5011)
Treynor J L, Black F
Portfolio selection using special information under
the assumptions of the diagonal model, with
mean-variance portfolio objectives, and without
constraints
(in Szego G P and Shell K eds., Mathematical
methods in investment and finance. N-Holland,
1972.)

(5012)
Tsiang S C
The rationale of the mean-standard deviation
analysis, skewness preference and the demand for
money
AER 1972 JUN VOL 62 p 354-371.

(5013)
Breen W J, Jackson R
An efficient algorithm for solving large-scale
portfolio problems
JFQA 1971 JAN VOL 6 p 627-638.

(5014)
Cheng P L
Efficient portfolio selection beyond the Markowitz
frontier
JFQA 1971 DEC VOL 6 p 1207-1234.

(5015)
Frankfurter G M, Phillips H E, Seagle J P
Portfolio selection: the effects of uncertain means,
variances, and covariances
JFQA 1971 DEC VOL 6 p 1251-1262.

(5016)
Hakansson N H
Capital growth and the mean-variance approach
to portfolio selection
JFQA 1971 JAN VOL 6 p 517-558.

(5017)
Hodges S D, Moore P G
Mathematical models in portfolio selection
JBF 1971 SPRING VOL 3.

(5018)
Jones-Lee M W
Some portfolio adjustment theorems for the use
of non-negativity constraints on security holdings
JF 1971 JUN VOL 26 p 763-776.

(5019)
Kalymon B A
Estimation risk in the portfolio selection model
JFQA 1971 JAN VOL 6 p 559-582.

(5020)
Levy H, Sarnat M
A note on portfolio selection and investors'
wealth
JFQA 1971 JAN VOL 6 p 639-642.

(5021)
Levy H, Sarnat M
Two-period portfolio selection and investor
discount rates
JF 1971 JUN VOL 26 p 757-762.

(5022)
Sharpe W F
A linear programming approximation for the
general portfolio analysis problem
JFQA 1971 DEC VOL 6 p 1263-1276.

(5023)
Sharpe W F
Portfolio theory and capital markets
McGraw, 1971.

(5024)
Stevens G V G
Two problems in portfolio analysis: conditional
and multiplicative random variables
JFQA 1971 DEC VOL 6 p 1235-1250.

(5025)
Wippern R F
Utility implications of portfolio selection and
performance appraisal models
JFQA 1971 JUN VOL 6 p 913-924.

(5026)
Alderfer C P, Bierman H Jr
Choices with risk: beyond the mean and variance
JB 1970 JUL VOL 43 p 341-353.

(5027)
Blume M E
Portfolio theory: a step toward its practical
application
JB 1970 APR VOL 43 p 152-173.

(5028)
Evans J L
An analysis of portfolio maintenance strategies
JF 1970 JUN VOL 25 p 561-572.

(5029)
Fried J S
Forecasting and probability distributions for
models of portfolio selection
JF 1970 JUN VOL 25 p 539-554.

(5030)
Hanoch G, Levy H
Efficient portfolio selection with quadratic and
cubic utility
JB 1970 APR VOL 43 p 181-189.

(5031)
Hodges S D, Brealey R A
Using the Sharpe model
Investment Analyst 1970 SEP VOL 27 p 41-50.

(5032)
Levy H, Hanoch G
Relative effectiveness of efficiency criteria for
portfolio selection
JFQA 1970 MAR VOL 5 p 63-76.

(5033)
Levy H, Sarnat M
Alternative efficiency criteria: an empirical
analysis
JF 1970 DEC VOL 25 p 1153-1158.

(5034)
Levy H, Sarnat M
Portfolio selection and investor's utility: a
graphical analysis
AE 1970 VOL 2 p 113-120.

(5035)
Miller N C, Whitman M v N
A mean-variance analysis of United States
long-term portfolio foreign investment
QJE 1970 MAY VOL 84 p 175-196.

(5036)
Pogue G A
An extension of the Markowitz portfolio selection
model to include variable transactions costs, short
sales, leverage policies and taxes
JF 1970 DEC VOL 25 p 1005-1028.

(5037)
Bickel S H
Minimum variance and optimal asymptotic
portfolios
MSci 1969 NOV VOL 16 p 221-226.

(5038)
Feldstein M
Mean-variance analysis in the theory of liquidity
preference and portfolio selection
REStud 1969 JAN VOL 36.

(5039)
Roll R
Bias in fitting the Sharpe model to time series
data
JFQA 1969 SEP VOL 4 p 271-289.

(5040)
Smith K V
Stock price and economic indexes for generating efficient portfolios
JB 1969 JUL VOL 42 p 326-336.

(5041)
Douglas A J
A theory of saving and portfolio selection
REStud 1968 OCT VOL 35 p 453-463.

(5042)
Friend I, Vickers D
Re-evaluation of alternative portfolio selection models
JB 1968 APR VOL 41 p 174-179.

(5043)
Smith K V
Alternative procedures for revising investment portfolios
JFQA 1968 DEC VOL 3 p 371-403.

(5044)
Cohen K J, Pogue J A
An empirical evaluation of alternative portfolio-selection models
JB 1967 APR VOL 40 p 166-193.

(5045)
Hester D D
Efficient portfolios with short sales and margin holdings
(in Hester D D and Tobin J eds., Risk aversion and portfolio choice. Wiley, 1967.)

(5046)
Hester D D, Tobin J eds.
Studies of portfolio behavior
Wiley, 1967..

(5047)**Hicks J R**
The pure theory of portfolio selection
(in Hicks J R, Critical essays in monetary theory. Oxford U Pr, 1967.)

(5048)
Pye G
Portfolio selection and security prices
REStat 1967 FEB VOL 49 p 111-115.

(5049)
Renshaw E F
Portfolio balance models in perspective: some generalizations that can be derived from the two-asset case
JFQA 1967 JUN VOL 2 p 123-149.

(5050)
Samuelson P A
Efficient portfolio selection for Pareto-Levy investments
JFQA 1967 JUN VOL 2 p 107-122.

(5051)
Sharpe W F
A linear programming algorithm for mutual fund portfolio selection
MSci 1967 MAR VOL 13 p 499-510.

(5052)
Sharpe W F
Portfolio analysis
JFQA 1967 JUN VOL 2 p 76-84.

(5053)
Smith K V
A transition model for portfolio revision
JF 1967 SEP VOL 22 p 425-439.

(5054)
Wallingford B A
A survey and comparison of portfolio selection models
JFQA 1967 JUN VOL 2 p 85-106.

(5055)
Baumol W J
Mathematical analysis of portfolio selection
FAJ 1966 SEP-OCT VOL 22 p 95-99.

(5056)
Pain N R
A case study in mathematical programming of portfolio selection
Applied Statistics 1966 VOL 15 p 24-36.

(5057)
Tobin J
The theory of portfolio selection
(in Hahn F H and Brechling F P R eds., The theory of interest rates. Macmillan Int, 1966.)

(5058)
Fama E F
Portfolio analysis in a stable Paretian market
MSci 1965 JAN VOL 11 p 404-419.

(5059)
Penner R G
A note on portfolio selection and taxation
REStud 1964 JAN VOL 31 p 83-86.

(5060)
Baumol W J
An expected gain-confidence limit criterion for
portfolio selection
MSci 1963 OCT VOL 9 p 174-182.

(5061)
Sharpe W F
Addendum to 'A simplified model for portfolio
analysis'
MSci 1963 APR VOL 9 p 498.

(5062)
Sharpe W F
A simplified model for portfolio analysis
MSci 1963 JAN VOL 9 p 277-293.

(5063)
Farrar D E
The investment decision under uncertainty
P-H, 1962.

(5064)
Markowitz H M
Portfolio selection: efficient diversification of
investments
Wiley, 1959.

(5065)
Markowitz H M
The optimization of a quadratic function subject
to linear constraints
Naval Research Logistics Quarterly 1956
MAR-JUN p 111-133.

(5066)
Martin A D Jr
Mathematical programming of portfolio selections
MSci 1955 JAN VOL 1 p 152-166.

(5067)
Markowitz H M
Portfolio selection
JF 1952 MAR VOL 7 p 77-91.

12.21   Delegated fund management

(5068)
Bailey J V, Arnott R D
Cluster analysis and manager selection
FAJ 1986 MAR-APR VOL 42 p 20-28.

(5069)
Bhattacharya S, Pfleiderer P
Delegated portfolio management
JET 1985 JUN VOL 36:1 p 1-25.

(5070)
Barry C B, Starks L T
Investment management and risk sharing with
multiple managers
JF 1984 JUN VOL 39:2 p 477-491.

(5071)
Sharpe W F
Decentralized investment management
JF 1981 MAY VOL 36:2 p 217-234.

(5072)
Ferguson R
Do inventory funds make sense
FAJ 1978 MAY-JUN p 38-45.

(5073)
Wagner W H, Zipkin C A
Better performance via inventory funds
FAJ 1978 MAY-JUN p 34-37.

12.22   Passive management and index funds

(5074)
Rudd A
Optimal selection of passive portfolios
FIN MGMT 1980 SPRING VOL 9 p 57.

(5075)
Ryan J C, Kritzman M
Catch 500: the irony in indexing
JPM 1980 WINTER VOL 6:2 p 30-35.

(5076)
Burgess R C, O'Dell B T
An empirical examination of index efficiency:
Implications for index funds
JFQA 1978 MAR VOL 13 p 93.

(5077)
Calderwood S
The truth about index funds
FAJ 1977 JUL-AUG p 36-47.

(5078)
Kahn I
Lemmings always lose
FAJ 1977 MAY-JUN p 27-30.

(5079)
Wilson P N, Cummin R I
Saving management and transaction costs
FAJ 1977 MAR-APR p 58-62.

(5080)
Good W R, Ferguson R, Treynor J L
An investor's guide to the index fund controversy
FAJ 1976 NOV-DEC VOL 32 p 27-36.

12.3   Safety-first and chance-constrained models

(5081)
Bawa V S
Safety-first, stochastic dominance and optimal
portfolio choice
JFQA 1978 JUN VOL 13 p 255.

(5082)
Arzac E R
Utility analysis of chance-constrained portfolio
selection: A correction
JFQA 1977 JUN VOL 12 p 321.

(5083)
Arzac E R, Bawa V S
Portfolio choice and equilibrium in capital
markets with safety-first investors
JFE 1977 VOL 4 p 277.

(5084)
Arzac E R
Utility analysis of chance-constrained portfolio
selection
JFQA 1974 DEC VOL 9 p 993.

(5085)
Levy H, Sarnat M
Safety first--an expected utility principle
JFQA 1972 JUN VOL 7 p 1829-1834.

(5086)
Pyle D H, Turnovsky S J
Risk aversion in chance constrained portfolio
selection
MSci 1971 NOV VOL 18 p 218-225.

(5087)
Pyle D H, Turnovsky S J
Safety-first and expected utility maximization in
mean-standard deviation portfolio analysis
REStat 1970 FEB VOL 52 p 75-81.

(5088)
Agnew N H et al.
An application of chance constrained
programming to portfolio selection in a casualty
insurance firm
MSci 1969 JUN VOL 15 p B512-B520.

(5089)
Roy A D
Safety first and the holding of assets
Em 1952 JUL VOL 20 p 431-449.

12.4   Dynamic portfolio models

(5090)
Cox J C, Huang C-F
Optimal consumption and portfolio policies when
asset prices follow a diffusion process
JET 1989 OCT VOL 49:1 p 33-83.

(5091)
Gandhi D K, Rashid M, Riener K D
Intertemporal resolution of uncertainty and portfolio behavior
FR 1989 AUG VOL 24:3 p 491-498.

(5092)
Dybvig P H
Inefficient dynamic portfolio strategies or how to throw away a million dollars in the stock market
RFS 1988 SPRING VOL 1:1 p 67-88.

(5093)
Brown D P
Multiperiod financial planning
MSci 1987 JUL VOL 33:7 p 848-875.

(5094)
Labadie P
Comparative dynamics and risk premia in an overlapping generations model
REStud 1986 VOL 53 p 139.

(5095)
Franke G
Conditions for myopic valuation and serial independence of the market excess return in discrete time models
JF 1984 JUN VOL 39:2 p 425-442.

(5096)
Lai T-Y, Boness A J
Investment in the long run
FR 1984 NOV VOL 19:4.

(5097)
Davies J B
Uncertain lifetime, consumption and dissaving in retirement
JPE 1981 VOL 89 p 561.

(5098)
Owen P D
Dynamic models of portfolio behavior: A general integrated model incorporating sequencing effects
AER 1981 VOL 71 p 231-238.

(5099)
Ulph D, Hemming R
Uncertain lifetime, imperfect insurance markets and the valuation of pension wealth
REStud 1980 VOL 47 p 587..

(5100)**Abrams R A, Karmarkar U S**
Infinite horizon investment - consumption policies
MSci 1979 OCT VOL 25:10 p 1005-1013.

(5101)
Constantinides G M
A note on the suboptimality of dollar-cost averaging as an investment policy
JFQA 1979 JUN VOL 14 p 443.

(5102)
Foldes L
Optimal saving and risk in continuous time
REStud 1978 VOL 45 p 39.

(5103)
Purvis D D
Dynamic models of portfolio behavior: More on pitfalls in financial model building
AER 1978 VOL 68 p 403-409.

(5104)
Levhari D, Mirman L J
Savings and consumption with an uncertain horizon
JPE 1977 VOL 85 p 265.

(5105)
Burness H S
A note on consistent naive intertemporal decision making and an application to the case of uncertain lifetime
REStud 1976 VOL 43 p 547.

(5106)
Fama E F
Multiperiod consumption investment decisions: A correction
AER 1976 VOL 66 p 723-730.

(5107)
Philippatos G C, Hayya J
Multiperiod portfolio analysis and the inefficiency of the market portfolio
JF 1976 VOL 31 p 1115.

(5108)
Cox J C
Portfolio choice and saving in an optimal consumption-leisure plan
REStud 1975 VOL 42 p 105.

(5109)
Miller B L
Optimal portfolio decision making where the horizon is infinite
MSci 1975 OCT VOL 22:2 p 220-225.

(5110)
Rader T
"Turnpike" theory with (under) consumption
REStud 1975 VOL 42 p 155.

(5111)
Richard S F
Optimal consumption, portfolio and life insurance rules for an uncertain lived individual in a continuous time model
JFE 1975 VOL 2 p 187.

(5112)
Ross S A
Portfolio turnpike theorems for constant policies
JFE 1974 VOL 1 p 171.

(5113)
Arditti F D, Grinold R C, Levy H
The investment-consumption decision under capital rationing: An efficient set analysis
REStud 1973 VOL 40 p 367.

(5114)
Pye G
Lifetime portfolio selection in continuous time for a multiplicative class of utility functions
AER 1973 VOL 63 p 1013-1016.

(5115)
Leland H E
On turnpike portfolios
(in Szego G P and Shell K eds., Mathematical methods in investment and finance. N-Holland, 1972.)

(5116)
Stevens G V G
On Tobin's multiperiod portfolio theorem
REStud 1972 VOL 39 p 461.

(5117)
Hakansson N H
Multi-period mean-variance analysis: toward a general theory of portfolio choice
JF 1971 SEP VOL 26 p 857-884.

(5118)
Hakansson N H
On optimal myopic portfolio policies with and without serial correlation of yields
JB 1971 JUL VOL 44 p 324-334.

(5119)
Holbrook R, Stafford F
The propensity to consume separate types of income: a generalized permanent income hypothesis
Em 1971 JAN VOL 39 p 1-22.

(5120)
Mirman L J
Uncertainty and optimal consumption decisions
Em 1971 JAN VOL 36 p 177-183.

(5121)
Pye G
Minimax policies for selling an asset and dollar averaging
MSci 1971 MAR VOL 17 p 379-393.

(5122)
Fama E F
Multi-period consumption-investment decisions
AER 1970 MAR VOL 60 p 163-174.

(5123)
Hakansson N H
Optimal investment and consumption strategies under risk for a class of utility functions
Em 1970 SEP VOL 38 p 587-607.

(5124)
Pogue G A
An inter-temporal model for investment management
JBR 1970 SPRING VOL 1:1 p 17-34.

(5125)
Black F
Lifetime investment strategies for individuals
Paper for the Seminar on the Analysis of Security Prices, U of Chicago, NOV 1969.

(5126)
Hakansson N H
Optimal investment and consumption strategies under risk, an uncertain lifetime and insurance
IntER 1969 OCT VOL 10 p 443-466.

(5127)
Merton R C
Lifetime portfolio selection under uncertainty
REStat 1969 AUG VOL 51 p 247-257.

(5128)
Samuelson P A
Lifetime portfolio selection by dynamic stochastic programming
REStat 1969 AUG VOL 51 p 239-246.

(5129)
Sandmo A
Capital risk, consumption and portfolio choice
Em 1969 OCT VOL 37 p 586-599.

(5130)
Mossin J
Optimal multiperiod portfolio policies
JB 1968 APR VOL 41 p 215-229.

(5131)
Sandmo A
Portfolio choice in a theory of saving
SJE 1968 VOL 70 p 106-122.

(5132)
Dince R R
Portfolio income: a test of a formula plan
JFQA 1966 SEP VOL 1 p 90-107.

(5133)
Dince R R
Another view of formula planning
JF 1964 DEC VOL 19 p 678-688.

(5134)
Naslund B, Whinston A
A model of multi-period investment under uncertainty
MSci 1962 JAN VOL 8 p 184-200.

(5135)
Phelps E S
The accumulation of risky capital: a sequential utility analysis
Em 1962 OCT VOL 30 p 729-743.

(5136)
Modigliani F, Brumberg R
Utility analysis and the consumption function: an interpretation of cross section data
(in Kurihara K ed., Post-Keynesian economics. Rutgers U Pr, 1954.)

12.41   Growth-optimal model

(5137)
Grauer R R
A comparison of growth optimal and mean variance investment policies
JFQA 1981 MAR VOL 16:1 p 1-21.

(5138)
Maier S F, Peterson D W, Vander Weide J H
Monte Carlo investigation of characteristics of optimal geometric mean portfolios
JFQA 1977 JUN VOL 12 p 215.

(5139)
Vander Weide J H, Peterson D W, Maier S F
A strategy which maximizes the geometric mean return on portfolio investments
MSci 1977 AUG VOL 23:12 p 1117-1123.

(5140)
Hakansson N H, Miller B L
Compound-return mean variance efficient portfolios never risk ruin
MSci 1976 VOL 22:12 p 391.

(5141)
Markowitz H M
Investment for the long run: New evidence for an old rule
JF 1976 VOL 31 p 1273.

(5142)
Elton E J, Gruber M J
On the maximization of the geometric mean with lognormal return distribution: Note
MSci 1975 AUG VOL 21:12 p 483.

(5143)
Kraus A, Litzenberger R H
Market equilibrium in a multiperiod state preference model with logarithmic utility
JF 1975 VOL 30 p 1213.

(5144)
Goldman M B
A negative report on the "near optimality" of the max-expected-log policy as applied to bounded utilities for long lived programs
JFE 1974 VOL 1 p 97.

(5145)
Hakansson N H
Convergence to isoelastic utility and policy in multiperiod portfolio choice
JFE 1974 VOL 1 p 201.

(5146)
Merton R C, Samuelson P A
Fallacy of the log-normal approximation to optimal portfolio decision-making over many periods
JFE 1974 VOL 1 p 67.

(5147)
Morris J
The logarithmic investor's decision to acquire costly information
MSci 1974 DEC VOL 21:4 p 383-391.

(5148)
Bicksler J L, Thorp E O
The capital growth model: An empirical investigation
JFQA 1973 MAR VOL 8:2 p 273- 288.

(5149)
Roll R
Evidence on the "growth-optimum" model
JF 1973 VOL 28 p 551.

(5150)
Ziemba W T
Note on optimal growth portfolios when yields are serially correlated
JFQA 1972 SEP VOL 7 p 1995.

(5151)
Litzenberger R H, Budd A P
A note on geometric mean portfolio selection and the market price of equities
JFQA 1971 DEC VOL 6 p 1263-1276.

(5152)
Samuelson P A
The "fallacy" of maximizing the geometric mean in long sequences of investing or gambling
Proceedings National Academy of Science 1971 OCT p 2493-2496..

(5153)**Hakansson N H**
Optimal growth portfolios when yields are serially correlated
REStat 1970 NOV VOL 52 p 385-394.

(5154)
Latane H A, Young W E
Test of portfolio building rules
JF 1969 SEP VOL 24 p 595-612.

(5155)
Young W E, Trent R H
Geometric mean approximations of individual security and portfolio performance
JFQA 1969 JUN VOL 4 p 179-200.

(5156)
Latane H A, Tuttle D L
Criteria for portfolio building
JF 1967 SEP VOL 22 p 360-361.

(5157)
Latane H A
Investment criteria--a three asset portfolio balance model
REStat 1963 NOV VOL 45 p 427-430.

(5158)
Breimann L
Investment policies for expanding businesses optimal in a long-run sense
Naval Research Logistics Quarterly 1960 DEC VOL 7 p 647-651.

(5159)
Latane H A
Criteria for choice among risky ventures
JPE 1959 APR VOL 67 p 144-155.

12.5 Asset allocation decisions

(5160)
Perold A F, Sharpe W F
Dynamic strategies for asset allocation
FAJ 1988 JAN-FEB VOL 44 p 16-27.

(5161)
Joehnk M D ed.
Asset allocation for institutional portfolios
Institute of Chartered Financial Analysts, 1987.

(5162)
Leibowitz M L
Liability returns: a new look at asset allocation
JPM 1987 WINTER VOL 13:2 p 11-18.

(5163)
Leibowitz M L
A new perspective on asset allocation
Research Foundation of the Institute of Chartered
Financial Analysts, 1987.

(5164)
Sharpe W F
Integrated asset allocation
FAJ 1987 SEP-OCT VOL 43 p 25-32.

(5165)
Brinson G P, Hood L R, Beebower G L
Determinants of portfolio performance
FAJ 1986 JUL-AUG VOL 42 p 39-44.

(5166)
Arnott R D
The pension sponsor's view of asset allocation
FAJ 1985 SEP-OCT VOL 41 p 17-23.

(5167)
Perez R, Malley S
Asset allocation and the social security system
FIN MGMT 1983 SPRING VOL 12 p 29-35.

(5168)
Michaud R O
Risk policy and long-term investment
JFQA 1981 JUN VOL 16:2 p 147-167

(5169)
Smith R F, Richards T M
Asset mix and investment strategy
FAJ 1976 MAR-APR p 67.

12.51 Passive asset allocation strategies

(5170)
Bostock P, Woolley P, Duffy M
Duration-based asset allocation
FAJ 1989 JAN-FEB VOL 45 p 53-60.

(5171)
Fong H G, Vasicek O A
Forecast-free international asset allocation
FAJ 1989 MAR-APR VOL 45 p 29-33.

(5172)
Leibowitz M L, Langetieg T C
Shortfall risk and the asset allocation decision: a
simulation analysis of stock and bond risk profiles
JPM 1989 FALL VOL 16:1 p 61-68.

(5173)
Solnik B H, Noetzlin B
Optimal international asset allocation
JPM 1982 FALL VOL 9:1 p 11-21.

(5174)
Lewis A L
The Ibbotson-Sinquefield simulation made easy
JB 1980 APR VOL 53:2 p 205-214

12.52 Active asset allocation strategies

(5175)
Arnott R D, Hendriksson R D
A disciplined approach to global asset allocation
FAJ 1989 MAR-APR VOL 45 p 17-28.

(5176)
Farrell J L Jr
A fundamental forecast approach to superior asset
allocation
FAJ 1989 MAY-JUN VOL 45 p 32-37.

(5177)
Vandell R F, Stevens J L
Evidence of superior performance from timing
JPM 1989 SPRING VOL 15:3 p 38-42.

(5178)
Arnott R D, Fabozzi F J
Asset allocation: A handbook of portfolio
policies, strategies and tactics
Chicago: Probus Publishing, 1988.

(5179)
Benari Y
An asset allocation paradigm
JPM 1988 WINTER VOL 14:2 p 47-51.

(5180)
Einhorn S G, Shangquan P
Using the dividend discount model for asset
allocation
FAJ 1984 MAY-JUN VOL 40 p 30-33.

(5181)
Arnott R D, Von Germeten J N
Systematic asset allocation
FAJ 1983 NOV-DEC VOL 39 p 31-39.

(5182)
Fielitz B D, Muller F L
The asset allocation decision
FAJ 1983 JUL-AUG VOL 39 p 44-51.

(5183)
Fong H G
An asset allocation framework
JPM 1980 WINTER VOL 6:2 p 58-66.

(5184)
Kritzman M, Ryan J C
A short-term approach to asset allocation
JPM 1980 FALL VOL 7:1 p 45-49.

13 Equilibrium prices of risky assets

(5185)
Nabi I
Investment in segmented capital markets
QJE 1989 AUG VOL 104:3 p 453-462.

(5186)
Nielsen L T
Asset market equilibrium with short selling
REStud 1989 VOL 56 p 467.

(5187)
Weil P
The equity premium puzzle and the risk-free rate
puzzle
JME 1989 VOL 24 p 401.

(5188)
Epstein L G
Risk aversion and asset prices
JME 1988 VOL 22:2 p 179-192.

(5189)
Mehra R, Prescott E C
The equity risk premium: a solution?
JME 1988 VOL 22:1 p 133-136.

(5190)
Rietz T A
The equity risk premium: a solution
JME 1988 VOL 22:1 p 117-132.

(5191)
Wei K C J
An asset-pricing theory unifying the CAPM and
APT
JF 1988 SEP VOL 43:4 p 881-892.

(5192)
Ehrhardt M C
A mean-variance derivation of a multifactor
equilibrium model
JFQA 1987 JUN VOL 22:2 p 227-236.

(5193)
French K R, Schwert G W, Stambaugh R F
Expected stock returns and volatility
JFE 1987 VOL 19 p 3-29.

(5194)
Harrington D R
Modern portfolio theory, the capital asset pricing
model, and arbitrage pricing theory: a user's guide
P-H, 1987.

(5195)
Williams A W
The formation of price forecasts in experimental
markets
JMCB 1987 FEB VOL 19:1 p 1-18.

(5196)
Chua J H, Schnabel J A
Nonpecuniary benefits and asset market
equilibrium
FR 1986 MAY VOL 21:2.

(5197)
Constantinides G M
Capital market equilibrium with transaction costs
JPE 1986 VOL 94 p 842.

(5198)
Dybvig P H, Ross S A
Tax clienteles and asset pricing
JF 1986 JUL VOL 41:3 p 751-763.

(5199)
Brown D P, Gibbons M R
A simple econometric approach for utility-based
asset pricing models
JF 1985 JUN VOL 40:2 p 359-381.

(5200)
Garman M B
Towards a semigroup pricing theory
JF 1985 JUL VOL 40:3 p 847-862

(5201)
Mehra R, Prescott E C
The equity premium: a puzzle
JME 1985 VOL 15 p 145-161.

(5202)
Bohren O
The validity of conventional valuation models
under multiperiod uncertainty
JBFA 1984 VOL 11:2 p 199.

(5203)
Diermeier J J, Ibbotson R G, Siegel L B
The supply of capital market returns
FAJ 1984 MAR-APR VOL 40 p 74-80.

(5204)
Ibbotson R G, Diermeier J J, Siegel L B
The demand for capital market returns: A new
equilibrium theory
FAJ 1984 JAN-FEB VOL 40 p 22-33.

(5205)
Fernholz R, Shay B
Stochastic portfolio theory and stock market
equilibrium
JF 1982 MAY VOL 37:2 p 615-624.

(5206)**Karady G G**
The effect of temporal risk aversion on liquidity
preference
JFE 1982 VOL 10 p 467.

(5207)
Peterson P P, Peterson D R
Divergence of opinion and return
JFR 1982 SUMMER 1.

(5208)
Ryan R J
Capital market theory - a case study in
methodological conflict
JBFA 1982 WINTER VOL 9:4 p 443.

(5209)
Boatsman J R, Baskin E F
Asset valuation with incomplete markets
AR 1981 JAN VOL 56:1 p 38-53.

(5210)
Garman M B, Ohlson J A
Valuation of risky assets in arbitrage-free
economies with transactions costs
JFE 1981 VOL 9 p 271.

(5211)
Holthausen D M
A risk-return model with risk and return
measured as deviations from a target return
AER 1981 VOL 71 p 182-188.

(5212)
LeRoy S F, La Civita C J
Risk aversion and the dispersion of asset prices
JB 1981 OCT VOL 54:4 p 535-547.

(5213)
Mayshar J
Transaction costs and the pricing of assets
JF 1981 JUN VOL 36:3 p 583-597

(5214)
Schmalensee R
Risk and return on long-lived tangible assets
JFE 1981 VOL 9 p 185.

(5215)
Cheng P L
Divergent rates, financial restrictions and relative
prices in capital market equilibrium
JFQA 1980 SEP VOL 15 p 509.

(5216)
Hilliard J E
Asset pricing under a subset of linear risk
tolerance functions and log-normal market returns
JFQA 1980 DEC VOL 15:5 p 1041-1061

(5217)
Jen F C, Lin W T
Consumption, investment, market price of risk
and the risk-free rate
JFQA 1980 DEC VOL 15 p 1025.

(5218)
Kira D, Ziemba W T
The demand for a risky asset
MSci 1980 NOV VOL 26:11 p 1158-1165.

(5219)
Owen J, Rabinovitch R
The cost of information and equilibrium in the
capital asset market
JFQA 1980 SEP VOL 15 P 497.

(5220)
Gregory D D
Multiplicative risk premium
JFQA 1978 DEC VOL 13 p 947.

(5221)
Lee C F, Lloyd W P
Block recursive systems in asset pricing models:
An extension
JF 1978 VOL 33 p 640.

(5222)
Bar-Yosef S, Mesnick R
On some definitional problems with the method
of certainty equivalents
JF 1977 VOL 32 p 1729.

(5223)
Bawa V S, Lindenberg E B
Capital market equilibrium in a mean-lower
partial moment framework
JFE 1977 VOL 5 p 189.

(5224)
Brenner M, Subrahmanyam M G
Intra-equilibrium and inter-equilibrium analysis in
capital market theory: A clarification
JF 1977 VOL 32 p 1313.

(5225)
Hammond J D, Melander E R, Shilling N
Risk, return and the capital market: The insurer
case
JFQA 1976 MAR VOL 11 p 115.

(5226)
Lloyd W P, Lee C F
Block recursive systems in asset pricing models
JF 1976 VOL 31 p 1101.

(5227)
Boyer M, Storoy S, Thore S
Equilibrium in linear capital market networks
JF 1975 VOL 30 p 1197.

(5228)
Caperaa P, Eeckhoudt L
Delayed risk and risk premiums
JFE 1975 VOL 2 p 309.

(5229)
Friend I, Blume M E
The demand for risky assets
AER 1975 DEC VOL 65:5 p 900-922.

(5230)
Gooding A E
Quantification of investors' perceptions of
common stocks: Risk and return dimensions
JF 1975 VOL 30 p 1301.

(5231)
Ingersoll J
Multidimensional security pricing
JFQA 1975 DEC VOL 10 p 785.

(5232)
Roberts G S
Endogenous endowments and capital asset prices
JF 1975 VOL 30 p 155.

(5233)
Jaffe J F, Merville L J
Stock price dependencies and the valuation of
risky assets with discontinuous temporal returns
JF 1974 VOL 29 p 1437.

(5234)
Kumar P
Market equilibrium and corporation finance:
Some issues
JF 1974 VOL 29 p1175.

(5235)
Brennan M J
An approach to the valuation of uncertain income
streams
JF 1973 VOL 28 p 661.

(5236)
Huntsman B
Natural behavior toward risk and the question of
value determination
JFQA 1973 MAR VOL 8:2 p 335-350.

(5237)
Levy H
The demand for assets under conditions of risk
JF 1973 VOL 28 p 79.

(5238)
Long J B Jr
Wealth, welfare and the price of risk
JF 1972 MAY VOL 27 p 419-433.

(5239)
Hammonds T M
Discounting for risk
QREB 1971 VOL 11:3 p 77.

(5240)
Koch J V
The homogeneity asumption and financial asset functions
QREB 1969 VOL 9:4 p 57.

(5241)
Soldofsky R M, Biderman R
Yield-risk measurements of the performance of common stocks
JFQA 1968 MAR VOL 3 p 59-74.

13.1 Capital asset pricing model

(5242)
Giovannini A, Jorion P
The time variation of risk and return in the foreign exchange and stock markets
JF 1989 JUN VOL 44:2 p 307-326.

(5243)
Harlow W V, Rao R K S
Asset pricing in a generalized mean-lower partial moment framework: theory and evidence
JFQA 1989 SEP VOL 24:3 p 285-312.

(5244)
Kandel S, Stambaugh R F
A mean-variance framework for tests of asset pricing models
RFS 1989 VOL 2:2 p 125-156.

(5245)
Lai T-Y
An equilibrium model of asset pricing with progressive personal taxes
JFQA 1989 MAR VOL 24:1 p 117-128.

(5246)
Wheatley S M
A critique of latent variable tests of asset pricing models
JFE 1989 VOL 23 p 325.

(5247)
Ang J S, Lai T-Y
Functional forms of the capital asset pricing model under different market risk regimes
FR 1988 AUG VOL 23:3 p 345-350.

(5248)
Barr G D, Knight R F
Some geometrical characteristics of the risk-return plane
JBFA 1988 AUTUMN VOL 15:3 p 437-446.

(5249)
Carroll C, Wei K C J
Risk, return, and equilibrium: an extension
JB 1988 VOL 61 p 485.

(5250)
Chan K C, Chen N-F
An unconditional asset-pricing test and the role of firm size as an instrumental variable for risk
JF 1988 JUN VOL 43:2 p 309-326.

(5251)
Chang P
Economies of scope, synergy, and the CAPM
JFR 1988 FALL VOL 11:3 p 255-263.

(5252)
Coles J L, Loewenstein U
Equilibrium pricing and portfolio composition in the presence of uncertain parameters
JFE 1988 VOL 22 p 279.

(5253)
Garven J A
CML to SML: An alternative approach
JBFA 1988 SUMMER VOL 15:2 p 283-288.

(5254)
Kroll Y, Levy H, Rapoport A
Experimental tests of the separation theorem and the capital asset pricing model
AER 1988 JUN VOL 78:3 p 500-519.

(5255)
Lewis K K
Inflation risk and asset market disturbances: the mean-variance model revisited
JIMF 1988 SEP VOL 7:3 p 273-288.

(5256)
Miller H P
The CAPM - a separation theorem or an explanation of German share prices?
MIR 1988 VOL 28:1 p 73-80.

(5257)
Nielsen L T
Uniqueness of equilibrium in the classical capital asset pricing model
JFQA 1988 SEP VOL 23 p 329.

(5258)
Rubio G
Further international evidence on asset pricing: the case of the Spanish capital market
JBankF 1988 VOL 12 p 221-242..

(5259) **Ferson W E, Kandel S, Stambaugh R F**
Tests of asset pricing with time-varying expected risk premiums and market betas
JF 1987 JUN VOL 42:2 p 201-220.

(5260)
Gibbons M R, Shanken J
Subperiod aggregation and the power of multivariate tests of portfolio efficiency
JFE 1987 VOL 19 p 389-394.

(5261)
Kandel S, Stambaugh R F
On correlations and inferences about mean-variance efficiency
JFE 1987 VOL 18 p 61-90.

(5262)
Levy H, Levy A
Equilibrium under uncertain inflation: a discrete time approach
JFQA 1987 SEP VOL 22:3 p 285-297.

(5263)
MacKinlay A C
On multivariate tests of the CAPM
JFE 1987 VOL 18 p 341-371.

(5264)
Saunders E M
Forecasting the price of risk within the context of the capital asset pricing model with market index implied standard deviations
MF 1987 VOL 13:2 p 16-19.

(5265)
Shanken J
Multivariate proxies and asset pricing relations: living with the Roll critique
JFE 1987 VOL 18 p 91-110.

(5266)
Tew B V, Reid D W
More evidence on expected value-variance analysis versus direct utility maximization
JFR 1987 FALL VOL 10:3 p 249-257.

(5267)
Burnie D A
Capital asset prices and the Friedman hypothesis of inflation
JBFA 1986 VOL 13:4 p 519.

(5268)
Green R C
Benchmark portfolio inefficiency and deviations from the Security Market Line
JF 1986 JUN VOL 41:2 p 295-311.

(5269)
Kandel S
The geometry of the maximum likelihood estimator of the zero-beta return
JF 1986 JUN VOL 41:2 p 339-346.

(5270)
Lakonishok J, Shapiro A C
Systematic risk, total risk and size as determinants of stock market returns
JBankF 1986 VOL 10 p 115.

(5271)
Shanken J
On the exclusion of assets from tests of the mean variance efficiency of the market portfolio : an extension
JF 1986 JUN VOL 41:2 p 331-339.

(5272)
Shanken J
Testing portfolio efficiency when the zero-beta rate is unknown: a note
JF 1986 MAR VOL 41:1 p 269-276.

(5273)
Stultz R M
Asset pricing and expected inflation
JF 1986 MAR VOL 41:1 p 209-223.

(5274)
Tinic S M, West R R
Risk, return and equilibrium: A revisit
JPE 1986 VOL 94 p 126.

(5275)
Amsler C E, Schmidt P
A Monte Carlo investigation of the accuracy of
multivariate CAPM tests
JFE 1985 VOL 14 p 359.

(5276)
Bergman Y Z
Time preference and capital asset pricing models.
JFE 1985 VOL 14:1 p 145-159.

(5277)
Best M J, Grauter R R
Capital asset pricing compatible with observed
market value weights
JF 1985 MAR VOL 40:1 p 85-103.

(5278)
Brennan M J, Schwartz E S
Asset pricing in a small economy: A test of the
omitted assets model
(in Spremann K ed., Survey of developments in
modern finance. Springer, 1985.)

(5279)
Frankel J A
Portfolio shares as "beta breakers"
JPM 1985 SUMMER VOL 11:4 p 18-23.

(5280)
Gibbons M R, Ferson W
Testing asset pricing models with changing
expectations and an unobservable market portfolio
JFE 1985 VOL 14 p 217.

(5281)
Huffman G W
Adjustment costs and capital asset pricing
JF 1985 JUL VOL 40:3 p 691-709.

(5282)
Jobson J D, Korkie B
Some tests of linear asset pricing with
multivariate normality
Canadian Journal of Administrative Sciences 1985
JUN VOL 2 p 114-138.

(5283)
Kwon Y K
Derivation of the capital asset pricing model
without normality or quadratic preference : a note
JF 1985 DEC VOL 40:5 p 1505-1509.

(5284)
Roll R
A note on the geometry of Shanken's CSR T2
test for mean\variance efficiency
JFE 1985 VOL 14 p 349.

(5285)
Sareewiwatthana P, Malone R P
Market behavior and the capital asset pricing
model in the securities exchange of Thailand : an
empirical application
JBFA 1985 AUTUMN VOL 12:3 p 439-452

(5286)
Schnabel J A
On cash demands, dividend yields and the CAPM
JBusR 1985 JUNE VOL 13:3.

(5287)
Sears R S, Wei K C J
Asset pricing higher moments and the market risk
premium : a note
JF 1985 SEP VOL 40:4 p 1251-1253.

(5288)
Elton E J, Gruber M J
Non-standard C.A.P.M.'s and the market portfolio
JF 1984 JUL VOL 39:3 p 911-924.

(5289)
Giaccotto C
A note on tests of the Capital Asset Pricing
Model
FR 1984 MAR VOL 19:1.

(5290)
Kandel S
On the exclusion of assets from tests of the mean
variance efficiency of the market portfolio
JF 1984 MAR VOL 39:1 p 63-75.

(5291)
Schnabel J A
Short sales restrictions and the security market
line
JBusR 1984 VOL 12 p 87-96.

(5292)
Van Zijl T
A new statement of the extended capital asset
pricing model
AJM 1984 DEC VOL 9 p 67-88.

(5293)
Brown S J, Weinstein M I
A new approach to testing asset pricing models :
the bilinear paradigm
JF 1983 JUN VOL 38:3 p 711-743.

(5294)
Gilster J E
Capital market equilibrium with divergent
investment horizon length assumptions
JFQA 1983 JUN VOL 18:2 p 257-268.

(5295)
Hawawini G A, Michel P A, Viallet C J
An assessment of the risk and return of French
common stocks
JBFA 1983 AUTUMN VOL 10:3 p 333-350.

(5296)
Jarrow R A, Rudd A
A comparison of the APT and CAPA: A note
JBankF 1983 VOL 7 p 295.

(5297)
Markowitz H M
Nonnegative or not nonnegative : a question
about CAPMs
JF 1983 MAY VOL 38:2 p 283-295.

(5298)
McDonald B
Functional forms and the capital asset pricing
model
JFQA 1983 SEP VOL 18:3 p 319-329.

(5299)
Stambaugh R F
Testing the CAPM with broader market indexes:
A problem of mean-deficiency
JBankF 1983 VOL 7 p 5.

(5300)
Stapleton R C, Subrahmanyam M G
The market model and capital asset pricing theory
: a note
JF 1983 DEC VOL 38:5 p 1637-1642.

(5301)
Casabona P A, Vora A
The bias of conventional risk premiums in
empirical tests of the capital asset pricing model
FIN MGMT 1982 SUMMER VOL 11 p 90.

(5302)
Chen S-N
An examination of risk-return relationship in bull
and bear markets using time-varying betas
JFQA 1982 JUN VOL 17:2 p 265-286.

(5303)
Fabozzi F J, Francis J C, Lee C F
Specification error random coefficient and the
risk-return relationship
QREB 1982 SPRING VOL 22:1 p 23-31.

(5304)
Gibbons M R
Multivariate tests of financial models: A new
approach
JFE 1982 VOL 10 p 3.

(5305)
Kryzanowski L, Chau T M
Asset pricing models when the number of
securities held is constrained : a comparison and
reconciliation of the Mao and Levy models
JFQA 1982 MAR VOL 17:1 p 63-73.

(5306)
Levy H
A test of the CAPM via a confidence level
approach
JPM 1982 FALL VOL 9:1 p 56-61.

(5307)
Losq E, Chateau J P D
A generalization of the CAPM based on a
property of the covariance operator
JFQA 1982 DEC VOL 17:5 p 783-797.

(5308)
Michener R W
Variance bounds in a simple model of asset
pricing
JPE 1982 VOL 90 p 166.

(5309)
Mullins D
Does the capital asset pricing model work?
HBR 1982 JAN-FEB VOL 60:1 p 105-114.

(5310)
Nantell T J, Price K, Price B
Mean-lower partial moment asset pricing model
: some empirical evidence.
JFQA 1982 DEC VOL 17:5 p 763-782.

(5311)
Stambaugh R F
On the exclusion of assets from tests of the
two-parameter model: A sensitivity analysis
JFE 1982 VOL 10:3 p 237-268..

(5312)**Aivazian V A, Callen J L**
The "unanimity" literature and the security market
line criterion: The additive risk case
JBFA 1981 SUMMER VOL 8:2 p 177-184

(5313)
Fuller R J
Capital asset pricing theories - Evolution and new
frontiers
Research Foundation of the Institute of Chartered
Financial Analysts, 1981.

(5314)
Grauer R R
Investment policy implications of the capital asset
pricing model
JF 1981 MAR VOL 36:1 p 127-141.

(5315)
Johnson J M, Lanser H P
Dividend risk measurement and tests of the
CAPM
JPM 1981 WINTER VOL 7:2 p 50-54.

(5316)
Levy H
The CAPM and the investment horizon
JPM 1981 WINTER VOL 7:2 p 32-40.

(5317)
Partington G H
Financial decisions, the cost(s) of capital and the
capital asset pricing model
JBFA 1981 SPRING VOL 8:1 p 97-112.

(5318)
Reinganum M R
A new empirical perspective on the CAPM
JFQA 1981 NOV VOL 16:4 p 439-462.

(5319)
Rosenberg B
The capital asset pricing model and the market
model
JPM 1981 WINTER VOL 7:2 p 5-16.

(5320)
Berry R H, Dyson R G
On the negative risk premium for risk adjusted
discount rates
JBFA 1980 AUTUMN VOL 7:3 p 427-436.

(5321)
Cheng P L, Grauer R R
An alternative test of the capital asset pricing
model
AER 1980 VOL 70 p 660-671.

(5322)
Harris R G
A general equilibrium analysis of the capital asset
pricing model
JFQA 1980 MAR VOL 15 p 99.

(5323)
Lee C F, Chen S N
A random coefficient model for reexamining
risk-decomposition method and risk-return
relationship test
QREB 1980 WINTER VOL 20:4 p 58-69

(5324)
Levy H
The capital asset pricing model, inflation and the
investment horizon: The Israeli experience
JFQA 1980 SEP VOL 15 p 561.

(5325)
Levy H
The CAPM and beta in an imperfect market
JPM 1980 WINTER VOL 6:2 p 5-11.

(5326)
Milne F, Smith C Jr
Capital asset pricing with proportional transaction
costs
JFQA 1980 JUN VOL 15 p 253.

(5327)
Pyun C S
A note on capital asset pricing model under uncertain inflation
JFQA 1980 JUN VOL 15 p 425.

(5328)
Bachrach B, Galai D
The risk-return relationship and stock prices
JFQA 1979 JUN VOL 14 p 421.

(5329)
Brown S J
The effect of estimation risk on capital market equilibrium
JFQA 1979 JUN VOL 14 p 215.

(5330)
Brown S L
Autocorrelation, market imperfections and the CAPM
JFQA 1979 DEC VOL 14 p 1027.

(5331)
Findlay M C III
Operating decisions and the CAPM
JBFA 1979 SUMMER VOL 6:2 p 131-144.

(5332)
Fowler D J, Rorke C H
Capital budgeting, capital asset pricing and externalities
JBFA 1979 SUMMER VOL 6:2 p 145-156.

(5333)
Mayers D, Rice E M
Measuring portfolio performance and the empirical content of asset pricing models.
JFE 1979 MAR VOL 7:1 p 3-28.

(5334)
Mayshar J
Transaction costs in a model of capital market equilibrium
JPE 1979 VOL 87 p 673.

(5335)
McEnally R W, Upton D E
A reexamination of the ex post risk-return tradeoff on common stocks
JFQA 1979 JUN VOL 14 p 395.

(5336)
Perrakis S
Capital budgeting and timing uncertainty within the CAPM
FIN MGMT 1979 AUTUMN VOL 8 p 32.

(5337)
Singer R F
Endogenous marginal income tax rates investor behavior and capital asset pricing model
JF 1979 JUL VOL 34:3 p 609-616.

(5338)
Theobald M
A note on variable transactions costs, the capital asset pricing model and the corporate dividend decision
JBFA 1979 SPRING VOL 6:1 p 9-16.

(5339)
Trauring M
A capital asset pricing model with investors' taxes and three categories of investment income
JFQA 1979 SEP VOL 14 p 537.

(5340)
Barry C B
Effects of uncertain and nonstationary parameters upon capital market equilibrium conditions
JFQA 1978 SEP VOL 13 p 419.

(5341)
Foster G
Asset pricing models: Further tests
JFQA 1978 MAR VOL 13 p 39.

(5342)
Friend I, Westerfield R, Granito M
New evidence on the capital asset pricing model.
JF 1978 JUN VOL 33:3 p 903-920.

(5343)
Goldberg M A, Vora A
Bivariate spectral analysis of the capital asset pricing model
JFQA 1978 SEP VOL 13 p 435.

(5344)
Gooding A E
Perceived risk and capital asset pricing
JF 1978 VOL 33 p 1401.

(5345)
Grauer R R
Generalized two parameter asset pricing models:
Some empirical evidence
JFE 1978 VOL 6 p 11-32.

(5346)
Greenberg E, Marshall W J, Yawitz J B
The technology of risk and return
AER 1978 VOL 68 p 241-251.

(5347)
Holthausen D M, Hughes J S
Commodity returns and capital asset pricing
FIN MGMT 1978 SUMMER VOL 7 p 37.

(5348)
Levy H
Equilibrium in an imperfect market: A constraint
on the number of securities in the portfolio
AER 1978 VOL 68 p 643-658.

(5349)
Long S W
Risk premium curve vs. capital market line:
differences explained
FIN MGMT 1978 SPRING VOL 7 p 60.

(5350)
Rendleman R J Jr
Ranking errors in CAPM capital budgeting
applications
FIN MGMT 1978 WINTER VOL 7 p 40.

(5351)
Ross S A
The current status of the capital asset pricing
model (CAPM)
JF 1978 JUN VOL 33:3 p 885-901.

(5352)
Smith K V
The effect of intervaling on estimating parameters
of the capital asset pricing model
JFQA 1978 JUN VOL 13 p 313.

(5353)
Alexander G J
An algorithmic approach to deriving the
minimum-variance zero-beta portfolio
JFE 1977 VOL 4 p 231.

(5354)
Brigham E F, Crum R L
On the use of the CAPM in public utility rate
cases
FIN MGMT 1977 SUMMER VOL 6 p 7.

(5355)
Laughhunn D J, Sprecher R
Probability of loss and the capital asset pricing
model
FIN MGMT 1977 SPRING VOL 6 p 18.

(5356)
Levhari D, Levy H
The capital asset pricing model and the
investment horizon
REStat 1977 FEB VOL 59:1 p 92-104.

(5357)
Myers S C, Turnbull S M
Captal budgeting and the capital asset pricing
model: good news and bad news
JF 1977 MAY VOL 32:2 p 321-332.

(5358)
Roll R
A critique of the asset pricing theory's tests; Part
1: On past and potential testability of the theory
JFE 1977 VOL 4 p 129.

(5359)
Ross S A
The capital asset pricing model [CAPM]
short-sale restrictions and related issues
JF 1977 VOL 32 p 177.

(5360)
Sharpe W F
The capital asset pricing model: A 'multi-beta'
interpretation
(in Levy H and Sarnat M eds., Financial decision
making under uncertainty. Academic Pr, 1977.)

(5361)
Turnbull S M
Market imperfections and the capital asset pricing
model
JBFA 1977 AUTUMN VOL 4:3 p 327-338.

(5362)
Turnbull S M
Market value and systematic risk
JF 1977 VOL 32 p 1125.

(5363)
Williams J T
Capital asset prices with heterogeneous beliefs
JFE 1977 VOL 5 p 219.

(5364)
Ball R J, Brown P, Officer R
Asset pricing in the Australian industrial equity
market
AJM 1976 APR..

(5365)**Brenner M**
A note on risk, return and equilibrium: Empirical
tests
JPE 1976 VOL 84 p 407.

(5366)
Gonedes N J
Capital market equilibrium for a class of
heterogenous expectations in a two-parameter
world
JF 1976 VOL 31 p 1.

(5367)
Grinyer J R
The cost of equity, the CAPM and management
objectives under uncertainty
JBFA 1976 WINTER VOL 3:4 p 101-122.

(5368)
Hagerman R L, Kim E H
Capital asset pricing level changes
JFQA 1976 SEP VOL 11 p 381.

(5369)
Jahankhani A
E-V and E-S capital asset pricing models: Some
empirical tests
JFQA 1976 NOV VOL 11.

(5370)
Lee C F
Investment horizon and the functional form of
the capital asset pricing model
REStat 1976 AUG VOL 58:3 p 356-363.

(5371)
Lee C F, Lloyd W P
The capital asset pricing model expressed as a
recursive system: An empirical investigation
JFQA 1976 JUN VOL 11 p 237.

(5372)
Haugen R A, Heins A J
Risk and the rate of return on financial assets:
Some old wine in new bottles
JFQA 1975 DEC VOL 10 p 775.

(5373)
Jensen M C
Tests of capital market theory and implications of
the evidence
Research Foundation of the Institute of Chartered
Financial Analysts, 1975.

(5374)
Jones-Lee M W, Poskitt D S
An existence proof for equilibrium in a capital
asset market
RBFA 1975 AUTUMN VOL 2:3 p 349-360.

(5375)
Morgan I G
Prediction of return with the minimum variance
zero-beta portfolio
JFE 1975 VOL 2 p 361.

(5376)
Fama E F, MacBeth J D
Long-term growth in a short-term market
JF 1974 VOL 29 p 857.

(5377)
Hogan W W, Warren J M
Toward the development of an equilibrium
capital-market model based on semivariance
JFQA 1974 JAN VOL 9 p 1.

(5378)
McEnally R W
A note on the return behavior of high risk
common stocks
JF 1974 VOL 29 p 199.

(5379)
Modigliani F, Pogue G A
An introduction to risk and return
FAJ 1974 MAR-APR VOL 30 p 68-80.

(5380)
Modigliani F, Pogue G A
An introduction to risk and return - II
FAJ 1974 MAY-JUN VOL 30 p 69-86.

(5381)
Pettit R R, Westerfield R
Using the capital asset pricing model and the
market model to predict security returns
JFQA 1974 SEP VOL 9 p 579.

(5382)
Fama E F, MacBeth J D
Risk, return and equilibrium: empirical tests
JPE 1973 MAY-JUN VOL 81:3 p 607-636.

(5383)
Friend I
A new look at the capital asset pricing model
JF 1973 VOL 28 p 19.

(5384)
Sharpe W F
Bonds versus stocks: Some lessons from capital
market theory
FAJ 1973 NOV-DEC VOL 29 p 74-80.

(5385)
Tsiang S C
Risk, return and portfolio analysis
JPE 1973 VOL 81 p 748.

(5386)
Weston J F
Investment decisions using the capital asset
pricing model
FIN MGMT 1973 SPRING VOL 2 p 25.

(5387)
Black F
Capital market equilibrium with restricted
borrowing
JB 1972 JUL VOL 45 p 444-455.

(5388)
Heckerman D G
Portfolio selection and the structure of capital
asset prices when relative prices of consumption
goods may change
JF 1972 MAR VOL 27 p 47-60.

(5389)
Jensen M C
Capital markets, theory and evidence
BellJ 1972 FALL VOL 3:2 p 357-398.

(5390)
Jensen M C
The foundations and current state of capital
market theory
(in Jensen M C ed., Studies in the theory of
capital markets. Praeger, 1972.)

(5391)
Jensen M C, Scholes M
The capital asset pricing model: some empirical
tests
(in Jensen M C ed., Studies in the theory of
capital markets. Praeger, 1972.)

(5392)
Jensen M C ed.
Studies in the theory of capital markets
Praeger, 1972.

(5393)
Litzenberger R H, Budd A P
Secular trends in risk premiums
JF 1972 SEP VOL 27 p 857-864.

(5394)
Miller M H, Scholes M
Rates of return in relation to risk: a
re-examination of some recent findings
(in Jensen M C ed., Studies in the theory of
capital markets. Praeger, 1972.)

(5395)
Reilly F K
Evidence regarding a segmented stock market
JF 1972 JUN VOL 27 p 607-626.

(5396)
Sharpe W F, Cooper G M
Risk-return class of New York Stock Exchange
common stocks, 1931-1967
FAJ 1972 MAR-APR VOL 28 p 46ff.

(5397)
Brennan M J
Capital market equilibrium with divergent
borrowing and lending rates
JFQA 1971 DEC VOL 6 p 1197-1206.

(5398)
Fama E F
Risk, return and equilibrium
JPE 1971 JAN-FEB VOL 79 p 30-55.

(5399)
Lintner J
The effects of short selling and margin requirements in perfect capital markets
JFQA 1971 DEC VOL 6 p 1173-1196.

(5400)
Gentry J A, Pike J R
An empirical study of the risk-return hypothesis using common stock portfolios of life insurance companies
JFQA 1970 JUN VOL 5 p 179-186.

(5401)
Lintner J
The market price of risk, size of market and investor's risk aversion
REStat 1970 FEB VOL 52 p 87-99.

(5402)
Stone B K
Risk, return and equilibrium: a general single-period theory of asset selection and capital-market equilibrium
MIT Pr, 1970.

(5403)
Upson R B, Jessup P F
Risk-return relationships in regional securites
JFQA 1970 JAN VOL 4 p 677-696.

(5404)
Adler M
On the risk-return trade-off in the valuation of assets
JFQA 1969 DEC VOL 4 p 493-512.

(5405)
Douglas J W
Risk in the equity market: an empirical appraisal of market efficiency
YEE 1969 SPRING VOL 9 p 3-45.

(5406)
Jones-Lee M W
A risk model of equilibrium equity price determination
Journal of Economic Studies 1969 NOV VOL 4.

(5407)
Mossin J
Security pricing and investment criteria in competitive markets
AER 1969 DEC VOL 59 p 749-756.

(5408)
Robichek A A
Risk and the value of securities
JFQA 1969 DEC VOL 4 p 513-538.

(5409)
Fama E F
Risk, return and equilibrium: some clarifying comments
JF 1968 MAR VOL 23 p 29-40.

(5410)
Arditti F D
Risk and the required return on equity
JF 1967 MAR VOL 22 p 19-36.

(5411)
Schrock N W
Asset choice under uncertainty with borrowing introduced
WEJ 1967 MAR p 201-209.

(5412)
Summers R
A peek at the trade off relationship between expected return and risk
QJE 1967 MAY VOL 81 p 437-456.

(5413)
Mossin J
Equilibrium in a capital asset market
Em 1966 OCT VOL 34 p 768-783.

(5414)
Lintner J
Security prices and risk; the theory and a comparative analysis of AT&T and leading industrials
Paper at the conference on 'The economics of regulated public utilities', sponsored by the Bell System and the U of Chicago Business School, Jun 1965.

(5415)
Lintner J
Security prices, risk and maximal gains from diversification
JF 1965 DEC VOL 20 p 587-615.

(5416)
Lintner J
The valuation of risk assets and the selection of risky investments in stock portfolios and capital budgets
REStat 1965 FEB VOL 47 p 13-37.

(5417)
Sharpe W F
Risk aversion in the stock market: some empirical evidence
JF 1965 SEP VOL 20 p 416-422.

(5418)
Sharpe W F
Capital asset prices: a theory of market equilibrium under conditions of risk
JF 1964 SEP VOL 19 p 425-442.

(5419)
Treynor J L
Towards a theory of market value of risky assets
Unp ms, 1961.

13.11 Intertemporal asset pricing

(5420)
Breeden D T, Gibbons M R, Litzenberger R H
Empirical tests of the consumption-oriented CAPM
JF 1989 JUN VOL 44:2 p 231-262.

(5421)
Rubio G
An empirical evaluation of the intertemporal capital asset pricing model: the stock market in Spain
JBFA 1989 WINTER VOL 16:5 p 729.

(5422)
Scott L O
Estimating the marginal rate of substitution in the intertemporal capital asset pricing model
REStat 1989 VOL 71 p 365.

(5423)
Bollerslev T, Engle R F, Wooldridge J M
A capital asset pricing model with time-varying covariances
JPE 1988 FEB VOL 96:1 p 116-131.

(5424)
Kazemi H B
An alternative testable form of consumption CAPM
JF 1988 MAR VOL 43:1 p 61-70.

(5425)
Wheatley S
Some tests of the consumption-based asset pricing model
JME 1988 VOL 22:2 p 193-216.

(5426)
Bosshardt D I
A model of intertemporal discount rates in the presence of real and inflationary autocorrelations
JF 1987 SEP VOL 42:4 p 1049-1070.

(5427)
Ferson W E, Merrick J J Jr
Non-stationarity and stage-of-the-business-cycle effects in consumption-based asset pricing relations
JFE 1987 VOL 18 p 127-146.

(5428)
Breeden D T
Consumption, production, inflation and interest rates: A synthesis
JFE 1986 VOL 15 p 3.

(5429)
Jagannathan R
An investigation of commodity futures prices using the consumption-based intertemporal capital asset pricing model
JF 1985 MAR VOL 40:1 p 175-191.

(5430)
Donaldson J B, Mehra R
Comparative dynamics of an equilibrium intertemporal asset pricing model
REStud 1984 VOL 51 p 491.

(5431)
Grinols E L
Production and risk leveling in the intertemporal capital asset pricing model
JF 1984 DEC VOL 39:5 p 1571-1595.

(5432)
Blume M E
The pricing of capital assets in a multiperiod world
JBankF 1983 VOL 7 p 31.

(5433)
Hansen L P, Singleton K J
Stochastic consumption, risk aversion and the temporal behavior of asset returns
JPE 1983 VOL 91 p 249.

(5434)
Constantinides G M
Intertemporal asset pricing with heterogeneous consumers and without demand aggregation
JB 1982 APR VOL 55:2 p 253-267.

(5435)
Grossman S J, Shiller R J
Consumption correlatedness and risk measurement in economies with non-traded assets and heterogeneous information
JFE 1982 VOL 10 p 195.

(5436)
Cornell B
The consumption based asset pricing model: A note on potential tests and applications
JFE 1981 VOL 9 p 103.

(5437)
Jennings R H, Starks L T, Fellingham J L
An equilibrium model of asset trading with sequential information arrival.
JF 1981 MAR VOL 36:1 p 143-161.

(5438)
Schipper K, Thompson R
Common stocks as hedges against shifts in the consumption or investment opportunity set
JB 1981 APR VOL 54:2 p 305-328.

(5439)
Constantinides G M
Admissible uncertainty in the intertemporal asset pricing model
JFE 1980 VOL 8 p 71-86.

(5440)
Baldwin C Y, Meyer R F
Liquidity preference under uncertainty: A model of dynamic investment in illiquid opportunities
JFE 1979 VOL 7 p 347-374.

(5441)
Breeden D T
An intertemporal asset pricing model with stochastic consumption and investment opportunities
JFE 1979 SEP VOL 7:3 p 265-296.

(5442)
Fama E F, MacBeth J D
Tests of the multiperiod two-parameter model
JFE 1974 VOL 1 p 43.

13.12 Pricing with non-marketable assets

(5443)
Brown D P
The implications of nonmarketable income for consumption-based models of asset pricing
JF 1988 SEP VOL 43:4 p 867-880.

(5444)
Holmstrom B
The cost of capital in nonmarketed firms
QJE 1981 VOL 95 p 765-773.

(5445)
Stapleton R C, Subrahmanyam M G
Marketability of assets and the price of risk
JFQA 1979 MAR VOL 14 p 1.

(5446)
Brito N O
Marketability restrictions and the valuation of
capital assets under uncertainty
JF 1977 VOL 32 p 1109.

(5447)
Fama E F, Schwert G W
Human capital and capital market equilibrium
JFE 1977 VOL 4 p 95.

(5448)
Landskroner Y
Nonmarketable assets and the determinants of the
market price of risk
REStat 1977 NOV VOL 59:4 p 482-492.

(5449)
Mayers D
Nonmarketable assets, market segmentation and
the level of asset prices
JFQA 1976 MAR VOL 11 p 1.

(5450)
Mayers D
Non-marketable   assets   and   capital   market
equilibrium under uncertainty
(in Jensen M C ed., Studies in the theory of
capital markets. Praeger, 1972.)

13.13 Asset pricing with three moments

(5451)
Lim K-G
A new test of the three-moment capital asset
pricing model
JFQA 1989 JUN VOL 24:2 p 205-216.

(5452)
Conine T E Jr, Tamarkin M
Implications of skewness in returns for utilities'
cost of equity capital
FIN MGMT 1985 WINTER VOL 14 p 66..

(5453)**Kraus A, Litzenberger R H**
On   the   distributional   conditions   for   a

consumption-oriented three moment CAPM
JF 1983 DEC VOL 38:5 p 1381-1391.

(5454)
Friend I, Westerfield R
Co-skewness and capital asset pricing
JF 1980 SEP VOL 35:4 p 897-915.

(5455)
Lee C F
Functional   form,   skewness   effect   and   the
risk-return relationship
JFQA 1977 MAR VOL 12 p 55.

(5456)
Kraus A, Litzenberger R H
Skewness preference and the valuation of risk
assets
JF 1976 VOL 31 p 1085.

13.14 International asset pricing

(5457)
Brennan M J, Solnik B
International risk sharing and capital mobility
JIMF 1989 VOL 8 p 359.

(5458)
Hietala P T
Asset pricing in partially segmented markets:
evidence from the Finnish market
JF 1989 JUL VOL 44:3 p 697-718.

(5459)
Alexander G J, Eun C S, Janakiramanan S
International listings and stock returns: some
empirical evidence
JFQA 1988 JUN VOL 23:2 p 135-152.

(5460)
Stockman A C, Hernandez D A
Exchange   controls,   capital   controls,   and
international financial markets
AER 1988 JUN VOL 78:3 p 362-374.

(5461)
Wheatley S
Some tests of international equity integration
JFE 1988 VOL 21 p 177.

(5462)
Hirst J
Restrictions on outward portfolio investment and
domestic equity markets
Managerial and Decision Economics 1987
SPRING p 75-80.

(5463)
Stulz R M
An equilibrium model of exchange rate
determination and asset pricing with nontraded
goods and imperfect information
JPE 1987 VOL 95 p 1024-1040.

(5464)
Cooper I A, Kaplanis E
Costs to crossborder investment and international
equity market equilibrium
(in Edwards J et al. eds., Recent developments in
corporate finance. Cambridge U Pr, 1986.)

(5465)
Eun C S, Janakiramanan S
A model of international asset pricing with a
constraint on the foreign equity ownership
JF 1986 SEP VOL 41:4 p 897-914.

(5466)
Jorion P, Schwartz E
Integration vs segmentation in the Canadian
Stock Market
JF 1986 JUL VOL 41:3 p 603-616.

(5467)
Errunza V R, Losq E
International asset pricing under mild
segmentation: theory and test
JF 1985 MAR VOL 40:1 p 105-124.

(5468)
Mantell E H
How to measure expected returns on foreign
investment
JPM 1984 WINTER VOL 10:2 p 38-43.

(5469)
Stultz R M
The pricing of capital assets in an international
setting: An introduction
JIBS 1984 SUMMER.

(5470)
Adler M, Dumas B
International portfolio choice and corporation
finance : a synthesis
JF 1983 JUN VOL 38:3 p 925-984

(5471)
Hodrick R J
International asset pricing model with
time-varying risk premia
JIntE 1981 NOV p 573-577.

(5472)
Stulz R M
On the effects of barriers to international
investment
JF 1981 SEP VOL 36:4 p 923-934.

(5473)
Stulz R M
A model of international asset pricing
JFE 1981 VOL 9 p 383.

(5474)
Sercu P
A generalization of the international asset pricing
model
Review of the French Finance Association 1980
VOL 1.

(5475)
Senbet L W
International capital market equilibrium and the
multinational firm financing and investment
policies
JFQA 1979 SEP VOL 14 p 455.

(5476)
Elliott J W
The expected return to equity and international
asset prices
JFQA 1978 DEC VOL 13 p 987.

(5477)
Solnik B
Testing international asset pricing: some
pessimistic views
JF 1977 MAY VOL 32:2 p 503-511.

(5478)
Stehle R
An empirical test of the alternative hypotheses of national and international pricing of risky assets
JF 1977 MAY VOL 32:2 p 493-502.

(5479)
Grauer F L A, Litzenberger R H, Stehle R E
Sharing rules and equilibrium in an international capital market under uncertainty
JFE 1976 VOL 3 p 233.

(5480)
Subrahmanyam M G
On the optimality of international capital market integration
JFE 1975 VOL 2 p 3.

(5481)
Black F
International capital market equilibrium with investment barriers
JFE 1974 VOL 1 p 337.

(5482)
Kouri P J K, Porter M G
International capital flows and portfolio equilibrium
JPE 1974 VOL 82 p 443.

(5483)
Solnik B H
An equilibrium model of the international capital market
JET 1974 AUG VOL 8:4 p 500-524.

(5484)
Cohn R A, Pringle J J
Imperfections in international financial markets: Implications for risk premia and the cost of capital to firms
JF 1973 VOL 28 p 59.

13.2 Arbitrage pricing theory

(5485)
Hamao Y
An empirical examination of the Arbitrage Pricing Theory using Japanese data
Japan and the World Economy 1989 JAN.

(5486)
Latham M
The arbitrage pricing theory and supershares
JF 1989 JUN VOL 44:2 p 263-282.

(5487)
Born J A, Moser J T
An investigation into the role of the portfolio in the arbitrage pricing theory
FR 1988 AUG VOL 23:3 p 287-300.

(5488)
Burmeister E, McElroy M B
Joint estimation of factor sensitivities and risk premia for the arbitrage pricing theory
JF 1988 JUL VOL 43:3 p 721-733.

(5489)
Connor G, Korajczyk R A
Risk and return in an equilibrium APT: Application of a new test methodology
JFE 1988 VOL 21 p 255.

(5490)
Jarrow R A
Preferences, continuity, and the arbitrage pricing theory
RFS 1988 SUMMER VOL 1:2 p 159-172.

(5491)
Lehmann B N, Modest D M
The empirical foundations of the arbitrage pricing theory
JFE 1988 VOL 21 p 213.

(5492)
McElroy M B, Burmeister E
Arbitrage pricing theory as a restricted nonlinear multivariate regression model: ITNLSUR estimates
Journal of Business and Economic Statistics 1988 JAN VOL 6 p 29-42.

(5493)
Tieman J
Exact arbitrage pricing and the minimum variance frontier
JF 1988 JUN VOL 43:2 p 327-338.

(5494)
Abeysekera S P, Mahajan A
A test of the APT in pricing UK stocks
JBFA 1987 AUTUMN VOL 14:3 p 377-391.

(5495)
Chang J S K, Shanker L
Option pricing and the arbitrage pricing theory
JFR 1987 SPRING VOL 10:1 p 1-16.

(5496)
Christofi A C, Philippatos G C
An empirical investigation of the international
arbitrage pricing theory
MIR 1987 VOL 27:1 p 13-22.

(5497)
Coggin T D, Hunter J E
A meta-analysis of spicing "risk" factors in APT
JPM 1987 FALL VOL 14:1 p 35-38.

(5498)
Ehrhardt M C
Arbitrage pricing models: the sufficient number of
factors and equilibrium conditions
JFR 1987 VOL 10:2 p 111-120.

(5499)
Ehrhardt M C, Jordan J V, Walkling R A
An application of arbitrage pricing theory to
futures markets: test of normal backwardation
JFM 1987 FEB VOL 7:1 p 21-34.

(5500)
Gultekin M N, Gultekin N B
Stock return anomalies and the tests of the APT
JF 1987 DEC VOL 42:5 p 1213-1224.

(5501)
Huberman G, Kandel S, Stambaugh R F
Mimicking portfolios and exact arbitrage pricing
JF 1987 MAR VOL 42:1 p 1-9.

(5502)
Pettway R H, Jordan B D
APT vc. CAPM estimates on the
return-generating function parameters for
regulated public utilities
JFR 1987 VOL 10:3 p 227-238.

(5503)
Beggs J J
A simple exposition of the Arbitrage Pricing
Theory approximation
AJM 1986 JUN VOL 11 p 13-22.

(5504)
Burmeister E, Wall K D
The arbitrage pricing theory and macroeconomic
factor measures
FR 1986 FEB VOL 21:1 p 1-20.

(5505)
Cho D C, Eun C S, Senbet L W
International arbitrage pricing theory : an
empirical investigation
JF 1986 JUN VOL 41:2 p 313-329..

(5506)**Connor G, Korajczyk R A**
Performance measurement with the Arbitrage
Pricing Theory: a new framework for analysis
JFE 1986 MAR VOL 15:3 p 373-394.

(5507)
Diacogiannis G P
Arbitrage pricing model : a critical examination of
its empirical applicability for the London Stock
Exchange
JBFA 1986 WINTER VOL 13:4 p 489-504

(5508)
Jarrow R A
The relationship between arbitrage and first order
stochastic dominance
JF 1986 SEP VOL 41:4 p 915-921.

(5509)
Luedecke B P
Arbitrage pricing, factor structure, eigenvectors
and all that - an exposition
AJM 1986 JUN VOL 11 p 67-86.

(5510)
Prisman E Z
Valuation of risky assets in arbitrage free
economies with frictions
JF 1986 JUL VOL 41:3 p 545-560.

(5511)
Trzcinka C
On the number of factors in the arbitrage pricing model
JF 1986 JUN VOL 41:2 p 347-368.

(5512)
Barone-Adesi G
Arbitrage equilibrium with skewed asset returns
JFQA 1985 SEP VOL 20:3 p 299-313.

(5513)
Dhrymes P J
New tests of the APT and their implications
JF 1985 JUL VOL 40:3 p 659-675.

(5514)
Dhrymes P J, Friend I, Gultekin N B
An empirical examination of the implications of arbitrage pricing theory
JBankF 1985 VOL 9 p 73.

(5515)
Dybvig P H, Ross S H
Yes, the APT is testable
JF 1985 SEP VOL 40:4 p 1173-1188.

(5516)
Gultekin N B, Rogalski R J
Government bond returns measurement of interest rate risk and the arbitrage pricing theory
JF 1985 MAR VOL 40:1 p 43-61.

(5517)
McElroy M B, Wall K D
Two estimators for the APT model when factors are measured
Economics Letters 1985 VOL 19 p 271-275.

(5518)
Raveh A
A note on factor analysis and arbitrage pricing theory
JBankF 1985 VOL 9 p 317.

(5519)
Bower D H, Bower R S, Logue D E
Arbitrage pricing theory and utility stock returns.
JF 1984 SEP VOL 39:4 p 1041-1054

(5520)
Bower D H, Bower R S, Logue D E
A primer on arbitrage pricing theory
MCFJ 1984 FALL VOL 2 p 31-40.

(5521)
Cho D C
On testing the arbitrage pricing theory : inter-battery factor analysis
JF 1984 DEC VOL 39:5 p 1485-1502.

(5522)
Cho D C, Elton E E, Gruber M J
On the robustness of the Roll and Ross arbitrage price theory
JFQA 1984 MAR VOL 19:1 p 1-10.

(5523)
Dhrymes P
Arbitrage pricing theory
JPM 1984 SUMMER VOL 10-4 p 35-44.

(5524)
Dhrymes P J, Friend I, Gultekin N B
A critical reexamination of the empirical evidence on the arbitrage pricing theory
JF 1984 JUN VOL 39:2 p 323-346.

(5525)
Ingersoll J E
Some results in the theory of arbitrage pricing
JF 1984 SEP VOL 39:4 p 1021-1039.

(5526)
Litzenberger R H, Rolfo J
Arbitrage pricing, transaction costs and taxation of capital gains: a study of government bonds with the same maturity date
JFE 1984 VOL 13 p 337-351.

(5527)
Roll R, Ross S A
The arbitrage pricing theory approach to strategic portfolio planning
FAJ 1984 MAY-JUN VOL 40 p 14-29.

(5528)
Chamberlain G
Funds, factors and diversification in arbitrage pricing models
Em 1983 SEP VOL 51 p 1305-1323.

(5529)
Chen N-F
Some empirical tests of the theory of arbitrage pricing
JF 1983 DEC VOL 38:5 p 1393-1414.

(5530)
Chen N-F, Ingersoll J E
Exact pricing in linear factor models with finitely many assets: a note
JF 1983 JUN VOL 38:3 p 985-988.

(5531)
Dybvig P H
An explicit bound on individual assets' deviations from APT pricing in a finite economy.
JFE 1983 DEC VOL 12:4 p 483-496.

(5532)
Elton E J, Gruber M J, Rentzler J C
The arbitrage pricing model and returns on assets under uncertain inflation
JF 1983 MAY VOL 38:2 p 525-537.

(5533)
Grinblatt M S, Titman S
Factor pricing in a finite economy
JFE 1983 VOL 12 p 497-507.

(5534)
Jarrow R A, Rudd A
A comparison of the APT and CAPM: A note
JBankF 1983 VOL 7 p 295.

(5535)
Solnik B H
International arbitrage pricing theory
JF 1983 MAY VOL 38:2 p 449-457.

(5536)
Stambaugh R F
Arbitrage pricing with information
JFE 1983 VOL 12:3 p 357-369.

(5537)
Fogler H R
Common sense on CAPM, APT, and correlated residuals
JPM 1982 SUMMER VOL 8:4 p 20-28.

(5538)
Jobson J D
A multivariate linear regression test for the arbitrage pricing theory
JF 1982 SEP VOL 37:4 p 1037-1042.

(5539)
Shanken J
The arbitrage pricing theory: is it testable
JF 1982 DEC VOL 37:5 p 1129-1140.

(5540)
Morris R C, Pope P F
The Jensen measure of portfolio performance in an arbitrage pricing theory context
JBFA 1981 SUMMER VOL 8:2 p 203-220.

(5541)
Reinganum M R
The arbitrage pricing theory: some empirical results
JF 1981 MAY VOL 36:2 p 313-321.

(5542)
Ohlson J A, Garman M B
A dynamic equilibrium for the Ross arbitrage model
JF 1980 JUN VOL 25:3 p 675-684.

(5543)
Roll R, Ross S A
An empirical investigation of the arbitrage pricing theory
JF 1980 DEC VOL 35:5 p 1073-1103.

(5544)
Ross S A
The arbitrage theory of capital asset pricing
JET 1976 DEC VOL 13:3 p 341-360.

(5545)
Ross S A
Return, risk and arbitrage
(in Friend I and Bicksler J eds., Studies in risk and return. Ballinger Publishing, 1975.)

13.3 Accounting measures of the reward for risk

(5546)
Norgaard R L
Evaluating intercorporate risk, returns, and trends
JFQA 1971 SEP VOL 6 p 1069-1082.

(5547)
Fisher I, Hall G R
Risk and corporate rates of return
QJE 1969 FEB VOL 83 p 79-92.

(5548)
Conrad G R, Plotkin I H
Risk/return: U.S. industry pattern
HBR 1968 MAR-APR VOL 46 p 90-99.

(5549)
Cootner P H, Holland D M
Risk and rate of return. Rev ed
MIT Pr, 1964.

(5550)
Florence P S
Reward for risk-bearing by shareholders in large companies
JIE 1957 VOL 5 p 81-111.

14 Measurement of investment performance

(5551)
ari R A
Wall Street week recommendations: yes or no
JPM 1987 FALL VOL 14:1 p 74-76.

(5552)
Chua J H, Woodward R S
J. M. Keynes' investment performance: a note
JF 1983 MAR VOL 38:1 p 232-235.

(5553)
Christner R, Stover R
Performance of institutionally held common
stocks, 1969-73: a new perspective
QREB 1976 VOL 16:2 p 51.

(5554)
Mincer J ed.
Economic forecasts and expectations: analyses of
forecasting behavior and performance
(Dist by Columbia U Pr) Natl Bur Econ Res,
1969.

14.1 Portfolio performance

(5555)
Ippolito R A
Efficiency with costly information: a study of
mutual fund performance, 1965-1984
QJE 1989 FEB VOL 104:1 p 1-24.

(5556)
Beckers S
Performance measurement and performance
attribution in less than efficient markets: A case
study
(in Dimson E ed., Stock market anomalies.
Cambridge U Pr, 1988.)

(5557)
Brooks R, Hand J
Evaluating the performance of stock portfolios
with index futures contracts
JFM 1988 FEB VOL 8:1 p 33-46.

(5558)
Chen N-F, Copeland T E, Mayers D
A comparison of single and multifactor portfolio
performance methodologies
(in Dimson E ed., Stock market anomalies.
Cambridge U Pr, 1988.).

(5559)**Lockwood L J, Kadiyala K R**
Measuring investment performance with a
stochastic parameter regression model
JBankF 1988 VOL 12:3 p 457-468.

(5560)
Chen N-F, Copeland T E, Mayers D
A comparison of single and multifactor portfolio
performance methodologies
JFQA 1987 DEC VOL 22:4 p 401-417.

(5561)
Garland J P
Taxable portfolios: value and performance
JPM 1987 WINTER VOL 13:2 p 19-25.

(5562)
Hagigi M, Kluger B
Safety-first: an alternative performance measure
JPM 1987 SUMMER VOL 13:4 p 34-40.

(5563)
Hagigi M, Kluger B
Assessing risk and return of pension funds'
portfolios by the Telser safety-first approach
JBFA 1987 VOL 14:2 p 241.

(5564)
Ippolito R A, Turner J A
Turnover, fees and pension plan performance
FAJ 1987 NOV-DEC VOL 43 p 16-26.

(5565)
Lehmann B N, Modest D M
Mutual fund performance evaluation : a
comparison of Benchmarks and Benchmark
comparisons
JF 1987 JUN VOL 42:2 p 233-265.

(5566)
Moses E A, Cheyney J M, Veit E T
A new and more complete performance measure
JPM 1987 SUMMER VOL 13:4 p 24-33.

(5567)
Mossavar-Rahmani S
Customized benchmarks in structured management
JPM 1987 SUMMER VOL 13:4 p 65-68.

(5568)
Sengupta J K, Sfeir R E
Evaluation of investment portfolios: some tests of robustness and diversification
AE 1987 FEB VOL 19:2 p 179-190.

(5569)
Brinson G P, Diermeier J J, Schlarbaum G G
A composite portfolio benchmark for pension plans
FAJ 1986 MAR-APR VOL 42 p 15-24.

(5570)
Chen S-N, Lee C F
The effects of the sample size, the investment horizon and market conditions on the validity of composite performance measures: a generalization
MSci 1986 NOV VOL 32:11 p 1410-1421.

(5571)
Connor G, Korajczyk R A
Performance measurement with the Arbitrage Pricing Theory: a new framework for analysis
JFE 1986 MAR VOL 15:3 p 373-394.

(5572)
Elton E J, Gruber M J, Grossman S
Discrete expectational data and portfolio performance
JF 1986 JUL VOL 41:3 p 699-714

(5573)
Gressis N, Philippatos G C, Vlahos G
Net selectivity as a component measure of investment performance
FR 1986 FEB VOL 21:1.

(5574)
Prakash A J, Bear R M
A simplifying performance measure recognizing skewness
FR 1986 FEB VOL 21:1.

(5575)
Brinson G P, Fachler N
Measuring non-U.S. equity portfolio performance
JPM 1985 SPRING VOL 11:3 p 73.

(5576)
Dybvig P H, Ross S A
The analytics of performance measurement using a security market line
JF 1985 JUN VOL 40:2 p 401-416.

(5577)
Dybvig P H, Ross S A
Differential information and performance measurement using a security market line
JF 1985 JUN VOL 40:2 p 383-399.

(5578)
Jobson J D, Korkie B
On the Jensen measure and marginal improvements in portfolio performance : a note
JF 1984 MAR VOL 39:1 p 245-251.

(5579)
Levy H
Measuring risk and performance over alternative investment horizons
FAJ 1984 MAR-APR VOL 40 p 61-68.

(5580)
Dunn P C, Theisen R D
How consistently do active managers win?
JPM 1983 SUMMER VOL 9:4 p 47-53.

(5581)
Kritzman M
Can bond managers perform consistently?
JPM 1983 SUMMER VOL 9:4 p 54.

(5582)
Woodward R S
The performance of UK closed-end funds : a comparison of the various ranking criteria
JBFA 1983 AUTUMN VOL 10:3 p 419-427

(5583)
Appleyard A R, Strong N, Walker M
Mutual fund performance in the context of models of equilibrium capital asset pricing
JBFA 1982 AUTUMN VOL 9:3 p 289-295

(5584)
Jobson J D, Korkie B
Potential performance and tests of portfolio efficiency
JFE 1982 VOL 10 p 433-466.

(5585)
Nagorniak J J
Risk adjusted equity performance measurement
JF 1982 MAY VOL 37:2 p 555-561.

(5586)
Nowakowski C A
International performance measurement
CJWB 1982 SUMMER VOL 17:2 p 53-57.

(5587)
Shawky H A
An update on mutual funds: better grades
JPM 1982 WINTER VOL 8:2 p 29-34.

(5588)
Calvet A L, Lefoll J
Performance and systematic risk stability of Canadian mutual funds under inflation
JBFA 1981 SUMMER VOL 8:2 p 279-289.

(5589)
Chen S-N, Lee C F
The sampling relationship between Sharpe's performance measure and its risk proxy: sample size, investment horizon and market conditions.
MSci 1981 JUN VOL 27:6 p 607-618.

(5590)
Ferri M G, Oberhelman H D
How well do money market funds perform?
JPM 1981 SPRING VOL 7:3 p 18-26.

(5591)
Ferri M G, Oberhelman H D
A study of the management of money market mutual funds, 1975-1980
FIN MGMT 1981 AUTUMN VOL 10 p 24-29.

(5592)
Jobson J D, Korkie B M
Performance hypothesis testing with the Sharpe and Treynor measures
JF 1981 SEP VOL 36:4 p 889-908.

(5593)
Lakonishok J
Performance of mutual funds versus their expenses
JBR 1981 SUMMER VOL 12:2.

(5594)
Morris R C, Pope P F
The Jensen measure of portfolio performance in an arbitrage pricing theory context
JBFA 1981 SUMMER VOL 8:2 p 203-220.

(5595)
Roll R
Performance evaluation and benchmark errors (II)
JPM 1981 WINTER VOL 7:2 p 17-22.

(5596)
Bogle J C, Twardowski J M
Institutional investment performance compared: Banks, investment counselors, insurance companies and mutual funds
FAJ 1980 JAN-FEB VOL 36 p 33-41.

(5597)
Brightman J S, Haslanger B L
Past investment performance seductive but deceptive
JPM 1980 WINTER VOL 6:2 p 43-45.

(5598)
Dietz P O, Fogler H R, Hardy D J
The challenge of analyzing bond portfolio returns
JPM 1980 SPRING VOL 6:3 p 53-58.

(5599)
Ferguson R
Performance measurement doesn't make sense
FAJ 1980 MAY-JUN p 59-70.

(5600)
Fielitz B D, Greene M T
Shortcomings in performance evaluation via MPT
JPM 1980 SUMMER VOL 6:4 p 13-19.

(5601)
Gressis N, Miller T W
Nonstationarity and evaluation of mutual fund performance
JFQA 1980 SEP VOL 15 p 639.

(5602)
Hymans C, Mulligan J
The measurement of portfolio performance: an
introduction
Kluwer, 1980.

(5603)
Murphy J M
Why no one can tell who's winning
FAJ 1980 MAY-JUN p 49-58.

(5604)
Peterson D, Rice M L
A note on ambiguity in portfolio performance
measures
JF 1980 DEC VOL 35:5 p 1251-1256.

(5605)
Roll R
Performance evaluation and benchmark errors (I)
JPM 1980 SUMMER VOL 6:4 p 5-12.

(5606)
Saunders A, Ward C, Woodward R
Stochastic dominance and the performance of U
K unit trusts
JFQA 1980 JUN VOL 15 p 323.

(5607)
Tehranian H
Empirical studies in porfolio performance using
higher degrees of stochastic dominance
JF 1980 MAR VOL 35:1 p 159-171.

(5608)
Verrecchia R E
The Mayers-Rice conjecture: A counterexample
JFE 1980 VOL 8 p 87.

(5609)
Williams A III
The bond market line: measuring risk and reward
JPM 1980 SUMMER VOL 6:4 p 62-64.

(5610)
Ang J S, Chua J H
Composite measures for the evaluation of
investment performance
JFQA 1979 JUN VOL 14 p 361.

(5611)
Cornell B
Asymmetric   information   and   portfolio
performance measurement
JFE 1979 DEC VOL 7:4 p 381-390..

(5612)**Lease R C, Lewellen W G, Schlarbaum G
G**
Investment performance and investor behavior
JFQA 1979 MAR VOL 14 p 29.

(5613)
Mayers D, Rice E M
Measuring   portfolio   performance   and   the
empirical content of asset pricing models.
JFE 1979 MAR VOL 7:1 p 3-28.

(5614)
Peasnell K V, Skerratt L C L, Taylor P A
An arbitrage rationale for tests of mutual fund
performance
JBFA 1979 AUTUMN VOL 6:3 p 373-400.

(5615)
Ang J S
A note on the leverage effect on portfolio
performance measures
JFQA 1978 SEP VOL 13 p 567.

(5616)
Gehr A K, Miller R E
Sample size bias and Sharpe's performance
measure: A note
JFQA 1978 DEC VOL 13 p 943.

(5617)
Jen F C, Lee C F
Effects of measurement errors on systematic risk
and performance measure of a portfolio
JFQA 1978 JUN VOL 13 p 299.

(5618)
Kim T
An assessment of the performance of mutual fund
management: 1969-1975
JFQA 1978 SEP VOL 13 p 385.

(5619)
Kon S J, Jen F C
Estimation of time-varying systematic risk and performance for mutual fund portfolios: An application of switching regression
JF 1978 VOL 33 p 457.

(5620)
Roll R
Ambiguity when performance is measured by the securities market line
JF 1978 VOL 33 p 1051.

(5621)
Schlarbaum G G, Lewellen W G, Lease R C
The common stock-portfolio performance record of the individual investor
JF 1978 VOL 33 p 429.

(5622)
Shick R A, Trieschmann J S
Some future evidence on the performance of property-liability insurance companies' stock portfolios
JFQA 1978 MAR VOL 13 p 157.

(5623)
Stover R D, Alexander G J
Bank managed equity common trust funds. A performance analysis
JBR 1978 WINTER VOL 8:4.

(5624)
Beebower G L, Bergstrom G L
Pension performance 1966-1975
FAJ 1977 MAY-JUN p 31-42.

(5625)
Bell P W
Portfolio reports for client and manager
FAJ 1977 MAY-JUNE p 56-61.

(5626)
Bloomfield T, Leftwich R, Long J B Jr
Portfolio strategies and performance
JFE 1977 VOL 5 p 201.

(5627)
Grant D
Portfolio performance and the "cost" of timing decisions
JF 1977 VOL 32 p 837.

(5628)
Meyer J
Further applications of stochastic dominance to mutual fund performance
JFQA 1977 JUN VOL 12 p 235.

(5629)
Barnea A, Logue D E
Stock trading and portfolio performance
JBR 1976 SUMMER VOL 7 p 150-157.

(5630)
Vooheis F L
How well do banks manage pooled pension portfolios?
FAJ 1976 SEP-OCT VOL 32 p 35-40.

(5631)
Ward C W R, Saunders A
U K unit trust performance 1964-74.
JBFA 1976 WINTER VOL 3:4 p 83-100.

(5632)
Gentry J A
Capital market line theory, insurance company portfolio performance, and empirical anomalies
QREB 1975 VOL 15:1 p 7.

(5633)
Matulich S
Portfolio performance with lending or borrowing
JBFA 1975 AUTUMN VOL 2:3 p 341-348.

(5634)
Garand J J
Fixed income portfolio performance: a discussion of the issues
JBR 1974 WINTER VOL 4:4 p 280-297.

(5635)
Joy O M, Porter R B
Stochastic dominance and mutual fund performance
JFQA 1974 JAN VOL 9 p 25.

(5636)
Parker G G C, Stewart S S
Risk and investment performance
FAJ 1974 MAY-JUN VOL 30 p 49-52.

(5637)
Schlarbaum G G
The investment performance of the common stock portfolios of property-liability insurance companies
JFQA 1974 JAN VOL 9 p 89.

(5638)
Klemkosky R C
The bias in composite performance measures
JFQA 1973 JUN VOL 8:3 p 505-516.

(5639)
McDonald J G
French mutual fund performance: Evaluation of internationally-diversified portfolios
JF 1973 VOL 28 p 1161.

(5640)
Fama E F
Components of investment performance
JF 1972 JUN VOL 27 p 551-568.

(5641)
Jensen M C
Optimal utilization of market forecasts and the evaluation of investment portfolio performance
(in Szego G P and Shell K eds., Mathematical methods in investment and finance. N-Holland, 1972.)

(5642)
Levy H
Portfolio performance and the investment horizon
MSci 1972 AUG VOL 18 p B645-B653.

(5643)
Rothstein M
On geometric and arithmetic portfolio performance indexes
JFQA 1972 SEP VOL 7 p 1983.

(5644)
Sarnat M
A note on the prediction of portfolio performance from ex post data
JF 1972 SEP VOL 27 p 903-906.

(5645)
Williamson P J
Measurement and forecasting of mutual fund performance: Choosing an investment strategy
FAJ 1972 NOV-DEC VOL 28 p 78-91.

(5646)
Arditti F D
Another look at mutual fund performance
JFQA 1971 JUN VOL 6 p 909-912.

(5647)
Gray K B Jr
Measuring investment performance: the time-weighted rate-appropriate measure of manager performance
JBR 1971 AUTUMN VOL 2:3.

(5648)
Carlson R S
Aggregate performance of mutual funds
JFQA 1970 MAR VOL 5 p 1-32.

(5649)
Friend I, Blume M E
Measurement of portfolio performance under uncertainty
AER 1970 SEP VOL 60 p 561-575.

(5650)
Gaumnitz J E
Appraising performance of investment portfolios
JF 1970 JUN VOL 25 p 555-560.

(5651)
Mills H D
On the measurement of fund performance
JF 1970 DEC VOL 25 p 1125-1132.

(5652)
Robinson R S
Measuring the risk dimension of investment performance
JF 1970 MAY VOL 25 p 455-468.

(5653)
Spitz A E
Mutual fund performance and cash inflows
AE 1970 AUG VOL 2 p 141-145.

(5654)
Bower R S, Wippern R F
Risk-return measurement in portfolio selection and performance appraisal models: progress report
JFQA 1969 DEC VOL 4 p 417-448.

(5655)
Simon J L
Does 'good portfolio management' exist?
MSci 1969 FEB VOL 15 p B308-B319.

(5656)
Smith K V, Tito D A
Risk-return measures of ex post portfolio performance
JFQA 1969 DEC VOL 4 p 449-472.

(5657)
Bank Administration Institute
Measuring the investment performance of pension funds
BAI, 1968.

(5658)
Bauman W S
Evaluation of prospective investment performance
JF 1968 MAY VOL 23 p 276-295.

(5659)
Cohen K J, Pogue J A
Some comments concerning mutual fund versus random portfolio performance
JB 1968 APR VOL 41 p 180-190.

(5660)
Dietz P O
Components of a measurement model: rate of return, risk and timing
JF 1968 MAY VOL 23 p 267-275.

(5661)
Jensen M C
The performance of mutual funds in the period 1945-64
JF 1968 MAY VOL 23 p 389-416.

(5662)
Levy R A
Measurement of investment performance
JFQA 1968 MAR VOL 3 p 35-57.

(5663)
Cohen K J, Elton E J
Inter-temporal portfolio analysis based on simulation of joint returns
MSci 1967 SEP VOL 13 p 5-18.

(5664)
Wood R N
Measurement of investment performance
Alexander, 1967..

(5665)**Dietz P O**
Pension funds: measuring investment performance
Free Pr, 1966.

(5666)
Horowitz I
The reward-to-variability ratio and mutual fund performance
JB 1966 OCT VOL 39 p 485-488.

(5667)
Jensen M C
Risk, the pricing of capital assets, and the evaluation of investment portfolios
JB 1966 APR VOL 42 p 167-247.

(5668)
Sharpe W F
Mutual fund performance
JB 1966 JAN VOL 39 p 119-138.

(5669)
Friend I, Vickers D
Portfolio selection and investment performance
JF 1965 SEP VOL 20 p 391-415.

(5670)
Horowitz I
A model for mutual fund evaluation
IMR 1965 SPRING VOL 6 p 81-92.

(5671)
Horowitz I
A rating of mutual fund managements' investment ability
IMR 1965 FALL VOL 7 p 65-76.

(5672)
Treynor J L
How to rate management of investment funds
HBR 1965 JAN-FEB VOL 43 p 63-75.

(5673)
Wood R N
Measuring the investment yield of pension funds
Alexander, 1965.

(5674)
Horowitz I
The varying (?) quality of investment trust
management
JASA 1963 DEC VOL 58 p 1011-1032.

(5675)
Horowitz I, Higgins H B
Some   factors   affecting   investment   fund
performance
QREB 1963 SPRING VOL 3 p 41-50.

(5676)
Mead S B
Mutual   fund   and   investment   company
performance in the 1950's
Mich St U Busn, 1962.

14.11 Performance-linked fees

(5677)
Cohen S I, Starks L T
Estimation risk and incentive contracts for
portfolio managers
MSci 1988 VOL 34 p 1067.

(5678)
Davanzo L E, Nesbitt S L
Performance fees for investment management
FAJ 1987 JAN-FEB VOL 43 p 14-20.

(5679)
Grinold R, Rudd A
Incentive fees: Who wins? Who loses?
FAJ 1987 JAN-FEB VOL 43 p 27-38.

(5680)
Kritzman M
Incentive fees: Some problems and some solutions
FAJ 1987 JAN-FEB VOL 43 p 21-26.

(5681)
Record E E, Tynan M A
Incentive fees: The basic issues
FAJ 1987 JAN-FEB VOL 43 p 39-43.

(5682)
Starks L T
Performance incentive fees: An agency theoretic
approach
JFQA 1987 MAR VOL 22 p 17-32.

(5683)
Modigliani F, Pogue G
Alternative   investment   performance   fee
arrangements and implications for SEC regulatory
policy
BellJ 1975 SPRING VOL 6:1 p 127-160.

(5684)
McWilliams J D
A closer look at incentive fees for bank managed
pension funds
JBR 1973 WINTER VOL 3:4 p 238-246.

(5685)
Williams G P Jr
An incentive plan for bank managed pension
funds
JBR 1971 SPRING VOL 2:1.

(5686)
Fiske H S
Performance fees: should a manager get a piece
of the action?
II 1968 MAR VOL 2 p 23ff.

14.2 Measuring market-timing

(5687)
Clarke R G, FitzGerald M T, Berent P
Market timing with imperfect information
FAJ 1989 NOV-DEC VOL 45 p 27-36.

(5688)
Kane A, Marks S G
Performance evaluation of market timers: Theory
and evidence
JFQA 1988 DEC VOL 23 p 425.

(5689)
Cumby R E, Modest D M
Testing for market timing ability: a framework for
forecast evaluation
JFE 1987 VOL 19 p 169-189.

(5690)
Admati A R
On timing and selectivity
JF 1986 JUL VOL 41:3 p 715-732

(5691)
Breen W, Jagannathan R, Ofer A R
Correcting for heteroscedasticity in tests for
market timing ability.
JB 1986 OCT VOL 59:4 p 585-598

(5692)
Jagannathan R, Korajczyk R A
Assessing the market timing performance of
managed portfolios
JB 1986 APR VOL 59:2 p 217-235.

(5693)
Chang E C, Lewellen W G
Market timing and mutual fund investment
performance
JB 1984 JAN VOL 57:1 p 57-72.

(5694)
Henriksson R D
Market timing and mutual fund performance : an
empirical investigation
JB 1984 JAN VOL 57:1 p 73-96.

(5695)
Kon S J
The market-timing performance of mutual fund
managers
JB 1983 JUL VOL 56:3 p 323-347.

(5696)
Veit E T, Cheney J M
Are mutual funds market timers?
JPM 1982 WINTER VOL 8:2 p 35-42.

(5697)
Henriksson R D, Merton R C
On market timing and investment performance 2.
Statistical procedures for evaluating forecasting
skills
JB 1981 OCT VOL 54:4 p 513-533.

(5698)
Merton R C
On market timing and investment performance. 1.
An equilibrium theory of value for market
forecasts
JB 1981 JUL VOL 54:3 p 363-406.

(5699)
Treynor J L, Mazuy K
Can mutual funds outguess the market?
HBR 1966 JUL-AUG VOL 44 p 131-136.

14.3 Forecasts of stock returns

(5700)
Dokko Y, Edelstein R H
How well do economists forecast stock market
prices? A study of the Livingston surveys
AER 1989 VOL 79:4 p 865-871.

(5701)
Hall T W, Tsay J J
An evaluation of the performance of portfolios
selected from Value Line rank one stocks
JFR 1988 FALL VOL 11:3 p 227-240.

(5702)
Tezel A
The Value Line stock rankings and the option
model implied standard deviations
JFR 1988 FALL VOL 11:3 p 215-226.

(5703)
Vander Weide J H, Carleton W T
Investor growth expectations: analysts vs. history
JPM 1988 SPRING VOL 14:3 p 78-83.

(5704)
Bowlin L, Rozeff M S
Do specialists' short sales predict returns?
JPM 1987 SPRING VOL 13:3 p 59-63.

(5705)
Muller F L, Fielitz B D
Standard & Poor's quality rankings revisited
JPM 1987 SPRING VOL 13:3 p 64-68.

(5706)
Dimson E, Marsh P
Event study methodologies and the size effect. The case of UK press recommendations
JFE 1986 SEP VOL 17:1 p 113-142.

(5707)
Dimson E, Marsh P
An analysis of brokers' and analysts' unpublished forecasts of UK stock returns
JF 1984 DEC VOL 39:5 p 1257-1292.

(5708)
Elton E J, Gruber M J, Gultekin M N
Professional expectations: accuracy and diagnosis of errors
JFQA 1984 DEC VOL 19:4 p 351-363

(5709)
Pearce D K
An empirical analysis of expected stock price movements
JMCB 1984 AUG VOL 16:3 p 317-327.

(5710)
Bjerring J H, Lakonishok J, Vermaelen T
Stock prices and financial analysts' recommendations
JF 1983 MAR VOL 38:1 p 187-204.

(5711)
Coggin T D
Problems in measuring the quality of investment information: The perils of the information coefficient
FAJ 1983 MAY-JUN VOL 39 p 25-34.

(5712)
Copeland T E, Mayers D
The Value Line enigma (1965-1978): A case study of performance evaluation issues
JFE 1982 NOV VOL 10:3 p 289-321.

(5713)
Ambachtsheer K P, Farrell J L
Can active management add value?
FAJ 1979 NOV-DEC VOL 35 p 39-48.

(5714)
Brown L D, Rozeff M S
Adaptive expectations time-series models and analyst forecast revision
JAR 1979 AUTUMN VOL 17:2 p 341-351

(5715)
Groth J C, Lewellen W G, Schlarbaum G G at al.
How good are brokers' recommendations?
FAJ 1979 JAN-FEB VOL 35:1 p 32-40.

(5716)
Groth J C
Investor objectives, stock recommendations, and abnormal returns
QREB 1978 VOL 18:2 p 55.

(5717)
Korschot B C
Measuring research analysts' performance
FAJ 1978 JUL-AUG p 41-46..

(5718) **Neave E H, Wiginton J C**
Evaluating security performance forecasts
MSci 1976 DEC VOL 23:4 p 371-379.

(5719)
Barnea A, Logue D E
Evaluating the forecasts of a security analyst
FIN MGMT 1973 SUMMER VOL 2 p 38.

(5720)
Kaplan R S, Weil R L
Risk and the Value Line contest
FAJ 1973 JUL-AUG VOL 29 p 56-62.

(5721)
Logue D E, Tuttle D
Brokerage house investment advice
FR 1973.

(5722)
Mastrapasqua F, Bolten S
A note on financial analyst evaluation
JF 1973 VOL 28 p 707.

(5723)
Ambachtsheer K P
Portfolio theory and the security analyst
FAJ 1972 NOV-DEC VOL 28 p 53-57.

(5724)
Firth M
The performance of share recommendations made
by investment analysts and the effects on market
efficiency
JBF 1972 SUMMER VOL 4 p 58.

(5725)
Neave E H, Nachman D C
The   framework   for   evaluating   securities
performance forecasts
JBR 1971 SUMMER VOL 2:2.

(5726)
Hausman W H
A note on "The Value Line contest: a test of the
predictability of stock price changes"
JB 1969 JUL VOL 42 p 317-320.

(5727)
Money Which
Share tipsters
Money Which 1968 SEP.

(5728)
Shelton J P
The   Value   Line   contest: a   test   of   the
predictibility of stock price changes
JB 1967 JUL VOL 40 p 251-269.

(5729)
Stoffels J D
Stock recommendations by investment advisory
services: immediate effects on market pricing
FAJ 1966 MAR-APR VOL 22 p 77-86.

(5730)
Colker S S
An   analysis   of   security   recommendations   by
brokerage houses
QREB 1963 SUMMER VOL 3 p 19-28.

(5731)
Ruff R T
The effect of selection & recommendation of a
stock of the month
FAJ 1963 MAR-APR VOL 19 p 41-43.

(5732)
Ferber R
Short-run effects of stock market services on
stock prices
JF 1958 MAR VOL 13 p 80-95.

(5733)
Cowles A
Stock market forecasting
Em 1944 JUL-OCT VOL 12 p 206-214.

(5734)
Cowles A
Can stock market forecasters forecast?
Em 1933 JUL.

15 Valuation of common stocks

(5735)
Fishman M J, Hagerty K M
Disclosure decisions by firms and the competition
for price efficiency
JF 1989 JUL VOL 44:3 p 633-646.

(5736)
Titman S, Warga A
Stock returns as predictors of interest rates and
inflation
JFQA 1989 MAR VOL 24:1 p 47-58.

(5737)
Desmond G M, Marcello J A
Handbook of small business valuation formulas
Marina del Rey, Ca.: Valuation Press, 1988.

(5738)
Fama E F, French K R
Permanent and temporary components of stock
prices
JPE 1988 APR VOL 96:2 p 246-273.

(5739)
Sherrerd K F ed.
Equity markets and valuation methods
Institute of Chartered Financial Analysts, 1988.

(5740)
Woolridge J R
Competitive decline: is a myopic stock market to
blame?
JACF 1988 SPRING VOL 1 p 26-36.

(5741)
Johnson L D
Growth prospects and share prices: a systematic
view
JPM 1987 WINTER VOL 13:2 p 58-60.

(5742)
Kane A, Marks S G
The rocking horse analyst
JPM 1987 SPRING VOL 13:3 p 32-37.

(5743)
Lee C J
Fundamental analysis and the stock market
JBFA 1987 SPRING VOL 14:1 p 131-141.

(5744)
Rappaport A
Stock market signals to managers
HBR 1987 NOV-DEC VOL 65:6 p 57-62.

(5745)
Kaufman R T, Jacoby R A
The stock market and the productivity slowdown:
international evidence
REStat 1986 VOL 68 p 18.

(5746)
Chugh L C, Meador J W
The stock valuation process; The analysts' view
FAJ 1984 NOV-DEC VOL 40 p 41-48.

(5747)
Huang R D, Kracaw W A
Stock market returns and real activity: a note
JF 1984 MAR VOL 39:1 p 267-273.

(5748)
Oppenheimer H R
A test of Ben Graham's stock selection criteria
FAJ 1984 SEP-OCT VOL 40:5 p 68-74.

(5749)
Varian H R
Nonparametric   tests   of   models   of
investor-behavior
JFQA 1983 SEP VOL 18:3 p 269-278

(5750)
Venezia I
A Bayesian approach to the optimal growth
period problem: a note
JF 1983 MAR VOL 38:1 p 237-246

(5751)
Vandell R F, Finn M T
Portfolio objective: win big, lose little!
JPM 1982 SUMMER VOL 8:4 p 37-45.

(5752)
Rappaport A
Selecting strategies that create shareholder value
HBR 1981 MAY-JUN VOL 59:3 p 139-149.

(5753)
Beaver W H, Lambert R, Morse D
The information content of security prices
JAE 1980 VOL p 3-28.

(5754)
Edesess M, Hambrecht G A
Scenario forecasting: necessity, not choice
JPM 1980 SPRING VOL 6:3 p 10-15.

(5755)
Stanley K L, Lewellen W G, Schlarbaum G G
Investor response' to investment research
JPM 1980 SUMMER VOL 6:4 p 20-27.

(5756)
Long M S, Racette G
Stochastic demand and the equity capitalization
rate
JBFA 1979 WINTER VOL 6:4 p 475-494.

(5757)
Ciccolo J
Money, equity values and income
JMCB 1978 FEB VOL 10:1 p 46-64.

(5758)
Fortune
The irrational one-tier stock market
F 1978 JUL 2 VOL 98 p 72-78.

(5759)
Schall L D, Kerr H S
The validity of existing capitalization methods
EE 1978 FALL VOL 24:1 p 29-35.

(5760)
Schweser C
Multidimensional security pricing: A correction
JFQA 1978 MAR VOL 13 p 177.

(5761)
Sennetti J T
On Bernoulli, Sharpe, financial risk and the St.
Petersburg paradox
JF 1976 VOL 31 p 960.

(5762)
Bernstein L A
In defense of fundamental investment analysis
FAJ 1975 JAN-FEB VOL 31 p 57-61.

(5763)
Firth M
Investment analysis: techniques of appraising the
British stock market
Har-Row, 1975.

(5764)
Pazner E A, Razin A
On expected value vs. expected future value
JF 1975 VOL 30 p 875.

(5765)
Foster E M
Common stock investment
Lexington Bks, 1974.

(5766)
Rubinstein M E
The fundamental theorem of parameter-preference
security valuation
JFQA 1973 JAN VOL 8:1 p 61-70.

(5767)
Beaver W H, Dukes R E
Interperiod tax allocation, earnings expectations
and the behavior of security prices
AR 1972 APR VOL 47 p 320-332.

(5768)
Elliott J W
Control, size, growth and financial performance in
the firm
JFQA 1972 JAN VOL 7 p 1309-1320.

(5769)
Slovic P
Psychological study of human judgment:
implications for investment decision making
JF 1972 SEP VOL 27 p 779-800.

(5770)
Slovic P, Fleissner D, Baumann W S
Analysing the use of information in investment
decision making: a methodological proposal
JB 1972 APR VOL 45 p 283-301..

(5771)**Mao J C T**
Security pricing in an imperfect capital market
JFQA 1971 SEP VOL 6 p 1105-1116.

(5772)
Smith R G E
Uncertainty, information and investment decisions
JF 1971 MAR VOL 26 p 67-82.

(5773)
Boness A J, Jen F C
A model of information diffusion, stock market
behavior, and equilibrium price
JFQA 1970 SEP VOL 5 p 279-296.

(5774)
Stitzel T E
Investing in intrastate issues of common stock
JFQA 1970 JAN VOL 4 p 697-706.

(5775)
Hubbard C L, Hawkins C A
Theory of valuation
Intext, 1969.

(5776)
West D A
The investor in a changing economy
P-H, 1968.

(5777)
Helfert E A
Valuation: concepts and practice
Wadsworth Pub, 1966.

(5778)
Robichek A A, Myers S C
Valuation of the firm: effects of uncertainty in the
market context
JF 1966 MAY VOL 21 p 215-227.

(5779)
Rose A M
A social psychological approach to the study of
the stock market
Kyk 1966 VOL 19 p 267-287.

(5780)
Hirschmann W B, Brauweiler J R
Investment analysis: coping with change
HBR 1965 MAY-JUN VOL 43 p 62-72.

(5781)
Gordon M J
Security and investment: theory and evidence
JF 1964 DEC VOL 19 p 607-618.

(5782)
Gordon M J
The investment, financing and valuation of the
corporation
Irwin, 1964.

(5783)
Ortner R
The concept of yield on common stock
JF 1964 MAY VOL 19 p 186-198.

(5784)
Lutz F A, Hague D C eds.
The theory of capital
Macmillan, 1963.

(5785)
Wyckoff P
The psychology of stock market timing
P-H, 1963.

(5786)
Gordon M J
The savings, investment and valuation of a
corporation
REStat 1962 FEB VOL 44 p 37-51.

(5787)
Gordon M J
Security and a financial theory of investment
QJE 1960 AUG VOL 74 p 472-492.

(5788)
Florence P S
Tests of the validity of some stock-exchange
folk-lore
Three Banks Review 1958 MAR VOL 37 p 3-20.

(5789)
Walker W B
A re-examination of common stocks as long term
investments
Anthoensen, 1954.

(5790)
Johnson L R, Shapiro E, O'Meara J
Valuation of closely-held stock for federal tax
purposes: approach to an objective method
University of Pennsylvania Law Review 1951
NOV VOL 100 p 166-195.

(5791)
Lutz F A, Lutz V C
The theory of investment of the firm
Princeton U Pr, 1951.

(5792)
Brown B
Common-stock price ratios and long-term interest rates
JB 1948 JUL VOL 21 p 180-182.

(5793)
Crum W S
Corporate size and earning power
Harvard U Pr, 1939.

(5794)
Williams J B
The theory of investment value
Harvard U Pr, 1938.

(5795)
Kulp C A
The discounting of dividends by the stock market
U of Pa Pr, 1924.

15.1 Determinants of stock prices

(5796)
Abowd J M
The effect of wage bargains on the stock market value of the firm
AER 1989 VOL 79:4 p 774-809.

(5797)
Arnott R D, Kelso C M Jr, Kiscadden S
Forecasting factor returns: an intriguing possibility
JPM 1989 FALL VOL 16:1 p 28-35.

(5798)
Bosch J-C, Hirschey M
The valuation effects of corporate name changes
FIN MGMT 1989 WINTER VOL 18 p 64-73.

(5799)
Emanuel D M
Asset revaluations and share price revisions
JBFA 1989 SPRING VOL 16:2 p 213.

(5800)
Jones R C
Group rotation from the bottom up
JPM 1989 SUMMER VOL 15:4 p 32-38.

(5801)
Leibowitz M L, Sorenson E H, Arnott R D
A total differential approach to equity duration
FAJ 1989 SEP-OCT VOL 45 p 30-37.

(5802)
Solt M E, Statman M
Good companies, bad stocks
JPM 1989 SUMMER VOL 15:4 p 39-44.

(5803)
Statman M, Sepe J F
Project termination announcements and the market value of the firm
FIN MGMT 1989 WINTER VOL 18 p 74-81.

(5804)
Zbesko J
Determinants of performance in the bull market
JPM 1989 WINTER VOL 15:2 p 38-44.

(5805)
Reinganum M R
The anatomy of a stock market winner
FAJ 1988 MAR-APR VOL 44 p 16-28.

(5806)
Reinganum M R
Selecting superior securities
Research Foundation of the Institute of Chartered Financial Analysts, 1988.

(5807)
Solt M E, Statman M
How useful is the sentiment index?
FAJ 1988 SEP-OCT VOL 44 p 45-55.

(5808)
Estep T
Security analysis and stock selection: turning financial information into return forecasts
FAJ 1987 JUL-AUG VOL 43 p 34-43.

(5809)
Senchak A J, Martin J D
The relative performance of the PSR and PER
investment strategies
FAJ 1987 MAR-APR VOL 43 p 46-56.

(5810)
Keim D B, Stambaugh R F
Predicting returns in the stock and bond markets.
JFE 1986 DEC VOL 17:2 p 357-390

(5811)
Litzenberger R H, Ronn E I
A utility-based model of common stock price
movements
JF 1986 MAR VOL 41:1 p 67-92.

(5812)
Oppenheimer H R
Ben Graham's net current asset values: A
performance update
FAJ 1986 MAR-APR VOL 42 p 40-47.

(5813)
Rappaport A
The affordable dividend approach to equity
valuation
FAJ 1986 JUL-AUG VOL 42 p 52-58.

(5814)
Shleifer A
Do demand curves for stocks slope down?
JF 1986 JUL VOL 41:3 p 579-590.

(5815)
Sorensen E H, Burke T
Portfolio returns from active industry group
rotation
FAJ 1986 SEP-OCT VOL 42 p 43-50.

(5816)
Arnott R D
The use and misuse of consensus earnings
JPM 1985 SPRING VOL 11:3 p 18-27.

(5817)
Arnott R D, Copeland W A
The business cycle and security selection
FAJ 1985 MAR-APR VOL 41 p 26-33.

(5818)
Eastaway N A, Booth H
Share valuation cases
Butterworth, 1985.

(5819)
Huang R D
Common stock returns and presidential elections
FAJ 1985 MAR-APR VOL 41 p 58-61.

(5820)
Morris V F
Central value in review
JPM 1985 FALL VOL 12:1 p 44-49.

(5821)
Pakes A
On patents R & D and the stock market rate of
return
JPE 1985 VOL 93 p 390.

(5822)
Bower R S, Bower D H
The Salomon brothers electric utility model :
Another challenge to market efficiency
FAJ 1984 SEP-OCT VOL 40:5 p 57-67.

(5823)
Casabona P A, Fabozzi F J, Francis J C
How to apply duration to equity analysis
JPM 1984 WINTER VOL 10:2 p 52-59..

(5824)**Gordon M J, Gould L I**
Comparison of the DCF and HPR measures of
the yield on common shares
FIN MGMT 1984 WINTER VOL 13 p 40-48.

(5825)
Granatelli A, Martin J D
Management quality and investment performance
FAJ 1984 NOV-DEC VOL 40 p 72-74.

(5826)
Kon S J
Models of stock returns - a comparison.
JF 1984 MAR VOL 39:1 p 147-165

(5827)
Shiller R J
Stock prices and social dynamics
Brookings Papers on Economic Activity 1984 NO
2 p 457-498.

(5828)
Brush J S, Boles K E
The predictive power in relative strength and CAPM
JPM 1983 SUMMER VOL 9:4 p 20-23.

(5829)
Fabozzi F J, Fonfeder R, Casabona P
An empirical examination of the impact of limited review on equity prices
JBFA 1983 VOL 10:1 p 127.

(5830)
Goodman D A, Peavy J W
Industry relative price-earnings ratios as indicators of investment returns
FAJ 1983 JUL-AUG VOL 39 p 60-66.

(5831)
Lerner E M, Theerathorn P
The returns of different investment strategies
JPM 1983 SUMMER VOL 9:4 p 26-28.

(5832)
Agmon T, Findlay M C
Domestic political risk and stock valuation
FAJ 1982 NOV-DEC VOL 38 p 74-76.

(5833)
Arbel A, Jaggi B
Market information assimilation related to extreme daily price jumps
FAJ 1982 NOV-DEC VOL 38 p 60-67.

(5834)
Bierman H Jr
Toward a constant price-earnings ratio
FAJ 1982 SEP-OCT VOL 38 p 62-65.

(5835)
Chance D M
Interest sensitivity and dividend yields
JPM 1982 WINTER VOL 8:2 p 69.

(5836)
Merrett A J, Newbould G D
CEPS: the illlusion of corporate growth
JPM 1982 FALL VOL 9:1 p 5-10.

(5837)
Rosenberg B
The current state and future of investment research
FAJ 1982 JAN-FEB p 43-51.

(5838)
Stancill J M
Does the market know your company's real worth?
HBR 1982 SEP-OCT VOL 60:5 p 42-50.

(5839)
Gipson J H
Investing in a zero sum economy
JPM 1981 SUMMER VOL 7:4 p 15-16.

(5840)
Piper T R, Fruhan W E
Is your stock worth its market price?
HBR 1981 MAY-JUN VOL 59:3 p 124-132.

(5841)
Joehnk M D, Petty J W III
The interest sensitivity of common stock prices
JPM 1980 WINTER VOL 6:4 p 19-25.

(5842)
Easman W S Jr, Falkenstein A, Weil R L
Sustainable income and stock returns
FAJ 1979 SEP-OCT p 44-49.

(5843)
Kirshner D, Udinsky J H
A comparison of relative predictive power for financial models of rates of return
JFQA 1979 JUN VOL 14 p 293.

(5844)
Beaver W H, Morse D
What determines price-earnings ratios?
FAJ 1978 JUL-AUG p 65-76.

(5845)
Boyd J H, Schonfeld E P
The effect of financial press advertising on stock prices
FIN MGMT 1977 SUMMER VOL 6 p 42.

(5846)
Kraft J, Kraft A
Determinants of common stock prices: a time series analysis
JF 1977 MAY VOL 32:2 p 417-426.

(5847)
Umstead D A
Forecasting stock market prices
JF 1977 MAY VOL 32:2 p 427-441.

(5848)
Burgess R C, Johnson K H
The effects of sampling fluctuations on the required inputs of security analysis
JFQA 1976 DEC VOL 11 p 847.

(5849)
Baker H K, Haslem J A
Toward the development of client-specified valuation models
JF 1974 VOL 29 p 1255.

(5850)
Bell F W
The relation of the structure of common stock prices to historical, expectational and industrial variables
JF 1974 VOL 29 p 187.

(5851)
Chung P S
An investigation of the firm effects influence in the analysis of earnings to price ratios of industrial common stocks
JFQA 1974 DEC VOL 9 p 1009.

(5852)
Haugen R A, Kumar P
The traditional approach to valuing levered-growth stocks
JFQA 1974 DEC VOL 9 p 1031.

(5853)
Cohen S, Smyth D J
Some determinants of price/earnings ratios of industrial common stock
QREB 1973 VOL 13:4 p 49.

(5854)
Dennis C N
An investigation into the effects of independent investor relations firms on common stock prices
JF 1973 VOL 28 p 373.

(5855)
Winkler R L
Bayesian models for forecasting future security prices
JFQA 1973 JUN VOL 8:3 p 387-406.

(5856)
Bierman H Jr, Hass J E
Normative stock price models
JFQA 1971 SEP VOL 6 p 1135-1146.

(5857)
Litzenberger R H, Joy O M, Jones C P
Ordinal predictions and the selection of common stocks
JFQA 1971 SEP VOL 6 p 1059-1068.

(5858)
Robichek A A, Bogue M C
A note on the behavior of expected price/earnings ratios over time
JF 1971 JUN VOL 26 p 731-736.

(5859)
Keenan W M
The state of the finance field methodology models of equity valuation: the great Serm bubble
JF 1970 MAY VOL 25 p 243-274.

(5860)
Bower R S, Bower D H
Risk and the valuation of common stock
JPE 1969 MAY-JUN VOL 77 p 349-362.

(5861)
Green P E, Maheshwari A
Common stock perception and preference: an application of multi-dimensional scaling
JB 1969 OCT VOL 42 p 439-457.

(5862)
Breen W J, Savage J
Portfolio distributions and tests of security selection models
JF 1968 DEC VOL 23 p 805-819.

(5863)
Nerlove M
Factors affecting differences among rates of return
on investments in individual common stocks
REStat 1968 AUG VOL 50 p 312-331.

(5864)
Niederhoffer V
Alphabetical properties of stock prices
FAJ 1968 MAR-APR VOL 24 p 105-111.

(5865)
Staubus G J
Earnings periods for common share analysis
JB 1968 OCT VOL 41 p 472-476.

(5866)
Ahlers D M
SEM: a security evaluation model
(in Cohen K J and Hammer F S eds., Analytical
methods in banking. Irwin, 1966.)

(5867)
Stevenson R A
The variability of common stock quality ratings
FAJ 1966 NOV-DEC VOL 22 p 97-101.

(5868)
Whitbeck V S, Kisor M
A new tool in investment decision-making
FAJ 1963 MAY-JUN VOL 19 p 55-62.

(5869)
Scott M F G
Relative share prices and yields
OEP 1962 OCT VOL 14 p 218-250.

(5870)
Benishay H
Variability in earnings-price ratios of corporate
equities
AER 1961 MAR VOL 51 p 81-94.

(5871)
Fisher G R
Some factors influencing share prices
EJ 1961 MAR VOL 71 p 121-141.

(5872)
Walter J E
A discriminant function for earnings-price ratios
of large industrial corporations
REStat 1959 FEB VOL 41 p 44-52.

(5873)
Morgan E V, Taylor C
The relationship between size of joint stock
companies and the yield of their shares
Ec 1957 VOL 24 p 116-127.

(5874)
Latane H A
Price changes in equity securities
JF 1954 SEP VOL 9 p 252-264.

15.11   Monetary policy and stock prices

(5875)
Foote W G
The rationality and efficiency of stock price
relative to money announcement information
FR 1989 MAY VOL 24:2 p 281-298.

(5876)
Schirm D C, Sheehan R G, Ferri M G
Financial market responses to Treasury debt
announcements
JMCB 1989 VOL 21 p 394-400..

(5877)**Bailey W**
Money supply announcements and the ex ante
volatility of asset prices
JMCB 1988 NOV VOL 20:4 p 611-620.

(5878)
Friedman M
Money and the stock market
JPE 1988 APR VOL 96:2 p 221-245.

(5879)
Hafer R W
The response of stock prices to changes in weekly
money and the discount rate
F R Bk St Louis Rev 1986 VOL 68:3.

(5880)
Loderer C, Lys T, Schweizer U
Daily monetary impulses and security prices
JME 1986 VOL 18 p 33.

(5881)
Solnik B H
Stock prices and monetary variables : The
international evidence
FAJ 1984 MAR-APR VOL 40:2 p 69-73.

(5882)
Pearce D K, Roley V V
The reaction of stock prices to unanticipated
changes in money : a note
JF 1983 SEP VOL 38:4 p 1323-1333.

(5883)
Davidson L S, Froyen R T
Monetary policy and stock returns: are stock
markets efficient?
F R Bk St Louis Rev 1982 VOL 64:3.

(5884)
Singh S P, Talwar P P
Monetary and fiscal policies and stock prices
JBFA 1982 SPRING VOL 9:1 p 75-91

(5885)
Sorensen E H
Rational expectations and the impact of money
upon stock prices.
JFQA 1982 DEC VOL 17:5 p 649-662.

(5886)
Rogalski R J, Vinso J D
Stock returns, money supply and the direction of
causality
JF 1977 VOL 32 p 1017.

(5887)
Wright F J
Monetary policy and the stock market
FAJ 1976 MAY-JUN VOL 32 p 27-34.

(5888)
Rozeff M S
The money supply and the stock market
FAJ 1975 SEP-OCT VOL 31 p 18-27.

(5889)
Cooper R V L
Efficient capital markets and the quantity theory
of money
JF 1974 VOL 29 p887.

(5890)
Gupta M C
Money supply and stock prices: A probabilistic
approach
JFQA 1974 JAN VOL 9 p 57.

(5891)
Rozeff M S
Money and stock prices: Market efficiency and the
lag in effect of monetary policy
JFE 1974 VOL 1 p 245.

(5892)
Budd A P, Litzenberger R H
Changes in the supply of money, the firm's
market value and cost of capital
JF 1973 VOL 28 p 49.

(5893)
Hamburger M J, Kochin L A
Money and stock prices: the channels of influence
JF 1972 MAY VOL 27 p 231-250.

(5894)
Homa K E, Jaffee D M
The supply of money and common stock
JF 1971 DEC VOL 26 p 1045-1066.

(5895)
Keran M W
Expectations, money and the stock market
F R Bk St Louis Rev 1971 JAN p 16-31.

(5896)
Sprinkel B W
Money and stock prices
Irwin, 1964.

15.2 Dividend-discount models

(5897)
Gordon D A, Gordon M J, Gould L I
Choice among methods of estimating share yield
JPM 1989 SPRING VOL 15:3 p 50-55.

(5898)
Timme S G, Eisemann P C
On the use of consensus forecasts of growth in the constant growth model: the case of electric utilities
FIN MGMT 1989 WINTER VOL 18 p 23-35.

(5899)
Darrat A F
On fiscal policy and the stock market
JMCB 1988 AUG VOL 20:3 p 353-363.

(5900)
Jacobs B I, Levy K N
On the value of " Value "
FAJ 1988 JUL-AUG VOL 44 p 47-62.

(5901)
Campbell J Y, Shiller R J
Cointegration and tests of present value models
JPE 1987 OCT VOL 95:5 p 1062-1088.

(5902)
Gurney R
Share valuation manual
Gower, 1987.

(5903)
Yagil J
Growth risk and the yield on common stocks in the context of the dividend-growth model
JBFA 1986 SUMMER VOL 13:2 p 251-256

(5904)
Donnelly B
The dividend model comes into its own
II 1985 MAR p 77-82.

(5905)
Estep P W
A new method for valuing common stocks
FAJ 1985 NOV-DEC VOL 41 p 26-34.

(5906)
Farrell J L
The dividend discount model: A primer
FAJ 1985 NOV-DEC VOL 41 p 16-25.

(5907)
Fielitz B D, Muller F L
A simplified approach to common stock valuation
FAJ 1985 NOV-DEC VOL 41 p 35-41.

(5908)
Michaud R O
A scenario-dependent dividend discount model: Bridging the gap between top-down investment information and bottom-up forecasts
FAJ 1985 NOV-DEC VOL 41 p 49-59.

(5909)
Rie D
How trustworthy is your valuation model?
FAJ 1985 NOV-DEC VOL 41 p 42-48.

(5910)
Scott L O
The present value model of stock prices: regression tests and Monte Carlo results
REStat 1985 VOL 67 p 599.

(5911)
Sorensen E H, Williamson D A
Some evidence on the value of dividend discount models
FAJ 1985 NOV-DEC VOL 41 p 60-69.

(5912)
Ferguson R, Lynn R
A security market plane approach to stock selection
FAJ 1984 SEP-OCT VOL 40:5 p 75-80.

(5913)
Fuller R J, Hsia C C
A simplified common stock valuation model
FAJ 1984 SEP-OCT VOL 40:5 p 49-56.

(5914)
Eastaway N A, Booth H
Practical share valuation
Butterworth, 1983.

(5915)
Estep T, Hanson N, Johnson C
Sources of value and risk in common stocks
JPM 1983 SUMMER VOL 9:4 p 5-13.

(5916)
Avera W, Fairchild B
On the use of security analysts' growth projections in the DCF model
(in Earnings regulation under inflation. Institute for Study of Regulation, Washington D.C., 1982.)

(5917)
Cragg J G, Malkiel B G
Expectations and the structure of share prices
U of Chicago Pr, 1982.

(5918)
Michaud R O, Davis P L
Valuation model bias and the scale structure of
dividend discount returns
JF 1982 MAY VOL 37:2 p 563-573

(5919)
Smith G
A simple model for estimating intrinsic value
JPM 1982 SUMMER VOL 8:4 p 46.

(5920)
McWilliams J D, Wei J
Some like to-matoes and some like to-matoes
JPM 1981 SUMMER VOL 7:4 p 43-47

(5921)
Fouse W L
Risk and liquidity revisited
FAJ 1977 JAN-FEB p 40-45.

(5922)
Hagaman T C, Jensen A E
Investment value: a reference point for analysts
FAJ 1977 MAR-APR p 63.

(5923)
Fouse W L
Risk and liquidity: The keys to stock price
behavior
FAJ 1976 MAY-JUN VOL 32 p 35-45.

(5924)
Granger C W J
Some consequences of the valuation model when
expectations are taken to be optimum forecasts
JF 1975 VOL 30 p 135.

(5925)
Jahnke W W
The growth stock mania revisited
FAJ 1975 JAN-FEB VOL 31 p 42-44.

(5926)
Jahnke W W
What's behind stock prices?
FAJ 1975 SEP-OCT VOL 31 p 69-76.

(5927)
Stone B K
The conformity of stock values based on
discounted dividends to a fair-return process
BellJ 1975 Vol 6:2 p 698-702.

(5928)
Taylor W
A note on Mao's growth stock-investment
opportunities approach
JF 1974 VOL 29 p 1573.

(5929)
Warren J M
A note on the algebraic equivalence of the Holt
and Malkiel models of share valuation
JF 1974 VOL 29 p 1007..

(5930)Jahnke W W
The growth stock mania
FAJ 1973 MAY-JUN VOL 29 p 65-69.

(5931)
Bierman H Jr, Downes D H, Hass J E
Closed-form stock price models
JFQA 1972 JUN VOL 7 p 1797-1808.

(5932)
Bower D H, Bower R S
Test of a stock valuation model
JF 1970 MAY VOL 25 p 483-492.

(5933)
Malkiel B G, Cragg J G
Expectations and the structure of share prices
AER 1970 SEP VOL 60 p 601-617.

(5934)
Merrett A J
Valuation of ordinary shares
Gower, 1970.

(5935)
Hakansson N H
On the dividend capitalization model under
uncertainty
JFQA 1969 MAR VOL 4 p 65-87.

(5936)
Bierman H Jr
The growth period decision
MSci 1968 FEB VOL 14 p B302-B309.

(5937)
Sloane W R, Reisman A
Stock   evaluation   theory: classification,
reconciliation and general model
JFQA 1968 JUN VOL 3 p 171-203.

(5938)
Mao J C T
The valuation of growth stocks
JF 1966 MAR VOL 21 p 95-102.

(5939)
Soldofsky R M
The industry of bond tables and stock valuation
models
JF 1966 MAR VOL 21 p 103-111.

(5940)
Bosland C C
Valuation theories and decisions of the Securities
and Exchange Commission
Simmons-B, 1964.

(5941)
Malkiel B G
Equity yields, growth and the structure of share
prices
AER 1963 DEC VOL 53 p 1004-1031.

(5942)
Holt C C
The influence of growth duration on share prices
JF 1962 SEP VOL 17 p 465-475.

(5943)
Clendenin J C
Theory and technique of growth stock valuation
UCLA Busn, 1957.

(5944)
Durand D
Growth stocks and the Petersburg paradox
JF 1957 SEP VOL 12 p 348-363.

(5945)
Clendenin J C, Van Cleave M
Growth and common stock values
JF 1954 SEP VOL 9 p 365-376.

(5946)
Eiteman W J, Smith F P
Common stock values and yields
U of Mich Pr, 1953.

15.3   Valuation of the market

(5947)
Asprem M
Stock prices, asset portfolios and macroeconomic
variables in ten European countries
JBankF 1989 SEP VOL 13:4-5 p 589-612.

(5948)
Cutler D M, Poterba J M, Summers L H
What moves stock prices?
JPM 1989 SPRING VOL 15:3 p 4-12.

(5949)
Gray W S
The anatomy of a stock market forecast
JPM 1989 FALL VOL 16:1 p 36-44.

(5950)
Harvey C R
Forecasts of economic growth from the bond and
stock market
FAJ 1989 SEP-OCT VOL 45 p 38-45.

(5951)
Wasserfallen W
Macroeconomic news and the stock market:
evidence from Europe
JBankF 1989 SEP VOL 13:4-5 p 613-626.

(5952)
McMillin W D, Laumas G S
The impact of anticipated and unanticipated
policy actions on the stock market
AE 1988 MAR VOL 20:3 p 375-384.

(5953)
Pindyck R S
Risk aversion and determinants of stock market
behavior
REStat 1988 VOL 70 p 183.

(5954)
Sorensen E H, Arnott R D
The risk premium and stock market performance
JPM 1988 SUMMER VOL 14:4 p 50-55.

(5955)
Chua J H, Woodward R S, To E C
Potential gains from stock market timing in
Canada
FAJ 1987 SEP-OCT VOL 43 p 50-56.

(5956)
Giovannini A, Jorion P
Interest rates and risk premia in the stock market
and in the foreign exchange market
JIMF 1987 MAR VOL 6:1 p 107-124.

(5957)
Bolten S E, Long S W
A note on cyclical and dynamic aspects of stock
market price cycles
FR 1986 FEB VOL 21:1.

(5958)
Cox W M
Government debt and the stock market
F R Bk Dallas Ec Rev 1986 SEP.

(5959)
Mankiw N G
The equity premium and the concentration of
aggregate shocks
JFE 1986 VOL 17 p 211.

(5960)
Pferfer P E
Market timing and risk reduction
JFQA 1985 DEC VOL 20:4 p 451-459.

(5961)
Renshaw E F
A risk premium model for market timing
JPM 1985 SUMMER VOL 11:4 p 33-35.

(5962)
Scott L O
The stationarity of the conditional mean of real
rates of return on common stocks: an empirical
investigation
JFQA 1984 JUN VOL 19:2 p 217-230.

(5963)
Shiller R J
Theories of aggregate stock price movements
JPM 1984 WINTER VOL 10:2 p 28-37.

(5964)
Klemkosky R C, Jun K W
The monetary impact on return variability and
market risk premia.
JFQA 1982 DEC VOL 17:5 p 663-681.

(5965)
Blanchard O J
Output, the stock market and interest rates
AER 1981 VOL 71 p 132-143.

(5966)
Luksetich W A, Riley W B
The market prefers republicans: Myth or reality
JFQA 1980 SEP VOL15 p 541.

(5967)
Merton R C
On estimating the expected return on the market:
An exploratory investigation
JFE 1980 VOL 8 p 323-361.

(5968)
Grant D
Market timing and portfolio management
JF 1978 VOL 33 p 1119.

(5969)
Hess A C
The riskless rate of interest and the market price
of risk: A correction
QJE 1978 VOL 92 p 689.

(5970)
McWilliams J D
The benefits and costs of timing equity
investments
JBR 1976 SPRING VOL 7:1.

(5971)
Hess A C
Interest and the market price of risk
QJE 1975 VOL 89 p 444.

(5972)
Sharpe W F
Likely gains from market timing
FAJ 1975 MAR-APR VOL 31 p 60-69.

(5973)
Apilado V P, Heathcotte B
The predictive content of some leading economic
indicators for future stock prices
JFQA 1974 MAR VOL 9 p 247.

(5974)
McDonald J G, Osborne A E Jr
Forecasting the market return on common stocks
JBFA 1974 SUMMER VOL 1:2 p 217-238.

(5975)
Jennings E H, Soldofsky R M
Risk-premium curves: empirical evidence on their
changing positions, 1950 to 1970
QREB 1973 VOL 13:1 p 49.

(5976)
Makridakis S G, Wheelwright S C
World events and their non-influence on stock
prices
JBF 1972 WINTER VOL 4:4 p 10-14.

(5977)
Niederhoffer V
The analysis of world events and stock prices
JB 1971 APR VOL 44 p 193-219.

(5978)
Walsh C F, Simonton G
The confidence index as a stock market indicator
JBR 1971 SUMMER VOL 2:2.

(5979)
Arena J J
Postwar stock market changes and consumer
spending
REStat 1965 NOV VOL 47 p 379-391.

(5980)
Cottle S, Whitman W T
Corporate earning power and market valuation,
1935-1955
Duke, 1959.

(5981)
Lamberton D L
Economic growth and stock prices: the Australian
experience
JB 1958 JUL VOL 31 p 200-212.

(5982)
Friend I, Parker S
A new slant on the stock market
F 1956 SEP VOL 68..

(5983)**Solomon E**
Economic growth and common-stock value
JB 1955 JUL VOL 28 p 213-221.

16 Accounting information and valuation

(5984)
Castagna A D, Matolcsy Z P
The marginal information content of selected
items in financial statements
JBFA 1989 SUMMER VOL 16:3 p 317.

(5985)
Barlev B, Denny W, Levy H
Using accounting data for portfolio management
JPM 1988 SPRING VOL 14:3 p 70-77.

(5986)
Bernstein L A
Financial statement analysis: theory, application
and interpretation. 4th ed
Irwin, 1988.

(5987)
Estep T
Security analysis and stock selection: turning
financial information into return forecasts
FAJ 1987 JUL-AUG VOL 43 p 34-43.

(5988)
Foster G
Financial statement analysis. 2nd ed
P-H, 1986.

(5989)
Rappaport A
Creating shareholder value: the new standard for
business performance
Free Pr, 1986.

(5990)
Gombola M J, Ketz J E
A caveat on measuring cash flow and solvency
FAJ 1983 SEP-OCT VOL 39 p 66-72.

(5991)
Barlev B, Levy H
The information content of accounting data and
the management of security portfolios
JBFA 1981 SUMMER VOL 8:2 p 221-248.

(5992)
Barth J R, Cordes J J
Optimal financial disclosure with and without
SEC regulation
QREB 1980 SPRING VOL 20:1 p 30-41

(5993)
Emmanuel C R, Pick R H
The predictive ability of U K segment reports
RBFA 1980 SUMMER VOL 7:2 p 201-218.

(5994)
Ball R J, Watts R
Some additional evidence on survival biases
JF 1979 MAR VOL 34:1 p 197-206

(5995)
Ohlson J A
Risk, return, security-valuation and the stochastic
behavior of accounting numbers
JFQA 1979 JUN VOL 14 p 317.

(5996)
Bernstein P W
Competition comes to accounting
F 1978 JUL 1 VOL 98 p 88-96.

(5997)
Foster T W, Vickrey D
The incremental information content of the 10-K
AR 1978 OCT VOL 53:4 p 921-934.

(5998)
Kaplan R S
The information content of financial numbers: A
survey of empirical evidence
(in Abdel-Khalik A R and Keller T F eds.,
Impact of accounting research on practice and
disclosure. Duke U Pr, 1978.)

(5999)
Lev B
Financial statement analysis
P-H, 1978.

(6000)
Spicer B H
Market risk, accounting data and companies'
pollution control records
JBFA 1978 SPRING VOL 5:1 p 67-84.

(6001)
Walker E W, Petty J W
Financial differences between large and small
firms
FIN MGMT 1978 WINTER VOL 7 p 61.

(6002)
Winsen J K
A reformulation of the API approach to
evaluating accounting income numbers
JFQA 1977 SEP VOL 12 p 499.

(6003)
Brandon C H, Jarrett J E
Evaluating accounting forecasts
JBFA 1976 AUTUMN VOL 3:3 p 67-78.

(6004)
Gonedes N J
Information-production and capital market
equilibrium
JF 1975 VOL 30 p 841.

(6005)
Kennedy H A
A behavioral study of the usefulness of four
financial ratios
JAR 1975 SPRING VOL 13:1 p 97-116.

(6006)
Emery J T
Efficient capital markets and the information
content of accounting numbers
JFQA 1974 MAR VOL 9 p 139.

(6007)
Marcis R G, Smith V K
Efficient estimation of multivariate financial
relationships
JF 1974 VOL 29 p 1415.

(6008)
Davis E G, Dunn D M, Williams W H
Ambiguities in the cross-section analysis of per
share financial data
JF 1973 VOL 28 p 1241.

(6009)
Patz D H, Boatzman J R
Accounting principle formulation in an efficient
markets environment
JAR 1972 AUTUMN VOL 10:2 p 392-403.

(6010)
Murphy J E Jr, Nelson J R
Random and nonrandom relationships among
financial variables: a financial model
JFQA 1971 MAR VOL 6 p 875-886.

(6011)
Whittington G
The prediction of profitability and other studies
of company behaviour
Cambridge U Pr, 1971.

(6012)
Pankoff L D, Virgil R L
Some preliminary findings from a laboratory
experiment on the usefulness of financial
accounting information to security analysts
ERA 1970 p 1-61.

(6013)
Theil H
The use of information theory concepts in the
analysis of financial statements
MSci 1969 MAY VOL 15 p 459-481.

(6014)
Singh A, Whittington G
Growth, profitability and valuation: a study of
United Kingdom quoted companies
Cambridge U Pr, 1968.

16.1 Accounting standards

(6015)
Dhaliwal D S
The effect of the firm's business risk on the
choice of accounting methods
JBFA 1988 SUMMER VOL 15:2 p 289.

(6016)
Worthy F S
Manipulating profits : how it's done
F 1984 JUN 25 VOL 109:13 p 34-38

(6017)
Zeghal D
Firm size and the informational content of
financial statements
JFQA 1984 SEP VOL 19:3 p 299-310.

(6018)
Zeghal D
Timeliness of accounting reports and their
informational content on the capital market
JBFA 1984 AUTUMN VOL 11:3 p 367-380

(6019)
Buzby S L, Falk H
Demand for social responsibility information by
university investors
AR 1979 JAN VOL 54:1 p 23-37.

(6020)
Collins D W, Simonds R R
SEC line-of-business disclosure and market risk
adjustments
JAR 1979 AUTUMN VOL 17:2 p 352-383.

(6021)
Lev B
The impact of accounting regulation on the stock
market: the case of oil and gas companies
AR 1979 JUL VOL 54:3 p 485-503.

(6022)
Gonedes N J
Corporate signaling external accounting and
capital market equilibrium: evidence on dividends
income and extraordinary items
JAR 1978 SPRING VOL 16:1 p 26-79.

(6023)
Harrison T
Different market reactions to discretionary and
nondiscretionary accounting changes
JAR 1977 SPRING VOL 15:1 p 84-107.

(6024)
Horwitz B, Kolodny R
Line of business reporting and security prices: an
analysis of an SEC disclosure rule
BellJ 1977 SPRING VOL 8:1 p 234-249.

(6025)
Watts R L
Corporate financial statements, a product of the
market and political processes
AJM 1977 VOL 2 p 53-75.

(6026)
Wright W F
Financial information processing models: an
empirical study
AR 1977 JUL VOL 52:3 p 676-689.

(6027)
Cassidy D B
Investor evaluation of accounting information:
some additional empirical evidence
JAR 1976 AUTUMN VOL 14:2 p 212-229.

(6028)
Deakin E B
Accounting reports, policy interventions and the
behavior of securities returns
AR 1976 JUL VOL 51:3 p 590-603.

(6029)
Stanga K G
Disclosure in published annual reports
FIN MGMT 1976 WINTER VOL 5 p 42.

(6030)
Eskew R K
An examination of the association between
accounting and share price data in the extractive
petroleum industry
AR 1975 APR VOL 50:2 p 316-324.

(6031)
Falk H, Ophir T
The influence of differences in accounting policies
on investment decisions
JAR 1973 SPRING VOL 11:1 p 108-116.

(6032)
Gonedes N J
Efficient capital markets and external accounting
AR 1972 JAN VOL 47.

(6033)
Spacek L
Business success requires an understanding of
unsolved problems of accounting and financial
reporting
Address presented at Harvard U, Sep 1959.

16.11   Effect of changes in accounting standards

(6034)
Knight R F, Affleck-Graves J F
Further evidence on the market reponse to LIFO
adoptions
JBFA 1988 SUMMER VOL 15:2 p 169-184.

(6035)
Brownlee E R ed.
The impact of FAS 87 on investment analysis and
portfolio management
Institute of Chartered Financial Analysts, 1987..

(6036)**Garlicki T D, Fabozzi F J, Fonfeder R**
The impact of earnings under FASB 52 on equity
returns
FIN MGMT 1987 AUTUMN VOL 16 p 36-44.

(6037)
Finnerty J D
The stock market's reaction to the switch from
flow-through to normalization
FIN MGMT 1982 WINTER VOL 11 p 36-47.

(6038)
Gheyara K, Boatsman J
Market reaction to the 1976 replacement cost
disclosures
JAE 1980 AUG VOL 2 p 107-126.

(6039)
Watts R L, Zimmerman J L
On the irrelevance of replacement cost disclosures
for security prices
JAE 1980 AUG VOL 2 p 98-106.

(6040)
Abdel-Khalik A R, McKeown C
Understanding accounting changes in an efficient
market: evidence of differential reaction
AR 1978 OCT VOL 53:4 p 851-868.

(6041)
Hong H, Kaplan R S, Mandelker G
Pooling vs. purchase: the effects of accounting for
mergers on stock prices
AR 1978 JAN VOL 53:1 p 31-47.

(6042)
Ng D S, Winsen J
Investor behavior and changes in accounting
methods
JFQA 1976 DEC VOL 11 p 873.

(6043)
Ortman R F
The effects on investment analysis of alternative
reporting procedure for diversified firms
AR 1975 APR VOL 50:2 p 298-304.

(6044)
Sunder S
Stock price and risk related to accounting changes
in inventory valuation
AR 1975 APR VOL 50:2 p 305-315.

(6045)
Kaplan R S, Roll R
Accounting changes and stock prices
FAJ 1973 JAN-FEB VOL 29 p 48-53.

(6046)
Ball R J
Risk, return and disequilibrium: an application to
changes in accounting techniques
JF 1972 MAY VOL 27 p 343-354.

(6047)
Kaplan R S, Roll R
Investor evaluation of accounting information:
some empirical evidence
JB 1972 APR VOL 45 p 225-257.

(6048)
Gonedes N J
Some evidence on investor actions and accounting
messages [Parts 1-2]
AR 1971 APR VOL 46 p 320-328; AR 1971 JUL
VOL 46 p 535-551.

(6049)
Mlynarczyk F A Jr
An empirical study of accounting methods and
stock prices
ERA 1969 p 63-89.

(6050)
Benston G J
Published corporate accounting data and stock
prices
ERA 1967 p 1-54.

(6051)
Jensen R E
An experimental design for study of effects of
accounting variations in decision making
JAR 1966 AUTUMN VOL 4 p 224-238.

(6052)
Jaenicke H R
Management's choice to purchase or pool
AR 1962 OCT VOL 37 p 758-765.

16.111   Inflation accounting

(6053)
Mahapatra S, Chase M J, Rodgers W
Information interaction effects of inflation adjusted accounting data on individual decision-maker's sophistication and risk preference
JBFA 1989 WINTER VOL 16:5 p 635.

(6054)
Dharan B G
The association between corporate dividends and current cost disclosures
JBFA 1988 SUMMER VOL 15:2 p 215-230.

(6055)
Brayshaw R E, Miro A R O
The information content of inflation-adjusted financial statements
JBFA 1985 VOL 12:2 p 249.

(6056)
Bar-Yosef S, Lev B
Historical cost earnings versus inflation-adjusted earnings in the dividend decision
FAJ 1983 MAR-APR VOL 39 p 41-51.

(6057)
Beaver W H, Griffin P A, Landsman W R
How well does replacement cost income explain stock return?
FAJ 1983 MAR-APR VOL 39 p 26-32.

(6058)
Ketz J E
Are constant dollar disclosures informative?
FAJ 1983 MAR-APR VOL 39 p 52-55.

(6059)
Morris M H, McDonald B
Asset pricing and financial reporting with changing prices
JBFA 1982 AUTUMN VOL 9:3 p 383.

(6060)
Beaver W H
Interpreting disclosures of the effects of changing prices
FAJ 1981 SEP-OCT VOL 37 p 45-56.

(6061)
Ro B T
The disclosure of replacement cost accounting data and its effects on transaction volumes
AR 1981 JAN VOL 56:1 p 70-84.

(6062)
Beaver W H
Accounting for inflation in an efficient market
International Journal of Accounting 1979 p 21-42.

(6063)
Brooks L D, Buckmaster D
The impact of price changes on accounting incomes: Holding gains and losses on monetary assets and liabilities
FIN MGMT 1977 AUTUMN VOL 6 p 60.

(6064)
Brooks L D, Buckmaster D
The impact of price changes on accounting income
FIN MGMT 1975 SPRING VOL 4 p 32.

(6065)
Smith R E, Reilly F K
Price-level accounting and financial analysis
FIN MGMT 1975 SUMMER VOL 4 p 21.

(6066)
Heintz J A
Price level restated: financial statements and investment decision making
AR 1973 OCT VOL 48:4 p 679-689.

16.112   Accounting for international transactions

(6067)
Prodhan B K
Geographical segment disclosure and multinational risk profile
JBFA 1986 SPRING VOL 13:1 p 15-37

(6068)
Beaver W H, Wolfson M
Foreign currency translation gains and losses: What effect do they have and what do they mean?
FAJ 1984 MAR-APR VOL 40 p 28-37.

(6069)
Wyman H E
Analysis of gains or losses from foreign monetary items: an application of purchasing power parity concepts
AR 1976 JUL VOL 51:3 p 545-558.

(6070)
Aliber R Z, Stickney C P
Accounting measures of foreign exchange exposure: the long and short of it
AR 1975 JAN VOL 50:1 p 44-57.

16.12 Auditing

(6071)
Craswell A T
Studies of the information content of qualified audit reports
JBFA 1985 VOL 12:1 p 93.

(6072)
Shevlin T J, Whittred G
Audit qualifications and share prices: Further evidence
AJM 1984 JUN VOL 9 p 37-52.

(6073)
Watts R L, Zimmerman J L
Agency problems, auditing, and the theory of the firm: some evidence
JLE 1983 VOL 26:3 p 613-634.

(6074)
DeAngelo L
Auditor independence, "low bailing", and disclosure regulation
JAE 1981 VOL 3 p 113-127.

(6075)
Firth M
Qualified audit reports and bank lending decisions
JBR 1979 WINTER VOL 9:4.

(6076)
Firth M
Qualified audit reports: their impact on investment decisions
AR 1978 JUL VOL 53:3 p 642-650.

(6077)
Ng D S
An information economics analysis of financial reporting and external auditing
AR 1978 OCT VOL 53:4 p 910-920.

(6078)
Schwarzbach H
The role of independent audit reports in commercial bank business loan decision making: a study of Rhode Island banks
JBR 1978 WINTER VOL 8:4.

(6079)
Lavin D, Libby R
The effect of the perceived independence of the auditor on the loan decision
JBR 1977 SUMMER VOL 8:2.

(6080)
Carpenter C G, Strawser R H
Displacement of auditors when clients go public
Journal of Accountancy 1971 p 55-58.

(6081)
Burton J C, Roberts W
A study of auditor changes
Journal of Accountancy 1967 p 31-36.

16.2 Accounting earnings

(6082)
Silhan P A
Using quarterly sales and margins to predict corporate earnings: a time-series perspective
JBFA 1989 SPRING VOL 16:1 p 131.

(6083)
Arnott R D
The use and misuse of consensus earnings
JPM 1985 SPRING VOL 11:3 p 18-27.

(6084)
Harl J E, Bresser R K
On the assessment of corporate productivity changes and their impact on financial performance
Omega 1984 VOL 12:4 p 363-370

(6085)
Hawkins E H, Chamberlin S C, Daniel W E
Earnings expectations and security prices
FAJ 1984 SEP-OCT VOL 40:5 p 24-38.

(6086)
Brandon C H, Jarrett J, Khumuwala S
On the predictability of growth in earnings per
share
JBFA 1983 AUTUMN VOL 10:3 p 373-388

(6087)
Rosen S
Authority, control and the distribution of earnings
BellJ 1982 AUTUMN VOL 13:2 p 311.

(6088)
Watts R L
Does it pay to manipulate EPS?
CFQ 1982 SPRING VOL 1 p 8-26..

(6089)**Lee C F, Zumwalt J K**
Associations between alternative accounting
profitability measures and security returns
JFQA 1981 MAR VOL 16:1 p 71-93.

(6090)
Black F
The magic in earnings: Economic earnings versus
accounting earnings
FAJ 1980 NOV-DEC VOL 36 p 19-25.

(6091)
Beaver W H, Clarke R, Wright W F
The association between unsystematic security
returns and the magnitude of earnings forecast
errors.
JAR 1979 AUTUMN VOL 17:2 p 316-340.

(6092)
Bernstein L A, Siegel J G
The concept of earnings quality
FAJ 1979 JUL-AUG VOL 35 p 72-78.

(6093)
Ehrbar A F
Unraveling the mysteries of corporate profits
F 1979 AUG 27 VOL 100:4 p 90-96

(6094)
Spraakman G P
The sensitivity of earnings per share growth to
some of its financial components
FIN MGMT 1979 WINTER VOL 6 p 41.

(6095)
Hagaman T C, Marks H J
Earnings stability: key to the equity market
JBR 1975 AUTUMN VOL 6:3.

(6096)
Shank J K, Burnell M
Smooth your earnings growth rate
HBR 1974 JAN-FEB VOL 52:1 p 136-141.

(6097)
Stern J M
Earnings per share don't count
FAJ 1974 JUL-AUG VOL 30 p 39-43.

(6098)
Bernstein P L
Advice to managers: watch earnings, not the
ticker tape
HBR 1973 JAN-FEB VOL 51:1 p 63-69.

(6099)
Bodenhorn D
A cash-flow concept of profit
JF 1964 MAR VOL 19 p 16-31.

(6100)
Fellner W
Profit as the risk-taker's surplus: a probabilistic
theory
REStat 1963 MAY VOL 45 p 173-184.

16.21 Measurement of earnings

(6101)
Craig D, Johnson G, Joy M
Accounting methods and P/E ratios
FAJ 1987 MAR-APR VOL 43 p 41-45.

(6102)
King R D
The effect of convertible bond equity values on
dilution and leverage
AR 1984 JUL VOL 59:3 p 419-431.

(6103)
Siegel J G
The "quality of earnings" concept - a survey
FAJ 1982 MAR-APR p 60-68.

(6104)
Beaver W H, Demski J S
The nature of income measurement
AR 1979 JAN VOL 54:1 p 38-46.

(6105)
Rice S J
The information content of fully diluted earnings
per share
AR 1978 APR VOL 53:2 p 429-438.

(6106)
Kratchman S H, Malcolm R E et al.
An intra industry comparison of alternative
income concepts and relative performance
evaluations
AR 1974 OCT VOL 49:4 p 682-689.

(6107)
Beaver W H, Dukes R E
Interperiod tax allocation, earnings expectations
and the behavior of security prices
AR 1972 APR VOL 47 p 320-332.

(6108)
Treynor J L
The trouble with earnings
FAJ 1972 SEP-OCT VOL 28 p 41-43.

(6109)
Simmons J K, Gray J
An investigation of the effect of differing
accounting frameworks on the prediction of net
income
AR 1969 OCT VOL 44 p 757-776.

(6110)
Werner F
A study of the predictive significance of two
income measures
JAR 1969 SPRING VOL 7 p 123-136.

(6111)
Greenball M N
Evaluation of the usefulness to investors of
different accounting estimators of earnings: a
simulation approach
ERA 1968 p 27-58.

16.22 Behavior of earnings

(6112)
Roberts C B
Forecasting earnings using geographical segment
data: some UK evidence
Journal of International Financial Management &
Accounting 1989 SUMMER VOL 1:2 p 130-151.

(6113)
Schwalbach J, Grasshoff U, Mahmood T
The dynamics of corporate profits
EER 1989 VOL 33 p 1625.

(6114)
Bathke A W
The relationship between time-series models and
the security market's expectation of quarterly
earnings
AR 1984 APR VOL 59:2 p 163-176.

(6115)
Lev B
Some economic determinants of time-series
properties of earnings
JAE 1983 APR VOL 5 p 31-48.

(6116)
Eckel N
An EPS forecasting model utilizing
macroeconomic performance expectations
FAJ 1982 MAY-JUN p 68.

(6117)
Firth M
Some time series properties of corporate earnings
in New Zealand: a note
JBFA 1982 AUTUMN VOL 9:3 p 353-359

(6118)
Hopwood W S, McKeown J C, Newbold P
Power transformations in time-series models of
quarterly earnings per share
AR 1981 OCT VOL 56:4 p 927-933.

(6119)
Khumawala S B, Polhemus N W, Liao W M
The predictability of quarterly cash flows
JBFA 1981 WINTER VOL 8:4 p 493-510.

(6120)
Brooks L D, Buckmaster D
First difference signals and accounting income
time series properties
JBFA 1980 AUTUMN VOL 7:3 p 437-454.

(6121)
Chant P D
On the predictability of earnings per share
behavior
JF 1980 MAR VOL 35:1 p 13-29.

(6122)
Deschamps B, Mehta D R
Predictive ability and descriptive validity of
earnings forecasting models
JF 1980 SEP VOL 35:4 p 933-949.

(6123)
Ruland W
On the choice of simple extrapolative model
forecasts of annual earnings
FIN MGMT 1980 SUMMER VOL 9 p 30.

(6124)
Brown L D, Rozeff M S
The predictive value of interim reports for
improving forecasts of future quarterly earnings
AR 1979 JUL VOL 54:3 p 585-591.

(6125)
Brown L D, Rozeff M S
Univariate time-series models of quarterly
accounting earnings per share: a proposed model
JAR 1979 SPRING VOL 17:1 p 179-189.

(6126)
Lorek K S
Predicting annual net earnings with quarterly
earnings time-series models
JAR 1979 SPRING VOL 17:1 p 190-204.

(6127)
Ruland W
The time series of earnings for forecast reporting
and nonreporting firms
JBFA 1979 SUMMER VOL 6:2 p 187-201

(6128)
Lorek K S, McKeown J C
The effect on predictive ability of reducing the
number of observations on a time-series analysis
of quarterly earnings data
JAR 1978 SPRING VOL 16:1 p 204-214.

(6129)
Albrecht W S, Lookabill L L, McKeown J C
The time series properties of annual earnings
JAR 1977 AUTUMN VOL 15:2 p 226-244.

(6130)
Salamon G L, Smith E D
Additional evidence on the time series properties
of reported earnings per share
JF 1977 VOL 32 p 1795.

(6131)
Watts R L, Leftwich R W
The time series of annual accounting earnings
JAR 1977 AUTUMN VOL 15:2 p 253-271.

(6132)
Brooks L D, Buckmaster D A
Further evidence of the time series properties of
accounting income
JF 1976 VOL 31 p 1359.

(6133)
Collins D W
Predicting earnings with sub-entity data: some
further evidence
JAR 1976 SPRING VOL 14:1 p 163-177.

(6134)
Larsen R A, Murphy J E
New insight into changes in earnings per share
FAJ 1975 MAR-APR VOL 31 p 77-83.

(6135)
Magee R P
Industry WIK: commonalities in earnings
JAR 1974 AUTUMN VOL 12:2 p 270-287.

(6136)
Gentry J A, Pyhrr S A
Simulating an EPS growth model
FIN MGMT 1973 SUMMER VOL 2 p 68.

(6137)
Ball R J, Watts R
Some time series properties of accounting income
JFA 1972 JUN VOL 27 p 663-682.

(6138)
Brown P, Kennelly J W
The informational content of quarterly earnings:
an extension and some further evidence
JB 1972 JUL VOL 45 p 403-415.

(6139)
Levin J
Growth rates - The bigger they come the harder
they fall
FAJ 1972 NOV-DEC VOL 28 p 71-77.

(6140)
Brealey R A
Some implications of the co-movement of
American company earnings
AE 1971 VOL 3 p 183-196.

(6141)
Kinney W R
Predicting earnings: entity versus subentity data
JAR 1971 SPRING VOL 9 p 127-136..

(6142)**Newell G E**
Revisions of reported quarterly earnings
JB 1971 JUL VOL 44 p 282-285.

(6143)
Beaver W H
The time series behavior of earnings
ERA 1970 p 62-107.

(6144)
Edwards C E, Hilton J G
Some comments on short-run earnings fluctuation
bias
JFQA 1970 JUN VOL 5 p 187-202.

(6145)
Green D Jr, Segall J E
Return of Strawman
JB 1970 JAN VOL 43 p 63-65.

(6146)
Niederhoffer V
The predictive content of first-quarter earnings
reports
JB 1970 JAN VOL 43 p 60-62.

(6147)
Lintner J, Glauber R R
Further observations on higgledy piggledy growth
Paper for the Seminar on the Analysis of Security
Prices, U of Chicago, May 1969.

(6148)
Brown P, Niederhoffer V
The predictive content of quarterly earnings
JB 1968 OCT VOL 41 p 488-497.

(6149)
Ball R J, Brown P
Some preliminary findings on the association
between the earnings of a firm, its industry and
the economy
ERA 1967 p 55-57.

(6150)
Green D Jr, Segall J E
The predictive power of first-quarter earnings
reports
JB 1967 JAN VOL 40 p 44-55.

(6151)
Lintner J, Glauber R R
Higgledy piggledy growth in America
Paper for the Seminar on the Analysis of Security
Prices, U of Chicago, May 1967.

(6152)
Little I M D, Rayner A C
Higgledy piggledy growth again
Blackwell, 1966.

(6153)
Andersen T A
Trends in profit sensitivity
JF 1963 DEC VOL 18 p 637-646.

(6154)
Little I M D
Higgledy piggledy growth
Oxford U: Institute of Economics and Statistics
Bulletin 1962 NOV VOL 24 p 387-412.

16.23 Earnings forecasts

(6155)
Fraser D R, Kannan S
The risk implications of forecast errors of bank earnings, 1976-1986.
JFR 1989 FALL VOL 12:3 p 261.

(6156)
Hassell J M, Jennings R H, Lasser D J
Management earnings forecasts: their usefulness as a source of firm-specific information to security analysts
JFR 1988 WINTER VOL 11:4 p 303-320.

(6157)
Brown L D, Richardson G D, Schwager S J
An information interpretation of financial analyst superiority in forecasting earnings
JAR 1987 SPRING VOL 25:1 p 49-67.

(6158)
Jennings R
Unsystematic security price movements, management earnings forecasts and revision in consensus analyst earnings forecasts
JAR 1987 SPRING VOL 25:1 p 90-110.

(6159)
Benesh G A, Peterson P P
On the relation between earnings changes, analysts' forecasts and stock price fluctuations
FAJ 1986 MAR-APR VOL 42 p 29-39.

(6160)
Harris R S
Using analysts' growth forecasts to estimate shareholder required rates of return
FIN MGMT 1986 SPRING VOL 15 p 58-67.

(6161)
Ajinkya B B, Gift M J
Dispersion of financial analysts' earnings forecasts and the (option model) implied standard deviations of stock returns
JF 1985 DEC VOL 40:5 p 1353-1365.

(6162)
Jennings R H
Reaction of financial analysts to management earnings forecasts
Research Foundation of the Institute of Chartered Financial Analysts, 1985.

(6163)
Moyer C, Chatfield R, Kelly G
The accuracy of long term earnings forecasts in the electric utility industry
International Journal of Forecasting 1985 FALL VOL 7.

(6164)
Penham S H
A comparison of the information content of insider trading and management earnings forecasts
JFQA 1985 MAR VOL 20:1 p 1-17.

(6165)
Givoly D, Lakonishok J
Properties of analysts' forecasts of earnings: A review and analysis of the research
Journal of Accounting Literature 1984 VOL 3.

(6166)
Givoly D, Lakonishok J
The quality of analysts's forecasts of earnings
FAJ 1984 SEP-OCT VOL 40 p 40-48.

(6167)
Kerrigan T J
When forecasting earnings, it pays to watch forecasts
JPM 1984 SUMMER VOL 10:4 p 19.

(6168)
Klemkosky R C, Miller W P
When forecasting earnings, it pays to be right!
JPM 1984 SUMMER VOL 10:4 p 13-18.

(6169)
Kodde D A, Schreuder H
Forecasting corporate revenue and profit : time-series models versus management and analysts
JBFA 1984 AUTUMN VOL 11:3 p 381-395

(6170)
Penman S H
The predictive content of earnings forecasts and dividends
JF 1983 VOL 38:4 p 1181-1199.

(6171)
Coggin D, Hunter J
Analysts' forecasts nearer actual than statistical models
Journal of Business Forecasting 1981.

(6172)
Brown L D, Rozeff M S
Analysts can forecast accurately!
JPM 1980 SPRING VOL 6:3 p 31-34.

(6173)
Jaggi B, Grier P
A comparative analysis of forecast disclosing and non-disclosing firms
FIN MGMT 1980 SUMMER VOL 9 p 38.

(6174)
Nichols D R, Tsay J J, Larkin P D
Investor trading responses to differing characteristics of voluntarily disclosed earnings forecasts
AR 1979 APR VOL 54:2 p 376.

(6175)
Nichols D R, Tsay J J
Security price reactions to long-range executive earnings forecasts
JAR 1979 SPRING VOL 17:1 p 140-155.

(6176)
Zacks L
EPS forecasts - accuracy is not enough
FAJ 1979 MAR-APR VOL 35 p 53-55.

(6177)
Abdel-Khalik A R, Espejo J
Expectations data and the predictive value of interim reporting
JAR 1978 SPRING VOL 16:1 p 1-13.

(6178)
Brown L D, Rozeff M S
The superiority of analyst forecasts as measures of expectations: evidence from earnings
JF 1978 VOL 33 p 1.

(6179)
Crichfield T, Dyckman T, Lakonishok J
An evaluation of security analysts' forecasts
AR 1978 JUL VOL 53:3 p 651-668.

(6180)
Fuller R J, Metcalf R W
How analysts use management forecasts
FAJ 1978 MAR-APR p 55-57.

(6181)
Imhoff E A
The representativeness of management earnings forecasts
AR 1978 OCT VOL 53:4 p 836-850.

(6182)
Jaggi B
A note on the information content of corporate annual earnings forecasts
AR 1978 OCT VOL 53:4 p 961-969.

(6183)
Jaggi B
Comparative accuracy of management's annual earnings forecast
FIN MGMT 1978 WINTER VOL 7 p 24.

(6184)
Roenfeldt R L, Cooley P L
Predicting corporate profitability for investment selection
JBFA 1978 SPRING VOL 5:1 p 57-65.

(6185)
Ruland W
The accuracy of forecasts by management and by financial analysts
AR 1978 APR VOL 53:2 p 439-447.

(6186)
Pan J, Nichols D R, Joy O M
Sales forecasting practices of large U S industrial firms
FIN MGMT 1977 AUTUMN VOL 6 p 72.

(6187)
Richards R M, Benjamin J J, Strawser R H
An examination of the accuracy of earnings forecasts
FIN MGMT 1977 AUTUMN VOL 6 p 78.

(6188)
Basi B A, Carey K J et al.
A comparison of the accuracy of corporate and
security analysts' forecasts of earnings
AR 1976 APR VOL 51:2 p 244-254.

(6189)
Ferris K R
The apparent effects of profit forecast disclosure
on   managerial   behaviour: An   empirical
examination
JBFA 1976 AUTUMN VOL 3:3 p 53-66.

(6190)
Patell J M
Corporate forecasts of earnings per share and
stock price behavior: empirical tests
JAR 1976 AUTUMN VOL 14:2 p 246-276.

(6191)
Johnson T E, Schmitt T G
Effectiveness of earnings per share forecasts
FIN MGMT 1974 SUMMER VOL 3 p 64.

(6192)
Clark J J, Elgers P
Forecasted   income   statements: an   investor
perspective
AR 1973 OCT VOL 48:4 p 668-678.

(6193)
Foster G
Stock market reaction to estimates of earnings
per share by company officials
JAR 1973 SPRING VOL 11:1 p 25-37.

(6194)
Ricketts D E, Barrett M J
Corporate operating income forecasting ability
FIN MGMT 1973 SUMMER VOL 2 p 53..

(6195)**Dev S, Webb M**
The accuracy of company profit forecasts
JBF 1972 AUTUMN VOL 4 p 26-39.

(6196)
Elton E J, Gruber M J
Earnings   estimates   and   the   accuracy   of
expectational data
MSci 1972 VOL 18 p B409-B424.

(6197)
Daily R A
The feasibility of reporting forecasted information
AR 1971 OCT VOL 46:4 p 686.

(6198)
McEnally R W
An investigation of the extrapolative determinants
of short-run earnings expectations
JFQA 1971 MAR VOL 6 p 687-706.

(6199)
Cragg J G, Malkiel B G
The consensus and accuracy of some predictions
of the growth of corporate earnings
JF 1968 MAR VOL 23 p 67-84.

16.24 Earnings announcements and stock returns

(6200)
Chang S J, Chen S-N
Stock price adjustment to earnings and dividend
surprises
QREB 1989 VOL 29:1 p 68.

(6201)
Falk H, Levy H
Market   reaction   to   quarterly   earnings'
announcements: a stochastic dominance based test
of market efficiency
MSci 1989 VOL 35 p 425.

(6202)
Kross W, Schroeder D A
Firm prominence and the differential information
content of quarterly earnings announcements
JBFA 1989 SPRING VOL 16:1 p 55.

(6203)
Campbell J Y, Shiller R J
Stock prices, earnings, and expected dividends
JF 1988 JUL VOL 43:3 p 661-676.

(6204)
Chari V V, Jagannathan R, Ofer A R
Seasonalities in security returns: the case of
earnings announcements
JFE 1988 VOL 21 p 101-122.

(6205)
Givoly D, Lakonishok J
Divergence of earnings expectations: The effect on
stock market response to earnings signals
(in Dimson E ed., Stock market anomalies.
Cambridge U Pr, 1988.)

(6206)
Woodruff C S, Senchak A J Jr
Intradaily price-volume adjustments of NYSE
stocks to unexpected earnings
JF 1988 JUN VOL 43:2 p 467-492.

(6207)
Hughes J S, Ricks W E
Associations between forecast errors and excess
returns near to earnings announcements
AR 1987 JAN VOL 62:1 p 158-175.

(6208)
Penman S H
The distribution of earnings news over time and
seasonalities in aggregate stock returns
JFE 1987 JUN VOL 18:2 p 199-228.

(6209)
Rendleman R J Jr, Jones C P, Latane H A
Further insight into the standardized unexpected
earnings anomaly: size and serial correlation
effects
FR 1987 FEB VOL 22:1.

(6210)
Banz R W, Breen W J
Sample-dependent results using accounting and
market data : some evidence
JF 1986 SEP VOL 41:4 p 779-793

(6211)
Jennings R, Starks L
Earnings announcements stock price adjustment
and the existence of option markets
JF 1986 MAR VOL 41:1 p 107-125.

(6212)
Venkatesh P C, Chiang R
Information asymmetry and the dealer's bid-ask
spread : a case study of earnings and dividend
announcements
JF 1986 DEC VOL 41:5 p 1089-1102.

(6213)
Beaver W H, Ryan S G
How well do statement No. 33 earnings explain
stock returns
FAJ 1985 SEP-OCT VOL 41 p 66-71.

(6214)
Calley N O, Chambers D R, Woolridge J R
A note on standardized unexpected earnings: the
case of the electric utility industry
FR 1985 FEB VOL 20:1.

(6215)
Jones P C, Rendleman R J Jr, Latane H A
Earnings announcements: pre-and-post responses
JPM 1985 SPRING VOL 11:3 p 28-33.

(6216)
Foster G, Olsen C, Shevlin T
Earnings releases anomalies and behavior of
security returns
AR 1984 OCT VOL 59:4 p 574-603.

(6217)
Jones C P, Rendleman R J Jr, Latane H
Stock returns and SUEs during the 1970s
JPM 1984 WINTER VOL 10:2 p 18-22.

(6218)
Kane A, Lee Y K, Marcus A
Earnings and dividend announcements : is there
a corroboration effect?
JF 1984 SEP VOL 39:4 p 1091-1099

(6219)
Patell J M, Wolfson M A
The intraday speed of adjustment of stock prices
to earnings and dividend announcements
JFE 1984 VOL 13 p 223-252.

(6220)
Kross W
Profitability, earnings announcement time lags and
stock prices
JBFA 1982 AUTUMN VOL 9:3 p 313-328.

(6221)
Rendleman R J Jr, Jones C P, Latane H A
Empirical anomalies based on unexpected
earnings and the importance of risk adjustments
JFE 1982 NOV VOL 10:3 p 269-287.

(6222)
Bidwell C M III
SUE/PE revista
JPM 1981 WINTER VOL 7:2 p 85.

(6223)
Nichols W D, Brown S L
Assimilating earnings and split information: Is the
capital market becoming more efficient?
JFE 1981 VOL 9 p 309.

(6224)
Aharony J, Swary I
Quarterly dividend and earnings announcements
and stockholders' returns: an empirical analysis
JF 1980 MAR VOL 35:1 p 1-21.

(6225)
Latane H A, Jones C P
Standardized unexpected earnings 1971-77
JF 1979 JUN VOL 34:3 p 717-724.

(6226)
Brown S L
Earnings changes, stock prices and market
efficiency
JF 1978 VOL 33 p 17.

(6227)
Watts R L
Systematic "abnormal" returns after quarterly
earnings announcements
JFE 1978 VOL 6 p 127-150.

(6228)
Joy O M, Litzenberger R H, McEnally R W
The adjustment of stock prices to announcements
of unanticipated changes in quarterly earnings
JAR 1977 AUTUMN VOL 15:2 p 207-225.

(6229)
Latane H A, Jones C P
Standardized unexpected earnings: A progress
report
JF 1977 VOL 32 p 1457.

(6230)
Collins D W
SEC product-line reporting and market efficiency
JFE 1975 VOL 2 p 125.

(6231)
Horwitz B, Young A
Extraordinary gains and losses and security prices
QREB 1974 VOL 14:4 p 101.

(6232)
Jones C P
Earnings trends and investment selection
FAJ 1973 MAR-APR VOL 29 p 79-83.

(6233)
Jorden R J
An empirical investigation of the adjustment of
stock prices to new quarterly earnings information
JFQA 1973 SEP VOL 8:4 p 609-620.

(6234)
Niederhoffer V, Regan P J
Earnings changes, analysts' forecasts and stock
prices
FAJ 1972 MAY-JUN VOL 28 p 65-71.

(6235)
Revsine L
Predictive ability, market prices and operating
flows
AR 1971 JUL VOL 46 p 480-489.

(6236)
Brown P
The impact of the annual net profit report on the
stock market
The Australian Accountant 1970 JUL p 277-283.

(6237)
Jones C P, Litzenberger R H
Quarterly earnings reports and intermediate stock
price trends
JF 1970 MAR VOL 25 p 143-148.

(6238)
Latane H A, Joy O M, Jones C P
Quarterly data, sort-rank routines, and security
evaluation
JB 1970 OCT VOL 43 p 427-438.

(6239)
Jones C P, Litzenberger R H
Earnings seasonality and stock prices
FAJ 1969 NOV-DEC VOL 25 p 57-59.

(6240)
Ball R J, Brown P
An empirical evaluation of accounting income numbers
JAR 1968 AUTUMN VOL 6 p 159-178.

(6241)
Beaver W H
The information content of annual earnings announcements
ERA 1968 p 67-100.

(6242)
Latane H A, Tuttle D L
An analysis of common stock price ratios
SEJ 1967 JAN VOL 33 p 343-354.

(6243)
O'Donnell J L
Relationships between reported earnings and stock prices in the electric utility industry
AR 1965 JAN VOL 40 p 135-143.

(6244)
Ashley J W
Stock prices and changes in earnings and dividends: some empirical results
JPE 1962 FEB VOL 70 p 82-85.

16.25   Firm size and profitability

(6245)
Marcus M
Profitability and size of the firm: some further evidence
REStat 1969 FEB VOL 51 p 104-107.

(6246)
Samuels J M, Smyth D J
Profits, variability of profits and firm size
Ec 1968 MAY VOL 35 p 127-139.

(6247)
Hall M, Weiss L W
Firm size and profitability
REStat 1967 AUG VOL 49 p 319-331..

(6248)**Quandt R E**
On the size distribution of firms
AER 1966 JUN VOL 56 p 416-432.

(6249)
Stekler H O
The variability of profitability with size of firm, 1947-1958
JASA 1964 DEC VOL 59 p 1183-1193.

(6250)
Stekler H O
Profitability and the size of firm
U of Cal Pr, 1963.

(6251)
Osborn R C
The relative profitability of large, medium sized and small business
AR 1956 OCT.

(6252)
Osborn R C
Efficiency and profitability in relation to size
HBR 1951 MAR VOL 29 p 82-94.

(6253)
Alexander S S
The effect of size of manufacturing corporations on the distribution of rate of return
REStat 1949 AUG VOL 17 p 229-235.

(6254)
Somers H B
A comparison of rates of earnings of large scale and small scale industries
QJE 1932 MAY VOL 46 p 465-479.

16.26   Accounting rates of return

(6255)
De Villiers J U
Inflation, asset structure and the discrepancy between accounting and true return
JBFA 1989 AUTUMN VOL 16:4 p 493.

(6256)
Gordon L A, Stark A W
Accounting and economic rates of return: a note on depreciation and other accruals
JBFA 1989 SUMMER VOL 16:3 p 425.

(6257)
Bank of England
Trends in real rates of return
BEQB 1988 VOL 28 p 376-381.

(6258)
Bierman H Jr
Beyond cash flow ROI
MCFJ 1988 WINTER VOL 5 p 36-39.

(6259)
Stanton P
Accounting rates of return as measures of
post-merger performance
AJM 1987 DEC VOL 12.

(6260)
Salamon G L
Accounting rates of return
AER 1985 VOL 75 p 495-504.

(6261)
Holland D M, Myers S C
Trends in corporate profitability and capital costs
in the United States
(in Holland D M ed., Measuring profitability and
capital costs. Lexington Bks, 1984.)

(6262)
Holland D M ed
Measuring profitability and capital costs
Lexington Bks, 1984.

(6263)
Hosek W R, Zahn F
A comparison of aggregate measures of real rate
of interest and the real rate of return on capital
QREB 1984 AUTUMN VOL 24:3 p 58-71

(6264)
Luckett P F
ARR vs. IRR: a review and an analysis
JBFA 1984 VOL 11:2 p 213.

(6265)
Fisher M, McGowan J J
On the misuse of accounting rates of return to
infer monopoly profits
AER 1983 VOL 73 p 82-97.

(6266)
Henrici S
The perversity, peril and pathos of ROI
FAJ 1983 SEP-OCT VOL 39 p 79-80.

(6267)
Salmi T
Estimating the internal rate of return from
published financial statements
JBFA 1982 SPRING VOL 9:1 p 63-74.

(6268)
Fraumeni B M, Jorgenson D W
Rates of return by industrial sector in the United
States, 1948-76
AER 1980 VOL 80 P+P p 326-330.

(6269)
Holland D M, Myers S C
Profitability and capital costs for manufacturing
corporations and all nonfinancial corporations
AER 1980 VOL 80 P+P p 320-325.

(6270)
Branch B
The impact of operating decisions on ROI
dynamics
FIN MGMT 1978 WINTER VOL 7 p 54.

(6271)
Gordon L A
Further thoughts on the accounting rate of return
vs. the economic rate of return
JBFA 1977 SPRING VOL 4:1 p 133-134.

(6272)
Gordon L A
Further thoughts on the accounting rate of return
vs. the economic rate of return
JBFA 1977 SPRING VOL 4:1 p 133-134.

(6273)
Kay J A
Accountants too could be happy in a golden age:
The accountant's rate of profit and the internal
rate of return
OEP 1976 VOL 28 p 447-460.

(6274)
Stephen F H
On deriving the internal rate of return from the accountant's rate of return
JBFA 1976 SUMMER VOL 3:2 p 147-150.

(6275)
Carey K J
Persistence of profitability
FIN MGMT 1974 SUMMER VOL 3 p 43.

(6276)
Gordon L A
Accounting rate of return vs. economic rate of return
JBFA 1974 AUTUMN VOL 1:3 p 343-356.

(6277)
Solomon E, Laya J C
Measuring profitability
P-H, 1969.

(6278)
Solomon E, Laya J
Measurement of company profitability: Some systematic errors in the accounting rate of return
(in Robichek A A ed., Financial research and management decisions. Wiley, 1967.)

(6279)
Harcourt G C
The accountant in a golden age
(OEP 1965; reprinted in Parker R H and Harcourt G C eds., Readings in the concept and measurement of income. Cambridge U Pr, 1969.)

(6280)
Stigler G J
Capital and rates of return in manufacturing
(Dist by Princeton U Pr) Natl Bur Econ Res, 1963.

16.3 Balance sheet information

(6281)
Bodenhorn D
Balance sheet items as the present value of future cash flows
JBFA 1984 VOL 11:4 p 493.

(6282)
Stowe J D, Watson C J, Robertson T D
Relationships between the two sides of the balance sheet: a canonical correlation analysis.
JF 1980 SEP VOL 35:4 p 973-980.

16.4 Financial ratios

(6283)
Kolari J, McInish T H, Saniga E M
A note on the distribution types of financial ratios in the commercial banking industry
JBankF 1989 JUL VOL 13:3 p 463-472.

(6284)
Barnes P
The analysis and use of financial ratios: a review article
JBFA 1987 VOL 14:4 p 449.

(6285)
Dun & Bradstreet
Key business ratios: 1: 1983/84/85
Dun & Bradstreet, 1987.

(6286)
Ezzamel M, Mar-Molinero C, Beecher A
On the distributional properties of financial ratios
JBFA 1987 VOL 14:4 p 463.

(6287)
O'Brien T J, Vanderheiden P A
Empirical measurement of operating leverage for growing firms
FIN MGMT 1987 SUMMER VOL 16 p 45-53.

(6288)
So J C
Some empirical evidence on the outliers and the non-normal distribution of financial ratios
JBFA 1987 VOL 14:4 p 483.

(6289)
Buijink W, Jegers M
Cross-sectional distributional properties of financial ratios in Belgian manufacturing industries: aggregation effects and persistence over time
JBFA 1986 VOL 13:3 p 337.

(6290)
McLeay S
Student's t and the distribution of financial ratios
JBFA 1986 VOL 13:2 p 209.

(6291)
McDonald B, Morris M H
The statistical validity of the ratio method in
financial analysis: an empirical examination
JBFA 1984 VOL 11:1 p 89.

(6292)
Rege U P
Accounting ratios to locate take-over targets
JBFA 1984 VOL 11:3 p 301.

(6293)
Gombola M J, Ketz J E
Financial ratio patterns in retail and
manufacturing organizations
FIN MGMT 1983 SUMMER VOL 12 p 45.

(6294)
Barnes P
Methodological implications of non-normally
distributed financial ratios
JBFA 1982 SPRING VOL 9:1 p 51.

(6295)
Chen K H, Shimerda T A
An empirical analysis of useful financial ratios
FIN MGMT 1981 SPRING VOL 10 p 51-60.

(6296)
Pohlman R A, Hollinger R D
Information redundancy in sets of financial ratios
JBFA 1981 WINTER VOL 8:4 p 511.

(6297)
Johnson W B
The cross-sectional stability of financial ratio
patterns
JFQA 1979 DEC VOL 14 p 1035.

(6298)
Laurent C R
Improving the efficiency and effectiveness of
financial ratio analysis
JBFA 1979 AUTUMN VOL 6:3 p 401.

(6299)
Walker M C, Stowe J D, Moriarity S
Decomposition analysis of financial statements
JBFA 1979 SUMMER VOL 6:2 p 173-186.

(6300)
Belkaoui A
Financial ratios as predictors of Canadian
takeovers
JBFA 1978 SPRING VOL 5:1 p 93-108..

(6301)**Johnson W B**
The cross-sectional stability of financial patterns
JBFA 1978 SUMMER VOL 5:2 p 207-214.

(6302)
Ricketts D, Stover R
An examination of commercial bank financial
ratios
JBR 1978 SUMMER VOL 9:2.

(6303)
Bird R G, McHugh A J
Financial ratios - an empirical study
JBFA 1977 SPRING VOL 4:1 p 29-46.

(6304)
Fadel H
The predictive power of financial ratios in the
British construction industry
JBFA 1977 AUTUMN VOL 4:3 p 339-354.

(6305)
Castagna A D, Matolcsy Z P
Financial ratios as predictors of company
acquisitions
Journal of the Securities Industry of Australia
DEC 1976 p 6-10.

(6306)
Lev B
Decomposition measures for financial analysis
FIN MGMT 1973 SPRING VOL 2 p 56.

(6307)
Sorter G H, Benston G
Appraising the defensive portion of a firm: the
interval measure
AR 1960 OCT VOL 35 p 633-640.

17 Interest rates

(6308)
Giaccotto C
Compounding and discounting with stochastic interest rates
JBFA 1989 WINTER VOL 16:5 p 745.

(6309)
Lauterbach B
Consumption volatility, production volatility, spot-rate volatility, and the returns on Treasury bills and bonds
JFE 1989 SEP VOL 24:1 p 155-180.

(6310)
Barsky R B et al.
The worldwide change in the behavior of interest rates and prices in 1914: comments
EER 1988 VOL 32:5.

(6311)
Clinton K
Transaction costs and covered interest arbitrage: theory and evidence
JPE 1988 APR VOL 96:2 p 358-370.

(6312)
Kasman B, Pigott C
Interest rate divergences among the major industrial nations
F R Bk New York Q Rev 1988 AUTUMN VOL 13:3.

(6313)
Giovannini A, Jorion P
Interest rates and risk premia in the stock market and in the foreign exchange market
JIMF 1987 MAR VOL 6:1 p 107-124.

(6314)
Johnson L J, Brick J R, Price K
The interest rate sensitivity of equity prices with respect to systematic risk and leverage
JBusR 1987 FEB VOL 15:1 p 85-92.

(6315)
Dothan M U, Feldman D
Equilibrium interest rates and multiperiod bonds in a partially observable economy
JF 1986 JUN VOL 41:2 p 369-382.

(6316)
Dotsey M, King R G
Informational implications of interest rate rules
AER 1986 VOL 76 p 33-42.

(6317)
Wenninger J
Responsiveness of interest rate spreads and deposit flows to changes in market rates
F R Bk New York Q Rev 1986 AUTUMN VOL 11:3.

(6318)
Rapping L A, Pulley L B
Speculation, deregulation and the interest rate
AER 1985 VOL 75 P+P p108-113.

(6319)
Shapiro A C
Nominal contracting in a world of uncertainty
JBankF 1983 VOL 7 p 69.

(6320)
Chance D M
Interest sensitivity and dividend yields
JPM 1982 WINTER VOL 8:2 p 69.

(6321)
Constantinides G M, Ingersoll J E
Tax effects and bond prices
JF 1982 MAY VOL 37:2 p 349-352.

(6322)
Rao R K S
The impact of yield changes on the systematic risk of bonds
JFQA 1982 MAR VOL 17:1 p 115-127.

(6323)
Blanchard O J
Output, the stock market and interest rates
AER 1981 VOL 71 p 132-143.

(6324)
Brown K H
Effects of changes in the discount rate on the foreign exchange value of the dollar: 1973 to 1978.
QJE 1981 VOL 96 p 551.

(6325)
Price K, Brick J R
Daily interest rate relationships
JMCB 1980 MAY VOL 12:2 p 215-220.

(6326)
Roley V V
The role of commercial banks' portfolio behavior
in the determination of Treasury security yields
JMCB 1980 MAY VOL 12:2 p 353-369.

(6327)
Fama E F, Farber A
Money, bonds and foreign exchange
AER 1979 VOL 69 p 639-649.

(6328)
Friedman B M
Substitution and expectation effects on long term
borrowing behavior and long term interest rates
JMCB 1979 MAY VOL 11:2 p 131-150.

(6329)
Craine R N, Pierce J L
Interest rate risk
JFQA 1978 NOV VOL 13 p 719.

(6330)
Jaffe J F
Corporate taxes, inflation, the rate of interest and
the return of equity
JFQA 1978 MAR VOL 13 p 55.

(6331)
Keown A J, Martin J D
Interest rate sensitivity and portfolio risk
JFQA 1977 JUN VOL 12 p 181.

(6332)
Krainer R E
Interest rates, leverage and investor rationality
JFQA 1977 MAR VOL 12 p 1.

(6333)
Lloyd W P, Shick R A
A test of Stone's two-index model of return
JFQA 1977 SEP VOL 12 p 363.

(6334)
Stone B K
Systematic interest-rate risk in a two-index model
of returns
JFQA 1974 NOV VOL 9 p 709.

(6335)
Guttentag J M ed.
Essays on interest rates, Vol 2
(Dist by Columbia U Pr) Natl Bur Econ Res,
1971.

(6336)
Kellison S G
The theory of interest
Irwin, 1970.

(6337)
Van Horne J C
The function and analysis of capital market rates
P-H, 1970.

(6338)
Guttentag J M, Cagan P eds.
Essays on interest rates, Vol 1
(Dist by Columbia U Pr) Natl Bur Econ Res,
1969.

(6339)
Hahn F H, Brechling F P R eds.
The theory of interest rates
Macmillan Int, 1966.

(6340)
Conard J W
An introduction to the theory of interest
U of Cal Pr, 1959.

(6341)
Sauvain H C
Changing interest rates and investment portfolio
JF 1959 MAY VOL 14 p 230-244.

(6342)
Keynes J M
A treatise on money
Macmillan Int, 1930.

17.1 Level of interest rates

(6343)
Dwyer G P Jr, Hafer R W
Interest rates and economic announcements
F R Bk St Louis Rev 1989 MAR-APR VOL 71:2.

(6344)
O'Connell J
Sterilization and interest rates
JIMF 1988 DEC VOL 7:4 p 425-428.

(6345)
Evans P
Do budget deficits raise nominal interest rates?
evidence from six countries
JME 1987 VOL 20 p 281.

(6346)
McCallum B T
Some issues concerning interest rate pegging,
price level determinancy and the real bills
doctrine
JME 1986 VOL 17 p 135.

(6347)
Penati A
The sources of the movements in interest rates:
An empirical investigation
JBankF 1986 VOL 10 p 343.

(6348)
Sweeney R J, Warga A D
The pricing of interest-rate risk : evidence from
the stock market
JF 1986 JUN VOL 41:2 p 393-410

(6349)
Bodie Z, Kane A, McDonald R
Why haven't nominal rates declined
FAJ 1984 MAR-APR VOL 40 p 16-27.

(6350)
Campbell J Y, Shiller R J
A simple account of the behavior of long-term
interest rates
AER 1984 VOL 74 P+P p 44-48.

(6351)
Hendershott P H
Expectations surprises and treasury bill rates :
1960-82
JF 1984 JUL VOL 39:3 p 685-698.

(6352)
Sundaresan M
Consumption and equilibrium interest rates in
stochastic production economies
JF 1984 MAR VOL 39:1 p 77-92.

(6353)
Bennett P
Reactions to discount rate cuts
F R Bk New York Q Rev 1983 AUTUMN VOL
8:3..

(6354)**Carmichael J, Stebbing P W**
Fisher's paradox and the theory of interest
AER 1983 VOL 73 p 619-630.

(6355)
Dewald W
Federal deficits and real interest rates: Theory
and evidence
Federal Reserve Bank of Atlanta Economic
Review 1983 JAN p 20-29.

(6356)
Slovin M B, Sushka M E
Money, interest rates and risk
JME 1983 VOL 12 p 475.

(6357)
Sundaresan M
Constant absolute risk aversion preferences and
constant equilibrium interest rates
JF 1983 MAR VOL 38:1 p 205-212.

(6358)
Lucas R
Interest rates and currency prices in a two-country
world
JME 1982 VOL 10 p 335.

(6359)
Wihlborg C
Interest rates, exchange rate adjustments and
currency risks: an empirical study 1967-1975
JMCB 1982 FEB VOL 14:1 p 58-75.

(6360)
Evans P
Why have interest rates been so volatile?
F R Bk San Francisco Ec Rev 1981 SUMMER.

(6361)
Pesando J E
On forecasting interest rates: an efficient markets
perspective
JME 1981 VOL 8 p 305.

(6362)
Santoni G J, Stone C C
What really happened to interest rates?: a
longer-run analysis
F R Bk St Louis Rev 1981 VOL 63:9.

(6363)
Throop A W
Interest rate forecasts and market efficiency
F R Bk San Francisco Ec Rev 1981 SPRING.

(6364)
Friedman B M
Survey evidence on the "rationality" of interest
rate expectations
JME 1980 OCT VOL 6 p 453-465.

(6365)
Friedman B M, Roley V V
Models of long-term interest rate determination
JPM 1980 SPRING VOL 6:3 p 35-45.

(6366)
Beja A
State preference and the riskless interest rate: a
Markov model of capital markets
REStud 1979 JUL VOL 46:144 p 435-446.

(6367)
Elliot J W, Baier J R
Econometric models and current interest rates:
how well do they predict future rates
JF 1979 SEP VOL 34:4 p 975-986.

(6368)
Boskin M J
Taxation, saving and the rate of interest
JPE 1978 VOL 86 p S3.

(6369)
Neftci S, Sargent T J
A little bit of evidence on the natural rate
hypothesis from the U S
JME 1978 VOL 4 p 315.

(6370)
Lombra R E, Torto R G
Discount rate changes and announcement effects
QJE 1977 VOL 91 p 171.

(6371)
Burger A E
An explanation of movements in short-term
interest rates
F R Bk St Louis Rev 1976 VOL 58:7.

(6372)
Pesando J E
Alternative models of the determination of
nominal interest rates: the Canadian evidence
JMCB 1976 MAY VOL 8:2 p 209-218.

(6373)
Laffer A B, Zecher R
Some evidence on the formation, efficiency and
accuracy of anticipations of nominal yields
JME 1975 VOL 1 p 327.

(6374)
Zwick B
The interest-induced wealth effect and the
behavior of real and nominal interest rates
JF 1974 VOL 29 p 1425.

(6375)
Feldstein M, Chamberlain G
Multimarket expectations and the rate of interest
JMCB 1973 NOV VOL 5:4 p 873-902.

(6376)
Prell M J
How well do the experts forecast interest rates?
F R Bk Kansas City Mo Rev 1973 SEP-OCT.

(6377)
Pierson G
Why have interest rates risen?
REStat 1971 FEB VOL 53 p 89-100.

(6378)
Bonello F J
The formulation of expected interest rates: an examination of alternative hypotheses
Mich St U Busn, 1970.

(6379)
Feldstein M, Eckstein O
The fundamental determinants of the interest rate
REStat 1970 NOV VOL 52 p 363-375.

(6380)
Sandmo A
Equilibrium and efficiency in loan markets
Ec 1970 FEB VOL 37 p 23-38.

(6381)
Weil R L
Realized interest rates and bondholders' returns
AER 1970 JUN VOL 60 p 502-511.

(6382)
Homer S, Johannesen R I Jr
The price of money, 1946-1969: an analytical study of United States and foreign interest rates
Rutgers U Pr, 1969.

(6383)
Lee T H
Alternative interest rates and the demand for money: the empirical evidence
AER 1967 DEC VOL 57 p 1168-1181.

(6384)
OECD Committee for Invisible Transactions
Capitals markets study: structure of interest rates in some OECD countries
OECD, 1967.

(6385)
Modigliani F, Sutch R
Innovations in interest rate policy
AER 1966 MAY VOL 56 p 178-197.

(6386)
Freund W C, Zinbarg E D
Application of flow of funds to interest-rate forecasting
JF 1963 MAY VOL 18 p 231-248.

(6387)
Homer S
A history of interest rates
Rutgers U Pr, 1963.

(6388)
Horwich G
Real assets and the theory of interest
JPE 1962 APR VOL 70 p 157-169.

(6389)
Spencer M H
Studies in the determination of specific interest rates
EE 1962 OCT-NOV VOL 8 p 17-32.

(6390)
Lerner A P
A note on the rate of interest and the value of assets
EJ 1961 SEP VOL 71 p 539-543.

(6391)
Samuelson P A
An exact consumption-loan model of interest with or without the social contrivance of money
JPE 1958 DEC VOL 66 p 467-482.

(6392)
Robinson J
Forecasting interest rates
JB 1954 JAN VOL 27 p 87-100.

(6393)
Robinson J
The rate of interest
Em 1951 APR VOL 19 p 92-111.

(6394)
Hicks J R
Mr. Hawtrey on bank rates and the long term rate on interest
MS 1939 VOL 10:1 p 21-37.

(6395)
Hawtrey R G
A century of bank rates
Longman, 1938.

(6396)
Fisher I
The theory of interest: as determined by impatience to spend income and opportunity to invest it
Kelly, 1930.

17.11 Time series properties of interest rates

(6397)
Faig M
Seasonal fluctuations and the demand for money
QJE 1989 NOV VOL 104:4 p 847-862.

(6398)
Sanders A B, Unal H
On the intertemporal behavior of the short-term rate of interest
JFQA 1988 DEC VOL 23 p 417.

(6399)
Sharp K P
Tests of US short and long interest rate seasonality
REStat 1988 VOL 70 p 177.

(6400)
Clark T A
Interest rate seasonals and the federal reserve
JPE 1986 VOL 94 p 76.

(6401)
Miron J A
Financial panics, the seasonality of the nominal interest rate, and the founding of the Fed
AER 1986 VOL 76 p 125-140.

(6402)
Smirlock M
Seasonality and bond market returns
JPM 1985 SPRING VOL 11:3 p 42-44.

(6403)
Singleton K J
A latent time series model of the cyclical behavior of interest rates
IntER 1980 OCT VOL 21:3 p 559-575.

(6404)
Pesando J E
On the random walk characteristics of short and long term interest rates in an efficient market
JMCB 1979 NOV VOL 11:4 p 457-466.

(6405)
Zwick B
Interest rate variability, government securities dealers and the stability of financial markets
JME 1979 VOL 5 p 365.

(6406)
Brick J R, Thompson H E
Time series analysis of interest rates: Some additional evidence
JF 1978 VOL 33 p 93..

(6407)**Porsius P**
Spectral analysis of the structure of interest rates in the Netherlands
JME 1977 VOL 3 p 191.

(6408)
Smith V K, Marcis R G
A time series analysis of post-accord interest rates
JF 1972 JUN VOL 27 p 589-606.

(6409)
Diller S
The seasonal variation of interest rates
Natl Bur Econ Res, 1969.

(6410)
Cagan P
Changes in the cyclical behavior of interest rates (Dist by Columbia U Pr) Natl Bur Econ Res, 1966.

(6411)
Cagan P
Changes in the cyclical behavior of interest rates
REStat 1966 AUG VOL 48 p 219-250.

(6412)
Holland T E
Cyclical movements of interest rates, 1948-61
JB 1964 OCT VOL 37 p 364-369.

(6413)
Federal Reserve Bank of St Louis
The seasonal pattern of interest rates
F R Bk St Louis Rev 1960 NOV.

17.12 Monetary policy and interest rates

(6414)
Belongia M T, Hafer R W, Sheehan R G
On the temporal stability of the interest
rate-weekly money relationship
REStat 1988 VOL 70 p 516.

(6415)
Cook T, Hahn T
The information content of discount rate
announcements and their effect on market
interest rates
JMCB 1988 MAY VOL 20:2 p 167-180.

(6416)
Pesando J E, Plourde A
The October 1979 change in the US monetary
regime : its impact on the forecastability of
Canadian interest rates
JF 1988 MAR VOL 43:1 p 217-240.

(6417)
Robinson K J
The effect of monetary policy on long-term
interest rates: further evidence from an
efficient-markets approach
F R Bk Dallas Ec Rev 1988 MAR.

(6418)
Thornton D L
The effect of monetary policy on short-term
interest rates
F R Bk St Louis Rev 1988 MAY-JUN VOL 70:3.

(6419)
Campbell J Y
Money announcements, the demand for bank
reserves, and the behavior of the federal funds
rate within the statement week
JMCB 1987 FEB VOL 19:1 p 56-67.

(6420)
Deaves R, Melino A, Pesando J E
The response of interest rates to the federal
reserve's weekly monetary announcements: the
"puzzle" of anticipated money
JME 1987 VOL 19 p 393.

(6421)
Hardouvelis G A
Reserves announcements and interest rates : does
monetary policy matter?
JF 1987 JUN VOL 42:2 p 407-422.

(6422)
Girton L, Nattress D
Monetary innovations and interest rates
JMCB 1985 AUG VOL 17:3 p 289-297.

(6423)
Loeys J G
Changing interest rate responses to money
announcements: 1977-1983
JME 1985 VOL 15 p 323.

(6424)
Siegel J J
Money supply announcements and interest rates:
does monetary policy matter
JME 1985 VOL 15 p 163.

(6425)
Engel C, Frankel J
Why interest rates react to money
announcements: an explanation from the foreign
exchange market
JME 1984 VOL 13 p 31.

(6426)
Roley V V, Walsh C E
Unanticipated money and interest rates
AER 1984 VOL 74 P+P p 49-54.

(6427)
Anderson R, Ando A, Enzler J
Interaction between fiscal and monetary policy
and the real rate of interest
AER 1983 VOL 73 P+P p 55-60.

(6428)
Cornell B
Money supply announcements and interest rates: another view
JB 1983 JAN VOL 56:1 p 1-23.

(6429)
Cornell B
The money supply announcements puzzle: Review and interpretation
AER 1983 VOL 73 p 644-657.

(6430)
Figlewski S, Urich T
Optimal aggregation of money supply forecasts : accuracy profitability and market efficiency
JF 1983 JUN VOL 38:3 p 695-710.

(6431)
Nichols D A, Small D H, Webster C E Jr
Why interest rates rise when an unexpectedly large money stock is announced
AER 1983 VOL 73 p 383-387.

(6432)
Roley V V
The response of short term interest rates to weekly money announcements
JMCB 1983 AUG VOL 15:3 p 344-354.

(6433)
Hafer R W, Hein S E
Monetary policy and short-term real rates of interest
F R Bk St Louis Rev 1982 VOL 64:3.

(6434)
Urich T J
The information content of weekly money supply announcements
JME 1982 VOL 10 p 73.

(6435)
Mishkin F S
Monetary policy and long-term interest rates: an efficient markets approach
JME 1981 VOL 7 p 29.

(6436)
Grauer F L A, Litzenberger R H
Monetary rules and the nominal rate of interest under uncertainty
JME 1980 VOL 6 p 277.

(6437)
Cornell B
Do money supply announcements affect short term interest rates?
JMCB 1979 FEB VOL 11:1 p 80-86.

(6438)
Blejer M I
Money and the nominal interest rate in an inflationary economy: an empirical test
JPE 1978 VOL 86 p 529.

(6439)
Friedman B M
Financial flow variables and the short-run determination of long-term interest rates
JPE 1977 VOL 85 p 661.

(6440)
Marcis R G, Smith V K
Monetary activity and interest rates: a return visit
QREB 1977 VOL 17:3 p 84.

(6441)
Darby M R
The financial and tax effects of monetary policy on interest rates
Economic Inquiry 1975 JUN VOL 13 p 266-276.

(6442)
Smith V K, Marcis R G
Monetary activity and interest rates: a spectral analysis
QREB 1973 VOL 13:2 p 69.

(6443)
Carr J, Smith L B
Money supply, interest rates, and the yield curve
JMCB 1972 AUG VOL 4:3 p 582-594.

(6444)
Laidler D
The rate of interest and the demand for money--some empirical evidence
JPE 1966 DEC VOL 74 p 543-555.

17.13 Real interest rates and inflation

(6445)
Groenewold N
The adjustment of the real interest rate to inflation
AE 1989 VOL 21:7 p 947.

(6446)
Kelly W A Jr, Miles J A
Capital structure theory and the Fisher effect
FR 1989 FEB VOL 24:1 p 53-74.

(6447)
MacDonald R, Murphy P D
Testing for the long run relationship between nominal interest rates and inflation using cointegration techniques
AE 1989 VOL 21:4 p 439-448.

(6448)
Makin J H, Couch K A
Saving, pension contributions, and the real interest rate
REStat 1989 VOL 71 p 401.

(6449)
Viren M
The long-run relationship between interest rates and inflation: some cross-country evidence
JBankF 1989 SEP VOL 13:4-5 p 571-588.

(6450)
Bank of England
Trends in real interest rates
BEQB 1988 VOL 28 p 225-231.

(6451)
Barth J R, Bradley M D
On interest rates, inflationary expectations and tax rates
JBankF 1988 VOL 12:2 p 215-220.

(6452)
Lahiri K, Teigland C, Zaporowski M
Interest rates and the subjective probability distribution of inflation forecasts
JMCB 1988 MAY VOL 20:2 p 233-248.

(6453)
Rose A K
Is the real interest rate stable?
JF 1988 DEC VOL 43:5 p 1095-1112.

(6454)
Shome D K, Smith S D, Pinkerton J M
The purchasing power of money and nominal interest rates: a re-examination
JF 1988 DEC VOL 43:5 p 1113-1126.

(6455)
Barsky R B
The Fisher hypothesis and the forecastability and persistence of inflation
JME 1987 VOL 19 p 3.

(6456)
Carrington S, Crouch R
Interest rate differentials on short-term securities and rational expectations of inflation
JBankF 1987 VOL 11 p 571-579.

(6457)
Carrington S, Crouch R
A theorem on interest rate differentials, risk and anticipated inflation
AE 1987 DEC VOL 19:12 p 1675-1684.

(6458)
Connock M, Hillier H
Long bond yields and inflation rates in OECD countries: a cross section study
AE 1987 MAR VOL 19:3 p 407-416.

(6459)
Hochman S, Palmon O
Expected inflation and the real rates of interest on taxable and tax exempt bonds
JMCB 1987 FEB VOL 19:1 p 90-103..

(6460)**Mankiw N G**
Government purchases and real interest rates
JPE 1987 VOL 95 p 407.

(6461)
Melnik A, Plaut S E
Interest rate indexation and the pricing of loan commitment contracts
JBankF 1987 VOL 11 p 137-145.

(6462)
Walsh C E
Three questions concerning nominal and real interest rates
F R Bk San Francisco Ec Rev 1987 FALL.

(6463)
Barthold T A, Dougan W R
The Fisher hypothesis under different monetary regimes
REStat 1986 VOL 68 p 674.

(6464)
Cornell B, French K R
Commodity own rates, real interest rates and money supply announcements
JME 1986 VOL 18 p 3.

(6465)
Hansson I, Stuart C
The Fisher hypothesis and international capital markets
JPE 1986 VOL 94 p 1330.

(6466)
Lee C-W J, Petruzzi C R
The Gibson paradox and the monetary standard
REStat 1986 VOL 68 p 189.

(6467)
Merrick J J Jr, Saunders A
International expected real interest rates: new tests of the parity hypothesis and US fiscal policy effects
JME 1986 VOL 18 p 313.

(6468)
Plessner Y, Shalit H
Inflation, the level of investment, and interest rates
EER 1986 VOL 30:6.

(6469)
Summers L H
Estimating the long-run relationship between interest rates and inflation: a response to McCallum
JME 1986 VOL 18 p 77.

(6470)
Arak M, Kreicher L
The real rate of interest: inferences from the new UK indexed gilts
IntER 1985 JUN VOL 26:2 p 399-408.

(6471)
Beranek W, Humphrey T M, Timberlake R H Jr
Fisher, Thornton, and the analysis of the inflation premium
JMCB 1985 AUG VOL 17:3 p 371-377.

(6472)
Cohen D
Inflation, wealth and interest rates in an intertemporal optimizing model
JME 1985 VOL 16 p 73.

(6473)
Day T E
Expected inflation and the real rate of interest: A note
JBankF 1985 VOL 9 p 491.

(6474)
Eddy A, Seifert B
Inflation, the Fisher hypothesis, and long-term bonds
FR 1985 FEB VOL 20:1.

(6475)
Granziol M J
Direct price controls as a source of instability in the interest rate/inflation rate relationship
JBankF 1985 VOL 9 p 275.

(6476)
Hoffman D L, Schlagenhauf D E
Real interest rates, anticipated inflation, and unanticipated money: a multi-country study
REStat 1985 VOL 67 p 284.

(6477)
Mark N C
A note on international real interest rate differentials
REStat 1985 VOL 67 p 481.

(6478)
Mitchell D W
Expected inflation and interest rates in a multi-asset model : a note
JF 1985 JUN VOL 40:2 p 595-599.

(6479)
Peel D A, Pope P F
Testing the Fisherian hypothesis : some methodological issues and further evidence for the UK
JBFA 1985 SUMMER VOL 12:2 p 297-311

(6480)
Holland A S
Real interest rates: what accounts for their recent rise?
F R Bk St Louis Rev 1984 VOL 66:10.

(6481)
Huizinga J, Mishkin F S
Inflation and real interest rates on assets with different risk characteristics
JF 1984 JUL VOL 39:3 p 699-714.

(6482)
Kelly W A Jr, Miles J A
Darby and Fisher: resolution of a paradox
FR 1984 MAR VOL 19:1.

(6483)
Lahiri K, Zaporowski M
A note on the variability of real interest rates, business cycles and the Livingston data
JBankF 1984 VOL 8 p 483.

(6484)
McMillan T E, Buck L E, Deegan J
The "Fisher Theorem" - an illusion, but whose?
FAJ 1984 NOV-DEC VOL 40 p 63-71.

(6485)
Mishkin F S
Are real interest rates equal across countries? An empirical investigation of international parity conditions
JF 1984 DEC VOL 39:5 p 1345-1357.

(6486)
Papadia F
Estimates of ex ante real rates of interest in the EEC countries and in the United States, 1973-82
JMCB 1984 AUG VOL 16:3 p 335-344.

(6487)
Pigott C
Indicators of long-term real interest rates
F R Bk San Francisco Ec Rev 1984 WINTER.

(6488)
Saunders A, Tress R B
On the constancy of the international real rate of interest
JME 1984 VOL 13 p 113.

(6489)
VanderHoff J
Evidence on the varying effect of expected inflation on interest rates
REStat 1984 VOL 66 p 477.

(6490)
Yun Y S
The effects of inflation and income taxes on interest rates : some new evidence
JFQA 1984 DEC VOL 19:4 p 425-448.

(6491)
Benninga S, Protopapadakis A
Real and nominal interest rates under uncertainty: The Fisher theorem and the term structure
JPE 1983 VOL 91 p 856.

(6492)
Ferri M G, Goldstein S J, Chew I K
Interest rates and the announcement of inflation
FIN MGMT 1983 AUTUMN VOL 12 p 52.

(6493)
Ferson W E
Expectations of real interest rates and aggregate consumption : empirical tests
JFQA 1983 DEC VOL 18:4 p 477-497.

(6494)
Fried J, Howitt P
The effects of inflation on real interest rates
AER 1983 VOL 73 p 968-980.

(6495)
Kane A, Rosenthal L, Ljung G
Tests of the Fisher hypothesis with international data : theory and evidence
JF 1983 MAY VOL 38:2 p 539-551.

(6496)
Lerman Z
Inflation and the structure of interest rates
Research in Finance 1983 VOL 4.

(6497)
Miles J A
Taxes and the Fisher effect: a clarifying analysis
JF 1983 MAR VOL 38:1 p 49-65.

(6498)
Peek J, Wilcox J A
The postwar stability of the Fisher effect
JF 1983 VOL 38:4 p 1111-1124.

(6499)
Summers L H
The non-adjustment of nominal interest rates: A study of the Fisher effect
(in Tobin J ed., Macroeconomics, prices, and quantities: Essays in honour of Arthur M. Okun. Blackwell, 1983.)

(6500)
Wilcox A
Why real interest rates were so low in the 1970's
AER 1983 VOL 73 p 44-53.

(6501)
Wilcox J A
The missing Fisher effect on nominal interest rates in the 1950s
REStat 1983 VOL 65 p 644.

(6502)
Wood J H
Interest rates and inflation: an old and unexplained relationship
F R Bk Dallas Ec Rev 1983 JAN.

(6503)
Fama E F, Gibbons M R
Inflation, real returns and capital investment
JME 1982 VOL 9 p 297-323.

(6504)
Frankel J A
A technique for extracting a measure of expected inflation from the interest rate term structure
REStat 1982 VOL 64 p 135.

(6505)
Gandolfi A E
Inflation taxation and interest rates
JF 1982 JUN VOL 37:3 p 797-807.

(6506)
Peek J
Interest rates, income taxes and anticipated inflation
AER 1982 VOL 72 p 980-991.

(6507)
Bomberger W A, Frazer W J
Interest rates uncertainty and the Livingston data
JF 1981 JUN VOL 36:3 p 661-675.

(6508)
Brown W W, Santoni G J
Unreal estimates of the real rate of interest
F R Bk St Louis Rev 1981 VOL 63:1.

(6509)
Cumby R E, Obstfield M
A note on exchange-rate expectations and nominal interest differentials: a test of the Fisher hypothesis
JF 1981 JUN VOL 36:3 p 697-703.

(6510)
Dwyer G P Jr
Are expectations of inflation rational? or is variation of the expected real interest rate unpredictable?
JME 1981 VOL 8 p 59.

(6511)
Leuthold S C
Interest rates, inflation and deflation
FAJ 1981 JAN-FEB VOL 37 p 28-41.

(6512)
Nielsen N C
Inflation and taxation: Nominal and real rates of return
JME 1981 MAR VOL 7 p 261-270..

(6513)**Turnbull S M**

Measurement of the real rate of interest and related problems in a world of uncertainty
JMCB 1981 MAY VOL 13:2 p 177-191.

(6514)
Cargill T F, Meyer R A
The term structure of inflationary expectations and market efficiency
JF 1980 MAR VOL 35:1 p 57-70.

(6515)
Friedman B M
Price inflation, portfolio choice and nominal interest rates
AER 1980 VOL 70 p 32-48.

(6516)
Martins M A C
A nominal theory of the nominal rate of interest and the price level
JPE 1980 VOL 80 p 174.

(6517)
Barnea A, Dotan A, Lakonishok J
The effect of price level uncertainty on the determination of nominal interest rates: Some empirical evidence
Southern Economic Journal 1979 OCT VOL 46 p 609-614.

(6518)
Brealey R A
Inflation and the real value of government assets
FAJ 1979 JAN-FEB p 18-22.

(6519)
Holmes A B, Kwast M L
Interest rates and inflationary expectations: tests for structural change 1952-1976
JF 1979 JUN VOL 34:3 p 733-741.

(6520)
Leiderman L
Interest rates as predictors of inflation in a high-inflation semi-industrialised economy
JF 1979 SEP VOL 34:4 p 1019-1025.

(6521)
Levi M D, Makin J H
Fisher Phillips Friedman and the measured impact of inflation on interest
JF 1979 MAR VOL 34:1 p 35-52.

(6522)
Garbade K, Wachtel P
Time variation in the relationship between inflation and interest rates
JME 1978 VOL 4 p 755.

(6523)
Levi M D, Makin J H
Anticipated inflation and interest rates: Further interpretation of findings on the Fisher equation
AER 1978 VOL 68 p 801-812.

(6524)
Makin J H
Anticipated inflation and interest rates in an open economy
JMCB 1978 AUG VOL 10:3 p 275-289.

(6525)
Amihud Y, Barnea A
A note on Fisher hypothesis and price level uncertainty
JFQA 1977 SEP VOL 12 p 525.

(6526)
Bomberger W A, Makinen G E
The Fisher effect: Graphical treatment and some econometric implications
JF 1977 VOL 32 p 719.

(6527)
Cargill T F, Meyer R C
Intertemporal stability of the relationship between interest rates and price changes
JF 1977 VOL 32 p 1001.

(6528)
Fama E F
Interest rates and inflation: The message in the entrails
AER 1977 VOL 67 p 487-486.

(6529)
Fama E F, Schwert G W
Asset returns and inflation
JFE 1977 VOL 5 p 115.

(6530)
Nelson C R, Schwert G W
On testing the hypothesis that the real rate of interest is constant
AER 1977 VOL 67 p 478-486.

(6531)
Shiller R J, Siegel J J
The Gibson paradox and historical movements in
real interest rates
JPE 1977 VOL 85 p 891.

(6532)
Bassie V L
The real rate of interest: a thesis in pseudoscience
QREB 1976 VOL 16:4 p 7.

(6533)
Eden B
On the specification of the demand for money:
The real rate of return versus the rate of inflation
JPE 1976 VOL 84 p 1353.

(6534)
Fama E F
Inflation uncertainty and expected returns on
Treasury bills
JPE 1976 JUN VOL 84:3 p 427-448.

(6535)
Feldstein M
Inflation, income taxes and the rate of interest: A
theoretical analysis
AER 1976 VOL 66 p 809-820.

(6536)
Gandolfi A E
Taxation and the "Fisher effect"
JF 1976 VOL 31 p 1127.

(6537)
Lahiri K
Inflationary expectations: Their formation and
interest rate effects
AER 1976 VOL 66 p 124-131.

(6538)
Anderson P A, Sargent T, Thislethwaite C
The response of interest rates to expected
inflation in the MPS model
JME 1975 VOL 1 p 111.

(6539)
Archer S H, Choate G M
Irving Fisher, inflation and the nominal rate of
interest
JFQA 1975 NOV VOL 10 p 675.

(6540)
Fama E F
Short-term interest rates as predictors of inflation
AER 1975 VOL 65 p 269-282.

(6541)
Hess P J, Bicksler J L
Capital asset prices versus time series models as
predictors of inflation: The expected real rate of
interest and market efficiency
JFE 1975 VOL 2 p 341.

(6542)
Visco I
Inflation and the rate of interest
QJE 1975 VOL 89 p 303.

(6543)
Grinyer J R
An extension of Fisher's model
JBF 1973 SPRING VOL 5:1 p 13-23.

(6544)
LeRoy S F
Interest rates and the inflation premium
F R Bk Kansas City Mo Rev 1973 MAY.

(6545)
Roll R
Assets, money, and commodity price inflation
under uncertainty demand theory
JMCB 1973 NOV VOL 5:4 p 903-923.

(6546)
Santomero A M
A note on interest rates and prices in general
equilibrium
JF 1973 VOL 28 p 997.

(6547)
Silveira A M
Interest rate and rapid inflation, the evidence
from the Brazilian economy
JMCB 1973 AUG VOL 5:3 p 794-805.

(6548)
Steindl F G
Price expectations and interest rates
JMCB 1973 NOV VOL 5:4 p 939-946.

(6549)
Talley R J
A "real" explanation of interest rate movements
QREB 1973 VOL 13:4 p 7.

(6550)
Gibson W E
Interest rates and inflationary expectations: New
evidence
AER 1972 VOL 62 p 854-865.

(6551)
Karni E
Inflation and real interest rate: A long-term
analysis
JPE 1972 VOL 80 p 365.

(6552)
Pyle D H
Observed price expectations and interest rates
REStat 1972 AUG VOL 54 p 275-280.

(6553)
Roll R
Interest rates on monetary assets and commodity
price index changes
JF 1972 MAY VOL 27 p 251-278.

(6554)
Sargent T J
Anticipated inflation and nominal interest
QJE 1972 VOL 86 p 212.

(6555)
Feldstein M
Inflation, specification bias and the impact of
interest rates
JPE 1970 NOV-DEC VOL 78 p 1325-1339.

(6556)
Gibson W E
Price expectations effects on interest rates
JF 1970 MAR VOL 25 p 19-34.

(6557)
Gupta S B
The portfolio balance theory of the expected rate
of change of prices
REStud 1970 APR VOL 37 p 187-203.

(6558)
Hicks J R
Inflation and interest
BNLQR 1970 SEP VOL 23 p 261-275.

(6559)
Sargent T J
Commodity price expectations and the interest
rate
QJE 1969 FEB VOL 83 p 127-140.

(6560)
Yohe W P, Karnosky D W
Interest rates and price level changes, 1952-69
F R Bk St Louis Rev 1969 DEC.

(6561)
Ball R J
Inflation and the theory of money
Allen, 1964.

(6562)
Meiselman D
Bond yields and the price level: the Gibson
paradox regained
(in Carson D ed., Banking and monetary studies.
Irwin, 1963.)

(6563)
Mundell R
Inflation and real interest
JPE 1963 JUN VOL 71 p 280-283.

(6564)
Kennedy C M
Inflation and the bond rate
OEP 1960 OCT VOL 12 p 269-273.

17.2   Term structure of interest rates

(6565)
Brooks R, Levy H, Livingston M
The coupon effect on term premiums
JFR 1989 SPRING VOL 12:1 p 15-22..

(6566)**Feldman D**
The term structure of interest rates in a partially
observable economy
JF 1989 JUL VOL 44:3 p 789.

(6567)
Johnson B D, Meyer K R
Managing yield curve risk in an index environment
FAJ 1989 NOV-DEC VOL 45 p 51-59.

(6568)
Longstaff F A
A nonlinear general equilibrium model of the term structure of interest rates
JFE 1989 VOL 23 p 195.

(6569)
Poitras G
Do changes in debt maturity composition affect the term structure? Some Canadian evidence
AE 1989 VOL 21:4 p 553.

(6570)
Turnovsky S J
Term structure of interest rates and the effects of macroeconomic policy
JMCB 1989 VOL 21 p 321-347.

(6571)
Babbel D F
Interest rate dynamics and the term structure: A note
JBankF 1988 VOL 12:3 p 401-418.

(6572)
Dermody J C, Prisman E Z
Term structure multiplicity and clientele in markets with transactions costs and taxes
JF 1988 SEP VOL 43:4 p 893-912.

(6573)
Dialynas C P
Bond yield spreads revisited
JPM 1988 WINTER VOL 14:2 p 57-62.

(6574)
Harvey C R
The real term structure and consumption growth
JFE 1988 VOL 22 p 305.

(6575)
Kool C J M, Tatom J A
International linkages in the term structure of interest rates
F R Bk St Louis Rev 1988 JUL-AUG VOL 70:4.

(6576)
Kugler P
An empirical note on the term structure and interest rate stabilization policies
QJE 1988 VOL 103 p 789.

(6577)
Nelson C R, Siegel A F
Long-term behavior of yield curves
JFQA 1988 MAR VOL 23 p 105-110.

(6578)
Campbell J Y
Stock returns and the term structure
JFE 1987 JUN VOL 18:2 p 373-399.

(6579)
Kolari J W
An analytical model of risky yield curves
JFR 1987 VOL 10:4 p 295-304.

(6580)
Kroll R
The term structure of Eurodollar interest rates and its relationship to the UK treasury-bill market
JIMF 1987 SEP VOL 6:3 p 339-354.

(6581)
Livingston M
Flattening of bond yield curves
JFR 1987 SPRING VOL 10:1 p 17-24.

(6582)
Oldfield G S, Rogalski R J
The stochastic properties of term-structure movements
JME 1987 VOL 19 p 229.

(6583)
Plosser C I
Fiscal policy and the term structure
JME 1987 VOL 20 p 343.

(6584)
Takagi S
Transactions costs and the term structure of interest rates in the OTC bond market in Japan
JMCB 1987 NOV VOL 19:4 p 515-527.

(6585)
Benninga S, Protopapadakis A
General equilibrium properties of the term structure of interest rates
JFE 1986 VOL 15 p 389.

(6586)
Dunn K B, Singleton K J
Modeling the term structure of interest rates under non-separable utility and durability of goods.
JFE 1986 VOL 17:1 p 27-35.

(6587)
Jaffee D M
Term structure intermediation by depository institutions
JBankF 1986 VOL 10 p 309.

(6588)
Mankiw N G, Miron J A
The changing behavior of the term structure of interest rates
QJE 1986 VOL 101 p 211.

(6589)
Clark S J
The effects of government expenditure on the term structure of interest rates
JMCB 1985 AUG VOL 17:3 p 397-400.

(6590)
Hwang H S
The term structure of interest rates in money demand: a reevaluation
JMCB 1985 AUG VOL 17:3 p 391-396.

(6591)
Kanemasu H, Litzenberger R H, Rolfo J
Pricing U.S. Treasury securites with tax effects using the likelihood function
Finance 1985 VOL 6:2.

(6592)
Bisignano J
Monetary policy regimes and international term structures of interest rates
F R Bk San Francisco Ec Rev 1984 FALL.

(6593)
Cargill T F, Meyer R A
Municipal interest rates and the term structure and inflationary expectations
FR 1984 MAY p 135-152.

(6594)
Turnovsky S J, Miller M H
The effects of government expenditure on the term structure of interest rates
JMCB 1984 FEB VOL 16:1 p 16-33.

(6595)
Kidwell D S, Koch T W
Market segmentation and the term structure of municipal yields
JMCB 1983 FEB VOL 15:1 p 40-55.

(6596)
Mascaro A, Meltzer A H
Long and short-term interest rates in a risky world
JME 1983 VOL 12 p 485

(6597)
Sorensen E H
Who puts the slope in the municipal yield curve?
JPM 1983 SUMMER VOL 9:4 p 61.

(6598)
Bisignano J
Consumption, the term structure of interest rates and inflation: an international comparison
F R Bk San Francisco Ec Rev 1982 SUMMER.

(6599)
Park S
Spot and forward rates in the Canadian treasury bill market
JFE 1982 VOL 10 p 107.

(6600)
Dyl E A, Joehnk M D
Riding the yield curve: does it work?
JPM 1981 SPRING VOL 7:3 p 13-17.

(6601)
Roley V V
The determinants of the treasury security yield curve
JF 1981 DEC VOL 36:5 p 1103-1126.

(6602)
Hartman R C
The term structure of interest rates and the demand for investment
QJE 1980 VOL 94 p 591.

(6603)
Langetieg T C
A multivariate model of term structure
JF 1980 MAR VOL 35:1 p 71-97.

(6604)
Lee W Y, Maness T S, Tuttle D L
Nonspeculative behavior and the term structure
JFQA 1980 MAR VOL 15 p 53.

(6605)
Mishkin F S
Is the preferred-habitat model of the term structure inconsistent with financial market efficiency?
JPE 1980 VOL 88 p 406.

(6606)
Singleton K J
Maturity specific disturbances and the term structure of interest rates
JMCB 1980 NOV VOL 12:4 p 603-614.

(6607)
de Vries G H
The influence of debt management on the term-structure of interest rates
De Economist 1979 VOL 127:2.

(6608)
Phillips L, Pippenger J
The term structure of interest rates in the MIT PENN SSRC model: reality or illusion?
JMCB 1979 MAY VOL 11:2 p 151-164.

(6609)
Sargent T J
A note on the estimation of the rational expectations model of the term structure
JME 1979 VOL 5 p 133-143.

(6610)
Amihud Y
Uncertainty in future interest rates and the term structure
JBFA 1978 SPRING VOL 5:1 p 49-56

(6611)
Cornell B
Monetary policy, inflation forecasting and the term structure of interest rates
JF 1978 VOL 33 p 117.

(6612)
Dothan L U
On the term structure of interest rates
JFE 1978 VOL 6 p 59-69.

(6613)
Caks J
The coupon effect on yield to maturity
JF 1977 VOL 32 p 103.

(6614)
Schaefer S M
The problem with redemption yields
FAJ 1977 JUL-AUG p 59.

(6615)
Cramer R H, Seifet J A
Measuring the impact of maturity on expected return and risk
JBR 1976 AUTUMN VOL 7:3.

(6616)
Echols M E, Elliott J W
Rational expectations in a disequilibrium model of the term structure
AER 1976 MAR VOL 66:1 p 28-44.

(6617)
Hendershott P H
A tax cut in a multiple security model: Crowding out, pulling in and the term structure of interest rates
JF 1976 VOL 31 p 1185.

(6618)
Phillips L, Pippenger J
Preferred habitat vs. efficient market: a test of alternative hypotheses
F R Bk St Louis Rev 1976 VOL 58:5..

(6619)**Long J B Jr**
Stock prices, inflation and the term structure of interest rates
JFE 1974 VOL 1 p 131.

(6620)
Gray J M
New evidence on the term structure of interest rates: 1884-1900
JF 1973 VOL 28 p 635.

(6621)
Shiller R J
Rational expectations and the term structure of interest rates
JMCB 1973 AUG VOL 5:3 p 856-859.

(6622)
Sinkey J F Jr
The term structure of interest rates
JMCB 1973 FEB VOL 5:1 p 192-200.

(6623)
Carr J, Smith L B
Money supply, interest rates, and the yield curve
JMCB 1972 AUG VOL 4:3 p 582-594.

(6624)
Homer S, Leibowitz M L
Inside the yield book: new tools for bond market strategy
P-H, 1972.

(6625)
Peters D H
Coupon rate of return
FIN MGMT 1972 WINTER VOL 1 p 25.

(6626)
Terrell W T, Frazer W J
Interest rates, portfolio behavior and marketable government securities
JF 1972 MAR VOL 27 p 1-36.

(6627)
Malkiel B G
The term structure of interest rates: Theory, empirical evidence and applications
McCaleb-Seiler, 1970.

(6628)
Rowan D C, O'Brien R J
Expectations, the interest rate structure and debt policy
(in Hilton K and Heathfield D F, The econometric study of the United Kingdom. Macmillan Int, 1970.)

(6629)
Mauer L J
Commercial bank maturity demand for United States government securities and the determinants of the term structure of interest rates
JFQA 1969 MAR VOL 4 p 37-52.

(6630)
Wood J H
Expectations and the demand for bonds
AER 1969 SEP VOL 59 p 522-530.

(6631)
Walters A A
The demand for money, expectations, and short and long rates
(in Wolfe J N ed., Value, capital and growth. Edinburgh U Pr, 1968.)

(6632)
Ben-Shanar H
The structure of interest rates, government financing and economic growth
Kyk 1967 VOL 20 p 492-500.

(6633)
Ford J L, Stark T
Long- and short-term interest rates
Blackwell, 1967.

(6634)
Grossman H I
Risk aversion, financial intermediation and the term structure of interest rates
JF 1967 DEC VOL 22 p 611-622.

(6635)
Wallace N
Term structure of interest rates and the maturity composition of the federal debt
JF 1967 MAY VOL 22 p 301-312.

(6636)
Fand D I
A time-series analysis of the "bills-only" theory of interest rates
REStat 1966 NOV VOL 48 p 361-371.

(6637)
Paish F W
Long-term and short-term interest rates in the
United Kingdom
Manchester U Pr, 1966.

(6638)
Pye G
A Markov model of the term structure
QJE 1966 FEB VOL 80 p 60-72.

(6639)
Struble F M
The current debate on the term structure of
interest rates
F R Bk Kansas City Mo Rev 1966 JAN-FEB.

(6640)
Kessel R A
The cyclical behavior of the term structure of
interest rates
(Dist by Columbia U Pr) Natl Bur Econ Res,
1965.

(6641)
Van Horne J C
Interest-rate risk and the term structure of
interest rates
JPE 1965 AUG VOL 73 p 344-351.

(6642)
Luckett D G
Bills only: a critical appraisal
REStat 1960 AUG VOL 41 p 301-306.

(6643)
Young R A, Yager C A
The economics of "bills preferably"
QJE 1960 AUG VOL 74 p 341-373.

(6644)
Walker C E
Federal reserve policy and the structure of
interest rates on government securities
QJE 1954 FEB VOL 68 p 19-42.

(6645)
Segall J E
The effect of maturity on price fluctuations
JB 1950 VOL 29 p 202-206.

(6646)
Lusher D W
The structure of interest rates and the Keynesian
theory of interest
JPE 1942 APR VOL 50 p 272-279.

17.21   Measurement of term structure

(6647)
Cecchetti S G
The case of the negative nominal interest rates:
new estimates of the term structure of interest
rates during the Great Depression
JPE 1988 DEC VOL 96:6 p 1111-1141.

(6648)
Hardouvelis G A
The predictive power of the term structure during
recent monetary regimes
JF 1988 JUN VOL 43:2 p 339-356.

(6649)
Rowe T D, Lawler T A, Cook T Q
Treasury bill versus private money market yield
curves
F R Bk Richmond Ec Rev 1986 VOL 72:4.

(6650)
Boyle P P
Prices instead of yields to model the term
structure
Finance 1985 VOL 6:2.

(6651)
Shea G S
Interest rate term structure estimation with
exponential splines : a note
JF 1985 MAR VOL 40:1 p 319-325.

(6652)
Chambers D R, Carleton W T, Waldman D W
A new approach to estimation of the term
structure of interest rates
JFQA 1984 SEP VOL 19:3 p 233-252.

(6653)
Jordan J V
Tax effects in term structure estimation
JF 1984 JUN VOL 39:2 p 393-406.

(6654)
Shea G S
Pitfalls in smoothing interest rate term structure data: equilibrium models and spline approximations
JFQA 1984 SEP VOL 19:3 p 253-269.

(6655)
Livingston M, Jain S
Flattening of bond yield curves for long maturities
JF 1982 MAR VOL 37:1 p 157-167.

(6656)
Dobson S W
Estimating term structure equations with individual bond data
JF 1978 VOL 33 p 75.

(6657)
Bank of England
Yield curves for gilt-edged stocks: a further modification
BEQB 1976 VOL 16 p 212.

(6658)
Carleton W T, Cooper I A
Estimation and uses of the term structure of interest rates
JF 1976 VOL 31 p 1067.

(6659)
Echols M E, Elliott J W
A quantitative yield curve model for estimating the term structure of interest rates
JFQA 1976 MAR VOL 11 p 87.

(6660)
Echols M E, Elliott J W
Measuring the shoulder of the yield curve
JBR 1975 WINTER VOL 5:4.

(6661)
McCulloch J H
An estimate of the liquidity premium
JPE 1975 FEB VOL 83:1 p 95-120.

(6662)
Cargill T F, Meyer R A
Estimating term structure phenomena from data aggregated over time
JMCB 1974 NOV VOL 6:4 p 503-516.

(6663)
Bank of England
Yield curves for gilt-edged stocks: further investigation
BEQB 1973 VOL 13 p 315-326.

(6664)
McCulloch J H
Measuring the term structure of interest rates
JB 1971 JAN VOL 44 p 19-31.

(6665)
Masera R S
Least-squares construction of the yield curves for Italian government securities, 1957-1967 [Parts 1-2]
BNLQR 1969 DEC VOL 22 p 347-371; BNLQR 1970 MAR VOL 23 p 82-102.

(6666)
Granger C W J, Rees H J B
Spectral analysis of the term structure of interest rates
REStat 1968 JAN VOL 50.

(6667)
Cohen K J, Kramer R L, Waugh W H
Regression yield curves for U.S. Government securities
MSci 1966 DEC VOL 13 p B168-B175.

(6668)
Durand D
A quarterly series of corporate basic yields 1952-1957 and some attendant reservations
JF 1958 SEP VOL 13 p 348-356.

(6669)
Durand D, Winn W J
Basic yields of bonds 1920-1947: their measurement and pattern
Natl Bur Econ Res, 1947.

(6670)
Durand D
Basic yields of corporate bonds 1900-1942
Natl Bur Econ Res, 1942.

17.22   Duration and immunization

(6671)
Chen C R
The impact of maturity and yield effects on the systemic risk of bonds
JBFA 1989 AUTUMN VOL 16:4 p 565..

(6672)**Bierwag G O, Kaufman G G**
Durations of non-default-free securities
FAJ 1988 JUL-AUG VOL 44 p 39-47.

(6673)
Bierwag G O, Kaufman G G, Latta C M
Duration models: a taxonomy
JPM 1988 FALL VOL 15:1 p 50-54.

(6674)
Chambers D R, Carleton W T, McEnally R W
Immunizing default-free bond portfolios with a duration vector
JFQA 1988 MAR VOL 23:1 p 89-104.

(6675)
Fong H G, Tang E M P
Immunized bond portfolios in portfolio protection
JPM 1988 WINTER VOL 14:2 p 63-68.

(6676)
Hegde S P, Nunn K P Jr
Non-infinitesimal rate changes and Macaulay duration
JPM 1988 WINTER VOL 14:2 p 69-73.

(6677)
Prisman E Z, Shores M R
Duration measures for specific term structure estimations and applications to bond portfolio immunization
JBankF 1988 VOL 12:3 p 493-504.

(6678)
Simonson D G, Stock D
Tax-adjusted duration for amortizing debt instruments
JFQA 1988 SEP VOL 23 p 313.

(6679)
Bierwag G O
Bond returns, discrete stochastic processes, and duration
JFR 1987 VOL 10:3 p 191-210.

(6680)
Bierwag G O, Kaufman G G, Latta C M
The usefulness of duration: response to critics
JPM 1987 WINTER VOL 13:2 p 48-52.

(6681)
Yawitz J B, Kaufold H, Macirowski T
The pricing and duration of floating rate bonds
JPM 1987 SUMMER VOL 13:4 p 49-56.

(6682)
Leibowitz M L
The dedicated bond portfolio in pension funds - Part 1: motivations and basics
FAJ 1986 JAN-FEB p 69.

(6683)
Leibowitz M L
The dedicated bond portfolio in pension funds - Part II: Immunization, horizon matching and contingent procedures
FAJ 1986 MAR-APR VOL 42 p 47-57.

(6684)
Morgan G E
Floating rate securities and immunization : some further results
JFQA 1986 MAR VOL 21:1 p 87-94.

(6685)
Prisman E Z
Immunization as a maxmin strategy: A new look
JBankF 1986 VOL 10 p 491.

(6686)
Alexander G J, Resnick B G
Using linear and goal programming to immunize bond portfolios
JBankF 1985 VOL 9 p 35.

(6687)
Bierwag G O, Kaufman G G
Duration gap for financial institutions
FAJ 1985 MAR-APR VOL 41 p 68-71.

(6688)
McEnally R W
Rethinking our thinking about interest rates
FAJ 1985 MAR-APR VOL 41 p 62-67.

(6689)
Babcock G C
Duration as a link between yield and value
JPM 1984 SUMMER VOL 10:4 p 58-65.

(6690)
Benesh G A, Colec S E
A simplified approach for calculating bond duration
FR 1984 NOV VOL 19:4.

(6691)
Casabona P A, Fabozzi F J, Francis J C
How to apply duration to equity analysis
JPM 1984 WINTER VOL 10:2 p 52-59.

(6692)
Chua J H
A closed-form formula for calculating bond duration
FAJ 1984 MAY-JUN VOL 40:3 p 76-78.

(6693)
Fong H G, Vasicek O A
A risk minimizing strategy for portfolio immunization
JF 1984 DEC VOL 39:5 p 1541-1546.

(6694)
Fuller R J, Settle J W
Determinants of duration and bond volatility
JPM 1984 SUMMER VOL 10:4 p 66.

(6695)
Little P K
Negative cash flows duration and immunization : a note
JF 1984 MAR VOL 39:1 p 283-288.

(6696)
Schaefer S
Immunisation and duration: a review of theory, performance, and applications
MCFJ 1984 FALL VOL 2 p 41-58.

(6697)
Bierwag G O, Kaufman G G, Toevs A
Immunization strategies for funding multiple liabilities.
JFQA 1983 MAR VOL 18:1 p 113-123.

(6698)
Bierwag G O, Kaufman G G, Toevs A eds.
Innovations in portfolio management: Duration analysis and immunization
JAI Pr, 1983.

(6699)
Bierwag G O, Kaufman G G, Toevs A
Bond portfolio immunization and stochastic process risk
JBR 1983 WINTER VOL 13:4.

(6700)
Bierwag G O, Kaufman G G, Toevs A
Duration: Its development and use in bond portfolio management
FAJ 1983 JUL-AUG VOL 39 p 15-36.

(6701)
Chance D M
Floating rate notes and immunization
JFQA 1983 SEP VOL 18:3 p 365-380.

(6702)
Fong H G, Vasicek O
The tradeoff between return and risk in immunized portfolios
FAJ 1983 SEP-OCT VOL 39 p 73-78.

(6703)
Ingersoll J E
Is immunization feasible? Evidence from the CRSP data
(in Bierwag G O, Kaufman G G and Toevs A eds., Innovations in bond portfolio management: duration analysis and immunization. JAI Pr, 1983.)

(6704)
Khang C
A dynamic global portfolio immunization strategy in the world of multiple interest rate changes : a dynamic immunization and minimax strategy
JFQA 1983 SEP VOL 18:3 p 355-363.

(6705)
Leibowitz M L, Weinberger A
Contingent immunization - Part II: Problem areas
FAJ 1983 JAN-FEB VOL 39 p 35-50.

(6706)
Nelson J, Schaefer S M
The dynamics of the term structure and
alternative portfolio immunization strategies
(in Bierwag G O, Kaufman G G and Toevs A
eds., Innovations in bond portfolio management:
duration analysis and immunization. JAI Pr,
1983.)

(6707)
Bierwag G O, Kaufman G G, Toevs A
Single factor duration models in a discrete
general equilibrium framework
JF 1982 MAY VOL 37:2 p 325-338.

(6708)
Kolb R W, Gay G D
Immunizing bond portfolios with interest rate
futures
FIN MGMT 1982 SUMMER VOL 11 p 81-89.

(6709)
Leibowitz M L, Weinberger A
Contingent immunization - Part I: Risk control
procedures
FAJ 1982 NOV-DEC VOL 38 p 17-32.

(6710)
Marshall W S, Yawitz J B
Lower bounds on portfolio performance : an
extension of the immunization strategy
JFQA 1982 MAR VOL 17:1 p 101-113.

(6711)
Dietz P O, Fogler H R, Rivers A U
Duration, nonlinearity and bond portfolio
performance
JPM 1981 SPRING VOL 7:3 p 37-41.

(6712)
Gushee C H
How to immunize a bond investment
FAJ 1981 MAR-APR VOL 37 p 44-51.

(6713)
Hessel C A, Huffman L
The effect of taxation on immunization rules and
duration estimation
JF 1981 DEC VOL 36:5 p 1127-1142.

(6714)
Haugen R A, Wichern D W
The term of a risk-free security
JFQA 1980 MAR VOL 15 p 41.

(6715)
McEnally R W
How to neutralize reinvestment rate risk
JPM 1980 SPRING VOL 6:3 p 59-63.

(6716)
Reilly F K, Sidhu R S
The many uses of bond duration
FAJ 1980 JUL-AUG VOL 36:4 p 58-72.

(6717)
Bierwag G O, Khang C
An immunization strategy is a minimax strategy
JF 1979 MAY VOL 34:2 p 389-399.

(6718)
Cox J C, Ingersoll J E, Ross S A
Duration and the measurement of basis risk
JB 1979 JAN VOL 52:1 p 51-61.

(6719)
Livingston M
Measuring bond price volatility
JFQA 1979 JUN VOL 14 p 343.

(6720)
Bierwag G O, Kaufman G G, Khang C
Duration and bonds
JFQA 1978 NOV VOL 13 p 671.

(6721)
Bradley C E, Joehnk M D, Fogler H R
The price elasticity of discounted bonds: Some
empirical evidence
JFQA 1978 SEP VOL 13 p 559.

(6722)
Ingersoll J E, Skelton J, Weil R L
Duration forty years later
JFQA 1978 NOV VOL 13 p 627.

(6723)
Lanstein R, Sharpe W F
Duration and security risk
JFQA 1978 NOV VOL 13 p 653.

(6724)
Livingston M
Duration and risk assessment for bonds and common stocks: A note
JF 1978 VOL 33 p 293..

(6725)**Bierwag G O**
Immunization, duration and the term structure of interest rates
JFQA 1977 DEC VOL 12 p 725.

(6726)
Cooper I A
Asset changes, interest rate changes and duration
JFQA 1977 DEC VOL 12 p 701.

(6727)
Hodges S D, Schaefer S M
A model for bond portfolio improvement
JFQA 1977 JUN VOL 12 p 243.

(6728)
Livingston M, Caks J
A note regarding a "duration" fallacy
JF 1977 VOL 32 p 185.

(6729)
Yawitz J B
The relative importance of duration and yield volatility on bond price volatility
JMCB 1977 FEB VOL 9:1 p 97-102.

(6730)
Boquist J A, Racette G A, Schlarbaum G G
Duration and risk assessment for bonds and common stocks
JF 1975 VOL 30 p 1360.

(6731)
Yawitz J B, Hempel G H, Marshall W J
The use of average maturity as a risk proxy in investment portfolios
JF 1975 MAY VOL 30:2 p 325-333.

(6732)
Carr J L, Halpern P J, McCallum J S
Correcting the yield curve: A re-interpretation of the duration problem
JF 1974 VOL 29 p 17.22

(6733)
Grove M A
On "duration" and the optimal maturity structure of the balance sheet
BellJ 1974 AUTUMN VOL 5:2 p 696-709.

(6734)
Hopewell M H, Kaufman G G
Bond price volatility and term to maturity: A generalized respecification
AER 1973 VOL 63 p 749-753.

(6735)
Fisher L, Weil R L
Coping with the risk of interest rate fluctuations; returns to bondholders from naive and optimal strategies
JB 1971 OCT VOL 44 p 408-431.

(6736)
Reddington F M
Review of the principles of life office evaluation
Journal of the Institute of Actuaries 1952 VOL 78 p 286-315.

(6737)
Macaulay F R
Some theoretical problems suggested by the movements of interest rates, bond yields and stock prices in the United States since 1856
Natl Bur Econ Res, 1938.

17.23 Factor models of term structure

(6738)
Bliss R R Jr, Ronn E I
Arbitrage-based estimation of nonstationary shifts in the term structure of interest rates
JF 1989 JUL VOL 44:3 p 591-610.

(6739)
Ahn C M, Thompson H E
Jump-diffusion processes and the term structure
of interest rates
JF 1988 MAR VOL 43:1 p 155-174.

(6740)
Brown S J, Dybvig P H
The empirical implications of the Cox Ingersoll
Ross Theory of the term structure of interest
rates
JF 1986 JUL VOL 41:3 p 617-632.

(6741)
Cox J C, Ingersoll J E, Ross S A
A theory of the term structure of interest rates
Em 1985 MAY VOL 53.

(6742)
Schaefer S M, Schwartz E S
A two-factor model of the term structure : an
approximate analytical solution
JFQA 1984 DEC VOL 19:4 p 413-424.

(6743)
Brennan M J, Schwartz E S
Duration bond pricing and portfolio performance
(in Bierwag G O, Kaufman G G and Toevs A
eds., Innovations in bond portfolio management:
duration analysis and immunization. JAI Pr,
1983.)

(6744)
Marsh T A, Rosenfeld E R
Stochastic processes for interest rates and
equilibrium bond prices
JF 1983 MAY VOL 38:2 p 635-647.

(6745)
Brennan M J, Schwartz E S
An equilibrium model of bond pricing and a test
of market efficiency
JFQA 1982 SEP VOL 17:3 p 301-329.

(6746)
Brennan M J, Schwartz E S
Bond pricing and market efficiency
FAJ 1982 SEP-OCT VOL 38 p 49-56.

(6747)
Vasicek O A, Fong G
Term structure modelling
JF 1982 MAY VOL 37:2 p 339-348.

(6748)
Brennan M J, Schwartz E S
Conditional predictions of bond prices and
returns
JF 1980 MAY VOL 35:2 p 405-419.

(6749)
Marsh T
Equilibrium   term   structure   models: test
methodology
JF 1980 MAY VOL 35:2 p 421-438.

(6750)
Ayres H F, Barry J Y
The equilibrium yield curve for government
securities
FAJ 1979 MAY-JUN VOL 35 p 31-40.

(6751)
Richard S F
An arbitrage model of the term structure of
interest rates
JFE 1978 VOL 6 p 33-57.

(6752)
Vasicek O A
An equilibrium characterization of the term
structure
JFE 1977 VOL 5 p 177.

17.24   Expectations theory and term premia

(6753)
Backus D K, Gregory A W, Zin S E
Risk premiums in the term structure: evidence
from artificial economies
JME 1989 VOL 24 p 371.

(6754)
Froot K A
New hope for the expectations hypothesis of the
term structure of interest rates
JF 1989 JUN VOL 44:2 p 283-306.

(6755)
Lee B-S
A nonlinear expectations model of the term structure of interest rates with time-varying risk premia
JMCB 1989 VOL 21 p 348-367.

(6756)
Levy H, Brooks R
An empirical analysis of term premiums using stochastic dominance
JBankF 1989 MAY VOL 13:2 p 245-260.

(6757)
Walz D T, Spencer R W
The informational content of forward rates: further evidence
JFR 1989 SPRING VOL 12:1 p 69-82.

(6758)
Belongia M T, Koedijk K G
Testing the expectations model of the term structure: some conjectures on the effects of institutional changes
F R Bk St Louis Rev 1988 SEP-OCT VOL 70:5.

(6759)
Chiang T C
The forward rate as a predictor of the future spot rate - a stochastic coefficient approach
JMCB 1988 MAY VOL 20:2 p 212-232.

(6760)
Heuson A J
The term premia relationship implicit in the term structure of treasury bills
JFR 1988 VOL 11:1 p 13-20.

(6761)
Stambaugh R F
The information in forward rates: implications for models of the term structure
JFE 1988 VOL 21 p 41-70.

(6762)
Engle R F, Lilien D M, Robins R P
Estimating time varying risk premia in the term structure: The ARCH-M model
Em 1987 MAR VOL 55 p 391-407.

(6763)
Fama E F, Bliss R R
The information in long-maturity forward rates
AER 1987 SEP VOL 77:4 p 680-692.

(6764)
McCulloch J H
The monotonicity of the term premium: a closer look
JFE 1987 VOL 18 p 185-192.

(6765)
Campbell J Y
A defense of traditional hypotheses about the term structure of interest rates
JF 1986 MAR VOL 41:1 p 183-193.

(6766)
Fama E F
Term premiums and default premiums in money markets.
JFE 1986 SEP VOL 17:1 p 175-196.

(6767)
Gilles C, Leroy S F
A note on the local expectations hypothesis : a discrete-time exposition
JF 1986 SEP VOL 41:4 p 975-979.

(6768)
Hsieh D A, Leiderman L
Portfolio implications of empirical rejections of the expectations hypothesis
REStat 1986 VOL 68 p 680.

(6769)
Walsh C E
A rational expectations model of term premia with some implications for empirical asset demand equations
JF 1985 MAR VOL 40:1 p 63-83.

(6770)
Fama E F
The information in the term structure
JFE 1984 VOL 13 p 509-528.

(6771)
Fama E F
Term premiums in bond returns
JFE 1984 VOL 13 p 529-546.

(6772)
Logue D E, Sweeney R J
Term premia on euro rates
JF 1984 JUL VOL 39:3 p 747-757.

(6773)
Jones D S, Vance R V
Rational expectations and the expectations model
of the term structure: A test using weekly data
JME 1983 SEP VOL 12 p 453-465.

(6774)
Pesando J E
On expectations, term premiums and the volatility
of long-term interest rates
JME 1983 VOL 12 p 467.

(6775)
Levy H
The yield curve and expected inflation
FAJ 1982 NOV-DEC VOL 38 p 37-44.

(6776)
Startz R
Do forecast errors or term premia really make
the difference between long and short rates?
JFE 1982 VOL 10:3 p 323-329.

(6777)
Cox J C, Ingersoll J E, Ross S A
A reexamination of traditional hypotheses about
the term structure of interest rates
JF 1981 SEP VOL 36:4 p 769-799..

(6778)**Lorie H R**
Another look at liquidity preference
QJE 1980 VOL 94 p 167.

(6779)
Roberts G S
Term premiums in the term structure of interest
rates
JMCB 1980 MAY VOL 12:2 p 184-197.

(6780)
Singleton K J
Expectations models of the term structure and
implied variance bounds
JPE 1980 VOL 88 p 1159.

(6781)
Baldwin C Y, Meyer R F
Liquidity preference under uncertainty: A model
of dynamic investment in illiquid opportunities
JFE 1979 VOL 7 p 347-374.

(6782)
Friedman B M
Interest rate expectations versus forward rates:
evidence from an expectations survey
JF 1979 SEP VOL 34:4 p 945-973.

(6783)
Heller H R, Khan M S
The demand for money and the term structure of
interest rates
JPE 1979 VOL 87 p 109.

(6784)
Sargent T J
A note on maximum likelihood estimation of the
rational expectations model of the term structure
JME 1979 VOL 5 p 133.

(6785)
Shiller R J
The volatility of long-term interest rates and
expectations models of the term structure
JPE 1979 VOL 87 p 1190.

(6786)
Brealey R, Schaefer S
Term structure and uncertain inflation
JF 1977 MAY VOL 32:2 p 277-290.

(6787)
Burger A E, Lang R W, Rasche R H
The Treasury bill futures market and market
expectations of interest rates
F R Bk St Louis Rev 1977 VOL 59:6.

(6788)
Elliott J W, Echols M E
Expected yield curve movements and rational
term structure expectations: an empirical note
JMCB 1977 FEB VOL 9:1 p 90-96.

(6789)
Dobson S W, Sutch R C, Vanderford D E
An evaluation of alternative empirical models of
the term structure of interest rates
JF 1976 VOL 31 p 1035.

(6790)
Fama E F
Forward rates as predictors of future spot rates
JFE 1976 VOL 3 p 361.

(6791)
Cargill T F
The term structure of interest rates: A test of the expectations hypothesis
JF 1975 VOL 30 p 761.

(6792)
McCallum J S
The expected holding period return, uncertainty and the term structure of interest rates
JF 1975 MAY VOL 30:2 p 307-324.

(6793)
Pesando J E
Determinants of term premiums in the market for United States Treasury Bills
JF 1975 VOL 30 p 1317.

(6794)
Santomero A M
The error-learning hypothesis and the term structure of interest rates in Eurodollars
JF 1975 VOL 30 p 773.

(6795)
Olsen R A
The effect of interest-rate risk on liquidity premiums: An empirical investigation
JFQA 1974 NOV VOL 9 p 901.

(6796)
Ben-Shahar J H B, Cukierman A
The term-structure of interest rates and expectations of price-increase and devaluation
JF 1973 VOL 28 p 567.

(6797)
Masera R S
The term structure of interest rates: an expectations model tested on post-war Italian data
Clarendon, 1972.

(6798)
Nelson C R
The term structure of interest rates
Basic, 1972.

(6799)
Diller S
The expectations component of the term structure
(in Guttentag J M ed., Essays on interest rates, vol 2. (Dist by Columbia U Pr) Natl Bur Econ Res, 1971.)

(6800)
Hamburger M J
Expectations, long-term interest rates and monetary policy in the United Kingdom
BEQB 1971 SEP VOL 11 p 354-372.

(6801)
Roll R
Investment diversification and bond maturity
JF 1971 MAR VOL 26 p 51-56.

(6802)
Sargent T J
Expectations at the short end of the yield curve: an application of Macaulay's test
(in Guttentag J M ed., Essays on interest rates, vol 2. (Dist by Columbia U Pr) Natl Bur Econ Res, 1971.)

(6803)
Buse A
Expectations, prices, coupons and yields
JF 1970 SEP VOL 25 p 809-818.

(6804)
Kane E J
The term structure of interest rates: an attempt to reconcile teaching with practice
JF 1970 MAY VOL 25 p 361-374.

(6805)
Nelson C R
A model of the term structure of interest rates
JASA 1970 SEP VOL 65 p 1163-1179.

(6806)
Pierson G
Effect of economic policy on the term structure of interest rates
REStat 1970 FEB VOL 52 p 1-11.

(6807)
Roll R
The behavior of interest rates: an application of
the efficient market model to U.S. Treasury bills
Basic, 1970.

(6808)
Diller S
Expectations in the term structure of interest
rates
(in Mincer J ed., Economic forecasts and
expectations. Natl Bur Econ Res, 1969.)

(6809)
Krainer R E
Liquidity preference and stock market speculation
JFQA 1969 MAR VOL 4 p 89-98.

(6810)
Malkiel B G, Kane E J
Expectations and interest rates: a cross-sectional
test of the error-learning hypothesis
JPE 1969 JUL-AUG VOL 77 p 453-470.

(6811)
Bierwag G O, Grove M A
A model of the term structure of interest rates
REStat 1967 FEB VOL 49 p 50-62.

(6812)
Buse A
Interest rates, the Meiselman model and random
numbers
JPE 1967 FEB VOL 75 p 49-62.

(6813)
Green H A J
Uncertainty and the "expectations hypothesis"
REStud 1967 OCT VOL 34 p 387-398.

(6814)
Kane E J, Malkiel B G
The term structure of interest rates: an analysis of
a survey of interest rate expectations
REStat 1967 AUG VOL 49 p 343-355.

(6815)
Luckett D G
Multi-period expectations and the term structure
of interest rates
QJE 1967 MAY VOL 81 p 321-329.

(6816)
Modigliani F, Sutch R
Debt management and the term structure of
interest rates
JPE 1967 AUG VOL 75 Suppl p 569-589.

(6817)
Telser L G
A critique of some recent empirical research on
the explanation of the term structure of interest
rates
JPE 1967 AUG VOL 75 Suppl p 546-561.

(6818)
Fisher D
Expectations, the term structure of interest rates
and recent British experience
Ec 1966 AUG VOL 46 p 319-329.

(6819)
Malkiel B G
The term structure of interest rates: expectations
and behavior patterns
Princeton U Pr, 1966.

(6820)
Van Horne J C
Interest-rate expectations, the shape of the yield
curve, and monetary policy
REStat 1966 MAY VOL 48 p 211-215.

(6821)
Weaver A R H
The uncertainty of the expectations theory of the
term structure of interest rates
WEJ 1966 VOL 4 p 122-134.

(6822)
Culbertson J M
The interest rate structure: towards completion of
the classical system
(in Hahn F H and Brechling F P R eds., The
theory of interest rates. Macmillan Int, 1965.)

(6823)
Michaelsen J B
The term structure of interest rates and
holding-period yields on government securities
JF 1965 SEP VOL 20 p 444-463.

(6824)
Scott R H
Liquidity and the term structure of interest rates
QJE 1965 FEB VOL 79 p 135-145.

(6825)
Grant J A G
Meiselman on the structure of interest rates: a
British test
Ec 1964 FEB VOL 44 p 51-71.

(6826)
Malkiel B G
The term structure of interest rates
AER 1964 MAY VOL 54 p 532-543.

(6827)
Wood J H
The expectations hypothesis, the yield curve and
monetary policy
QJE 1964 AUG VOL 78 p 457-470.

(6828)
Freeman J F
Liquidity preference and loanable funds: a new
approach to the problem
EJ 1963 DEC VOL 73 p 681-688.

(6829)
Wood J H
Expectations, errors, and the term structure of
interest rates
JPE 1963 APR VOL 71 p 160-171.

(6830)
Malkiel B G
Expectations, bond prices and the term structure
of interest rates
QJE 1962 MAY VOL 76 p 197-218..

(6831)**Meiselman D**
The term structure of interest rates
P-H, 1962.

(6832)
Goode R, Birnham E A
The relation between long-term and short-term
interest rates in the United States
IMF 1959 OCT p 224-243.

(6833)
Luckett D G
Professor Lutz and the structure of interest rates
QJE 1959 FEB VOL 73 p 131-144.

(6834)
Culbertson J M
The term structure of interest rates
QJE 1957 NOV VOL 71 p 485-517.

(6835)
Lutz F A
The structure of interest rates
QJE 1940-1941 VOL 55 p 36-63.

17.25   Tax and term structure

(6836)
Torous W N
Differential taxation and the equilibrium structure
of interest rates
JBankF 1985 VOL 9 p 363.

(6837)
Jordan J V
Tax effects in term structure estimation
JF 1984 JUN VOL 39:2 p 393-406.

(6838)
Litzenberger R H, Rolfo J
An international study of tax effects on
government bonds
JF 1984 MAR VOL 39:1 p 1-22.

(6839)
Schaefer S M
Tax-induced clientele effects in the market for
British Government Securities: Placing bounds on
security values in an incomplete market
JFE 1982 VOL 10 p 121.

(6840)
Schaefer S M
Measuring a tax specific term structure of interest
rates in the market for British government
securities
EJ 1981 JUN VOL 91.

(6841)
Livingston M
Bond taxation and the shape of the yield-to-maturity curve
JF 1979 MAR VOL 34:1 p 189-196.

(6842)
Livingston M
Taxation and bond market equilibrium in a world of uncertain future interest rates
JFQA 1979 MAR VOL 14 p 11.

(6843)
Shiller R J, Modigliani F
Coupon and tax effects on new and seasoned bond yields and the measurement of the cost of debt capital.
JFE 1979 SEP VOL 7:3 p 297-318

(6844)
McCulloch J H
The tax-adjusted yield curve
JF 1975 VOL 30 p 811.

(6845)
Colin J W, Dyl E A
Calculation of tax effective yields: a correction
JFQA 1971 SEP VOL 6 p 1163-1164.

(6846)
Robichek A A, Niebuhr W D
Tax-induced bias in reported Treasury yields
JF 1970 DEC VOL 25 p 1081-1090.

(6847)
Pye G
On the tax structure of interest rates
QJE 1969 NOV VOL 83 p 562-579.

(6848)
Federal Reserve Bank of Kansas City
Taxes and the term structure of yields
F R Bk Kansas City Mo Rev 1960 DEC.

17.3   Default premia

(6849)
Gardner M J, Mills D L
Evaluating the likelihood of default on delinquent loans
FIN MGMT 1989 WINTER VOL 18 p 55-63.

(6850)
Lamy R E, Thompson G R
Risk premia and the pricing of primary issue bonds
JBankF 1988 DEC VOL 12:4 p 585-602.

(6851)
Rodriguez R J
Default risk, yield spreads, and time to maturity
JFQA 1988 MAR VOL 23:1 p 111-117.

(6852)
Fons J S
The default premium and corporate bond experience
JF 1987 MAR VOL 42:1 p 81-97.

(6853)
Chiang R, Kolb R W
An analytical model of the relationship between maturity and bonds risk differentials
FR 1986 MAY VOL 21:2.

(6854)
Fama E F
Term premiums and default premiums in money markets.
JFE 1986 SEP VOL 17:1 p 175-196.

(6855)
Gehrlein W V, McIntosh T H
Cyclical variability of bond risk premia: A note
JBankF 1985 VOL 9 p 157.

(6856)
Weinstein M I
The equity component of corporate bonds
JPM 1985 SPRING VOL 11:3 p 37-41.

(6857)
Yawitz J B, Maloney K J, Ederington L H
Taxes, default risk and yield spreads
JF 1985 SEP VOL 40:4 p 1127-1140.

(6858)
Liu P, Thakor A V
Interest yields, credit ratings, and economic characteristics of state bonds: an empirical analysis
JMCB 1984 AUG VOL 16:3 p 344-351.

(6859)
Molho L E
Loan rates as a selective credit control
JBankF 1984 VOL 8 p 79.

(6860)
Pitts C G C, Selby M J P
The pricing of corporate debt : a further note
JF 1983 SEP VOL 38:4 p 1311-1313.

(6861)
Pozdena R J, Iben B
Pricing debt instruments: the options approach
F R Bk San Francisco Ec Rev 1983 SUMMER.

(6862)
Feder G, Ross K
Risk assessments and risk premiums in the Eurodollar market
JF 1982 JUN VOL 37:3 p 679-691.

(6863)
Kolari J W, Apilado V P
Bond risk premiums, financial data and the effects of market segmentation
JBFA 1982 SUMMER VOL 9:2 p 207-218.

(6864)
Lawler T A
Default, risk, and yield spreads: a clarification
JPM 1982 SUMMER VOL 8:4 p 65-66.

(6865)
Arzac E R, Schwartz R A, Whitcomb D K
The leverage structure of interest rates
JMCB 1981 FEB VOL 13:1 p 72-88.

(6866)
Kidwell D S, Trzcinka C A
The risk structure of interest rates and the Penn-Central crisis
JF 1979 JUN VOL 34:3 p 751-760.

(6867)
Benson E D, Rogowski R J
The cyclical behavior of risk spreads on new municipal issues
JMCB 1978 AUG VOL 10:3 p 348-362.

(6868)
Ferri M G
An empirical examination of the determinants of bond yield spreads
FIN MGMT 1978 AUTUMN VOL 7 p 40.

(6869)
Meyer K R
Yield spreads and interest rate levels
FAJ 1978 NOV-DEC p 58-63.

(6870)
Tezel A
A note on bond risk differential
JFQA 1978 SEP VOL 13 p 573.

(6871)
Davis S I
How risky is international lending?
HBR 1977 JAN-FEB VOL 55:1 p 135-143.

(6872)
Melton W C
Recent behavior of the risk structure of bond yields
F R Bk New York Q Rev 1977 SUMMER VOL 2.

(6873)
Yawitz J B
An analytical model of interest rate differentials and different default recoveries
JFQA 1977 SEP VOL 12 p 481.

(6874)
Bierman H Jr, Hass J E
An analytical model of bond risk differentials
JFQA 1975 DEC VOL 10 p 757.

(6875)
Jaffee D M
Cyclical variations in the risk structure of interest rates
JME 1975 VOL 1 p 309

(6876)
Ederington L H
The yield spread on new issues of corporate
bonds
JF 1974 VOL 29 p 1531.

(6877)
Pye G
Gauging the default premium
FAJ 1974 JAN-FEB VOL 30 p 49-52.

(6878)
Silvers J B
An alternative to the yield spread as a measure of
risk
JF 1973 VOL 28 p 933.

(6879)
Soldofsky R M, Miller R L
Risk premium curves for different classes of
long-term securities, 1950-1966
JF 1969 JUN VOL 24 p 429-445.

(6880)
Baxter N D
Marketability, default risk and yields on money
market instruments
JFQA 1968 MAR VOL 3 p 75-86.

(6881)
Atkinson T R
Trends in corporate bond quality
(Dist by Columbia U Pr) Natl Bur Econ Res,
1967.

(6882)
Johnson R E
Term structures of corporate bond yields as a
function of risk of default
JF 1967 MAY VOL 22 p 313-345.

(6883)
Sloane P E
Determinants of bond yield differentials,
1954-1959
YEE 1963 SPRING VOL 3 p 3-55..

(6884)**Fraine H G, Mills R H**
Effect of defaults and credit deterioration on
yields of corporate bonds
JB 1961 SEP VOL 34 p 423-434.

(6885)
Brimmer A F
Credit conditions and price determination in the
corporate bond market
JF 1960 SEP VOL 15 p 353-370.

(6886)
Fisher L
Determinants of risk premiums on corporate
bonds
JPE 1959 JUN VOL 67 p 217-237.

(6887)
Hickman W B
Corporate bond quality and investor experience
Natl Bur Econ Res and Princeton U, 1958.

(6888)
Hickman W B
Corporate bonds: quality and investment
performance
Natl Bur Econ Res, 1957.

17.31 Bond ratings

(6889)
Gentry J A, Whitford D T, Newbold P
Predicting industrial bond ratings with a probit
model and funds flow components
FR 1988 AUG VOL 23:3 p 269-286.

(6890)
Hsueh L P, Kidwell D S
Bond ratings: Are two better than one?
FIN MGMT 1988 SPRING VOL 17 p 46-53.

(6891)
Perry L G, Liu P, Evans D A
Modified bond ratings: further evidence on the
effect of split ratings on corporate bond yields
JBFA 1988 SUMMER VOL 15:2 p 231-242.

(6892)
Wood D, Piesse J
The information value of failure predictions in
credit assessment
JBankF 1988 VOL 12 p 275-292.

(6893)
Zaima J K, McCarthy J
The impact of bond rating changes on common stocks and bonds: tests of the wealth redistribution hypothesis
FR 1988 NOV VOL 23:4 p 483-498.

(6894)
Ederington L H, Yawitz J B, Roberts B E
The informational content of bond ratings
JFR 1987 FALL VOL 10:3 p 211-226.

(6895)
Liu P, Moore W T
The impact of split bond ratings on risk premia
FR 1987 FEB VOL 22:1.

(6896)
Ogden J P
Determinants of the ratings and yields on corporate bonds: tests of the contingent claims model
JFR 1987 VOL 10:4 p 329-340.

(6897)
Ederington L H
Why split ratings occur
FIN MGMT 1986 SPRING VOL 15 p 37-47.

(6898)
Holthausen R W, Leftwich R W
The effect of bond rating changes on common stock prices
JFE 1986 SEP VOL 17:1 p 57-89.

(6899)
Billingsley R S, Lamy R E, Marr M W
Split ratings and bond re-offering yields
FIN MGMT 1985 SUMMER VOL 14 p 59-65.

(6900)
Ederington L H
Classification models and bond ratings
FR 1985 NOV VOL 20:4.

(6901)
Glascock J L, Davidson W N III
The effect of bond deratings on bank stock returns
JBR 1985 AUTUMN VOL 16:3 p 120-127.

(6902)
Billingsley R S, Fraser D R
Determinants of bank holding company debt ratings
FR 1984 MAR VOL 19:1.

(6903)
Cluff G S, Farnham P G
Standard & Poor vs Moody's : which city characteristics influence municipal bond ratings?
QREB 1984 AUTUMN VOL 24:3 p 72-94

(6904)
Belkaoui A
Industrial bonds and the rating process
Quorum Bks, 1983.

(6905)
Bhandari S B, Soldofsky R M, Boe W J
What's in a change in an industrial bond rating?
JBusR 1983 VOL 11 p 91-106.

(6906)
Ingram R W, Brooks L D, Copeland R M
The information content of municipal bond rating changes : a note
JF 1983 JUN VOL 38:3 p 997-1003.

(6907)
Martin L J, Henderson G V
On bond ratings and pension obligations : a note.
JFQA 1983 DEC VOL 18:4 p 463-470

(6908)
Morse D, Deely C
Regional differences in municipal bond ratings
FAJ 1983 NOV-DEC VOL 39 p 54-59.

(6909)
Altman E I
Computerized bond rating replication: worthwhile or futile?
JBR 1982 WINTER VOL 12:4.

(6910)
Griffin P A, Sanvicente A Z
Common stock returns and rating changes : a methodological comparison
JF 1982 MAR VOL 37:1 p 103-119.

(6911)
Morris R B
Fundamental factors affecting electric utility bond ratings: A quantitative approach
FAJ 1982 SEP-OCT VOL 38 p 59-61.

(6912)
Stock D, Robertson T
Improved techniques for predicting municipal bond ratings
JBR 1981 AUTUMN VOL 12:3.

(6913)
Wakeman L M
The real function of bond rating agencies
CFQ 1981 FALL VOL 1 p 18-26.

(6914)
Ferri M G, Martin C G
The cyclical pattern in corporate bond quality
JPM 1980 WINTER VOL 6:2 p 26-29.

(6915)
McAdams L
How to anticipate utility bond rating changes
JPM 1980 FALL VOL 7:1 p 56-60.

(6916)
Sorensen E H
Bond ratings versus market risk premiums
JPM 1980 SPRING VOL 6:3 p 64.

(6917)
Bhandari S B, Soldofsky R M, Boe W J
Bond quality rating changes for electric utilities: A multivariate analysis
FIN MGMT 1979 SPRING VOL 8 p 74.

(6918)
Edelman R B
The impact on electric utility bond ratings of substituting debt for preferred stock
FIN MGMT 1979 SPRING VOL 8 p 51.

(6919)
Kaplan R S, Urwitz G
Statistical models of bond ratings: a methodological inquiry.
JB 1979 APR VOL 52:2 p 231-261.

(6920)
Pinches G E, Singleton J C, Jahankhani A
Fixed coverage as a determinant of electric utility bond ratings
FIN MGMT 1978 SUMMER VOL 7 p 45.

(6921)
Pinches G E, Singleton J C
The adjustment of stock prices to bond rating changes
JF 1978 VOL 33 p 29.

(6922)
Fraser D R, Richards R M
Further evidence on the informational value of bond-rating changes
QREB 1977 VOL 17:3 p 73.

(6923)
Michel A J
Municipal bond ratings: A discriminant analysis approach
JFQA 1977 NOV VOL 12 p 587.

(6924)
Weinstein M I
The effect of a rating change announcement on bond price
JFE 1977 VOL 5 p 329.

(6925)
Hettenhouse G W, Sartoris W L
An analysis of the informational value of bond-rating changes
QREB 1976 VOL 16:2 p 65.

(6926)
Reilly F K, Joehnk M D
The association between market-determined risk measures for bonds and bond ratings
JF 1976 VOL 31 p 1287.

(6927)
Sherwood H C
How corporate and municipal debt is rated
Wiley, 1976.

(6928)
Ang J S, Patel K A
Empirical research on capital markets bond rating methods: Comparison and validation
JF 1975 MAY VOL 30:2 p 631-640.

(6929)
Belkaoui A
Industrial bond ratings: A new look
FIN MGMT 1975 AUTUMN VOL 4 p 44.

(6930)
Pinches G E, Mingo K A
The role of subordination and industrial bond
ratings
JF 1975 VOL 30 p 201.

(6931)
Pinches G E, Mingo K A
A multivariate analysis of industrial bond ratings
JF 1973 VOL 28 p 1.

(6932)
West R R
Bond ratings, bond yields, and financial
regulation: some findings
JLE 1973 VOL 16 p 159.

(6933)
Hoffland D L
The price-rating structure of the municipal bond
market
FAJ 1972 MAR-APR VOL 28 p 65-70.

(6934)
Pogue T F, Soldofsky R M
What's in a bond rating?
JFQA 1969 JUN VOL 4 p 201-228.

(6935)
Horton J J Jr
Statistical classification of municipal bonds
JBR 1970 AUTUMN VOL 1:3 p 29-40.

(6936)
West R R
An alternative approach to predicting bond
ratings
JAR 1970 SPRING VOL 8 p 118-125..

(6937)**Horton J J Jr**
A statistical rating index for municipal bonds
FAJ 1969 MAR-APR VOL 25 p 72-75.

(6938)
Packer S R
Municipal bond ratings
FAJ 1968 JUL-AUG VOL 24 p 93-97.

(6939)
Riehle R C
Moody's municipal ratings
FAJ 1968 MAY-JUN VOL 24 p 71-73.

(6940)
Horrigan J O
The determination of long-term credit standing
with financial ratios
ERA 1966.

17.32 Credit rationing

(6941)
Stiglitz J E, Weiss A
Credit rationing and collateral
(in Edwards J et al. eds., Recent developments in
corporate finance. Cambridge U Pr, 1986.)

(6942)
Bester H
Screening vs. rationing in credit markets with
imperfect information
AER 1985 VOL 75 p 850-855.

(6943)
Gale D, Hellwig M
Incentive-compatible   debt   contracts: The
one-period problem
REStud 1985 VOL 52 p 647-664.

(6944)
Guttentag J M, Herring R J
Credit rationing and financial disorder
JF 1984 DEC VOL 39:5 p 1359-1382.

(6945)
Allen F
Credit rationing and payment incentives
REStud 1983 VOL 50 p 639.

(6946)
Hansen R S, Thatcher J G
On the nature of credit demand and credit
rationing in competitive credit markets
JBankF 1983 VOL 7 p 273.

(6947)
Koskela E
Credit rationing and non-price loan terms: A re-examination
JBankF 1983 VOL 7 p 405.

(6948)
Thakor A V, Callaway R
Costly information production equilibria in the bank credit market with applications to credit rationing
JFQA 1983 JUN VOL 18:2 p 229-256.

(6949)
Wette H C
Collateral in credit rationing in markets with imperfect information: Note
AER 1983 VOL 73 p 442-445.

(6950)
Blackwell N R, Santomero A M
Bank credit rationing and the customer relation
JME 1982 VOL 9 p 121.

(6951)
Arzac E R, Schwartz R A, Whitcomb D K
A theory and test of credit rationing: Some further results
AER 1981 VOL 71 p 735-737.

(6952)
Stiglitz J E, Weiss A
Credit rationing in markets with imperfect information
AER 1981 VOL 71 p 393-410.

(6953)
Fried J, Howitt P
Credit rationing and implicit contract theory
JMCB 1980 AUG VOL 12:3 p 471-487.

(6954)
Keeton W R
Equilibrium credit rationing
Garland, 1979.

(6955)
Sealey C W Jr
Credit rationing in the commercial loan market: estimates of a structural model under conditions of disequilibrium
JF 1979 JUN VOL 34:3 p 689-702.

(6956)
Baltensperger E
Credit rationing
JMCB 1978 MAY VOL 10:2 p 170-183.

(6957)
Kalay A, Rabinovitch R
On individual loans pricing, credit rationing and interest rate regulation
JF 1978 VOL 33 p 1071.

(6958)
Russell T, Jaffee D M
Imperfect information, uncertainty and credit rationing
QJE 1976 VOL 90 p 651.

(6959)
Harris D G
Credit rationing at commercial banks
JMCB 1974 MAY VOL 6:2 p 227-240.

(6960)
Smith V L
A theory and test of credit rationing: Some generalizations
AER 1972 VOL 62 p 477-483.

(6961)
Jaffee D M
Credit rationing and the commercial loan market: an econometric study of the commercial loan market
Wiley, 1971.

18 Debt and preferred stock

(6962)
Sarig O, Warga A
Bond price data and bond market liquidity
JFQA 1989 SEP VOL 24:3 p 267-378.

(6963)
Benari Y
A bond market timing model
JPM 1988 FALL VOL 15:1 p 45-49.

(6964)
Horvath P A
A measurement of the errors in intra-period compounding and bond valuation: a short extension
FR 1988 AUG VOL 23:3 p 359-364.

(6965)
Takagi S
Recent developments in Japan's bond and money markets
Journal of Japanese and International Economics 1988 VOL 2 p 63-91.

(6966)
Taylor R W
The valuation of semiannual bonds between interest payment dates
FR 1988 AUG VOL 23:3 p 365-368.

(6967)
Fabozzi F J, Pollack I M eds.
Handbook of fixed income securities. 2nd ed
Dow Jones-Irwin, 1987.

(6968)
Lindley J T, Helms B P, Haddad M
A measurement of the errors in intra-period compounding and bond valuation
FR 1987 FEB VOL 22:1.

(6969)
Rose S
Extending the loan-sales revolution
MCFJ 1987 FALL VOL 5 p 64-66.

(6970)
Stigum M, Fabozzi F J
The Dow Jones-Irwin guide to bond and money market investments
Dow Jones-Irwin, 1987.

(6971)
Keim D B, Stambaugh R F
Predicting returns in the stock and bond markets.
JFE 1986 DEC VOL 17:2 p 357-390

(6972)
Frankel J A
Portfolio crowding out empirically estimated
QJE 1985 VOL 100 Suppl p 1041-1065.

(6973)
Institute of Chartered Financial Analysts
CFA readings in fixed-income securities analysis
Institute of Chartered Financial Analysts, 1985.

(6974)
Webb D C
Imperfect information and credit market equilibrium
EER 1984 VOL 26:1-2.

(6975)
Carmichael J
On Barro's theorem of debt neutrality: The irrelevance of net wealth
AER 1982 VOL 72 p 202-213.

(6976)
Kuroda A
Is the Japanese bond market rational and efficient?
JPM 1982 FALL VOL 9:1 p 46-51.

(6977)
Sorensen E H
On the seasoning process of new bonds: some are more seasoned than others
JFQA 1982 JUN VOL 17:2 p 195-208.

(6978)
Darst D M
The handbook of the bond and money markets
McGraw, 1981.

(6979)
McEnally R W
What causes bond prices to change?
JPM 1981 SPRING VOL 7:3 p 5-12.

(6980)
Jenkins J W
Taxes, margining and bond selection
FAJ 1980 MAY-JUN p 41-48.

(6981)
Jaffe J F, Mandelker G
Inflation and the holding period returns on bonds
JFQA 1979 DEC VOL 14 p 959.

(6982)
Tyndall D G
The value of participation in a loan contract
FAJ 1979 JAN-FEB p 68.

(6983)
Kaufman G G
Measuring risk and return for bonds: a new
approach
JBR 1978 SUMMER VOL 9:2.

(6984)
Pesando J E
On the efficiency of the bond market: some
Canadian evidence
JPE 1978 VOL 86 p 1057.

(6985)
Brooks L D
Stochastic dominance tests for selecting acceptable
debt issuance strategies
MSci 1976 AUG VOL 22:12 p 477.

(6986)
Smith V L
The borrower-lender relationship
AER 1976 JUN VOL 66:3 p 406-407.

(6987)
Handorf W C
Flexible debt financing
FIN MGMT 1974 SUMMER VOL 3 p 17.

(6988)
Kichline J L, Laub P M, Stevens G V
Obtaining the yield on a standard bond from a
sample of bonds with heterogeneous
characteristics
F R Bul 1973 VOL 59:5.

(6989)
Conard J W, Frankena M W
The yield spread between new and seasoned
corporate bonds, 1952-63
(in Guttentag J M and Cagan P eds., Essays on
interest rates, vol 1. (Dist by Columbia U Pr)
Natl Bur Econ Res, 1969.).

(6990)**Schilbred C M**
Bond evaluation as a decision under certainty,
risk or uncertainty
SJE 1968 MAY VOL 70 p 43-56.

(6991)
Thompson E A
Debt instruments in both macroeconomic theory
and capital theory
AER 1967 DEC VOL 57 p 1196-1210.

(6992)
Bierman H Jr
The bond issue size decision
JFQA 1966 DEC VOL 1 p 1-14.

(6993)
Puu T
A simple graphic method for estimating the yield
of bonds
(in Hahn F H and Brechling F P R eds., The
theory of interest rates. Macmillan Int, 1966.)

(6994)
Fullerton D H
The bond market in Canada
Carswell, 1962.

(6995)
Durand D, Winn W J
Basic yields of bonds 1926-1947: their
measurement and pattern
Natl Bur Econ Res, 1948.

18.1 Debt portfolio management

(6996)
Hakanoglu E, Kopprasch R, Roman E
Constant proportion portfolio insurance for
fixed-income investment
JPM 1989 SUMMER VOL 15:4 p 58-66.

(6997)
Maloney K J, Logue D E
Neglected complexities in structured bond portfolios
JPM 1989 WINTER VOL 15:2 p 59-68.

(6998)
Granito M R
The problem with bond index funds
JPM 1987 SUMMER VOL 13:4 p 41-48.

(6999)
Pieptea D R
Leveraged bond portfolio optimization under uncertainty
FR 1987 FEB VOL 22:1.

(7000)
Ronn E I
A new linear programming approach to bond portfolio management
JFQA 1987 DEC VOL 22 p 439.

(7001)
Barnes T, Johnson K, Shannon D
A test of fixed-income strategies
JPM 1984 WINTER VOL 10:2 p 60-65.

(7002)
Fong H G, Fabozzi F J
Fixed income portfolio management
Dow Jones-Irwin, 1985.

(7003)
Fong H G, Fabozzi F J
How to enhance bond returns with naive strategies
JPM 1985 SUMMER VOL 11:4 P 57.

(7004)
Heaney W J, Cheng P L
Continuous maturity diversification of default-free bond portfolios and a generalization of efficient diversification
JF 1984 SEP VOL 34:4 p 1101-1117.

(7005)
Platt R B, Latainer G D
Risk-return tradeoffs of contingent insurance strategies for active bond portfolios
FAJ 1984 MAY-JUN VOL 40:3 p 34-39.

(7006)
Kritzman M
Can bond managers perform consistently?
JPM 1983 SUMMER VOL 9:4 p 54.

(7007)
Tuttle D L ed.
The revolution in techniques for managing bond portfolios
Institute of Chartered Financial Analysts, 1983.

(7008)
Stock D
Does active management of municipal bond portfolios pay?
JPM 1982 WINTER VOL 8:2 p 51-55.

(7009)
Bierwag G O, Kaufman G G, Schweitzer R
The art of risk management in bond portfolios
JPM 1981 SPRING VOL 7:3 p 27-36.

(7010)
Gouldey B K, Gray G J
Implementing mean-variance theory in the selection of U S government bond portfolios
JBR 1981 AUTUMN VOL 12:3.

(7011)
Lewellen W G, Emery D R
On the matter of parity among financial obligations
JF 1981 MAR VOL 36:1 p 97-113

(7012)
Dietz P O, Fogler H R, Hardy D J
The challenge of analyzing bond portfolio returns
JPM 1980 SPRING VOL 6:3 p 53-58.

(7013)
Fong H G
Bond portfolio analysis and selection
Research Foundation of the Institute of Chartered Financial Analysts, 1980.

(7014)
Williams A III
The bond market line: measuring risk and reward
JPM 1980 SUMMER VOL 6:4 p 62-64.

(7015)
Gross W H
Coupon valuation and interest rate cycles
FAJ 1979 JUL-AUG VOL 35 p 68-71.

(7016)
Leibowitz M L
The horizon annuity
FAJ 1979 MAY-JUN VOL 35 p 68-74.

(7017)
Magee H R, Roberts G S
On portfolio theory, holding period assumptions
and bond maturity diversification
FIN MGMT 1979 WINTER VOL 8 p 68.

(7018)
Bierwag G O, Kaufman G
Bond portfolio strategy simulations: Critique
JFQA 1978 SEP VOL 13 p 519.

(7019)
Lane M
Applying risk/return analysis to short-term
fixed-income portfolios
JBR 1978 SPRING VOL 9:1.

(7020)
Fabozzi F J, Garlicki T D
Advances in bond analysis and portfolio strategies
Probus, 1987.

(7021)
Fogler H R, Groves W A, Richardson J G
Bond portfolio strategies, returns and skewness: A
note
JFQA 1977 MAR VOL 12 p 127.

(7022)
Yawitz J B, Hempel G H, Marshall W J
A risk-return approach to the selection of optimal
government bond portfolios
FIN MGMT 1976 AUTUMN VOL 5 p 36.

(7023)
Ang J S, Balcha D
Bond swap profitability
JBR 1975 AUTUMN VOL 6:3.

(7024)
Bradley S P, Crane D B
Simulation of bond portfolio strategies: laddered
vs. barbell maturity structure
JBR 1975 SUMMER VOL 6:2.

(7025)
Cramer R H, Hawk S L
The consideration of coupon levels, taxes,
reinvestment rates and maturity in the investment
management of financial institutions
JFQA 1975 MAR VOL 10 p 67.

(7026)
Bradley S P, Crane D B
A dynamic model for bond portfolio management
MSci 1972 OCT VOL 19:2 p 139-151.

(7027)
Watson R D
Tests of maturity structures of commercial bank
government securities portfolios: a simulation
approach
JBR 1972 SPRING VOL 3:1 p 34-46.

(7028)
Evans M D
Arbitrage in domestic securities in the U.S.
Parker Pub, 1965.

(7029)
Cheng P L
Optimum bond portfolio selection
MSci 1962 JUL VOL 8 p 490-499.

(7030)
Latane H A
Portfolio balance--the demand for money, bonds,
and stock
SEJ 1962 OCT VOL 29 p 71-76.

18.2 Issuers of debt and preferred stock

(7031)
Skelton J L
Relative risk in municipal and corporate debt
JF 1983 MAY VOL 38:2 p 625-634.

18.21 Central government and agency debt

(7032)
Cox W M, Lown C S
The capital gains and losses on US government debt: 1942-1987
REStat 1989 VOL 71 p 1.

(7033)
Puglisi D J, D'Souza R E
A note on fiscal agent pricing of federal agency debt
JBankF 1989 MAY VOL 13:2 p 311-320.

(7034)
Wann P
Inside the US Treasury market
Woodhead-Faulkner, 1989.

(7035)
Wormell J ed.
The gilt-edged market compendium
London & International Publishers, 1989.

(7036)
Appelt T, Schulman E
The government of Canada bond market: Is it efficiently priced?
Canadian Investment Review 1988 FALL VOL 1 p 63-72.

(7037)
Schwartz E, Van Order R
Valuing the implicit guarantees of the Federal National Mortgage Association
Journal of Real Estate Finance and Economics 1988 VOL 1.

(7038)
Conroy R M, Rendleman R J Jr
A test of market efficiency in government bonds
JPM 1987 SUMMER VOL 13:4 p 57-64.

(7039)
Mayers D, Smith C W
Death and taxes: the market for flower bonds
JF 1987 JUL VOL 42:3 p 685-698.

(7040)
Phillips P
Inside the new gilt-edged market. 2nd ed
Woodhead-Faulkner, 1987.

(7041)
Cox W M
Government debt and the stock market
F R Bk Dallas Ec Rev 1986 SEP.

(7042)
Bank of England
The future structure of the gilt-edged market
BEQB 1985 VOL 25 p 250..

(7043)**Fortune**
The troubled market in Federal securities
F 1985 MAY 13 VOL 111:10 p 46-53.

(7044)
Gultekin N B, Rogalski R J
Government bond returns measurement of interest rate risk and the arbitrage pricing theory
JF 1985 MAR VOL 40:1 p 43-61.

(7045)
Wormell J
The gilt-edged market
Allen, 1985.

(7046)
Hirschhorn E
Rational expectations and the effects of government debt
JME 1984 VOL 14 p 55.

(7047)
Litzenberger R H, Rolfo J
Arbitrage pricing, transaction costs and taxation of capital gains: a study of government bonds with the same maturity date
JFE 1984 VOL 13 p 337-351.

(7048)
Cox W M, Hirschorn E
The market value of U S government debt: monthly 1942-1984
JME 1983 VOL 11 p 261.

(7049)
Van Horne J C, Heaton H B
Government security dealers' positions information and interest-rate expectations: a note
JF 1983 DEC VOL 38:5 p 1643-1649.

(7050)
McCallum J S
Return and risk in the Canadian federal bond market
JBR 1982 SPRING VOL 13:1.

(7051)
Plosser C I
Government financing decisions and asset returns
JME 1982 VOL 9 p 325.

(7052)
McCallum J S
The empirical impact of changes in government on bond yields
JBR 1981 WINTER VOL 11:4.

(7053)
Seater J J
The market value of outstanding government debt, 1919-1975
JME 1981 VOL 8 p 85.

(7054)
Barry J Y, Ayres H F
A theory of the U S treasury market equilibrium
MSci 1980 JUN VOL 26:6 p 539-569.

(7055)
Bildersee J S
Bid ask price spreads in the agency bond market
JMCB 1979 MAY VOL 11:2 p 209-213.

(7056)
Resler D H, Lang R W
Federal agency debt: another side of federal borrowing
F R Bk St Louis Rev 1979 VOL 61:11.

(7057)
Stevens N A
Government debt financing - its effects in view of tax discounting
F R Bk St Louis Rev 1979 VOL 61:7.

(7058)
Banks L
The market for agency securities
F R Bk New York Q Rev 1978 SPRING VOL 3:1.

(7059)
Bildersee J S
U.S. government and agency securities: an analysis of yield spreads and performance
JB 1978 JUL VOL 51:3 p 499-520.

(7060)
Garbade K D
Electronic quotation systems and the market for government securities
F R Bk New York Q Rev 1978 SUMMER VOL 3:2.

(7061)
Garbade K D, Hunt J F
Risk premiums on federal agency debt
JF 1978 VOL 33 p 105.

(7062)
Grant D, Whaley R
Transactions costs on government bonds: a respecification
JB 1978 JAN VOL 51:1 p 57-64.

(7063)
Bildersee J S
Price spreads, performance and the seasoning of new treasury and agency bond issues
JFQA 1977 SEP VOL 12 p 433.

(7064)
Garbade K D, Silber W L
Price dispersion in the government securities market
JPE 1976 AUG VOL 84:4 p 721-740.

(7065)
Barro R J
Are Government bonds net wealth?
JPE 1974 VOL 82 p 1095.

(7066)
de Swardt C J
Some problems in the South African gilt-edged stock market
Finance and Trade Review 1974-75 VOL 11:2-3.

(7067)
Wolf C R
Bank preferences and government security yields
QJE 1971 MAY VOL 85 p 283-303.

(7068)
Kramer R L
Arbitrage in U.S. Government bonds: a management science approach
JBR 1970 SUMMER VOL 1:2 p 30-44.

(7069)
Wolf C R
A model for selecting commercial bank government security portfolios
REStat 1969 FEB VOL 51 p 40-52.

(7070)
Scott I O Jr
Government securities markets
McGraw, 1965.

(7071)
Berney R E
The auction of long-term government securities
JF 1964 SEP VOL 19 p 470-482.

(7072)
Federal Reserve Bank of New York
The financing of goverment securities dealers
F R Bk New York Mo Rev 1964 JUN.

(7073)
Bloch E
Short cycles in corporate demand for government securities
AER 1963 DEC VOL 53 p 1058-1077.

(7074)
Goldstein H N
Should the Treasury auction long-term securities?
JF 1962 SEP VOL 17 p 444-464.

(7075)
Federal Reserve Bank of Kansas City
Corporate participation in the government securities market
F R Bk Kansas City Mo Rev 1960 DEC.

18.22 Municipal debt

(7076)
Kochin L A, Parks R W
Was the tax-exempt bond market inefficient or were future expected tax rates negative?
JF 1988 SEP VOL 43:4 p 913-932.

(7077)
Trim T D ed.
The municipal bond market: New rules, new opportunities, and new strategies
Institute of Chartered Financial Analysts, 1988.

(7078)
Kidwell D S, Sorenson E H, Wachowichz J M
Estimating the signaling benefits of debt insurance: the case of municipal bonds
JFQA 1987 SEP VOL 22:3 p 299-313.

(7079)
Nauss R M
Generating optimal true interest cost bids for new municipal bond competitive issues
JBankF 1987 VOL 11 p 329-343.

(7080)
Peavy J W III, Hempel G H
The effect of the WPPSS crisis on the tax-exempt bond
JFR 1987 VOL 10:3 p 239-248.

(7081)
Van Horne J C
Call risk and municipal bonds
JPM 1987 WINTER VOL 13:2 p 53-57.

(7082)
Buser S A, Hess P J
Empirical determinants of the relative yields on taxable and tax-exempt securities
JFE 1986 VOL 17 p 335.

(7083)
Elmer P I
Preferred stock arbitrage of municipal bond market segmentation
FR 1986 NOV VOL 21:4.

(7084)
Heaton H
The relative yields on taxable and tax exempt debt
JMCB 1986 NOV VOL 18:4 p 482-494.

(7085)
Nauss R M
True interest cost in municipal bond bidding : an
integer programming approach
MSci 1986 JUL VOL 32:7 p 870-877.

(7086)
Poterba J M
Explaining the yield spread between taxable and
tax-exempt bonds: The role of expected tax policy
(in Rosen H S ed., Studies in state and local
public finance. U of Washington Pr, 1986.)

(7087)
Trzcinka C
Risk, segmentation, and the municipal term
structure
FR 1986 NOV VOL 21:4.

(7088)
Walter J R
Short-term municipal securities
F R Bk Richmond Ec Rev 1986 VOL 72:6.

(7089)
Proctor A J, Rappaport J N
Federal tax reform and the regional character of
the municipal bond market
F R Bk New York Q Rev 1985 AUTUMN VOL
10:3.

(7090)
Bierwag G O, Kaufman G G, Leonard P H
Interest rate effects of commercial bank
underwriting of municipal revenue bonds:
Additional evidence
JBankF 1984 VOL 8 p 35.

(7091)
Cargill T F, Meyer R A
Municipal interest rates and the term structure
and inflationary expectations
FR 1984 MAY p 135-152.

(7092)
Cluff G S, Farnham P G
Standard & Poor vs Moody's : which city
characteristics influence municipal bond ratings?
QREB 1984 AUTUMN VOL 24:3 p 72-94

(7093)
Forbes R W, Leonard P A
The effects of statutory portfolio constraints on
tax exempt interest rates
JMCB 1984 FEB VOL 16:1 p 93-99.

(7094)
Joehnk M D, Kidwell D S
The impact of market uncertainty on municipal
bond underwriting spread
FIN MGMT 1984 SPRING VOL 13 p 37-44.

(7095)
Liu P, Thakor A V
Interest yields, credit ratings, and economic
characteristics of state bonds: an empirical
analysis
JMCB 1984 AUG VOL 16:3 p 344-351..

(7096)**Robbins E H**
Pricing municipal debt
JFQA 1984 DEC VOL 19:4 p 467-483.

(7097)
Stock D, Schrems E L
Municipal bond demand premiums and bond
price volatility : a note
JF 1984 JUN VOL 39:2 p 535-539.

(7098)
Arak M, Guentner K
The market for tax exempt issues: Why are the
yields so high?
NTJ 1983 JUN VOL 36 p 145-161.

(7099)
Ingram R W, Brooks L D, Copeland R M
The information content of municipal bond rating
changes : a note
JF 1983 JUN VOL 38:3 p 997-1003.

(7100)
Kidwell D S, Koch T W
Market segmentation and the term structure of
municipal yields
JMCB 1983 FEB VOL 15:1 p 40-55.

(7101)
Kidwell D S, Rogowski R J
State bond bank issues: Method of sale and
market acceptance over time
FIN MGMT 1983 SUMMER VOL 12 p 15-20.

(7102)
Kidwell D S, Sorensen E H
Pricing of municipal bond underwritings: It may
pay to invest when underwriters don't
FAJ 1983 MAR-APR VOL 39 p 58-64.

(7103)
Kidwell D S, Trzcinka C A
The impact of the New York city fiscal crisis on
the interest cost of new issue municipal bonds.
JFQA 1983 SEP VOL 18:3 p 381-399

(7104)
Leonard P A
Variations in municipal bond default risk premia
by term-to-maturity
JBusR 1983 VOL 11 p 523-530.

(7105)
Proctor A J, Donahoo K K
Commercial bank investment in municipal
securities
F R Bk New York Q Rev 1983-84 WINTER
VOL 8:4.

(7106)
Skelton J L
Banks, firms and the relative pricing of
tax-exempt and taxable bonds.
JFE 1983 NOV VOL 12:3 p 343-355.

(7107)
Sorensen E H
Who puts the slope in the municipal yield curve?
JPM 1983 SUMMER VOL 9:4 p 61.

(7108)
Arditti F D, Livingston M
The relative price volatility of taxable and
non-taxable bonds: a note
JF 1982 JUN VOL 37:3 p 877-881.

(7109)
Beek D C
Rethinking tax-exempt financing for state and
local governments
F R Bk New York Q Rev 1982 AUTUMN VOL
7:3.

(7110)
Braswell R C, Reinhart W J, Hasselback J R
The tax treatment of municipal discount bonds:
Correction of a fallacy
FIN MGMT 1982 SPRING VOL 11 p 77.

(7111)
Cole C W, Millar J A
The impact of municipal bond banking on
municipal interest costs
FIN MGMT 1982 VOL 11 p 70-76.

(7112)
Cook T Q
Determinants of individual tax-exempt bond
yields: A survey of the evidence
F R Bk Richmond Ec Rev 1982 MAY-JUN p
14-39.

(7113)
Kaufman G G
The tax treatment of municipal discount bonds:
Rebuttal and expansion
FIN MGMT 1982 WINTER VOL 11 p 48-51.

(7114)
Kidwell D S, Koch T W
The behavior of the interest rate differential
between tax-exempt revenue and general
obligation bonds: a test of risk preferences and
market segmentation
JF 1982 MAR VOL 37:1 p 73-85.

(7115)
Kidwell D S, Koch T W
Why and when do revenue bonds yield more than
GOs?
JPM 1982 SUMMER VOL 8:4 p 51-56.

(7116)
Livingston M
The pricing of municipal bonds
JFQA 1982 JUN VOL 17:2 p 179-193.

(7117)
Stock D
Does active management of municipal bond portfolios pay?
JPM 1982 WINTER VOL 8:2 p 51-55.

(7118)
Treynor J L
On the quality of municipal bonds
FAJ 1982 MAY-JUN p 25-31.

(7119)
Trzcinka C
The pricing of tax-exempt bonds and the Miller hypothesis
JF 1982 SEP VOL 37:4 p 907-923.

(7120)
Kaufman G G
Municipal bond underwriting: market structure
JBR 1981 SPRING VOL 12:1.

(7121)
Leibowitz M L
Volatility in tax-exempt bonds: A theoretical model
FAJ 1981 NOV-DEC VOL 37 p 31-53.

(7122)
Mallman T L
Volatility in municipal bonds: Estimating and using volatility factors
FAJ 1981 NOV-DEC VOL 37 p 54-60.

(7123)
Nauss R M, Keeler B R
Minimizing net interest cost in municipal bond bidding
MSci 1981 APR VOL 27:4 p 365-376.

(7124)
Nauss R M, Keeler B R
Optimizing municipal bond bids
JBR 1981 AUTUMN VOL 12:3.

(7125)
Stock D, Robertson T
Improved techniques for predicting municipal bond ratings
JBR 1981 AUTUMN VOL 12:3.

(7126)
Campbell T S
On the extent of segmentation in the municipal securities market
JMCB 1980 FEB VOL 12:1 p 71-83.

(7127)
Hendershott P H, Koch T W
The demand for tax-exempt securities by financial institutions
JF 1980 JUN VOL 25:3 p 717-727.

(7128)
Higgins W W, Moore B J
Market structure versus information costs as determinants of underwriters' spreads on municipal bonds
JFQA 1980 MAR VOL 15 p 85.

(7129)
Rogowski R J
Underwriting competition and issuer borrowing costs in the municipal revenue bond market
JBR 1980 WINTER VOL 10:4.

(7130)
Sorensen E H
An analysis of the relationship between underwriter spread and the pricing of municipal bonds
JFQA 1980 JUN VOL 15 p 435..

(7131)**Mussa M L, Kormendi R C**
The taxation of municipal bonds
American Enterprise Institute for Public Policy Research, 1979.

(7132)
Osteryoung J S, Braswell R C, Blevins D R
PIC: An alternative approach to accepting bids on local and state government bonds
FIN MGMT 1979 SUMMER VOL 8 p 36.

(7133)
Babad Y M, Speer P D
Optimization of the arbitrage process in advance refunding of municipal bonds
MSci 1978 VOL 24 p 987-1000.

(7134)
Benson E D, Rogowski R J
The cyclical behavior of risk spreads on new
municipal issues
JMCB 1978 AUG VOL 10:3 p 348-362.

(7135)
Hopewell M H, Kaufman G G
The incidence of excess interest costs paid by
municipalities in the competitive sale of bonds
JME 1978 VOL 4 p 281.

(7136)
Yawitz J B
Risk premia on municipal bonds
JFQA 1978 SEP VOL 13 p 475.

(7137)
Butler A D, Warren S A
An optimal temporary loan model for state
borrowers
JF 1977 VOL 32 p 1305.

(7138)
Hopewell M H, Kaufman G G
Commercial bank bidding on municipal bonds:
New evidence
JF 1977 VOL 32 p 1647.

(7139)
Michel A J
Municipal bond ratings: A discriminant analysis
approach
JFQA 1977 NOV VOL 12 p 587.

(7140)
Dyl E A, Joehnk M D
Refunding tax exempt bonds
FIN MGMT 1976 SUMMER VOL 5 p 59.

(7141)
Hopewell M H, Kaufman G G
The cost of inefficient coupons on municipal
bonds
JFQA 1974 MAR VOL 9 p 155.

(7142)
Freimer M
Note on "Municipal bond coupon schedules with
limitations on the number of coupons"
MSci 1973 AUG VOL 19:12 p 379.

(7143)
Hempel G H
An evaluation of municipal "bankruptcy" laws and
procedures
JF 1973 VOL 28 p 1339.

(7144)
Hempel G H
Quantitative borrower characteristics associated
with defaults on municipal general obligations
JF 1973 VOL 28 p 523.

(7145)
Bierman H Jr
Alternative debt bids by state and local
governments
FIN MGMT 1972 WINTER VOL 1 p 51.

(7146)
Hastie K L
Determinants of municipal bond yields
JFQA 1972 JUN VOL 7 p 1729-1748.

(7147)
Hoffland D L
The price-rating structure of the municipal bond
market
FAJ 1972 MAR-APR VOL 28 p 65-70.

(7148)
Rao M R, Weingartner H M
Note on optimal municipal bond coupon
schedules: maximum difference between the
highest and lowest coupon
JBR 1972 SPRING VOL 3:1 p 63-64.

(7149)
Weingartner H M
Municipal bond coupon schedules with limitations
on the number of coupons
MSci 1972 DEC VOL 19:4 p 369-380.

(7150)
Hempel G H
The postwar quality of state and local debt
Columbia U Pr, 1971.

(7151)
Kessel R A
A study of the effects of competition in the
tax-exempt bond market
JPE 1971 JUL-AUG VOL 79 p 706-738.

(7152)
Horton J J Jr
Statistical classification of municipal bonds
JBR 1970 AUTUMN VOL 1:3 p 29-40.

(7153)
Robinson R I
Postwar market for state and local government
securities
Princeton U Pr, 1970.

(7154)
Horton J J Jr
A statistical rating index for municipal bonds
FAJ 1969 MAR-APR VOL 25 p 72-75.

(7155)
Calvert G L ed.
Fundamentals of municipal bonds. 7th ed
Inv Bankers, 1968.

(7156)
Packer S R
Municipal bond ratings
FAJ 1968 JUL-AUG VOL 24 p 93-97.

(7157)
Riehle R C
Moody's municipal ratings
FAJ 1968 MAY-JUN VOL 24 p 71-73.

(7158)
Smith W P
Commercial bank entry into revenue bond
underwriting: an appraisal of the public benefits
of S 1306
Washington, DC: Dept of Banking and Currency,
Office of the Controller of the Currency, 1967.

(7159)
West R R
Determinants of underwriters' spreads on tax
exempt issues
JFQA 1967 SEP VOL 2 p 241-264.

(7160)
Cohen K J, Hammer F S
Optimal level debt schedules for municipal bonds
MSci 1966 NOV VOL 13 p 161-166.

(7161)
West R R
More on the effects of municipal bond
monopsony
JB 1966 APR VOL 39 p 305-308.

(7162)
Cohen K J, Hammer F S
Optimal coupon schedules for municipal bonds
MSci 1965 SEP VOL 12 p 68-82.

(7163)
Diamond P A
On the cost of tax-exempt bonds
JPE 1965 AUG VOL 73 p 399-403.

(7164)
West R R
New issue concession on municipal bonds: a case
of monopolistic pricing
JB 1965 APR VOL 38 p 135-148.

(7165)
West R R
Should commercial banks be allowed to
underwrite municipal bonds?
NBR 1965 SEP VOL 3 p 35-44.

(7166)
Heins A J
The interest rate differential between revenue
bonds and general obligations: a regression model
NTJ 1962 DEC VOL 15 p 399-405.

(7167)
Gottlieb M
Cyclical timing of municipal bond issues
QREB 1961 MAY VOL 1 p 67-75.

18.23 Corporate debt

(7168)
Goodman L S, Cohen A H
Pay-in-kind debentures: an innovation
JPM 1989 WINTER VOL 15:2 p 9-16.

(7169)
Hsueh L P, Chandy P R
An examination of the yield spreads between insured and uninsured debt
JFR 1989 FALL VOL 12:3 p 235-244.

(7170)
Kim J-H, Stover R D
The role of bank letters of credit in corporate tax-exempt financing
FIN MGMT 1987 SPRING VOL 16 p 31-37.

(7171)
Lovata L M, Nichols W D, Philipich K L
Defeasing discounted debt: An economic analysis
FIN MGMT 1987 SPRING VOL 16 p 41-45.

(7172)
Ogden J P
Determinants of the relative interest rate sensitivities of corporate bonds
FIN MGMT 1987 SPRING VOL 16 p 22-30.

(7173)
Fung W K H, Rudd A
Pricing new corporate bond issues : an analysis of issue cost and seasoning effects
JF 1986 JUL VOL 41:3 p 633-644.

(7174)
Finnerty J E, Nunn K P Jr
Comparative yield spreads on US corporate bonds and $Eurobonds
FAJ 1985 JUL-AUG VOL 41:4 p 68-73.

(7175)
Peterson P P, Peterson D R, Ang J S
The extinguishment of debt through in-substance defeasance
FIN MGMT 1985 SPRING VOL 14 p 59-67.

(7176)
Gatti J F
Risk and return on corporate bonds : a synthesis
QREB 1983 SUMMER VOL 23:2 p 53-70

(7177)
Altman E I, Tubiana P S
The multi-firm bond issue: A fund-raising financial instrument
FIN MGMT 1981 SUMMER VOL 10 p 23-33.

(7178)
Bank of England
The UK corporate bond market
BEQB 1981 VOL 21 p 54-58.

(7179)
Boardman C M, McEnally R W
Factors affecting seasoned corporate bond prices.
JFQA 1981 JUN VOL 16:2 p 207-226

(7180)
Edmonds C P, Lloyd W P
Industrial development bond financing
FE 1981 APR VOL 49:4 p 42-50.

(7181)
Sorensen E H, Wert J E
A new tool for estimating new issue bond yields
JPM 1981 SPRING VOL 7:3 p 42-45.

(7182)
Weinstein M I
The systematic risk of corporate bonds
JFQA 1981 SEP VOL 16:3 p 257-278.

(7183)
Alexander G J
Applying the market model to long-term corporate bonds
JFQA 1980 DEC VOL 15 p 1063-1080..

(7184)**Dyl E A, Sawaya W J**
The bond issue size decision revisited
FIN MGMT 1979 WINTER VOL 8 p 60.

(7185)
Caks J
Corporate debt decisions: A new analytical framework
JF 1978 VOL 33 p 1297.

(7186)
Jarrow R A
The relationship between yield, risk and return of corporate bonds
JF 1978 VOL 33 p 1235.

(7187)
Weinstein M I
The seasoning process of new corporate bond issues
JF 1978 VOL 33 p 1343.

(7188)
Lindvall J R
New issue corporate bonds, seasoned market
efficiency and yield spreads
JF 1977 VOL 32 p 1057.

(7189)
Zwick B
The market for corporate bonds
F R Bk New York Q Rev 1977 AUTUMN VOL
2.

(7190)
Morris J R
A model for corporate debt maturity decisions
JFQA 1976 SEP VOL 11 p 339.

(7191)
Morris J R
On corporate debt maturity strategies
JF 1976 VOL 31 p 29.

(7192)
Joehnk M D, Nielsen J F
Return and risk characteristics of speculative
grade bonds
QREB 1975 VOL 15:1 p 27.

(7193)
Kichline J L, Laub P M, Deck B
Yields on recently offered corporate bonds
F R Bul 1973 VOL 59:5.

(7194)
Litzenberger R H, Rutenberg D P
Size and timing of corporate bond flotations
JFQA 1972 JAN VOL 7 p 1343-1360.

(7195)
Wilbur W L
Return and risk characteristics of high-grade
bonds
QREB 1972 VOL 12:3 p 45.

(7196)
Peters J R
Economics of the Canadian corporate bond
market
McGill-Queens U Pr, 1971.

(7197)
Tuttle D L, Wilbur W L
A multivariate time-series investigation of annual
returns on highest grade corporate bonds
JFQA 1971 MAR VOL 6 p 707-722.

(7198)
Wilbur W L
A theoretical and empirical study of holding
period yields on highest grade corporate bonds
U of NC, 1967.

(7199)
Cohan A B
Yields on new underwritten corporate bonds,
1935-58
JF 1964 DEC VOL 17 p 585-605.

(7200)
Herzog J P
Investor experience in corporate securities
JF 1964 MAR VOL 19 p 46-62.

(7201)
Kaplan M
Yields on recently issued corporate bonds: a new
index
JF 1962 MAR VOL 17 p 81-109.

(7202)
Hickman W B
Statistical measures of corporate bond financing
since 1900
(Dist by Princeton U Pr) Natl Bur Econ Res,
1960.

(7203)
Shapiro E
The postwar market for corporate securities:
1946-55
JF 1959 MAY VOL 14 p 196-217.

(7204)
Hickman W B
The volume of corporate bond financing since
1900
Princeton U Pr, 1953.

(7205)
Hickman W B
Trends and cycles in corporate bond financing
Natl Bur Econ Res, 1950.

(7206)
National Bureau of Economic Research
Corporate bond project: organisation and methods. Parts 1-5
Natl Bur Econ Res, 1942-1944.

18.3 Terms and conditions of debt and preferred

(7207)
Pecchenino R A
The loan contract: mechanism of financial control
EJ 1988 MAR VOL 98:389 p 126-137.

(7208)
Eaton J
Lending with costly enforcement of repayment and potential fraud
JBankF 1986 VOL 10 p 281.

(7209)
Dietrich J R, Deitrick J W
Bond exchanges in the airline industry : analyzing public disclosures
AR 1985 JAN VOL 60:1 p 109-126.

(7210)
Baker K R, Vander Weide J H
The bond scheduling problem of the multi-subsidiary holding company
MSci 1982 JUL VOL 28:7 p 738-748.

(7211)
Boettcher J H, Sotelino F B
A look at the variable-maturity loan
HBR 1982 MAY-JUN VOL 60:3 p 80-86

(7212)
Thakor A V
An exploration of competitive signalling equilibria with "third party" information production: the case of debt insurance
JF 1982 JUN VOL 37:3 p 717-739.

(7213)
Findlay M C III, Williams E E, Gordon L A
Toward more adequate measures of lender protection
FIN MGMT 1975 AUTUMN VOL 4 p 54.

18.31 Seniority, security and debt covenants

(7214)
Leeth J D, Scott J A
The incidence of secured debt: evidence from the small business community
JFQA 1989 SEP VOL 24:3 p 379-394.

(7215)
Berlin M, Loeys J
Bond covenants and delegated monitoring
JF 1988 JUN VOL 43:2 p 397-412.

(7216)
Chan Y S, Thakor A V
Collateral and competitive equilibria with moral hazard and private information
JF 1987 JUN VOL 42:2 p 345-363.

(7217)
Malitz I
On financial contracting: The determinants of bond covenants
FIN MGMT 1986 SUMMER VOL 15 p 18-25.

(7218)
Business Week
Takeovers and buyouts clobber blue chip bondholders
Business Week 1985 NOV 11 p 113.

(7219)
Chan Y S, Kanatas G
Asymmetric valuations and the role of collateral in loan agreements
JMCB 1985 FEB VOL 17:1 p 84-95.

(7220)
John K, Kalay A
Informational content of optimal debt contracts
(in Altman E and Subrahmanyam M eds., Recent advances in corporate finance. Irwin, 1985.)

(7221)
Plaut S E
The theory of collateral
JBankF 1985 VOL 9 p 401.

(7222)
Stulz R M, Johnson H
An analysis of secured debt
JFE 1985 DEC VOL 14:4 p 501-521.

(7223)
Roberts G S, Viscione J A
The impact of seniority and security covenants on
bond yields : a note
JF 1984 DEC VOL 39:5 p 1597-1600.

(7224)
Brauer G A
Evidence of the market value of me-first rules
FIN MGMT 1983 SPRING VOL 12 p 11-18.

(7225)
Ho T S Y, Singer R F
Bond indenture provisions and the risk of
corporate debt.
JFE 1982 DEC VOL 10:4 p 375-406.

(7226)
Kalay A
Stockholder-bondholder conflict and dividend
constraints
JFE 1982 VOL 10 p 211.

(7227)
Mason S P, Bhattacharya S
Risky debt, jump processes and safety covenants
JFE 1981 VOL 9 p 281.

(7228)
Smith C W Jr, Warner J B
On financial contracting. An analysis of bond
covenants.
JFE 1979 JUN VOL 7:2 p 117-161

(7229)
Kim E H, McConnell J J, Greenwood P R
Capital structure rearrangements and me-first
rules in an efficient capital market
JF 1977 VOL 32 p 789.

(7230)
Quill G D, Cresci J C, Shuter B D
Some considerations about secured lending
JCBL 1977 APR VOL 59 p 41-56.

(7231)
Barro R J
The loan market collateral, and rates of interest
JMCB 1976 NOV VOL 8:4 p 439-456.

(7232)
Quarles J C
The floating lien
JCBL 1970 NOV VOL 53 p 51-58.

(7233)
Dennon L E
The security agreement
JCBL 1968 FEB VOL 50 p 32-40.

(7234)
Van Horne J C
A linear programming approach to evaluating
restrictions under bond indenture or loan
agreement
JFQA 1966 JUN VOL 1 p 68-83.

(7235)
Johnson R W
Subordinated debentures: debt that serves as
equity
JF 1955 MAR VOL 10 p 1-16.

18.32 Sinking funds and serial bonds

(7236)
Kidwell D S, Marr M W, Ogden J P
The effect of a sinking fund on the reoffering
yields of new public utility bonds
JFR 1989 SPRING VOL 12:1 p 1-14..

(7237)**Gombola M J, Nunn K P Jr**
Valuation of the preferred stock sinking fund
feature: a time-series approach
JFR 1988 VOL 11:1 p 33-42.

(7238)
Ogden J P
A rationale for the sinking-fund provision in a
quasicompetitive corporate-bond market
JBusR 1988 MAY VOL 16:3 p 197-208.

(7239)
Dunn K B, Spatt C S
A strategic analysis of sinking fund bonds
JFE 1984 SEP VOL 13:3 p 399-423.

(7240)
Ho T S Y, Singer R F
The value of corporate debt with a sinking-fund
provision
JB 1984 JUL VOL 57:3 p 315-336.

(7241)
McDaniel W R
Sinking fund preferred stock
FIN MGMT 1984 SPRING VOL 45.

(7242)
Kalotay A J
Sinking funds and the realized cost of debt
FIN MGMT 1982 SPRING VOL 11 p 43-54.

(7243)
Sorensen E H, Hawlins C A
The demand for preferred stock with sinking
funds and without: a note
JF 1982 MAR VOL 37:1 p 237-241.

(7244)
Kalotay A J
On the management of sinking funds
FIN MGMT 1981 SUMMER VOL 10 p 34-40.

(7245)
Laiderman R
The sinking fund bond game
FAJ 1980 NOV-DEC VOL 36:6 p 33-36.

(7246)
Bierwag G O
Optimal TIC bids on serial bond issues
MSci 1976 VOL 22 p 1175-1185.

(7247)
Demetriou P A
The present value of investments in sinking funds
MSci 1967 JAN VOL 13 p 336-343.

(7248)
Jen F C, Wert J E
The effect of sinking fund provisions on corporate
bond yields
FAJ 1967 MAR-APR VOL 23 p 125-131.

(7249)
Thompson F C, Norgaard R L
Sinking funds
Fin Exec, 1967.

(7250)
Jen F C, Wert J E
Imputed yields of sinking fund bonds and the
term structure of interest rates
JF 1966 DEC VOL 21 p 697-714.

18.33 Callable and retractable bonds

(7251)
Narayanan M P, Lim S-P
On the call provision in corporate zero-coupon
bonds
JFQA 1989 MAR VOL 24:1 p 91-104.

(7252)
Spivey M F
The cost of including a call provision in
municipal debt contracts
JFR 1989 FALL VOL 12:3 p 203-216.

(7253)
Dunetz M L, Mahoney J M
Using duration and convexity in the analysis of
callable bonds
FAJ 1988 MAY-JUN VOL 44 p 53-73.

(7254)
Allen D S, Lamy R E, Thompson G R
Agency costs and alternative call provisions: An
empirical investigation
FIN MGMT 1987 WINTER VOL 16 p 37-44.

(7255)
Emery D R, Hoffmeister J R, Spahr R W
The case for indexing a bond's call price
FIN MGMT 1987 AUTUMN VOL 16 p 57-64.

(7256)
Van Horne J C
Call risk and municipal bonds
JPM 1987 WINTER VOL 13:2 p 53-57.

(7257)
Chatfield R E, Moyer R C
"Putting" away bond risk: An empirical examination of the value of the put option on bonds
FIN MGMT 1986 SUMMER VOL 15 p 26-33.

(7258)
Robbins E H, Schatzberg J D
Callable bonds : a risk-reducing signalling mechanism
JF 1986 SEP VOL 41:4 p 935-949.

(7259)
Vu J D
An empirical investigation of calls of non-convertible bonds
JFE 1986 JUN VOL 16:2 p 235-265

(7260)
Brick I E, Wallingford B A
The relative tax benefits of alternative call features in corporate debt
JFQA 1985 MAR VOL 20:1 p 95-105.

(7261)
Thatcher J S
The choice of call provision terms : evidence of the existence of agency costs of debt
JF 1985 JUN VOL 40:2 p 549-561.

(7262)
Toevs A
Interest rate risk and uncertain lives
JPM 1985 SPRING VOL 11:3 p 45-56.

(7263)
Galai D
Pricing of optional bonds
JBankF 1983 VOL 7 p 323.

(7264)
Kraus A
An analysis of call provisions and the corporate refunding provision
MCFJ 1983 SPRING VOL 1 p 46-60.

(7265)
Brennan M J, Schwartz E S
Savings bonds: Valuation and optimal redemption strategies
(in Sharpe W F and Cootner C M eds., Financial economics: Essays in honor of Paul Cootner. P-H, 1982.)

(7266)
Yawitz J B, Marshall W J
Measuring the effect of callability on bond yields
JMCB 1981 FEB VOL 13:1 p 60-71.

(7267)
Ananthanarayanan A L, Schwartz E S
Retractable and extendible bonds: the Canadian experience
JF 1980 MAR VOL 35:1 p 31-47.

(7268)
Barnea A
A rationale for debt maturity structure and call provisions in the agency theoretic framework
JF 1980 DEC VOL 35:5 p 1223-1234.

(7269)
McCallum J S
The Canadian conversion loan: a remembrance
JBR 1980 SPRING VOL 11:1.

(7270)
Van Horne J C
Called bonds: how does the investor fare?
JPM 1980 SUMMER VOL 6:4 p 58-61.

(7271)
Dipchand C R, Hanrahan J R
Exit and exchange option values of Government of Canada "retractable" bonds
FIN MGMT 1979 AUTUMN VOL 8 p 62.

(7272)
Bodie Z, Friedman B M
Interest rate uncertainty and the value of bond call protection
JPE 1978 VOL 86 p 19-43.

(7273)
Bodie Z, Taggart R A
Future investment opportunities and the value of the call provision on a bond
JF 1978 VOL 33 p 1187.

(7274)
Brennan M J, Schwartz E S
Savings bonds, retractable bonds and callable
bonds
JFE 1977 VOL 5 p 67.

(7275)
Elton E J, Gruber M J
The economic value of the call option
JF 1972 SEP VOL 27 p 891-902.

(7276)
Frankena M W
The influence of call provisions and coupon rate
on the yields of corporate bonds
(in Guttentag J M ed., Essays on interest rates,
vol 2. (Dist by Columbia U Pr) Natl Bur Econ
Res, 1971.)

(7277)
Jen F C, Wert J E
Effect of call risk on corporate yields
JF 1967 DEC VOL 22 p 637-651.

(7278)
Pye G
Value of call deferment on a bond: some
empirical results
JF 1967 DEC VOL 22 p 623-636.

(7279)
Jen F C, Wert J E
The value of the deferred call privilege
NBR 1966 MAR.

(7280)
Pye G
The value of a call option on a bond
JPE 1966 APR VOL 74 p 200-205.

(7281)
Hess A C, Winn W J
The value of the call privilege
JF 1959 MAY VOL 14 p 182-195.

18.34 Bond refunding

(7282)
Fischer E O, Heinkel R, Zechner J
Dynamic recapitalization policies and the role of
call premia and issue discounts
JFQA 1989 DEC VOL 24:4 p 427-446.

(7283)
Maris B A
Analysis of bond refunding with overlapping
interest
JBFA 1989 AUTUMN VOL 16:4 p 587.

(7284)
Finnerty J D, Kalotay A J, Farrell F X
The financial manager's guide to evaluating bond
refunding opportunities
Ballinger, 1988.

(7285)
Livingston M
Measuring the benefit of a bond refunding: The
problem of nonmarketable call options
FIN MGMT 1987 SPRING VOL 16 p 38-40.

(7286)
Finnerty J D
Refunding discounted debt : a clarifying analysis
JFQA 1986 MAR VOL 21:1 p 95-106.

(7287)
Finnerty J D
Refunding high-coupon debt
MCFJ 1986 WINTER VOL 3 p 59-74.

(7288)
Kim S-H
The effect of refunding decisions on the
relationship between interest rates and stock
prices : an empirical test
JBFA 1986 AUTUMN VOL 13:3 p 405-424

(7289)
Dietrich J R
Effects of early bond refundings: An empirical
investigation of security returns
JAE 1984 VOL 6 p 67-96..

(7290)**Emery D R, Lewellen W G**
Refunding noncallable debt
JFQA 1984 MAR VOL 19:1 p 73-82.

(7291)
Finnerty J D
An illustrated guide to bond refunding analysis
Research Foundation of the Institute of Chartered
Financial Analysts, 1984.

(7292)
Finnerty J D
Preferred stock refunding analysis: Synthesis and
extension
FIN MGMT 1984 AUTUMN VOL 13 p 22-28.

(7293)
Kalotay A J
Refunding   considerations   under   rate-based
regulation
FIN MGMT 1984 AUTUMN VOL 13 p 11-14.

(7294)
Finnerty J D
Evaluating   the   economics   of   refunding
high-coupon sinking-fund debt
FIN MGMT 1983 SPING VOL 12 p 5-11.

(7295)
Kalotay A J
On the structure and valuation of debt refundings
FIN MGMT 1982 SPRING VOL 11 p 41-42.

(7296)
Harris R S
The refunding of discounted debt: An adjusted
present value analysis
FIN MGMT 1980 WINTER VOL 9 p 7.

(7297)
Riener K D
Financial structure effects of bond refunding
FIN MGMT 1980 SUMMER VOL 9 p 18.

(7298)
Boyce W M, Kalotay A J
Optimum bond calling and refunding
Interfaces 1979 NOV VOL 9 p 36-49.

(7299)
Laber G
Implications of discount rates and financing
assumptions for bond refunding decisions
FIN MGMT 1979 SPRING VOL 8 p 7.

(7300)
Babad Y M, Speer P D
Optimization of the arbitrage process in advance
refunding of municipal bonds
MSci 1978 VOL 24 p 987-1000.

(7301)
Emery D R
Overlapping   interest   in   bond   refunding: A
reconsideration
FIN MGMT 1978 SUMMER VOL 7 p 19.

(7302)
Kalotay A J
On the advanced refunding of discounted debt
FIN MGMT 1978 SUMMER VOL 7 p 14

(7303)
Laber G
Repurchases of bonds through tender offers:
Implications for shareholder wealth
FIN MGMT 1978 SUMMER VOL 7 p 7.

(7304)
Dyl E A, Joehnk M D
Effect of latest IRS regulations on advance
refundings
FIN MGMT 1977 SUMMER VOL 6 p 71.

(7305)
Ofer A R, Taggart R A Jr
Bond refunding: A clarifying analysis
JF 1977 VOL 32 p 21.

(7306)
Yawitz J B, Anderson J A
The effect of bond refunding on share-holder
wealth
JF 1977 VOL 32 p 1738.

(7307)
Ziese C H, Taylor R K
Advance refunding: a practitioner's perspective
FIN MGMT 1977 SUMMER VOL 6 p 73

(7308)
Dyl E A, Joehnk M D
Refunding tax exempt bonds
FIN MGMT 1976 SUMMER VOL 5 p 59.

(7309)
Ang J S
The two faces of bond refunding
JF 1975 VOL 30 p 869.

(7310)
Friedman Y, Zvi L
Planning and forecast horizons for the bond
refunding problem: Note
MSci 1975 JUL VOL 20:11 p 1332.

(7311)
Bierman H Jr, Barnea A
Expected short-term interest rates in bond
refunding
FIN MGMT 1974 SPRING VOL 3 p 75.

(7312)
Johnson R, Klein R
Corporate motives in repurchases of discounted
bonds
FIN MGMT 1974 AUTUMN VOL 3 p 44.

(7313)
Kolodny R
The refunding decision in near perfect markets
JF 1974 VOL 29 p 1467.

(7314)
Mayor T H, McCoin K G
The rate of discount in bond refunding
FIN MGMT 1974 AUTUMN VOL 3 p 54.

(7315)
Sibley A M
Some evidence on the cash flow effects of bond
refunding
FIN MGMT 1974 AUTUMN VOL 3 p 50.

(7316)
Kraus A
The bond refunding decision in an efficient
market
JFQA 1973 DEC VOL 8:5 p 793-806.

(7317)
Bierman H Jr
The bond refunding decision
FIN MGMT 1972 SUMMER VOL 1 p 27.

(7318)
Bryan W R
Treasury advanced refundings: An empirical
investigation
JFQA 1972 DEC VOL 7 p 2139.

(7319)
Kalymon B A
Bond refunding with stochastic interest rates
MSci 1971 NOV VOL 18 p 171-183.

(7320)
Weingartner H M
Optimal timing of bond refunding
MSci 1967 MAR VOL 13 p 511-524.

(7321)
Bierman H Jr
The bond refunding decision as a Markov process
MSci 1966 AUG VOL 12 p B545-B551.

(7322)
Bowlin O D
The refunding decision
JF 1966 MAR VOL 21 p 55-68.

18.35 Securitization

(7323)
Donaldson T H
Credit risk and exposure in securitization and
transactions
Macmillan, 1989.

(7324)
Acheson M W, Halstead D W
Trends in securitization - private and public
JACF 1988 FALL VOL 1 p 52-60.

(7325)
Bryan L L
Structured securitized credit: A superior
technology for lending
JACF 1988 FALL VOL 1 p 6-20.

(7326)
Goldberg C J, Rogers K
An introduction to asset backed securities
JACF 1988 FALL VOL 1 p 20-31.

(7327)
Goldberg H H
Asset securitization and corporate financial health
JACF 1988 FALL VOL 1 p 45-51.

(7328)
Ocampo J M, Rosenthal J A
The future of credit securitization and the
financial services industry
JACF 1988 FALL VOL 1 p 90-100.

(7329)
Rosenberg R M, Kravitt J H P
Legal issues in securitization
JACF 1988 FALL VOL 1 p 52-60.

(7330)
Rosenthal J A, Ocampo J M
Analyzing the economic benefits of securitized
credit
JACF 1988 FALL VOL 1 p 32-44.

(7331)
Cumming C
The economics of securitization
F R Bk New York Q Rev 1987 AUTUMN VOL
12:3.

(7332)
Rose S
Rethinking securitization
MCFJ 1987 FALL VOL 5 p 62-63.

18.4 Types of debt and preferred

(7333)
Biger N, Israel R
A note on the pricing of double choice bonds
JBankF 1989 MAY VOL 13:2 p 181-190.

(7334)
Christensen P O, Nielsen J A
The bond-type effect on yield to maturity
Scandanavian Journal of Economics 1987 VOL
89:2 p 193-208.

(7335)
McEnally R W ed.
Innovations in fixed-income instruments and
markets
Institute of Chartered Financial Analysts, 1987.

(7336)
Zahn H E
Financial innovations: glossary of new hedging
and financing instruments: English - German
Frankfurt am Main: Fritz Knapp, 1986.

(7337)
West R R
When is a GIC not a GIC?
FAJ 1983 JAN-FEB VOL 39 p 24-26.

(7338)
Livingston M
The pricing of premium bonds
JFQA 1979 SEP VOL 14 p 517.

(7339)
Darst D M
The complete bond book: a guide to all types of
fixed-income securities
McGraw, 1975.

18.41 Privately placed debt

(7340)
Blackwell D W, Kidwell D S
An investigation of cost differences between
public sales and private placements
JFE 1988 VOL 22 p 253.

(7341)
Cabanilla N B
Directly-placed bonds: a test of market efficiency
JPM 1984 WINTER VOL 10:2 p 72.

(7342)
Lund H A et al., eds.
Private placements: national and international
markets
Euromoney Publications, 1984..

(7343)**Zwick B**
Yields on privately-placed corporate bonds
JF 1980 MAR VOL 35:1 p 23-29.

(7344)
Zinbarg E D
The private placement loan agreement
FAJ 1975 JUL-AUG VOL 31 p 33-35.

(7345)
Cohan A B
Yields on corporate debt directly placed
(Dist by Columbia U Pr) Natl Bur Econ Res, 1967.

(7346)
Federal Reserve Bank of Cleveland
Direct placement of corporate debt
F R Bk Cleveland Mo Bus Rev 1965 MAR.

(7347)
Cohan A B
Private placements and public offerings: market shares since 1935
U of NC Busn, 1961.

(7348)
Soldofsky R M
The size and maturity of direct-placement loans
JF 1960 MAR VOL 15 p 32-44.

(7349)
Conklin G T Jr
Direct placements
JF 1951 JUN VOL 6 p 85-118.

(7350)
Corey E R
Direct placement of corporate securities
Harvard Busn, 1951.

18.42 Eurobonds and foreign bonds

(7351)
Bowe M A
Eurobonds
Dow Jones-Irwin, 1989.

(7352)
Ingrams L ed.
Intenational bond portfolio management
Euromoney Publications, 1989.

(7353)
Fisher F G
Eurobonds
Euromoney Publications, 1988.

(7354)
Gallant P
The Eurobond market
Woodhead-Faulkner, 1988.

(7355)
Kim Y C, Stulz R M
The Eurobond market and corporate financial policy: A test of the clientele hypothesis
JFE 1988 VOL 22 p 189.

(7356)
Marr W, Trimble J
The persistent borrowing advantage of Eurodollar bonds: a plausible explanation
JACF 1988 SUMMER VOL 1 p 65-70.

(7357)
Mason R
Innovations in the structure of international securities
Credit Suisse First Boston, SEP 1986.

(7358)
McEnally R W ed.
International bonds and currencies
Institute of Chartered Financial Analysts, 1986.

(7359)
Finnerty J E, Nunn K P Jr
Comparative yield spreads on US corporate bonds and $Eurobonds
FAJ 1985 JUL-AUG VOL 41:4 p 68-73.

(7360)
Kidwell D S, Marr M W, Thompson G R
Eurodollar bonds: Alternative financing for U S companies
FIN MGMT 1985 WINTER VOL 14 p 18-27.

(7361)
Kerr I M et al.
A history of the Eurobond market: the first 21 years
Euromoney Publications, 1984.

(7362)
Adler M, Dumas B
The exposure of long-term foreign currency bonds
JFQA 1980 NOV VOL 15 p 973-994.

(7363)
Finnerty J E, Schneeweis T, Hegde S P
Interest rates in the $Eurobond market
JFQA 1980 SEP VOL 15 p 743.

(7364)
Folks W R, Advani R
Raising funds with foreign currency
FE 1980 FEB VOL 48 p 44-49.

(7365)
Geisst C R
Raising international capital: international bond
markets and the European institutions
Saxon House, 1980.

(7366)
Mendelsohn M S
Money on the move: the modern international
capital market
McGraw, 1980.

(7367)
Donnerstag H C, Thorn P ed.
The eurobond market
Financial Times, 1975.

(7368)
Solnik B H, Grall J
Eurobonds: determining the demand for capital
and the international interest rate structure
JBR 1975 WINTER VOL 5:4.

(7369)
Park Y S
The euro-bond market: function and structure
Praeger, 1974.

(7370)
Cheng H-S
International bond issues of the less-developed
countries: diagnosis and prescription
Iowa St U Pr, 1969.

(7371)
Einzig P
The Eurobond market
Macmillan Int, 1969.

(7372)
Chown J F, Valentine R
The international bond market in the 1960s: its
development and operation
Praeger, 1968.

(7373)
Williams D
Foreign currency issues on European security
markets
IMF 1967 MAR VOL 14 p 43-79.

18.43   Floating rate notes

(7374)
Finnerty J D
Measuring the duration of a floating-rate bond
JPM 1989 SUMMER VOL 15:4 p 67-72.

(7375)
Smith D J
The pricing of bull and bear floating rate notes:
an application of financial engineering
FIN MGMT 1988 WINTER VOL 17 p 72-81.

(7376)
Ogden J P
An analysis of yield curve notes
JF 1987 MAR VOL 42:1 p 99-110.

(7377)
Wilson R S
Domestic floating-rate and adjustable-rate debt
securities
(in Fabozzi F J and Pollack I M eds., Handbook
of fixed income securities, 2nd ed. Dow
Jones-Irwin, 1987.)

(7378)
Morgan G E
Floating rate securities and immunization : some
further results
JFQA 1986 MAR VOL 21:1 p 87-94.

(7379)
Ramaswamy K, Sundaresan S M
The valuation of floating-rate instruments: Theory
and evidence
JFE 1986 VOL 17 p 251.

(7380)
Rowley I, Neuhaus H
How caps and floors can influence desired cash
flows
Euromoney Corporate Finance JUL 1986.

(7381)
Bank of England
The international market for floating-rate
instruments
BEQB 1984 VOL 24 p 337-345.

(7382)
Chance D M
Floating rate notes and immunization
JFQA 1983 SEP VOL 18:3 p 365-380.

(7383)
Fortune
Let's not sink floating rates
F 1983 JUN 13 VOL 107:12 p 87-98.

(7384)
Santomero A M
Fixed versus variable rate loans
JF 1983 DEC VOL 38:5 p 1363-1380.

(7385)
Agmon T, Ofer A R
Variable rate debt instruments and corporate debt
policy
JF 1981 MAR VOL 36:1 p 113-125.

(7386)
Cornell B
The future of floating rate bonds
CFQ 1981 FALL VOL 1 p 27-38.

(7387)
Cox J C, Ingersoll J E, Ross S A
An analysis of variable rate loan contracts
JF 1980 MAY VOL 35:2 p 389-403.

(7388)
Marks K R, Law W A
Hedging against inflation with floating-rate notes
HBR 1980 MAR-APR VOL 58:2 p 106-112.

(7389)
Von Furstenberg G M
The equilibrium spread between variable rates and
fixed rates on long-term financing instruments
JFQA 1973 DEC VOL 8:5 p 807-820.

18.44   Indexed bonds and commodity bonds

(7390)
Hochman S, Palmon O
A tax-induced clientele for index-linked corporate
bonds
JF 1988 DEC VOL 43:5 p 1257-1264.

(7391)
Lessard D R
Recapitalizing Third-World debt: toward a new
vision of commercial financing for less-developed
countries
MCFJ 1987 FALL VOL 5 p 6-21.

(7392)
Boschen J F
The information content of indexed bonds
JMCB 1986 FEB VOL 18:1 p 76-87.

(7393)
Bootle R P
Index-linked gilts: a practical investment guide
Woodhead-Faulkner, 1985.

(7394)
Eden B
Indexation and related issues: a review essay
JME 1985 VOL 16 p 259.

(7395)
Huberman G, Schwert G W
Information aggregation, inflation and the pricing
of indexed bonds
JPE 1985 VOL 93 p 92..

(7396)**Peled D**
Stochastic inflation and government provision of
indexed bonds

JME 1985 VOL 15 p 291.

(7397)
Babbel D F
Real immunization with indexed bonds
FAJ 1984 NOV-DEC VOL 40 p 49-55.

(7398)
O'Hara M
Commodity bonds and consumption risks
JF 1984 MAR VOL 39:1 p 193-206.

(7399)
Budd N
The future of commodity-indexed financing
HBR 1983 JUL-AUG VOL 61:4 p 44-50.

(7400)
Dornbusch R, Simonson M H eds.
Inflation, debt and indexation
MIT Pr, 1983.

(7401)
Fischer S
Indexing and inflation
JME 1983 VOL 12 p 519.

(7402)
Fischer S
On the nonexistence of privately issued index
bonds in the US capital market
(in Dornbusch R and Simonson M H eds.,
Inflation, debt and indexation. MIT Pr, 1983.)

(7403)
Levhari D
The effects of government intermediation in the
indexed bonds market on consumer behavior
(in Dornbusch R and Simonson M H eds.,
Inflation, debt and indexation. MIT Pr, 1983.)

(7404)
Rutterford J
Index-linked gilts
NWBQR 1983 NOV p 2-17.

(7405)
Schwartz E S
The pricing of commodity-linked bonds
JF 1982 MAY VOL 37:2 p 525-541.

(7406)
White D L
Next in corporate finance : index-linked loans?
HBR 1981 SEP-OCT VOL 59:5 p 14-22.

(7407)
McCulloch J H
The ban on indexed bonds, 1933-77
AER 1980 VOL 70 p 1018-1021.

(7408)
Bhattacharya S
Welfare and savings effects of indexation
JMCB 1979 MAY VOL 11:2 p 192-201.

(7409)
Liviatan N, Levhari D
Risk and the theory of indexed bonds
AER 1977 JUN VOL 67:3 p 366-375.

(7410)
Siegel J J, Warner J B
Indexation, the risk-free asset and capital market
equilibrium
JF 1977 VOL 32 p 1101.

(7411)
Bicksler J L, Hess P J
More on purchasing power risk, portfolio analysis
and the case for index linked bonds
JMCB 1976 MAY VOL 8:2 p 265-266.

(7412)
Ragazzi G
Index linking and general welfare
JMCB 1976 MAY VOL 8:2 p 261-263.

(7413)
Tanzi V
Inflation indexation and interest income taxation
BNLQR 1976 p 54-76.

(7414)
Fischer S
The demand for index bonds
JPE 1975 JUN VOL 83:3 p 509-534.

(7415)
Yang J-H
The case for and against indexation: an attempt
at perspective
F R Bk St Louis Rev 1974 VOL 56:10.

(7416)
OECD
Indexation of fixed-interest securities: report by
the Committee on Financial Markets
OECD, 1973.

(7417)
Sarnat M
Purchasing power risk, portfolio analysis, and the
case for index linked bonds
JMCB 1973 AUG VOL 5:3 p 836-845.

(7418)
Mullineaux D J
Inflation insurance an "escalator clause" for
securities?
F R Bk Bus Rev Philadelphia 1972 OCT.

(7419)
Eagly R V
On government issuance of an index bond
Public Finance 1967 VOL 22 p 268-284.

(7420)
Robson P
Index-linked bonds
REStud 1960 OCT VOL 28 p 57-68.

18.45   Original issue discount bonds

(7421)
Narayanan M P, Lim S-P
On the call provision in corporate zero-coupon
bonds
JFQA 1989 MAR VOL 24:1 p 91-104.

(7422)
Nichols D R
The new Dow Jones-Irwin guide to zero coupon
investments
Dow Jones-Irwin, 1989.

(7423)
Braswell R C, Marks B, Reinhart W J et al.
The effect of term structure and taxes on the
issuance of discount bonds
FIN MGMT 1988 WINTER VOL 17 p 92.

(7424)
Gilmer R H Jnr., Stock D R
Yield volatilty of discount coupon bonds
JFR 1988 FALL VOL 11:3 p 189-200.

(7425)
Rosen L R
Investing in zero coupon bonds: all about CATS,
STRIPS, TIGRs, LIONS, TRs, and TBRs
Wiley, 1986.

(7426)
Stock D
The analytics of tax effects in discount bond
valuation
FR 1986 NOV VOL 21:4.

(7427)
Arak M
Profit opportunities with old OIDs
JPM 1985 SPRING VOL 11:3 p 63-66.

(7428)
Finnerty J D
Zero coupon bond arbitrage: An illustration of
the regulatory dialetic at work
FIN MGMT 1985 WINTER VOL 14 p 13-17.

(7429)
Schaefer S M
Less is more: the attractions of zero coupon bond
financing
The Treasurer 1985 OCT p 21-26.

(7430)
Arak M, Silver A
The value of the tax teatment of original-issue
deep-discount bonds : a note
JF 1984 MAR VOL 39:1 p 253-259.

(7431)
Hills J
Deep discount bonds - or how to get an
interest-free loan
FS 1984 VOL 5:3.

(7432)
Kalotay A J
An analysis of original issue discount bonds
FIN MGMT 1984 AUTUMN VOL 13 p 29-38.

(7433)
Roll R
After-tax investment results from long-term vs short-term discount coupon bonds
FAJ 1984 JAN-FEB VOL 40:1 p 43-54

(7434)
Yawitz J B, Maloney K J
Evaluating the decision to issue original issue discount bonds: Term structure and tax effects
FIN MGMT 1983 WINTER VOL 12 p 36-46.

(7435)
Kalotay A J
Innovations in corporate finance: Deep discount private placements
FIN MGMT 1982 SPRING VOL 11 p 55-57.

(7436)
Silver A
Original issue deep discount bonds
F R Bk New York Q Rev 1981-82 WINTER VOL 6:4.

(7437)
Woolridge J R, Gray G
Are original-issue discount bonds here to stay?
HBR 1982 MAY-JUN VOL 60:3 p 54-60.

(7438)
Pyle D H
Is deep discount debt financing a bargain?
CFQ 1981 FALL VOL 1 p 39-61.

(7439)
Harper W K, Berger P D et al.
How about original issue, deep discount bonds?
HBR 1975 SEP-OCT VOL 53:5 p 8, 12, 16.

18.46   Junk bonds

(7440)
Howe J T
Junk bonds: Analysis and portfolio strategies
Chicago: Probus Publishing, 1988.

(7441)
Perry K J, Taggart R A
The growing role of junk bonds
JACF 1988 SPRING VOL 1 p 37-45.

(7442)
Altman E I
The anatomy of the high-yield bond market
FAJ 1987 JUL-AUG VOL 43 p 12-25.

(7443)
Altman E I, Nammacher S A
Investing in junk bonds: inside the high yield debt market
Wiley, 1987.

(7444)
Blume M E, Keim D B
Lower-grade bonds: their risk and returns
FAJ 1987 JUL-AUG VOL 43 p 26-33.

(7445)
Weinstein M I
A curmudgeon's view of junk bonds
JPM 1987 SPRING VOL 13:3 p 76-80.

(7446)
Worthy F
The coming defaults in junk bonds
F 1987 MAR 16 VOL 115:6 p 20-27.

(7447)
Bookstaber R M, Jacob D P
The composite hedge : Controlling the credit risk of high-yield bonds
FAJ 1986 MAR-APR VOL 42:2 p 25-36.

(7448)
Altman E I, Nammacher S A
The default rate experience on high yield corporate debt
FAJ 1985 JUL-AUG VOL 41 p 25-41.

18.47   Income bonds

(7449)
McConnell J J, Schlarbaum G G
The income bond puzzle
CFQ 1982 SUMMER VOL 1 p 8-28.

(7450)
McConnell J J, Schlarbaum G G
Returns risks and pricing of income bonds 1956-76 (does money have an odor?)
JB 1981 JAN VOL 54:1 p 33-63.

(7451)
McConnell J J, Schlarbaum G G
Evidence on the impact of exchange offers on security prices: the case of income bonds
JB 1981 JAN VOL 54:1 p 65-85.

(7452)
McConnell J J, Schlarbaum G G
Another foray into the backwaters of the market
JPM 1980 FALL VOL 7:1 p 61-65.

(7453)
Brown B
Why companies should consider income bonds
FE 1967 OCT VOL 35 p 74-78.

(7454)
Halford F A
Income bonds
FAJ 1964 JAN-FEB VOL 20 p 73-79.

(7455)
Robbins S M
A bigger role for income bonds
HBR 1955 NOV-DEC VOL 33 p 100-115.

18.48 Preferred stock

(7456)
Linn S C, Pinegar J M
The effect of issuing preferred stock on common and preferred stockholder wealth
JFE 1988 VOL 22 p 155.

(7457)
Hetherington N S
High return and low risk in called preferreds
JPM 1987 SPRING VOL 13:3 p 81-82.

(7458)
Elmer P I
Preferred stock arbitrage of municipal bond market segmentation
FR 1986 NOV VOL 21:4.

(7459)
Pinegar J M, Lease R C
The impact of preferred-for-common exchange offers on firm value
JF 1986 SEP VOL 41:4 p 795-814.

(7460)
Finnerty J D
Preferred stock refunding analysis: Synthesis and extension
FIN MGMT 1984 AUTUMN VOL 13 p 22-28.

(7461)
McDaniel W R
Sinking fund preferred stock
FIN MGMT 1984 SPRING VOL 45.

(7462)
Emanuel D C
A theoretical model for valuing preferred stock
JF 1983 VOL 38:4 p 1133-1155.

(7463)
Rosenfeld J
The effect of common-stock dividend reductions on the returns of non-convertible preferred stocks : a note
JF 1983 JUN VOL 38:3 p 1019-1024.

(7464)
Sorensen E H, Hawlins C A
The demand for preferred stock with sinking funds and without: a note
JF 1982 MAR VOL 37:1 p 237-241.

(7465)
Joehnk M D, Bowlin O D, Petty J W III
Preferred dividend rolls: A viable strategy for corporate money managers?
FIN MGMT 1980 SUMMER VOL 9 p 78.

(7466)
Bildersee J S
Some aspects of the performance of non-convertible preferred stocks
JF 1973 VOL 28 p 1187.

(7467)
Stevenson R A
Retirement of non-callable preferred stock
JF 1970 DEC VOL 25 p 1143-1152.

(7468)
Fischer D E, Wilt G A Jr
Non-convertible preferred stock as a financing instrument, 1950-1965
JF 1968 SEP VOL 23 p 611-624.

(7469)
Donaldson G
In defense of preferred stock
HBR 1962 JUL-AUG VOL 40 p 123-136.

(7470)
Fergusson D A
Preferred stock valuation in recapitalizations
JF 1958 MAR VOL 13 p 48-69.

(7471)
Fergusson D A
Recent developments in preferred stock financing
JF 1952 SEP VOL 7 p 447-462.

18.481 Floating rate preferred

(7472)
Mavrides L P
Development of the variable rate preferred stock
market
EJOR 1987 JUN VOL 30:1 p 6-12.

18.482 Auction rate preferred

(7473)
Alderson M J, Brown K C, Lummer S L
Dutch auction rate preferred stock
FIN MGMT 1987 SUMMER VOL 16 p 68.

(7474)
Winger B J, Chen C R, Martin J D
Adjustable rate preferred stock
FIN MGMT 1986 SPRING VOL 15 p 48-57.

18.5 Bank lending

(7475)
Clarke P S
Managing problem loans
Dow Jones-Irwin, 1989.

(7476)
Forbes S M, Mayne L S
A friction model of the prime
JBankF 1989 MAR VOL 13:1 p 127-136.

(7477)
Greenbaum S I, Kanatas G, Venezia I
Equilibrium loan pricing under the bank-client
relationship
JBankF 1989 MAY VOL 13:2 p 221-236.

(7478)
Lang W W, Nakamura L I
Information losses in a dynamic model of credit
JF 1989 JUL VOL 44:3 p 731-746.

(7479)
Sundaram A K
Syndications in sovereign lending
JIMF 1989 VOL 8 p 451.

(7480)
Duchessi P, Shawky H, Seagle J P
A knowledge-engineered system for commercial
loan decisions
FIN MGMT 1988 AUTUMN VOL 17 p 57-66.

(7481)
James C
The use of loan sales and standby letters of credit
by commercial banks
JME 1988 VOL 22:3 p 395-422.

(7482)
James C, Wier P
Are bank loans different?: some evidence from
the stock market
JACF 1988 SUMMER VOL 1 p 46-54.

(7483)
Milde H, Riley J G
Signaling in credit markets
QJE 1988 FEB VOL 103:1 p 101-130.

(7484)
Shaw M J, Gentry J A
Using an expert system with inductive learning to
evaluate business loans
FIN MGMT 1988 AUTUMN VOL 17 p 45-56.

(7485)
Boot A, Thakor A V, Udell G F
Competition,   risk   neutrality   and   loan
commitments
JBankF 1987 VOL 11 p 449-471.

(7486)
Melnik A, Plaut S E
Interest rate indexation and the pricing of loan
commitment contracts
JBankF 1987 VOL 11 p 137-145.

(7487)
Thakor A V, Udell G F
An economic rationale for the pricing structure of
bank loan commitments
JBankF 1987 VOL 11 p 271-289.

(7488)
Edwards S
The pricing of bonds and bank loans in
international markets: an empirical analysis of
developing countries' foreign borrowing
EER 1986 VOL 30:3.

(7489)
Lieber Z, Orgler Y E
Optimal borrowing and bank lending policies: An
interactive approach
JBankF 1986 VOL 10 p 255.

(7490)
Melnik A, Plaut S E
Loans commitment contracts, terms of lending
and credit allocation
JF 1986 JUN VOL 41:2 p 425-435.

(7491)
Melnik A, Plaut S E
The economics of loan commitment contracts:
Credit pricing and utilization
JBankF 1986 VOL 10 p 267.

(7492)
Viscione J A
How long should you borrow short term?
HBR 1986 MAR-APR VOL 64:2 p 20-24.

(7493)
Brady T F
Changes in loan pricing and business lending at
commercial banks
F R Bul 1985 VOL 71:1.

(7494)
Churchill N C, Lewis V L
Profitability of small-business lending
JBR 1985 SUMMER VOL 16:2 p 63-71.

(7495)
Do T Q, Chateau J P B
A geometrical exposition of the credit setting
strategies of the banking firm under loan rate
uncertainty
Finance 1985 VOL 6:1.

(7496)
Goldberg M A, Lloyd-Davis P R
Standby letters of credit: are banks overextending
themselves?
JBR 1985 SPRING VOL 16:1 p 28-39.

(7497)
Kling J L
The dynamic behavior of business loans and the
prime rate
JBankF 1985 VOL 9 p 421.

(7498)
Osano H, Tsutsui Y
Implicit contracts in the Japanese bank loan
market.
JFQA 1985 JUN VOL 20:2 p 211-229

(7499)
Brau E, Williams R C
Recent multilateral debt restructurings with
official and bank creditors
IMF, 1983.

(7500)
Costa J E Ricart i, Greenbaum S I
Bank forward lending : a note
JF 1983 SEP VOL 38:4 p 1315-1322.

(7501)
Donaldson T H
Understanding corporate credit: the lending banker's viewpoint
Macmillan, 1983.@

(7502)**James C**
Pricing alternatives for loan commitments: a note
JBR 1983 WINTER VOL 13:4.

(7503)
Manage N D
Further evidence on estimating regulated personal loan market relationships
QREB 1983 WINTER VOL 23:4 p 63-80

(7504)
Slovin M B, Sushka M E
A model of the commercial loan rate
JF 1983 DEC VOL 38:5 p 1583-1596.

(7505)
Stiglitz J E, Weiss A
Incentive effects of termination: Applications to the credit and labor markets
AER 1983 VOL 73 p 912-927.

(7506)
United Nations.   Centre on Transnational Corporations
Issues in negotiating international loan agreements with transnational banks
New York: United Nations, 1983.

(7507)
Wood J H
Familiar developments in bank loan markets
F R Bk Dallas Ec Rev 1983 NOV.

(7508)
Arnold J H
How to negotiate a term loan
HBR 1982 MAR-APR VOL 60:2 p 131-138.

(7509)
Cramer R H, Sterk W E
The present value approach to commercial loan pricing
JBR 1982 WINTER VOL 12:4.

(7510)
Deshmukh S D, Greenbaum S I, Kanatas G
Bank forward lending in alternative funding environments
JF 1982 SEP VOL 37:4 p 925-940.

(7511)
Donaldson J A, Donaldson T H
The medium-term loan market
Macmillan, 1982.

(7512)
Hawkins G D
An analysis of revolving credit agreements
JFE 1982 VOL 10 p 59.

(7513)
James C
An analysis of bank loan rate indexation
JF 1982 JUN VOL 37:3 p 809-825.

(7514)
Krasker W S
Hedging on loans linked to the prime
HBR 1982 MAY-JUN VOL 60:3 p 66-68.

(7515)
McDonald R P
International syndicated loans
Euromoney Publications, 1982.

(7516)
Seiders D F
Interest rates and terms on construction loans at commercial banks
F R Bul 1982 VOL 68:7.

(7517)
Vittas D, Brown R
Bank lending and industrial investments: a response to recent criticisms
Banking Information Service, 1982.

(7518)
Williamson J
The lending policies of the International Monetary Fund
Washington, DC: Institute for International Economics, 1982.

(7519)
Gisselquist D
The political economics of international bank lending
Praeger, 1981.

(7520)
Goldberg M A
The impact of regulatory and monetary factors on bank loan charges
JFQA 1981 JUN VOL 16:2 p 227-246.

(7521)
McCabe G M, Blackwell J M
The hedging strategy: a new approach to spread management banking and commercial lending
JBR 1981 SUMMER VOL 12:2.

(7522)
Peterson R L, Ginsberg M D
Determinants of commercial bank auto loan rates
JBR 1981 SPRING VOL 12:1.

(7523)
Trepeta W T
Changes in bank lending practices, 1979-81
F R Bul 1981 VOL 67:9.

(7524)
Altman E I
Commercial bank lending: Process, credit scoring and costs of errors in lending
JFQA 1980 NOV VOL 15 p 813.

(7525)
Bank of England
Conditions in the syndicated medium-term eurocredit market
BEQB 1980 VOL 20 p 311-318.

(7526)
Black H, Schweitzer R L
Discrimination in the lending decision: home improvement loans
JBR 1980 AUTUMN VOL 11:3.

(7527)
Smith C W Jr
On the theory of financial contracting: The personal loan market
JME 1980 JUL VOL 6 p 333-357.

(7528)
Ang J S, Chua J, Bowling C
The profiles of late paying customer loan borrowers: an exploratory study
JMCB 1979 MAY VOL 11:2 p 222-226.

(7529)
Bartter B J, Rendleman R J Jr
Fee-based pricing of fixed rate bank loan commitments
FIN MGMT 1979 SPRING VOL 8 p 13.

(7530)
Brady T F
Changes in bank lending practices, 1977-79
F R Bul 1979 VOL 65:10.

(7531)
Burstein N R
Effects on the credit markets of the abolition of holder-in-due-course
FIN MGMT 1979 WINTER VOL 8 p 19.

(7532)
Cowen S S, Page A L
Factors affecting the performance of loans to minority small businessmen: a case study
JBR 1979 AUTUMN VOL 10:3.

(7533)
Hester D D
Customer relationships and terms of loans: evidence from a pilot survey
JMCB 1979 AUG VOL 11:3 p 349-357.

(7534)
Lloyd-Davies P R
Survey of standby letters of credit
F R Bul 1979 VOL 65:9.

(7535)
Campbell T S
A model for the market lines of credit
JF 1978 VOL 33 p 231.

(7536)
LeCompte M A
International loan syndications, the Securities Acts, and the duties of a lead bank
VLR 1978 VOL 64:6 p 897-919.

(7537)
Benston G J
The impact of maturity regulation on high
interest rate lenders and borrowers
JFE 1977 VOL 4 p 23.

(7538)
Boltz P W
Survey of terms of bank lending
F R Bul 1977 VOL 63:5.

(7539)
Hoehenwarter W P
Method for evaluation of the economic
characteristics of loan portfolios
JBR 1976 WINTER VOL 6:4.

(7540)
Beighley H P, McCall A S
Market power and structure and commercial bank
installment lending
JMCB 1975 NOV VOL 7:4 p 449-467.

(7541)
Wood J H
Commercial bank loan and investment behaviour
Wiley, 1975.

(7542)
Oliver B L
Selected insights on bankers' loan decisions
JBR 1974 WINTER VOL 4:4 p 311-313.

(7543)
Berger P D, Harper W K
Determination of an optimal revolving credit
agreement
JFQA 1973 JUN VOL 8:3 p 491-498.

(7544)
Melitz J, Pardue M
The demand and supply of commercial bank loans
JMCB 1973 MAY VOL 5:2 p 688-692.

(7545)
Crane D B, White W L
Who benefits from a floating prime rate?
HBR 1972 JAN-FEB VOL 50:1 p 121ff.

(7546)
Stone B K
The cost of bank loans
JFQA 1972 DEC VOL 7 p 2077.

(7547)
Eisenbeis R A
Local banking markets for business loans
JBR 1971 SUMMER VOL 2:2.

(7548)
Hayes D A
Bank lending policies, domestic and international
Bureau of Business Research, U of Michigan,
1971.

(7549)
Saulnier R J
Industrial banking companies and their credit
practices
Natl Bur Econ Res, 1940.

18.6 Money market

(7550)
Dowding M, Mackinnon N
The sterling money market
IFR, 1989.

(7551)
Bank of England
Bank of England operations in the sterling money
market
BEQB 1988 VOL 28 p 391.

(7552)
Stigum M
After the trade: dealer and clearing bank
operations in money market and government
securities
Dow Jones-Irwin, 1988.

(7553)
Dotsey M
The Australian money market and the operations
of the Reserve Bank of Australia: a comparative
analysis
F R Bk Richmond Ec Rev 1987 VOL 73:5.

(7554)
Halttunen H
The money market in Finland
Kansallis-Osake-Pankki Economic Review 1987 1
p 5-12..

(7555)Ogden J P
The end of the month as a preferred habitat: a
test of operational efficiency in the money market
JFQA 1987 SEP VOL 22:3 p 329-343.

(7556)
Fabozzi F J, Thurston T B
State taxes and reserve requirements as major
determinants of yield spreads among money
market instruments.
JFQA 1986 DEC VOL 21:4 p 427-436.

(7557)
Thornton D L
The discount rate and market interest rates:
theory and evidence
F R Bk St Louis Rev 1986 VOL 68:7.

(7558)
Stigum M
The money market. Rev ed
Dow Jones-Irwin, 1983.

(7559)
Bank of England
The role of the Bank of England in the money
market
BEQB 1982 VOL 22 p 86-94.

(7560)
Glasgo P W, Landes W J, Thompson A F
Bank discount, coupon equivalent and compound
yields
FIN MGMT 1982 AUTUMN VOL 11 p 80.

(7561)
Cook T Q, Summers B J eds.
Instruments of the money market. 5th ed
Federal Reserve Bank of Richmond, 1981.

(7562)
Gattl J F, Mills J R, McTagget P J
The feasibility of small denomination consumer
note issues as a source of funds for non-financial
borrowers
FIN MGMT 1981 AUTUMN VOL 10 p 41-53.

(7563)
Shaw E R
The London money market. 3rd ed
Heinemann, 1981.

(7564)
Wallace N
A Modigliani-Miller theorem for open-market
operations
AER 1981 VOL 71 p 267-274.

(7565)
Ferri M G, Gaines J P
A study of yield spreads in the money markets:
1971-1978
FIN MGMT 1980 AUTUMN VOL 9 p 52.

(7566)
Fildes R A, Fitzgerald M D
Efficiency and premiums in the short term money
market
JMCB 1980 NOV VOL 12:4 p 615-629.

(7567)
Kobrin D, Stott V
Negotiable instruments
Anderson Keenan Publishing, 1980.

(7568)
Levich R M
Tests of forecasting models and market efficiency
in the international money market
(in Frenkel J A and Johnson H G eds., The
economics of exchange rates: Selected studies.
Addison-Wes, 1978.)

(7569)
Puglisi D J
Yield movements in the money market: evidence
and implications
QREB 1978 VOL 18:2 p 106.

(7570)
Thomson T D, Pierce J L et al.
A monthly money market model
JMCB 1975 NOV VOL 7:4 p 411-431.

(7571)
Cohen B C
Money market development and the demand for
money
JFQA 1971 SEP VOL 6 p 1155-1158.

(7572)
Goodhart C A E
The New York money market and the finance of trade, 1900-1913
Harvard U Pr, 1969.

(7573)
Scammell W M
The London discount market
Elek, 1968.

(7574)
Wilson J S G
Monetary policy and the development of money markets
Allen, 1966.

(7575)
Stone R W
The changing structure of the money markets
JF 1965 MAY VOL 20 p 229-238.

(7576)
Brimmer A F
Foreign banking institutions in the United States money market
REStat 1962 FEB VOL 44 p 76-81.

(7577)
Reierson R L
New forces in the money market
JF 1962 MAY VOL 17 p 220-229.

(7578)
Wilson J S G
The new money markets
LBR 1962 APR VOL 64 p 31-45.

(7579)
Nadler M, Heller S, Shipman S S
The money market and its institutions
Ronald, 1955.

(7580)
Riefler W W
Money rates and money markets in the United States
Har-Row, 1930.

18.61 Treasury bills

(7581)
Simon D P
Expectations and risk in the Treasury bill market: an instrumental variables approach
JFQA 1989 SEP VOL 24:3 p 357-366.

(7582)
Zivney T L, Marcus R D
The day the United States defaulted on Treasury bills
FR 1989 AUG VOL 24:3 p 475-490.

(7583)
Park S Y, Reinganum M R
The puzzling price behavior of Treasury bills that mature at the turn of calendar months
JFE 1986 JUN VOL 16:2 p 267-283.

(7584)
Ferri M G, Goldstein S J, Oberhelman H D
The performance of the when-issued market for t bills
JPM 1985 SPRING VOL 11:3 p 57-62.

(7585)
Simpson W G, Ireland T C
The impact of financial futures on the cash market for treasury bills
JFQA 1985 SEP VOL 20:3 p 371-379.

(7586)
Oldfield G S, Rogalski R J
Treasury bills and common stock returns
JF 1981 MAY VOL 36:2 p 337-350.

(7587)
Scott J, Wolf C
Bidding on treasury bills
JPM 1980 SPRING VOL 6:3 p 46-52.

(7588)
Capozza D R, Cornell B
Treasury bill pricing in the spot and futures markets
REStat 1979 NOV VOL 61:4 p 513-520.

(7589)
Sivesind C M
Noncompetitive tenders in Treasury auctions: how much do they affect savings flows?
F R Bk New York Q Rev 1978 AUTUMN VOL 3:3.

(7590)
Senchack A Jr, Heep D M
Auction profits in the treasury bill market
FIN MGMT 1975 SUMMER VOL 4 p 45.

(7591)
Bolten S
Treasury Bill auction procedures: An empirical investigation
JF 1973 VOL 28 p 577.

(7592)
Mullineaux D J
Deposit rate ceilings and noncompetitive bidding for US Treasury bill
JMCB 1973 FEB VOL 5:1 p 201-212.

(7593)
Griffiths B
The determination of the Treasury bill tender rate
Ec 1971 MAY VOL 38 p 180-191.

(7594)
Rieber M
Bids, bid patterns and collusion in the auction market for Treasury bills
JLE 1967 OCT VOL 10 p 149-168.

(7595)
Rieber M
Collusion in the auction market for Treasury bills
JPE 1964 OCT VOL 72 p 509-512.

(7596)
Brimmer A F
Price determination in the United States Treasury bills market
REStat 1962 MAY VOL 44 p 178-183.

(7597)
Goldstein H N
The Friedman proposal for auctioning Treasury bills
JPE 1962 AUG VOL 70 p 386-392.

(7598)
Scott I O Jr
The changing significance of Treasury bill obligations in commercial bank portfolios
JF 1957 MAY VOL 12 p 213-222.

18.62 Federal funds

(7599)
Cook T, Hahn T
The effect of changes in the federal funds rate target on market interest rates in the 1970s
JME 1989 VOL 24 p 331.

(7600)
Simon D P
The rationality of federal funds rate expectations: evidence from a survey
JMCB 1989 VOL 21 p 388-393.

(7601)
Barrett W B, Slovin M B, Sushka M E
Reserve regulation and recourse as a source of risk premia in the federal funds market
JBankF 1988 DEC VOL 12:4 p 575-584.

(7602)
Hoffmeister J R, Spindt P A
The micromechanics of the federal funds market: Implications for day-of-the-week effects in funds rate variability
JFQA 1988 DEC VOL 23 p 401.

(7603)
Saunders A, Urich T
The effects of shifts in monetary policy and reserve accounting regimes on bank reserve management behavior in the federal funds market
JBankF 1988 DEC VOL 12:4 p 523-536.

(7604)
Saunders A, Urich T
Weekly variation in the Federal funds market: The weekend game and other effects
(in Dimson E ed., Stock market anomalies. Cambridge U Pr, 1988.)

(7605)
Cosimano T F
The federal funds market under bank deregulation
JMCB 1987 AUG VOL 19:3 p 326-339.

(7606)
Allen L, Saunders A
The large-small bank dichotomy in the Federal
Funds market
JBankF 1986 VOL 10 p 219.

(7607)
Dyl E A, Hoffmeister J R
Efficiency and volatility in the federal funds
market
JBR 1985 WINTER VOL 15:4..

(7608)**Ho T S Y, Saunders A**
A micro model of the federal funds market
JF 1985 JUL VOL 40:3 p 977-990.

(7609)
Vogt M G, Hanna R S
Variation of the federal funds rate and bank
reserve management
JBR 1984 AUTUMN VOL 15:3.

(7610)
Clayman C F, Severn A K
The effect of random disturbances in float on the
federal fund rate
JBR 1979 SPRING VOL 10:1.

(7611)
Bryan W R, Gallagher T J
The role of the federal funds market
JMCB 1978 FEB VOL 10:1 p 102-104.

(7612)
Platt R B
The interest rate on federal funds: an empirical
approach
JF 1970 JUN VOL 25 p 585-598.

(7613)
Nichols D M
Trading in federal funds
Washington, DC: Board of Governors, Federal
Reserve System, 1965.

(7614)
Willis P B
The federal funds market
The Federal Reserve Bank of Boston, 1964.

(7615)
Federal Reserve Bank of Cleveland
Trading in federal funds
F R Bk Cleveland Mo Bus Rev 1961 OCT.

(7616)
Federal Reserve Bank of St Louis
The federal funds market
F R Bk St Louis Rev 1960 APR.

(7617)
Federal Reserve System
The federal funds market
Washington, DC: Board of Governors, 1959.

(7618)
Turner B
The federal funds market
P-H, 1931.

18.63 Bankers' acceptances

(7619)
Shovlin H P
Bills of exchange and other negotiable
instruments: a handbook of effective practice
Woodhead-Faulkner, 1988.

(7620)
Melton W C, Mahr J M
Bankers' acceptances
F R Bk New York Q Rev 1981 SUMMER VOL
6:2.

(7621)
Federal Reserve Bank of Chicago
Bankers' acceptance used more widely
F R Bk Chicago Bus Cond 1965 MAY p 9-16.

18.64 Certificates of deposit

(7622)
Cargill T F
CAMEL ratings and the CD market
JFSR 1989 VOL 3:4 p 347-358.

(7623)
Hannan T H, Hanweck G A
Bank insolvency risk and the market for large
certificates of deposit
JMCB 1988 MAY VOL 20:2 p 203-211.

(7624)
Lawler T A
Reserve requirements and the structure of the CD
market: a note
JF 1981 SEP VOL 36:4 p 935-940.

(7625)
Slovin M B, Sushka M E
An economic model of the market for negotiable
certificates of deposit
JME 1979 VOL 5 p 551.

(7626)
Melton W C
The market for large negotiable CDs
F R Bk New York Q Rev 1977-78 WINTER
VOL 2:4.

(7627)
Crane D B
A study of interest rate spreads in the 1974 CD
market
JBR 1976 AUTUMN VOL 7:3.

(7628)
Crane D B
Lessons from the 1974 CD market
HBR 1975 NOV-DEC VOL 53:6 p 73-79.

(7629)
Bank of England
Sterling certificates of deposit and the inter-bank
market
BEQB 1973 VOL 13 p 308-314.

(7630)
Cohan S B
The determinants of supply and demand for
certificates of deposit
JMCB 1973 FEB VOL 5:1 p 100-112.

(7631)
Heth M
The CD in American banking: retrospect and
prospect
BNLQR 1968 MAR VOL 21 p 48-74.

(7632)
Federal Reserve Bank of New York
Certificate of deposits
F R Bk New York Mo Rev 1963 JUN p 82-87.

(7633)
Law W, Crum C
New trend in finance, the negotiable certificate of
deposit
HBR 1963 JAN-FEB VOL 41 p 113-126.

18.65 Commercial paper and underwritten europaper

(7634)
Calomiris C W
The motivations for loan commitments backing
commercial paper: a comment on: "Commercial
paper, bank reserve requirements, and the
informational role of loan commitments"
JBankF 1989 MAY VOL 13:2 p 271-278.

(7635)
Lackman C L
Forecasting commercial paper rates
JBFA 1988 WINTER VOL 15:4 p 499-521.

(7636)
Mitchell C
The sterling commercial paper market
Woodhead-Faulkner, 1988.

(7637)
Slovin M B, Sushka M E, Hudson C D
Corporate commercial paper, note issuance
facilities, and shareholder wealth
JIMF 1988 SEP VOL 7:3 p 289-302.

(7638)
Bank of England
Commercial paper markets: an international survey
BEQB 1987 VOL 27 p 46-53.

(7639)
Bank of England
The early development of the sterling commercial paper market
BEQB 1987 VOL 27 p 527-532.

(7640)
Bullock G
Euronotes and Euro-commercial paper
Butterworth, 1987.

(7641)
Felix R ed.
Commercial paper
Euromoney Publications, 1987.

(7642)
McCauley R N, Hargraves L A
Eurocommercial paper and U.S. commercial paper: converging money markets?
F R Bk New York Q Rev 1987 AUTUMN VOL 12:3..

(7643)Nott J
Sterling commercial paper: a guide for issuers and investors
Economist Publications, 1987.

(7644)
International Financing Review
Note issuance and Eurocommercial paper facilities. 3rd ed
IFR Publishing, 1986.

(7645)
Perry L G, Cronan T P
A note on rank transformation discriminant analysis: An alternative procedure for classifying bank holding company commercial paper ratings
JBankF 1986 VOL 10 p 605.

(7646)
Peavy J W III, Edgar S M
An expanded commercial paper rating scale : classification of industrial issuers
JBFA 1984 AUTUMN VOL 11:3 p 397-407.

(7647)
Peavy J W III, Edgar S M
A multiple discriminant analysis of BHC commercial paper ratings
JBankF 1983 VOL 7 p 161.

(7648)
Stanton H G, Rickard J A
The true cost of borrowing under a commercial bill
AJM 1983 DEC VOL 8 p 95-104.

(7649)
Hurley E M
The commercial paper market since the mid-Seventies
F R Bul 1982 VOL 68:6.

(7650)
Judd J P
Competition between the commercial paper market and commercial banks
F R Bk San Francisco Ec Rev 1979 WINTER.

(7651)
Hurley E M
The commercial paper market
F R Bul 1977 VOL 63:6.

(7652)
Schadrack F C Jr
Demand and supply in the commercial paper market
JF 1970 SEP VOL 25 p 837-852.

(7653)
Cloos G W
A larger role for commercial paper
F R Bk Chicago Bus Cond 1968 DEC p 2-12.

(7654)
Johnston R
Rebirth of commercial paper
F R Bk San Francisco Mo Rev 1968 JUL p 137-142.

(7655)
Struble F M
The commercial paper boom in perspective
F R Bk Kansas City Mo Rev 1968 NOV p 3-10.

(7656)
Selden R T
Trends and cycles in the commercial paper market
(Dist by Columbia U Pr) Natl Bur Econ Res, 1963.

18.66 Repurchase agreements

(7657)
Bowsher N N
Repurchase agreements
F R Bk St Louis Rev 1979 VOL 61:9.

(7658)
Smith W J
Repurchase agreements and federal funds
F R Bul 1978 VOL 64:5.

(7659)
Lucas C M, Jones M T, Thurston T B
Federal funds and repurchase agreements
F R Bk New York Q Rev 1977 SUMMER VOL 2.

18.67 International money market

(7660)
Davis E P
Instability in the euromarkets and the economic theory of financial crisis
Bank of England, 1989.

(7661)
Gibson H D
The Eurocurrency markets, domestic financial policy and international instability
Macmillan, 1989.

(7662)
Campbell J Y, Clarida R H
The term structure of euro-market interest rates: an empirical investigation
JME 1987 VOL 19 p 25.

(7663)
Savvides A
Bank loan rate indexation in the eurocurrency market
JIMF 1987 SEP VOL 6:3 p 355-372.

(7664)
Bank of England
Arbitrage between the spot and futures markets for eurodollars
BEQB 1985 VOL 25 p 559-569.

(7665)
Cornell B, Sand O C
The value of base rate options in the eurocredit market
JBR 1985 SPRING VOL 16:1 p 22-27.

(7666)
Savona P, Sutija G eds.
Eurodollars and international banking
Macmillan, 1985.

(7667)
Thottathil P
A note on eurodollar borrowing by U S banks: derivation of reg D equation
JBR 1985 SPRING VOL 16:1 p 40-44.

(7668)
Bernauer K
The Asian dollar market
F R Bk San Francisco Ec Rev 1983 WINTER.

(7669)
Logue D E, Senbet L W
External currency market equilibrium and its implications for regulation of the eurocurrency market
JF 1983 MAY VOL 38:2 p 435-449.

(7670)
Terrell H S, Mills R H
International banking facilities and the eurodollar market
F R Bul 1983 VOL 69:8.

(7671)
Feder G, Ross K
Risk assessments and risk premiums in the Eurodollar market
JF 1982 JUN VOL 37:3 p 679-691.

(7672)
Johnston R B
The economics of the Euro-market: history,
theory and policy
Macmillan, 1982.

(7673)
Kreicher L L
Eurodollar arbitrage
F R Bk New York Q Rev 1982 SUMMER VOL
7:2.

(7674)
McInish T H, Puglisi D J
The efficiency of the international money markets
JBFA 1982 SUMMER VOL 9:2 p 167-177

(7675)
Coats W L
The weekend Eurodollar game
JF 1981 JUN VOL 36:3 p 649-659.

(7676)
Goodman L S
The pricing of syndicated eurocurrency credits
F R Bk New York Q Rev 1980 SUMMER VOL
5:2.

(7677)
Mendelsohn M S
Money on the move: the modern international
capital market
McGraw, 1980.

(7678)
Angelini A, Eng M, Lees F A
International lending, risk and the Euromarkets
Macmillan, 1979.

(7679)
Bank of England
Some   aspects   of   the   determination   of
euro-currency interest rates
BEQB 1979 VOL 19 p 35-46.

(7680)
Frydl E J
The debate over regulating the eurocurrency
markets
F R Bk New York Q Rev 1979-80 WINTER
VOL 4:4.

(7681)
Meade N, Finney M J
Analysis of the choice between domestic and
foreign loan facilities
Omega 1979 VOL 7:2 p 333-338.

(7682)
Dufey G, Giddy I H
The international money market
P-H, 1978.

(7683)
Dufey G, Giddy I H
Measuring the eurocurrency market
JBR 1978 AUTUMN VOL 9:3.

(7684)
Moya H
Euro-yen bond issues: a growing market?
FD 1978 VOL 15:4.

(7685)
Agmon T, Barnea A
Transaction costs and marketability services in the
eurocurrency money market
JME 1977 VOL 3 p 359.

(7686)
Einzig P, Quinn B S
The Euro-dollar system: practice and theory of
international interest rates. 6th ed
Macmillan, 1977.

(7687)
Feder G, Just R E
An analysis of credit terms in the eurodollar
market
EER 1977 VOL 9:2.

(7688)
Freedman C
A model of the eurodollar market
JME 1977 VOL 3 p 139.

(7689)
Freedman C
The euro-dollar market: a review of five recent
studies
JME 1977 VOL 3 p 467.

(7690)
Bank of England
Controlling the euro-markets
BEQB 1976 VOL 16 p 74-77.

(7691)
Hewson J, Sakakibara E
A general equilibrium approach to the Eurodollar
market
JMCB 1976 AUG VOL 8:3 p 297-323.

(7692)
Findlay M C III, Kleinschmidt E J
Error-learning in the Eurodollar market
JFQA 1975 SEP VOL 10 p 429.

(7693)
Hewson J, Sakakibara E
The eurocurrency markets and their implications:
a "new" view of international monetary problems
and monetary reform
Lexington Bks, 1975.

(7694)
Hewson J, Sakakibara E
The effect of U S controls on U S commercial
bank borrowing in the Euro-dollar market
JF 1975 VOL 30 p 1101.

(7695)
Hewson J, Sakakibara E
A qualitative analysis of Euro-currency controls
JF 1975 MAY VOL 30:2 p 377-400..

(7696)**Quinn B S**
The new euromarkets: a theoretical and practical
study of international financing in the eurobond,
eurocurrency and related financial markets
Macmillan, 1975.

(7697)
Bank of England
The London dollar certificate of deposit
BEQB 1973 VOL 13 p 446-452.

(7698)
Bell G
The Euro-dollar market and the international
financial system
Macmillan, 1973.

(7699)
Lee B E
The Euro-dollar multiplier
JF 1973 VOL 28 p 867.

(7700)
Makin J H
Identifying a reserve base for the Euro-Dollar
system
JF 1973 VOL 28 p 609.

(7701)
Einzig P
Parallel money markets. 2 vols
Macmillan, 1972.

(7702)
Clendenning E W
The euro-dollar market
Clarendon, 1970.

(7703)
Chalmers E
Readings in the euro-dollar
Griffith, 1969.

(7704)
Einzig P
The euro-dollar market. 2nd ed
Macmillan, 1969.

(7705)
Madden J T, Nadler M
The international money markets
Greenwood, 1968.

(7706)
Swoboda A K
The Euro-dollar market: an interpretation
Princeton U Intl Fin, Feb 1968.

(7707)
Hendershott P H
Structure of international interest rates: the US
Treasury bill rate and the Eurodollar deposit rate
JF 1967 SEP VOL 22 p 455-465.

(7708)
Klopstock F H
The international money market: structure, scope
and instruments
JF 1965 MAY VOL 20 p 182-208.

(7709)
Einzig P
Some recent changes in the Euro-dollar system
JF 1964 SEP VOL 19 p 443-449.

(7710)
Holmes A R, Klopstock F H
The market for dollar deposits in Europe
F R Bk New York Mo Rev 1960.

19 Options

(7711)
Cavalla N M
GNI handbook of traded options
Macmillan, 1989.

(7712)
Chance D M
An introduction to options and futures
Dryden Pr, 1989.

(7713)
Choie K S, Novomestky F
Replication of long-term with short-term options
JPM 1989 WINTER VOL 15:2 p 17-19.

(7714)
Hull J
Options, futures and other derivative securities
P-H, 1989.

(7715)
IFR Publishing
Financial futures and options: recent developments
IFR Publishing, 1989.

(7716)
Kishimoto N
Pricing contingent claims under interest rate and asset price risk
JF 1989 JUL VOL 44:3 p 571-590.

(7717)
Miskovic M
Futures and options: a practical guide for institutional investors
Longman, 1989.

(7718)
Block S B, Gallagher T J
How much do bank trust departments use derivatives?
JPM 1988 FALL VOL 15:1 p 12-15.

(7719)
Gastineau G L
The options manual. 3rd ed
McGraw, 1988.

(7720)
Marshall J F
Futures and options contracting: Theory and practice
SW Pub, 1988.

(7721)
Nachman D C
Spanning and completeness with options
RFS 1988 FALL VOL 1:3 p 311-328.

(7722)
OECD
New financial instruments: disclosure and accounting
OECD, 1988.

(7723)
Walmsley J
The new financial instruments: an investor's guide
Wiley, 1988.

(7724)
Bookstaber R M
Option pricing and investment strategies
Chicago: Probus Publishing, 1987.

(7725)
Evnine J, Henriksson R
Asset allocation and options
JPM 1987 FALL VOL 14:1 p 56-61.

(7726)
Koziol J D
A handbook for professional futures and options traders
Wiley, 1987.

(7727)
Livingston M
The delivery option on forward contracts.
JFQA 1987 MAR VOL 22:1 p 79-87.

(7728)
Ritchken P H
Options: theory, strategy, and applications
Scott, Foresman, 1987.

(7729)
Rubinstein M
Derivative assets analysis
JEP 1987 VOL 1:2 p 73-94.

(7730)
Smith C
Option strategies: profit-making techniques for stock, stock index, and commodity options
Wiley, 1987..

(7731)**Smith D J**
Putting the cap on options
Euromoney Corporate Finance JAN 1987.

(7732)
Ward C W R
Returns from the Indexed Mortgage: an Option Pricing Model approach
JBFA 1987 SPRING VOL 14:1 p 109-120.

(7733)
Wolf A, Castelino M, Francis J
Hedging mispriced options
JFM 1987 APR VOL 7:2 p 147-156.

(7734)
Brown K C, Lummer S L
A re-examination of the covered call option strategy for corporate cash management
FIN MGMT 1986 SUMMER VOL 15 p 13-17.

(7735)
Jennings R, Starks L
Earnings announcements stock price adjustment and the existence of option markets
JF 1986 MAR VOL 41:1 p 107-125.

(7736)
Laufman P
Handbook of futures markets: commodity, financial stock indices and options
Wiley, 1986.

(7737)
McMillan L G
Options as a strategic investment: a comprehensive analysis of listed option strategies. 2nd ed
New York Institute of Finance, 1986.

(7738)
Petruzzi C R
An options approach to setting risk adjusted hurdle rates
EE 1986 SPRING VOL 31:3 p 237-248.

(7739)
Pettit R R, Singer R F
Instant option betas
FAJ 1986 SEP-OCT VOL 42 p 51-62.

(7740)
Schachter B
A note on the welfare consequences of new option markets
JF 1986 MAR VOL 41:1 p 263-267.

(7741)
Smith A L H
Trading financial options
Butterworth, 1986.

(7742)
Billingsley R S, Chance D M
Options market efficiency and the box spread strategy
FR 1985 NOV VOL 20:4.

(7743)
Bookstaber R M, Clarke R
Problems in evaluating the performance of portfolios with options
FAJ 1985 JAN-FEB VOL 41:1 p 48-62.

(7744)
Chen N-F, Johnson H
Hedging options
JFE 1985 VOL 14:2 p 317-321.

(7745)
Cox J C, Rubinstein M
Options markets
P-H, 1985.

(7746)
Fortune
Who's winning in the options boom
F 1985 MAR 18 VOL 111:6 p 91-95.

(7747)
Garman M B
The duration of option portfolios.
JFE 1985 VOL 14:2 p 309-315.

(7748)
Henin C G, Rentz W F
Subjective stochastic dominance put writing and
stock purchases with extensions to option pricing
and portfolio composition
MSci 1985 AUG VOL 31:8 p 919-927.

(7749)
Mason S P, Merton R C
The role of contingent claims analysis in
corporate finance
(in Altman E and Subrahmanyam M eds., Recent
advances in corporate finance. Irwin, 1985.)

(7750)
Sarig O H
On mergers, divestments and options: a note
JFQA 1985 SEP VOL 20:3 p 385-389.

(7751)
Bookstaber R M, Clarke R
Option portfolio strategies : measurement and
evaluation
JB 1984 OCT VOL 57:4 p 469-492.

(7752)
Brown K C, Lummer S L
The cash management implications of a hedged
dividend capture strategy
FIN MGMT 1984 WINTER VOL 13 p 7-17.

(7753)
Eckardt W L Jr, Williams S L
The complete options indexes
FAJ 1984 JUL-AUG VOL 40:4 p 48-57.

(7754)
Fischer D E ed.
Options and futures: New route to risk/return
management
Institute of Chartered Financial Analysts, 1984.

(7755)
Foster C, Van Order R
An option-based model of mortgage default
HFR 1984 VOL 3:4.

(7756)
Henin C G, Rentz W F
Call purchases, stock purchases and subjective
stochastic dominance
JBFA 1984 SPRING VOL 11:1 p 127-138.

(7757)
Levy H, Levy A
Ordering uncertain options under inflation : a
note
JF 1984 SEP VOL 39:4 p 1223-1229.

(7758)
Pozdena R J, Iben B
Pricing mortgages: an options approach
F R Bk San Francisco Ec Rev 1984 SPRING.

(7759)
Rubinstein M
A simple formula for the expected rate of return
of an option over a finite holding period
JF 1984 DEC VOL 39:5 p 1503-1509.

(7760)
Baesel J B, Shows G, Thorp E
The cost of liquidity services in listed options : a
note
JF 1983 JUN VOL 38:3 p 989-995.

(7761)
Bookstaber R M, Clarke R
An algorithm to calculate the return distribution
of portfolios with option positions
MSci 1983 APR VOL 29:4 p 419-429.

(7762)
Bookstaber R M, Clarke R G
Option strategies for institutional investment
management: a guide for improving portfolio
performance
Addison-Wes, 1983.

(7763)
Courtadon G, Merrick J J
The option pricing model and the valuation of
corporate securities
MCFJ 1983 FALL VOL 1 p 43-57.

(7764)
Galai D
The components of the return from hedging
options against stocks
JB 1983 JAN VOL 56:1 p 45-54.

(7765)
Sears R S, Trennepohl G
Diversification and skewness in option portfolios
JFR 1983 FALL VOL 6 p 199-212.

(7766)
Weinstein M I
Bond systematic risk and the option pricing model
JF 1983 DEC VOL 38:5 p 1415-1429.

(7767)
Merton R C, Scholes M, Gladstein M L
The returns and risks of alternative put-option portfolio investment strategies
JB 1982 JAN VOL 55:1 p 1-55.

(7768)
Sears R S, Trennepohl G L
Measuring portfolio risk in options
JFQA 1982 SEP VOL 17:3 p 391-409.

(7769)
Bookstaber R M, Clarke R
Options can alter portfolio return distributions
JPM 1981 SPRING VOL 7:3 p 63-70.

(7770)
Haugen R A, Senbet L W
Resolving the agency problems of external capital through options
JF 1981 JUN VOL 36:3 p 629-647.

(7771)
John K
Efficient funds in a financial market with options: a new irrelevance proposition
JF 1981 JUN VOL 36:3 p 685-695.

(7772)
Rendleman R J Jr
Optimal long-run option investment strategies
FIN MGMT 1981 SPRING VOL 10 p 61-76.

(7773)
Rudd A
Using options to increase reward and decrease risk
JBR 1981 AUTUMN VOL 12:3.

(7774)
Arditti F D, John K
Spanning the state space with options
JFQA 1980 MAR VOL 15 p 1.

(7775)
Slivka R T
Risk and return for option investment strategies
FAJ 1980 SEP-OCT VOL 36 p 67-73.

(7776)
Veit E T, Avey M L, Corley J L
The role of stock options in the bank trust departments: fifth Federal Reserve District banks
JBR 1980 WINTER VOL 10:4.

(7777)
Murray R F
A new role for options
JFQA 1979 NOV VOL 14 p 895.

(7778)
Rubinstein M
An economic evaluation of organized options markets
Journal of Comparative Corporate Law and Securities Regulation 1979 VOL 2 p 49-64.

(7779)
Banz R W, Miller M H
Prices for state-contingent claims: some estimates and applications
JB 1978 OCT VOL 51:4 p 653-672.

(7780)
Levy H, Kroll Y
Ordering uncertain options with borrowing and lending
JF 1978 VOL 33 p 553.

(7781)
Merton R C, Scholes M, Gladstein M L
The returns and risk of alternative call option portfolio investment strategies.
JB 1978 APR VOL 51:2 p 183-242.

(7782)
Boyle P P
Options: A Monte Carlo approach
JFE 1977 VOL 4 p 323.

(7783)
Findlay M C III, Capozza D R
The variable rate mortgage and risk in the mortgage market: an option theory perspective
JMCB 1977 MAY VOL 9:2 p 356-364..

(7784)**Henim C G, Ryan P J**

Options: theory and practice
Lexington Bks, 1977.

(7785)
Garman M B
An algebra for evaluating hedge portfolios
JFE 1976 VOL 3 p 403.

(7786)
Ross S A
Options and efficiency
QJE 1976 FEB VOL 90 p 75-89.

(7787)
Welham P
Investing in share options, warrants and convertibles
Woodhead-Faulkner, 1975.

(7788)
Puglisi D J
A rationale for option buying behavior: Theory and evidence
QREB 1974 SPRING VOL 14:1 p 55-66.

(7789)
McGugan J R, King W R
Security option strategy under risk aversion: An analysis
JFQA 1973 JAN VOL 8:1 p 1-16.

(7790)
Schmalensee R
Option demand and consumer's surplus: Valuing price changes under uncertainty
AER 1972 VOL 62 p 813-824.

(7791)
Malkiel B G, Quandt R E
Strategies and rational decisions in the securities options market
MIT Pr, 1969.

(7792)
Hausman W H, White W L
Theory of option strategy under risk aversion
JFQA 1968 SEP VOL 3 p 343-358.

(7793)
Hayes S L III
New interest in incentive financing
HBR 1966 JUL-AUG VOL 44 p 99-112.

(7794)
Holland D M, Lewellen W G
Probing the record of stock options
HBR 1962 MAR-APR VOL 40 p 132-150.

(7795)
Franklin C B, Colberg M R
Puts and calls: a factual survey
JF 1958 MAR VOL 13 p 21-34.

(7796)
Hardee C
Stock options and the "insider trading" provisions of the Securities Exchange Act
HLR 1952 VOL 65.

(7797)
Higgins L R
The put-and-call
Effingham, 1906.

(7798)
Bachelier L
Theorie de la speculation. Docteur des Sciences Mathematiques diss, University of Paris, 1900. Originally published in Annales de l'Ecole Normale Superieure, Sec. 3, 1900, p 21-86. English translation by Boness A J, Theory of speculation
(in Cootner P H ed., The random character of stock market prices. MIT Pr, 1964.)

19.1   Option valuation

(7799)
Boyle P P, Evnine J, Gibbs S
Numerical evaluation of multivariate contingent claims
RFS 1989 VOL 2:2 p 241-250.

(7800)
Boyle P P, Turnbull S M
Pricing and hedging capped options
JFM 1989 VOL 9:1 p 41-54.

(7801)
Chang S J, Chen S-N
A study of call price behavior under a stationary return generating process
FR 1989 AUG VOL 24:3 p 335-354.

(7802)
Choi D F S, Ward C W R
The reconciliation of the Smith's and Jarrow and
Rudd's option sensitivity formulae: a teaching
note
FR 1989 AUG VOL 24:3 p 507.

(7803)
Madan D B, Milne F, Shefrin H
The multinomial option pricing model and its
Brownian and Poisson limits
RFS 1989 VOL 2:2 p 251-266.

(7804)
Rabinovitch R
Pricing stock and bond options when the
default-free rate is stochastic
JFQA 1989 DEC VOL 24:4 p 447-458.

(7805)
Aase K
Contingent claims valuation when the security
price is a combination of an Ito process and a
random point process
Stochastic Processes and their Applications 1988
VOL 28 p 185-220.

(7806)
Hull J, White A
The use of the control variate technique in option
pricing
JFQA 1988 SEP VOL 23 p 237.

(7807)
Turnbull S M
Option valuation
Dryden Pr, 1988.

(7808)
Bhattacharya M
Price changes of related securities: The case of
call options and stocks
JFQA 1987 MAR VOL 22 p 1-15.

(7809)
Chang J S K, Shanker L
Option pricing and the arbitrage pricing theory
JFR 1987 SPRING VOL 10:1 p 1-16.

(7810)
Jacob D P, Lord G, Tilley J A
A generalized framework for pricing contingent
cash flows
FIN MGMT 1987 AUTUMN VOL 16 p 5-14.

(7811)
Johnson H, Stulz R
The pricing of options with default risk
JF 1987 JUN VOL 42:2 p 267-280.

(7812)
Lo A W
Statistical tests of contingent-claims asset-pricing
models: A new methodology
JFE 1986 VOL 17 p 143.

(7813)
Marcus A J, Modest D M
The valuation of a random number of put options
: an application of agricultural price supports.
JFQA 1986 MAR VOL 21:1 p 73-86

(7814)
O'Brien T J, Selby M J P
Option pricing theory and asset expectations: a
review and discussion in tribute to James Boness
FR 1986 NOV VOL 21:4 p 399-418.

(7815)
Stoll H R, Whaley R E
The new option instruments: Arbitrageable
linkages and valuation
Advances in Futures and Options Research 1986
VOL 1 p 25-62.

(7816)
Geske R, Shastri K
Valuation by approximation : a comparison of
alternative option valuation techniques
JFQA 1985 MAR VOL 20:1 p 45-71.

(7817)
Muller S
Arbitrage pricing of contingent claims
Springer-Verlag, 1985.

(7818)
Bensoussan A
On the theory of option pricing
Acta Applicandae Mathematicae 1984 VOL 2 p
139-158..

(7819)**Borch K**
A note on option prices
FR 1984 MAR VOL 19:1.

(7820)
Conine T E Jr, Tamarkin M
A pedagogic note on the derivation of the
comparative statics of the option pricing model
FR 1984 NOV VOL 19:4.

(7821)
McDonald R, Siegel D
Option pricing when the underlying asset earns a
below-equilibrium rate of return : a note
JF 1984 MAR VOL 39:1 p 261-265.

(7822)
Brenner M ed.
Option pricing: theory and applications
Heath, 1983.

(7823)
Castagna A D, Matolcsy Z P
The evaluation of traded options pricing models
in Australia
JBFA 1983 SUMMER VOL 10:2 p 225-234

(7824)
Cox J C, Rubinstein M
A survey of alternative option pricing models
(in Brenner M ed., Option pricing. Heath, 1983.)

(7825)
French D W
Black-Scholes vs Kassouf option pricing : an
empirical comparison
JBFA 1983 AUTUMN VOL 10:3 p 395-408

(7826)
Jarrow R A, Rudd A
Tests of an approximate option-valuation formula
(in Brenner M ed., Option pricing. Heath, 1983.)

(7827)
Jarrow R A, Rudd A
Option pricing
Dow Jones-Irwin, 1983.

(7828)
Rubinstein M
Displaced diffusion option pricing
JF 1983 MAR VOL 38:1 p 213-217.

(7829)
Sterk W E
Comparative performance of the Black-Scholes
and Roll-Geske-Whaley option pricing models
JFQA 1983 SEP VOL 18:3 p 345-354.

(7830)
Courtadon G
A more accurate finite difference approximation
for the valuation of options
JFQA 1982 DEC VOL 17:5 p 697-725.

(7831)
Jarrow R A, Rudd A
Approximate option valuation for arbitary
stochastic processes
JFE 1982 VOL 10 p 347.

(7832)
Bhattacharya S
Notes on multiperiod valuation and the pricing of
options
JF 1981 MAR VOL 36:1 p 163-180.

(7833)
Rao R K S
Modern option pricing models: A dichotomous
classification
JFR 1981 SPRING VOL 4 p 33-44.

(7834)
Rubinstein M, Leland H E
Replicating options with positions in stock and
cash
FAJ 1981 JUL-AUG p 63.

(7835)
Goldman H B, Sosin H B, Gatto M A
Path dependent options: "buy at the low sell at
the high"
JF 1979 DEC VOL 34:5 p 1111-1127.

(7836)
Gleit A
Valuation of general contingent claims: Existence, uniqueness and comparisons of solutions
JFE 1978 VOL 6 p 71-87.

(7837)
Merton R C
On the pricing of contingent claims and the Modigliani-Miller theorem
JFE 1977 VOL 5 p 241.

(7838)
Weygandt J J
Valuation of stock option contracts
AR 1977 JAN VOL 52:1 p 40-51.

(7839)
Kassouf S T
The lag structure of option price
Journal of Econometrics 1976 NOV VOL 4 p 303-310.

(7840)
Rubinstein M
The valuation of uncertain income streams and the pricing of options
BellJ 1976 AUTUMN VOL 7:2 p 407-425.

(7841)
Smith C W Jr
Option pricing: A review
JFE 1976 VOL 3 p 3.

(7842)
Black F
Fact and fantasy in the use of options
FAJ 1975 JUL-AUG VOL 31 p 36-41.

(7843)
Bierman H Jr
The valuation of stock options
JFQA 1967 SEP VOL 2 p 327-334.

(7844)
Taylor H M
Evaluating a call option and optimal timing strategy on the stock market
MSci 1967 SEP VOL 14 p 111-120.

(7845)
Thorp E O, Kassouf S T
Beat the market: a scientific stock market system
Random, 1967.

(7846)
Boness A J
Elements of a theory of stock option value
JPE 1964 APR VOL 72 p 163-175.

(7847)
Kruizenga R J
Comment on 'Puts and calls: a factual survey'
JF 1959 MAR VOL 14 p 67-70.

19.11   Bounds on option value

(7848)
Ritchken P, Kuo S
On stochastic dominance and decreasing absolute risk averse option pricing bounds
MSci 1989 VOL 35 p 51.

(7849)
Chance D M
Boundary condition tests of bid and ask prices of index call options
JFR 1988 VOL 11:1 p 21-32.

(7850)
Loudon G F
Put call parity theory: Evidence from the Big Australian
AJM 1988 JUN VOL 13 p 53-68.

(7851)
Lo A W
Semi-parametric upper bounds for option prices and expected payoffs
JFE 1987 VOL 19 p 373-387.

(7852)
Sachdeva K
On the equality of two lower bounds on the call price : a note
JFQA 1986 JUN VOL 21:2 p 235-237.

(7853)
Levy H
Upper and lower bounds of put and call options
value: stochastic dominance approach
JF 1985 SEP VOL 40:4 p 1197-1217.

(7854)
Ritchken P H
On option pricing bound
JF 1985 SEP VOL 40:4 p 1219-1233.

(7855)
Ryan P J, Perrakis S
Option pricing bounds in discrete time
JF 1984 JUN VOL 39:2 p 519-525.

(7856)
Klemkosky R C, Resnick B G
An ex ante analysis of put-call parity.
JFE 1980 DEC VOL 8:4 p 363-378

(7857)
Galai D
A convexity test for traded options
QREB 1979 VOL 19:2 p 83.

(7858)
Stoll H R
The relationship between put and call option
prices
JF 1969 DEC VOL 24 p 801-824.

19.12   Black-Scholes and binomial valuation models

(7859)
Black F
How we came up with the option formula
JPM 1989 WINTER VOL 15:2 p 4-8.

(7860)
Finucane T J
Black-Scholes approximations of call option prices
with stochastic volatilities: a note
JFQA 1989 DEC VOL 24:4 p 527-532.

(7861)
Levy H, Yoder J A
Applying the Black-Scholes model after large
market shocks
JPM 1989 FALL VOL 16:1 p 103.

(7862)
Duffie D
An extension of the Black-Scholes model of
security valuation
JET 1988 OCT VOL 46:1 p 194-204.

(7863)
Schroder M
Adapting the binomial model to value options on
assets with fixed-cash payouts
FAJ 1988 NOV-DEC VOL 44 p 54-62.

(7864)
Bick A
On the consistency of the Black-Scholes model
with a general equilibrium framework
JFQA 1987 SEP VOL 22 p 259-275.

(7865)
Butler J S, Schachter B
Unbiased estimation of the Black-Scholes formula
JFE 1986 VOL 15 p 341.

(7866)
Garven J R
A pedagogic note on the derivation of the
Black-Scholes option pricing formula
FR 1986 MAY VOL 21:2.

(7867)
Stapleton R C, Subrahmanyam M G
The valuation of options when asset returns are
generated by a binomial process
JF 1984 DEC VOL 39:5 p 1525-1539.

(7868)
Hsia C-C
On binomial option pricing
JFR 1983 SPRING VOL 6 p 41-50.

(7869)
Kreps D M
Multiperiod securities and the efficient allocation
of risk: A comment on the Black-Scholes option
pricing model
(in McCall J J ed., The economics of information
and uncertainty. U of Chicago Pr, 1982.)

(7870)
Bhattacharya M
Empirical properties of the Black-Scholes formula
under ideal conditions
JFQA 1980 DEC VOL 15 p 1081.

(7871)
Cox J C, Ross S A, Rubinstein M
Option pricing: a simplified approach
JFE 1979 SEP VOL 7:3 p 229-263..

(7872)**Rendelman R J Jr, Bartter B J**
Two-state option pricing
JF 1979 DEC VOL 34:5 p 1093-1110.

(7873)
Galai D
On the Boness and Black-Scholes models for
valuation of call options
JFQA 1978 MAR VOL 13 p 15.

(7874)
Dimson E
Option valuation nomograms
FAJ 1977 NOV-DEC p 71.

(7875)
Black F, Scholes M
The pricing of options and corporate liabilities
JPE 1973 MAY-JUN VOL 81:3 p 637-654.

(7876)
Merton R C
The theory of rational option pricing
BellJ 1973 SPRING VOL 4:1 p 141-183.

(7877)
Thorp E O
Extensions of the Black-Scholes option model
Proceedings of the 39th Session of the
International Statistical Institute AUG 1973 p
1029-1036.

19.13   Option valuation with changing variance

(7878)
Schroder M
Computing the constant elasticity of variance
option pricing formula
JF 1989 MAR VOL 44:1 p 211-220.

(7879)
Tucker A L, Peterson D R, Scott E
Tests of the Black-Scholes and constant elasticity
of variance currency call option valuation models
JFR 1988 FALL VOL 11:3 p 201-214.

(7880)
Hull J, White A
The pricing of options on assets with stochastic
volatilities
JF 1987 JUN VOL 42:2 p 281-300.

(7881)
Johnson H, Shanno D
Option pricing when the variance is changing
JFQA 1987 JUN VOL 22 p 143.

(7882)
Scott L O
Option pricing when the variance changes
randomly: Theory, estimation and an application
JFQA 1987 DEC VOL 22 p 419.

(7883)
Wiggins J B
Option values under stochastic volatility: theory
and empirical estimates
JFE 1987 VOL 19 p 351-372.

(7884)
Ang J S, Peterson D R
Empirical properties of the elasticity coefficient in
the constant elasticity of variance model
FR 1984 NOV VOL 19:4.

(7885)
Emanuel D C, MacBeth J D
Further results on the constant elasticity of
variance call option pricing model
JFQA 1982 NOV VOL 17:4 p 533-554.

(7886)
Beckers S
The constant elasticity of variance model and its
implications for option pricing
JF 1980 JUN VOL 25:3 p 661-673.

(7887)
MacBeth J D, Merville L J
Tests of the Black-Scholes and Cox call option
valuation models
JF 1980 MAY VOL 35:2 p 285-303.

19.14   Option valuation with jump
processes

(7888)
Akgiray V, Booth G
Stock price processes with discontinuous time
paths: an empirical examination
FR 1986 MAY VOL 21:2.

(7889)
Page F H, Sanders A B
A general derivation of the Jump Process Option
Pricing Formula.
JFQA 1986 DEC VOL 21:4 p 437-446.

(7890)
Ball C A, Torous W N
On jumps in common stock prices and their
impact on call option pricing
JF 1985 MAR VOL 40:1 p 155-173.

(7891)
Jones E P
Option arbitrage and strategy with large price
changes
JFE 1984 MAR VOL 13:1 p 91-113.

(7892)
Ball C A, Torous W N
A simplified jump process for common stock
returns
JFQA 1983 MAR VOL 18:1 p 53-65.

(7893)
Brennan M J, Schwartz E S
Finite difference methods and jump processes
arising in the pricing of contingent claims: A
synthesis
JFQA 1978 SEP VOL 13 p 461.

(7894)
Cox J C, Ross S A
The valuation of options for alternative stochastic
processes
JFE 1976 VOL 3 p 145.

(7895)
Merton R C
Option pricing when underlying stock returns are
discontinuous
JFE 1976 VOL 3 p 125.

19.15   Discrete-time option models

(7896)
Omberg E
Efficient discrete time jump process models in
option pricing
JFQA 1988 JUN VOL 23:2 p 161-174.

(7897)
O'Brien T J
A discrete time option model dependent on
expected return : a note
JF 1986 JUN VOL 41:2 p 515-520.

(7898)
Stapleton R C, Subrahmanyam M G
The valuation of multivariate contingent claims in
discrete time models
JF 1984 MAR VOL 39:1 p 207-228.

(7899)
Lee W Y, Rao R K S, Auchmuty J F G
Option pricing in a lognormal securities market
with discrete trading
JFE 1981 VOL 9 p 75-101.

(7900)
Boyle P P, Emanuel D
Discretely adjusted option hedges.
JFE 1980 SEP VOL 8:3 p 259-282

(7901)
Brennan M J
The pricing of contingent claims in discrete time
models
JF 1979 MAR VOL 34:1 p 53-68.

19.16   Option valuation with costly rebalancing

(7902)
Ritchken P H, Kuo S
Option bounds with finite revision opportunities
JF 1988 JUN VOL 43:2 p 301-308.

(7903)
Leland H E
Option pricing and replication with transactions
costs
JF 1985 DEC VOL 40:5 p 1283-1301.

(7904)
Gilster J E, Lee W
The effects of transaction costs and different
borrowing and lending rates on the option pricing
model : a note
JF 1984 SEP VOL 39:4 p 1215-1221.

(7905)
Ho T S Y, Macris R G
Dealer bid-ask quotes and transaction prices : an
empirical study of some AMEX options
JF 1984 MAR VOL 39:1 p 23-45.

(7906)
Phillips S M, Smith C W Jr
Trading costs for listed options: The implications
for market efficiency.
JFE 1980 JUN VOL 8:2 p 179-201.

19.2 Complex options

(7907)
Carr P
The   valuation   of   sequential   exchange
opportunities
JF 1988 DEC VOL 43:5 p 1235-1256.

(7908)
Johnson H
Options on the maximum or the minimum of
several assets
JFQA 1987 SEP VOL 22:3 p 277-283.

(7909)
Stulz R M
Options on the minimum or the maximum of two
risky assets: Analysis and applications
JFE 1982 VOL 10 p 161.

(7910)
Fischer S
Call option pricing when the exercise price is
uncertain and the valuation of index bonds
JF 1978 VOL 33 p 169.

(7911)
Margrabe W
The value of an option to exchange one asset for
another
JF 1978 VOL 33 p 177.

19.21 Compound options

(7912)
Schroder M
A reduction method applicable to compound
option formulas
MSci 1989 VOL 35 p 823.

(7913)
Boyle P P
A lattice framework for option pricing with two
state variables
JFQA 1988 MAR VOL 23:1 p 1-12.

(7914)
Selby M J P, Hodges S D
On the evaluation of compound options
MSci 1987 MAR VOL 33:3 p 347-355.

(7915)
Brealey R A, Hodges S D, Selby M J P
The risk of bank loan portfolios
(in Brenner M ed., Option pricing. Heath, 1983.)

(7916)
Geske R
The valuation of compound options
JFE 1979 VOL 7 p 63-81.

(7917)
Geske R
The valuation of corporate liabilities as compound options
JFQA 1977 NOV VOL 12 p 541.

19.22   American puts

(7918)
Blomeyer E C, Johnson H
An empirical examination of the pricing of American put options
JFQA 1988 MAR VOL 23:1 p 13-22.

(7919)
Grinblatt M S, Johnson H
A put option paradox
JFQA 1988 MAR VOL 23:1 p 23-26.

(7920)
Barone-Adesi G, Whaley R E
Efficient analytic approximation of American option values.
JF 1987 JUN VOL 42:2 p 301-320.

(7921)
Blomeyer E C
An analytic approximation for the American put price for options on stocks with dividends
JFQA 1986 JUN VOL 21:2 p 229-233.

(7922)
Brill E A, Harriff R B
Pricing American options: Managing risk with early exercise
FAJ 1986 MAR-APR VOL 42 p 48-55.

(7923)
MacMillan L W
Analytic approximation for the American put option
Advances in Futures and Options Research 1986 VOL 1 p 119-139.

(7924)
Geske R, Shastri K
The early exercise of American puts
JBankF 1985 VOL 9 p 207..

(7925)**Geske R, Johnson H E**
The American put option valued analytically
JF 1984 DEC VOL 39:5 p 1511-1524.

(7926)
Johnson H E
An analytic approximation for the American put price
JFQA 1983 MAR VOL 18:1 p 141-148.

(7927)
Eckardt W L Jr
The American put: Computational issues and value comparisons
FIN MGMT 1982 AUTUMN VOL 11 p 42-52.

(7928)
Farkas K L, Hoskins R E
Testing a valuation model for American puts
FIN MGMT 1979 AUTUMN VOL 8 p 51.

(7929)
Brennan M J, Schwartz E S
The valuation of American put options
JF 1977 MAY VOL 32:2 p 449-462.

19.23   Options on dividend-paying assets

(7930)
Barone-Adesi G, Whaley R E
The valuation of American call options and the expected ex-dividend stock price decline
JFE 1986 SEP VOL 17:1 p 91-111.

(7931)
Kaplanis C P
Options taxes and ex-dividend day behavior
JF 1986 JUN VOL 41:2 p 411-424.

(7932)
Geske R, Roll R
On valuing American call options with the Black-Scholes European formula
JF 1984 JUN VOL 39:2 p 443-455.

(7933)
Geske R, Roll R, Shastri K
Over-the-counter   option   market   dividend
protection and "biases" in the Black-Scholes
model : a note
JF 1983 SEP VOL 38:4 p 1271-1277.

(7934)
Sterk W E
Option pricing: Dividends   and   the   in-and
out-of-the-money bias
FIN MGMT 1983 WINTER VOL 12 p 47-54.

(7935)
Whaley R E
On the valuation of American call options on
stocks with known dividends
JFE 1981 VOL 9 p 207.

(7936)
Geske R
A note on an analytical valuation formula for
unprotected American call options on stocks with
known dividends
JFE 1979 VOL 7 p 375.

(7937)
Geske R
The pricing of options with stochastic dividend
yield
JF 1978 VOL 33 p 617.

(7938)
Merton R C
An analytic valuation formula for unprotected
American call options on stocks with known
dividends
JFE 1977 VOL 5 p 251.

19.24 Options on futures and forwards

(7939)
Brenner M, Courtadon G, Subrahmanyam M
Options on stock indices and options on futures
JBankF 1989 SEP VOL 13:4-5 p 773-782.

(7940)
Gay G D, Kolb R W, Yung K
Trader rationality in the exercise of futures
options
JFE 1989 VOL 23 p 339.

(7941)
Blomeyer E C, Boyd J C
Empirical tests of boundary conditions for options
on treasury bond futures contracts
JFM 1988 APR VOL 8:2 p 185-198.

(7942)
Wilson W W, Fung H-G, Ricks M
Option price behavior in grain futures markets
JFM 1988 FEB VOL 8:1 p 47-66.

(7943)
Bailey W R D
An empirical investigation of the market for
Comex gold futures options
JF 1987 DEC VOL 42:5 p 1187-1194.

(7944)
Jordan J V, Seale W E, McCabe N C
Transaction data tests of the Black Model for
soybean futures options
JFM 1987 OCT VOL 7:5 p 535-554.

(7945)
Webb R I
A note on volatility and pricing of futures options
during choppy markets
JFM 1987 JUN VOL 7:3 p 333-338.

(7946)
Ball C A, Torous W N
Futures options and the volatility of futures prices
JF 1986 SEP VOL 41:4 p 857-870.

(7947)
Kuprianov A
Options on short-term interest rate futures
F R Bk Richmond Ec Rev 1986 VOL 72:6.

(7948)
Shastri K, Tandon K
An empirical test of a valuation model for
American options on futures contracts
JFQA 1986 DEC VOL 21:4 p 377-392.

(7949)
Whaley R E
Valuation of American futures options : theory and empirical tests
JF 1986 MAR VOL 41:1 p 127-150.

(7950)
Whaley R E
On valuing American futures options
FAJ 1986 MAY-JUN VOL 42 p 49-59.

(7951)
Brenner M, Courtadon G, Subrahmanyam M
Options on the spot and options on futures
JF 1985 DEC VOL 40:5 p 1303-1317.

(7952)
Ramaswamy K, Sundaresan S M
The valuation of options on futures contracts
JF 1985 DEC VOL 40:5 p 1319-1340.

(7953)
Belongia M T, Gregory T H
Are options on treasury bond futures priced efficiently?
F R Bk St Louis Rev 1984 VOL 66:1.

(7954)
Figlewski S, Fitzgerald M D
Options on commodity futures: Recent experience in the London market
(in Brenner M ed., Option pricing. Heath, 1983.)

(7955)
Kim Y Y, Meyer J E
An autoregressive forecast of the world sugar future option market
JFQA 1975 DEC VOL 10 p 821

19.25 Options on bonds and interest rates

(7956)
Dattatreya R E, Fabozzi F J
A simplified model for valuing debt options
JPM 1989 SPRING VOL 15:3 p 64-73.

(7957)
Jamshidian F
An exact bond option formula
JF 1989 MAR VOL 44:1 p 205-210.

(7958)
Maloney K J, Byrne M J
An equilibrium debt option pricing model in discrete time
JBankF 1989 JUL VOL 13:3 p 421-442.

(7959)
Barnhill T M, Seale W E
Optimal exercise of the switching option in treasury bond arbitrages
JFM 1988 OCT VOL 8:5 p 517-532.

(7960)
Finucane T J
Options on US Treasury coupon issues
FR 1988 NOV VOL 23:4 p 403-426.

(7961)
Overdahl J A
The early exercise of options on Treasury bond futures
JFQA 1988 DEC VOL 23 p 437.

(7962)
Arak M, Goodman L S
Treasury bond futures: valuing the delivery options
JFM 1987 JUN VOL 7:3 p 269-286.

(7963)
Schaefer S M, Schwartz E S
Time-dependent variance and the pricing of bond options
JF 1987 DEC VOL 42:5 p 1113-1128.

(7964)
Block S B, Gallagher T J
The use of interest rate futures and options by corporate financial managers
FIN MGMT 1986 AUTUMN VOL 15 p 73.

(7965)
Dietrich-Campbell B, Schwartz E
Valuing debt options. Empirical evidence.
JFE 1986 JUL VOL 16:3 p 321-343

(7966)
Ho T S Y, Leo S B
Term structure movements and pricing interest rate contingent claims.
JF 1986 DEC VOL 41:5 p 1011-1029.

(7967)
Kane A, Marcus A J
Valuation and optimal exercise of the wild card option in the treasury bond futures market
JF 1986 MAR VOL 41:1 p 195-207.

(7968)
Kane A, Marcus A J
The quality option in the Treasury bond futures market: An empirical assessment
JFM 1986 SUMMER VOL 6 p 231-248.

(7969)
Benninga S, Smirlock M
An empirical analysis of the delivery option, marking to market and the pricing of treasury bond futures
JFM 1985 FALL VOL 5.

(7970)
Fabozzi F J ed.
Winning the interest game: A guide to debt options
Chicago: Probus Publishing, 1985.

(7971)
Pitts M
An introduction to the pricing of options on debt instruments
(in Fabozzi F J ed., Winning the interest game: A guide to debt options. Probus Publishing, 1985.)

(7972)
Brennan M J, Schwartz E S
Alternative methods for valuing debt options
Finance 1984 JUL VOL 5 p 583-607.

(7973)
Eckardt W L
Equivalent delivery procedures for GNMA futures contracts and options
JFM 1984 SPRING VOL 4 p 75-85.

(7974)
Ball C A, Torous W N
Bond price dynamics and options.
JFQA 1983 DEC VOL 18:4 p 517-531

(7975)
Brennan M J, Schwartz E S
Alternative methods of valuing debt options
Finance 1983 OCT VOL 4 p 119-137.

(7976)
Burton T E
Observations on the theory of option pricing on debt instruments
(in Brenner M ed., Option pricing. Heath, 1983.)

(7977)
Courtadon G
The pricing of options on default-free bonds
JFQA 1982 MAR VOL 17:1 p 75-100..

(7978)**Parkinson M**
The valuation of GNMA options
FAJ 1982 SEP-OCT VOL 38 p 66-76.

(7979)
Bartter B J, Rendleman R J Jr
The pricing of options on debt securities
JFQA 1980 MAR VOL 15 p 11.

19.3 Variances in option valuation

(7980)
Choi J Y, Shastri K
Bid-ask spreads and volatility estimates: the implications for option pricing
JBankF 1989 MAY VOL 13:2 p 207-220.

(7981)
Skinner D J
Options markets and stock return volatility
JFE 1989 VOL 23 p 61.

(7982)
Ajinkya B B, Gift M J
Dispersion of financial analysts' earnings forecasts and the (option model) implied standard deviations of stock returns
JF 1985 DEC VOL 40:5 p 1353-1365.

(7983)
Brenner M, Galai D
On measuring the risk of common stocks implied
by options prices: a note
JFQA 1984 DEC VOL 19:4 p 403-412.

(7984)
Jagannathan R
Call options and the risk of underlying securities
JFE 1984 VOL 13 p 425-434.

(7985)
Manaster S, Koehler G
The calculation of implied variances from the
Black-Scholes model: a note
JF 1982 MAR VOL 37:1 p 227-230.

(7986)
Boyle P P, Ananthanarayanan A L
The impact of variance estimation in option
valuation models
JFE 1979 VOL 5 p 375.

(7987)
Galai D, Masulis R W
The option pricing model and the risk factor of
stock
JFE 1976 VOL 3 p 53.

19.31 Implied variances

(7988)
Finucane T J
A simple linear weighting scheme for
Black-Scholes implied volatilities - a note
JBankF 1989 MAY VOL 13:2 p 321-326.

(7989)
Klein L S, Peterson D R
Investor expectations of volatility increases around
large stock splits as implied in call option premia
JFR 1988 VOL 11:1 p 71-80.

(7990)
Brenner M, Galai D
On the prediction of the implied standard
deviation
Advances in Futures and Options Research 1987
SEP.

(7991)
Heaton H
Volatilities implied by options premia: a test of
market efficiency
FR 1986 FEB VOL 21:1.

(7992)
Schmalensee R, Trippi R R
Common stock volatility expectations implicit by
option premia
JF 1978 VOL 33 p 129.

19.4 Options classed by underlying asset/ empirical studies

(7993)
Barone E, Cuoco D
The Italian market for "premium" contracts: an
application of option pricing theory
JBankF 1989 SEP VOL 13:4-5 p 709-743.

(7994)
French D W, Martin L J
The measurement of option mispricing
JBankF 1988 DEC VOL 12:4 p 537-550.

(7995)
Kane A, Marcus A J
The delivery option on forward contracts: A note
JFQA 1988 SEP VOL 23 p 337.

(7996)
Selby M J P, Franks J R, Karki J P
Loan guarantees, wealth transfers and incentives
to invest
JIE 1988 VOL 37 p 47-65.

(7997)
Ronn E I, Verma A K
Pricing risk-adjusted deposit insurance : an
optionbased model
JF 1986 SEP VOL 41:4 p 871-895.

(7998)
Tilley J A, Latainer G D
A synthetic option framework for asset allocation
FAJ 1985 MAY-JUN VOL 41 p 32-43.

(7999)
Beckers S
On the efficiency of the gold options market
JBankF 1984 VOL 8 p 459.

(8000)
Gay G D, Manaster S
The quality option implicit in futures contracts
JFE 1984 SEP VOL 13:3 p 353-370.

(8001)
Galai D
A survey of empirical tests of option pricing
models
(in Brenner M ed., Option pricing. Heath, 1983.)

(8002)
Hoag J W
The valuation of commodity options
(in Brenner M ed., Option pricing. Heath, 1983.)

(8003)
Camerer C
The pricing and social value of commodity
options
FAJ 1982 JAN-FEB p 62-67.

(8004)
Courtadon G
A note on the premium market of the Paris
Stock Exchange
JBankF 1982 DEC VOL 6 p 561-564.

(8005)
Gatto M A, Geske R, Litzenberger R
Mutual fund insurance
JFE 1980 VOL 8 p 283-317.

(8006)
Sosin H B
On the valuation of Federal loan guarantees to
corporations
JF 1980 DEC VOL 35:5 p 1209-1221

(8007)
Brennan M J, Schwartz E S
Alternative investment strategies for the insurers
of equity linked life insurance policies with an
asset value guarantee
JB 1979 JAN VOL 52:1 p 63-93.

(8008)
Brennan M J, Schwartz E S
Pricing and investment strategies for guaranteed
equity-linked life insurance
Irwin, 1979.

(8009)
Garman M B
The pricing of supershares.
JFE 1978 MAR VOL 6:1 p 3-10.

(8010)
Hakansson N H
The Superfund: Efficient paths toward efficient
capital markets in large and small countries
(in Levy H and Sarnat M eds., Financial decision
making under uncertainty. Academic Pr, 1977.)

(8011)
Brennan M J, Schwartz E S
The pricing of equity-linked life insurance policies
with an asset value guarantee
JFE 1976 VOL 3 p 195.

(8012)
Hakansson N H
The purchasing power fund: A new kind of
financial intermediary
FAJ 1976 NOV-DEC VOL 32 p 49-59.

(8013)
Smith C W Jr, Zimmerman J
Valuing employee stock option plans using option
pricing models
JAR 1976 AUTUMN VOL 14 p 357-364.

19.41   Options markets

(8014)
Anthony J H
The interrelation of stock and options market
trading-volume data
JF 1988 SEP VOL 43:4 p 949-964.

(8015)
Labuszewski J, Sinquefield J C
Inside the commodity option markets
Wiley, 1985.

(8016)
Swanson J E
The European option markets: a new approach to investment
Kluwer, 1984.

(8017)
Goodman L S
New options markets
F R Bk New York Q Rev 1983 AUTUMN VOL 8:3.

(8018)
Asay M R
A note on the design of commodity option contracts
JFM 1982 SPRING VOL 2 p 1-7.

19.411   Common stock options

(8019)
Bansal V K, Pruitt S W, Wei K C J
An empirical reexamination of the impact of CBOE option initiation on the volatility and trading volume of the underlying equities: 1973-1986
FR 1989 FEB VOL 24:1 p 19-30.

(8020)
Brown R L
Adjusting option contracts to reflect capitalisation changes
JBFA 1989 SPRING VOL 16:2 p 247.

(8021)
Cotner J S, Horrell J F
An analysis of index option pricing
JFM 1989 VOL 9:5 p 449-460.

(8022)
Hexton R
Dealing in traded options
P-H, 1989.

(8023)
Neal R
Potential competition and actual competition in equity options
JF 1987 JUL VOL 42:3 p 511-531.

(8024)
Rao R P, Ma C K
The effect of call-option-listing announcement on shareholder wealth
JBusR 1987 OCT VOL 15:5 p 449.

(8025)
Strong R A, Andrew W P
Further evidence of the influence of option expiration on the underlying common stock
JBusR 1987 AUG VOL 15:4 p 291-302.

(8026)
Gemmill G
The forecasting performance of stock options on the London Traded Options Market
JBFA 1986 WINTER VOL 13:4 p 535-546

(8027)
Bookstaber R M
The use of options in performance structuring
JPM 1985 SUMMER VOL 11:4 p 36-51.

(8028)
Chance D M, Ferris S P
The CBOE call option index: a historical record
JPM 1985 FALL VOL 12:1 p 75.

(8029)
Halpern P J, Turnbull S M
Empirical tests of boundary conditions for Toronto Stock Exchange options
JF 1985 JUN VOL 40:2 p 481-500.

(8030)
Ritchken P H
Enhancing mean-variance analysis with options
JPM 1985 SPRING VOL 11:3 p 67-72.

(8031)**Rubinstein M**
Nonparametric tests of alternative option pricing models using all reported trades and quotes on the 30 most active CBOE option classes from August 23 1976 through August 31 1978
JF 1985 JUN VOL 40:2 p 455-480.

(8032)
Evnine J, Rudd A
Option portfolio risk analysis
JPM 1984 WINTER VOL 10:2 p 23-27.

(8033)
Gastineau G L, Madansky A
Some comments on the CBOE Call Options Index
FAJ 1984 JUL-AUG VOL 40:4 p 58-67.

(8034)
Bhattacharya M
Transactions data tests of efficiency of the Chicago Board options exchange
JFE 1983 AUG VOL 12:2 p 161-185.

(8035)
Blomeyer E C, Klemkosky R C
Tests of market efficiency for American call options
(in Brenner M ed., Option pricing. Heath, 1983.)

(8036)
Brown R L, Shevlin T J
Modelling option prices in Australia using the Black-Scholes model
AJM 1983 JUN VOL 8 p 1-20.

(8037)
Brown R L, Shevlin T J
Stock market efficiency and price predictions implicit in option trading
AJM 1983 DEC VOL 8 p 71-94.

(8038)
Chamberlain G
Trading in options: an investor's guide to making high profits in the traded options market. 2nd ed
Woodhead-Faulkner, 1982.

(8039)
Gultekin N B, Rogalski R, Tinic S M
Option pricing model estimates: Some empirical results
FIN MGMT 1982 SPRING VOL 11 p 58-69.

(8040)
Manaster S, Rendleman R J
Option prices as predictors of equilibrium stock prices
JF 1982 SEP VOL 37:4 p 1043-1057.

(8041)
Whaley R E
Valuation of American call options on dividend-paying stocks: Empirical tests
JFE 1982 VOL 10 p 29.

(8042)
Bookstaber R M
Observed option mispricing and the nonsimultaneity of stock and option quotations
JB 1981 JAN VOL 54:1 p 141-155.

(8043)
Mueller P A
Covered options: An alternative investment strategy
FIN MGMT 1981 AUTUMN VOL 10 p 64-71.

(8044)
Slivka R T
Call option spreading
JPM 1981 SPRING VOL 7:3 p 71.

(8045)
Trennepohl G L
A comparison of listed option premiums and Black and Scholes model prices: 1973-1979
JFR 1981 SPRING VOL 4 p 11-20.

(8046)
Trennepohl G L, Dukes W P
An empirical test of option writing and buying strategies utilizing in-the-money and out-of-the-money contracts
JBFA 1981 SUMMER VOL 8:2 p 185-199

(8047)
Arnott R D
Modeling portfolios with options: risks and returns
JPM 1980 FALL VOL 7:1 p 66-73.

(8048)
Klemkosky R C, Maness T S
The impact of options on the underlying securities
JPM 1980 WINTER VOL 6:2 p 12-18.

(8049)
Phillips S M, Smith C W Jr
Trading costs for listed options: The implications
for market efficiency.
JFE 1980 JUN VOL 8:2 p 179-201.

(8050)
Yates J W Jr, Kopprasch R W Jr
Writing covered call options: profits and risks
JPM 1980 FALL VOL 7:1 p 74.

(8051)
Galai D
A proposal for indexes for traded call options
JF 1979 DEC VOL 34:5 p 1157-1172.

(8052)
Galai D
A convexity test for traded options
QREB 1979 SUMMER VOL 19 p 83-90.

(8053)
Gastineau G L, Madansky A
Simulation is no guide to option strategies
FAJ 1979 SEP-OCT p 61.

(8054)
Hayes S L III, Tennenaum M E
The impact of listed options on the underlying
shares
FIN MGMT 1979 WINTER VOL 8 p 72.

(8055)
Klemkosky R C, Resnick B G
Put-call parity and market efficiency
JF 1979 DEC VOL 34:5 p 1141-1155.

(8056)
Patell J M, Wolfson M A
Anticipated information releases reflected in call
option prices
JAE 1979 AUG VOL 1 p 117-140.

(8057)
Securities and Exchange Commission
Report of the special study of the options
markets
US Govt, 1979.

(8058)
Trennepohl G L, Dukes W P
Return and risk from listed option investment
JFR 1979 SPRING VOL 2 p 37-49.

(8059)
Chiras D P, Manaster S
The information content of option prices and a
test of market efficiency.
JFE 1978 JUN-SEP VOL 6:2-3 p 212-234.

(8060)
Finnerty J E
The Chicago Board Options Exchange and market
efficiency
JFQA 1978 MAR VOL 13 p 29.

(8061)
Galai D
Empirical tests of boundary conditions for CBOE
(Chicago Board Options Exchange) options
JFE 1978 JUN-SEP VOL 6:2-3 p 187-211.

(8062)
Garbade K D, Kaicher M M
Exchange-traded options on common stock
F R Bk New York Q Rev 1978-79 WINTER
VOL 3:4.

(8063)
Gombola M J, Roenfeldt R L, Cooley P L
Spreading strategies in CBOE options: Evidence
on market performance
JFR 1978 WINTER VOL 1 p 33-44.

(8064)
Klemkosky R C
The impact of option expirations on stock prices
JFQA 1978 SEP VOL 13 p 507.

(8065)
Fuller R J
Factors which influence listed call option prices
RBER 1977-78 WINTER VOL 13 p 21-34..

(8066)**Gastineau G L**
An index of listed option premiums
FAJ 1977 MAY-JUN p 70.

(8067)
Trennepohl G L, Dukes W P
An empirical test of option writing strategies
RBER 1977 FALL VOL 13 p 48-58.

(8068)
Trippi R R
A test of option market efficiency using a
random-walk valuation model
Journal of Economics and Business 1977
WINTER VOL 29 p 93-98.

(8069)
Panton D
Chicago Board call options as predictors of
common stock price changes
Journal of Econometrics 1976 VOL 4 p 101-113.

(8070)
Hettenhouse G W, Puglisi D J
Investor experience with put and call options
FAJ 1975 JUL-AUG VOL 31 p 53-72.

(8071)
Reback R
Risk and return in CBOE and AMEX option
trading
FAJ 1975 JUL-AUG VOL 31 p 42-52.

(8072)
Gould J P, Galai D
Transactions costs and the relationship between
put and call prices
JFE 1974 VOL 1 p 105.

(8073)
King W R, McGuigan J
Evaluating alternative stock option timing
strategies
JFQA 1974 SEP VOL 9 p 567.

(8074)
Jensen M C, Scholes M
The valuation of option contracts and a test of
market efficiency
JF 1972 MAY VOL 27 p 399-417.

(8075)
Boness A J
Some evidence on the profitability of trading in
put and call options
(in Cootner P H ed., The random character of
stock market prices. MIT Pr, 1964.)

(8076)
Katz R C
The profitability of put and call option writing
IMR 1963 FALL VOL 5 p 55-69.

(8077)
Securities and Exchange Commission
Report on put and call options
US Govt, 1961.

(8078)
Platt S D, Rosen D A
Put and call options under section 16 of the
Securities Exchange Act
Yale Law Journal 1960 APR.

19.412 Stock index options

(8079)
Alderson M J, Zivney T L
Optimal cross-hedge portfolios for hedging stock
index options
JFM 1989 VOL 9:1 p 67-76.

(8080)
Bailey W, Stulz R M
The pricing of stock index options in a general
equilibrium model
JFQA 1989 MAR VOL 24:1 p 1-12.

(8081)
Brooks R
Investment decision making with index futures
and index futures options
JFM 1989 VOL 9:2 p 143-162.

(8082)
Cakici N, Eytan T H, Harpaz G
American vs. European options on the Value
Line Index
JFM 1988 JUN VOL 8:3 p 373-388.

(8083)
Day T E, Lewis C M
The behavior of the volatility implicit in the prices of stock index options
JFE 1988 VOL 22 p 103.

(8084)
King S R, Remolona E M
The pricing and hedging of market index deposits
F R Bk New York Q Rev 1987 SUMMER VOL 12:2.

(8085)
Kling A
How the stock market can learn to live with index futures and options
FAJ 1987 SEP-OCT VOL 43 p 33-39.

(8086)
Luskin D L
Index options and futures: the complete guide
Wiley, 1987.

(8087)
Stoll H R, Whaley R E
Expiration day effects of index options and futures
NYU, 1987.

(8088)
Eytan T H, Harpaz G
The pricing of futures and options contracts on the Value Line index
JF 1986 SEP VOL 41:4 p 843-855.

(8089)
Zivney T L, Alderson M J
Hedged dividend capture with stock index options
FIN MGMT 1986 SUMMER VOL 15 p 5-12.

(8090)
Evnine J, Rudd A
Index options : the early evidence
JF 1985 JUL VOL 40:3 p 743-756.

19.413 Currency options

(8091)
Adams P D, Wyatt S B
On the pricing of European and American foreign currency options: a clarification
JIMF 1989 VOL 8 p 305.

(8092)
Buttler H-J
An expository note on the valuation of foreign exchange options
JIMF 1989 VOL 8 p 295.

(8093)
Chesney M, Scott L
Pricing European currency options: a comparison of the modified Black-Scholes model and a random variance model
JFQA 1989 SEP VOL 24:3 p 267-284.

(8094)
Clasing H
Currency options
Dow Jones-Irwin, 1989.

(8095)
Jorion P, Stoughton N M
An empirical investigation of the early exercise premium of foreign currency options
JFM 1989 VOL 9:5 p 365-376.

(8096)
Briys E, Crouhy M
Creating and pricing hybrid foreign currency options
FIN MGMT 1988 WINTER VOL 17 p 59-65.

(8097)
Lyons R K
Test of the foreign exchange risk premium using the expected second moments implied by option pricing
JIMF 1988 MAR VOL 7:1 p 91-108.

(8098)
Ogden J P, Tucker A L
The relative valuation of American currency spot and futures options: Theory and empirical tests
JFQA 1988 DEC VOL 23 p 351.

(8099)
Sutton W
The currency options handbook
Woodhead-Faulkner, 1988.

(8100)
Adams P D, Wyatt S B
Biases in option prices: evidence from the foreign
currency option market
JBankF 1987 VOL 11 p 549-562.

(8101)
Adams P D, Wyatt S B
On the pricing of European and American
foreign currency call options
JIMF 1987 SEP VOL 6:3 p 315-338.

(8102)
Bodurtha J N Jr, Courtadon G R
Tests of an American option pricing model on
the foreign currency options market
JFQA 1987 JUN VOL 22 p 153.

(8103)
Hull J, White A
Hedging the risks from writing foreign currency
options
JIMF 1987 JUN VOL 6:2 p 131-152.

(8104)
Ogden J P, Tucker A L
Empirical tests of the efficiency of the currency
futures options markets
JFM 1987 DEC VOL 7:6 p 695-704.

(8105)
Shastri K, Tandon K
Valuation of American options on foreign
currency
JBankF 1987 VOL 11 p 245-269.

(8106)
Shastri K, Wethyavivorn K
The valuation of currency options for alternate
stochastic processes
JFR 1987 VOL 10:4 p 283-294.

(8107)
Sondermann D
Currency options: hedging and social value
EER 1987 VOL 31:1-2.

(8108)
Tucker A L
Foreign exchange option prices as predictors of
equilibrium forward exchange rates
JIMF 1987 SEP VOL 6:3 p 283-295.

(8109)
Bodurtha J N Jr, Courtadon G R
Efficiency tests of the foreign currency options
market.
JF 1986 MAR VOL 41:1 p 151-162.

(8110)
Johnson L J
Foreign-currency options, ex ante exchange-rate
volatility, and market efficiency: an empirical test
FR 1986 NOV VOL 21:4.

(8111)
Shastri K, Tandon K
Valuation of foreign currency options: some
empirical tests
JFQA 1986 JUN VOL 21:2 p 145-160.

(8112)
Coggan P ed.
Currency options
Gee, 1985.

(8113)
Yang H C
A note on currency option pricing models
JBFA 1985 AUTUMN VOL 12:3 p 429-438

(8114)
Biger N, Hull J
The valuation of currency options
FIN MGMT 1983 SPRING VOL 12 p 24-28.

(8115)
Garman M B, Kohlhagen S W
Foreign currency option values
JIMF 1983 DEC VOL 2 p 231-237.

(8116)
Giddy I H
Foreign exchange options
JFM 1983 SUMMER VOL 3 p 143-166.

(8117)
Giddy I H
The foreign exchange option as a hedging tool
MCFJ 1983 FALL VOL 1 p 32-42.

(8118)
Grabbe J O
The pricing of call and put options on foreign exchange
JIMF 1983 DEC VOL 2 p 239-253..

(8119)**Feiger G, Jacquillat B**
Currency option bonds puts and calls on spot exchange and the hedging of contingent foreign earnings
JF 1979 DEC VOL 34:5 p 1129-1139.

19.42 Portfolio insurance

(8120)
Bird R, Dennis D, Tippett M
A stop loss approach to portfolio insurance
JPM 1988 FALL VOL 15:1 p 35-40.

(8121)
Black F, Jones R
Simplifying portfolio insurance for corporate pension plans
JPM 1988 SUMMER VOL 14:4 p 33-37.

(8122)
Bookstaber R M, Langsam J A
Portfolio insurance trading rules
JFM 1988 FEB VOL 8:1 p 15-32.

(8123)
Bradley D P, Walsh M
Portfolio insurance and the U K stock market
JBFA 1988 SPRING VOL 15:1 p 67-76.

(8124)
Brennan M J, Schwartz E S
Time-invariant portfolio insurance strategies
JF 1988 JUN VOL 43:2 p 283-300.

(8125)
Dreher W A
Does portfolio insurance ever make sense
JPM 1988 SUMMER VOL 14:4 p 25-32.

(8126)
Estep T, Kritzman M
TIPP: time invariant portfolio protection
JPM 1988 SUMMER VOL 14:4 p 38-42.

(8127)
Grossman S J
Insurance seen and unseen: the impact on markets
JPM 1988 SUMMER VOL 14:4 p 5-8.

(8128)
Merrick J R Jr
Portfolio insurance with stock index futures
JFM 1988 AUG VOL 8:4 p 441-456.

(8129)
O'Brien T J
Portfolio insurance mechanics
JPM 1988 SPRING VOL 14:3 p 40-47.

(8130)
Trennepohl G L, Booth J R, Tehranian H
An empirical analysis of insured portfolio strategies using listed options
JFR 1988 VOL 11:1 p 1-12.

(8131)
Zhu Y, Kavee R C
Performances of portfolio insurance strategies
JPM 1988 SPRING VOL 14:3 p 48-54.

(8132)
Black F, Jones R
Simplifying portfolio insurance
JPM 1987 FALL VOL 14:1 p 48-51.

(8133)
Clarke R G, Arnott R D
The cost of portfolio insurance: tradeoffs and choices
FAJ 1987 NOV-DEC VOL 43 p 35-47.

(8134)
Garcia C B, Gould F J
An empirical study of portfolio insurance
FAJ 1987 JUL-AUG VOL 43 p 44-54.

(8135)
Rendleman R J Jr, McEnally R W
Assessing the costs of portfolio insurance
FAJ 1987 MAY-JUN VOL 43:3 p 27-37.

(8136)
Ferguson R
How to beat the S&P 500 (without losing sleep)
FAJ 1986 MAR-APR VOL 42 p 37-46.

(8137)
Benninga S, Blume M
On the optimality of portfolio insurance
JF 1985 DEC VOL 40:5 p 1341-1352.

(8138)
Rubinstein M
Alternative paths to portfolio insurance
FAJ 1985 JUL-AUG VOL 41 p 42-52.

(8139)
Platt R B, Latainer G D
Risk-return tradeoffs of contingent insurance strategies for active bond portfolios
FAJ 1984 MAY-JUN VOL 40 p 34-40.

(8140)
Brennan M J, Solanki R
Optimal portfolio insurance
JFQA 1981 SEP VOL 16:3 p 279-300.

(8141)
Leland H E
Who should buy portfolio insurance
JF 1980 MAY VOL 35:2 p 581-596.

(8142)
Goldman M B, Sosin H B, Shepp L A
On contingent claims that insure ex-post optimal stock market timing
JF 1979 MAY VOL 34:2 p 401-414

(8143)
Pozen R C
When to purchase a protective put
FAJ 1978 JUL-AUG p 47-60.

(8144)
Boyle P P, Schwartz E S
Equilibrium prices of guarantees under equity-linked contracts
Journal of Risk and Insurance 1977 DEC VOL 44 p 639-680.

19.43 Real options

(8145)
Conine T E Jr, Jensen O W, Tamarkin M
On optimal output in an option pricing framework
JBFA 1988 SPRING VOL 15:1 p 21-26.

(8146)
Paddock J L, Siegel D R, Smith J L
Option valuation of claims on real assets: The case of offshore petroleum leases
QJE 1988 AUG VOL 103:3 p 479-508.

(8147)
Kensinger J W
Adding the value of active management into the capital budgeting equation
MCFJ 1987 SPRING VOL 5 p 31-42.

(8148)
Seigel D R, Smith J L, Paddock J L
Valuing offshore oil properties with option pricing models
MCFJ 1987 SPRING VOL 5 p 22-30.

(8149)
Trigeorgis L, Mason S P
Valuing managerial flexibility
MCFJ 1987 SPRING VOL 5 p 14-21.

(8150)
Brennan M J, Schwartz E S
Evaluating natural resource investments
JB 1985 APR VOL 58:2 p 135-157.

(8151)
Brennan M J, Schwartz E S
A new approach to evaluating natural resource investments
MCFJ 1985 SPRING VOL 3 p 37-47.

(8152)
Kester W C
Today's options for tomorrow's growth
HBR 1984 MAR-APR VOL 62:2 p 153-160.

(8153)
Myers S C
Finance theory and financial strategy
Interfaces 1984 JAN-FEB VOL 14 p 126-137.

(8154)
Lee W Y, Martin J D, Senchack A J
The case for using options to evaluate salvage values in financial leases
FIN MGMT 1982 AUTUMN VOL 11 p 33-41.

(8155)
Rao R K S, Martin J D
Another look at the use of options pricing theory to evaluate real asset investment opportunities
JBFA 1981 AUTUMN VOL 8:3 p 421-429

(8156)
Emery D R, Parr P C, Mokkelbost P B
An investigation of real investment decision making with the options pricing model
JBFA 1978 WINTER VOL 5:4 p 363-370.

19.431 Abandonment options

(8157)
Deily M E
Investment activity and the exit decision
REStat 1988 VOL 70 p 595.

(8158)
McDonald R, Siegel D
Investment and valuation of firms when there is an option to shut down
IntER 1985 JUN VOL 26 p 331-349.

(8159)
Bonini C P
Capital investment under uncertainty with abandonment options
JFQA 1977 MAR VOL 12 p 39.

(8160)
Joy O M
Abandonment values and abandonment decisions: A clarification
JF 1976 VOL 31 p 1225.

(8161)
Robichek A A, Van Horne J C
Abandonment value and capital budgeting
JF 1967 DEC VOL 22 p 577-589.

(8162)
Shillinglaw G
Profit analysis for abandonment decision
(in Solomon E ed., The management of corporate capital. Free Pr, 1959.)

19.432 Options to invest

(8163)
Lee C J
Capital budgeting under uncertainty: The issue of optimal timing
JBFA 1988 SUMMER VOL 15:2 p 155-168.

(8164)
Majd S, Pindyck R S
Time to build, option value, and investment decisions
JFE 1987 VOL 18 p 7-27.

(8165)
McDonald R, Siegel D
The value of waiting to invest
QJE 1986 VOL 101 p 707.

(8166)
Senner M
Japanese Euroderivatives
Euromoney Publications, 1989.

(8167)
Chen A H, Kensinger J W
Puttable stock: A new innovation in equity financing
FIN MGMT 1988 SPRING VOL 17 p 27-37.

(8168)
Luskin D L
The marketplace for "composite assets"
JPM 1987 FALL VOL 14:1 p 12-19.

(8169)
Rice S J
The information content of fully diluted earnings per share
AR 1978 APR VOL 53:2 p 429-438.

(8170)
Leibowitz M L
Convertible securities
FAJ 1974 NOV-DEC VOL 30 p 57-67.

20.1 Convertible bonds and preferred

(8171)
Altman E I
The convertible debt market: are returns worth the risk?
FAJ 1989 JUL-AUG VOL 45 p 23-31..

(8172)**Beatty R P, Lee C F, Chen K C**
On the non-stationarity of convertible bond betas: theory and evidence
QREB 1988 VOL 28:3 p 15.

(8173)
Ma C K, Rao R P, Weinraub H J
The seasonality in convertible bond markets: a stock effect or a bond effect?
JFR 1988 WINTER VOL 11:4 p 335-348.

(8174)
Hoffmeister J R, Hays P A, Kelley G D
Conditions affecting the timing of convertible bond sales
JBusR 1987 FEB VOL 15:1 p 101.

(8175)
Janjigian V
The leverage changing consequences of convertible debt financing
FIN MGMT 1987 AUTUMN VOL 16 p 15-21.

(8176)
Finnerty J D
The case for issuing synthetic convertible bonds
MCFJ 1986 FALL VOL 4 p 73-82.

(8177)
Jones E P, Mason S P
Equity-linked debt
MCFJ 1986 WINTER VOL 3 p 46-58.

(8178)
McConnell J J, Schwartz E S
LYON taming
JF 1986 JUL VOL 41:3 p 561-577.

(8179)
Marr M W, Thompson G R
Primary market pricing of convertible preferred stock
QREB 1985 SPRING VOL 25:2 p 73-80

(8180)
Dann L Y, Mikkelson W H
Convertible debt issuance, capital structure change and financing-related information: some new evidence
JFE 1984 JUN VOL 13:2 p 157-186.

(8181)
King R D
The effect of convertible bond equity values on dilution and leverage
AR 1984 JUL VOL 59:3 p 419-431.

(8182)
Marr M W, Thompson G R
The pricing of new convertible bond issues
FIN MGMT 1984 SUMMER VOL 13 p 31-37.

(8183)
Brennan M J, Schwartz E S
The case for convertibles
CFQ 1982 SPRING VOL 1 p 27-46.

(8184)
Stevenson R A
Deep-discount convertible bonds:an analysis
JPM 1982 SUMMER VOL 8:4 p 57-64.

(8185)
Soldofsky R M
The risk-return performance of convertibles
JPM 1981 WINTER VOL 7:2 p 80-84.

(8186)
Bierman H Jr
Convertible bonds as investments
FAJ 1980 MAR-APR VOL 36 p 59-62.

(8187)
Brennan M J, Schwartz E S
Analyzing convertible bonds
JFQA 1980 NOV VOL 15 p 907.

(8188)
Alexander G J, Stover R D, Kuhnav D B
Market timing strategies in convertible debt
financing
JF 1979 MAR VOL 34:1 p 143-155.

(8189)
Alexander G J, Stover R D
Pricing in the new issue convertible debt market
FIN MGMT 1977 AUTUMN VOL 6 p 35.

(8190)
Brennan M J, Schwartz E S
Convertible bonds: Valuation and optimal
strategies for call and conversion
JF 1977 VOL 32 p 1699.

(8191)
Hoffmeister J R
Use of convertible debt in the early 1970s: a
reevaluation of corporate motives
QREB 1977 VOL 17:2 p 23.

(8192)
Ingersoll J E
A contingent-claim valuation of convertible
securities
JFE 1977 VOL 4 p 289.

(8193)
Bond F M
Yields on convertible securities: 1969-1974
JBFA 1976 SUMMER VOL 3:2 p 83-114.

(8194)
Frankle A W, Hawkins C A
Beta coefficients for convertible bonds
JF 1975 VOL 30 p 207.

(8195)
Dawson S M
Timing interest payments for convertible bonds
FIN MGMT 1974 SUMMER VOL 3 p 14.

(8196)
Frank W G, Kroncke C O
Classifying conversions of convertible debentures
over four years
FIN MGMT 1974 SUMMER VOL 3 p 33.

(8197)
Jennings E H
An estimate of convertible bond premiums
JFQA 1974 JAN VOL 9 p 33.

(8198)
Skerratt L C L
The price determination of convertible loan stock:
A U K model
JBFA 1974 AUTUMN VOL 1:3 p 429-444.

(8199)
Lewellen W G, Racette G A
Convertible debt financing
JFQA 1973 DEC VOL 8:5 p 777-792.

(8200)
Walter J E, Que A V
The valuation of convertible bonds
JF 1973 VOL 28 p 713.

(8201)
Brealey R A, Hodges S D
The valuation of British convertibles
(in Szego G P and Shell K eds., Mathematical
methods in investment and finance. N-Holland,
1972.)

(8202)
Groth S C
The trouble with convertibles
FAJ 1972 NOV-DEC VOL 28 p 92-100.

(8203)
Frank W G, Weygandt J T
A prediction model for convertible debentures
JAR 1971 SPRING VOL 9 p 116-126.

(8204)
Sprecher C R
A note on financing mergers with convertible
preferred stock
JF 1971 JUN VOL 26 p 683-686.

(8205)
Pinches G E
Financing with convertible preferred stock,
1960-1967
JF 1970 MAR VOL 25 p 53-63.

(8206)
Vinson C E
Pricing practices in the primary convertible bond
market
QREB 1970 VOL 10:2 p 47.

(8207)
Weil R L, Segal J E, Green D Jr
Premiums on convertible bonds
JF 1968 JUN VOL 23 p 445-463.

(8208)
Baumol W J, Malkiel B G, Quandt R E
The valuation of convertible securities
QJE 1966 FEB VOL 80 p 48-59.

(8209)
Brigham E F
An analysis of convertible debentures: theory and
some empirical evidence
JF 1966 MAR VOL 21 p 35-54.

(8210)
Kassouf S T
The evaluation of convertible securities
Analytical Inv, 1966.

(8211)
Kaplan S A
Piercing the corporate boilerplate: anti-dilution
clauses in convertible securities
University of Chicago Law Review 1965
AUTUMN VOL 33 p 1-30.

(8212)
Poensgen O H
The valuation of convertible bonds [Parts 1-2]
IMR 1965 FALL VOL 7 p 77-92; IMR 1966
SPRING VOL 7 p 83-98.

(8213)
Broman K L
The use of convertible subordinated debentures by
industrial firms, 1949-1959
QREB 1963 SPRING VOL 3 p 65-75.

(8214)
Pilcher J C
Raising capital with convertible securities
U of Mich Pr, 1955.

20.11 Call provisions on convertibles

(8215)
Dunn K B, Eades K M
Voluntary conversion of convertible securities and
the optimal call strategy
JFE 1989 VOL 23 p 273.

(8216)
Ofer A R, Natarajan A
Convertible call policies: an empirical analysis of
an information-signalling hypothesis
JFE 1987 VOL 19 p 91-108.

(8217)
Harris M, Raviv A
A sequential signalling model of convertible debt
call policy
JF 1985 DEC VOL 40:5 p 1263-1281.

(8218)
Mikkelson W H
Convertible calls and stock price declines
FAJ 1985 JAN-FEB VOL 41:1 p 63-69.

(8219)
Mikkelson W H
Convertible calls and security returns
JFE 1981 VOL 9 p 237.

(8220)
Alexander G J, Stover R D
The effect of forced conversions on common
stock prices
FIN MGMT 1980 SPRING VOL 9 p 39.

(8221)
Ingersoll J
An examination of corporate call policies on
convertible securities
JF 1977 MAY VOL 32:2 p 463-478.

(8222)
Bacon P W, Winn E L
The impact of forced conversion on stock prices
JF 1969 DEC VOL 24 p 871-874.

20.2   Warrants

(8223)
Ferri M G, Moore S B, Schirm D C
The listing, size, and value of equity warrants
FR 1989 FEB VOL 24:1 p 135-146.

(8224)
Folks W R, Ferri M G
Equity-linked cross-currency international financial
instruments: a study of the pricing of
euro-warrants
MF 1987 VOL 13:1 p 23-26..

(8225)Green R C
Investment incentives, debt, and warrants
JFE 1984 MAR VOL 13:1 p 115-136.

(8226)
Kudla R J
A note on resolving agency problems through
warrants
JBFA 1984 SPRING VOL 11:1 p 67-71

(8227)
Sinkey J F Jr, Miles J A
The use of warrants in the bail out of First
Pennsylvania Bank: An application of option
pricing
FIN MGMT 1982 AUTUMN VOL 11 p 27-32.

(8228)
Kim M K, Young A
Rewards and risks from warrant hedging
JPM 1980 SUMMER VOL 6:4 p 65-68.

(8229)
Galai D, Schneller M I
Pricing of warrants and the value of the firm
JF 1978 VOL 33 p 1333.

(8230)
Hilliard J E, Leitch R A
Analysis of the warrant hedge in a stable paretian
market
JFQA 1977 MAR VOL 12 p 85.

(8231)
Rogalski R J
Trading in warrants by mechanical systems
JF 1977 VOL 32 p 87.

(8232)
Schwartz E S
The valuation of warrants: Implementing a new
approach
JFE 1977 VOL 4 p 79.

(8233)
Stone B K
Warrant financing
JFQA 1976 MAR VOL 11 p 143.

(8234)
Leabo D A, Rogalski R J
Warrant price movements and the efficient
market model
JF 1975 VOL 30 p 163.

(8235)
Horrigan J O
Some hypotheses on the valuation of stock
warrants
JBFA 1974 SUMMER VOL 1:2 p 239-249.

(8236)
Rush D R, Melicher R W
An empirical examination of factors which influence warrant prices
JF 1974 VOL 29 p 1449.

(8237)
Bierman H Jr
The cost of warrants
JFQA 1973 JUN VOL 8:3 p 499-505.

(8238)
Post L A
Yield to early maturity: An important factor with usable bonds
FAJ 1973 NOV-DEC VOL 29 p 70-73.

(8239)
Chen A H
A model of warrant pricing in a dynamic market
JF 1970 DEC VOL 25 p 1041-1060.

(8240)
Hayes S L III, Reiling H B
Sophisticated financing tool: the warrant
HBR 1969 JAN-FEB VOL 47 p 137-150.

(8241)
Kassouf S T
An econometric model for option price with implications for investors' expectations and audacity
Em 1969 OCT VOL 37 p 685-694.

(8242)
Samuelson P A, Merton R C
A complete model of warrant pricing that maximises utility
IMR 1969 WINTER VOL 10 p 17-46.

(8243)
Van Horne J C
Warrant valuation in relation to volatility and opportunity costs
IMR 1969 SPRING VOL 10 p 19-32.

(8244)
Kassouf S T
Stock price random walks: some supporting evidence
REStat 1968 MAY VOL 50 p 275-278.

(8245)
Kassouf S T
Warrant price behavior, 1945-1964
FAJ 1968 JAN-FEB VOL 24 p 123-126.

(8246)
Shelton J P
The relation of the price of a warrant to the price of the associated stock [Parts 1-2]
FAJ 1967 MAY-JUN VOL 23 p 143-151; FAJ 1967 JUL-AUG VOL 23 p 88-99.

(8247)
Samuelson P A
Rational theory of warrant pricing
IMR 1965 SPRING VOL 6 p 13-31.

(8248)
Ayres H F
Risk aversion in the warrant markets
IMR 1963 FALL VOL 4 p 45-53.

(8249)
Cheng P L, Savage D T
Short-run manipulative aspects of common stock warrants
QREB 1963 SUMMMER VOL 3 p 102-107.

(8250)
Sprenkle C M
Warrant prices as indicators of expectations and preferences
YEE 1961 FALL VOL 1 p 179-231.

20.21 Warrant exercise policy

(8251)
Ferri M G, Moore S B, Schirm D C
Investor expectations about callable warrants
JPM 1988 SPRING VOL 14:3 p 84-86.

(8252)
Spatt C S, Sterbenz F P
Warrant exercise, dividends, and reinvestment policy
JF 1988 JUN VOL 43:2 p 493-506.

(8253)
Constantinides G M
Warrant exercise and bond conversion in competitive markets
JFE 1984 VOL 13 p 371-397.

(8254)
Emanuel D C
Warrant valuation and exercise strategy
JFE 1983 VOL 12 p 211-235.

21 Hedging instruments: futures and forwards

(8255)
Carter C A
Arbitrage opportunities between thin and liquid futures markets
JFM 1989 VOL 9:4 p 347-354.

(8256)
Chance D M
An introduction to options and futures
Dryden Pr, 1989.

(8257)
Demers F, Demers M
A privately revealing rational expectations equilibrium for the futures market
EER 1989 VOL 33 p 663.

(8258)
Duffie D
Futures markets
P-H, 1989.

(8259)
Goldenberg D H
Memory and equilibrium futures prices
JFM 1989 VOL 9:3 p 199-214.

(8260)
Hegde S P
On the value of the implicit delivery options
JFM 1989 VOL 9:5 p 421-438.

(8261)
IFR Publishing
Financial futures and options: recent developments
IFR Publishing, 1989.

(8262)
Levy A
A note on the relationship between forward and futures contracts
JFM 1989 VOL 9:2 p 171-174.

(8263)
Lien D-H D
Cash settlement provisions on futures contracts
JFM 1989 VOL 9:3 p 263-270.

(8264)
Lien D-H D
Optimal settlement specification on futures contracts
JFM 1989 VOL 9:4 p 355-358.

(8265)
Miskovic M
Futures and options: a practical guide for institutional investors
Longman, 1989.

(8266)
Poitras G
Optimal futures spread positions
JFM 1989 VOL 9:2 p 123-134.

(8267)
Bick A
Producing derivative assets with forward contracts
JFQA 1988 JUN VOL 23:2 p 153-160.

(8268)
Block S B, Gallagher T J
How much do bank trust departments use derivatives?
JPM 1988 FALL VOL 15:1 p 12-15.

(8269)
Bookstaber R M, Gold J
In search of the liability asset
FAJ 1988 JAN-FEB VOL 44 p 70-80.

(8270)
Brown K C, Smith D J
Recent innovations in interest rate risk management and the reintermediation of commercial banking
FIN MGMT 1988 WINTER VOL 17 p 45-58.

(8271)
Edwards F R, Neftci S N
Extreme price movements and margin levels in futures markets
JFM 1988 VOL 8:6 p 639-656.

(8272)
Finnerty J D
Financial engineering in corporate finance: an overview
FIN MGMT 1988 WINTER VOL 17 p 14-33.

(8273)
Goldenberg D H
Trading frictions and futures price movements
JFQA 1988 DEC VOL 23 p 465.

(8274)
Institute of Chartered Financial Analysts
CFA readings in derivative securities
Institute of Chartered Financial Analysts, 1988.

(8275)
Lukac L P, Brorsen B W, Irwin S H
A test of futures market disequilibrium using
twelve different technical trading systems
AE 1988 MAY VOL 20:5 p 623-640.

(8276)
Maberly E D
The other Friday "bull" effect: a chance
occurrence or the harbinger of yet another
puzzling anomaly? A note!
JFM 1988 VOL 8:6 p 723-724.

(8277)
Marshall J F
Futures and options contracting: Theory and
practice
SW Pub, 1988..

(8278)**Monroe M A**
Indeterminacy of price and quantity in futures
markets
JFM 1988 OCT VOL 8:5 p 575-588.

(8279)
OECD
New financial instruments: disclosure and
accounting
OECD, 1988.

(8280)
Redhead K, Hughes S
Financial risk management
Gower, 1988.

(8281)
Walmsley J
The new financial instruments: an investor's guide
Wiley, 1988.

(8282)
Ehrhardt M C, Jordan J V, Walkling R A
An application of arbitrage pricing theory to
futures markets: test of normal backwardation
JFM 1987 FEB VOL 7:1 p 21-34.

(8283)
Gay G D, Kim T-H
An investigation into seasonality in the futures
market
JFM 1987 APR VOL 7:2 p 169-182.

(8284)
Hartzmark M L
Returns to individual traders of futures: aggregate
results
JPE 1987 DEC VOL 95:6 p 1292-1306.

(8285)
Kamara A, Siegel A F
Optimal hedging in futures markets with multiple
delivery specifications
JF 1987 SEP VOL 42:4 p 1007-1021.

(8286)
Kawaller I G
A note: debunking the myth of the risk free
return
JFM 1987 JUN VOL 7:3 p 327-332.

(8287)
Koziol J D
A handbook for professional futures and options
traders
Wiley, 1987.

(8288)
Livingston M
The delivery option on forward contracts.
JFQA 1987 MAR VOL 22:1 p 79-87.

(8289)
Martell T F, Wolf A S
Determinants of trading volume in futures
markets
JFM 1987 JUN VOL 7:3 p 233-244.

(8290)
Nermuth M
Futures markets, information structures, and the
allocation of resources: an introduction
EER 1987 VOL 31:1-2.

(8291)
Smithson C W
A LEGO approach to engineering: an introduction to forwards, futures, swaps, and options
MCFJ 1987 WINTER VOL 4 p 16-28.

(8292)
Williams J
Futures markets: a consequence of risk aversion or transaction costs?
JPE 1987 OCT VOL 95:5 p 1000-1023.

(8293)
Brennan M J
A theory of price limits in futures markets
JFE 1986 JUN VOL 16:2 p 213-233.

(8294)
Gay G D, Manaster S
Implicit delivery options and optimal delivery strategies for financial futures contracts
JFE 1986 VOL 15 p 41.

(8295)
Goss B A ed.
Futures markets: their establishment and performance
Croom Helm, 1986.

(8296)
Laufman P
Handbook of futures markets: Commodity, financial stock indices and options
Wiley, 1986.

(8297)
Milonas N T
Liquidity and price variability in futures markets
FR 1986 MAY VOL 21:2.

(8298)
Stein J L
The economics of futures markets
Blackwell, 1986.

(8299)
Williams J
The economic function of futures markets
Cambridge U Pr, 1986.

(8300)
Zahn H E
Financial innovations: glossary of new hedging and financing instruments: English - German
Frankfurt am Main: Fritz Knapp, 1986.

(8301)
Belongia M T, Santoni G J
Cash flow or present value: what's lurking behind that hedge?
F R Bk St Louis Rev 1985 VOL 67:1.

(8302)
Chang E C
Return to speculators and the theory of normal backwardation
JF 1985 MAR VOL 40:1 p 193-208.

(8303)
Peck A E ed.
Futures markets: regulatory issues
Washington, DC: American Enterprise Institute for Public Policy Research, 1985.

(8304)
Stahl D O
Bankruptcies in temporary equilibrium forward markets with and without institutional restrictions
REStud 1985 VOL 52 p 459.

(8305)
Turnovsky S J, Campbell R B
The stabilizing and welfare properties of futures markets: a simulation approach
IntER 1985 JUN VOL 26:2 p 277-303.

(8306)
Brannel P P, Ulveling E F
Considering an informational role for a futures market
REStud 1984 VOL 51 p 33.

(8307)
Forsythe R, Palfrey T R, Plott C R
Futures markets and informational efficiency : a laboratory examination.
JF 1984 SEP VOL 39:4 p 955-981

(8308)
Gay G D, Manaster S
The quality option implicit in futures contracts
JFE 1984 SEP VOL 13:3 p 353-370.

(8309)
Kamara A
The behavior of futures prices: A review of theory and evidence
FAJ 1984 JUL-AUG VOL 40 p 68-75.

(8310)
Kaufman P J
Handbook of futures markets: commodity, financial, stock index, and options
Wiley, 1984.

(8311)
Magill M J P
Understanding futures markets
Empirica 1984 VOL 11:2.

(8312)
Marcus A J, Modest D M
Futures markets and production decisions
JPE 1984 VOL 92 p 409.

(8313)
Silber W L
Marketmaker behavior in an auction market : an analysis of scalpers in future markets
JF 1984 SEP VOL 39:4 p 937-953.

(8314)
Anderson R W, Danthine J P
The time pattern of hedging and the volatility of future prices
REStud 1983 VOL 50 p 249.

(8315)
Carter C A, Rausser G C, Schmitz A
Efficient asset portfolios and the theory of normal backwardation
JPE 1983 VOL 91 p 319.

(8316)
French K R
A comparison of futures and forward prices
JFE 1983 VOL 12 p 311-342.

(8317)
Garbade K D, Silber W L
Price movements and price discovery in futures and cash markets
REStat 1983 VOL 65 p 289.

(8318)
Baesel J B, Grant D
Optimal sequential futures trading
JFQA 1982 DEC VOL 17:5 p 683-695.

(8319)
Burns J M
Electronic trading in futures markets
FAJ 1982 JAN-FEB p 33-42.

(8320)
Houthakker H S
The regulation of financial and other futures markets
JF 1982 MAY VOL 37:2 p 481-491.

(8321)
Cox J C, Ingersoll J E, Ross S A
The relation between forward prices and future prices
JFE 1981 VOL 9 p 321.

(8322)
Jarrow R A, Oldfield G S
Forward contracts and futures contracts
JFE 1981 VOL 9 p 373.

(8323)
Moriarty E, Phillips S, Tosini P
A comparison of options and futures in the management of portfolio risk
FAJ 1981 JAN-FEB VOL 37 p 61-67.

(8324)
Richard S F, Sundaresan M
A continuous time equilibrium model of forward prices and futures prices in a multigood economy
JFE 1981 VOL 9 p 347.

(8325)
Shefrin H M
Transaction costs, uncertainty and generally inactive futures markets
REStud 1981 JAN VOL 48 p 131-138.

(8326)
Feder G, Just R, Schmitz A
Futures markets and the theory of the firm under price uncertainty
QJE 1980 MAR VOL 94 p 317-328.

(8327)
Grauer F L A, Litzenberger R H
The pricing of commodity futures contracts nominal bonds and other risky assets under commodity price uncertainty
JF 1979 MAR VOL 34:1 p 69-83.

(8328)
Townsend R M
On the optimality of forward markets
AER 1978 VOL 68 p 54-66.

(8329)
Grossman S J
The existence of futures markets, noisy rational expectations and informational externalities
REStud 1977 VOL 44 p 431.

(8330)
Peterson R L
Investor preferences for futures straddles
JFQA 1977 MAR VOL 12 p 105..

(8331)**Telser L G, Higinbotham H N**
Organized futures markets: costs and benefits
JPE 1977 OCT VOL 85:5 p 969-1000.

(8332)
Cox C C
Futures trading and market information
JPE 1976 VOL 84 p 1215.

(8333)
Peck A E
Futures markets, supply response and price stability
QJE 1976 VOL 90 p 407.

(8334)
Mehr R I, Hedges B A
Risk management: concepts and applications
Irwin, 1974.

(8335)
Cootner P H
Speculation and hedging
FRIS 1967 VOL 7 Suppl p 65-105.

(8336)
Phillips J
The theory and practice of futures trading
Review of Marketing and Agricultural Economics 1966 JUN.

(8337)
Working H
New concepts concerning futures markets and prices
AER 1962 JUN VOL 52 p 431-459.

(8338)
Cootner P H
Common elements in futures markets for commodities and bonds
AER 1961 MAY VOL 51 p 173-183.

(8339)
Cootner P H
Returns to speculators: Telser versus Keynes
JPE 1960 AUG VOL 68 p 396-404.

(8340)
Johnson L L
The theory of hedging and speculation in commodity futures
REStud 1960 JUN VOL 27 p 139-151.

(8341)
Peston M H, Yamey B S
Inter-temporal price relationships with forward markets: a method of analysis
Ec 1960 NOV VOL 27 p 355-367.

(8342)
Working H
Speculation on hedging markets
FRIS 1960 MAY VOL 1 p 185-220.

(8343)
Houthakker H S
Restatement of the theory of normal backwardation
Cowles Foundation Discussion Paper, No 44, 18 DEC 1957.

(8344)
Hawtrey R G
A symposium on the theory of the forward market: III Mr. Kaldor on the forward market
REStud 1940 JUN VOL 7 p 196-205.

(8345)
Kaldor N
A note on the theory of the forward markets
REStud 1939 OCT VOL 7 p 196-201.

21.1 Hedging

(8346)
Castelino M G
Basis volatility: implications for hedging
JFR 1989 SUMMER VOL 12:2 p 157-172.

(8347)
Eldor R, Pines D, Schwartz A
Determinants of an individual's demand for
hedging instruments
JFM 1989 VOL 9:2 p 135-142.

(8348)
Grant D, Eaker M
Complex hedges: how well do they work?
JFM 1989 VOL 9:1 p 15-28.

(8349)
Howcroft B, Storey C
Management and control of currency and interest
rate risk
Woodhead-Faulkner, 1989.

(8350)
Lindahl M
Measuring hedging effectiveness with R2 [R
squared]: a note
JFM 1989 VOL 9:5 p 469.

(8351)
Miller S E, Kahl K H
Performance of estimated hedging ratios under
yield uncertainty
JFM 1989 VOL 9:4 p 307-320.

(8352)
Adler M, Detemple J
Hedging with futures in an intertemporal
portfolio context
JFM 1988 JUN VOL 8:3 p 249-270.

(8353)
Adler M, Detemple J B
On the optimal hedge of a nontraded cash
position
JF 1988 MAR VOL 43:1 p 143-154.

(8354)
Brodt A I
Optimal bank asset and liability management with
financial futures
JFM 1988 AUG VOL 8:4 p 457-482.

(8355)
Cecchetti S G, Cumby R E, Figlewski S
Estimation of the optimal futures hedges
REStat 1988 VOL 70 p 623.

(8356)
Fortin M, Khoury N T
Effectiveness of hedging interest rate risks and
stock market risks with financial futures
JFM 1988 JUN VOL 8:3 p 319-334.

(8357)
Saunders A, Sienkiewicz S
The hedging performance of ECU futures
contracts
JFM 1988 JUN VOL 8:3 p 335-352.

(8358)
Schroeder T C, Hayenga M L
Comparison of selective hedging and options
strategies in cattle feedlot risk management
JFM 1988 APR VOL 8:2 p 141-156.

(8359)
Anderson G, Chiang R
Interest rate risk hedging for due-on sale
mortgages with early termination
JFR 1987 VOL 10:2 p 133-142.

(8360)
Anderson G, Chiang R
Interest rate risk hedging for due-on-sale
mortgages with early termination
JFR 1987 SUMMER VOL 10:2 p 133-142.

(8361)
Belongia M T, Santoni G J
Interest rate risk, market value, and hedging
financial portfolios
JFR 1987 VOL 10:1 p 47-56.

(8362)
Bond G E, Thompson S R, Lee B M S
Application of a simplified hedging rule
JFM 1987 FEB VOL 7:1 p 65-72.

(8363)
Doukas J
The performance of Euromoney Currency Report
hedging recommendations
AE 1987 JUN VOL 19:6 p 845-852.

(8364)
Eaker M R, Grant D M
Cross-hedging foreign currency risk
JIMF 1987 MAR VOL 6:1 p 85-106.

(8365)
Gjerde O
Measuring hedging effectiveness in a traditional
one-periodic portfolio framework
JFM 1987 DEC VOL 7:6 p 663-674.

(8366)
Grumball C
Managing interest rate risk
Woodhead-Faulkner, 1987.

(8367)
Kenyon D, Clay J
Analysis of profit margin hedging strategies for
hog producers
JFM 1987 APR VOL 7:2 p 183-202.

(8368)
Koppenhaver G D, Lee C F
Alternative instruments for hedging inflation risk
in the banking industry
JFM 1987 DEC VOL 7:6 p 619-636.

(8369)
Leuthold R M, Peterson P E
A portfolio approach to optimal hedging for a
commercial cattle feedlot
JFM 1987 APR VOL 7:2 p 119-134.

(8370)
Sheales T C, Tomek W G
Hedging Australian wheat exports using futures
markets
JFM 1987 OCT VOL 7:5 p 519-534.

(8371)
Witt H J, Schroeder T C, Hayenga M L
Comparison of analytical approaches for
estimating hedge ratios for agricultural
commodities
JFM 1987 APR VOL 7:2 p 135-146.

(8372)
Bell D E, Krasker W S
Estimating hedge ratios
FIN MGMT 1986 SUMMER VOL 15 p 34-39.

(8373)
Figlewski S, John K, Merrick J
Hedging with financial futures for institutional
investors: From theory to practice
Ballinger, 1986.

(8374)
Morgan G E III, Smith S D
Basis risk partial takedown and hedging by
financial intermediaries
JBankF 1986 VOL 10 p 467.

(8375)
Platt R B et al.
Controlling interest rate risk: new techniques and
applications for money management
Wiley, 1986.

(8376)
Doherty N A
Corporate risk management: A financial
exposition
McGraw, 1985.

(8377)
Kraster W S
Sequential hedging
MSci 1985 JUN VOL 31:6 p 657-663.

(8378)
Shapiro A C, Titman S
An integrated approach to corporate risk
management
MCFJ 1985 SUMMER VOL 3 p 41-56.

(8379)
Grant D
Rolling the hedge forward: An extension
FIN MGMT 1984 WINTER VOL 13 p 26-28.

(8380)
Howard C T, D'Antonio L J
A risk-return measure of hedging effectiveness
JFQA 1984 MAR VOL 19:1 p 101-112.

(8381)
Stulz R M
Optimal hedging policies.
JFQA 1984 JUN VOL 19:2 p 127-140

(8382)
Gay G D, Kolb R, Chiang R
Interest rate hedging: An empirical test of
alternative strategies
JFR 1983 MAR VOL 6.

(8383)
Anderson R W, Danthine J-P
Hedging and joint-production: theory and
illustrations
JF 1980 MAY VOL 35:2 p 487-501..

(8384)**Telser L G**
Safety-first and hedging
REStud 1955-1956 VOL 23 p 1-16.

(8385)
Working H
Futures trading and hedging
AER 1953 JUN VOL 43 p 314-343.

(8386)
Working H
Hedging reconsidered
JFarmE 1953 NOV VOL 35 p 314-343.

21.2 Financial futures

(8387)
Carroll B L
Financial futures trading
Butterworth, 1989.

(8388)
Chiang R, Lasser D J
Tax timing options on futures contracts and the
1981 Economic Recovery Act
FR 1989 FEB VOL 24:1 p 75-92.

(8389)
Yano A S
Configurations for arbitrage using financial futures
contracts
JFM 1989 VOL 9:5 p 439-448.

(8390)
Chu C-C
A risk premium under uncertain inflation: the
inflation futures evidence
JFM 1988 JUN VOL 8:3 p 353-364.

(8391)
Elam E W, Dixon B L
Examining the validity of a test of futures market
efficiency
JFM 1988 JUN VOL 8:3 p 365-372.

(8392)
Gehr A K Jr
Undated futures markets
JFM 1988 FEB VOL 8:1 p 89-98.

(8393)
Hill J M, Jain A, Wood R A Jr
Insurance: volatility risk and futures mispricing
JPM 1988 WINTER VOL 14:2 p 23-29.

(8394)
Kolb R W
Understanding futures markets. 2nd ed
Scott, Foresman, 1988.

(8395)
Merrick J J Jr
Hedging with mispriced futures
JFQA 1988 DEC VOL 23 p 451.

(8396)
Morgan G E, Shome D K, Smith S D
Optimal futures positions for large banking firms
JF 1988 MAR VOL 43:1 p 175-196.

(8397)
Danthine J-P
Financial and futures markets: introduction
EER 1987 VOL 31:1-2.

(8398)
Doukas J, Rahman A
Unit roots tests: Evidence from the foreign
exchange futures market
JFQA 1987 MAR VOL 22 p 101-108.

(8399)
Glassman D
The efficiency of foreign exchange futures markets
in turbulent and non-turbulent periods
JFM 1987 JUN VOL 7:3 p 245-268.

(8400)
White F L, Stein W L
New off-exchange futures-related instrumentss:
modern day "bucket shops" or legitimate products
JFM 1987 JUN VOL 7:3 p 341-344.

(8401)
Kaufman P J ed.
Concise handbook of futures markets: money
management, forecasting, and the markets
Wiley, 1986.

(8402)
Schwarz E M, Hill J, Schneeweis T
Financial futures: fundamentals, strategies, and
applications
Irwin, 1986.

(8403)
Sharda R, Musser K D
Financial futures hedging via goal programming
MSci 1986 AUG VOL 32:8 p 933-947.

(8404)
Atchison M D, DeMong R F, Kling J L
New financial instruments: A descriptive guide
Research Foundation of the Institute of Chartered
Financial Analysts, 1985.

(8405)
Elton E J, Gruber M J, Rentzler J C
Employing financial futures to increase the return
of near cash (Treasury Bill) investments.
MSci 1985 MAR VOL 31:3 p 293-300.

(8406)
Kolb R W, Gay G D, Hunter W C
Liquidity requirements for financial futures
investments
FAJ 1985 MAY-JUN VOL 41 p 60-68.

(8407)
Kolb R W, Gay G eds.
Interest rate and stock index futures and options
Charlottesville, Va.: Financial Analysts Research
Foundation, 1985.

(8408)
Koppenhaver G D
Bank funding risks risk aversion and the choice of
futures hedging instruments
JF 1985 MAR VOL 40:1 p 241-255.

(8409)
Fortune
Big new players in financial futures
F 1984 SEP 17 VOL 110:6 p 79-86.

(8410)
Friedman M
Financial futures markets and tabular standards
JPE 1984 VOL 92 p 165.

(8411)
Kolb R W, Gay G D
Interest rate and stock index futures and options:
Characteristics, valuation and portfolio strategies
Research Foundation of the Institute of Chartered
Financial Analysts, 1984.

(8412)
Powers M
Inside the financial futures markets. 2nd ed
Wiley, 1984.

(8413)
Rothstein N H, Little J M eds.
Handbook of financial futures: a guide for
investors and professional financial managers
McGraw, 1984.

(8414)
Brown B, Geisst C R
Financial futures markets
Macmillan, 1983.

(8415)
Fitzgerald M D
Financial futures
Euromoney Publications, 1983.

(8416)
Kolb R W, Morin R A, Gay G D
Regulation regulatory lag and the use of futures
markets
JF 1983 MAY VOL 38:2 p 405-418.

(8417)
Kilcollin T E
Difference systems in financial futures markets
JF 1982 DEC VOL 37:5 p 1183-1197.

(8418)
Leibowitz M L
The analysis of value and volatility in financial
futures
NYU, 1982.

(8419)
Fortune
Banks should look to the futures
F 1981 APR 20 VOL 103:8 p 185-192.

(8420)
Ederington L H
Living with inflation: A proposal for new futures
and options markets
FAJ 1980 JAN-FEB VOL 36 p 42-48.

(8421)
Kane E J
Market incompleteness and divergences between
forward and futures interest rates
JF 1980 MAY VOL 35:2 p 221-234.

(8422)
Ederington L H
The hedging performance of the new futures
markets
JF 1979 MAR VOL 34:1 p 157-170.

(8423)
Stevens N A
A mortgage futures market: its development, uses,
benefits, and costs
F R Bk St Louis Rev 1976 VOL 58:4.

(8424)
Goshay R C, Sandor R L
An inquiry into the feasibility of a reinsurance
futures market
JBF 1973 SUMMER VOL 5:2 p 56.

(8425)
Lovell M C, Vogel R C
A CPI futures market
JPE 1973 JUL-AUG VOL 81:4 p 1009-1016.

21.21 Stock index futures

(8426)
Bailey W
The market for Japanese index futures: some
preliminary evidence
JFM 1989 VOL 9:4 p 283-296.

(8427)
Brenner M, Subrahmanyam M G, Uno J
The behavior of prices in the Nikkei spot and
futures market
JFE 1989 VOL 23 p 363.

(8428)
Brooks R
Investment decision making with index futures
and index futures options
JFM 1989 VOL 9:2 p 143-162.

(8429)
Maberly E D
The relationship between stock indices and stock
index futures from 3:00-3:15: a note
JFM 1989 VOL 9:3 p 271.

(8430)
Merrick J J J Jr
Early unwindings and rollovers of stock index
futures arbitrage programs: analysis and
implications for predicting expiration day effects
JFM 1989 VOL 9:2 p 101-112.

(8431)
Billingsley R S, Chance D M
The pricing and performance of stock index
futures spreads
JFM 1988 JUN VOL 8:3 p 303-318.

(8432)
Brooks R, Hand J
Evaluating the performance of stock portfolios
with index futures contracts
JFM 1988 FEB VOL 8:1 p 33-46.

(8433)
Edwards F R
Futures trading and cash market volatility: stock
index and index rate futures
JFM 1988 AUG VOL 8:4 p 421-440.

(8434)
Edwards F R
Does futures trading increase stock market
volatility
FAJ 1988 JAN-FEB VOL 44 p 63-69.

(8435)
Finnerty J E, Park H Y
How to profit from program trading
JPM 1988 WINTER VOL 14:2 p 40-46.

(8436)
Gould F J
Stock index futures: the arbitrage cycle and
portfolio investment
FAJ 1988 JAN-FEB VOL 44 p 48-62..

(8437)Grossman S J
Program trading and stock and futures price
volatility
JFM 1988 AUG VOL 8:4 p 413-420.

(8438)
Kawaller I G, Koch P D, Koch T W
The relationship between the S&P 500 index and
S&P 500 index futures prices
F R Bk Atlanta Ec Rev 1988 VOL 73:3.

(8439)
Kawaller I G, Koch T W
Managing cash flow risk in stock index futures:
the tail hedge
JPM 1988 FALL VOL 15:1 p 41-44.

(8440)
MacKinlay A C, Ramaswamy K
Index-futures arbitrage and the behavior of stock
index futures prices
RFS 1988 SUMMER VOL 1:2 p 137-158.

(8441)
Saunders E M, Mahajan A
An empirical examination of composite stock
index futures pricing
JFM 1988 APR VOL 8:2 p 210-228.

(8442)
Stoll H R
Index futures, program trading, and stock market
procedures
JFM 1988 AUG VOL 8:4 p 391-412.

(8443)
Stoll H R
Portfolio trading
JPM 1988 SUMMER VOL 14:4 p 20-24.

(8444)
Stoll H R, Whaley R E
Volatility and futures: message versus messenger
JPM 1988 WINTER VOL 14:2 p 20-22.

(8445)
Chang J S K, Loo J C H
Marking-to-market, stochastic interest rates and
discounts on stock index futures
JFM 1987 FEB VOL 7:1 p 15-20.

(8446)
Dubofsky D A
Hedging dividend capture strategies with stock
index futures
JFM 1987 OCT VOL 7:5 p 471-482.

(8447)
Graham D, Jennings R
Systematic risk, dividend yield and the hedging
performance of stock index futures
JFM 1987 FEB VOL 7:1 p 1-14.

(8448)
Herbst A F, McCormack J P, West E N
Investigation of a lead-lag relationship between
spot indices and their futures contracts
JFM 1987 AUG VOL 7:4 p 373-382.

(8449)
Kawaller I G, Koch P D, Koch T W
The temporal price relationship between S&P 500
Futures and the S&P 500 index
JF 1987 DEC VOL 42:5 p 1309-1330.

(8450)
Kling A
How the stock market can learn to live with
index futures and options
FAJ 1987 SEP-OCT VOL 43 p 33-39.

(8451)
Luskin D L
Index options and futures: the complete guide
Wiley, 1987.

(8452)
Maberly E D
An analysis of trading and nontrading period returns for the Value Line Composite Index; spot versus futures: a note
JFM 1987 OCT VOL 7:5 p 497-500.

(8453)
Merrick J J Jr
Volume determination in stock and stock index futures markets: an analysis of arbitrage and volatility effects
JFM 1987 OCT VOL 7:5 p 483-496.

(8454)
Stoll H R, Whaley R E
Expiration day effects of index options and futures
NYU, 1987.

(8455)
Stoll H R, Whaley R E
Program trading and expiration-day effects
FAJ 1987 MAR-APR VOL 43 p 16-28.

(8456)
Dyl E A, Maberly E D
The weekly pattern in stock index futures: a further note
JF 1986 DEC VOL 41:5 p 1149-1155.

(8457)
Eytan T H, Harpaz G
The pricing of futures and options contracts on the Value Line index
JF 1986 SEP VOL 41:4 p 843-855.

(8458)
Bowers J, Twite G
Arbitrage opportunities in the Australian share price index futures contract
AJM 1985 DEC VOL 10 p 1-30.

(8459)
Cornell B
The weekly pattern in stock returns : cash versus futures : a note
JF 1985 JUN VOL 40:2 p 583-588.

(8460)
Figlewski S
Hedging with stock index futures: Theory and application in a new market
JFM 1985 SUMMER VOL 5 p 183-199.

(8461)
Peters E
The growing efficiency in index-futures markets
JPM 1985 SUMMER VOL 11:4 p 52-56.

(8462)
Fabozzi F J, Kipnis G M eds.
Stock index futures
Dow Jones-Irwin, 1984.

(8463)
Figlewski S
Hedging performance and basis risk in stock index futures
JF 1984 JUL VOL 39:3 p 657-669.

(8464)
Figlewski S
Explaining the early discounts on stock index futures : The case for disequilibrium
FAJ 1984 JUL-AUG VOL 40:4 p 43-47.

(8465)
Hill J N, Schneeweis T
Reducing volatility with financial futures
FAJ 1984 NOV-DEC VOL 40:6 p 34-40.

(8466)
Modest D M
On the pricing of stock index futures.
JPM 1984 SUMMER VOL 10:4 p 51-57.

(8467)
Weiner N S
Stock index futures: a guide for traders, investors, and analysts
Wiley, 1984.

(8468)
Cornell B, French K
The pricing of stock index futures
JFM 1983 SPRING VOL p 1-14.

(8469)
Cornell B, French K R
Taxes and the pricing of stock index futures
JF 1983 JUN VOL 38:3 p 675-694.

(8470)
Gastineau G L, Madansky A
S & P 500 stock index futures evaluation tables
FAJ 1983 NOV-DEC VOL 39:6 p 68-76.

(8471)
Modest D, Sundaresan M
The relationship between spot and futures prices
in stock index futures markets: Some preliminary
evidence
JFM 1983 SUMMER VOL 3 p 15-41.

(8472)
Zeckhauser R, Niederhoffer V
The performance of market index futures
contracts
FAJ 1983 JAN-FEB VOL 39 p 59-65.

(8473)
Figlewski S, Kon S J
Portfolio management with stock index futures
FAJ 1982 JAN-FEB p 52-61.

(8474)
Grant D
Market index futures contracts: some thoughts on
delivery dates
FAJ 1982 MAY-JUN p 60-63.

(8475)
Niederhoffer V, Zeckhauser R
Market index futures contracts
FAJ 1980 JAN-FEB VOL 36 p 49-55.

21.22 Bond and bill futures

(8476)
Gagnon L, Mensah S, Blinder E
Hedging Canadian corporate debt: a comparative
study of the hedging effectiveness of Canadian
and US bond futures
JFM 1989 VOL 9:1 p 29-40.

(8477)
Hilliard J E, Jordan S D
Hedging interest rate risk with futures portfolios
under full-rank assumptions
JFQA 1989 JUN VOL 24:2 p 217-240.

(8478)
Ma C K, Rao R P, Sears R S
Limit moves and price resolution: the case of the
Treasury bond futures market
JFM 1989 VOL 9:4 p 321-336.

(8479)
Macdonald S S, Hein S E
Future rates and forward rates as predictors of
near-term Treasury bill rates
JFM 1989 VOL 9:3 p 249-262.

(8480)
Viswanath P V
Taxes and the futures-forward price difference in
the 91-day T-bill market
JMCB 1989 VOL 21 p 190-205.

(8481)
Allen L, Thurston T
Cash-futures arbitrage and forward-futures spreads
in the treasury bill market
JFM 1988 OCT VOL 8:5 p 563-574.

(8482)
Heaton H
On the possible tax-driven arbitrage opportunities
in the new municipal bonds futures contract
JFM 1988 JUN VOL 8:3 p 291-302.

(8483)
Hegde S P
An empirical analysis of implicit delivery options
in the Treasury bond futures contract
JBankF 1988 VOL 12:3 p 469-492.

(8484)
Labarge K P
Daily trading estimates for treasury bond futures
contract prices
JFM 1988 OCT VOL 8:5 p 533-562.

(8485)
MacDonald S S, Peterson R L, Koch T W
Using futures to improve treasury bill
performance
JFM 1988 APR VOL 8:2 p 167-184.

(8486)
Arak M, Fischer P, Goodman L
The municipal-treasury futures spread
JFM 1987 AUG VOL 7:4 p 355-372.

(8487)
Arak M, Goodman L S
Treasury bond futures: valuing the delivery
options
JFM 1987 JUN VOL 7:3 p 269-286.

(8488)
Barnhill T M, Jordan J V, Scale W E
Maturity and refunding effects on Treasury-bond
futures price variance
JFR 1987 SUMMER VOL 10:2 p 121-131.

(8489)
Batkin C A
Hedging mortgage-backed securities with treasury
bond futures
JFM 1987 DEC VOL 7:6 p 675-694..

(8490)**Bhattacharya A K**
Option expirations and treasury bond futures
prices
JFM 1987 FEB VOL 7:1 p 49-64.

(8491)
Hegde S P
The forecast performance of Treasury bond
futures contracts
JBFA 1987 SUMMER VOL 14:2 p 291-304.

(8492)
Lasser D J
Influence of Treasury bill futures trading on the
primary sale of the deliverable Treasury bill
FR 1987 NOV VOL 22:4.

(8493)
Livingston M
The effect of coupon level on treasury bond
futures delivery
JFM 1987 JUN VOL 7:3 p 303-310.

(8494)
Rzepczynski M S
Risk premiums in financial futures markets: the
case of treasury bond futures
JFM 1987 DEC VOL 7:6 p 653-662.

(8495)
Woodward R S
Interest rate arbitrage using the forwards and
futures markets, 1977-1985.
AE 1987 OCT VOL 19:10 p 1329-1336.

(8496)
Block S B, Gallagher T J
The use of interest rate futures and options by
corporate financial managers
FIN MGMT 1986 AUTUMN VOL 15 p 73.

(8497)
Kane A, Marcus A J
The quality option in the Treasury bond futures
market: An empirical assessment
JFM 1986 SUMMER VOL 6 p 231-248.

(8498)
Kane A, Marcus A J
Valuation and optimal exercise of the wild card
option in the treasury bond futures market
JF 1986 MAR VOL 41:1 p 195-207.

(8499)
Kobold K
Interest rate futures markets and capital market
theory: theoretical concepts and empirical
evidence
Berlin: Walter de Gruyter, 1986.

(8500)
Kuprianov A
Short-term interest rate futures
F R Bk Richmond Ec Rev 1986 VOL 72:5.

(8501)
Bank of England
Arbitrage between the spot and futures markets
for eurodollars
BEQB 1985 VOL 25 p 559-569.

(8502)
Benninga S, Smirlock M
An empirical analysis of the delivery option,
marking to market and the pricing of treasury
bond futures
JFM 1985 FALL VOL 5.

(8503)
Gendreau B C
Carrying costs and treasury bill futures
JPM 1985 FALL VOL 12:1 p 58-64.

(8504)
Hegde S P, Nunn K P Jr
A multivariate analysis of the cross-hedging
performance of T-bond and GNMA futures
markets
FR 1985 MAY VOL 20:2.

(8505)
Simpson W G, Ireland T C
The impact of financial futures on the cash
market for treasury bills
JFQA 1985 SEP VOL 20:3 p 371-379.

(8506)
Belongia M T, Santoni G J
Hedging interest rate risk with financial futures:
some basic principles
F R Bk St Louis Rev 1984 VOL 66:8.

(8507)
Booth J R, Smith R L II, Stolz R W
Use of interest rate futures by financial
institutions
JBR 1984 SPRING VOL 15:1.

(8508)
Eckardt W L
Equivalent delivery procedures for GNMA futures
contracts and options
JFM 1984 SPRING VOL 4 p 75-85.

(8509)
Elton E J, Gruber M J, Rentzler J
Intra-day tests of the efficiency of the treasury bill
futures market
REStat 1984 VOL 66 p 129.

(8510)
Hilliard J E
Hedging interest rate risk with futures portfolios
under term structure effects
JF 1984 DEC VOL 39:5 p 1547-1569.

(8511)
McCarty D E, Osteryoung J S, Roberts G S
Riding a hedged yield curve with Treasury bill
futures
JBR 1984 WINTER VOL 14:4.

(8512)
Draper D W
Financial futures for hedging long-term debt.
HBR 1983 MAR-APR VOL 61:2 p 172-176.

(8513)
Ho T S Y, Saunders A
Fixed rate loan commitments, take-down risk, and
the dynamics of hedging with futures
JFQA 1983 DEC VOL 18:4 p 499-516.

(8514)
Jacobs R L
Fixed rate lending and interest rate futures
hedging
JBR 1983 AUTUMN VOL 14:3.

(8515)
Koppenhaver G D
A T-bill futures hedging strategy for banks
F R Bk Dallas Ec Rev 1983 MAR.

(8516)
McCabe G M, Franckle C T
The effectiveness of rolling the hedge forward in
the Treasury Bill futures market
FIN MGMT 1983 SUMMER VOL 12 p 2129.

(8517)
Trainer F H
The uses of treasury bond futures in fixed-income
portfolio management
FAJ 1983 JAN-FEB VOL 39 p 27-34.

(8518)
Bearman A E
Treasury bill futures and determinants of the bid-ask spreads
QREB 1982 SUMMER VOL 22:2 p 84-100

(8519)
Gay G D ed., Kolb R W
Interest rate futures: concepts and issues
Dame, 1982.

(8520)
Kolb R W
Interest rate futures: a comprehensive introduction
Dame, 1982.

(8521)
Kolb R W, Gay G D
Immunizing bond portfolios with interest rate futures
FIN MGMT 1982 SUMMER VOL 11 p 81-89.

(8522)
Putnam B H
Managing interest rate risk: An introduction to financial futures and options
CFQ 1982 SPRING VOL 1 p 88-113.

(8523)
Cornell B
Taxes and the pricing of treasury bill futures contracts : a note
JF 1981 DEC VOL 36:5 p 1169-1176.

(8524)
Figlewski S
Futures trading and volatility in the GNMA market
JF 1981 MAY VOL 36:2 p 445-456.

(8525)
Kolb R A, Chiang R
Improving hedging performance using interest rate futures
FIN MGMT 1981 AUTUMN VOL 10 p 72-79.

(8526)
Leibowitz M L
A yield basis for financial futures
FAJ 1981 JAN-FEB VOL 37 p 42-51.

(8527)
Leventen A C
Financial futures and the revitalization of the fixed rate loan
CJWB 1981 FALL VOL 16:3 p 43-52.

(8528)
Dale C, Workman R
The arc sine law and the treasury bill futures market
FAJ 1980 NOV-DEC VOL 36 p 71-75.

(8529)
Jacobs R L, Jones R A
The treasury-bill futures market
JPE 1980 VOL 88 p 699.

(8530)
Loosigian A M
Interest rate futures
Dow Jones, 1980.

(8531)
Arak M, McCurdy C J
Interest rate futures
F R Bk New York Q Rev 1979-80 WINTER VOL 4:4.

(8532)
Capozza D R, Cornell B
Treasury bill pricing in the spot and futures markets
REStat 1979 NOV VOL 61:4 p 513-520.

(8533)
Arditti F D
Interest rate futures: an intermediate stage toward efficient risk reallocation
JBR 1978 AUTUMN VOL 9:3.

(8534)
Froewiss K C
GNMA futures: stabilizing or destabilizing?
F R Bk San Francisco Ec Rev 1978 SPRING.

(8535)
Lang R W, Rasche R H
A comparison of yields on futures contracts and implied forward rates
F R Bk St Louis Rev 1978 VOL 60:12.

(8536)
Poole W
Using T-bill futures to gauge interest-rate expectations
F R Bk San Francisco Ec Rev 1978 SPRING.

(8537)
Burger A E, Lang R W, Rasche R H
The Treasury bill futures market and market expectations of interest rates
F R Bk St Louis Rev 1977 VOL 59:6.

(8538)
Bacon P W, Williams R
Interest rate futures trading: New tool for the financial manager
FIN MGMT 1976 SPRING VOL 5 p 32.

21.3   Commodity futures

(8539)
Abken P A
An analysis of intra-market spreads in heating oil futures
JFM 1989 VOL 9:1 p 77.

(8540)
Aspel D, Cogen J, Rabin M
Hedging long term commodity swaps with futures
Global Finance Journal 1989 VOL 1:1.

(8541)
Boyle P P
The quality option and timing option in futures contracts
JF 1989 MAR VOL 44:1 p 101-114.

(8542)
Brorsen B W
Liquidity costs and scalping returns in the corn futures markets
JFM 1989 VOL 9:3 p 225-236..

(8543)**Brorsen B W, Oellermann C M, Farris P L**
The live cattle futures market and daily cash price movements
JFM 1989 VOL 9:4 p 273-282.

(8544)
Dalal A J, Arshanapalli B G
Effects of expected cash and futures prices on hedging and production: comments and extensions
JFM 1989 VOL 9:4 p 337-346.

(8545)
Hirschliefer D
Determinants of hedging and risk premia in commodity futures markets
JFQA 1989 SEP VOL 24:3 p 313-332.

(8546)
Kahl K H, Hudson M A, Ward C E
Cash settlement issues for live cattle futures contracts
JFM 1989 VOL 9:3 p 237-248.

(8547)
Lauterbach B, Monroe M
Evidence on the effect of information and noise trading on intraday gold futures returns
JFM 1989 VOL 9:4 p 297-306.

(8548)
Lien D-H D
Optimal hedging and spreading on wheat futures markets
JFM 1989 VOL 9:2 p 163-170.

(8549)
Ma C W
Forecasting efficiency of energy futures prices
JFM 1989 VOL 9:5 p 393-420.

(8550)
Murphy J A, Hilliard J E
An investigation into the equilibrium structure of the commodity futures market anomaly
FR 1989 FEB VOL 24:1 p 1-18.

(8551)
Oellermann C M, Brorsen B W, Farris P L
Price discovery for feeder cattle
JFM 1989 VOL 9:2 p 113-122.

(8552)
Schaede U
Forwards and futures in Tokugawa-period Japan: a new perspective on the Dojima rice market
JBankF 1989 SEP VOL 13:4-5 p 487-514.

(8553)
Shalen C T
The optimal maturity of hedges and participation
of hedgers in futures and forward markets
JFM 1989 VOL 9:3 p 215-224.

(8554)
Stewart T H ed.
Trading in futures
Woodhead-Faulkner, 1989.

(8555)
Barnhardt S W
Commodity futures prices and economic news: an
examination under alternative monetary regimes
JFM 1988 AUG VOL 8:4 p 483-510.

(8556)
Cornew R W
Commodity pool operators and their pools:
expenses and profitability
JFM 1988 OCT VOL 8:5 p 617-637.

(8557)
Edwards F R, Ma C
Commodity pool performance: is the information
contained in pool prospectuses useful
JFM 1988 OCT VOL 8:5 p 589-616.

(8558)
Elam E W, Vaught D
Risk and return in cattle and hog futures
JFM 1988 FEB VOL 8:1 p 79-87.

(8559)
Fort R, Quirk J
Normal backwardation and the inventory effect
JPE 1988 FEB VOL 96:1 p 81-99.

(8560)
Hirshleifer D
Risk, futures pricing, and the organization of
production in commodity markets
JPE 1988 DEC VOL 96:6 p 1206-1220.

(8561)
Hirshleifer D
Residual risk, trading costs, and commodity
futures risk premia
RFS 1988 SUMMER VOL 1:2 p 173.

(8562)
Kuhn B A
A note: do futures prices always reflect the
cheapest deliverable grade of the commodity
JFM 1988 FEB VOL 8:1 p 99-102.

(8563)
Lien D-H D
Hedger response to multiple grades of delivery on
futures markets
JFM 1988 VOL 8:6 p 687-702.

(8564)
Lukac L P, Brorsen B W, Irwin S H
Similarity of computer guided technical trading
systems
JFM 1988 FEB VOL 8:1 p 1-14.

(8565)
Ma C K, Soenen L A
Arbitrage opportunities in metal futures markets
JFM 1988 APR VOL 8:2 p 199-209.

(8566)
Oellermann C M, Farris P L
Note on trader concentration effects in feeder
cattle futures and comparison with live cattle
JFM 1988 FEB VOL 8:1 p 103-114.

(8567)
Aggarwal R, Sundararaghavan P S
Efficiency of the silver futures market: an
empirical study using daily data
JBankF 1987 VOL 11 p 49-64.

(8568)
Bohi D R, Toman M A
Futures trading and oil market conditions
JFM 1987 APR VOL 7:2 p 203-222.

(8569)
Chen K C, Sears R S, Tzang D-N
Oil prices and energy futures
JFM 1987 OCT VOL 7:5 p 501-518.

(8570)
Hudson M A, Leuthold R M, Sarassoro G F
Commodity futures price changes: recent evidence
for wheat, soybeans and live cattle
JFM 1987 JUN VOL 7:3 p 287-302.

(8571)
Irwin S H, Brorsen B W
A note on the factors affecting technical trading
system returns
JFM 1987 OCT VOL 7:5 p 591-596.

(8572)
Kenyon D, Kling K, Jordan J
Factors affecting agricultural futures price
variance
JFM 1987 FEB VOL 7:1 p 73-92.

(8573)
Labys W C
Primary commodity markets and models: an
international bibliography
Avebury, 1987.

(8574)
Lein D-H D
The inventory effect in commodity futures
markets: an empirical study
JFM 1987 DEC VOL 7:6 p 637-652.

(8575)
Malick W M, Ward R W
Stock effects and seasonality in the FCOJ futures
basis
JFM 1987 APR VOL 7:2 p 157-168.

(8576)
Markham J W
The history of commodity futures trading and its
regulation
Praeger, 1987.

(8577)
Milonas N T
The effects of USDA crop announcements on
commodity prices
JFM 1987 OCT VOL 7:5 p 571-590.

(8578)
Overdahl J A
The use of crude oil futures by the governments
of oil-producing states
JFM 1987 DEC VOL 7:6 p 603-618.

(8579)
Pruitt S W, Tawarangkoon W, Wei K C J
Chernobyl, commodities and chaos: an
examination of the reaction of commodity futures
prices to evolving information
JFM 1987 OCT VOL 7:5 p 555-570.

(8580)
Shaviro F W
An analysis of cash and futures prices in the
delivery period of maturing contracts in the coffee
"C" market, 1972-1981
JFM 1987 AUG VOL 7:4 p 413-442.

(8581)
So J C
Commodity futures risk premium and unstable
systematic risk
JFM 1987 JUN VOL 7:3 p 311-326.

(8582)
Tueting W F, King C Q
Funds protections: an overview of what happens
when a commodity broker becomes insolvent
JFM 1987 FEB VOL 7:1 p 93-102.

(8583)
Bank of England
The commodity futures market
BEQB 1986 VOL 26 p 216-224.

(8584)
Fesharaki F, Razavi H
Spot oil, netbacks and petroleum futures: the
emergence of a new oil market
Economist Intelligence Unit, 1986.

(8585)
Herbst A F
Commodity futures: markets, methods of analysis,
and management of risk
Wiley, 1986.

(8586)
Kahl K H, Tomek W G
Forward-pricing models for futures markets: some
statistical and interpretive issues
FRIS 1986 VOL 20:1.

(8587)
Murphy J J
Technical analysis of the futures markets: a
comprehensive guide to trading methods and
applications
New York Institute of Finance, 1986.

(8588)
Jagannathan R
An investigation of commodity futures prices
using the consumption-based intertemporal capital
asset pricing model
JF 1985 MAR VOL 40:1 p 175-191.

(8589)
Lee C F, Leuthold R M, Cordier J E
The stock market and the commodity futures
market: Diversification and arbitrage potential
FAJ 1985 JUL-AUG VOL 41 p 53-60.

(8590)
Nicholas D
Commodities futures trading: a guide to
information sources and computerized services
Mansell, 1985.

(8591)
Strohmaier J S, Dahl R P
Price relationships between wheat futures markets:
implications for hedging
FRIS 1985 VOL 19:3.

(8592)
Wasendorf R R
Commodities trading: the essential primer
Dow Jones-Irwin, 1985.

(8593)
Yamey B S et al.
How commodity futures markets work
Trade Policy Research Centre, 1985.

(8594)
Anderson R W ed.
The industrial organization of futures markets
Lexington Bks, 1984.

(8595)
Britto R
The simultaneous determination of spot and
futures prices in a simple model with production
risk
QJE 1984 VOL 99 p 351..

(8596)**Gunnin R**
Petroleum futures trading: Practical appliations by
the trade
Review of Research in Futures Trading 1984
VOL 3 p 129-144.

(8597)
Hazuka T B
Consumption   betas   and   backwardation   in
commodity markets
JF 1984 JUL VOL 39:3 p 647-657.

(8598)
Ho T S Y
Intertemporal commodity futures hedging and the
production decision
JF 1984 JUN VOL 39:2 p 351-376.

(8599)
Anderson R W, Danthine J P
Hedger diversity in futures markets
EJ 1983 JUN VOL 93 p 370-389.

(8600)
Kawai M
Price volatility of storable commodities under
rational expectations in spot and futures markets
IntER 1983 JUN VOL 24:2 p 435-459.

(8601)
Kawai M
Spot   and   futures   prices   of   nonstorable
commodities under rational expectations
QJE 1983 VOL 98 p 235.

(8602)
Protopapadakis A, Stoll H R
Spot and futures prices and the law of one price
JF 1983 DEC VOL 38:5 p 1431-1455.

(8603)
Asay M R
A note on the design of commodity option
contracts
JFM 1982 SPRING VOL 2 p 1-7.

(8604)
Gray R W, Peck A E
The Chicago wheat futures market: recent problems in historical perspective
FRIS 1981 VOL 18:1 p 89-115.

(8605)
Telser L G
Why there are organized futures markets
JLE 1981 VOL 24:1 p 1.

(8606)
Bodie Z, Rosansky V I
Risk and return in commodity futures
FAJ 1980 MAY-JUN p 27-40.

(8607)
Breeden D T
Consumption risk in futures markets
JF 1980 MAY VOL 35:2 p 503-520.

(8608)
Rolfo J
Optimal hedging under price and quantity uncertainty: The case of a cocoa producer
JPE 1980 VOL 88 p 100.

(8609)
Peck A E
Reflections of hedging on futures market activity
FRIS 1979-80 VOL 17:3.

(8610)
Stoll H R
Commodity futures and spot price determination and hedging in capital market equilibrium
JFQA 1979 NOV VOL 14 p 873.

(8611)
Tomek W G
Futures trading and market information: some new evidence
FRIS 1979-80 VOL 17:3.

(8612)
Goss B A, Yamey B S eds.
Economics of futures trading: readings. 2nd ed
Macmillan, 1978.

(8613)
Harris S et al.
Analysis of commodity markets for policy purposes
Trade Policy Research Centre, 1978.

(8614)
Watling T F, Morley J
Successful commodity futures trading: how you can make money in commodity markets
Business Bks, 1978.

(8615)
Black F
The pricing of commodity contracts
JFE 1976 VOL 3 p 167.

(8616)
Cargill T F, Rausser G C
Temporal price behavior in commodity futures markets
JF 1975 VOL 30 p 1043.

(8617)
Gold G
Modern commodity futures trading. 7th ed
New York: Commodity Research Bureau, 1975.

(8618)
Labys W C ed.
Quantitative models of commodity markets
Ballinger, 1975.

(8619)
Dusak K
Futures trading and investor returns: an investigation of commodity market risk premium
JPE 1973 NOV-DEC VOL 81:6 p 1387-1406.

(8620)
Kroll S, Shishko I
The commodity futures market guide
Har-Row, 1973.

(8621)
Sandor R L
Innovation by an exchange: a case study of the development of the plywood futures contract
JLE 1973 VOL 16 p 119.

(8622)
Bear R M
Margin levels and the behavior of futures prices
JFQA 1972 SEP VOL 7 p 1907.

(8623)
Leuthold R M
Random walk and price trends: the live cattle
futures market
JF 1972 SEP VOL 27 p 879-890.

(8624)
Gray R W, Rutledge D
The economics of commodity futures markets: A
survey
Review of Marketing and Agricultural Economics
1971 VOL 39.

(8625)
Labys W C, Granger C W J
Speculation, hedging and commodity price
forecasts
Heath, 1970.

(8626)
Poole W
McKinnon on futures markets and buffer stocks
JPE 1970 SEP-OCT VOL 78 p 1185-1190.

(8627)
Stevenson R A, Bear R M
Commodity futures: trends or random walks?
JF 1970 MAR VOL 25 p 65-81.

(8628)
Ehrich R L
Cash-futures price relationships for live beef cattle
American Journal of Agricultural Economics 1969
FEB VOL 51 p 26-39.

(8629)
Teweles R J, Harlow C V, Stone H L
The commodity futures trading guide
McGraw, 1969.

(8630)
Snape R H
Price relationships on the Sydney wool futures
market
Ec 1968 MAY VOL 35.

(8631)
Larson A B
Price prediction on the egg futures market
FRIS 1967 VOL 7 Suppl p 49-64.

(8632)
McKinnon R
Futures markets, buffer stocks, and income
stability for primary producers
JPE 1967 DEC VOL 75 p 844-861.

(8633)
Rockwell C S
Normal backwardation, forecasting and the return
to commodity futures traders
FRIS 1967 VOL 7 Suppl p 107-130.

(8634)
Telser L G
The supply of speculative services in wheat, corn
and soybeans
FRIS 1967 VOL 7 Suppl p 131-176.

(8635)
Working H
Tests of a theory concerning floor trading on
commodity exchanges
FRIS 1967 VOL 7 Suppl p 5-48.

(8636)
Weymar F H
The supply of storage revisited
AER 1966 DEC VOL 56 p 1226-1234.

(8637)
Smidt S
A test of the serial independence of price changes
in soybean futures
FRIS 1965 VOL 5 p 117-136.

(8638)
Snape R H, Yamey B S
Test of the effectiveness of hedging
JPE 1965 OCT VOL 73 p 540-544.

(8639)
Venkataramanan L S
The theory of futures trading
Asia, 1965.

(8640)
Gray W R
The attack upon potato futures trading in the
United States
FRIS 1964 VOL 4 p 97-121.

(8641)
Gray W R
Fundamental price behavior characteristics in
commodity futures
Futures Trading Seminar, Mimir, 1963.

(8642)
Working H
Futures markets under renewed attack
FRIS 1963 FEB VOL 5 p 13-24.

(8643)
Gray W R
The relationship among three futures markets: an
example of the importance of speculation
FRIS 1961 FEB VOL 2 p 21-32.

(8644)
Gray W R
The search for a risk premium
JPE 1961 JUN VOL 69 p 250-260.

(8645)
Houthakker H S
Systematic and random elements in short-term
price movements
AER 1961 MAR VOL 51 p 164-172.

(8646)
Larson A B
Estimation of hedging and speculative positions in
futures markets
FRIS 1961 NOV VOL 2 p 203-212.

(8647)
Stein J L
The simultaneous determination of spot and
future prices
AER 1961 DEC VOL 51 p 1012-1025.

(8648)
Gray W R
The characteristic bias in some thin futures
markets
FRIS 1960 NOV VOL 1 p 296-312..

(8649) **Larson A B**

Measurement of a random process in futures
prices
FRIS 1960 NOV VOL 1 p 313-324.

(8650)
Working H
Price effects of futures trading
FRIS 1960 FEB VOL 1 p 3-31.

(8651)
Houthakker H S
The scope and limits of futures trading
(in Abromovitz M ed., Allocation of economic
resources. Stanford U Pr, 1959.)

(8652)
Telser L G
Futures trading and the storage of cotton and
wheat
JPE 1958 JUN VOL 66 p 233-255.

(8653)
Brennan M J
The supply of storage
AER 1957 MAR VOL 47 p 50-72.

(8654)
Houthakker H S
Can speculators forecast prices?
REStat 1957 MAY VOL 39 p 143-151.

(8655)
Johnson L L
Price instability, hedging and trade volume in the
coffee market
JPE 1957 AUG VOL 65.

(8656)
Houthakker H S
Commodity futures IV: an empirical test of the
theory of normal backwardation
Cowles Commission Discussion Paper, Economics,
No 2124, 22 JUN 1955.

(8657)
Working H
Price effects of scalping and day trading
Proceedings of the Chicago Board of Trade
Annual Symposium 1954 p 114-139.

(8658)
Working H
Whose markets? Evidence on some aspects of futures trading
JM 1954 JUL VOL 19.

(8659)
Graf T F
Hedging--how effective is it?
JFarmE 1953 AUG VOL 35 p 398-413.

(8660)
Houthakker H S, Telser L G
Commodity futures II: gains and losses of hedgers and futures speculators
Cowles Commission Discussion Paper, Economics, No 2090, 7 DEC 1952.

(8661)
Yamey B S
An investigation of hedging on an organized produce exchange
MS 1951 SEP VOL 19.

(8662)
Schultz T W
Spot and futures prices as production guides
AER 1949 MAY VOL 39.

(8663)
Howell L D
Analysis of hedging and other operations in grain futures
US Dept of Agriculture Technical Bulletin No 971 1948 AUG.

(8664)
Vaile R
Inverse carrying charges in futures markets
JFarmE 1948 AUG VOL 30 p 574-575.

(8665)
Working H
Theory of the inverse carrying charge in futures markets
JFarmE 1948 VOL 30 p 1-28.

(8666)
Johnson D G
Forward prices for agriculture
U of Chicago Pr, 1947.

(8667)
Vance L
Grain market forces in the light of inverse carrying charges
JFarmE 1946 NOV VOL 28 p 1036-1040.

(8668)
Blau G
Some aspects of the theory of futures trading
REStud 1944 VOL 12

(8669)
Vaile R
Cash and futures price of corn
JM 1944 JUL VOL 9.

(8670)
Working H
Quotations on commodity futures as price forecasts
Em 1942 VOL 10 p 30-52.

(8671)
Hoos S, Working H
Price relations of Liverpool wheat futures with special reference to the December-March spread
Wheat 1940 NOV VOL 16 p 101-143.

(8672)
Williams J B
Speculation and the carryover
QJE 1936 MAY VOL 50.

(8673)
Irwin H S
Seasonal cycles in aggregates of wheat futures contracts
JPE 1935 VOL 43 p 278-288.

(8674)
Working H
Price relations between July and September wheat futures at Chicago since 1885
Wheat 1933 p 187-238.

(8675)
Emery H C
Legislation against futures
Political Science Quarterly 1895 MAR.

21.4 Swaps

(8676)
Das S
Swap financing: interest rate and currency swaps, LTFX, FRAs, caps, floors and collars: structures, pricing, applications and markets
IFR Publishing, 1989.

(8677)
Kawaller I G
Interest rate swaps versus Eurodollar strips
FAJ 1989 SEP-OCT VOL 45 p 55-61.

(8678)
Wall L D
Interest rate swaps in an agency theoretic model with uncertain interest rates
JBankF 1989 MAY VOL 13:2 p 261-270.

(8679)
Wall L D, Pringle J J
Alternative explanations of interest rate swaps: a theoretical and empirical analysis
FIN MGMT 1989 SUMMER VOL 18 p 59-73.

(8680)
Arak M, Estrella A, Goodman L
Interest rate swaps: An alternative explanation
FIN MGMT 1988 SUMMER VOL 17 p 12-18.

(8681)
Henderson S K, Price J A M
Currency and interest rate swaps. 2nd ed
Butterworth, 1988.

(8682)
Smith C W Jr, Smithson C W, Wakeman L M
The market for interest rate swaps
FIN MGMT 1988 WINTER VOL 17 p 34-44.

(8683)
Smith D J
Measuring the gains from "arbitraging" the swap market
FE 1988 MAR-APR.

(8684)
Wall L D, Pringle J J
Interest rate swaps: a review of the issues
F R Bk Atlanta Ec Rev 1988 VOL 73:6.

(8685)
Bank of England
Recent developments in the swap market
BEQB 1987 VOL 27 p 66-80.

(8686)
Felgran S D
Interest rate swaps: Use, risk, and prices
New England Economic Review 1987 NOV-DEC.

(8687)
Gooch A C, Klein L B
Swap agreement documentation: annotated sample agreements for interest rate exchange; currency exchange; master interest rate exchange; swap confirmations
Euromoney Publications, 1987.

(8688)
Stillet D
Unravelling the asset swap
Euromoney Corporate Finance APR 1987.

(8689)
Turnbull S M
Swaps: A zero sum game?
FIN MGMT 1987 SPRING VOL 16 p 15-21.

(8690)
Antl B ed.
Swap finance
Euromoney Publications, 1986.

(8691)
Bicksler J L, Chen A H
An economic analysis of interest rate swaps
JF 1986 JUL VOL 41:3 p 645-655.

(8692)
International Financing Review
Inside the swap market. 2nd ed
IFR Publishing, 1986.

(8693)
Mahajan A, Mehta D
Swaps, expectations and exchange rates
JBankF 1986 VOL 10 p 7.

(8694)
Smith C W Jr, Smithson C W, Wakeman L M
The evolving market for swaps
MCFJ 1986 WINTER VOL 3 p 20-32.

(8695)
Arnold T S
How to do interest rate swaps
HBR 1984 SEP-OCT VOL 62:5 p 96-101.

(8696)
Mitello F C
Swap financing, a new approach to international
transactions
FE 1984 OCT VOL 52.

22 Capital expenditures

(8697)
Chaney P K
Moral hazard and capital budgeting
JFR 1989 SUMMER VOL 12:2 p 113-128.

(8698)
Conine T E Jr, Jensen O W, Tamarkin M
On optimal production and the market to book
ratio given limited shareholder diversification
MSci 1989 VOL 35 p 1004.

(8699)
Woods J C, Randall M R
The net present value of future investment
opportunities: its impact on shareholder wealth
and implications for capital budgeting theory
FIN MGMT 1989 SUMMER VOL 18 p 85-92.

(8700)
Pindyck R S
Irreversible investment, capacity choice, and the
value of the firm
AER 1988 VOL 78:5 p 969-985.

(8701)
Mamer J W, Shogan A W
A constrained capital budgeting problem with
applications to repair kit selection
MSci 1987 JUN VOL 33:6 p 800-809.

(8702)
Mott G
Investment appraisal for managers: a guide to
profit planning. 2nd ed
Gower, 1987.

(8703)
Bromiley P
Corporate capital investment: a behavioral
approach
Cambridge U Pr, 1986.

(8704)
Buser S A
La Place transforms as present value rules : a
note
JF 1986 MAR VOL 41:1 p 243-247.

(8705)
Law W A
A corporation is more than its stock
HBR 1986 MAY-JUN VOL 64:3 p 80-83.

(8706)
Hodder J E, Riggs H E
Pitfalls in evaluating risky projects
HBR 1985 JAN-FEB VOL 63:1 p 128-135.

(8707)
Horvath P A
A pedagogic note on intra-period compounding
and discounting
FR 1985 FEB VOL 20:1.

(8708)
McConnell J J, Muscarella C J
Corporate capital expenditure decisions and the
market value of the firm
JFE 1985 VOL 14 p 399.

(8709)
Mikkelson W H, Ruback R S
An empirical analysis of the interfirm equity
investment process
JFE 1985 DEC VOL 14 p 523-553.

(8710)
Shapiro A C
Corporate strategy and the capital budgeting
decision
MCFJ 1985 SPRING VOL 3 p 22-36.

(8711)
Williams J T
Trading and valuing depreciable assets
JFE 1985 VOL 14 p 283.

(8712)
Bernanke B S
Irreversibility, uncertainty and cyclical investment
QJE 1983 VOL 98 p 85.

(8713)
Prastacos G P
Optimal sequential investment decisions
MSci 1983 JAN VOL 29:1 p 118-134.

(8714)
Armstrong R D, Cook W D, Kung D S
Capital budgeting and Lagrangian relaxation : a
case study
Omega 1982 VOL 10:3 p 321-327.

(8715)
Grant E L, Ireson W G, Leavenworth R S
Principles of engineering economy. 7th ed
Ronald, 1982.

(8716)
Greenberg J S
Investment decisions: the influence of risk and
other factors
AMA, 1982.

(8717)
Herbst A F
Capital budgeting
Har-Row, 1982.

(8718)
Rivers R, Oxner T H
A network simulation for budgeting
Omega 1982 VOL 10:2 p 135-155.

(8719)
Crum R L, Derkinderen F G J eds.
Capital budgeting under conditions of uncertainty
Martinus Nijhoff, 1981.

(8720)
Quirin G D, Wiginton J C
Analyzing capital expenditures
Irwin, 1981.

(8721)
Beranek W
The AB procedure and capital budgeting
JFQA 1980 JUN VOL 15 p 391.

(8722)
Greene M T, Fielitz B D
Long-term dependence and least squares
regression in investment analysis
MSci 1980 OCT VOL 26:10 p 1031-1038.

(8723)
von Ungern Sternberg T
Current profits and investment behavior
BellJ 1980 AUTUMN VOL 11:2 p 745-748.

(8724)
Kim M K
Inflationary effects in the capital investment
process: an empirical examination
JF 1979 SEP VOL 34:4 p 941-950.

(8725)
Venezia I, Brenner M
The optimal duration of growth investments and
search
JB 1979 JUL VOL 52:3 p 393-407

(8726)
Felsen J
Cybernetic approach to investment decision
making
Omega 1978 VOL 6:3 p 237-247

(8727)
Roenfeldt R L, Cooley P L
Predicting corporate profitability for investment
selection
JBFA 1978 SPRING VOL 5:1 p 57-65.

(8728)
Yawitz J B
Externalities and risk investments
JF 1977 VOL 32 p 1143.

(8729)
Carsberg B V, Hope A
Business investment decisions under inflation:
theory and practice
ICAEW, 1976.

(8730)
Sampson A A
Liquidity constraints on investment and dividends
JBFA 1976 SUMMER VOL 3:2 p 131-142.

(8731)
Bierman H Jr, Smidt S
The capital budgeting decision: economic analysis
and financing of investment projects. 4th ed
Collier Macmillan, 1975.

(8732)
Blume M E, Friend I
Risk investment strategy and the long run rates of
return
REStat 1974 AUG VOL 56:3 p 259-269.

(8733)
Henry C
Investment decisions under uncertainty: The
"irreversibility effect"
AER 1974 VOL 64 p 1006-1012.

(8734)
Osteryoung J
Capital budgeting: Long-term asset selection
Columbus, Ohio: Grid, 1974.

(8735)
Krouse C G
On the theory of optimal investment, dividends
and growth in the firm
AER 1973 VOL 63 p 269-279.

(8736)
Merrett A J, Sykes A
Capital budgeting and company finance. 2nd ed
Longman, 1973..

(8737)Merrett A J, Sykes A
The finance and analysis of capital projects. 2nd
ed
Longman, 1973.

(8738)
Smith G W
Engineering   economy: analysis   of   capital
expenditures. 2nd ed
Iowa St U Pr, 1973.

(8739)
Bierman H Jr, Hausman W H
The resolution of investment uncertainty through
time
MSci 1972 AUG VOL 18 p B654-B662.

(8740)
Boness A J
Capital budgeting: the public and private sectors
Longman, 1972.

(8741)
Hillman R H
How to redeploy assets
HBR 1971 NOV-DEC VOL 49:6 p 95.

(8742)
Jean W H
The analytical theory of finance: a study of the
investment decision process of the individual and
the firm
HR & W, 1970.

(8743)
Johnson R W
Capital budgeting
Wadsworth Pub, 1970.

(8744)
Oakford R V
Capital budgeting--a quantitative evaluation of
investment alternatives
Ronald, 1970.

(8745)
Murdick R G, Deming D D
The management of capital expenditures
McGraw, 1968.

(8746)
DeGarmo E P
Engineering economy. 4th ed
Macmillan, 1967.

(8747)
Diggory T G, Wade E
Capital expenditure
Anbar, 1967.

(8748)
Ijiri Y
On the convergence of periodic reinvestments by
an amount equal to depreciation
MSci 1967 JAN VOL 13 p 321-335.

(8749)
Quirin G D
The capital expenditure decision
Irwin, 1967.

(8750)
Terborgh G W
Business investment management
Machinery and Allied Products Institute and
Council for Technological Advancement, 1967.

(8751)
Alberts W W
Capital investment by the firm in plant and
equipment
JF 1966 MAY VOL 21 p 178-201.

(8752)
Jack A B
The capital expenditure function
MS 1966 MAY VOL 34 p 133-158.

(8753)
Vickers D
Profitability and reinvestment rates: a note on the
Gordon paradox
JB 1966 JUL VOL 39 p 366-370.

(8754)
Iglehart D L
Capital accumulation and production for the firm:
optimal dynamic policies
MSci 1965 NOV VOL 11.

(8755)
Williams B R,   Scott W P
Investment proposals and decisions
Allen, 1965.

(8756)
Dyckman T R
On the investment decision
AR 1964 APR VOL 39 p 285-295.

(8757)
Harvard Business Review
Capital investment decisions [15 articles reprinted
from Harvard Business Reviews, 1954 to 1964]
Harvard U, 1964.

(8758)
Taylor G A
Managerial and engineering economy: economic
decision-making
Van N-Rein, 1964.

(8759)
Theil H
Optimal decision rules for government and
industry
N Holland, 1964.

(8760)
Solomon M B Jr
Investment decisions in small business
U of Ky Pr, 1963.

(8761)
Gort M
Systematic errors in budgeting capital outlays
REStat 1962 FEB VOL 44 p 72-75.

(8762)
Vandell R F,   Vancil R F
Cases in capital budgeting
Irwin, 1962.

(8763)
Sunbury D H,   Thompson G C
Improving control over capital expenditures
Natl Ind Conf Bd, Conference Board Business
Record 1961 OCT VOL 18 p 22-33.

(8764)
Walker R G
The judgment factor in investment decisions
HBR 1961 MAR-APR VOL 39 p 93-99.

(8765)
Whyte L G
Some basic principles of investment
Cambridge U Pr, 1961.

(8766)
Dean J
Management of capital expenditures
U of Tex Busn, 1960.

(8767)
Terborgh G W
Studies in the analysis of business investment
projects
Machinery and Allied Products Institute and
Council for Technological Advancement, 1960-61.

(8768)
Bodenhorn D
On the problem of capital budgeting
JF 1959 DEC VOL 14 p 473-492.

(8769)
Terborgh G W
An introduction to business investment analysis
Machinery and Allied Products Institute and
Council for Technological Advancement, 1958.

(8770)
Bierman H Jr, Smidt S
Capital budgeting and the problem of reinvesting cash proceeds
JB 1957 OCT VOL 30 p 276-279.

(8771)
Hill H G Jr
Capital expenditures management
JB 1955 OCT VOL 28 p 285-290.

(8772)
Mayer T, Sonenblum S
Lead times for fixed investment
REStat 1955 AUG VOL 37 p 300-304.

22.1   Aggregate capital expenditure

(8773)
Craine R
Risky business: the allocation of capital
JME 1989 VOL 23 p 201.

(8774)
Moon P, Hodges S
Implications of the recent tax changes for corporate capital investment
JBFA 1989 SPRING VOL 16:1 p 25.

(8775)
Mullins M, Wadhwani S B
The effect of the stock market on investment: a comparative study
EER 1989 VOL 33 p 939.

(8776)
Angell R J
The effect of the Tax Reform Act on capital investment decisions
FIN MGMT 1988 WINTER VOL 17 p 82-86.

(8777)
Farimani M, Buongiorno J, Thompson H E
A financial model of investment, with an application to the paper industry
AE 1988 JUN VOL 20:6 p 767-784.

(8778)
Ferris S P, Makhija A K
Inflation effect on corporate capital investment
JBusR 1988 MAY VOL 16:3 p 251-260.

(8779)
Bar-Yosef S, Callen J L, Livnat J
Autoregressive modeling of earnings-investment causality
JF 1987 MAR VOL 42:1 p 11-28.

(8780)
Moore M L, Steece B M, Swenson C W
An analysis of the impact of state income tax rates and bases on foreign investment
AR 1987 OCT VOL 62:4 p 671-685.

(8781)
Fullerton D, Henderson Y K
Long-run effects of the accelerated cost recovery system
REStat 1985 VOL 67 p 363.

(8782)
Bernanke B S
The determinants of investment: Another look
AER 1983 VOL 73 P+P p 71-75.

(8783)
Fama E F, Gibbons M R
Inflation, real returns and capital investment
JME 1982 VOL 9 p 297-323.

(8784)
Anderson G J
A new approach to the empirical investigation of investment expenditures
EJ 1981 MAR VOL 91:361 p 88-105.

(8785)
Usher D ed.
The measurement of capital
U of Chicago Pr, 1980.

(8786)
Wunder H F
Tax incentives and the investment function of electric utilities
EE 1979 FALL VOL 25:1 p 39-51.

(8787)
Eisner R
Factors in business investment
Ballinger, 1978.

(8788)
Palash C J
Tax policy: its impact on investment incentives
F R Bk New York Q Rev 1978 SUMMER VOL
3:2.

(8789)
Scheinkman J A
Stability of separable Hamiltonians and
investment theory
REStud 1978 OCT VOL 45 p 559-574.

(8790)Tatom J A, Turley J E
Inflation and taxes: disincentives for capital
formation
F R Bk St Louis Rev 1978 VOL 60:1.

(8791)
Corcoran P J
Inflation, taxes, and corporate investment
incentives
F R Bk New York Q Rev 1977 AUTUMN VOL
2.

(8792)
Cowing T G, Smith V K
A note on the variability of the replacement
investment capital stock ratio
REStat 1977 MAY VOL 59:2 p 238-243.

(8793)
Birch E M, Siebert C D
Uncertainty, permanent demand, and investment
behavior
AER 1976 MAR VOL 66:1 p 15-27.

(8794)
Craine R
Investment adjustment costs and uncertainty
IntER 1975 OCT VOL 16:3 p 648-661.

(8795)
Gardner R, Sheldon R
Financial conditions and the time path of
equipment expenditures
REStat 1975 MAY VOL 57:2 p 164-170.

(8796)
Sandmo A
Investment incentives and the corporate income
tax
JPE 1974 VOL 82 p 287.

(8797)
Elliott J W
Theories of corporate investment behavior
revisited
AER 1973 VOL 63 p 195-208.

(8798)
Poindexter J C, Jones C P
The effect of recent tax policy changes on
manufacturing investment
QREB 1973 VOL 13:4 p 79.

(8799)
Summer M T
Investment and corporate taxation
JPE 1973 VOL 81 p 982.

(8800)
Thomas R
The change in corporation tax and the incentive
to invest
JBF 1973 SPRING VOL 5:1 p 69-75.

(8801)
Jorgenson D W
Investment behavior and the production function
BellJ 1972 SPRING VOL 3:1 p 220-251.

(8802)
Jorgenson D W, Hunter J, Nadir M I
The predictive performance of economic models
of quarterly investment behavior
Em 1970 MAR VOL 38 p 213-224.

(8803)
Jorgenson D W, Siebert C D
A comparison of alternative theories of corporate
investment behavior
AER 1968 SEP VOL 58 p 681-772.

(8804)
Jorgenson D W, Siebert C D
Optimal capital accumulation and corporate
investment behavior
JPE 1968 NOV-DEC VOL 76 p 1123-1151.

(8805)
Evans M K
A study of industry investment decisions
REStat 1967 MAY VOL 49 p 151-164.

(8806)
Ferber R ed.
Determinants of investment behavior: a conference of the Universities National Bureau Committee for Economic Research
Natl Bur Econ Res, 1967.

(8807)
Gould J P
Market value and the theory of investment of the firm
AER 1967 SEP VOL 57 p 910-913.

(8808)
Anderson W H L
Corporate finance and fixed investment: an econometric study
Harvard Busn, 1964.

(8809)
Hammer F S
The demand for physical capital: application of a wealth model
P-H, 1964.

(8810)
Meyer J R, Glauber R R
Investment decisions, economic forecasting and public policy
Harvard Busn, 1964.

(8811)
Jorgenson D W
Capital theory and investment behavior
AER 1963 MAY VOL 53 p 247-259.

(8812)
Kuh E
Capital stock growth: a micro-econometric approach
N Holland, 1963.

(8813)
Haavelmo T
A study in the theory of investment
U of Chicago Pr, 1960.

(8814)
Kuh E
Capital theory and capital budgeting
Met 1960 AUG-DEC VOL 12 p 64-80.

(8815)
Meyer J R, Kuh E
The investment decision: an empirical study
Harvard U Pr, 1957.

(8816)
White W H
Interest inelasticity of investment demand: the case from business attitude surveys re-examined
AER 1956 SEP VOL 46 p 565-587.

(8817)
Hoover E M
Some institutional factors in business investment decisions
AER 1954 MAY VOL 44 p 201-213.

22.11   Tobin's q

(8818)
Ben-Horim M, Callen J L
The cost of capital, Macaulay's duration, and Tobin's q
JFR 1989 SUMMER VOL 12:2 p 143-156.

(8819)
McFarland H
Evaluating q as an alternative to the rate of return in measuring profitability
REStat 1988 VOL 70 p 614.

(8820)
Montgomery C A, Wernerfelt B
Diversification, Ricardian rents, and Tobin's q
RandJ 1988 WINTER VOL 19:4 p 623.

(8821)
Nguyen T-H, Bernier G
Beta and q in a simultaneous framework with pooled data
REStat 1988 VOL 70 p 520.

(8822)
Chirinko R S
Tobin's Q and financial policy
JME 1987 VOL 19 p 69

(8823)
Jose M L, Nichols L M, Stevens J L
Contributions of diversification, promotion, and
R&D to the value of multiproduct firms: A
Tobin's q approach
FIN MGMT 1986 WINTER VOL 15 p 33-42.

(8824)
Stevens J L
Tobin's q ratio, monopoly earnings, risk and
dividend policy
JBusR 1986 JUNE VOL 14:3 p 213-224.

(8825)
Edwards J S S, Keen M J
Taxes, investment and Q
REStud 1985 VOL 52 p 665.

(8826)
Wildasin D E
The q theory of investment with many capital
goods
AER 1984 VOL 74 p 203-210.

(8827)
Abel A B
Dynamic effects of permanent and temporary tax
policies in a q model of investment
JME 1982 VOL 9 p 353

(8828)
Chappell H W, Cheng D C
Expectations, Tobin's q and investment: a note
JF 1982 MAR VOL 37:1 p 231-236.

(8829)
Lindenberg E B, Ross S A
Tobin's q ratio and industrial organization
JB 1981 JAN VOL 54:1 p 1-32.

(8830)
Ciccolo J, Fromm G
"q," corporate investment, and balance sheet
behavior
JMCB 1980 MAY VOL 12:2 p 294-307.

(8831)
Yoshikawa H
On the "q" theory of investment
AER 1980 VOL 70 p 739-743.

(8832)
Ciccolo J, Fromm G
"q" and the theory of investment
JF 1979 MAY VOL 34:2 p 535-547.

(8833)
**Malkiel B G, Von Furstenberg G M, Watson H
S**
Expectations, Tobin's q and industry investment
JF 1979 MAY VOL 34:2 p 549-561.

(8834)
Von Furstenberg G M
Corporate investment: Does market valuation
really matter?
Brookings Papers on Economic Activity 1977 NO
2 p 347-397.

22.2 Organization and determinants of a firm's capital expenditures

(8835)
Cooper K, Richards R M
Investing the Alaskan project cash flows: The
Sohio experience
FIN MGMT 1988 SUMMER VOL 17 p 58-70.

(8836)
Marsh P, Barwise T P, Thomas K et al.
Managing strategic investment decisions in large
diversified companies
(in Pettigrew A M ed., Competitiveness and the
management process. Blackwell, 1988.)

(8837)
Pohlman R A, Santiago E S, Markel F L
Cash flow estimation practices of large firms
FIN MGMT 1988 SUMMER VOL 17 p 71-79.

(8838)
Fazzari S M, Athey M J
Asymmetric information, financing constraints and
investment
REStat 1987 VOL 69 p 481.

(8839)
Pruitt S W, Gitman L J
Capital budgeting forecast biases: Evidence from the Fortune 500
FIN MGMT 1987 SPRING VOL 16 p 46-51.

(8840)
Statman M, Caldwell D
Applying behavioral finance to capital budgeting: Project terminations
FIN MGMT 1987 WINTER VOL 16 p 7-15.

(8841)
Bower J L
Managing the resource allocation process: a study of corporate planning and investment. Rev ed
Harvard Bus Pr, 1986.

(8842)
Dotan A, Ovadia A
A capital-budgeting decision-the case of a multinational corporation operating in high inflation countries
JBusR 1986 OCT VOL 14:5 p 403-410..

(8843)**Farragher E J**
Capital budgeting practices of non-industrial firms
EE 1986 SUMMER VOL 31:4 p 293-302.

(8844)
Ghemawat P, Caves R E
Capital commitment and profitability : an empirical investigation.
OEP 1986 NOV VOL 38 Suppl p 94-110.

(8845)
Hodder J E
Evaluation of manufacturing investments: A comparison of U S and Japanese practices
FIN MGMT 1986 SPRING VOL 15 p 17-24.

(8846)
Kennedy J A, Sugden K F
Ritual and reality in capital budgeting
Management Accounting 1986 FEB p 34-37.

(8847)
Ross M
Capital budgeting practices of twelve large manufacturers
FIN MGMT 1986 WINTER VOL 15 p 15-22.

(8848)
White B E, Smith G W
Comparing the effectiveness of ten capital investment ranking criteria
EE 1986 WINTER VOL 31:2 p 151-163.

(8849)
Canada J R, Miller N P
Review of surveys on use of capital investment evaluation techniques
EE 1985 WINTER VOL 30:2 p 193-200.

(8850)
Johnson S B
Motivating division managers to select tax incentive compatible investments
EE 1985 SUMMER VOL 30:4 p 329-346.

(8851)
Logue D E, Tapley T C
Performance monitoring and the timing of cash flows
FIN MGMT 1985 AUTUMN VOL 14 p 34-39.

(8852)
Statman M, Tyebjee T T
Optimistic capital budgeting forecasts: An experiment
FIN MGMT 1985 AUTUMN VOL 14 p 27-33.

(8853)
Kim S-H, Crick T, Farragher E J
Foreign capital budgeting practices used by the US and non-US multinational companies
EE 1984 SPRING VOL 29:3 p 207-215.

(8854)
Klammer T P, Walker A C
The continuing increase in the use of sophisticated capital budgeting techniques
CMR 1984 FALL p 137-148.

(8855)
Scott D F Jr, Petty J W II
Capital budgeting practices in large American firms: a retrospective analysis and synthesis
FR 1984 MAR VOL 19:1.

(8856)
Stanley M T, Block S B
A survey of multinational capital budgeting
FR 1984 MAR VOL 19:1.

(8857)
Larcker D F
The association between performance plan adoption and corporate capital investment
JAE 1983 APR VOL 5 p 3-30.

(8858)
Runyon L R
Capital expenditure decision making in small firms
JBusR 1983 VOL 11 p 389-397.

(8859)
Sharon E M
The budget-limit effect on the delegation of the capital budgeting authority: the case of sequential and frequent investment decisions
MSci 1983 MAR VOL 29:3 p 289-299.

(8860)
Kim S-H
An empirical study on the relationship between capital budgeting practices and earnings performance
EE 1982 SPRING VOL 27:3 p 185-196.

(8861)
Pinches G E
Myopia, capital budgeting and decision making
FIN MGMT 1982 AUTUMN VOL 11 p 6-19.

(8862)
Kelly M W
Foreign investment evaluation practices of US multinational corporations
UMI Research Pr, 1981.

(8863)
Scapens R W, Sale J T
Performance measurement and formal capital expenditure controls in divisionalized companies
JBFA 1981 AUTUMN VOL 8 p 389-420.

(8864)
Aggarwal R
Corporate use of sophisticated capital budgeting techniques: A strategic perspective and a critique of survey results
Interfaces 1980 APR p 31-34.

(8865)
Oblak D J, Helm R J
Survey and analysis of capital budgeting methods used by multinationals
FIN MGMT 1980 WINTER VOL 9 p 37.

(8866)
Rosenblatt M J
A survey and analysis of capital budgeting decision processes in multi-division firms
EE 1980 SUMMER VOL 25:4 p 259-273.

(8867)
Clark J J, Hindelang T J, Pritchard R D
Capital budgeting: Planning and control of capital expenditures
P-H, 1979.

(8868)
Obel B, Vander Weide J H
On the decentralized capital budgeting problem under uncertainty
MSci 1979 SEP VOL 25:9 p 873-883.

(8869)
Sharon E M
Decentralization of the capital budgeting authority
MSci 1979 JAN VOL 25:1 p 31-42.

(8870)
Beardsley G, Mansfield E
A note on the accuracy of industrial forecasts of the profitability of new products and processes
JB 1978 JAN VOL 51:1 p 127-135.

(8871)
Brown K C
The rate of return of selected investment projects
JF 1978 VOL 33 p 1250.

(8872)
Nickell S J
The investment decisions of firms
Cambridge U Pr, 1978.

(8873)
Reece J S, Cool W R
Measuring investment center performance
HBR 1978 MAR-APR VOL 56:3 p 28-176.

(8874)
Schall L D, Sundem G L, Geijsbeek W R Jr
Survey and analysis of capital budgeting methods
JF 1978 VOL 33 p 281.

(8875)
Gitman L J, Forrester J R Jr
A survey of capital budgeting techniques used by
major U S firms
FIN MGMT 1977 AUTUMN VOL 6 p 66.

(8876)
Nickell S
Uncertainty and lags in the investment decisions
of firms
REStud 1977 VOL 44 p 249.

(8877)
Schwartz S L, Vertinsky I
Multi attribute investment decisions: a study of
R&D project selection
MSci 1977 NOV VOL 24:3 p 285-301.

(8878)
Curley A J
Reconciling investment planning and accounting
control mechanisms
JBFA 1976 AUTUMN VOL 3:3 p 17-28.

(8879)
Maier S F, Vander Weide J H
Capital budgeting in the decentralized firm
MSci 1976 DEC VOL 23:4 p 433-443.

(8880)
King P
Is the emphasis of capital budgeting theory
misplaced?
JBFA 1975 SPRING VOL 2:1 p 69-82.

(8881)
Litzenberger R H, Joy J M
Decentralized capital budgeting decisions and
shareholder wealth maximization
JF 1975 VOL 30 p 993.

(8882)
Sundem G L
Evaluating capital budgeting models in simulated
environments
JF 1975 VOL 30 p 977.

(8883)
Brown K C
A note on the apparent bias of net revenue
estimates for capital investment projects
JF 1974 VOL 29 p 1215.

(8884)
Hastie K L
One businessman's view of capital budgeting
FIN MGMT 1974 WINTER VOL 3 p 36.

(8885)
Baker J C, Beardsley L J
Multinational companies' use of risk evaluation
and profit measurement for capital budgeting
decisions
JBF 1973 SPRING VOL 5:1 p 38-44.

(8886)
Brigham E F, Pettway R H
Capital budgeting by utilities
FIN MGMT 1973 AUTUMN VOL 2 p 11.

(8887)
Kim S-H, Farragher E J
Current capital budgeting practices
Management Accounting 1973 SUMMER p 17-23.

(8888)
Rockley L E
Investment for profitability: an analysis of the
policies and practices of UK and international
companies
Business Bks, 1973.

(8889)
Trivoli G W
Evaluation of pollution control expenditures by
leading corporations
FIN MGMT 1973 WINTER VOL 2 p 19.

(8890)
Klammer T P
Empirical evidence of the adoption of
sophisticated capital budgeting techniques
JB 1972 JUL VOL 45 p 387-397.

(8891)
Mao J C T
Survey of capital budgeting: theory and practice
JF 1970 MAY VOL 25 p 349-360.

(8892)
Rockley L E
Capital investment decisions: a manual for profit planning
Business Bks, 1968.

(8893)
Aharoni Y
The foreign investment decision process
Harvard Bus, 1966.

(8894)
Christy G A
Capital budgeting: current practices and their efficiency
Oregon Busn, 1966.

(8895)
Soldofsky R M
Capital budgeting practices in small manufacturing companies
(in Luckett D G ed., Studies in the factor markets for small business firms. Small Business Administration, Washington, DC, 1964.).

(8896)**Wright R W**
Investment decision in industry
Chapman, 1964.

(8897)
Istvan D F
Capital-expenditures decisions: how they are made in large corporations
Ind U Busn Res, 1961.

(8898)
Eisner R
Determinants of capital expenditures: an interview study
U of Ill Bur of Busn, 1956.

(8899)
Norton F E
Administrative organization in capital budgeting
JB 1955 OCT VOL 28 p 291-295.

(8900)
Dean J
Capital budgeting; top-management policy on plant, equipment, and product development
Columbia U Pr, 1951.

22.3 Criteria for capital expenditures

(8901)
Ang J S, Lai T-Y
A simple rule for multinational capital budgeting
Global Finance Journal 1989 VOL 1:1.

(8902)
Barwise P, Marsh P R, Wensley R
Must finance and strategy clash?
HBR 1989 SEP-OCT p 85-90.

(8903)
Bierman H Jr
Implementing capital budgeting techniques
Ballinger, 1988.

(8904)
Mills D E
Preemptive investment timing
RandJ 1988 SPRING VOL 19:1 p 114-122.

(8905)
Myers S C
Notes on an expert system for capital budgeting
FIN MGMT 1988 AUTUMN VOL 17 p 23-31.

(8906)
Ang J S
Tax asymmetries and the optimal investment decision in the firm
EE 1987 WINTER VOL 32:2 p 135-161.

(8907)
Benzion U, Yagil J
On the discounting formula for a stream of independent risky cash flows
EE 1987 SUMMER VOL 32:4 p 337-345.

(8908)
Burns M R
New evidence on the value additivity principle
JFQA 1987 MAR VOL 22:1 p 65-77.

(8909)
Miller E M
The competitive market assumption and capital budgeting criteria
FIN MGMT 1987 WINTER VOL 16 p 22-28.

(8910)
Taggart R A
Allocating capital among a firm's divisons: hurdle
rates vs budgets
JFR 1987 FALL VOL 10:3 p 177-189.

(8911)
Thompson R A, Thuesen G J
Applications of dynamic investment criteria for
capital budgeting decisions
EE 1987 FALL VOL 33:1 p 59-86.

(8912)
Downs T W
The user cost and capital budgeting
FR 1986 MAY VOL 21:2.

(8913)
Langetieg T C
Stochastic control of corporate investment when
output affects future prices
JFQA 1986 SEP VOL 21:3 p 239-263

(8914)
Leung L C, Tanchoco J M A
Alternative methods for cash flow modeling
EE 1986 SUMMER VOL 31:4 p 303-316.

(8915)
Pike R, Dobbins R
Investment decisions and financial strategy
Philip Allan, 1986.

(8916)
Gandhi D K, Hausmann R Jr, Saunders A
On syndicate sharing rules for unanimous project
rankings
JBankF 1985 VOL 9 p 517.

(8917)
Ikoku C U
Economic analysis and investment decisions
Wiley, 1985.

(8918)
Thanassoulis E
Selecting a suitable solution method for a multi
objective programming capital budgeting problem
JBFA 1985 AUTUMN VOL 12:3 p 453-471

(8919)
Thompson R A, Thuesen G J
Dynamic investment criteria for capital budgeting
decisions
EE 1985 FALL VOL 31:1 p 1-26.

(8920)
Bernhard R H
Risk-adjusted values timing of uncertainty
resolution and the measurement of project worth
JFQA 1984 MAR VOL 19:1 p 83-99

(8921)
Brick I E, Weaver D G
A comparison of capital budgeting techniques in
identifying profitable investments
FIN MGMT 1984 WINTER VOL 13 p 29-39.

(8922)
Giaccotto C
A simplified approach to risk analysis in capital
budgeting with serially correlated cash flow
EE 1984 SUMMER VOL 29:4 p 273-286.

(8923)
Harpaz G, Thomadakis S B
Project valuation with imperfect information
EE 1984 WINTER VOL 29:2 p 101-112.

(8924)
Kroll Y
The analysis of risky investment: A
state-contingent approach
JBankF 1984 VOL 8 p 509.

(8925)
Arzac E R
A mechanism for the allocation of corporate
investment
JFQA 1983 JUN VOL 18:2 p 175-188

(8926)
Cogger K O
A goal seeking investment model
MSci 1983 SEP VOL 29:9 p 1027-1036.

(8927)
Greenberg R, Kim S K, Manes R
Optimal exploitation of a stock resource
EE 1983 SUMMER VOL 28:4 p 293-310.

(8928)
Grimlund R A, Capettini R
Sign tests for actual investments with latter period
net cash outflows
JBFA 1983 SPRING VOL 10:1 p 83-104

(8929)
Matsumoto K
The present value of cash flow generated under
the double-declining -balance method with
switching to the straight-line method : a
pedagogic note
EE 1983 WINTER VOL 28:2 p 148-157.

(8930)
Moore W T, Chen S N
The value of perfect information in capital
budgeting decisions with unknown cash flow
parameters
EE 1983 FALL VOL 29:1 p 41-51.

(8931)
Shapiro A C
International capital budgeting
MCFJ 1983 SPRING VOL 1 p 26-45.

(8932)
Warr P G
Domestic resource cost as an investment criterion
OEP 1983 JUL VOL 35:2 p 302-306.

(8933)
Weigand R
International investments: weighing the incentives
HBR 1983 JUL-AUG VOL 61:4 p 146-152.

(8934)
Wilkes F M
Capital budgeting techniques. 2nd ed
Wiley, 1983.

(8935)
Bodie Z
"Compound-interest" depreciation in capital
investment
HBR 1982 MAY-JUN VOL 60:3 p 58-60.

(8936)
Booth L D
Correct procedures for the evaluation of risky
cash outflows
JFQA 1982 JUN VOL 17:2 p 287-300.

(8937)
Eilon S, Cosmetatos G P
The effect of investment on unit cost and on
profit
Omega 1982 VOL 10:1 p 35-42

(8938)
Oakford R V, Salazar A
The arithmetic of inflation corrections in
evaluating 'real' present worths
EE 1982 WINTER VOL 27:2 p 127-143.

(8939)
Salamon G L
Cash recovery rates and measures of firm
profitability
AR 1982 APR VOL 57:2 p 292-302.

(8940)
Spahr R W
Basic uncertainty in capital budgeting : stochastic
reinvestment rates
EE 1982 SUMMER VOL 27:4 p 275-289.

(8941)
Tanchoco J M A, Buck J R, Egbelu P J
Analysis of capital expenditure projects with
uncertain discrete cash flows
Omega 1982 VOL 10:3 p 299-307.

(8942)
Devarajan S, Fisher A C
Hotelling's "Economics of exhaustible resources":
Fifty years later
JEL 1981 MAR VOL 19 p 65-73.

(8943)
Durand D
Comprehensiveness in capital budgeting
FIN MGMT 1981 WINTER VOL 10 p 7-13.

(8944)
Gehr A K Jr
Risk-adjusted capital budgeting using arbitrage
FIN MGMT 1981 WINTER VOL 10 p 14-19.

(8945)
Kalymon B A
Methods of large project assessment given
uncertainty in future energy pricing
MSci 1981 APR VOL 27:4 p 377-395.

(8946)
Newton J K
Computer modelling for project evaluation
Omega 1981 VOL 9:3 p 281-286.

(8947)
Dothan U, Williams J
Term-risk structures and the valuation of projects
JFQA 1980 NOV VOL 15 p 875.

(8948)
Fuller R J, Kim S-H
Inter-temporal correlation of cash flows and the
risk of multi-period investment projects
JFQA 1980 DEC VOL 15 p 1149-1162..

(8949)**Landau H J**
On comparison of cash flow streams
MSci 1980 DEC VOL 26:12 p 1218-1226

(8950)
Pettway G H
A return on capital measure - better than DCF?
HBR 1980 MAY-JUN VOL 58:3 p 34-36.

(8951)
Schall L D, Sundem G L
Capital budgeting methods and risk: A further
analysis
FIN MGMT 1980 SPRING VOL 9 p 7.

(8952)
Sunder S
Corporate capital investment, accounting methods
and earnings: a test of the control hypothesis
JF 1980 MAY VOL 35:2 p 553-568

(8953)
Weston J F, Chen N F
A note on capital budgeting and the three R's
FIN MGMT 1980 SPRING VOL 9 p 12.

(8954)
Ang J S, Chua J H, Sellers R
Generating cash flow estimates: An actual study
using the Delphi techniques
FIN MGMT 1979 SPRING VOL 8 p 64.

(8955)
Baron D P
Investment policy, optimality, and the
mean-variance model
JF 1979 MAR VOL 34:1 p 207-232.

(8956)
Blatt J M
Investment evaluation under uncertainty
FIN MGMT 1979 SUMMER VOL 8 p 66.

(8957)
Blocher E, Stickney C
Duration and risk assessments in capital
budgeting
AR 1979 JAN VOL 54:1 p 180-188.

(8958)
Briston R J, Liversidge J
A practical approach to business investment
decisions
Macmillan, 1979.

(8959)
Fowler D J, Rorke C H
Capital budgeting, capital asset pricing and
externalities
JBFA 1979 SUMMER VOL 6:2 p 145-156.

(8960)
Johnson J M
Optimal tax lives of depreciable assets
FIN MGMT 1979 AUTUMN VOL 8 p 27.

(8961)
Park C S, Thuesen G J
Combining the concepts of uncertainty resolution
and project balance for capital allocation
decisions
EE 1979 WINTER VOL 24:2 p 109-127.

(8962)
Perrakis S
Capital budgeting and timing uncertainty within
the CAPM
FIN MGMT 1979 AUTUMN VOL 8 p 32.

(8963)
Baum S, Carlson R C, Jucker J V
Some problems in applying the continuous portfolio selection model to the discrete capital budgeting problem
JFQA 1978 JUN VOL 13 p 333.

(8964)
Beedles W L
Evaluating negative benefits
JFQA 1977 MAR VOL 13 p 173.

(8965)
Beranek W
Some new capital budgeting theorems
JFQA 1978 DEC VOL 13 p 809.

(8966)
Bhattacharya S
Project valuation with mean-reverting cash flow streams
JF 1978 VOL 33 p 1317.

(8967)
Bierman H Jr, Rao V R
Investment decisions with sampling
FIN MGMT 1978 AUTUMN VOL 7 p 19.

(8968)
Constantinides G M
Market risk adjustment in project valuation
JF 1978 VOL 33 p 603.

(8969)
Cyert R M, DeGroot M H, Holt C A
Sequential investment decisions with Bayesian learning
MSci 1978 VOL 24 p 712-718.

(8970)
Hong H, Rappaport A
Debt capacity, optimal capital structure and capital budgeting analysis
FIN MGMT 1978 AUTUMN VOL 7 p 7.

(8971)
Miller E M
Uncertainty induced bias in capital budgeting
FIN MGMT 1978 AUTUMN VOL 7 p 12.

(8972)
OECD
A management approach to project appraisal and evaluation: with special reference to non-directly productive products
OECD, 1978.

(8973)
Rendleman R J Jr
Ranking errors in CAPM capital budgeting applications
FIN MGMT 1978 WINTER VOL 7 p 40.

(8974)
Rosenthal R E
The variance of present worth of cash flows under uncertain timing
EE 1978 SPRING VOL 23:3 p 163-170.

(8975)
Ross S A
A simple approach to the valuation of risky streams
JB 1978 JUL VOL 51:3 p 453-475.

(8976)
Senbet L W, Thompson H E
The equivalence of alternative mean-variance capital budgeting models
JF 1978 VOL 33 p 395.

(8977)
Shapiro A C
Capital budgeting for the multinational corporation
FIN MGMT 1978 SPRING VOL 7 p 7.

(8978)
Bailey A D Jr, Jensen D L
General price level adjustments in the capital budgeting decision
FIN MGMT 1977 SPRING VOL 6 p 26.

(8979)
Ben-Shahar H, Werner F M
Multiperiod capital budgeting under uncertainty: A suggested application
JFQA 1977 DEC VOL 12 p 859.

(8980)
Bernardo J J, Lanser H P
A capital budgeting decision model with subjective criteria
JFQA 1977 JUN VOL 12 p 261.

(8981)
Myers S C, Turnbull S M
Captal budgeting and the capital asset pricing model: good news and bad news
JF 1977 MAY VOL 32:2 p 321-332.

(8982)
Marsh P, Brealey R A
The use of imperfect forecasts in capital investment decisions
(in Proceedings of the European Finance Association, N Holland, 1976.)

(8983)
Martin J D, Scott D F Jr
Debt capacity and the capital budgeting decision
FIN MGMT 1976 SUMMER VOL 5 p 7.

(8984)
Nelson C K
Inflation and capital budgeting
JF 1976 VOL 31 p 923.

(8985)
Perrakis S, Sahin I
On risky investments with random timing of cash returns and fixed planning horizon
MSci 1976 VOL 22 p 799-809.

(8986)
Treynor J L, Black F
Corporate investment decisions
(in Myers S C ed., Modern developments in financial management. Praeger, 1976.)

(8987)
Trivoli G W
Project investment analysis and anticipated government mandated expenditures
FIN MGMT 1976 WINTER VOL 5 p 18.

(8988)
Chateau J-P D
The capital budgeting problem under conflicting financial policies
JBFA 1975 SPRING VOL 2:1 p 83-104.

(8989)
Cooley P L, Roenfeldt R L, Chew I-K
Capital budgeting procedures under inflation
FIN MGMT 1975 WINTER VOL 4 p 18.

(8990)
Searby F W
Return to return on investment
HBR 1975 MAR-APR VOL 53:2 p 113-119.

(8991)
Carsberg B V
Analysis for investment decisions
Accountancy Age Books, 1974.

(8992)
Edwards C E, Goodwin J S
Tax shields from depreciation allowances: a further examination
QREB 1974 VOL 14:4 p 116.

(8993)
Flavell R B, Salkin G R
A sequential analysis of large-scale investment projects
JBFA 1974 SPRING VOL 1:1 p 75-92.

(8994)
Grinyer J R
Relevant criterion rates in capital budgeting
JBFA 1974 AUTUMN VOL 1:3 p 357-374.

(8995)
Lee S M, Lerro A J
Capital budgeting for multiple objectives
FIN MGMT 1974 SPRING VOL 3 p 58.

(8996)
Spies R R
The dynamics of corporate capital budgeting
JF 1974 VOL 29 p 829.

(8997)
Sundem G L
Evaluating simplified capital budgeting models using a time state preference metric
AR 1974 APR VOL 49:2 p 306-320.

(8998)
Trippi R R
Conventional and unconventional methods for evaluating investments
FIN MGMT 1974 AUTUMN VOL 3 p 31.

(8999)
Barron M J
Investment decisions under uncertainty
JBF 1973 SPRING VOL 5:1 p 3-9.

(9000)
Bierman H Jr, Hass J E
Capital budgeting under uncertainty: A reformulation
JF 1973 VOL 28 p 119.

(9001)
Durand D
Indices of profitability as aids to judgement in capital budgeting
JBR 1973 WINTER VOL 3:4 p 200-219..

(9002)**Merville L J, Tavis L A**
A generalized model for capital investment
JF 1973 VOL 28 p 109.

(9003)
Scholefield N H, McBain N S, Bagwell J
The effects of inflation on investment appraisal
JBF 1973 SUMMER VOL 5:2 p 39-48.

(9004)
Barnea A
A note on the cash-flow approach to valuation and depreciation of productive assets
JFQA 1972 JUN VOL 7 p 1841.

(9005)
Fogler H R
Overkill in capital budgeting technique?
FIN MGMT 1972 SPRING VOL 1 p 92.

(9006)
Folger H R
Ranking techniques and capital budgeting
AR 1972 JAN VOL 47:1 p 134.

(9007)
Frost P A, Schall L D
Ramsey's investment criterion
JPE 1972 VOL 80 p 803.

(9008)
Hawkins C J, Pearce D W
Capital investment appraisal
Macmillan, 1972.

(9009)
Keeley R H, Westerfield R
A problem in probability distribution techniques for capital budgeting
JF 1972 JUN VOL 27 p 703-710.

(9010)
Lusk E J
Discriminant analysis as applied to the resource allocation decision
AR 1972 JUL VOL 47:3 p 567-574.

(9011)
Meyers S L
Avoiding depreciation influences on investment decisions
FIN MGMT 1972 WINTER VOL 1 p 17.

(9012)
Pye G
Capital gains taxation, dividends, and capital budgeting
QJE 1972 VOL 86 p 226.

(9013)
Walter J E
Investment planning under variable price changes
FIN MGMT 1972 WINTER VOL 1 p 36.

(9014)
Laughhunn D J, Peterson D E
Computational experience with capital expenditure programming models under risk
JBF 1971 WINTER VOL 3 p 43-48.

(9015)
Peterson D E, Laughhunn D J
Capital expenditure programming and some alternative approaches to risk
MSci 1971 JAN VOL 17 p 320-336.

(9016)
Stapleton R C
Portfolio analysis, stock valuation and capital budgeting decision rules for risky projects
JF 1971 MAR VOL 26 p 95-118.

(9017)
Uyar K M
Certainty equivalent and investment behavior under risk
QREB 1971 VOL 11:4.

(9018)
Whitmore G A, Darkazanli S
A linear risk constraint in capital budgeting
MSci 1971 DEC VOL 18 p B155-B157.

(9019)
Hammonds T M, Padberg D I
The risk factor in investment decisions
JASA 1970 JUN VOL 65 p 602-612.

(9020)
Kabak I W, Owen J
Random variables, the time value of money and capital expenditures
MSci 1970 NOV VOL 17 p 142-145.

(9021)
Litzenberger R H, Budd A P
Corporate investment criteria and the valuation of risk assets
JFQA 1970 DEC VOL 5 p 395-420.

(9022)
Mao J C T
Models of capital budgeting, E-V vs E-S
JFQA 1970 JAN VOL 4 p 657-676.

(9023)
Reutlinger S
Techniques for project appraisal under uncertainty
Johns Hopkins, 1970.

(9024)
Sunley E M Jr
Alternatives to the investment tax credit
QREB 1970 VOL 10:4 p 31.

(9025)
Fleischer G A
Capital allocation theory: the study of investment decisions
Appleton, 1969.

(9026)
Jean W H
Capital budgeting: the economic evaluation of investment projects
Intext, 1969.

(9027)
Moag J S, Lerner E M
Capital budgeting decisions under imperfect market conditions--a systems framework
JF 1969 SEP VOL 24 p 613-622.

(9028)
Sunley E M Jr
The present value of depreciation allowances
QREB 1969 VOL 9:4 p 77.

(9029)
Townsend E C
Investment and uncertainty: a practical guide
Oliver, 1969.

(9030)
Van Horne J C
The analysis of uncertainty resolutions in capital budgeting for new products
MSci 1969 APR VOL 15 p B376-B386.

(9031)
Ziemba W T
A myopic capital budgeting model
JFQA 1969 SEP VOL 4 p 305-328.

(9032)
Gupta S K, Rosenhead J
Robustness in sequential investment decisions
MSci 1968 OCT VOL 15 p B18-B29.

(9033)
Hanssman F
Operations research techniques for capital investment
Wiley, 1968.

(9034)
Jeynes P H
Profitability and economic choice
Iowa St U Pr, 1968.

(9035)
Manne A S
Optimal dividend and investment policies for a self financing business enterprise
MSci 1968 NOV VOL 15 p 119-129.

(9036)
Myers S C
Procedures for capital budgeting under uncertainty
IMR 1968 SPRING VOL 9 p 1-20.

(9037)
Tuttle D L, Litzenberger R H
Capital budgeting under uncertainty
Southern Journal of Business 1968 APR p 119-131.

(9038)
Tuttle D L, Litzenberger R H
Leverage, diversification and capital market effects on a risk-adjusted capital budgeting framework
JF 1968 JUN VOL 23 p 427-443.

(9039)
Vaughn D E, Bennett H
Adjusting for risk in the capital budget of a growth-oriented company
JFQA 1968 DEC VOL 3 p 445-462.

(9040)
Hastie K L
The determination of optimal investment policy
MSci 1967 AUG VOL 13 B757-B774.

(9041)
Manne A S ed.
Investments for capacity expansion: size, location and time phasing
Allen, 1967.

(9042)
Mathur G
Investment criteria in a platinum age
OEP 1967 JUL VOL 19 p 199-214.

(9043)
Mayer R R
Financial analysis of investment alternatives
Allyn, 1966.

(9044)
Solomon M B Jr
Uncertainty and its effect on capital investment analysis
MSci 1966 APR VOL 12 p B334-B339.

(9045)
Van Horne J C
Capital-budgeting decisions involving combinations of risky investments
MSci 1966 OCT VOL 13 p B84-B92.

(9046)
Williams A C, Nassar J I
Financial measurement of capital investments
MSci 1966 JUL VOL 12 p 851-864.

(9047)
Adelson R M
Criteria for capital investment: an approach through decision theory
Operational Research Quarterly 1965 MAR VOL 16 p 19-50.

(9048)
Gaver D P
Models for appraising investments yielding stochastic returns
MSci 1965 JUL VOL 11 p 815-830.

(9049)
Teichroew D, Robichek A A, Montalbano M
An analysis of criteria for investment and financing decisions under certainty
MSci 1965 NOV VOL 11 p 151-179.

(9050)
Wright J F
Some further comments on the ambiguity and usefulness of marginal efficiency as an investment criterion
OEP 1965 MAR VOL 17 p 81-89.

(9051)
Lerner E M, Carleton W T
The integration of capital budgeting and stock valuation
AER 1964 SEP VOL 54 p 681-702.

(9052)
Kaufman G M
Sequential investment analysis under uncertainty
JB 1963 JAN VOL 36 p 39-65.

(9053)
Marglin S A
Approaches to dynamic investment planning
N Holland, 1963.

(9054)
Wright J F
Notes on the marginal efficiency of capital
OEP 1963 JUL VOL 15 p 124-129..

(9055)**Reisman A, Buffa E S**
A general model for investment policy
MSci 1962 APR VOL 8 p 304-310.

(9056)
Davidson S, Drake D F
Capital budgeting and the "best" tax depreciation
method
JB 1961 OCT VOL 34 p 442-452.

(9057)
Fisher J L
A class of stochastic investment problems
OR 1961 JAN-FEB VOL 9 p 53-65.

(9058)
Haring J E
The investment horizon
Met 1961 AUG VOL 13 p 77-93.

(9059)
Hetrick J C
Mathematical models in capital budgeting
HBR 1961 JAN-FEB VOL 39 p 49-64.

(9060)
Sobotka S P, Schnabel C
Linear programming as a device for predicting
market value: Prices of used commercial aircraft,
1959-65
JB 1961 JAN VOL 34 p 10-30.

(9061)
Bailey M J
Formal criteria for investment decisions
JPE 1959 OCT VOL 67 p 476-488.

(9062)
Shillinglaw G
Residual values in investment analysis
(in Solomon E ed., The management of corporate
capital. Free Pr, 1959.)

(9063)
Wright J F
The marginal efficiency of capital
EJ 1959 DEC VOL 69 p 813-816.

(9064)
McLean J G
How to evaluate new capital investments
HBR 1958 NOV-DEC VOL 36 p 59-69.

(9065)
Renshaw E F
A note on the arithmetic of capital budgeting
decisions
JB 1957 JUL VOL 30 p 193-201.

(9066)
Solomon E
The arithmetic of capital budgeting decisions
JB 1956 APR VOL 29 p 124-129.

(9067)
Anthony R N
Re: depreciation in investment decisions
HBR 1955 JAN-FEB VOL 33 p 75-76.

(9068)
Shillinglaw G
Residual values in investment analysis
JB 1955 OCT VOL 28 p 275-284.

22.31   Discounted cash flow techniques

(9069)
Black F
A simple discounting rule
FIN MGMT 1988 SUMMER VOL 17 p 7-11.

(9070)
McDaniel W R, McCarty D E, Jessell K A
Discounted cash flow with explicit reinvestment
rates: tutorial and extension
FR 1988 AUG VOL 23:3 p 369.

(9071)
Sick G A
Multi-period risky project valuation: A mean-variance certainty-equivalence approach
(in Lee C F ed., Advances in Financial Planning and Forecasting, VOL 3. JAI Press, 1987.)

(9072)
Sick G A
A certainty-equivalent approach to capital budgeting
FIN MGMT 1986 WINTER VOL 15 p 23-32.

(9073)
Lohmann J R, Oakford R V
Errors in present worth evaluations attributable to the end-of-year and mid-year cash flow conventions
EE 1984 SUMMER VOL 29:4 p 303-309.

(9074)
Logue D E, West R R
Discounted cash flow analysis: A response to the critics
National Productivity Review 1983 VOL 3 p 233-241.

(9075)
Ang J S, Lewellen W G
Risk adjustment in capital investment project evaluations
FIN MGMT 1982 SUMMER VOL 11 p 5-14.

(9076)
Gurnani C
Present worth analysis of deterministic periodic cash flows
EE 1982 WINTER VOL 27:2 p 101-126.

(9077)
Hayes R H, Garvin D A
Managing as if tomorrow mattered
HBR 1982 MAY-JUN VOL 60:3 p 71-79.

(9078)
Rappaport A, Taggart R A Jr
Evaluation of capital expenditure proposals under inflation
FIN MGMT 1982 SPRING VOL 11 p 5-13.

(9079)
Wilkes F M
Stochastic interest rates and investment appraisal
JBFA 1979 AUTUMN VOL 6:3 p 347-354.

(9080)
Brick J R, Thompson H E
The economic life of an investment and the appropriate discount rate
JFQA 1978 DEC VOL 13 p 831.

(9081)
Bierman H Jr
Some old and new ideas on capital budgeting: A reconciliation of present value capital budgeting and accounting
FIN MGMT 1977 SUMMER VOL 6 p 52.

(9082)
Fama E F
Risk-adjusted discount rates and capital budgeting under uncertainty
JFE 1977 VOL 5 p 3.

(9083)
Beranek W
The cost of capital, capital budgeting and the maximization of shareholder wealth
JFQA 1975 MAR VOL 10 p 1.

(9084)
Bierman H Jr, Smidt S
Application of the capital asset pricing model to multi-period investments
JBFA 1975 AUTUMN VOL 2:3 p 327-340.

(9085)
Mare-de-la R F
An investigation into the discounting formulae used in capital budeting models
JBFA 1975 SUMMER VOL 2:2 p 203-218.

(9086)
Arditti F D
A note on discounting the components of an income stream
JF 1974 VOL 29 p 995.

(9087)
Weston J F
Investment decisions using the capital asset pricing model
FIN MGMT 1973 SPRING VOL 2 p 25.

(9088)
Wright F K
The relationship between present value and value to the owner
JBF 1973 SUMMER VOL 5:2 p 19-25.

(9089)
Donaldson G
Strategic hurdle rates for capital investment
HBR 1972 MAR-APR VOL 50:2 p 50-58.

(9090)
Bierman H Jr
Discounted cash flows, price level adjustments and expectations
AR 1971 OCT VOL 46 p 693-699.

(9091)
Hamada R S
Investment decisions with a general equilibrium mean-variance approach
QJE 1971 NOV VOL 85.

(9092)
Jean W H
Terminal value or present value in capital budgeting programs
JFQA 1971 JAN VOL 6 p 649-652.

(9093)
Lerner E M, Rappaport A
Limit DCF in capital budgeting
HBR 1968 SEP-OCT VOL 46 p 133-139.

(9094)
Wright J F
Discounted cash flow
McGraw, 1968.

(9095)
Masse P
Optimal investment decisions: rules for action and criteria for choice
P-H, 1962.

(9096)
Hirshleifer J
Risk, the discount rate, and investment decisions
AER 1961 MAY VOL 51 p 112-120.

(9097)
Hirshleifer J
On the theory of optimal investment decisions
JPE 1958 AUG VOL 66 p 329-352.

22.311   Internal rate of return

(9098)
Cannaday R E, Colwell P F, Paley H
Relevant and irrelevant internal rates of return
EE 1986 FALL VOL 32:1 p 17-38.

(9099)
Gronchi S
On investment criteria based on the internal rate of return
OEP 1986 MAR VOL 38:1 p 174-180.

(9100)
Howe K M
Reinvestment rate assumptions in dscounted cash flow models
EE 1985 FALL VOL 31:1 p 43-49.

(9101)
Ward T L
Internal rates of return : a linear systems theoretic view
EE 1985 WINTER VOL 30:2 p 135-156.

(9102)
Wohl M
A new ordering procedure and set of decision rules for the internal rate of return method
EE 1985 SUMMER VOL 30:4 p 363-386.

(9103)
Beidleman C R
Discounted cash flow reinvestment rate assumptions
EE 1984 WINTER VOL 29:2 p 127-139.

(9104)
Panton D B, Verdini W A
On implementing the Sturm-Kaplan for counting
internal rates of return
EE 1984 SUMMER VOL 29:4 p 300-302.

(9105)
Russell A M, Rickard J A
An algorithm for determining unique nonnegative
internal rates of return
JBFA 1984 AUTUMN VOL 11:3 p 355-365

(9106)
Faro C de
On implementing the Sturm-Kaplan procedure for
counting internal rates of return
EE 1983 SUMMER VOL 28:4 p 322-325.

(9107)
Salmi T
Estimating the internal rate of return from
published financial statements
JBFA 1982 SPRING VOL 9:1 p 63-74..

(9108)**Dorfman R**
The meaning of internal rates of return
JF 1981 DEC VOL 36:5 p 1011-1021.

(9109)
Bernhard R H
A simplification and an extension of the
Bernhard-deFaro sufficient condition for a unique
non-negative internal rate of return
JFQA 1980 MAR VOL 15 p 201.

(9110)
Bernhard R H, Norstrom C J
A further note on unrecovered investment,
uniqueness of the internal rate and the question
of project acceptability
JFQA 1980 JUN VOL 15 p 421.

(9111)
Rapp B
The internal rate of return method - a critical
study
Engineering Costs and Production Economics
1980.

(9112)
Wilkes F M
On multiple rates of return
JBFA 1980 WINTER VOL 7:4 p 569-584.

(9113)
Bernhard R H
A more general sufficient condition for a unique
nonnegative internal rate of return
JFQA 1979 JUN VOL 14 p 337.

(9114)
Faro C de, Soares L
A flexible sufficient condition for a unique
nonnegative internal rate of return
EE 1978 WINTER VOL 23:2 p 117-127.

(9115)
Herbst A
The unique real internal rate of return: Caveat
emptor!
JFQA 1978 JUN VOL 13 p 363.

(9116)
Hsaio F S T, Smith W J
An analytical approach to sensitivity analysis of
the internal rate of return model
JF 1978 VOL 33 p 645.

(9117)
Longbottom D A, Wiper L
Necessary conditions for the existence of multiple
rates in the use of internal rate of return
JBFA 1978 WINTER VOL 5:4 p295-306.

(9118)
Bernhard R H
Unrecovered investment, uniqueness of the
internal rate and the question of project
acceptability
JFQA 1977 MAR VOL 12 p 33.

(9119)
Stephen F H
On deriving the internal rate of return from the
accountant's rate of return
JBFA 1976 SUMMER VOL 3:2 p 147-150.

(9120)
Arditti F D
The reinvestment assumption in the internal rate of return
JBF 1973 SPRING VOL 5:1 p 1-2.

(9121)
Doenges R C
The "reinvestment problem" in a practical perspective
FIN MGMT 1972 SPRING VOL 1 p 85.

(9122)
Dudley C L Jr
A note on reinvestment assumptions in choosing between net present value and internal rate of return
JF 1972 SEP VOL 27 p 907-916.

(9123)
Norstrom C J
A sufficient condition for a unique nonnegative internal rate of return
JFQA 1972 JUN VOL 7 p 1835-1840.

(9124)
Arrow K J, Levhari D
Uniqueness of the internal rate of return with variable life of investments
EJ 1969 SEP VOL 79 p 560-566.

(9125)
Sarnat M, Levy H
The relationship of rules of thumb to the internal rate of return: a restatement and generalization
JF 1969 JUN VOL 24 p 479-490.

(9126)
Bernhard R H
On the consistency of the Soper and Sturm-Kaplan conditions for uniqueness of the internal rate of return
Journal of Industrial Engineering 1967 AUG VOL 18 p 498.

(9127)
Jean W H
On multiple rates of return
JF 1968 MAR VOL 23 p 187-191.

(9128)
Kaplan S
Computer algorithms for finding exact rates of return
JB 1967 OCT VOL 40 p 389-392.

(9129)
Weingartner H M
The generalized rate of return
JFQA 1966 SEP VOL 1 p 1-29.

(9130)
Kaplan S
A note on a method for precisely determining the uniqueness or non-uniqueness of the internal rate of return for a proposed investment
Journal of Industrial Engineering 1965 JAN-FEB VOL 16.

(9131)
Merrett A J
Net present value versus the internal rate of return yet again
Scottish Journal of Political Economy 1965 FEB VOL 12 p 116-118.

(9132)
Teichroew D, Robichek A A, Montalbano M
Mathematical analysis of rates of return under certainty
MSci 1965 JAN VOL 11 p 395-403.

(9133)
Turvey R
Present value versus internal rate of return: an essay in the theory of the third best
EJ 1963 MAR VOL 73 p 93-98.

(9134)
Alchian A A
The rate of return, Fisher's rate of return over cost and Keynes' internal rate of return
AER 1955 DEC VOL 45 p 938-943.

(9135)
Lorie J H, Savage L J
Three problems in rationing capital
JB 1955 OCT VOL 28 p 229-239.

(9136)
Samuelson P A
Some aspects of the pure theory of capital
QJE 1937 VOL 51 p 469-496.

22.312   Profitability index

(9137)
Hoskins C G
Benefit-cost ratio ranking for size disparity
problems
JBFA 1977 SUMMER VOL 4:2 p 229-232.

(9138)
Hoskins C G
Benefit-cost ratios versus net present value:
Revisited
JBFA 1974 SUMMER VOL 1:2 p 249-266.

(9139)
Schwab B, Lusztig P
A comparative analysis of the net present value
and the benefit-cost ratio as measures of the
economic desirability of investments
JF 1969 JUN VOL 24 p 507-516.

22.32   Other criteria

(9140)
Hoskins C G
Capital budgeting decision rules for risky projects
derived from a capital market model based on
semivariance
EE 1978 SUMMER VOL 23:4 p 211-222.

(9141)
Sealey C W Jr
Utility maximisation and programming models for
capital budgeting
JBFA 1978 AUTUMN VOL 5:3 p 355-366.

(9142)
Longbottom D A, Wiper L
Capital appraisal and the case for average rate of
return
JBFA 1977 WINTER VOL 4:4 p 419-426.

(9143)
Osteryoung J S, Scott E, Roberts G S
Selecting capital projects with the coefficient of
variation
FIN MGMT 1977 SUMMER VOL 6 p 65.

(9144)
Bey R P, Porter R B, Lewis D C
The development of a mean-semivariance
approach to capital budgeting
JFQA 1975 NOV VOL 10 p 639.

(9145)
Hawkins C A, Adams R A
A goal programming model for capital budgeting
FIN MGMT 1974 SPRING VOL 3 p 52.

(9146)
Hanssman F
Probability of survival as an investment criterion
MSci 1968 SEP VOL 15 p 33-48.

(9147)
Kennedy M
A critique of game theory for capital budgeting
NAA Bulletin 1963 MAY VOL 44.

(9148)
Nelson W G
Could game theory help capital budgeting?
NAA Bulletin 1962 JUN VOL 43.

(9149)
Dryden M M
The MAPI urgency rating as an investment
ranking criterion
JB 1960 OCT VOL 33 p 327-341.

22.321   Payback

(9150)
Prakash A J, Dandapani K, Karels G V
Simple resource allocation rules
JBFA 1988 AUTUMN VOL 15:3 p 447.

(9151)
Narayanan M P
Observability and the payback criterion
JB 1985 JUL VOL 58:3 p 309-323.

(9152)
Statman M, Sepe J F
Managerial incentive plans and the use of the payback method
JBFA 1984 SPRING VOL 11:1 p 61-65

(9153)
Boardman C M, Reinhart W J, Celec S E
The role of the payback period in the theory and application of duration to capital budgeting
JBFA 1982 WINTER VOL 9:4 p 511-522.

(9154)
Statman M
The persistence of the payback method : a principal-agent perspective
EE 1982 WINTER VOL 27:2 p 95-100.

(9155)
Hoskins C G, Mumey G A
Payback: a maligned method of asset ranking?
EE 1979 FALL VOL 25:1 p 53-65.

(9156)
Durand D
Payout period, time spread and duration: aids to judgement in capital budgeting
JBR 1974 SPRING VOL 5:1 p 20-34.

(9157)
Lewellen W G, Lanser H P, McConnell J J
Payback substitutes for discounted cash flow
FIN MGMT 1973 SUMMER VOL 2 p 17.

(9158)
Mendelson M
A comment on payback
JFQA 1971 SEP VOL 6 p 1159-1160.

(9159)
Weingartner H M
Some new views on the payback period and capital budgeting decisions
MSci 1969 AUG VOL 15 p B594-B607.

(9160)
Levy H
A note on the payback method
JFQA 1968 DEC VOL 3 p 433-444..

(9161) **Gordon M J**
The pay-off period and the rate of profit
JB 1955 OCT VOL 28.

22.4   Constraints on capital expenditures

(9162)
Hayes J W
Discount rates in linear programming formulations of the capital budgeting problem
EE 1984 WINTER VOL 29:2 p 113-126.

(9163)
Ederington L H, Henry W R
On costs of capital in programming approaches to capital budgeting
JFQA 1979 DEC VOL 14 p 1019.

(9164)
Rychel D F
Capital budgeting with mixed integer linear programming: An application
FIN MGMT 1977 WINTER VOL 6 p 43.

(9165)
Galai D
A note on Cord's method of allocating funds to investment projects
MSci 1975 AUG VOL 21:12 p 1466.

(9166)
Gear A E, Lockett G
Multistage capital budeting under uncertainty
JFQA 1975 MAR VOL 10 p 21.

(9167)
Whitmore G A, Darkazanli S
A linear risk constraint in capital budgeting
MSci 1971 DEC VOL 18 p B155-B157.

(9168)
Mao J C T, Wallingford B A
An extension of Lawler and Bell's method of discrete optimization with examples from capital budgeting
MSci 1968 OCT VOL 15 p B51-B60.

(9169)
Byrne R, Charnes A, Cooper W W et al.
A chance constrained approach to capital budeting with portfolio type payback and liquidity constraints and horizon posture controls
JFQA 1967 DEC VOL 2 p 339-364.

(9170)
Kaplan S
Solution of the Lorie-Savage and similar integer programming problems by the generalized Lagrange multiplier method
OR 1966 NOV-DEC VOL 14 p 1130-1136.

(9171)
Naslund B
A model of capital budgeting under risk
JB 1966 APR VOL 39 p 257-271.

(9172)
Cord J
A method of allocating funds to investment projects when returns are subject to uncertainty
MSci 1964 JAN VOL 10 p 335-341.

22.41   Capital rationing

(9173)
Trivoli G W, McDaniel W R
Uncertainty, capital immobility and capital rationing in the investment decision
JBFA 1987 SUMMER VOL 14:2 p 215-228.

(9174)
Antle R, Eppen G D
Capital rationing and organizational slack in capital budgeting
MSci 1985 FEB VOL 31:2 p 163-174.

(9175)
Pike R
The capital budgeting behaviour and corporate characteristics of capital constrained firms
JBFA 1983 WINTER VOL 10:4 p 663-671

(9176)
Forsyth J D, Owen D C
Capital rationing methods
(in Crum R L and Derkinderen F G J eds., Capital budgeting under conditions of uncertainty. Martinus Nijhoff, 1981.)

(9177)
Lohmann J R, Oakford R V
A decision procedure for capital rationing investment and borrowing decisions
EE 1981 SUMMER VOL 26:4 p 275-292.

(9178)
Oakford R V, Salazar A
The long term effectiveness of "exact" and approximate capital rationing procedures under uncertainty and incomplete information
JBFA 1981 SPRING VOL: 8:1 p 113-137

(9179)
Bhaskar K N
Linear programming and capital budgeting: the financing problem
JBFA 1978 SUMMER VOL 5:2 p 159-194.

(9180)
Bradley S P, Frey S C Jr
Equivalent mathematical programming models of pure capital rationing
JFQA 1978 JUN VOL 13 p 345.

(9181)
Weingartner H M
Capital rationing: n authors in search of a plot
JF 1977 VOL 32 p 1403.

(9182)
Bhaskar K N
Linear programming and capital budgeting: A reappraisal
JBFA 1976 AUTUMN VOL 3:3 p 29-40.

(9183)
Norstrom C J
A comment on two simple decision rules in capital rationing
RFBA 1976 SUMMER VOL 3:2 p 63-70.

(9184)
Bhaskar K N
Borrowing and lending in a mathematical programming model of capital budgeting
JBFA 1974 SUMMER VOL 1:2 p 267-318.

(9185)
Burton R M, Damon W W
On the existence of a cost of capital under pure capital rationing
JF 1974 VOL 29 p 1165.

(9186)
Forsyth J D, Laughunn D J
Rationing capital in a telephone company
FIN MGMT 1974 AUTUMN VOL 3 p 36.

(9187)
Hughes J S, Lewellen W G
Programming solutions to capital rationing problems
JBFA 1974 SPRING VOL 1:1 p 55-74.

(9188)
Ma R, Tydeman J
Project selection criteria, wealth maximization and capital rationing
JBF 1972 WINTER VOL 4:4 p 34-43.

(9189)
Myers S C
A note on linear programming and capital budgeting
JF 1972 MAR VOL 27 p 89-92.

(9190)
Elton E J
Capital rationing and external discount rates
JF 1970 JUN VOL 25 p 573-584.

(9191)
Bernhard R H
Mathematical programming models for capital budgeting--a survey, generalization and critique
JFQA 1969 JUN VOL 4 p 111-158.

(9192)
Carleton W T
Linear programming and capital budgeting models: a new interpretation
JF 1969 DEC VOL 24 p 825-833.

(9193)
Weingartner M H
Mathematical programming and the analysis of capital budgeting problems - with three related articles
Markham Publishing Co., 1967.

(9194)
Weingartner H M
Criteria for programming investment project selection
JIE 1966 NOV VOL 15 p 65-76.

(9195)
Baumol W J, Quandt R E
Investment and discount rates under capital rationing--a programming approach
EJ 1965 JUN VOL 75 p 317-329.

(9196)
Charnes A, Cooper W W, Miller M H
Application of linear programming to financial budgeting and the costing of funds
JB 1959 JAN VOL 32 p 20-46.

22.42 Interdependent projects

(9197)
Kwan C C Y, Yuan Y
Optimal sequential selection in capital budgeting: A shortcut
FIN MGMT 1988 SPRING VOL 17 p 54-59.

(9198)
Meyer R L, Besley S, Longstreet J R
An examination of capital budgeting decision alternatives for mutually exclusive investment with unequal lives
JBFA 1988 AUTUMN VOL 15:3 p 415-426.

(9199)
Rucker R R, Leffler K B
To harvest or not to harvest? An analysis of cutting behavior on federal timber sales contracts
REStat 1988 VOL 70 p 207.

(9200)
Leung L C, Tanchoco J M A
Multiple machine replacement within an integrated system framework
EE 1987 WINTER VOL 32:2 p 89-114.

(9201)
Srinivasan V, Kim Y H
Evaluating interrelated capital projects: an alternative framework
EE 1987 FALL VOL 33:1 p 13-30.

(9202)
Lummer S L
Equivalent real annual costs : Evaluating investment alternatives with unequal lives under inflation
EE 1986 SUMMER VOL 31:4 p 317-326.

(9203)
Luxhoj J T, Jones M S
A framework for replacement modeling assumptions
EE 1986 FALL VOL 32:1 p 39-49.

(9204)
Howe K M, McCabe G M
On optimal asset abandonment and replacement.
JFQA 1983 SEP VOL 18:3 p 295-305

(9205)
Schwartz E, McNamara J R
The optimal replacement cycle given an efficient resale market for used assets
EE 1983 WINTER VOL 28:2 p 91-100.

(9206)
Baldwin C Y
Optimal sequential investment when capital is not readily reversible
JF 1982 JUN VOL 37:3 p 763-782.

(9207)
Emery G W
Some guidelines for evaluating capital investment alternatives with unequal lives
FIN MGMT 1982 SPRING VOL 11 p 14-19.

(9208)
Boucher T O
A mixed-integer programming planning model for optimal investment and financing in segmented international capital markets
EE 1981 FALL VOL 27:1 p 1-28.

(9209)
Findlay M C III, Williams E E
The problem of "unequal lives" reconsidered
JBFA 1981 SUMMER VOL 8:2 p 161-164

(9210)
Emery D R, Gaumnitz J E
Asset growth, abandonment value and the replacement decision of like-for-like capital assets
JFQA 1980 JUN VOL 15 p 407.

(9211)
Berry R H, Dyson R G
A mathematical programming approach to taxation induced interdependencies in investment appraisal
JBFA 1979 WINTER VOL 6:4 p 425-441

(9212)
Bacon P W
The evaluation of mutually exclusive investments
FIN MGMT 1977 SUMMER VOL 6 p 55.

(9213)
Goldwerger J, Paroush J
Capital budgeting of interdependent projects: activity analysis approach
MSci 1977 JUL VOL 23:11 p 1242-1246.

(9214)**Thompson H E**
Mathematical programming, the capital asset pricing model and capital budgeting of interrelated projects
JF 1976 VOL 31 p 125.

(9215)
Malcolmson J M
Replacement and the rental value of capital equipment subject to obsolescence
JET 1975 FEB VOL 10:1 p 24-41.

(9216)
Nickell S
A closer look at replacement investment
JET 1975 FEB VOL 10:1 p 54-88.

(9217)
Trippi R R, Khumawala B M
Solution of the multi-asset finite horizon investment renewal problem
MSci 1975 JUN VOL 21:10 p 1156-1163.

(9218)
Brumelle S L, Schwab B
Capital budgeting with uncertain future opportunities: A Markovian approach
JFQA 1973 JAN VOL 8:1 p 111-122.

(9219)
Gould J R
On investment criteria for mutually exclusive projects
Ec 1972 FEB VOL 39 p 70-77.

(9220)
Lusztig P A, Schwab B
A note on the application of linear programming to capital budgeting
JFQA 1968 DEC VOL 3 p 427-432.

(9221)
Weingartner H M
Capital budgeting of interrelated projects: survey and synthesis
MSci 1966 MAR VOL 12 p 485-516.

(9222)
Cheng P L, Shelton J P
A contribution to the theory of capital budgeting--the multi-investment case
JF 1963 DEC VOL 18 p 622-636.

22.5   Public projects and cost-benefit analysis

(9223)
Burgess D F
Complementarity and the discount rate for public investment
QJE 1988 VOL 103 p 527.

(9224)
Khan A
Capital budgeting practices in large US cities
EE 1987 FALL VOL 33:1 p 1-12.

(9225)
National Economic Development Council
Investment in the public sector built infrastructure: NEDC papers
NEDO, 1985.

(9226)
Officer R R
Financial targeting for public enterprise: The criterion of a rate of return to capital
AJM 1985 DEC VOL 10.

(9227)
Bridger G A, Winpenny J T
Planning development projects: a practical guide to the choice and appraisal of public sector investments
HMSO, 1983.

(9228)
Treasury
Investment appraisal in the public sector
HMSO, 1982.

(9229)
Christiansen V
Evaluation of public projects under optimal taxation
REStud 1981 JUL VOL 48:3 NO 153 p 447-458.

(9230)
Graham D A
Cost-benefit analysis under uncertainty
AER 1981 VOL 71 p 715-725.

(9231)
Mendelsohn R
The choice of discount rates for public projects
AER 1981 VOL 71 p 239-241.

(9232)
Pearce D W, Nash C A
The social appraisal of projects: a text in cost-benefit analysis
Macmillan, 1981.

(9233)
Hansen J R
Guide to practical project appraisal: social benefit-cost analysis in developing countries
United Nations, 1978.

(9234)
Irvin G
Modern cost-benefit methods: an introduction to financial, economic and social appraisal of development projects
Macmillan, 1978.

(9235)
Keown A J, Martin J D
Capital budgeting in the public sector: A zero-one goal programming approach
FIN MGMT 1978 SUMMER VOL 7 p 21.

(9236)
Stapleton R C, Subrahmanyam M G
Capital market equilibrium in a mixed economy, optimal public sector investment decision rules and the social rate of discount
QJE 1978 VOL 92 p 399.

(9237)
Keown A J, Martin J D
An integer goal programming model for capital budgeting in hospitals
FIN MGMT 1976 AUTUMN VOL 5 p 28.

(9238)
Wacht R F, Whitford D T
A goal programming model for capital investment analysis in non-profit hospitals
FIN MGMT 1976 SUMMER VOL 5 p 37.

(9239)
Bradford D F
Constraints on government investment opportunities and the choice of discount rate
AER 1975 VOL 65 p 887-899.

(9240)
Frost M J
How to use cost benefit analysis in project appraisal
Gower, 1975.

(9241)
Furst R W, Bauerschmidt A D
Review article: The financial management of hospitals
FIN MGMT 1975 SPRING VOL 4 p 25.

(9242)
James E
A note on uncertainty and the evaluation of public investment decisions
AER 1975 VOL 65 p 200-205.

(9243)
Little I M D, Mirrlees J A
Project appraisal and planning for development
Heinemann, 1974.

(9244)
Jackman H W
Financing public hospitals in Ontario: a case study in rationing of capital budget
MSci 1973 DEC VOL 20:4 p 645-655.

(9245)
Shapiro D L
Can public investment have a positive rate of return?
JPE 1973 MAR-APR VOL 81:2 p 401-413.

(9246)
Williams J D, Rakich J S
Investment evaluation in hospitals
FIN MGMT 1973 SUMMER VOL 2 p 30.

(9247)
Bailey M J, Jensen M C
Risk and the discount rate for public investment
(in Jensen M C ed., Studies in the theory of capital markets. Praeger, 1972.)

(9248)
Dasgupta P et al.
Guidelines for project evaluation
United Nations, 1972.

(9249)
Knobel R J, Longest B B Jr
Cost-benefit assumptions in analysis for hospitals
FIN MGMT 1972 SPRING VOL 1 p 63.

(9250)
Arrow K J, Lind R C
Uncertainty and the evaluation of public investment decisions
AER 1970 JUN VOL 60 p 364-378.

(9251)
Schwartz E
The cost of capital and investment criteria in the public sector
JF 1970 MAR VOL 25 p 135-142.

(9252)
Arrow K J
Discounting and public investment criteria
(in Kneese A V and Smith S C eds., Water Research. Baltimore, 1966.)

(9253)
Arrow K J
Criteria for social investment
Water Resources Research 1965 VOL 1 p 1-8.

(9254)
Mao J C T
Efficiency in public urban renewal expenditures
through capital budgeting
U of Cal, 1965.

(9255)
Samuelson P A
Principles of efficiency: discussion
AER 1964 MAY VOL 54 p 93-96.

22.6 Risk analysis of capital expenditures

(9256)
Kim S-H, Elsaid H H
Estimation of periodic standard deviations under
the PERT and derivation of probabilistic
information
JBFA 1988 WINTER VOL 15:4 p 557-572.

(9257)
Cooper D F, Chapman C B
Risk analysis for large projects: models, methods
and cases
Wiley, 1987.

(9258)
Park C S
The Mellin transform in probabilistic cash flow
modelling
EE 1987 WINTER VOL 32:2 p 115-134.

(9259)
Shashua L, Goldschmidt Y
Break-even analysis under inflation
EE 1987 WINTER VOL 32:2 p 79-88.

(9260)
Balachandran B V, Nagarajan A J, Rappaport A
Threshold margins for creating economic value
FIN MGMT 1986 SPRING VOL 15 p 68-77.

(9261)
Buck J R, Askin R G
Partial means in the economic risk analysis of
projects
EE 1986 SPRING VOL 31:3 p 189-212.

(9262)
Levy H, Brooks R
Financial break-even analysis and the value of the
firm
FIN MGMT 1986 AUTUMN VOL 15 p 22-26.

(9263)
Kim S-H, Elsaid H H
Safety margin allocation and risk assessment
under the NPV method
JBFA 1985 SPRING VOL 12:1 p 133-144

(9264)
Hertz D B, Thomas H
Risk analysis and its applications
Wiley, 1983.

(9265)
Chen S-N, Moore W T
Investment decisions under uncertainty :
application of estimation risk in the Hillier
approach
JFQA 1982 SEP VOL 17:3 p 425-440

(9266)
Cozzolino J M
Controlling risk in capital budgeting: a practical
use of utility theory for measurement and control
of petroleum exploration risk
EE 1980 VOL 25:3 p 161-186..

(9267)**Hull J C**
The evaluation of risk in business investment
Pergamon, 1980.

(9268)
Lere J C
Deterministic net present value as an
approximation of expected net present value
JBFA 1980 SUMMER VOL 7:2 p 245-259

(9269)
Ekern S
On the inadequacy of a probabilistic internal rate
of return
JBFA 1979 SUMMER VOL 6:2 p 229-238.

(9270)
Hertz D B
Risk analysis in capital investment
HBR 1979 SEP-OCT VOL 57:5 p 169-181.

(9271)
Hull J C
The interpretation of the output from a sensitivity
analysis in investment appraisal
JBFA 1978 SPRING VOL 5:1 p 109-122.

(9272)
Hax A C, Wiig K M
The use of decision analysis in capital investment
problems
SMR 1976 WINTER VOL 17 p 19-48.

(9273)
Whisler W D
Sensitivity analysis of rates of return
JF 1976 VOL 31 p 63.

(9274)
Fairley W B, Jacoby H D
Investment analysis using the probability
distribution of the internal rate of return
MSci 1975 AUG VOL 21:12 p 1428-1437.

(9275)
Robichek A A
Interpreting the results of risk analysis
JF 1975 VOL 30 p 1384.

(9276)
Joy O M, Bradley J O
A note on sensitivity analysis of rates of return
JF 1973 VOL 28 p 1255.

(9277)
Reinhardt U E
Break-even analysis for Lockheed's Tri-star: An
application of financial theory
JF 1973 VOL 28 p 821.

(9278)
Carter E E
What are the risks in risk analysis?
HBR 1972 JUL-AUG VOL 50:4 p 72-82.

(9279)
Lewellen W G, Long M S
Simulation vs. single-value estimates in capital
expenditure analysis
Decision Sciences 1972 VOL 3 p 19-34.

(9280)
Byrne R F et al.
Studies in budgeting
N Holland, 1971.

(9281)
Hillier F S
The evaluation of risky interrelated investments
N Holland, 1969.

(9282)
Hertz D B
Investment policies that pay off
HBR 1968 JAN-FEB VOL 46 p 96-103.

(9283)
Salazar R C, Sen S K
A simulation model of capital budgeting under
uncertainty
MSci 1968 DEC VOL 15 p B161-B179.

(9284)
Hespos R F, Strassman P A
Stochastic decision trees for the analysis of
investment decisions
MSci 1965 AUG VOL 12 p B244-B259.

(9285)
Hillier F S
Supplement to the derivation of probabilistic
information for the evaluation of risky
investments
MSci 1965 JAN VOL 11 p 485-487.

(9286)
Hertz D B
Risk analysis in capital investment
HBR 1964 JAN-FEB VOL 42 p 95-106.

(9287)
Hillier F S
Derivation of probabilistic information for the
evaluation of risky investments
MSci 1963 APR VOL 9 p 443-457.

23 Cost of capital

(9288)
Ashton D J
The cost of capital and the imputation tax system
JBFA 1989 SPRING VOL 16:1 p 75.

(9289)
Benzion U, Rapoport A, Yagil J
Discount rates inferred from decisions: an
experimental study
MSci 1989 VOL 35 p 270.

(9290)
Butler J S, Schachter B
The investment decision: estimation risk and risk
adjusted discount rates
FIN MGMT 1989 WINTER VOL 18 p 13-22.

(9291)
Harris R S, O'Brien T J, Wakeman D
Divisional cost-of-capital estimation for
multi-industry firms
FIN MGMT 1989 SUMMER VOL 18 p 74-84.

(9292)
Harris F H deB
Capital intensity and the firm's cost of capital
REStat 1988 VOL 70 p 587.

(9293)
Shome D K, Smith S D
An econometric analysis of equity costs and risk
premiums in the electric utility industry:
1971-1985
FR 1988 NOV VOL 23:4 p 439-452.

(9294)
Auerbach A J
The Tax Reform Act of 1986 and the cost of
capital
JEP 1987 VOL 1:1 p 73-86.

(9295)
Friend I, Tokutsu I
The cost of capital to corporations in Japan and
the USA
JBankF 1987 VOL 11 p 313-327.

(9296)
Arnold J H
Assessing capital risk : you can't be too
conservative
HBR 1986 SEP-OCT VOL 64:5 p 113-121

(9297)
Hull J C
A note on the risk-adjusted discount rate method
JBFA 1986 AUTUMN VOL 13:3 p 445-450

(9298)
Mayer C
Corporation tax, finance and the cost of capital
REStud 1986 VOL 53 p 93.

(9299)
Petruzzi C R
An options approach to setting risk adjusted
hurdle rates
EE 1986 SPRING VOL 31:3 p 237-248.

(9300)
Ruback R S
Calculating the market value of riskless cash flows
JFE 1986 MAR VOL 15:3 p 323-339.

(9301)
Zhu Y, Friend I
The effects of different taxes on risky and
risk-free investment and on the cost of capital
JF 1986 MAR VOL 41:1 p 53-66.

(9302)
Brigham E F, Shome D K, Vinson S R
The risk premium approach to measuring a
utility's cost of equity
FIN MGMT 1985 SPRING VOL 14 p 33-45.

(9303)
Chen K C, Davidson W N III
A note on the cost of equity when dividend
changes are level gradients
EE 1985 WINTER VOL 30:2 p 182-190.

(9304)
Conine T E Jr, Tamarkin M
Divisional cost of capital estimation adjusting for
leverage
FIN MGMT 1985 SPRING VOL 14 p 54-58.

(9305)
Riener K D
A pedagogic note on the cost of capital with
personal taxes and risky debt
FR 1985 MAY VOL 20:2.

(9306)
Siegel J J
The application of the DCF methodology for determining the cost of equity capital
FIN MGMT 1985 SPRING VOL 14 p 46-53.

(9307)
Beedles W L
Some notes on the cost of new equity
JBFA 1984 SUMMER VOL 11:2 p 245-251

(9308)
Haley C W
Valuation and risk-adjusted discount rates
JBFA 1984 AUTUMN VOL 11:3 p 347-353

(9309)
Linke C M, Zumwalt J K
Estimation biases in discounted cash flow analyses of equity capital cost in rate regulation
FIN MGMT 1984 AUTUMN VOL 13 p 15-21.

(9310)
Mehta D R, Curley M D, Fung H-G
Inflation, cost of capital and capital budgeting procedures
FIN MGMT 1984 WINTER VOL 13 p 48.

(9311)
Moore W T, Jose M L
An alternative approach to computing the after-tax cost of debt
EE 1984 WINTER VOL 29:2 p 150-155.

(9312)
Bierman H Jr, Hass J E
Investment cut-off rates and dividend policy
FIN MGMT 1983 WINTER VOL 12 p 19-24.

(9313)
Bohren O
Bounding certainty equivalent factors and risk adjusted discount rates
JBFA 1983 SPRING VOL 10:1 p 139-146

(9314)
Corcoran P J
The cost of capital: an update
F R Bk New York Q Rev 1983 AUTUMN VOL 8:3.

(9315)
Greenfield R L, Randall M R, Wood J C
Financial leverage and use of the net present value investment criterion
FIN MGMT 1983 AUTUMN VOL 12 p 40-44.

(9316)
Vickers D
A note on the marginal cost of debt capital
JBFA 1983 WINTER VOL 10:4 p 673-676

(9317)
Chambers D R, Harris R S, Pringle J J
Treatment of financing mix in analyzing investment opportunities
FIN MGMT 1982 SUMMER VOL 11 p 24-41.

(9318)
Corcoran P J, Sahling L G
The cost of capital: how high is it?
F R Bk New York Q Rev 1982 SUMMER VOL 7:2.

(9319)
Fitzpatrick D
Does the negative risk premium really exist?
PUF 1982 JUL 8 p 27-33..

(9320)**Gitman L J, Mercurio V A**
Cost of capital techniques used by major U S firms: Survey and analysis of Fortune's 1000
FIN MGMT 1982 WINTER VOL 11 p 21-29.

(9321)
Gup B E, Norwood S W III
Divisional cost of capital: A practical approach
FIN MGMT 1982 SPRING VOL 11 p 20-24.

(9322)
Rhee S G, McCarthy F L
Corporate debt capacity and capital budgeting analysis
FIN MGMT 1982 SUMMER VOL 11 p 42-50.

(9323)
Rhyne R G
Can the capital asset pricing model give reliable estimates of the cost of equity?
PUF 1982 NOV 25 p 21-26.

(9324)
Senbet L W, Thompson H E
Growth and risk
JFQA 1982 SEP VOL 17:3 p 331-340

(9325)
Taylor G, Peake C
A utility's cost of common stock equity may be
less than its cost rate for new debt
PUF 1982 JUN 24 p 23-30.

(9326)
Yagil J
On valuation, beta, and the cost of equity capital
: a note
JFQA 1982 SEP VOL 17:3 p 441-449.

(9327)
Fuller R J, Kerr H S
Estimating the divisional cost of capital : an
analysis of the pure-play technique
JF 1981 DEC VOL 36:5 p 997-1009.

(9328)
Holmstrom B
The cost of capital in nonmarketed firms
QJE 1981 VOL 95 p 765-773.

(9329)
Partington G H
Financial decisions, the cost(s) of capital and the
capital asset pricing model
JBFA 1981 SPRING VOL 8:1 p 97-112.

(9330)
Sharp G P, Guzman-Garza A
Borrowing interest rate as a function of the
debt-equity ratio in capital budgeting models
EE 1981 SUMMER VOL 26:4 p 293-315.

(9331)
Vickers D
The marginal efficiency of (money) capital
JBFA 1981 SUMMER VOL 8:2 p 165-176

(9332)
Berry R H, Dyson R G
On the negative risk premium for risk adjusted
discount rates
JBFA 1980 AUTUMN VOL 7:3 p 427-436.

(9333)
Booth L D
Capital structure taxes and the cost of capital
QREB 1980 AUTUMN VOL 20:3 p 86-98

(9334)
Elliott J W
The cost of capital and US capital investment: a
test of alternative concepts
JF 1980 SEP VOL 35:4 p 981-999.

(9335)
Van Horne J C
An application of the CAPM to divisional
required returns
FIN MGMT 1980 SPRING VOL 9 p 14.

(9336)
Aivazian V A, Callen J L
Investment, market structure and the cost of
capital
JF 1979 MAR VOL 34:1 p 85-92

(9337)
Auerbach A J
Wealth maximization and the cost of capital
QJE 1979 VOL 93 p 433.

(9338)
Dhaliwal D S, Spicer B H, Vickrey D
The quality of disclosure and the cost of capital
JBFA 1979 SUMMER VOL 6:2 p 245.

(9339)
Everett J E, Schwab B
On the proper adjustment for risk through
discount rates in a mean-variance framework
FIN MGMT 1979 SUMMER VOL 8 p 61.

(9340)
Ezzamel M A
Divisional cost of capital and the measurement of
divisional performance
JBFA 1979 AUTUMN VOL 6:3 p 307-320.

(9341)
Ezzell J R, Porter R B
Correct specification of the cost of capital and net
present value
FIN MGMT 1979 SUMMER VOL 8 p 13.

(9342)
Long M S, Racette G
Stochastic demand and the equity capitalization rate
JBFA 1979 WINTER VOL 6:4 p 475-494.

(9343)
Williams E E, Findlay M C III
Capital budgeting, cost of capital and ex ante static equilibrium
JBFA 1979 WINTER VOL 6:4 p 455-473.

(9344)
Arditti F D, Pinkerton J M
The valuation and the cost of capital of the levered firm with growth opportunities
JF 1978 VOL 33 p 65.

(9345)
Gordon M J, Gould L I
The cost of equity capital with personal income taxes and flotation costs
JF 1978 VOL 33 p 1201.

(9346)
Haley C W, Schall L D
Problems with the concept of the cost of capital
JFQA 1978 DEC VOL 13 p 847.

(9347)
Jaffe J F
Corporate taxes, inflation, the rate of interest and the return of equity
JFQA 1978 MAR VOL 13 p 55.

(9348)
Jarrett J E
Estimating the cost of capital for a division of a firm and the allocation problem in accounting
JBFA 1978 SPRING VOL 5:1 p 39-48.

(9349)
Keane S M
The cost of capital as a financial decision tool
JBFA 1978 AUTUMN VOL 5:3 p 339-354.

(9350)
Oso J B
The proper role of the tax-adjusted cost of capital in present value studies
EE 1978 FALL VOL 24:1 p 1-12.

(9351)
Schwab B
Conceptual problems in the use of risk-adjusted discount rates with disaggregated cash flows
JBFA 1978 WINTER VOL 5:4 p 281-293

(9352)
Sullivan T G
The cost of capital and the market power of firms
REStat 1978 MAY VOL 60:2 p 209-217.

(9353)
Vickers D
Realism and relevance in the cost of money capital
OEP 1978 MAR VOL 30:1 p 102-116.

(9354)
Hayes S L III
Capital commitments and the high cost of money
HBR 1977 MAY-JUN VOL 55:3 p 155-161.

(9355)
Keane S M
The irrelevance of the firm's cost of capital as an investment decision tool
JBFA 1977 SUMMER VOL 4:2 p 201-216.

(9356)
Lewellen W G
Some observations on risk-adjusted discount rates
JF 1977 VOL 32 p 1331.

(9357)
Lewellen W G, McConnell J J
Tax reform, firm valuation and capital costs
FIN MGMT 1977 WINTER VOL 6 p 59.

(9358)
Taggart R A
Capital budeting and the financing decision: An exposition
FIN MGMT 1977 SUMMER VOL 6 p 59.

(9359)
Zanker F W A
The cost of capital for debt-financed investments
JBFA 1977 AUTUMN VOL 4:3 p 277-284.

(9360)
Bank of England
The cost of capital, finance and investment
BEQB 1976 VOL 16 p 193-205.

(9361)
Brealey R A, Hodges S D, Capron D
The return on alternative sources of finance
REStat 1976 VOL 58 p 469.

(9362)
Findlay M C III, Gooding A E, Weaver W Q Jr
On the relevant risk for determining capital
expenditure hurdle rates
FIN MGMT 1976 WINTER VOL 5 p 9.

(9363)
Grinyer J R
The cost of equity, the CAPM and management
objectives under uncertainty
JBFA 1976 WINTER VOL 3:4 p 101-122.

(9364)
Groves R E V, Samuels J M
A note on the cost of retained earnings and
deferred taxes in the U K
JBFA 1976 WINTER VOL 3:4 p 143-150.

(9365)
Henderson G V Jr
On capitalization rates for riskless streams
JF 1976 VOL 31 p 1491.

(9366)
Keenan M, Maldonado R M
The redundancy of earnings leverage in a cost of
capital decision framework
JBFA 1976 SUMMER VOL 3:2 p 43-56.

(9367)
Lawrenz D W
The effects of corporate taxation on the cost of
equity capital
FIN MGMT 1976 SPRING VOL 5 p 53.

(9368)
Lewellen W G
The cost of capital
Kendall-Hunt, 1976.

(9369)
Bower R S, Jenks J M
Divisional screening rates
FIN MGMT 1975 AUTUMN VOL 4 p 42.

(9370)
Brigham E F
Hurdle rates for screening capital expenditure
proposals
FIN MGMT 1975 AUTUMN VOL 4 p 17.

(9371)
Petry G H
Empirical evidence on cost of capital weights
FIN MGMT 1975 WINTER VOL 4 p 58.

(9372)
Adler M
The cost of capital and valuation of a two-country
firm
JF 1974 VOL 29 p 119..

(9373)**Burton R M, Damon W W**
On the existence of a cost of capital under pure
capital rationing
JF 1974 VOL 29 p 1165.

(9374)
Gordon M J, Halpern P J
Cost of capital for a division of a firm
JF 1974 VOL 29 p 1153.

(9375)
Haegert L
An analysis of the Kuhn-Tucker conditions of
stochastic programming with reference to the
estimate of discount rate and risk premia
JBFA 1974 AUTUMN VOL 1:3 p 319-334.

(9376)
Keane S M
The cost of capital and the relevance of
nondiversifiable risk
JBFA 1974 SPRING VOL 1:1 p 129-144.

(9377)
King M A
Taxation and the cost of capital
REStud 1974 VOL 41 p 21.

(9378)
Lewellen W G
A conceptual reappraisal of cost of capital
FIN MGMT 1974 WINTER VOL 3 p 63.

(9379)
Arditti F D, Tysseland M S
Three ways to present the marginal cost of capital
FIN MGMT 1973 SUMMER VOL 2 p 63.

(9380)
Bernstein P I
What rate of return can you "reasonably expect"?
JF 1973 VOL 28 p 273.

(9381)
Elton E J, Gruber M J
Asset selection with changing capital structure
JFQA 1973 JUN VOL 8:3 p 459-474.

(9382)
Rubinstein M E
A mean-variance synthesis of corporate financial
theory
JF 1973 VOL 28 p 167.

(9383)
Tepper I
Revealed preference methods and the pure theory
of the cost of capital
JF 1973 VOL 28 p 35.

(9384)
Grinyer J R
The cost of equity capital
JBF 1972 WINTER VOL 4:4 p 44-52.

(9385)
Litzenberger R H, Rao C U
Portfolio theory and industrial cost-of-capital
estimates
JFQA 1972 MAR VOL 7 p 1443-1462.

(9386)
Whittington G
The profitability of retained earnings
REStat 1972 MAY VOL 54 p 152-160.

(9387)
Litzenberger R H, Joy O M
Target rates of return and corporate asset and
liability structure under uncertainty
JFQA 1971 MAR VOL 6 p 675-686.

(9388)
Magen S D
Cost of capital and dividend policies in
commercial banks
JFQA 1971 MAR VOL 6 p 733-746.

(9389)
Baumol W J, Heim P, Malkiel B G et al.
Earning retention, new capital and the growth of
firms
REStat 1970 NOV VOL 52 p 345-355.

(9390)
Sampson A A
Measuring the rate of return on capital
JF 1969 MAR VOL 24 p 61-74.

(9391)
Brigham E F, Gordon M J
Leverage, dividend policy, and the cost of capital
JF 1968 MAR VOL 23 p 85-103.

(9392)
Baumol W J, Malkiel B G
The firm's optimal debt-equity combination and
the cost of capital
QJE 1967 NOV VOL 81 p 547-578.

(9393)
Krainer R E
Interest rates, investment decisions and external
financing
OEP 1966 NOV VOL 18 p 304-312.

(9394)
Merrett A J, Sykes A
Rates of return standards: the cost of capital
Accountancy 1966 JAN VOL 77 p 7-14.

(9395)
Robichek A A, Myers S C
Conceptual problems in the use of risk adjusted
discount rates
JF 1966 DEC VOL 21 p 727-730.

23.1   Adjusted cost of capital formulas

(9396)
Solow R M
Capital theory and the rate of return
Chicago: Rand McNally, 1965.

(9397)
Boness A J
A pedagogic note on the cost of capital
JF 1964 MAR VOL 19 p 99-106.

(9398)
Lintner J
The cost of capital and optimal financing of corporate growth
JF 1963 MAY VOL 18 p 302-310.

(9399)
Weston J F
A test of cost of capital propositions
SEJ 1963 OCT VOL 30 p 105-112.

(9400)
Ravenscroft E A
Return on investment: fit the method to your need
HBR 1960 MAR-APR VOL 38 p 97-109.

(9401)
Gordon M J, Shapiro E
Capital equipment analysis: the required rate of profit
MSci 1956 OCT VOL 3 p 102-110.

(9402)
Solomon E
Measuring a company's cost of capital
JB 1955 OCT VOL 28 p 240-252.

(9403)
Soule R P
Trends in the cost of capital
HBR 1953 MAR-APR VOL 31 p 33-47.

(9404)
Durand D
Cost of debt and equity funds for business: trends and problems of measurement
(in Conference on Research in Business Finance, Natl Bur Econ Res, 1952.)

23.1   Adjusted cost of capital formulas

(9405)
Miller M H, Modigliani F
Some estimates of the cost of capital to the electric utility industry, 1954-57
AER 1966 JUN VOL 56 p 333-391.

(9406)
Modigliani F, Miller M H
Corporate income taxes and the cost of capital: a correction
AER 1963 JUN VOL 53 p 433-443.

23.11   Weighted-average cost of capital

(9407)
Wirth A, Wright F K
New-issue costs and project evaluation : Ezzell and Porter revisited
JBFA 1987 AUTUMN VOL 14:3 p 393-407.

(9408)
Brigham E F, Tapley T C
Financial leverage and use of the net present value investment criterion: A re-examination
FIN MGMT 1985 SUMMER VOL 14 p 48-52.

(9409)
Golbe D L, Schacher B
The net present value rule and an algorithm for maintaining a constant debt-equity ratio
FIN MGMT 1985 SUMMER VOL 14 p 53-58.

(9410)
Miles J A, Ezzell J R
The weighted average cost of capital, perfect capital markets and project life: A clarification
JFQA 1980 SEP VOL 15 p 719.

(9411)
Henderson G V Jr
In defense of the weighted average cost of capital
FIN MGMT 1979 AUTUMN VOL 8 p 57.

(9412)
Levacic R, Rebmann-Huber A
The tax-deductibility of interest payments and the
weighted average cost of capital once again
JBFA 1979 SPRING VOL 6:1 p 101-110.

(9413)
Shapiro A C
In defense of the traditional weighted average
cost of capital as a cutoff rate
FIN MGMT 1979 SUMMER VOL 8 p 22.

(9414)
Arditti F D, Levy H
The weighted average cost of capital as a cutoff
rate: A critical analysis of the classical textbook
weighted average
FIN MGMT 1977 AUTUMN p 24.

(9415)
Beranek W
The weighted average cost of capital and
shareholder wealth maximization
JFQA 1977 MAR VOL 12 p 17.

(9416)
Findlay M C III
The weighted average cost of capital and finite
flows
JBFA 1977 SUMMER VOL 4:2 p 217-228.

(9417)
Ezzell J R, Porter R B
Flotation costs and the weighted average cost of
capital
JFQA 1976 SEP VOL 11 p 403.

(9418)
Keane S M
The tax-deductibility of interest payments and the
weighted average cost of capital
JBFA 1976 WINTER VOL 3:4 p 53-62.

(9419)
Beranek W
A little more on the weighted average cost of
capital
JFQA 1975 DEC VOL 10 p 892.

(9420)
Nantell T J, Carlson C R
The cost of capital as a weighted average
JF 1975 VOL 30 p 1343.

(9421)
Arditti F D
The weighted average cost of capital: Some
questions on its definition, interpretation and use
JF 1973 VOL 28 p 1001.

(9422)
Brennan M J
A new look at the weighted average cost of
capital
JBF 1973 SPRING VOL 5:1 p 24-30.

(9423)
Reilly R R, Wecker W E
On the weighted average cost of capital
JFQA 1973 JAN VOL 8:1 p 123-126.

23.2 Adjusted present value

(9424)
Lessard D R
Evaluating foreign projects - An adjusted present
value approach
(in Lessard D R ed., International financial
management: Theory and application, 2nd ed.
Wiley, 1986.)

(9425)
Howe K M, Patterson J H
Capital investment decisions under economies of
scale in flotation costs
FIN MGMT 1985 AUTUMN VOL 14 p 61-69..

(9426)**Miles J A, Ezzell J R**
Reformulating tax shield valuation : a note
JF 1985 DEC VOL 40:5 p 1485-1492.

(9427)
Ezzell J R, Kelly W A Jr
An APV analysis of capital budgeting under
inflation
FIN MGMT 1984 AUTUMN VOL 13 p 49.

(9428)
Hubbard C M
Flotation costs in capital budgeting: A note on
the tax effects
FIN MGMT 1984 SUMMER VOL 13 p 38-40.

(9429)
Howe K M
A note on flotation costs and capital budgeting
FIN MGMT 1982 WINTER VOL 11 p 30-33.

(9430)
Harris R S
The refunding of discounted debt: An adjusted
present value analysis
FIN MGMT 1980 WINTER VOL 9 p 7.

(9431)
Myers S C
Interactions of corporate financing and investment
decisions - implications for capital budgeting
JF 1974 VOL 29 p 23.2

24 New securities issues

(9432)
Lamoureux C G, Wansley J W
The pricing of when-issued securities
FR 1989 MAY VOL 24:2 p 183-198.

(9433)
Powell J L
Issues and offers of company securities: the new
regimes
Sweet, 1988.

(9434)
Smith C W Jr
Raising capital: Theory and evidence
MCFJ 1986 SPRING VOL 4 p 6-22.

(9435)
Dealers' Digest Inc.
Five year directory of corporate financing
1980-1984, ed. A V Ricotta
New York: Mason Slaine, 1985.

(9436)
Jarrell G A
The economic effects of federal regulation of the
market for new security issues
JLE 1981 VOL 24:3 p 613.

(9437)
Finnerty J E
Corporate stock issue and repurchase
FIN MGMT 1975 AUTUMN VOL 4 p 62.

(9438)
Cragg J G, Baxter N D
The issuing of corporate securities
JPE 1970 NOV-DEC VOL 78 p 1310-1324.

(9439)
Friend I
Investment banking and the new issues market:
summary volume
U of Pa, Wharton School of Finance, 1965.

(9440)
Nevin E
Some reflections on the New York new issue
market
OEP 1961 FEB VOL 13 p 84-102.

(9441)
Welfling W
Financing business enterprise
New York: American Institute of Banking, 1960.

24.1 Venture capital

(9442)
Golis C
Enterprise and venture capital: an entrepreneurs'
and investors' handbook
Allen, 1989.

(9443)
Lorenz T
Venture capital today: a practical guide to the
venture capital market. 2nd ed
Woodhead-Faulkner, 1989.

(9444)
Morris J K, Isenstein S eds.
Pratt's guide to venture capital sources. 13th ed
Needham, MA: Venture Economics, 1989.

(9445)
Peat Marwick McLintock
Venture capital in Europe: 1989 ECVA yearbook
Peat Marwick McLintock, 1989.

(9446)
Stoy Hayward
Guide to venture capital 1989
Stoy Hayward, 1989.

(9447)
Gladstone D
Venture capital handbook. Rev ed
P-H, 1988.

(9448)
Lloyd S E
Guide to European venture capital sources. 2nd
ed
Venture Economics, 1988.

(9449)
Macdonald M
Venture capital: Its coming of age in Canada
Canadian Investment Review 1988 FALL VOL 1
p 81-86.

(9450)
Ormerod J, Burns I
Raising venture capital in the UK
Butterworth, 1988.

(9451)
Sahlman W A
Aspects of financial contracting in venture capital
JACF 1988 SUMMER VOL 1 p 23-36.

(9452)
Bleicher K, Paul H
The external corporate venture capital fund-a
valuable vehicle for growth
Long Range Planning 1987 DEC VOL 20:6 p
64-70.

(9453)
Clark R
Venture capital in Britain, America and Japan
Croom Helm, 1987.

(9454)
Henderson J W
Obtaining venture financing: principles and
practices
Heath, 1987.

(9455)
Ramirez A
Foreign affairs of a venture capitalist
F 1987 FEB 2 VOL 115:3 p 68-72

(9456)
Schilit W K
How to obtain venture capital
Business Horizons 1987 MAY-JUN VOL 30:3 p
76-81.

(9457)
Siskos J, Zopounidis C
The evaluation criteria of the venture capital
investment activity : An interactive assessment
EJOR 1987 SEP VOL 31:3 p 304-313.

(9458)
Torpey W J, Viscione J A
Mezzanine money for smaller businesses
HBR 1987 MAY-JUN VOL 65:3 p 116-122.

(9459)
Doran A, Hoyle M
Lending to small firms: a study of appraisal and
monitoring methods: a report
NEDO, 1986.

(9460)
**National Economic Development Council. Cttee
on Finance for Industry**
External capital for small firms: a review of recent
developments
NEDO, 1986.

(9461)
OECD
Venture capital: context, development and policies
OECD, 1986.

(9462)
Stancill J M
How much money does your new venture need?
HBR 1986 MAY-JUN VOL 64:3 p 122-139.

(9463)
Sykes H B
Lessons from a new ventures program
HBR 1986 MAY-JUN VOL 64:3 p 69-74.

(9464)
Block Z, MacMillan I C
Milestones for successful venture planning
HBR 1985 SEP-OCT VOL 63:5 p 184-196.

(9465)
Commission of the European Communities
Improving venture capital opportunities in
Europe: proceedings of a symposium held in
Luxembourg, 3-5 October 1984
Kogan Page, 1985.

(9466)
Hector G
A tough slog for venture capitalists
F 1985 JUN 10 VOL 111:12 p 74-80.

(9467)
Pettit R R, Singer R F
Small business finance: A research agenda
FIN MGMT 1985 AUTUMN VOL 14 p 47-60.

(9468)
Silver A D
Venture capital: the complete guide for investors
Wiley, 1985.

(9469)
Alexander T
Venture capitalists' private bets
F 1984 APR 30 VOL 109:9 p 75-84.

(9470)
Bank of England
Venture capital in the United Kingdom
BEQB 1984 VOL 24 p 207-211.

(9471)
Branch B
Special offerings and market efficiency
FR 1984 MAR VOL 19:1.

(9472)
Lipper A, Ryan G
Venture's guide to investing in private companies:
a financing manual for the entrepreneurial
investor
Dow Jones-Irwin, 1984.

(9473)
Tyebjee T T, Bruno A V
A model of venture capitalist investment activity
MSci 1984 SEP VOL 30:9 p 1051-1066.

(9474)
Chan Y S
On the positive role of financial intermediation in
allocation of venture capital in a market with
imperfect information
JF 1983 DEC VOL 38:5 p 1543-1568.

(9475)
Hardymon G F, De Nino M J, Salter M S
When corporate venture capital doesn't work
HBR 1983 MAY-JUN VOL 61:3 p 114-120.

(9476)
Martin J D, Petty J W
An analysis of the performance of publicly traded
venture capital companies
JFQA 1983 SEP VOL 18:3 p 401-410.

(9477)
Bank of England
Venture capital
BEQB 1982 VOL 22 p 511-513.

(9478)
Bates J, Hally D L
The financing of small business. 3rd ed
Sweet, 1982..

(9479)**Dizard J W**
Do we have too many venture capitalists?
F 1982 OCT 4 VOL 106:7 p 106-119.

(9480)
Jarrett M, Wright M
New initiatives in the financing of smaller firms
NWBQR 1982 AUG p 40-52.

(9481)
Kinross J B
Fifty years in the city: financing small business
John Murray, 1982.

(9482)
Pence C C
How venture capitalists make investment decisions
UMI Research Pr, 1982.

(9483)
Timmons J A, Gumpert D A
Discard many old rules about getting venture
capital
HBR 1982 JAN-FEB VOL 60:1 p 152-156.

(9484)
Huntsman B, Hoban J P Jr
Investment in new enterprise: Some empirical
observations on risk, return, and market structure
FIN MGMT 1980 SUMMER VOL 9 p 44.

(9485)
Cooper I A, Carleton W T
Dynamics of borrower - lender interaction:
partitioning final payoff in venture capital finance
JF 1979 MAY VOL 34:2 p 517-531.

(9486)
Gumpert D E
Venture capital becoming more widely available
HBR 1979 JAN-FEB VOL 57:1 p 178-182.

(9487)
Fortune
The woes of investors in private corporations
F 1978 AUG 3 VOL 98 p 189-192.

(9488)
Coutarelli S A
Venture capital in Europe
Praeger, 1977.

(9489)
United States. Department of Commerce
An analysis of venture capital market
imperfections
Washington, DC: Department of Commerce, 1976.

(9490)
Osborn R C
Providing risk capital for small business:
experience of the SBICs
QREB 1975 VOL 15:1 p 77.

(9491)
Dominguez J R
Venture capital
Lexington Bks, 1974.

(9492)
Osborn R C
The supply of equity capital by the SBICs
QREB 1973 VOL 13:1 p 69.

(9493)
Hooper C N
SBA's business loan program: retrospect and
prospect
JBR 1971 AUTUMN VOL 2:3.

(9494)
**Trade and Industry, Dept. of,   Committee of
Inquiry on Small Firms**
Financial facilities for small firms: a study by
Economists Advisory Group
HMSO, 1971.

(9495)
Flink S J
Equity financing for small business
Simmons-B, 1962.

(9496)
Summers G W
Financing and initial operations of new firms
P-H, 1962.

(9497)
Weaver R A Jr
Equity financing for the small firm
HBR 1956 MAR-APR VOL 34 p 91-102.

24.2   Initial public offerings

(9498)
Affleck-Graves J,   Miller R E
Regulatory and procedural effects on the
underpricing of initial public offerings
JFR 1989 FALL VOL 12:3 p 193-202.

(9499)
Allen F,   Faulhaber G R
Signaling by underpricing in the IPO market
JFE 1989 VOL 23 p 303.

(9500)
Bower N L
Firm value and the choice of offering method in
initial public offerings
JF 1989 JUL VOL 44:3 p 647-662.

(9501)
Elton E J,   Gruber M J,   Rentzler J
New public offerings, information, and investor
rationality: the case of publicly offered commodity
funds
JB 1989 VOL 62:1 p 1-16.

(9502)
Gale I,   Stiglitz J E
The information content of initial public offerings
JF 1989 JUN VOL 44:2 p 469.

(9503)
Grinblatt M,   Hwang C Y
Signalling and the pricing of new issues
JF 1989 JUN VOL 44:2 p 393-420.

(9504)
Hegde S P, Miller R E
Market-making in initial public offerings of common stocks: an empirical analysis
JFQA 1989 MAR VOL 24:1 p 75-90.

(9505)
Koh F, Walter T
A direct test of Rock's model of the pricing of unseasoned issues
JFE 1989 VOL 23 p 251.

(9506)
Krinsky I, Rotenberg W
Signalling and the valuation of unseasoned new issues revisited
JFQA 1989 JUN VOL 24:2 p 257.

(9507)
Muscarella C J, Vetsuypens M R
A simple test of Baron's model of IPO underpricing
JFE 1989 SEP VOL 24:1 p 125-136.

(9508)
Muscarella C J, Vetsuypens M R
The underpricing of "second" initial public offerings
JFR 1989 FALL VOL 12:3 p 183-192.

(9509)
Simon C J
The effect of the 1933 Securities Act on investor information and the performance of new issues
AER 1989 VOL 79:3 p 295-318.

(9510)
Ward C
Guide to company flotation
Director Books, 1989.

(9511)
Weiss K
The post-offering price performance of closed-end funds
FIN MGMT 1989 AUTUMN VOL 18 p 57-67.

(9512)
Welch I
Seasoned offerings, imitation costs, and the undrpricing of initial public offerings
JF 1989 JUN VOL 44:2 p 421-450.

(9513)
Dawson S M, Reiner N
Raising capital with initial public share issues in Germany: 1977-1985
MIR 1988 VOL 28:1 p 64-72.

(9514)
Finn F J, Higham R
The performance of unseasoned new equity issues-cum-stock exchange listings in Australia
JBankF 1988 VOL 12:3 p 333-352.

(9515)
Ibbotson R G, Sindelar J L, Ritter J R
Initial public offerings
JACF 1988 SUMMER VOL 1 p 37-45.

(9516)
Johnson J M, Miller R E
Investment banker prestige and the underpricing of initial public offerings
FIN MGMT 1988 SUMMER VOL 17 p 19-29.

(9517)
Krinsky I, Rotenberg W
The valuation of initial public offers
Contemporary Accounting Research 1988.

(9518)
Loderer C, Zimmermann H
Stock offerings in a different institutional setting: The Swiss case 1973-1983
JBankF 1988 VOL 12:3 p 353-376.

(9519)
Muscarella C J
Price performance of initial public offerings of master limited partnership units
FR 1988 NOV VOL 23:4 p 513.

(9520)
Tinic S M
Anatomy of initial public offerings of common stock
JF 1988 SEP VOL 43:4 p 789-822.

(9521)
Chalk A, Peavy J W
Initial public offerings: Daily returns, offering types and the price effect
FAJ 1987 SEP-OCT VOL 43 p 65-69.

(9522)
Chalk A J, Peavy J W
Why you'll never get a "hot" new issue
AAII Journal 1987 MAR VOL 9 p 16-20.

(9523)
Dawson S M
Secondary stock market performance of initial
public offers Hong Kong Singapore and Malaysia
: 1978-1984
JBFA 1987 SPRING VOL 14:1 p 65-76.

(9524)
Jog V M, Riding A L
Underpricing in Canadian IPOs
FAJ 1987 NOV-DEC VOL 43 p 48-55.

(9525)
Miller R E, Reilly F K
An examination of mispricing, returns and
uncertainty for inital public offerings
FIN MGMT 1987 SUMMER VOL 16 p 33-38.

(9526)
Ritter J R
The costs of going public
JFE 1987 VOL 19 p 269-281.

(9527)
Bank of England
New issue costs and methods in the UK equity
market
BEQB 1986 VOL 26 p 532-542.

(9528)
De Ridder A
Access to the stock market: an empirical study of
the efficiency of the British and the Swedish
primary markets
Stockholm: Federation of Swedish Industries,
1986.

(9529)
Ellis J
Why initial public offers are bad bets
Money Magazine 1986 APR p 175-186.

(9530)
Uttal B
Inside the deal that made Bill Gates $350,000,000
F 1986 JUL 21.

(9531)
Arnold J L
Exempt offerings : going public privately.
HBR 1985 JAN-FEB VOL 63:1 p 16-30..

(9532)**Stern R L, Bornstein P**
Why new issues are lousy investments
Forbes 1985 DEC 2 VOL 136 p 152-190.

(9533)
Neuberger B M, La Chapelle C A
Unseasoned new issue price performance on three
tiers: 1975-1980
FIN MGMT 1983 AUTUMN VOL 12 p 23-28.

(9534)
Schneider C W, Manko J, Kant R
Going public: Practice, procedure, and
consequences
Packard Press, 1983.

(9535)
Downes D H, Heinkel R
Signaling and the valuation of unseasoned new
issues
JF 1982 MAR VOL 37:1 p 1-10.

(9536)
Buckland R, Herbert P J, Yeomans K A
Price discount on new equity issues in the UK
and their relationship to investor subscription in
the period 1965-75
JBFA 1981 SPRING VOL 8:1 p 79-95

(9537)
Block S, Stanley M
The financial characteristics and price movement
patterns of companies approaching the
unseasoned securities market in the late 1970's
FIN MGMT 1980 WINTER VOL 9 p 30.

(9538)
Reilly F K
New issues revisited
FIN MGMT 1977 WINTER VOL 6 p 28.

(9539)
Vaughan G D, Grinyer P H
From private to public: an analysis of the choices,
problems and performance of newly floated
companies, 1966-1974
Woodhead-Faulkner, 1977.

(9540)
Davis E W, Yeomans K A
Market discount on new issues of equity: The
influence of firm size, method of issue and market
volatility
JBFA 1976 WINTER VOL 3:4 p 27-42.

(9541)
Bear R M, Curley A J
Unseasoned equity financing
JFQA 1975 JUN VOL 10 p 311.

(9542)
Ibbotson R G
Price performance of common stock new issues
JFE 1975 VOL 2 p 235.

(9543)
Ibbotson R G, Jaffe J J
"Hot Issue" markets
JF 1975 VOL 30 p 1027.

(9544)
Davis E W, Yeomans K A
Company finance and the capital market: a study
of the effects of firm size
Cambridge U Pr, 1974.

(9545)
Hammond C T, Newberger B M
A study of underwriters' experience with
unseasoned new issues
JFQA 1974 MAR VOL 9 p 165.

(9546)
Reilly F K
Further evidence on short-run results for new
issue investors
JFQA 1973 JAN VOL 8:1 p 83-90.

(9547)
Logue D E
Risk-adjusted performance of unseasoned common
stock offerings
QREB 1972 VOL 12:4 p 67.

(9548)
McDonald J G, Fisher A K
New issue stock price behavior
JF 1972 MAR VOL 27 p 92-102.

(9549)
Robinson G J
Going public--successful securities underwriting.
2nd ed
Boardman, 1971.

(9550)
Shaw D C
The performance of primary common stock
offerings: a Canadian comparison
JF 1971 DEC VOL 26 p 1101-1114.

(9551)
Brown J M
Post-offering experience of companies going
public
JB 1970 JAN VOL 43 p 10-18.

(9552)
Stoll H R, Curley A J
Small business and the new issues market for
equities
JFQA 1970 SEP VOL 5 p 309-322.

(9553)
Merrett A J, Howe M, Newbould G D
Equity issues and the London capital market
Longman, 1967.

(9554)
Merrett A J, Newbould G D
The comparative efficiency of methods of issues
MS 1966 JAN VOL 34 p 1-14.

(9555)
Goldstein H N
Should the Treasury auction long-term securities?
JF 1962 SEP VOL 17 p 444-464.

(9556)
Klein S
How to play the new issues game
F 1962 JAN VOL 74.

(9557)
Winter E L
A complete guide to making a public stock
offering
P-H, 1962.

(9558)
Henderson R F
The new issue market and the finance of industry
Bowes, 1951.

24.3 Issues of debt and seasoned stock issues

(9559)
Keeley M C
The stock price effects of bank holding company securities issuance
F R Bk San Francisco Ec Rev 1989 WINTER NO 1.

(9560)
Giammarino R, Lewis T
A theory of negotiated equity financing
RFS 1988 FALL VOL 1:3 p 265-288.

(9561)
Mikkelson W H, Partch M M
Withdrawn security offerings
JFQA 1988 JUN VOL 23:2 p 119-134.

(9562)
Bhagat S, Brickley J A, Lease R C
The authorization of additional common stock: An empirical investigation
FIN MGMT 1986 AUTUMN VOL 15 p 45-53.

(9563)
Hansen R
Evaluating the costs of a new equity issue
MCFJ 1986 SPRING VOL 4 p 42-55.

(9564)
Heinkel R, Schwartz E
Precommitment to equity financing choices in a world of asymmetric information
(in Edwards J et al. eds., Recent developments in corporate finance. Cambridge U Pr, 1986.)

(9565)
Heinkel R, Schwartz E S
Rights versus underwritten offerings : an asymmetric information approach
JF 1986 MAR VOL 41:1 p 1-18.

(9566)
Dorton K J
Auctioning new issues of corporate securities
VLR 1985 VOL 71:8 p 1381-1410.

(9567)
Kidwell D S, Rogowski R J
State bond bank issues: Method of sale and market acceptance over time
FIN MGMT 1983 SUMMER VOL 12 p 15-20.

(9568)
Rice M L, McEnally R W
Hedging possibilities in the flotation of debt securities
FIN MGMT 1979 WINTER VOL 8 p 12.

24.31 Price effects

(9569)
Polonchek J, Slovin M B, Sushka M E
Valuation effects of commercial bank securities offerings: a test of the information hypothesis
JBankF 1989 JUL VOL 13:3 p 443-462.

(9570)
Wansley J W, Dhillon U S
Determinants of valuation effects for security offerings of commercial bank holding companies
JFR 1989 FALL VOL 12:3 p 217-234.

(9571)
Barclay M J, Litzenberger R H
Announcement effects of new equity issues and the use of intraday price data
JFE 1988 VOL 21 p 71-100.

(9572)
Wasserfallen W, Wydler D
Underpricing of newly issued bonds: evidence from the Swiss capital market
JF 1988 DEC VOL 43:5 p 1177-1192.

(9573)
Berglund T, Liljeblom E, Wahlroos B
Stock price reactions to announcements of stock dividends and rights issues: a test of liquidity and signalling hypotheses on the Helsinki Stock Exchange
Finance 1987 VOL 8:2.

(9574)
Kalay A, Shimrat A
Firm value and seasoned equity issues: price pressure, wealth redistribution, or negative information
JFE 1987 VOL 19 p 109-126.

(9575)
Asquith P, Mullins D
Equity issues and offering dilution
(in Edwards J et al. eds., Recent developments in corporate finance. Cambridge U Pr, 1986.)

(9576)
Asquith P, Mullins D W Jr
Equity issues and offering dilution
JFE 1986 VOL 15 p 61.

(9577)
Eckbo B E
Valuation effects of corporate debt offerings
JFE 1986 VOL 15 p 119.

(9578)
Krasker W S
Stock price movements in response to stock issues under asymmetric information
JF 1986 MAR VOL 41:1 p 93-105.

(9579)
Masulis R W, Korwar A N
Seasoned equity offerings: An empirical investigation
JFE 1986 VOL 15 p 91.

(9580)
Mikkelson W H, Partch M M
Valuation effects of security offerings and the issuance process
JFE 1986 VOL 15 p 31.

(9581)
Mikkelson W H, Partch M M
Stock price effects and costs of secondary distributions.
JFE 1985 VOL 14:2 p 165-194.

(9582)
Parsons J E, Raviv A
Underpricing of seasoned issues
JFE 1985 VOL 14 p 377.

(9583)
Pettway R H, Radcliffe R C
Impacts of new equity sales upon electric utility share prices
FIN MGMT 1985 SPRING VOL 14 p 16-26.

(9584)
Hess A C, Frost P A
Tests for price effects of new issues of seasoned securities
JF 1982 MAR VOL 37:1 p 11-25.

(9585)
Martin J D, Richards R M
The seasoning process for corporate bonds
FIN MGMT 1981 SUMMER VOL 10 p 41-48.

(9586)
Lusztig P A, White R W
The price effects of rights offering
JFQA 1980 MAR VOL 15 p 25.

(9587)
Marsh P
Equity rights issues and the efficiency of the UK stock market
JF 1979 SEP VOL 34:4 p 839-862.

(9588)
Korsvold P E
Price behaviour of new debt issues and channelling efficiency in three European capital markets
JBF 1972 WINTER VOL 4:4 p 1-9.

(9589)
Reilly F K, Hatfield K
Experience with new stock issues
FAJ 1969 SEP-OCT VOL 25 p 73-82.

(9590)
Investment Bankers Association of America
A study of the market effects of cash equity financing, Jan 1, 1958-Jun 30, 1960.
Report of the Industrial Securities Committee, 1960.

(9591)
Dolley J C
The price-effect of stock right issues
JB 1934 APR VOL 7 p 133-160.

24.32   Issue costs

(9592)
Wirth A, Wright F K
New-issue costs and project evaluation : Ezzell
and Porter revisited
JBFA 1987 AUTUMN VOL 14:3 p 393-407.

(9593)
Howe K M, Patterson J H
Capital investment decisions under economies of
scale in flotation costs
FIN MGMT 1985 AUTUMN VOL 14 p 61-69.

(9594)
Hubbard C M
Flotation costs in capital budgeting: A note on
the tax effects
FIN MGMT 1984 SUMMER VOL 13 p 38-40.

(9595)
Howe K M
A note on flotation costs and capital budgeting
FIN MGMT 1982 WINTER VOL 11 p 30-33.

(9596)
Ezzell J R, Porter R B
Flotation costs and the weighted average cost of
capital
JFQA 1976 SEP VOL 11 p 403.

(9597)
Johnson K B, Morton T G, Findlay M C III
An analysis of the flotation cost of corporate
quasi-equity securities, 1971-1972.
FIN MGMT 1975 WINTER VOL 4 p 12.

(9598)
Johnson K B, Morton T G, Findlay M C III
A empirical analysis of the flotation cost of
corporate securities 1971-1972
JF 1975 VOL 30 p 1129.

(9599)
Van Horne J C
Implied fixed costs of long-term debt issues
JFQA 1973 DEC VOL 8:5 p 821-834.

(9600)
Karna A S
The cost of private versus public debt issues
FIN MGMT 1972 SUMMER VOL 1 p 65.

(9601)
Cohan A B
Cost of flotation of long-term corporate debt
since 1935
U of NC Busn, 1961.

(9602)
Securities and Exchange Commission
Cost of flotation of corporate securities,
1951-1955
US Govt, 1957.

24.33   Shelf registration

(9603)
Foster F D
Syndicate size, spreads and market power during
the introduction of shelf registration
JF 1989 MAR VOL 44:1 p 195-204.

(9604)
Kadapakkam P-R, Kon S J
The value of shelf registration for new debt issues
JB 1989 VOL 62:2 p 271-292.

(9605)
Thatcher J S, Thatcher J G
Timing performance and the flotation of
shelf-registered bonds
FIN MGMT 1988 SPRING VOL 17 p 16-26.

(9606)
Kidwell D S, Marr M W, Thompson G R
Shelf registration: competition and market
flexibility
JLE 1987 VOL 30:1 p 181.

(9607)
Moore N H, Peterson D R, Peterson P P
Shelf registrations and shareholder wealth : a
comparison of shelf and traditional equity
offerings
JF 1986 JUN VOL 41:2 p 451-463.

(9608)
Rogowski R J, Sorensen E H
Deregulation in investment banking: Shelf
registration, structure and performance
FIN MGMT 1985 SPRING VOL 14 p 5-15.

(9609)
Banoff B A
Regulatory subsidies, efficient markets, and shelf
registration: an analysis of Rule 415
VLR 1984 VOL 70:2 p 135-185.

(9610)
Bhagat S
The evidence on shelf registration
MCFJ 1984 SPRING VOL 2 p 6-12.

(9611)
Fox M B
Shelf registration, integrated disclosure, and
underwriter due diligence: an economic analysis
VLR 1984 VOL 70:5 p 1005-1034.

(9612)
Kidwell D S, Marr M W, Thompson G R
SEC rule 415: the ultimate competitive bid
JFQA 1984 JUN VOL 19:2 p 183-195.

24.34 Pre-emptive rights

(9613)
Hansen R S
The demise of the rights issue
RFS 1988 FALL VOL 1:3 p 289-310.

(9614)
Bank of England
Pre-emption rights
BEQB 1987 VOL 27 p 545-549.

(9615)
Hansen R S, Pinkerton J M, Ma T
On the rightholders' subscription to the
underwritten rights offering
JBankF 1986 VOL 10 p 595.

(9616)
Berglund T, Wahlroos B
The efficiency of the Finnish market for rights
issues : an application of the Black-Scholes model
JBFA 1985 SPRING VOL 12:1 p 151-164

(9617)
Bhagat S
The effect of pre-emptive right amendments on
shareholder wealth
JFE 1983 NOV VOL 12:3 p 289-310.

(9618)
Hansen R S, Pinkerton J M
Direct equity financing: a resolution of a paradox
JF 1982 JUN VOL 37:3 p 651-665.

(9619)
Weston C R
The information content of rights trading
JBFA 1978 SPRING VOL 5:1 p 65-92..

(9620)**Dipchand C R**
The Canadian experience with inherent stock
splits of right issues
FIN MGMT 1977 SUMMER VOL 6 p 34.

(9621)
Smith C W Jr
Alternative methods for raising capital: Rights
versus underwritten offerings
JFE 1977 VOL 5 p 273.

(9622)
Weston C R
Adjustment to future dividend rates in the
prediction of ex-rights prices
JBFA 1974 AUTUMN VOL 1:3 p 335-342.

(9623)
Thompson H E
A note on the value of rights in estimating the
investor capitalization rate
JF 1973 VOL 28 p 157.

(9624)
Wakoff G I
On shareholders' indifference to the proceeds
price in preemptive rights offerings
JFQA 1973 DEC VOL 8:5 p 835-836.

(9625)
Bacon P W
The subscription price in rights offerings
FIN MGMT 1972 SUMMER VOL 1 p 59.

(9626)
Edge S K
Sources of funds from rights issues and their cost
Journal of Economic Studies 1965 WINTER.

(9627)
Beranek W
Common stock financing, book values and stock
rights: the theory and the evidence
U of Wisc Busn, 1961.

(9628)
Leffler G L
Stock rights
B 1957 SEP 16 p 15ff.

(9629)
Archer S H
The theoretical value of a stock right
JF 1956 SEP VOL 11 p 363-366.

(9630)
Evans G H Jr
The theoretical value of a stock right
JF 1955 MAR VOL 10 p 55-61.

24.4 Underwriting

(9631)
Marr M W, Rogowski R W, Trimble J L
The competitive effects of US and Japanese
commercial bank participation in Eurobond
underwriting
FIN MGMT 1989 WINTER VOL 18 p 47-54.

(9632)
Pugel T A, White L J
An empirical analysis of the underwriting spreads
on initial public offerings
QREB 1988 VOL 28:4 p 6.

(9633)
Hansen R S, Fuller B R, Janjigian V
The over-allotment option and equity financing
flotation costs: An empirical investigation
FIN MGMT 1987 SUMMER VOL 16 p 24-32.

(9634)
Beatty R P, Ritter J R
Investment banking, reputation and the
underpricing of initial public offerings
JFE 1986 VOL 15 p 213.

(9635)
Booth J R, Smith R L II
Capital raising, underwriting and the certification
hypothesis
JFE 1986 VOL 15 p 261.

(9636)
Booth J R, Smith R L II
The certification role of the investment banker in
new issue pricing
MCFJ 1986 SPRING VOL 4 p 56-63.

(9637)
Rogowski R J, Sorensen E H
Evaluating your investment banker's performance
in bond offerings
MCFJ 1986 SPRING VOL 4 p 33-41.

(9638)
Smith C W Jr
Investment banking and the capital acquisition
process
JFE 1986 VOL 15 p 3.

(9639)
Giddy I H
Is equity underwriting risky for commercial bank
affiliates?
(in Walter I ed., Deregulating Wall Street:
Commercial bank penetration of the corporate
securities market. Wiley, 1985.)

(9640)
Junimura M, Iihara Y
Valuation of underwriting agreements for raising
capital in the Japanese capital market
JFQA 1985 JUN VOL 20:2 p 231-241.

(9641)
Bierwag G O, Kaufman G G, Leonard P H
Interest rate effects of commercial bank underwriting of municipal revenue bonds: Additional evidence
JBankF 1984 VOL 8 p 35.

(9642)
Harvard Law Review
Restrictions on bank underwriting of corporate securities: a proposal for more permissive regulation
HLR 1984 VOL 97:3 p 720-738.

(9643)
Joehnk M D, Kidwell D S
The impact of market uncertainty on municipal bond underwriting spread
FIN MGMT 1984 SPRING VOL 13 p 37-44.

(9644)
Choi D, Strong R A
The pricing of when-issued common stock : a note
JF 1983 SEP VOL 38:4 p 1293-1298.

(9645)
Baron D P
A model of the demand for investment banking advising and distribution services for new issues
JF 1982 SEP VOL 37:4 p 955-976.

(9646)
Downes D H, Heinkel R
Signaling and the valuation of unseasoned new issues
JF 1982 MAR VOL 37:1 p 1-10.

(9647)
Kaufman G G
Municipal bond underwriting: market structure
JBR 1981 SPRING VOL 12:1.

(9648)
Baron D P, Holmstrom B
The investment banking contract for new issues under asymmetric information: delegation and the incentive problem
JF 1980 DEC VOL 35:5 p 1115-1138.

(9649)
Higgins W W, Moore B J
Market structure versus information costs as determinants of underwriters' spreads on municipal bonds
JFQA 1980 MAR VOL 15 p 85.

(9650)
Marsh P
Valuation of underwriting agreements for UK rights issues
JF 1980 JUN VOL 25:3 p 693-716.

(9651)
Rogowski R J
Underwriting competition and issuer borrowing costs in the municipal revenue bond market
JBR 1980 WINTER VOL 10:4.

(9652)
Sorensen E H
An analysis of the relationship between underwriter spread and the pricing of municipal bonds
JFQA 1980 JUN VOL 15 p 435.

(9653)
Guzzardi W
The bomb IBM dropped on Wall Street
F 1979 NOV VOL 100 p 52-56.

(9654)
Logue D E, Rogalski R J
Does it pay to shop for your bond underwriter?
HBR 1979 JUL-AUG VOL 57:4 p 111-117.

(9655)
Ederington L H
Bidding for securities: the effect on the issuer's interest costs
JB 1978 OCT VOL 51:4 p 673-686.

(9656)
Mandelker G, Raviv A
Investment banking: An economic analysis of optimal underwriting contracts
JF 1977 VOL 32 p 683.

(9657)
Ederington L H
Uncertainty, competition and costs in corporate
bond underwriting
JFE 1975 VOL 2 p 71.

(9658)
Friend I, Longstreet J R, Mendelson M et al.
Investment banking and the new issues market
World Pub, 1967.

(9659)
Friend I, Herman E S
The S.E.C. through a glass darkly
JB 1964 OCT VOL 37 p 382-405.

24.41   Competitive versus negotiated underwriting

(9660)
Smith R L
The choice of issuance procedure and the cost of
competitive and negotiated underwriting : an
examination of the impact of rule 50
JF 1987 JUL VOL 42:3 p 703-720.

(9661)
Bhagat S
The effect of management's choice between
negotiated and competitive equity offerings on
shareholder wealth
JFQA 1986 JUN VOL 21:2 p 181-196.

(9662)
Bhagat S, Frost P A
Issuing costs to existing shareholders in
competitive and negotiated underwritten public
utility equity offerings
JFE 1986 VOL 15 p 233.

(9663)
Kidwell D S, Marr M W
Preferred stock : the impact of credit market
conditions on competitive versus negotiated sales
QREB 1986 WINTER VOL 26:4 p 35-50

(9664)
Maese J E
Competitive versus negotiated municipal revenue
bond issues: An investigation of underpricing
FIN MGMT 1985 SPRING VOL 14 p 26-32.

(9665)
Hays P A, Kidwell D S, Marr M W
The effect of market uncertainty on negotiated
and competitively underwritten public utility
bonds
FR 1984 NOV VOL 19:4.

(9666)
Braswell R C, Nosari E J, Sumners D L
A comparison of the true interest costs of
competitive and negotiated underwritings in the
municipal bond market: a note
JMCB 1983 FEB VOL 15:1 p 102-106.

(9667)
Fabozzi F J, West R R
Negotiated versus competitive underwritings of
public utility bonds: just one more time
JFQA 1981 SEP VOL 16:3 p 323-339.

(9668)
Joehnk M D, Kidwell D S
Comparative costs of competitive and negotiated
underwritings in the state and local bond market
JF 1979 JUN VOL 34:3 p 725-731.

(9669)
Sorensen E H
Negotiated   municipal   bond   underwritings:
implications for efficiency
JMCB 1979 AUG VOL 11:3 p 366-370.

(9670)
Cooperman D, Parker G G C
Competitive bidding in the underwriting of public
utilities securities
JFQA 1978 DEC VOL 13 p 885.

(9671)
Fabozzi F J, LiCalzi G M
Negotiated versus competitive underwriting of
corporate bonds, 1974-76
QREB 1978 VOL 18:3 p 109.

(9672)
Hopewell M H, Kaufman G G
The incidence of excess interest costs paid by
municipalities in the competitive sale of bonds
JME 1978 VOL 4 p 281..

(9673)**Logue D E, Jarrow R A**
Negotiation vs. competitive bidding in the sale of
securities by public utilities
FIN MGMT 1978 AUTUMN VOL 7 p 31.

(9674)
Ederington L H
Negotiated versus competitive underwritings of
corporate bonds
JF 1976 VOL 31 p 17.

(9675)
Tallman G D, Rush D F, Melicher R W
Competitive versus negotiated underwriting costs
for regulated industries
FIN MGMT 1974 SUMMER VOL 3 p 49.

(9676)
Christenson C J
Strategic aspects of competitive bidding for
corporate securities
Harvard Busn, 1965.

(9677)
Percus J, Quinto L
The application of linear programming to
competitive bond bidding
Em 1956 OCT VOL 24 p 413-429.

25 Splits and stock dividends

(9678)
Liljeblom E
The informational impact of announcements of stock dividends and stock splits
JBFA 1989 WINTER VOL 16:5 p 681.

(9679)
Berglund T, Liljeblom E, Wahlroos B
Stock price reactions to announcements of stock dividends and rights issues: a test of liquidity and signalling hypotheses on the Helsinki Stock Exchange
Finance 1987 VOL 8:2.

(9680)
Lakonishok J, Lev B
Stock splits and stock dividends: why, who and when
JF 1987 SEP VOL 42:4 p 913-932.

(9681)
Elgers P T, Murray D
Financial characteristics related to managements' stock split and stock dividend decisions
JBFA 1985 WINTER VOL 12:4 p 543-551

(9682)
Grinblatt M S, Masulis R W, Titman S
The valuation effects of stock splits and stock dividends
JFE 1984 VOL 13 p 461-490.

(9683)
Nichols W D
Semantics and capital market efficiency: testing the market's reaction to the naming of stock distributions as splits
JBusR 1983 VOL 11 p 11-20.

(9684)
Sosin H B
Neutral recapitalizations: Predictions and tests concerning valuation and welfare
JF 1978 VOL 33 p 1228.

(9685)
Millar J A
Split or dividend: do the words really matter?
AR 1977 JAN VOL 52:1 p 52-55.

(9686)
Millar J A, Fielitz B D
Stock-split and stock-dividend decisions
FIN MGMT 1973 WINTER VOL 2 p 35.

25.1 Stock splits

(9687)
Brennan M J, Copeland T E
Stock splits, stock prices and transaction costs
JFE 1988 VOL 22 p 83.

(9688)
Klein L S, Peterson D R
Investor expectations of volatility increases around large stock splits as implied in call option premia
JFR 1988 VOL 11:1 p 71-80.

(9689)
Lamoureux C G, Poon P
The market reaction to stock splits
JF 1987 DEC VOL 42:5 p 1347-1370.

(9690)
Sloan R G
Bonus issues, share splits and ex-day share price behaviour: Australian evidence
AJM 1987 DEC VOL 12 p 227-291.

(9691)
Ohlson J A, Penman S H
Volatility increases subsequent to stock splits: An empirical aberration
JFE 1985 VOL 14 p 251.

(9692)
Reilly F K, Gustavson S G
Investing in options on stocks announcing splits
FR 1985 MAY VOL 20:2.

(9693)
Spudeck R E, Moyer R C
Reverse splits and shareholder wealth: The impact of commissions
FIN MGMT 1985 WINTER VOL 14 p 52-56.

(9694)
Woolridge J R, Chambers D R
Reverse splits and shareholder wealth
FIN MGMT 1983 AUTUMN VOL 12 p 5-15.

(9695)
Copeland T E
The evidence against stock splits
CFQ 1981 FALL VOL 1 p 8-17.

(9696)
Nichols W D, Brown S L
Assimilating earnings and split information: Is the
capital market becoming more efficient?
JFE 1981 VOL 9 p 309.

(9697)
Reilly F K, Drzycimski E F
Short-run profits from stock splits
FIN MGMT 1981 SUMMER VOL 10 p 64.

(9698)
Baker W K, Gallagher P L
Management's view of stock splits
FIN MGMT 1980 SUMMER VOL 9 p 73.

(9699)
Copeland T E
Liquidity changes following stock splits
JF 1979 MAR VOL 34:1 p 115-141.

(9700)
Radcliffe R C, Gillespie W G
The price impact of reverse splits
FAJ 1979 JAN-FEB p 63-67.

(9701)
Charest G
Split information, stock returns and market
efficiency
JFE 1978 JUN-SEP VOL 6:2-3 p 265-296.

(9702)
Bar-Yosef S, Brown L D
A reexamination of stock splits using moving
betas
JF 1977 VOL 32 p 1069.

(9703)
Dipchand C R
The Canadian experience with inherent stock
splits of right issues
FIN MGMT 1977 SUMMER VOL 6 p 34.

(9704)
Firth M
An empirical investigation of the impact of the
announcements of capitalisation issues on share
prices
JBFA 1977 SPRING VOL 4:1 p 47-60.

(9705)
Finn F J
Stock splits: prior and subsequent price
relationships
JBFA 1974 SPRING VOL 1:1 p 93-108.

(9706)
West R R, Brouillette A B
Reverse stock splits--harbinger of bad times or
valid management technique?
FE 1970 JAN p 12-17.

(9707)
Fama E F, Fisher L, Jensen M C
The adjustment of stock prices to new
information
IntER 1969 FEB VOL 10 p 1-21..

(9708)**Johnson K B**
Stock splits and price change
JF 1966 DEC VOL 21 p 675-686.

(9709)
Merjos A
Reverse stock splits
B 1962 MAY 28.

(9710)
Barker C A
Stock splits in a bull market
HBR 1957 MAY-JUN VOL 35 p 72-79.

(9711)
Barker C A
Effective stock splits
HBR 1956 JAN-FEB VOL 34 p 101-106.

25.2 Stock dividends

(9712)
Woolridge J R
Ex-date stock price adjustment to stock dividends:
a note
JF 1983 MAR VOL 38:1 p 247-255.

(9713)
Eisemann P C, Moses E A
Stock dividends: management's view
FAJ 1978 JUL-AUG p 77.

(9714)
Foster T W, Vickrey D
The information content of stock dividend
announcements
AR 1978 APR VOL 53:2 p 360-370.

(9715)
Sussman M R
The stock dividend
U of Mich Busn Res, 1962.

(9716)
Sosnick S H
Stock dividends are lemons, not melons
CMR 1961 WINTER VOL 3 p 61-82.

(9717)
Seghers P D, Reinhart W J, Nimaroff S
Essentially equivalent to a dividend
Ronald, 1960.

(9718)
Barker C A
Price changes of stock dividend shares at
ex-dividend dates
JF 1959 SEP VOL 14 p 373-378.

(9719)
Barker C A
Evaluation of stock dividends
HBR 1958 JUL-AUG VOL 36 p 99-114.

(9720)
Green D Jr
Taxable stock dividends
JB 1953 OCT VOL 26 p 224-230.

(9721)
Bothwell J C Jr
Periodic stock dividends
HBR 1950 JAN VOL 28 p 89-100.

(9722)
Livermore S
Value of stock dividends
AER 1930 DEC VOL 20 p 687-691.

26 Cash dividends

(9723)
Scholes M S, Wolfson M A
Decentralized investment banking: the case of discount, dividend-reinvestment and stock-purchase plans
JFE 1989 SEP VOL 24:1 p 7-36.

(9724)
Shiller R J
Comovements in stock prices and comovements in dividends
JF 1989 JUL VOL 44:3 p 719-730.

(9725)
Goldberg M A, Vora A
Dividend yield, regulation, and the return on U.S. public utility stocks
JBFA 1985 VOL 12:1 p 47.

(9726)
Dielman T E, Oppenheimer H R
An examination of investor behavior during periods of large dividend changes
JFQA 1984 JUN VOL 19:2 p 197-216.

(9727)
Fung W K H, Theobald M F
Dividends and debt under alternative tax systems.
JFQA 1984 MAR VOL 19:1 p 59-72

(9728)
Penman S H
The predictive content of earnings forecasts and dividends
JF 1983 VOL 38:4 p 1181-1199.

(9729)
Smirlock M, Marshall W
An examination of the empirical relationship between the dividend and investment decisions : a note
JF 1983 DEC VOL 38:5 p 1659-1667.

(9730)
Chance D M
Interest sensitivity and dividend yields
JPM 1982 WINTER VOL 8:2 p 69.

(9731)
John K, Kalay A
Costly contracting and optimal payout constraints
JF 1982 MAY VOL 37:2 p 457-476.

(9732)
Johnson J M, Lanser H P
Dividend risk measurement and tests of the CAPM
JPM 1981 WINTER VOL 7:2 p 50-54.

(9733)
Baker H K, Seippel W H
Dividend reinvestment plans win wide currency
HBR 1980 NOV-DEC VOL 58:6 p 182-186.

(9734)
DeAngelo H, Masulis R W
Leverage and dividend irrelevancy under corporate and personal taxation
JF 1980 MAY VOL 35:2 p 453-467.

(9735)
Mehta D R
The influence of dividends, growth, and leverage on share prices in the electric utility industry: an econometric study
JFQA 1980 DEC VOL 15:5 p 1163.

(9736)
Litzenberger R H, Van Horne J C
Elimination of the double taxation of dividends and corporate financial policy
JF 1978 JUN VOL 33:3 p 737-757.

(9737)
Keane S M
Dividends and the resolution of uncertainty
JBFA 1974 AUTUMN VOL 1:3 p 389-394.

(9738)
Pettway R H, Malone R P
Automatic dividend reinvestment plans of nonfinancial corporations
FIN MGMT 1973 WINTER VOL 2 p 11.

26.1 Determinants of dividends

(9739)
Chowdhury G, Miles D K
Modelling companies' debt and dividend decisions with company accounts data
AE 1989 VOL 21:11 p 1483-1508.

(9740)
Lambert R A, Lanen W N, Larcker D F
Executive stock option plans and corporate dividend policy
JFQA 1989 DEC VOL 24:4 p 409-426.

(9741)
Partington G H
Variables influencing dividend policy in Australia: survey results
JBFA 1989 SPRING VOL 16:2 p 165.

(9742)
Thompson L, Watson R
Historic cost earnings, current cost earnings and the dividend decision
JBFA 1989 SPRING VOL 16:1 p 1.

(9743)
Born J A, Moser J T, Officer D T
Changes in dividend policy and subsequent earnings
JPM 1988 SUMMER VOL 14:4 p 56-62.

(9744)
Dharan B G
The association between corporate dividends and current cost disclosures
JBFA 1988 SUMMER VOL 15:2 p 215-230.

(9745)
Oppenheimer H R, Dielman T E
Firm dividend policy and insider activity: Some empirical results
JBFA 1988 WINTER VOL 15:4 p 525-542.

(9746)
Marsh T A, Merton R C
Dividend behavior for the aggregate stock market
JB 1987 JAN VOL 60:1 p 1-40.

(9747)
Wansley J W, Lane W R
A financial profile of the dividend initiating firm
JBFA 1987 AUTUMN VOL 14:3 p 425-436.

(9748)
Eddy A, Seifert B
Dividend changes of financially weak firms
FR 1986 NOV VOL 21:4.

(9749)
Lobo G J, Nair R D, Song I M
Additional evidence on the information content of dividends
JBFA 1986 WINTER VOL 13:4 p 597-608

(9750)
Michel A J, Shaked I
Country and industry influence on dividend policy : evidence from Japan and the USA
JBFA 1986 AUTUMN VOL 13:3 p 365-381

(9751)
Shiller R J
The Marsh-Merton model of managers' smoothing of dividends
AER 1986 VOL 76 p 499-503.

(9752)
Stevens J L
Tobin's q ratio, monopoly earnings, risk and dividend policy
JBusR 1986 JUNE VOL 14:3 p 213-224.

(9753)
Partington G H
Dividend policy and its relationship to investment and financing policies : empirical evidence
JBFA 1985 WINTER VOL 12:4 p 531-542

(9754)
Jalilvand A, Harris R S
Corporate behavior in adjusting to capital structure and dividend targets : an econometric study
JF 1984 MAR VOL 39:1 p 127-145.

(9755)
Riding A L
The information content of dividends : another test
JBFA 1984 SUMMER VOL 11:2 p 163-176

(9756)
Kennedy W F, Scott D F Jr
Some observations on the dividend policies of large commercial banks
JBR 1983 WINTER VOL 13:4.

(9757)
Rozeff M S
Growth, beta and agency costs as determinants of dividend payout ratios
JFR 1982 FALL VOL 5 p 249-259.

(9758)
Rozeff M S
How corporations set their dividend-payout ratios
CFQ 1982 WINTER VOL 1 p 68-83.

(9759)
Davidson I
An optimal control theory framework for dividend determination and the implications for intertemporal dividend change
JBFA 1980 VOL 7:4 p 527-540

(9760)
Mayne L S
Bank dividend policy and holding company affiliation
JFQA 1980 JUN VOL 15 p 469..

(9761)**Michel A J**
Industry influence on dividend policy
FIN MGMT 1979 AUTUMN VOL 8 p 22.

(9762)
Taylor P A
The information content of dividends hypothesis: Back to the drawing board?
JBFA 1979 WINTER VOL 6:4 p 495-526.

(9763)
Theobald M
Intertemporal dividend models - an empirical analysis using recent U K data
JBFA 1978 SPRING VOL 5:1 p 123.

(9764)
Sampson A A
Liquidity constraints on investment and dividends
JBFA 1976 SUMMER VOL 3:2 p 131-142.

(9765)
Cupta M C, Walker D A
Dividend disbursal practices in commercial banking
JFQA 1975 SEP VOL 10 p 515.

(9766)
Jacquillat B, McDonald J G, Nussenbaum M
Dividend investment and financing decisions: Empirical evidence on French firms
JFQA 1975 DEC VOL 10 p 791.

(9767)
Fama E F
The empirical relationships between the dividend and investment decisions of firms
AER 1974 VOL 64 p 304-318.

(9768)
Pogue T F
A cross-section study of the relationship between dividends and investment
YEE 1971 VOL 11 p 181-218.

(9769)
Feldstein M
Corporate taxation and dividend behavior
REStud 1970 JAN VOL 37 p 57-72.

(9770)
Fama E F, Babiak H
Dividend policy: an empirical analysis
JASA 1968 DEC VOL 63 p 1132-1161.

(9771)
Dhrymes P J, Kurz M
Investment dividend, and external finance behavior of firms
(in Ferber R ed., Determinants of investment behavior. Natl Bur Econ Res, 1967.)

(9772)
Jaakelainen V
Growth of earnings and dividend distribution policy
SJE 1967 SEP VOL 69 p 184-195.

(9773)
Turnovsky S J
The allocation of corporate profits between dividends and retained earnings
REStat 1967 NOV VOL 49 p 583-589.

(9774)
Brittain J A
Corporate dividend policy
Brookings, 1966.

(9775)
Borch K
Dividend policies
Statsokonomist Tiddskrift 1965 DEC VOL 79 p
183-201.

(9776)
Brittain J A
The tax structure and corporate dividend policy
AER 1964 MAY VOL 54 p 272-287.

(9777)
Dhrymes P J, Kurz M
On the dividend policy of electric utilities
REStat 1964 FEB VOL 46 p 76-81.

(9778)
Dobrovolsky S P
Corporate income retention, 1915-1943
Natl Bur Econ Res, 1962.

(9779)
Holland D M
Dividends under the income tax
Princeton U Pr, 1962.

(9780)
Cox E B
Changes in the size distribution of dividend
income
JASA 1961 JUN VOL 56 p 150-260.

(9781)
Stevens G
Corporation dividend payout ratios and target
ratios
Cowles Foundation Discussion Paper, Cowles
Commission for Research in Economics, Dept of
Economics, Yale U, 1961.

(9782)
Darling P G
The influence of expectations and liquidity on
dividend policy
JPE 1957 JUN VOL 65 p 209-224.

(9783)
Lintner J
Distribution of incomes of corporations among
dividends, retained earnings and taxes
AER 1956 MAY VOL 46 p 97-113.

(9784)
Darling P G
A surrogative measure of business confidence and
its relation to stock prices
JF 1955 DEC VOL 10 p 442-458.

(9785)
Lintner J
The determinants of corporate savings
(in Heller W W et al., Savings in the modern
economy. U of Minn Pr, 1953.)

26.2 Dividend announcements

(9786)
Chang S J, Chen S-N
Stock price adjustment to earnings and dividend
surprises
QREB 1989 VOL 29:1 p 68.

(9787)
Lang L H P, Litzenberger R H
Dividend announcements: cash flow signalling vs.
free cash flow hypothesis
JFE 1989 SEP VOL 24:1 p 181-192.

(9788)
Venkatesh P C
The impact of dividend initiation on the
information content of earnings announcements
and returns volatility
JB 1989 VOL 62:2 p 175-198.

(9789)
Aharony J, Falk H, Swary I
Information content of dividend increases: The
case of regulated utilities
JBFA 1988 AUTUMN VOL 15:3 p 401-414.

(9790)
Born J A
Insider ownership and signals evidence from
dividend initiation announcement effects
FIN MGMT 1988 SPRING VOL 17 p 38-45.

(9791)
Eddy A, Seifert B
Firm size and dividend announcements
JFR 1988 WINTER VOL 11:4 p 295-302.

(9792)
Ghosh C, Woolridge J R
An analysis of shareholder reaction to dividend cuts and omissions
JFR 1988 WINTER VOL 11:4 p 281-294.

(9793)
Healy P M, Palepu K G
Earnings information conveyed by dividend initiations and omissions
JFE 1988 VOL 21 p 149.

(9794)
Jayaraman N, Shastri K
The valuation impacts of specially designated dividends
JFQA 1988 SEP VOL 23 p 301.

(9795)
West K D
Dividend innovations and stock price volatility
Em 1988 JAN VOL 56 p 37-61.

(9796)
Kalay A, Loewenstein U
The informational content of the timing of dividend announcements.
JFE 1986 JUL VOL 16:3 p 373-388

(9797)
Venkatesh P C, Chiang R
Information asymmetry and the dealer's bid-ask spread : a case study of earnings and dividend announcements
JF 1986 DEC VOL 41:5 p 1089-1102.

(9798)
Eades K M, Hess P J, Kim E H
Market rationality and dividend announcements
JFE 1985 DEC VOL 14:4 p 581-604.

(9799)
Kalay A, Loewenstein U
Predictable events and excess returns: The case of dividend announcements
JFE 1985 VOL 14 p 423.

(9800)
Woolridge J R, Gosh C
Dividend cuts: do they always signal bad news?
MCFJ 1985 SUMMER VOL 3 p 20-32.

(9801)
Cole J A
Are dividend surprises independently important?
JPM 1984 SUMMER VOL 10:4 p 45-50.

(9802)
Handjinicolaou G, Kalay A
Wealth redistributions or changes in firm value. An analysis of returns to bondholders and stockholders around dividend announcements.
JFE 1984 VOL 13 p 35-63.

(9803)
Kane A, Lee Y K, Marcus A
Earnings and dividend announcements : is there a corroboration effect?
JF 1984 SEP VOL 39:4 p 1091-1099

(9804)
Patell J M, Wolfson M A
The intraday speed of adjustment of stock prices to earnings and dividend announcements
JFE 1984 VOL 13 p 223-252.

(9805)
Asquith P, Mullins D W
The impact of initiating dividend payments on shareholders wealth
JB 1983 JAN VOL 56:1 p 77-96.

(9806)
Divecha A, Morse D
Market responses to dividend increases and changes in payout ratios
JFQA 1983 JUN VOL 18:2 p 163-173.

(9807)
Keen H Jr
The impact of a dividend cut announcement on bank share prices
JBR 1983 WINTER VOL 13:4.

(9808)
Rosenfeld J
The effect of common-stock dividend reductions on the returns of non-convertible preferred stocks : a note
JF 1983 JUN VOL 38:3 p 1019-1024.

(9809)
Woolridge J R
Dividend changes and security prices
JF 1983 DEC VOL 38:5 p 1607-1615.

(9810)
Kwan C C Y
Efficient market tests of the informational content
of dividend announcements : critique and
extension
JFQA 1981 JUN VOL 16:2 p 193-206.

(9811)
Charest G
Dividend information, stock returns and market
efficiency.
JFE 1978 JUN-SEP VOL 6:2-3 p 297-330.

(9812)
Ashley J W
Stock prices and changes in earnings and
dividends: some empirical results
JPE 1962 FEB VOL 70 p 82-85.

26.3 Dividend policy

(9813)
Bagwell L S, Shoven J B
Cash distributions to shareholders
JEP 1989 SUMMER VOL 3:3 p 129-140..

(9814)**Crutchley C E, Hansen R S**
A test of the agency theory of managerial
ownership, corporate leverage, and corporate
dividends
FIN MGMT 1989 WINTER VOL 18 p 36-46.

(9815)
Durand D
Afterthoughts on a controversy with MM, plus
new thoughts on growth and the cost of capital
FIN MGMT 1989 SUMMER VOL 18 p 12-18.

(9816)
Gordon M J
Corporate finance under the MM theorems
FIN MGMT 1989 SUMMER VOL 18 p 19-28.

(9817)
Jose M L, Stevens J L
Capital market valuation of dividend policy
JBFA 1989 WINTER VOL 16:5 p 651.

(9818)
Weston J F
What MM have wrought
FIN MGMT 1989 SUMMER VOL 18 p 29-38.

(9819)
Bailey W
Canada's dual class shares: further evidence on
the market value of cash dividends
JF 1988 DEC VOL 43:5 p 1143-1160.

(9820)
Barclay M J, Smith C W Jr
Corporate payout policy: Cash dividends versus
open-market repurchases
JFE 1988 VOL 22 p 61.

(9821)
Castanias R, Chung K-Y, Johnson H
Dividend spreads
JB 1988 VOL 61 p 299.

(9822)
Crockett J, Friend I
Dividend policy in perspective: can theory explain
behavior?
REStat 1988 VOL 70 p 603.

(9823)
Fama E F, French K R
Dividend yields and expected stocks returns
JFE 1988 VOL 22 p 3.

(9824)
Franks J R, Landskroner Y
Dividends, taxes and financial intermediaries
Studies in Banking and Finance 1988 VOL 5.

(9825)
Masulis R W, Trueman B
Corporate investment and dividend decisions
under differential personal taxation
JFQA 1988 DEC VOL 23 p 369.

(9826)
Moore W T, Sartoris W L
On the existence of a dividend clientele in the market for electric utility stocks
QREB 1988 VOL 28:1 p 88.

(9827)
Miller M H
Behavioral rationality in finance: the case of dividends
MCFJ 1987 WINTER VOL 4 p 6-15.

(9828)
Ofer A R, Thakor A V
A theory of stock price responses to alternative corporate cash disbursement methods: stock repurchases and dividends
JF 1987 JUN VOL 42:2 p 365.

(9829)
Vanthienen L, Vermaelen T
The effect of personal taxes on common stock prices: the case of a Belgian tax reform
JBankF 1987 VOL 11 p 223-244.

(9830)
Brown K C, Lummer S L
Hedged dividend capture
MCFJ 1986 FALL VOL 4 p 65-72.

(9831)
Gilmer R H Jr, Lee C F
Empirical tests of Granger's propositions on the dividend effect controversy
REStat 1986 VOL 68 p 351.

(9832)
Lee C F, Chang H
Dividend policy and capital market theory: a generalized error components model approach
JBusR 1986 VOL 14:2 p 177-188.

(9833)
Poterba J M
The market valuation of cash dividends: The Citizens Utilities case reconsidered
JFE 1986 VOL 15 p 395.

(9834)
Richardson G, Sefcik S E, Thompson R
A test of dividend irrelevance using volume reactions to a change in dividend policy
JFE 1986 DEC VOL 17:2 p 313-333

(9835)
Baker H K, Farrelly G E, Edelman R B
A survey of management views on dividend policy
FIN MGMT 1985 AUTUMN VOL 14 p 78.

(9836)
Moore W T, Sartoris W L
Dividends and taxes: another look at the electric utility industry
FR 1985 FEB VOL 20:1.

(9837)
Nakamura A, Nakamura M
Rational expectations and the firm's dividend behavior
REStat 1985 VOL 67 p 606.

(9838)
Peterson P P, Peterson D R, Ang J S
Direct evidence on the marginal rate of taxation on dividend income
JFE 1985 VOL 14 p 267.

(9839)
Easterbrook F H
Two agency-cost explanations of dividends
AER 1984 VOL 74 p 650-659.

(9840)
Edwards J
Does dividend policy matter?
FS 1984 VOL 5:1.

(9841)
Poterba J M, Summers L H
New evidence that taxes affect the valuation of dividends
JF 1984 DEC VOL 39:5 p 1397-1415.

(9842)
Shefrin H M, Statman M
Explaining investor preference for cash dividends
JFE 1984 VOL 13 p 253-282.

(9843)
Bierman H Jr, Hass J E
Investment cut-off rates and dividend policy
FIN MGMT 1983 WINTER VOL 12 p 19-24.

(9844)
Brealey R A
Does dividend policy matter?
MCFJ 1983 SPRING VOL 1 p 17-25.

(9845)
Elton E J, Gruber M J, Rentzler J C
A simple examination of the empirical
relationship between dividend yields and
deviations from the CAPM
JBankF 1983 VOL 7 p 135.

(9846)
Feldstein M, Green J
Why do companies pay dividends?
AER 1983 VOL 73 p 17-30.

(9847)
Hakansson N H
To pay or not to pay dividends
JF 1982 MAY VOL 37:2 p 415-428.

(9848)
Hakansson N H
Unravelling the dividend puzzle
CFQ 1982 WINTER VOL 1 p 84-99.

(9849)
Hess P J
The dividend debate: 20 years of discusion
CFQ 1982 WINTER VOL 1 p 19-39.

(9850)
Litzenberger R H, Ramaswamy K
The effects of dividends on common stock prices
: tax effects or information effects
JF 1982 MAY VOL 37:2 p 429-443.

(9851)
Miller M H
Can management use dividend policy to influence
the value of the firm
CFQ 1982 WINTER VOL 1 p 8-18.

(9852)
Miller M H, Scholes M
Dividends and taxes: Some empirical evidence
JPE 1982 VOL 90 p 1118-1141.

(9853)
Modigliani F
Debt dividend policy, taxes, inflation and market
valuation.
JF 1982 MAY VOL 37:2 p 255-273.

(9854)
Morgan I G
Dividends and capital asset prices
JF 1982 SEP VOL 37:4 p 1071-1086.

(9855)
Ballentine J G
Dividend policy and tax incidence in a growing
economy
QJE 1981 VOL 95 p 781.

(9856)
Feenberg D
Does the investment interest limitation explain
the existence of dividends?
JFE 1981 VOL 9 p 265.

(9857)
Fischel D R
The law and economics of dividend policy
VLR 1981 VOL 67:4 p 699-726.

(9858)
Hayes L S
Fresh evidence that dividends don't matter
F 1981 MAY 4 p 351-354.

(9859)
Blume M E
Stock returns and dividend yields: some more
evidence
REStat 1980 NOV VOL 62:4 p 567-577.

(9860)
Brudney V
Dividends, discretion, and disclosure
VLR 1980 VOL 66:1 p 85-129.

(9861)
Dehez P
Employment and dividend policy of the firm under risk
REStud 1980 VOL 47 p 503.

(9862)
Deschamps B, Mehta D R, Walker M C
The influence of dividends, growth, and leverage on share prices in the electric utility industry: An econometric study
JFQA 1980 DEC VOL 15 p 1163.

(9863)
Gordon R H, Bradford D F
Taxation and the stock market valuation of capital gains and dividends: Theory and empirical results
Journal of Public Economics 1980 OCT VOL 14 p 109-136.

(9864)
Litzenberger R H, Ramaswamy K
Dividends short selling restrictions tax - induced investor clienteles and market equilibrium
JF 1980 MAY VOL 35:2 p 469-485.

(9865)
Morgan I G
Dividends and stock price behavior in Canada
Journal of Business Administration 1980 FALL VOL 12 p 91-106.

(9866)
Mukhergee T K, Austin L M
An empirical investigation of small bank stock valuation and dividend policy
FIN MGMT 1980 SPRING VOL 9 p 27..

(9867)**Chateau J-P D**
Dividend policy revisited: within- and out-of-sample tests
JBFA 1979 AUTUMN VOL 6:3 p 355-372.

(9868)
Elton E J, Gruber M J
Taxes and portfolio composition.
JFE 1979 DEC VOL 6:4 p 399-410.

(9869)
Litzenberger R H, Ramaswamy K
The effect of personal taxes and dividends on capital asset prices. Theory and empirical evidence.
JFE 1979 JUN VOL 7:2 p 163-195.

(9870)
Price L N
Growth or yield: The choice depends on your tax rate
FAJ 1979 JUL-AUG VOL 35 p 57-67.

(9871)
Theobald M
A note on variable transactions costs, the capital asset pricing model and the corporate dividend decision
JBFA 1979 SPRING VOL 6:1 p 9-16.

(9872)
Lewellen W G, Stanley K L, Lease R C
Some direct evidence on the dividend clientele phenomenon
JF 1978 VOL 33 p 1385.

(9873)
Long J B Jr
The market valuation of cash dividends: A case to consider
JFE 1978 VOL 6 p 235.

(9874)
Miller M H, Scholes M
Dividends and taxes
JFE 1978 VOL 6 p 333-364.

(9875)
Khoury N T, Smith K V
Dividend policy and the capital gains tax in Canada
Journal of Business Administration 1977 SPRING VOL 8:2 p 19-38.

(9876)
Pettit R R
Taxes, transactions costs and the clientele effect of dividends
JFE 1977 VOL 5 p 419.

(9877)
Stapleton R C, Subrahmanyam M G
Market imperfections, capital market equlibrium,
and corporation finance
JF 1977 MAY VOL 32:2 p 307-320.

(9878)
Wilkes F M
Dividend policy and investment appraisal in
imperfect capital markets
JBFA 1977 SUMMER VOL 4:2 p 187-200.

(9879)
Arditti F D, Levy H, Sarnat M
Taxes, uncertainty and optimal dividend policy
FIN MGMT 1976 SPRING VOL 5 p 46.

(9880)
Bar-Yosef S, Kolodny R
Dividend policy and capital market theory
REStat 1976 MAY VOL 58:2 p 181-190.

(9881)
Groves R E V, Samuels J M
A note on the cost of retained earnings and
deferred taxes in the U K
JBFA 1976 WINTER VOL 3:4 p 143-150.

(9882)
Henderson G V Jr
Shareholder taxation and the required rate of
return on internally generated funds
FIN MGMT 1976 SUMMER VOL 5 p 25.

(9883)
Lee C F
Functional form and the dividend effect in the
electric utility industry
JF 1976 VOL 31 p 1881.

(9884)
Rubinstein M
The irrelevancy of dividend policy in an
Arrow-Debreu economy
JF 1976 VOL 31 p 1229.

(9885)
Sharpe W F, Sosin H B
Risk, return and yield on common stocks
FAJ 1976 MAR-APR p 33-42.

(9886)
Grabowski H G, Mueller D C
Life cycle effects on corporate returns on
retentions
REStat 1975 NOV VOL 57:4 p 400-409.

(9887)
Wrightsman D, Horrigan J O
Retention, risk of success and the price of stock
JF 1975 VOL 30 p 1357.

(9888)
Black F, Scholes M
The effects of dividend yield and dividend policy
on common stock prices and returns
JFE 1974 VOL 1 p 1.

(9889)
Higgins R C
Growth, dividend policy and capital costs in the
electric utility industry
JF 1974 VOL 29 p 1189.

(9890)
Ryan T M
Dividend policy and market valuation in British
industry
JBFA 1974 AUTUMN VOL 1:3 p 415-428.

(9891)
Brealey R A
A note on dividends and debt under the new
taxation
JBF 1973 SPRING VOL 5:1 p 66-68.

(9892)
Krouse C G
On the theory of optimal investment, dividends
and growth in the firm
AER 1973 VOL 63 p 269-279.

(9893)
Feldstein M
Corporate taxation and dividend behaviour: A
reply and extension
REStud 1972 VOL 39 p 235.

(9894)
Higgins R C
The corporate dividend-saving decision
JFQA 1972 MAR VOL 7 p 1527.

(9895)
Higgins R C
Dividend policy and increasing discount rates: A clarification
JFQA 1972 JUN VOL 7 p 1757.

(9896)
Pye G
Capital gains taxation, dividends, and capital budgeting
QJE 1972 VOL 86 p 226.

(9897)
Wallingford B A
An inter-temporal approach to the optimization of dividend policy with predetermined investments
JF 1972 JUN VOL 27 p 627-636.

(9898)
Brennan M J
A note on dividend irrelevance and the Gordon valuation model
JF 1971 DEC VOL 26 p 1115-1122.

(9899)
Krainer R E
A pedagogic note on dividend policy
JFQA 1971 SEP VOL 6 p 1147-1154.

(9900)
Magen S D
Cost of capital and dividend policies in commercial banks
JFQA 1971 MAR VOL 6 p 733-746.

(9901)
Van Horne J C, McDonald J G
Dividend policy and new equity financing
JF 1971 MAY VOL 26 p 507-520.

(9902)
Brigham E F, Gordon M J
Leverage, dividend policy, and the cost of capital
JF 1968 MAR VOL 23 p 85-103.

(9903)
Loomis C J
A case for dropping dividends
F 1968 JUN 15 p 181 ff.

(9904)
Manne A S
Optimal dividend and investment policies for a self financing business enterprise
MSci 1968 NOV VOL 15 p 119-129.

(9905)
West R R, Bierman H Jr
Corporate dividend policy and preemptive security issues
JB 1968 JAN VOL 41 p 71-75.

(9906)
Diamond J J
Earnings distribution and the evaluation of shares: some recent evidence
JFQA 1967 MAR VOL 2 p 14-29.

(9907)
Walter J E
Dividend policy and enterprise valuation
Wadsworth Pub, 1967.

(9908)
Wilson R
A Pareto-optimal dividend policy
MSci 1967 MAY VOL 13 p 756-764.

(9909)
Woods D H, Brigham E F
Stockholder distribution decisions: share repurchases or dividends
JFQA 1966 MAR VOL 1 p 15-25.

(9910)
Rubner A
The ensnared shareholder
Macmillan Int, 1965.

(9911)
Friend I, Puckett M
Dividends and stock prices
AER 1964 SEP VOL 54 p 656-682.

(9912)
Lintner J
Optimal dividends and corporate growth under uncertainty
QJE 1964 FEB VOL 78 p 68-71.

(9913)
Baumol W J
On dividend policy and market imperfection
JB 1963 JAN VOL 36 p 112-115.

(9914)
Miller M H, Modigliani F
Dividend policy and market valuation: a reply
JB 1963 JAN VOL 36 p 116-119.

(9915)
Walter J E
Dividend policy: its influence on the value of the
enterprise
JF 1963 MAY VOL 18 p 280-291.

(9916)
Lintner J
Dividends, earnings, leverage, stock prices and the
supply of capital to corporations
REStat 1962 AUG VOL 44 p 243-269.

(9917)
Miller M H, Modigliani F
Dividend policy, growth, and the valuation of
shares
JB 1961 OCT VOL 34 p 411-433.

(9918)
Gordon M J
The optimum dividend rate
(in Scind Verhulst M eds., Management science,
models and techniques. Pergamon, 1960.)

(9919)
Gordon M J
Dividends, earnings and stock prices
REStat 1959 MAY VOL 41 p 99-105..

(9920)**Porterfield J T S**
Dividends, dilution, and delusion
HBR 1959 NOV-DEC VOL 37 p 56-61.

(9921)
Dobrovolsky S P
Economics of corporate internal and external
financing
JF 1958 MAR VOL 13 p 35-47.

(9922)
Walter J E
Dividend policies and common stock prices
JF 1956 MAR VOL 11 p 29-41.

(9923)
Harkavy O
The relationship between retained earnings and
common stock prices for large listed corporations
JF 1953 SEP VOL 8 p 283-297.

26.31   Signalling models of dividend policy

(9924)
Kumar P
Shareholder-manager conflict and the information
content of dividends
RFS 1988 SUMMER VOL 1:2 p 111-136.

(9925)
Williams J
Efficient signalling with dividends, investment, and
stock repurchases
JF 1988 JUL VOL 43:3 p 737-748.

(9926)
Ambarish R, John K, Williams J
Efficient signalling with dividends and investments
JF 1987 JUN VOL 42:2 p 321-343.

(9927)
Ofer A R, Siegel D R
Corporate financial policy information and market
expectations : An empirical investigation of
dividends
JF 1987 SEP VOL 42:4 p 889-911.

(9928)
Asquith P, Mullins D W Jr
Signalling with dividends, stock repurchases and
equity issues
FIN MGMT 1986 AUTUMN VOL 15 p 27-44.

(9929)
Bar-Yosef S, Huffman L
The information content of dividends : a
signalling approach.
JFQA 1986 MAR VOL 21:1 p 47-58

(9930)
Makhija A K, Thompson H E
Some aspects of equilibrium for a cross section of
firms signalling profitability with dividends : a
note
JF 1986 MAR VOL 41:1 p 249-253.

(9931)
Miller M H
The informational content of dividends
(in Bossons J, Dornbusch R, Fischer S eds.,
Macroeconomics: Essays in honor of Franco
Modigliani. MIT Pr, 1986.)

(9932)
John K, Williams J
Dividends dilution and taxes : a signalling
equilibrium
JF 1985 SEP VOL 40:4 p 1053-1070.

(9933)
Miller M H, Rock K
Dividend policy under asymmetric information
JF 1985 SEP VOL 40:4 p 1031-1051.

(9934)
Brickley J A
Shareholder wealth, information signaling and the
specially designated dividend: An empirical study
JFE 1983 VOL 12 p 187-209.

(9935)
Eades K M
Empirical evidence on dividends as a signal of
firm value
JFQA 1982 NOV VOL 17:4 p 471-502.

(9936)
Bhattacharya S
Nondissipative signaling structures and dividend
policy
QJE 1981 VOL 95 p 1-24.

(9937)
Kalay A
Signaling, information content and the reluctance
to cut dividends
JFQA 1980 NOV VOL 15 p 855.

(9938)
Bhattacharya S
Imperfect information, dividend policy, and "the
bird in the hand" policy
BellJ 1979 SPRING VOL 10:1 p 259-270.

26.4 Ex-dividend price behavior

(9939)
Grammatikos T
Dividend stripping, risk exposure, and the effect
of the 1984 Tax Reform Act of the ex-dividend
day behavior
JB 1989 VOL 62:2 p 157-174.

(9940)
Fehrs D H, Benesh G A, Peterson D R
Evidence of a relation between stock price
reactions around cash dividend changes and yields
JFR 1988 VOL 11:2 p 111-124.

(9941)
Heath D C, Jarrow R A
Ex-dividend stock price behavior and arbitrage
opportunities
JB 1988 VOL 61 p 95.

(9942)
Karpoff J M, Walkling R A
Short-term trading around ex-dividend days:
Additional evidence
JFE 1988 VOL 21 p 291.

(9943)
Barclay M J
Dividends, taxes, and common stock prices: the
ex-dividend day behavior of common stock prices
before the income tax
JFE 1987 VOL 19 p 31-44.

(9944)
Barone-Adesi G, Whaley R E
The valuation of American call options and the
expected ex-dividend stock price decline
JFE 1986 SEP VOL 17:1 p 91-111.

(9945)
Brown P, Walter T
Ex-dividend behaviour of Australian share prices
AJM 1986 DEC VOL 11 p 117-138.

(9946)
Lakonishok J, Vermaelen T
Tax-induced trading around ex-dividend days
JFE 1986 JUL VOL 16:3 p 287-319

(9947)
Booth L D, Johnston D J
The ex-dividend day behavior of Canadian stock
prices : tax changes and clientele effects.
JF 1984 JUN VOL 39:2 p 457-476.

(9948)
Eades K M, Hess P J, Kim E H
On interpreting security returns during the
ex-dividend period
JFE 1984 MAR VOL 13:1 p 3-34.

(9949)
Lakonishok J, Vermaelen T
Tax reform and ex-dividend day behavior
JF 1983 VOL 38:4 p 1157-1179.

(9950)
Hess P J
The ex-dividend day behavior of stock returns :
further evidence on tax effects
JF 1982 MAY VOL 37:2 p 445-456.

(9951)
Kalay A
The ex-dividend day behavior of stock prices : a
re-examination of the clientele effect
JF 1982 SEP VOL 37:4 p 1059-1070.

(9952)
Finnerty J D
The behavior of electric utility common stock
prices near the ex-dividend date
FIN MGMT 1981 WINTER VOL 10 p 59-69.

(9953)
Elton E J, Gruber M J
Marginal stockholder tax rates and the clientele
effect
REStat 1970 FEB VOL 52 p 68-74.

(9954)
Woods I R
Price behavior of ordinary shares on ex div dates
on the Johannesburg Stock Exchange, July 1, 1959
to June 30, 1961
South African Journal of Economics 1963 MAR
VOL 31 p 38-59.

(9955)
Durand D, May A M
The ex-dividend behavior of American Telephone
and Telegraph stock
JF 1960 MAR VOL 11 p 19-31.

(9956)
Campbell J A, Beranek W
Stock price behavior on ex-dividend dates
JF 1955 DEC VOL 10 p 425-429.

27 Company financing and capital structure

(9957)
Copp A
Financing your business
Croner, 1989.

(9958)
Kelly W A Jr, Miles J A
Capital structure theory and the Fisher effect
FR 1989 FEB VOL 24:1 p 53-74.

(9959)
Benninga S, Talmor E
The interaction of corporate and government
financing in general equilibrium
JB 1988 VOL 61 p 233.

(9960)
Bhandari L C
Debt/equity ratio and expected common stock
returns: empirical evidence
JF 1988 JUN VOL 43:2 p 507-528.

(9961)
Billingsley R S, Lamy R E Jr, Thompson G R
The choice among debt, equity, and convertible
bonds
JFR 1988 VOL 11:1 p 43-56.

(9962)
Cornell B, Shapiro A C
Financing corporate growth
JACF 1988 SUMMER VOL 1 p 6-22.

(9963)
Deshpande S D, Philippatos G C
Leverage decisions and the effect of corporate
Eurobond offerings
AE 1988 JUL VOL 20:7 p 901-916.

(9964)
Ford J
The indebted society: credit and default in the
1980s
Routledge, 1988.

(9965)
Hilton A
Debt/equity swaps: costs, benefits and prospects
Financial Times Business Information, 1988.

(9966)
Narayanaswamy C R
A mean-variance synthesis of corporate financial
theory: a note
JF 1988 JUN VOL 43:2 p 529-530.

(9967)
Prezas A P
Interactions of the firm's real and financial
decisions
AE 1988 APR VOL 20:4 p 551-560.

(9968)
Ravid S A
On interactions of production and financial
decisions
FIN MGMT 1988 AUTUMN VOL 17 p 87-99.

(9969)
Williamson O E
Corporate finance and corporate governance
JF 1988 JUL VOL 43:3 p 567-592.

(9970)
Baldwin C Y
Competing for capital in a global environment
MCFJ 1987 SPRING VOL 5 p 43-64.

(9971)
Fung W K H, Theobald M F
Taxes, unequal access, public debt and corporate
financial policy in the United Kingdom
JBankF 1987 VOL 11 p 67-78.

(9972)
Prezas A P
Effects of debt on the degrees of operating and
financial leverage
FIN MGMT 1987 SUMMER VOL 16 p 39-44..

(9973)**Williams J**
Perquisites, risk, and capital structure
JF 1987 MAR VOL 42:1 p 29-48.

(9974)
Friedman B M ed.
Financing corporate capital formation
U of Chicago Pr, 1986.

(9975)
Lewellen W G, Emery D R
Corporate debt management and the value of the firm.
JFQA 1986 DEC VOL 21:4 p 415-426.

(9976)
Shapiro A C
Guidelines for long-term corporate financing strategy
MCFJ 1986 WINTER VOL 3 p 6-19.

(9977)
Strebel P
Managing the information cost of financing
CJWB 1986 SUMMER VOL 21:2 p 39-45.

(9978)
John K, Kalay A
Informational content of optimal debt contracts
(in Altman E and Subrahmanyam M eds., Recent advances in corporate finance. Irwin, 1985.)

(9979)
Kane A, Marcus A J, McDonald R L
Debt policy and the rate of return premium to leverage
JFQA 1985 DEC VOL 20:4 p 479-499.

(9980)
Kolodny R, Suhler D R
Changes in capital structure, new equity issues and scale effects
JFR 1985 SUMMER VOL 8 p 127-136.

(9981)
Long M, Malitz I
Investment patterns and financial leverage
(in Friedman B ed., Corporate capital structures in the United States. U of Chicago Pr, 1985.)

(9982)
Long M, Malitz I
The investment-financing nexus: some empirical evidence
MCFJ 1985 FALL VOL 3 p 53-59.

(9983)
Fung W K H, Theobald M F
Dividends and debt under alternative tax systems.
JFQA 1984 MAR VOL 19:1 p 59-72

(9984)
Huberman G
External financing and liquidity
JF 1984 JUL VOL 39:3 p 895-910

(9985)
Shrieves R E, Pashley M M
Evidence on the association between mergers and capital structure
FIN MGMT 1984 AUTUMN VOL 13 p 39-48.

(9986)
Huffman L
Operating leverage, financial leverage and equity risk
JBankF 1983 VOL 7 p 197.

(9987)
New York Stock Exchange
The financial health of U.S. corporations: Current assessment and future prospects
New York Stock Exchange Office of Economic Research, March 1983.

(9988)
Orgler Y E, Taggart R A Jr
Implications of corporate capital structure theory for banking institutions
JMCB 1983 MAY VOL 15:2 p 212-221.

(9989)
Townsend R M
Financial structure and economic activity
AER 1983 VOL 73 p 895-911.

(9990)
Bar-Yosef S
Corporate financial policies: an analysis of interaction
EER 1982 VOL 17:2.

(9991)
Kornbluth S H, Vinso J D
Capital structure and the financing of the multinational corporation: fractional multiobjective approach
JFQA 1982 JUN VOL 17:2 p 147-178.

(9992)
Seitz N
Shareholder goals, firm goals and firm financing
decisions
FIN MGMT 1982 AUTUMN VOL 11 p 20-26.

(9993)
Gordon R H, Malkiel B G
Corporation finance
(in Aaron H J and Pechman J A eds., How taxes
affect economic behavior. Brookings, 1981.)

(9994)
Johnson D J
The behavior of financial structure and
sustainable growth in an inflationary environment
FIN MGMT 1981 AUTUMN VOL 10 p 30-35.

(9995)
Taggart R A
Rate-of-return regulation and utility capital
structure decisions
JF 1981 MAY VOL 36:2 p 383-393.

(9996)
Friedman B M
The financing must come - but from where?
HBR 1980 SEP-OCT VOL 58:5 p 52-56.

(9997)
Gup B E
The financial consequences of corporate growth
JF 1980 DEC VOL 35:5 p 1257-1265

(9998)
Martin D R, Sloane W R
Financial leverage: A more precise approach
JBFA 1980 WINTER VOL 7:4 p 585-590.

(9999)
Mehta D R
The influence of dividends, growth, and leverage
on share prices in the electric utility industry: an
econometric study
JFQA 1980 DEC VOL 15:5 p 1163.

(10000)
Campbell T S
Optimal investment financing decisions and the
value of confidentiality
JFQA 1979 DEC VOL 14 p 913.

(10001)
Carrington J C, Edwards G T
Financing industrial investment
Macmillan, 1979.

(10002)
Feldstein M, Green J, Sheshinski E
Corporate financial policy and taxation in a
growing economy
QJE 1979 VOL 93 p 411.

(10003)
Gahlon J H, Stover R D
Diversification, financial leverage and
conglomerate systematic risk
JFQA 1979 DEC VOL 14 p 999.

(10004)
Gritta R D
The effect of financial leverage on air-carrier
earnings: A break-even analysis
FIN MGMT 1979 SUMMER VOL 8 p 53.

(10005)
Turnbull S M
Debt capacity
JF 1979 SEP VOL 34:4 p 931-940.

(10006)
Donaldson G
New framework for corporate debt policy
HBR 1978 SEP-OCT VOL 56:5 p 149-164.

(10007)
Feldstein M, Green J, Sheshinski E
Inflation and taxes in a growing economy with
debt and equity finance
JPE 1978 VOL 86 Suppl p 53.

(10008)
Sethi S P
Optimal equity and financing model of Krouse
and Lee: Corrections and extensions
JFQA 1978 SEP VOL 13 p 487.

(10009)
Severn A K, Meinster D R
The use of multicurrency financing by the
financial manager
FIN MGMT 1978 WINTER VOL 7 p 45.

(10010)
Shapiro A C
Financial structure and cost of capital in the multinational corporation
JFQA 1978 JUN VOL 13 p 211.

(10011)
Yohn F O Jr
Recent developments in corporate finance
F R Bul 1978 VOL 64:6.

(10012)
Briscoe G, Hawks G
Long-term debt and realisable gains in shareholder wealth: An empirical study
JBFA 1976 SPRING VOL 3:1 p 125-136.

(10013)
Martin J D, Scott D F Jr
Debt capacity and the capital budgeting decision
FIN MGMT 1976 SUMMER VOL 5 p 7.

(10014)
Perrakis S
A note on optimal equity financing of the corporation
JFQA 1976 MAR VOL 11 p 157.

(10015)
Silvers J B
Liquidity, risk and duration patterns in corporate financing
FIN MGMT 1976 AUTUMN VOL 5 p 54.

(10016)
de Faro C, Jucker J V
The selection of international borrowing sources
JFQA 1975 SEP VOL 10 p 381.

(10017)
Haugen R A, Wichern D W
The intricate relationship between financial leverage and the stability of stock prices
JF 1975 VOL 30 p 1283

(10018)
Jacquillat B, McDonald J G, Nussenbaum M
Dividend investment and financing decisions: Empirical evidence on French firms
JFQA 1975 DEC VOL 10 p 791.

(10019)
Reilly F K
A three tier stock market in corporate financing
FIN MGMT 1975 AUTUMN VOL 4 p 7.

(10020)
Carleton W T, Kendall G, Tandon S
Application of the decomposition principle to the capital problem in a decentralized firm
JF 1974 VOL 29 p 815.

(10021)
Naumann-Etienne R
A framework for financial decisions in multinational corporations - summary of recent research
JFQA 1974 NOV VOL 9 p 859.

(10022)
Sullivan T G
Market, power, profitability and financial leverage
JF 1974 VOL 29 p 1407.

(10023)
Vickers D
Disequilibrium structures and financing decisions in the firm
JBFA 1974 AUTUMN VOL 1:3 p 375-388.

(10024)
Braun M E
Planning the debt mix: A linear programming approach
JBF 1973 SUMMER VOL 5:2 p 26-31.

(10025)
Breen W J, Lerner E M
Corporate financial strategies and market measures of risk and return
JF 1973 VOL 28 p 339..

(10026)**Elton E J, Gruber M J**
Asset selection with changing capital structure
JFQA 1973 JUN VOL 8:3 p 459-474.

(10027)
Gupta M C
Optimal financing policy for a firm with uncertain fund requirements
JFQA 1973 DEC VOL 8:5 p 731.

(10028)
Inselbag I
Financing decisions and the theory of the firm
JFQA 1973 DEC VOL 8:5 p 763-776.

(10029)
Krouse C G, Lee W Y
Optimal equity financing of the corporation
JFQA 1973 SEP VOL 8:4 p 539-564.

(10030)
Rubinstein M E
Corporate financial policy in segmented securities
markets
JFQA 1973 DEC VOL 8:5 p 749-762.

(10031)
Berg G H, Tucker J M
Techniques for arranging hospital financing
FIN MGMT 1972 SPRING VOL 1 p 48.

(10032)
Scanlon J H
Bell System financial policies
FIN MGMT 1972 SUMMER VOL 1 p 16.

(10033)
Scott D F Jr
Evidence on the importance of financial structure
FIN MGMT 1972 SUMMER VOL 1 p 45.

(10034)
Schall L D
Firm financial structure and investment
JFQA 1971 JUN VOL 6 p 925-942.

(10035)
DeFelice F
Security and investment: more evidence
JF 1970 SEP VOL 25 p 803-808.

(10036)
Haslem J A
Leverage effects on corporate earnings
Arizona Review 1970 MAR VOL 19 p 7-11.

(10037)
Turnovsky S J
Financial structure and the theory of production
JF 1970 DEC VOL 25 p 1061-1080.

(10038)
Morgan B W
Corporate   debt   and   stockholder   portfolio
selection
YEE 1967 FALL VOL 7 p 210-261.

(10039)
Lerner E M, Carleton W T
Financing decisions of the firm
JF 1966 MAY VOL 21 p 202-214.

(10040)
Brownlee O H, Scott I O
Utility, liquidity and debt management
Em 1963 JUL VOL 31 p 349-362.

(10041)
Miller M H
The   corporation   income   tax   and   corporate
financial policies
(in The Commission on Money and Credit,
Stabilization Policies. P-H, 1963.)

(10042)
Donaldson G
Corporate debt capacity: a study of corporate debt
policy and the determination of corporate debt
capacity
Harvard Busn, 1961.

(10043)
Hunt P
A proposal for precise definitions of 'trading on
the equity' and 'leverage'
JF 1961 SEP VOL 16 p 377-386.

(10044)
Weston J F
Norms for debt levels
JF 1954 MAY VOL 9 p 124-135.

(10045)
Jacoby N H, Weston J F
Factors influencing managerial decisions in
determining forms of business financing: an
exploratory study
Conference on Research in Business Finance.
Natl Bur Econ Res, 1952.

27.1   Descriptive studies of capital structure

(10046)
Allen D E, Mizuno H
The determinants of corporate capital structure: Japanese evidence
AE 1989 VOL 21:5 p 569-586.

(10047)
Chowdhury G, Miles D K
Modelling companies' debt and dividend decisions with company accounts data
AE 1989 VOL 21:11 p 1483-1508.

(10048)
Chung K H
Debt and risk: a technical note
JBFA 1989 WINTER VOL 16:5 p 719.

(10049)
Bank of England
The financial behaviour of industrial and commercial companies, 1970-86
BEQB 1988 VOL 28 p 75-82.

(10050)
Fatemi A M
The effect of international diversification on corporate financing policy
JBusR 1988 JAN VOL 16:1 p 17-30.

(10051)
Johnson D
The currency denomination of long-term debt in the Canadian corporate sector: an empirical analysis
JIMF 1988 MAR VOL 7:1 p 77-90.

(10052)
Maksimovic V
Capital structure in repeated oligopolies
RandJ 1988 AUTUMN VOL 19:3 p 389-407.

(10053)
Titman S, Wessels R
The determinants of capital structure choice
JF 1988 MAR VOL 43:1 p 1-20.

(10054)
Wall L D
Leverage ratios of US nonfinancial corporations
F R Bk Atlanta Ec Rev 1988 VOL 73:3.

(10055)
Aggarwal R, Baliga G
Capital structure among Latin American companies
MF 1987 VOL 13:1 p 3-11

(10056)
Bank of England
Companies' long-term financial decisions; dividends and debt
BEQB 1987 VOL 27 p 261.

(10057)
Friend I, Hasbrouck J
Determinants of capital structure
(in Chen A ed., Research in Finance, Vol. 7. JAI Pr, 1987.)

(10058)
Taggart R A
Corporate financing: Too much debt?
FAJ 1986 MAY-JUN VOL 42 p 35-42.

(10059)
Friedman B M ed.
Corporate capital structures in the United States
U of Chicago Pr, 1985.

(10060)
Hochman S, Palmon O
The impact of inflation on the aggregate debt-asset ratio
JF 1985 SEP VOL 40:4 p 1115-1125.

(10061)
Labich K
Is business taking on too much debt?
F 1985 JUL 22 VOL 112:2 p 58-61

(10062)
Michel A J, Shaked I
Japanese leverage: Myth or reality
FAJ 1985 JUL-AUG VOL 41 p 61-67.

(10063)
Misawa M
Financing Japanese investments in the United
States: Case studies of a large and
medium-sized-firm
FIN MGMT 1985 WINTER VOL 14 p 5-12.

(10064)
Bank of England
Business finance in the United Kingdom and
Germany
BEQB 1984 VOL 24 p 368.

(10065)
Jalilvand A, Harris R S
Corporate behavior in adjusting to capital
structure and dividend targets : an econometric
study
JF 1984 MAR VOL 39:1 p 127-145.

(10066)
White B
International differences in gearing : how
important are they?
NWBQR 1984 NOV p 14-25.

(10067)
Collins J M, Sekely W S
The relationship of headquarters country and
industry classification to financial structure
FIN MGMT 1983 AUTUMN VOL 12 p 45-51.

(10068)
Peterson P P, Benesh G A
A reexamination of the empirical relationship
between investment and financing decisions
JFQA 1983 DEC VOL 18:4 p 439-453

(10069)
Bowen R M, Daley L A, Huber C C Jr
Leverage measures and industrial classification:
Review and additional evidence
FIN MGMT 1982 WINTER VOL 11 p 10-20.

(10070)
Friedman B M ed.
The changing roles of debt and equity in
financing U.S. capital formation
U of Chicago Pr, 1982.

(10071)
Marsh P
The choice between equity and debt : an
empirical study
JF 1982 MAR VOL 37:1 p 121-144.

(10072)
Scott D F Jr, Johnson D J
Financing policies and practices in large
corporations
FIN MGMT 1982 SUMMER VOL 11 p 51-59.

(10073)
Bank of England
The financing of Japanese industry
BEQB 1981 VOL 21 p 510-518.

(10074)
Kuroda I, Oritani Y
A reexamination of the unique features of Japan's
corporate financial structure
Japanese Economic Studies 1980 SUMMER VOL
8.

(10075)
Mains N E
Recent corporate financing patterns
F R Bul 1980 VOL 66:9.

(10076)
Errunza V R
Determinants of financial structure in the central
American common market
FIN MGMT 1979 AUTUMN VOL 8 p 72.

(10077)
Ferri M G, Jones W H
Determinants of financial structure: a new
methodological approach
JF 1979 DEC VOL 34:3 p 631-644.

(10078)
Litzenberger R H, Sosin H B
A comparison of capital structure decisions of
regulated and nonregulated firms
FIN MGMT 1978 AUTUMN VOL 7 p 17..

(10079)**Thomas W A**
The finance of British industry 1918-1976
Methuen, 1978.

(10080)
Taggart R A
A model of corporate financing decisions
JF 1977 VOL 32 p 1467.

(10081)
Ang J S
The intertemporal behavior of corporate debt policy
JFQA 1976 NOV VOL 11.

(10082)
Melicher R W, Rush D F, Winn D N
Industry concentration, financial structure and profitability
FIN MGMT 1976 AUTUMN VOL 5 p 48.

(10083)
Albach H
The development of the capital structure of German companies
JBFA 1975 AUTUMN VOL 2:3 p 281-294.

(10084)
Belkaoui A
A Canadian survey of financial structure
FIN MGMT 1975 SPRING VOL 4 p 74.

(10085)
Coates J H, Woolley P K
Corporate gearing in the EEC
JBFA 1975 SPRING VOL 2:1 p 1-18.

(10086)
Scott D F Jr, Martin J D
Industry influence on financial structure
FIN MGMT 1975 SPRING VOL 4 p 67.

(10087)
Stonehill A I, Beekhuisen T, Wright R
Financial goals and debt ratio determinants: A survey of practice in five countries
FIN MGMT 1975 AUTUMN VOL 4 p 27.

(10088)
Taub A J
Determinants of the firm's capital structure
REStat 1975 NOV VOL 57:4 p 410-416.

(10089)
Beekhuisen T, Toy N, Stonehill A
A comparative international study of growth, profitability and risk as determinants of corporate debt ratios in the manufacturing sector
JFQA 1974 NOV VOL 9 p 875.

(10090)
Hurdle G J
Leverage, risk, market structure and profitability
REStat 1974 NOV VOL 56:4 p 478-485.

(10091)
Martin J D, Scott D F Jr
A discriminant analysis of the corporate debt-equity decision
FIN MGMT 1974 WINTER VOL 3 p 71.

(10092)
Remmers L, Stonehill A, Wright R
Industry and size as debt ratio determinants in manufacturing internationally
FIN MGMT 1974 SUMMER VOL 3 p 24.

(10093)
Baker S A
Risk, leverage and profitability: an industry analysis
REStat 1973 NOV VOL 55:4 p 503-507.

(10094)
Pinches G E, Mingo K A, Caruthers J K
The stability of financial patterns in industrial organizations
JF 1973 VOL 28 p 389.

(10095)
Boot J C G, Frankfurter G M
The dynamics of corporate debt management, decision rules and some empirical evidence
JFQA 1972 SEP VOL 7 p 1957.

(10096)
Melberg W F
Benishayan time series as models for debt processes over time
AR 1972 JAN VOL 47:1 p 116.

(10097)
Robbins S M, Stobaugh R B
Financing foreign affiliates
FIN MGMT 1972 WINTER VOL 1 p 56.

(10098)
Walls E L Jr
Hospital dependency on long-term debt
FIN MGMT 1972 SPRING VOL 1 p 42.

(10099)
Whittington G
The profitability of retained earnings
REStat 1972 MAY VOL 54 p 152-160.

(10100)
Baxter N D, Cragg J G
Corporate choices among long-term financing
instruments
REStat 1970 AUG VOL 52 p 225-235.

(10101)
Gupta M C
The effect of size, growth, and industry on the
financial structure of manufacturing companies
JF 1969 JAN VOL 24 p 517-529.

(10102)
Harkins E P, Walsh F J Jr
Corporate debt management
Natl Ind Conf Bd, 1968.

(10103)
Childs J F
Long-term financing
P-H, 1965.

(10104)
Walter J E
The use of borrowed funds
JB 1955 APR VOL 28 p 138-147.

27.2 Optimal capital structure

(10105)
Barton S L, Hill N C, Sundaram S
An empirical test of stakeholder theory
predictions of capital structure
FIN MGMT 1989 SPRING VOL 18 p 36-44.

(10106)
Baskin J
An empirical investigation of the pecking order
hypothesis
FIN MGMT 1989 SPRING VOL 18 p 26-35.

(10107)
Chatterjee S, Scott J H Jr
Explaining differences in corporate capital
structure: theory and new evidence
JBankF 1989 MAY VOL 13:2 p 283-310.

(10108)
Choi J J, Fabozzi F J, Yaari U
Optimum corporate leverage with risky debt: a
demand approach
JFR 1989 SUMMER VOL 12:2 p 129-142.

(10109)
Cornett M M, Travlos N G
Information associated with debt-for-equity and
equity-for-debt exchange offers
JF 1989 JUN VOL 44:2 p 451-468.

(10110)
Errunza V R, Moreau A F
Debt-for-equity swaps under a rational
expectations equilibrium
JF 1989 JUL VOL 44:3 p 663-680.

(10111)
Fischer E O, Heinkel R, Zechner J
Dynamic capital structure choice: theory and tests
JF 1989 MAR VOL 44:1 p 19-40.

(10112)
Gordon M J
Corporate finance under the MM theorems
FIN MGMT 1989 SUMMER VOL 18 p 19-28.

(10113)
Pinegar J M, Wilbricht L
What managers think of capital structure theory:
a survey
FIN MGMT 1989 WINTER VOL 18 p 82.

(10114)
Sugrue T F, Scherr F C
An empirical test of Ross's cash flow beta theory
of capital structure
FR 1989 AUG VOL 24:3 p 355-370.

(10115)
Weston J F
What MM have wrought
FIN MGMT 1989 SUMMER VOL 18 p 29-38.

(10116)
Anstaett K W, McCrary D P, Monahan S T
Practical debt policy considerations for growth
companies: a case study approach
JACF 1988 SUMMER VOL 1 p 71-78.

(10117)
Bhattacharya S
Corporate finance and the legacy of Miller and
Modigliani
JEP 1988 VOL 2:4 p 135-148.

(10118)
DeMarzo P M
An extension of the Modigliani-Miller theorem to
stochastic economies with incomplete markets and
interdependent securities
JET 1988 AUG VOL 45:2 p 353-369.

(10119)
Howe J S, Shilling J D
Capital structure theory and REIT security
offerings
JF 1988 SEP VOL 43:4 p 983.

(10120)
Masulis R W
The debt/equity choice
Ballinger, 1988.

(10121)
Miller M H
The Modigliani-Miller propositions after thirty
years
JEP 1988 VOL 2:4 p 99-120.

(10122)
Modigliani F
MM - past, present and future
JEP 1988 VOL 2:4 p 149-158.

(10123)
Ross S A
Comment on the Modigliani-Miller propositions
JEP 1988 VOL 2:4 p 127-134.

(10124)
Stiglitz J E
Why financial structure matters
JEP 1988 VOL 2:4 p 121-126.

(10125)
Scherr F C
A multiperiod mean-variance model of optimal
capital structure
FR 1987 FEB VOL 22:1.

(10126)
Ashton R K
Personal leverage v corporate leverage : an
extension to the debate
JBFA 1986 WINTER VOL 13:4 p 619-626

(10127)
Litzenberger R H
Some observations on capital structure and the
impact of recent recapitalizations on share prices.
JFQA 1986 MAR VOL 21:1 p 59-71

(10128)
Myers S C
The capital structure puzzle
MCFJ 1985 FALL VOL 3 p 6-18.

(10129)
Peavy J W III, Scott J A
The effect of stock for debt swaps on security
returns
FR 1985 NOV VOL 20:4.

(10130)
Peavy J W III, Scott J A
A closer look at stock-for-debt swaps
FAJ 1985 MAY-JUN VOL 41 p 44-50.

(10131)
Spence M A
Capital structure and the corporation's product
market environment
(in Friedman B ed., Corporate capital structures
in the United States. U of Chicago Pr, 1985.).

(10132)**Titman S**
The effect of forward markets on the debt-equity
mix of investor portfolios and the optimal capital
structure of firms.
JFQA 1985 MAR VOL 20:1 p 19-27.

(10133)
Bradley M, Jarrell G A, Kim E H
On the existence of an optimal capital structure
: theory and evidence
JF 1984 JUL VOL 39:3 p 857-880.

(10134)
Brennan M J,   Schwartz E S
Optimal financial policy and firm valuation
JF 1984 JUL VOL 39:3 p 593-609

(10135)
Jones E P,   Mason S P,   Rosenfeld E
Contingent claims analysis of corporate capital
structures : an empirical investigation
JF 1984 JUL VOL 39:3 p 611-627

(10136)
Myers S C
The capital structure puzzle
JF 1984 JUL VOL 39:3 p 575-592.

(10137)
Senbet L W,   Taggart R A
Capital structure equilibrium under market
imperfections and incompleteness
JF 1984 MAR VOL 39:1 p 93-103.

(10138)
Alberts W W,   Hite G L
The Modigliani-Miller leverage equation
considered in a product market context.
JFQA 1983 DEC VOL 18:4 p 425-437.

(10139)
Brick I E,   Mellon W G,   Surkis J
Optimal capital structure: A multi-period
programming model for use in financial planning
JBankF 1983 VOL 7 p 45.

(10140)
Hochman S,   Palmon O
The irrelevance of capital structure for the impact
of inflation on investment
JF 1983 JUN VOL 38:3 p 785-794.

(10141)
Maloney K J,   Marshall W J,   Yawitz J B
The effect of risk on the firm's optimal capital
stock : a note
JF 1983 SEP VOL 38:4 p 1279-1284

(10142)
Masulis R W
The impact of capital structure change on firm
value: some estimates
JF 1983 MAR VOL 38:1 p 107-126.

(10143)
Myers S C
The search for optimal capital structure
MCFJ 1983 SPRING VOL 1 p 6-16.

(10144)
Modigliani F
Debt dividend policy, taxes, inflation and market
valuation.
JF 1982 MAY VOL 37:2 p 255-273.

(10145)
Piper T R,   Weinhold W A
How much debt is right for your company?
HBR 1982 JUL-AUG VOL 60:4 p 106-114.

(10146)
Barnea A,   Haugen R A,   Senbet L W
An equilibrium analysis of debt financing under
costly tax arbitrage and agency problems
JF 1981 JUN VOL 36:3 p 569-581.

(10147)
Hong H K
Finance mix and capital structure
JBFA 1981 WINTER VOL 8:4 p 485-491.

(10148)
Shelton J
Equal access and Miller's equilibrium.
JFQA 1981 NOV VOL 16:4 p 603-623.

(10149)
Aivazian V A,   Callen J L
Corporate leverage and growth: the
game-theoretic issues.
JFE 1980 DEC VOL 8:4 p 379-399

(10150)
Booth L D
Capital structure taxes and the cost of capital
QREB 1980 AUTUMN VOL 20:3 p 86-98

(10151)
Deschamps B,   Mehta D R,   Walker M C
The influence of dividends, growth, and leverage
on share prices in the electric utility industry: An
econometric study
JFQA 1980 DEC VOL 15 p 1163.

(10152)
Flath D, Knoeber C R
Taxes, failure costs and optimal industry capital structure: an empirical test.
JF 1980 MAR VOL 35 p 99-117.

(10153)
Masulis R W
The effects of capital structure change on security prices: A study of exchange offers
JFE 1980 VOL 8 p 139-178.

(10154)
Chen A H, Kim E H
Theories of corporate debt policy: a synthesis
JF 1979 MAY VOL 34:2 p 371-384.

(10155)
Appelbaum E, Harris R G
Optimal capital policy with bounded investment plans
IntER 1978 FEB VOL 19:1 p 103-114.

(10156)
Becher J
General proof of Modigliani-Miller propositions I and II using parameter-preference theory
JFQA 1978 MAR VOL 13 p 65.

(10157)
Fama E F
The effects of a firm's investment and financing decisions on the welfare of its security holders
AER 1978 JUN VOL 68:3 p 272-284

(10158)
Hong H, Rappaport A
Debt capacity, optimal capital structure and capital budgeting analysis
FIN MGMT 1978 AUTUMN VOL 7 p 7.

(10159)
Kim E H
A mean-variance theory of optimal capital structure and corporate debt capacity
JF 1978 VOL 33 p 45.

(10160)
Arditti F D, Levi H, Sarnat M
Taxes, capital structure, and the cost of capital: some extensions
QREB 1977 VOL 17:2 p 89.

(10161)
Carleton W T, Silberman I H
Joint determination of rate of return and capital structure: An econometric analysis
JF 1977 VOL 32 p 811.

(10162)
Dickinson J P, Kyuno K
Corporate valuation: A reconciliation of the Miller-Modigliani and traditionalist views
JBFA 1977 SUMMER VOL 4:2 p 177-186.

(10163)
Gonzales N, Litzenberger R, Rolfo J
On mean variance models of capital structure and the absurdity of their predictions
JFQA 1977 JUN VOL 12 p 165.

(10164)
Hite G L
Leverage output effects and the M-M theorems
JFE 1977 VOL 4 p 177.

(10165)
Krainer R E
Interest rates, leverage and investor rationality
JFQA 1977 MAR VOL 12 p 1.

(10166)
Bourn M
The "gain" on borrowing
JBFA 1976 SPRING VOL 3:1 p 167-182.

(10167)
Watson R D, Oldfield G S, Santomero A M
A symposium on the capital structure of banks
FIN MGMT 1976 WINTER VOL 5 P 53.

(10168)
Baron D P
Firm valuation, corporate taxes and default risk
JF 1975 VOL 30 p 1251.

(10169)
Jones C P, Joy O M
Leverage and the valuation of risk assets: an empirical test
QREB 1975 VOL 15:4 p 81.

(10170)
Kumar P
Growth stocks and corporate capital structure theory
JF 1975 MAY VOL 30:2 p 532-547.

(10171)
Lev B, Pekelman D
A multiperiod adjustment model for the firm's capital structure
JF 1975 VOL 30 p 75.

(10172)
Lloyd-Davies P R
Optimal financial policy in imperfect markets
JFQA 1975 SEP VOL 10 p 457.

(10173)
Love D A
The use and abuse of leverage
FAJ 1975 MAR-APR VOL 31 p 51-59.

(10174)
Senchack J Jr
The firm's optimal financing policies: Solution, equilibrium and stability
JFQA 1975 NOV VOL 10 p 543.

(10175)
Shalit S S
On the mathematics of financial leverage
FIN MGMT 1975 SPRING VOL 4 p 57.

(10176)
Keller T F, Person R J
Optimal financial structure, cost of capital and the lease-or-buy decision
JBFA 1974 AUTUMN VOL 1:3 p 405-414.

(10177)
Brealey R A
A note on dividends and debt under the new taxation
JBF 1973 SPRING VOL 5:1 p 66-68.

(10178)
Kraus A, Litzenberger R H
A state-preference model of optimal financial leverage
JF 1973 VOL 28 p 911.

(10179)
Levy H, Arditti F D
Valuation, leverage and the cost of capital in the case of depreciable assets
JF 1973 VOL 28 p 687.

(10180)
Robichek A A, Higgins R C, Kinsman M
The effect of leverage on the cost of equity capital of electric utility firms
JF 1973 VOL 28 p 353.

(10181)
Chen A H, Boness A J, Jatusipitak S
On relations among stock price behavior and changes in the capital structure of the firm
JFQA 1972 SEP VOL 7 p 1967.

(10182)
Rao N K
Equivalent-risk class hypothesis: An empirical study
JFQA 1972 JUN VOL 7 p 1763-1772.

(10183)
Haugen R A, Pappas J L
Equilibrium in the pricing of capital assets, risk-bearing debt instruments and the question of optimal capital structure
JFQA 1971 JUN VOL 6 p 943-954.

(10184)
Resek R W
Multidimensional risk and the Modigliani-Miller hypothesis
JF 1970 MAR-APR VOL 25 p 47-51..

(10185)**Tinsley P A**
Capital structure, precautionary balances, and valuation of the firm: the problem of financial risk
JFQA 1970 MAR VOL 5 p 33-64.

(10186)
Vickers D
The cost of capital and the structure of the firm
JF 1970 MAR VOL 25 p 35-46.

(10187)
Borch K
The capital structure of a firm
SJE 1969 MAR VOL 71.

(10188)
Hamada R S
Portfolio analysis, market equilibrium and corporation finance
JF 1969 MAR VOL 24 p 13-31.

(10189)
Mumey G A
Theory of financial structure
HR & W, 1969.

(10190)
Sarma L, Rao K
Leverage and the value of the firm
JF 1969 SEP VOL 24 p 673-677.

(10191)
Stiglitz J E
A re-examination of the Modigliani-Miller theorem
AER 1969 DEC VOL 59 p 784-793.

(10192)
Ben-Shanar H
Capital structure and the cost of capital
JF 1968 SEP VOL 23 p 639-653.

(10193)
Brigham E F, Gordon M J
Leverage, dividend policy, and the cost of capital
JF 1968 MAR VOL 23 p 85-103.

(10194)
Baumol W J, Malkiel B G
The firm's optimal debt-equity combination and the cost of capital
QJE 1967 NOV VOL 81 p 547-578.

(10195)
Schwartz E, Aronson J R
Some surrogate evidence in support of the concept of optimal financial structure
JF 1967 MAR VOL 22 p 10-18.

(10196)
Vickers D
Elasticity of capital supply, monopsonistic discrimination and optimal capital structure
JF 1967 MAR VOL 22 p 1-9.

(10197)
Haley C W
A note on the cost of debt
JFQA 1966 DEC VOL 1 p 72-93.

(10198)
Miller M H, Modigliani F
Some estimates of the cost of capital to the electric utility industry, 1954-57
AER 1966 JUN VOL 56 p 333-391.

(10199)
Robichek A A, Myers S C
Problems in the theory of optimal capital structure
JFQA 1966 JUN VOL 1 p 1-35.

(10200)
Wippern R F
Financial structure and the value of the firm
JF 1966 DEC VOL 21 p 615-634.

(10201)
Wippern R F
A note on the equivalent risk class assumption
EE 1966 SPRING p 13-22.

(10202)
Wright F K, Young I C, Barton A D
The effect of financial structure on the market value of companies
Australian Economic Papers 1966 JUN p 21-34.

(10203)
Robichek A A, Myers S C
Optimal financing decisions
P-H, 1965.

(10204)
Robichek A A, Teichroew D, Jones J M
Optimal short-term financing decision
MSci 1965 SEP VOL 12 p 1-36.

(10205)
Barges A
The effect of capital structure on the cost of capital: a test and evaluation of the Modigliani and Miller propositions
P-H, 1963.

(10206)
Gordon M J
Optimal investment and financing policy
JF 1963 MAY VOL 18 p 264-272.

(10207)
Solomon E
Leverage and the cost of capital
JF 1963 MAY VOL 18 p 273-279.

(10208)
Miller M H, Modigliani F
The cost of capital, corporation finance and the
theory of investment: reply
AER 1959 SEP VOL 49 p 655-668.

(10209)
Schwartz E
Theory of the capital structure of the firm
JF 1959 MAR VOL 14 p 18-39.

(10210)
Modigliani F, Miller M H
The cost of capital, corporation finance and the
theory of investment
AER 1958 JUN VOL 48 p 261-297.

27.21 Tax and capital structure

(10211)
Dammon R M, Senbet L W
The effect of taxes and depreciation on corporate
investment and financial leverage
JF 1988 JUN VOL 43:2 p 357-374.

(10212)
Emery D R, Gehr A K Jr
Tax option, capital structure and Miller
equilibrium: A numerical illustration
FIN MGMT 1988 SUMMER VOL 17 p 30-40.

(10213)
Fazzari S M, Hubbard R G, Petersen B
Investment, financing decisions, and tax policy
AER 1988 MAY VOL 78:2 p 200-205.

(10214)
Lewellen W G, Mauer D C
Tax options and corporate capital structures
JFQA 1988 DEC VOL 23 p 387.

(10215)
Barnea A, Talmor E, Haugen R A
Debt and taxes: a multiperiod investigation
JBankF 1987 VOL 11 p 79-97.

(10216)
Ben-Horim M, Hochman S, Palmon O
The impact of the 1986 Tax Reform Act on
corporate financial policy
FIN MGMT 1987 AUTUMN VOL 16 p 29-35.

(10217)
Brick I E, Fisher L
Effects of classifying equity or debt on the value
of the firm under tax asymmetry
JFQA 1987 DEC VOL 22:4 p 383-399.

(10218)
Cheung J K
Depreciation debt and equilibrium tax rates: a
reconsideration
QREB 1987 SPRING VOL 27:1 p 6-15.

(10219)
Davis A H R
Effective tax rates as determinants of Canadian
capital structure
FIN MGMT 1987 AUTUMN VOL 16 p 22-28.

(10220)
Fung W K H, Theobald M F
Taxes, unequal access, public debt and corporate
financial policy in the United Kingdom
JBankF 1987 VOL 11 p 67-78.

(10221)
Hamada R S
Differential taxes and the structure of equilibrium
rates of return: Managerial implications and
remaining conundrums
(in Lee C F ed., Advances in Financial Planning,
VOL 2. JAI Press, 1987.)

(10222)
Kim E H
Optimal capital structure in Miller's equilibrium
(in Bhattacharya S and Constantinides eds.,
Frontiers of financial theory. Rowman and
Littlefield, 1987.)

(10223)
Mauer D C, Lewellen W G
Debt management under corporate and personal taxation
JF 1987 DEC VOL 42:5 p 1275-1292.

(10224)
Pozdena R J
Tax policy and corporate capital structure
F R Bk San Francisco Ec Rev 1987 FALL.

(10225)
Rangazas P, Abdullah D
Taxes and the corporate sector debt ratio: Some time series evidence
REStat 1987 VOL 69 p 357.

(10226)
Zechner J, Swoboda P
The critical implicit tax rate and capital structure
JBankF 1986 VOL 10 p 327.

(10227)
Ang J S, Peterson D, Peterson P
Marginal rates: evidence from nontaxable corporate bonds: a note
JF 1985 MAR VOL 40:1 p 327-332.

(10228)
Jordan B D, Pettway R H
The pricing of short-term debt and the Miller hypothesis : a note
JF 1985 JUN VOL 40:2 p 589-594.

(10229)
Patterson C S
Debt and taxes : empirical evidence
JBFA 1985 SUMMER VOL 12:2 p 187-206

(10230)
Ross S A
Debt and taxes and uncertainty
JF 1985 JUL VOL 40:3 p 637-658.

(10231)
Rutterford J
An international perspective on the capital structure puzzle
MCFJ 1985 FALL VOL 3 p 60-72.

(10232)
Boquist J A, Moore W T
Inter-industry leverage differences and the DeAngelo-Masulis tax shield hypothesis
FIN MGMT 1984 SPRING VOL 13 p 5-9.

(10233)
Jaffe J F, Westerfield R
Leverage and the value of a firm under a progressive income tax: A correction and extension
JBankF 1984 VOL 8 p 491.

(10234)
Kane A, Marcus A J, McDonald R L
How big is the tax advantage to debt?
JF 1984 JUL VOL 39:3 p 841-855.

(10235)
Auerbach A J
Taxation, corporate financial policy and the cost of capital.
JEL 1983 SEP VOL 21:3 p 905-940.

(10236)
Auerbach A J, King M A
Taxation, portfolio choice, and debt equity ratios: a general equilibrium model
QJE 1983 NOV VOL 98:4 p 587-609.

(10237)
Cordes J J, Sheffrin S M
Estimating the tax advantage of corporate debt
JF 1983 MAR VOL 38:1 p 95-105..

(10238)**Harris J M, Roenfeldt R L, Cooley P L**
Evidence of financial leverage clienteles
JF 1983 VOL 38:4 p 1125-1132.

(10239)
Franks J R, Pringle J J
Debt financing corporate financial intermediaries and firm valuation
JF 1982 JUN VOL 37:3 p 751-761.

(10240)
Kim E H
Miller's equilibrium shareholder leverage clienteles and optimal capital structure
JF 1982 MAY VOL 37:2 p 301-319.

(10241)
Trzcinka C
The pricing of tax-exempt bonds and the Miller hypothesis
JF 1982 SEP VOL 37:4 p 907-923.

(10242)
Brealey R A, Young C M
Debt taxes and leasing: a note
JF 1980 DEC VOL 35:5 p 1245-1250.

(10243)
DeAngelo H, Masulis R W
Optimal capital structure under corporate and personal taxation
JFE 1980 MAR VOL 8:1 p 3-29.

(10244)
Schneller M I
Taxes and the optimal capital structure of the firm
JF 1980 MAR VOL 35:1 p 119-127.

(10245)
Taggart R A
Taxes and corporate capital structure in an incomplete market
JF 1980 JUN VOL 25:3 p 645-659.

(10246)
Bierman H Jr, Oldfield G S
Corporate debt and corporate taxes
JF 1979 SEP VOL 34:4 p 951-956.

(10247)
Kim E H, Lewellen W G, McConnell J J
Financial leverage clienteles: theory and evidence.
JFE 1979 MAR VOL 7:1 p 84-109

(10248)
Wrightsman D
Tax shield valuation and the capital structure decision
JF 1978 VOL 33 p 650.

(10249)
Miller M H
Debt and taxes
JF 1977 MAY VOL 32:2 p 261-276.

(10250)
Archer S
Holding gains, deferred taxation and capital structure
JBFA 1976 WINTER VOL 3:4 p 151-168.

(10251)
Modigliani F, Miller M H
Corporate income taxes and the cost of capital: a correction
AER 1963 JUN VOL 53 p 433-443.

27.22 Imperfect information, moral hazard and capital structure

(10252)
Aghion P, Bolton P
The financial structure of the firm and the problem of control
EER 1989 VOL 33 p 286.

(10253)
Crutchley C E, Hansen R S
A test of the agency theory of managerial ownership, corporate leverage, and corporate dividends
FIN MGMT 1989 WINTER VOL 18 p 36-46.

(10254)
Dann L Y, DeAngelo H
Corporate financial policy and corporate control: a study of defensive adjustments in asset and ownership structure
JFE 1988 VOL 20 p 87-128.

(10255)
Friend I, Lang L H P
An empirical test of the impact of managerial self-interest on corporate capital structure
JF 1988 JUN VOL 43:2 p 271-282.

(10256)
Harris M, Raviv A
Corporate control contests and capital structure
JFE 1988 VOL 20 p 55-86.

(10257)
Narayanan M P
Debt versus equity under asymmetric information
JFQA 1988 MAR VOL 23:1 p 39-52.

(10258)
Shah S, Thakor A V
Private versus public ownership: investment, ownership distribution, and optimality
JF 1988 MAR VOL 43:1 p 41-60.

(10259)
Wedig G, Sloan F A, Hassan M
Capital structure, ownership, and capital payment policy: the case of hospitals
JF 1988 MAR VOL 43:1 p 21-40.

(10260)
Blazenko G W
Managerial preference asymmetric information and financial structure
JF 1987 SEP VOL 42:4 p 839-862.

(10261)
Bradford W D
The issue decision of manager-owners under information asymmetry
JF 1987 DEC VOL 42:5 p 1245-1260.

(10262)
Brennan M J, Kraus A
Efficient financing under asymmetric information
JF 1987 DEC VOL 42:5 p 1224-1244.

(10263)
John K
Risk-shifting incentives and signalling through corporate capital structure
JF 1987 JUL VOL 42:3 p 623-641.

(10264)
Darrough M N, Stoughton N M
Moral hazard and adverse selection : the question of financial structure
JF 1986 JUN VOL 41:2 p 501-513.

(10265)
Flannery M J
Asymmetric information and risky debt maturity choice
JF 1986 MAR VOL 41:1 p 19-37

(10266)
Green R C, Talmor E
Asset subsitition and the agency costs of debt financing
JBankF 1986 VOL 10 p 391.

(10267)
Kim W S, Sorensen E H
Evidence on the impact of the agency costs of debt on corporate debt policy
JFQA 1986 JUN VOL 21:2 p 131-144.

(10268)
Myers S C, Majluf N S
Corporate financing and investment decisions when firms have information that investors do not have
JFE 1984 VOL 13 p 187.

(10269)
Lee W L, Thakor A V, Vora G
Screening market signalling and capital structure theory
JF 1983 DEC VOL 38:5 p 1507-1518.

(10270)
Grossman S J, Hart D
Corporate capital structure and managerial incentives
(in Friedman B ed., Corporate capital structures in the United States. U of Chicago Pr, 1982.)

(10271)
Grossman S J, Hart O
Corporate financial structure and managerial incentives
(in McCall J J ed., The economics of information and uncertainty. U of Chicago Pr, 1982.)

(10272)
Gupta K
Determinants of corporate borrowing: A note
JFE 1982 VOL 10 p 115.

(10273)
Heinkel R
A theory of capital structure relevance under imperfect information
JF 1982 DEC VOL 37:5 p 1141-1150.

(10274)
Barnea A, Haugen R A, Senbet L W
Market imperfections, agency problems and capital structure: A review
FIN MGMT 1981 SUMMER VOL 10 p 7-22.

(10275)
Myers S C
Determinants of corporate borrowing
JFE 1977 VOL 5 p 147.

(10276)
Ross S A
The determination of financial structure: the
incentive signalling approach
BellJ 1977 SPRING VOL 8:1 p 23-41.

27.23   Bankruptcy and capital structure

(10277)
Haugen R A, Senbet L W
Bankruptcy and agency costs: their significance to
the theory of optimal capital structure
JFQA 1988 MAR VOL 23:1 p 27-38.

(10278)
Moore W T
Asset composition bankruptcy costs and the firm's
choice of capital structure
QREB 1986 WINTER VOL 26:4 p 51-61

(10279)
Titman S
The effect of capital structure on a firm's
liquidation decision
JFE 1984 VOL 13 p 137-151.

(10280)
Castanias R
Bankruptcy risk and optimal capital structure
JF 1983 DEC VOL 38:5 p 1617-1635.

(10281)
Castanias R
Bankruptcy risk and optimal capital structure
JF 1983 DEC VOL 38:5 p 1617-1635.

(10282)
Greenfield R L, Randall M R, Wood J C
Financial leverage and use of the net present
value investment criterion
FIN MGMT 1983 AUTUMN VOL 12 p 40-44.

(10283)
Lohmann J R, Oakford R V
The effects of borrowing on the rate of growth of
capital and the risk of ruin of a firm
JBFA 1982 SUMMER VOL 9:2 p 219-237

(10284)
Hellwig M F
Bankruptcy, limited liability and the
Modigliani-Miller theorem
AER 1981 VOL 71 p 155-170.

(10285)
Feder G
A note on debt, assets and lending under default
risk
JFQA 1980 MAR VOL 15 p 191.

(10286)
Boisjoly R, Lee W
Optimal financial policies under threat of
bankruptcy
JFQA 1978 NOV VOL 13 p 783

(10287)
Haugen R A, Senbet L W
The insignificance of bankruptcy costs to the
theory of optimal capital structure
JF 1978 MAY VOL 33:2 p 383-394.

(10288)
Rendleman R J Jr
Effects of default risk on the firm's investment
and financing decisions
FIN MGMT 1978 SPRING VOL 7 p 45.

(10289)
Arbel A, Kolodny R, Lakonishok J
The relationship between risk of default and
return on equity: An empirical investigation
JFQA 1977 NOV VOL 12 p 615.

(10290)
Scott J H Jr
Bankruptcy, secured debt and optimal capital
structure
JF 1977 VOL 32 p 1..

(10291)**Baron D P**
Default risk and the Modigliani-Miller theorem:
A synthesis
AER 1976 VOL 66 p 204-212.

(10292)
Hagen K P
Default risk, homemade leverage and the Modigliani-Miller theorem: Note
AER 1976 VOL 66 p 199-203.

(10293)
Bierman H Jr, Chopra K, Thomas J
Ruin considerations: Optimal working capital and capital structure
JFQA 1975 MAR VOL 10 p 119.

(10294)
Cheng P L
Default risk, scale and the homemade leverage theorem: Note
AER 1975 VOL 65 p 768-790.

(10295)
Milne F
Choice over asset economies: Default risk and corporate leverage
JFE 1975 VOL 2 p 165.

(10296)
Stapleton R C
A note on default risk, leverage and the M-M theorem
JFE 1975 VOL 2 p 377.

(10297)
Baron D P
Default risk, homemade leverage and the Modigliani-Miller theorem
AER 1974 VOL 64 p 176-182.

(10298)
Bierman H Jr, Thomas L J
Ruin considerations and debt issuance
JFQA 1972 JAN VOL 7 p 1361-1378.

(10299)
Smith V L
Default risk, scale, and the homemade leverage theorem
AER 1972 MAR VOL 62 p 66-76.

(10300)
Bierman H Jr
Risk and the addition of debt to the capital structure
JFQA 1968 DEC VOL 3 p 415-426.

(10301)
Baxter N D
Leverage, risk of ruin and the cost of capital
JF 1967 SEP VOL 22 p 395-403.

(10302)
Quirk J P
The capital structure of firms and the risk of failure
IntER 1961 MAY VOL 2 p 210-228.

28 Leasing and project finance

(10303)
De Metz R
Off balance sheet finance
Graham & Trotman, 1985.

28.1 Leasing

(10304)
Finucane T J
Some empirical evidence on the use of financial leases
JFR 1988 WINTER VOL 11:4 p 321-334.

(10305)
Isom T A et al.
The handbook of equipment leasing
Salt Lake City, UT: Amembal & Isom, 1988.

(10306)
Loewenstein M A, McClure J E
Taxes and financial leasing
QREB 1988 VOL 28:1 p 21.

(10307)
Mayes D G, Nicholas C S
The economic impact of leasing
Macmillan, 1988.

(10308)
Moody C E Jr, Kruvant W J
Joint bidding, entry, and the price of OCS leases
RandJ 1988 SUMMER VOL 19:2 p 276-284.

(10309)
Nevitt P K, Fabozzi F J
Equipment leasing. 3rd ed
Dow Jones-Irwin, 1988.

(10310)
Paddock J L, Siegel D R, Smith J L
Option valuation of claims on real assets: The case of offshore petroleum leases
QJE 1988 AUG VOL 103:3 p 479-508.

(10311)
Smith J L, Siegel D R, Cheng C S A
Failure of the net profit share leasing experiment for offshore petroleum resources
REStat 1988 VOL 70 p 199.

(10312)
Bayless M E, Diltz J D
Capital leasing and corporate borrowing
EE 1987 SUMMER VOL 32:4 p 281-302.

(10313)
Brick I E, Fung W, Subrahmanyam M
Leasing and financial intermediation: Comparative tax advantages
FIN MGMT 1987 SPRING VOL 16 p 55.

(10314)
Weingartner H M
Leasing, asset lives and uncertainty: Guides to decision making
FIN MGMT 1987 SUMMER VOL 16 p 5-12.

(10315)
Bayless M E, Diltz J D
An empirical study of the debt displacement effects of leasing
FIN MGMT 1986 WINTER VOL 15 p 53-60.

(10316)
Engelbrecht-Wiggins R, Dougherty E L, Lohrenz J
A model for the distribution of the number of bids on federal offshore oil leases
MSci 1986 SEP VOL 32:9 p 1087-1094.

(10317)
Gilley O W, Karels G V, Leone R P
Uncertainty experience and the "Winner's Curse" in OCS lease bidding
MSci 1986 JUN VOL 32:6 p 673-682.

(10318)
Bank of England
Developments in leasing
BEQB 1985 VOL 25 p 582-585.

(10319)
Clark T M ed.
Leasing finance
Euromoney Publications, 1985.

(10320)
Smith C W Jr, Wakeman L M
Determinants of corporate leasing policy
JF 1985 JUL VOL 40:3 p 895-910.

(10321)
Ang J S, Peterson P P
The leasing puzzle
JF 1984 SEP VOL 39:4 p 1055-1065.

(10322)
Hochman S, Rabinovitch R
Financial leasing under inflation
FIN MGMT 1984 SPRING VOL 13 p 17-26.

(10323)
Moore W T, Chen S N
The decision to lease or purchase under
uncertainty : a Bayesian approach
EE 1984 SPRING VOL 29:3 p 195-206.

(10324)
Young C M
The competitiveness of lease markets: an
empirical investigation of the UK local authority
lease market
JBFA 1984 VOL 11:2 p 189.

(10325)
Marks B R
Calculating the rate of return on a leveraged lease
- a constant leverage approach
JBR 1983 WINTER VOL 13:4.

(10326)
O'Brien T J, Nunnally B H Jr
A 1982 survey of corporate leasing analysis
FIN MGMT 1983 SUMMER VOL 12 p 30-36.

(10327)
Rieder M L, Wagner R R, Remer D S
Case study : an economic cost model for using an
airplane via lease-back ownership or rental
arrangements
EE 1983 WINTER VOL 28:2 p 101-130.

(10328)
Warren A C Jr, Auerbach A J
Tax policy and equipment leasing after TEFRA
HLR 1983 VOL 96:7 p 1579-1598.

(10329)
Cheung J K
The association between lease disclosure and the
lessee's systematic risk
JBFA 1982 AUTUMN VOL 9:3 p 297.

(10330)
Harvard Law Review
"Safe harbor" as tax reform: taxpayer election of
lease treatment
HLR 1982 VOL 95:7 p 1648-1668.

(10331)
Hughes J S, Vander Weide J H
Incentive considerations in the reporting of
leveraged leases
JBR 1982 SPRING VOL 13:1.

(10332)
Hull J C
The bargaining positions of the parties to a lease
agreement
FIN MGMT 1982 AUTUMN VOL 11 p 71-79.

(10333)
Lee T K
Resource information policy and federal resource
leasing
BellJ 1982 AUTUMN VOL 13:2 p 561-568.

(10334)
Lee W Y, Martin J D, Senchack A J
The case for using options to evaluate salvage
values in financial leases
FIN MGMT 1982 AUTUMN VOL 11 p 33-41.

(10335)
Smith B D
Planning models in the leasing industry
Omega 1982 VOL 10:4 p 345-351.

(10336)
Smith B D
Accelerated debt repayment in leveraged leases
FIN MGMT 1982 SUMMER VOL 11 p 73- 80.

(10337)
Willis M A
Leasing - a financial option for states and
localities?
F R Bk New York Q Rev 1981-82 WINTER
VOL 6:4.

(10338)
Capettini R, Toole H
Designing leveraged leases: A mixed integer linear
programming approach
FIN MGMT 1981 AUTUMN VOL 10 p 15-23.

(10339)
Crawford P J, Harper C P, McConnell J J
Further evidence on the terms of financial leases
FIN MGMT 1981 AUTUMN VOL 10 p 7-14.

(10340)
Laros M A
Leverage leasing: optimizing the lessee's
decisionmaking process
FE 1981 DEC VOL 49:12 p 18-25.

(10341)
Levy H, Landskroner Y
Lease financing : cost versus liquidity
EE 1981 FALL VOL 27:1 p 59-69.

(10342)
Bank of England
Equipment leasing
BEQB 1980 VOL 20 p 304-310.

(10343)
Bowman R G
The debt equivalence of leases: an empirical
investigation
AR 1980 APR VOL 55:2 p 237-253..

(10344)**Davey P J**
Leasing: experiences and expectations
New York: Conference Board, 1980.

(10345)
Flath D
The economics of short-term leasing
Economic Inquiry 1980 APR VOL 18 p 247-249.

(10346)
Park C S
Case study: Buy vs lease decision of automobiles
EE 1980 FALL VOL 26:1 p 53-74.

(10347)
Allen C L, Martin J D, Anderson P F
Debt-capacity and the lease-purchase problem: a
sensitivity analysis
EE 1979 WINTER VOL 24:2 p 87-108.

(10348)
Franks J R, Hodges S D
The role of leasing in capital investment
NWBQR 1979 AUG p 20-31.

(10349)
Roenfeldt R L, Henry J B
Lease/cost measurement of hospital equipment
under cost-based reimbursment
FIN MGMT 1979 SUMMER VOL 8 p 24.

(10350)
Ashton D J
The reasons for leasing - a mathematical
programming framework
JBFA 1978 SUMMER VOL 5:2 p 233-252.

(10351)
Clark T M
Leasing
McGraw, 1978.

(10352)
Kim E H, Lewellen W G, McConnell J J
Sale-and-leaseback agreements and enterprise
valuation
JFQA 1978 DEC VOL 13 p 871.

(10353)
Leland H E
Optimal risk sharing and the leasing of natural
resources, with application to oil and gas leasing
on the OCS
QJE 1978 VOL 78 p 413.

(10354)
Ro B T
The disclosure of capitalized lease information
and stock prices
JAR 1978 AUTUMN VOL 16:2 p 315-340.

(10355)
Anderson P G, Martin J D
Lease vs. purchase decisions: A survey of current
practice
FIN MGMT 1977 SPRING VOL 6 p 41.

(10356)
Long M S
Leasing and the cost of capital
JFQA 1977 NOV VOL 12 p 579.

(10357)
Sorensen I W, Johnson R E
Equipment financial leasing practices and costs:
An empirical study
FIN MGMT 1977 SPRING VOL 6 p 33.

(10358)
Fawthrop R A, Terry B
The evaluation of an integrated investment and lease-financing decision
JBFA 1976 AUTUMN VOL 3:3 p 79-112.

(10359)
Lewellen W G, Long M S, McConnell J J
Asset leasing in competitive capital markets
JF 1976 VOL 31 p 787.

(10360)
Miller M H, Upton C W
Leasing, buying and the cost of capital services
JF 1976 VOL 31 p 761.

(10361)
Sykes A
The lease-buy decision: a survey of current practice in 202 companies
British Institute of Management, 1976.

(10362)
Fawthrop R A, Terry B
Debt management and the use of leasing finance in U K corporate financing strategies
JBFA 1975 AUTUMN VOL 2:3 p 295-314.

(10363)
Horton W L, Gross H S
Opportunities for commercial banks in the business lease/instalment loan market
JBR 1974 SUMMER VOL 5:2 p 125-128.

(10364)
Bower R S
Issues in lease financing
FIN MGMT 1973 WINTER VOL 2 p 25.

(10365)
Roenfeldt R L, Osteryoung J S
Analysis of financial leases
FIN MGMT 1973 SPRING VOL 2 p 74.

(10366)
Vanderwicken P
Powerful logic of the leasing boom
F 1973 NOV VOL 87 p 132-161.

(10367)
Mitchell G B
After-tax cost of leasing
AR 1970 APR VOL 45 p 308-314.

(10368)
Hamel H G
Leasing in industry
Natl Ind Conf Bd, 1968.

(10369)
Pettway R H
Interest rates on direct leases and secured term loans
NBR 1966 JUN VOL 3 p 533-537.

28.11   Lease valuation

(10370)
Bierman H Jr
Buy versus lease with an alternative minimum tax
FIN MGMT 1988 WINTER VOL 17 p 87-91.

(10371)
Franks J R, Hodges S D
Lease valuation when taxable earnings are a scarce resource
JF 1987 SEP VOL 42:4 p 987-1005.

(10372)
Schall L D
Analytic issues in lease vs. purchase decisions
FIN MGMT 1987 SUMMER VOL 16:2 p 17-20.

(10373)
Schallheim J S, Johnson R E, Lease R C
The determinants of yields on financial leasing contracts
JFE 1987 VOL 19 p 45-67.

(10374)
Heaton H
Corporate taxation and leasing
JFQA 1986 SEP VOL 21:3 p 351-359.

(10375)
Hodges S D
The valuation of variable rate leases
FIN MGMT 1985 SPRING VOL 14 p 68-74.

(10376)
Schall L D
The evaluation of lease financing opportunities
MCFJ 1985 SPRING VOL 3 p 48-65.

(10377)
Wolfson M A
Tax incentive and risk-sharing issues in the allocation of property rights : the generalized lease-or-buy problem
JB 1985 APR VOL 58:2 p 159-171.

(10378)
Steele A
Difference equation solutions to the valuation of lease contracts
JFQA 1984 SEP VOL 19:3 p 311-328.

(10379)
Ezzell J R, Miles J A
Analyzing leases with the after-tax cost of debt
JBusR 1983 VOL 11 p 489-500.

(10380)
Fabozzi F J, Yaari U
Valuation of safe harbor tax benefit transfer leases
JF 1983 MAY VOL 38:2 p 595-606.

(10381)
McConnell J J, Schallheim J S
Valuation of asset leasing contracts
JFE 1983 VOL 12 p 237-261.

(10382)
Copeland T E, Weston J F
A note on the evaluation of cancellable operating leases
FIN MGMT 1982 SUMMER VOL 11 p 60-67.

(10383)
Flavell R B, Salkin G R
A model of a lessor
Omega 1982 VOL 10:4 p 413-431.

(10384)
Grimlund R A, Capettini R
A note on the evaluation of leveraged leases and other investments
FIN MGMT 1982 SUMMER VOL 11 p 68-72.

(10385)
Long M S
Using a before or after tax discount rate in the lease-buy decision
EE 1981 SUMMER VOL 26:4 p 263-274.

(10386)
Athanasopoulos P J, Bacon P W
The evaluation of leveraged leases
FIN MGMT 1980 SPRING VOL 9 p 76.

(10387)
Brealey R A, Young C M
Debt taxes and leasing: a note
JF 1980 DEC VOL 35:5 p 1245-1250.

(10388)
Hull J C, Hubbard G L
Lease evaluation in the U K : Current theory and practice
JBFA 1980 WINTER VOL 7:4 p 619-638.

(10389)
Idol C R
A note on specifying debt displacement and tax shield borrowing opportunities in financial lease valuation models
FIN MGMT 1980 SUMMER VOL 9 p 24.

(10390)
Levy H, Sarnat M
Leasing, borrowing and financial risk
FIN MGMT 1979 WINTER VOL 8 p 47.

(10391)
Franks J R, Hodges S D
Valuation of financial lease contracts: A note
JF 1978 VOL 33 p 657.

(10392)
Gaumnitz J E, Ford A
The lease or sell decision
FIN MGMT 1978 WINTER VOL 7 p 69.

(10393)
Perg W F
Leveraged leasing: The problem of changing leverage
FIN MGMT 1978 AUTUMN VOL 7 p 47.

(10394)
Dyl E A, Martin S A Jr
Setting terms for leveraged leases
FIN MGMT 1977 WINTER VOL 6 p 20.

(10395)
Myers S C, Dill D A, Bautista A J
Valuation of financial lease contracts
JF 1976 VOL 31 p 799.

(10396)
Ofer A R
The evaluation of the lease versus purchase
alternatives
FIN MGMT 1976 SUMMER VOL 5 p 67..

(10397)**Cooper K, Strawser R H**
Evaluation of capital investment projects involving
asset leases
FIN MGMT 1975 SPRING VOL 4 p 44.

(10398)
Honig L E, Coley S C
An after-tax equivalent payment approach to
conventional lease analysis
FIN MGMT 1975 WINTER VOL 4 p 28.

(10399)
Moyer R C
Lease evaluation and the investment tax credit: A
framework for analysis
FIN MGMT 1975 SUMMER VOL 4 p 39.

(10400)
Chasteen L G
Implicit factors in the evaluation of lease vs buy
alternatives: a reply
AR 1974 OCT VOL 49:4 p 809-811.

(10401)
Gordon M J
A general solution to the buy or lease decision:
A pedagogical note
JF 1974 VOL 29 p 245.

(10402)
Keller T F, Person R J
Optimal financial structure, cost of capital and
the lease-or-buy decision
JBFA 1974 AUTUMN VOL 1:3 p 405-414.

(10403)
Schall L D
The lease-or-buy and asset acquisition decisions
JF 1974 VOL 29 p 1203.

(10404)
Chasteen L G
Implicit factors in the evaluation of lease vs buy
alternatives
AR 1973 OCT VOL 48:4 p 764-767.

(10405)
Nantell T J
Equivalence of lease vs. buy analyses
FIN MGMT 1973 AUTUMN VOL 2 p 61.

(10406)
Sartoris W L, Paul R S
Lease evaluation-another capital budgeting
decision
FIN MGMT 1973 SUMMER VOL 2 p 46.

(10407)
Smith P R
A straightforward approach to leveraged leasing
JCBL 1973 JUL p 19-39.

(10408)
Wiar R C
Economic implications of multiple rates of return
in The Leveraged Lease Context
JF 1973 VOL 28 p 1275.

(10409)
Johnson R W, Lewellen W G
Analysis of the lease-or-buy decision
JF 1972 SEP VOL 27 p 815-824.

(10410)
Bower R S, Herringer F C, Williamson J P
Lease evaluation
AR 1966 APR VOL 41 p 257-265.

(10411)
Vancil R F
Lease or borrow--new method of analysis
HBR 1961 SEP VOL 39 p 122-136.

28.2 Project finance

(10412)
Nevitt P K
Project financing. 5th ed
Euromoney Publications, 1989.

(10413)
Kensinger J W, Martin J D
Project finance: Raising money the old-fashioned
way
JACF 1988 FALL VOL 1 p 69-81.

(10414)
Shah S, Thakor A V
Optimal capital structure and project financing
JET 1987 AUG VOL 42:2 p 209-243.

(10415)
Wynant L
Essential elements of project financing
HBR 1980 MAY-JUN VOL 58:3 p 165-173.

(10416)
Phillips P D, Groth J C, Richards R M
Financing the Alaskan project: The experience of
Sohio
FIN MGMT 1979 AUTUMN VOL 8 p 7.

(10417)
Brozozowski L J, Turner L D, Olsen E E
Project financing evaluation: a simulation
approach
JBR 1977 SPRING VOL 8:1.

29 Financial planning

(10418)
Asch D, Kaye G R
Financial planning: modelling methods and techniques
Kogan Page, 1989.

(10419)
Martin J D, Morgan G E
Financial planning where the firm's demand for funds is nonstationary and stochastic
MSci 1988 VOL 34 p 1054.

(10420)
Bryant J W ed.
Financial modelling in corporate management. 2nd ed
Wiley, 1987.

(10421)
Grubmann N
Besmod : A strategic balance sheet simulation model
EJOR 1987 JUN VOL 30:1 p 30-34.

(10422)
Kester G W
A note on solving the balancing problem
FIN MGMT 1987 SPRING VOL 16 p 52-54.

(10423)
Kornbluth J S H, Salkin G R
The management of corporate financial assets: applications of mathematical programming models
Academic Pr, 1987.

(10424)
Sandberg C M, Lewellen W G, Stanley K L
Financial strategy: planning and managing the corporate leverage position
SMJ 1987 JAN-FEB VOL 8:1 p 15-24.

(10425)
Donaldson G
Strategy for financial mobility. Rev ed
Harvard Bus Pr, 1986.

(10426)
Donaldson G
Financial goals and strategic consequences
HBR 1985 MAY-JUN VOL 63:3 p 57-66.

(10427)
Lee C F ed.
Advances in financial planning
JAI Pr, 1984.

(10428)
Brick I E, Mellon W G, Surkis J
Optimal capital structure: A multi-period programming model for use in financial planning
JBankF 1983 VOL 7 p 45.

(10429)
Donaldson G, Lorsch J W
Decision making at the top
Basic, 1983.

(10430)
Ellsworth R R
Subordinate financial policy to corporate strategy
HBR 1983 NOV-DEC VOL 61:6 p 170-182.

(10431)
Sherwood D
Financial modelling: a practical guide
Gee, 1983.

(10432)
Wright B J
Total financial planning
AMA, 1983.

(10433)
Grawoig D E, Hubbard C L
Strategic financial planning with simulation
Petrocelli Books, 1982.

(10434)
Raine P S, Flavell R B, Salkin G R
A likelihood control system for use with formal planning models
JBFA 1981 SUMMER VOL 8:2 p 249-266

(10435)
Kvanli A H
Financial planning using goal programming
Omega 1980 VOL 8:2 p 207-218.

(10436)
LaForge R L, Wood D R Jr
Use of operations research in the planning activities of large US banks
JBR 1980 AUTUMN VOL 11:3.

(10437)
Timmons J A
A business plan is more than a financing device
HBR 1980 MAR-APR VOL 58:2 p 28-34.

(10438)
Crum R L, Klingman D D, Tavis L A
Implementation of large-scale financial planning
models: Solution efficient transformations
JFQA 1979 MAR VOL 14 p 137.

(10439)
Fruhan W E
Financial strategy: Studies in the creation,
transfer, and destruction of shareholder value
Irwin, 1979.

(10440)
Greenlaw P S et al.
Finanism: a financial management simulation. 2nd
ed
West Pub, 1979.

(10441)
Carleton W T, Machado E L
Financial planning in a regulated enviroment
JFQA 1978 NOV VOL 13 p 759.

(10442)
Grinyer P H, Wooller J
Corporate models today - a new tool for financial
management. 2nd ed
London: Institute of Chartered Accountants, 1978.

(10443)
Kottas J F, Lau A H-L, Lau H-S
A general approach to stochastic management
planning models: an overview
AR 1978 APR VOL 53:2 p 389-401.

(10444)
Sealey C W Jr
Financial planning with multiple objectives
FIN MGMT 1978 WINTER VOL 7 p 17.

(10445)
Merville L J, Tavis L A
Financial planning in a decentralized firm under
conditions of competitive capital markets
FIN MGMT 1977 AUTUMN VOL 6 p 17.

(10446)
Meyer H I
Corporate financial planning models
Wiley, 1977.

(10447)
Naylor T H, Schauland H
A survey of users of corporate planning models
MSci 1976 AUG VOL 22:12 p 927.

(10448)
Smith G, Brainard W
The value of a priori information in estimating a
financial model
JF 1976 VOL 31 p 1299.

(10449)
Taylor B W III, Moore L J
A simulation approach to planning bank projects
JBR 1976 AUTUMN VOL 7:3..

(10450)**Arzac E R**
Structural planning under controllable business
risk
JF 1975 VOL 30 p 1229.

(10451)
Carlson P G
Planning, growth, and the efficient use of capital
FIN MGMT 1975 SUMMER VOL 4 p 27

(10452)
Lyneis J M
Designing financial policies to deal with limited
financial resources
FIN MGMT 1975 SPRING VOL 4 p 13.

(10453)
Powell J R P, Vergin R C
A heuristic model for planning corporate
financing
FIN MGMT 1975 SUMMER VOL 4 p 13.

(10454)
Traenkle J W, Cox E B, Bullard J A
The use of financial models in business
Fin Exec, 1975.

(10455)
Frank W G
Solving financial planning problems using input output models
AR 1974 APR VOL 49:2 p 371-376.

(10456)
Herendeen J B
Alternative models of the corporate enterprise: growth maximization and value maximization
QREB 1974 VOL 14:4 p 59.

(10457)
Merville L J, Tavis L A
Long range financial planning
FIN MGMT 1974 SUMMER VOL 3 p 56.

(10458)
Tavis L A, Merville L J
A total real asset planning system
JFQA 1974 JAN VOL 9 p 107.

(10459)
Branch B
Corporate objectives and market performance
FIN MGMT 1973 SUMMER VOL 2 p 24.

(10460)
Carleton W T, Dick C L Jr, Downes D H
Financial policy models: Theory and practice
JFQA 1973 DEC VOL 8:5 p 691-710.

(10461)
Nicholson E A, Litschert R L
Long range planning in banking: ten cases in the U S and Britain
JBR 1973 SPRING VOL 4:1.

(10462)
Robinson R S
BANKMOD: an interactive simulation aid for bank financial planning
JBR 1973 AUTUMN VOL 4:3 p 212-224.

(10463)
Snider W D
Building an on-line financial planning model
JBR 1973 AUTUMN VOL 4:3 p 232-238.

(10464)
Thomson M R
Forecasting for financial planning
JBR 1973 AUTUMN VOL 4:3 p 225-231.

(10465)
Chambers D J
Dividend plans and balance sheet management
JBF 1972 AUTUMN VOL 4 p 17-25.

(10466)
Elliott J W
Forecasting and analysis of corporate financial performance with an econometric model of the firm
JFQA 1972 MAR VOL 7 p 1499-1526.

(10467)
Krouse C G
A model for aggregate financial planning
MSci 1972 VOL 18 p B555-B566.

(10468)
Logue D E, Merville L J
Financial policy and market expectations
FIN MGMT 1972 SUMMER VOL 1 p 37.

(10469)
Pogue G A, Bussard R N
A linear programming model for short-term financial planning under uncertainty
SMR 1972 SPRING VOL 13 p 69-99.

(10470)
Jacobs D P, Lerner E M, Moag J S
Guidelines for designing bank planning models and information systems
JBR 1971 SPRING VOL 2:1.

(10471)
Warren J M, Shelton J P
A simultaneous equation approach to financial planning
JF 1971 DEC VOL 26 p 1123-1142.

(10472)
Carleton W T
An analytical model for long-range financial planning
JF 1970 MAY VOL 25 p 291-315.

(10473)
Schrieber A N ed.
Corporate simulation models
U of Washington Pr, 1970.

(10474)
Gershefski G W
Building a corporate financial model
HBR 1969 JUL-AUG VOL 47 p 61-72.

(10475)
Childs J F
Profit goals and capital management
P-H, 1968.

(10476)
Carleton W T, Lerner E M
Measuring corporate profit opportunities
JFQA 1967 SEP VOL 2 p 225-240.

(10477)
Chambers D J
Programming the allocation of funds subject to
restrictions on reported results
Operational Research Quarterly 1967 DEC VOL
18 p 407-432.

(10478)
Moag J S, Carleton W T, Lerner E M
Defining the finance function: a systems approach
JF 1967 DEC VOL 22 p 543-555.

(10479)
Mattessich R
Simulation of a firm through a budget computer
program
Irwin, 1964.

(10480)
Ijiri Y, Levy F K, Lyon R C
A linear programming model for budgeting and
financial planning
JAR 1963 AUTUMN VOL 1 p 198-212.

(10481)
Mattessich R
Budgeting models and system simulation
AR 1961 JUL VOL 36 p 384-397.

30 Working capital

(10482)
Hampton J J, Wagner C L
Working capital management
Wiley, 1989.

(10483)
Gentry J A
State of the art of short-run financial
management
FIN MGMT 1988 SUMMER VOL 17 p 41-57.

(10484)
Hill N C, Sartoris W L
Short-term financial management
Macmillan, 1988

(10485)
Beranek W
An historical perspective of research and practice
in working capital management
(in Kim Y H ed., Advances in working capital
management. Addison-Wes, 1987.)

(10486)
Bank of England
Companies' short-term financial decisions
BEQB 1986 VOL 26 p 78.

(10487)
Gilmer R H Jr
The optimal level of liquid assests: An empirical
test
FIN MGMT 1985 WINTER VOL 14 p 39-43.

(10488)
Kroll Y
On the differences between accrual accounting
figures and cash flows: The case of working
capital
FIN MGMT 1985 SPRING VOL 14 p 75.

(10489)
Vander Weide J H, Maier S F
Managing corporate liquidity: An introduction to
working capital management
Wiley, 1985.

(10490)
Gentry J A, Newbold P, Whitford D T
Bankruptcy, working capital and funds flow
components
Managerial Finance 1984 VOL 10:3-4 p 26-39.

(10491)
Kallberg J G, Parkinson K
Current asset management
Wiley-Interscience, 1984.

(10492)
Sartoris W L, Hill N C
A generalized cash flow approach to short-term
financial decisions
JF 1983 MAY VOL 38:2 p 349-360

(10493)
Smith K V ed.
Readings on the management of working capital
West Pub, 1980.

(10494)
Goldman R I
Look to receivables and other assets to obtain
working capital
HBR 1979 NOV-DEC VOL 57:6 p 206-216.

(10495)
Lambrix R J, Singhvi S S
Managing the working capital cycle
FE 1979 JUN VOL 47 p 32-41.

(10496)
Maier S F, Vander Weide J H
A practical approach to short-run financial
planning
FIN MGMT 1978 WINTER VOL 7 p 10.

(10497)
Yardini E E
A portfolio-balance model of corporate working
capital
JF 1978 VOL 33 p 535.

(10498)
Simonson D G
Funds management by state treasurers: Direct vs.
socio-economic returns
FIN MGMT 1977 WINTER VVOL 6 p 51.

(10499)
Folks W R Jr
The analysis of short-term cross-border financing
decisions
FIN MGMT 1976 AUTUMN VOL 5 p 19.

(10500)
Gitman L J
Estimating corporate liquidity requirements: A
simplified approach
FR 1974 p 79-88.

(10501)
Mehta D R
Working capital management
P-H, 1974.

(10502)
Sartoris W L, Spruill M L
Goal   programming   and   working   capital
management
FIN MGMT 1974 SPRING VOL 3 p 67..

(10503)**Aigner D J, Sprenkle C M**
On optimal financing of cyclical cash needs
JF 1973 VOL 28 p 1249.

(10504)
Haley C W, Higgins R C
Inventory policy and trade credit financing
MSci 1973 DEC VOL 20:4 p 464-471.

(10505)
Merville L J, Tavis L A
Optimal   working   capital   policies: A
chance-constrained programming approach
JFQA 1973 JAN VOL 8:1 p 47-60.

(10506)
Shapiro A C
Optimal inventory and credit-granting strategies
under inflation and devaluation
JFQA 1973 JAN VOL 8:1 p 37-46.

(10507)
Stancil J M
The management of working capital
Intext, 1971.

(10508)
Beranek W
Working capital management
Wadsworth Pub, 1966.

(10509)
Heston A W
An empirical study of cash, securities, and other
current accounts of large corporations
YEE 1962 SPRING VOL 2 p 116-168.

30.1   Cash management

(10510)
Soenen A, Aggarwal R
Cash and foreign exchange management: theory
and corporate practice in three countries
JBFA 1989 WINTER VOL 16:5 p 599.

(10511)
Back P L
Corporate cash management
Woodhead-Faulkner, 1988.

(10512)
Davis H A
Changing priorities in corporate cash management
FE 1987 VOL 3:1 p 18-21.

(10513)
Gallinger G W, Healey P B
Liquidity analysis and management
Addison-Wes, 1987.

(10514)
Vickers D
Money capital in the theory of the firm: a
preliminary analysis
Cambridge U Pr, 1987.

(10515)
Brown K C, Lummer S L
A re-examination of the covered call option
strategy for corporate cash management
FIN MGMT 1986 SUMMER VOL 15 p 13-17.

(10516)
Lanser H P, Halloran J A
Evaluating cash flow systems under growth
FR 1986 MAY VOL 21:2.

(10517)
Soenen L A
International cash management: a study of the practices of U.K. based companies
JBusR 1986 AUG VOL 14:4 p 345-354.

(10518)
Srinivasan V, Kim Y H
Deterministic cash flow management : state of the art and research directions
Omega 1986 VOL 14:2 p 145-166.

(10519)
Ferguson D M, Hill N C
Cash flow timeline management: The next frontier of cash management
JCM 1985 MAY-JUN VOL 5 p 12-22.

(10520)
Hill N C, Emery G W, Sartoris W L
Essentials of cash management: A study guide
National Corporate Cash Management Association, 1985.

(10521)
Kamath R R, Khaksari S, Meier H H
Management of excess cash: Practices and developments
FIN MGMT 1985 AUTUMN VOL 14 p 70-77.

(10522)
Kawaller I J
How and why to hedge a short-term portfolio
JCM 1985 JAN-FEB VOL 5 p 26-30.

(10523)
Brown K C, Lummer S L
The cash management implications of a hedged dividend capture strategy
FIN MGMT 1984 WINTER VOL 13 p 7-17.

(10524)
Dotsey M
An investigation of cash management practices and their effects on the demand for money
F R Bk Richmond Ec Rev 1984 VOL 70:5.

(10525)
Beehler P J
Contemporary cash management
Irwin, 1983.

(10526)
Carter J N
Bank evaluation
JCM 1983 OCT-NOV VOL 3 p 10-20.

(10527)
Cohen A M
Treasury terminal systems and cash management information support
JCM 1983 AUG-SEP VOL 3 p 9-18.

(10528)
Morris J R
The role of cash balances in firm valuation
JFQA 1983 DEC VOL 18:4 p 533-545.

(10529)
Stone B K
The design of a company's banking system
JF 1983 MAY VOL 38:2 p 373-385.

(10530)
Bank of England
Recent changes in the use of cash
BEQB 1982 VOL 22 p 519-529.

(10531)
Beehler P J
Cash management: principles and practices for the '80s
New York: AMACOM, 1980.

(10532)
Richards V D, Laughlin E J
A cash conversion cycle approach to liquidity analysis
FIN MGMT 1980 SPRING VOL 9 p 32.

(10533)
Gitman L J, Moses E A, White I T
An assessment of corporate cash management practices
FIN MGMT 1979 SPRING VOL 8 p 32.

(10534)
Dyment J J
International cash management
HBR 1978 MAR-APR VOL 56:3 p 143-150.

(10535)
Hunt A L
Corporate cash management; including electronic funds transfer
New York: AMACOM, 1978.

(10536)
Jaffe R S
A singular cash management problem
FE 1978 MAY VOL 46:5 p 44-46

(10537)
Mao J C T, Sarndal C E
Cash management: theory and practice
JBFA 1978 AUTUMN VOL 5:3 p 329-338.

(10538)
Campbell T S, Brendsel L
The impact of compensating balance requirements on the cash balances of manufacturing corporations: An empirical study
JF 1977 VOL 32 p 31.

(10539)
Pulliam K P
A liquidity portfolio management strategy approach
JBR 1977 SPRING VOL 8:1.

(10540)
Graves P E
Wealth and cash asset proportions
JMCB 1976 NOV VOL 8:4 p 487-496.

(10541)
Prindl A
Guidelines for MNC money managers
HBR 1976 JAN-FEB VOL 54:1 p 73-80.

(10542)
Shapiro A C
International cash management - the determination of multicurrency cash balances
JFQA 1976 DEC VOL 11 p 893.

(10543)
Homonoff R, Mullins D W
Cash management
Lexington Bks, 1975.

(10544)
Koot R S
A factor analytic approach to an empirical definition of money
JF 1975 VOL 30 p 1081.

(10545)
Ben Zion U
The cost of capital and the demand for money by firms
JMCB 1974 MAY VOL 6:2 p 263-269.

(10546)
Bain A D, Harris A G, Makower M S
The management of liquid assets in general insurance companies
JBF 1973 SPRING VOL 5:1 p 52-65.

(10547)
Marcis R G, Smith V K
The demand for liquid asset balances by U S manufacturing corporations: 1959-1970.
JFQA 1973 MAR VOL 8:2 p 207-218.

(10548)
Desalvo A
Cash management converts dollars into working assets
HBR 1972 MAY-JUN VOL 50:3 p 92-100.

(10549)
Crouch R L
Tobin vs Keynes on liquidity preference
REStat 1971 NOV VOL 53 p 368-371.

(10550)
Komar R I
Developing a liquidity management model
JBR 1971 SPRING VOL 2:1.

(10551)
Orr D
Cash management and the demand for money
Praeger, 1971.

(10552)
Cohen B C
Economies of scale and cash balances
JBR 1970 SUMMER VOL 1:2 p 45-48.

(10553)
Frost P A
Banking services, minimum cash balances and the firm's demand for money
JF 1970 DEC VOL 25 p 1029-1039.

(10554)
Hill R W
Cash management techniques
AMA, 1970.

(10555)
Orgler Y E
Cash management: Methods and models
Wadsworth Pub, 1970..

(10556)**King A M**
Increasing the productivity of the company cash
P-H, 1969.

(10557)
Mock E J
The investment of corporate cash
Management Services 1967 SEP-OCT VOL 4.

(10558)
Patinkin D
An indirect-utility approach to the theory of money, assets and savings
(in Hahn F H and Brechling F P R eds., The theory of interest rates. Macmillan Int, 1966.)

(10559)
Whalen E L
Extension of the Baumol-Tobin approach to the transactions demand for cash
JF 1965 MAR VOL 23 p 113-134.

(10560)
Patinkin D
Money, interest and prices. 2nd ed
Har-Row, 1964.

(10561)
Duesenberry J S
The portfolio approach to the demand for money and other assets
REStat 1963 FEB VOL 45 Suppl p 9-24.

(10562)
McCall J J
Difference between the personal demand for money and the business demand for money
JPE 1960 AUG VOL 68 p 358-368.

30.11 Optimal cash balances and money demand

(10563)
Smith G W
Transactions demand for money with a stochastic, time-varying interest rate
REStud 1989 VOL 56 p 623.

(10564)
Beckman S R, Foreman J N
An experimental test of the Baumol-Tobin transactions demand for money
JMCB 1988 AUG VOL 20:3 p 291-305.

(10565)
Outreville J F
The long-run and short-run demand for cash balances: the case of insurance companies
QREB 1988 VOL 28:4 p 78.

(10566)
Gijlswijk V van
Evaluating the interest aspect of cash management
EJOR 1987 JUN VOL 30:1 p 85-88.

(10567)
Warschauer T, Cherin A
Optimal liquidity in personal financial planning
FR 1987 NOV VOL 22:4.

(10568)
Feenstra R C
Functional equivalence between liquidity costs and the utility of money
JME 1986 VOL 17 p 271.

(10569)
Smith G W
A dynamic Baumol-Tobin model of money demand
REStud 1986 VOL 53 p 465.

(10570)
Vickson R G
Simple optimal policy for cash management : the
average balance requirement case
JFQA 1985 SEP VOL 20:3 p 353-369.

(10571)
Wirth A
A note: a cash management model allowing for
overdrafts
JBFA 1984 WINTER VOL 11:4 p 557-561.

(10572)
Batlin C A, Hinko S
A game theoretic approach to cash management
JB 1982 JUL VOL 55:3 p 367-381.

(10573)
Levy H, Sarnat M
Risk inflation and liquidity performance : a
simulation of the portfolio demand for money
QREB 1982 SPRING VOL 22:1 p 7-22

(10574)
Punter A
Optimal cash management under conditions of
uncertainty
JBFA 1982 AUTUMN VOL 9:3 p 329-340

(10575)
Frenkel J A, Jovanovic B
On transactions and precautionary demand for
money
QJE 1981 VOL 95 p 25.

(10576)
Chen A H
Effects of purchasing power risk on portfolio
demand for money
JFQA 1979 JUN VOL 14 p 243.

(10577)
Frenkel J A
Further evidence on expectations and the demand
for money during the German hyperinflation
JME 1979 VOL 5 p 81.

(10578)
Salemi M K
Adaptive expectations, rational expectations and
money demand in hyperinflation Germany
JME 1979 VOL 5 p 593.

(10579)
Clower R W, Howitt P W
The transactions theory of the demand for money:
A reconsideration
JPE 1978 VOL 86 p 449.

(10580)
Moosa S A
Portfolio balance and the demand for money: a
test of some alternative hypotheses
QREB 1978 VOL 18:3 p 41.

(10581)
Policano A J, Choi E K
The effects of relative price changes on the
household's demand for money
JME 1978 VOL 4 p 743.

(10582)
Ahsan S M
Relative risk-aversion and the demand for cash
balances
JF 1977 VOL 32 p 769.

(10583)
Moosa S A
Dynamic portfolio-balance behavior of time
deposits and "money"
JF 1977 VOL 32 p 709.

(10584)
Anderson R E
The individual's transactions demand for money:
a utility maximization approach
JME 1976 VOL 2 p 237.

(10585)
Barro R J
Integral contraints and aggregation in an
inventory model of money demand
JF 1976 VOL 31 p 77.

(10586)
Constantinides G M
Stochastic cash management with fixed and
proportional transaction costs
MSci 1976 AUG VOL 22:12 p 1320-1331.

(10587)
Cropper M L
A state-preference approach to the precautionary demand for money
AER 1976 VOL 66 p 388-394.

(10588)
Harris M
Optimal planning under transaction costs: the demand for money and other assets
JET 1976 APR VOL 12:2 p 298-314.

(10589)
Mullins D, Homonoff R
Applications of inventory cash management models
(in Myers S C ed., Modern developments in financial management. Praeger, 1976.)

(10590)
Budin M, Van Handel R J
A rule-of-thumb theory of cash holdings by firm
JFQA 1975 MAR VOL 10 p 85.

(10591)
Chen A H, Kim E H, Kon S J
Cash demand, liquidation costs and capital market equilibrium under uncertainty
JFE 1975 VOL 2 p 293.

(10592)
Hausman W H, Sanchez Bell A
The stochastic cash balance problem with average compensating balance requirements
MSci 1975 APR VOL 21:8 p 849-857.

(10593)
Hausman W H, Sanchez-Bell A
The stochastic cash balance problem with average compensating balance requirements
MSci 1975 AUG VOL 21:12 p 849.

(10594)
Wilbratte B J
Some essential differences in the demand for money by households and by firms
JF 1975 VOL 30 p 1091.

(10595)
Chen A H, Jen F C, Zionts S
The joint determination of portfolio and transaction demand for money
JF 1974 VOL 29 p 175.

(10596)
Daellenbach H G
Are cash management optimization models worthwhile
JFQA 1974 SEP VOL 9 p 607.

(10597)
Lewis K A
A note on the interest elasticity of the transactions demand for cash
JF 1974 VOL 29 p 1149.

(10598)
Orr D
A note on the uselessness of transaction demand models
JF 1974 VOL 29 p 1565.

(10599)
Srinivasan V
A transshipment model for cash management decisions
MSci 1974 VOL 20 p 1350-1363.

(10600)
Heyman D P
A model for cash balance management
MSci 1973 AUG VOL 19:12 p 1407.

(10601)
Karni E
The transactions demand for cash: incorporation of the value of time into the inventory approach
JPE 1973 SEP-OCT VOL 81:5 p 1216-1225.

(10602)
Lockyer K G
Cash as an item of stock
JBF 1973 SPRING VOL 5:1 p 44-51.

(10603)
Pesek B P
Equilibrium level of transaction services of money
JF 1973 VOL 28 p 647.

(10604)
Porteus E L
Equivalent formulations of the stochastic cash
balance problem
MSci 1973 JUL VOL 19:11 p 250.

(10605)
Chen A H, Jen F C, Zionts S
Portfolio models with stochastic cash demands
MSci 1972 NOV VOL 19:3 p 319-332.

(10606)
Porteus E L, Neave E H
The stochastic cash balance problem with charges
levied against the balance
MSci 1972 JUL VOL 18:11 p 600.

(10607)
Stone B K
The use of forecasts and smoothing in
control-limit models for cash management
FIN MGMT SPRING 1972 VOL 1 p 72.

(10608)
Eppen G D, Fama E F
Three asset cash balance and dynamic portfolio
problems
MSci 1971 JAN VOL 17 p 320-336..

(10609)**Falero F Jr, Campbell D L**
Additional evidence on the demand for money
QREB 1971 VOL 11:2 p 7.

(10610)
Saving T R
Transactions costs and the demand for money
AER 1971 JUN VOL 61 p 407-420.

(10611)
Neave E H
The stochastic cash balance problem with fixed
costs for increases and decreases
MSci 1970 MAR VOL 16 p 472-490.

(10612)
Sastry A S R
The effect of credit on transactions demand for
cash
JF 1970 SEP VOL 25 p 777-781.

(10613)
Eppen G D, Fama E F
Cash balance and simple dynamic portfolio
problems with proportional costs
IntER 1969 JUN VOL 10 p 119-133.

(10614)
Orgler Y E
An unequal-period model for cash management
decisions
MSci 1969 OCT VOL 16 p B77-B92.

(10615)
Sprenkle C M
The uselessness of transactions demand models
JF 1969 DEC VOL 24 p 835-847.

(10616)
Calman R F
Linear programming and cash management--cash
alpha
MIT Pr, 1968.

(10617)
Eppen G D, Fama E F
Solutions for cash balance and simple dynamic
portfolio problems
JB 1968 JAN VOL 41 p 94-112.

(10618)
Girgis N M
Optimal cash balance levels
MSci 1968 NOV VOL 15 p 130-140.

(10619)
Miller M H, Orr D
The demand for money by firms: extensions of
analytical results
JF 1968 DEC VOL 23 p 735-759.

(10620)
Archer S H
A model for the determination of firm cash
balances
JFQA 1966 MAR VOL 1 p 1-11.

(10621)
Baumol W J
The transactions demand for cash: an inventory
theoretic approach
QJE 1966 FEB VOL 80 p 48-59.

(10622)
Miller M H, Orr D
A model of the demand for money by firms
QJE 1966 AUG VOL 80 p 413-435.

(10623)
Orgler Y E
Joint demand and time deposits: an application of
inventory control
NBR 1966 SEP VOL 4 p 73-80.

(10624)
Tobin J
The interest elasticity of transactions demand for
cash
REStat 1956 AUG VOL 38 p 241-247.

30.12 Forecasting sources and uses of cash

(10625)
Stone B K, Miller T W
Daily cash forecasting with multiplicative models
of cash flow patterns
FIN MGMT 1987 WINTER VOL 16 p 45-54.

(10626)
Miller T W, Stone B K
Daily cash forecasting and seasonal resolution :
alternative models and techniques for using the
distribution approach.
JFQA 1985 SEP VOL 20:3 p 335-351.

(10627)
Chand S, Morton T E
A perfect planning horizon procedure for a
deterministic cash flow balance.
MSci 1982 JUN VOL 28:6 p 652-669.

(10628)
Cale B T, Branch B
Cash flow analysis: more important than ever
HBR 1981 JUL-AUG VOL 59:4 p 131-136.

(10629)
Emery G W
Some empirical evidence on the properties of
daily cash flow
FIN MGMT 1981 SPRING VOL 10 p 21-28.

(10630)
Khumawala S B, Polhemus N W, Liao W M
The predictability of quarterly cash flows
JBFA 1981 WINTER VOL 8:4 p 493-510.

(10631)
Maier S F, Robinson D W, Vander Weide J H
A short-term disbursement forecasting model
FIN MGMT 1981 SPRING VOL 10 p 9-20.

(10632)
Stone B K, Miller T
Daily cash flow forecasting: A structural
framework
JCM 1981 VOL 1 p 35-50.

(10633)
Scott D F Jr, Moore L J, Saint-Denis A
Implementation of a cash budget simulator at Air
Cananda
FIN MGMT 1979 SUMMER VOL 8 p 46.

(10634)
Stone B K, Wood R A
Daily cash forecasting: A simple method for
implementing the distribution approach
FIN MGMT 1977 AUTUMN VOL 6 p 40.

(10635)
Tennent M
Practical liquidity management: a means to
financial strength in companies
Gower, 1976.

(10636)
Stone B K
Cash planning and credit-line determination with
a financial statement simulator: A cash report on
short-term financial planning
JFQA 1973 DEC VOL 8:5 p 711-730.

30.13 Cash collection and disbursement

(10637)
Anvari M
Cash transfer scheduling for concentrating
noncentral receipts
MSci 1987 JAN VOL 33:1 p 25-38.

(10638)
Anvari M
Efficient scheduling of cross-border cash transfers
FIN MGMT 1986 SUMMER VOL 15 p 40-49.

(10639)
Liang M-Y
Bank float, mail float and the definition of money
JBankF 1986 VOL 10 p 533.

(10640)
Orgler Y E, Tauman Y
A game theoretic approach to collections and disbursements
MSci 1986 AUG VOL 32:8 p 1029-1039.

(10641)
Anvari M
Alternative cash concentration systems in Canada: An example of national banking
JCM 1983 JUN-JUL VOL 3 p 48-58.

(10642)
Ferguson D M
Optimize your firm's lockbox selection system
FE 1983 APR VOL 51:4 p 8-19.

(10643)
Maier S F, Vander Weide J H
What lockbox and disbursement models really do
JF 1983 MAY VOL 38:2 p 361-371.

(10644)
Ross I
What's new about this boom
F 1983 MAY 30 VOL 107:11 p 50-55.

(10645)
Ross I
The race is to the slow payer
F 1983 APR 18 VOL 107:8 p 111-116.

(10646)
Brandon M B
Contemporary disbursing practices and products: A survey
JCM 1982 MAR VOL 2 p 26-39.

(10647)
Ferguson D M, Maier S F
Disbursement system design for the 1980s
JCM 1982 NOV VOL 2 p 56-69.

(10648)
Fielitz B D, White D L
An evaluation and linking of alternative solution procedures for the lock box location problem
JBR 1982 SPRING VOL 13:1.

(10649)
Stone B K, Hill N C
Alternative cash transfer mechanisms and methods: Evaluation frameworks
JBR 1982 SPRING VOL 13 p 7-16.

(10650)
Batlin C A, Hinke S
Lockbox management and value maximization
FIN MGMT 1981 WINTER VOL 10 p 39-44.

(10651)
Haag L H
Using money funds for business disbursing accounts
JCM 1981 OCT VOL 1 p 51-54.

(10652)
Stone B K, Hill N C
The design of a cash concentration system.
JFQA 1981 SEP VOL 16:3 p 301-322

(10653)
Anvari M, Mohan N
A computerized cash concentration system
Omega 1980 VOL 8:4 p 459-464.

(10654)
Stone B K
Lock box selection and collection-system design: objective function validity
JBR 1980 WINTER VOL 10:4.

(10655)
Stone B K, Hill N C
Cash transfer scheduling for efficient cash concentration
FIN MGMT 1980 AUTUMN VOL 9 p 35.

(10656)
Nauss R M, Markland R E
Solving lock box location problems
FIN MGMT 1979 SPRING VOL 8 p 21.

(10657)
Geyer G A
Balance reporting: an important new cash management tool
FE 1978 NOV VOL 46:11 p 38-44.

(10658)
Cornuejols G, Fisher M L, Nemhauser G L
Location of bank accounts to optimize float: an analytic study of exact and approximate algorithms
MSci 1977 VOL 23 p 789-810.

(10659)
Hathaway D D
Managing balances in lock box accounts
JBR 1977 SPRING VOL 8:1.

(10660)
Gitman L J, Forrester D K, Forrester J R Jr
Maximizing cash disbursement float
FIN MGMT 1976 SUMMER VOL 5 p 15.

(10661)
Maier S F, Vander Weide J H
A unified location model for cash disbursements and lock-box collections
JBR 1976 SUMMER VOL 7:2..

(10662)**Maier S F, Vander Weide J H**
The lock-box location problem: a practical reformulation
JBR 1974 SUMMER VOL 5:2 p 92-95.

(10663)
Shanker R J, Zoltners A A
The corporate payment problem
JBR 1972 SPRING VOL 3:1 p 47-53.

(10664)
Kraus A, Janssen C, McAdams A
The lock-box location problem
JBR 1970 AUTUMN VOL 1:3 p 50-58.

30.2 Inventories

(10665)
Ashton R K
Stockholding costs and stockholding policies: a field test
JBFA 1989 AUTUMN VOL 16:4 p 575.

(10666)
Prodhan B K, Harris M C
Systematic risk and the discretionary disclosure of geographical segments: an empirical investigation of US multinationals
JBFA 1989 AUTUMN VOL 16:4 p 467.

(10667)
Knight R F, Affleck-Graves J F
Further evidence on the market reponse to LIFO adoptions
JBFA 1988 SUMMER VOL 15:2 p 169-184.

(10668)
Guth M A S
Functional form in finished goods inventory investment
JMCB 1987 AUG VOL 19:3 p 396-401.

(10669)
Bivin D G
Inventories and interest rates: A critique of the buffer stock model
AER 1986 VOL 76 p 168-176.

(10670)
Kim Y H, Philippatos G C, Chung K H
Evaluating investment in inventory policy : A net present value framework
EE 1986 WINTER VOL 31:2 p 119-136.

(10671)
McDaniel W R
The economic ordering quantity problem and wealth maximization
FR 1986 NOV VOL 21:4.

(10672)
West K D
A variance bounds test of the linear quadratic inventory model
JPE 1986 VOL 94 p 374.

(10673)
Abel A B
Inventories, stockouts and production smoothing
REStud 1985 VOL 52 p 283.

(10674)
Biddle G C, Martin R K
Tax-cutting inventory management
MCFJ 1985 SUMMER VOL 3 p 33-40.

(10675)
Brown R M
On carrying costs and the EOQ model: a pedagogical note
FR 1985 NOV VOL 20:4.

(10676)
Azoury K S, Miller B L
A comparison of the optimal ordering levels of Bayesian and non-Bayesian inventory models
MSci 1984 AUG VOL 30:8 p 993-1003.

(10677)
Eichenbaum M
Rational expectations and the smoothing properties of inventories of finished goods
JME 1984 VOL 14 p 71.

(10678)
Akhtar M A
Effects of interest rates and inflation on aggregate inventory investment in the United States
AER 1983 VOL 73 p 319-328.

(10679)
Eichenbaum M
A rational expectations equilibrium model of inventories of finished goods and employment
JME 1983 VOL 12 p 259.

(10680)
Hall R W
Zero inventories
Dow Jones-Irwin, 1983.

(10681)
Arvan L, Mooses L N
Inventory investment and the theory of the firm
AER 1982 VOL 72 p 186-193.

(10682)
Blinder A S, Fischer S
Inventories, rational expectations and the business cycle
JME 1981 VOL 8 p 277.

(10683)
Irvine F O Jr
Retail inventory investment and the cost of capital
AER 1981 VOL 71 p 633-648.

(10684)
Irvine F O Jr
Merchant wholesaler inventory investment and the cost of capital
AER 1981 VOL 71 P+P p 23-29.

(10685)
Maccini L J, Rossana R J
Investment in finished goods inventories: An analysis of adjustment speeds
AER 1981 VOL 71 P+P p 17-22.

(10686)
Brooks L D
Risk-return criteria and optimal inventory stocks
EE 1980 SUMMER VOL 25:4 p 275-299.

(10687)
Lieberman C
Inventory demand and cost of capital effects
REStat 1980 AUG VOL 62:3 p 348-356.

(10688)
Barbosa L C, Friedman M
Deterministic inventory lot-size models - a general root law
MSci 1978 DEC VOL 24:16 p 819.

(10689)
Bryant J
Relative prices and inventory investment
JME 1978 VOL 4 p 85.

(10690)
Gould J P
Inventories and stochastic demand: equilibrium models of the firm and industry
JB 1978 JAN VOL 51:1 p 1-42.

(10691)
Morton T E
The nonstationary infinite horizon inventory problem
MSci 1978 DEC VOL 24:16 p 1474.

(10692)
Nahmias S
On ordering perishable inventory when both demand and lifetime are random
MSci 1978 DEC VOL 24:16 p 82.

(10693)
Johnson G D, Thompson H E
Optimality of myopic inventory policies for
certain dependent demand processes
MSci 1975 JUL VOL 21:11 p 1303.

(10694)
Sunder S
Stock price and risk related to accounting changes
in inventory valuation
AR 1975 APR VOL 50:2 p 305-315.

(10695)
Gross D, Harris C M
Continuous-review (s,S) inventory models with
state-dependent leadtimes
MSci 1973 JUL VOL 19:11 p 567.

(10696)
Iglehart D L, Morey R C
Inventory systems with imperfect asset information
MSci 1972 AUG VOL 18:12 p B-388.

(10697)
McCallum B T
Inventory holdings, rational expectations and the
law of supply and demand
JPE 1972 VOL 80 p 386.

(10698)
Oral M, Salvador M S, Reisman A
On the evaluation of shortage costs for inventory
control of finished goods
MSci 1972 AUG VOL 18:12 p 344.

(10699)
Pierskalla W P, Roach C D
Optimal issuing policies for perishable inventory
MSci 1972 VOL 18:11 p 603.

(10700)
Simmons D M
Optimal inventory policies under a hierarchy of
setup costs
MSci 1972 AUG VOL 18:12 p B-591.

30.3 Credit

(10701)
Stanford R E
Optimizing profits from a system of accounts
receivable
MSci 1989 VOL 35 p 1227.

(10702)
Strong J S
The market valuation of credit market debt
JMCB 1989 VOL 21 p 307-320.

(10703)
Briggs D, Edwards B
Credit insurance: how to reduce the risks of trade
credit
Woodhead-Faulkner, 1988.

(10704)
Bryan L L
The credit bomb in our financial system
HBR 1987 JAN-FEB VOL 65:1 p 45-51.

(10705)
Smith J K
Trade credit and information asymmetry
JF 1987 SEP VOL 42:4 p 863-872.

(10706)
Lam C H, Chen A H
A note on optimal credit and pricing policy under
uncertainty : a contingent-claims approach
JF 1986 DEC VOL 41:5 p 1141-1148.

(10707)
Chiplin B, Wright M
Inter-industry differences in the response of trade
credit to changes in monetary policy
JBFA 1985 SUMMER VOL 12:2 p 221-248

(10708)
Edwards H ed.
Credit management handbook. 2nd ed
Gower, 1985.

(10709)
Brick I E, Fung W K H
The effect of taxes on the trade credit decision
FIN MGMT 1984 SUMMER VOL 13 p 24-30.

(10710)
Emery G W
A pure financial explanation for trade credit
JFQA 1984 SEP VOL 19:3 p 271-285.

(10711)
Goddard M
Effective credit management: a practical guide
Graham & Trotman, 1984.

(10712)
Ben-Horim M, Levy H
Management of accounts receivable under
inflation
FIN MGMT 1983 SPRING VOL 12 p 42.

(10713)
Heath R J
Summary findings of survey of credit management
practices of medium sized United Kingdom
companies
Control Data Business Advisors, 1983.

(10714)
Ferris J S
A transactions theory of trade credit use
QJE 1981 VOL 96 p 243-270..

(10715)**Popell S D**
Effectively manage receivables to cut costs
HBR 1981 JAN-FEB VOL 59:1 p 58-64.

(10716)
Sachdeva K S, Gitman L J
Accounts receivable decisions in a capital
budgeting framework
FIN MGMT 1981 WINTER VOL 10 p 45-49.

(10717)
Brosky J J
The implicit cost of trade credit and theory of
optimal terms of sale
New York: Credit Research Foundation, 1979.

(10718)
Kim Y H, Atkins J C
Evaluating investments in accounts receivable: A
maximizing framework
JF 1978 VOL 33 p 403.

(10719)
Dyl E A
Another look at the evaluation of investment in
accounts receivable
FIN MGMT 1977 WINTER VOL 6 p 67.

(10720)
O'Brien J M
On the incidence of selective credit and related
policies in a multi-asset framework
JF 1977 VOL 32 p 1539.

(10721)
Walia T S
Explicit and implicit cost of changes in the level
of accounts receivable
FIN MGMT 1977 WINTER VOL 6 p 75.

(10722)
Oh J S
Opportunity cost in the evaluation of investment
in accounts receivable
FIN MGMT 1976 SUMMER VOL 5 p 32.

(10723)
Benz G V
International trade credit management: a 22
country survey of effective credit practices
Gower, 1975.

(10724)
Lieber Z, Orgler Y E
An integrated model for accounts receivable
management
MSci 1975 OCT VOL 22:2 p 212-219.

(10725)
Davis E W, Yeomans K A
Company finance and the capital market: a study
of the effects of firm size
Cambridge U Pr, 1974.

(10726)
Herbst A F
A factor analysis approach to determining the
relative endogeneity of trade credit
JF 1974 VOL 29 p 1087.

(10727)
Hutson T G, Butterworth J
Management of trade credit. 2nd ed
Gower, 1974.

(10728)
Schwartz R A
An economic model of trade credit
JFQA 1974 SEP VOL 9 p 643.

(10729)
Freitas L
Monitoring accounts receivable
Management Accounting 1973 SEP p 18-21.

(10730)
Cole R H
Consumer and commercial credit management.
4th ed
Irwin, 1972.

(10731)
Miller D E, Relkin D B
Improving credit practice
AMA, 1971.

(10732)
Daniels F, Legg S, Yueille E C
Accounts receivable and related inventory
financing
JCBL 1970 JUL VOL 53 p 38-53.

(10733)
Beckman T N, Foster R S
Credits and collections: management and theory.
8th ed
McGraw, 1969.

(10734)
Nadiri M I
The determinants of trade credit in the US total
manufacturing sector
Em 1969 JUL VOL 37 p 408-423.

(10735)
Levy F K
An application of heuristic problem solving to
accounts receivable management
MSci 1966 FEB VOL 12 p B236-B244.

30.31   Credit instruments

(10736)
Shovlin H P
Bills of exchange and other negotiable
instruments: a handbook of effective practice
Woodhead-Faulkner, 1988.

(10737)
Kim J-H, Stover R D
The role of bank letters of credit in corporate
tax-exempt financing
FIN MGMT 1987 SPRING VOL 16 p 31-37.

(10738)
Rowe M
Letters of credit
Euromoney Publications, 1985.

(10739)
Stancill J M
Domestic uses of letters of credit
HBR 1979 SEP-OCT VOL 57:5 p 196-202.

30.32   Credit analysis

(10740)
Wood D
The information value of failure predictions in
credit assessment
JBankF 1988 VOL 12:2 p 275-292.

(10741)
Bathory A
The analysis of credit: foundations and
development of corporate credit assessment
McGraw, 1987.

(10742)
Infocheck comp.
Macmillan's top 100,000 company credit ratings:
1987
Macmillan, 1987.

(10743)
Hessol G
Financial management and credit ratings
MCFJ 1985 FALL VOL 3 p 49-52.

(10744)
Kolesar P, Showers J L
A robust credit screening model using categorical data
MSci 1985 FEB VOL 31:2 p 123-133.

(10745)
Backer M, Gosman M L
The use of financial ratios in credit downgrade decisions
FIN MGMT 1980 SPRING VOL 9 p 53.

(10746)
Nulty P
An upstart takes on Dun & Bradstreet
F 1979 APR 9 p 98-100.

(10747)
Long M S
Credit screening system selection
JFQA 1976 JUN VOL 11 p 313.

(10748)
Bower R S, Lessard D R
An operational approach to risk-screening
JF 1973 VOL 28 p 321.

(10749)
Lane S
Submarginal credit risk classification
JFQA 1972 JAN VOL 7 p 1379.

(10750)
Smith P F
Measuring risk on consumer installment credit
MSci 1964 NOV VOL 11 p 327-340.

30.33   Credit decisions

(10751)
Srinivasan V, Kim Y H
Designing expert financial systems: A case study of corporate credit management
FIN MGMT 1988 AUTUMN VOL 17 p 32-44.

(10752)
Srinivasan V, Kim Y H
Credit granting : a comparative analysis of classification procedures
JF 1987 JUL VOL 42:3 p 665-681.

(10753)
Miles J A, Varma R
Using financial market data to make trade credit decisions
JBFA 1986 WINTER VOL 13:4 p 505-518

(10754)
Besley S, Osteryoung J S
Survey of current practices in establishing trade-credit limits
FR 1985 FEB VOL 20:1.

(10755)
Stowe J D
An integer programming solution for the optimal credit investigation/credit granting sequence
FIN MGMT 1985 SUMMER VOL 14 p 66.

(10756)
Ben-Horim M, Levy H
Inflation and the trade credit period
MSci 1982 JUN VOL 28:6 p 646-651.

(10757)
Halloran J A, Lanser H P
The credit policy decision in an inflationary enviroment
FIN MGMT 1981 WINTER VOL 10 p 31-38.

(10758)
Eisenbeis R A
Selection and disclosure of reasons for adverse action in credit-granting systems
F R Bul 1980 VOL 66:9.

(10759)
Schwartz R A, Whitcomb T
The trade credit decision
(in Bicksler J ed., Handbook of financial economics. N Holland, 1980.)

(10760)
Hill N C, Riener K D
Determining the cash discount in the firm's credit policy
FIN MGMT 1979 SPRING VOL 8 p 68.

(10761)
Fortune
The persistent myth of redlining
F 1978 MAR 5 VOL 97 p 66-69.

(10762)
Dirickx Y M I, Wakeman L E
An extension of the Bierman-Hausman model for
credit granting
MSci 1976 VOL 22 p 1229-1237.

(10763)
Liebman L H
A Markov decision model for selecting optimal
credit control policies
MSci 1972 AUG VOL 18:12 p B-519.

(10764)
Wrightsman D
Optimal credit terms for accounts receivable
QREB 1969 VOL 9:2 p 59.

30.34   Credit collection/ factoring

(10765)
Business Marketing Services
Awareness of and attitudes towards factoring
BMSL, 1988.

(10766)
Gallinger G W, Ifflander A J
Monitoring accounts receivable using variance
analysis
FIN MGMT 1986 WINTER VOL 15 p 69.

(10767)
Gentry J A, De La Garza J M
A generalized model for monitoring accounts
receivable
FIN MGMT 1985 WINTER VOL 14 p 28-38..

(10768)**Boldin R J, Feeney P D**
The increased importance of factoring
FE 1981 APR VOL 49:4 p 19-21

(10769)
Shim J K
Estimating cash collection rates from credit sales:
A lagged regression approach
FIN MGMT 1981 WINTER VOL 10 p 28-30.

(10770)
Copeland T E, Khoury N T
A theory of credit extensions with default risk and
systematic risk
EE 1980 FALL VOL 26:1 p 35-52.

(10771)
Carpenter M D, Miller J E
A reliable framework for monitoring accounts
receivable
FIN MGMT 1979 WINTER VOL 8 p 37.

(10772)
Stancill J M
Is your bad debt expense too low?
HBR 1979 MAY-JUN VOL 57:3 p 6-7.

(10773)
Corcoran A W
The use of exponentially-smoothed transition
matrices to improve forecasting of cash flows
from accounts receivable
MSci 1978 MAR VOL 24:7 p 732-739.

(10774)
Moskowitz L A
Modern factoring and commercial finance
Thomas Y. Crowell, 1977.

(10775)
Forman M, Gilbert J
Factoring and finance
Heinemann, 1976.

(10776)
Stone B K
The payments-pattern approach to the forecasting
and control of accounts receivable
FIN MGMT 1976 AUTUMN VOL 5 p 65.

(10777)
Lewellen W G, Edmister R O
A general model for accounts-receivable analysis
and control
JFQA 1973 MAR VOL 8:2 p 195-206.

(10778)
Abraham A B
Factoring: The new frontier for commercial banks
JCBL 1971 APR p 32-43.

30.35   Consumer credit

(10779)
Kon S J, Thatcher J G
The effect of bankruptcy laws on the valuation of risky consumer debt
FR 1989 AUG VOL 24:3 p 371-396.

(10780)
Sullivan A C, Worden D D
Deregulation, tax reform, and the use of consumer credit
JFSR 1989 VOL 3:1 p 75.

(10781)
Peterson R L, Black D A
Consumer credit search
JMCB 1984 NOV VOL 16:4 p 527-535.

(10782)
Weber E A
Instalment credit for autos: a literature survey of sources, terms and demand effects
JBR 1984 SPRING VOL 15:1.

(10783)
Kalberg J G, Saunders A
Markov chain approaches to the analysis of payment behavior of retail credit customers
FIN MGMT 1983 SUMMER VOL 12 p 5-14.

(10784)
Peterson R L
Usury laws and consumer credit : a note
JF 1983 SEP VOL 38:4 p 1299-1304.

(10785)
Murphy N B
Economies of scale in the cost of compliance with consumer credit protection laws: the case of the implementation of the Equal Credit Opportunity Act of 1974
JBR 1980 WINTER VOL 10:4.

(10786)
Wiginton J C
A note on the comparison of logit and discriminant models of consumer credit behavior
JFQA 1980 SEP VOL 15 p 757.

(10787)
Bellenger D N, Robertson D H, Greenberg B A
Female attitudes toward the use of credit vs. cash
JBR 1979 SPRING VOL 10:1.

(10788)
Davis J
Protecting consumers from overdisclosure and gobbledygook: an empirical look at the simplification of consumer-credit contracts
VLR 1977 VOL 63:6 p 841-920.

(10789)
Eastwood D B, Anderson R
Consumer credit and consumer demand for automobiles
JF 1976 VOL 31 p 113.

(10790)
Peterson R L
The impact of general credit restraint on the supply of commercial bank consumer installment credit
JMCB 1976 NOV VOL 8:4 p 527-535.

(10791)
Dunkelberg W C, Smiley R H
Subsidies in the use of revolving credit
JMCB 1975 NOV VOL 7:4 p 469-490.

(10792)
Mayo O G ed.
Consumer credit control
Gower, 1971.

(10793)
Orgler Y E
Evaluation of bank consumer loans with credit scoring models
JBR 1971 SPRING VOL 2:1.

30.36   Finance of foreign trade

(10794)
Ball J, Knight M eds.
Export finance: 1989
Euromoney Publications, 1989.

(10795)
Clarke B W ed.
Handbook of international credit management
Gower, 1989.

(10796)
Perry E W
Practical export trade finance
Dow Jones-Irwin, 1989.

(10797)
Dillon K B et al.
Officially supported export credits: developments
and prospects
IMF, 1988.

(10798)
Euromoney
Forfaiting
Euromoney 1988 FEB SUPPL.

(10799)
Gmur C J ed.
Trade financing. 2nd ed
Euromoney Publications, 1986.

(10800)
Kingman-Brundage J, Schulz S A
The fundamentals of trade finance: the ins and
outs of import-export financing
Wiley, 1986.

(10801)
Venedikan H M, Warfield G A
Export-import financing. 2nd ed
Wiley, 1986.

(10802)
Dunn A, Knight M
Export finance
Euromoney Publications, 1982..

(10803)**OECD**
The export credit financing systems in OECD
member countries
OECD, 1982.

(10804)
Fortune
Export-import follies
F 1980 AUG 25 VOL 102:4 p 74-77.

(10805)
Export Credits Guarantee Department
Insurance facilities of the British Government's
Export Credits Guarantee Department: ECGD
Service
ECGD, 1975.

31 Mergers and corporate restructuring

(10806)
Black B S, Grundfest J A
Shareholder gains from takeovers and restructurings
JACF 1988 SPRING VOL 1 p 5-15.

(10807)
Kensinger J W, Martin J D
The quiet restructuring
JACF 1988 SPRING VOL 1 p 16-25.

(10808)
Murray M J, Reid F C
Financial style and corporate control
JACF 1988 SPRING VOL 1 p 76-84.

(10809)
Stern J M, Stewart G B, Chew D H eds.
Corporate restructuring and executive compensation
Ballinger, 1988.

(10810)
Stewart G B, Glassman D M
The motives and methods of corporate restructuring [Parts I and II]
JACF 1988 SPRING VOL 1 p 85-99; SUMMER VOL 1 p 79-88.

(10811)
Brickley J A, Dark F H
The choice of organizational form: The case of franchising
JFE 1987 VOL 18 p 401.

(10812)
Kensinger J W, Martin J D
R&D limited partnership financing and the new tax law
MCFJ 1987 WINTER VOL 4 p 44-54.

(10813)
Mendelson H
Consolidation, fragmentation and market performance
JFQA 1987 JUN VOL 22 p 189.

(10814)
Kensinger J W, Martin J D
Royalty trusts, master partnerships, and other organizational means of "unfirming" the firm
MCFJ 1986 SUMMER VOL 4 p 72-80.

(10815)
Martin J, Kensinger J
An economic analysis of R&D limited partnerships
MCFJ 1986 WINTER VOL 3 p 33-45.

(10816)
Hite G L, Owers J E
The restructuring of corporate America: an overview
MCFJ 1984 SUMMER VOL 2 p 6-16.

(10817)
Garbade K D, Silber W L, White L J
Market reaction to the filing of antitrust suits: an aggregate and cross-sectional analysis
REStat 1982 VOL 64 p 686.

31.1   Mergers and corporate combinations

(10818)
American Management Association
Tying the corporate knot: an American Management Association research report on the effects of mergers and acquisitions
AMA, 1989.

(10819)
Angear T R, Dewhurst J eds.
How to buy a company
Director Books, 1989.

(10820)
Fairburn J A, Kay J A eds.
Mergers and merger policy
Oxford U Pr, 1989.

(10821)
Hill Samuel Bank Ltd
Mergers, acquisitions and alternative corporate strategies
Mercury Books, 1989.

(10822)
IFR Publishing
International mergers and acquisitions
IFR Publishing, 1989.

(10823)
Pearson B
Successful acquisition of unquoted companies: a practical guide. 3rd ed
Gower, 1989.

(10824)
Sneath C G, Adler H S
Guide to acquisitions in the US
Butterworth, 1989.

(10825)
Auerbach A J ed.
Corporate takeovers: causes and consequences
U of Chicago Pr, 1988.

(10826)
Bagnoli M, Lipman B L
Successful takeovers without exclusion
RFS 1988 SPRING VOL 1:1 p 89.

(10827)
Brown C, Medoff J L
The impact of firm acquisitions on labor
(in Auerbach A J ed., Corporate takeovers: Causes and consequences. U of Chicago Pr, 1988.)

(10828)
Business International
Making acquisitions work: lessons from companies' successes and mistakes
Geneva: Business International, 1988.

(10829)
Chakrabarti A K, Clark J J, Chiang T C
Trend and stochastic movements in US merger activity
QREB 1988 VOL 28:2 p 6.

(10830)
Cooke T E
International mergers and acquisitions
Blackwell, 1988.

(10831)
Jensen M C
Takeovers: their causes and consequences
JEP 1988 VOL 2:1 p 21-48.

(10832)
Johnson J R
Takeover
Grafton Books, 1988.

(10833)
Morck R, Schleifer A, Vishny R W
Characteristics of targets of hostile and friendly takeovers
(in Auerbach A J ed., Corporate takeovers: Causes and consequences. U of Chicago Pr, 1988.)

(10834)
OECD
International mergers and competition policy
OECD, 1988.

(10835)
Roy A
Optimal acquisition fraction and a theory for partial acquisitions
JBFA 1988 WINTER VOL 15:4 p 543-556.

(10836)
Scharfstein D
The disciplinary role of takeovers
REStud 1988 VOL 54 p 183.

(10837)
Shleifer A, Vishny R W
Value maximization and the acquisition process
JEP 1988 VOL 2:1 p 7-20.

(10838)
Simmons M et al.
Successful mergers: planning, strategy and execution
Waterlow Publishers, 1988.

(10839)
Stallworthy E A, Kharbanda O P
Takeovers, acquisitions and mergers: strategies for rescuing companies in distress
Kogan Page, 1988.

(10840)
Stein J C
Takeover threats and managerial myopia
JPE 1988 FEB VOL 96:1 p 61-80.

(10841)
Auerbach A J ed.
Mergers and acquisitions
U of Chicago Pr, 1987.

(10842)
Chapman D R, Junor C W
Inflation firm control-type and vulnerability to
takeover
OEP 1987 SEP VOL 39:3 p 500-515.

(10843)
Chiplin B, Wright M
The logic of mergers: the competitive market in
corporate control in theory and practice
Inst Econ Aff, 1987.

(10844)
Dickie R, Michel A, Shaked I
The winner's curse in the merger game
Journal of General Management 1987 SPRING
VOL 12:3 p 32-51.

(10845)
Fallon I, Srodes J
Takeovers
Hamilton, 1987.

(10846)
Fisher F M
Horizontal mergers: triage and treatment
JEP 1987 VOL 1:2 p 23-40.

(10847)
Lubatkin M
Merger strategies and stockholder value
SMJ 1987 JAN-FEB VOL 8:1 p 39-53.

(10848)
Moore T
How the 12 top raiders rate
F 1987 SEP 28 VOL 116:7 p 32-38

(10849)
Rock M L ed.
Mergers and acquisitions handbook
McGraw, 1987.

(10850)
Schmalensee R
Horizontal merger policy: problems and changes
JEP 1987 VOL 1:2 p 41-54.

(10851)
Singh H, Montgomery C A
Corporate acquisition strategies and economic
performance
SMJ 1987 JUL-AUG VOL 8:4 p 377-386.

(10852)
Tully S
Europe's takeover kings
F 1987 JUL 20 VOL 116:2 p 63-66.

(10853)
Varaiya N P, Ferris K R
Overpaying in corporate takeovers: The winner's
curse
FAJ 1987 MAY-JUN VOL 43 p 64-71.

(10854)
White L J
Antitrust and merger policy: review and critique
JEP 1987 VOL 1:2 p 13-22.

(10855)
Wiener D P
Deals of the year
F 1987 FEB 2 VOL 115:3 p 56-61.

(10856)**Boesky I F, Madrick J ed.**
Merger mania: arbitrage: Wall Street's best kept
money-making secret
Bodley Head, 1986.

(10857)
Brown K C, Raymond M V
Risk arbitrage and the prediction of successful
corporate takeovers
FIN MGMT 1986 AUTUMN VOL 15 p 54-63.

(10858)
Brown P, Horin A
Assessing competition in the market for corporate
control: Australian evidence
AJM 1986 JUN VOL 11 p 23-50.

(10859)
Cooke T E
Mergers and acquisitions
Blackwell, 1986.

(10860)
Earl P, Fisher F G
International mergers and acquisitions
Euromoney Publications, 1986.

(10861)
Giammarino R M, Heinkel R L
A model of dynamic takeover behaviour
JF 1986 JUN VOL 41:2 p 465-480.

(10862)
Hirschey M
Mergers, buyouts and fakeouts
AER 1986 VOL 76 P+P p 317-322.

(10863)
Jemison D B, Sitkin S B
Acquisitions : the process can be a problem
HBR 1986 MAR-APR VOL 64:2 p 107-116.

(10864)
Jensen M C
The takeover controversy: analysis and evidence
MCFJ 1986 SUMMER VOL 4 p 6-32.

(10865)
John T A
Mergers and investment incentives
JFQA 1986 DEC VOL 21:4 p 393-413.

(10866)
Main J
Companies that float from owner to owner
F 1986 APR 28 VOL 113:9 p 28-34.

(10867)
Moir C
The acquisitive streak: an analysis of the takeover
and merger boom
Hutchinson, 1986.

(10868)
Palepu K
Predicting takeover targets: A methodological and
empirical analysis
JAE 1986 MAR VOL 8 p 3-36.

(10869)
Petre P
Merger fees that bend the mind
F 1986 JAN 20 VOL 113:2 p 14-19

(10870)
Steindel C
Tax reform and the merger and acquisition
market: the repeal of General Utilities
F R Bk New York Q Rev 1986 AUTUMN VOL
11:3.

(10871)
Castagna A D, Matolcsy Z P
Accounting ratios and models of takeover target
screens: Some empirical evidence
AJM 1985 JUN VOL 10 p 1-16.

(10872)
Clayton R J, Beranek W
Disassociations and legal combinations
FIN MGMT 1985 SUMMER VOL 14 p 24-28.

(10873)
Davidson I R
Takeovers : partitioning of gains and Pareto
improvement in a rational market with
asymmetric information
JBFA 1985 AUTUMN VOL 12:3 p 373-385

(10874)
Davidson K M
Megamergers: corporate America's billion-dollar
takeovers
Ballinger, 1985.

(10875)
DeMong R F, Peavy J W
Takeovers and shareholders: The mounting
controversy
Research Foundation of the Institute of Chartered
Financial Analysts, 1985.

(10876)
Eckbo B E, Weir P
Antimerger policy under the Hart-Scott-Rodino
Act: a reexamination of the market power
hypothesis
JLE 1985 VOL 28:1 p 119-150.

(10877)
Fairburn J A
British merger policy
FS 1985 VOL 6:1.

(10878)
Fogg J G
Takeovers : last chance for self-restraint
HBR 1985 NOV-DEC VOL 63:6 p 30-40.

(10879)
Mueller D C
Mergers and market share
REStat 1985 VOL 67 p 259.

(10880)
O'Conor C W
Packaging your business for sale
HBR 1985 MAR-APR VOL 63:2 p 52-58.

(10881)
Ott M, Santoni G J
Mergers and takeovers - the value of predators'
information
F R Bk St Louis Rev 1985 VOL 67:10.

(10882)
Roy A
Partial acquisition strategies for business
combinations
FIN MGMT 1985 SUMMER VOL 14 p 16-23.

(10883)
Sarig O H
On mergers, divestments and options: a note
JFQA 1985 SEP VOL 20:3 p 385-389.

(10884)
Dietrich J K, Sorensen E
An application of logit analysis to prediction of
merger targets
JBusR 1984 VOL 12 p 393-402.

(10885)
Kumar M S
Growth, acquisition and investment: an analysis of
the growth of industrial firms and their overseas
activities
Cambridge U Pr, 1984.

(10886)
OECD
Merger policies and recent trends in mergers
OECD, 1984.

(10887)
Rege U P
Accounting ratios to locate take-over targets
JBFA 1984 VOL 11:3 p 301.

(10888)
Ruback R S
An economic view of the market for corporate
control
Delaware Journal of Corporate Law 1984 VOL 9
p 613-625.

(10889)
Shrieves R E, Pashley M M
Evidence on the association between mergers and
capital structure
FIN MGMT 1984 AUTUMN VOL 13 p 39-48.

(10890)
Shughart W F III, Tollison R D
The random character of merger activity
RandJ 1984 WINTER VOL 15:4 p 500-509.

(10891)
Bradley M
The economic consequences of mergers and
tender offers
MCFJ 1983 WINTER VOL 1 p 17-28.

(10892)
Dodd P
The market for corporate control: A review of the
evidence
MCFJ 1983 SUMMER VOL 1 p 6-20.

(10893)
Foster G
Comments on M&A analysis and the role of
investment bankers
MCFJ 1983 WINTER VOL 1 p 36-38.

(10894)
Halpern P J
Corporate acquisitions : a theory of special cases?
a review of event studies applied to acquisitions
JF 1983 MAY VOL 38:2 p 297-317.

(10895)
Hetherington N S
Taking the risk out of risk arbitrage
JPM 1983 SUMMER VOL 9:4 p 24-25.

(10896)
Lev B
Observations on the merger phenomenon and a
review of the evidence
MCFJ 1983 WINTER VOL 1 p 6-16.

(10897)
Lewellen W G, Ferri M G
Strategies for the merger game: Management and
the market
FIN MGMT 1983 WINTER VOL 12 p 25-35.

(10898)
Melicher R W, Ledolter J, D'Antonio L J
A time series analysis of aggregate merger activity
REStat 1983 VOL 65 p 423.

(10899)
Myers S C
The evaluation of an acquisition target
MCFJ 1983 WINTER VOL 1 p 39-48.

(10900)
Rappaport A
Program overview: what we know and don't know
about mergers
MCFJ 1983 WINTER VOL 1 p 63-67.

(10901)
Stillman R
Examining antitrust policy towards horizontal
mergers
JFE 1983 APR VOL 11 p 225-240.

(10902)
Swary I
Bank acquisition of non-bank firms: An empirical
analysis of administrative decisions
JBankF 1983 VOL 7 p 213.

(10903)
Weston J F
The rules for successful mergers
MCFJ 1983 WINTER VOL 1 p 49-50.

(10904)
Keenan M, White L J eds.
Mergers and acquisitions: current problems in
perspective
Lexington Bks, 1982.

(10905)
Knight W J L
The acquisition of private companies. 3rd ed
Oyez Longman, 1982.

(10906)
Weston J F
Trends in anti-trust policy
CFQ 1982 SPRING VOL 1 p 66-87.

(10907)
Grossman S J, Hart O D
The allocational role of takeover bids in
situations of asymmetric information
JF 1981 MAY VOL 36:2 p 253-270.

(10908)
Keown A J, Pinkerton J M
Merger announcements and insider trading
activity: an empirical investigation
JF 1981 SEP VOL 36:4 p 855-869..

(10909)**Madden G P**
Potential corporate takeovers and market
efficiency : a note
JF 1981 DEC VOL 36:5 p 1191-1197.

(10910)
Cowling K et al.
Mergers and economic performance
Cambridge U Pr, 1980.

(10911)
Dodd P
Merger proposals, management discretion and
stockholder wealth.
JFE 1980 JUN VOL 8:2 p 105-137.

(10912)
Haugen R A, Langetieg T C, Wichern D W
Merger and stock-holder risk
JFQA 1980 SEP VOL 15 P 689.

(10913)
Mueller D C ed.
Determinants and effects of mergers: an
international comparison
Oelgeschlager, Gunn & Hain, 1980.

(10914)
Rappaport A
Strategic analysis for more profitable acquisitions
HBR 1979 JUL-AUG VOL 57:4 p 99-110.

(10915)
Belkaoui A
Financial ratios as predictors of Canadian takeovers
JBFA 1978 SPRING VOL 5:1 p 93-108.

(10916)
Ehbar A F
Kennecott after the battle
F 1978 JUN 15 p 124-130.

(10917)
Ferris K R, Melnik A, Rappaport A
Factors influencing the pricing of stock repurchase tenders
QREB 1978 VOL 18:1 p 31.

(10918)
Hong H, Kaplan R S, Mandelker G
Pooling vs. purchase: the effects of accounting for mergers on stock prices
AR 1978 JAN VOL 53:1 p 31-47.

(10919)
Hart O D
Take-over bids and stock market equilibrium
JET 1977 OCT VOL 16:1 p 53-83.

(10920)
Kim E H, McConnell J J
Corporate merger and the co-insurance of corporate debt
JF 1977 MAY VOL 32:2 p 349-365.

(10921)
Belkaoui A
The entropy law, information decomposition measures and corporate takeover
JBFA 1976 AUTUMN VOL 3:3 p 41-52.

(10922)
Castagna A D, Matolcsy Z P
Financial ratios as predictors of company acquisitions
Journal of the Securities Industry of Australia DEC 1976 p 6-10.

(10923)
Moon R W
Business mergers and take-over bids: a study of the post-war pattern of amalgamations and reconstructions of companies. 5th ed
Gee, 1976.

(10924)
Rosenberg M, Young A
The performance of common stocks subsequent to repurchase by recent tender offers
QREB 1976 VOL 16:1 p 109.

(10925)
Adler M, Dumas B
Optimal international acquisitions
JF 1975 VOL 30 p 1.

(10926)
Appleyard A R, Yarrow G K
The relationship between take-over activity and share valuation
JF 1975 VOL 30 p 1239.

(10927)
Kuehn D
Takeovers and the theory of the firm: an empirical analysis for the UK 1957-1969
Macmillan, 1975.

(10928)
Rhoades S A
Clarification of the potential competition doctrine in bank merger analysis
JBR 1975 SPRING VOL 6:1.

(10929)
Stapleton R C
The acquisition decision as a capital budgeting problem
JBFA 1975 SUMMER VOL 2:2 p 187-202.

(10930)
Franks J R, Miles R, Bagwell J
A review of acquisition valuation models
JBFA 1974 SPRING VOL 1:1 p 35-54.

(10931)
OECD
Mergers and competition policy: report of the Committee of experts on restrictive business practices
OECD, 1974.

(10932)
Beman L
What we learned from the great merger frenzy
F 1973 APR p 70ff.

(10933)
Dalton J A, Esposito L
The impact of liquidity on merger activity
QREB 1973 VOL 13:1 p 15.

(10934)
Institute of Economic Affairs
Mergers, takeovers and the structure of industry: ten papers on economics, law, rules
Inst Econ Aff, 1973.

(10935)
Lorange P
Anatomy of a complex merger: A case study and analysis
JBF 1973 SUMMER VOL 5:2 p 32-38.

(10936)
Reid S R
Petroleum mergers, multinational investments refining capacity and performance in the energy crisis
FIN MGMT 1973 WINTER VOL 2 p 50.

(10937)
Stevens D L
Financial characteristics of merged firms: A multivariate analysis
JFQA 1973 MAR VOL 8:2 p 149-158.

(10938)
Doctoroff M
Company mergers and takeovers, how the game is played in Australia
Gower, 1972.

(10939)
Lev B, Mandelker G
The microeconomic consequences of corporate mergers
JB 1972 JAN VOL 45 p 85-104.

(10940)
Reinhardt U E
Mergers and consolidations: A corporate financial approach
Morristown, NJ: General Learning Press, 1972.

(10941)
Ryden B
Mergers in Swedish industry: an empirical analysis of corporate mergers in Swedish industry, 1946-69
Stockholm: Industrial Institute for Economic and Social Research, 1972.

(10942)
Samuels J M ed.
Readings on mergers and takeovers
Elek, 1972.

(10943)
Schick R A
The analysis of mergers and acquisitions
JF 1972 MAY VOL 27 p 495-502.

(10944)
Stiglitz J E
Some aspects of the pure theory of corporate finance, bankruptcies and take-overs
BellJ 1972 FALL VOL 3:2 p 458-482.

(10945)
Jervis F R
The economics of mergers
Routledge, 1971.

(10946)
Ramanathan K V, Rappaport A
Size, growth rates and merger valuation
AR 1971 OCT VOL 46 p 733-745.

(10947)
Simkowitz M, Monroe R J
A discriminant analysis function for conglomerate targets
Southern Journal of Business 1971 NOV p 1-16.

(10948)
Singh A
Take-overs: their relevance to the stock market and the theory of the firm
Cambridge U Pr, 1971.

(10949)
Hindley B
Industrial merger and public policy
Inst Econ Aff, 1970.

(10950)
MacDougal G E, Malek F V
Master plan for merger negotiations
HBR 1970 JAN-FEB VOL 48 p 71-82.

(10951)
Newbould G D
Management and merger activity
Guthstead, 1970.

(10952)
Woods D H, Caverly T A
Development of a linear programming model for the analysis of merger/acquisition situations
JFQA 1970 JAN VOL 4 p 627-642.

(10953)
Eis C
The 1919-1930 merger movement in American industry
JLE 1969 OCT VOL 12 p 267-296.

(10954)
Harvey J L, Newgarden A eds.
Management guides to mergers and acquisitions
Wiley-Interscience, 1969.

(10955)
Hunter A
Mergers and industry concentration in Britain
BNLQR 1969 DEC VOL 22 p 372-394.

(10956)
Kramer A
Mergers and acquisitions
New York, Practising Law Institute, 1969.

(10957)
Krekel N R A et al.
Mergers: a European approach to technique
Business Bks, 1969.

(10958)
Hutchinson G S ed.
The business of acquisitions and mergers
Presidents, 1968.

(10959)
Linowes D F
Managing growth through acquisition
AMA, 1968.

(10960)
Mossin J
Merger agreements: some game-theoretic considerations
JB 1968 OCT VOL 41 p 460-471.

(10961)
Pratten C F
The merger boom in manufacturing industry
LBR 1968 OCT VOL 90 p 39-55..

(10962)**Reid S R**
Mergers, managers and the economy
McGraw, 1968.

(10963)
Silberman I H
A note on merger valuation
JF 1968 JUN VOL 23 p 528-534.

(10964)
Wyatt A R, Kieso D E
Mergers, acquisitions and consolidations
Intext, 1968.

(10965)
Hichens A
Valuing a company for acquisition
Investment Analyst 1967 MAY VOL 17 p 3-10.

(10966)
Reeves J P
Tax aspects of corporate mergers, exchanges, redemptions, liquidations, and reorganisations
Vantage, 1967.

(10967)
Short R A
Business mergers: how and when to transact them
P-H, 1967.

(10968)
Alberts W W, Segall J E
The corporate merger
U of Chicago Pr, 1966.

(10969)
Hennessy J H
Acquiring and merging businesses
P-H, 1966.

(10970)
National Industrial Conference Board
Mergers and markets: an economic analysis of the
first fifteen years under the Merger Act of 1950.
5th ed
Natl Ind Conf Bd, 1966.

(10971)
Parker W M
Business combinations and accounting valuation
JAR 1966 AUTUMN VOL 4 p 149-154.

(10972)
Stacey N A H
Mergers in modern business
Hutchinson, 1966.

(10973)
Manne H G
Mergers and the market for corporate control
JPE 1965 APR VOL 73 p 110-120.

(10974)
Mosich A N
Impact of merger accounting on post-merger
financial records
Management Accounting 1965 DEC VOL 97 p
21-28.

(10975)
Wakefield B R
Mergers and acquisitions
HBR 1965 SEP-OCT VOL 43 p 6ff.

(10976)
Weiss L W
An evaluation of mergers in six industries
REStat 1965 MAY VOL 47 p 172-181.

(10977)
Young G R et al.
Mergers and acquisitions: planning and action
Routledge, 1965.

(10978)
Scharf C A
Techniques for buying, selling and merging
businesses
P-H, 1964.

(10979)
Drayton C I Jr, Emerson C, Griswald J D
Mergers and acquisitions: planning and action
Fin Exec, 1963.

(10980)
Heflebower R B
Corporate mergers: policy and economic analysis
QJE 1963 NOV VOL 77 p 537-558.

(10981)
McCarthy G D
Acquisitions and mergers
Ronald, 1963.

(10982)
Sapienza S R
Business combinations: a case study
AR 1963 JAN VOL 91 p 91-101.

(10983)
Healy K T
The merger movement in transportation
AER 1962 MAY VOL 52 p 436-444.

(10984)
Jaenicke H R
Management's choice to purchase or pool
AR 1962 OCT VOL 37 p 758-765.

(10985)
Mace M L, Montgomery G E Jr
Management problems of corporate acquisitions
Harvard Busn, 1962.

(10986)
National Industrial Conference Board
Bibliography on diversification and mergers
Natl Ind Conf Bd, 1962.

(10987)
McCarthy G D
Premeditated merger
HBR 1961 JAN-FEB VOL 39 p 74-82.

(10988)
Sapienza S R
Distinguishing between purchase and pooling
Journal of Accountancy 1961 JUN VOL 111 p
35-40.

(10989)
Kottke F J
Mergers of large manufacturing companies: 1951
to 1959.
REStat 1959 NOV VOL 41 p 430-433.

(10990)
Nelson R L
Merger   movements   in   American   industry
1895-1956
(Dist by Princeton U Pr) Natl Bur Econ Res,
1959.

(10991)
Cook P L
Effects of mergers: six studies
Allen, 1958.

(10992)
Sommers H M
Estate taxes and business mergers
JF 1958 MAY VOL 13 p 201-210.

(10993)
Stigler G J
The statistics of monopoly and merger
JPE 1956 FEB VOL 64 p 33-40.

(10994)
Kaplan A D H
The current merger movement analysed
HBR 1955 MAY-JUN VOL 33 p 391-398.

(10995)
Nutter G W
Growth by merger
JASA 1954 SEP VOL 49 p 448-466.

(10996)
Weston J F
The role of mergers in the growth of large firms
U of Cal Pr, 1953.

(10997)
Weston J F
The recent merger movement
JB 1952 JAN VOL 25 p 30-38.

(10998)
Butters J K, Lintner J, Cary W L
Effects of taxation on corporate mergers
Harvard Busn, 1951.

(10999)
Stigler G J
Monopoly and oligopoly by merger
AER 1950 MAY VOL 40.

31.11   Motivation

(11000)
Lang L H P, Stulz R M, Walkling R A
Managerial performance, Tobin's q, and the gains
from successful tender offers
JFE 1989 SEP VOL 24:1 p 137-154.

(11001)
Lewellen W, Loderer C, Rosenfeld A
Mergers, executive risk reduction, and stockholder
wealth
JFQA 1989 DEC VOL 24:4 p 459-472.

(11002)
Mitchell M L, Mulherin J H
The stock price response to pension terminations
and the relation of terminations with corporate
takeovers
FIN MGMT 1989 AUTUMN VOL 18 p 41-56.

(11003)
Bruner R F
The use of excess cash and debt capacity as a
motive for merger
JFQA 1988 JUN VOL 23:2 p 199-218.

(11004)
Gilson R J, Scholes M, Wolfson M A
Taxation and the dynamics of corporate control:
The uncertain case for tax-motivated acquisitions
(in Coffee J, Lowenstein L and Rose-Ackerman
S eds., Knights, raiders and targets: The impact of
the hostile takeover. Oxford U Pr, 1988.)

(11005)
Griffin J M
A test of the free cash flow hypothesis: results
from the petroleum industry
REStat 1988 VOL 70 p 76.

(11006)
Horn H, Wolinsky A
Bilateral monopolies and incentives for merger
RandJ 1988 AUTUMN VOL 19:3 p 408-419.

(11007)
Maloney M T, McCormick R E
Excess capacity, cyclical production, and merger
motives: some evidence from the capital markets
JLE 1988 VOL 31:2 p 321-350.

(11008)
Salinger M A
Vertical mergers and market foreclosure
QJE 1988 MAY VOL 103:2 p 335-356.

(11009)
Auerbach A J, Reishus D
Taxes and the merger decision
(in Coffee J and Lowenstein L eds., Takeovers
and contests for corporate control. Oxford U Pr,
1987.)

(11010)
Brickley J A, James C M
The takeover market, corporate board
composition, and ownership structure: the case of
banking
JLE 1987 VOL 30:1 p 161-180.

(11011)
Moore N H, Pruitt S W
The market pricing of net operating loss
carryforwards : implications of the tax motivations
of mergers
JFR 1987 SUMMER VOL 10:2 p 153-160.

(11012)
Crossman S J, Hart O D
The costs and benefits of ownership: A theory of
vertical and lateral integration
JPE 1986 VOL 94 p 691.

(11013)
Jensen M C
Agency costs of free cash flow, corporate finance
and takeovers
AER 1986 VOL 76 P+P p 323-329.

(11014)
Roll R
The hubris hypothesis of corporate takeovers
JB 1986 APR VOL 59:2 p 197-216..

(11015)**Bierman H Jr**
A neglected tax incentive for mergers
FIN MGMT 1985 SUMMER VOL 14 p 29-32.

(11016)
Bittlingmayer G
Did antitrust policy cause the great merger wave?
JLE 1985 VOL 28:1 p 77-118.

(11017)
Eckbo B E
Mergers and the market concentration doctrine :
evidence from the capital market
JB 1985 JUL VOL 58:3 p 325-349.

(11018)
Hasbrouck J
The characteristics of takeover targets q and other
measures
JBankF 1985 VOL 9 p 351.

(11019)
Lewellen W G, Loderer C, Rosenfeld A
Merger decisions and executive stock ownership
JAE 1985 APR VOL 7 p 209-232.

(11020)
Mikkelson W H, Ruback R S
Takeovers and managerial compensation: A
discussion
JAE 1985 APR VOL 7 p 233-238.

(11021)
Ashton D J, Atkins D R
A partial theory of takeover bids
JF 1984 MAR VOL 39:1 p 167-183.

(11022)
Larcker D F
Managerial incentives in mergers and their effect
on shareholder wealth
MCFJ 1983 WINTER VOL 1 p 29-35.

(11023)
Shrieves R E, Stevens D L
Bankruptcy avoidance as a motive for merger
JFQA 1979 SEP VOL 14 p 501.

(11024)
Melicher R W, Rush D F, Winn D N
Degree of industry concentration and market
risk-return performance
JFQA 1976 NOV VOL 11.

(11025)
Schmalensee R
A note on the theory of vertical integration
JPE 1973 VOL 81 p 442.

(11026)
Jackson R
The consideration of economies in merger cases
JB 1970 OCT VOL 43 p 439-447.

(11027)
Gort M
An economic disturbance theory of mergers
QJE 1969 NOV VOL 83 p 624-642.

(11028)
Kuehn D A
Stock market valuation and acquisitions: an
empirical test of one component of managerial
utility
JIE 1969 APR VOL 17 p 132-144.

31.12 Conglomerate mergers and firm diversification

(11029)
Amit R, Livnat J
Efficient corporate diversification: methods and
implications
MSci 1989 VOL 35 p 879.

(11030)
Amit R H, Livnat J
Corporate diversification
Dow Jones-Irwin, 1989.

(11031)
Lee W B, Cooperman E S
Conglomerates in the the 1980s: a performance
appraisal
FIN MGMT 1989 SPRING VOL 18 p 45-54.

(11032)
Aron D J
Ability, moral hazard, firm size and diversification
RandJ 1988 SPRING VOL 19:1 p 72-87.

(11033)
Board J, Sutcliffe C
Forced diversification
QREB 1988 VOL 28:3 p 43.

(11034)
Kudla R J, Dhatt M S
An empirical test of operating synergism
JBFA 1988 AUTUMN VOL 15:3 p 427-436.

(11035)
Jahera J S Jr, Lloyd W P, Page D E
Firm diversification and financial performance
QREB 1987 SPRING VOL 27:1 p 51-62.

(11036)
Jahera J S Jr, Lloyd W P, Page D E
The relationship between financial performance
and stock market based measures of corporate
diversification
FR 1987 NOV VOL 22:4.

(11037)
Lloyd W P, Hand J H, Modani N K
The effect of the degree of ownership control on firm diversification, market value and merger activity
JBusR 1987 AUG VOL VOL 15:4 p 303-312.

(11038)
Hill C, Pickering J
Conglomerate mergers, internal organization and competition policy
International Review of Law and Economics 1986 VOL 6 p 59-75.

(11039)
Rosenthal L, Sullivan T G
Some estimates of the impact of corporate diversification on the valuation and leverage of USA firms : estimates from 1972 data
JBFA 1985 SUMMER VOL 12:2 p 275-284

(11040)
Lam C H, Boudreaux K J
Conglomerate merger wealth redistribution and debt : a note
JF 1984 MAR VOL 39:1 p 275-281.

(11041)
Michel A J, Shaked I
Does business diversification affect performance
FIN MGMT 1984 WINTER VOL 13 p 18-25.

(11042)
Benston G L
Conglomerate mergers: Causes, consequences and remedies
American Enterprise Institute for Public Policy Research, 1980.

(11043)
Biggadike R
The risky business of diversification
HBR 1979 MAY-JUN VOL 57:3 p 103-111.

(11044)
Gahlon J H, Stover R D
Diversification, financial leverage and conglomerate systematic risk
JFQA 1979 DEC VOL 14 p 999.

(11045)
Salter M S, Weinhold W A
Diversification through acquisition: strategies for creating economic value
Free Pr, 1979.

(11046)
Azzi C
Conglomerate mergers, default risk and homemade mutal funds
AER 1978 VOL 68 p 161-172.

(11047)
Salter M S, Weinhold W A
Diversification via acquisition; creating value
HBR 1978 JUL-AUG VOL 56:4 p 166-176.

(11048)
Lee L W
Co-insurance and conglomerate merger
JF 1977 VOL 32 p 1527.

(11049)
Scott J H Jr
On the theory of conglomerate mergers
JF 1977 VOL 32 p 1235.

(11050)
Mason R H, Goudzwaard M B
Performance of conglomerate firms: A portfolio approach
JF 1976 VOL 31 p 39.

(11051)
Copeland R M, Holzmann O J, Hayya J
Income measures of conglomerate performance
QREB 1975 VOL 15:3 p 67.

(11052)
Higgins R C, Schall L D
Corporate bankruptcy and conglomerate merger
JF 1975 VOL 30 p 93.

(11053)
Hughes J S, Logue D E, Sweeney R J
Corporate international diversification and market assigned measures of risk and diversification
JFQA 1975 NOV VOL 10 p 627.

(11054)
Fielitz B D
Indirect versus direct diversification
FIN MGMT 1974 WINTER VOL 3 p 54.

(11055)
Joehnk M D, Nielsen J F
The effects of conglomerate merger activity on systematic risk
JFQA 1974 MAR VOL 9 p 215.

(11056)
Melicher R W, Rush D F
Evidence on the acquisition-related performance of conglomerate firms
JF 1974 VOL 29 p 141.

(11057)
Goldberg L G
The effect of conglomerate mergers on competition
JLE 1973 VOL 16 p 137.

(11058)
Melicher R W, Rush D F
The performance of conglomerate firms: recent risk and return experience
JF 1973 VOL 28 p 381.

(11059)
Melnek A, Pollatschek M A
Debt capacity, diversification and conglomerate mergers
JF 1973 VOL 28 p 1263.

(11060)
Rhoades S A
The effect of diversification on industry profit performance in 241 manufacturing industries, 1963
REStat 1973 MAY VOL 55:2 p 146-155.

(11061)
U.S. Federal Trade Commission
Economic report on conglomerate merger performance
US Govt, NOV 1972.

(11062)
Weston J F, Smith K V, Shrieves R E
Conglomerate performance using the capital asset pricing model
REStat 1972 NOV VOL 54:4 p 357-363.

(11063)
Celler Committee Staff Report
Investigation of conglomerate corporations
US Govt, JUN 1, 1971.

(11064)
Lewellen W G
A pure financial rationale for the conglomerate merger
JF 1971 MAY VOL 26 p 521-537.

(11065)
Lynch H H
Financial performance of conglomerates
Harvard Busn, 1971.

(11066)
Levy H, Sarnat M
Diversification, portfolio analysis and the uneasy case for conglomerate mergers
JF 1970 SEP VOL 25 p 795-802.

(11067)
Lorie J H, Halpern P
Conglomerates: the rhetoric and the evidence
JLE 1970 APR VOL 13 p 149-166..

(11068)Shapiro D L
Conglomerate mergers and optimal investment policy
JFQA 1970 JAN VOL 4 p 643-656.

(11069)
Weston J F
Diversification and merger trends
Business Economics 1970 JAN p 50-57.

(11070)
Goudzwaard M B
Conglomerate mergers, convertibles, and cash dividends
QREB 1969 VOL 9:1 p 53.

(11071)
Mead W J
Instantaneous profit as a conglomerate merger motive
WEJ 1969 DEC p 295-306.

(11072)
Mueller D C
A theory of conglomerate mergers
QJE 1969 NOV VOL 83 p 643-659.

(11073)
Smith K V, Schreiner J C
A portfolio analysis of conglomerate
diversification
JF 1969 JUN VOL 35 p 413-427.

(11074)
Westerfield R
The capital asset pricing model: an analysis of the
performance of conglomerates
U of Pa Pr, 1969.

(11075)
Narver J C
Conglomerate mergers and market competition
U of Cal Pr, 1967.

(11076)
O'Hanlon T
The odd news about conglomerates
F 1967 JUN 15 p 175-177.

(11077)
West R R
"Homemade" diversification vs. corporate
diversification
JFQA 1967 DEC VOL 2 p 417-420.

(11078)
Turner D F
Conglomerate mergers and section 7 of the
Clayton Act
HLR 1965 MAY VOL 78 p 1313-1395.

(11079)
Gort M
Diversification and integration in American
industry
Princeton U Pr, 1962.

31.13 Wealth effects of mergers

(11080)
Franks J R, Harris R S
Shareholder wealth effects of corporate takeovers:
the U.K. experience 1955-1985
JFE 1989 VOL 23 p 225.

(11081)
Hayn C
Tax attributes as determinants of shareholder
gains in corporate acquisitions
JFE 1989 VOL 23 p 121.

(11082)
Jarrell G A, Poulsen A B
The returns to acquiring firms in tender offers:
evidence from three decades
FIN MGMT 1989 AUTUMN VOL 18 p 12-19.

(11083)
Nathan K S, O'Keefe T B
The rise in takeover premiums: an exploratory
study
JFE 1989 VOL 23 p 101.

(11084)
Scanlon K P, Trifts J W, Pettway R H
Impacts of relative size and industrial relatedness
on returns to shareholders of acquiring firms
JFR 1989 SUMMER VOL 12:2 p 103-112.

(11085)
Ang J S, Tucker A L
The shareholder wealth effects of corporate
greenmail
JFR 1988 WINTER VOL 11:4 p 265-280.

(11086)
Bradley M, Desai A, Kim E H
Synergistic gains from corporate acquisitions and
their division between the stockholders of target
and acquiring firms
JFE 1988 VOL 21 p 3-40.

(11087)
Doukas J, Travlos N G
The effect of corporate multinationalism on
shareholders' wealth: evidence from international
acquisitions
JF 1988 DEC VOL 43:5 p 1161-1176.

(11088)
Forbes W
Stock exchange reactions to Monopoly and Merger Commission reports
AE 1988 JUL VOL 20:7 p 929-938.

(11089)
Kaufman D J Jr
Factors affecting the magnitude of premiums paid to target-firm shareholders in corporate acquisitions
FR 1988 NOV VOL 23:4 p 465-482.

(11090)
Michel A J, Shaked I
Corporate takeovers: Excess returns and the multiple bidding phenomena
JBFA 1988 SUMMER VOL 15:2 p 263-274.

(11091)
Stoughton N M
The information content of corporate merger and acquisition offers
JFQA 1988 JUN VOL 23:2 p 175-198.

(11092)
Allen P R, Sirmans C F
An analysis of gains to acquiring firm's shareholders: the special case of REITs
JFE 1987 VOL 18 p 175-184.

(11093)
Calvet A L, Lefoll J
Information asymmetry and wealth effect of Canadian corporate acquisitions
FR 1987 NOV VOL 22:4.

(11094)
Casey R, Dodd P, Dolan P
Takeovers and corporate raiders: Empirical evidence from extended event studies
AJM 1987 DEC VOL 12 p 201-220.

(11095)
Dechow P
The share market's assessment of initial acquisitions by seven controversial investors
AJM 1987 JUN VOL 12 p 23-48.

(11096)
Huang Y-S, Walkling R A
Target abnormal returns associated with acquisition announcements: payment, acquisition form, and managerial resistance
JFE 1987 VOL 19 p 329-349.

(11097)
James C, Wier P
Returns to acquirers and competition in the acquisition market : the case of banking
JPE 1987 APR VOL 95:2 p 355-370.

(11098)
Stanton P
Accounting rates of return as measures of post-merger performance
AJM 1987 DEC VOL 12.

(11099)
Wansley J W, Lane W R, Yang H C
Gains to bidder firms in cash and securities transactions
FR 1987 NOV VOL 22:4.

(11100)
Weidenbaum M, Vogt S
Takeovers and stockholders : winners and losers
CMR 1987 SUMMER VOL 29:4 p 157-168.

(11101)
Yagil J
An exchange ratio determination model for mergers: a note
FR 1987 FEB VOL 22:1.

(11102)
Amihud Y, Dodd P, Weinstein M
Conglomerate mergers, managerial motives and stockholder wealth
JBankF 1986 VOL 10 p 401.

(11103)
Dennis D K, McConnell J J
Corporate mergers and security returns
JFE 1986 JUN VOL 16:2 p 143-187.

(11104)
Pettway R H, Yamada T
Mergers in Japan and their impacts upon stockholders' wealth
FIN MGMT 1986 WINTER VOL 15 p 43-52.

(11105)
Dodds J C, Quek J P
Effect of mergers on the share price movement of
the acquiring firms : a UK study
JBFA 1985 SUMMER VOL 12:2 p 285-296

(11106)
Holderness C G, Sheehan D P
Raiders or saviors? The evidence on six
controversial investors
JFE 1985 DEC VOL 14:4 p 555-579.

(11107)
Jarrell G A
The wealth effects of litigation by targets: do
interests diverge in a merge?
JLE 1985 VOL 28:1 p 151-178.

(11108)
Malatesta P H, Thompson R
Partially anticipated events: A model of stock
price reactions with an application to corporate
acquisitions
JFE 1985 VOL 14 p 237.

(11109)
Atoncic M A, Bennett P
Financial consequences of mergers
F R Bk New York Q Rev 1984 SPRING VOL
9:1.

(11110)
Walter T S
Australian takeovers: Capital market efficiency
and shareholder risk and return
AJM 1984 JUN VOL 9 p 63-120.

(11111)
Asquith P
Merger bids, uncertainty, and stockholder returns.
JFE 1983 APR VOL 11 p 51-83.

(11112)
Asquith P, Bruner R F, Mullins D W Jr
The gains to bidding firms from merger
JFE 1983 APR VOL 11 p 121-139.

(11113)
Eckbo B E
Horizontal mergers, collusion, and stockholder
wealth.
JFE 1983 APR VOL 11 p 241-273

(11114)
Eger C E
An empirical test of the redistribution effect in
pure exchange mergers.
JFQA 1983 DEC VOL 18:4 p 547-572

(11115)
Jensen M C, Ruback R S
The market for corporate control : the scientific
evidence.
JFE 1983 APR VOL 11 p 5-50

(11116)
Malatesta P H
The wealth effect of merger activity and the
objective functions of merging firms
JFE 1983 VOL 11 p 155.

(11117)
Ruback R S
Assessing competition in the market for corporate
acquisitions
JFE 1983 APR VOL 11 p 141-153.

(11118)
Ruback R S
The Cities Service takeover : a case study
JF 1983 MAY VOL 38:2 p 319-330.

(11119)
Schipper K, Thompson R
Evidence on the capitalized value of merger
activity for acquiring firms.
JFE 1983 APR VOL 11 p 85-119

(11120)
Wansley J W, Lane W R, Yang H C
Shareholder returns to USA acquired firms in
foreign and domestic acquisitions
JBFA 1983 WINTER VOL 10:4 p 647-656.

(11121)**Wansley J W, Lane W R, Yang H C**
Abnormal returns to acquired firms by type of
acquisition and method of payment
FIN MGMT 1983 AUTUMN VOL 12 p 16-22.

(11122)
Wansley J W, Roenfeldt R L, Cooley P L
Abnormal returns from merger profiles.
JFQA 1983 JUN VOL 18:2 p 149-162.

(11123)
Weston J F, Chung K S
Do mergers make money?
Mergers & Acquisitions 1983 FALL p 40-48.

(11124)
Bradley M
The economic effects of acquisitions by tender
offer
CFQ 1982 SUMMER VOL 1 p 44-62.

(11125)
Gagnon J-M et al.
Stock market behaviour of merging firms: the
Belgian experience
EER 1982 VOL 17:2.

(11126)
Hoshino Y
The performance of corporate mergers in Japan
JBFA 1982 SUMER VOL 9:2 p 153.

(11127)
Ruback R S
The Conoco takeover and stockholder returns
SMR 1982 WINTER VOL 23 p 13-33.

(11128)
Elgers P T, Clark J J
Merger types and shareholder returns: Additional
evidence
FIN MGMT 1980 SUMMER VOL 9 p 66.

(11129)
Firth M
Takeovers, shareholder returns and the theory of
the firm
QJE 1980 VOL 94 p 235.

(11130)
Firth M
Synergism in mergers: Some British results
JF 1978 VOL 33 p 670.

(11131)
Kummer D R, Hoffmeister J R
Valuation consequences of cash tender offers
JF 1978 VOL 33 p 505.

(11132)
Langetieg T C
An application of a three-factor performance
index to measure stockholder gains from merger
JFE 1978 DEC VOL 6:4 p 365-383.

(11133)
Dodd P, Ruback R
Tender offers and stockholder returns: An
empirical analysis
JFE 1977 VOL 5 p 351.

(11134)
Franks J R, Broyles J E, Hecht M J
An industry study of the profitability of mergers
in the United Kingdom
JF 1977 VOL 32 p 1513.

(11135)
Meeks G
Disappointing marriage: a study of the gains from
merger
Cambridge U Pr, 1977.

(11136)
Firth M
Share prices and mergers: a study of stock market
efficiency
Saxon House, 1976.

(11137)
Balog J
Why the stock market reacts the way it does to
announcements of mergers and acquisitions
FAJ 1975 MAR-APR VOL 31 p 84-88.

(11138)
Haugen R A, Langetieg T C
An empirical test for synergism in merger
JF 1975 VOL 30 p 1003.

(11139)
Mandelker G
Risk and return: The case of merging firms
JFE 1974 VOL 1 p 303.

(11140)
Shick R A, Jen F C
Merger benefits to shareholders of acquiring firms
FIN MGMT 1974 WINTER VOL 3 p 45.

(11141)
Nielsen J F, Melicher R W
A financial analysis of acquisition and merger premiums
JFQA 1973 MAR VOL 8:2 p 139-148.

(11142)
Haugen R A, Udell J G
Rates of return to stockholders of acquired companies
JFQA 1972 JAN VOL 7 p 1387-1398.

(11143)
Gort M, Hogarty T F
New evidence on mergers
JLE 1970 APR VOL 13 p 167-184.

(11144)
Hogarty T F
The profitability of corporate mergers
JF 1970 JUL VOL 43 p 317-327.

(11145)
Johnson H W, Simon J L
The success of mergers: the case of advertising agencies
Oxford U: Institute of Economics and Statistics Bulletin 1969 VOL 31 p 139-144.

(11146)
Segall J E
Merging for fun and profit
IMR 1968 WINTER VOL 9 p 17-30.

(11147)
Kelly E M
The profitability of growth through mergers
Pa St U, Center for Research of the College of Business Administration, 1967.

(11148)
Kitching J
Why do mergers miscarry?
HBR 1967 NOV-DEC VOL 45 p 84-101.

(11149)
Cohen K J, Reid S R
The benefits and costs of bank mergers
JFQA 1966 DEC VOL 1 p 15-57.

(11150)
Dellenbarger L E Jr
Common stock valuation in industrial mergers
U of Fla Pr, 1966.

(11151)
Merjos A
Broken mergers: a security analyst adds up the gains and losses
B 1966 MAR 21 VOL 36 p 5ff.

(11152)
Dellenbarger L E Jr
A study of relative common equity values in fifty mergers of listed industrial corporations, 1950-57.
JF 1963 SEP VOL 18 p 564-565.

(11153)
Markham J W
Survey of the evidence and findings on mergers
(Dist by Princeton U Pr) Natl Bur Econ Res, 1955.

(11154)
Livermore S
The success of industrial mergers
QJE 1935 NOV VOL 49 p 68-95.

(11155)
Dewing A S
A statistical test of the success of consolidations
QJE 1921 NOV VOL 36 p 84-101.

31.14 Tender offers, takeover defenses and merger regulation

(11156)
Bebchuk L A
Takeover bids below the expected value of minority shares
JFQA 1989 JUN VOL 24:2 p 171-184.

(11157)
Fishman M J
Preemptive bidding and the role of the medium of exchange in acquisitions
JF 1989 MAR VOL 44:1 p 41-58.

(11158)
Giliberto S M, Varaiya N P
The winner's curse and bidder competition in acquisitions: evidence from failed bank auctions
JF 1989 MAR VOL 44:1 p 59-76.

(11159)
Mitchell M L, Netter J M
Triggering the 1987 stock market crash: antitakeover provisions in the proposed House Ways and Means bill
JFE 1989 SEP VOL 24:1 p 37-68.

(11160)
Netter J M, Poulsen A B
State corporation laws and shareholders: the recent experience
FIN MGMT 1989 AUTUMN VOL 18 p 29-40.

(11161)
Ryngaert M D
Firm valuation, takeover defenses, and the Delaware Supreme Court
FIN MGMT 1989 AUTUMN VOL 18 p 20-28.

(11162)
Brickley J A, Lease R C, Smith C W Jr
Ownership structure and voting on antitakeover amendments
JFE 1988 VOL 20 p 267-292.

(11163)
Brown D T
The construction of tender offers: capital gains taxes and the free rider problem
JB 1988 VOL 61 p 183.

(11164)
Coffee J, Lowenstein L, Ackerman S R
Knights, raiders and targets
Oxford U Pr, 1988.

(11165)
Dann L Y, DeAngelo H
Corporate financial policy and corporate control: a study of defensive adjustments in asset and ownership structure
JFE 1988 VOL 20 p 87-128.

(11166)
Fabozzi F J, Ferri M G, Fabozzi T D
A note on unsuccessful tender offers and stockholder returns
JF 1988 DEC VOL 43:5 p 1275-1284.

(11167)
Fishman M J
A theory of preemptive takeover bidding
RandJ 1988 SPRING VOL 19:1.

(11168)
Harris M, Raviv A
Corporate control contests and capital structure
JFE 1988 VOL 20 p 55-86.

(11169)
Jarrell G A, Poulsen A B
Dual-class recapitalizations as antitakeover mechanisms: the recent evidence
JFE 1988 VOL 20 p 129-152.

(11170)
Kamma S, Weintrop J, Weir P
Investors' perceptions of the Delaware Supreme Court decision in Unocal v. Mesa
JFE 1988 VOL 20 p 419-430.

(11171)
Malatesta P H, Walkling R A
Poison pill securities: stockholder wealth, profitability and ownership structure
JFE 1988 VOL 20 p 347-376.

(11172)
Pound J
The information effects of takeover bids and resistance
JFE 1988 VOL 22 p 207.

(11173)
Ruback R S
Coercive dual-class exchange offers
JFE 1988 VOL 20 p 153-174..

(11174)**Ryngaert M**
The effect of poison pill securities on shareholder wealth
JFE 1988 VOL 20 p 377-418.

(11175)
Schumann L
State regulation of takeovers and shareholder wealth: the case of New York's 1985 takeover statutes
RandJ 1988 WINTER VOL 19:4 p 557-567.

(11176)
Bhagat S, Brickley J A, Loewenstein U
The pricing effects of interfirm cash tender offers
JF 1987 SEP VOL 42:4 p 965-986.

(11177)
Bishop S, Dodd P
Partial takeovers: Are they coercive?
AJM 1987 JUN VOL 12 p 9-22.

(11178)
Comment R, Jarrell G A
Two-tier and negotiated tender offers: the imprisonment of the free-riding shareholder
JFE 1987 VOL 19 p 283-310.

(11179)
Green C
Mergers in Canada and Canada's new merger law
Antitrust Bulletin 1987 SPRING VOL 32:1 p 253-273.

(11180)
Jarrell G A, Poulsen A B
Shark repellents and stock prices: the effects of antitakeover amendments since 1980
JFE 1987 VOL 19 p 127-168.

(11181)
Jorde T M
Coping with the merger guidlines and the government's "fix-it-first" approach: a modest appeal for more information
Antitrust Bulletin 1987 FALL VOL 32:3 p 565-578.

(11182)
Kosnik R D
Greenmail : a study of board performance in corporate governance
Administrative Science Quarterly 1987 JUN VOL 32:2 p 163-185

(11183)
Pound J
The effects of antitakeover amendments on takeover activity: some direct evidence
JLE 1987 VOL 30:2 p 353-368.

(11184)
Carney W J
Two-tier tender offers and shark repellants
MCFJ 1986 SUMMER VOL 4 p 48-56.

(11185)
Casey R, Eddey P H
Defence strategies of listed companies under the takeover code
AJM 1986 DEC VOL 11 p 153-172.

(11186)
Jarrell G A, Poulsen A B
Shark repellants and poison pills: stockholder protection - from the good guys or the bad guys?
MCFJ 1986 SUMMER VOL 4 p 39-47.

(11187)
Knoeber C R
Golden parachutes, shark repellents and hostile tender offers
AER 1986 VOL 76 p 155-167.

(11188)
Loomis C J
The comeuppance of Carl Icahn
F 1986 FEB 17 VOL 113:4 p 14-21

(11189)
Millstein I M
Takeover reform : common sense from the common law.
HBR 1986 JUL-AUG VOL 64:4 p 16-19.

(11190)
Samuelson W, Rosenthal L
Price movements as indicators of tender offer success
JF 1986 JUN VOL 41:2 p 481-499.

(11191)
Shleifer A, Vishny R W
Greenmail, white knights and shareholders' interest
RandJ 1986 AUTUMN VOL 17:3 p 293-309.

(11192)
Walkling R A, Long M S
Strategic issues in cash tender offers: predicting bid premiums, probability of success, and target management's response
MCFJ 1986 SUMMER VOL 4 p 57-65.

(11193)
Harvard Law Review
Greenmail: targeted stock repurchases and the management-entrenchment hypothesis
HLR 1985 VOL 98:5 p 1045-1065.

(11194)
Holderness C G, Sheehan D P
Why corporate raiders are good news for stockholders
MCFJ 1985 SUMMER VOL 3 p 6-19.

(11195)
Kesner I F, Dalton D R
Antitakeover tactics: Management 42, stockholders 0
Business Horizons 1985 SEP-OCT p 17-25.

(11196)
Panel on Take-overs and Mergers
The City code on take-overs and mergers and the rules governing substantial acquisitions of shares
The Panel, 1985.

(11197)
Saul R S
Hostile takeovers : what should be done?
HBR 1985 SEP-OCT VOL 63:5 p 18-24.

(11198)
Smiley R H, Stewart S D
White knights and takeover bids
FAJ 1985 JAN-FEB VOL 41 p 19-26.

(11199)
Walkling R A
Predicting tender offer success : a logistic analysis
JFQA 1985 DEC VOL 20:4 p 461-478.

(11200)
Walkling R A, Edmister R O
Determinants of tender offer premiums
FAJ 1985 JAN-FEB VOL 41 p 27-37.

(11201)
Boorsten P
A review of the revised merger guidelines
The Antitrust Bulletin 1984 WINTER p 613-652.

(11202)
Fortune
When paying off a raider benefits the shareholders
F 1984 APR 30 VOL 109:9 p 88-90.

(11203)
Baron D P
Tender offers and management resistance
JF 1983 MAY VOL 38:2 p 331-343.

(11204)
Bradley M, Desai A, Kim E H
The rationale behind interfirm tender offers: information or synergy?
JFE 1983 APR VOL 11 p 183-206

(11205)
DeAngelo H, Rice E M
Antitakeover charter amendments and stockholder wealth
JFE 1983 APR VOL 11 p 329-360.

(11206)
Linn S C, McConnell J J
An empirical investigation of the impact of "antitakeover" amendments on common stock prices
JFE 1983 APR VOL 11 p 361-399.

(11207)
Wier P
The costs of antimerger lawsuits: Evidence from the stock market
JFE 1983 VOL 11 p 207-224.

(11208)
Easterbrook F H, Fischel D R
The proper role of a target's management in responding to a tender offer
HLR 1981 VOL 94:6 p 1161-1204.

(11209)
Hoffmeister J R, Dyl E A
Predicting outcomes of cash tender offers
FIN MGMT 1981 WINTER VOL 10 p 50-58.

(11210)
Bradley M
Interfirm tender offers and the market for corporate control
JB 1980 OCT VOL 53:4 p 345-376.

(11211)
Grossman S J, Hart O D
Disclosure laws and takeover bids.
JF 1980 MAY VOL 35:2 p 323-334.

(11212)
Jarrell G A, Bradley M
The economic effects of federal and state regulation of cash tender offers
JLE 1980 VOL 23:2 p 371.

(11213)
Johnston A
The City take-over code
Oxford U Pr, 1980.

(11214)
Harvard Law Review
Bank financing of hostile takeovers of borrowers: Washington Steel Corp. v. TW Corp.
HLR 1979 VOL 93:2 p 440-451.

(11215)
Aranow E R, Berlstein G
Development in tender offers for corporate control
Columbia U Pr, 1977.

(11216)
Harvard Law Review
Fairness standards for SEC approval of mergers - Collins v. SEC
HLR 1976 VOL 90:2 p 453-462.

(11217)
Austin D V
The financial management of tender offer takeovers
FIN MGMT 1974 SPRING VOL 3 p 37.

(11218)
Aranow E R, Einhorn H A
Tender offers for corporate control
Columbia U Pr, 1973.

(11219)
Snyder G L
Take-over tactic: Tender offering for options on the common stock
FAJ 1973 JUL-AUG VOL 29 p 30-40.

31.15 Leveraged buyouts and buyins

(11220)
Burrough B, Helyar J
Barbarians at the gate: the fall of RJR Nabisco
Jonathan Cape, 1990.

(11221)
Kaplan S
Management buyouts: evidence on taxes as a source of value
JF 1989 JUL VOL 44:3 p 611-632.

(11222)
Amihud Y
Management buyouts
Dow Jones-Irwin, 1988.

(11223)
Bruner R F, Paine L S
Management buyouts and managerial ethics
CMR 1988 WINTER VOL 30:2 p 89-106.

(11224)
Green S
The incentive effects of ownership and control in management buy-outs
Long Range Planning 1988 FEB VOL 21:1 p 26-34.

(11225)
Kleiman R T
Shareholder gains from leveraged cash-outs
JACF 1988 SPRING VOL 1 p 46-53.

(11226)
Schleifer A, Summers L H
Breach of trust in corporate takeovers
(in Auerbach A J ed., Corporate takeovers: Causes and consequences. U of Chicago Pr, 1988.).

(11227)**DeAngelo H, DeAngelo L**
Management buyouts of publicly traded corporations

FAJ 1987 MAY-JUN VOL 43 p 38-49.

(11228)
Maupin R J
Financial and stock market variables as predictors
of management buyouts
SMJ 1987 JUL-AUG VOL 8:4 p 319-327.

(11229)
Thompson R S, Wright M
Markets to hierarchies and back again: The
implications of management buy-outs for factor
supply
Journal of Economic Studies 1987 VOL 14:3 p
1-22.

(11230)
Torabzadeh K M, Bertin W J
Leveraged buyouts and shareholder returns
JFR 1987 VOL 10:4 p 313-320.

(11231)
Hanney J
The management buy-out: An offer you can't
refuse!
Omega 1986 VOL 14:2 p 119-134.

(11232)
Lowenstein L
No more cozy management buyouts
HBR 1986 JAN-FEB VOL 64:1 p 147-156.

(11233)
Bradley K, Gelb A
Employee buyouts of troubled companies
HBR 1985 SEP-OCT VOL 63:5 p 121-130.

(11234)
Lowenstein L
Management buy-outs
Columbia Law Review 1985 VOL 85 p 730-784.

(11235)
McComas M
After the buyout life isn't easy
F 1985 DEC 9 VOL 112:13 p 48-53

(11236)
Wright M, Coyne J
Management buy-outs
Croom Helm, 1985.

(11237)
Fortune
How the champs do leveraged buyouts
F 1984 JAN 23 VOL 109:2 p 70-78.

(11238)
Mason L
Structuring and financial management buyouts
San Diego, CA: Buyout Publications, 1984.

(11239)
Maupin R J, Bidwell C M, Ortegren A K
An empirical investigation of the characteristics of
publicly-quoted corporations which change to
closely-held ownership through management
buyouts
JBFA 1984 WINTER VOL 11:4 p 435-450

(11240)
Ferenbach C
Leveraged buyouts: a new capital market in
evolution
MCFJ 1983 WINTER VOL 1 p 56-62.

(11241)
Wallner N, Greve J T
Leveraged buyouts: a review of the state of the
art
San Diego, CA: Buyout Publications, 1983.

(11242)
Gargiulo A F, Levine S J
The leveraged buyout
AMA, 1982.

(11243)
Coleman R
Overview of leveraged buyouts
(in Lee S and Colman R eds., Handbook of
mergers, acquisitions and buyouts. P-H, 1981.)

(11244)
Ross I
What happens when the employees buy the
company
F 1980 JUN 2 VOL 101:11 p 108-111.

(11245)
Wallner N
Leveraged buyouts: a review of the state of the
art, part II
Mergers & Acquisitions 1980 WINTER p 16-26.

(11246)
Gilbert F S
Financing the leveraged buy-out through the acquired assets
HBR 1978 JUL-AUG VOL 56:4 p 8-16.

31.16 Exchange medium in mergers

(11247)
Hansen R G
A theory for the choice of exchange medium in mergers and acquisitions
JB 1987 JAN VOL 60:1 p 75-95.

(11248)
Travlos N G
Corporate takeover bids methods of payment and bidding firms' stock returns
JF 1987 SEP VOL 42:4 p 943-963.

(11249)
Carleton W T
An empirical analysis of the role of the medium of exchange in mergers
JF 1983 JUN VOL 38:3 p 813-826.

31.17 Joint ventures

(11250)
Darrough M N, Stoughton N M
A bargaining approach to profit sharing in joint ventures
JB 1989 VOL 62:2 p 237-270.

(11251)
McConnell J J, Nantell T J
Corporate combinations and common stock returns : the case of joint ventures
JF 1985 JUN VOL 40:2 p 519-536

31.2 Divestitures and spin-offs

(11252)
Glassman D M
Spin-offs and spin-outs: Using "securitization" to beat the bureaucracy
JACF 1988 FALL VOL 1 p 82-89.

(11253)
Kudla R J, McInish T H
Divergence of opinion and corporate spin-offs
QREB 1988 VOL 28:2 p 20-29.

(11254)
Chastain C E
Divestiture : antidote to merger mania
Business Horizons 1987 NOV-DEC VOL 30:6 p 43-49.

(11255)
Davidson W N III, McDonald J L
Evidence of the effect on shareholder wealth of corporate spinoffs: the creation of royalty trusts
JFR 1987 VOL 10:4 p 321-328.

(11256)
Hite G L, Owers J E, Rogers R C
The market for interfirm asset sales: partial sell-offs and total liqidations
JFE 1987 VOL 18 p 229-252.

(11257)
Sicherman N W, Pettway R H
Acquisition of divested assets and shareholders' wealth
JF 1987 DEC VOL 42:5 p 1261-1274.

(11258)
Alexander G J, Benson P G, Gunderson E W
Asset redeployment: Trans World corporation's spinoff of TWA
FIN MGMT 1986 SUMMER VOL 15 p 50.

(11259)
Chen A H, Merville L J
An analysis of divestiture effects resulting from deregulation
JF 1986 DEC VOL 41:5 p 997-1010.

(11260)
Coyne J, Wright M eds.
Divestment and strategic change
Philip Allan, 1986.

(11261)
Hearth D, Zaima J K
Divestiture uncertainty and shareholder wealth :
evidence from the USA (1975-1982)
JBFA 1986 SPRING VOL 13:1 p 71-85.

(11262)**Klein A**
The timing and substance of divestiture
announcements : individual simultaneous and
cumulative effects
JF 1986 JUL VOL 41:3 p 685-697.

(11263)
Schipper K, Smith A
A comparison of equity carve-outs and seasoned
equity offerings: Share price effects and corporate
restructuring
JFE 1986 VOL 15 p 153.

(11264)
Schipper K, Smith A
Equity carve-outs
MCFJ 1986 SPRING VOL 4 p 23-32.

(11265)
Jain P C
The effect of voluntary sell-off announcements on
shareholder wealth
JF 1985 MAR VOL 40:1 p 209-224.

(11266)
Toy S
Splitting up: the other side of merger mania
Business Week 1985 JUL 1 p 50-55.

(11267)
Alexander G J, Benson P G, Kampmeyer J M
Investigating the valuation effects of
announcements of voluntary corporate selloffs
JF 1984 JUN VOL 39:2 p 503-517.

(11268)
Hearth D, Zaima J K
Voluntary corporate divestitures and value
FIN MGMT 1984 SPRING VOL 13 p 10-16.

(11269)
Linn S C, Rozeff M S
The corporate sell-off
MCFJ 1984 SUMMER VOL 2 p 17-26.

(11270)
Rosenfeld J D
Additional evidence on the relation between
divestiture announcements and shareholder wealth
JF 1984 DEC VOL 39:5 p 1437-1448.

(11271)
Schipper K, Smith A
The corporate spin-off phenomenon
MCFJ 1984 SUMMER VOL 2 p 27-34.

(11272)
Hite G L, Owers J E
Security price reactions around corporate spin-off
announcements.
JFE 1983 DEC VOL 12:4 p 409-436.

(11273)
Kudla R J, McInish T H
Valuation consequences of corporate spin-offs
RBER 1983 WINTER VOL 18 p 71-77.

(11274)
Miles J A, Rosenfeld J D
The effect of voluntary spin-off announcements
on shareholder wealth
JF 1983 DEC VOL 38:5 p 1597-1606.

(11275)
Rosenfield D B, Shapiro R D, Butler D A
Optimal strategies for selling an asset
MSci 1983 SEP VOL 29:9 p 1051-1061

(11276)
Schipper K
The evidence of divestitures, going private
proposals, and spin-offs
MCFJ 1983 WINTER VOL 1 p 51-55.

(11277)
Schipper K, Smith A
Effects of recontracting on shareholder wealth :
the case of voluntary spin-offs
JFE 1983 DEC VOL 12:4 p 437-467.

(11278)
Ehrbar A F
Splitting up RCA
F 1982 MAR 22 VOL 105:6 p 62-76.

(11279)
Bernstein P W
Who buys corporate losers
F 1981 JAN 26 p 60-66.

(11280)
Wilson B D
Disinvestment of foreign subsidiaries
UMI Research Pr, 1980.

(11281)
Boudreaux K J
Divestiture and share price
JFQA 1975 NOV VOL 10 p 619.

31.3 Stock repurchase

(11282)
Davidson W N III, Garrison S H
The stock market reaction to significant tender
offer repurchases of stock: size and purpose
perspective
FR 1989 FEB VOL 24:1 p 93-108.

(11283)
Scholes M S, Wolfson M A
Decentralized investment banking: the case of
discount, dividend-reinvestment and
stock-purchase plans
JFE 1989 SEP VOL 24:1 p 7-36.

(11284)
Wansley J W, Lane W R, Sarkar S
Managements' view on share repurchase and
tender offer premiums
FIN MGMT 1989 AUTUMN VOL 18 p 97.

(11285)
Bank of England
Share repurchase by quoted companies
BEQB 1988 VOL 28 p 382.

(11286)
Barclay M J, Smith C W Jr
Corporate payout policy: Cash dividends versus
open-market repurchases
JFE 1988 VOL 22 p 61.

(11287)
Klein A, Rosenfeld J
The impact of targeted share repurchases on the
wealth of non-participating shareholders
JFR 1988 VOL 11:2 p 89-98.

(11288)
Klein A, Rosenfeld J
Targeted share repurchases and top management
changes
JFE 1988 VOL 20 p 493-506.

(11289)
Williams J
Efficient signalling with dividends, investment, and
stock repurchases
JF 1988 JUL VOL 43:3 p 737-748.

(11290)
Ofer A R, Thakor A V
A theory of stock price responses to alternative
corporate cash disbursement methods: stock
repurchases and dividends
JF 1987 JUN VOL 42:2 p 365.

(11291)
Wyatt M
Company acquisition of own shares. 2nd ed
Longman, 1986.

(11292)
Bhagat S, Brickley J A, Lease R C
Incentive effects of stock purchase plans
JFE 1985 VOL 14 p 195.

(11293)
Billingsley R S, Thompson G R
Determinants of stock repurchases by bank
holding companies
JBR 1985 AUTUMN VOL 16:3 p 128-145.

(11294)
Loomis C J
Beating the market by buying back stock
F 1985 APR 29 VOL 111:9 p 20-26

(11295)
Vermaelen T
Repurchase tender offers, signaling and managerial incentives
JFQA 1984 JUN VOL 19:2 p 163-181.

(11296)
Bradley M, Wakeman L M
The wealth effects of targeted share repurchases.
JFE 1983 APR VOL 11 p 301-328

(11297)
Dann L Y, DeAngelo H
Standstill agreements, privately negotiated stock repurchases, and the market for corporate control
JFE 1983 APR VOL 11 p 275-300.

(11298)
Dann L Y
Common stock repurchases: what do they really accomplish?
CFQ 1982 SUMMER VOL 1 p 29-43.

(11299)
Dann L Y
Common stock repurchases: An analysis of returns to bondholders and stockholders
JFE 1981 VOL 9 p 113.

(11300)
Vermaelen T
Common stock repurchases and market signalling: An empirical study
JFE 1981 VOL 9 p 139.

(11301)
Baker H K, Rheinstein C
Tender offers to buy back odd-lot holdings of stock
HBR 1980 SEP-OCT VOL 58:5 p 66-70.

(11302)
Dielman T, Nantell T J, Wright R L
Price effects of stock repurchasing: A random coefficient regression approach
JFQA 1980 MAR VOL 15 p 175.

(11303)
Masulis R W
Stock repurchase by tender offer: an analysis of the causes of common stock price changes
JF 1980 MAY VOL 35:2 p 305-321.

(11304)
Stewart S S Jr
Should a corporation repurchase its own stocks?
JF 1976 VOL 31 p 911.

(11305)
Finnerty J E
Corporate stock issue and repurchase
FIN MGMT 1975 AUTUMN VOL 4 p 62.

(11306)
Norgaard R, Norgaard C
A critical examination of share repurchase
FIN MGMT 1974 SPRING VOL 3 p 44.

(11307)
Ellis C D, Young A E
The repurchase of common stock
Ronald, 1971.

(11308)
Elton E J, Gruber M J
The cost of retained earnings--implications of share repurchase
IMR 1968 SPRING VOL 9 p 87-104.

(11309)
Elton E J, Gruber M J
The effect of share repurchases on the value of the firm
JF 1968 MAR VOL 23 p 135-149.

(11310)
Marshall W S, Young A E
A mathematical model for re-acquisition of small shareholdings
JFQA 1968 DEC VOL 3 p 463-470.

(11311)
Guthart L A
Why companies are buying back their own stock
FAJ 1967 MAR-APR VOL 23 p 105-110.

(11312)
Bierman H Jr, West R R
Acquisition of common stock by the corporate issuer
JF 1966 DEC VOL 21 p 687-696.

(11313)
Woods D H, Brigham E F
Stockholder distribution decisions: share repurchases or dividends
JFQA 1966 MAR VOL 1 p 15-25.

(11314)
Ellis C D
Repurchase stock to revitalize equity
HBR 1965 JUL-AUG VOL 43 p 119-128..

(11315)**Guthart L A**
More companies are buying back their stock
HBR 1965 MAR-APR VOL 43 p 41-53, 172.

(11316)
Merjos A
Into the Treasury
B 1964 AUG 17 p 9-12.

(11317)
Merjos A
Treasury stock: many companies are regular buyers of their own shares
B 1960 AUG 29 p 11-12.

31.31 Exchange offers

(11318)
Cornett M M, Travlos N G
Information associated with debt-for-equity and equity-for-debt exchange offers
JF 1989 JUN VOL 44:2 p 451-468.

(11319)
Errunza V R, Moreau A F
Debt-for-equity swaps under a rational expectations equilibrium
JF 1989 JUL VOL 44:3 p 663-680.

(11320)
Helpman E
The simple analytics of debt-equity swaps
AER 1989 VOL 79:3 p 440-451.

(11321)
Rubin S M
Debt equity swaps in the 1990s. 2 vols
Economist Publications, 1989.

(11322)
Hilton A
Debt/equity swaps: costs, benefits and prospects
Financial Times Business Information, 1988.

(11323)
Rubin S M
Guide to debt equity swaps
Economist, 1987.

(11324)
Finnerty J D
Stock-for-dept swaps and shareholder returns
FIN MGMT 1985 AUTUMN VOL 14 p 5-17.

(11325)
Peavy J W III, Scott J A
The effect of stock for debt swaps on security returns
FR 1985 NOV VOL 20:4.

(11326)
Peavy J W III, Scott J A
A closer look at stock-for-debt swaps
FAJ 1985 MAY-JUN VOL 41 p 44-50.

(11327)
Rogers R C, Murphy N B, Owers J E
Financial innovation, balance sheet cosmetics and market response: the case of equity-for-debt exchanges in banking
JBR 1985 AUTUMN VOL 16:3 p 145-149.

(11328)
Rogers R C, Owers J E
Equity for debt exchanges and stockholder wealth
FIN MGMT 1985 AUTUMN VOL 14 p 18-26.

(11329)
Scott J A, Hempel G H, Peavy J W III
The effect of stock-for-debt swaps on bank holding companies
JBankF 1985 VOL 9 p 233.

(11330)
Brooks L D
Stock-bond swaps in regulated utilities
FIN MGMT 1984 AUTUMN VOL 13 p 5-10.

(11331)
Bierman H Jr
The debt-equity swap
MCFJ 1983 FALL VOL 1 p 58-63.

(11332)
Masulis R W
The impact of capital structure change on firm value: some estimates
JF 1983 MAR VOL 38:1 p 107-126.

(11333)
Masulis R W
The effects of capital structure change on security prices: A study of exchange offers
JFE 1980 VOL 8 p 139-178.

31.4 Going private

(11334)
Lehn K, Poulsen A
Free cash flow and stockholder gains in going private transactions
JF 1989 JUL VOL 44:3 p 771-788.

(11335)
Marais L, Schipper K, Smith A
Wealth effects of going private for senior securities
JFE 1989 VOL 23 p 155.

(11336)
DeAngelo H, DeAngelo L, Rice E M
Going private: the effects of a change in corporate ownership structure
MCFJ 1984 SUMMER VOL 2 p 35-42.

(11337)
DeAngelo H, DeAngelo L, Rice E M
Going private: minority freezeouts and stockholder wealth
JLE 1984 VOL 27:2 p 367-402.

(11338)
Fortune
Carl Lindner's disappearing act (American Financial has gone private)
F 1981 JUL 13 VOL 104:1 p 85-96.

(11339)
Schnepper J A
"Going private" and the minority shareholders
FAJ 1978 MAR-APR

31.5 Partnerships

(11340)
Moore W T, Christensen D G, Roenfeldt R L
Equity valuation effects of forming master limited partnerships
JFE 1989 SEP VOL 24:1 p 107-124.

(11341)
Farrell J, Scotchmer S
Partnerships
QJE 1988 VOL 103 p 279.

(11342)
Muscarella C J
Price performance of initial public offerings of master limited partnership units
FR 1988 NOV VOL 23:4 p 513.

(11343)
Collins J M, Bey R P
The master limited partnership: An alternative to the corporation
FIN MGMT 1986 WINTER VOL 15 p 5-14.

(11344)
Mayers D, Smith C W
Ownership structure and control. The mutualization of stock life insurance companies
JFE 1986 MAY VOL 16:1 p 73-98.

31.6 Nationalization and privatization

(11345)
Phillips-Patrick F J
The effect of asset and ownership structure on political risk: some evidence from Mitterand's election in France
JBankF 1989 SEP VOL 13:4-5 p 651-674.

(11346)
Grout P A
Employee share ownership and privatisation : some theoretical issues
EJ 1988 VOL 98:390 CONFERENCE PAPERS SUPPL p 97-104.

(11347)
Blankart C B
Limits to privatization
EER 1987 VOL 31:1-2.

(11348)
Bos D
Privatization of public enterprises
EER 1987 VOL 31:1-2.

(11349)
Thompson D J
Privatization in the U.K.: deregulation and the advantage of incumbency
EER 1987 VOL 31:1-2.

(11350)
Langohr H W, Viallet C J
Compensation and wealth transfers in the French nationalizations 1981-1982
JFE 1986 DEC VOL 17:2 p 273-312.

(11351)
Trades Union Congress
Stripping our assets: the City's privatisation killing
TUC, 1985.

(11352)
Heald D
Privatisation: analysing its appeal and limitations
FS 1984 VOL 5:1.

(11353)
Sharpe T
Privatisation, regulation and competition
FS 1984 VOL 5:1.

(11354)
Minns R, Thornley J
State shareholding: the role of local and regional authorities
Macmillan, 1978.

(11355)
Long N V
Resource extraction under the uncertainty about possible nationalization
JET 1975 FEB VOL 10:1 p 42-53.

31.7 Bankruptcy and liquidation

(11356)
D'Aveni R A
Dependability and organizational bankruptcy: an application of agency and prospect theory
MSci 1989 VOL 35 p 1120.

(11357)
Franks J R, Torous W N
An empirical investigation of U.S. firms in reorganization
JF 1989 JUL VOL 44:3 p 747-770.

(11358)
Giammarino R M
The resolution of financial distress
RFS 1989 VOL 2:1 p 25-48.

(11359)
Johnson D J
The risk behavior of equity firms approaching bankruptcy
JFR 1989 SPRING VOL 12:1 p 33-50.

(11360)
Kim E H, Schatzberg J
Voluntary liquidations: causes and consequences
MCFJ 1988 WINTER VOL 5 p 30-35.

(11361)
Luckett C A
Personal bankruptcies
F R Bul 1988 SEP VOL 74:9.

(11362)
Balderston F E
Facade and self-deception in the deteriorating financial firm
CMR 1987 WINTER VOL 29:2 p 101-111.

(11363)
Kim E H, Schatzberg J D
Voluntary corporate liquidations
JFE 1987 VOL 19 p 311-328.

(11364)
Williamson S D
Financial intermediation, business failures and
real business cycles
JPE 1987 VOL 95 p 1196.

(11365)
Jackson T H
The logic and limits of bankruptcy law
Harvard U Pr, 1986.

(11366)
Morrison R
Business   opportunities   from   corporate
bankruptcies
Wiley, 1985.

(11367)
Gentry J A, Newbold P, Whitford D T
Bankruptcy, working capital and funds flow
components
Managerial Finance 1984 VOL 10:3-4 p 26-39..

(11368)**Titman S**
The effect of capital structure on a firm's
liquidation decision
JFE 1984 VOL 13 p 137-151.

(11369)
White M J
Bankruptcy liquidation and reorganization
(in Logue D ed., Handbook of modern finance.
Warren, Gorham, and Lamont, 1984.)

(11370)
Allen F
The prevention of default
JF 1981 MAY VOL 36:2 p 271-276

(11371)
Ang J S, Chua J H
Corporate bankruptcy and job losses among top
level managers
FIN MGMT 1981 WINTER VOL 10 p 70-74.

(11372)
Golbe D L
The   effects   of   imminent   bankruptcy   on
stockholder risk preferences and behavior
BellJ 1981 SPRING VOL 12:1 p 321-328.

(11373)
Mittman L, Morrison R W
Bankruptcies: assets often can be picked up at
bargain prices
HBR 1981 JUL-AUG VOL 59:4 p 155-160.

(11374)
Bank of England
Corporate insolvency
BEQB 1980 VOL 20 p 430-436.

(11375)
Lippman S A, McCall J J, Winston W L
Constant absolute risk aversion bankruptcy and
wealth-dependent decisions.
JB 1980 JUL VOL 53:3 p 285-296.

(11376)
Benninga S
Competitive equilibrium with bankruptcy in a
sequence of markets
IntER 1979 OCT VOL 20:3 p 557-575.

(11377)
Clark R C
The duties of the corporate debtor to its creditors
HLR 1977 VOL 90:3 p 505-562.

(11378)
Warner J B
Bankruptcy, absolute priority and the pricing of
risky debt claims
JFE 1977 VOL 4 p 239.

(11379)
Argenti J
Corporate collapse: the causes and symptoms
McGraw, 1976.

(11380)
Higgins R C, Schall L D
Corporate bankruptcy and conglomerate merger
JF 1975 VOL 30 p 93.

(11381)
Deeson A F L
Great company crashes
W. Foulsham & Co., 1972.

(11382)
Stiglitz J E
Some aspects of the pure theory of corporate finance, bankruptcies and take-overs
BellJ 1972 FALL VOL 3:2 p 458-482.

(11383)
Gordon M J
Towards a theory of financial distress
JF 1971 MAY VOL 26 p 347-356.

31.71   Bankruptcy prediction

(11384)
Aziz A, Lawson G H
Cash flow reporting and financial distress models: testing of hypotheses
FIN MGMT 1989 SPRING VOL 18 p 55-63.

(11385)
BarNiv R, Raveh A
Identifying financial distress: a new nonparametric approach
JBFA 1989 SUMMER VOL 16:3 p 361.

(11386)
Booth P, Hutchinson P
Distinguishing between failing and growing firms: a note on the use of decomposition measure
JBFA 1989 SPRING VOL 16:2 p 267.

(11387)
Aharony J, Swary I
A note on corporate bankruptcy and the market model risk measures
JBFA 1988 SUMMER VOL 15:2 p 275-282.

(11388)
Elmer P J, Borowski D M
An expert system approach to financial analysis: The case of S&L bankruptcy
FIN MGMT 1988 AUTUMN VOL 17 p 66-76.

(11389)
Zavgren C V, Friedman G E
Are bankruptcy prediction models worthwhile? An application in securities analysis
MIR 1988 VOL 28:1 p 34-44.

(11390)
Abrams B A, Huang C J
Predicting bank failures: the role of structure in affecting recent failure experiences in the USA
AE 1987 OCT VOL 19:10 p 1291-1302.

(11391)
Betts J, Belhoul D
The effectiveness of incorporating stability measures in company failure models
JBFA 1987 AUTUMN VOL 14:3 p 323-334

(11392)
Crapp H R, Stevenson M
Development of a method to assess the relevant variables and the probability of financial distress
AJM 1987 DEC VOL 12 p 221-236.

(11393)
Gentry J A, Newbold P, Whitford D T
Funds flow components, financial ratios, and bankruptcy
JBFA 1987 VOL 14:4 p 595.

(11394)
Gombola M J, Haskins M E, Ketz J E
Cash flow in bankruptcy prediction
FIN MGMT 1987 WINTER VOL 16 p 55-65.

(11395)
Houghton K A, Woodliff D R
Financial ratios: the prediction of corporate 'success' and failure
JBFA 1987 VOL 14:4 p 537.

(11396)
Karels G V, Prakash A J
Multivariate normality and forecasting of business bankruptcy
JBFA 1987 VOL 14:4 p 573.

(11397)
Keasey K, Watson R
Non-financial symptoms and the prediction of small company failure : a test of Argenti's hypotheses
JBFA 1987 AUTUMN VOL 14:3 p 335-354.

(11398)
Lau A H L
A five-state financial distress prediction model
JAR 1987 SPRING VOL 25:1 p 127-138.

(11399)
Michel A J, Shaked I
Airline deregulation and the probability of air carrier insolvency
FR 1987 FEB VOL 22:1.

(11400)
Queen M, Roll R
Firm mortality: Using market indicators to predict survival
FAJ 1987 MAY-JUN VOL 43 p 9-26.

(11401)
Rushinek A, Rushinek S F
Using financial ratios to predict insolvency
JBusR 1987 FEB VOL 15:1 p 93-100.

(11402)
Lawrence E C, Bear R M
Corporate bankruptcy prediction and the impact of leases
JBFA 1986 WINTER VOL 13:4 p 571-585

(11403)
Frydman H, Altman E I, Kao D L
Introducing recursive partitioning for financial classification : The case of financial distress
JF 1985 MAR VOL 40:1 p 269-291.

(11404)
Gentry J A, Newbold P, Whitford D T
Predicting bankruptcy: If cash flow's not the bottom line, what is?
FAJ 1985 SEP-OCT VOL 41 p 47-58.

(11405)
Kharbanda O P, Stallworthy E A
Corporate failure: prediction, panacea and prevention
McGraw, 1985.

(11406)
Zavgren C V
Assessing the vulnerability to failure of American industrial firms : a logistic analysis
JBFA 1985 SPRING VOL 12:1 p 19-45

(11407)
Altman E I
Introduction: Company and country risk models
JBankF 1984 VOL 8 p 151.

(11408)
Altman E I
The success of business failure prediction models: An international survey
JBankF 1984 VOL 8 p 171.

(11409)
Appetiti S
Identifying unsound firms in Italy: An attempt to use trend variables
JBankF 1984 VOL 8 p 269.

(11410)
Argenti J
Predicting corporate failure
ICAEW, 1984.

(11411)
Giroux G A, Wiggins C E
An events approach to corporate bankruptcy
JBR 1984 AUTUMN VOL 15:3.

(11412)
Izan H Y
Corporate distress in Australia
JBankF 1984 VOL 8 p 303.

(11413)
Lincoln M
An empirical study of the usefulness of accounting ratios to describe levels of insolvency risk
JBankF 1984 VOL 8 p 321.

(11414)
Marcus A J, Shaked I
The relationship between accounting measures and prospective probabilities of insolvency: an application to the banking industry
FR 1984 MAR VOL 19:1.

(11415)
Micha B
Analysis of business failures in France
JBankF 1984 VOL 8 p 281.

(11416)
Saini K G, Bates P S
A survey of the quantitative approaches to
country risk analysis
JBankF 1984 VOL 8 p 341.

(11417)
Schmidt R
Early warning of debt rescheduling
JBankF 1984 VOL 8 p 357.

(11418)
Taffler R J
Empirical models for the monitoring of U K
corporations
JBankF 1984 VOL 8 p 199.

(11419)
Takahashi K, Kurokawa Y, Watase K
Corporate bankruptcy prediction in Japan
JBankF 1984 VOL 8 p 229.

(11420)
Tamari M
The use of a bankruptcy forecasting model to
analyze corporate behavior in Israel
JBankF 1984 VOL 8 p 293..

(11421)**Von Stein J H, Ziegler W**
The prognosis and surveillance of risks from
commercial credit borrowers
JBankF 1984 VOL 8 p 249.

(11422)
Altman E I
Corporate financial distress: a complete guide to
predicting, avoiding and dealing with bankruptcy
Wiley, 1983.

(11423)
Altman E I, Spivack J
Predicting bankruptcy: The Value Line relative
financial strength system vs. the zeta bankruptcy
classification approach
FAJ 1983 NOV-DEC VOL 39 p 60-67.

(11424)
Booth P J
Decomposition measures and the prediction of
financial failure
JBFA 1983 SPRING VOL 10:1 p 67-82

(11425)
Hennawy R H A El, Morris R C
The significance of base year in developing failure
prediction models
JBFA 1983 SUMMER VOL 10:2 p 209-224

(11426)
Richardson F M, Davidson L F
An exploration into bankruptcy discriminant
model sensitivity
JBFA 1983 VOL 10:2 p 195.

(11427)
Taffler R J
The assessment of company solvency and
performance using a statistical model
Accounting and Business Research 1982 VOL 52
p 295-307.

(11428)
Taffler R J
Forecasting company failure in the UK using
discriminant analysis and financial ratio data
JRSS Series A 1982 VOL 145 p 342-358.

(11429)
Walker R G, Wilkins T, Zimmer I
The effect of consolidated statements on loan
officers' assessments of ability to repay
AJM 1982 DEC VOL 7.

(11430)
Castagna A D, Matolcsy Z P
The market characteristics of failed companies:
Extensions and further evidence
JBFA 1981 WINTER VOL 8:4 p 467.

(11431)
Scapens R W, Ryan R J, Fletcher L
Explaining corporate failure: a catastrophe theory
approach
JBFA 1981 SPRING VOL 8:1 p 1-26

(11432)
Collins R A
An empirical comparison of bankruptcy prediction
models
FIN MGMT 1980 SUMMER VOL 9 p 52.

(11433)
Dambolena I G, Khoury S J
Ratio stability and corporate failure
JF 1980 SEP VOL 35:4 p 1017-1026.

(11434)
Largay J A, Stickney C P
Cash flows, ratio analysis and the W.T. Grant
Company bankruptcy
FAJ 1980 JUL-AUG VOL 36 p 51-54.

(11435)
Ohlson J A
Financial ratios and the probabilistic prediction of
bankruptcy
JAR 1980 SPRING VOL 18:1 p 109-131.

(11436)
Norton C L, Smith R E
A comparison of general price level and historical
cost financial statements in the prediction of
bankruptcy
AR 1979 JAN VOL 54:1 p 72-87.

(11437)
Vinso J D
A determination of the risk of ruin
JFQA 1979 MAR VOL 14 p 77.

(11438)
Altman E I
Examining Moyer's re-examination of forecasting
financial failure
FIN MGMT 1978 WINTER VOL 7 p 76.

(11439)
Altman E I, Eisenbeis R A
Financial applications of discriminant analysis: A
clarification
JFQA 1978 MAR VOL 13 p 185.

(11440)
Moyer R C
Forecasting financial failure: A re-examination
FIN MGMT 1977 SPRING VOL 6 p 11.

(11441)
Joy O M, Tollefson J O
On the financial applications of discriminant
analysis
JFQA 1975 DEC VOL 10 p 723.

(11442)
Libby R
Accounting ratios and the prediction of failure:
some behavioral evidence
JAR 1975 SPRING VOL 13:1 p 150-161.

(11443)
Altman E I, Margain M, Schlosser M
Financial and statistical analysis for commercial
loan evaluation: A French experience
JFQA 1974 MAR VOL 9 p 195.

(11444)
Altman E I
Predicting railroad bankruptcies in America
BellJ 1973 SPRING VOL 4:1 p 184-211.

(11445)
Edmister R O
An empirical test of financial ratio analysis for
small business failure prediction
JFQA 1972 MAR VOL 7 p 1477-1494.

(11446)
Meyer P A, Pifer H W
Prediction of bank failures
JF 1970 SEP VOL 25 p 853-868.

(11447)
Altman E I
Financial ratios, discriminant analysis and the
prediction of corporate bankruptcy
JF 1968 SEP VOL 23 p 589-609.

(11448)
Beaver W H
Financial ratios and predictors of failure
JAR 1966 Suppl (Empirical Research in
Accounting: Selected Studies) p 77-111.

31.72   Bankruptcy procedures

(11449)
Brown D T
Claimholder incentive conflicts in reorganization:
the role of bankruptcy law
RFS 1989 VOL 2:1 p 109.

(11450)
White M J
The corporate bankruptcy decision
JEP 1989 SPRING VOL 3:2 p 129-152.

(11451)
Boyes W J, Faith R L
Some effects of the Bankruptcy Reform Act of
1978
JLE 1986 VOL 29:1 p 139-150.

(11452)
Scott J A, Smith T C
The effect of the Bankruptcy Reform Act of 1978
on small business loan pricing
JFE 1986 MAY VOL 16:1 p 119-140

(11453)
Cork K, Weiss G A eds.
European insolvency practitioners' handbook: the
AEPPC compendium of insolvency law and
practice
Macmillan, 1984.

(11454)
Shepard L
Personal failures and the Bankruptcy Reform Act
of 1978
JLE 1984 VOL 27:2 p 419.

(11455)
Aivazian V A, Callen J L
Reorganization in bankruptcy and the issue of
strategic risk
JBank F 1983 VOL 7 p 119.

(11456)
Baldwin C Y, Mason S P
The resolution of claims in financial distress : the
case of Massey Ferguson
JF 1983 MAY VOL 38:2 p 505-516.

(11457)
LoPucki L
The debtor in full control - systems failure under
Chapter 11 of the Bankruptcy Code?
American Bankruptcy Law Journal 1983 SPRING
VOL 57 p 99-126.

(11458)
Ang J S, Chua J H
Coalitions, the me first rule, and the liquidation
decision
BellJ 1980 SPRING VOL 11:1 p 355-359.

(11459)
Levine R L, Sherman H D
Trade-offs in the new bankruptcy law
HBR 1980 MAR-APR VOL 58:2 p 46-52.

(11460)
White M J
Public policy toward bankruptcy: me first and
other priority rules
BellJ 1980 AUTUMN VOL 11:2 p 550-564.

(11461)
Bulow J I, Shoven J B
The bankruptcy decision
BellJ 1978 AUTUMN VOL 9:2 p 437-456.

(11462)
Van Horne J C
Optimal initiation of bankruptcy proceedings by
debt holders
JF 1976 VOL 31 p 897.

(11463)
Pye G, Tezel A
Optimal foreclosure policies
MSci 1974 OCT VOL 21:2 p 141-147.

31.73   Bankruptcy costs

(11464)
Cutler D M, Summers L H
The costs of conflict resolution and financial
distress: evidence from the Texaco-Pennzoil
litigation
RandJ 1988 SUMMER VOL 19:2 p 157-172.

(11465)
Robertson D K, Tress R B
Bankruptcy costs: Evidence from small-firm liquidations
AJM 1985 JUN VOL 10 p 49-60.

(11466)
Altman E I
A further empirical investigation of the bankruptcy cost question
JF 1984 SEP VOL 39:4 p 1067-1089.

(11467)
Kalaba R E
Estimation of implicit bankruptcy costs
JF 1984 JUL VOL 39:3 p 629-645.

(11468)
White M J
Bankruptcy costs and the new bankruptcy code
JF 1983 MAY VOL 38:2 p 477-488.

(11469)
Ang J S, Chua J H, McConnell J J
The administrative costs of corporate bankruptcy: a note
JF 1982 MAR VOL 37:1 p 219-226.

(11470)
Warner J B
Bankruptcy costs: some evidence
JF 1977 MAY VOL 32:2 p 337-348.

31.74 Effect of bankruptcy on security returns

(11471)
Hradsky G T, Long R D
High-yield default losses and the return performance of bankrupt debt
FAJ 1989 JUL-AUG VOL 45 p 38-49.

(11472)
Morse D, Shaw W
Investing in bankrupt firms
JF 1988 DEC VOL 43:5 p 1193-1206.

(11473)
Zavgren C V, Dugan M T, Reeve J M
The association between probabilities of bankruptcy and market responses a test of market anticipation
JBFA 1988 SPRING VOL 15:1 p 27-46..

(11474)**Skantz T R, Marchesini R**
The effect of voluntary corporate liquidation on shareholder wealth
JFR 1987 SPRING VOL 10:1 p 65-75.

(11475)
Fraser D R, Richards R M
The Penn Square failure and the inefficient market
JPM 1985 SPRING VOL 11:3 p 34-36.

(11476)
Katz S, Lilien S, Nelson B
Stock market behavior around bankruptcy model distress and recovery predictions
FAJ 1985 JAN-FEB VOL 41:1 p 70-74.

(11477)
Clark T A, Weinstein M I
The behavior of the common stock of bankrupt firms
JF 1983 MAY VOL 38:2 p 489-504.

(11478)
Hennawy R H A El, Morris R C
Market anticipation of corporate failure in the UK
JBFA 1983 AUTUMN VOL 10:3 p 359-372

(11479)
Altman E I, Brenner M
Information effects and stock market response to signs of firm deterioration
JFQA 1981 MAR VOL 16:1 p 35-51

(11480)
Aharony J, Jones C P, Swary I
An analysis of risk and return characteristics of corporate bankruptcy using capital market data
JF 1980 SEP VOL 35:4 p 1001-1016.

(11481)
Altman E I
Corporate bankruptcy potential, stockholder returns and share valuation
JF 1969 DEC VOL 24 p 887-900.

(11482)
Beaver W H
Market prices, financial ratios and the prediction of failure
JAR 1968 AUTUMN VOL 6 p 179-192.

(11483)
Beesley M E, Littlechild S C
The regulation of privatized monopolies in the United Kingdom
RandJ 1989 AUTUMN VOL 20:3 p 454.

(11484)
Braeutigam R R, Panzar J C
Diversification incentives under "price-based" and "cost-based" regulation
RandJ 1989 AUTUMN VOL 20:3 p 373-391.

(11485)
Lewis T R, Sappington D E M
Regulatory options and price-cap regulation
RandJ 1989 AUTUMN VOL 20:3 p 405-416.

(11486)
Mathios A D, Rogers R P
Theimpact of alternative forms of state regulation of AT&T on direct-dial, long-distance telephone rates
RandJ 1989 AUTUMN VOL 20:3 p 437-453.

(11487)
Prager R A
Using stock price data to measure the effects of regulation: the Interstate Commerce Act and the railroad industry
RandJ 1989 SUMMER VOL 20:2 p 280.

(11488)
Ronen J, Srinidhi B
Depreciation policies in regulated companies: which policies are the most efficient?
MSci 1989 VOL 35 p 515.

(11489)
Schmalensee R
Good regulatory regimes
RandJ 1989 AUTUMN VOL 20:3 p 417-436.

(11490)
Sibley D
Asymmetric information, incentives and price-cap regulation
RandJ 1989 AUTUMN VOL 20:3 p 392-404.

(11491)
Baron D P
Regulation and legislative choice
RandJ 1988 AUTUMN VOL 19:3 p 467-477.

(11492)
Lewis T R, Sappington D E M
Regulating a monopolist with unknown demand
AER 1989 VOL 78:5 p 986-998.

(11493)
Lewis T R, Sappington D E M
Regulating a monopolist with unknown demand and cost functions
RandJ 1988 AUTUMN VOL 19:3 p 438-457.

(11494)
Mayo J W, Flynn J E
The effects of regulation on R & D: theory and evidence
JB 1988 VOL 61 p 321.

(11495)
Wallace M S, Watson S B, Yandle B
Environmental regulation: a financial market test
QREB 1988 VOL 28:1 p 69.

(11496)
Demski J S, Sappington D E M
Hierarchical regulatory control
RandJ 1987 AUTUMN VOL 18:3 p 369-383.

(11497)
Schipper K, Thompson R, Weil R L
Disentangling interrelated effects of regulatory changes on shareholder wealth: the case of motor carrier deregulation
JLE 1987 VOL 30:1 p 67-100.

(11498)
Eckel C C, Vermaelen T
Internal regulation: the effects of government ownership on the value of the firm
JLE 1986 VOL 29:2 p 381-404.

(11499)
Smith R T, Bradley M, Jarrell G
Studying firm-specific effects of regulation with stock market data: an application to oil price regulation
RandJ 1986 WINTER VOL 17:4 p 467-489.

(11500)
Kolbe A L, Myers S C, Tye W B
Regulation and capital formation in the oil pipeline industry
Transportation Journal 1984 SPRING.

(11501)
Smith L D
Quantifying risk for establishing rates of return in
regulated industries
EE 1983 SUMMER VOL 28:4 p 267-292.

(11502)
Brennan M J, Schwartz E S
Regulation and corporate investment policy
JF 1982 MAY VOL 37:2 p 289-300.

(11503)
Gelhorn E, Pierce R J
Regulated industries
West Pub, 1982.

(11504)
Howe K M, Rasmussen E F
Public utility economics and finance
P-H, 1982.

(11505)
Tussing A R, Barlow C C
The decline and fall of regulation in the natural
gas industry
Energy Journal 1982 VOL 3:4.

(11506)
Fromm G ed.
Studies in public regulation
MIT Pr, 1981.

(11507)
Marshall W J, Yawitz J B, Greenberg E
Optimal regulation under uncertainty
JF 1981 SEP VOL 36:4 p 909-921.

(11508)
Schwert G W
Using financial data to measure effects of
regulation
JLE 1981 VOL 24:1 p 121.

(11509)
Edwards F R
Managerial objectives in regulated industries:
expense-preference behavior in banking
JPE 1977 FEB VOL 85:1 p 147-162.

(11510)
Peltzman S
Toward a more general theory of regulation
JLE 1976 VOL 19 p 211.

(11511)
Elton E J, Gruber M J, Lieber Z
Financial models of regulated firms valuation,
optimum investment and financing for the firm
subject to regulation
JF 1975 MAY VOL 30:2 p 401-426.

(11512)
McNicol D L
The comparative statics properties of the theory
of the regulated firm
BellJ 1973 AUTUMN VOL 4:2 p 428-453.

32.1   Utilities

(11513)
Chandy P R, Karafiath I
The effect of the WPPSS crisis on utility common
stock returns
JBFA 1989 AUTUMN VOL 16:4 p 531.

(11514)
Nelson J P, Roberts M J
Ramsey numbers and the role of competing
interest groups in electric utility regulation
QREB 1989 AUTUMN VOL 29:3 p 21-42.

(11515)
Prager R A
The effects of regulatory policies on the cost of
debt for electric utilities: an empirical
investigation
JB 1989 VOL 62:1 p 33-54.

(11516)
Aharony J, Falk H, Swary I
Information content of dividend increases: The
case of regulated utilities
JBFA 1988 AUTUMN VOL 15:3 p 401-414.

(11517)
Evans L, Garber S
Public-utility regulators are only human: a
positive theory of rational constraints
AER 1988 VOL 78:3 p 444-462.

(11518)
Fraser D R, Kolari J W, Uselton G C
Intraindustry risk changes in the electric utility industry since Three-Mile-Island
JBusR 1988 MAY VOL 16:3 p 225-234.

(11519)
Gort M, Wall R A
Foresight and public utility regulation
JPE 1988 FEB VOL 96:1 p 177-188.

(11520)
Schmidt R H
Deregulating electric utilities: issues and implications
F R Bk Dallas Ec Rev 1987 SEP.

(11521)
Barrett W B, Heuson A J, Kolb R W
The effect of Three Mile Island on utility bond risk premia : a note
JF 1986 MAR VOL 41:1 p 255-261.

(11522)
Binder J J
Measuring the effects of regulation with stock price data
RandJ 1985 SUMMER VOL 16:2 p 167-183.

(11523)
Brigham E F, Shome D K, Vinson S R
The risk premium approach to measuring a utility's cost of equity
FIN MGMT 1985 SPRING VOL 14 p 33-45.

(11524)
Pettway R H, Radcliffe R C
Impacts of new equity sales upon electric utility share prices
FIN MGMT 1985 SPRING VOL 14 p 16-26.

(11525)
Baron D P, Besanko D
Regulation, asymmetric information and auditing
RandJ 1984 WINTER VOL 15:4 p 447-470.

(11526)
Beedles W L
Electric utility returns and the market model
JBusR 1984 VOL 12 p 463-480..

(11527)Bower D H, Bower R S, Logue D E
Arbitrage pricing theory and utility stock returns.

JF 1984 SEP VOL 39:4 p 1041-1054

(11528)
Nelson R A
Regulation, capital vintage, and technical change in the electric utility industry
REStat 1984 VOL 66 p 59.

(11529)
Patterson C S
The financing objectives of large U S electric utilities
FIN MGMT 1984 SUMMER VOL 13 p 15-23.

(11530)
Bowen R M, Castanias R P, Daley L A
Intra-industry effects of the accident at Three Mile Island
JFQA 1983 MAR VOL 18:1 p 87-111

(11531)
Hill J, Schneeweis T
The effect of Three Mile Island on electric utility stock prices : a note.
JF 1983 SEP VOL 38:4 p 1285-1292.

(11532)
Patterson C S
The effects of leverage on the revenue requirements of public utilities
FIN MGMT 1983 AUTUMN VOL 12 p 29-39.

(11533)
Finnerty J D
The stock market's reaction to the switch from flow-through to normalization
FIN MGMT 1982 WINTER VOL 11 p 36-47.

(11534)
Bowen R M
Valuation of earnings components in the electric utility industry
AR 1981 JAN VOL 56:1 p 1-22.

(11535)
Finnerty J D
The behavior of electric utility common stock prices near the ex-dividend date
FIN MGMT 1981 WINTER VOL 10 p 59-69.

(11536)
Deschamps B, Mehta D R, Walker M C
The influence of dividends, growth, and leverage on share prices in the electric utility industry: An econometric study
JFQA 1980 DEC VOL 15 p 1163.

(11537)
McAdams L
How to anticipate utility bond rating changes
JPM 1980 FALL VOL 7:1 p 56-60.

(11538)
Trebing H M
Structural change and regulatory reform in the utilities industries
AER 1980 VOL 70 P+P p 388-392.

(11539)
Berndt E R, Sharp K C, Watkins G C
Utility bond rates and tax normalization
JF 1979 DEC VOL 34:5 p 1211-1220.

(11540)
Bhandari S B, Soldofsky R M, Boe W J
Bond quality rating changes for electric utilities: A multivariate analysis
FIN MGMT 1979 SPRING VOL 8 p 74.

(11541)
Edelman R B
The impact on electric utility bond ratings of substituting debt for preferred stock
FIN MGMT 1979 SPRING VOL 8 p 51.

(11542)
Frankfurter G, Strauss R, Young A
Utility equities and the allocation of capital resources
QREB 1979 VOL 19:4 p 45.

(11543)
Gandhi D K, Tysseland M S
Depreciation, inflation, and capital formation in public utilities: one possible approach toward a solution
QREB 1979 VOL 19:1 p 99.

(11544)
Loeb M, Magat W A
A decentralized method for utility regulation
JLE 1979 VOL 22:2 p 399.

(11545)
Gilster J E Jr, Linke C M
More on the estimation of beta for public utilities: Biases resulting from structural shifts in true beta
FIN MGMT 1978 AUTUMN VOL 7 p 60.

(11546)
Brigham E F, Pettway R H
Capital budgeting by utilities
FIN MGMT 1973 AUTUMN VOL 2 p 11.

(11547)
Koller R H II
Why regulate utilities?   To control price discrimination
JLE 1973 VOL 16 p 191.

(11548)
Myers S C
A simple model of firm behavior under regulation and uncertainty
BellJ 1973 SPRING VOL 4:1 p 304-315.

(11549)
Areeda P E
Antitrust laws and public utility regulation
BellJ 1972 SPRING VOL 3:1 p 42-57.

(11550)
Miller M H, Modigliani F
Some estimates of the cost of capital to the electric utility industry, 1954-57
AER 1966 JUN VOL 56 p 333-391.

(11551)
Lerner E M, Carleton W T
The capital structure problem of a regulated public utility
PUF 1965 JUL 8 VOL 76 p 24-32.

(11552)
Bosland C C
The valuation of public utility enterprises by the Securities and Exchange Commission
JF 1961 MAR VOL 16 p 52-64.

32.11   Rate regulation

(11553)
Bussa R G, Linke C M, Zumwalt J K
Rate of return - rate base issues in utility
regulation
EE 1987 SPRING VOL 32:3 p 231-245.

(11554)
Goldenberg D H
Market power and the required return to electric
utilities
FR 1987 FEB VOL 22:1.

(11555)
Linke C M, Zumwalt J K
The irrelevance of compounding frequency in
determining a utility's cost of equity
FIN MGMT 1987 AUTUMN VOL 16 p 65.

(11556)
Rothwell G S, Eastman K A
A note on allowed and realized rates of return on
the US electric utility industry
JIE 1987 SEP VOL 36:1 p 105-110.

(11557)
Marcus A J
Depreciation rules and rate shock in rate of
return regulation
FIN MGMT 1986 WINTER VOL 15 p 61-68.

(11558)
Goldberg M A, Vora A
Dividend yield, regulation, and the return on U.S.
public utility stocks
JBFA 1985 VOL 12:1 p 47.

(11559)
Kolbe A L, Lincoln R A, Read J A
Determining the cost of capital for utility
investments
(in Kydes A S and Geraghty D M eds., Energy
markets in the longer term: Planning under
uncertainty. N Holland, 1985.)

(11560)
Kolbe A L, Myers S C, Tye W B
Inflation and the rate of return regulation
(in Research in Transportation Economics, Vol 2.
JAI Press, 1985.)

(11561)
Revsine L
Hedonism and rate shock
MCFJ 1985 SUMMER VOL 3 p 57-64.

(11562)
Soldofsky R A
Return premiums on utility common stocks
QREB 1985 SPRING VOL 25:2 p 60-72.

(11563)
Greenwald B C
Rate base selection and the structure of
regulation
RandJ 1984 SPRING VOL 15:1 p 85-98.

(11564)
Kalotay A J
Refunding   considerations   under   rate-based
regulation
FIN MGMT 1984 AUTUMN VOL 13 p 11-14.

(11565)
Kolbe A L, Read J A, Hall G R
Estimating the rate of return to public utilities
MIT Pr, 1984.

(11566)
Linke C M, Zumwalt J K
Estimation biases in discounted cash flow analyses
of equity capital cost in rate regulation
FIN MGMT 1984 AUTUMN VOL 13 p 15-21.

(11567)
Dukes W, Chandy P R
Rate of return and risk for public utilities
PUF 1983 SEP 1 p 35-41.

(11568)
Roll R, Ross S A
Regulation, the capital asset pricing model and
the arbitrage pricing theory
PUF 1983 MAY 26 p 22-28.

(11569)
Brennan M J, Schwartz E S
Consistent regulatory policy under uncertainty
BellJ 1982 AUTUMN VOL 13:2 p 506-540.

(11570)
Foster J R, Holmberg S R
Earnings regulation under inflation
Washington, DC: The Institute for Study of
Regulation, 1982.

(11571)
Sherman R, Visscher M
Rate-of-return regulation and two-part tariffs
QJE 1982 VOL 97 p 27.

(11572)
Arzac E R, Marcus M
Flotation cost allowance in rate of return
regulation : a note
JF 1981 DEC VOL 36:5 p 1199-1202.

(11573)
Cooley P L
A review of the use of beta in regulatory
proceedings
FIN MGMT 1981 WINTER VOL 10 p 75-81.

(11574)
Taggart R A
Rate-of-return regulation and utility capital
structure decisions
JF 1981 MAY VOL 36:2 p 383-393.

(11575)
Clarke R G
The effect of fuel adjustment clauses on the
systematic risk and market values of electric
utilities
JF 1980 MAY VOL 35:2 p 347-358.

(11576)
Das S P
On the effect of rate-of-return regulation under
uncertainty
AER 1980 VOL 70 p 456-460.

(11577)
Greenwald B C
Admissable rate bases fair rates of return and the
structure of regulation
JF 1980 MAY VOL 35:2 p 359-368.

(11578)
Harrington D R
The changing use of the capital asset pricing
model in utility regulation
PUF 1980 FEB 14 p 28-30.

(11579)
Hyman L S, Egan J M
The utility stock market: Regulation, risk and
beta
PUF 1980 FEB 14 p 21-27..

(11580)**Litzenberger R H, Ramaswamy K, Sosin
H B**
On the CAPM approach to the estimation of a
public utility's cost of equity capital
JF 1980 MAY VOL 35:2 p 369-387.

(11581)
Thompson H E
Estimating the cost of equity capital for electric
utilities: 1958-1976
BellJ 1979 AUTUMN VOL 10:2 p 619-635.

(11582)
Clarke R G
The impact of a fuel adjustment clause on the
regulated firm's value and cost of capital
JFQA 1978 NOV VOL 13 p 745.

(11583)
Hagerman R L, Ratchford B T
Some determinants of allowed rates of return on
equity to electric utilities
BellJ 1978 SPRING VOL 9:1 p 46-55.

(11584)
Panzar J C, Sibley D S
Public utility pricing under risk: The case of
self-rationing
AER 1978 VOL 68 p 888-895.

(11585)
Pettway R H
On the use of beta in regulatory proceedings: an
empirical examination
BellJ 1978 SPRING VOL 9:1 p 239-248.

(11586)
Brigham E F, Crum R L
On the use of the CAPM in public utility rate cases
FIN MGMT 1977 SUMMER VOL 6 p 7.

(11587)
Gordon M J
Comparison of historical cost and general price level adjusted cost rate base regulation
JF 1977 VOL 32 p 1501.

(11588)
Howe K M
Public utility valuation and cost-of-capital models: some regulatory and economic considerations
QREB 1977 VOL 17:4 p 57.

(11589)
Callen J, Mathewson G F, Mohring H
The benefits and costs of rate of return regulation
AER 1976 VOL 66 p 290-297.

(11590)
Hagerman R L
Finance theory in rate hearings
FIN MGMT 1976 SPRING VOL 5 p 18.

(11591)
Keran M W
Inflation, regulation, and utility stock prices
BellJ 1976 SPRING VOL 7:1 p 268-280.

(11592)
Peles Y C, Stein J L
The effect of rate of return regulation is highly sensitive to the nature of the uncertainty
AER 1976 JUN VOL 66:3 p 278-289.

(11593)
West D A, Eubank A A
An automatic cost of capital adjustment model for regulating public utilities
FIN MGMT 1976 SPRING VOL 5 p 23.

(11594)
Kennedy T E
Incentive pricing and utility regulation
QJE 1975 VOL 89 p 311.

(11595)
Leland H E
Regulation of natural monopolies and the fair rate of return
BellJ 1974 SPRING VOL 5:1 p 3-15.

(11596)
Schmalensee R
Examining the costs and benefits of utility regulation
QREB 1974 VOL 14:2 p 51.

(11597)
Davis B E, Sparrow F T
Valuation models in regulation
BellJ 1972 FALL VOL 3:2 p 544-568.

(11598)
Mann P C, Seifried E J
Pricing in the case of publicly owned electric utilities
QREB 1972 VOL 12:2 p 77.

(11599)
Myers S C
The application of finance theory to public utility rate cases
BellJ 1972 SPRING VOL 3:1 p 58-97.

(11600)
Elton E J, Gruber M J
Valuation and the cost of capital for regulated industries
JF 1971 JUN VOL 26 p 661-670.

(11601)
Litzenberger R H, Rao C U
Estimates of the marginal rate of time preference and average risk aversion of investors in electric utility shares, 1960-1966
BellJ 1971 SPRING p 265-277.

32.111 Regulatory lag

(11602)
Carleton W T, Chambers D R, Lakonishok J
Inflation risk and regulatory lag
JF 1983 MAY VOL 38:2 p 419-431.

(11603)
John K, Saunders A
Asymmetry of information regulatory lags and
optimal incentive contracts : theory and evidence
JF 1983 MAY VOL 38:2 p 391-404.

(11604)
Kolb R W, Morin R A, Gay G D
Regulation regulatory lag and the use of futures
markets
JF 1983 MAY VOL 38:2 p 405-418.

(11605)
Elton E J, Gruber M J
Optimal investment & financing patterns for a
firm subject to regulation with a lag
JF 1977 VOL 32 p 1485.

32.12   Investment and pricing

(11606)
Braeutigam R R
An analysis of fully distributed cost pricing in
regulated industries
BellJ 1980 SPRING VOL 11:1 p 182-196.

(11607)
Livingstone J L, Sherali A D
Construction work in progress in the public utility
rate base: The effect of multiple projects and
growth
FIN MGMT 1979 SPRING VOL 8 p 42.

(11608)
Peck S C
Alternative investment models for firms in the
electric utilities field
BellJ 1974 AUTUMN VOL 5:2 p 420-458.

33 Foreign exchange

(11609)
Bank of England
The market in foreign exchange in London
BEQB 1989 NOV VOL 29:4 p 531-535.

(11610)
Douch N
The economics of foreign exchange: a practical
market approach
Woodhead-Faulkner, 1989.

(11611)
Miller M et al, eds.
Blueprints for exchange-rate management
Academic Press, 1989.

(11612)
Flight H, Lee-Swan B
All you need to know about exchange rates
Sidgwick & Jackson, 1988.

(11613)
Haynes S E
Identification of interest rates and international
capital flows
REStat 1988 VOL 70 p 103.

(11614)
Kenen P B
Managing exchange rates
Routledge, 1988.

(11615)
Gerlach S
Exchange rates: a review essay
JME 1987 VOL 19 p 137.

(11616)
Swanson P E
Capital market integration over the past decade:
the case of the US dollar
JIMF 1987 JUN VOL 6:2 p 215-226.

(11617)
Bank of England
The market for foreign exchange in London
BEQB 1986 VOL 26 p 379-382.

(11618)
Coninx R G F
Foreign exchange dealer's handbook. 2nd ed
Woodhead-Faulkner, 1986.

(11619)
Kettell B, Hodson D
A businessman's guide to the foreign exchange
market
Graham & Trotman, 1985.

(11620)
Andrews M D
Recent trends in the U.S. foreign exchange
market
F R Bk New York Q Rev 1984 SUMMER VOL
9:2.

(11621)
Choi J J
Consumption basket, exchange risk, and asset
demand
JFQA 1984 SEP VOL 19:3 p 287-298.

(11622)
Chrystal K A
A guide to foreign exchange markets
F R Bk St Louis Rev 1984 VOL 66:3.

(11623)
Engel C, Frankel J
Why interest rates react to money
announcements: an explanation from the foreign
exchange market
JME 1984 VOL 13 p 31.

(11624)
Lewellen W G, Ang J S
Inflation, currency exchange rates and the
international securities market
JBusR 1984 VOL 12 p 97-114.

(11625)
Shapiro A C
Currency risk and relative price risk
JFQA 1984 DEC VOL 19:4 p 365-373.

(11626)
Weisweiller R
Introduction to foreign exchange. 2nd ed
Woodhead-Faulkner, 1984.

(11627)
Bell S, Kettell B
Foreign exchange handbook
Graham & Trotman, 1983.

(11628)
Logue D E, Senbet L W
External currency market equilibrium and its implications for regulation of the eurocurrency market
JF 1983 MAY VOL 38:2 p 435-449.

(11629)
Riehl H, Rodriguez R M
Foreign exchange and money markets
McGraw, 1983.

(11630)
Walmsley J
The foreign exchange handbook: a user's guide
Wiley, 1983.

(11631)
Goodman L S
Bank foreign exchange operations: a portfolio approach
JMCB 1982 FEB VOL 14:1 p 84-91.

(11632)
Lucas R
Interest rates and currency prices in a two-country world
JME 1982 VOL 10 p 335..

(11633)**Callier P**
One way arbitrage foreign exchange and securities markets : a note
JF 1981 DEC VOL 36:5 p 1177-1189.

(11634)
Eaker M R
The numeraire problem and foreign exchange risk
JF 1981 MAY VOL 36:2 p 419-426.

(11635)
Revey P A
Evolution and growth of the United States foreign exchange market
F R Bk New York Q Rev 1981 AUTUMN VOL 6:3.

(11636)
Bank of England
The foreign exchange market in London
BEQB 1980 VOL 20 p 437.

(11637)
Coninx R G F
Foreign exchange today. Rev ed
Woodhead-Faulkner, 1980.

(11638)
Cornell B
The denomination of foreign trade contracts once again
JFQA 1980 NOV VOL 15 p 933.

(11639)
Fama E F, Farber A
Money, bonds and foreign exchange
AER 1979 VOL 69 p 639-649.

(11640)
Aliber R Z
Exchange risk and corporate international finance
Macmillan, 1978.

(11641)
Frenkel J A, Johnson H G eds.
Economics of exchange rates: selected studies
Addison-Wes, 1978.

(11642)
Mehra R
On the financing and investment decisions of multinational firms in the presence of exchange risk
JFQA 1978 JUN VOL 13 p 227.

(11643)
Sunder S
Accuracy of exchange valuation rules
JAR 1978 AUTUMN VOL 16:2 p 341-367.

(11644)
Bowers D A
A warning note on empirical research using foreign exchange rates
JFQA 1977 JUN VOL 12 p 315.

(11645)
Enders W
Portfolio balance and exchange rate stability
JMCB 1977 AUG VOL 9:3 p 491-499.

(11646)
McCallum B T
The role of speculation in the Canadian forward exchange market: some estimates assuming rational expectations
REStat 1977 MAY VOL 59:2 p 145-151.

(11647)
Riehl H, Rodriguez R M
Foreign exchange markets: a guide to foreign currency operations
McGraw, 1977.

(11648)
Westerfield J
Empirical properties of foreign exchange rates under fixed and floating regimes
JME 1977 SPRING VOL 3.

(11649)
Shapiro A C
Exchange rate changes, inflation and the value of the multinational corporation
JF 1975 MAY VOL 30:2 p 485-502.

(11650)
Heckerman D
On the effects of exchange risk
JIntE 1973 NOV p 379-387.

(11651)
Hayes D J
Translating foreign currencies
HBR 1972 JAN-FEB VOL 50:1 p 6ff.

(11652)
Canterbery E R
A theory of foreign exchange speculation under alternative systems
JPE 1971 MAY-JUN VOL 79 p 407-436.

(11653)
Evitt H E
A manual of foreign exchange. 7th ed by Raymond F Pither
Pitman, 1971.

(11654)
Einzig P
A textbook of foreign exchange. 2nd ed
Macmillan, 1969.

(11655)
Feldstein M
Uncertainty and forward exchange speculation
REStat 1968 MAY VOL 50 p 182-192.

(11656)
Obst N P
A connection between speculation and stability in the foreign exchange market
SEJ 1967 JUL VOL 34 p 146-149.

(11657)
Stein J L
The nature and efficiency of the foreign exchange market
Princeton U Intl Fin, Oct 1962.

(11658)
Tsiang S C
A theory of foreign-exchange speculation under a floating exchange system
JPE 1958 OCT VOL 66 p 399-418.

33.1   Foreign exchange systems

(11659)
Bentley P ed.
A world guide to exchange control regulations 1989. Vol 1: Arab Gulf States to Japan; Vol 2: Kenya to Zaire
Euromoney Publications, 1989.

(11660)
Greenwood J, Williamson S D
International financial intermediation and aggregate fluctuations under alternative exchange-rate regimes
JME 1989 VOL 23 p 401.

(11661)
Wasserfallen W
Flexible exchange rates: a closer look
JME 1989 VOL 23 p 511.

(11662)
McKibbin W J, Sachs J D
Comparing the global performance of alternative exchange arrangements
JIMF 1988 DEC VOL 7:4 p 387-410.

(11663)
Stockman A C, Hernandez D A
Exchange controls, capital controls, and international financial markets
AER 1988 JUN VOL 78:3 p 362-374.

(11664)
Levich R M
ECU: The European Currency Unit
Euromoney Publications, 1987.

(11665)
Levich R M, Sommariva A eds.
The ECU market: current developments and future prospects of the European Currency Unit
Lexington Bks, 1987.

(11666)
Pozo S
The ECU as international money
JIMF 1987 JUN VOL 6:2 p 195-206.

(11667)
Brooks S et al.
The exchange rate environment
Croom Helm, 1986.

(11668)
Makin J H, Sauer R D
Exchange rate determination with changes in the policy regime: the yen/dollar rate
REStat 1986 VOL 68 p 164.

(11669)
Goedhuys D ed.
The foreign exchange market in the 1980s: the views of market participants
New York: Group of Thirty, 1985.

(11670)
Aschauer D, Greenwood J
A further exploration in the theory of exchange rate regimes
JPE 1983 VOL 91 p 868.

(11671)
Williamson J
The exchange rate system
Washington, DC: Institute for International Economics, 1983.

(11672)
Blin J M et al.
Flexible exchange rates and international business
British-North American Committee, 1981.

(11673)
Helpman E
An exploration in the theory of exchange-rate regimes
JPE 1981 VOL 89 p 865.

(11674)
White B B, Woodbury J R III
Exchange rate systems and international capital market integration
JMCB 1980 MAY VOL 12:2 p 175-183.

(11675)
Pardee S E
How well are the exchange markets functioning?
F R Bk New York Q Rev 1979 SPRING VOL 4:1.

(11676)
Bank of England
The investment currency market
BEQB 1976 VOL 16 p 314-322.

(11677)
Turnovsky S J
The relative stability of alternative exchange rate systems in the presence of random disturbances
JMCB 1976 FEB VOL 8:1 p 29-50.

(11678)
Fountain J
Premium dollars
FAJ 1975 MAR-APR VOL 31 p 70-76.

(11679)
Sohmen E
Flexible exchange rates. Theory and controversy.
Rev ed
U of Chicago Pr, 1969.

(11680)
Stein J L
The optimum foreign exchange market
AER 1963 JUN VOL 53 p 384-402.

33.2 Behavior of spot exchange rates

(11681)
Baillie R T, Bollerslev T
Common stochastic trends in a system of exchange rates
JF 1989 MAR VOL 44:1 p 167-182.

(11682)
Delbecque B
Exchange-rate dynamics in a model with imperfect capital mobility and asset substitutability
EER 1989 VOL 33 p 1161.

(11683)
Frankel J
Flexible exchange rates: experience versus theory
JPM 1989 WINTER VOL 15:2 p 45-54.

(11684)
Gavin M
The stock market and exchange-rate dynamics
JIMF 1989 VOL 8 p 181.

(11685)
Giovannini A, Jorion P
The time variation of risk and return in the foreign exchange and stock markets
JF 1989 JUN VOL 44:2 p 307-326..

(11686)**Guidotti P E**
Exchange rate determination, interest rates, and an integrative approach to the demand for money
JIMF 1989 VOL 8 p 29.

(11687)
Hakkio C, Rush M
Market efficiency and cointegration: an application to the sterling and deutschemark exchange markets
JIMF 1989 VOL 8 p 75.

(11688)
Hodrick R J
Risk, uncertainty, and exchange rates
JME 1989 VOL 23 p 433.

(11689)
Isaac A G
Exchange rate volatility and currency substitution
JIMF 1989 VOL 8 p 277.

(11690)
Koedijk K, Schotman P
Dominant real exchange rate movements
JIMF 1989 VOL 8 p 517.

(11691)
Kritzman M
Serial dependence in currency returns: investment implications
JPM 1989 FALL VOL 16:1 p 96-102.

(11692)
Krugman P R
Exchange-rate instability
MIT Pr, 1989.

(11693)
Lewis K K
Changing beliefs and systematic rational forecast errors with evidence from foreign exchange
AER 1989 VOL 79:4 p 621-636.

(11694)
Lewis K K
Can learning affect exchange-rate behavior? The case of the dollar in the early 1980's
JME 1989 VOL 23 p 79.

(11695)
Raymond A J, Weil G
Diversification benefits and exchange-rate changes
JBFA 1989 AUTUMN VOL 16:4 p 455.

(11696)
Reagan P B, Stulz R M
Contracts, delivery lags, and currency risk
JIMF 1989 VOL 8 p 89.

(11697)
Thornton D L
The effect of unanticipated money on the money and foreign exchange markets
JIMF 1989 VOL 8 p 573.

(11698)
Akgiray V, Booth G G
Mixed diffusion-jump process modeling of exchange rate movements
REStat 1988 VOL 70 p 631.

(11699)
Blackburn K
Collapsing exchange rate regimes and exchange
rate dynamics: some further examples
JIMF 1988 DEC VOL 7:4 p 373-386.

(11700)
Canarella G, Pollard S K
Efficiency in foreign exchange markets: a vector
autoregression approach
JIMF 1988 SEP VOL 7:3 p 331-346.

(11701)
MacDonald R
Floating exchange rates: theories and evidence
Unwin Hyman, 1988.

(11702)
Marini G
Flexible exchange rates and stabilizing speculation
JIMF 1988 JUN VOL 7:2 p 251-257.

(11703)
Tabellini G
Learning and the volatility of exchange rates
JIMF 1988 JUN VOL 7:2 p 243-250.

(11704)
Tygier C
Basic handbook of foreign exchange: a guide to
foreign exchange dealing. 2nd ed
Euromoney Publications, 1988.

(11705)
Wasserfallen W
The behavior of flexible exchange rates: evidence
and implications
FAJ 1988 SEP-OCT VOL 44 p 36-44.

(11706)
Ahking F W, Miller S M
A comparison of the stochastic processes of
structural and time-series exchange-rate models
REStat 1987 VOL 69 p 496.

(11707)
Dornbusch R
Exchange rates and prices
AER 1987 VOL 77 p 93-106.

(11708)
Frankel J A, Stock J J
Regression vs. volatility tests of the efficiency of
foreign exchange markets
JIMF 1987 MAR VOL 6:1 p 31-48.

(11709)
Fratianni M, Hur H-D, Kang H
Random walk and monetary causality in five
exchange markets
JIMF 1987 DEC VOL 6:4 p 505-514.

(11710)
Macdonald R, Ta G
The Singapore dollar: tests of the efficient
markets hypothesis and the role of news
AE 1987 MAY VOL 19:5 p 569-580.

(11711)
Stulz R M
An   equilibrium   model   of   exchange   rate
determination and asset pricing with nontraded
goods and imperfect information
JPE 1987 VOL 95 p 1024-1040.

(11712)
Woo W T
Some evidence of speculative bubbles in the
foreign exchange markets
JMCB 1987 NOV VOL 19:4 p 499-514.

(11713)
Chiang T C
On the predictors of the future spot rates - a
multi-currency analysis
FR 1986 FEB VOL 21:1.

(11714)
Glick R
Real exchange rates, imperfect information, and
economic disturbances
F R Bk San Francisco Ec Rev 1986 FALL.

(11715)
Kenen P B, Rodrik D
Measuring and analyzing the effects of short-term
volatility in real exchange rates
REStat 1986 VOL 68 p 311.

(11716)
Batten D S, Thornton D L
The discount rate, interest rates and foreign exchange rates: an analysis with daily data
F R Bk St Louis Rev 1985 VOL 67:2.

(11717)
Nowak M
Black markets in foreign exchange
FD 1985 VOL 22:1.

(11718)
Tandon K, Simaan Y
The reaction of effective exchange rates to information about inflation
FR 1985 MAY VOL 20:2.

(11719)
Wasserfallen W, Zimmermann H
The behavior of intra-daily exchange rates
JBankF 1985 VOL 9 p 55.

(11720)
Bank of England
The variability of exchange rates: measurement and effects
BEQB 1984 VOL 24 p 346-349.

(11721)
Bilson J F O, Marston R C
Exchange rate theory and practice
U of Chicago Pr, 1984.

(11722)
Rose A K, Selody J G
Exchange market efficiency: a semi-strong test using multiple markets and daily data
REStat 1984 VOL 66 p 669.

(11723)
Bhandari J S
An alternative theory of exchange rate dynamics
QJE 1983 VOL 98 p 337.

(11724)
Frankel J A
Estimation of portfolio-balanced functions that are mean-variance optimizing: the mark and the dollar
EER 1983 VOL 23:3.

(11725)
Krueger A O
Exchange-rate determination
Cambridge U Pr, 1983.

(11726)
Madura J
Empirical measurement of exchange rate betas
JPM 1983 SUMMER VOL 9:4 p 43-46.

(11727)
Hakkio C S
Exchange rate determination and the demand for money
REStat 1982 VOL 64 p 681.

(11728)
McFarland J W, Pettit R R, Sung S K
The distribution of foreign exchange price changes: trading day effects and risk measurement
JF 1982 JUN VOL 37:3 p 693-715.

(11729)
Mussa M
A model of exchange rate dynamics
JPE 1982 VOL 90 p 74.

(11730)
Pigott C
The influence of real factors on exchange rates
F R Bk San Francisco Ec Rev 1982 WINTER.

(11731)
Saurman D S
Transactions costs, foreign exchange demands, and the expected rates of change of exchange rates
JMCB 1982 FEB VOL 14:1 p 20-32.

(11732)
Wihlborg C
Interest rates, exchange rate adjustments and currency risks: an empirical study 1967-1975
JMCB 1982 FEB VOL 14:1 p 58-75.

(11733)
Brown K H
Effects of changes in the discount rate on the foreign exchange value of the dollar: 1973 to 1978.
QJE 1981 VOL 96 p 551.

(11734)
Gupta S
A note on the efficiency of black markets in foreign currencies
JF 1981 JUN VOL 36:3 p 705-710.

(11735)
Kareken J, Wallace N
On the indeterminacy of equilibrium exchange rates
QJE 1981 VOL 96 p 207.

(11736)
Longworth D
Testing the efficiency of the Canadian-U.S. exchange market under the assumption of no risk premium
JF 1981 MAR VOL 36:1 p 43-49.

(11737)
Garman M B, Kohlgen S W
Inflation and foreign exchange rates under production and monetary uncertainty
JFQA 1980 NOV VOL 15 p 949.

(11738)
Rodriguez C A
The role of trade flows in exchange rate determination: a rational expectations approach
JPE 1980 VOL 88 p 1148..

(11739)**Stockman A C**
A theory of exchange rate determination
JPE 1980 VOL 88 p 673.

(11740)
Throop A W
Managed floating and the independence of interest rates
F R Bk San Francisco Ec Rev 1980 SUMMER.

(11741)
Deardorff A V
One-way arbitrage and its implications for the foreign exchange markets
JPE 1979 VOL 87 p 351.

(11742)
Levich R M
On the efficiency of markets for foreign exchange
(in Dornbusch R and Frenkel J A eds., International economic policy: An assessment of theory and evidence. Johns Hopkins U Pr, 1979.)

(11743)
Mudd D R
Do rising U.S. interest rates imply a stronger dollar?
F R Bk St Louis Rev 1979 VOL 61:6.

(11744)
Mussa M
Empirical regularities in the behavior of exchange rates and theories of the foreign exchange market
(in Brunner K and Meltzer A H eds., Policies for employment, prices and exchange rates. N Holland, 1979.)

(11745)
Wilson C A
Anticipated shocks and exchange rate dynamics
JPE 1979 VOL 87 p 639.

(11746)
Makin J H
Portfolio theory and the problem of foreign exchange risk
JF 1978 VOL 33 p 517.

(11747)
Branson W H, Halttunen H, Masson P
Exchange rates in the short run: the dollar-Deutschemark rate
EER 1977 VOL 10 p 303.

(11748)
Brittain B
Tests of theories of exchange rate determination
JF 1977 MAY VOL 32:2 p 519.

(11749)
Burt J, Kaen F R, Booth G G
The behavior of foreign exchange spot prices
JF 1977 VOL 32 p 1325.

(11750)
Farber A, Roll R, Solnik B
An empirical study of exchange risk under fixed
and flexible exchange rates
JME 1977 SPRING VOL 3.

(11751)
Kohlhagen S W
The stability of exchange rate expectations and
Canadian flows
JF 1977 VOL 32 p 1657.

(11752)
Logue D E, Sweeney R J
"White-noise" in imperfect markets: The case of
the Franc/Dollar exchange rate
JF 1977 VOL 32 p 761.

(11753)
Roll R, Solnik B
A pure foreign exchange asset pricing model
JIntE 1977 MAY VOL 7 p 161-179.

(11754)
Westerfield J M
An examination of foreign exchange risk under
fixed and floating rate regimes
JIntE 1977 VOL 7 p 181-200.

(11755)
Giddy I H
An integrated theory of exchange rate equilibrium
JFQA 1976 DEC VOL 11 p 883.

(11756)
Fieleke N S
Exchange-rate flexibility and the efficiency of the
foreign-exchange markets
JFQA 1975 SEP VOL 10 p 409.

(11757)
Giddy I H, Dufey G
The random behavior of flexible exchange rates:
Implications for forecasting
JIBS 1975 SPRING VOL 6.

(11758)
Lewis K A, Breen F F
Empirical issues in the demand for currency: A
multinational study
JF 1975 VOL 30 p 1065.

(11759)
Arndt S W
International short term capital movements: a
distributed lag model of speculation in foreign
exchange
Em 1968 JAN VOL 36 p 59-70.

(11760)
Glahe F R
An empirical study of the foreign exchange
market: test of a theory
Princeton U Pr, 1967.

(11761)
Poole W
Speculative prices as random walks: an analysis of
ten time series of flexible exchange rates
SEJ 1967 APR VOL 33 p 468-478.

33.21 Purchasing power parity

(11762)
McNown R, Wallace M S
National price levels, purchasing power parity,
and cointegration: a test of four high inflation
economies
JIMF 1989 VOL 8 p 533.

(11763)
Benninga S, Protopapasakis A
The equilibrium pricing of exchange rates and
assets when trade takes time
JIMF 1988 JUN VOL 7:2 p 129-150.

(11764)
Dornbusch R
Exchange rates and inflation
MIT Pr, 1988.

(11765)
McClure J H
PPP, interest rate parities, and the modified
Fisher effect in the presence of tax agreements: a
comment
JIMF 1988 SEP VOL 7:3 p 347-350.

(11766)
Taylor M P
An empirical examination of long-run purchasing
power parity using cointegration techniques
AE 1988 OCT VOL 20:10 p 1369-1382.

(11767)
Taylor M P, McMahon P C
Long-run purchasing power parity in the 1920s
EER 1988 VOL 32:1.

(11768)
Edison H J
Purchasing power parity in the long run: a test of
the dollar/pound exchange rate (1890-1978)
JMCB 1987 AUG VOL 19:3 p 376-387.

(11769)
Huang R D
Expectations of exchange rates and differential
inflation rates : further evidence on purchasing
power parity in efficient markets
JF 1987 MAR VOL 42:1 p 69-79.

(11770)
Takagi S
Testing the multilateral version of purchasing
power parity: an application to Burma and Jordan
under the SDR peg, 1981-5
AE 1987 MAR VOL 19:3 p 367-380.

(11771)
Pippenger J
Arbitrage and efficient markets interpretations of
purchasing power parity: theory and evidence
F R Bk San Francisco Ec Rev 1986 WINTER.

(11772)
Booth G G, Duggan J E, Koveos P E
Deviations from purchasing power parity, relative
inflation, and exchange rates: the recent
experience
FR 1985 MAY VOL 20:2.

(11773)
Davutyan N, Pippenger J
Purchasing power parity did not collapse during
the 1970's
AER 1985 VOL 75 p 1151-1158.

(11774)
Koveos P, Seifert B
Purchasing power parity and black markets
FIN MGMT 1985 AUTUMN VOL 14 p 40-46.

(11775)
Bilson J F O
Purchasing power parity as a trading strategy.
JF 1984 JUL VOL 39:3 p 715-725.

(11776)
Junge G
Purchasing power parity in the 1920s and the
1970s: a note
EER 1984 VOL 26:1-2.

(11777)
Koh A T
Money shocks and deviations from purchasing
power parity
JME 1984 VOL 14 p 105.

(11778)
Miller S
Purchasing power parity and relative price
variability: evidence from the 1970s
EER 1984 VOL 26:3.

(11779)
Adler M, Lehmann B
Deviations from purchasing power parity in the
long run
JF 1983 DEC VOL 38:5 p 1471-1487.

(11780)
Shapiro A C
What does purchasing power parity mean?
JIMF 1983 DEC VOL 2 p 295-318.

(11781)
Blejer M I, Hillman A L
A proposition on short-run departures from the
law-of-one-price: unanticipated   inflation,
relative-price dispersion, and commodity arbitrage
EER 1982 VOL 17:1.

(11782)
Crouhy-Veyrac L, Crouhy M, Melitz J
More about the law of one price
EER 1982 VOL 18:3.

(11783)
Officer L H
Purchasing power parity and exchange rates: theory, evidence and relevance
JAI Pr, 1982.

(11784)
Barrett R N
Purchasing power parity and the equilibrium exchange rate
JMCB 1981 MAY VOL 13:2 p 227-233.

(11785)
Eun C S
Global purchasing power view of exchange risk
JFQA 1981 DEC VOL 16:5 p 639-650.

(11786)
Frenkel J A
The collapse of purchasing power parities during the 1970s
EER 1981 VOL 16 p 145-165.

(11787)
Niehans J
Static deviations from purchasing-power parity
JME 1981 VOL 7 p 57.

(11788)
Cornell B
Inflation, relative price changes and exchange risk
FIN MGMT 1980 AUTUMN VOL 9 p 30.

(11789)
Prakken J L
The exchange rate and domestic inflation
F R Bk New York Q Rev 1979 SUMMER VOL 4:2.

(11790)
Roll R
Violations of the "law of one price" and their implications for differentially denominated assets
(in Sarnat M and Szego S eds., International finance and trade. Ballinger, 1979.)

(11791)
Kyle J F
Financial assets non-traded goods and devaluation
REStud 1978 FEB VOL 45:139 p 155-163..

(11792)**Chen C-N**
Currency denominations and the price level

JPE 1976 VOL 84 p 179.

(11793)
Officer L H
The purchasing power parity theory of exchange rates: A review article
IMF 1976 MAR.

(11794)
Wyman H E
Analysis of gains or losses from foreign monetary items: an application of purchasing power parity concepts
AR 1976 JUL VOL 51:3 p 545-558.

(11795)
Holmes J M
The purchasing power parity theory: In defense of Gustav Cassel as a modern theorist
JPE 1967 OCT VOL 75 p 686-695.

(11796)
Balassa B
The purchasing power parity doctrine: A reappraisal
JPE 1964 DEC VOL 72 p 584-596.

(11797)
Cassel G
The present situation of the foreign exchanges
EJ 1916 VOL 26 p 62-65.

33.22 Exchange rate forecasts

(11798)
Froot K A, Ito T
On the consistency of short-run and long-run exchange rate expectations
JIMF 1989 VOL 8 p 487.

(11799)
Pesaran M H
Consistency of short-term and long-term expectations
JIMF 1989 VOL 8 p 511.

(11800)
Schinasi G J, Swamy P A V B
The out-of-sample forecasting performance of exchange rate models when coefficients are allowed to change
JIMF 1989 VOL 8 p 375.

(11801)
Manzur M
How much are exchange rate forecasts worth?
AJM 1988 JUN VOL 13 p 93-114.

(11802)
Wolff C C P
Exchange rates, innovations and forecasting
JIMF 1988 MAR VOL 7:1 p 49-62.

(11803)
Dudley L
Explaining forecasting bias: the case of real exchange rate variance
AE 1987 SEP VOL 19:9 p 1249-1260.

(11804)
Sweeney R J
Beating the foreign exchange market
JF 1986 MAR VOL 41:1 p 163-182.

(11805)
Levich R M
Evaluating the performance of the forecasters
(in Ensor R ed., The management of foreign exchange risk, 2nd ed. Euromoney Publications, 1982.)

(11806)
Levich R M
How to compare chance with forecasting expertise
Euromoney 1981 AUG p 61-78.

(11807)
Levich R M
Analyzing the accuracy of foreign exchange advisory services: Theory and evidence
(in Levich R and Wihlborg C eds., Exchange risk and exposure. Heath, 1980.)

(11808)
Goodman S H
Foreign exchange rate forecasting techniques: implications for business and policy
JF 1979 MAY VOL 34:2 p 415-427.

(11809)
Serfall W D Jr
You can't outguess the foreign exchange market
HBR 1976 MAR-APR VOL 54:2 p 134-137.

33.3 Currency forwards and futures

(11810)
Braga F S, Martin L J, Meilke K D
Cross hedging the Italian lira/US dollar exchange rate with Deutsch mark futures
JFM 1989 VOL 9:2 p 87-100.

(11811)
Callen J L, Chan M W L, Kwan C C Y
Spot and forward exchange rates: a causality analysis
JBFA 1989 SPRING VOL 16:1 p 105.

(11812)
Froot K A, Frankel J A
Forward discount bias: is it an exchange risk premium?
QJE 1989 FEB VOL 104:1 p 139-162.

(11813)
Garman M
Immunizing foreign exchange contracts against swap rate and volatility risks
Journal of International Financial Management & Accounting 1989 SPRING VOL 1:1 p 41-54.

(11814)
Herbst A F, Kare D D, Caples S C
Hedging effectiveness and minimum risk hedge ratios in the presence of autocorrelation: foreign currency futures
JFM 1989 VOL 9:3 p 185-198.

(11815)
Huang R D
An analysis of intertemporal pricing for forward exchange contracts
JF 1989 MAR VOL 44:1 p 183-194.

(11816)
Levine R
The pricing of forward exchange rates
JIMF 1989 VOL 8 p 163.

(11817)
Chrystal K A, Thornton D L
On the informational content of spot and forward
exchange rates
JIMF 1988 SEP VOL 7:3 p 321-330.

(11818)
Eytan T H, Harpaz G, Krull S
The pricing of dollar index futures contracts
JFM 1988 APR VOL 8:2 p 127-140.

(11819)
Hammer J A
Hedging and risk aversion in the foreign currency
market
JFM 1988 VOL 8:6 p 657-686.

(11820)
Lypny G J
Hedging foreign exchange risk with currency
futures: portfolio effects
JFM 1988 VOL 8:6 p 703-716.

(11821)
Peterson D R, Tucker A L
Implied spot rates as predictors of currency
returns: a note
JF 1988 MAR VOL 43:1 p 247-258.

(11822)
Quirk P J et al.
Policies for developing forward foreign exchange
markets
Washington, DC: International Monetary Fund,
1988.

(11823)
Doukas J, Rahman A
Unit roots tests: Evidence from the foreign
exchange futures market
JFQA 1987 MAR VOL 22 p 101-108.

(11824)
Garbers H
A misspecification analysis of the relationship
between spot and forward exchange rates
EER 1987 VOL 31:7.

(11825)
Ramaswamy K, Sundaresan S M
The pricing of derivative assets in foreign
exchange markets
(in Khoury S and Gosh A eds., Recent
developments in international banking and
finance. Lexington Bks, 1987.)

(11826)
Tucker A L
Foreign exchange option prices as predictors of
equilibrium forward exchange rates
JIMF 1987 SEP VOL 6:3 p 283-295.

(11827)
Grammatikos T
Intervalling effects and the hedging performance
of foreign currency futures
FR 1986 FEB VOL 21:1.

(11828)
Ott M, Veugelers P T W M
Forward exchange rates in efficient markets: the
effects of news and changes in monetary policy
regimes
F R Bk St Louis Rev 1986 VOL 68:6.

(11829)
Thomas L R
A winning strategy for currency-futures
speculation
JPM 1985 FALL VOL 12:1 p 65-69.

(11830)
Eaton J, Turnovsky S J
The forward exchange market, speculation and
exchange market intervention
QJE 1984 VOL 99 p 45.

(11831)
Yang H C
The value of a forward contract in foreign
currencies
JBFA 1984 WINTER VOL 11:4 p 575-577

(11832)
Brown B
The forward market in foreign exchange: a study
in market-making, arbitrage and speculation
Croom Helm, 1983.

(11833)
Maldonado R, Saunders A
Foreign exchange futures and the law of one price
FIN MGMT 1983 SPRING VOL 12 p 19-23.

(11834)
Levis M
The behaviour of the Australian forward exchange market
AJM 1982 JUN VOL 7 p 61-74.

(11835)
Cornell B, Reinganum M R
Forward and future prices: evidence from the foreign exchange markets
JF 1981 DEC VOL 36:5 p 1035-1045.

(11836)
Phaup E D
A reinterpretation of the modern theory of forward exchange rates
JMCB 1981 NOV VOL 13:4 p 477-484.

(11837)
Krasker W S
The "peso problem" in testing the efficiency of forward exchange markets
JME 1980 VOL 6 p 269

(11838)
Stein J L
The dynamics of spot and forward prices in an efficient foreign exchange market with rational expectations
AER 1980 VOL 70 p 565-583.

(11839)
Levi M D
Underutilization of forward markets or rational behaviour
JF 1979 SEP VOL 34:4 p 1013-1017.

(11840)
Bilson J F O
Rational expectations and the exchange rate
(in Frenkel J A and Johnson H G eds., The economics of exchange rates: Selected studies. Addison-Wes, 1978.)

(11841)
Levich R M
Tests of forecasting models and market efficiency in the international money market
(in Frenkel J A and Johnson H G eds., The economics of exchange rates: Selected studies. Addison-Wes, 1978.)

(11842)
Frenkel J A
The forward exchange rate, expectations and the demand for money: The German hyperinflation
AER 1977 VOL 67 p 653-670.

(11843)
Messina R J, Oldfield G S
Forward exchange price determination in continuous time
JFQA 1977 SEP VOL 12 p 473.

(11844)
Adler M, Dumas B
Portfolio choice and the demand for forward exchange
AER 1976 VOL 66 P+P p 332-339..

(11845)**Folks W R Jr**
The optimal level of forward exchange transactions
JFQA 1973 JAN VOL 8:1 P 105-110.

(11846)
Upson R B
Random walk and forward exchange rates: A spectral analysis
JFQA 1972 SEP VOL 7 p 1897.

(11847)
Stoll H R
An empirical study of the forward exchange market under fixed and flexible exchange rate systems
Canadian Journal of Economics 1968 FEB VOL 1 p 55-78.

(11848)
Einzig P
A dynamic theory of forward exchange. 2nd ed
Macmillan, 1967.

(11849)
Frevert P W
A theoretical model of the forward exchange
[Parts 1-2]
IntER 1967 JUN VOL 8 p 307-326; IntER 1967
OCT VOL 8 p 153-167.

(11850)
Grubel H G
Forward exchange, speculation and the
international flow of capital
Stanford U Pr, 1966.

(11851)
Sohmen E
The theory of forward exchange
International Finance Section, Dept of
Economics, Princeton U, 1966.

(11852)
Grubel H G
Profits from forward exchange speculation
QJE 1965 MAY VOL 79 p 248-262.

(11853)
Goldstein H N
The implications of triangular arbitrage for
forward exchange policy
JF 1964 SEP VOL 19 p 544-551.

(11854)
Aliber R Z
More about counter-speculation in the forward
exchange markets
JPE 1963 DEC VOL 71 p 589-590.

(11855)
Grubel H G
A neglected aspect of forward exchange theory
and policy
JF 1963 SEP VOL 18 p 537-548.

(11856)
Auten J H
Counter-speculation and the forward exchange
market
JPE 1961 FEB VOL 69 p 49-55.

(11857)
Auten J H
Monetary policy and the forward exchange market
JF 1961 DEC VOL 16 p 546-558.

33.31 Term premia

(11858)
Cornell B
The impact of data errors on measurement of
foreign exchange risk premium
JIMF 1989 VOL 8 p 147.

(11859)
Sibert A
The risk premium in the foreign exchange market
JMCB 1989 VOL 21 p 49-65.

(11860)
Bomhoff E J, Koedijk K G
Bilateral exchange rates and risk premia
JIMF 1988 JUN VOL 7:2 p 205-220.

(11861)
Boyer R S, Adams F C
Forward premia and risk premia in a simple
model of exchange rate determination
JMCB 1988 NOV VOL 20:4 p 633-644.

(11862)
Frankel J A
Recent estimates of time-variation in the
conditional variance and in the exchange risk
premium
JIMF 1988 MAR VOL 7:1 p 115-125.

(11863)
Giovannini A, Jorion P
Foreign exchange risk premia volatility once again
JIMF 1988 MAR VOL 7:1 p 111-114.

(11864)
Lyons R K
Test of the foreign exchange risk premium using
the expected second moments implied by option
pricing
JIMF 1988 MAR VOL 7:1 p 91-108.

(11865)
Mark N C
Time-varying betas and risk premia in the pricing
of forward foreign exchange contracts
JFE 1988 VOL 22 p 335.

(11866)
Pagan A
A note on the magnitude of risk premia
JIMF 1988 MAR VOL 7:1 p 109-110.

(11867)
Giovannini A, Jorion P
Interest rates and risk premia in the stock market
and in the foreign exchange market
JIMF 1987 MAR VOL 6:1 p 107-124.

(11868)
Koedijk K G, Ott M
Risk aversion, efficient markets and the forward
exchange rate
F R Bk St Louis Rev 1987 VOL 69:10.

(11869)
Woolf C P
Forward foreign exchange rates, expected spot
rates and premia : a signal extraction approach.
JF 1987 JUN VOL 42:2 p 395-406.

(11870)
Hodrick R J
The covariation of risk premiums and expected
future spot exchange rates
JIMF 1986 MAR VOL 5 p 5-21.

(11871)
Domowitz I, Hakkio C S
Conditional variance and the risk premium in the
foreign exchange market
JIntE 1985 AUG VOL 19 p 47-66.

(11872)
Korajczyk R A
The pricing of forward contracts for foreign
exchange
JPE 1985 VOL 93 p 346-368.

(11873)
Mark N C
On time varying risk premia in the foreign
exchange market: an econometric analysis
JME 1985 VOL 16 p 3.

(11874)
Fama E F
Forward and spot exchange rates
JME 1984 VOL 14 p 319.

(11875)
Hodrick R J, Srivastava S
An investigation of risk and return in forward
foreign exchange
JIMF 1984 APR VOL 3 p 5-29.

(11876)
Hsieh D A
Tests of rational expectations and no risk
premium in forward exchange markets
JIntE 1984 AUG VOL 17 p 173-184.

(11877)
Agmon T, Arad R
Currency-related risk and risk premium in the
world's currency market
EER 1983 VOL 22:3.

(11878)
Hansen L P, Hodrick R J
Risk-averse speculation in the forward foreign
exchange market: and econometric analysis of
linear models
(in Frenkel J A ed., Exchange rates and
international macroeconomics. U of Chicago Pr,
1983.)

(11879)
Frankel J A
In search of the exchange risk premium: a six
currency test assuming mean-variance optimization
JIMF 1982 VOL 1 p 255-274.

(11880)
Jacobs R L
The effect of errors in variables on tests for a risk
premium in forward exchange rates
JF 1982 JUN VOL 37:3 p 667-677.

(11881)
Hakkio C S
Expectations and the forward exchange rate
IntER 1981 OCT VOL 22:3 p 663-678.

(11882)
Hakkio C S
The term structure of the forward premium
JME 1981 VOL 8 p 41.

(11883)
Hansen L P, Hodrick R J
Forward exchange rates as optimal predictors of future spot rates: An econometric analysis
JPE 1980 VOL 88 p 829.

(11884)
Cornell B
Spot rates, forward rates and exchange market efficiency
JFE 1977 VOL 5 p 55

33.32 Interest rate parity

(11885)
Clinton K
Transaction costs and covered interest arbitrage: theory and evidence
JPE 1988 APR VOL 96:2 p 358-370.

(11886)
Cumby R E
Is it risk? explaining deviations from uncovered interest parity
JME 1988 VOL 22:2 p 279-300.

(11887)
Poitras G
Arbitrage boundaries, Treasury bills, and covered interest parity
JIMF 1988 DEC VOL 7:4 p 429-446.

(11888)
Bahmani-Oskooee M, Bas S P
Transaction costs and the interest parity theorem
JPE 1985 VOL 93 p 793.

(11889)
Browne F X
Departures from interest rate parity: Further evidence
JBankF 1983 VOL 7 p 253.

(11890)
Dooley M P, Isard P
Capital controls, political risk and deviations from interest-rate parity
JPE 1980 VOL 88 p 370.

(11891)
Kupferman M, Levi M D
Taxation and interest rate parity
FAJ 1978 JUL-AUG p 61-64.

(11892)
Allen W A
A note on uncertainty, transaction costs and interest parity
JME 1977 VOL 3 p 367.

(11893)
Frenkel J A, Levich R M
Transaction costs and interest arbitrage: tranquil versus turbulent periods
JPE 1977 DEC VOL 85:6 p 1209-1226.

(11894)
Agmon T, Bronfield S
The international mobility of short-term covered arbitrage capital
JBFA 1975 SUMMER VOL 2:2 p 269-280.

(11895)
Frenkel J A, Levich R M
Covered interest arbitrage: Unexploited profits?
JPE 1975 VOL 83 p 325.

(11896)
Aliber R Z
The interest rate parity theorem: a reinterpretation
JPE 1973 NOV-DEC VOL 81:6 p 1451-1459.

(11897)
Frenkel J A
Elasticities and the interest parity theory
JPE 1973 MAY-JUN VOL 81:3 p 741-747..

(11898)**Van Belle J J**
Spot rates, forward rates, and the interest rate differentials
JMCB 1973 NOV VOL 5:4 p 997-999.

(11899)
Siegel J J
Risk, interest and forward exchange
QJE 1972 VOL 86 p 303.

(11900)
Branson W H
The minimum covered interest differential needed
for international arbitrage activity
JPE 1969 NOV-DEC VOL 77 p 1028-1035.

(11901)
White W H
Interest rate differences, forward exchange
mechanism and scope for short-term capital
movements
IMF 1963 NOV.

33.4 Managing foreign exchange risk

(11902)
Black F
Universal hedging: optimizing currency risk and
reward in international equity portfolios
FAJ 1989 JUL-AUG VOL 45 p 16-22.

(11903)
Kritzman M
A simple solution for optimal currency hedging
FAJ 1989 NOV-DEC VOL 45 p 47-50.

(11904)
Soenen A, Aggarwal R
Cash and foreign exchange management: theory
and corporate practice in three countries
JBFA 1989 WINTER VOL 16:5 p 599.

(11905)
Thomas L R
The performance of currency-hedged foreign
bonds
FAJ 1989 MAY-JUN VOL 45 p 25-31.

(11906)
Khoury S J, Chan K H
Hedging foreign exchange risk: selecting the
optimal tool
MCFJ 1988 WINTER VOL 5 p 40-52.

(11907)
Perold A F, Schulman E C
The free lunch in currency hedging: implications
for investment policy and performance standards
FAJ 1988 MAY-JUN VOL 44 p 45-52.

(11908)
Pfeil E von
Effective control of currency risks: a practical,
comprehensive guide
Macmillan, 1988.

(11909)
Donaldson J A
Corporate currency risk: a reappraisal. 2nd ed
Financial Times Business Information, 1987.

(11910)
Glassman D
Exchange rate risk and transaction costs: evidence
from bid-ask spreads
JIMF 1987 DEC VOL 6:4 p 479-490.

(11911)
Ross D et al.
International treasury management
Woodhead-Faulkner, 1987.

(11912)
Abuaf N
The nature and management of foreign exchange
risk
MCFJ 1986 FALL VOL 4 p 30-44.

(11913)
Chown J F
Tax efficient forex management
Professional Publishing, 1986.

(11914)
Flood E Jr, Lessard D R
On the measurement of operating exposure to
exchange rates: A conceptual approach
FIN MGMT 1986 SPRING VOL 15 p 25-36.

(11915)
Grammatikos T, Saunders A, Swary I
Returns and risks of US bank foreign currency
activities
JF 1986 JUL VOL 41:3 p 671-683.

(11916)
Hekman C R
Don't blame currency values for strategic errors
MCFJ 1986 FALL VOL 4 p 45-55.

(11917)
Kaufold H, Smirlock M
Managing corporate exchange and interest rate
exposure
FIN MGMT 1986 AUTUMN VOL 15 p 64-72.

(11918)
Lessard D R
Finance and global competition: exploiting
financial scope and coping with volatile exchange
rates
MCFJ 1986 FALL VOL 4 p 6-29.

(11919)
Bhandari J S ed.
Exchange rate management under uncertainty
MIT Pr, 1985.

(11920)
Eaker M R, Grant D
Optimal hedging of uncertain and long-term
foreign exchange exposure
JBankF 1985 VOL 9 p 221.

(11921)
Heckman C R
A financial model of foreign exchange exposure
JIBS 1985 SUMMER.

(11922)
Madura J, Reiff W
A hedge strategy for international portfolios
JPM 1985 FALL VOL 12:1 p 70-74.

(11923)
Shapiro A C
Currency risk and country risk in international
banking
JF 1985 JUL VOL 40:3 p 881-893.

(11924)
Adler M, Dumas B
Exposure to currency risk: Definition and
measurement
FIN MGMT 1984 SUMMER VOL 13 p 41-50.

(11925)
Garner C K, Shapiro A
A practical method of assessing foreign exchange
risk
MCFJ 1984 FALL VOL 2 p 6-17.

(11926)
Lessard D R, Sharp D
Measuring the performance of operations subject
to fluctuating exchange rates
MCFJ 1984 FALL VOL 2 p 18-30.

(11927)
Banker P
You are the best judge of foreign risks
HBR 1983 MAR-APR VOL 61:2 p 157-165.

(11928)
Cornell B, Shapiro A C
Managing foreign exchange risks
MCFJ 1983 FALL VOL 1 p 16-31.

(11929)
Dufey G, Srinivasulu S L
The case for corporate management of foreign
exchange risk
FIN MGMT 1983 WINTER VOL 12 p 54-62.

(11930)
Hekman C R
Measuring foreign exchange exposure: A practical
theory and its application
FAJ 1983 SEP-OCT VOL 39 p 59-65.

(11931)
Herring R J ed.
Managing foreign exchange risk
Cambridge U Pr, 1983.

(11932)
Business International
New directions in managing currency risk:
changing corporate strategies and systems under
FAS No. 52
New York: Business International, 1982.

(11933)
Ensor R ed.
The management of foreign exchange risk
Euromoney Publications, 1982.

(11934)
Errunza V R, Senbet L W
The effects of international operations on the
market value of the firm: theory and evidence
JF 1981 MAY VOL 36:2 p 401-417

(11935)
Fieleke N S
Foreign-currency positioning by U.S. firms: some
new evidence
REStat 1981 FEB VOL 63:1 p 35-42.

(11936)
Kenyon A
Currency risk management
Wiley, 1981.

(11937)
Levy H
Optimal portfolio of foreign currencies with
borrowing and lending
JMCB 1981 AUG VOL 13:3 p 325-341.

(11938)
Naslund B
Exchange rate variations and the behavior of the
purchasing department.
Omega 1981 VOL 9:4 p 365-370.

(11939)
Rodriguez R M
Corporate exchange risk management: theme and
aberrations
JF 1981 MAY VOL 36:2 p 427-439.

(11940)
Srinivasulu S L
Strategic response to foreign exchange risks
CJWB 1981 SPRING VOL 16:1 p 13-23.

(11941)
Aggarwal R
The management of foreign exchange: Optimal
policies of a multinational company
New York: Arno, 1980.

(11942)
Antl B ed.
Currency risk and the corporation
Euromoney Publications, 1980.

(11943)
Eaker M R
Denomination   decision   for   multinational
transactions
FIN MGMT 1980 AUTUMN VOL 9 p 23.

(11944)
Levich R M,   Wihlborg C G eds.
Exchange risk and exposure: current developments
in international financial management
Lexington Bks, 1980.

(11945)
McRae T W,   Walker D P
Foreign exchange management
P-H, 1980.

(11946)
Rodriguez R M
Foreign exchange in US multinationals
Lexington Bks, 1980.

(11947)
Calderon-Rossell J R
Covering   foreign   exchange   risks   of   single
transactions
FIN MGMT 1979 AUTUMN VOL 8 p 78.

(11948)
Christofides N,   Hewins R D,   Salkin G R
Graph theoretic approaches to foreign exchange
operations
JFQA 1979 SEP VOL 14 p 481.

(11949)
Soenen L A
A portfolio model for foreign exchange exposure
management
Omega 1979 VOL 7:2 p 339-344.

(11950)
Soenen L A
Foreign   exchange   management: a   portfolio
approach
Alphen aan den Rijn, Netherlands: Sijthoff &
Noordhoff, 1979..

(11951)**Soenen L A**
Efficient market implications for foreign exchange
exposure management
De Economist 1979 VOL 127:2.

(11952)
Folks W R Jr
Optimal   foreign   borrowing   strategies   with
operations in forward exchange markets
JFQA 1978 JUN VOL 13 p 245.

(11953)
Levy H, Sarnat M
Exchange rate risk and the optimal diversification
of foreign currency holdings
JMCB 1978 NOV VOL 10:4 p 453-463.

(11954)
Schwab B, Lusztig P
Apportioning foreign exchange risk through the
use of third currencies
FIN MGMT 1978 AUTUMN VOL 7 p 25.

(11955)
Giddy I H
Exchange risk: Whose view?
FIN MGMT 1977 SUMMER VOL 6 p 23.

(11956)
Lessard D R, Lorange P
Currency changes and management control:
resolving the centralization/decentralization
dilemma
AR 1977 JUL VOL 52:3 p 628-637.

(11957)
Logue D E, Oldfield G S
Managing foreign assets when foreign exchange
markets are efficient
FIN MGMT 1977 SUMMER VOL 6 p 16.

(11958)
Denis J
How well does the international monetary market
track the interbank forward market?
FAJ 1976 JAN-FEB VOL 32 p 50-54.

(11959)
Robichek A A, Eaker M R
Debt denomination and exchange risk in
international capital markets
FIN MGMT 1976 AUTUMN VOL 5 p 11.

(11960)
Shapiro A C, Rutenberg D P
Managing exchange risks in a floating world
FIN MGMT 1976 SUMMER VOL 5 p 48.

(11961)
Aliber R Z
Exchange risk, political risk, and investor demand
for external currency deposits
JMCB 1975 MAY VOL 7:2 p 161.

(11962)
Imai Y
Exchange rate risk protection in international
business
JFQA 1975 SEP VOL 10 p 447.

(11963)
Ankrom R K
Top level approach to the foreign exchange
problem
HBR 1974 JUL-AUG VOL 52:4 p 79-90.

(11964)
Rodriguez R M
Management of foreign exchange risk in the U S
multinationals
JFQA 1974 NOV VOL 9 p 849.

(11965)
Shapiro A C, Rutenberg D P
When to hedge against devaluation
MSci 1974 AUG VOL 20:12 p 1514-1530.

(11966)
Dufey G
Corporate finance and exchange rate variations
FIN MGMT 1972 SUMMER VOL 1 p 51.

(11967)
Folks W R Jr
Decision analysis for exchange risk management
FIN MGMT 1972 WINTER VOL 1 p 101.

(11968)
Hoyt N H Jr
The management of currency exchange risk by the
Singer company
FIN MGMT 1972 SPRING VOL 1 p 13.

(11969)
Lietaer B A
Financial management of foreign exchange
MIT Pr, 1971.

34 Real estate

(11970)
Brueggeman W B, Fisher J D, Stone L D
Real estate finance. 8th ed
Irwin, 1989.

(11971)
Conroy R, Miles M
Commercial forestland in the pension portfolio:
the biological beta
FAJ 1989 SEP-OCT VOL 45 p 46-54.

(11972)
Green J
Property development: a bibliography
Joseph Clarke, 1989.

(11973)
Greer G
The new Dow Jones-Irwin guide to real estate
investing
Dow Jones-Irwin, 1989.

(11974)
Sa-Aadu J, Sirmans C F, Benjamin J D
Financing and house prices
JFR 1989 SPRING VOL 12:1 p 83-92.

(11975)
Allen R H
Real estate investment strategy. 3rd ed
SW Pub, 1988.

(11976)
Hartzell D J, Shulman D G, Langetieg T C
A look at real estate duration
JPM 1988 FALL VOL 15:1 p 16-24.

(11977)
Shenkel W M
Real estate finance
Irwin, 1988.

(11978)
Froland C
What determines cap rates on real estate
JPM 1987 SUMMER VOL 13:4 p 77-82.

(11979)
Smith H C, Corgel J B
Real estate perspectives
Irwin, 1987.

(11980)
Webb J R, Rubens J A
How much in real estate? a surprising answer
JPM 1987 SPRING VOL 13:3 p 10-14.

(11981)
Wurtzebach C H, Miles M E
Modern real estate. 3rd ed
Wiley, 1987.

(11982)
Sale T S ed.
Real estate investing
Institute of Chartered Financial Analysts, 1986.

(11983)
Throop A W
Financial deregulation, interest rates, and the
housing cycle
F R Bk San Francisco Ec Rev 1986 SUMMER.

(11984)
Fogler H R
20% in real estate: can theory justify it?
JPM 1984 WINTER VOL 10:2 p 6-13.

(11985)
Fraser W D
Principles of property investment and pricing
Macmillan, 1984.

(11986)
Neidich D, Steinberg T M
Corporate real estate : source of new equity?
HBR 1984 JUL-AUG VOL 62:4 p 76-83.

(11987)
Shenkel W M
Modern real estate principles. 3rd ed
Irwin, 1984.

(11988)
Hendershott P H, Hu S C
The allocation of capital between residential and
nonresidential uses : taxes inflation and capital
market constraints
JF 1983 JUN VOL 38:3 p795-812.

(11989)
Sirmans G S, Smith S D, Sirmans C F
Assumption financing and selling price of
single-family homes.
JFQA 1983 SEP VOL 18:3 p 307-318.

(11990)
Miles M, Esty A
How well do commingled real estate funds perform?
JPM 1982 WINTER VOL 8:2 p 62-68.

(11991)
Titman S
The effects of anticipated inflation on housing market equilibrium
JF 1982 JUN VOL 37:3 p 827-842.

(11992)
Ward C W R
Arbitrage and investment in commercial property
JBFA 1982 SPRING VOL 9:1 p 93-108

(11993)
Webb J R, Curcio R J
Interest rate illusions and real property purchases
JPM 1982 SUMMER VOL 8:4 p 67.

(11994)
Hein S E, Lamb J C Jr
Why the medium-priced home costs so much
F R Bk St Louis Rev 1981 VOL 63:6.

(11995)
Coyne T J, Goulet W M, Picconi M J
Residential real estate versus financial assets
JPM 1980 FALL VOL 7:1 p 20-24.

(11996)
Gau G W, Kohlhepp D B
The financial planning and management of real estate developments
FIN MGMT 1980 SPRING VOL 9 p 46.

(11997)
Kau J B, Keenan D
The theory of housing and interest rates
JFQA 1980 NOV VOL 15 p 833.

(11998)
Brueggeman W B, Peiser R B
Housing choice and relative tenure prices
JFQA 1979 NOV VOL 14 p 735.

(11999)
Edelstein R H
An appraisal of residential property tax regressivity
JFQA 1979 NOV VOL 14 p 753.

(12000)
Noland C W
Assessing hedonic indexes for housing
JFQA 1979 NOV VOL 14 p 783.

(12001)
Aldrich P C, Upton K
Real estate investment for pension funds
HBR 1977 MAY-JUN VOL 55:3 p 14-16.

(12002)
Trippi R R
Estimating the relationship between price and time to sale for investment property
MSci 1977 APR VOL 23:8 p 838-842.

(12003)
Zerbst R H, Brueggeman W B
FHA and V A mortgage discount points and housing prices
JF 1977 VOL 32 p 1766..

(12004)**Hayes S L I, Harlan L M**
Caveat emptor in real estate equities
HBR 1972 MAR-APR VOL 50:2 p 86ff.

(12005)
Pellatt P G K
The analysis of real estate investments under uncertainty
JF 1972 MAY VOL 27 p 459-472.

(12006)
Friedman H C
Real estate investment and portfolio theory
JFQA 1971 MAR VOL 6 p 861-874.

(12007)
Kinnard W N
Income property valuation: principles and techniques of appraising income-producing real estate
Heath, 1971.

(12008)
Hanford L D
Analysis and management of investment property
Inst Real Est Mgmt, 1970.

(12009)
Ring A A
The valuation of real estate. 2nd ed
P-H, 1970.

(12010)
Hoagland H E, Stone L D
Real estate finance. 4th ed
Irwin, 1969.

(12011)
Unger M A
Real estate: principles and practices. 4th ed
SW Pub, 1969.

(12012)
Wendt P F, Cerf A R
Real estate investment analysis and taxation
McGraw, 1969.

(12013)
Hayes S L III, Harlan L M
Real estate as a corporate investment
HBR 1967 JUL-AUG VOL 45 p 144-160.

(12014)
McMichael S L, O'Keefe P T
How to finance real estate. 3rd ed
P-H, 1967.

(12015)
Hanford L D
Investing in real estate
Inst Real Est Mgmt, 1966.

(12016)
Ricks R B, Weston J F
Land as a growth investment
FAJ 1966 JUL-AUG VOL 22 p 69-78.

(12017)
Maisel S J
Financing real estate
McGraw, 1965.

(12018)
Kahn S R, Case F E, Schimmel A
Real estate appraisal and investment
Ronald, 1963.

(12019)
Vidger L P
Selected cases and problems in real estate
Wadsworth Pub, 1963.

(12020)
Ratcliff R U
Real estate analysis
McGraw, 1961.

(12021)
Turvey R
The economics of real property: an analysis of
property values and patterns of use
Allen, 1957.

34.1 Real estate market

(12022)
Baum A, Crosby N
Property investment appraisal
Routledge, 1988.

(12023)
Chinloy P
Real estate: Investment and financial strategy
Kluwer Academic, 1988.

(12024)
Firstenberg P M, Ross S A, Zisler R C
Real estate: the whole story
JPM 1988 SPRING VOL 14:3 p 22-34.

(12025)
Kaufman H M
FNMA'S role in deregulated markets: implications
from past behavior
JMCB 1988 NOV VOL 20:4 p 673.

(12026)
Corcoran P J
Explaining the commercial real estate market
JPM 1987 SPRING VOL 13:3 p 15-21.

(12027)
Grissom T V, Kuhle J L, Walther C H
Diversification works in real estate, too
JPM 1987 WINTER VOL 13:2 p 66-71.

(12028)
Irwin S H, Landa D
Real estate, futures, and gold as portfolio assets
JPM 1987 FALL VOL 14:1 p 29-34.

(12029)
Sirmans G S, Sirmans C F
The historical perspective of real estate returns
JPM 1987 SPRING VOL 13:3 p 22-31.

(12030)
Brown K C, Brown D J
Using order statistics to estimate real estate bid
distributions
MSci 1986 MAR VOL 32:3 p 289-297.

(12031)
Goodwin T H
Inflation, risk, taxes, and the demand for
owner-occupied housing
REStat 1986 VOL 68 p 197.

(12032)
Fogler H R, Granito M R, Smith L R
A theoretical analysis of real estate returns
JF 1985 JUL VOL 40:3 p 711-721.

(12033)
McIntosh A P J, Sykes S G
A guide to institutional property investment
Macmillan, 1985.

(12034)
Thom R
The relationship between housing starts and
mortgage availability
REStat 1985 VOL 67 p 693.

(12035)
Gau G W
Weak form tests of the efficiency of real estate
investment markets
FR 1984 NOV VOL 19:4.

(12036)
Patel R C, Olsen R A
Financial determinants of systematic risk in real
estate investment trusts
JBusR 1984 VOL 12 p 481-482.

(12037)
Freund J L
The housing market: recent developments and
underlying trends
F R Bul 1983 VOL 69:2.

(12038)
Ebrill L P, Possen U M
Inflation and the taxation of equity in
corporations and owner occupied housing
JMCB 1982 FEB VOL 14:1 p 33-47.

(12039)
Summers L H
Inflation, the stock market and owner-occupied
housing
AER 1981 VOL 71 P+P p 429.

(12040)
Hoag J W
Towards indices of real estate value and return
JF 1980 MAY VOL 35:2 p 569-580.

(12041)
Pozdena R J
Inflation expectations and the housing market
F R Bk San Francisco Ec Rev 1980 FALL.

(12042)
Webb J R, Sirmans C F
Yields and risk measures for real estate, 1966-77
JPM 1980 FALL VOL 7:1 p 14-19.

(12043)
Barras R
The returns from office development and
investment
Centre for Environmental Studies, 1979.

(12044)
Follain J R Jr
A study of the demand for housing by low versus
high income households
JFQA 1979 NOV VOL 14 p 769.

(12045)
Smith K V, Schulman D
The performance of equity real estate investment trusts
FAJ 1976 SEP-OCT VOL 32 p 61-66.

(12046)
Arcelus F, Meltzer A H
The markets for housing and housing services
JMCB 1973 FEB VOL 5:1 p 78-99.

(12047)
Swan C
The markets for housing and housing services: comment
JMCB 1973 NOV VOL 5:4 p 960-972.

(12048)
Ricks R B
Imputed returns on real estate financed with life insurance company loans
JF 1969 DEC VOL 24 p 921-937.

(12049)
Jones O
Private secondary market facilities
JF 1968 MAY VOL 23 p 359-366.

(12050)
Kost W E
Rates of return for farm real estate and common stock
American Journal of Agricultural Economics 1968 MAY VOL 50 p 213-224.

(12051)
Wendt P F, Wong S N
Investment performance: common stocks versus apartment houses
JF 1965 DEC VOL 20 p 633-646.

(12052)
Morgan E V
The structure of property ownership in Great Britain
Clarendon, 1960.

34.2 Mortgages

(12053)
Chari V V, Jagannathan R
Adverse selection in a model of real estate lending
JF 1989 JUN VOL 44:2 p 499-508.

(12054)
Corcoran P J
Commercial mortgages: measuring risk and return
JPM 1989 WINTER VOL 15:2 p 69.

(12055)
Titman S, Torous W
Valuing commercial mortgages: an empirical investigation of the contingent-claims approach to pricing risky debt
JF 1989 JUN VOL 44:2 p 345-374.

(12056)
Berk J, Roll R
Adjustable rate mortgages
Journal of Real Estate Finance and Economics 1988 VOL 1..

(12057)**Dunn K B, Spatt C S**
Private information and incentives: Implications for mortgage contract terms and pricing
Journal of Real Estate Finance and Economics 1988 VOL 1.

(12058)
Hendershott P H, Van Order R
Pricing mortgages: An interpretation of the model and results
Journal of Financial Services Research 1988 VOL 1.

(12059)
Heuson A J
Mortgage terminations and pool characteristics: some additional evidence
JFR 1988 VOL 11:2 p 143-152.

(12060)
Anderson G, Chiang R
Interest rate risk hedging for due-on-sale mortgages with early termination
JFR 1987 SUMMER VOL 10:2 p 133-142.

(12061)
Boleat M, Coles A
The mortgage market
Allen, 1987.

(12062)
Kau J B, Keenan D C, Muller W J III
The valuation and securitization of commercial
and multifamily mortgages
JBankF 1987 VOL 11 p 525-546.

(12063)
Park C S
Case study: alternative home-mortgage financing
instruments
EE 1987 FALL VOL 33:1 p 31-58.

(12064)
Quigley J M
Interest rate variations, mortgage prepayments
and household mobility
REStat 1987 VOL 69 p 636.

(12065)
Shilling J D, Sirmans C F
Pricing fast-pay mortgages: some simulation
results
JFR 1987 SPRING VOL 10:1 p 25-32.

(12066)
Tuchman J N
Latest innovations in the US mortgage market
Economist Publications, 1987.

(12067)
Green J, Shoven J B
The effects of interest rates on mortgage
prepayments
JMCB 1986 FEB VOL 18:1 p 41-59.

(12068)
Tuchman J N
Innovation in the US mortgage market to 1990
Economist Intelligence Unit, 1986.

(12069)
Bank of England
The housing finance market: recent growth in
perspective
BEQB 1985 VOL 25 p 80.

(12070)
Dunn K B, Spatt C S
An analysis of mortgage contracting: prepayment
penalties and the due-on-sale clause
JF 1985 MAR VOL 40:1 p 293-308.

(12071)
Alm J, Follain J R
Alternative mortgage instruments, the tilt
problem, and consumer welfare.
JFQA 1984 MAR VOL 19:1 p 113-126

(12072)
Buser S A, Hendershott P H
Pricing default-free fixed-rate mortgages
HFR 1984 VOL 3:4.

(12073)
Capozza D R, Gau G W
The pricing and implementation of mortgage rate
insurance
HFR 1984 VOL 3:4.

(12074)
Cunningham D F, Hendershott P H
Pricing FHA mortgage default insurance
HFR 1984 VOL 3:4.

(12075)
Eskridge W N Jr
One hundred years of ineptitude: the need for
mortgage rules consonant with the economic and
psychological dynamics of the home sale and loan
transaction
VLR 1984 VOL 70:6 p 1083-1218.

(12076)
Foster C, Van Order R
An option-based model of mortgage default
HFR 1984 VOL 3:4.

(12077)
French D W, Haney R L Jr
Pricing the shared-appreciation mortgage in a
stochastic environment
HFR 1984 VOL 3:4.

(12078)
Pozdena R J, Iben B
Pricing mortgages: an options approach
F R Bk San Francisco Ec Rev 1984 SPRING.

(12079)
Campbell T S, Dietrich J K
The determinants of default on insured
conventional residential mortgage loans
JF 1983 DEC VOL 38:5 p 1569-1581.

(12080)
Mayer T, Nathan H
Mortgage rates and regulation Q: a note
JMCB 1983 FEB VOL 15:1 p 107-115.

(12081)
Bank of England
Mortgage lending and the housing market
BEQB 1982 VOL 22 p 390-398.

(12082)
Jones M T
Mortgage designs, inflation and real interest rates
F R Bk New York Q Rev 1982 SPRING VOL
7:1.

(12083)
Luckett C
Recent developments in the mortgage and
consumer credit markets
F R Bul 1982 VOL 68:5.

(12084)
Warner A E, Ingram F J
A test for discrimination in a mortgage market
JBR 1982 SUMMER VOL 13:2.

(12085)
Webb B G
Borrower risk under alternative mortgage
instruments
JF 1982 MAR VOL 37:1 p 169-183.

(12086)
Benston G J
Mortgage redlining research: a review and critical
analysis
JBR 1981 SPRING VOL 12:1.

(12087)
Gilbert R A
Will the removal of regulation Q raise mortgage
interest rates?
F R Bk St Louis Rev 1981 VOL 63:10.

(12088)
Kaufman H M, Schlagenhauf D E
FNMA auction results as a forecaster of
residential mortgage yields
JMCB 1981 AUG VOL 13:3 p 352-364.

(12089)
Ostas J R
The Federal Home Loan Bank system: cause or
cure for disintermediation?
JME 1981 VOL 8 p 231.

(12090)
Rose J T, Rutz R D
Organizational form and risk in bank affiliated
mortgage companies
JMCB 1981 AUG VOL 13:3 p 375-380.

(12091)
Seiders D F
Changing patterns of housing finance
F R Bul 1981 VOL 67:6..

(12092)**Kent R J**
Credit rationing and the home mortgage market
JMCB 1980 AUG VOL 12:3 p 488-501.

(12093)
McNulty J E
A reexamination of the problem of state usury
ceilings: the impact in the mortgage market
QREB 1980 SPRING VOL 20:1 p 16-29

(12094)
Benston G J, Horsky D
Redlining and the demand for mortgages in the
central city and suburbs
JBR 1979 SUMMER VOL 10:2.

(12095)
Kearl J R
Inflation, mortgages and housing
JPE 1979 VOL 87 p 1115.

(12096)
Gau G W
A taxonomic model for the risk-rating of
residential mortgages
JB 1978 OCT VOL 51:4 p 687-706.

(12097)
Vandell K D
Default risk under alternative mortgage instruments
JF 1978 VOL 33 p 1279.

(12098)
Curley A J, Guttentag J M
Value and yield risk on outstanding insured residential mortgages
JF 1977 MAY VOL 32:2 p 403-411.

(12099)
Kaufman H M
An analysis of the behavior of federal mortgage market agencies
JMCB 1977 MAY VOL 9:2 p 349-355.

(12100)
McConnell J J
Price distortions induced by the revenue of federally sponsored mortgage loan programs
JF 1977 VOL 32 p 1201.

(12101)
Ostas J R
Regional differences in mortgage financing costs: A reexamination
JF 1977 VOL 32 p 1774.

(12102)
Smith L B
An analysis of the effects of the removal of the yield ceilings on federally insured mortgages in Canada
JF 1977 VOL 32 p 195.

(12103)
Fisher R M, McConnell J J eds.
Research topics in mortgage markets
Purdue U, 1976.

(12104)
McConnell J J
Valuation of a mortgage company's servicing portfolio
JFQA 1976 SEP VOL 11 p 433.

(12105)
Ostas J R
Effects of usury ceilings in the mortgage market
JF 1976 VOL 31 p 821.

(12106)
Stevens N A
A mortgage futures market: its development, uses, benefits, and costs
F R Bk St Louis Rev 1976 VOL 58:4.

(12107)
Kane E J
Costs and benefits of the proposed tax credit on residential mortgage income
JBR 1975 SUMMER VOL 6:2.

(12108)
Ostas J R, Zahn F
Interest and non-interest credit rationing in the mortgage market
JME 1975 VOL 1 p 187.

(12109)
Meltzer A H
Credit availability and economic decisions: Some evidence from the mortgage and housing markets
JF 1974 VOL 29 p 763.

(12110)
Robins P K
The effects of state usury ceilings on single family homebuilding
JF 1974 VOL 29 p 227.

(12111)
Von Furstenberg G M, Green R J
Home mortgage delinquencies: A cohort analysis
JF 1974 VOL 29 p 1545.

(12112)
Clauretie T M
Interest rates, the business demand for funds and the residential mortgage market: A sectoral econometric study
JF 1973 VOL 28 p 1313.

(12113)
Rakes G K
A numerical credit evaluation model for residential mortgages
QREB 1973 VOL 13:3 p 73.

(12114)
Boorman J T, Peterson M O
The Hunt Commission and the mortgage market:
an appraisal
JBR 1972 AUTUMN VOL 3:3 p 155-165.

(12115)
Lusztig P, Nicol R E G, Schwab B
An alternative in mortgage lending
QREB 1972 VOL 12:1 p 31.

(12116)
Williamson J P
Mortgage loan extensions after an interest rate
change: a problem in blended interest rates
JBR 1972 SUMMER VOL 3:2.

(12117)
Smith L B
Housing and mortgage markets in Canada
Bank of Canada, 1970.

(12118)
Edwards E E
Changing character of the real estate mortgage
markets
JF 1964 MAY VOL 19 p 313-320.

(12119)
Page A N
The variation of mortgage interest rates
JB 1964 JUL VOL 37 p 280-294.

34.21   Fixed- versus variable-rate mortgages

(12120)
Heuson A J
Offering rates on fixed- and adjustable-rate
mortgage loans
FR 1989 FEB VOL 24:1 p 147.

(12121)
Dhillon U S, Shilling J D, Sirmans C F
Choosing between fixed and adjustable rate
mortgages
JMCB 1987 MAY VOL 19:2 p 260-267.

(12122)
Ward C W R
Returns from the Indexed Mortgage: an Option
Pricing Model approach
JBFA 1987 SPRING VOL 14:1 p 109-120.

(12123)
Ott R A
The duration of an adjustable-rate mortgage and
the impact of the index
JF 1986 SEP VOL 41:4 p 923-933.

(12124)
Stutzer M J, Roberds W
Adjustable rate mortgages: increasing efficiency
more than housing activity
F R Bk Minneapolis Q Rev 1985 VOL 9:3.

(12125)
Hess A G
Variable rate mortgages : Confusion of means and
ends
FAJ 1984 JAN-FEB VOL 40:1 p 67-70

(12126)
Page D E, Sirmans C F
Yield differences on fixed and adjustable rate
mortgages
QREB 1984 AUTUMN VOL 24:3 p 18-28

(12127)
Statman M
Fixed rate or index-linked mortgages from the
borrower's point of view : a note
JFQA 1982 SEP VOL 17:3 p 451-457.

(12128)
Baesel J B, Biger N
The allocation of risk: Some implications of fixed
versus index-linked mortgages
JFQA 1980 JUN VOL 15 p 457.

(12129)
Melton W C
Graduated payment mortgages
F R Bk New York Q Rev 1980 SPRING VOL
5:1.

(12130)
Melton W C, Heidt D L
Variable rate mortgages
F R Bk New York Q Rev 1979 SUMMER VOL
4:2.

(12131)
Findlay M C III, Capozza D R
The variable rate mortgage and risk in the
mortgage market: an option theory perspective
JMCB 1977 MAY VOL 9:2 p 356-364.

(12132)
Kaufman G G
Variable rate residential mortgages: the early
experience from California
F R Bk San Francisco Ec Rev 1976 SUMMER.

(12133)
Cassidy H J, McElhone J
The pricing of variable rate mortgages
FIN MGMT 1975 WINTER VOL 4 p 37.

(12134)
Gambs C M
Variable rate mortgages: their potential in the
United States
JMCB 1975 MAY VOL 7:2 p 245-251.

(12135)
Millar J A, Stansell S R
Variable rate mortgage experience of the farm
credit system
FIN MGMT 1975 WINTER VOL 4 p 46.

(12136)
Kaufman G G
The questionable benefit of variable-rate
mortgages
QREB 1973 VOL 13:3 p 43.

(12137)
Krupnick A J
Variable-rate mortgages: econ or bane?
F R Bk Bus Rev Philadelphia 1972 SEP.

34.22   Mortgage-backed securities

(12138)
Boyle P P
Valuing Canadian mortgage-backed securities
FAJ 1989 MAY-JUN VOL 45 p 55-60.

(12139)
Richard S F, Roll R
Prepayments on fixed-rate mortgage-backed
securities
JPM 1989 SPRING VOL 15:3 p 74.

(12140)
Schwartz E S, Torous W N
Prepayment and the valuation of mortgage-backed
securities
JF 1989 JUN VOL 44:2 p 375-392.

(12141)
Roulac S E
Real estate securities valuation
JPM 1988 SPRING VOL 14:3 p 35-39.

(12142)
Fabozzi F J ed.
New developments in mortgage-backed securities
Institute of Chartered Financial Analysts, 1985.

(12143)
Gainer W J
Mortgage revenue bonds: their costs outweigh
their benefits to homebuyers
HFR 1984 VOL 3:4.

(12144)
Dunn K B, Singleton K J
An empirical analysis of the pricing of
mortgage-backed securities
JF 1983 MAY VOL 38:2 p 613-623..

(12145)**Black D G, Garbade K D, Silber W L**
The impact of the GNMA pass-through program
on FHA mortgage costs
JF 1981 MAY VOL 36:2 p 457-469.

(12146)
Dunn K B, McConnell J J
Valuation of GNMA mortgage-backed securities
JF 1981 JUN VOL 36:3 p 599-616.

(12147)
Dunn K B, McConnell J J
A comparison of alternative models for pricing GNMA mortgage-backed securities
JF 1981 MAY VOL 36:2 p 4781.

(12148)
Dunn K B, McConnell J J
Rate of return indexes for GNMA securities
JPM 1981 WINTER VOL 7:2 p 65-74.

(12149)
Kaufman H M
FNMA and its relationship to the mortgage market
JBR 1981 AUTUMN VOL 12:3.

(12150)
Lamle H R
Ginnie Mae: age equals beauty
JPM 1981 WINTER VOL 7:2 p 75-79.

(12151)
Miles M, Sears R S
An econometric approach to the FNMA free market system auction.
JFQA 1981 JUN VOL 16:2 p 177-192.

(12152)
Seiders D F
The GNMA-guaranteed pass-through security: market development and implications for the growth and stability of home mortgage lending
F R Bul 1979 VOL 65:12.

(12153)
Sivesind C M
Mortgage-backed securities: the revolution in real estate finance
F R Bk New York Q Rev 1979 AUTUMN VOL 4:3.

(12154)
Haney R L Jr
Analysis of yield spreads between Ginnie Mae pass-throughs and Aaa corporate bonds
FIN MGMT 1978 SPRING VOL 7 p 17.

(12155)
McConnell J J
Mortgage company bids on the GNMA auctions
JBR 1977 WINTER VOL 7:4.

(12156)
Haney R L Jr
An empirical investigation of the relative attractiveness of the GNMA pass-through security
QREB 1976 VOL 16:4 p 79.

35 Commodity markets and exhaustible resources

(12157)
Leuthold R M, Garcia P, Adam B D
An examination of the necessary and sufficient
conditions for market efficiency: the case of hogs
AE 1989 VOL 21:2 p 193-204.

(12158)
MacDonald R, Taylor M P
Rational expectations, risk and efficiency in the
London Metal Exchange: an empirical analysis
AE 1989 VOL 21:2 p 143-154.

(12159)
Wilson W W
Price discovery and hedging in the sunflower
market
JFM 1989 VOL 9:5 p 377-392.

(12160)
Wright B D, Williams J C
A theory of negative prices for storage
JFM 1989 VOL 9:1 p 1-14.

(12161)
Anderson R W, Gilbert C L
Commodity agreements and commodity markets
: lessons from Tin
EJ 1988 MAR VOL 98:389 p 1-15.

(12162)
Chang E C
A monthly effect in commodity price changes: a
note
JFM 1988 VOL 8:6 p 717-722.

(12163)
Fama E F, French K R
Business cycles and the behavior of metals prices
JF 1988 DEC VOL 43:5 p 1075-1094.

(12164)
International Monetary Fund
Primary commodities: market developments and
outlook
IMF, 1988.

(12165)
MacAvoy P W
Explaining metals prices
Kluwer Academic, 1988.

(12166)
Thurman W N
Speculative carryover: an empirical examination of
the US refined copper market
RandJ 1988 AUTUMN VOL 19:3 p 420-437.

(12167)
Bernard V L, Frecka T J
Commodity contracts and common stocks as
hedges against relative consumer price risk
JFQ 1987 JUN VOL 22 p 169.

(12168)
Bopp A E, Sitzer S
Are petroleum prices good predictors of cash
value
JFM 1987 DEC VOL 7:6 p 705-720.

(12169)
Buckley J ed.
Guide to world commodity markets: physical,
futures and options trading. 5th ed
Kogan Page, 1986.

(12170)
Canarella G, Pollard S K
The "efficiency" of the London Metal Exchange:
A test with overlapping and non-overlapping data
JBankF 1986 VOL 10 p 575.

(12171)
Miller M H, Upton C W
The pricing of oil and gas : some further results
JF 1985 JUL VOL 40:3 p 1009-1020.

(12172)
Pring M J ed.
McGraw-Hill handbook of commodities and
futures
McGraw, 1985.

(12173)
Roll R
Orange juice and weather
AER 1984 VOL 74 p 861-880.

(12174)
Ackley G
Commodities and capital: Prices and quantities
AER 1983 VOL 73 p 1-16.

(12175)
Atkin M J ed.
ICCH commodities and financial futures yearbook
1983/4
Landell Mills Commodities Studies, 1983.

(12176)
Gibson-Jarvis R
The London Metal Exchange: a commodity
market. 2nd ed
Woodhead-Faulkner, 1983.

(12177)
Granger C W J
Trading in commodities. 4th ed
Woodhead-Faulkner, 1983.

(12178)
Camerer C
The pricing and social value of commodity
options
FAJ 1982 JAN-FEB p 62-67.

(12179)
Fortune
Who guards whom at the commodity exchange
F 1980 JUL 28 VOL 102:2 p 38-42.

(12180)
OECD
The instability of agricultural commodity markets
OECD, 1980.

(12181)
Ehrbar A F
High stakes in the silver game
F 1979 DEC 17 VOL 100:12 p 57-59

(12182)
Goodwin G, Mayall J eds.
A new international commodity regime
Croom Helm, nd [c1979]

(12183)
Adams F G, Klein S A eds.
Stabilizing world commodity markets: analysis,
practice and policy
Lexington Bks, 1978.

(12184)
Holthausen D M, Hughes J S
Commodity returns and capital asset pricing
FIN MGMT 1978 SUMMER VOL 7 p 37.

(12185)
Barty-King H
The Baltic Exchange: the history of a unique
market
Hutchinson Benham, 1977.

(12186)
Warr P G
On the shadow pricing of traded commodities
JPE 1977 AUG VOL 85:4 p 865-872.

(12187)
**Graham D A, Jennergren L P, Peterson D W et
al.**
Trader-commodity parity theorems
JET 1976 JUN VOL 12:3 p 443-454.

(12188)
OECD
Study of trends in world supply and demand of
major agricultural commodities
OECD, 1976.

(12189)
Bank of England
UK commodity markets
BEQB 1975 VOL 15 p 244.

(12190)
Rees G L
Britain's commodity markets
Elek, 1972.

(12191)
Labys W C, Rees H J B, Elliott C M
Copper price behaviour and the London Metal
Exchange
AE 1971 JUN VOL 3 p 99-114.

(12192)
Labys W C, Granger C W J
Speculation, hedging and commodity price
forecasts
Heath, 1970.

(12193)
Radetzki M
International commodity market arrangements: a study of the effects of post-war commodity agreements and compensatory finance schemes
Hurst, 1970.

(12194)
Weymar F H
The dynamics of the world cocoa market
MIT Pr, 1968.

(12195)
Kogiku K C
A model of the raw materials market
IntER 1967 FEB VOL 8 p 116-120.

(12196)
Nimrod V L, Bower R S
Commodities and computers
JFQA 1967 MAR VOL 2 p 58-73.

(12197)
Miller N C
The great salad oil swindle
Gollancz, 1966..

(12198)**Houck J P**
A statistical model of the demand for soybeans
JFarmE 1964 MAY VOL 46 p 366-374.

(12199)
Smidt S, Johnson A
Expectations and information: a study of pork inventory behavior
Graduate School of Business and Public Administration, Cornell U, 1962.

(12200)
Working H
Cycles in wheat prices
Wheat 1931 NOV VOL 7.

(12201)
Working H
Financial results of speculative holdings in wheat
Wheat 1931 JUL VOL 7.

35.1 Gold

(12202)
Frank M, Stengos T
Measuring the strangeness of gold and silver rates of return
REStud 1989 VOL 56 p 553.

(12203)
Jaffe J F
Gold and gold stocks as investments for institutional portfolios
FAJ 1989 MAR-APR VOL 45 p 53-59.

(12204)
Aggarwal R, Soenen L A
The nature and efficiency of the gold market
JPM 1988 SPRING VOL 14:3 p 18-21.

(12205)
Poitras G
"Golden turtle tracks": in search of unexploited profits in gold spreads
JFM 1987 AUG VOL 7:4 p 397-412.

(12206)
Ball C A, Tschoegl A E
The degree of price resolution: The case of the gold market
JFM 1985 SPRING VOL 5 p 29-43.

(12207)
Beckers S
On the efficiency of the gold options market
JBankF 1984 VOL 8 p 459.

(12208)
Beckers S, Soenen L
Gold : more attractive to non-US than to US investors?
JBFA 1984 SPRING VOL 11:1 p 107-112

(12209)
Herbst A F
Gold versus US common stocks: Some evidence on inflation hedge performance and cyclical behavior
FAJ 1983 JAN-FEB VOL 39 p 66-74.

(12210)
Carter K J, Affleck-Graves J F, Money A H
Are gold shares better than gold for diversification?
JPM 1982 FALL VOL 9:1 p 52-55.

(12211)
Chua J H, Woodward R S
Gold as an inflation hedge: A comparative study of six major industrial countries
JBFA 1982 SUMMER VOL 9:2 p 191-197.

(12212)
Solt M E, Swanson P J
On the efficiency of the markets for gold and silver.
JB 1981 JUL VOL 54:3 p 453-478

(12213)
Sarnoff P
Trading in gold
Woodhead-Faulkner, 1980.

(12214)
Mayer M
The message from the gold markets
F 1979 NOV 5 VOL 100:9 p 55-72

(12215)
Tarasanar H
Recent developments on the gold front
F R Bk Bus Rev Philadelphia 1973 NOV.

(12216)
Frankel S H
Investment and the return to equity capital in the South African gold mining industry 1887 - 1965: an international comparison
Blackwell, 1967.

35.2 Economics of exhaustible resources

(12217)
Morck R, Schwartz E, Stangeland D
The valuation of forestry resources under stochastic prices and inventories
JFQA 1989 DEC VOL 24:4 p 473-488.

(12218)
Stensland G, Tjostheim D
Optimal investments using empirical dynamic programming with application to natural resources
JB 1989 VOL 62:1 p 99-120.

(12219)
Schmidt R H
Hotelling's rule repealed? An examination of exhaustible resource pricing
F R Bk San Francisco Ec Rev 1988 FALL NO 4.

(12220)
Livernois J R, Uhler R S
Extraction costs and the economics of nonrenewable-resources
JPE 1987 VOL 95 p 195.

(12221)
Brennan M J, Schwartz E S
Evaluating natural resource investments
JB 1985 APR VOL 58:2 p 135-157.

(12222)
Farrow S
Testing the efficiency of extraction from a stock resource
JPE 1985 VOL 93 p 452.

(12223)
Miller M H, Upton C W
A test of the Hotelling valuation principle
JPE 1985 VOL 93 p 1-25.

(12224)
Farzin Y H
The effect of the discount rate on depletion of exhaustible resources
JPE 1984 VOL 92 p 841.

(12225)
Pindyck R S
Uncertainty in the theory of renewable resource markets
REStud 1984 VOL 51 p 289.

(12226)
Eswaran M, Lewis T R, Heapes T
On the nonexistence of market equilibria in exhaustible resource markets with decreasing costs
JPE 1983 VOL 91 p 154.

(12227)
Dasgupta P, Gilbert R J, Stiglitz J E
Invention and innovation under alternative market structures: The case of natural resources
REStud 1982 VOL 49 p 567.

(12228)
Devarajan S, Fisher A C
Hotelling's "Economics of exhaustible resources":
Fifty years later
JEL 1981 MAR VOL 19 p 65-73.

(12229)
Levhari D, Pindyck R S
The pricing of durable exhaustible resources
QJE 1981 VOL 96 p 365.

(12230)
Mitra T
Some results on the optimal depletion of exhaustible resources under negative discounting
REStud 1981 JUL VOL 48:3 NO 153 p 521-532.

(12231)
Cropper M L, Weinstein M C, Zeckhauser R J
The optimal consumption of depletable natural resources: An elaboration, correction, and extension
QJE 1978 VOL 92 p 337.

(12232)
Hoel M
Resource extraction when a future substitute has an uncertain cost
REStud 1978 VOL 45 p 637.

(12233)
Kamien M I, Schwartz N L
Optimal exhaustible resource deplection with endogenous technical change
REStud 1978 VOL 45 p 179.

(12234)
Loury G C
The optimal exploitation of an unknown reserve
REStud 1978 VOL 45 p 621.

(12235)
Gilbert R J
Resource extraction with differential information
AER 1977 VOL 67 P+P p 250-254.

(12236)
Haurie A, Hung N M
Turnpike properties for the optimal use of a natural resource
REStud 1977 VOL 44 p 329.

(12237)
Weinstein M C, Zeckhauser R J
Optimal consumption of depletable resources
QJE 1975 VOL 89 p 371.

36 Other speculative markets

(12238)
Baumol W J
Unnatural value: or art investment as floating crap game
AER 1986 VOL 76 P+P p 10-14.

(12239)
Amoako-Adu B, Marmer H, Yagil J
The efficiency of certain speculative markets and gambler behavior
Journal of Economics and Business 1985 DEC VOL 37 p 365-378.

(12240)
Kane A
Coins: anatomy of a fad asset
JPM 1984 WINTER VOL 10:2 p 44-51.

(12241)
Taylor W M
The estimation of quality-adjusted rates of return in stamp auctions
JF 1983 VOL 38:4 p 1095-1110.

(12242)
Jaeger E
To save or savor: The rate of return to storing wine
JPE 1981 VOL 89 p 584.

(12243)
Penn R E
The economics of the market in modern prints
JPM 1980 FALL VOL 7:1 p 25-35.

(12244)
Krasker W S
The rate of return to storing wines
JPE 1979 VOL 87 p 1363.

(12245)
Duthy R
Alternative investment
Michael Joseph, 1978.

(12246)
Stein J P
The monetary appreciation of paintings
JPE 1977 OCT VOL 85:5 p 1021-1035.

36.1 Wagers

(12247)
Hausch D B, Ziemba W T eds.
Efficiency of racetracking
Academic Pr, 1989.

(12248)
Gandar J, Zuber R, O'Brien T
Testing rationality in the points spread betting market
JF 1988 SEP VOL 43:4 p 995.

(12249)
Sauer R D, Brajer V, Ferris S P
Hold your bets: another look at the efficiency of the gambling market for National Football League games
JPE 1988 FEB VOL 96:1 p 206-213.

(12250)
Thaler R H, Ziemba W T
Anomalies: Parimutuel betting markets: racetracks and lotteries
JEP 1988 VOL 2:2 p 161-174..

(12251)**Smith D J**
Risk-efficient lottery bets
JPM 1987 FALL VOL 14:1 p 25-28.

(12252)
Amoako-Adu B, Marmer H, Yagil J
The efficiency of certain speculative markets and gambler behavior
Journal of Economics and Business 1985 DEC VOL 37 p 365-378.

(12253)
Zuber R A, Gandar J M, Bowers B D
Beating the spread: Testing the efficiency of the gambling market for National Football League Games
JPE 1985 VOL 93 p 800.

(12254)
Tuckwell R H
Determinants of betting turnover
AJM 1984 DEC VOL 9 p 59-66.

(12255)
Ziemba W T, Hausch D B
Beat the racetrack
HarBraceJ, 1984.

(12256)
Gilovich T
Biased evaluation and persistence in gambling
Journal of Personality and Social Psychology 1983
JUN VOL 44 p 1110-1126.

(12257)
Asch P, Malkiel B G, Quandt R E
Racetrack betting and informed behavior
JFE 1982 VOL 10 p 187.

(12258)
Bassett G W Jr
Point spreads versus odds
JPE 1981 VOL 89 p 752.

(12259)
Hausch D B, Ziemba W T, Rubinstein M
Efficiency of the market for racetrack betting.
MSci 1981 DEC VOL 27:12 p 1435-1452

(12260)
Figlewski S
Subjective information and market efficiency in a
betting market
JPE 1979 VOL 87 p 75.

(12261)
Snyder W W
Horse racing: Testing the efficient markets model
JF 1978 VOL 33 p 1109.

(12262)
Tryfos P et al.
Winning strategies for wagering on National
Football League games
MSci 1978 APR VOL 24 p 809-818.

(12263)
Ali M M
Probability and utility estimates for racetrack
bettors
JPE 1977 AUG VOL 85 p 803-815.

(12264)
Canes M E
The market for pro football betting
(in Eadington W R ed., Gambling and society:
Interdisciplinary studies on the subject of
gambling. Charles C. Thomas, Springfield, Ill.,
1976.)

(12265)
Gruen A
An inquiry into the economics of race-track
gambling
JPE 1976 VOL 84 p 169-178.

(12266)
Smith V L
Economic theory of wager markets
WEJ 1971 SEP VOL 9 p 242-255.

(12267)
Pankoff L D
Market efficiency and football betting
JB 1968 APR VOL 41 p 203-214.

(12268)
Griffith R M
A footnote of horse race betting
Transactions Kentucky Academy of Science 1961
VOL 22 p 78-81.

(12269)
Griffith R M
Odd adjustments by American horse-race bettors
AJP 1949 APR VOL 62 p 290-294.

37 Human capital

(12270)
De Meza D, Webb D C
Labour turnover, job-specific skills and efficiency in a search model
QJE 1987 VOL 102 p 281.

(12271)
Greenwald B C
Adverse selection in the labour market
REStud 1986 VOL 53 p 325.

(12272)
Waldman M
Job assignments, signalling and efficiency
RandJ 1984 SUMMER VOL 15:2 p 255-270.

(12273)
Carmichael L
Firm-specific human capital and promotion ladders
BellJ 1983 SPRING VOL 14:1 p 251-258

(12274)
Cothren R
Job search and implicit contracts
JPE 1983 VOL 91 p 494.

(12275)
Stiglitz J E, Weiss A
Incentive effects of termination: Applications to the credit and labor markets
AER 1983 VOL 73 p 912-927.

(12276)
Galenson D W
The market evaluation of human capital: The case of indentured servitude
JPE 1981 VOL 89 p 446.

(12277)
Graham J W
An explanation for the correlation of stocks of nonhuman capital with investment in human capital
AER 1981 VOL 71 p 248-255.

(12278)
Guasch J L, Weiss A
Self-selection in the labor market
AER 1981 VOL 71 p 275-284.

(12279)
Hashimoto M
Firm-specific human capital as a shared investment
AER 1981 VOL 71 p 475-482.

(12280)
Eaton J, Rosen H S
Taxation, human capital and uncertainty
AER 1980 VOL 70 p 705-715.

(12281)
Liberman J
Human capital and the financial capital market
JB 1980 APR VOL 53:2 p 165-191.

(12282)
Rorke C H
On the portfolio effects of nonmarketable assets: Government transfers and human capital payments
JFQA 1979 JUN VOL 14 p 167.

(12283)
Williams J T
Risk human capital and the investor's portfolio
JB 1978 JAN VOL 51:1 p 65-89.

(12284)
Riley J G
Information, screening and human capital
AER 1976 VOL 66 P+P p 254-260.

(12285)
Salop J, Salop S
Self-selection and turnover in the labor market
QJE 1976 VOL 90 p 619-627..

(12286)**Spence M**
Competition in salaries and signaling prerequisites for jobs
QJE 1976 VOL 90 p 51.

(12287)
Becker G S
Human capital: a theoretical and empirical analysis, with special reference to education. 2nd ed
Natl Bur Econ Res, 1975.

(12288)
Holt G
Human capital investment under constrained
optimization
QREB 1975 VOL 15:1 p 47.

(12289)
Levhari D, Weiss Y
The effect of risk on the investment in human
capital
AER 1974 VOL 64 p 950-963.

(12290)
Mayers D
Portfolio theory, job choice and the equilibrium
structure of expected wages
JFE 1974 VOL 1 p 23.

(12291)
Razin A
Optimum investment in human capital
REStud 1972 VOL 39 p 455.

(12292)
Lindsay C M
Measuring human capital returns
JPE 1971 NOV-DEC VOL 79:6 p 1195.

(12293)
Cutler D M
Tax reform and the stock market: an asset price approach
AER 1988 VOL 78:5 p 1107-1117.

(12294)
Downs T, Tehranian H
Predicting stock price responses to tax policy changes
AER 1988 VOL 78:5 p 1118-1130.

(12295)
Emery D R, Lewellen W G, Mauer D C
Tax-timing options, leverage, and the choice of corporate form
JFR 1988 VOL 11:2 p 99-110.

(12296)
Dammon R M, Green R C
Tax arbitrage and the existence of equilibrium prices for financial assets
JF 1987 DEC VOL 42:5 p 1143-1166.

(12297)
Feldstein M ed.
The effects of taxation on capital accumulation
U of Chicago Pr, 1987.

(12298)
Feldstein M ed.
Taxes and capital formation
U of Chicago Pr, 1987.

(12299)
Hamada R S
Differential taxes and the structure of equilibrium rates of return: Managerial implications and remaining conundrums
(in Lee C F ed., Advances in Financial Planning, VOL 2. JAI Press, 1987.)

(12300)
Shevlin T
Taxes and off-balance sheet financing: research and development limited partnership
AR 1987 JUL VOL 62:3 p 480-509.

(12301)
Auerbach A J
The dynamic effects of tax law asymmetries
REStud 1986 VOL 53 p 205.

(12302)
Dybvig P H, Ross S A
Tax clienteles and asset pricing
JF 1986 JUL VOL 41:3 p 751-763.

(12303)
Haugen R A, Senbet L W
Corporate finance and taxes: A review
FIN MGMT 1986 AUTUMN VOL 15 p 5-21.

(12304)
Zhu Y, Friend I
The effects of different taxes on risky and risk-free investment and on the cost of capital
JF 1986 MAR VOL 41:1 p 53-66.

(12305)
Edwards J S S, Keen M J
Taxes, investment and Q
REStud 1985 VOL 52 p 665.

(12306)
Bulow J I, Summers L H
The taxation of risky assets
JPE 1984 VOL 92 p 20.

(12307)
Gordon R H
Inflation, taxation and corporate behavior
QJE 1984 VOL 99 p 313.

(12308)
Amoako-Adu B
The Canadian tax reform and its effect on stock prices : a note
JF 1983 DEC VOL 38:5 p 1669-1675.

(12309)
Auerbach A J
Taxation, corporate financial policy and the cost of capital.
JEL 1983 SEP VOL 21:3 p 905-940.

(12310)
Feldstein M
Inflation, tax rules and capital formation
U of Chicago Pr, 1983.

(12311)
Miles J A
Taxes and the Fisher effect: a clarifying analysis
JF 1983 MAR VOL 38:1 p 49-65.

(12312)
Abel A B
Dynamic effects of permanent and temporary tax
policies in a q model of investment
JME 1982 VOL 9 p 353

(12313)
Kanniainen V
Unanticipated inflation, taxation and common
stocks
JBFA 1982 WINTER VOL 9:4 p 459-469.

(12314)
Pointon J
Taxation and mathematical programming
JBFA 1982 SPRING VOL 9:1 p 43-50

(12315)
Seater J J
Are future taxes discounted?
JMCB 1982 AUG VOL 14:3 p 376-389.

(12316)
Sebenius J K, Stan P J E
Risk-spreading properties of common tax and
contract instruments
BellJ 1982 AUTUMN VOL 13:2 p 555-560.

(12317)
Treynor J L
The fiscal burden
FAJ 1982 SEP-OCT VOL 38 p 17-26.

(12318)
Aaron H J, Pechman J A eds.
How taxes affect economic behavior
Brookings, 1981.

(12319)
Abel A B
Taxes, inflation and the durability of capital
JPE 1981 VOL 89 p 548.

(12320)
Baron D P, Forsythe R
Uncertainty and the theory of tax incidence in a
stock market economy
IntER 1981 OCT VOL 22:3 p 567-576.

(12321)
Nielsen N C
Inflation and taxation: Nominal and real rates of
return
JME 1981 MAR VOL 7 p 261-270.

(12322)
Vandell R F, Pontius M L
The impact of tax status on stock selection
JPM 1981 SUMMER VOL 7:4 p 35-42.

(12323)
Warren A
The relation and integration of individual and
corporate income taxes
HLR 1981 VOL 94:4 p 717-800.

(12324)
Ballentine J G, McLure C E Jr
Taxation and corporate financial policy
QJE 1980 VOL 94 p 351.

(12325)
Feldstein M
Inflation, tax rules and the stock market
JME 1980 VOL 6 p 309.

(12326)
Feldstein M, Slemrod J
Personal taxation, portfolio choice and the effect
of the corporation income tax
JPE 1980 VOL 88 p 854-866.

(12327)
Horst T
A note on the optimal taxation of international
investment income
QJE 1980 VOL 94 p 793.

(12328)
Jenkins J W
Taxes, margining and bond selection
FAJ 1980 MAY-JUN p 41-48.

(12329)
Auerbach A J
The optimal taxation of heterogeneous capital
QJE 1979 VOL 93 p 589.

(12330)
Everett J E, Dickinson J P
Some aspects of inflation, tax and the investing borrower
JBFA 1979 WINTER VOL 6:4 p 527-538.

(12331)
Feldstein M, Green J, Sheshinski E
Corporate financial policy and taxation in a growing economy
QJE 1979 VOL 93 p 411.

(12332)
Hamada R S
Financial theory and taxation in an inflationary world: some public policy issues
JF 1979 MAY VOL 34:2 p 347-369.

(12333)
Livingston M
Taxation and bond market equilibrium in a world of uncertain future interest rates
JFQA 1979 MAR VOL 14 p 11.

(12334)
Rickwood C P, Groves R E V
Tax and the integration of finance and investment
JBFA 1979 SUMMER VOL 6:2 p 157-171

(12335)
Scott J H Jr
The tax effects of investment in marketable securities on firm valuation
JF 1979 MAY VOL 34:2 p 307-324.

(12336)
Tanner J E
An empirical investigation of tax discounting
JMCB 1979 MAY VOL 11:2 p 214-218.

(12337)
Boskin M J
Taxation, saving and the rate of interest
JPE 1978 VOL 86 p S3.

(12338)
Browning E K
The burden of taxation
JPE 1978 VOL 86 p 649..

(12339)Feldstein M, Green J, Sheshinski E
Inflation and taxes in a growing economy with debt and equity finance

JPE 1978 VOL 86 Suppl p 53.

(12340)
Palash C J
Tax policy: its impact on investment incentives
F R Bk New York Q Rev 1978 SUMMER VOL 3:2.

(12341)
Siegel J J
Notes on optimal taxation and the optimal rate of inflation
JME 1978 VOL 4 p 297.

(12342)
Hong H
Inflationary tax effects on the assets of business corporations
FIN MGMT 1977 AUTUMN VOL 6 p 51.

(12343)
Lewellen W G, McConnell J J
Tax reform, firm valuation and capital costs
FIN MGMT 1977 WINTER VOL 6 p 59.

(12344)
Sandmo A
Portfolio theory, asset demand and taxation: Comparative statics with many assets
REStud 1977 VOL 44 p 369.

(12345)
King M A
Taxation and the cost of capital
REStud 1974 VOL 41 p 21.

(12346)
Sandmo A
A note on the structure of optimal taxation
AER 1974 VOL 64 p 701-706.

(12347)
Bergstrom T
A note on efficient taxation
JPE 1973 VOL 81 p 187.

(12348)
Baumol W J
On taxation and the control of externalities
AER 1972 VOL 62 p 307-322.

(12349)
Oakland W H
Corporate earnings and tax shifting in U.S.
manufacturing, 1930-1968.
REStat 1972 AUG VOL 54 p 235-244.

(12350)
Stiglitz J E
Taxation, risk taking and the allocation of
investment in a competitive economy
(in Jensen M C ed., Studies in the theory of
capital markets. Praeger, 1972.)

(12351)
Feldstein M, Flemming J S
Tax policy, corporate saving and investment
behaviour in Britain
REStud 1971 VOL 38 p 415-434.

(12352)
Feldstein M
The effects of taxation on risk taking
JPE 1969 JUL-AUG VOL 77 p 755-764.

(12353)
Shibata A N
Effects of taxation on risk taking
AER 1969 MAY VOL 59 p 553-561.

(12354)
Mossin J
Taxation and risk-taking: an expected utility
approach
Ec 1968 FEB VOL 35 p 74-82.

(12355)
Naslund B
Some effects of taxes on risk-taking
REStat 1968 VOL 35 p 289-306.

(12356)
Bierwag G O, Grove M A
Portfolio selection and taxation
OEP 1967 JUL VOL 19 p 215-221.

(12357)
Hall R E, Jorgenson D W
Tax policy and investment behavior
AER 1967 JUN VOL 57 p 391-414.

(12358)
Richter M K
Cardinal utility, portfolio selection and taxation
REStud 1960 JUN VOL 27 p 152-166.

(12359)
Brown E C
Mr. Kaldor on taxation and risk-bearing
REStud 1957 VOL 25 p 49-52.

(12360)
Butters J K
Taxation incentives and financial capacity
AER 1954 MAY VOL 44 p 504-519.

(12361)
Streeten P
The effect of taxation on risk bearing
OEP 1953 VOL 5 p 271-287.

(12362)
Domar E D, Musgrave R A
Proportional income taxation and risk-taking
QJE 1944 MAY VOL 58 p 388-422.

38.1 Capital gains tax

(12363)
Fullerton D, Henderson Y K
The marginal excess burden of different capital
tax instruments
REStat 1989 VOL 71 p 435.

(12364)
Gordon R H, Wilson J D
Measuring the efficiency cost of taxing risky
capital income
AER 1989 VOL 79:3 p 427-439.

(12365)
Balcer Y, Judd K L
Effects of capital gains taxation on life-cycle
investment and portfolio management
JF 1987 JUL VOL 42:3 p 743-758.

(12366)
Severn A D, Mills J C, Copeland B L Jr
Capital gains taxes after tax reform
JPM 1987 SPRING VOL 13:3 p 69-75.

(12367)
Lakonishok J, Smidt S
Volume for winners and losers : taxation and other motives for stock trading
JF 1986 SEP VOL 41:4 p 951-974.

(12368)
Ortmeyer D L, Peek J
An ex ante view of household portfolio choice: the role of expected capital gains
REStat 1986 VOL 68 p 207.

(12369)
Slemrod J
Stock transaction volume and the 1978 capital gains tax reduction
Public Finance Quarterly 1986 VOL 14 p 3-16.

(12370)
Branch B, Chang K
Tax-loss trading, is the game over or have the rules changed?
FR 1985 FEB VOL 20:1.

(12371)
Ball R J
The natural taxation of capital gains and losses when income is taxed
JBankF 1984 VOL 8 p 471.

(12372)
Constantinides G M
Optimal stock trading with personal taxes: implications for prices and the abnormal January returns
JFE 1984 VOL 13 p 65-89.

(12373)
Constantinides G M, Ingersoll J E Jr
Optimal bond trading with personal taxes
JFE 1984 VOL 13 p 299-335.

(12374)
Brown P, Keim D B, Kleidon A W et al.
Stock return seasonalities and the tax-loss selling hypothesis : analysis of the arguments and Australian evidence.
JFE 1983 JUN VOL 12:1 p 105-127.

(12375)
Stiglitz J E
Some aspects of the taxation of capital gains
Journal of Public Economics 1983 VOL 21 p 257-294.

(12376)
Palmon D, Yaari U
Retention and tax avoidance: A clarification
FIN MGMT 1981 SPRING VOL 10 p 29-36.

(12377)
Boskin M J, Shoven J B
Issues in the taxation of capital income in the United States
AER 1980 VOL 70 P+P p 164-170.

(12378)
Constantinides G M, Scholes M
Optimal liquidation of assets in the presence of personal taxes: implications for asset pricing
JF 1980 MAY VOL 35:2 p 439-452.

(12379)
Dyl E A
A state preference model of capital gains taxation
JFQA 1979 SEP VOL 14 p 529.

(12380)
Feldstein M, Summers L
Inflation and the taxation of capital gains in the corporate sector
NTJ 1979 DEC VOL 32 p 445-470.

(12381)
Dyl E A
Short selling and the capital gains tax
FAJ 1978 MAR-APR p 61-64.

(12382)
Feldstein M, Slemrod J
How inflation distorts the taxation of capital gains
HBR 1978 SEP-OCT VOL 56:5 p 2022.

(12383)
Green J, Sheshinski E
Optimal capital gains taxation under limited information
JPE 1978 VOL 86 p 1143.

(12384)
Stevens N A
Taxation of capital gains: principle versus practice
F R Bk St Louis Rev 1978 VOL 60:10.

(12385)
Ahsan S M
Capital gains and risk taking
QJE 1975 VOL 89 p 151.

(12386)
Mantell E H
The effects of tax exemption of capital gains on
demand for risky investments
QREB 1975 VOL 15:4 p 93.

(12387)
Haugen R A, Wichern D W
The diametric effects of the capital gains tax on
the stability of stock prices
JF 1973 VOL 28 p 987.

(12388)
Pye G
Preferential tax treatment of capital gains, optimal
dividend policy, and capital budgeting
QJE 1972 MAY VOL 86 p 226-242.

(12389)
Pye G
Capital gains taxation, dividends, and capital
budgeting
QJE 1972 VOL 86 p 226.

(12390)
McClung N
The distribution of capital gain on corporate
shares by holding time
REStat 1966 OCT VOL 48 p 40-50.

(12391)
Merrett A J
The capital gains tax
LBR 1965 OCT VOL 78 p 1-14..

(12392)**Malkiel B G, Kane E J**
U.S. tax law and the locked-in effect
NTJ 1963 DEC VOL 16 p 389-396.

(12393)
Holt C C, Shelton J P
The lock-in effect of the capital gains tax
NTJ 1962 DEC VOL 15 p 337-352.

(12394)
Shelton J P
Influence of the six-month capital gains rules on
short term transactions
FAJ 1962 SEP-OCT VOL 18 p 99-101.

(12395)
Sprinkel B W, West B K
Effects of capital gains taxes on investment
decisions
JB 1962 APR VOL 35 p 122-134.

(12396)
Holt C C, Shelton J P
The implications of the capital gains tax for
investment decision
JF 1961 DEC VOL 16 p 559-580.

(12397)
Steiger W
The taxation of unrealized capital gains and
losses: a statistical study
NTJ 1957 SEP VOL 10.

(12398)
Gemmill R F
The effect of the capital gains tax on asset prices
NTJ 1956 VOL 9.

38.2   Personal income tax

(12399)
Barth J R, Bradley M D
On interest rates, inflationary expectations and tax
rates
JBankF 1988 VOL 12:2 p 215-220.

(12400)
Bey R P, Collins J M
The relationship between before- and after-tax
yields on financial assets
FR 1988 AUG VOL 23:3 p 313-332.

(12401)
Dammon R M
A security market and capital structure equilibrium under uncertainty with progressive personal taxes
(in Chen A ed., Research in finance, Vol 7. JAI Pr, 1987.)

(12402)
Rashid M, Amoako-Adu B
Personal taxes, inflation and market valuation
JFR 1987 VOL 10:4 p 341-352.

(12403)
Vanthienen L, Vermaelen T
The effect of personal taxes on common stock prices: the case of a Belgian tax reform
JBankF 1987 VOL 11 p 223-244.

(12404)
Dymits L, Murray M L
Another look at implied tax rates
JBankF 1986 VOL 10 p 133.

(12405)
Hubbard R G
Personal taxation, pension wealth, and portfolio composition
REStat 1985 VOL 67 p 53.

(12406)
Talmor E
Personal tax considerations in portfolio construction : tilting the optimal portfolio selection
QREB 1985 AUTUMN VOL 25:3 p 55-71

(12407)
Peek J
Interest rates, income taxes and anticipated inflation
AER 1982 VOL 72 p 980-991.

(12408)
Schaefer S M
Taxes and security market equilibrium
(in Sharpe W F and Cootner C M eds., Financial economics: Essays in honor of Paul Cootner. P-H, 1982.)

(12409)
Vandell R F, Stevens J L
Personal taxes and equity security pricing
FIN MGMT 1982 SPRING VOL 11 p 31-40.

(12410)
Eaton J, Rosen H S
Taxation, human capital and uncertainty
AER 1980 VOL 70 p 705-715.

(12411)
Feldstein M
The welfare cost of capital income taxation
JPE 1978 VOL 86 Suppl p 29.

(12412)
Shoven J B
The incidence and efficiency effects of taxes on income from capital
JPE 1976 VOL 84 p 1261.

(12413)
Broome J
An important theorem on income tax
REStud 1975 VOL 42 p 649.

(12414)
Lepper S J
Effects of alternative tax structures on individuals' holdings of financial assets
(in Hester D D and Tobin J eds., Risk aversion and portfolio choice. Wiley, 1967.)

(12415)
Jolivet V
The weighted average marginal tax rate on dividends received by individuals in the U.S.
AER 1966 JUN VOL 56 p 473-477.

(12416)
Holland D M
The income-tax burden on stockholders
(Dist by Princeton U Pr) Natl Bur Econ Res, 1958.

(12417)
Butters J K, Thompson L E, Bollinger L L
Effects of taxation on investments by individuals
Harvard Busn, 1953.

38.3   Corporate tax

(12418)
Gravelle J G, Kotlikoff L J
The incidence and efficiency costs of corporate
taxation when corporate and noncorporate firms
produce the same good
JPE 1989 VOL 97 p 749.

(12419)
Angell R J
The effect of the Tax Reform Act on capital
investment decisions
FIN MGMT 1988 WINTER VOL 17 p 82-86.

(12420)
Auerbach A J, Hines J R Jr
Investment tax incentives and frequent tax reforms
AER 1988 MAY VOL 78:2 p 211-216.

(12421)
Mintz J M
An empirical estimate of corporate tax
refundability and effective tax rates
QJE 1988 VOL 103 p 225.

(12422)
Ang J S
Tax asymmetries and the optimal investment
decision in the firm
EE 1987 WINTER VOL 32:2 p 135-161.

(12423)
Heaton H
On the bias of the corporate tax against high-risk
projects
JFQA 1987 SEP VOL 22 p 365-371.

(12424)
Alworth J
A cost of capital approach to the taxation of
foreign direct investment income
(in Edwards J et al. eds., Recent developments in
corporate finance. Cambridge U Pr, 1986.)

(12425)
Green R C, Talmor E
Effects of asymmetric taxation on the scale of
corporate investment
(in Edwards J et al. eds., Recent developments in
corporate finance. Cambridge U Pr, 1986.)

(12426)
Mayer C
Corporation tax, finance and the cost of capital
REStud 1986 VOL 53 p 93.

(12427)
Angell R J
Depreciable basis/ITC decisions when the ITC is
deferred
FIN MGMT 1985 SUMMER VOL 14 p 43-47.

(12428)
Gordon R H
Taxation of corporate capital income: Tax
revenues versus tax distortions
QJE 1985 VOL 100 p 1.

(12429)
Green R C, Talmor E
The structure and incentive effects of corporate
tax liabilities
JF 1985 SEP VOL 40:4 p 1095-1114.

(12430)
Maloney K J, Selling T I
Simplifying tax simplification: An analysis of its
impact on the profitability of capital investment
FIN MGMT 1985 SUMMER VOL 14 p 33-42.

(12431)
Auerbach A J
Welfare aspects of current U S corporate taxation
AER 1983 VOL 73 P+P p 76-81.

(12432)
Brenner M, Venezia I
The effects of inflation and taxes on growth
investments and replacement policies
JF 1983 DEC VOL 38:5 p 1519-1528.

(12433)
Cooper I A, Franks J R
The interaction of financial and investment
decisions when the firm has unused tax credits
JF 1983 MAY VOL 38:2 p 571-583.

(12434)
Angell R J, Wingler T R
A note on expensing versus depreciating under
the accelerated cost recovery system
FIN MGMT 1982 WINTER VOL 11 p 34-35.

(12435)
Auerbach A J
Inflation and the tax treatment of firm behavior
AER 1981 VOL 71 P+P p 419-423.

(12436)
Caks J
Sense and nonsense about depreciation
FIN MGMT 1981 AUTUMN VOL 10 p 80-86.

(12437)
Cordes J J, Sheffrin S M
Taxation and the sectoral allocation of capital in
the U.S.
NTJ 1981 VOL 34 p 419-432.

(12438)
Fullerton D, King A R, Shoven J B
Corporate tax integration in the United states: A
general equilibrium approach
AER 1981 VOL 71 p 677-691.

(12439)
Kopcke R W
Inflation, corporate income taxation and the
demand for capital assets
JPE 1981 VOL 89 p 122-131.

(12440)
Malcomson J M
Corporate tax policy and the service life of capital
equipment
REStud 1981 APR VOL 48:2 NO 152 p 311-316.

(12441)
Mintz J M
Some additional results on investment risk taking
and full loss offset corporate taxation with
interest deductibility
QJE 1981 VOL 96 p 631.

(12442)
Wunder H F
Tax incentives and the investment function of
electric utilities
EE 1979 FALL VOL 25:1 p 39-51.

(12443)
Ballentine J G
The incidence of a corporation income tax in a
growing economy
JPE 1978 VOL 86 P 863

(12444)
Boadway R
Investment incentives corporate taxation and
efficiency in the allocation of capital
EJ 1978 SEP VOL 88:351 p 470-481..

(12445) **Jaffe J F**
A note on taxation and investment
JF 1978 VOL 33 p 1439.

(12446)
Jaffe J F
Corporate taxes, inflation, the rate of interest and
the return of equity
JFQA 1978 MAR VOL 13 p 55.

(12447)
Tatom J A, Turley J E
Inflation and taxes: disincentives for capital
formation
F R Bk St Louis Rev 1978 VOL 60:1.

(12448)
Akhtar M A
Taxation of corporate income: some European
approaches
F R Bk New York Q Rev 1977 SUMMER VOL
2.

(12449)
Corcoran P J
Inflation, taxes, and corporate investment
incentives
F R Bk New York Q Rev 1977 AUTUMN VOL
2.

(12450)
Lawrenz D W
The effects of corporate taxation on the cost of
equity capital
FIN MGMT 1976 SPRING VOL 5 p 53.

(12451)
Stiglitz J E
The corporation tax
Journal of Public Economics 1976 VOL 5 p
303-311.

(12452)
Sandmo A
Investment incentives and the corporate income
tax
JPE 1974 VOL 82 p 287.

(12453)
Brealey R A
A note on dividends and debt under the new
taxation
JBF 1973 SPRING VOL 5:1 p 66-68.

(12454)
Comiskey E E, Hasselback J R
Analyzing the profit-tax relationship
FIN MGMT 1973 WINTER VOL 2 p 57.

(12455)
Summer M T
Investment and corporate taxation
JPE 1973 VOL 81 p 982.

(12456)
Thomas R
The change in corporation tax and the incentive
to invest
JBF 1973 SPRING VOL 5:1 p 69-75.

(12457)
Musgrave P B
International tax division base and the
multinational corporation
Public Finance 1972 VOL 27 p 394-413.

(12458)
Cragg J G, Harburger A C, Mieszkowski P
Empirical evidence on the incidence of the
corporation income tax
JPE 1967 DEC VOL 75 p 811-821.

(12459)
Samuelson P A
Tax deductibility of economic depreciation to
insure invariant valuations
JPE 1964 VOL 72 p 604-606.

(12460)
Krzyzaniak M, Musgrave R A
The shifting of the corporation income tax: an
empirical study of its short run effect upon the
rate of return
Johns Hopkins, 1963.

(12461)
Miller M H
The corporation income tax and corporate
financial policies
(in The Commission on Money and Credit,
Stabilization Policies. P-H, 1963.)

(12462)
Harberger A C
The incidence of the corporation income tax
JPE 1962 JUN VOL 70 p 215-240.

(12463)
Clark C D
A note on investment activities and the graduated
corporate tax
JF 1957 MAR VOL 12 p 44-50.

(12464)
Smith D T
Corporate taxation and common stock financing
NTJ 1953 SEP VOL 6 p 209-225.

(12465)
Smith D T
Effects of taxation: corporate financial policy
Harvard Busn, 1952.

39 Inflation

(12466)
Stockton D J, Struckmeyer C S
Tests of the specification and predictive accuracy
of nonnested models of inflation
REStat 1989 VOL 71 p 275.

(12467)
Benabou R
Search, price setting and inflation
REStud 1988 VOL 55 p 353.

(12468)
Chu C-C
A risk premium under uncertain inflation: the
inflation futures evidence
JFM 1988 JUN VOL 8:3 p 353-364.

(12469)
Jonung L, Laidler D
Are perceptions of inflation rational?   Some
evidence from Sweden
AER 1988 VOL 78:5 p 1080-1087.

(12470)
Green S
Theories of inflation: a review essay
JME 1987 VOL 20 p 169.

(12471)
Lewellen W G, Kracaw W A
Inflation, corporate growth and corporate leverage
FIN MGMT 1987 WINTER VOL 16 p 29-36.

(12472)
Kantor L G
Inflation uncertainty and real economic activity:
an alternative approach
REStat 1986 VOL 68 p 493.

(12473)
Gordon R H
Inflation, taxation and corporate behavior
QJE 1984 VOL 99 p 313.

(12474)
Engle R F
Estimates of the variance of U.S. inflation based
upon the ARCH model
JMCB 1983 AUG VOL 15:3 p 286-301.

(12475)
Hochman S, Palmon O
The irrelevance of capital structure for the impact
of inflation on investment
JF 1983 JUN VOL 38:3 p 785-794.

(12476)
Pagan A R, Hall A D, Trivedi P K
Assessing the variability of inflation
REStud 1983 VOL 50 p 585.

(12477)
Ben-Horim M, Levy H
Inflation and the trade credit period
MSci 1982 JUN VOL 28:6 p 646-651.

(12478)
Chua J H, Woodward R S
Gold as an inflation hedge: A comparative study
of six major industrial countries
JBFA 1982 SUMMER VOL 9:2 p 191-197.

(12479)
Fama E F
Inflation output and money
JB 1982 APR VOL 55:2 p 201-231.

(12480)
Hall R E ed.
Inflation: causes and effects
U of Chicago Pr, 1982.

(12481)
Morris M H, McDonald B
Asset pricing and financial reporting with
changing prices
JBFA 1982 AUTUMN VOL 9:3 p 383.

(12482)
Feldstein M
Private pensions and inflation
AER 1981 VOL 71 P+P p 424-428.

(12483)
Kane E J
Accelerating inflation technological innovation
and the decreasing effectiveness of banking
regulation
JF 1981 MAY VOL 36:2 p 355-367.

(12484)
Kopcke R W
Inflation, corporate income taxation and the demand for capital assets
JPE 1981 VOL 89 p 122-131.

(12485)
Landskroner Y, Liviatan N
Risk premia and the sources of inflation
JMCB 1981 MAY VOL 13:2 p 205-214.

(12486)
McCallum B T
Price level determinacy with an interest rate policy rule and rational expectations
JME 1981 VOL 8 p 319.

(12487)
Arrow K J
Real and nominal magnitudes in economics
JFQA 1980 NOV VOL 15 p 773.

(12488)
Everett J E, Dickinson J P
Some aspects of inflation, tax and the investing borrower
JBFA 1979 WINTER VOL 6:4 p 527-538.

(12489)
Frenkel J A
Further evidence on expectations and the demand for money during the German hyperinflation
JME 1979 VOL 5 p 81.

(12490)
Goodman D E, McMahon W W
Predicting inflation rates with changing oil prices
QREB 1979 VOL 19:2 p 35.

(12491)
Jaffe J F, Mandelker G
Inflation and the holding period returns on bonds
JFQA 1979 DEC VOL 14 p 959.

(12492)
Pearce D K
Comparing survey and rational measures of expected inflation: forecast performance and interest rate effects
JMCB 1979 NOV VOL 11:4 p 447-456.

(12493)
Salemi M K
Adaptive expectations, rational expectations and money demand in hyperinflation Germany
JME 1979 VOL 5 p 593.

(12494)
Scadding J L
Estimating the underlying inflation rate
F R Bk San Francisco Ec Rev 1979 SPRING.

(12495)
Feldstein M, Green J, Sheshinski E
Inflation and taxes in a growing economy with debt and equity finance
JPE 1978 VOL 86 Suppl p 53.

(12496)
Feldstein M, Slemrod J
How inflation distorts the taxation of capital gains
HBR 1978 SEP-OCT VOL 56:5 p 2022.

(12497)
Sarnat M ed.
Inflation and the capital markets
Ballinger, 1978..

(12498)**Siegel J J**
Notes on optimal taxation and the optimal rate of inflation
JME 1978 VOL 4 p 297.

(12499)
Solnik B H
Inflation and optimal portfolio choices
JFQA 1978 DEC VOL 13 p 903.

(12500)
Balbach R
The effects of changes in inflationary expectations
F R Bk St Louis Rev 1977 VOL 59:4.

(12501)
Frenkel J A
The forward exchange rate, expectations and the demand for money: The German hyperinflation
AER 1977 VOL 67 p 653-670.

(12502)
Hong H
Inflationary tax effects on the assets of business corporations
FIN MGMT 1977 AUTUMN VOL 6 p 51.

(12503)
Bisignano J
Inflation and the efficiency of capital markets
F R Bk San Francisco Ec Rev 1976 SUMMER.

(12504)
Keran M W
Inflation, regulation, and utility stock prices
BellJ 1976 SPRING VOL 7:1 p 268-280.

(12505)
Yeager L
Bootstrap inflation
JF 1976 VOL 31 p 103.

(12506)
Cowan T K
The maintenance of financial viability under inflationary conditions: A planning model
JBFA 1975 AUTUMN VOL 2:3 p 361-372.

(12507)
Francis D R
The origin and impact of inflation
F R Bk St Louis Rev 1975 VOL 57:12.

(12508)
Gordon R J
The demand for and supply of inflation
JLE 1975 VOL 18 p 807.

(12509)
Gramm W P
Inflation: its cause and cure
F R Bk St Louis Rev 1975 VOL 57:2.

(12510)
Helbling H H, Turley J E
A primer on inflation: its conception, its costs, its consequences
F R Bk St Louis Rev 1975 VOL 57:1.

(12511)
Karnosky D S
A primer on the consumer price index
F R Bk St Louis Rev 1974 VOL 56:7.

(12512)
Lovell M C, Vogel R C
A CPI futures market
JPE 1973 JUL-AUG VOL 81:4 p 1009-1016.

(12513)
Bierman H Jr
Discounted cash flows, price level adjustments and expectations
AR 1971 OCT VOL 46 p 693-699.

(12514)
Kessel R A, Alchian A A
Effects of inflation
JPE 1962 DEC VOL 70 p 521-537.

39.1 Inflation expectations

(12515)
Batchelor R A, Dua P
Household versus economist forecasts of inflation: a reassessment
JMCB 1989 VOL 21 p 252-257.

(12516)
Patterson K D
Modelling price expectations
AE 1989 VOL 21:4 p 413.

(12517)
Mehra Y P
The forecast performance of alternative models of inflation
F R Bk Richmond Ec Rev 1988 SEP-OCT VOL 74:5.

(12518)
Throop A W
An evaluation of alternative measures of expected inflation
F R Bk San Francisco Ec Rev 1988 SUMMER NO 3.

(12519)
Webb R H
Commodity prices as predictors of aggregate price change
F R Bk Richmond Ec Rev 1988 NOV-DEC VOL 74:6.

(12520)
Leonard D C, Solt M E
Stock market signals of changes in expected inflation
JFR 1987 VOL 10:1 p 57-64.

(12521)
Pearce D K
Short term inflation expectations: evidence from a monthly survey
JMCB 1987 AUG VOL 19:3 p 388-395.

(12522)
Stockton D J, Glassman J E
An evaluation of the forecast performance of alternative models of inflation
REStat 1987 VOL 69 p 108.

(12523)
Bryan M F, Gavin W T
Models of inflation expectations formation: a comparison of household and economist forecasts
JMCB 1986 NOV VOL 18:4 p 539-544.

(12524)
Burmeister E, Hamilton J
Estimation of unobserved expected monthly inflation using Kalman filtering
Journal of Business and Economic Statistics 1986 APR VOL 4 p 147-160.

(12525)
Cukierman A
Measuring inflationary expectations: a review essay
JME 1986 VOL 17 p 315.

(12526)
Schroeter J R, Smith S L
A reexamination of the rationality of the Livingston price expectations: a note
JMCB 1986 MAY VOL 18:2 p 239-246.

(12527)
Thies C F
Business price expectations: 1947-83
JMCB 1986 AUG VOL 18:3 p 336-354.

(12528)
Hamilton J D
Uncovering financial market expectations of inflation
JPE 1985 VOL 93 p 1224.

(12529)
Hvidding J M
Models of inflation expectations formation
JMCB 1985 NOV VOL 17:4 p 534-538.

(12530)
Fama E F, Gibbons M R
A comparison of inflation forecasts
JME 1984 VOL 13 p 327.

(12531)
Fishe R P H
On testing hypotheses using the Livingston price expectations data
JMCB 1984 NOV VOL 16:4 p 520-527.

(12532)
VanderHoff J
A "rational" explanation for "irrational" forecasts of inflation
JME 1984 VOL 13 p 387.

(12533)
Gramlich E M
Models of inflation expectations formation: a comparison of household and economist forecasts
JMCB 1983 MAY VOL 15:2 p 155-173.

(12534)
Papadia F
Rationality of inflationary expectations in the European Economic Communities countries
Empirical Economics 1983 VOL 8:3-4.

(12535)
Engle R F
Autoregressive conditional hetereroscedasticity with estimates of the variance of United Kingdom inflation
Em 1982 JUL VOL 50 p 987-1008.

(12536)
Frankel J A
A technique for extracting a measure of expected inflation from the interest rate term structure
REStat 1982 VOL 64 p 135.

(12537)
Jonung L
Perceived and expected rates of inflation in Sweden
AER 1981 VOL 71 p 961-968.

(12538)
Hafer R W, Resler D H
The "rationality" of survey-based inflation forecasts
F R Bk St Louis Rev 1980 VOL 62:9.

(12539)
Pigott C
Expectations, money, and the forecasting of inflation
F R Bk San Francisco Ec Rev 1980 SPRING.

(12540)
Resler D H
The formation and inflation expectations
F R Bk St Louis Rev 1980 VOL 62:4.

(12541)
Cukierman A, Wachtel P
Differential inflationary expectations and the variability of the rate of inflation: Theory and evidence
AER 1979 VOL 69 p 595-609.

(12542)
Carlson J
A study of price forecasts
Annals of Economic and Social Measurement 1977 WINTER VOL 6 p 27-53.

(12543)
Fackler J, Stanhouse B
Rationality of the Michigan price expectations data
JMCB 1977 NOV VOL 9:4 p 662-666.

(12544)
Khan M S
The variability of expectations in hyperinflations
JPE 1977 VOL 85 p 817.

(12545)
Valentine T J
The demand for money and price expectations in Australia
JF 1977 VOL 32 p 735.

(12546)
Frankel J A
Inflation and the formation of expectations
JME 1975 VOL 1 p 403.

(12547)
Mussa M
Adaptive and regressive expectations in a rational model of the inflationary process
JME 1975 VOL 1 p 423.

(12548)
Pesando J E
A note on the rationality of the Livingston price expectations
JPE 1975 VOL 83 p 849.

(12549)
Severn A K
Further evidence on the formation of price expectations
QREB 1973 VOL 13:4 p 27.

(12550)
Van Horne J C
Expected inflation implied by capital market rates
JF 1973 VOL 28 p 301.

39.2 Inflation and risky asset returns

(12551)
Dokko Y
Are changes in inflation expectations capitalized into stock prices? A micro-firm test for the nominal contracting hypothesis
REStat 1989 VOL 71 p 309.

(12552)
Ely D P, Robinson K J
The stock market and inflation: a synthesis of the theory and evidence
F R Bk Dallas Ec Rev 1989 MAR.

(12553)
Labadie P
Stochastic inflation and the equity premium
JME 1989 VOL 24 p 277.

(12554)
Ma C K, Ellis M E
Selecting industries as inflation hedges
JPM 1989 SUMMER VOL 15:4 p 45-48.

(12555)
McDevitt C L
The role of the nominal tax system in the
common stock returns/expected inflation
relationship
JME 1989 VOL 24 p 93.

(12556)
Titman S, Warga A
Stock returns as predictors of interest rates and
inflation
JFQA 1989 MAR VOL 24:1 p 47-58.

(12557)
Chen S-N
Estimation risk and the demand for risky assets
under uncertain inflation: heterogeneous versus
homogeneous expectations
QREB 1988 VOL 28:2 p 30.

(12558)
Estep A, Hanson N
The valuation of financial assets in inflation
(in Fabozzi F ed., Selected topics in investment
management. Ballinger, 1988.)

(12559)
Lewis K K
Inflation risk and asset market disturbances: the
mean-variance model revisited
JIMF 1988 SEP VOL 7:3 p 273-288.

(12560)
Loo J C H
Common stock returns, expected inflation, and
the rational expectations hypothesis
JFR 1988 VOL 11:2 p 165-171.

(12561)
Pearce D K, Roley V V
Firm characteristics, unanticipated inflation and
stock returns
JF 1988 SEP VOL 43:4 p 965-982.

(12562)
Peel D A, Pope P F
Stock returns and expected inflation in the U K:
Some new evidence
JBFA 1988 WINTER VOL 15:4 p 459-468.

(12563)
Bernard V L, Frecka T J
Commodity contracts and common stocks as
hedges against relative consumer price risk
JFQ 1987 JUN VOL 22 p 169.

(12564)
Chang E C, Pinegar J M
Risk and inflation
JFQA 1987 MAR VOL 22 p 89-99.

(12565)
Howe K M
Does inflationary change affect capital asset life?
FIN MGMT 1987 SUMMER VOL 16 p 63-67.

(12566)
Howe K M, Lapan H
Inflation and asset life : The Darby versus the
Fisher effect
JFQA 1987 JUN VOL 22:2 p 249-258.

(12567)
Jones C P, Wilson J W
Stocks, bonds, paper, and inflation: 1870-1985
JPM 1987 FALL VOL 14:1 p 20-24.

(12568)
Kaul G
Stock returns and inflation: the role of the
monetary sector
JFE 1987 JUN VOL 18:2 p 253-276.

(12569)
Levy H, Levy A
Equilibrium under uncertain inflation: a discrete
time approach
JFQA 1987 SEP VOL 22:3 p 285-297.

(12570)
Bernard V L
Unanticipated inflation and the value of the firm
JFE 1986 VOL 15 p 285-321.

(12571)
Burnie D A
Capital asset prices and the Friedman hypothesis
of inflation
JBFA 1986 VOL 13:4 p 519.

(12572)
Chang R P, Rhee S G
Does the stock market react to announcements of
the producer price index?
FR 1986 FEB VOL 21:1.

(12573)
Matolcsy Z P
The distributive nominal and real micro effects of
inflation on security returns: Some Australian
evidence
JBankF 1986 VOL 10 p 361.

(12574)
Smirlock M
Inflation announcements and financial market
reaction: evidence from the long-term bond
market
REStat 1986 VOL 68 p 329.

(12575)
Stultz R M
Asset pricing and expected inflation
JF 1986 MAR VOL 41:1 p 209-223.

(12576)
Wahlroos B, Berglund T
Stock returns, inflationary expectations and real
activity: New evidence
JBankF 1986 VOL 10 p 377.

(12577)
Benderly J, Zwick B
Inflation, real balances, output and real stock
returns
AER 1985 VOL 75 p 1115-1123.

(12578)
Canto V A, Findlay M C, Reinganum M R
Inflation, money and stock prices: an alternative
interpretation
FR 1985 FEB VOL 20:1.

(12579)
Jaffe J F
Inflation, the interest rate, and the required
return on equity.
JFQA 1985 MAR VOL 20:1 p 29-44.

(12580)
Day T E
Real stock returns and inflation
JF 1984 JUN VOL 39:2 p 493-502.

(12581)
Hasbrouck J
Stock returns inflation and economic activity : the
survey evidence
JF 1984 DEC VOL 39:5 p 1293-1310.

(12582)
Kanniainen V, Kurikka V
On the effects of inflation in the stock market :
empirical evidence with Finnish data 1968-1981
JBFA 1984 SUMMER VOL 11:2 p 139-150

(12583)
Pindyck R S
Risk, inflation and the stock market
AER 1984 VOL 74 p 335-351.

(12584)
French K R, Ruback R S, Schwert G W
Effects of nominal contracting on stock returns
JPE 1983 VOL 91 p 70.

(12585)
Geske R, Roll R
The fiscal and monetary linkage between stock
returns and inflation
JF 1983 MAR VOL 38:1 p 1-33.

(12586)
Gordon M J
The impact of real factors and inflation on the
performance of the U.S. stock market from 1960
to 1980
JF 1983 MAY VOL 38:2 p 553-563.

(12587)
Gultekin N B
Stock market returns and inflation forecasts
JF 1983 JUN VOL 38:3 p 663-673

(12588)
Gultekin N B
Stock market returns and inflation: evidence from other countries
JF 1983 MAR VOL 38:1 p 49-65

(12589)
Solnik B H
The relation between stock prices and inflationary expectations: the international evidence
JF 1983 MAR VOL 38:1 p 35-46.

(12590)
Copeland B L
Inflation, interest rates and equity risk premia
FAJ 1982 MAY-JUN p 32-44.

(12591)
Ebrill L P, Possen U M
Inflation and the taxation of equity in corporations and owner occupied housing
JMCB 1982 FEB VOL 14:1 p 33-47.

(12592)
Gertler M, Grinols E L
Unemployment, inflation, and common stock returns
JMCB 1982 MAY VOL 14:2 p 216-233.

(12593)
Kanniainen V
Unanticipated inflation, taxation and common stocks
JBFA 1982 WINTER VOL 9:4 p 459-469.

(12594)
Ruback R S
The effect of discretionary price control decisions on equity values
JFE 1982 VOL 10 p 83.

(12595)
Arak M
Inflation and stock values: is our tax structure the villain?
F R Bk New York Q Rev 1980-81 WINTER VOL 5:4.

(12596)
Auerbach A J
Inflation and the tax treatment of firm behavior
AER 1981 VOL 71 P+P p 419-423.

(12597)
Cohn R A, Lessard D R
The effect of inflation on stock prices: international evidence
JF 1981 MAY VOL 36:2 p 277-289.

(12598)
Fama E F
Stock returns, real activity, inflation and money
AER 1981 VOL 71 p 545-565.

(12599)
Fuller R J, Petry G H
Inflation, return on equity and, stock prices
JPM 1981 SUMMER VOL 7:4 p 19-25.

(12600)
Higgins R C
Sustainable growth under inflation
FIN MGMT 1981 AUTUMN VOL 10 p 36-40.

(12601)
Johnson D J
The behavior of financial structure and sustainable growth in an inflationary environment
FIN MGMT 1981 AUTUMN VOL 10 p 30-35.

(12602)
Schwert G W
The adjustment of stock prices to information about inflation
JF 1981 MAR VOL 36:1 p 15-29.

(12603)
Summers L H
Inflation, the stock market and owner-occupied housing
AER 1981 VOL 71 P+P p 429..

(12604)**Bloom R**
Inflation gains and losses on monetary items: an empirical test
JBFA 1980 VOL 7:4 p 603-618

(12605)
Feldstein M
Inflation, tax rules and the stock market
JME 1980 VOL 6 p 309.

(12606)
Feldstein M
Inflation and the stock market
AER 1980 VOL 70 p 839-847.

(12607)
Levy H
The capital asset pricing model, inflation and the
investment horizon: The Israeli experience
JFQA 1980 SEP VOL 15 p 561.

(12608)
Modani N K, Cooley P L, Roenfeldt R L
Covariation of risk measures under inflation
JBFA 1980 AUTUMN VOL 7:3 p 393-400.

(12609)
Moore B
Equity values and inflation: the importance of
dividends
LBR 1980 JUL 137 p 1-15

(12610)
Pozdena R J
Inflation expectations and the housing market
F R Bk San Francisco Ec Rev 1980 FALL.

(12611)
Pyun C S
A note on capital asset pricing model under
uncertain inflation
JFQA 1980 JUN VOL 15 p 425.

(12612)
Brealey R A
Inflation and the real value of government assets
FAJ 1979 JAN-FEB p 18-22.

(12613)
Firth M
The relationship between stock market returns
and rates of inflation
JF 1979 JUN VOL 34:3 p 743-749.

(12614)
Modigliani F, Cohn R A
Inflation, rational valuation and the market
FAJ 1979 MAR-APR VOL 35 p 24-44.

(12615)
Saunders A
Expected inflation, unexpected inflation and the
return on UK shares 1961-1973
JBFA 1978 AUTUMN VOL 5:3 p 309-320.

(12616)
Hong H
Inflation and the market value of the firm:
Theory and tests
JF 1977 VOL 32 p 1031.

(12617)
Meltzer A H
Anticipated inflation and unanticipated price
change
JMCB 1977 FEB VOL 9:1 p 182-205.

(12618)
Rozeff M S
The association between firm risk and wealth
transfers due to inflation
JFQA 1977 JUN VOL 12 p 151.

(12619)
Biger N
Portfolio selection and purchasing power risk -
recent Canadian experience
JFQA 1976 JUN VOL 11 p 251.

(12620)
Bradford W D
Monetary position, unanticipated inflation, and
changes in the value of the firm
QREB 1976 VOL 16:4 p 47.

(12621)
Friend I, Landskroner Y, Losq E
The demand for risky assets under uncertain
inflation
JF 1976 VOL 31 p 1287.

(12622)
Gordon M J, Halpern P J
Bond share yield spreads under uncertain inflation
AER 1976 SEP VOL 66:4 p 559-565.

(12623)
Johnson G L, Reilly F K, Smith R E
A correction and update regarding individual
common stocks as inflation hedges
JFQA 1975 DEC VOL 10 p 871.

(12624)
Jollineau R W, Singh S P
Inflation and the profitability of firms in Canada
JBFA 1975 SPRING VOL 2:1 p 105-120.

(12625)
Lintner J
Presidential address: Inflation and security returns
JF 1975 MAY VOL 30:2 p 259-280.

(12626)
Mussa M
Equities, interest, and the stability of the inflationary process
JMCB 1975 NOV VOL 7:4 p 433-448.

(12627)
Long J B Jr
Stock prices, inflation and the term structure of interest rates
JFE 1974 VOL 1 p 131.

(12628)
Brinson G P
The synergistic impact of taxes and inflation on investment return
FAJ 1973 MAR-APR VOL 29 p 74-75.

(12629)
Oudet B A
The variation of the return on stocks in periods of inflation
JFQA 1973 MAR VOL 8:2 p 247-258.

(12630)
Johnson G L, Reilly F K, Smith R E
Individual common stocks as inflation hedges
JFQA 1971 JUN VOL 6 p 1015-1024.

(12631)
Nichols D A
A note on inflation and common stock values
JF 1968 SEP VOL 23 p 655-657.

(12632)
Alchian A A, Kessel R A
Redistribution of wealth through inflation
Science 1959 SEP 4 VOL 130 p 535-539.

(12633)
Clendenin J C
Price-level variations and the tenets of high grade investment
JF 1959 MAY VOL 14 p 245-262.

39.3   Inflation and financial decisions

(12634)
Agmon T, Horesh R
Inflation, disinflation, and corporate financial decisions
Heath, 1988.

(12635)
Ferris S P, Makhija A K
Inflation effect on corporate capital investment
JBusR 1988 MAY VOL 16:3 p 251-260.

(12636)
Baldwin C Y, Ruback R S
Inflation uncertainty and investment.
JF 1986 JUL VOL 41:3 p 657-669.

(12637)
Hochman S, Palmon O
The impact of inflation on the aggregate debt-asset ratio
JF 1985 SEP VOL 40:4 p 1115-1125.

(12638)
Landskroner Y, Ruthenberg D
Optimal bank behavior under uncertain inflation
JF 1985 SEP VOL 40:4 p 1159-1171.

(12639)
Ezzell J R, Kelly W A Jr
An APV analysis of capital budgeting under inflation
FIN MGMT 1984 AUTUMN VOL 13 p 49.

(12640)
Mehta D R, Curley M D, Fung H-G
Inflation, cost of capital and capital budgeting procedures
FIN MGMT 1984 WINTER VOL 13 p 48.

(12641)
Schall L D
Taxes, inflation and corporate financial policy
JF 1984 MAR VOL 39:1 p 105-126.

(12642)
Brenner M, Venezia I
The effects of inflation and taxes on growth investments and replacement policies
JF 1983 DEC VOL 38:5 p 1519-1528.

(12643)
Feldstein M
Inflation, tax rules and capital formation
U of Chicago Pr, 1983.

(12644)
Shashua L, Goldschmidt Y
Tools for financial management: emphasis on inflation
Lexington Bks, 1983.

(12645)
Fama E F, Gibbons M R
Inflation, real returns and capital investment
JME 1982 VOL 9 p 297-323.

(12646)
Rappaport A, Taggart R A Jr
Evaluation of capital expenditure proposals under inflation
FIN MGMT 1982 SPRING VOL 11 p 5-13.

(12647)
Bodie V
An innovation for stable real retirement income
JPM 1980 FALL VOL 7:1 p 5-13.

(12648)
Leuthold S C
The myths of inflation and investing
Crain Books, 1980.

(12649)
Auerbach A J
Inflation and the choice of asset life
JPE 1979 VOL 87 p 621.

(12650)
Jaffe J F
Corporate taxes, inflation, the rate of interest and the return of equity
JFQA 1978 MAR VOL 13 p 55.

(12651)
Tatom J A, Turley J E
Inflation and taxes: disincentives for capital formation
F R Bk St Louis Rev 1978 VOL 60:1.

(12652)
Corcoran P J
Inflation, taxes, and corporate investment incentives
F R Bk New York Q Rev 1977 AUTUMN VOL 2.

(12653)
Von Furstenberg G M, Malkiel B G
Financial analysis in an inflationary environment
JF 1977 MAY VOL 32:2 p 575-587.

(12654)
Chen A H, Boness J A
Effects of uncertain inflation on the investment and financing decisions of a firm
JF 1975 MAY VOL 30:2 p 469-484.

(12655)
Cooley P L, Roenfeldt R L, Chew I-K
Capital budgeting procedures under inflation
FIN MGMT 1975 WINTER VOL 4 p 18.

(12656)
Scholefield N H, McBain N S, Bagwell J
The effects of inflation on investment appraisal
JBF 1973 SUMMER VOL 5:2 p 39-48..

(12657)**Van Horne J C**
A note on biases in capital budgeting introduced by inflation
JFQA 1971 JAN VOL 6 p 653-658.

(12658)
Foster E M
The impact of inflation on capital budgeting decisions
QREB 1970 VOL 10:3 p 19.

(12659)
Mathews R
Inflation and company finance
<u>AR 1960 JAN VOL 35 p 8-18</u>.

40 Econometrics and statistics

(12660)
Skomp S E, Cronan T P, Seaver W L
On application of the rank transformation discrimination method to financial problems
FR 1986 NOV VOL 21:4.

(12661)
Tauchen G
Statistical properties of GMM estimates of structural parameters using financial market data
Journal of Business and Economic Statistics 1986 OCT VOL 4 p 372-375.

(12662)
Judge G G et al.
The theory and practice of econometrics. 2nd ed
Wiley, 1985.

(12663)
Johnston J
Econometric methods. 3rd ed
McGraw, 1984.

(12664)
Hansen L P
Large sample properties of generalized method of moments estimators
Em 1982 JUL VOL 50 p 1029-1054.

(12665)
Hansen L P, Singleton K J
Generalized instrumental variables estimation of nonlinear expectations models
Em 1982 SEP VOL 50 p 1269-1286.

(12666)
Altman E I, Avery R B, Eisenbeis R A et al.
Applications of classification techniques in business, banking and finance
JAI Pr, 1981.

(12667)
Beaver W H
Econometric properties of alternative security return methods
JAR 1981 SPRING VOL 19:1 p 163-184.

(12668)
Altman E I, Eisenbeis R A
Financial applications of discriminant analysis: A clarification
JFQA 1978 MAR VOL 13 p 185.

(12669)
Dhrymes P J
Mathematics for econometrics
Springer, 1978

(12670)
Eisenbeis R A
Pitfalls in the application of discriminant analysis in business, finance and economics
JF 1977 VOL 32 p 875.

(12671)
Intrilagator M
Econometric models, techniques and applications
McGraw, 1977.

(12672)
Maddala G S
Econometrics
McGraw, 1977.

(12673)
Lindgren B W
Statistical theory. 3rd ed
Macmillan, 1976.

(12674)
Joy O M, Tollefson J O
On the financial applications of discriminant analysis
JFQA 1975 DEC VOL 10 p 723.

(12675)
Kmenta J
Elements of econometrics
Macmillan, 1971

(12676)
Theil H
Principles of econometrics
Wiley, 1971.

(12677)
Theil H
Applied economic forecasting
N Holland, 1966.

(12678)
Goldberger A S
Econometric theory
Wiley, 1964

(12679)
Savage L J
The foundations of statistics
Wiley, 1954.

40.1 Non-parametric statistics

(12680)
Daniel W W
Applied nonparametric statistics
HM, 1978.

(12681)
Siegel S
Nonparametric statistics
McGraw, 1956.

40.2 Regression analysis

(12682)
Froot K A
Consistent covariance matrix estimation with cross-sectional dependence and heteroskedasticity in financial data
JFQA 1989 SEP VOL 24:3 p 333-356.

(12683)
Ingram F J, Frazier E L
Alternative multivariate tests in limited dependent variable models: an empirical assessment
JFQA 1982 JUN VOL 17:2 p 227-241

(12684)
Zellner A
An efficient method of estimating seemingly unrelated regressions and tests for aggregation bias
JASA 1982 JUN p 348-368.

(12685)
Kon S J, Lau W P
Specification tests for portfolio regression parameter stationarity and the implication for empirical research
JF 1979 MAY VOL 34:2 p 451-465

(12686)
Chang H-S, Cheng F L
Using pooled time-series and cross-section data to test the firm and time effects in financial analyses
JFQA 1977 SEP VOL 12 p 457.

(12687)
Brown R L, Durbin J, Evans J M
Techniques for testing the constancy of regression relationships over time
JRSS Series B 1975 VOL 37 p 149-192.

(12688)
Rao C R
Linear statistical inference and its applications
Wiley, 1973

(12689)
Brown K C
The significance of dummy variables in multiple regressions involving financial and economic data
JF 1968 JUN VOL 23 p 515-517.

(12690)
Graybill F A
An introduction to linear statistical models
McGraw, 1961.

40.21 Heteroscedasticity/ ARCH models

(12691)
Bollerslev T
A conditionally heteroskedastic time series model for speculative prices and rates of return
REStat 1987 VOL 69 p 542.

(12692)
Duncan G
Estimation and inference for heteroscedastic systems of equations
IntER 1983 OCT VOL 24 p 559-566.

(12693)
Engle R F
Estimates of the variance of U.S. inflation based upon the ARCH model
JMCB 1983 AUG VOL 15:3 p 286-301.

(12694)
Hsieh D A
A heteroscedasticity-consistent covariance matrix
estimator for time series regressions
Journal of Econometrics 1983 AUG VOL 22.

(12695)
Engle R F
Autoregressive conditional hetereroscedasticity
with estimates of the variance of United Kingdom
inflation
Em 1982 JUL VOL 50 p 987-1008.

(12696)
Koenker R
A   note   on   Studentizing   a   test   for
heteroscedasticity
Journal of Econometrics 1981 SEP VOL 17 p
107-112.

(12697)
White H
A heteroscedasticity-consistent covariance matrix
estimator and a direct test for heteroscedasticity
Em 1980 MAY VOL 48 p 817-838.

(12698)
Breusch T, Pagan A
A single test for heteroscedasticity and random
coefficient variation
Em 1979 SEP VOL 47 p 1287-1294.

(12699)
Wichern D W, Miller R B, Hsu D A
Changes of variance in first-order autoregressive
time series models - with an application
JRSS Series C 1976 VOL 25 p 248-256.

40.3   Time series methodology

(12700)
Granger C W J, Newbold P
Forecasting economic time series
Academic Pr, 1977.

(12701)
Box G E P, Jenkins G M
Time series analysis, forecasting and control
Holden-Day, 1976

(12702)
Daniels H E
Autocorrelation between first differences of
mid-ranges
Em 1966 JAN VOL 34 p 215-219.

(12703)
Waud R N
Small sample bias due to misspecification in the
"partial adjustment" and "adaptive expectation"
models
JASA 1966 DEC VOL 61 p 1130-1152.

(12704)
Working H
A random difference series for use in the analysis
of time series
JASA 1934 MAR VOL 29 p 11-24.

40.4   Frequency distributions

(12705)
Jean W H, Helms B P
Geometric mean approximations
JFQA 1983 SEP VOL 18:3 p 287-293

(12706)
Huang C C, Wehrung D A, Ziemba W T
A homogeneous distribution problem with
applications to finance
MSci 1977 AUG VOL 23:12 p 297.

(12707)
Aitchison J, Brown J A C
The lognormal distribution
Cambridge U Pr, 1957.

40.41   Stable paretian distributions

(12708)
Blattberg R, Sargent T
Regression   analysis   with   non-Gaussian
disturbances: some sampling results
Em 1971 MAY VOL 39 p 501-510.

(12709)
Fama E F, Roll R
Parameter estimates for symmetric stable distributions
JASA 1971 JUN VOL 66 p 331-338..

(12710)**Fama E F, Roll R**
Some properties of symmetric stable distributions
JASA 1968 SEP VOL 63 p 817-836.

(12711)
Gnedenko B V, Kolmogorov A N
Limit distributions for sums of independent random variables
Addison-Wes, 1968.

(12712)
Mandelbrot B
New methods in statistical economics
JPE 1963 OCT VOL 71 p 421-440.

(12713)
Mandelbrot B
The stable Paretian income distribution when the apparent exponent is near two
IntER 1963 JAN VOL 4 p 111-115.

(12714)
Wise J
Linear estimators for linear regression systems having infinite residual variances
Paper presented to the Berkeley-Stanford Mathematical Economics Seminar, OCT 1963.

(12715)
Mandelbrot B
Paretian distributions and income maximization
QJE 1962 FEB VOL 76 p 57-85.

40.5 Stochastic processes

(12716)
Malliaris A G, Brock W A
Stochastic methods in economics and finance
N Holland, 1982.

(12717)
Ikeda N, Watanabe S
Stochastic differential equations and diffusion processes
N Holland, 1981.

(12718)
Kamien M I, Schwartz N L
Dynamic optimization: The calculus of variations and optimal control in economics and management
N Holland, 1981.

(12719)
Karlin S, Taylor H M
A second course in stochastic processes
Academic Pr, 1981.

(12720)
Hall P, Heyde C C
Martingale limit theory and its application
Academic Pr, 1980.

(12721)
Smith G D
Numerical solutions of partial differential equations: finite difference methods
Oxford U Pr, 1978.

(12722)
Karlin S, Taylor H M
A first course in stochastic processes
Academic Pr, 1975.

(12723)
Ziemba W T, Vickson R G eds.
Stochastic optimization models in finance
Academic Pr, 1975.

(12724)
Arnold L
Stochastic differential equations: theory and applications
Wiley, 1974

(12725)
Intrilagator M
Mathematical optimization and economic theory
P-H, 1971.

(12726)
Abramowitz M,   Stegun I A
Handbook of mathematical functions
Dover Publications, 1970.

(12727)
Cox D,   Miller H
The theory of stochastic processes
Wiley, 1968.

(12728)
Kushner H
Stochastic stability and control
Academic Pr, 1967.

AUTHOR INDEX

Miller M et al, eds. (11611)
Miller M H (37), (1401), (1708), (1959), (5394), (6594), (7779), (9196), (9405), (9406), (9827), (9851), (9852), (9874), (9914), (9917), (9931), (9933), (10041), (10121), (10198), (10208), (10210), (10249), (10251), (10360), (10619), (10622), (11550), (12171), (12223), (12461)
Miller M H et al (1942)
Miller N C (5035), (12197)
Miller N P (8849)
Miller R B (2366), (2816), (3400), (12699)
Miller R E (2603), (5616), (9498), (9504), (9516), (9525)
Miller R J (2352), (2699)
Miller R L (2278), (6879)
Miller R M (923)
Miller S (11778)
Miller S E (8351)
Miller S M (626), (2491), (11706)
Miller T (10632)
Miller T W (3529), (5601), (10625), (10626)
Miller W P (6168)
Millon-Cornett M H (2660)
Mills C C eds. (3610)
Mills D E (8904)
Mills D L (1326), (2100), (6849)
Mills H D (5651)
Mills J C (12366)
Mills J R (7562)
Mills R H (6884), (7670)
Millstein I M (11189)
Milne F (814), (919), (958), (1350), (1909), (5326), (7803), (10295)
Milnor J (701)
Milonas N T (8297), (8577)
Milutinovich J S (2392)
Minami W N (2549)
Mincer J ed. (5554)
Minford P (1637)
Mingo J J (2406), (2555), (2635), (2702), (2705), (2707), (2787)
Mingo K A (6930), (6931), (10094)
Minns R (11354)
Mintz J M (12421), (12441)
Mirman L J (586), (632), (997), (5104), (5120)
Miro A R O (6055)
Miron J A (2674), (6401), (6588)
Mirrlees J A (9243)
Misawa M (10063)
Mishkin F S (2258), (6435), (6481), (6485), (6605)
Miskovic M (7717), (8265)
Misra L (3988)
Mitchell C (7636)
Mitchell D W (2719), (2933), (6478)
Mitchell G B (10367)

Mitchell J (3078)
Mitchell K (2869)
Mitchell M L (1928), (1929), (3572), (11002), (11159)
Mitchell P L (3986)
Mitchell W C (4270)
Mitello F C (8696)
Mitra T (4799), (12230)
Mitrusi A (1791)
Mittman L (11373)
Mizuno H (10046)
Mlynarczyk F A Jr (6049)
Moag J S (2807), (2833), (9027), (10470), (10478)
Mock E J (321), (368), (10557)
Mock E J ed. (409), (414)
Mock E J et al. (427)
Modani N K (4420), (11037), (12608)
Modest D (8471)
Modest D M (5491), (5565), (5689), (7813), (8312), (8466)
Modigliani F (5136), (5379), (5380), (5683), (6385), (6816), (6843), (9405), (9406), (9853), (9914), (9917), (10122), (10144), (10198), (10208), (10210), (10251), (11550), (12614)
Moffett M (3163)
Moffitt M (466)
Mohan N (10653)
Mohindru R K (2405)
Mohr R M (4498), (4528)
Mohring H (11589)
Moir C (10867)
Mokkelbost P B (4494), (8156)
Molho L E (6859)
Monahan J P (3713)
Monahan K B (3713)
Monahan S T (10116)
Money A H (12210)
Money Which (3982), (5727)
Monroe M (8547)
Monroe M A (8278)
Monroe R J (3471), (10947)
Montalbano M (9049), (9132)
Montgomery C A (8820), (10851)
Montgomery G E Jr (10985)
Monti M et al. (1530)
Moody C E Jr (10308)
Mookerjee R (3750)
Mookherjee D (1159), (1282)
Moon P (8774)
Moon R W (10923)
Moondra S L (2393)
Moore A B (3907)
Moore B (12609)
Moore B J (654), (1364), (7128), (9649)
Moore H A (1400)
Moore J (1130)
Moore J H H (1126), (1132)
Moore J S (242), (283)

Moore L J (75), (2397), (10449), (10633)
Moore M L (8780)
Moore N H (9607), (11011)
Moore P G (4417), (4426), (5017)
Moore S B (8223), (8251)
Moore T (10848)
Moore T G (1902)
Moore W R (2421)
Moore W T (4534), (4883), (6895), (8930), (9265), (9311), (9826), (9836), (10232), (10278), (10323), (11340)
Moosa S A (10580), (10583)
Mooses L N (10681)
Moran M (2259)
Moran M J (3281)
Morck R (1227), (1233), (3648), (3649), (10833), (12217)
Morck R and Taggart R A (3594)
Moreau A F (10110), (11319)
Morey R C (10696)
Morgan B W (10038)
Morgan E V (1555), (1577), (5873), (12052)
Morgan E V eds. (1369)
Morgan E V et al. (1545)
Morgan G E (1701), (2114), (2743), (2909), (2951), (3064), (6684), (7378), (8396), (10419)
Morgan G E III (8374)
Morgan I G (3974), (4385), (4805), (5375), (9854), (9865)
Morgan J (1666)
Morgenstern O (703), (3873), (3906), (3909)
Moriarity S (6299)
Moriarty E (8323)
Morin R A (575), (8416), (11604)
Morley J (8614)
Morris J (67), (5147)
Morris J K (9444)
Morris J R (7190), (7191), (10528)
Morris M H (6059), (6291), (12481)
Morris R B (6911)
Morris R C (3083), (5540), (5594), (11425), (11478)
Morris R D (3139), (3150)
Morris V F (5820)
Morrison G R (2850)
Morrison R (11366)
Morrison R W (11373)
Morse D (1814), (3940), (4002), (5753), (5844), (6908), (9806), (11472)
Morse J N (4623)
Morton J E (1402)
Morton T E (10627), (10691)
Morton T G (2153), (9597), (9598)
Moseidjord A (2082)
Moser J T (5487), (9743)
Moses E A (422), (4148), (5566), (9713), (10533)

813

817